HISTORY

OF THE

BURGH OF DUMFRIES

HISTORY

OF THE

BURGH OF DUMFRIES,

WITH NOTICES OF NITHSDALE, ANNANDALE
AND THE WESTERN BORDER

BY

WILLIAM McDOWALL,

WITH A SUPPLEMENTARY CHAPTER BY
ALFRED TRUCKELL

FOURTH REVISED EDITION
With additional notes

DUMFRIES;
T.C. Farries & Co. Limited in
association with Royal Burgh of Dumfries
OCTOCENTENARY COMMITTEE OF
NITHSDALE DISTRICT COUNCIL

THE ARMS OF THE ANCIENT
ROYAL BURGH OF DUMFRIES

© T C Farries & Co Ltd
Irongray Road, Lockside,
Dumfries

ISBN 0 948278 01 3

Reprinted in Great Britain by
Penwell Ltd, Parkwood, Callington, Cornwall

Bound by Booth Bookbinders, Mabe, Cornwall

Castle Street, Dumfries from an
original watercolour by
Joseph Watson, 1863
Reproduced by kind permission
of Dumfries Burgh Museum

PREFACE

The year 1986 marks the 800th Anniversary of the founding of the Royal
Burgh of Dumfries. Although with the introduction of the Local
Government (Scotland) Act, 1973 the Royal Burgh of Dumfries ceased to
exist on 15th May, 1975, one of its successors, Nithsdale District
Council, decided that the occasion should be marked in a variety of ways.
With this in mind the District Council set up an Octocentenary
Committee to oversee the celebrations. The Committee recognised it
would be appropriate that, if possible, McDowall's History of Dumfries
should be updated and republished.

It was felt that there is no better and more knowledgeable person to
undertake this task than Mr. Alfred Truckell, MBE., MA., former
Curator of Dumfries Museum and well known local historian.

Nithsdale District Council is proud to be associated with the updating
of McDowall's History of Dumfries and is confident that the latest
volume will be of considerable worth not only locally but to all who have
an interest in the unique history of the town.

WILLIAM W. JAPP

CHIEF EXECUTIVE,

NITHSDALE DISTRICT COUNCIL

1986

ERRATA

P.433.—For "and lift" read "ane list."
P.548, line 22.—For "M'Briar" read "M'Brair."
P.659.—For "Magisgrove" read "Mavisgrove."
P.762.—Read: Rev. David Mackie was inducted; translated Partick in
October, 1900.
P.776.—For "Closeburn" read "Keir."
P.833.—For "T.D. Weir" read "J.D. Weir".

CHAPTER I.

WILLIAM McDOWALL WROTE HIS HISTORY OF DUMFRIES AT KINGHOLM LODGE IN SIX MONTHS IN 1867, IN THE MIDST OF HIS DUTIES AS A BUSY NEWSPAPER EDITOR.

IT IS AN EXCEPTIONALLY GOOD LOCAL HISTORY, MAKING VERY FULL USE OF THE SOURCES AT ITS AUTHOR'S DISPOSAL, AND WRITTEN IN VIGOROUS MID-NINETEENTH CENTURY JOURNALESE.

HIS ATTITUDES AND INTERESTS ARE, OF COURSE, THOSE OF HIS PERIOD: AND THE EDITIONS OF 1872 AND 1906, WHILE BRINGING THE HISTORY UP TO DATE, RETAIN THESE.

THE 1972 EDITION IS THAT OF 1906 PLUS A MUCH TOO BRIEF INTRODUCTORY CHAPTER.

IT WAS GENERALLY FELT THAT THIS WAS INADEQUATE, AND ALSO THAT McDOWALL'S VERY WEAK INDEX SHOULD BE STRENGTHENED: THE PRESENT INTRODUCTORY CHAPTER AND REVISED AND ENLARGED INDEX IS THE ANSWER.

THIS NEW CHAPTER HAS TWO MAIN PURPOSES: TO ADD INFORMATION McDOWALL DID NOT HAVE: AND TO BRING THE HISTORY FROM 1906 TO 1985.

THE Ordovician and Silurian rocks making up much of the South of Scotland were laid down as fine mud at the bottom of a deep oceanic trench along a mountainous coast, in what we would term a subduction zone, around and just short of 400 million years ago. There followed a highly volcanic period, when the granite magma which has become the Criffel massif and the Burnswark Lavas were intruded—a period of mainly desert conditions in our area: then came the long quiet period of the Carboniferous, laying down coal beds which still survive as near Dumfries as Powillimont. The climate was tropical and our area alternated many times between shallow coastal sea, with coral reefs, and swampy coastal jungle. This in its turn was followed by the Permian desert period, some fifty million years from around 200 to around 150 million years ago: this gave us the characteristic Dumfries Basin red sandstone and breccia.

The last Ice Ages have effectively removed any later rocks apart from a few igneous dykes: our present landscape is a product of the last twenty-five thousand years or so. While there was open steppe certainly within fifteen miles of Dumfries twelve thousand-odd years ago the ice came down again (moraines near Auldgirth may have forced the Nith out of its broad old valley (now Lochar Moss) and made it pirate the Cluden valley), and probably did not finally clear our area till around ten thousand years ago, when the sea level was 120 feet below that of the present, leaving much of the Solway dry land.

Archaeological finds show us that man was already in the area between eight and ten thousand years ago: the first farmers were already clearing land around Dumfries by somewhere around 3600 B.C., when the sea was just beginning to withdraw from a level twenty five feet above its present level: at its highest the Nith where Dumfries is now had been permanent seawater and the Lochar Moss a bay of the sea. The farmers brought the art of pottery making with them, and a simple form of weaving too. By a little before 2000 B.C. bronze-users were in our district and the next twelve or thirteen hundred years show a heavy occupation of the Dumfries district—there are several groups of urn burials within the area of the town—one where the Midsteeple now stands, another at Palmerston, another in Goldie Park, another in Hamilton Starke park: stone axe-hammers, flint scrapers, and flint 'slug-knives' of this period have been common finds within the town. While metal was still little known, around 2100 B.C., stone axes hewed out a dugout canoe which was found a few years ago beside the Lochar on Catherinefield farm: it had plied the marshy lakes which had followed the recently-retreated sea.

By the Iron Age, say 2,500 years ago, there were forts at Kirkland Plantation and the Midsteeple hill or the one at the Academy Street end of Loreburn Street, or on Chapel Hill.

By around 81 A.D. the Romans came to our area, planting their forts, planned like little Hellenistic cities, over our area—far closer than we had thought until the aerial photograph discoveries of the dry Summer of 1984—and linking them with roads, one of which, coming along the Wardlaw-Bankend-Trohoughton ridge from the Roman harbour at Caerlaverock, runs down near the Bankend Road, through the garden of Mountainhall, and, as St Michael Street-High Street-Academy Street-Edinburgh Road, runs through the town.

The Romans were in the area until near 100 A.D., probably sporadically from then on, and fully in occupation again from 151 until around 158: the nearest site to yield large amounts of pottery and some metal, including figurines, is the mid-second-century site at Carzield four miles North of the town: Dalswinton a few miles further North saw intense occupation in both the first and second centuries: but it is likely that the Romans used the excellent fords in and near Dumfries.

Coin finds suggest that there was Roman influence in the area until near the end of the Roman Empire: the large dug-grave cemetery within the great Iron Age fort at Trohoughton two miles South of Dumfries, overlooking the head of ocean navigation on the Nith, almost certainly started within Roman times and shows very early Christianity in our area—it seems that the rampart of the same fort yielded the pre-Christian Celtic head now in Dumfries Museum.

The earliest Christian inscriptions in Galloway, at Kirkmadrine and Whithorn to the South-West of Dumfries, relate to the period just after the formal withdrawal of imperial Roman power from Britain: the enshrouded burials above a cremation cemetery at Whithorn are perhaps a little earlier. The Civitas Carvettiorum, comprising much of North-West England, with Luguvallium-Caerluel-Carlisle as its capital, seems to have evolved into the Welsh-speaking principality of Rheged-Yrechwydd (The Strand) which covered both shores of the Solway-Dunragit near Stranraer seems to contain the root Rheged, just as Rochdale in Lancashire may. Urbgen (City-Born-he was probably born in Carlisle) who flourished in the late 500's, was the most famous ruler of Rheged: his bard was Taliessin. The area containing Dumfries passed from Welsh rule with the marriage of Urien's great-grand-daughter Rhienmelth (Queen or Princess Lightning) to Osuiu of Northumbria around 632. This transfer seems to have been mainly peaceful though Mote of Mark between Rockcliffe and Kippford some 20 miles S.S.W. of Dumfries, was taken by storm about this time and Aethilifrida whose name was scratched in runes on a bone comb there may have been wife or daughter of one of the Northumbrian victors.

Northumbrian influence seems to have extended rapidly after this: the name of Terregles was fossilized by the change from Welsh to English around 675: some time between 650 and 700 the Ruthwell Cross was erected, that great symbol of the power of the Northumbrian Empire and of the Church of Rome: its Lay of the Rood is the earliest poem in the English language—and of a far more varied and flexible form than the stilted later Anglo-Saxon poetry. The name of the religious site at Trohoughton remained Welsh: it seems to have already passed out of use by the time English came in.

The Angles were village builders: and it seems most likely that it was at some time in the 700's that a village grew up on the Roman road on the well-drained Dumfries ridge, protected by moss, river, and the smaller Lore and Mill burns.

Around the mid-500's Irish missionaries were passing through our area: the pecked crosses at Foregirth, eight miles North, and Ruthwell, ten miles East, of the town attest their activities: a century or more later, Holywood-Sancta Nemore, Sacro Bosco, the Holy Grove, may have been the Anglian Minster for Lower Nithsdale, as Closeburn was for mid-Nithsdale and Glencairn for that valley: the two latter have yielded Northumbrian crosses: Durrisdeer, which yielded another, may have been a small minster, and Kirkconnel, with its 10th-11th century crosses, a slightly later one.

The Irish missionaries had left a few Old Irish names in the area—Slewcairn in Southwick, Kimkerrick in Kirkbean, Annatland at Newabbey, possibly Relichill in the Ae valley: for a time English names dominated: then in the later 800's came the Norse, scattering such names as Eggerness, Almorness, Heston, Southwick, and Southerness, and in the following century the Gallghaidheal, speaking a rather Irish form of Gaelic, and Danish-speakers from the Danelaw in Northern England, giving such names as Lockerbie, Waterbeck, Foregirth, Tinwald (where presumably the local Ting or assembly was held), Tundergarth, Mouswald, and Torthorwald (Thorvaldr's castle): at the same time developed Highland Gaelic was coming into the North and East of our area as the Kings of Scots extended their power South: the Battle of Brunanburh (Burnswark, related in the stirring saga incorporated in the Anglo-Saxon Chronicle) involved Norsemen from Ireland, West Saxons from the South of England, Scots from the North, and Strathclyde Welsh and took place in 932. This was the period described in the Inquisition of Prince David, compiled between 1117 and 1124, when "different peoples, speaking different tongues, some of them not Christians, and not aggreeing well among themselves" came into our area.

The Gallghaidheal—the Galwegians—occupied much of S.W. Scotland: an English chronicler describes Carlisle as being "on the frontier of Galloway": the Galloway Ditch was on Kershopemuir in Cumberland above the Liddell water: and Prince David, according to the English chroniclers, "took Annandale out of Galloway and gave it to Robert de Brus".The grant of Annandale to Bruce dates to 1123 or 1124: and in that grant Dunegal of Stranid is mentioned as Bruce's neighbour to the West. Dunegal has a Welsh name—the modern Welsh form would be Dyfnwal—and the grant to Brus of "Estrahanent"—Ystrad Annant—gives, like the Inquisition, so many Welsh place-names as to show that Lower Annandale at least was Welsh-speaking at this date. Stranid, the Eastern principality of Galloway—Fergus or Feregus held the Western part—seems to have been shading from Welsh towards Gaelic as Dunegal's son Duuenald, though named after him, took the Gaelic form—Donald—of the name. Another of Dunegal's sons was named Radulf: and now we come back to Dumfries.

Dumfries first appears in writing in or as near as may be to 1160 in a grant by Radulf son of Dunegal of as much land "at Donfres" as two oxen could plough in a day to the Hospice of St. Peter at York—York being the religious centre of the old Northumbria. The witnesses to this, the first Dumfries document, tell us a good deal about the people of our area at that time, just before feudalism. They are Gilchrist, son of Brun (Servant of Christ, son of Brown—a Gaelic-named son of an Anglo-Saxon-named father)—Gilendonrut Bretnach—Servant of (an indecipherable saint's name), the Briton—that is, he was probably a Welsh speaker—Gilcomgal MacGilblaan—Servant of St. Connel, son of the servant of St. Blane—Udard son of Uttu, both names probably Anglo-Saxon, and Waldev son of Gilchrist. Waldev, the last-named, may be the son of the first-named, and may also be the Walleve (spelling of names was very fluid), Dean of Dumfries, who witnessed a Bruce agreement with the Bishop of Glasgow in 1189—all the more likely as it was desirable, where possible, to have at least one cleric among the witnesses when the grant was to a religious house. Udard in the list is probably Udard de Hodelm, of an old Carlisle family: he supported Brus in Annandale, and was the ancestor of the Carlyles of Hoddam and, later, Torthorwald.

Radulf also granted, to Kelso Abbey, a piece of land between the road to the church of St. Blane (near Bankend) and the road which goes round a certain rock which is called Greneham (the Craigs).

There is one reference to the immediate surroundings of Dumfries, which as it lies between 1158 and 1164 is very close in time to Radulf's. This is a grant by Uchtred of Galloway—evidently a close kinsman, possibly a full cousin, of Radulf—of a ploughland and a toft in Troqueer to the Hospice of St. Peter at York. Radulf's son Lochlan ("The Norseman" in Gaelic), who seems to have died young without issue, and Gilla Chad (possibly the Gillecatfar—servant of St. Catfarch—a Welsh saint—foster-brother of Uchtred, who witnesses several of Uchtred's charters), and Gilla Mor—probably the Gillemore Albanach ("The Scotsman", who appears in other Uchtred witness lists—all witness this document. The fact that this grant also is to the same recipient as Radulf's makes it certain that there is some connection between the two—it looks as if the two were acting in concert.

Radulf died some time in 1164-5 and the Holme Cultram Chartulary shows that much of what had been his territory in and to South and East of Dumfries, as far as the boundary of Cummertrees parish, was in Crown hands by not long after.

The next mention of the town comes some ten years later: King William the Lion confirmed certain rights of teinds to the Bishopric of Glasgow, and the writ was granted "apud Dunfres"—at Dumfries: it can be dated by the witnesses to 1174-5—none of the witnesses seems to be local, all being members of the King's entourage.

We now come to three important documents which seem from the witnesses to have been very close in time to each other. One, dated "at Gretna" grants 2½ ploughlands in the territory of Dumfries and Conheath to the Hospice of St. Peter at York—as in the two earlier local grants: another grants to the church of Glasgow "that toft at Dumfries which is between the old castlestead and the church, viz., from the castlestead to the cemetery of the church". The third confirms to the Abbey of Kelso the church of Dumfries, with lands and tithes and all oblations, and the chapel of St. Thomas in that burgh, and the toft belonging to that chapel. This gift was made "at Dunfres". The "in that burgh" is the first mention of the town's status as a royal burgh. In his paper "The Burghal Origins of Dumfries" in the Transactions of the Dumfries and Galloway Natural History and Antiquarian Society for 1912 the late Dr. George Neilson, one of the finest historians this area has produced, made out a convincing case for June-July 1186, when

Henry II of England, William the Lion, and Roland of Galloway were settling the Galloway question, with a dazzling entourage of notables, somewhere in the Gretna area—already effectively the border between the two kingdoms: many of the notables and high clergy attesting the documents would of necessity be there. As Neilson pointed out, an "old castlestead" implied a new castlestead, which could only be the King's: and a Royal castle, and a church in the King's hands to give, implied a Royal burgh.

However Dr. Neilson's dating has recently been put in doubt, as it has been discovered that one of the notable clerics witnessing the documents was in Rome for some time around that date. So the nearest we can come at present for the date on which Dumfries achieved Burghal status is in the bracket from 1174-5 for something around ten years thereafter.

As for the other information contained in these documents, the Chapel of St. Thomas was on Chapel Hill between High Street and Queensberry Street: William the Lion was a devotee of the cult of St. Thomas à Becket—it seems likely that he had known him personally—so it is likely that he founded the chapel. The document does not call it a new chapel, so that it may have been in existence for a few years. The "Old Castlestead" has usually be equated with the small Motte beside the Kingholm Road Entrance to Castledykes park, part of the rock on which it stands cut away for the road: it was formerly called "Paradise"—the name for a herb-garden: it could have been an infeudation—a grant to a knight—of Radulf's time. The only thing against this identification is that the distance from the churchyard is rather great—"toft" usually means a small piece of land.

The next mention of the town is the presence of Walleve, mentioned previously, witnessing a Bruce agreement with the Bishop of Glasgow in 1189: he is named as Dean of Dumfries. Still in the ecclesiastical field, about or just after 1200 Ralph the dean of Dumfries presented his nephew Martin to the living of St. Michael's church, and in support of his claim produced certain charters which he had in his possession. The case went before a board of arbitrators consisting of the Bishop of St. Andrews and two assessors and although they decided in favour of Kelso they allowed Martin to retain the church during his lifetime, provided he paid a reasonable rent to Kelso. This strongly suggests that William had made his grant to Kelso in forgetfulness or ignorance of earlier contradictory grants—possibly by Radulf? The arbitrators clearly thought Ralph and Martin had some case. St. Michael's church seems to be one of a small group, all on sharp hillocks near the sea or tidal water, in the Hebrides, West Highlands, Dumfries, South Wales, S.E. Ireland, Cornwall and Brittany, and all associated with a harvest festival and horse-racing—suggesting an Iron Age deity whose functions approximated to those of the archangel and whose shrines were adapted by the early missionaries following the same sea routes as their Iron Age predecessors—St. Michael's Mount and Mont St. Michel are obvious examples: so that, if as the evidence suggests, we accept a pre-William

the Lion date of foundation for St. Michael's Church in Dumfries, so that
the name is not one of the rash of St. Michael dedications so favoured by
the Normanisers, then a church in Dumfries may go well back into the
Dark Ages—remembering also that it stands above a good ford carrying
an ancient cross-country route over the Nith.

Church and castle—two of the three feudal elements. The third, the
mill, was almost certainly in existence by the time the town is first
mentioned as a burgh, but is not mentioned until the next century. One
of these mentions, the Adam the Miller murder case, is now dated to
1256 as near as may be. Richard, son of Robert, son of Elias, and Adam
the Miller met in the churchyard of St. Michael's after Mass on the first
Tuesday after the Festival of St. Michael, probably in 1256. They
quarrelled, and Adam called Richard a Galuvet—a Galloway man "That
is to say, a thief". On the following Thursday a woman ran up to Adam
while he was standing in his own doorway and cried, "Take yourself
away: for behold Richard is here". Adam replied that he would not take
himself away, he had a knife as sharp as Richard's, went into his house,
returned with a long knife, and attacked Richard as he passed. Richard
drew his sword in self-defence, using the flat of the blade: Adam attacked
with his left arm: the two closed: and in the struggle Adam was fatally
wounded. Richard, charged with murder, was tried in the Castle of
Dumfries, on the Monday after the Feast of Saints Fabian and
Sebastian, by a tribunal consisting of the King's baillies, a jury of 13
burgesses, and a number of barons: the burgesses were Adam Long,
Adam Mille, Hugh Schereman, Roger Wytewell, Richard Haket, Walter
Faccinger, Thom Scut, Robert Muner, Thom Calui, Robert Boys,
William Scot, William the Skinner, and Henry the Dyer. The enquiry
found that Richard had not intended to kill Adam: that Richard was an
honourable man and Adam a man of ill repute: and so granted an
honourable discharge to Richard.

Here we have a list of Dumfries men, very different in character from
the mainly Celtic and pre-feudal witnesses to Radulf's grant, and
including tradesmen.

The other mention of the Mill is in an agreement betwen Kelso Abbey
and Roger Wytwele, burgess of Dumfries, leasing to Wytwele "the whole
of these lands which Malcolm, the son of Uchtred of Travereglis, held
from the formerly named inheritance of William, the son of Bele, with
tofts and crofts in the territory and town of Dumfries . . . as they lie, viz.,
between the lands of St. John, which lie beside the cemetery of the
mother church of Dumfries on the north side, and so by the road which
leads from the town of Dumfries towards the Castle as far as the road
which leads towards the Chapel of St. Lawrence of Keldwood on the
south side, and so towards the east beside the Crown land as far as the
Dumfries Burn which falls into the mill pond of Dumfries"—a stretch of
land which, if not the same, must lie adjacent to William the Lion's grant
tot the church of Glasgow.

Castle, church, mill: there was another element in the second half of the
1100's—defence, of which the planting of the Royal Castle at Castle-

dykes was probably the last phase. The unusual number of mottes and motte-like structures about Dumfries—the great troop-mustering motte at Troqueer just across the ford from Castledykes, the small early motte at Castledykes, the motte-like structure which existed until recently in the curve of the road at the Western end of the old ford just above the Caul, Lochside Mote, the motte-like structure at Lady Chapel Knowe, Terregles, the probable motte at Castlehill near the Castle-Douglas road—one of the thickest concentrations of such structures anywhere—must relate to the uneasy relationship between Galloway and the Scottish crown.

The last building relating to the building of the King's Castle is the Chapel of our Lady at Castledykes, first mentioned just after 1200 but almost certain, given the needs of the time, to be contemporary with the Castle: it stood all through the Middle Ages and long outlasted the Reformation, seeing use as a warehouse, and standing till the early 1700's.

The next building for which we have an approximate date is the Convent of the Greyfriars of Dumfries, founded in 1264/65: the King's Castle had probably been a timber building in its first phase, for we hear of Master Peter, a mason, being paid £20—quite a large sum—towards work done on the Castle in 1265, and this fits in well with the construction of stone castles elsewhere in our area. The Greyfriars were probably established in the town by Derbforgaill—the Gaelic means something like "daughter of the oath", or "daughter of the covenant"—we know it better in its Latinised form Dervorguilla—daughter of Alan, the last man to bear the title of King of Galloway, and wife, and later widow of John Balliol of Barnard Castle, with Buittle Castle as her Galloway seat—of her ten children, one was King of Scotland and one ancestor of the Dukes of Parma, and her grandson, Edward Balliol was also King of Scotland. Although the Bridge is first attributed to her in 1746 by Robert Edgar the historian there is no reason to doubt the tradition he quotes that the first, wooden, stage, which should date somewhere between 1260 and 1280, was her benefaction: she also of course founded Sweetheart Abbey six miles from the town, on an old religious site, in 1273.

Although the Grammar School of Dumfries is not mentioned until 1330, when the Rector pays the town's taxes to Edward III at Berwick, it is most unlikely that it was founded in the very troublous times which had followed since the death of King Alexander III: so here is another likely benefaction of the same period as the friary and the bridge.

In fact, the sixties and seventies were a golden age in Dumfries: the submission of Magnus the last Norse King of Man to King Alexander of Scotland at Dumfries in 1263 was a major political event: a Royal mint was established at Dumfries minting beautiful coins, some of them bearing the name of the moneyer, "Walter on Fres": it has been suggested that the fine bronze Common Seal matrix of Dumfries, bearing the figure of St. Michael, dates to this period: the Bridge, the Friary, very probably the School: indeed the high point of the mediaeval town: and a number of documents tell us about the town and its people during this period.

Adam, the son of Henry, of Dumfries, gave Kelso Abbey those lands that he acquired by his lawful emancipation in Dumfries—the lands which Robert the Locksmith, Roger the shoemaker, Walter the butcher (more trades!), Ralph the merchant, Alan the son of Emma, Adam Summerswain, and Alan of Bodha held of him. Thomas the parson of Troqueer is mentioned in the time of Alan of Galloway, who died in 1235. Roger Grindegret of Dumfries granted Holm Cultram Abbey a toft in "Dunfres" between the land of Nicholas the butcher and the land of Henry the Locksmith, Robert the son of William de Moffat grants a toft and a croft in the "villa" of Troqueer next the toft of Hugh the son of Norman, as freely as Walter de Burgh did to the same monastery, Richard the son of Lestelin gave a toft in the Western part of Dumfries between the land of Robert the son of Avelin and the land of Radulph called William Peter's son, of the same size as the other crofts round it. Michael the son of Matthew gives the toft in Dumfries which Henry the Locksmith formerly held of Michael's father and which R---le Fleming held of Michael. William Grindegreth of Dumfries grants to Lanercost for the good of the souls of himself and his wife Alice, his parents and all his ancestors a stone of wax or four pounds from his houses between the houses of John Grindergret his brother on the one side and the house of Michael Geargun. Among the witnesses are J. Grindegret, Uchtred of Terregles, and Robert Luggespick burgess of Dumfries.

This grant is later than the others and must date to about 1290.

Ecclesiastical litigation gives us the name of Magister Adam, vicar of Dumfries in 1250: Melrose Abbey, which owned Bruntscarth, Auchencrieff and Dargavel, in the parish of Dumfries, but outside the Burgh, took him to arbitration over the tithes on these lands: he had to give up his claim in return for three marks annually from the Abbey.

Dumfries folk were already travelling about: on April 24th, 1256, a case was heard regarding a murder in Corbridge, Northumbria: John of Dumfries, Adam of Dumfries, and Eva his wife, were lodged in William le Despenser's house in Corbridge, and a strife arose between them for Adam's wife. Adam struck John with a knife in the belly, causing instant death. He and his wife forthwith fled to Rowbyry church, confessed the deed, and abjured the kingdom, before the coroner. Their chattells were ten pence, for which the sheriff was to answer: and the vill of Corbridge was fined for not taking them.

Late on the night of 19th March 1286 something happened which signalled the end of the long period of prosperity and rapid progress which had lasted since the second half of the 1100's: King Alexander and his horse went over a cliff in the black dark near Kinghorn, hurrying home from a council in Edinburgh Castle to his young wife of a few months, Joleta daughter of the count of Dreux, the end of a very prosperous reign of thirty-seven years. "When Alexander our King wes deid, Then wes our gowd all turned to leid".

So now we come to a different source of information. In 1288 the watchman and gatekeeper of the Castle were paid, as a gratuity, £1-12/-, on account of extra watching by reason of the war raised by Robert de Brus and his son the Earl of Carrick (this was the revolt by the Elder Brus). The Castle was in English hands most of the time from 1291 to 1313 and the careful book-keeping of King Edward's accountants ("Rex Avarus, "Le Roi Coveytous", had to keep close control of the costs of his military ventures) has left us a wealth of detail—how many men-at-arms, squires, valets, horses (described individually), crossbows, crossbow quarrels, stockfish, wine, projectile weapons. We also have King Edward's accounts for the strengthening of the castle—largely by the erection of a great ditch and pele—in 1300. From all this material we will select items specifically relating to the town and its people. On the 29th November 1291, for instance, Sir. William de Boyville, Warden of the Castle, acknowledged having received £8 from the Burgh by the hands of Robert de Nam, a burgess. A receipt of 12th March 1292 is witnessed by John of the Stone House—probably that which shows up on the aerial photograph of the Stonehouse Loaning just outside the town and can just be discerned as a low mound beside the road. On 10th December 1292 King Edward wrote to John de Twynholm farmer of the Burgh of Dumfries regarding eighteen pounds of arrears. In 1300 the Minor Friars of Dumfries were paid six shillings for the King's support for three days on his arrival in the town in June: on 10th July the King made an oblation of seven shillings at the great altar of the Minor Friars (the abecediary from the lectern beside the altar is in Dumfries Museum). On 16th July, after the siege of Caerlaverock, the King made another offering in the church. On 24th October the King made his oblation of seven shillings in his own chapel in the town "for the good report which he heard from the parts of Galloway", and again on the 28th, in the church of the Minor Friars, being the feast of Simon and Jude, he gave seven shillings. On 1st November the feast of All Saints was celebrated in the presence of the King and of Lord Edward the King's son, in the church of the Minor Friars of Dumfries, when he made his usual offering of six shillings. On the same day the Minor Friars were paid five shillings and four pence for the King's board for four days of his stay there in October, by the hands of William of Annan. The Queen and the Court arrived in Dumfries on the 17th October, and remained until the end of the month. On 24th October Robert de Belton was paid 4/3d for money paid by him to various porters carrying timber from the water near Dumfries to the peel of the same place: some of the workers were imported from Northumberland but this particular item probably refers to Dumfries people. Adam de Boulton and David Arplyn, who are mentioned as "prepositi" (Provosts—usually the King's Baillie and the Burgh Baillie) may well have been English appointees. In 1304 John de Heyton, who held a mortgage on the 12 tofts in and near to the town belonging to the Knights Hospitallers of St. John of Jerusalem, called "Our Lady's Tofts", was illegally disseised by the English sheriff in champerty with Mathew de Terregles. On Hayton's petition Friar Ralph de Lindesee, Warden of the Hospital, was sent to Dumfries to hold an enquiry. One or more of the tofts adjoined the north side of the cemetery of St. Michael's. The land of Spitlefields near Conheath was probably one of these tofts. "Homines burgi de Dunfres" are mentioned in the lost Exchequer rolls for 1291 as rendering accounts. William Jargon—the same surname as the earlier "Geargun"—appears to have been a baillie in 1304: the entry in Bain's "Calendar" is a complaint that Sir Maheu the Redman, Sheriff of Dumfries, imprisoned Jargon, impressed all the carts around Dumfries, and carried off William's corn to the value of 10 marks and more, and charged Jargon and others who had had seisin of their lands from the King for getting possession of them. William Jargon was in the King's service guarding the peace of the town when he saw Sir Mathew's outrages, and was going to complain to the Guardian and Treasurer when Sir Mathew seized his horse and still keeps it. Sir Mathew took all the beasts that came to the market one day, to the number of 100 oxen and cows, and exacted fines before handing them back (this is the literal "blackmail"): five cows he sent to Stirling and two of them came from a poor stranger.

In September 1297 Sir William Wallace, according to Blind Harry, came to Dumfries after riding through Durrisdeer, Morton and Closeburn, where a fracas took place, past Lochar Moss to the shore near Cockpool where a pitched fight occurred on the sand—all this just after his defeat of the English at Stirling Bridge on 11th September. The vengeful English reoccupation of the Castle in 1288 lasted for seven years: and in that time 1300 was the highlight for the town and district.

The Solway was filled in Summer and Autumn with the English fleet of 95 ships, furnished by the Cinque Ports, under Command of Gervaise Allard himself, Lord High Admiral of the Ocean-Sea (at the end of the season the King presented him with a fine white horse: Allard, prudent man, rode it home to the channel coast—he was taking no risks!) Edward's fleet was based on the old Roman harbours of Maryport and, especially, Skinburness: there is a suggestion that some of the supplies for his siege of Caerlaverock in August 1300 were landed at the Roman harbour there, which on a high tide could still muster six feet of water—enough for the shallow-draft grain ships—and timber was evidently being rafted up the Nith for his pele at Castledyes later in the Autumn. The fleet accompanied the King as he marched his army West along the Galloway coast as far as Glenluce. The great gathering of the nobility of England and Western Europe attested, with blasons, in the verse "Siege de Karlaverok" by Edward's clerical minstrel, had besieged and finally taken the castle, with the aid of the great machines "Cat" and "Berefrey" brought from Lochmaben Castle. The siege ended, the Archbishop of Canterbury himself, Robert of Winchelsea, carrying Papal orders to Edward to cease hostilities who had lingered for weeks at Bowness, refused transport by the King who knew too well what order he carried and finally, brave and desperate, got a local man to guide him over the dangerous fords in the firth and across to Caerlaverock where he finally handed the order to the King who agreed with bad grace (the campaign being after all successfully concluded) to cease fighting. Did he pass through Dumfries, eight miles away, at some stage on his return? We do not know: the Royal accounts say nothing: the King would give no hospitality to this emissary of a Church with which he was on very bad terms because of his wish to tax Church property. The names of the ships of his supporting fleet are known—such as Annete, Blakebat, Blithe, Chevaler, Grace Dieu, Godelyne, Godeyere, Holy Spirit, Holy Rood, Mariote, St. Edmund, St. Edward, St. Thomas, Waynepayne and so on: the St. Edward cog of Winchelsea was armoured with a "hurdicium".

King Edward's principal business in Dumfries in the Autumn of 1300 was the massive refortification of the Castle. He had been much about the town since June, when he stayed with the Friars: on 7th June he was in the town again: the Queen and the Court arrived in Dumfries on 17th October, and remained until the end of the month. They journeyed in the company of a squadron of foot soldiers, leaving Carlisle on Saturday, 15th October, on which day they came in sight of Dumfries. From 5th September to 23rd November a great force of labourers and tradesmen dug a great ditch, built a massive wooden stockade or pele with wooden turrets, assembled in Inglewood in Cumberland: labour was brought mainly from Northumberland; masons reinforced the stonework of the Castle proper under Master Edward de Appleby and eleven journeymen. All the King's ordinary activities were carried on during his time in Dumfries: in the end of October he sent his cofferer from Dumfries to Carlisle to meet the French ambassadors who were conducting a truce with Scotland, and paid their expences for several days at Annan. The Lord Treasurer of England attended personally at Dumfries in November for settling the accounts for the work on the Castle—in fact, many of the most notable personalities of the English realm were in the Castle during these hectic Autumn days—and some must have been boarded out in the town.

The capture and execution of Wallace in 1305 put an end to Scottish resistance for the time, and the English occupation of Dumfries Castle, with its detailed accounts of supplies, garrison and armaments, runs on smoothly until the events of 10th February 1306, when Bruce killed Comyn of Dalswinton, the "Red Comyn", Bruce's cousin, at the High Altar of the church of the Grey Friars. King Edward certainly knew of the murder before 24th February, and sent two clerics North to find out just what had happened (his letter turned up in the English Record Office at Somerset House only a few years ago: their report has not yet been found). On the same day he ordered Sir James de Dalelegh to secure the peace and quiet of the King's lieges in the area.

As for the events in Dumfries, tradition has it that Bruce seized a horse—Comyn's, according to one account, though his own should have been handy—and galloped to the Castle, taking it and hoisting his standard. It is said that the justiciary court was sitting—this might well be why both Bruce and Comyn were both in Dumfries—and Comyn may have been doing his castleward duty too, as a knight of the shire-and Bruce probably obtained entry as of right: he obviously reached the Castle, about a mile from the Greyfriars, before news of the murder had got there. With the Castle he took Edward's Constable, Sir Richard Siward of Tibbers in mid-Nithsdale.

Considering that Bruce's murder of Comyn is one of the key events in Scottish history, we know very little definite (in the absence of the report to Edward) about what really happened. The Chronicle of Lanercost, compiled between 1333 and 1336—that is between 27 and 30 years after the event—simply says that the Red Comyn and his uncle were slain by Bruce: the Scala Chronicle, written after 1355 by Sir Thomas Gray when he lay a prisoner in Edinburgh Castle, and based on the recollections of Gray's father, affirms that Bruce struck Comyn with his dagger, and that others (un-named) struck him down before the altar. Barbour finished his poem, "The Bruce" in 1375, having been born before 1320: he says that Bruce met Comyn at the high altar "then with a knife on that very spot reft the life out of him. Others too were slain of much account. Nevertheless some say that the strife befell otherwise". Fordun wrote his Chronicle between 1363 and 1385. He says the wounded Comyn was laid by the friars behind the altar and when asked by them whether he could live replied "I can". His foes, hearing this, gave him another wound, and then he was taken away from this world. Wyntoun, who wrote his rhyming Chronicle between 1420 and 1424, refers briefly to the knifing of Comyn by Bruce, but gives no further details. Buchanan's "Liber Pluscardinensis", written in 1461, says that the friars dragged the wounded Comyn into the vestry behind the altar. James Lindsay of Kilpatrick, a cousin and dear friend of Bruce, finding that Comyn was not dead but only wounded, asked him if he could recover. On his saying yes Lindsay killed him. Walter Bower writing his Scotichronicon in 1447 had named two of the murderers—James Lindsay and Kirkpatrick; Mylne's MS, written before 1548, says that James Lindsay and Roger Kirkpatrick despatched Comyn and his uncle. They had been waiting with horses at the gate of the cemetery of the Friary, and it was only when Bruce emerged from the Church that they went into action. Major's History, printed in 1521, follows the Liber Pluscardinensis but names the two followers as "Lord John Lindsay and Lord Roger Kirkpatrick". George Buchanan, writing his History in 1578, mentions both James Lindsay and Roger Kirkpatrick as with Bruce, but declares that Lindsay alone went back into the church to assure Comyn's death. There was no Roger Kirkpatrick in the cadet Closeburn branch at or near this time: Sir Roger de Kirkpatrick of that Ilk—that is, of Auchencas above Beattock in Annandale—was on the English side throughout this episode and had English help in modernising his castle: his young as yet un-knighted son Roger might have been concerned in the affair.

I have treated this incident at length, because of its importance.

The Castle of Dumfries was retaken for Edward by Gilbert McDowall and his Galloway men on 3rd March from Bruce's men who had held it for three weeks. On the recapture of the Castle a stocktaking showed that Bruce's men had lost or destroyed 9 casks of wine, 2 casks of honey, 221 quarters of salt, and 182 horse shoes. There was great activity in the Castle again: and the Castle accounts and correspondence continue until its surrender to Bruce on 7th February, 1313: it is likely that it was systematically destroyed by him soon after, as Sir Eustace Maxwell, in his tax return of 1335, showed Castledykes as waste.

Later in 1306 Sir Christopher Seton, a Yorkshire knight married to Bruce's sister Christiana, who had been betrayed by his host when he took refuge in Loch Doon Castle, was hung as a traitor at the Dumfries place of execution on the hillock where St. Mary's Church now stands: the date was shortly before 4th October. In November 1323 King Robert endowed the Chapel of the Holy Rood, known later as the Chrystal Chapel, on the spot where his brother-in-law had been executed—hanging was the punishment of traitors, nobles being beheaded. We now enter a period of scant documentation: but homage lists and taxation receipts often give us information on local people: thus, early in the Edwardian period, Alianore, Prioress of the convent of Benedictine Nuns at Lincluden (probably founded by Uchtred around 1160) presented herself at Berwick-on-Tweed to swear fealty to Edward on 28th August 1296. Similarly, on 7th March, 1330, at Berwick, the account of the Provost of Dromfres was paid into the Exchequer by "Master John, Rector of the Church Schools"—the earliest mention of Dumfries Grammar School.

Dumfries passed into English hands again when on 23rd November 1332 King Edward Balliol surrendered most of South Scotland to Edward III of England: and it is clear that the town was in English hands for a good part of the time until 1354. In 1330, and 1331, we have the accounts of the "prepositi" of Dumfries (there were usually two, one for the crown or superior, and one for the town: the "King's Bailie", one of the prepositi, later developed into the provost). In 1357 another Provost, un-named, is met with and the same record mentions the Common Seal of the Burgh. Most of the mid-century was a very bad time for Dumfries: the Black Death reached the area near the beginning of 1350 and there was a second virulent outbreak in 1361. The town was burnt by the English in December 1345 and again in 1384, on the latter occasion by the Earl of Nottingham.

Left without a castle by the demolition of Castledykes, the town had to have some central strong-point in these times of war and famine, and the New Wark, which stood near the centre of what is now Queensberry Square—the 1912 underground urinal remembered by many Dumfries people was on its site—seems to have been the town's answer. It was a massive structure 85 feet long by 49½ feet wide, with an internal area of 467 square yards, and with thick walls of great strength.

It contained a large room known in later times as "the consistorie chamber" and may have functioned as a civic meeting place as well as a strong point. There are few records from these dark and difficult days (from the beginning of the century villages such as Kirkconnel at Springkell, Carruthers, Brattles, and cattle and sheep ranches such as Unthank, had been going out of occupation and many parish churches falling into ruin: English forces sweeping across burning the harvest in the barns, driving off the cattle, population sinking dramatically in the countryside) but the New Wark was most probably built between the 1360's and the 1390's. It does not seem to have stood alone, for the Mid-Raw was built in line with it, and separated from it by a narrow lane, seemingly about the same time. This is the compact block, originally with the gables to the street and the passages between the houses controlled by iron yetts—gates—highly defensive, in fact, between Queensberry Street and High Street, running North to what is now Chapel Street. The New Wark and the Mid-Raw formed the first intrusion into the wide central space which served as market-place and arms-mustering area (hence the name "Rattenraw" for the part of High Street near the mouth of Chapel Street).

Mention of the Common Seal in the 1350's, New Wark and Mid Raw shortly after: plague, famine and war or no, the town seems to have shown remarkable tenacity and determination to survive and progress: customs duties were being collected at Dumfries in 1330 and 1331—sure evidence of sea trade: French painted jug fragments from the Saintonge near Bordeaux have been found at Caerlaverock, Kirkcudbright and Dunrod. The considerable amount of pottery found by the writer under the Gas-House Close in the early 1970's runs from the late 1100's on, with the bulk of material in the 13th, 14th and 15th centuries, and including some probably imported pieces.

Robert the Third's Charter of 28th April, 1395, seems to recognise and reward the town's viability. Was it a confirmation of an earlier charter? It does not say, and charters of this date usually do state if they are confirming or extending an earlier right or replacing a lost or destroyed charter: if we had not known of the reference to Dumfries as a Burgh in the late 1100's we would have assumed that this was the town's first charter. Even the Robert II Charter has only come down to us in a copy of about 1560, 170 years later. Many places have traditions of charters by King Robert Bruce: Dumfries, so intimately linked with him, has none, though tradition does say that he granted the town the Kingholm, and he granted the Greyfriars extensive peat-cutting rights in the Lochar Moss (and possibly the town also) and fishing rights in the Nith.

There are a few records of local people during this disturbed century: in 1347, on the Monday before St. Mark's day, there was an Inquisition at Dumfreis before John de la More under-sheriff of Dumfries, by William son of Matilda, John of Dumfries, Malcolm MacConyng, Padin Smolan, Malcolm Mackenn', Henry Demester, John Milner, William, son of Roger, John Lange, Alan of Barnard Castle (Dumfries was in English hands at the time), Martin Milner, Thomas son of Bridoc, and Adam Macayne, jurors. The inquest found that Henry de Malton, father of John de Malton, was seized in the whole manor of Kirkpatrick juxta Travereglis, also of Dalscone and Ellisland in the Nith valley, and that Thomas de Malton was the lawful heir of the said Henry. Malton is an English name, not local, and it looks very much as if we have here an example of the English practice, well attested in Annandale at this time, of granting land to Englishmen.

Another source gives us Andrew McBrair, bailie of Dumfries in 1384—the first of this family, later so prominent in the town's affairs, to be named.

While through much of the 1300's sources on Dumfries are scanty indeed, in the next century the picture begins to improve markedly. Conditions remained difficult: the town was burnt probably in 1415-16 and certainly in 1448 and 1482 by the English: the plague "bot rameid (without cure) for thare war nane that tuk it bot deit within 24 houris" first reached Scotland at Dumfries (probably by sea) in 1439: yet even so the century seems to have been one of fairly steady progress. The Bridge is mentioned in the confirmation of 16th January 1425/6, by Princess Margaret, Lady of Galloway and Annandale, Countess of Touraine, of the Bridge Dues to the Greyfriars (done "apud le Tref", "at Threave", by Margaret's clerk McGilhauch, then or later parson of Parton): it figures again in the Papal Dispensation of 1431-32 granting relaxation of a year and forty days of enjoined penance to penitents who give alms "towards the building of the bridge which has been recently begun over the River Nith near the Burgh of Dumfries, in the Diocese of Glasgow, by the burgesses and inhabitants of these parts, and also for amplification of the Chapel of St. Mary the Virgin (the Greyfriars chapel) founded near the said bridge". On 4th January 1452-3 James, Earl of Douglas, confirmed by charter to the Friars the right to levy toll at the bridge. The Douglases had to render as blanch rent for the Lordship of Galloway a red rose at the Feast of St. John the Baptist, as had the McCullochs of Kirkmabreck. When James II passed through the town on his way to Threave in 1455 he seems to have taken up the question of putting the bridge into good order, for in 1456 Magister John Oliver, Vicar of Kirkbean, was appointed Master of Works for the bridge, receiving £6-13-4 from the King: the work dragged on for several years: in 1464 the Vicar obtained a remission of £11-5-10 from the fermes of Dumfries for the Bridge work: the remission was reduced to £6-13-4 in 1465 "for this year only".

Princess Margaret of the 1425/6 remission brought Tournois masons to decorate Lincluden Collegiate Church in the fine florid French Late Gothic style in the 1420's and '30's—a timber has been ring-dated to 1431.

The New Wark appears in a sasine to Robert McBrair, burgess, and, later, Provost, in "diverss annual rents and tenements within the Burgh, with the advocation and donation of the New Wark, etc.", dated 5th November 1442. This is the first record of it but there is no suggestion that it is a new building. The Tolbooth must have been built between 1473 (the last surviving Burgh Court extract) and 1481, when the next extract states that the Burgh Court was held in the Tolbooth: no earlier extract mentions it. This Tolbooth survived, strengthened and altered in 1718, until 1935: it occupied what is now the uphill end of the block partly occupied by Messrs. Burton: its hall latterly housed the printing establishment of Hannavy and McMunn: older Dumfriesians will remember this, and the "Rainbow Stairs" or "Rainbow Steps" which were in earlier times the site of Royal proclamations and the like. The term "rainbow" was used because the double steps had the form of a rainbow.

The McBrair family, first appearing in 1384, is clearly in the saddle during this century: Robert McBrair seems to have been provost most of the time between 1453 and 1477: his father Herbert McBrair died prior to June 1444. Nicholas, Robert's son, seems to have been Provost from 1484 till 1512. A John McBrair is witness to the 1444 document.

From the records of Middelburg in Holland we hear of Provost Nicholas McBrair and other Dumfries merchants arranging a large deal over wool in Edinburgh in 1492: there had been a customer for Dumfries port as early as 1330-31, but the next reference to customs accounts is in 1463-4: Robert McBrair, Provost, took office as customer on 12th July 1463: he stated that "before this account no great custom arose in Dumfries". Duty on wool and cloth (remember, it was mainly exports, not imports, which were taxed at this time) in the first year amounted to £52-5/-, half of which was remitted by the Lords of Council to "the merchants of Brittany coming to Dumfries, to induce them and others like them to come to these parts"—which does rather suggest that overseas trade had been weak for some time. In the next three years only one ship exported goods from Dumfries and the duty collected was no more than £7. This is the last shipping record until 1505; the 1492 transaction may have related to goods shipped from Bo'ness on the Firth of Forth.

On 16th January 1453 Provost Robert McBrair resigned in the hands of Bailie Andrew Nicolson of Dumfries all right in the acres and crofts belonging to him within the Burgh except the Barkerland, for a yearly payment by the town of £5 Scots. The witnesses, Dumfries men, included Alexander Martinson, William Broun, Adam Cordonar, Finlay McIlhaugh, Gilbert Walker, John Durand, John McBrair, Thomas McGray, Robert Glover, Patrick Corson, Herbert Newall and Thomas Davison. A feu charter by Baillies John Edgar and Andrew Nicolson, dated 22nd January 1453-4, to Provost Robert McBrair of the lands of Over-Netherwood, Nether-Netherwood and the Langholm, lying in the territory of the Burgh, between the ford called Blackford on the North and the Kelton spring on the South, the lands of Conheath-rig on the East, and the lands of the Laird of Betwixt-the-Waters on the West,

across the Nith, may represent the other side of the preceding transaction: McBrair gave up his lands within the Burgh proper, except Barkerland, in exchange for Netherwood. Thomas Finlai appears as Dean of Guild in connection with the original charter of the first document—Finlay, John Dougan, Michael Goldsmith, Nicolas Haliday and Robert Haliday, burgesses, witness the second document.

The Lord Treasurer's Accounts show King James III at the justice ayres in Dumfries in 1473 and 1488, and James IV in 1494: the cases dealt with are mainly of "depredations" by Border reivers and do not seem to include many townspeople. While the King was in Dumfries on the last day of February 1488 six quarters of velvet to cover a steel breastplate for the King, and broad-cloth for it, were purchased in the town for four pound thirteen shillings.

Although Lincluden, founded in the 12th century by Uchtred of Galloway as a convent of Benedictine nuns (and converted into a collegiate church in the 1390's by Archibald the Grim, using trumped-up charges of immorality to get rid of the nuns—Lady Blanche, the last prioress, is buried, uniquely, in the Cistercian monastery of Dundrennan—Archibald wanted to get a collegiate church the cheapest way he could)—is a mile or so from the mediaeval town, it was always much more closely connected with the town than Holywood Abbey, a mile further out. During this century its provosts were important men of state. There is a safe-conduct to England in 1404 for Elias, the first Provost of the College: his successor Alexander Cairns is shown in 1413 as Chancellor to the Duke of Touraine, Lord of Galloway: in 1410 he acted as a commissioner for negotiating a day of Border truce with the English: two years later he was one of an embassy appointed to go to France on state affairs—adverse winds prevented its going. John Cameron, the third Provost, was a man of great intellect and one of the most accomplished and ambitious clerics of his day. He had previously been secretary and confessor to the Duke of Touraine. Cameron attended the Council of Basle as one of the representatives of the Scottish Church. Soon afterwards he was appointed Keeper of the Great Seal and Auditor of the Exchequer. He left Lincluden to become Bishop of Glasgow and Chancellor of the Kingdom. John McGilhauch, Rector of Parton and secretary to the Duchess of Touraine, followed Cameron: his successor was John Halyburton. John Winchester held the Provostry until 1436 when he became Bishop of Moray. John Methven, a learned doctor of decretals, followed him. Made a Secretary of state during the minority of James II, he went to London with other plenipotentiaries during the war of 1438 and succeeded in negotiating a peace to last for nine years. He was succeeded in 1449 by James Lindsay of Covington: and it was in 1460, during his term of office, that Margaret of Anjou, Henry VI's Queen, stayed at Lincluden with her young son, and there met the Queen Mother of Scotland and the young James III: their deliberations continued for twelve days. Bailie Herbert Gledstanes of Dumfries submitted a note in his account rendered at Edinburgh the following year, which stated that 15/- was to be allowed to the accountant in his next account for a bed-cover and a pair of sheets lost at Lincluden when the Queen was there with the Queen of England: and allowance is accordingly made in the next audit. In 1465 Lindsay was appointed Keeper of the Privy Seal, and as such he and other magnates crossed the Border that year to hold a conference for the redress of grievances, with Commissioners from the English court. In 1483 David Livingstone became Provost: in the summer of 1488 he was followed by Andrew Stewart, a cadet of the House of Garlies. George Hepburn and William Stewart (the latter also of the Garlies family), succeeded him: beginning as Rector of Lochmaben this Stewart eventually became Bishop of Aberdeen and Lord Treasurer of Scotland.

Apart from the meeting of the Queens, the principal event connected with Lincluden during this century was the great meeting held at Lincluden on 18th December 1448 to revise and codify the statutes of Border Law and fix sites for warning beacons around the countryside: the meeting was called by Earl William Douglas as Warden of the West Border. The Border Laws, Leges Marchiarum, under which this area lived until the beginning of the 17th century, were an archaic Teutonic law code, going back probably to the tenth century, and the only law code in Europe under which death did not excuse attendance at a court— the body had to be taken to the court. It included trial by conflict, from which even highly-placed clerics were not excused.

The earliest surviving volume of Dumfries Burgh Court Records begins in 1506, but the extracts from an earlier volume made in 1509 for use in the dispute with Lord Crichton over Courts of Blood (assault and battery cases) carry us back to 16th May 1453: "The Burgh Court of Dumfries held the 16th day of the month of May 1453: suits called, the court affirmed, etc. The which day it is found by an inqueist that John of Aiken is in a bloodwit". The court of 16th March 1473 found that John of Lauder and David Maxwell were in a bloodwit and fined for the drawings of Andro Burnie's blood: doom was given by Mathew Padzane. The court of 23rd November 1473 found that Nycoll of Hutton is in the wrong and in the bloodwit in the action between Martin Potter and him. The court of 22nd November 147- finds Syme Donaldson's wife in an unlaw and bloodwit: the court of the 27th June, 1481, held in the Tolbooth, finds Robert Hamylton in an amerciament and bloodwit for drawing Donald McCredie's blood: Donald is to be recompensed within term of law, five shillings to be paid him within fifteen days and five by the Roodmass. Doom was given by Duncan Martinson. The court of 5th June 1482 found against John Milligan for troubling the town and drawing Farline's blood: doom was given by Jok Haliday. The court of last March 1483 ordained Thom Burnie that he did not strike Esot McGuilhauch nor drew her blood in the place where she and her husband Nicoll of Burnie dwelt. The Head Court of 17th January 1486 fines Thom of Hutton for the wrongous drawing of Robert of Hamilton's blood: doom given by Pawton of Corssane. The Whitsunday court of 21st May 1487 finds John

Bensone not guilty of coming upon John McCreye and striking him violently and drawing his blood and the said John is found guilty of bloodwit and fined. Gilbert Walker gave doom. The court of 13th November 1489 finds Isobell Mark offering to prove that Cristiane Herron wrongously struck her and drew her off a ladder when she was handing up thatch to Nycoll Anderson where he is thatching. The Guild Court held at 9a.m. on 22nd January 1489/90 orders Andrew Patrikson to acquit himself of striking Thom Wilson's wife or drawing her blood and taking a stand of hers. The court of 30th May 1493 fines Davie Black for the wrongous troubling of Thom Blackwood and drawing a knife to him: 20/- is to be paid to Blackwood: doom given by Robert Hamylton. The court of 16th November 1494 fines David Corsby for failing to acquit himself of 10/- to be paid by him to Besse Blackwood because he drew her blood: doom given by John of How.

Finally, one of the witnesses when Robert Lord Maxwell acquired a tenement near the present Castle Street in 1481—a site on and around which the Maxwells developed during the next century the "Maxwell's House" or "Castle", was "Master John Turnbull, Rector of the School of Dumfries"—150 years after the previous mention of a Rector of the School of Dumfries—the Master implies that he had a degree.

The century from 1500 was little smoother in its progress for Dumfries than the two preceding it: an accidental fire in 1504 caused extensive damage in the Burgh—the town obtained £20 remission from the Exchequer in part recompense for the "unexpected" fire which had destroyed among others the house of William Cunynhame who, in April 1501, and perhaps in September 1504, had entertained the King himself. The King granted him £13-6-8 from the fermes of Kirkcudbright to rebuild his house but it had not been completed when he returned in 1505 for then he rested in "John Coupan's chamir". Cunningham's house fronted on what is now Queensberry Square—it would look out then on the New Wark—and contained the famous Painted Chamber: in this house the Reformation was first preached in Dumfries in 1558, and in 1617 it held Royalty again, in the person of James VI and I. The town seems to have been burnt by the English in 1536 and 1542: the English occupation from December 1547 to March 1548, though troublesome, does not seem to have involved fire: a Royal pardon in the name of the child Queen Mary to over 200 Dumfriesians who swore loyalty to England at that time is in Dumfries museum: the English Warden, having heard that there were only "preestes and old women" in the town occupied it, garrisoned the castle (the New Wark, presumably) "and did spoyle and rifle the towne and left nothing in it that thei could carry away, but raised no fyre at that tyme". The "Castle" *could* have been the fine mansion built by the Maxwells in 1545 but it is unlikely. The English occupation of 1570, following on the Battle of Mid Locharwood (the town paid a surgeon to heal a townsman's nose injured in the conflict, in which the Baillies and burgesses had opposed the English force) caused the burning of a few houses: the Maxwells' fine house was destroyed as they favoured the Marian faction: the English were here in the cause of the young James VI. Both English occupations caused the loss of many webs of cloth—Dumfries was very much a textile town at this time, and Dumfries cloth was very clearly popular South of the Border! The last fire in the century was in 1599, coming at a time of plague and famine: James Broun, merchant burgess of Dumfries, complained on 10th June that William White of Wanlockhead had robbed him of £400 ready cash at the lead mines which in conjunction with "the lait unhappie fyre" in the Burgh whereby all his houses, biggings, goods etc. were destroyed, had brought him to "grit miserie and povertie".

The town may or may not have been affected by the plague raging in other parts of Scotland in 1549: certainly its Plague Regulations were entered in the back of the Burgh Court Book in 1548 or 1549—the quarantine area was on the Burgh Muir (Marchmount) beside the Gallows.

Both English occupations were politically inspired: the first was part of "The Rough Wooing" by which Henry VIII hoped to ensure the marriage of Mary Queen of Scots to his weakly son Edward Tudor: the second was an attempt to keep the Marian party, which under Lord Herries was very strong around Dumfries, under control: the 1570 occupation was managed as far as possible in such a way as to avoid harm to the townspeople, but the English took the bells of St. Michael's: on 14th December the Town Council borrowed "the great bell callit Marie and John" from Sweetheart Abbey, and did not return it, to the great dissatisfaction of Abbot Gilbert Broun.

A lively century, therefore, witnessing the Reformation and many other great changes: and a century which from its very beginning is liberally documented, for not only do we have the Lord Treasurer's Accounts, Privy Seal Registers, Register Great Seal, Register of the Convention of Royal Burghs, and similar national sources, but from 1506 we have the detailed almost day-by-day account of the Burgh Court Records which run with hardly a break from then on, and they, with their Town Council proceedings (including annual elections), royal edicts, auction lists of burgesses' possessions, creations of burgesses and the like, and the court proceedings themselves, give a most intimate view of the town and its people.

The first few folios of the Burgh Court records give us the dramatis personae, names most of which follow us through the records to the present day, though some disappear early: here they are, as they occur on the first seven folios of the first Court Book, in and just after 1506: Patrikson (now Paterson): Welsh: Wallis, Wallace, etc.: Prydoun: McBrayr: Ewart: Lawder: Carruthers: McClopine: McClarine: Glover: McCon: Hauch: McMasley: Edgar: Fergusson: McCulzane (now McWilliam): McGrath: Cunningham: Lorimer: McGilhaugh: Grierson: Millar: Maxwell: Martin: Connelson: Newall: Amuligane (Milligan): Durand: Wyld: Rae: McIlrewe: Rigg: McCarthe: Lockhart: Hairstanes: McBurnie: Barbour: Ramsay: Morin: Crosbie: Stewart: Oliver: McCleland: Hutcheon: Gledstaines: Muir: Dungalson: Lindsay: Dougane: Atkinson: Anderson: Atkin: Hunter: Baty: McGhie: Walker: Smith: Mckennan: Donald: Sloane: Gillespie: Tinning: Craik: Hamilton: Cawart: McKennan: McNaught: Morton: McGyrnan: Kirkpatrick: McGlidder: McCaskyn: Crow or Trow: McSkimming: McWhirk: Blackwood: Birkmyre: Shortrig: McCristin.

The first noted election, in October 1519, gives us, among the officers appointed, the Town Orator, Town Minstrel, Ale Cunnars (Ale Testers), and Lynors (for fixing boundaries).

On 5th October 1519 the Records show for the first time a man who became prominent in the town: Schir Herbert McBrair, chaplain, resigned his chaplainship of Our Lady Service in St. Michael's to Schir Hary Mersar: Schir Hary had "to sing and say in the queir with the laiff or the sangstars". In February 1519-20 Schir Hary was made a burgess of the town. There followed a dispute between Schir Hary and the tenant of Our Lady Place: Tom McKennan, the tenant, had failed to lend him a horse to ride to Glasgow or Edinburgh or where he pleased for each of the three years of the tack, for twenty days in each year as part of the rent: Tom Muirhead, McKennan's predecessor as tenant, claimed that McKennan had wrongously intromitted with the plums from the plum orchard in the Lady Yaird. On 10th July 1521 Tom McKennan's wife is charged to prove that she did not promise Schir Hary three shirts at the letting of the Yaird—so evidently, between plums, horse loan and shirts it was quite a problem collecting the chaplain's fees of Our Lady Service!

In May 1522 Schir Hary became joint tenant with four other priests in certain common lands, and in January 1524-25 he signed an agreement with the Council, in company with the curate, parish clerk, and four other priests, to keep the service in the parish church and the quire. On 24th July 1532 Schir Hary is granted a free burgess: and in effectuation of this, on 31st July 1532, John Martin is made burgess and the fee given to Schir Hary "For the play of gude fryday and vitsonday". On 2nd October 1532 Schir Hary, on handing over the "Lady Licht" was enjoined to leave the heirsses (the harrows—triangular harrow-like spiked frameworks which held the candles of the altar) in as good condition as he had received them. On 8th May 1533 Schir Hary receives 40/- from a new burgess for making a new banner for the town—probably for the Corpus Christi procession—and for making stone moulds for casting lead tokens (begging badges) for the poor, and for mending the Millburn Brig. In March 1533-34 a burgess fee is given to Schir Hary because he has made glass windows in Our Lady Aisle, the window of St. Andrew altar, and the St. Christopher Altar and shall make and renew two windows of Our Lady Piety altar, he bearing half the expence of making them. On 7th October 1535 the Burgh threatens to put him and his fellow chaplains out if they do not keep Divine Service according to their contract: however he is still Chaplain of Our Lady Service in 1536, when he makes claim to the rental of a property pertaining to the said service. On 21st April 1536-37 the town grants Schir Hary 10/- for making token-moulds and tokens "to the puyr folkis" at the town's command. On 21st May 1537 Schir hary is forbidden to act as procurator in law court cases: and on 30th May 1537 he is successful in the claim he raised in 1536 regarding a property rental. The first volume ends at this point and when the second surviving one takes up in 1561 there is no mention of him. The "schir" is simply the honorific for any priest—Chaucer's "Sir Priest".

Here, then, in a very small way, is the town's Renaissance Man—priest, playwright, smith, bridge-builder, lead-worker, banner-maker, window-maker, and would-be lawyer—if only his Passion Play had survived! Our area gave birth, of course, to a more famous Renaissance Man, at Eliock below Sanquhar, later in the same century—that Crichton nicknamed "The Admirable".

St. Michael's had, by the Reformation, eight chapels—the altar of St. Anna, founded in 1547 by the Tailor trade: the altar of St. Nicholas, of which the McBrairs were patrons, and the New Wark the endowment; the altar of the Blessed Virgin Mary: the altar of St. Gregory in the chapel dedicated to that Saint, founded by Magister Herbert Gledstanis, and endowed with land and a great stone house called "St. Grigor's Place" (the IHS stone in Dumfries Museum seems to have come from St. Gregory's Place, lying on the west side of John Rawlings Close) (that is, in the Munches Street area, adjacent to Queensberry Square): the Altar of St. John the Baptist: the Altar of St. Andrew, of which the Haliday family were patrons, and Schirs David and Patrick Wallace the chaplains: the Haliblude Altar, founded by the Cunyngham family—part of its endowment was the Rude House lying in the Millgait (Burns Street): the altar of St. Ninian—part of the endowments of this altar were called "Howesoun's Rent", probably the chaplainry without cure of souls, founded in the parish church by the late John Hawys, valued at 20 gold florins, of which Dom. John McBrenny (McBurnie) was chaplain in 1381. Cardinal Beaton elevated his Cross in the church in 1539. William Harlow, an Edinburgh tailor and lay preacher, was brought to the town in October 1558 by Alexander Stewart younger of Garlies, who had a house in the town—the Stewarts of Garlies had been much influenced by English Lollardism. On the morning of 23rd October Harlow preached first at Stewart's house and then moved on to the fore-hall of Robert Cunninghame's house—the famous "painted hall". The Dean of Nithsdale asked the civil authorities to intervene: Archibald Menzies challenged Harlow's authority to preach and David McGhie, notary, took letters against him, in Garlies' lodging, before Schir Patrick Wallace, Curate of Dumfries, and others. Wallace preached a sermon in St. Michael's against Harlow and his teachings, and Menzies asked Bailies David Cunningham and James Rig to arrest Harlow. They refused, and Menzies took instruments against them in St. Michael's.

Schir Patrick Wallace, who here appears as an antagonist ot reform, had been a chaplain in the town as early as 1543: from 1545 he is designated Curate of Dumfries. Antagonist or no, he appears on 21st

January 1561-2 as already Minister of Dumfries, and in fact it is evident
that for some years he and his successor ministered to both Catholic and
Reformed congregations, much to the disgust of the Assembly in
Edinburgh—but Dumfries never took too much thought on Edinburgh
opinion! His successor was the Rector of the Grammar School of
Dumfries. Schir John Turnor, exceptionally for the Grammar School not
an M.A., was "chapellane and sculemaister" on 19th February 1521-22,
and appears in various capacities up to 1545 at least; he may have
continued as schoolmaster also. We first hear of the schoolhouse in the
1548 Rental: it may have been in the same place, on the North side of
Chapel Street, with its gable to the street, for a considerable time before
this. It was a thatched single-storey building, probably of rubble and
puddled clay, 36 feet long, with its "yett" (door) in the gable end: there
was a back door also. Edgar, writing of the moving of the Schoolhouse in
about 1741, says it had stood in the same place for "nigh 200 years".
Master Ninian Dalzell was appointed Master of the Grammar School on
8th November 1558 by the Town Council, at ten merks per year, plus fees
for the pupils. There was to be no other grammar school in the Burgh.

Dalzell weathered the Reformation and continues to appear as
Schoolmaster. By 1567 he was Minister also, with a stipend of £40. In
c1570 Dalzell was accused of enticing people in the Burgh to Catholicism, and reading the Roman Catechism to his scholars, and was deposed
by the Assembly: however he made his peace and continued in both
capacities. The Assembly, in deposing him, had ordered one of the
"doctouris" (teachers) of the school to teach in his place: this shows that
there was more than one teacher under the rector. Dalzell had given up
the ministry of Dumfries to become (simultaneously) minister of
Caerlaverock, Torthorwald, Tynwald and Trailflat before 1574, with a
stipend of £46-13-4, (and this must have involved him in a great deal of
horse travel on the tracks of the time) but seems to have retained his
post as Rector of the Grammar School until his death on 21st April 1587,
and drew his half-yearly £5 as Rector up to that time. He left his books to
his close friend Abbot Gilbert Broun of Sweetheart Abbey—though he
had been Presbyterian Minister of five parishes in his time there was no
doubt where his sympathies lay!

As McDowell says, one of his pupils had been John Welsh, son of the
Laird of Collieston, and later the famous preacher of Ayr. Welsh
frequently ran away from the Grammar School: and in his later years at
the school he "left the school and his father's house and joined himself to
the thieves on the English Border—a reminder of the still disturbed times.

A "Scholemaister", un-named, received 20 merks for 1590-91: he may
have been Mr. Herbert Gledstanis, who graduated M.A. in 1590, and is in
office as schoolmaster in 1601: he became Minister of Caerlaverock and
still later of Troqueer.

One effect of the Reformation should be noted here: in place of a whole
group of clergy, mostly with Master of Arts degrees, the town suddenly
found itself with only one Minister: Friar Hume, Warden of the Grey

friars, became ringer of the church bell, of St. Mary of the Greyfriars, and was given a pension by the town: several of the other Catholic clergy were already papal notaries and took up work as lawyers; Schir Mark Carruthers, a chaplain, son of the Laird of Mouswald, was very prominent among these and his Protocol Book, which has survived, is a mine of information.

Peter Watson, who succeeded Dalzell in 1574 as Minister of Dumfries, was not local, and was a strong Presbyterian, and of fairly humble origins: for all of this he was heartily disliked locally: a Dumfries man broke into his house in his absence and told Mrs. Watson that she and her husband were "land lowperis" (interlopers) and "mischaivit beistis", and that he "wald cutt ane lug out of hir heid and cupill it to hir kirtill taill". A year or two later another man said that he "wald leiffer listen to the mekill devill of hell" preaching in St. Michael's than the Reverend Peter. The Burgh clearly did not greatly favour Presbyterianism, for when the Minister and Reader declined to hold a service on Christmas Day 1574, the inhabitants brought in a Reader of their own and held a service. On Christmas Day 1585 a procession—according to some accounts a civic procession led by the magistrates—marched from the town to Lincluden and celebrated Mass there with full pomp: this ties in with the evidence for a strong Catholic element in the town in the early 1600's.

John Little, Minister of Troqueer in 1562, seems to have been the pre-Reformation priest there too. John Knox preached in St. Michael's in 1562.

As for the two Christmas Day services, it has to be remembered that Christmas was done away with by the reformers: in the 1600's and 1700's we find courts and Town Council meetings held on 25th December and business going on normally, though a few references to "Yuill" linger on.

Trade figures largely during the century: in the 1520's there are several casual references in the Burgh Court Records to Dumfries-owned shipping wintering in the Urr estuary and unloading at Heston: the crew of one ship pled successfully that they had to throw several packs of wool overboard in a storm to save their lives: John Norroway (was he Norwegian?) is accused of neglecting Bailie Rig's ship in the Urr estuary and losing his anchor: a separate document relating to the case of the Grace of God, discharging her cargo "three miles bewest the Watter of Orr" in 1563 shows the Burgh's claim that it had held Customs rights as far West as Burnfoot of Dundrennan "tyme immemoriall, past memor of man" being accepted by the Court of Session in Edinburgh. The ship's master was Arnold Devencentiss and her supercargo Peter Purot. Hector Boece, writing in 1524, mentions Dumfries' trade with France, Spain, the Low Countries, Denmark and Germany, in wool and fine woolen cloth. A ship was wrecked off Carsethorn in 1540: in September 1562 a ship was being loaded at Carsethorn, already the town's outport, for Rochelle and Bordeaux: the Dumfries place-names Rochel (spelt

Rotchell since the 1870's) and Bilbow (the strip of land, extending up from the river, on which Dumfries Museum stands) commemorate Rochelle and Bilbao: both names are certainly not new when they are first casually mentioned just after 1600.

Archibald Douglas' account of the Customs of Dumfries for the 19 months preceding 22nd January 1579, for instance, showed that duty had been paid on 8 sacks and 19 stones of wool, 2 barrels of tar, 5 barrels of vinegar, 13½ barrels of "ploumdames" (prunes), 11 gross of leather laces, 10½ dozen blue bonnets, 1 dozen black bonnets, 19 dozen leather belts, 8 boxes of combs, 6 stones of lead, 4 stones of alum (as a mordant in dyeing cloth), 5 stones 5lb. of pepper and ginger, 4 gross of wool cards, 3 barrels of herrings, 52 stones of flax, 36 bolts of worsteads, 1½ barrels of oil, 96lbs. of hemp, 720 ells of linen cloth, 14 stones of brass and 7 dozen papers of pins. Some of this must have come from England as English imports were the only ones taxed at this time. Douglas had succeeded George Maxwell as custumar at Dumfries: by August 1581 James Geddes of Barnbauchle was custumar. The Burgh wanted rid of him, he being a country gentleman and no burgess, but he was still in office into the next century. Earlier in the century, Nicholl McBrair and William Cunningham had been appointed custumars in 1506, and recorded four ships in the next year. In 155- Provost John McBrair was appointed custumar of English goods imported at the Border. In 1563 Peter Rig was commissioned to collect foreign currency in the town for a trading venture to France: he collected 12 currencies—French crowns, Emperor crowns, heavy crowns, crowns of the sun, ducadouns, Spanish reals, angel nobles, "old English groats", French francs and sous, and so on.

Several times in the 1560's we find James Maxwell, Burgess of Rouen, figuring in the Burgh Court Book as collector for the tax raised in Scottish burghs "for the doun putting of the sextene deneris in the frank"—16 deniers in the franc—an exchange control operation initiated in the time of Marie of Guise: and Dumfries merchants figure also as burgesses of Calais, Dieppe, and Havre: Rochelle and Bordeaux seem to have been the town's principal trading partners: Bordeaux figures in the records as "Burdiehouss in Brattonye"—though Bordeaux was far from Britanny: Burdiehouse near Edinburgh was originally nicknamed for Queen Mary's French retainers who lived there.

Foreign trade is very apparent in the Dumfries Property lists which appear from 1563 to 1585 in the Court Records: when a burgess died intestate the Burgh sold his goods, charged a small fee for doing so, and divided the proceeds of the sale among the heirs, excepting any goods which were known to have been reserved to particular persons: these lists are valuable social documents, as the deceased are of every class and occupation: a priest: the town minstrel: a timber merchant: several cloth merchants: a smith: not only are the lists full of Continental cloths, French hats, imported luxuries like ginger, treacle, licquorice, olive oil, pepper, and tapestries—every house seems to have had several "arras verks", and the old ones went cheaply—what would an "old" tapestry of the 1560's be worth now!: but we hear of a silver "sposing ring" with "ane ruby stane", a silver maser, "ane sapher stane" and so on.

On 21st June we find the Gypsies making a first appearance in the town records: George Faw, Egiptiane, treated with some respect as a visiting foreign notable: "The which day in presence of the Provost, bailies and council of Dumfries convened in the tolbooth of the same James Hannow servant to George Faw egiptiane and Alexander Leiss Scotsman servant to Robert McCulloch burgess in Kirkcudbright upon a writing of the said George Faw sent with them to George Maxwell provost of Dumfries have received from Thomas Batie burgess of Dumfries a canopy of red taffaty, a velvet doublet of cam colour, a signet ring of gold, a sleeveless velvet coat, which the said Thomas Batie had from the said George Faw in security for a debt of twenty pounds thirty pence conform to the said George Faw's letter of the which sum the said Thomas granted him to have received, according to a just account, eighteen pounds ten shillings and so rests thirty shillings and thirty pence, for which he was retained as surety two small gold rings: and so the said Provost and bailies exonerated the said Thomas of the rest of the said sureties by deliverance of the same as above written at their commands: whereupon the said Thomas Batie required act and note in face of court". This, be it noted, some considerable time after the Act which made being a Gypsy a criminal offence!

Returning to the property lists, we find much detail on ordinary possessions—ploughs, harrows, "carrs" (sledges), lances, spears, arrows, arrowheads, bows, arrow bags (never called quivers), swords, hangers, breastplates, steel-bonnets and their coverings and linings, horses and horse tackle—"ane hors sadillit and brydillit" for example—cloth in great variety, much of it imported from the Continent, trades tools of all kinds including stevedores' pack-hooks—there is a mention in the 1530's of packs of goods being washed away from the Whitesands by a flood— musical instruments—a lute, a guitar, a "blawing horn", cymbals (the Dumfries Sheriff Court Book for the 1580's has among the scribbles on its flyleaf a bar of music "for the bussonis" in the old square notation, and a Wigtownshire lawyer's protocol book of the same period was bound in a page of plainsong for Easter Eve of around 1425, from Glenluce or Saulseat Abbeys). Another kind of information comes from a document engrossed in the Burgh Court Book of Dumfries on 27th July 1563: Archibald Welsche, Robert Maxwell, John Rule, John Welsche, James Birkmyre and Michael Birkmyre his son—all blacksmiths—for themselves, their servants and apprentices, fix prices for a very wide range of blacksmith work—plough parts, horseshoes, spades, shovels, yokes, crooks and swees, shackles, garden forks: nails: hoops for brew cauldrons: axes; augers: pinch-bars: fetter locks and so on: and the price of a peck of Sanquhar coal was to be eight pence. All in all, a good example of early trade guild practice in Dumfries.

Still on trade, Morocco leather, an obvious import, figures in the property lists, as does a seal skin and a roe fawn skin. At the beginning of the century, in 1501-04, the Lord Treasurer's Accounts show the King purchasing a heavy gold chain, scissors, and hawk accoutrements, with velvet and broad cloth to cover and line a steel breastplate, in the town.

A feature of the annual rounds of life in Dumfries was the May Play, during which Robin Hood and his lieutenant Little John, as Lords of Misrule, had absolute power in the town: there are references to this in 1534, 1536, 1537 and 1570: Thom Trustre was fined in 1570 for refusing to act Robin Hood for the year. During the May Play, which usually took place on the first weekend in May—the townsfolk wore green and were armed to the teeth. The Muckmen rode out to Dalskairth Wood near the town and "brought in the Simmer" in the form of leafy birch branches (as at Aberdeen in 1496 and St. Andrew's in 1432).

Another town festival was in the Autumn, when the horse-race and the Riding of the Marches, with throwing of apples to the children at the Tounheid Mote, more or less coincided with the Rood Fair and was near the date of the Annual Election of the Town Council. There are two specific references to the Rood Fair—held at the Feast of the Finding of the Holy Rood by St. Helena during the century—one referring to the Bailie Gluvis—a special fee for the Bailies for keeping order during the Fair—in 1521, when the Fair is mentioned as having taken place at the same time and place "Tyme immemorial, past memor of man", and another in the late 1560's objecting to the imposition of "Sheriff Gluvis" on a date regarded as different from that regarded as correct for the Fair "tyme immemoriall, past memor of man"—the same phrase as was used in the Grace of God customs rights case.

One of the most serious melees in the town during this turbulent century was that of 31st July 1508. This arose over the clash between Lord Crichton of Sanquhar, Sheriff of Nithsdale, and the town under Provost Nicholas McBrair over the town's right to hold Courts of Blood—that is, to try assault and battery cases in the Burgh Court, the Sheriff claiming that he alone had this right, while the Burgh quoted Minutes back to 1453, and 300 years of precedents, for its right. On the third day Lord Robert Crichton rode into the town with a strong body of horsemen and had his Depute, John Crichton of Hartwood, go to the Tolbooth and hold a court of "bloodwits". The Provost objected, Hartwood denied the Burgh's right, the Provost reaffirmed it and retired. In the street was Lord Maxwell and a large body of men and many of the lairds of the district. Weapons were drawn, and in a little while a wild melee of struggling men swung to and fro in the wide street. The Crichtons broke and fled. Three lairds were killed in the action and several men on each side, while there were several seriously injured. This became known as the "Battle of Whitesands", though all the evidence suggests that it started in the High Street.

As an example of the cases held in the Sheriff Court, Marioun Paris complained against George Scott dwelling in College of Lincluden and several others before the Sheriff, Lord Crichton, in Dumfries Tolbooth on

21st May 1500, claiming that they had come to her house, she being "at goddis pece", and "masterfully reft and made spouliatioun of eight score threaves of barley and oats, amounting to 3 chalders of Nithsdale measure, nine score creels of fuel, worth two merks: a feather bed with bolster and covering which were taken away to Lochmaben, worth £2-5/-: a stand bed and many other things"—a useful reminder of how unsettled even "peaceful" times were—when, for instance, the Abbot of Holywood's tenants had to petition for an interdict to prevent him calling them out so often on raids, as they could not get their farm work done.

This general insecurity is of course reflected in the Burgh's affairs: on 18th June 1522, for instance, the Council decided that each acre of common land should pay two terms rent in advance and "has ordained Thom McKnacht to receive the same to buy their guns and powder and all other things that is needful for the common profit."

The meeting of the "Secreit Consale" (Town Council affairs were of course secret, by common practice and under the town's traditional "auld and lovit sett" (constitution))—on 27th or 28th May 1523 tells us a good deal about this side of the Burgh affairs: exceptionally, it brings in Lord Maxwell, Earl of Nithsdale, as "oversman", presumably as Warden of the West Marches: the meeting was "Chosin and suorn befoir my Lord Maxwell": Maxwell and his "kin and friends" undertake to pursue any malefactor wanted by the bailies who has escaped from Dumfries: the Council also ordained that when the Common Bell (presented by William Carlyle Lord Torthorwald to St. Michael's Church in 1443, transferred to the Burgh in 1451, and now in Dumfries Museum, having been rung for 30 years at the Guid Nychburris festival) was rung all the inhabitants should come "incontinent" to the Tolbooth Stair, the bell only being rung for a great cause: also that every man be ready on the market day with his "gear"—armour and arms—upon him and sufficient weapons in his booth "redy to pas with the saids aldirman (provost) and bailies to resist ony partyss doand ony trouble within the toun'"—just as Wigtown town council ordained in 1513 that all the burgesses assemble fully armed "when the provost and bailies hes ony business ado". The earlier paragraph of the Dumfries meeting also rules that anyone resisting the bailies or their officers in the execution of their duties shall be imprisoned, banished, and lose their freedom as burgesses.

The Records give us several other accounts of civic activity of this kind: later in the century, for instance, we have the populace being summoned to build a defensive ditch: even women had to carry "mands" (baskets) of soil: watch and ward was kept up meticulously: "oversmen" or "quartermaisters" were appointed for each quarter of the town who were to have complete command in emergency, under the Provost and Bailies: from time to time the town was summoned by the King to provide armed men "bodin in feir of veir" (armed for war) to be sent to him at Linlithgow or some other place of tryst. Oddly enough, it is in this century that we have a woman burgess (one of the two known—the other is a century later): so far as can be checked she was allowed, exceptionally, to pay a substitute on the night watch: she seems (like her successor) to have been a widow carrying on her late husband's business. The town's military and other commitments seem to have strained its resources: on 5th April, 1524, when John McIlrewe, Common Barber, applied for a salary of 40/- Scots per year the town found that the common purse was "bot wyke and superexpendit": so instead of a salary he was granted the town's shop to shave in and John Barber and the other barbers in the town were forbidden the use of it.

The Tolbooth was slated quite early in the century and by the 1520's had a clock, which had to be protected by a sheet from meal-dust on market days. The Sandbed Miln and its cauld (weir) upstream at Stakeford are first mentioned in the late 1520's. The Prison was built by the town at the Privy Council's command and was probably completed by 1583: the 16th-century stones now built into the Midsteeple came from it, after most of a century in the summerhouse at Knockhill near Hoddam.

The religious houses do not figure very prominently during the century: Friar Robert Little, Warden of the Greyfriars, was one of Lord Herries' hostages hung at Carlisle when he changed sides in the midst of the Battle of Drumlanrig (12 were hung-hence Repentance Tower): Charles Hume, the last Warden, was like his predecessors an unassuming man who seems to have been well liked in the town: he was kept on to ring the bells of the Convent's Church of St. Mary after the Reformation: the Chapel of the Willies (Willows) on the Irish Street-Bank Street corner, known as the Rigs' Chapel, was in the hands of that family at the Reformation and an immigrant dyer, one Abercado, used it as a dye-house: he was most inefficient, repeatedly spoiling cloth, and was finally forbidden by the Town Council to practice his craft. Robert Douglas, Provost of Lincluden at the Reformation, was a domineering man who disposed of the College's lands without much regard for the wishes of the prebends. The Maxwell family built a fine mansion on their lands on and near the present site of Greyfriars' Church in 1545: this was destroyed by the English in 1570 and the still finer, semi-castellated mansion which arose in 1572 in its place made extensive use of the fabric of the Greyfriars' building adjacent and of the orchard and garden ground of the Friars. The Greyfriars' church of St. Mary was much used for arbitrations and other legal business, just as St. Michael's Church was the place fixed for a Dumfries man who had attacked a fellow-burgess with a knife to beg his pardon on bended knee, proferring the hilt of the knife to his victim. Finally, the Abbot of Holywood appears for several years after the Reformation in the Burgh Court Records, being pursued for the price of a pair of "brekis"—the breeches in question having presumably been purchased just before the Reformation and the Abbot finding difficulty, on his slightly reduced post-Reformation income, in raising the price!

The annual elections, fully recorded in the Court books, as previously mentioned, show the appointment of Council and officials such as ale

cunners, lynors, minstrel, and burgh orator: another appointment in
these lists is that of the byrlawmen or barleymen: these men held the
byrlaw—burgh law—court which dealt with disputes between townspeople: as described in 1519 it was a "curt of gud nychburrhede"—court
of good neighbourhood; and it was this reference that gave G.W. Shirley
the name for the Guid Nychburs festival which he and Darlison started
in 1932.

There are other sources of information useful in this century: these
include the Protocol Books of several local notaries—Herbert Anderson
and Mark Carruthers, from the 1530's, Cunningham and Anderson in
1560's and later: some of the Protocol Books—Carruthers' book, for
instance—tell us a good deal about Church furnishings and ceremonial at
the induction of a young priest at Lochmaben and—a final mercantile
touch—on 2nd February 1539-40 John Martin, Burgess of Dumfries,
William McBurnie, and Gilbert McCustin bind themselves to pay John
Neilson in Whithorn ten shillings a ton weight for building a ship in the
town of Dumfries, plus a bonus on completion.

The Property Lists show how well almost every individual was armed:
the Court Book carries from time to time Royal orders for Wapenschaws:
the Siller Gun, not actually presented until 1617 as a trophy for the
annual wapenschaw, seems almost certain nevertheless to have been
made in 1588 as all the other known examples are of that year and the
Provost's initials on the Gun suit that year and not 1617. The "Bairns'
Bow Butts", the archery range on the Whitesands just above the Sandy
Entry, figures in the Records during this century.

It is during this century also that we first hear of the town's efforts to
cobble the streets and to keep them clean: the lockman—executioner—is
appointed Swine Slayer, to kill pigs found loose on the streets: we hear in
the 1530's of "innocent barnis" herding pigs into St. Michael's
Churchyard, where they are "wirtand up the dede crocis and grene
gravis" and the long line of edicts about keeping geese, chickens, goats
and the like under control during the crop planting and growing season
begins. The Records also show us much of the town's agriculture: the
lands of Wolfgill, Barkerland, Kingholm and so on, under run-rig
cultivation or in fallow with the townspeoples' horses and cattle grazing
on them: the town's Royalties still extending in a wide aureole around it,
supporting it with food and fuel: the town's vigilance against intrusion
by neighbouring lairds as witness the important and interesting
Perambulation of the town's bounds with Carnsalloch in 1518, which
settled a dispute going back 40 years or more (a later Laird of
Carnsalloch was to signal his displeasure with the Burgh, around 1712,
by blocking the main Edinburgh Road just beyond Dalscone by felling
trees across it!) The Whitsunday tack lists, year by year until the late
1530's, show the townspeople renting their "sowmes" of the common
land and of the fishings: by the 1560's a good deal of these "tacks" had
been converted to feus. Council tenants often sold the "kindness"—that
is, the right of inheritance—of these tacks: the Council, usually in the

person of a bailie, had to approve the transaction.

There are several mentions of the Bridge during this century: by 1522 the Burgh had a "Brig Maister", appointed annually, and from then on part of the Burgesses' entry fees was allocated to the upkeep of the Brig. The Friars leased half the Brig dues to Edward Johnstone in Nunholm and, on his death, to his son John (the second lease dated 1557). The Burgh acquired this half from Johnstone's grand-daughter on 31st July 1623. The other half passed formally from the Friars to the Burgh in 1569 but had clearly been held by the Burgh in practice since at least 1522. In 1563 both Ports were repaired and the causeway sorted and, on 22nd March 1564, Thomas Barker was ordered "to make up the Cawsaye on the Brig". In 1576 repairs costing £200 were undertaken. An appeal was made to the Convention of Burghs on 10th September 1592 "for support for the reparing thair decayit Brig".

The Auld Brig has seen much pageantry and history in its day. The Douglases and McCullochs paying their blanch rent of a red rose: a succession of Stuart kings on grim business, humble (once barefoot) pilgrimage or in brilliant cavalcade with their Queens—last among them Mary Queen of Scots in 1563 with James VI and I in 1617: the cuirassed dragoons led by Claverhouse or Lagg thundering across in search of "Whigs" or returning with some doomed countryman: the Baillies and burgesses setting out to burn Kirkcudbright and massacre its inhabitants in the 1590's (trade rivalry—fortunately for Kirkcudbright the tide was in the surrounding ditch and the Dumfriesians could not cross): the five suspect witches dragged across tied hand and foot in the June dawn in 1671: Provost Maxwell fleeing in his shirt on a dark night in December 1688, his cloak bag full of Burgh and State papers—he was caught and handed over to the Privy Council: boys taking beer, cheese and rolls across to the Hebronites during the 1715 Rebellion: Robert Burns plodding over on his daily duties—the writer in July 1981 leading twenty-odd Lebanese lads at the gallop across the Bridge, they waving their cedar-tree flag and singing their national anthem—the first time the Bridge had seen *that*!

Returning to the theme of 16th-century Dumfries, the following "view" of the town around 1560 may be of use. Mediaeval towns had to support their inhabitants: so Dumfries, as a Royal Burgh, was surrounded by its Royalties, a wide aureole of farmland, moor and moss, on which the citizens grew their food, pastured their flocks, and gathered their peats, whins and bracken for fuel: the river fishings, in the town's possession, furnished a rich store of salmon. At the extremity of the royalties downstream, at Kelton, the humble but nutritious flounder was available. Peats, incidentally, could be dangerous to the unscrupulous—if you were caught stealing your neighbour's peats in the Moss or from his stack, a Town Council Act laid down that you were branded on the cheek with the key of the Town Clock heated red-hot in a fire of the stolen peats.

We begin, then, North of the town. The 1518 Perambulation with

Carnsalloch shows the boundary of the royalties, or commonalty, running by Dalscone, Dargavel, out into the Lochar Moss—the Burgh had the peat rights of the whole Moss south to Kelwood by grant of King Robert the Bruce—and by Craigs and Kelwood over the ridge to Keltonthorn. Already by 1560 some of this had been alienated, usually by exchange of feu: the town rentals of the 1520's and 30's still showed the burgesses taking their "sowms" of land annually at Kirkland Mote, Wolfgill, Barkerland, Hannay's Thorn (Noblehill) and on the Marchhill. A little later, in the 1560's, the town acquired the Friars' lands on Corbelly Hill on the West side of the river. Kelton was, incidentally, the highest point on the Nith to which ocean-going vessels from Rochelle or Bordeaux—the town's most usual trading partners—could come.

The town had grown up on the well-drained ridge of agricultural land protected by the Moss on the East, the river on the West, and the Mill Burn on the South, at several good fords across the river, and also on the Roman road up Nithsdale. Only from the North, along this road, was access by enemies fairly easy and it was to the muddy or lore (our modern Scots world "lair" for mud) Burn that the citizens were called in emergency—hence the town's slogan "A Loreburne". Coming round the town from North through East to South, the Martinton Ford crossed the river about a mile North of the town, near the Nunholm, which had belonged to the nuns of Lincluden across the river. From Dalscone Loch a stream flowed past the Sand Loch, passing the Auld or Merch-Hill Dyke (one of the town's earlier protective earthworks), to enter the Mill Burn near Milldamhead, at the near end of the Far Gallowrig. At the outer end of the Far Gallowrig was Hannay's Thorn, now Noblehill: beyond this was Locharmoss. The road to Nunholm and Martinton Ford ran out of the Tounheid Port, opposite the farther end of the Academy, past the Lochans, the Langlands (where the town's pottery kilns seem to have been—it is a windy ridge suitable for the purpose, outside the town for fire risk, and much pottery (and glazed trial-piece pebbles) has been found there), Cunninghill—there may have been a rabbit warren here at some time—the rabbit, the "cunning", was a domestic animal—and Creynlarimoss, part of the Braidmyre and across the Poindfield Burn. The Gallows Close, the modern Moffat and Edinburgh Road, left the town by Lochmabengate Port, on English Street, opposite the mouth of Shakespeare Street, passing the Laripott Bog, where Hoods Loaning is now, the Crystal Chapel on its hillock (St. Mary's Church is there now), opposite which a track left the road to go through the bog towards the Mill Burn: past the Craneberry Moss, then past the Watslacks Bog, where the S.M.T. Car Sales and Garage and the railway is now, past Punnershill, on past the Gallows Myre (always these bogs!), past the Gallows itself on the end of the Gallowrigg (the Gallows Flosh flowed down the other end of the Rigg to flow into the Mill Burn at Milldamhead), past the town quarantine area at Deidmanshirst, Gallowsmuir, Scabbit Isle and the Black Loch, later a haunt of curlers, with the Bane Loaning nearby, past the Greystanes Bronze Age stone

circle and Greystaneflatt beside the Black Loch, past the Auld or
Merchhill Dyke and the Dow Corse—the Dove Cross, now Dhucorse. To
the East of the town, towards Irvine Place and St. Joseph's Sports
Ground, lay the Berelandis—the Barley Lands—and the Barcarland,
where cloth was "barked" in pits fed by the Mill Burn, with a ditch
between them and the Moss. The Mill Burn itself rose between the First
and Second Craigs, on what is now Craigs Farm, in the Gore Loch, and
flowed as the Wolf Gill into the Gill ("Leech") Loch on Georgetown Road
(drained, like Dalscone, Sand, Black and Gore Lochs, College Loch and
Reid's Dub, during last century), through Barcarland, Berelandis and
Milldamheid—that is, through Irvine Place, under the railway line near
Eastfield Road S.M.T. depot and down Millburn Avenue, past today's
Government Buildings, under the railway near Bullock's Bridge, along
the embankment at the side of Broom's Road, by Robertson's Sawmill,
that is, the Watslacks bog—past the Laripotts Bog, where, in the middle
of the present Queen Street, the Lore Burn flowed into it—and so into
the Millhole Dam with its tanneries, kilns and bark-holes. The oval bog
opposite Tounheid Mote, where Catherine Street and Lower Rae Street
now lie—the Library basement still floods—had two outlets, one a small
stream running N.W. to enter the Nith just South of the Langlands, and
the Lore Burn flowing S.E. parallel to Yairdheids—Loreburn
Street—and crossing Lochmabengate (English Street) just outside the
Lochmabengate Port and running down Shakespeare Street and Brooke
Street to its junction with the Mill Burn under Queen Street. A still
shorter stream, the Gutter of Calsay, rose near the upper part of
Munches Street and ran down Bank Street. As it acquired a load of
smells passing through the Flesh Mercat it gave Bank Street or
Cawart's Vennel the name of the "Stinking Vennel".

Going South, the Cat Strand or Friezehole Runner, rising in a lochan
near the Berelandis, crossed St. Michael Street and ran through the
Goosedubs Bog between that street and the river to enter the river at the
lower end of the present Stank harbourage just below St. Michael's
Bridge: and the vigorously-flowing small stream which rose in Reid's
Dub (a dub was a particularly wet bog) ran through the ditch of
Castledykes castlestead (as it still does) and into the river just above
Castledykes gate.

Within the town there was a bog on the Plainstones in the central
space, opposite the English Street opening, near the Fish Corse Hill, and
another bog where Yairdheids (Loreburn Street), runs into
Lochmabengate (English Street).

The town was much hillier then than now—there was a hillock where
Johnstone and Clark's Works are now, at the Academy Street end of
Loreburn Street: the Chapel Hill between High Street and Queensberry
Street, behind Rankine's, was the highest of the town's hillocks: the
Girss Hill rose around the Mercat Corce, where the uphill end of the
Midsteeple block now is—evidently grassy, by its name—the Fish Corse
Hill rose about where the fountain now is on High Street, opposite the

mouth of English Street. There was a sharp hillock between High Street and Irish Street down towards Nith Place, and the Clerk Hill rose just outside the Kirkgate Port, between the mouth of Burns' Street and Broom's Road. The Aldermanhill was a little further South, where Aldermanhill House is, in the grounds of St. Joseph's College. Clerkhill was one of a group of ecclesiastical names surrounding St. Michael's Church: just behind the church was the Archdene Croft and, South of that, the Vicar Meadow, the Vicarage Lands, and the Glebe Lands. The Barnslaps, the pathway off St. Michael's Street with the town's barns along it, probably lay on the Vicar Meadow.

Returning to the river north of the town, there was a cauld or weir across the river opposite Tounheid Mote, just above the Stake Ford, a ford marked by stakes in the riverbed and one of the principal routes to the West, also at this time known by its older name of Poliwaddum—the Stream Wade. From the cauld ran a mill lade, down through the Over or Green Sandbeds which began about this point—the river was not so far in on the Dumfries side then—right down through the Nethersandbeds—the Whitesands—or Laigh Sandbeds—with the Bairns' Bow-Butts just above the present Sandy Entry, where the boys practised that necessary art, archery: down past the Willies—Willows, which bound the river-bank—at the foot of Bank Street—and on down what is now the Dock Park. Goods, such as salt herring in barrels, brought up the river by boat, with packs of cloth, were stacked on the Whitesands by the river and, occasionally, were swept away by floods: the Town Council frequently passed regulations forbidding laying heavy boxes, barrels or packs on the Willows lest they be damaged and the river bank weakened.

The Sandbedmiln stood just downstream from the end of Friars' Vennel: the mill lade from the Caul at Stakeford ran through the terminal pier of the Bridge, in the middle of the lane between Whitesands and Brewery Street, opposite the White Hart Hotel. Friars' Vennel was—and is—aligned, not on the Bridge, but on the excellent ford, now submerged by the water held back by the present Caul: after crossing the river the road swung round an earthwork just behind the site of the Old Bridge House, curving round to become the How Gate, the hollow way, the present Howgate Street.

Now for the town itself, high on its hogback ridge, well above flood water—the town did not extend below the Vennel-Irish Street crossing, the Freirport, until the 1560's, when the New Toun began to take shape and gradually worked down through the orchards of apples and plums which lay on the riverward side of Irish Street (the Irishgate). Coming in from the North through Tounheid Port, with Tounheid Mote, a good deal higher than it is now, looming above—it was the place where citizens settled arguments, the fiery Perilous John Newall saying "Alas, would I had thee on the Mote!"—and the mouth of Yairdheids, now Loreburn Street, part of the access road which as "Under the Yairds"—Irishgate or Irish Street and Shakespeare Street—the two sections were sometimes called the Barnraws-Shakespeare Street was Nether Barnraws—and

"Yairdheids"—encircled the town, taking the produce from the "yairds" behind the tenements on the main streets—each yaird had its gate on this back street, and the Toun Herd collected the stock from the yairds each morning to take it out to the common grazings: vegetables and some cereal crops were grown in the Yairds and pigs and hens kept there in the sowing and crop-growing season.

One passed a number of tenements on the West side of the road and the hillock at the mouth of Yairdheids and a few tenements on the East side—a rather down-at-heel quarter with several forges—derelict tenements here, as elsewhere in the town, were usually gifted by the Town Council to the Friars—then swung round into what is now Church Crescent, then dominated by the fine house built by the Maxwells, Lords Nithsdale, in 1545, which was to be replaced in 1572 after its destruction by the English in 1570 by a still more palatial structure—looking something like McClellan's House in Kirkcudbright—which later became known as the Maxwells' Castle and gave its name to Castle Street.

The track to the Stakeford passed on the riverward side of the Castle, past the Church of St. Mary, the church of the Community of Greyfriars, still in residence under their Warden, Charles Hume, and the orchard ground and gardens of the Friars. Going down the Vennel one passed the high gable-ends of the tenements on one's left and the conventual buildings of the Friars, in the same style, on the right, down to the Freirport—later, as the New Toun grew, to be moved to the middle of the Bridge to become the Brig Port—where the vehicle-passing place now is near the centre of the Bridge.

Returning to the broad central street, the King's High Street (or Cowgate), one comes out of the Vennel into the Rattonraw, that part of the street opposite the mouth of Chapel Street—the name suggests that the town's arms practice field had once been here—and, turning down the High Street, one passes on the left the compact highly-defensive block between High Street and Queensberry Street, known as the Midraw—the Hole i' the Wa' Inn is part of it and was certainly by the 1580's, if not before, already an alehouse—and on the right the tenements as far as Perrisoun's Herb Garden which lay about where the mouth of the Long Close is now. Past the Midraw one came to the Newark, a massive tower-castle type of building, something like Threave or Closeburn. Here, where Queensberry Square now is, under the shadow of the Newark, was the Mercat. The Mercat Corce seems to have been on the Northern slope of the Girss or Grass Hill, under the northern end of the shop forming the northern part of the Midsteeple—the Steeple still 150 years in the future.

To the East of the Mercat Square, near the Newark, lay several large tenements—St. Gregory's, St. Nicholas—the rents of which—like those of the Newark tenants—supported chaplainries or altarages in St. Michael's Church. On the South side of the Square, about where the present Electricity Showrooms are, stood the great Painted Hall of the Cunninghams which had housed Royalty at the beginning of the century, had more recently seen the first preaching of the Reformation in the town in 1558, and was to see Royalty in residence again in 1617.

Continuing South down the slope of the wide central space (no Midsteeple then), one passed the Tolbooth, built in the 1480's, with the Town Bell mounted in its chimney and the town clock which, for thirty years and more, had given the town its time. To the right Cawart's Vennel—Bank Street—ran stinking down towards the river: on its right side, just after crossing Irishgate, lay the Chapel of Our Lady of the Willies, just about to be converted to a dyeworks in the early post-Reformation years.

On down the Soutergate, passing the bog and thorn-tree and forge on the Plainstanes and, round the rise of the Fish Corce Hill, the mouth of Lochmabengate, the town's main route to the Northeast: and down Soutergate, past the hillock which rose over Nith Place, through the old Soutergate Port, to be demolished in the early 1600's. Where Nith Place is now, the Irishgate section of Under-the-Yairds swung round to become the present Shakespeare Street which continued to the Lochmabengate Port. Yairdheids or East Barnraws further up Lochmabengate, now Loreburn Street, continued the line.

Off Mill Hole, on the side away from the river, lay the Mill, the Millhole Dam and the tanneries and bark-holes and kilns associated with it. The Millgate took off behind the Mill and linked up with the main street again: for the Soutergate on crossing Milnburnbrig became the Kirkgate, which climbed the hill towards St. Michael's and passed the heavy bastle-house called the Penthouse-End protecting the Kirkgate Port-both of these lay at the Kirkgate (St. Michael Street) end of the Millgate (now Burns' Street). The Milnburnbrig existed well into the 1700's.

On then through the Port and up the hill, past Clerkhill, the Kirk with its fine square Gothic tower and its green churchyard where children had to be restrained from herding the town's pigs lest they root up the crosses and disturb the graves. Just before the Kirk was reached the footpath to the Moss, now Broom's road, took off. It passed the Laripotts or Corn Lands and Watslacks on its way along the Mill Burn. On down the main street, past the Goosedubs and over the Catstrand or Friezehole Runner—which ran through the Vicar Meadow, the Glebe Lands, and the Vicarage Lands. The Archdene Croft lay just behind the Church. On past the Castledykes with the town quarry where, when masons were available, stone was cut for the use of the citizens, and the Chapel of Our Lady of the Casteldikis, both on the right side of the road, and, on the left, a little above the road, the Pykit, or pointed, Cross, guarding the main road to Kirkblane, Bankend, and England. Below the road was the important crop and grazing land of Kingholm, with a ditch on its East side: above the road rose Kirkland Mote.

There, then, was the town—thatched roofs, central hearths, earth floors, cruck beams—pigs, geese, chickens, running the patchily cobbled streets with their central gutters and rooting in the midden-heaps beside the doors or close-mouths—for few doors opened on the main street as the half-timbered wattle-and-daub houses turned their gables to the street and were entered by wooden stairs up the closes. Filling the streets the colourful townsfolk and the drabber countrymen mingled: the Town Minstrel in his "blew reid and zallow" cloak: plaids and blue bonnets clashing with fashionable Elizabethan clothes: flamboyant Border reivers like "Reid-Cloak", chief of the Bloody Bells: townsmen, like Potter Lumisdaill, Evill Thom Maxwell and perilous John Newall, he of the quick temper: female worthies like Bessie "Half Dawark" Maxwell: all the men with hand ever ready on sword or quhinger, a full kit of weapons ready at their market stalls as the town regulations demanded: peat-stealers being dragged up to the tolbooth stairs to have their cheeks branded with the clock key heated red-hot in a fire of the stolen peats: the Trone, the municipal scales, standing at the Croce: legal announcements or Royal proclamations being made at the Tolbooth stairs, those "Rainbow Stairs" which survived till 1935—as, for example, when in the 1580's a Royal messenger brought a demand for several years of outstanding taxes: he was greeted by the Provost, indeed, on the Stairs, before the assembled townspeople, as re-enacted each year now at the Guid Nychburris Festival: but the Provost made as if to wipe his bottom with the paper, tore it up and threw it away—thus did the town treat its King and Government: but this time the King was strong enough and later the town had to pay a heavy fine *and* the taxes! and perhaps a small detachment of men fully armed—"Bodin in feir of veir"—being sent off at Royal request to rendezvous at Linlithgow as part of a royal host.

　　Having left the 16th century behind us, we start on the 17th. Even more markedly than the previous century, the hundred years from 1600 yield a wealth of source material—so much so that many books could be written on the history of Dumfries for this period, each covering a different field. The period starts with a gap in the Court Books, which fail in 1588 and do not take up again (this is simply a matter of decay and loss, of course), till about 1612: however the Privy Council Register yields a great deal and there is much in the way of property deeds, litigations and so on. In 1616 the Marriage Register begins: the Kirk Session Minutes, a positive mine of social material, take up in 1635 and run continuously from then on: the Presbytery Records run from 1628: the earliest of the trades minute-books starts in 1612: the Treasurer's Accounts, a very detailed source, begin in 1631 and are reasonably complete from then on. The Burgh Court Records continue in the old form, including Council business, from 1612 apparently until the 1630's: Town Council Minutes proper begin in 1643 and are continuous from then: there is a gap in the Burgh Court Records from 1636 but these begin again, now devoted entirely to Court business, from 1658, in massive volumes and run on through the next century. As mentioned above, the Incorporated Trades minute book begins in 1612: that of the Fleshers in 1658, the Glovers and Skinners in 1650: the Hammermen

have a sumary from 1601 although their detailed minutes only begin in
1703: the Shoemakers' minutes take up in 1658, and the Weavers in
1654. Loose documents—accounts, petitions, correspondence and so
on—begin to be abundant in 1650 and there are many thousands
thereafter—complete billetting bundles for the Dragoons in the 1670's
and 1680's: church seat dispositions: evidence of witnesses in court
cases: pharmacists' accounts—with such herbs as tussilago, horehound
and maidenhair prominent: application by the Lord of the Muckmen for
their annual beer money when they bring in the summer from Dalskairth
and hold their race: entry slips for horses running in the local races as
Stoop: an account for a wide variety of sweets, cakes, biscuits, figs and
other dried fruit from Carlisle: a letter from an Edinburgh Baillie to a
Dumfries Baillie reminding him that he is to send him three stone of
cheese for a "Dumfries Fry"—evidently a local speciality: notes in
shorthand on the back of a tailor's account: wine and boarding accounts
in great variety, with pipes and tobacco figuring strongly—they first
appear in the Treasurer's Accounts in the late 1640's: a reference in the
fragmentary Minute Book of the Company of Merchants Adventuring
from Dumfries in 1682, referring to the attack by the burgesses and
baillies of Kirkcudbright on the Company's ship "Adventure", returning
from Bordeaux laden with wine, in Balcary Bay: orders to the Council to
burn condemned witches: boxes of petitions, ranging from a claim by a
household for the value of blankets soiled by the blood of a dragoon
billeted on them who had cut his throat to appeals for better conditions
by prisoners: letters to Holland by Dr. Archibald and by Dumfries
Merchants, to the Scottish Factor in Holland: charity is paid to "ane
poor shipwracked Polonien": a clergyman, his wife and ten children are
helped on their way to the Tweed valley after being taken by French
privateers in the North Channel; a crippled woman "hurled in a barrow"
is given money to help her to Moffat to take the waters: a women begs
for surgical help for her son's acute gravel—"his yeard is like to volt fra
him": a clergyman, imprisoned as a Covenanter, is pardoned because
when the Dalry men cleared the prison he said he would not go until
properly released by the authorities: the Commissary Court Records
show in great detail the evidence against the many witches tried and
sentenced in the town: the Kirk Session Minutes show an apprentice lad
flogged through the streets and banished, after imprisonment, for
having come out on the street in his sister's clothes as a lark: an old
woman is imprisoned for "having held needless discourse anent the
purchase of a hen" on the Sabbath Day: eminent townspeople are heavily
fined for being married just across the Border and ordered to remarry:
the Sheriff Officer orders a woman to worship him on bended knee, or if
not him his staff of office, or if not it the Devil: pregnant unmarried girls
are pursued and arrested in case they flee the punishment for their sin:
the Accounts and loose documents give us a detailed picture of the
development of the Grammar School throughout the century—
thatching, benches, fetterlocks, the appointment in the 1640's of

Mathematics and Music teachers: school amateur dramatics—a performance of "Bellum Grammaticale", written in the 1630's by one of the
Annandale Irvings—the parts of speech of Latin grammar armed and
fighting on the stage, the performance put on in 1672: the Privy Council
tells us of the lively year of 1607—a man tries to strangle a boy with a
garter and throws him in the Mill Dam in March: the King's messenger
comes through the town in May, to find the inhabitants dressed in green
and armed for the May Play: a couple of Bailies' sons take up the cry "A
Loreburne", their fathers repeat it: shots are fired and horses wounded:
the Messenger and his men flee: church burials have been outlawed some
years before, a family break open the church door with tree-trunks and
bury a dead relation within, whereupon another family hurry home, grab
a corpse, and bury it, and a third family dig up an uncle and are about to
bury him when the Law finally turns up: Herbert Cunningham, Sheriff
and Town Clerk, composing himself in his pew in church for the service
when the Irvings break in, beat him, smash up his pew and cast it out in
the aisle: he gets it repaired and the following week the process is
repeated and he is threatened with death: two other cases of the same
thing, with different pew-holders and assailants, later in the year—life in
the town was certainly not dull. Customs records show us a lively
international trade from about 1612 through into the late twenties, when
the shipping records fail—cloth, wool and hides exported, mordants,
dried fruits, French hats, writing paper, sweets, fine cloth and clothing,
imported—plus timber, iron and brass. These records take up again in the
1660's with lively trade re-established—a wealth of information on
exports and imports, and Customs officers being ordered in 1685, the
Killing Time, to search ships about to leave the town's outport at
Carsethorn for any Covenanters who might be hiding aboard in an effort
to escape Lagg, who gives the order: very detailed expences for the
voyage in 1694 of the "Henrietta" of Lagghall, owned by Lagg and
captained by Robert Grierson, to and back from Liverpool, and of the
voyage of the "Fortune" of Whitehaven to Donaghadee in 1696, in the
famine years, for tallow and grain (these two in the loose Burgh
documents): the construction of a metalled wagon road, one of the first in
Scotland, from Dumfries to Carsethorn in the 1660's: the list could go on
for pages! The loose Burgh Documents have been listed in precis form by
the writer: deeds and processes have been calendared by the late Dr. R.C.
Reid. A complete rental of burgage lands for 1674 has been printed from
the manuscript in the Burgh Records.

      This, then, is the raw material, much of which was not accessible to
McDowall: what picture emerges of the town during this century?

      We find it in 1600 still with a strong Catholic element, and just
emerging from a succession of hard years of famine, fire and plague:
trade is picking up: the town has enough resilience in 1619 to weather the
disaster of the collapse of the Bridge and to repair it within a year from
its own resources. The Accounts give a lively picture of growing
prosperity during the 1630's: education, particularly, was advancing

rapidly in the town during this and the next decade. More troublous
times followed from 1638, the Burgh first on one side and then the other
in the long civil war: the end of 1650 and the beginning of 1651 was a
particularly black time, with large bodies of English troops passing
through, demanding billets and fodder and destroying as much as their
horses ate: the Welshman Colonel Alured who in May 1651 seized all the
town's cattle and held them until the town sent him ransom to Hawick
(this is the literal "blackmail") is typical of this time: the Town Council
Minutes give a picture of continuous military exactments, stents having
to be raised at a few days' notice or money borrowed at high interest and
on difficult conditions from local lairds: we see the Treasurer announcing
that the stent can at last be reduced a little and the very next day
another officer and his troop turns up and demands a large sum which
has to be met by borrowing. After 1650 things quieten down and though
there seems to be little external trade a measure of prosperity returns,
though the town did not relish what amounted to English rule, English
military occupation, and English law, all imposed under the
Commonwealth: the occupation force is never referred to as
Parliamentary, but always just as "The English Army" or "The English
soldiers", and the Council and Kirk Sessions do all they can to ostracise
the ordinary soldiers, though the officers must for expediency be
entertained to wine by the Provost.

   Just before the Restoration we find copies in the archives of letters
from General Monk: the earlier of them relates to a spy captured by the
Dumfries magistrates, the second thanks our support for Monk's intention to march South and restore the King. The Restoration of 1660, of a
monarch crowned in Scotland and regarded as a pillar of the Covenant at
first makes little difference in the town but within a couple of years all is
changed: the beloved Hugh Henderson, minister of St. Michael's since
1648, is expelled from his church, despite the Council's desperate
pleas—the whole Council even went formally to his house to make a last
effort at persuading him to make sufficient agreement with Government
policy anent church worship to enable him to stay on—along with his
son-in-law assistant Campbell: and suddenly, at the October Council
elections, we find a Major Carruthers attending to ensure that only the
right people are elected and ordering those elected to take action against
those who are not approved by Royal policy or who will not take the
Test, that very binding oath of subservience and recognition of the
King's absolute powers: within a few weeks more this arbitrary
interference is extended to the Trades, and a bailie is ordered by
Carruthers to attend the election of Trades deacons and ensure that only
the right people from the King's viewpoint are elected (and this was a
very ticklish situation as the Trades had always resisted any attempt by
the Council to interfere in their affairs): there was some resistance, rival
Deacons being elected by different factions: but the Trades knew the
Council was under Government coercion and eventually toed the line.
Thereafter for over 26 years the Town Council was virtually a cypher,

restricted to purely administrative measures, and we find it being forced, with obvious reluctance, to take such measures as exposing the heads of executed Covenanters on poles above the Brig-port.

The Glorious Revolution of December 1688 is particularly dramatic at Dumfries: immediately on the news reaching the town the Council appointed by the King—latterly even the annual Council elections had been suspended and a Catholic Provost, former Town Clerk John Maxwell, the laird of Barncleuch, appointed by King James—disappears, and we find the old Council of nearly thirty years before in control again, acting vigorously, calling the whole countryside to arms to stamp out the threat of Jacobite revolt, capturing Barncleuch fleeing across the Bridge at midnight in his shirt with his saddle-bag full of town and State papers, sending special couriers off to the Privy Council—resuming in full measure the autonomy which had been its from the Middle Ages until twenty-eight years before. Thereafter until the end of the century and after it retains this initiative.

The Kirk Session Minutes tell the same story: until the Royal pressure is applied in the early Summer of 1662 the Session is a vigorous body, largely identical in personnel with the Council, taking action not only within its own sphere but also often on matters properly Town Council ones—such as imprisonment—just as the Council often acted in matters properly Kirk Session—such as the case of the man accused of sharing a bed with three women: this is very obvious and clearly the members, serving on both bodies as they did, did not always distinguish over-nicely in which capacity they were acting. After that there is a considerable break and when the Session Minutes take up again they are lifeless and concerned only with minor cases of discipline: such matters as church attendance were now entirely out of their hands and under the aegis of the military. They too spring back to life, after a break, in early 1690, and thereafter are lively again: but they show one important change: where before 1662 the Session has been highly democratic, with the Minister merely its mouthpiece, from 1690 the Minister dominates the Session entirely—against his will—because the Elders of the Session all regard themselves as having been to some degree weak under the persecution while the Minister has been through the fire: and this is a permanent change.

Much more has been written, in addition to the evidence McDowall had, by such excellent writers as G.W. Shirley—"Fragmentary Notices of the Burgh School", for instance—on the 17th century: but we must now move on to the 18th century.

McDowall's sources here were much fuller and he used them to give a very full picture (incidentally the first "modern" description of our town and neighbourhood is that written for Sibbald in the 1680's by Dr. Archibald). Even so, there is much material still existing to which he did not have access: the great bulk of a ton or so of loose records and bound volumes in the Archives has still to be dealt with and will undoubtedly shed a great deal of fresh light. Three histories were written during this

century: Edgar's unknown "Mine Author", Edgar himself (1746), and
Dr. Burnside's near the end of the century. The Town Council Minutes
are complete, as are a number of special committee minutes, such as the
volume on the construction of the Midsteeple (and loose correspondence
and accounts add to the very complete documentation on this building
and on the new Town Mills), all the bound volumes of Accounts, Jail
Books from 1714, various Burgh Court Books, Porteous Rolls, Assizes of
Bread, and Police Commission books in full series: assessment rolls from
the beginning of the century onwards: the bound Shipping Impost Book
of 1750-62 plus annual bundles to the end of the century): Services of
Heirs from the 1750's: the bound Burgh Chartulary from the 1750's also
the Minute books of the Seven Trades Incorporation and of the
individual Trades. The Old Statistical Account of 1791-93 gives a full
account of the Burgh: Riddell's MS Notes on Dr. Burnside's MS., and
the notes of Copland of King's Grange, both supplementary to the
A.S.A., supply still further material. The Burgh plan appears in
reasonable detail on the General Roy map of 1753 (the Pont MS map of
1585 and the printed Pont of 1642 of course give no detail: Aglionby's
Platt of 1546 gives a schenatic view of the town and the rather
inaccurate print of the town some time between 1560 and 1600 does
contain some useful information): the town plan appears in the Taylor
and Skinner Itinerary in the 1780's, and on the Ainslie map of Galloway
in 1797—though the town is outside Galloway he gives a good deal of
detail: there is an excellent chart of the shipping approaches to Dumfries
compiled and published in 1742. Most of the dictionaries and gazetteers
of the century mention it—Malachy Postlethwaite's Commercial
Cyclopaedia of 1752, for instance, gives a good description, adding after
the town's name "The Scottish Liverpool"—this being a reference to the
town's vigorous shipping trade.

The town's first newspaper was "The Dumfries Mercury", a few
numbers of which are known, dating to April and May 1721, the earliest
numbered 12: under its title it bore "Containing an Account of the Most
Remarkable Occurrences"—it was the last known publication of the Rae
Press, and made Dumfries the first Scottish town other than those with
universities to publish a news-sheet. It is not yet known how long it ran.
Dumfries had four printing presses during the 18th century: Robert Rae,
1715-21: John Duncan (probable), 1723-27: Robert Jackson, 1773-1810:
Robert and Cuthbert McLachlan, 1784-1802: Rae's press was that of his
father, the Rev. Peter Rae of Kirkbride, Durrisdeer (who printed the
broadside against the Union of the Parliaments in 1706): it had to be
transferred to Dumfries under his son because of criticism of his
combining printing work with his ministry. The first book proper printed
at Kirkbride was in 1711. Robert Rae seems to have come to Dumfries in
late 1714 or early 1715—the Town Council gave the venture every
encouragement, including a free burgess-ship to Robert. In 1715 Robert
took on a printer named Steel and published six or perhaps seven items
during that year: the earliest seems to have been a reprint of Henry's

"Sober-mindedness Press'd Upon Young People": the year also saw a
sermon by the Annan minister and a quarto volume, author unknown, on
the Civil Authority: probably about September the press reprinted "The
New Exercise of Firelocks and Bayonets" in view of the Rebellion then
commencing. The last item of this year is "A Looking-Glass for
Ministers and Christians, or a True View of the Principles and Practices
of the Great Apstle (sic!) Paul". "The Loyal Garland, Composed of Three
Excellent New Songs" seems to date to this year too. The most notable
publication of the Rae Press was Peter Rae's "History of the Late
Revellion", printed in 1718, a fine thick volume which, read in
conjunction with the Town Council Minutes and the voluminous
Treasurer's Accounts and loose documents, gives a most detailed picture
of the town's vigorous reaction to the 1715 Rebellion. The first book of
music printed in Dumfries was Duncan's collection of psalm tunes,
engraved, printed and sold by him in 1723. Eighty-one items seem to
have been published in the town during the century. The Dumfries
Weekly Magazine, published by Jackson, began on Tuesday 16th March
1773 and ran until July 1777 when it changed, on 29th July, into the
Dumfries Weekly Journal, a four-page newspaper, with news and essays
but less of the essays, tales and poems which had taken up most of the
"Magazine". There are more or less complete files of these in the
Regional Library and the 18th century files, with the later ones, have
been indexed.

A diary which gives a good deal of incidental information on the town
is that of the Rev. Duncan, Minister of Lochfoot from the 1740's
onwards: the whereabouts of the original is not known at the time of
writing this but a considerable portion exists in copy form at the
Library. One very useful manuscript source for the last six years of the
century is the Diary of William Grierson, begun on 1st January 1794,
shortly after his 21st birthday: this gives a full picture of life in the town
as seen by a draper's son with a good education and wide interests: the
theatre: social events: military affairs: the visit of a menagerie of mainly
Australian birds: the attempted elopment of a bailie's daughter with a
sergent-major: weather: Town Council and Church politics: the
Philosophical Society: food scarcities and meal riots: a detailed account
of Burns' funeral—Grierson knew and admired him and in the next
century had much to do with the Mausoleum and the foundation of the
Burns Club: sports: the Siller Gun shooting: the town's reaction to
national events: public hangings: a girl serving as a soldier in the
Fencibles.

The Kirk Session, Synod and Presbytery Minutes are complete for this
century and give a wealth of information: birth, death, baptismal and
marriage records are reasonably full.

It will be seen therefore that the sources for the 18th century are of a
different order of magnitude to those for any earlier period: such things
as the Roup Book, running from the 1780's to 1801, which lists item by
item the contents of debtors' houses being sold up, with estimated and

actual prices, or the detailed shipping documents, give a virtually complete picture.

The town in 1700 still had much that was mediaeval about it—physically a quarter of its houses were ruinous: the town's reaction to the Jacobite threat in 1715 was the traditional one-massive ditching, re-erecting the town's gates—the "Ports"—calling in and paying and housing volunteers from all over the area, arranged by districts: the heretical followers of the Rev. Hepburn of Urr encamped on Corberry Hill across the river from the town and re-fortified the little Iron Age fort there (an account survives for sending beer, cheese, and rolls, by a boy, across the river to "Mr Hebron's men"): The Provost, in armour, rode to the Port at the crisis to repel the threatened attack: arms and ammunition were hastily gathered in or improvised—the Council had only a few months before disposed of its old stock of powder "in view of more peaceful times". Thirty years later all is changed: the 1745 rebellion is clearly regarded by the merchants who ruled the town as an unwelcome interference with trade: the mercantile philosophy of the century is dominant: there is complete reliance on the Government to keep trouble away—before, the town had always stood on its own—and no attempt at resistance is made: the town's stock of arms is hurriedly shifted from place to place and hidden: but no trained bands, no drilling: merely a lament at the interference with business and the hope that things will quickly return to normal.

Murderers' hands are still being exposed on spikes in the 1720's—there is a rather apologetic letter from an Edinburgh bailie in 1712 enclosing a pair of hands for exposure by the Burgh, from a Dumfries murderer just executed in Edinburgh. Conditions in the town's prison were still mediaeval: the jail petitions give a terrible picture: a minister lies in January in the vault with the clothes rotted off his back by the water dripping from the roof, and his legs eaten to the bone by the irons: another man begs to have his cell-mate shifted as the man is not only mad but also very verminous: a jail escape attempt in 1713, with the prisoner being dressed as a woman by his wife, clearly gave the Countess of Nithsdale, residing at Terregles, the idea for her famous rescue of her husband from the Tower of London two years later. There were several escape attempts: most prisoners were in for debt—quite small debts: a crofter from the Ae Valley complains that he has been held six months on a five shilling debt and that his creditor has taken over not only his croft but also his wife and family: a Dumfries man claims that when he came to visit a friend in prison he was himself arrested without any reason given and his watch taken: he still lies in prison (the jailor, Burgh Officers and Executioner, were often criminals in prison offered release if they took these detested posts): another prisoner, in jail for six weeks with little food, acknowledges the heinous nature of his crime—being a witness at a Border wedding—but asks to be released so that he can work to pay off his £100 fine: a young mother is hailed into prison for carrying live coals from one house to another—a breach of the stringent

fire regulations (twenty per cent of the houses in the centre of the town
had no chimneys and had central hearths with peats, bracken and whins
stacked alongside the fire, in 1722): her husband begs for her release
because she had left a small baby at home and is pregnant—but release is
refused. Elizabeth Lockhart, that incorrigible fire-raiser and mother-
beater, after repeated spells in prison from 1706 or so onwards, is at last
in 1718 taken by the Provost himself to Whitehaven and put on a ship for
America as an indentured labourer, he buying her straw for her bed, a
linen kerchief, and a pack of leaf tobacco for her solace—all duly charged
up to the Burgh, of course! A twelve-year-old girl petitions in 1712 that
on the death of her Father, the Burgh Treasurer, Irving of Gribton has
siezed his entire property, including the tenement the rents of which
were reserved for the support of herself and her younger sister, though
there was ample in the estate to satisfy all creditors and more: the
Council offers her fifteen pence as a once-for-all charity; six years later
she, just married to a prosperous young tradesman, sues Irving and gets
the property back. In 1702 the Jailor of Edinburgh prison complains that
a debtor of his in Dumfries Prison is being allowed to visit his
"Inamorada" and play "goff" (golf) on the Kingholm (there was a
bowling green beside the Maxwell's Castle wall by this time): in 1718 the
Burgh Court loose papers show a war in progress between the Jardines
and the Johnstones at Lockerbie and a Bewcastle cattle-reiver caught in
Wamphray Glen with 45 head of stolen cattle—eleven years after the Act
of Union and a hundred after James VI and I's pacification of the
Borders.

A shopkeeper beneath the Prison complains in 1712 that a "furious
madd person" has been kept for some months in the "Theaves Hole"
above his shop: that the entrance to his shop is blocked by people
gathering outside to speak to the lunatic and bait him to throw his plates
and stoups at them: and that as the man has no tub to ease nature in, as
the other prisoners do, urine and faeces are soaking through the ceiling
of his shop and making it and its goods "somewhat noisome" and
"damnified", to the detriment of his business. Lunatics were sometimes
escorted by the Burgh Officer across Bankend Bridge and abandoned
near Mid-Locharwoods—this seems to have been common practice in
Scotland—Ayr Burgh Officers in the 16th century took its lunatics out
thirteen miles, to the moors, and left them there.

The 1720's and 1740's saw Dumfries at its peak as a Transatlantic and
Continental trading port—for a time it had, through its outport at
Carsethorn, more American tobacco trade than Glasgow—as late as 1752
it was called the "Scottish Liverpool"—but as the century rolled on
legitimate foreign trade was weakened by intensive smuggling and by
the last decade was mainly coasting: the 1750-62 Impost Book shows
ships of 18 tons trading round the North of Scotland with the Continent
in winter, and 30-tonners crossing the Atlantic at the same season,
though most of the foreign trade was carried in ships of 150-odd to
300-odd tons. A trickle of emigrants passed to America via the ships

owned by local firms—the records of one of these firms exist in the charter chest of the Stewarts of Shambellie.

Dumfries Grammar School figures prominently throughout the century, under a succession of brilliant Rectors and talented teachers—its complex regulations, the twice-each-Sunday school procession to Church, the purchase of books, the repair in 1781 of the school's Gregorian reflector telescope.

Near the end of the century, in the 80's and 90's, we find O'Neill (of the Stoop resistance-to-the-pressgang case) petitioning in 1793 that his grown daughter be removed from the small cell where she is held with him and another man, a stranger, and transferred to the woman's part of the prison. The tenants of the houses fronting on Queensberry square complain in 1793 that all the town's rubbish is collected by the scavengers each morning and piled in the Square and not removed until afternoon: the teacher of the English class, housed because of lack of space in the Grammar School in a room overlooking the Fleshmarket complains that he cannot open the windows despite the heat of Summer because of the stench and the flies: the Rev. Burnside writes from his manse demanding that "this *abominable* Dungheap" be at once removed from out side the manse "Or else what are we to think of the Magistrates and Police of this town?" The Methodist minister writes in the 1780's asking permission to erect a chapel (at the head of Queen Street): a cotton manufacturer asks permission in 1786 to erect a cotton-mill on the river: there is a proposal as early as the 1760's to introduce gravitation water from Dalskairth to the town: the town held long to its old restrictive economy—a cooper was jailed, fined £100, and banished the town with his wife and six children in the 1760's for having practiced his trade without being a freeman: right through to the end of the century and beyond the Council insisted that traders and shopkeepers must be freemen and, if not freemen's sons, must pay stiffly for the privilege—and this is all the stranger in view of the town's cosmopolitan trading interests.

Crafts and skills multiplied greatly during the century—we hear of gun-barrel boring around 1712, an antique dealer in 1718, and so on. Stocking-weaving was becoming important from the late 1760's.

So much for the 18th century. McDowall, writing in 1867, had, in his position as a local man and a newspaper editor, very full information for his century: much exists that he did not use— William Grierson's diary up to 1809: James Murray the coalman of Greenbrae Loaning's day-by-day commentaries for the 1870's and 80's—he had been making them since the fifties but alas the earlier volumes do not seem to have survived: the Roup Lists, including the 1801 list of the stock of Maria Riddell's museum and library: maps: photographs.

The 18th-century Society of the Pantheon was followed by the Philosophical Society, of which Grierson was a member: the Burns' Club and the Mechanics' Institute in the 1820's: the Astronomical Society

(1835), and the Natural History and Antiquarian Society (1862).

Photography brought a new element into local recording—Crombie the architect was doing both studio and field photography from 1846 but the earliest which have survived, by various hands, are from the 1850's and 1860's: the number increases greatly after 1860, so that a vivid picture of the town, its people, trades and sports can be built up for the last forty years of the century from this source alone: and artists such as Costen Aitken and Jos. Watson (father of the famous "Tommy" Watson, vigorous radical editor of the "Standard") have left us a fine range of drawings and paintings of the streets, shipping, trades and people of the town from the thirties to the seventies of the century, while a few cover the period 1800-1830.

A print of around 1806 shows bathers among the willows on the Maxwelltown side of the river opposite Dockfoot, with a view upstream showing ships tied up along Whitesands and across the foot of the Caul. The river-bank on the Dumfries side is shown as natural merse. Another print of a few years later shows an earth embankment from Dockfoot up, and cattle wading in the river at Dockfoot. The advertisements in the "Courier" and "Journal" for emigrant ships from 1812 onwards bear little thumbnail prints of the ships concerned, some of them apparently accurate likenesses and not mere symbols.

Shipbuilding had been active on the Nith from 1732 at least, concentrating first at Kelton, where ships were certainly being built by the 1760's: by the early 1800's Glencaple was beginning to cut into Kelton's monopoly and from about 1812 Glencaple was producing ships up to 300-odd tons, although most were much smaller. Thomson's Packet was busy, with many others, in the Liverpool trade by the beginning of the century, and another Thomson family, from about 1812 onwards developed the three-legged Transatlantic trade, of emigrants and manufactured goods to Prince Edward Island and New Brunswick, with Richibucto, Miramichi and the Baie de Chaleur as the main debarcation points, and Canadian timber in ships built in Canada by Solway shipwrights taken out by the Thomson company—one brother in Dumfries, one in Liverpool and one in New Brunswick. From about 1812 we see a very rapid development of the emigrant trade—it is said that in 1851 from the port of Dumfries more than ten thousand people sailed for North America, more than seven thousand to Australia and more than four thousand to New Zealand—South-West Scotland played a large part in the settling of Otago province. As late as 1872 the entire village of the "Busy Bit", near Dunscore, emigrated to Sydney, New South Wales, villagers, schoolmaster, a nearby blacksmith, Clydesdale horses and all, from Carsethorn. By the end of the century the emigrant trade had moved to Glasgow and Liverpool, as had several local shipping firms, and local shipping was mainly coastal and on a reduced scale—the work, of course, of the railways. McDowall makes little of the 1848 Cholera epidemic in Dumfries, although it was nearly as severe as the 1832 one: the doctor sent down from Glasgow by the Public Health Board found the dead lying in the streets and deaths in the hundreds—and the Town Council, in direct opposition to its vigorous reaction in the 1832 Epidemic, taking no action at all, on the grounds that it had cost too much six years before!

Dumfries throughout the early part of the century had a distinct French presence. One result of the Napoleonic Wars was the influx of French officer prisoners of war to the area: these were well liked—they were on parole, and could move about locally: several married local girls. Our area already had a few French residents—Fountainbleau on the Lockerbie Road had been founded by Huguenots in the 1760's, and M. Perochon, another Huguenot, came to the town, probably from London, in the late 1790's. He was a man of substance, and built, first, a cottage on "Perochon's Loan" (or "the inclined plane"), the very steep foot road linking Kingholm Road and Glencaple Road a little upstream from Castledykes grounds, and then Castledykes House itself, a fine large mansion in Regency style, built in 1816: even the steel locks were handmade, beautiful examples of fine craftsmanship.

The second half of the century saw an influx of Germans into the town: Mogerley the pork butcher: Seiffert the jeweller: Konrad Ahrweiler (from East Prussia), the Hillenbrands (hairdressers, like Ahrweiler).

One incomer who lived a long time in the town and was very popular was a dark Madrasi, Krishnamurtha Razaloo, an Untouchable converted to Christianity, who came to Scotland as a manservant to a young Doctor of Dumfries origin, who returned to Scotland after service in India with the East India Company. He died young from illness contracted in India, and was buried in the midlands of Scotland, where he had been practicing, and left a small pension to his servant, who settled in his master's native town, where he lived for upwards of forty years—a member of St. Mary's congregation and of the bowling club. He used to pass up pennies on the ferrule of his umbrella to children sitting on the high wall of Dumfries Academy grounds on Academy Street, and in Summer he would walk the towpath to Glencaple gathering wild flowers on the way to present to a lady at Glencaple who gave him a basin of cool water to refresh his tired feet: Known as "Raja", or "Black Raja", he once terrified a drunk who met him in St. Michael Street one dark night: thinking him the "Black Man"—the Devil himself—the drunk bolted, put his foot down an open grating, and broke his leg.

Late in the century Abraham Appleton settled in Dumfries and his wife came from Riga to marry him unseen—the town's only, and very popular, Jewish family.

From the 1870's Italians were settling in Dumfries as icecream and fish-and-chip merchants: they too were quickly adopted into the community.

Changing the subject again: football in the modern sense took off in the town during the 1870's and rapidly cut into the older sports of bowling, quoits and curling: photographs exist from the late seventies onwards.

The 1890's saw a good deal of development in Dumfries—the major Dumfries Academy building was one item—and in 1896 the Town Council agreed to replace the gas lighting of the town, first installed in 1826, by electricity, though this did not actually happen till 1911.

And now we come to the present century. The rapid rate of change for which the 19th century was remarkable has of course continued—and even accentuated—in the 20th: the writer, 66 in 1985, can remember the Solway sailing schooners: he lived in the 1920's in Queensland Place, Pullman Terrace, on the Georgetown Road, in the upstairs flat: there was an outdoor sink on the landing at the stairhead: water had to be brought from the tap near the gate down the entry, a distance of perhaps thirty feet, and carried up the stairs: the dry privy was at the foot of the garden, some fifty feet from the stair foot: the privy backed on to a sleeper-enclosed midden which in Summer writhed with maggots which penetrated the privy wall in great numbers: the midden was emptied once a year by a farmer's cart in the field over the fence. The area was very quiet and rural: a mile or so out the road was the village of Georgetown, with naked children playing on the road bank and rows of little home-made cages outside the houses, made with wooden rods, and containing linnets and goldfinches birdlimed out on the Lochar Moss: while he lived at Queensland Place there was a case of bestiality (the "Scottish Crime") at Carthagena farm (a half-wit): and yet when one says "Georgetown Road" to a modern Dumfriesian his immediate vision is of a wide area of modern private housing—and this in one lifetime.

When the writer attended Nobelhill School on the Annan Road (from 1924) the headmaster, John White (Auld Jock and his Mongrel—a little terrier was always with him)—had commenced his teaching career at the old 1805 Gasstown School—what is now Gasstown Hall: the children from Georgetown came in barefoot the mile and a half or more to school from April to October, to save their footgear: most traffic on the Annan Road was still horsedrawn: Percival's Motor 'Bus came through a few times per day. The Writer's Father, walking to Carlisle on Saturday afternoons in 1913-14, felt that the main road was busy if he met more than two or three horse-drawn wagons and a very occasional motor-car—where now the A75 Eororoute has a non-stop procession of juggernaut lorries heading to and from Ireland. And that is another change—who walks to Carlisle now, or takes a walk round by Dalry and New Galloway, as the writer's Father did in the 1912-14 period? The writer knows of a Dalry man who into the 1930's stayed to the end of the Country Fair—the Wednesday of the Rood Fair—and when the Fair finished around 11p.m., walked home—some 28 miles.

Some people did not use Shanks' Pony: Toddy Tam, who farmed Seeside in Irongray, and did clog-dances at the Rood Fair for toddy, used to be put into his pony trap by his friends at the end of a convivial evening in Dumfries: the pony, slapped on the rump to start it off, trotted happily the six or so miles home, Tam blissfully asleep, joggling about in the trap, and fetching up at his own door, where his wife, alerted by the sound of the wheels and hoof-beats (there was less background noise then) awaited him: this, too, would be about 1912-13.

The rapid progress of the 1890's continued into the 1900's: Ewart Library in 1903, electricity lighting the streets by 1911, the large County Buildings going up between 1911 and 1915: "Tar Macadam" Macaulay as Provost pushing through the first tarred roads and streets (when any notable development of his term of office was mentioned the retired loom-tuner would say "It wis me pusht it furrit"—he was one of the best Provosts of this century, lack of education or no): the advent of the Drummond Car in 1909, and then the arrival of the great Arrol Johnston motor company in their new steel, glass and concrete factory at Heathhall in 1912: the first dirigible aircraft flying over the town in 1915: Sir Alan Cobham's flying circus coming annually from 1922: the formation of Dumfries Wireless Club in the same year (and the taking of the first aerial photograph of the town, by a young Dumfries Courier linotype operator taking a sixpenny flight with Cobham's Circus—this 1922 photograph is in Dumfries Museum)—Dumfries people were indeed living through rapid change.

There was another kind of change from previous centuries: for in the 20th century Dumfries has for the first time escaped the bubonic fever, the typhus, the smallpox, and the cholera which had marked the centuries before—though the 1919 influenza pandemic was bad enough, killing more people around the world than had the terrible 1914-18 War. Pulmonary tuberculosis—"consumption"—was endemic, not epidemic, but until the early 1950's it was still one of the greatest killers of young adults—especially young women—just as diptheria was the great killer of young children (it killed two of the writer's brothers), and pneumonia, the "Old Man's Friend", of the aged—Sir James Crichton-Browne the brain specialist and Joe Milligan the jeweller were among the latter.

The Smallpox Hospital, on the Craigs Road—a tin-roofed hut—became a tuberculosis hospital until the opening of the Sanatorium at Lochmaben around 1911: after this it lay derelict until occupied by down-and-out squatters, who finally around 1970 became enough of a nuisance for the building to be demolished and the squatters rehoused.

The demolitions of 1910-1930 saw the end of many narrow closes—the Beehive, Admiral Duncan, and Coffee closes in the Munches Street area for example: the demolitions of the 1950's and 1960's saw the disappearance of such picturesque names as "Tartan Raw" on Maxwell Street—it was built of red and white bricks. Sheepheid Raw—Pleasance Cottages—on the lane between Brooms Road and Annan Road—was so called because the hard-up nineteenth-century inhabitants used to have sheeps' heads singed in the furnaces of McKinnell's Foundry a few hundred yards away: and why the terrace on Brownrigg Loaning should be known as "Monkey Castle" the writer has never been able to discover. "Jock's Loaning" goes back into the nineteenth century: the writer's grandfather knew Jock, a retired county roadman who had a cottage on the loaning, and who did not approve at all of the young courting couples who frequented it on summer evenings: he would sally forth waving his stick and roaring whenever they appeared. Most names have a commonplace origin: the area on the riverward side of St. Michael Street between Moorhead's Hospital and Nithsdale Mill is still known as "The Bleachfield": prints early in the 19th century show it as just that and accounts for bleaching in the Burgh Records refer to it: but there has been no bleaching done there commercially for over a century—just as the tanneries and the basket-making and candle-making establishments in the Mill Hole went out of action between 1910 and 1914, as did the Ryedale claypits and brickworks in Maxwelltown: even the Maxwelltown cycle-racing track is now a grass-grown earthwork which visitors mistake for something prehistoric, though it was lively enough from the 1870's until around 1910.

The century began with a good many years in which there was always some sort of military or semi-military presence—Galloway Militia, Volunteers, Territorials, shooting at the Conhuith Targets, where the brick trenches and dugouts still stand, and where one can pick up flattened bullets: the annual camps on the Kingholm and in the hutments at Hannahfield: cavalry galloping up the ramp on the towpath a little way inside the Kingholm Lodge gate (the Museum has a fishing ticket for the Kingholm stretch issued by the Ministry of Defence—the Kingholm reverted to the Crown as ultimus haeres, having been sold by the town during the second of its two bankruptcies: it was allocated to the Ministry of Defence, and was not returned to the town until the early 1920's)—the military presence dropped away steadily—apart from the Second World War, of course—now military bands and trumpeters at the Guid Nychburris celebrations, visiting parachute teams, and the unobtrusive Territorial and cadet forces are all that is left plus the recruiting office, for heavy unemployment moves many young men to take up a military career.

The 20th century brought its crop of new people to Dumfries: the brilliant historian G.W. Shirley, appointed to the Burgh Library in 1903, and to the County Library in 1929: the talented theatrical manager Darlison, who came shortly after that to take over the Playhouse Cinema—he happened to share a railway compartment with Miss Gordon of Kenmuir Terrace on his way down from Edinburgh, and in that compartment, on that day, the Dumfries Guid of Players had its origin.

Much later, in 1932, Shirley and Darlison, historian and dramatic manager, founded the Guid Nychburris Festival, with the writer's father writing prologues and epilogues for the outdoor theatrical performances at Palmerston Park which at that time formed an important part of the proceedings.

Politics in the town have had less fire, less fierce commitment, in the 20th than in the 19th century: true, Shirley was a fervent Fabian, the "Standard" at the beginning of the century was still radical, evening classes in social studies were well patronised—and radicals such as

James Maxton and Keir Hardie (and suffragettes such as "General" Drummond) addressed rowdy meetings from the raised ground at the Dumfries end of the Suspension Bridge: but with the '14-'18 war much of the heat went out: the countryside was still Liberal Radical and the well-beloved and idealistic doctor "Joe" Hunter gave up his profession to become an M.P in Lloyd George's entourage in the early twenties: he was used shamelessly as a political hack by that ruthless politician and died comparatively young—and everyone felt that it was of a broken heart.

Lloyd George had a successful meeting in the Drill Hall: he and Ramsay MacDonald both figured in group photographs at Burns' Mausoleum. Now began a gradual turn to the Right. The "standard", edited by James Reid for the Misses Watson, Conservative daughters of the Radical editor "Tommy" Watson, became steadily more Conservative: the county town moved from Liberal to Nat. Lib., with "Punch", Sir Harry Fildes, as its capable and well-liked M.P., who had his head modelled in bronze by the late J.G. Jeffs, then assistant curator at Dumfries Museum: during an election campaign he and the writer's father, who needed to see Fildes on election business, pursued the vigorous M.P. around Dumfries from meeting to meeting, always arriving at a venue just after he had left for the next—Jeffs needed one more sitting—Jeffs finally bursting out characteristically "We'll hae tae set snares for the auld b---". Then from Nat. Lib. to Conservative, and our present able and respected Sir Hector Monro, farmer of Williamwood near Eaglesfield.

As for the Town Council and its successor the District Council, the change has been from a Council of individuals to a Council of party representatives, with a few independants surviving but usually tending to align with one or other of the parties. There were many notable individuals: conservative master painter and amateur pugilist Joseph Johnstone Glover, who served continuously for twelve years from the 1890's: radical Joseph Johnstone Macaulay, already mentioned—at the Convention of Royal Burghs he held up the procession for two and a half hours because Dumfries had not been given its proper place in the procession: Lord Lyon King at Arms had to be called in and decided in Dumfries' favour. Reviewing a company of troops about to leave for Europe outside the old Buccleuch Street General Post Office this lean, small, old man walked up and down the line, hand on chin, murmuring quite audibly, "Aye, ye're a gran' lot o' lads: some o' ye'll come back wi'oot an airm: some o' ye'll come back wi'oot a leg—an' some o' ye'll no' come back at a' "—not very encouraging, perhaps, but he did not know he was being heard—and it was only too true: the town lost so many of its fine young men in this and in the following war. During that first war, too, Senior Bailie Kelly was seeing troops off at the station: he said to them that he hoped that this regrettable conflict would soon be over so that trade could return to normal (most of his tin goods came from Germany): peppery, patriotic Bailie Kerr—Dr. Kerr—who was with him on the platform punched him on the jaw and knocked him down.

The advent of G.W. Shirley as Burgh Librarian and Darlison as Manager of the Playhouse Cinema (which took over the Mechanics' Hall), gave a considerable impetus to culture and the arts in the town in the years immediately following Shirley's arrival in 1903: the Guild of Players was founded: the Academy staff organised an ambitious series of school theatricals, of which photographs exist: elaborate galas and fetes were held to raise funds for various good causes, especially the Library which, though the building was erected with Andrew Carnegie's money, on land gifted by benefactress Jessie McKie of Moat House (the two of them opened it), and though the Mechanics' Institute passed on to it their large collection of books—mainly the library gifted to the Institute by the Rev. Dodds in the 1890's (this collection still formed an important part of the Ewart's lending stock well into the 1930's), was sadly under-financed by the Burgh—Shirley's book purchase allocation in the Annual Estimates was for very many years in succession five pounds a year. Shirley in particular was active in stimulating evening classes, in political subjects, literature, economics and languages—the writer's Father learnt German in the evening classes between about 1910 and 1914, from Gustav Emil Hugelshofer, the Academy's Swiss teacher of German and French—to such effect that in the 1939-45 War he ended up as an Army interpreter in French and German.

The 1914-18 War came to a shock to the educated younger generation of Dumfries, including the writer's Father, his colleagues in the Land Valuation Office in Castle Street, Shirley, and Darlison: as Father said, this was the 20th century: there had been no truly major European war ·since Napoleon: we were past that kind of thing: civilised people simply did not go to war any longer (and the British Parliament was against joining in only hours before we did). Shirley, Socialist and pacifist, joined an ambulance unit as a stretcher bearer and went right through the war: a group photograph of the Dumfries Local Defence Volunteers shows very young and elderly men, with a few in reserved occupations (the Museum has a Dumfries munition-worker at Gretna's badge—to ward off the White Feather), and, incongruously, in an officer's uniform, the dwarfish, twisted, large-headed figure of Darlison—who surely could not have marched (despite his severe physical handicaps he lived into his nineties).

There had been a great deal of social activity during the War—fetes, galas, all sorts of fund-raising activities to help the troops: large houses such as Broomlands were pressed into service as military hospitals: Belgian refugees came to the area and some stayed—Marie Baert of Douievale Cottage was in the writer's class at Noblehill and Mrs. Delahaye purveyed lemonade from her terrace home at the end of the Kissing-Gates path.

With the war ended, the general social activity continued: one feature of the 20's and 30's was the Police Concerts, usually held in the Lyceum

Cinema, where one could hear top-rank musical ensembles such as the Lener Quartet, first-rate violinists such as the little Jugoslav Dushko Jovanovitch who played brilliantly while standing on his head, lying on his back or doing the splits—light relief, yes, and a type of humour we in Dumfries were unfamiliar with—but he *still* played beautifully—or comedians such as Harry Lauder, Dave Willis, Will Fyfe and the like.

We forget, however, how simple much of life remained: the Lochvale Boys' Home boys in their grey tweed uniforms (when Father was young the Industrial School boys in *their* grey uniforms sold the firewood they had chopped from barrows in the street (the town's first swimming pool was in the Industrial School on Clerkhill behind Burns' house and remained in use for youth organisations into the thirties, existing into the late forties—long before the efforts which had been going on in the Town Council from 1906 resulted in the late fifties in the fine modern pool beside the river): the Police had a barrow for drunks but more often, in Father's youth, just dragged them along the gutters by their collars: and in his day there was a really horrible public privy projecting over the river (and discharging direct into it) down near Nith Place.

Well into the thirties, too, some of the closes were narrow and dirty: Father, returning in the early hours from McGowan Son and Brydon's office during an election campaign, seeing one of the typists safely home, stumbled over a body in the pitch dark in the close and said to the girl "Careful—there's a man on the ground here"—to which a slurred feminine voice from the ground riposted "Sh'not a man—Sh'a lady!" Father remembered also in the thirties, coming into the High Street from the Long Close in a summer dawn during an election campaign, meeting a wild rabbit in High Street—and the "Courier" reporters, coming up St. Michael's bridge early one morning, met a roe deer which bolted and got itself stuck in the tall privet hedge on the Rosefield Mills side of the road: the men hauled it out, pointed its nose towards Dalskairth, and let go—it never looked behind it.

Modern office staffs would not tolerate late night work—yet the Town Clerk's office where the writer worked from 1937 still at that time worked to between 12-30 and 2-30a.m. once a month to get the cyclostyled Council minutes out—Town Clerk, Depute, clerks, girls and all—and no extra pay. Girls in offices, by the way, are a 20th century phenomemon—Father remembered that when he was a young man it was not quite the thing for a girl to work in an office: it was understood that perhaps family financial necessity demanded it—but still, not quite the done thing.

Just as the first World War brought Belgians to the town, so the second left several nationalities behind—Germans, Norwegians, Poles, Ukrainians—it could be disconcerting, in the sixties, to 'phone the manager of Trimtree Limited at Mouswald Place a few miles out of town and hear him reply "Mr. Scott here—Scott, T,C,O,C,Z."

Anders Tomter, Norwegian manager of Ironhirst Peatworks in the Lochar Moss, had been here for years before the war, and his wife also—

she came from Vadsö N.E. Arctic Norway. Of the wartime Norwegians
(Dumfries was a Norwegian headquarters) Major Olaus Myrseth
founded his popular Folk Museum in Dumfries in 1950: Capt. Jahr the
distinguished philatelist also stayed on in Dumfries, is still an honoured
member of our community, and organised the 40th anniversary
exhibition at Dumfries Museum in 1980, commemorating the arrival of
the Norwegian Armed Forces in Dumfries in 1940—they had their
headquarters in "Norges Hus" opposite Burns' Statue, and King Olav
once reviewed them in Troqueer Road. The "Norges", many of them
former whalers, were very popular in Dumfries; many of them married
Dumfries girls, who come back from Norway from time to time to visit
family and friends: the town has kept up musical and football links with
Norway ever since and has an active branch of the Scoto—Norwegian
Society.

From the 1960's other ethnic groups have joined our town: there was a
long period after "Raja" Razaloo's death in the late 19th century when
no one from outside Europe lived in the town—a resplendent young
Indian nobleman might be seen at Shambellie gate: the Chinese Vice-
Consul reopened Dumfries Museum in 1935, with the finest exhibition of
Chinese and Japanese art material seen up to that time in Europe, from
the collections of the Jardine Matheson—connected families in
Dumfriesshire: a Negro came with the Rood Fair in the 1920's: then,
about 1937, the first Indian draper settled in town, an unassuming, quiet
man who rented a garden behind the Railway Mission on Greenbrae
Loaning, and grew what were to us at that time strange crops—maize
and unfamiliar vegetables—a neat and well-tended garden. From the
1960's more Indian drapers were to be seen: an Indian property agent
began buying up houses: Indians opened up shops and, in the 1970's,
restaurants—a hard-working, frugal-living group, who brought their
wives and children. Some came to the town as nurses or doctors at the
Infirmary or Crichton Royal—where there are also West Indian and
African staff residing in town.

The Chinese community of Hong Kong/New Territories origin, began
coming to Dumfries in the mid-sixties: all are in the restaurant or "take-
out" business, and many have their wives and families with them: they
also are quiet, law-abiding citizens.

Another smaller group is the Tibetans, attracted to the area because of
the Samye Ling Buddhist centre in Eskdale but residing in town.
Children of all these communities go to the town's schools and are
completely integrated.

Amusements are another social function which has changed greatly
from 1900. At that time the cinema was no more than a penny peepshow
at the Rood Fair: the Theatre Royal had sunk to rather cheap
variety—Jugglers, "spectacles" and the like: rather similar
entertainment could be seen at the Mechanics' Institute, though there
singers, instrumentalists and ensembles of national, and even
international reputation could still be seen from time to time. Then the

Playhouse Cinema took over the Mechanics' Hall and the Lyceum
Cinema opened: by the thirties the Playhouse Cinema closed and the
Regal Cinema opened and Darlison transferred to it: the writer can
remember old apple orchard where the Regal Cinema now is. The Theatre
Royal became the Electric Cinema (the "Auld Scratch", because of its
flea population) quite early in the century: the Lyceum opened a fine new
building and was in its turn demolished: and cinemas sank as television
took over, so that now there is only the Regal, a combined small cinema
and bingo hall. For a few years before the Second War a reputable
repertory company came to the Electric for several months in the year
and had audience enough to attract them for another year: and there the
wheel has turned again and under the Guild of Players it has now been
for many years again the Theatre Royal and fine amateur and
professional performances can be seen there; in the oldest theatre
building in Scotland.

The town has now for some time had its own, and very popular wireless
station, Radio Solway: and as this is being written it is announced that
the town is to have a small five kilometre range commercial station also.

One major event early in the century was the fire at the Town Hall in
1908: Father was a clerk with the town's Collector of Rates at that time,
across Buccleuch Street from the Town Hall, and wanted to go over to
help, but old Pringle, the Collector, told him to stay at his desk—Town
Hall on fire or no, the work had to go on! Fortunately, damage was
limited though the large oil painting of William and Mary presented to
the town by a local Jacobite laird for its kindness in imprisoning him
during the 1715 Rebellion (a tongue-in-cheek gift, needless to say) was
burnt: the hurried clearance during the fire led to the discovery in an
attic cupboard of the town's archives, going back to the Middle Ages:
these were immediately worked on by Shirley and Dr. R.C. Reid of
Cleughbrae and a whole new dimension added to our history—Dumfries
is indeed fortunate in having one of the most complete burgh archives in
Scotland.

One place in Dumfries which has changed greatly during the century is
the Whitesands: when the century started, and for two years later, the
cattle and horse markets still took place on it—a number of photographs
have survived recording the busy scene, the ostlers with their trousers
tied under the knee with "nickie tams" guarding the docile Clydesdales:
then the market moved into the recently vacated timber yards: it was the
Twenties before 'buses began to use the Sands as a stance (the writer
remembers the Carsethorn 'bus leaving from the King's Arms Yard, and
from Brewery Street). Speaking of transport, his father lifted him up on
the parapet of the Annan Road Bridge to see the serried ranks of engines
piled up in the goods yard, no smoke or steam coming from their
chimneys, silent, during the 1926 General Strike.

The Amalgamation of Dumfries and Maxwelltown as a result of the
1928 Local Government Act was a major event in the late twenties:
Maxwelltown Town Council burnt its current minute books and records

in the town hall fire rather than let them fall into the hands of the enemy across the river: Judge Hutchison was borne shoulder-high out Glasgow Road amid a cheering crowd for his efforts to retain Maxwelltown's independence. Linked to some degree with the Amalgamation was the building of St. Michael's Bridge: the writer crossed it when the river below could still be seen beneath its timbers, and was at its opening—and, well before that, had paddled in the river at the Stank and in the gravelly shallows at the grating-protected outlet of the channel under the Town Mills which fed the wheel which from 1911 had generated electricity.

The closeness of the two burghs had led to problems: the writer's Grandfather, cashier in Walker and Sharpe's law office at the Maxwelltown end of the New Bridge, was accosted at the Dumfries end of the bridge by an English gentleman who asked the way to Dumfries Railway Station: Grandfather gave him clear instructions: a couple of hours later the same man walked into the office a hundred yards from where they had last met: he had walked half a mile to Dumfries station, waited for the next train stopping at Maxwelltown Station, got off there, and walked a good half mile more to get to the office, not realising till he got there that he was just across the river from where he had been—and there was really no way for a stranger to know that those houses across the water were in a different town and county, for they appeared—and were—continuous with Dumfries. It was for this latter reason that Mr. Sharpe of the law firm built St. Clair Terrace on the Annan Road, so as to secure a £10 vote in Dumfries as well as in Maxwelltown, where he lived—which is why the writer's father, son of Sharpe's cashier, was born in St. Clair Terrace!

The mention of Judge Hutchison being borne out Glasgow Road by the crowd conveys something of the atmosphere in the local Town Councils: Hutchison later campaigned successfully on two occasions in the 1930's to stop the building of a swimming pool in Dumfries, and managed to stop the building of a town hall on to the Municipal Chambers when the building was modernised in 1931-32—both would have been on the wrong side of the river, from his viewpoint. David Brodie, Dumfries' first Catholic Provost, and a very competent and well-liked one, master-minded the Amalgamation negotiations. Though the Town Councillors were very much individuals Will Gray was a Socialist, Julia Jardine and Mrs. Shirley also Socialists, and Mrs. Charteries of Charteries and Spence of the tweed mills a staunch Conservative: the ladies behaved well enough but the constable on ceremonial guard at the Council Hall door had to be called in occasionally to pull the male councillors off each other—Judge Hutchison would have "Chay" Richardson (who built the first river bicycle and pedalled it up and down the Nith) by the throat or be belabouring him over the shoulders with his stick: and when "Chay" dropped dead no councillor would sit in his seat at the Council table for a year.

Dumfries has never flirted with extremism but for a few years in the late thirties there was quite a lively group of Mosley's Blackshirts in the town, holding parades (a photo has survived) in the Vennel: Mosley spoke to a crowded Drill Hall meeting: his men went up and down the aisles clubbing hecklers senseless with the steel balls on chains round their wrists: the police did not intervene.

Much has been said earlier of Dumfries shipping: at a fairly low level early in the century (the last ship berthed at Dockfoot in 1916) it sank further during the 1914-18 War and remained fairly low through the 1920's. Extensive dredging by the Nith Navigation Commission in the early thirties resulted in a marked comeback: through the later thirties traffic was running at 100-150 vessels through the Port each year (the writer photographed four vessels together at Kinghorn Quay in 1937): but the 1939-45 War dealt the final blow: only an occasional vessel comes to Glencaple now and the Nith Navigation Commission has been disbanded.

The field of housing and population distribution has seen major changes since 1906. The years before the First World War saw only gradual development though some ribbon development of private homes continued on the main roads: there was little change in the grim living conditions in the central part of the town, although the demolition of the cruck-framed Munches Street slum area was planned in 1913 and Municipal Terrace (reputed to be the first municipal housing in Scotland) was built in 1914 at the junction of Brooms Road and Annan Road.

The 1914-18 war affected Dumfries as it did every part of the country: Arrol Johnston changed to the manufacture of aeroplane engines, propellers and frames and machine-gun parts. MacGeorge's textile mill made army gloves, and many local people worked in the major munitions manufacturing and storage development outside town in the Eastriggs—Gretna area where the population jumped to around 20,000 from a parish total of just over 1200 in 1911, and fell as rapidly at the end of the war.

The period between the two World Wars saw a quickening pace of physical development in and around Dumfries. In 1923 Cresswell Housing Scheme was begun in open fields and built as a unit not as a mere ribbon development. This scheme marked the commencement of a long succession of major Council housing schemes which altered the whole shape of the town. The early 1920's also saw the beginning of a real attempt to clear the town's slum properties. The Munches Street warren of mean alleys was finally cleared and the fine new thoroughfare of Great King Street created in place of the narrow "Wide Entry". The late twenties saw the building of St. Michael's Bridge (1927-29), the first traffic bridge since 1791. Consequent upon this and the Amalgamation of Dumfries and Maxwelltown (1929), came the rapid growth from 1929 to 1939 of Municipal building schemes on the West bank of the river—Troqueer, Sandside, and the first part of Lincluden—plus rapid private building development on Pleasance Avenue between the West end of the newly built bridge and Newabbey Road: East of the river there was the Balmoral housing scheme between that Annan and Lockerbie roads, and much private building in that general area also.

The 1930's in common with the rest of the country were disastrous years industrially: Arrol-Johnston went into liquidation in 1928 and the works, after a few years winding up, finally closed in 1932: many of the skilled work force moved South to Coventry. The largest single unit in the town's textile industry, Messrs. Charteries and Spence's woollen mill, also closed in this period despite full order books as a result of a dispute among the partners, putting 600 girls out of work: however a heavy public building programme and the town's continued importance as a market centre for the countryside around cushioned the worst effects of the recession. The Carnation Milk Plant brought new industry to the town in 1934-35 and remains one of the large employers.

The second World War saw the town once again on a war footing: the former Arrol-Johnston factory at Heathhall was used as an R.A.F. store and an aerodrome was built at Tinwald Downs, site of the old race-course. The town was a headquarters of the Norwegian armed forces. Imperial Chemical Industries chemical explosives plant at Drungans, just outside the town, built in 1938-39, employed many people. Dumfries folk worked also in the other explosives factories at Powfoot and Daleattie.

Progress in the town was accelerated after the end of the War in 1945: business and industry began to recover a peacetime look: the North British Rubber Company (now Uniroyal) took over the former motor factory at Heathhall after the R.A.F. vacated it, due largely to the efforts of the late James Hutcheon, Town Clerk (whose wife and children had been in Gretna that night of the Masonic Dinner when many prominent Dumfries business men were killed by a random bomb—the pilot had known he was somewhere over the arms depots at Gretna—James was head of Air Raid Precautions and could not leave his post—it was the next day before he knew they were safe). I.C.I. built a large new factory beside the wartime Nobel plant at Drungans for the manufacture of Ardil, a synthetic fibre made from groundnut waste. Unhappily this enterprise was not a success but the factory was turned over to the manufacture of plastic film and has expanded considerably over the years. The traditional knitwear industry has continued despite fluctuations in trade but is no longer—as it was before the War—the leading industry of Dumfries. The progressive agriculture of S.W. Scotland still plays a major part in the economic life of the town, and the slaughterhouse in Dumfries, built in the 1930's, plays a key part in the export of dead meat from the area, not only to the customary markets of England and Scotland but also to the Continent of Europe. Not surprisingly for the centre of a milk-producing area, milk processing at the Carnation Milk Factory has become a very important feature of local industry. Although the bulk of production consists of the well-known tinned milk, some other milk-based foods are now being produced too, as well as "Coffee-Mate", a non-milk coffee whitener which one meets, for example, on the airlines between Britain and Israel. Here also the same company have a large can-making plant opened in the nineteen sixties. The servicing of the agriculture industry of today requires many skills and the commerce of the town has been diversified in many ways to meet its needs. Industrially, then, in the years since the War, Dumfries has had a fair measure of prosperity, not enjoying any great "booms" but avoiding the severe depression suffered by areas such as Upper Nithsdale dependent on traditional declining industry: though alas, the problem of lack of employment for the young, so severe everywhere, has not missed our town.

Dumfries is well supplied by hospitals, and soon after the 1939-45 War the modern Cresswell Maternity Hospital was built out of—and extended from—the old Poor Law Workhouse which had been taken over during the war: and in 1975 the huge modern Dumfries and Galloway Royal Infirmary, built on the former Crichton Royal Golf Course beside the Bankend Road, was opened—one of the most modern and efficient in Britain: it adjoins the Crichton Royal psychiatric hospital, which makes for ease in administration: the old Royal Infirmary building on St. Michael Street is now a geriatric hospital.

The pressure for houses to meet the early post-war need and to replace the old houses in tenements, back lands and vennels, led to a considerable expansion of the built-up area of the town and its boundaries. In 1947 the town took in another large area on the West side of the Nith between the river and Hardthorn Road and extending to Newbridge: much of this land was used for local authority houses, mostly at Lochside: land on Irongray Road was set aside for a small industrial estate and factory buildings built there: the pre-war Sandside housing development was extended and was soon separated only by a field or so from the extended Lincluden scheme which also considerably extended itself outwards to Jock's Loaning. The story of how Dumfries overcame a very difficult housing problem illustrated the effectiveness at that time of local democracy in action. The Burgh was credited with being the first local authority to complete its slum clearance. The major task finished, and with finance drying up, attention was by the 1970's concentrated on modernising houses now regarded as sub-standard: much of this is being done by owner-occupiers. In recent years, following Government legislation to encourage it, many municipal houses have been purchased by their tenants. At the same time as the major municipal housing effort was being made there was a great extension of private housing in such places as Castledykes and the much larger Georgetown Road—Craigs Road area: and local authority housing schemes were constructed at Kingholm and Glencaple. Outside the town proper major housing developments by the then County at Heathhall and Locharbriggs created a satellite dormitory suburb of great size.

So the Dumfries conurbation has grown four or five fold since 1906: and the universal use of motor cars means that people come in every day to work in Dumfries from as far afield as Kirkcudbright and Kirkconnel. The four or five fold increase in area covered does not mean that the

population has increased: it hovers between 29,000 and 30,000, a figure it
has held for a good many years—though this does not include Locharbriggs—Heathhall. Furthermore, since the 1929 Amalgamation a
substantial proportion of the population now lives West of the Nith.

Within the old town centre the greatest change has been the complete
demolition and rebuilding of the lower High Street, and the advent of the
great multiples—Boots, Menzies, W.H. Smith, Marks & Spencers,
Littlewoods, Presto, Low's, and the creation of the Co-Operative
Society's large supermarket. Building Society and Insurance offices
have ramified, and trades which did not exist in 1906—radio and
television shops, video shops, motor car parts and spares—have become
important—even the ubiquitous washing machine did not exist then: and
the filament street lighting which began to replace gas in 1911 has been
replaced by neon and sodium lighting: the Gas Works is closed, and a
large new petroleum-fuelled gas works built at Locharbriggs. New
houses have been accompanied by new school buildings: older schools
have been modernised and new ones built: Dumfries Academy has been
vastly extended: Dumfries High School left George Street for
Marchmount, the old premises housing a technical education
department: the great Dumfries and Galloway College of
Technology—the area's nearest thing to a University—at Locharbriggs
draws students from all over the South-West: in 1970 Maxwelltown
High School opened at Lochside: St. Joseph's College, since 1872 a
Catholic boarding and day school run by the Marist Brothers, is now an
interdenominational comprehensive secondary school: Cargenbridge
High School, built in the fifties, has been rather left behind by
developments elsewhere in the town. Twice during this century Dumfries
has laid claim to a University (it has been trying since the 1690's)
without success: but many still hope that one day the advantages and
claims of Dumfries will be recognised.

Since the war there has been a much greater emphasis on public
service for the aged, disabled, and less fortunate members of the
community. This has produced altered and new buildings on various
sites: a children's home on the site of Cresswell House: Moorheads
Hospital (1742) was transferred to the then Town Council following an
agreement with the Trustees and was then extended and modernised as
an old folks' home: the site of the old houses in Swans Vennel is now
occupied by flatlets for old people, with a resident nurse/supervisor, one
or more meals a day being supplied by Moorheads next door: although
Lincluden House was demolished after serving for a number of years as a
community centre, the name remains in a most modern old folks' home
completed in 1971: the Church of Scotland has a fine old folks' home in
George Street and there are now several Abbeyfield Homes for the
elderly in the town, while a few miles out of town the Cheshire Home at
Carnsalloch tends the severely handicapped. Administratively the
biggest change came in 1975 when the Royal Burgh of Dumfries was
merged into Nithsdale District, administered from the Municipal Cham-

bers in Buccleuch Street, and the County was replaced by Dumfries and Galloway Region. Culturally, the Ewart Library, once the Burgh, then the County, and now the Regional Library, caters for many interests and is the centre of the Library Service for the whole of Dumfries and Galloway: a fine modern Art Gallery opened at Gracefield in 1951: the Burgh Museum, now Dumfries Museum, is now greatly extended, with several professional staff and good conservation, study and teaching facilities, and is in charge of Burns' House, the Old Bridge House, and the Old Mill. The Dumfries and Galloway Natural History and Antiquarian Society, founded in 1862, is still vigorous and still publishes its valuable Transactions: and, especially in winter, there are many University Extra-Mural and other classes. Modern interest in travel has led to the establishment of several travel agents in the town: actual emigration, strong until 1914, dropped off sharply except for a boom in emigration to Australia in the late fifties—but many Dumfries families still boast close relations in Canada, U.S.A., Australia, S. Africa and New Zealand, and, particularly from the U.S.A., visits by family associations such as the McBrairs and Kirkpatricks having ancestors in this area have become commonplace.

McDowall always took great interest in the Churches of Dumfries: while there were very few changes from the time of his death until long after the appearance of the 1906 edition of his History, the mid-20th century has been a time of rapid movement in this field.

In 1906 there were twenty-one churches in Dumfries and Maxwelltown representing eight denominations—five Church of Scotland, seven United Free Church of Scotland, two Scottish Episcopal, one Roman Catholic, one Wesleyan, one Baptist, two Congregational and two Catholic Apostolic (Irvingite) as well as other small religious groups and a Corps of the Salvation Army.

In 1974 there were twenty-three places of worship representing twelve denominations—ten Church of Scotland, one United Free Church of Scotland, one Free Church of Scotland, two Scottish Episcopal, two Roman Catholic, one Methodist, one Baptist, one Congregational, one Salvation Army, one Christian Brethren, one Jehova's Witnesses, one Mormon, an interdenominational Mission hall on Greenbrae, and some other small religious groups, including the Christian Scientists and the Society of Friends. Since then the major changes have been the closure of Laurieknowe Church, the closure of the Methodist Church in Buccleuch Street (there is now no Methodist presence in Dumfries, for the first time since the 1780's), and the closure of the South Church, now absorbed by St. Michael's.

The town's small Muslim, Buddhist and Hindu communities have no places of worship though the Buddhists on Laurieknowe run a contemplation centre.

Various causes, including movement of population, and the Union of the Church of Scotland and the United Free Church of Scotland in 1929, led to changes in the older part of the town. In 1917 Waterloo Place

Congregational Church united with Irving Street Congregational Church: in 1924 Martyrs' United Free Church of Scotland was dissolved: in 1945 Buccleuch Street Church of Scotland was also dissolved, while in 1951 the South and Townhead congregations of the Church of Scotland united, the Townhead Church being subsequently sold, and, after reconstruction costing £22,500, being opened as the Dining Hall of Dumfries Academy (only a hundred yards or so away from the site of the wartime Nissen hut British Restaurant next to the Ewart Library). The Catholic Apostolic congregation in Queen Street ceased to exist, as did the smaller one near the foot of Maxwell Street in Maxwelltown: after housing a small congregation of the Elim Church for a few years the Queen Street building was demolished in 1966.

The rapid expansion of residential development on the West side of the Nith brought a need for new churches. The first to be opened was in Lincluden housing scheme in 1953 where a Hall Church, a dual purpose building, was erected for the Church of Scotland, the architect being Mr. Purdon Smith. In 1958 St. Teresa's, a handsome Roman Catholic church of modern style, with a large separate bell steeple (housing the bell from the little Virginhall Free Church further up Nithsdale), was built on Glasgow Street, Mr. John Sutherland being the architect. In 1962 a hall with belfry was built for the Church of Scotland at Lochside. This was followed in 1965 by a church in the shape of an irregular octagon. The church, linked to the hall, possesses a gallery for organ and choir. The architect was J.C. Miller. St. Ninian's Episcopal Church in Howgate Street closed in 1963 (it now houses Dumfries Operatic Society, and the Jehovah's Witness church has been built next door to it) and a new St. Ninian's opened in Lochside in 1967, Messrs. Morton and Fotheringham being the architects. The destruction by fire of St. Andrew's Pro-Cathedral, and the reduction of its status to that of a parish church, necessitated the building of a new church: this, completed in 1964, is of a style more removed than that of St. Teresa's from that of the nineteenth century, with a striking tent-type roof: the tall, angular steeple of the Cathedral has been kept as a free-standing bell-tower. The architects were Sutherland, Dickie, and Partners. A third striking building was completed in 1966 on a commanding position overlooking the Edinburgh Road where it leaves the river to cross the railway bridge: this is the Mormon Church, designed and built by one of the community from Utah.

Though the Benedictine Convent on Corbelly Hill ceased to run its school a few years ago the community of nuns is still there and at the time of writing this there is a proposal to create at the convent a small museum of monastic history in the area.

One of the greatest changes of the century has in fact been in the field of religion: whereas in 1906 the vast majority of the townspeople were regular churchgoers, now congregations other than the Catholic have dropped off severely and many people only attend churches for marriages, baptisms and the like: several of the town's undertakers have over the last twenty years created small funeral chapels. When the writer was a boy many houses kept their blinds down all day on Sunday: no housewife would be seen hanging out washing on that day: his Mother chided him if he whistled on Sunday: his Father remembered, as a boy of twelve, his Grandfather, seeing him reading "Treasure Island" on a Sunday, taking it from him and setting the Bible down before him, saying "read that—it's true"—novel—reading was frowned on. In the schools, on the other hand, religious teaching has been introduced during the century: in 1906 a good proportion of the Academy staff were proselytising atheists or agnostics: now most schools have morning prayers. There has been a tendency for the more fundamentalist churches to increase their strength.

History of Dumfries.

CHAPTER I.

DUMFRIESSHIRE, about whose chief town this work is principally
written, lies in an elliptical form on the north side of the Solway
Frith, its greater diameter extending about fifty miles, from the
mountain of Corsincon, in Ayrshire, to Liddel Moat, in Roxburghshire ; and its smaller diameter stretching from Loch Craig, on the
confines of Peeblesshire. to Caerlaverock Castle, on the Solway—a
distance of about thirty-two miles. It has a sea-shore of fully
twenty-one miles, running from the mouth of the river Nith to
that of the river Sark ; and its total circumference is one hundred
and seventy-four miles, not including the estuaries of the Nith,
the Lochar, the Annan, and the Sark :* its whole surface measuring 1098 square miles.

The county is separated from Kirkcudbrightshire for several
miles on the south-west by the water of Cairn, or Cluden ; and
from the point where that stream ceases to become its boundary-
line it is cinctured by a high mountain range, which breaks away
westward from Cumberland into the south of Scotland—the only
exception being an open part of Liddesdale that slopes smoothly
into the neighbouring shire of Roxburgh. At this exceptional
point a frontier is supplied by the Liddel, and afterwards by the
Liddel in conjunction with the Esk, till the line, coming overland
westward, touches the Sark, runs with that stream to the sea,
then follows the devious margin of the Solway till it terminates at
the estuary of the Nith ; the Sark becoming in its course not
simply the fringe of the county in that direction, but the small,
faint border-line which divides England from Scotland. Dum-

* Singer's Survey of Dumfriesshire, p. 2.

friesshire comprehends the districts of Nithsdale, Annandale, and Eskdale : which natural divisions nearly agree with the ancient jurisdictions that prevailed : the first having been governed as a sheriffship, the second as a stewartry, and the third as a regality. Its population, which was 39,788 in 1755, had risen to 75,878 in 1861, and been reduced chiefly by emigration from the rural districts, to 74,715 in 1871. There are fifty-three parishes in the synod of Dumfries, ten of which are in the stewartry of Kirkcudbright ; these ten, with seven that are in the county, making up the presbytery of Dumfries. The parish of Dumfries has an area of fifteen square miles : its population a hundred years ago was about 5500 ; at the beginning of the current century it was little more than 7000 ; it is now nearly double that amount *(a)*. Save the site of the burgh, and a low ridge of hills below it running nearly parallel with the river on to Caerlaverock, the parish presents a level surface ; agriculturally, its north and north-western sections are a reddish earth, having a freestone bottom ; the south-western consisting of a strong clay, with clay upon gravel where the lands are flat ; while the eastern forms part of a huge waste, Lochar Moss, regarding which it is proverbially said,

"First a wood, and then a sea,
Now a moss, and ay will be."

But the process of reclamation has gone on so rapidly of late as to lead us to hope that in this case the wilderness will, ere many years elapse, " blossom like the rose."

The Nith is the chief river of the county. Coming from its cradle among the mountains east of Dalmellington, in Ayrshire, it describes a south-westerly course, watering by the way the royal burgh of Sanquhar, at the head of the dale, and further down the ducal village of Thornhill, around which the country opens well up—spacious plains claiming with success ample room and verge from the highlands, that seem at points further north as if they wished to shut up the valley altogether. From an eminence westward of Thornhill the enormous mass of Drumlanrig Castle is seen looking down, says Robert Chambers, " with its innumerable windows upon the plain, like a great presiding idol "*—the embodied genius of feudalism. One of the barrier ridges northward is pierced by the narrow, gloomy pass of Enterkin, through which the sister vales of Nith and Clyde keep up precarious intercourse. Lower down, at Auldgirth Bridge, near Blackwood, the mountain ranges that environ the dale approach each other more closely, then recede, till round and below Dumfries a spacious plain, like that of " Lombardy in miniature," is formed ; differing chiefly from its beautiful Italian type in having a larger propor-

(a) In 1891 the population of the county was 74,308 ; and of the parish, including the burgh, 16,500.
* Picture of Scotland, p. 235.

tion of upland compared to its champaign country.* The Nith is swelled by numerous brooks at various stages of its course—its latest and greatest acquisition being the Cluden, a mile above Dumfries ; and about eight miles below the burgh the river falls into the Solway Frith : its entire course being forty-five miles.

An upland spot, where the counties of Lanark, Peebles, and Dumfries confront each other, gives birth to three streams, according to the popular rhyme,

> " The Annan, Tweed, and Clyde
> A' rise oot o' ae hill-side."

The Annan, after a somewhat rapid rush from its highland home, five miles above the pretty watering-place of Moffat, is joined two miles below that town by several tributaries ; it then proceeds more leisurely in a southerly direction down the dale to which it gives a name, and which, narrowed at first by rocks or ridges, expands into a wide, fertile basin, called the Howe of Annandale, studded with villages, and spangled by the nine lakes of Loch-maben ; Bruce's ancient burgh and the town of Lockerbie occupy-ing conspicuous situations on its western and eastern sides. Other rivulets, including the Dryfe, give increased volume to the stream below Lochmaben ; the valley narrowing again as the waters grow wider and deeper. When little more than a mile from the sea, it waters the second town in Dumfriesshire, the royal burgh of Annan ; the entire course of the river measuring nearly forty miles. The ancient stewartry of Annandale had a wider range than the valley of the Annan, as it comprised the tracts of country that lie eastward to the Sark, and westward along the Solway towards the Lochar.

Dumfriesshire is separated from England for fully a mile in extent by the Esk—which river, starting from the frontiers of Selkirkshire, takes a southern route, sweeps past the baronial town of Langholm, and after being a Scottish stream to the extent of thirty miles, enters Cumberland, passes by Longtown, then takes a westward turn, and falls, like its two sister rivers, into the Solway. The length of the Esk is nearly forty miles : part of its lower waters, meandering through the Debatable Land, constitutes a portion of the Western Border ; and often, as we shall have to notice, its waves ran red with blood to the sea, owing to its boun-dary position between two hostile nations.

Having given these brief sketches of Nithsdale, Annandale, and Eskdale, let us point out with a little more detail the position and aspect of the county town. Snugly built on the left bank of the river, eight miles above where it loses itself in the Solway, stands the royal burgh of Dumfries. When viewed from the neighbouring heights, especially those on the opposite Galloway side, the town with its environments forms a charming picture.

* Fullarton & Co.'s Gazetteer of Scotland, vol. i., p. 425.

The old burgh is seen lying nestled in the plain below, embosomed in umbrageous woods, while gentle acclivities or bolder elevations rise like the seats of an amphitheatre on every side. Hill and dale contrast finely with each other ; country and town seem linked in kindly fellowship—the handicraft creations of man mingling without harshness or abrupt transition with the inimitable works of Nature ; while here and there may be noticed a barren track or rugged peak, varying without impairing the attractiveness of the landscape. Nithsdale, with its queenly capital, looks indeed beautiful when seen at summer - tide from such a " coign of vantage," and all the more so owing to the red-sandstone of its buildings giving warmth and contrast to the prevailing green—the whole sight suggesting the appreciative words of Burns :

> " How lovely, Nith, thy fruitful vales,
>   Where spreading hawthorns gaily bloom ;
> How sweetly wind thy sloping dales,
>   Where lambkins wanton through the broom."

A range of hills far to the north, or left, is cleft by the river ; and one of the separated portions, passing eastward, terminates in the heights of Mouswald ; while the other, taking a western sweep, culminates in Criffel. Within the enclosure thus formed lies the oval-shaped strath itself ; and after marking its fertile fields, its " lown," sunny nooks, and its smiling groves, the eye rests with human interest on the spires and pinnacles, the tall chimneys and clustering domiciles just below, where a " link " of the Nith is seen lying like a miniature lake—all telling that a hive of industry, busy though small, has its homestead in these vernal bowers. *

The burgh, thus pleasantly situated, lies in the latitude of 55 degrees, 8 minutes, and 30 seconds, north ; its longitude being 3 degrees, 36 minutes, west. The population in 1861 was 12,347 : during the ten intervening years the inhabitants so increased that they numbered 13,710 when the census was taken on the 2nd of April, 1871. Maxwelltown, separated from its elder sister town by the river, and belonging to a different county, joins with it to form a parliamentary burgh, the constituency of which numbers 1717, while the municipal constituency of Dumfries amounts to 1194. (a)

Such, in brief, are the aspect and size of the burgh in 1872 ; and after this preliminary glance at it, and the district with which

---

* Visitor's Guide to Dumfries (second edition), p. 10.

(a) In 1891 the population of the Parliamentary burgh, which includes Maxwell-town, was 18,049 ; and of the royal burgh, which does not include Maxwelltown but is wider than the municipal boundary, 16,673. The population of Maxwelltown, included in the parliamentary burgh of Dumfries, was 4975. The population of the parish of Dumfries, exclusive of the burgh, was 4787 ; and of the parish of Troqueer, exclusive of Maxwelltown, 912. In 1898 the voters in the parliamentary burgh numbered 2404 (including 741 in Maxwelltown); and on the municipal roll for Dumfries 1663 males, 544 females. In the parish, exclusive of the burgh, the Parliamentary roll numbered 719 voters. On the Maxwelltown municipal roll there were 782 males and 200 females ; and in Troqueer (exclusive of Maxwelltown) the parliamentary voters (for the Stewartry) were 204.

it is associated, we must withdraw from the picture for a long while. Going far back into the misty depths of the past — the distant days of other years—we must endeavour to ascertain the origin of Dumfries—see how it looked in its embryo state, when its first rude buildings threw shadows on the rising beach, or were mirrored on the river's bosom ; then follow its varying fortunes—mark its growth and periods of temporary decadence— till we can reproduce the sketch just laid aside, of the burgh as it now is, and fill in a few details to render the likeness more complete.

No positive information has been obtained of the era and circumstances in which the town of Dumfries was founded. There are distant traces of its existence as far back as the eleventh century ; and it may be fairly inferred that it had its origin at a period much more remote—though we fear those writers who hold that it flourished as a place of distinction during the Roman occupation of North Britain would experience great difficulty in establishing their hypothesis. It is not unlikely that the Selgovæ, who inhabited Nithsdale and neighbouring districts at that time, and who, by means of their rude but strong forts, long resisted the legions of Agricola, may have raised some military works of a defensive nature on or near the site of Dumfries ; and it is more than probable that a castle of some kind formed the nucleus of the town. This is inferred from the etymology of the name, which, according to the learned Chalmers, is resolvable into two Gaelic terms, signifying a castle in the copse or brushwood.*

According to another theory, the name is a corruption of two words which mean the Friars' Hill ; those who favour this idea alleging that St. Ninian, by planting a religious house near the head of what is now the Friars' Vennel, at the close of the fourth century, became the virtual founder of the burgh ;† but Ninian, so far as is known, did not originate any monastic establishments in Nithsdale or elsewhere, and was simply a missionary or evangelist on a great scale. In the list of British towns given by the ancient historian Nennius, the name Caer Peris occurs, which some modern antiquarians—without any sufficient warrant, we think—suppose to have been transmuted by a change of dialect into Dumfries.‡ Others, again, fancy that Bede alludes to the town when he states that St. Wilfred, a zealous North of England bishop of the seventh century, held a synod "juxta fluvium Nidd." § But, if so, it is singular that so careful a chronicler as Bede did not denote the town in more specific terms. Most likely the Nidd he speaks of is the river of that name in Yorkshire.

* Caledonia, vol. iii., p. 44.   † MS. Lecture by Rev. H. Small, Dumfries.
‡ Paper read by Mr Skene before the Society of Antiquaries of Scotland, on the Early Frisian Settlements in Scotland.
§ Bede, Eccles. Hist., lib. v., cap. 20.

In connection with this question there is yet another hypothesis. When, in 1069, Malcolm Canmore and William the Conqueror held a conference respecting the claims of Edward
Altheling to the English Crown, they met at Abernithi—a term
which in the old British tongue means a port at the mouth of
the Nith. * Surely, it has been argued, the town thus characterised must have been Dumfries ; and therefore it must have
existed as a port in the kingdom of Strathclyde, if not in the
older province of Valentia. Unfortunately for this assumption,
the town is situated eight or nine miles distant from the sea ;
and we cannot suppose that the estuary of the river was higher
up in the eleventh century than it now is, whatever it may have
been in the pre-historic ages. Some forgotten village called
Abernithi may have, long since, looked out on the waters of
the Solway ; but that name could scarcely have been borne by
the burgh of whose origin we are in search.

In the earliest charter to the town still extant — that of
Robert III., dated 28th April, 1395—the appellation given is
"Burgi de Drumfreiss," a form of spelling which, with one " s "
omitted, continued in vogue till about 1780. During the reign
of Alexander III. and the long interregnum which followed, the
form nearly resembled that of the present day—the prefix being
generally Dun or Dum, rather than Drum : thus, in a contemporary representation made to the English Government respecting the slaughter of John Comyn in 1306, the locality is described
as " en l'eglise de Freres meneours de la ville de Dunfres ; " † and
later we read of the sheriff of Dumfries (vicecomes de Dunfres), as
well as of the sheriffdom or county (vicecomitatus) (a). Such
uncouth spellings of the name as Dounfres, Dunfreisch, Droon-
freisch, and Drumfriesche, occasionally occur in old documents ;
but the variations are never so great as to leave any doubt as to
the town that is meant ; and nearly all more or less embody the
idea of a " castle in the shrubbery," ‡ according to the etymology
of Chalmers, which we accept as preferable to any other that has
been suggested. § (b)

* Redpath's Border History, p. 63.
† Sir Francis Palgrave's Documents and Records Illustrative of the History of
Scotland, p. 335.
(a) Stevenson's Hist. Doc. ; Scot. II., 90. Mr M'Dowall's text has been altered
here to free it of some confusion.
‡ The only exception we have met with occurs in a Papal Bull issued against
Bruce in 1320, for the homicide of Comyn, which it stated to have been perpetrated in
the Minorite Church of " Dynifes."
§ Chalmers's words are: " This celebrated prefix *Dun* must necessarily have been
appropriated to some fortlet, or strength, according to the secondary signification of
that ancient word. The *phrys* of the British speech, and the kindred *phreas* of the
Scoto, signify shrubs ; and the Dun-fres must consequently mean the castle among
the shrubberies, or copsewood."—*Caledonia*, vol. iii., p. 45.
(b) Sir Herbert Maxwell quotes Prosper Aquitanus, who, writing in A.D. 455,
under the year 441, says : " Britain up to this time is brought widely under the dominion
of the Saxons by various conflicts and transactions." One of these settlements, says
Sir Herbert, " seems to have been fixed on the banks of the Nith, and in Dumfries is
preserved the name given to it by the Celtic population—*dun Fris*, the Frisians' fort."

Whilst we are unable to identify Dumfries with any organised community of Britons during the Roman period, there can be no doubt that the district in which it lies was for several centuries ruled over and deemed of much importance by the invading Romans. Apart from the written testimony on the subject, many traces of their presence in Dumfriesshire are still to be found ; coins, weapons, sepulchral remains, military earthworks, and roads being among the relics left by that conquering and civilising race of their lengthened sojourn in this part of Scotland. An interesting inquiry it would be to consider how far they intermingled with the aboriginal population, and left the impress of their genius on its living tide as well as on the material soil ; and we may fairly hazard the supposition that, though the Romans visited the territory of the Selgovæ as enemies, they in course of time became in numerous instances friends and relatives by marriage, as well as conquerors. Thus, not only could the Dumfriesians of a later date speak of their Celtic, British, Saxon, and Norman ancestors, but they might, in common with those of some other Scottish districts, have claimed blood relationship with the masters of the world. The Apostle Paul claimed rank and privilege as a Roman citizen on account of his birth at Tarsus ; and it is a curious fact that the Caledonian tribes in the south of Scotland were invested with the same rights by an edict of Antoninus Pius.

In all, twenty-one British tribes occupied North Britain during the first century of the Christian era, and remained for ages afterwards the chief occupiers of the soil. Five of them, including the Selgovæ, subdued by the arms and civilised by the arts of Rome, occupied the extensive range of country which stretched from the protecting Wall built by Antoninus Pius between the friths of Forth and Clyde, and the other Roman Wall erected by Adrian as a mural link between the Solway and the Tyne. This district was called the province of Valentia *(a)* by Theodosius, in honour of his imperial colleague Valens, and its inhabitants received freedom as well as civilisation from their Italian conquerors. That the subjugated people were treated generously is proved by the circumstance that they were, as we have said, made citizens of the empire ; and, as further evidence of the same fact, they were permitted to choose their own chief governor, or pendragon—whose rule, however, was often challenged by the district chiefs, though rarely interfered with by the Roman emperors—that is to say, we suppose, when the tribute due by the province was promptly paid.

But Dronfres occurs in one of the oldest charter references—Bain's Calendar II., No. 1606 (3)—in the 12th century, and it has been suggested to us that "Drumfres as an original form might naturally wear down to Dunfres, while Dunfres, if original, would not so naturally develop the Drum."

(a) The attribution of the name of Valentia has been questioned by modern scholars, and though not without classical vouchers is doubtful. In the view of one well-qualified to form an opinion on the point, Mr M'Dowall's "Roman picture is a good deal firmer than the state of the evidence warrants."

Late in the fourth century the masterful race who had
exercised a beneficial influence on Valentia took farewell of the
country. The empire, undermined by luxury, and harassed by
barbarous hordes from the north of Europe, was falling to pieces ;
and its ruler, Constantine, who for a time resided in Britain,
left its shores, taking with him the flower of his army—all the
forces belonging to Rome in various parts of the world being
needed for its defence. Then the Britons of Valentia, whom the
Romans had helped to protect when assailed by the Scots from
Ireland and their Caledonian neighbours in the north, found
themselves in an unenviable predicament. The sixteen aboriginal
tribes who had never acknowledged the Roman yoke, and remained
as barbarous as they were brave, did not relish the idea of being
shut out of the rich district that lay south of the Wall of Antonine.
Impelled by acquisitiveness and a love of adventure, a portion of
them, named Picts, sailed down the frith of Forth in their canoes
and curraghs ; whilst others, still more resolute, scaled the interposing wall ; and soon the Britons found, to their dismay, that
their hitherto happy district was overrun by painted savages,
carrying with them fire and sword. (a)

The Picts repeatedly ravaged Valentia in all its borders, and
doubtless the Nith was often stained by the blood they shed ; and
if, at this early period, as some of our chroniclers assert, the drum
or acclivity on which Dumfries now stands was occupied by a
fortress, there would, we may suppose, be many a fierce struggle
for its possession.

The Valentians were unable to shut out the invaders from
their territory ; and the latter, though powerful enough to plunder
and slay, were not sufficiently organised to take complete possession of the land. They were wild, marauding clans, held together
by common instincts rather than by a regular form of government,
or even the asserted supremacy of a ruling chief. It is probably
owing to this circumstance that the Britons of the far north, the
un-Romanized Caledonians or Picts (for these are probably the
same people under different names*), did not conquer the south of
Scotland. Had they done so, and established their authority over
the whole country, the tide of its civilisation would have been
rolled centuries backwards, and Scotland could scarcely ever, in
the nature of things, have occupied a high position in the scale of
nations. The brave defence made by the Selgovæ and their allies,
combined with the disorganisation of the Picts, kept Valentia from

(a) Gildas, the earliest of British historians (c. 516-570), says : " Foul hordes of
Picts and Scots, like tawny worms coming forth in the burning heat of noon out of
the deepest recesses of their holes, hastily land from their curraghs in which they
had crossed the Tithican Valley." Mr George Neilson, in his " Annals of the Solway,"
says of this expression of the British historian that " it has been considerably discussed.
Most probably it is an inflated term from classic Tethys, wife of the Ocean, a goddess
whose name was a metonyme for the sea. The 'Tithican Valley' thus points to the
Solway Strath."

* Caledonia, vol. ii., p 6.

being thrown back into barbarism, and saved the sceptre of the future kingdom for better hands—those of the Scots, a people of the same Celtic origin as the Britons. The Scots had long been settled in Ireland, and had frequently sent over to Galloway and other parts of Britain shoals of adventurers. Eventually, after subduing their Pictish rivals, they conquered the Britons also, and gave their rule and name to the entire country, from the promontory of Orcas to the Wall of Adrian—the new kingdom thus established including a large portion of the north of England.

We must, however, confine our attention at present to the fortunes of the primitive inhabitants of Dumfriesshire. Two of the tribes with whom they were associated, the Ottadini and Gadeni, though able to hold their own against the Picts, were subdued by the Saxons from Northumbria, who, after defeating them at the Battle of Cattraeth, occupied their territory, which lay between the Tweed and Forth. Thus Valentia came to be restricted to Teviotdale, Dumfriesshire, Galloway, Ayrshire, Renfrewshire, Strathclyde, and parts of Stirlingshire and Dumbartonshire. This district, still a very extensive one, was called Regnum Cambrense—the kingdom of Cumbria—and sometimes the kingdom of Strathclyde ; its metropolis being Alcluyd, which the Scoto-Irish subsequently called Dunbritton—the fortress of the Britons—hence the modern name of the town, Dumbarton. For at least a century after the Scots had established their supremacy over the rest of the country, the Strathclyde Britons maintained their independence. The Saxons and Danes sometimes invaded their territory ; and the former appear to have subdued a portion of it at the close of the seventh century, and to have partially colonised Dumfriesshire, or, as Chalmers says, to have scattered over it " a very thin settlement." *

A century later, however, we find members of their royal family intermarrying with those of the Scottish monarch—a proof that the Selgovæ and their kinsmen were still a powerful race. But gradually their strength became reduced, and their dominions circumscribed. The nuptial alliances made with the neighbouring sovereigns proved a new source of weakness to the dispirited Britons, as they were the means of introducing amongst them so many Scots that they could scarcely call the place their own. The strangers settled in great numbers throughout Galloway, and not a few of them passed from that province to the left bank of the Nith, till all the southern portion of Strathclyde seemed to be on the verge of a peaceful social revolution.

The Cumbrians were almost subdued by the new comers before they fairly realised their danger ; and, thoroughly jostled out of the territory which their race had colonised and occupied

* Caledonia, vol iii., p. 61.

for many centuries before the Christian era, they arranged with
Gregory, King of Scots, to leave it, and seek an asylum from their
British countrymen in Wales. Whilst on their sorrowful journey
southward, they were seized with home sickness—repented that
they had tamely yielded up their rich heritage, and resolved to
win it back or perish, rather than pine in exile. A report reached
them that the King of Scots had, after their departure, disbanded
his army, and was therefore defenceless — which news either
originated or confirmed their determination to retrace their steps.

Our historians do not exactly agree in their account of subsequent events ; but they concur in stating that, after the expatriated Britons had re-entered their territory, and plundered the
new settlers to a large extent, they heard with alarm that Gregory
had collected a considerable force, and was hastening to overtake
them. The tidings proved to be correct. The infuriated monarch
fell upon them at the place now occupied as Lochmaben : a brief
but sanguinary struggle ensued, which ended in the utter rout of
the Britons, Constantine their king falling among heaps of slain.
His followers who escaped the battle were slaughtered in the
pursuit, few of them being spared to tell the tale ; but the huge
tumuli, still visible at the scene of the contest,* tell of the terrible
carnage in which the vengeance of Gregory was slaked, and the
kingdom of Cumbria annihilated.†(a) After this decisive engagement, which took place in the year 890, the Britons existed no
more as a separate people in Scotland ; and the government of
that country began to be consolidated and directed by a single
sovereign.

It is not to be supposed, however, that the British element
was, by this memorable exodus and overthrow, entirely blotted
from the population of Dumfriesshire. Many of the Cumbrians
formed matrimonial alliances with the dominant Scots, and many
others would probably remain in the county while the great body
of their countrymen went on their forlorn expedition to Wales.
We think there is every reason to believe that the people who
lived in the district for eleven centuries at least, and were the first
to settle in it of which history takes notice, became nearly as
much as either the Scoto-Irish or the Saxons the progenitors of
the existing race ; and if they are thus in one sense continuing to
occupy a part of the soil which they long exclusively held, we
know that their language still survives in the names of rivers,
streams, mountains, and headlands, most of which in Dumfriesshire and Galloway are British : the nomenclature of the first
colonists thus remaining unchanged by the conflicts of race or the
flight of ages.

* Statistical Account, vol. iii., p. 241.
† Buchanan's History of Scotland, book vi., chap. xi. ; and Chalmers's Caledonia,
vol. iii., p. 61.
(a) For the alleged battle at Lochmaben there is not any really ancient historical
evidence ; and without this, that of the tumuli, which would be corroborative of the
other if the other existed, is inconclusive.

CHAPTER II.

FAINT notices—not very reliable, we fear—are given by pedigree-
makers respecting some Nithsdale families of this early time.
Nuath, son of Coel Godhebog, a Cumbrian prince who flourished
before 300, owned lands in Annandale and Clydesdale, it is said,
which were named, after him, Caer-nuath or Carnwath. If this
statement could be relied upon, it would be no very bold hypothesis to say that the river Nith also owes its name to the son of
Godhebog. One of Nuath's descendants of the fourth generation,
Loth, a Pictish king, formed a strong encampment along the base
of the Tynwald hills, which bore the appellation of Barloth. The
second son, Gwallon, built a chain of forts extending from Dryfesdale to the vicinity of Lochmaben, the designation of which is still
preserved in the existing farm of Galloberry. Gwallon's sister,
Thenelis, was the mother of the celebrated Kentigern, or St.
Mungo, whose name is retained by a Dumfriesshire parish.
Marken, or Marcus, brother of Loth, had a son named Kinder:
to him belonged the district which now forms the parish of Newabbey, and which was at first called after him, Loch Kinder. A
son of Kinder's, Yrein or Yrvin, owned lands in Eskdale, which
bore his name; and to him, it is said, the prolific family of the
Irvings, who ages afterwards flourished in Annandale, and often
held civic rule in Dumfries, owe their origin.*(a)
The long mythical line of Coel Godhebog, now brought down
to the sixth century, had already yielded saints as well as princes.
In or about 560 it produced a rival to Ossian, in the person of

* Barjarg Manuscripts.
(a) The genealogies are, as the author says, not very reliable.

Lywarch Hen, called by the genealogists "a great poet."* He, like Moore's young minstrel, bore both lyre and brand. He wrote poems and built fortresses, none of which survive, though the names of the latter, Castle Lywar in Eskdale and Caer Laurie in the Lothians, still linger on the tongue of tradition. Better than all, perhaps, he founded a wide-spread family, who inherit his name in its modern form, Laurie, which is still a common one in Dumfriesshire. This warrior-bard left two sons, one of whom, Lywarch-Ogg, is said to have settled down on the north shore of the Solway, within the region termed Carbantorigum by Ptolemy, and there, early in the seventh century, originated the greatest of the Nithsdale fortresses, Caer-Lywarch-Ogg—named after himself, and historically famous as the Castle of Caerlaverock.†

About eighty years after the era of this potentate, the Scoto-Irish begin to exercise a complete ascendancy. They have gone far to absorb both Picts and Britons, and are seen overspreading all the land south of the Forth and Clyde. "As a result," says Chalmers, "the whole of Galloway and Carrick becomes full of Scoto-Irish names of places, all imposed by the Irish colonists who settled in these countries at the end of the eight century, and who in subsequent times gradually overspread Kyle, the upper part of Strathclyde, and even pushed into Nithsdale and Eskdale." Our Dumfries progenitors of the eighth century spoke in the old British tongue, best represented by the modern Welsh ; but in the ninth century, and for a long period afterwards, their language was Gaelic, similar to that which is now used in the Highlands and some parts of Ireland.

As yet the boundary-line between Scotland and England was undefined. For centuries before the reign of Alexander II., a large portion of Saxon Cumberland—six manors, it is said—formed an integral part of the former kingdom, except for a short period, when William the Conqueror dispossessed its Scottish occupants and divided it among his followers, assigning large lands on the eastern side of the Esk to a knight named De Estonville, from whom they descended by marriage to the De Wakes. Besides, many rich estates attached to the Scottish Crown lay south of the Sark or Tweed ; and we know that after the death of Alexander III. an account was furnished of the monies yielded by manors that belonged to him in Tynedale and Cumberland, including those of Wark, Grindon, Penreth, Scotby, Carlton, Sowerby, Lang-

---

* The alleged poems of Lywarch Hen have been investigated lately by Mr Thomas Wright and others. These critics reject them all as spurious save one—"A Lament for Urien"—the rest being considered by them as Welsh inventions of the twelfth century.

† Grose seems half disposed to accredit this statement. His words are : "The castle [of Caerlaverock] is said to have been originally founded in the sixth century by Lewarch-Ogg, son of Lewarch-Hen, a famous British poet, and after him to have been called Caer-Lewarch-Ogg, which in the Gaelic signified the city or fortress of Lewarch-Ogg."—*Antiquities*, vol. i., p. 159.

wathby, and Salkeld.* If these circumstances led to frequent wars, they also facilitated the intercourse of the two peoples. Dumfriesshire had not become, as yet, a border county ; there was no broad line of demarcation between its Celtic inhabitants and the Anglo-Saxons further south : as a consequence, these races exercised considerable influence on each other ; and when Malcolm Canmore married an English princess, in 1069, this reciprocal influence was greatly enhanced. The Queen of Scots was followed to her new home by numerous relatives and domestics ; and the Norman Conquest of England, about the same period, drove thousands more of expatriated Saxons into North Britain, where they settled, and soon became a felt power in the country. *(a)*

Some of the Norman chiefs followed them, as we shall see, at a later period ; and the races who were at fierce antagonism in England manifested no such feeling towards each other when they met further north. Many families who subsequently played a distinguished part in Scottish public life were founded by these Saxon or Norman settlers, and some by a union of both. Especially was this the case in that portion of the kingdom to which this history relates.

As a result of the immigration, a new speech was heard everywhere on the banks of the Nith, and many other parts of southern Scotland. Before the end of the twelfth century, the Anglo-Saxon, or rather the Scoto-Saxon, mother of our modern Doric, became the ruling language : it silenced the Gaelic, or banished it beyond the Forth, just as the Gaelic had previously subdued the original tongue. About this time we begin to get a dim view of Dumfries ; but, before we endeavour to describe how at this early period it looked, glimmering in the mist of the ancient chroniclers, an additional word or two must be said as to its probable origin and fortunes in pre-historic times.

We have seen how the Britons of Nithsdale were harassed by the Picts or Caledonians ; and it is not unlikely that the latter, some time before the exodus under Constantine, may have planted down a rude fort of some kind on the site now occupied by Dum-

* Pipe Roll, 19 Edw. I., as published in Historical Documents 1286-1306, edited by the Rev. J. Stevenson.

(a) Mr George Neilson ("Annals of the Solway") traces the name of the frith to the ford across the mouth of the Esk—the chief ford between Scotland and England. The name is composed of two Norse words—"Sol," for mud, and "Vath" (or Anglo-Saxon ' Waeth "), for ford—meaning muddy ford. At the Scottish end of this passage stood and still stands the Clochmabenstane, or Lochmabenstane, where the warden courts were held for the West March. When the name Sulewath occurs in thirteenth century documents it refers to the Esk ford ; and it was not till later that it was applied first to the whole of the mouth of the Esk, and then to the arm of the sea that is now known as the frith. It was not, according to this authority, "until 1092, when William Rufus seized, restored, and occupied Carlisle, building a fort or castellum there, that the Solway took that place as the march between England and Scotland which it maintained throughout the reign of Henry I." On Henry's death, in 1135, David I. of Scotland successfully reasserted the Scottish claim to Cumbria, made Carlisle his residence, built its great keep, and heightened the city walls. During this period the Solway ceased to be a boundary of the realm of Scotland. But in 1157 Cumberland was ceded to Henry II. by Malcolm the Maiden, and "thenceforth the Solway became a vital part of the marches of the realms."

fries, with the view of securing a permanent footing in the district. They, however, never seem to have acquired a regular settlement on the left bank of the Nith ; and to their kinsmen of a later period, the Scoto-Irish, the credit must be given of having built the castle which originated the town. Our forefathers of that early time did not erect many castles of stone and lime ; and the defensive structure which, from its situation, conferred a name on the town that gradually grew up around it, was doubtless formed of oak, hewn down in some neighbouring forest—for there was nothing but brushwood on the somewhat barren and exposed eminence which received the castle for its crest. *(a)*

The existence of such a fortress at a very early period is beyond the reach of doubt. A charter by William the Lion, witnessed by David his brother and others, describes a toft or tenement at Dumfries as being between the castle and the church ; and another charter from the same monarch confers a piece of land similarly situated on Jocelyne, Bishop of Glasgow—the words used in the latter instance, "inter vetus Castellum et Ecclesiam," indicating that the castle, even at that period (about 1180), was an ancient building. Supposing it to have been at the date of the grant a hundred and eighty years old, this would carry us back to 1000 as the year when this particular castle was erected ; but long before that date a Selgovian fortlet on the same site may have been planted down and become the germ of the burgh. *(b)*

In considering a question of this kind, natural influences, in the absence of written documents, may sometimes be profitably consulted ; and in the case before us there are two which especially claim attention : the first, a defile or pass in the mountain range overlooking the town on the west, through which the Scoto-Irish from Galloway would proceed when entering Nithsdale ; and the second is the shallowing of the Nith just before the site of the town is reached rendering the stream easily fordable by persons crossing it in an opposite way from Cumberland.* That under such conditions as these, a small colony of Scoto-Irish should, in the ninth or tenth century, have been planted down on the left bank of the river, is highly probable ; and a few of the settlers may even have tenanted their rude cabins some time before a fortress rose to give a name and protection to their humble village.

We can easily fancy to ourselves a band of adventurous Celts taking possession of this favourable site, in spite of any opposition that may have been made to them by previous occupants. Crossing the Nith in their curraghs, or wading it at the fords, they would occupy at first only the drum, or low, shrub-covered hillside

---

(a) The early fortresses were earthworks, palisaded. The first of the Norman fortresses were motes.

(b) In some of the charters the word is *castellarium*. It is not an ancient building but an old site that is indicated.

* Dr. Burnside's MS. History of Dumfries.

--up which the oldest street of the burgh runs—in order to maintain close communication with their friends in Galloway. Eventually growing more confident, they would, we suppose, creep a little north and south, thus giving a cross-like form to their colony; and by-and-by build for their defence a peel-house, the progenitor of several future fortresses, at the top of the acclivity. Friars' Vennel, the street first referred to, is unquestionably the most ancient portion of the town ; and we are inclined to think that it and a small part of High Street, with a few adjoining outskirts, formed the Dumfries of the eleventh century. Soon afterwards, on being constituted a royal burgh, it must have expanded rapidly : the main thoroughfare running down nearly half a mile to the church of St. Michael, houses rising up in Lochmabengate, and all around the castle at the head of High Street, and forming as a whole no inconsiderable town. *(a)*

During a long epoch preceding the reign of Malcolm Canmore the district watered by the Nith had experienced many changes. The Britons, rude and idolatrous, were its primitive occupants. Then we find them comparatively civilised by their Roman conquerors, though still left by them in all the moral darkness of their original heathenism. The barrows, cairns, and remains of stone temples still to be seen in the district tell of a time when Druidism was the prevailing religion, and Christianity unknown. Before the Romans retired from Valentia, more potent civilisers appeared in it, who originated a beneficent influence that proved to be enduring. Ninian passing through Nithsdale bearing the

(a) The conclusion that Friars' Vennel is the oldest street proceeds on the assumption that both the castle and the monastery were towards the top of it. It is difficult to imagine two such establishments crowding upon each other there. Dr Burnside, in his manuscript history of Dumfries, places the castle at the opposite end of the town ; and he is borne out by documentary evidence that has since been brought to light.

The charter referred to by Mr M'Dowall places the castellum south of the church (of St. Michael), though his reference does not disclose that fact ; and when Bruce murdered Comyn in the monastery it is on record (Hemingburgh, ii., 266) that he mounted Comyn's horse and rode to the castle—which suggests that the castle was some distance off, and not merely round the corner.

Mr George Neilson, writing in the *Dumfries Standard* (May-June, 1899) on the origin of the burgh, shews that the earliest attribution of that status to Dumfries was in the year 1186, that in several deeds of William's of that period it is so referred to, and that both the castle and the burgh were creations of William. "On the wild Galloway frontier Dumfries castle had been built, and Dumfries burgh had been instituted, by King William, to help in keeping down and stopping the periodic outbreaks of the marauding Celt."

It is evident, as already indicated, that there was a castle of some sort before William's. There are references to the old site in his time. And in 1336 the reference is most distinct. There is a waste *mota castri* spoken of, with the kyngesholm beside it. (Bain's Calendar, iii., 318.) The Kingholm adjoins Castledykes, where William's castle was erected, and where the earlier castle stood.

In his admirable guide to Dumfries ("Dumfries and Round About"—1898) Mr W. Dickie quotes from several documents to bear out the view that Dumfries castle was at the south end of the town. Among others a manuscript report (Cottonian collection) to the English Government by a military officer (c. 1563-1566) regarding the defensive condition of Dumfries. It is there stated that "the auld castell of Drumfreis is fyve miles and a half within the mowthe of Nyth, standing upon the syde of the saime, very good for a forte. The platt and grounde thairof like to Roxburgh Castell. It may lett [obstruct] the towne and the bridge of Drumfreis, and receive boates of tenn tonnes as said is furth of Englonde." Dumfries itself, the writer goes on to say, "standeth six myles within the mouth of Nith, the head toun of the shyre. Lord Maxwell hath a fair house batteled within the toun, but not tentable or strong againis aine battery or gunnes."

gospel lamp, and irradiating the moral darkness of the district, is the finest picture we can think of in those early times. He it was who first denounced the Druidical rites and superstitution of its people, and called upon them to abandon their idolatrous groves and their altars, crimsoned at times with human blood, and embrace the new faith. This devoted apostle of the Selgovæ made many disciples, who had to endure the fires of persecution ; but the pure doctrines which he preached made steady progress in spite of all opposition. Ninian commenced his labours about the year 400 ; and before another century had elapsed nearly all the people of Valentia had been baptised. He founded a college at Whithorn, in Galloway, and Bede records that the first stone church in Britain was built by him at the same place, and appropriately called Candida Casa. The Scoto-Irish invaders of Valentia in the ninth century also professed Christianity, having been converted long before through the instrumentality of the Culdees under Columbia. Their intermixture with the Selgovæ, and ultimate ascendancy over them, were on the whole fruitful of good results.

When the Saxons came in thousands, and the Normans in hundreds, to the south of Scotland, as encouraged by Malcolm Canmore and succeeding sovereigns, another powerful impulse was given to the civilisation of the kingdom.

In the eleventh century we find the heterogeneous elements of the population so fused together that the inhabitants are not so much Britons, Picts, Scoto-Irish, or Saxons, as Scots, forming a nation, united under one common head, and their country taking a not unimportant position among the states of Europe. It is under such interesting circumstances as these that we get our first faint glimpses of Dumfries and Nithsdale—that we see the " castle " towering through the " brushwood," the cabins beginning to cluster round it, and the neighbourhood occupied by chiefs making some little figure in history, for which they were taken notice of by contemporary annalists or by the eye of tradition.

Even down till the death of David I., which took place in 1153, Nithsdale was still for the most part Celtic in its people and institutions. Its lord or chief, Dunegal, one of the Dougalls or M'Dowalls of Galloway,* ruled over the valley in patriarchial style—the feudal system not yet having forced its way into this portion of Scotland. All the land on which the town of Dumfries now stands, and many a fair rood besides, were, under the name of Stranith, held by Dunegal as their legal superior ; the inhabitants being recognised as the tenants of the soil, according to their real or supposed relationship to him as head of the clan. Probably the Castle of Dumfries was held by him for the Crown : he did not reside there, however, but at another stronghold situated fifteen

* Tytler's Hist. of Scotland, vol. i., p. 270 ; also, Nisbet's Heraldry, vol. i., p. 282.

miles further up the Nith—the Castle of Morton *--the hoary
ruins of which still remain, carrying the beholder eight centuries
back to an epoch and a people which present a striking contrast
to those of the present day.

Dunegal of Stranid appears as witness of the grant made by
David I. to Robert Brus, of Strathannand or Annandale, about
1124. When Dunegal died, his extensive possessions were divided
among four sons left by him, only two of whom, Randolph (or
Rodolph) and Duvenal, are specially noticed by the chroniclers of
the time.† Randolph, the eldest, who inherited the largest share
of Stranith, lived like his sire in the style of a petty king, at the
patrimonial castle, till the reign of William the Lion. This, the
second territorial magnate of Nithsdale mentioned in history,
acquired additional opulence by his marriage with the Lady
Bethoc, who brought him Bethoc-rule, Bugh-chester, and other
manors, in Teviotdale ; and from them sprang many illustrious
descendants, the chief of whom was the celebrated Thomas
Randolph, created Earl of Moray by Bruce, as a reward for his
patriotic services during the War of Independence. ‡

Dunegal's eldest son was no doubt superior of Dumfries :
as such, ˌhe granted a portion of land lying near the town to
the Abbey of Jedburgh, in 1147. Randolph had three sons—
Duncan, Gillespie (or Gillipatrick), and Dovenald—the last of
whom received from his father Sanchar, Ellioc, Dunscore, and
other lands in the district, and was slain while quite a youth at
the "Battle of the Standard." One of Dovenald's sons, Edgar,
who lived in the reigns of William the Lion and Alexander II.,
gave the Church of Morton to the Monastery of Kelso, and the
Churches of Dalgarnock and Dunscore to the Monastery of
Holywood, or Darcongall, which stood at a distance of three miles
from Dumfries. The children of this chief adopted the name
Edgar for the family—one of the earliest recorded instances of the
use of surnames in Nithsdale. His daughter, Affrica Edgar, who
inherited the parish of Dunscore, gave the fourth part of it to
Melrose Abbey ; § one of his sons, Richard, owned the Castle and
half of the barony of Sanquhar ; and a grandson, Donald, acquired
from David II. the captainship of the MacGowans, a numerous
clan then located in the district. Edgar is still a common name in
Dumfriesshire : one or two families who bear it have been settled
in the parish of Caerlaverock, on the Solway, for seven centuries ;
the common progenitor of all the Edgars having been the son of
Dovenald the Scoto-Irish chief.

While the Dunegal dynasty was becoming less powerful, but
before its influence finally disappeared, another Celtic family, the

---

* Grose's Antiquities, vol. i., p. 148.
† Douglas's Peerage, p. 498.   ‡ Caledonia, vol. iii., p. 72.
§ There is a farm in Dunscore called Edgarstown ; so named, perhaps, from having
been the residence of Affrica.

D

M'Dowalls, Lords of Galloway, from whom it originally sprang, became landholders in Nithsdale, and closely associated with its hamlet-capital. In the reign of David I., the lordship of Galloway was held by Fergus. Distinguished for his warlike achievements, he was still better known as a patron of such learning as the age produced, and as a promoter of religion. To him the Monasteries of Tongland, Whithorn, and Soulseat, the Priory of St. Mary's Isle, and the Abbey of Dundrennan, owed their origin ; * and it is believed that the revival, in 1154, of the Bishopric of Candida Casa, which included part of Dumfriesshire, was due to his munificence. † By marrying Elizabeth, illegitimate daughter of Henry I., Fergus acquired extensive lands in England, and under him Galloway, when not aiming at entire independence, kept up a closer connection with that monarch than with David I. ; just as Cumberland at the same period was a sort of debatable district, but more intimately allied to the Scottish than to the English crown.

Fergus left two sons, Uchtred and Gilbert, and one daughter, bearing, like the descendant of Dunegal previously mentioned, the singular name of Affrica, who, marrying Olave, King of Man, became the progenitor of all its succeeding sovereigns of the Norwegian line. The two sons of Fergus inherited his dominions between them : they were broad enough for both ; but Gilbert, a fierce, unscrupulous savage, wishing to be lord of the entire province, levied war upon his brother, surprised his Castle of Loch Fergus, near Kirkcudbright, and put him to death under circumstances of the most revolting cruelty. The unfortunate Uchtred founded the beautiful Abbey of Lincluden, near the confluence of the Cluden with the Nith, about a mile above Dumfries :‡ according to tradition, it eventually furnished a resting-place for his mutilated remains ; and its grey ruins still help to keep his memory green. Gilbert closed a life of turbulence eleven years after the fratricidal deed ; and Roland, son of the slaughtered Uchtred, claimed a right to succeed him, which he enforced by the sword.

At Roland's death his eldest son, Alan, became undisputed ruler of Galloway. By his marriage with Margaret, daughter of David, Earl of Huntingdon, and niece of William the Lion, he acquired a large addition to his territorial wealth. His position in Scotland was second only to that of the King ; and so extensive were his possessions in England, that the Scoto-Irish chief was recognised as an equal by the proudest of its Norman chivalry. When, in 1211, King John invaded Ireland, Lord Alan assisted him with both men and arms ; for which service he received from that monarch a grant of the Island of Ruglin, and lands in Ulster.

* Spottiswood's Religious Houses, chap. v., sect. 1.
† Murray's Literary History of Galloway.   ‡ Spottiswood, chap, xviii., sect. 2.

A few years afterwards we find him arrayed against his English
sovereign, combining with other barons to extort from John the
world-famous Magna Charta.* Alexander II. seems to have at
first been jealous of his powerful subject, and to have disapproved
of his proceedings in the sister country ; but when John
temporarily overcame the leaguers of the Charter, and Alan fled
northwards for protection, he was graciously received at the
Scottish Court, and made Chancellor of the kingdom. (a) It is a
curious circumstance that in the royal charter which confers upon
him this office he is called, not Prince or Lord of Galloway, but
simply " Alan of Dumfres "†—a clear proof that he had a large
proprietary interest in the town, ‡ and favouring the belief that
he resided in it occasionally, fraternising with his near kinsmen,
the descendants of Dunegal, some of whom still occupied a high
position in the district ; the most prominent being Thomas, son of
Rodolph, who died in 1261, and who was father of Thomas
Randolph of Stranid, and brother-in-law to King Robert Bruce.
Alan was three times married : by his first wife he had an only
child, married to Roger de Quincy, a Norman baron ; by his
second wife he had a son, who died without issue, and two
daughters, one of whom, Christian, wedded to William de Fortibus,
left no offspring ; the other was the far-famed Devorgilla, (b) born in
1213, of whom we shall have much to say in a subsequent chapter.
Dying without male issue, Alan was the last of his line who bore
rule over Galloway : sage, pious, and benevolent, he was one of the
best as well as the last of its ancient lords.

Respecting the other territorial chiefs of Celtic lineage who
flourished at an early period in Dumfriesshire, little is known.
Probably some of them, by acquiring French-looking surnames,
according to the courtly fashion which David I. encouraged, have
been lost sight of, and figure in history as Norman barons. Some
genealogists, as we have seen, find trace of a Nithsdale potentate
in the name Caerlaverock ; but the reputed builder of the great

* As showing the high position occupied by this Galloway lord in England, the names
of only four temporal peers have precedence of his name in Magna Charta, while eleven
names come after it. He appears in the document as " Alani de Galweia constabularii
Scotie."—*Rymer's Fœdera*, vol. i., p. 131.

(a) The purport of this passage is in part obscure and in part erroneous. If it is
meant that Alexander disapproved of Alan's attitude towards John, it must be a mistake. For Alexander was himself in arms against that sovereign, and clause 59 of
Magna Charta was in his favour.
    Again : Alexander did not make Alan of Galloway Chancellor. It was Master Alan
de Dunfres who occupied that office, and he received it, not from Alexander, but, in
1292, from Edward I. (Stevenson's Hist. Doc., Scot., i., 324). Master Alan, like his
immediate predecessor in the office, William de Dunfres, was probably an ecclesiastic.
It is not therefore " a curious circumstance " that Alan of Dumfries is not referred to
in the terms of his appointment to the Chancellorship as the Lord of Galloway.

† Calendars of Ancient Charters referred to in Nicholson's History of Galloway,
vol. i., p. 179.

‡ The volume of the Transactions of the Dumfriesshire and Galloway Natural
History and Antiquarian Society for 1864-5 contains an ingenious and interesting
paper on the connection of Alan, Lord of Galloway, with Dumfries, by Mr James
Starke, F.S.A., Scot.

(b) The name was Dervorgilla.

Border fortress has a somewhat shadowy aspect, like Ossian's heroes.

Not so Ruther, a genuine patriarch of the old Gaelic stock, who, dying in the reign of David I., left his name to the parish lands he possessed, Caer-Ruther, corrupted to Carruthers—a parish so called, now annexed to that of Middlebie, and signifying the town of Ruther. * Thomas, son of Robert Carruthers, received from David II. a grant of Musfold (Mouswald) ; and his son is witness to a charter in 1363. In 1426, Roger Carruthers received a charter from Archibald, Earl of Douglas, of Holmains, Little Dalton, and other contiguous lands ; and from him are descended the Carrutherses of Holmains, Warmanbie, and Dormont.

Here we may fittingly introduce the name of a great family with whose fortunes Nithsdale and Dumfries were most closely associated for centuries—the Maxwells : of a Scoto-Irish stock, according to some authorities ; cradled in Normandy, the nursery-land of heroes, say others. David, Earl of Cumberland, afterwards King of Scots, gave lands on the Tweed, near Kelso, to Maccus—a Celtic-sounding name, though his father, Unwyn, it is stated, claimed a Norman lineage. Here Maccus " erected a church for the service of God, a castle for himself, and a village and a mill for the convenience of his dependants ;" † calling the estate after himself, Maccusville, which in course of time became modified to Maxwell ; the family name, however, according to another theory, being traceable to the circumstance that the house built by Unwyn's son overlooked an eddy or " weil " in the river, which might have been known as the Weil of Maccus. (a) Sir John de Maccuswel, the grandson of this chief, acquired the barony of Caerlaverock, where he would doubtless build a stronghold of some kind, which, from its favourable position on the Solway, might be able to command the approaches to the kingdom in that direction. If Sir John be not the prototype of Lywarch-Ogg, he seems to have performed the castle-building services attributed by tradition to that hero ; and at all events the great Border fortress of Caerlaverock first became historical in the hands of the Maxwell family. The original patrimony on the Tweed remained in their keeping for centuries ; about 1250 the barony of Mearns, in Renfrewshire, was added to their other possessions ; and they acquired additional wealth and influence by Eugene de Maccuswell marrying the daughter of Roland, Lord of Galloway, which nuptial alliance would tend to strengthen their connection with Dumfries.

With the Maxwells are associated the old Celtic family of the Kirkconnells, who settled near the estuary of the Nith, on the

* Barjarg Manuscripts.
† Fraser's " Maxwells of Pollok," Preface, p. viii.
(a) It is now known with certainty that the name was Maccusweil—"weil" being the name for a pool of the river Tweed. (Sir Herbert Maxwell's " Dumfries and Gallo-way," p. 60.)

Galloway side, in the days of Malcolm Canmore ; taking their name from the lands they occupied, as was customary at that early period. John, Dominus de Kirkconnell, founded the Abbey of Holywood some time in the twelfth century ; * and about 1200 his supposed grandson, William Fitzmichael, granted a portion of the family patrimony to the monks of Holmcultram. † As Caerlaverock Castle, on the opposite shore of the Solway, was within sight of Kirkconnell Tower, their owners were near neighbours ; and what more natural than that their families should intermarry ? Accordingly, in course of time Aymer, nephew of the first Lord Maxwell, espoused Janet, the heiress of the Kirkconnells, and the name of the latter became merged in that of Maxwell. No fewer than five baronetcies were held by cadets of the Nithsdale Maxwells—namely, Springkell in Dumfriesshire, Cardoness and Monreith in Galloway, Calderwood in Lanarkshire, and Pollok in Renfrewshire.

For two centuries or more, no name was so much identified with the County as the illustrious one of Douglas :—

> " Hosts have been known at that dread sound to yield ;
> And Douglas dead, his name has won the field."

" Sholto Dhu-glass ! " (Behold the dark man !) said the Squire of Solvathius, King of Scots, on presenting to that monarch a swarthy stranger who had saved the royal life at a battle in the Western Isles. " ' Dhu-glass ' shall he be called," rejoined the grateful king ; " and for his gallant service this day he shall receive broad lands in Lanarkshire as a reward." If this tradition is to be relied upon, the saviour of Solvathius was the ancestor of the Douglasses ; but their historian, Hume of Godscroft, looking upon the tale as a fable, says : " We do not know them in the fountain, but in the stream ; not in the root, but in the stem : for we know not who was the first mean man that did raise himself above the vulgar." William of Dufglass, the first of the name on record, witnessed a charter by Joceline, Bishop of Glasgow, to the monks of Kelso, some time between 1170 and 1190. ‡ Passing over three generations, we reach the fifth head of the house and the first of the name who was associated with Dumfries—Sir William Douglas, who fought and bled with Wallace. He was father of the Good Sir James ·Douglas, the great warrior who commanded

---

* Dugdale's Monasticon, vol. ii., p. 1057.

† Cambden tells us that, about the year 946, " King Edmund, with the assistance of Lodine, King of Wales, spoiled Cumberland of all its riches, and having put out the eyes of Dunmaile, King of that county, granted it to Malcolm, King of Scots, to hold of him, to protect the northern part of England by sea and land against the incursions of his enemies ;" and the same historian states that the Abbey—" Ulme or Holme Cultraine "—was founded by David I., the owner of the territory as King of Scotland. According to the chronicle of Melrose, its origin was due to the son of that monarch, Prince Henry ; while some writers attribute it to Henry I. of England, and hold that the Scottish sovereign and his son were only among its earliest benefactors. The building was of immense size, second only in this respect to Furness Abbey ; but very little of it now remains to attest its former extent and magnificence.

‡ Douglas's Peerage, vol. i., p. 419.

the left wing of the patriotic army at Bannockburn, and who
fifteen years afterwards was slain by the Moors of Andalusia,
while on his way to deposit the heart of the "Hero-King" in the
Holy Sepulchre at Jerusalem.

The origin of the Scotts, like that of the Douglasses, is so remote that it cannot be traced with certainty. "Uchtredus filius
Scoti," are words which occur in a deed of inquisition regarding
the Church of Glasgow in the days of Alexander I., and which
seem to denote a Scoto-Irish knight residing in a district chiefly
occupied by people who were not Celts. Uchtred's son, Richard
le Scott, was witness to the foundation-charter of the Priory of
St. Andrew's, some time before 1158. * Richard is said to have
had two sons, one called after himself, who occupied the lands of
Murdochstone or Murdieston, in Clydesdale, from whom are
descended the Scotts of Buccleuch ; the other, Michael, who gave
rise to the Scotts of Balwearie. It was not till several centuries
afterwards that the noble family who have now a yearly rental
in Dumfriesshire of £79,000, † possessed a rood of land in the
County ; their first acquisition there having been, it is supposed,
when Sir Walter Scott of Kirkcup, who had some time before
bartered Murdieston for Branxholm, in Roxburghshire, received a
grant of part of the barony of Langholm from King James II., in
1459. ‡

A Celtic chief who possessed the lands of Crichton, in Mid-
Lothian, in the reign of Malcolm Canmore, borrowed his surname
from them ; and some of his descendants are traceable in Upper
Nithsdale about two centuries later. Thomas, supposed son of
Thurstanus de Crichton, swore fealty to Edward I. William, his
second son, acquired, by marriage with Isobel, daughter of Robert
de Ross (related to the Lord of the Isles), half of the barony of
Sanquhar. The other half having been purchased by his
successors, it became the chief title of the family. In 1633, the
direct descendant of the Mid-Lothian baron was created Viscount
of Ayr and Earl of Dumfries.

The Fergussons, another Celtic family, existed very early in
Dumfriesshire ; but whether they belonged to a sept of that name
which had its chief seat to the north of Dunkeld, or were
descended from some earlier settlers in the south, is not known.
Early in the fourteenth century, John of Crauford, son of the
Laird of Dalgarnock, granted a charter of lands in the parish of
Glencairn to his cousin, John Fergusson, "Dominus de Craigdarroch ;" and it is believed that the estate so called—which is
owned by them till this day—had been at that date in their

---

* Ibid, vol. i., p. 245.   † Valuation Roll of the County of Dumfries.

‡ So say some genealogists ; but, as the Retours of the period do not confirm the
statement, other authorities hold that this date is too early.

possession for several generations. * A branch of the family, the Fergussons of Isle, resided for many centuries in the neighbouring parish of Kirkmahoe. Their house, a fine specimen of a Scottish gentleman's domicile during the middle ages, is still to be seen entire, though untenanted, overlooking the patrimonial acres, and other ground full of historical and poetical interest—Dalswinton, Friars' Carse, the lands of Lag and Ellisland—on which we must not pause to dilate.

The Fergussons are literally " the sons of Fergus :" and in like manner another ancient Dumfriesshire family, the Griersons, are " the sons of Gregor ;" those of them who settled in Lag tracing their descent from Gilbert, second son of Malcolm, Dominus de MacGregor, who died in 1374.

Many Flemings were attracted to Scotland during the twelfth century : one of them, named Freskin, obtained the lands of Strathbrock, in Linlithgowshire, now termed Broxburn, as a reward for his valour against an insurgent band in Morayshire. Some time about 1130 he received a grant of land in that county ; and his descendants, settling there, assumed the name of de Moray or de Moravia. Such is the account given of the origin of the Murrays, who, in various branches, acquired a high position in Scotland. The Moryquhat, or Murraythwaite branch, flourished in Dumfriesshire during the thirteenth century. Sir William Murray of Cockpule, who lived in the reign of Alexander III., married Isobel, sister of Thomas Randolph, Earl of Moray. Their son, William, received a charter of the barony of Comlongan † and Ryvil, from his uncle Randolph. The family were ennobled about 1623, in the person of Sir John Murray of Lochmaben, created Earl of Annandale.

The boyhood of David I. was spent at the English Court. As Earl of Cumberland he was brought into familiar intercourse with the Norman barons ; and when he was called to succeed Alexander I., in 1124, many of them accompanied or followed him to Scotland. One of these was Gervase, son of Geoffry, Lord of Ridel, who received from the King estates in Roxburghshire. His descendant, Sir Walter Riddel (the second baronet), left five sons, the eldest of whom acquired lands in Glencairn, which he named Glenriddel, thus giving rise to the patronymic of a well-known Dumfriesshire family. He married Katherine, daughter of his neighbour, Sir Robert Grierson of Lag ; and by her had issue two sons, one of

---

* Not a few members of the Craigdarroch family acquired distinction as soldiers and lawyers : one of them in recent times figured as the hero of Burns's ballad, " The Whistle," on gaining which trophy he was thus addressed by the bard :—
> " Thy line, that have struggled for freedom with Bruce,
> Shall heroes and patriots ever produce :
> So thine be the laurel, and mine be the bay ;
> The field thou hast won, by yon bright god of day."

† According to Pennant, the great Lord Mansfield, a descendant of Murray of Cockpule, was born in Comlongan Castle.

whom espoused Jane, daughter of another local proprietor, Alexander Fergusson of Craigdarroch. Charteris is the surname of a very old Scottish family. Their origin is traced to William, son of the Earl of Charteris, in France, who went to England with the Norman conqueror. A son or grandson of William migrated northward in the reign of David I. Robert de Charteris acquired the lands of Amisfield or Hempis-field, in Tinwald, prior to 1175. His son, Walter, and grandson, Thomas, are mentioned in a donation to the Monastery of Kelso. Robert, son of Thomas, granted to the same monastery the patro-nage of two Dumfriesshire churches, by a charter in which his name appears in its Latinised form as Robert de Cornoto Miles. The manor-house of Amisfield, a quaint memorial of the olden time, is yet to be seen, situated about four miles north-east of Dumfries ;* and the family had a residence in the Burgh, which also, in a sadly altered form, survives.

Long before Walter(a) the Steward ascended the Scottish throne, in virtue of his marriage with Bruce's daughter Marjory, several members of the same family acquired lands in various parts of Scotland ; and when he took the surname of Stewart, they followed his example. One branch of the Stewarts settled in Nithsdale before the death of Alexander III. Soon afterwards we read of Sir Walter Stewart of Dalswinton : he acquired the lands of Garlies, in Wigtownshire. His direct descendant in the seven-teenth century, Sir Alexander Stewart, was ennobled under the title of Earl of Galloway. According to Pinkerton, the first of the Stewarts was a Norman knight named Alan, who obtained from William the Conqueror the barony of Oswestry, in Shropshire.

Ronaldus de Dinnistoun witnessed the inquisition made by David, when Prince of Cumberland, in 1116. *(b)* One of his female descendants shared the throne of Robert II. (the first of the Stewarts), and gave birth to a line of sovereigns : hence the family saying, "Kings came of us, not we of Kings." They obtained the barony of Glencairn from that monarch : a daughter of the house having married Sir William Cunningham of Kilmaurs, the descendant of a North of England family, he acquired with her the barony ; and their grandson, Alexander, became Earl of Glen-cairn—the first who wore the title. †

Roger de Mandeville, whose ancestor crossed from Normandy with its irresistible Duke, married Affrica, natural daughter of William the Lion ; obtaining with her the barony of Tynwald, and the temple-lands of Dalgarno and Closeburn—the latter of which,

---

* Robert Chalmers, in his picture of Scotland, p. 228, says : "[Amisfield Tower] is not large, and not in the least degree imposing ; but yet it is, without exception, the most curious specimen of the baronial tower now existing in Scotland.

(a) It was Walter's son Robert who ascended the throne as Robert II.

(b) The name does not appear in the Inquisition. (Reg. Epis. Glasguensis.)

† Douglas's Peerage, vol. i., p. 633 ; Barjarg MSS.

at her death, in 1233, were given by Alexander II. to Ivon Kirk-patrick. Roger de Mandeville, second of the name, was a competitor for the Crown in 1296. We read of John Mundville, notary at Dumfries in 1610 ; and the Mundells, who trace their origin to Roger the Norman, have still numerous representatives in the town and district. (a)

While William Rufus reigned in England, if not before, the Norman family of Heriz, descended from Count de Vendôme, resided at Wyverton, in Nottinghamshire, and they, too, were represented in the train of the Prince of Cumberland, when he went northward to become King of Scots. William de Heriz was witness to various royal charters, dating from 1175 to 1199. His descendant, Nigel, held lands in Selkirkshire so early as the reign of Alexander II. ; a charter from that monarch to the monks of Melrose describing certain property granted to them as extending " from the river Etreyich, by the rivulet of Tymeye, as far as the marches of Nigel de Heriz." Soon afterwards we find the family settling down in the Vale of Nith. Their head, William de Herris, swore fealty to Edward I. for his lands in Galloway ; and Robert, the son of William, is designated " Dominus de Nithsdale " in a charter granted to him, in 1323, by King Robert Bruce.*

During the reign of David I. no family held higher rank in Scotland than the De Morevilles, whose progenitor, Hugh, accom-panied him from Cumberland. The names of De Mantelent, Conyngham (ancestor of the Earls of Glencairn), De Thirlstane, Haig of Bemersyde, and St. Clair, appear in the list of their vassals. Henry St. Clair rose to be Earl of Orkney ; and by his marriage with "the Fair Maid of Nithsdale," daughter of the Black Douglas, became Sheriff of the district. Roland, Lord of Galloway, wedded Eliza De Moreville ; and her brother William, the next head of the house, dying without issue, their whole estates, with the office of High Constable held by them, devolved upon the M'Dowalls. (b)

Among the followers of Hugh de Moreville was a knight named Elsi or Eklis, who received from him a grant of Thirlstane. The daughter and heiress of Eklis married Richard de Mantelent, also of Norman blood. In course of time the original name was trans-ferred to lands owned by the family in Penpont ; and the family patronymic was changed to Maitland ; hence the Maitlands of Eccles, one of the most ancient houses in the South of Scotland.

Another very old family connected with Dumfries, the Hunters, trace their origin to Norman the Hunter, designated in the Notes

(a) Mandeville is not the same name as Mundeville. Sir Henry de Mundeville of Dumfriesshire (" del comite de Dunfres ") sealed the Ragman Roll, 1296.—Bain's Cal., ii., 198.
* Ibid, vol. i., p. 726.
(b) It is doubtful if the M'Dowalls can claim Roland and his successors as of their name.

E

on the Ragman's Roll as proprietor of Hunterston. John, the
seventh baron, by marrying the daughter of Sir William Douglas
of Drumlanrig, strengthened the relationship of his family with
the district.*

We find Walter de Carnoc the possessor of Drumgray and
Trailflat, in Annandale, early in the twelfth century ; Alexander
de Meyners, son of Robert, Chancellor of Scotland, holding the
lands of Durisdeer at the same period ; the Corbits, who held the
lordship of Millum, in Cumberland, under Henry III., passing
northward † in the succeeding reign, and founding several families,
one of whom settled in Dumfries ; and the Siwards, originally
Saxon, holding high offices in Nithsdale before and after the
outbreak of the Succession War.

During the reigns of Malcolm IV. and David I., the territory
which afterwards became famous as the Western Border, including
the Debatable Land, was held for the most part by two brothers
called Rosindale, who had followed the banner of the Norman
Duke. Guido de Rosindale, who owned possessions on both sides
of the Lower Liddel, manifested his devotional zeal by giving to
the monks of Jedburgh forty acres of land lying between the Esk
and the Liddel, throwing the fishings of the latter stream into the
grant. His brother, Turgot, was a still more bountiful son of the
Church. He founded a conventual establishment in Eskdale,
calling it " Domus de Religiosus de Liddall," endowing it richly,
and placing both house and lands under the superiority of Jedburgh. It afterwards came to be known as the Priory of Canonby,
owing to the canons residing within its walls. Another French
knight, Ranulph de Soulis, who swelled the train and won the
favour of King David, also obtained from him a large slice of
Liddesdale, where he erected a fortalice that originated the village
of Castleton. John de Soulis received from Bruce the baronies of
Kirkandrews, on the Esk, and of Torthorwald, near Dumfries.

Other names come up, which call for a more detailed genealogical notice ; those of Bruce, Baliol, and Comyn—all of Norman
lineage—all associated with great historical events—all closely
identified with Dumfries. The Bruces have been traced back to
Thebotaw, Duke of Sleswick, who lived in the eighth century, and
left an heir, Ouslin, by his wife Gundella, a German princess.
Reginald, a Danish lord, Eynor, Torfin, Lothar, Sygurt, all successive Earls of Orkney, form a continuation of the stem till the

---

* On the 26th of February, 1825, King George IV. granted liberty to the then head of
this ancient house, William Francis Hunter of Barjarg Tower, and of Lagan (both in
Dumfriesshire), and to Jane, his wife, only surviving child of Francis St. Aubyn of
Collen Mixton, Cornwall, by Jane, his wife, daughter and co-heir of Robert Arundell,
Esq., some time of Marozion, Cornwall, to assume the surname and arms of Arundell
with those of Hunter. The Arundells are of very remote antiquity, having occupied
for at least ten centuries an illustrious position in the West of England. The present
representative of both houses is W. F. Hunter Arundell, Esq., of Barjarg.

† Barjarg Manuscripts.

eighth head of the house is reached—Brusce, Earl of Caithness, whose mother was daughter to Malcolm II., King of Scots. Regenwald, son of Brusce, wedded Arlogia, daughter of Waldemar, Duke of Russia; their eldest son, Robert, built the castle of La Brusce, in Normandy, during the tenth century. The family, though ranked as Norman, were only so for one generation—and if the pedigree before us can be relied upon,* they were Scottish or Orcadian before being French; they were then English for two generations—Robert de Brusce, second of the name, coming to South Britain with William the Conqueror, becoming Lord of Skelton, in Yorkshire, and their son, Robert de Brus, accompanying David, Earl of Cumberland, into Scotland, settling down in that kingdom—a goodly plant, which, in the light of subsequent events, might be spoken of allegorically as the root of Freedom's tree.

Robert, about 1124, received from his royal friend and patron, David, a grant of Strathannand (Annandale), or Estrahannent, as it is termed in the charter. He was succeeded by a son of the same name, the second Baron of Annandale; and the son of the latter, also named Robert, on inheriting the estates was created Lord of Annandale. Dying without male issue, he was succeeded by his brother William, second Lord of Annandale. Robert de Brus, William's eldest son, fifth Baron and third Lord of Annandale, married Isabella, second daughter of David, Earl of Huntingdon, brother of William the Lion; and by this alliance with the royal house of Scotland founded the claim to the Crown made by his son Robert, the fourth Lord, in 1292. The grandson of the latter—the greatest of his race—restored the monarchy and reestablished the independence of Scotland, when both had been long trodden in the dust.

Soon after the Bruces settled in Annandale, the rival house of Baliol also received a grant of Scottish territory from David I., still retaining, however, their original English patrimony of Barnard Castle, Durham.† In the reign of William the Lion, Ingleram de Baliol married the heiress of Walter de Berkley, Chamberlain of Scotland; and Henry, the fruit of their union, succeeded to that influential office. Another scion of the original stock, John Baliol of Barnard Castle, married Devorgilla (a), daughter of Alan, Lord of

---

* Genealogy of the Bruces in Ord's History of Cleveland, as extended by the late Mr John Parker, principal extractor of the Court of Session. See the Rev. W. Graham's Lochmaben Five Hundred Years Ago, pp. 150-157.

† "Barnard Castle," saith old Leland, "standeth stately upon Tees." It is founded upon a very high rock, and its ruins impend over the river, including within the area a circuit of six acres and upwards. This once magnificent fortress derives its name from its founder, Barnard Baliol.—Note A to Rokeby.

(a) Mr Andrew Lang (" A History of Scotland ") gives the name as Devergoil or Deverguila. Sir Archibald H. Dunbar, Bart. ("Scottish Kings 1005-1625 "), gives it as Dervorgulla. Mr Neilson is of opinion that Dervorgilla is the correct form. It is evidently a Celtic name. O'Ruare's wife, whose carrying off by Dermot was the cause of the Conquest of Ireland, was called Dervorgilla. Lord Alan's famous daughter's name is therefore " an interesting connection of Celt and culture."

Galloway. This illustrious woman sometimes resided at her father's court, but more frequently at Fotheringay, in Northamptonshire, the seat of her maternal grandfather the Earl of Huntingdon. There the young Yorkshire baron wooed and won "the Lady of Fotheringay," as she was then usually termed—a most auspicious alliance in itself, but the source of much unhappiness to the country ; John, their only surviving son, entailing upon it a load of woes by becoming a competitor for the Crown, in virtue of his mother's descent from the eldest niece of William the Lion.

In many respects the Comyns resembled the two distinguished houses just noticed, having been like them Norman-French, afterwards English, finally Scottish, and also putting forth a claim to the disputed sceptre ; while all the three families, as we shall subsequently see, were vitally concerned in a foul tragedy with which the country rang, and the scene of which was an obscure vennel in the village-capital of Nithsdale. William Comyn was High Chancellor of Scotland for nine years, ending in 1142. His nephew, Richard, married Hexilda, granddaughter of King Donald-Bain ; and dying in 1189, was succeeded by his eldest son, William, who by his second marriage acquired the earldom of Buchan, and added the Highland territory of Badenoch to the other estates of the house. Richard Comyn, the fruit of the first marriage, died about 1249 ; his son, John Comyn the Red, became Justiciary of Galloway in 1258 ; while about the same period the connection of the family with the ancient province was further strengthened by the marriage of Alexander Comyn, Earl of Buchan, with Elizabeth, daughter of Roger de Quincey, the niece of Devorgilla. John was succeeded by his second son, John Comyn the Black, designated of Badenoch, which estate devolved upon him at the death of his uncle, the Earl of Monteith. The position and relationship acquired by this aspiring family in Galloway opened up the way to a still closer bond of union with its hereditary rulers, which was effected by the Black Comyn marrying Devorgilla's youngest daughter, Marjory ; and thus he became also the brother-in-law of John Baliol, afterwards King of Scotland. At his death, in 1299, he was succeeded by John, the second of the family that bore the surname of the Red.

The estate given by David I. to Robert Brus, third of the name, is described in the charter as " Estrahannent et totam terram a divisa Dunegal de Stranid, usque ad divisam Randulphi Meschines ;* that is to say, Annandale, and all the land lying between the Niths-dale property of Dunegal, and that of Randulph de Meschines, (a) Lord of Cumberland ; and the deed empowered him to hold and enjoy his castle there, with all the privileges pertaining to it

---

* The original document is in the British Museum.
(a) Not De Meschines. The word is le Meschin, and is old French for "the younger."

(suum castellum bene et honorifice, cum omnibus consuetudinibus
suis teneat et habeat)," in the same manner as Randulph did in
Carlisle and his other Cumbrian possessions. The extensive barony
of the Bruce was given to him on feudal terms ; he was to hold it
by the sword, and render in return military service to his sovereign. *(a)* That the knight might be able to fulfil these conditions,
he brought with him numerous Norman followers, some of whom
founded families in the district ; but it is not necessary to assume,
as has been hastily done by some historians, that he drove out all
the original holders of the soil, or that he even placed himself in
opposition to them as a class.

It has been generally supposed, too, that the Kirkpatricks were
strangers to Annandale till they acquired lands there as his
vassals ; but it is far more probable that they belonged to its old
Scoto-Irish or Scoto-Saxon population. Ivon, the first Kirkpatrick
of whom we read, may have been a young, landless soldier of
fortune when Bruce came into the district ; or he may, before that
time, have taken by right his surname from one or other of the
Dumfriesshire parishes that, as early as the tenth century, bore
the name of Kirkpatrick.* At all events, we think it probable
that he was a dweller in "Estrahannent" when it was first
erected into a barony. That Ivon was of good birth and family
may be inferred from the favour shown to him by his feudal
superior. Some time about 1160, he received from Bruce, second
baron of Annandale, a charter of the fishings of Bleatwood and
Yester ; and the words "testibus Ivon" are attached to a deed by
which the same nobleman granted the Torduff fishings of the
Solway to Abbot Everard and the fraternity of Holmcultram.†
At a later period he obtained the hand of Bruce's daughter,
Euphemia, in marriage—an honour which must have been flattering to his pride, and which bound his family to the Brucian
interest during the fearful struggle which ensued on the death of
Alexander III.

From that monarch's immediate predecessor, Ivon, when a
very old man, received a grant of the lands of Closeburn, the

(a) The tenure of Annandale comprehended many privileges and liberties, held,
as a jury said in 1304, "by the title of antiquity." (Bain's Cal., ii., No 1588.)
Technically, under David I. Annandale was held "in forest." (Bain's Cal., i., No. 29.)

* The parish of Kirkpatrick-Juxta was of old called Kilpatrick, from the dedica-
tion of its church to Patrick, the great apostle of Ireland, who appears to have been
equally well remembered by the Scoto-Irish of the south-west of Scotland. The
Gaelic *Kil*, signifying a church, was afterwards translated into the Anglo-Saxon *Kirk*.
In the fifteenth century the adjunct *juxta* appears to the name of this parish, in
order to distinguish it from Kirkpatrick-Fleming, in the east of Annandale.—
Caledonia, vol. iii., p. 181.

† The first of these charters exists among the Carlyle papers ; the second is entered
in the Register of Holmcultram Abbey. Both are undated ; but their dates may be
approximately determined by the date of another charter, by which William the Lion,
in the first year of his reign, grants lands in Canonby to Jedburgh Abbey, and to which
Abbot Everard is a witness.

charter being dated the 5th of August, 1232.*   Adam Kirkpatrick,
Lord of Closeburn, the son of this union, was alive in 1294. The
next head of the house, Stephen, is styled in the chartulary of
Kelso (1278), " Dominus Villæ de Closeburn, filius et hæres Domini
Ade de Kilpatrick, militis." In the same year he entered into an
engagement with the monks of Kelso, regarding a claim made by
them to the church of Closeburn. Stephen left two sons : Sir
Roger, famous in after times as the knight of the deadly dagger—
the " Maksiccar " Kirkpatrick—and Duncan, who married Isabel,
daughter and heiress of Sir David Torthorwald, who is mentioned
in the chartulary of Holmcultram as witness to a donation of one
merk out of the lands of Maybie, in 1289.   Nigel de Kilpatrike
(probably brother to Stephen) was imprisoned with other patriots
in the Castle of Kenilworth, in 1298. The family were related to
Wallace, as well as Bruce, if we are to believe Harry the Minstrel,
who says of Duncan, the founder of the Torthorwald branch :

> " Kyrkpatryk, that cruel was and keyne,
> In Esdaill wod that half yer he had been ;
> With Inglishmen he couth noch weill accord,
> Of Torthorowald he barron was and lord,
> Of kyn he was to Wallace' modvr ner." †

The Carliels, or Carlyles, who trace their descent from Crinan,
Abthane of Dunkeld (whose son, Maldred, married Beatric,
daughter of Malcolm II.), held lands in Annandale. like the
Kirkpatricks, under Robert Brus, its first lord, about 1185. They
also owned property in Cumberland, taking their surname, it is
believed, from its chief town, Carlisle. The eldest son of Uchtred,
son of Maldred, was Robert of Kinmount : his second son, Richard,
received the lands of Newbie-on-the-Moor from his grandfather.
Eudo de Carlyle, grandson of Richard, witnessed a charter to the
Monastery of Kelso about 1207.‡   The next head of the family,
Adam, had a charter of various lands in Annandale from William
de Brus, second Lord of that district, who died in 1215. Gilbert,
son of Adam, swore fealty to Edward I. in 1296. (a) William, grandson of Gilbert, rose so high in the favour of his liege lord, Bruce,
Earl of Carrick, that he gave him his daughter, Margaret, in
marriage : the chief of the Carlyles thus becoming brother-in-law
to the illustrious restorer of the monarchy. Their son obtained
a charter from his royal uncle of the lands of Colyn and Roucan,
lying near Dumfries, in which he is designated " William Karlo,

the King's sister's son." The head of this ancient house was, as we shall afterwards see, ennobled in 1470 as Lord Carlyle of Torthorwald.*

Another Annandale sept—the Jardines—held lands in the parish of Applegarth, before the Celtic element in the population was overlaid by that of the Saxons. Winfredus de Jardine, the first of the name on record, flourished prior to 1153 ; he having been a witness to various grants conferred, during the reign of David I., on the Abbeys of Aberbrothwick and Kelso. Members of this old house have at various times intermarried with the Charterises, Douglasses, and other patrician families of the district. †

At what period the great family of the Johnstones settled in Annandale has not been determined. The first trace that we find of them is in the reign of Alexander III., when Hugo de Johnstone owned lands in East Lothian, which he bequeathed to his son John, who gave a portion to them to the Monastery of Soltray, about 1285, "for the safety of his soul." His descendants, Thomas, Walter, Gilbert, and John, swore fealty to Edward I. in 1296—the last-mentioned baron being termed in the deed, "Chevalier of the County of Dumfries." It is more than likely, however, we think, that the Johnstones, as well as the Kirkpatricks, had long previously resided in Strathannand. The name is suggestive of a Saxon origin ; and the idea is a natural one that they either gave it to, or received it from, the parish of Johnstone, in Annandale.‡ (a)

---

* Douglas's Peerage, vol. i., p. 70. A fresh lustre has been cast upon this old Annandale family by the genius of one of its "latter day" members, Thomas Carlyle, the distinguished author.

† Sir William Jardine, Bart., the eminent naturalist, is the present head of the family.

‡ The parish of Johnstone, says Chalmers, derived its name from the village ; and the hamlet, from its having become in Scoto-Saxon times, the *tun*, or dwelling, of some person who was distinguished by the name of John. This place afterwards gave the surname to the family of Johnstone, who became a powerful clan in Annandale.— Caledonia, vol. iii., p. 179.

(a) There were Johnstones in Annandale before Hugo. Sir William Fraser says (Historical Manuscripts, Fifteenth Report, Appendix, Part ix. : "James Johnstone of that ilk and Knight of Dunskellie complains that on 6th April, 1585, certain Maxwells came to his house of the Lochwood and 'brint the place, mantioun and haill houss,' with all its contents, and 'brint and destroyit my chartour kist with my haill evidentis and wreittis, besyd uther jowellis.' . . . Though the charters of the Johnstone's which are still extant do not date further back than the year 1400, it can be proved from other records that they have held the lands of Johnstone and others in Annandale from the time of King William the Lion, and perhaps from the time of his grandfather King David the First. That bountiful monarch bestowed the whole of Annandale upon his friend and vassal Robert Bruce in 1124. The grant was renewed by King David at a later date, and repeated by his grandson King William the Lion, between 1165 and 1174. Not many years afterwards we find John, the founder of the family of Johnstone, giving his Christian name to his lands, whence his son Gilbert, between 1194 and 1220, took his surname. These facts are known from charters by members of the family of Bruce in the Record Office, London, and also in the muniment room at Drumlanrig, which record the existence of Gilbert, son of John, otherwise Gilbert of Jonistun (Johnstun or Johnston), between these dates."

CHAPTER III.

Now that we have supplied some information regarding the way
in which the district was peopled at various epochs, and introduced
the chief local actors in the great drama of real life which soon
afterwards opened in Nithsdale and Annandale, let us see how
Dumfries gradually threw off its hamlet garb, and acquired that
of a royal burgh. Before the town was chartered, it was in a
condition of complete dependence on its Celtic superiors, and
equally so on the feudal overlords who succeeded them in the days
of William the Lion. Nearly all the inhabitants were in a state of
absolute villanage, having no property in the soil, and owing any
immunities they possessed to the arbitrary will of their chief, who
in most matters was free to act as he pleased, though nominally
responsible to the Crown. He gave them the means of subsistence,
shelter, and protection ; in return for which they rendered him
military service, manual labour, and tributes in money or rural
produce. With the view of increasing their scanty resources, and
enabling them to bear increased exactions, trading privileges were
by-and-by conferred upon them ; and when, in the further development of the feudal system, all the land came to be legally recognised as royal property, the merchants and craftsmen obtained
the exclusive right to traffic and labour within the town and a
prescribed range of territory around it, for which favours they
furnished a revenue to the Crown, derived from rents, tolls, and
customs. (a)

To William the Lion, it is believed, the burgh was indebted
for its first charters. (b) He granted more than one—Chalmers says

(a) Norman feudalism meant subduing the Celt, and was largely a police or quasi-
military settlement.

(b) See p. 15, note (a). William the Lion was the great charterer of military
burghs. All the evidence points to its being he who gave a charter to Dumfries, but
there may have been no elaborate scheme of citizenship. "It is very interesting,"
writes Mr Neilson, "to see the Kingholm so near the old castle—a castle which was
even in the 15th century the head court at which the feudal rent of Galloway this side
the Cree was renderable to the Crown by the Earls of Douglas and Lords of Galloway.
(*Registrum Magni Sigilli*, 69.)"

"many "*—which were so drawn up as to indicate that he frequently resided in the town ; but, unfortunately, they were either lost or destroyed during the succession warfare.† The earlier of these documents would relate chiefly, if not solely, to subjects of trade and handicraft, and be silent as to the right of self-government. Judging from the charters granted by the same monarch to other burghs, those at first conferred by him on Dumfries merely improved the relationship in which the inhabitants stood to the King, by changing them from precarious tenants to fixed vassals, holding directly of the Crown ; they acquiring thereby a right of property in their tofts or tenements, for which they paid yearly rents, independently of their personal services.‡ Thus the burgh was a portion of the royal possessions, occupied by an aggregation of tenants, each paying his quota of maills or money tribute. At fixed periods, half-yearly or quarterly, the King's *ballivi*, or bailies, collected the rents from his vassals ; also the fines levied in the burgh courts, and other impositions called *exitus curiæ*, the issues of court, which equally belonged to the Crown.§

Afterwards the whole of these rents and issues were handed over, on short leases, to the bailies, or rather the community, for a specific sum ; and eventually a permanent arrangement was made, in virtue of which the community, by contracting to pay so many hundred merks yearly into the exchequer, acquired a perpetual heritable right to the royal maills and issues—the tenure of individual burgesses, however, continuing unaltered. Agreeably to feudal forms, this important change was effected by constituting the inhabitants holders of the burgh in feu-farm under the King ; a tenure that enabled their functionaries to enforce recovery and payment the same as if they had been appointed by the State.‖(a)

When, probably about 1190,(b) William raised Dumfries to the rank of a royal burgh, the charter of erection would, in addition to these property rights, confer the privilege of local government. The burgesses were thereby rendered freemen in a double sense : they were no longer tenants-at-will—dependent vassals ; they were the legally-constituted occupiers of their own burgh, and had the choice of their own rulers, who were amenable to them and the

---

* Caledonia, vol. iii., p. 136. † Ibid.

‡ Report of Royal Commissioners on the Municipal Corporations of Scotland, page 12.

§ Municipal Report, p. 12. ‖ Ibid, p. 12.

(a) In 1395 Robert III. let to the provost, bailies, burgesses, and community of the Burgh of Dumfres for ever the said burgh and to their successors in fee, with various liberties, tolls, &c., for a rent of £20. (*Registrum Magni Sigilli* ii., No. 635.) Prior to this the ferme paid or due was in the years stated as follows ; 1327, £18 13s 4d (paid) ; 1330, £30 (which was the sum at which they had been set by the Chamberlain-Exchequer Rolls, I., 302-3) ; 1331, £30 ; 1383 (paid), £24 1s ; 1384, £10 15s per annum—this smallness of the payment being due to the burning of the town ; 1385 and 1386, £21 10s (town still suffering from English devastation) ; 1424 and 1425 (when the charter was evidently in effect), £40 (per annum).

(b) Mr Neilson shews that the status of burgh was attributed to Dumfries as early as 1186.

F

general laws of the country. Accordingly, at Michaelmas, the
good men of the burgh—the "probi homines villæ fideles et bonæ
famæ" of the charter—met to exercise a totally new prerogative,
to elect magistrates, who, on being voted into office, swore "to
keep the customys of the toune, and that they sal nocht halde
lauch on ony man or woman for wrath, nor for haterent, nor for
drede or for love of ony man, bot throw ordinans, consaile, and
dome of gud men of the toune ;" swearing also " that nather for
radness, nor for luve, nor for haterent, nor for cosynage, nor for
tynsale of their silver," shall they fail to mete out justice to all
the lieges that are placed under their rule.*

Here, as in other royal burghs, the magistrates were at first
chosen by the whole burgesses.(a) Afterwards the practice crept in
of allowing the elective franchise to be exercised by a select few
only, who came to be known as the Council. That this body,
however it may have been constituted, usurped a power belonging
to the entire community, is sufficiently plain. In the "Statuta
Gilde," framed mainly for Berwick in the reign of Alexander II.,
it is provided that, in addition to the aldermen and bailies, there
shall be twenty-four " probi homines de melioribus et discretioribus
et fide dignioribus ejusdem burgi ad hoc electi," who, in the event
of a dispute, were to decide on whom the suffrages had fallen. In
some simple way, such as this, the popular vote may have been
gradually overridden, and ultimately set aside.†

Besides the merchants, artificers, and free farmers who resided
within the liberties of the town, there was a class of cottars whom
the royal charter did not reach. They remained in a condition of
absolute slavery, and could be sold with the land as readily as if
they had been cattle.‡ In course of time many of them acquired
their freedom by purchase or otherwise. The Crown, without
trying to set aside the law which made them bondsmen, did much
to promote their emancipation, and thus to strengthen the independence of the burgh, as a foil to the great barons of the neighbourhood, and to augment its resources, so that it might yield an
increasing revenue to the State. A vassal or slave who was so
fortunate as to purchase a house within any royal burgh, and
occupy it for a year and a day without being claimed by his
master, became a freeman for ever.§

While these changes were progressing in Dumfries, other
hamlets in the county, which rose also to be royal burghs, were

---

* Laws of the Burghs, chap. 70.

(a) Little is known as to how the magistrates were chosen at first. They are called
Provosts in the Exchequer Rolls ; though that may be a mistranslation of Prepositi,
which is the equivalent for reeves. However, as already noted, in 1395 the town had a
provost and bailies.

† Origin and Progress of Burghs in Scotland, by Joseph Irving, p. 10.

‡ Tytler's History of Scotland, vol. ii., p. 253.

§ Tytler, vol. ii., p. 301 ; M'Pherson's Annals of Commerce, vol. i., p. 307 ; Laws
of the Burghs, chap. 17.

rapidly ripening into towns. In the reign of David I., the territory of Sanchar, at the head of Nithsdale, was included in the demesnes of Dunegal, the Celtic chieftain. The word "Sean-caer," in that language, signifying " old fort," suggests the origin of the village— houses gathering for protection under the friendly shadow of some ancient pile ; their increase fostered by the erection on the same site of a baronial castle, at the end of the twelfth or beginning of the thirteenth century.*(a)* Through Strathannand meandered a pleasant stream, which, taking its name from the valley it watered, gave it in turn to a little town that rose upon the river's bank, about a mile above its flux into the Solway. Coin struck prior to 1249 bear the legends, " Johas on An," and "Thomas on An," which a high authority in numismatic lore considers apply tó Annan.*(b)* A mint, royal or baronial, may have been in operation at that town during the reign of Alexander II.; and whatever doubt may be entertained on this point, it is certain that Annan was a royal burgh when Bruce ascended the throne, in 1306. One of the predecessors of the Patriot-King erected a castle to protect the town and its port ; the fortress continuing for ages afterwards one of the Border strongholds. Pennant, when visiting the burgh in 1772, saw an interesting relic of this old feudal fortress—a stone, built into a garden wall, bearing the words, " Robert de Brus, Count de Carrick et Senieur du Val de Annan, 1300."†*(c)* From this inscription Chalmers concludes the castle was rebuilt in that year.‡

When the first Lord of Annandale settled in the district, he built a strong house for himself beside a group of lakes, which lay like sheets of silver on the green bosom of the valley. It was erected on the north-west of one of them—called for that reason the Castle Loch—and was the chief seat of the Bruces from about 1130 till 1306. Soon after the latter year, the ancient peel was superseded by a far more extensive fortress,*(d)* reared on a penin- sula on the south-east side of the same lake, occupying above six- teen acres, built in the massive Norman style, and surrounded by three deep fosses, fed with water from the lake : it was at once the largest and strongest castle in the district. That near the sheen

---

(a) Sir Herbert Maxwell says that Corda, one of the four towns assigned by Ptolemy to the Selgovæ, appears to have been Sanquhar, and to have possessed as a prefix the same syllable caer which the modern name bears as a suffix. In a note he adds : "Sanquhar—Gaelic, sean cathair (caher), old fortress." Mr Neilson, on the other hand, says : "The 'c' of caer does not exist in the real spelling even now. Quhar is whar (or where). Old spelling was Senewar. 'Old fort' is in my opinion un- tenable."

* Cardonell's Numismatæ Scotiæ, plate i., p. 44.

(b) Mr Neilson ("Old Annan" and Burgh Papers in *Dumfries Standard*) shews that though Annan did not become a royal burgh before the 14th century, if even so early as that, it yet possessed a certain burghal status in 1296, when it figures, together with Lochmaben, as *burgus* in a legal document.

† Tour, vol. iii., p. 84.

(c) The original castle would be a moat, not a stone structure, which would come later.

‡ Caledonia, vol. iii., p. 140.

(d) The peel was not constructed till 1298-9.

of these sparkling lakes, and under the shadow of these protecting castles, a village should spring up, was only natural. The name of the little town is mentioned in a charter granted by Robert I. to Thomas de Carruthers, of certain lands, the *reddendum* of which the king requires him to deliver, "at our manor of Lochmalban" —a term signifying, in the Celtic tongue, "the lake of the bald (or smooth) eminence," and referring probably to the mound on which the first Brucian fortress was erected.*(a)* The burgh of Lochmaben grew up and flourished under the fostering influence of that family ; and, according to tradition, was royally chartered by the greatest of the Bruces, soon after his accession to the throne. The family had two other residences in Annandale : Hoddom Castle, on the east bank of the Annan,* and Castle Malc, or Milk,*(b)* in the parish of St. Mungo ; the latter of which is mentioned in the chartulary of Glasgow, so early as 1179.

At this period—the middle of the twelfth century—the land of Scotland began to be partially divided into royalty and regality. Those parts distinguished by the term royalty were subject in criminal matters to the jurisdiction of the King and his judges ; while in those known as regalities, such as Eskdale, the barons or ecclesiastics to whom they had been given by the Crown, held their own courts for the trial of offenders.† Before Nithsdale was con-stituted a sheriffdom, it was periodically visited by the King's bailies or judges, who, sitting in Dumfries as the head town of the royalty, gave judgment in the cases brought before them.*(c)*

Of this practice a curious instance is recorded, so far back as the days of Malcolm IV.*(d)* It arose out of the following circum-stances. On the first Tuesday after the festival of St. Michael, the sacred fane at Dumfries, dedicated to the archangel of that name and patron of the town, was occupied with worshippers, two of whom—Richard, son of Robert, son of Elias, and Adam the Miller — met after mass in the burying-ground, in an angry spirit, quite at variance with the services of the day. Probably there had been a standing feud between them ; and whether from sheer malice, or because "the son of Robert" had made too free with some of the miller's goods, Adam saluted Richard with the

(a) "Lochmalban" is a mere clerical blunder of some enrolling clerk of the Great Seal Office. There is no "bold eminence" at Lochmaben. *Maibean* is Gaelic for bunch or cluster. ("Annals of the Solway.") The cluster of lochs around the town would therefore be correctly described by the name Lochmaben.

* Its site was on the farm of Hallyards, anciently Halguard ; the more modern Castle of Hoddom, the seat of the Kirkpatrick-Sharpes, was built on the west bank of the Annan, by John, Lord Herries.

(b) Castlemilc in 1170 ; Castlemilc in 1181. (Regis. Epis., Glas., pp, 23-50.)

† Tytler's History of Scotland. vol. ii., p. 246.

(c) It is almost certain that justice was first administered in Nithsdale after the constitution of Dumfries into a sheriffdom. That was probably under William the Lion ; though it may have been under his immediate predecessor.

(d) Mr M'Dowall's date is wrong, as Mr Neilson has shewn in his Burghs Papers Malcolm reigned from 1153 to 1165, long before Dumfries was a burgh or could have any burgess. Thomas Thomson and Cosmo Innes, the great legal antiquaries, place the deed after 1232 and before 1259, and Joseph Bain, the weightest living authority follows them.

opprobrious epithet of "Galloway thief,"(a) bidding him at the
same time begone from the place. Richard slunk away, either
afraid of his antagonist, or from a dread of incurring the guilt of
sacrilege by fighting with him in the churchyard; but he was probably heard muttering threats of vengeance, as, on the following
Thursday, a woman ran up to Adam while he was standing in his
own doorway, and cried, "Take yourself away; for, behold, Richard
is here!"—as if she had said, "the man you abused so much on
Tuesday last has come to return you hard knocks for bad words,
and you had better be off." But the bold miller replied, "I won't
take myself away : I have a knife as sharp as his own ;" saying
which, he entered the domicile, and re-appeared with a long knife,
seemingly bent on embowelling his enemy. There is no evidence
whatever to show that Richard's errand was revenge. He was
perhaps casually passing the miller's house at the time : at all
events, in the conflict that ensued he was not the assailant.
Attacked by the miller, he drew his sword in self-defence ; and
when he struck at all, it was with the flat side of the weapon.
Adam, bent on disabling his opponent, sought with his left arm to
ward off the sword that came between him and his wish. The men
closed in a life-and-death struggle, during which Adam the Miller
was thrust through, fatally wounded ; and Richard, the son of
Robert, was arraigned on a charge of murder.

The court which tried him sat in the Castle of Dumfries, on
the Monday after the Feast of Saints Fabian and Sebastian ; the
tribunal consisting of the king's bailies ("balivis") and a jury of
thirteen burgesses * ("fideles homines") ; the names of the latter,
in their Latinised form, being given thus : "Ade Long, Ade Mille,
Hugonis Schereman, Rogeri Wytewell, Ricardi Haket, Walteri
Faccinger, Thome Scut, Roberti Muner, Thome Calui, Roberti
Boys, Willelmy Scot, Willelmy Pellaparii, Henrici Tinctoris."
While Richard was placed at the bar charged with a capital offence,
the case assumed the form of an inquisition into the whole of its
circumstances ; and the jury were required, after hearing evidence,
to give a narrative of these as they understood them, in connection
with and explanatory of their verdict. Accordingly, the finding of
the jury set out with the statement that, at the time specified,
"Riccardum, filium Roberti, fili Elie," had met with the deceased,
"Adam Molendinarius," in "Cemeterio Sancti Michaelis ;" that the
latter had defamed the former in the manner we have described ;
and that, in the conflict two days afterwards, the panel did not
intend to slaughter the deceased, but said truth when he declared
at the time, "I take ye all to witness that I have not killed the

(a) Not "Galloway thief," but a term which implied that being a Galloway man
he was a thief. Dumfries at that time was strongly anti-Celtic.

* "It is probable," says Tytler, "although it cannot be affirmed with historical
certainty, that, even at this early age, the opinion of the majority of this jury of
thirteen decided the case, and that unanimity was not required."—History of Scotland,
vol. ii., p. 249.

miller, but that his death lies at his own door." For these reasons
the jury unanimously acquitted Richard ; finding, moreover, that
he had been "fidelem in omnibus aliüs," faithful in all things, and
that the miller, "furem esse et defamatum," was a man of bad
repute. The bailies concurring, the panel was honourably discharged.*(a)

Before the close of the century, Dumfries had become the seat
of a sheriff, who exercised a very extensive sway, stretching over
the stewartry of Kirkcudbright on the west, and the entire country
eastward bounded by the Esk.† About the year 1180, the judges
sitting in the burgh decided, that any one convicted of breaking
the king's peace in Galloway should forfeit twelve score of cows
and three bulls : ‡ a very appropriate fine, as the hornless dusky
herds which at a later date became famous were already common
in the district, and were the true representatives of its wealth.

The Church of Scotland for ages after its erection remained
comparatively pure and simple, unaffected by the peculiar tenets
of the Papacy, and independent of the Roman See. " Columba and
his disciples," says Bede, " would receive those things only which
are contained in the writings of the prophets, evangelists, and
apostles, diligently observing the works of faith and virtue." A
great change had, however, taken place at the time we have now
reached, brought about mainly by the Saxon and Norman immigrants. Gradually the simple, primitive rule of the Culdees
became supplanted by that of lordly prelates ; and the Church,
forgetting Iona, accepted the authority of Rome in matters of
doctrine, ritual, and government.

David I., of whom so much mention has been made, built up the
ecclesiastical establishment by such a lavish outlay that one of his
descendants characterised him as "a sore sanct to the Crown."
He revived the episcopate of Glasgow, placing under it the whole
churches of Dumfriesshire. By the inquisition of 1116 it was found
that the churches of " Abermelc, Drivesdale, and Hodelm," with
others in the county, belonged by right to that see ; and its
authority over the parishes of Eskdale, Ewisdale, Drivesdale,
Annandale, Glencairn, and Stranith, with a part of Cumberland,

---

* For the facts of this case, extraordinary in itself, and valuable as an illustration
of old times in Dumfries, we are indebted to the first volume of the Acts of the Scottish
Parliament, where they are briefly recorded in Latin.

(a) Historically (says Mr Neilson in his Burghs Papers) the value of the document
turns not a little on the important constitutional fact that although the man was
killed in the town the enquiry was conducted in the castle by the King's bailies ; the
oaths of upwards of thirteen citizens were taken ; and sworn along with them and expressly concurring were a number of barons. The sworn barons agreed in all respects
with the sworn burgesses. And all the burgesses and barons (the latter styled this
time not barones but alii baronie) declared that the said " Richard was faithful in all
things, while Adam had been a thief and of bad fame."

† Chalmers, in a note to Caledonia, vol. iii., p. 66, states that practically the sheriffdom came to have much narrower limits ; the local jurisdictions in Annandale and
Kirkcudbrightshire restricting it almost entirely to Nithsdale.

‡ The words of the Act are : " Gif ony Galowa man be convickit ouder be batal, or
be ony other way of the kingis pece brokin, the king sal haf of him xijxx. ky and iii
gatharionis, or for ilka gatharion ix. ky, the quilk are in numer xx. an vij."

was confirmed by Pope Alexander in 1178, by Pope Lucius in 1181, and by Pope Urban in 1186. Dumfries had at this early period, as already noticed, its parish church, dedicated to the patron saint of the town, St. Michael ; a chapel, dedicated to St. Thomas ; another, termed " Our Lady's Chapel ;" a third, of a more private character, connected with the castle ; and an hospital, situated about a mile from the Market Cross, in a southern direction. The erection of a religious house in Canonby has already been noticed. Another rose up in the tree-covered plains of Cluden, long a favourite haunt of the Druids. There grew the sacred grove in which their district priests held annual synod ; and the temple in which they sacrificed —a circle of huge, unhewn masses of rock still remains, nearly entire.* After these primitive worshippers had been scared away by the beams of a better faith that penetrated into their shady retreat, an ascetic enthusiast found in the deserted bowers a place of congenial retirement from the world :—

> " Unknown tb public view,
> From youth to age this reverend hermit grew ;"

leaving to his cell of sanctity, when he died, the name Darcongal, which signifies in the British and Scoto-Irish tongues, "the oak wood of Congal." In course of time the simple grotto of this half-forgotten recluse became the germ of an opposing structure, the Abbey of Darcongal or Holywood, which, as we have seen, was founded by John, Lord of Kirkconnell, ancestor of the Kirkconnell Maxwells.† A charter-seal of one of its earliest abbots, which still exists, bears the following inscription, dated 1264: " Sg. Abbot. Sacri Nemoris " (the Seal of the Abbot of the Sacred Grove). In a Bull of Pope Innocent III. the principal of the abbey has a similar designation ; but in the list of the lords who constituted the great Parliament at Brigham, in 1289, we find him resuming his old Celtic title, slightly Frenchified to Darwongvil.‡

Two officials directed the ecclesiastical system of the county under the bishop, or rather his archdeacon or surrogate : these were, the Dean of Dumfries or Nith, who ruled over the parishes in Nithsdale, those of Kirkmichael and Garval, in Annandale, and those of Terregles, Troqueer, Newabbey, Kirkpatrick-Durham, Kirkpatrick, Lochrutton, and Kirkgunzeon, lying in Galloway, westward of the river Urr ; and the Dean of Annandale, who had charge of all the parishes within that district except Kirkmichael and Garval, with those of Kirkandrews, Canonby, Morton, Wauchope, Stapelgorton, Westerkirk, Eskdalemuir, and Ewes, in Eskdale.

---

* These stones lie about a quarter of a mile south-west from the parish church of Holywood. Originally they were twelve in number ; but a gap was made in the oval circle which they formed by the removal of one of them half a century ago or more. They are all of coarse-grained greywaucke except one, which is of granite. The weight of the largest is estimated at nearly twelve tons.

† Dugdale, vol. ii., p. 1057, where John is mentioned as " Dominus de Kirkconnell fundavit Sacrum Boscum."

‡ Rymer's Fœdera, vol. i., p. 30.

CHAPTER IV.

EPOCH OF DEVORGILLA—SHE BUILDS A BRIDGE OVER THE NITH—SHE ALSO
FOUNDS A GREYFRIARS' MONASTERY IN THE BURGH, AND NEWABBEY IN
KIRKCUDBRIGHTSHIRE—BENEFICIAL EFFECTS OF THE BRIDGE UPON THE
TOWN—THE SEAL OF DEVORGILLA—HER DEATH AND BURIAL.

AT the period now reached—the middle of the thirteenth century
—Dumfries would probably have much fewer than two thousand
inhabitants. When Devorgilla * visited it after her marriage with
the Lord of Barnard Castle, it must have worn a very primitive
aspect ; and she would readily realise the loss to the inhabitants,
as well as the inconvenience to herself, caused by the want of a
bridge over the Nith to connect the town with Galloway. Her
family had possessions on both sides of the river—in England also,
not less than in Scotland—and as a ready means of communication
between them a bridge was needed ; and such a structure would
at the same time promote the well-being of a town in which she
began to take a deep interest. Impressed with this idea, she was
not long in giving effect to it. The Lady Devorgilla belonged to
one of the most opulent families in Europe : she was large-hearted
and liberal-minded up to the full measure of her wealth ; and no
greater boon could she have conferred on the Dumfriesians of that
and many after generations than by linking together the two sides
of Nithsdale. The river, a few miles above the town, when it
rolled past Dalswinton Castle—where her future kinsman, the
Black Comyn, resided—and the opposite territory of the Kirkpatricks, looked very much as it now does ; and it then laved the
abbey lands gifted by her ancestor, just as it now steals gently
past the ruined house of Uchtred ; but when it reached within a
stone-cast of the ridge crowned by the " Castle in the shrubbery,"
it took a wider sweep eastward than it does at present. Not that
the channel of the Nith near to and opposite the town has been
absolutely changed during the six centuries that have intervened.
On this point there is no small amount of popular misconception.
The bed of the river is still essentially the same ; but down till
the reign of William the Lion, its margin next the town had little
natural and no artificial embankment. As a consequence, the
upper sand-beds, or Green Sands, and the lower sand-beds, or
White Sands, were seriously encroached upon ; and a watery

---

* The lady's name is variously spelt : on her seal, preserved in Baliol College,
Oxford, it appears as " Dervorgille," the words added being "deballio Alani de
Galawad ;" sometimes it is written " Devorgille ;" in contemporary Latin documents it
generally appears as " Dervorgulla ;" at Oxford the style used is " Devorguilla."
Dugdale, appending the family name, calls her " Devorgilla Macdowall." [See note,
p. 27.]

dominion, more or less wide, was established over the Dock
Meadow, as far down as the other stronghold of the Comyns at
Castledykes—the high rock on which the fortress stood at this
point giving the encroaching element a westward curve, till the
river fringed an ancient mound on the Troqueer side, the mote-hill
from which Devorgilla's forefathers, as Lords of Galloway, must
often have administered brehon law to their vassals.*

The rocky bed of the Nith at Castledykes still impedes the
navigation ; (a) but it shot up higher, shallowing the water much
more in old times than at the present day ; and a flood in the
upper reaches therefore ebbed out at a very indolent pace. A spate
in the Nith was, for these reasons, a serious visitation, seeming
sometimes as if the Solway had advanced seven miles further
north ; the Vennel looking like a miniature canal, and the impetuous waves threatening to invade the row of little cabins which then
occupied the site of Irish Street. The tides, when high, had a range
only less extensive, depositing a vast accumulation of sand, which
still lies below the herbage of the Dock and houses that are now
beyond the sweep of the tidal flux and river. These statements
are further borne out by old sazines, which make the Nith the
boundary of certain gardens in St. Michael's Street. Under such
circumstances, the crossing of the river by boats or on horseback
must have been often dangerous, and sometimes impracticable,
though easily enough effected in these ways, or even by wading,
when the water was in its normal state.

The bridge was not the only fabric raised for behoof of the
town by Devorgilla. She was full of spiritual fervour ; and, quite
in accordance with the practice of her family and of the age, her
piety expressed itself in the erection of religious houses and the
endowment of monastic fraternities. The vast extent of her
wealth, and her desire, as she fondly thought, to store up a portion
of it in heaven, were proved to the world, when a convent at
Dundee—with which town she was connected through the Comyns
—another at Wigtown, the Greyfriars' Monastery at Dumfries, and
greatest of all, Newabbey in Kirkcudbrightshire, grew up at her
command. Baliol died in 1269 ; and we are inclined to think that
all these religious houses were erected after that date. Her
affection for him seems to have been unbounded : perhaps she
sought, by the building of such expansive fanes, to promote the
eternal well-being of her departed husband.

The dates of these erections are unknown, except in the case
of Newabbey, which, Fordun tells us, was built in 1275,† a period

* The Scoto-Irish colonists of Galloway and Nithsdale had, for a long period, no
written laws ; and cases were usually decided by the will of the brehon, or judge,
guided by traditional precedents.

(a) There was a ford at this point. Hence the two Motes—one on the Troqueer
side ; the other on the Dumfries side (at Castledykes). This arrangement historically
is found of frequent occurrence.

† Fordun, in the Scotichronicon, gives this date twice : vol. i., p. 474, and vol. ii,
p. 124.

G

when the decorated style of Gothic architecture was just beginning
to enrich the severer dignity of the early English. The abbey is of
this complex, transitional character ; and as the monastery was in
the early English style, no difficulty is felt in determining that it
came first into existence, and that it could scarcely have been built
later than, 1270—the probability being that it had a somewhat
earlier origin. There were no architects among the ordinary Celtic
or Saxon population of Dumfriesshire and Galloway competent to
design such buildings ; no masons able to fashion the materials, and
weave them, as it were, into the requisite shape. The Norman
nobles and yeomen, who had newly come into the country, had little
relish for such artistic or industrial pursuits : more liking had they
for "the pomp, pride, and circumstance of glorious war," and the
exuberant pleasures of the chase. When it entered into the mind
of Devorgilla, therefore, to dower her native district with goodly
temples dedicated to God's service, she had to bring artists and
operatives from a distance before her conceptions could be carried
into effect. The lady's wealth was a handmaid to her will, which,
like the talisman of Aladdin, brought agents at her call ready and
able to do the work assigned to them. There were building associations in France and Italy, formed for the very purpose of erecting, or assisting to erect, gorgeous religious structures adapted for
the sumptuous ritual of the Western Church.* (a) Some of these,
on being appealed to, would only be too glad to visit Nithsdale, in
order to realise the grand ideas of this bountiful princess and
dutiful daughter of Rome.

    In due time a band of foreign workmen would arrive at Dum-
fries ; and, probably, after completing their contract there, a portion
of them would be engaged on the greater undertaking further down
the river. There is no necessity, however, for supposing that all
the head and hand work employed on these buildings was furnished
from abroad. Some native churchmen may have co-operated with

* Tytler, in his History of Scotland, expresses his decided opinion that the magnificent ecclesiastical structures that rose up in the kingdom during the thirteenth
century were built by associations of French and Italian workmen, acting under the
auspices of the Papal Church. As connected with this subject, we may quote the
following curious inscription, cut on a tablet in Melrose Abbey :—

> " John Morow sum tym callit was I,
> And born in Parysse certanly ;
> And had in kepyng all masn werk
> Of Sant Androy's, the hye kyrk
> Of Glasgw, Melros, and Paslay,
> Of Nyddysdayll, and of Galway :
> I pray to God and Mari baith,
> And sweet Sanct John, to kep this haly kyrk fra scaith."

    It has been thought by some antiquaries that Murdo, as the name was at one
time read, or Morow, as the latest authority (Mr P. Macgregor Chalmers) reads it, was
the agent of one of the French or Italian building associations noticed above ; but Mr
Billings (author of the Antiquities of Scotland) is of opinion that the Melrose inscription cannot well be older than the sixteenth century, and that Morow or Murdo,
whose name indicates a Scottish origin, performed no work beyond repairs and
restorations.

    (a) The architectural culture of this country at the time referred to seems to be
somewhat underestimated in the text. In those days the Scots were quite capable of
building anything.

the foreign architects ; and Newabbey, at all events, manifests some features—such as the depression of the upper window of the transept—which are never found in French or Italian buildings of the same style and period.

The site selected for the abbey was an admirable one—a pleasant nook of land, laved by a mountain brook, which at a little distance loses itself in the Solway ; and there arose the marvellous pile which is still charming in its decay, though sadly changed since the wimpling rivulet and the surging sea sang responsive to the vesper melody of its inmates.

Its humble sister building, which has long since disappeared, was a monastic establishment belonging to an order founded by St. Francis of Assisi, who, from being a wild libertine, had become an ascetic devotee, and died in the odour of sanctity about the year 1230. When brooding sorrowfully over his wasted prime, he heard a sermon on Matthew x., 9, 10 : "Provide neither gold, nor silver, nor brass in your purses ; nor scrip for your journey, neither two coats, neither shoes, nor yet staves : for the workman is worthy of his meat." This discourse fixed the destiny of young Francis Bernardone—had a wonderful influence, too, as we shall afterwards see, on the fortunes of Scotland ; for, if he had not established a monastic order in consequence, there would probably have been no friary at Dumfries, and in that case no slaughter of Comyn ; and the pliant Lord of Annandale might never have grown into resolute heroism—never have ripened into the Bruce of Bannockburn. Francis, interpreting the Scriptural injunctions literally, gave up all his worldly goods, attired himself in coarse raiment, and wandering the country round, begged from man and prayed to Heaven by turns—one of the first specimens of a mendicant friar which Europe had ever seen. He obtained a numerous train of followers, formed an order on his own self-sacrificing model, which, in further proof of his humility, he named Fratres Minores—as if they were too contemptible to be put on a footing of equality with the other religious brotherhoods. Devorgilla, a devotee herself, cordially sympathised with these poor ascetics. She had conceived the idea of building and endowing a magnificent abbey for monks of a more patrician class—the Cistercians : she resolved first to found a house for the lowly Franciscans, the fame of whose virtues and sacrifices had often been sounded in her ears, and had won her warmest admiration.

This monastery, though a small building as compared with Newabbey, had a handsome external aspect. (*a*) In that respect it had no rival in Dumfries. The castle had more strength than ornament ; the smaller fortress southward of the town, belonging

(*a*) It was the initial principle of the Franciscan system to have everything humble ; and the suggestion that the house at Dumfries was elaborately ornate can rest only on a conjecture which is opposed to that principle.

to the Comyns, was a rough piece of masonry ; (a) and the primitive church, erected during the Scoto-Irish period, would be simply a square or oblong fabric, with probably a roof of thatch, and certainly with few pretensions to architectural beauty. The new religious house was erected westward of the castle, near the head of the oldest street—still called, on that account, the Friars' Vennel. It consisted of a range of cloisters, a refectory, a dormitory, with other necessary appendages ; and there was added to it a church, not commonplace, like the other church, but made up of nave and aisle, chancel and choir—all in the early English style, which prevailed for about eighty years after the disappearance of the Norman style, in the beginning of the thirteenth century.

Some time in the latter half of the same century, swarthy oreigners from the sunny south were seen mingling with the fair-complexioned Celts and Saxons of the town - *in*, but not *of*, the ordinary population. Their language, dress, and mode of life were alike strange : some of them spoke Norman-French, others the soft Italian tongue—in curious contrast to their rough attire, which consisted of a coarse grey gown, having a hood of the same stuff, and fastened at the waist with a hempen cord by way of girdle. These grotesque-looking strangers were the original Grey Friars, the primitive tenants of the Monastery in the Vennel. Afterwards they would be joined by numerous recluses from the neighbourhood ; and, when the foreign friars had acquired some knowledge of the native dialect, the order would enter upon its duties, which, as summarily expressed in the rules of its founder, were— " To live to preach, and beg to live."

But the liberal lady who brought the brethren to Dumfries did not wish them to interpret these words too literally : she fancied that a fixed income would be an acceptable addition to precarious doles given by the charitable ; and, accordingly, the house was endowed by her with the customs exacted at the bridge.* (b) The Nith was now no longer a wild, untrammelled, vagrant river, rioting wantonly over its eastern bank, playing at high jinks when it pleased, dashing its spray upon the lieges as they looked out of their little domiciles, and saying complacently to itself, " I shall have these encroaching houses down some day."

The river was bridged ; a beginning had been made of the embankment townward at the bottom of the Vennel ; and, though spring tides and lammas freshets still at times turned the stream into an inland sea, its destructive power was sensibly reduced, and,

(a) There is no evidence that the Castledykes Castle was not the Castle of Dumfries at that time, or that Comyn had anything to do with it. See note on page 15.

* Devorgilla had such interest at Court as enabled her also to get an occasional allowance for her poor fraters from Alexander III., as is shown in Historical Documents, 1286-1306, in vol. ii., p. 246, of which the following entries occur : " Dunfres, item in procuratione Fratrum Minorum, cxvijs." (£5 17s) ; " Item eisdem Fratribus Minoribus de Dunfres, vij*l*. xvj*s*." (£7 16s).

(b) There is no need to infer court influence for such doles. All the kings of Scotland kept them up. So did Edward I.

rage and foam as it might on such occasions, it could not get rid
of the curb put upon it, or break the bond of stone which rose
above its subject billows to unite Dumfriesshire with Galloway.
The bridge was a colossal one, of nine arches or more, having no
equal at that time in Scotland.* Some of the workmen, who
literally left their mark on the monastery, would probably be
employed in its construction also. Three years were spent, fully
five centuries afterwards, in erecting the new bridge over the
Nith ; and we may reasonably suppose that the building of the old
bridge would occupy a still longer period. This latter structure
helped to make Dumfries : it was thereby brought into a close
relationship with Galloway, and became an important station
on the leading highway between England and Scotland. The
founder of Dumfries is unknown ; its first royal patron was William
the Lion, and the person to whom it was indebted next to him in
mediæval times was Devorgilla. Before the charters and the bridge
a humble village—after them a thriving burgh.

Some time prior to 1282, when several other years had elapsed,
Devorgilla gave yet another proof of her extraordinary munificence,
by establishing Baliol College,† in the University of Oxford, so
called in memory of her deceased husband, who was rarely absent
from her thoughts.‡ The original deed embodying the statutes of
the foundation is still extant with an impression of Devorgilla's
seal attached—both precious relics.§ The impression of the seal—
a double one, reproduced on our title-page—is especially interest
ing. One side exhibits the arms of Baliol impaled with those of
Galloway ; ‖ the other a full-length figure, doubtless her own,
holding up the shields of both families, one in each hand, with two
more shields below—one consisting of three garbes, the other of
three piles conjoined in point, and representing respectively the
related houses of Chester and Huntingdon. Wyntoun, Prior of
Lochleven, states that Devorgilla was a comely personage—" rycht
pleasand of bewté ;" that

> " A bettyr ladye than she, wes nane,
>   In all the yle of Mare Bretane." ¶

Pity that some of the lines in this miniature likeness have been so
obliterated by " Time's effacing fingers," that the nobility of mind
which made her higher and richer far than her princely rank or her

---

* Appendix A.

   † The name of Devorgilla's husband appears in old Latin documents as " Johannis
de Balliolo "—hence the retention of the double " l " in the name at Oxford.

   ‡ The original building has long since disappeared, and in the existing College
there is nothing earlier than the middle of the fifteenth century. The foundation at
present comprises a master, twelve fellows, and fourteen scholars, besides exhibitioners.
—*Walk through Oxford*, p. 103.   § Appendix B.

   ‖ The lion rampant is the Galloway portion of the seal. " There are," says Nisbet,
" three old families of note in Galloway of the name of M'Dowall [Garthland, Logan, and
Freuch] claiming their descents from the old Lords of Galloway, and carrying their
arms as a tessera [token] of their descent.—*Heraldry*, vol. i., p. 283.

   ¶ Cronykil, Book viii., c. 8.

boundless wealth, is not seen imprinted on the features ; but the reflex of the eloquent eyes has been to some extent preserved, the soul of the sainted lady seeming, as it were, to look through them still, and through the mist of the long cycle that has intervened since she passed away from earth.

During her latter years Devorgilla seems to have resided chiefly in Huntingdonshire, on the lands she inherited from her father, and which she held as a fief from the Crown of Scotland. Her favourite abode was Kempstone, in the honour of Huntingdon, the ancient manor-house of which, we may be sure, was known far and wide as the dwelling-place of one who had throughout her lengthened widowhood been not less charitable than pious :—

> " So pious, as she had no time to spare
> For human thoughts, but was confined to prayer ;
> Yet in such charities she passed the day,
> 'Twas wondrous that she found an hour to pray."

At the venerable age of eighty years she breathed her last in the Vill de Kempstone, on "the Sabbath following the conversion of St Paul "—that is, the 29th of September (1289).* Her husband, John Baliol, died at his ancestral castle twenty years before that date, and was buried in its neighbourhood—all except the heart : which symbol of our emotional nature the sorrowful widow caused to be embalmed, and placed in a little ivory casket, which she kept beside her as a daily companion till the erection of Newabbey furnished for it a fitting shrine.† It was built in over the high altar of that magnificent monumental fane : hence the romantic name it ever afterwards bore—Dulce Cor, or Sweetheart Abbey. They brought the body of Devorgilla to her native Nithsdale, burying it within the walls of the abbey, and placing upon the lady's bosom

---

* " Dicunt etiam quod dicta Domina Devorgulla diem clausit extremum die Sabbati proxima post conversionem Sancto Pauli anno predicto." Extract from the declaration made by Hugo of St Edward, William Bernard, and others, appointed to value the lands and tenements owned by Devorgilla in Kempstone at the date of her demise. These, which formed but a very small portion of her property, were set down at £28 of annual value, made up as follows : " A certain chief messuage, worth, after deductions, 6s 8d per annum ; 360 acres of arable land in the barony, each acre worth 6d per annum ; 20½ acres of meadow, each worth 2s per annum ; 6 acres of separate pasture, each worth 12d ; rents paid by the freemen at the Feast of the Apostle St. Andrews, 36s, at the Feast of the Annunciation to the Blessed Mary, 21s, at the Feast of the Nativity of St. John the Baptist, 23s, and at the Feast of St. Michael, 21s ; twenty-one cottars (sulinarii), holding 17½ roods of land, whose work is worth £8 8s 4d per annum, contributing at the Feast of St. Michael for aid, 40s ; a certain small eel-pond (conegera), worth 6s 8d per annum ; a fishery in the Ouse, worth 10s per annum ; 40 acres of copsewood, the produce of which is worth 13s ; and a certain observatory (certus visis), worth 5s—Inquisitio post mortem, 18 Edw. I., No. 28, as given in *Historical Documents*, 1286-1306, pp. 123-4. (See Appendix C for more information regarding Devorgilla's effects.)

† " That ilk hart than, as men sayd,
Scho bawmyd, and gert it be layd
In-til a cophyn of evore,
That she gert be made there-for,
Annamalyd and perfectly dycht,
Lockyt and bwyndyn with sylver brycht ;
And alwayis quhan scho ghed till mete
That cophyne scho gert by hir sett ;
And till hyr Lord as in presens,
Ay to that she dyd reverens."

Wyntoun's Cronykι.

her husband's heart, in obedience to her dying wish ; another
affecting illustration of the strong love which made them one. A
tombstone, of which there is left no certain trace, marked the spot,
bearing upon it an inscription which, unlike most epitaphs, did not
recount one half of the virtues possessed by the lady who slept
below. The epitaph, composed by Hugh de Burgh, Prior of Lanercost, ran as follows :—

> " In Dervorvilla moritur sensata Sibilla,
> Cum Marthaque pia, contemplativa Maria ;
> Da Dervorvillam requie, Rex summe potiri
> Quam tegit iste lapis, cor pariterque viri."

Which lines have been translated thus, by some unknown hand :—

> In Devorgil a sybil sage doth die, as
> Mary contemplative, as Martha pious ;
> To her, oh deign, high King, rest to impart
> Whom this stone covers with her husband's heart.

CHAPTER V.

It is in the palmy days of Alexander III. that we find Dumfries
first associated with great historical events. In the reign of that
good and sagacious king, Scotland reached a condition of prosperity
to which it had never before attained. He encouraged commerce
and literature ; and, whilst cultivating with success the arts of
peace, he acquired fame and more substantial results by his prowess
in the field. Fighting at the head of his army, in 1263, he gained
a decisive victory over the Norwegian invaders under King Haco,
at Largs, in Ayrshire ; and, with the view of pushing his success,
he in the following year visited Dumfries, and there planned an
expedition against the Isle of Man, which originally belonged to
Scotland, but had for about a hundred and eighty years been
subject to the Crown of Norway. The King brought with him a
powerful force, which would be swelled, we may suppose, by the
vassals of the neighbouring chiefs, anxious to show fealty to their
feudal superior. When the Army of Mona, as it may be called,
was all duly equipped, it embarked in a squadron of vessels brought
to the estuary of the Nith for that purpose ; and, under the leadership of Alexander Stewart (progenitor of the royal family of that
name), and of John Comyn, Earl of Buchan, proceeded down the
Solway to its destination.* (a)

* Both Hector Boethius and Buchanan furnish accounts of this expedition.
According to the former historian, the fleet consisted of thirteen ships, manned by
five hundred mariners.

(a) The authorities quoted are untrustworthy on the point. It was after Haco's
death in Orkney that Man was invaded by Alexander's force. The isle was then ruled
by Magnus, son of Olaf, who was indisposed to shew fight, and tendered Man in
vassalage to the Scottish king. The expedition was persisted in, however, in spite of
promises, and Magnus hastened to Dumfries, to interview Alexander personally,
and do homage for his kingdom—undertaking feudal service with ten "pirate
galleys," five of them with four-and-twenty oars and five with twelve. This galley
service may have been the basis of a marine policy the continuance of which is
attested by Brucian west-coast charters. See Annals of the Solway.

It does not appear that the hostile fleet encountered any opposition. We read of no naval engagement introductory to the battles which took place on the soil of Man for the possession of the island. These, however, were numerous and obstinate—Guara, King of Man, under Haco, offering a desperate resistance. At length he was forced to yield ; and the expedition returned laden with the spoils of victory, after having subdued the island and appointed a viceroy over it, who engaged, by way of tribute, to maintain thirteen ships, with five hundred mariners, for the use of the Scottish monarch.

Other twenty prosperous years pass away, to be suceeded by more than twenty of desolation and trial. Dumfries was identified with the conquest of Man, and shared in the general well-being of the country ; and when, by the accidental death of Alexander III., its Augustan era was brought to a sudden close, the town and its neighbourhood experienced more than their share of the sufferings which ensued. The proximity of Dumfries to the dominions of the ambitious monarch who aimed at making Scotland a dependency of the English Crown, exposed the town to peculiar perils, rendering the interregnum a time of rapine and terror for the unfortunate inhabitants.

Alexander III. died childless, and his heiress and granddaughter, the Maiden of Norway, was an infant in a foreign land. For a long period the northern kingdom had been coveted by Edward I. of England ; and, with the view of getting it under his control, he sought to negotiate a nuptial alliance between the young Princess and his eldest son—a project which was favourably entertained by the Guardians of Scotland. The peers who acted in that capacity, together with many other nobles, including Robert de Brus, Alexander de Baliol, Richard Siward, Herbert de Maccuswel, and William de Douglas, met at Brigham in 1290, and there agreed to the proposed royal marriage. Some time before, however, the Bruces, mindful of their own interests, entered into what was termed a bond of mutual defence with certain other barons, the main object of which was to uphold the claims of Robert, fourth Earl of Annandale, to the crown.* So bent was the English monarch upon the match that was to give him a daughter-in-law dowered with a kingdom, that he despatched a ship of his own to bring her from Norway—" Noroway o'er the faem ;" but the child-bride with whose innocent life his guilty aspirations were bound up, and who stood between Scotland and the perplexities of a disputed succession, died on the voyage : thus was he placed under the necessity of abandoning his acquisitive policy, or of carrying it out by fraud and force. In an unhappy hour for Scotland and for himself he adopted the latter course. It is not necessary that we should narrate with minuteness how he schemed and acted—

* Historical Documents, vol. i., p. 22.

H

into what troubles he plunged the country, and how it was
eventually delivered out of them, and his ambition thoroughly
baffled ; but in order to understand the history of Dumfries, we
must pay some attention to the proceedings at this period, with
which it is inseparably bound up.

In the first scene of the evolving drama, the competitors for
the Crown—including John Baliol, Devorgilla's son, and Robert
Bruce—are discovered laying their respective claims before the
crafty English monarch as umpire. Each of them tries to make
the best of his own case ; and Baliol, not satisfied with such a
course, adopts the expedient of traducing his chief rival, Bruce.
In a paper laid before King Edward, he affirmed that when the
Bishops and other great men of Scotland had sworn to defend the
kingdom of their Lady the daughter of Norway, and keep the
peace of her land, Sir Robert Bruce, and the Earl of Carrick, his
son, after also doing fealty to her as their Lady liege, attacked
the Castle of Dumfries with fire and arms, and banners displayed,
expelling the forces of the Queen who held the same ; that thereupon Sir Robert advanced to the Castle of Buittle, and caused a
proclamation to be made by one Patrick M'Guffock, within the
bailery of the same fortress, warning certain loyal individuals
away from the district : the result being that good subjects
quitted the land or were banished therefrom.* How far these
allegations were correct cannot now be ascertained ; the " mutual
defence " compact entered into by the Bruces soon after the death
of Alexander III., proves that they paid little regard to his
heiress ; the probability, therefore, is that Baliol's tale was but an
exaggerated version of some real occurrence.

In the second scene, we find the royal umpire reducing the
competitors to these two ; to Bruce, as son of the second daughter
of William the Lion's brother, and Baliol, as grandson of the same
nobleman's eldest daughter. In the third, we see him selecting
Baliol as the more pliant of the two. In the fourth, we hear the
obsequious favourite acknowledge that he is but a vassal sovereign
to his patron Edward, the Lord Paramount of Scotland. And in
the fifth, the castles of the country, that had been given temporarily to that puissant monarch, as a pledge that his decision
would be accepted, are seen passing into the hands of the puppet
king, with Englishmen for their governors. The sad finale being
a virtual surrender of the nation's power, and a sacrifice of its
independence : which humiliation is symbolised by the breaking
of the Great Seal of Scotland into fragments.

Thus far the schemes of Edward bore rich fruit. He had
secured a great triumph, at little cost of treasure and with no loss
of blood ; diplomacy doing more for him than his predecessors

---

* Sir Francis Palgrave's Documents and Records Illustrative of the History of
Scotland, vol. i., Introduction, page 80.

had been able to accomplish by the sword. Well pleased with the issue, he withdrew for awhile from all direct personal interference with Scottish affairs, resolving, however, to take advantage of any circumstances that might arise to facilitate his complete conquest of the kingdom. Feeling secure as regards Baliol, Edward tried, with considerable success, to propitiate the family of the disappointed competitor. Among other favours, he remitted certain fees owing to the English Exchequer by the Lord of Annandale for lands in Essex ; also, sundry sums due to it by the Earl of Carrick ; and he gave the latter liberty to import corn, wine, and other necessaries (" blada vina, victuallis, et alia necessaria ") from Ireland.* Baliol's rival never fairly accepted Edward's settlement of the succession difficulty ; but it may be mentioned as a proof that there was no " bad blood " between them, that when Bruce, shortly before his death at Lochmaben in 1295, broke the forest laws, by " hunting the deer with hound and horn " in the royal chase of Essex, the fine of a hundred merks which he had incurred was remitted by the King.†

From the summer of 1291 till the autumn of 1295, the country occupied a position that was anomalous as well as degrading ; the Guardians, though they had sworn fealty to a foreign king, manifesting a show of independence for a long while afterwards ; King John figuring at times as *de facto* ruler ; while all financial matters were managed by Alexander de Baliol, his Chamberlain and near kinsman, and by Robert Heron, agent for the Lord Superior. Whilst the Guardians had full power, Walter de Curry was Governor of the Castle of Dumfries ; two strongholds in Galloway —those of Kirkcudbright and Wigtown—being also entrusted to his care ; but, towards the close of 1291, he had to give up his keys of office to William de Boyville, who was forthwith made custodier of the south-western fortresses. They were held by Curry for the Daughter of Norway, and on her demise, for the Guardians of the Scottish nation : mark what a change for the worse is revealed by this small document—a money receipt from the new keeper, addressed to Lord Alexander de Baliol : "William de Boyville, custos Castrorum de Dounfres, Kyrkcutbright, et Wyggetone, sends greetings. He acknowledges to have received sixty pounds sterling from the bailies of Dumfries (de ballivis burgi de Dounfres) for the sustentation of the garrisons in the castles aforesaid, by the hands of Roberti de Nam, burgess of the said burgh. . . . . acknowledging also that he holds the said castles for the most illustrious Lord Edward, King of England and Lord Superior of the Scottish kingdom !"‡

About this troublous period a second Alan of Dunfres is seen in the foreground : as he is also termed " Alani de Galwey " in

* Historical Documents, vol. i., p. 233.
† Historical Documents, vol. i., p. 422.　　　‡ Ibid, vol. i., p. 259.

contemporary writs, it may be fairly inferred that he was one of
Dunegal's descendants, or closely connected otherwise with the
first Alan of Dumfries, and the last Lord of Galloway. Alan the
second was Bishop of Caithness, and, like his supposed ancestor,
Chancellor of Scotland—an appointment held by him under the
Guardians, and also during the English conquest, till his death.
Of William de Dunfres we also catch at this time more than a
passing glimpse. He was probably the nephew of the Chancellor ;
had he been his son, he would have been termed William Fitz
Alan. He first appears as Clerk of the Rolls, when the country
was still free ; next as Rector of Kinross, when it was falling into
bondage ; last of all as Chancellor of Scotland, when, by the
death of Alan, that appointment was placed at the disposal of the
English monarch.(a) The language of the commission, dated the
27th of February, 1292, which confers this high honour on William
of Dumfries, is that of a man who has a will of his own, and
whose word makes law. It is addressed by King Edward to the
Bishop of Bath and Wells, whom he roundly scolds at the outset
for neglecting to take the steps previously required of him for
appointing " Magistro Willelmo de Dunfrys Chancellor of *our*
Kingdom of Scotland." The Bishop is then told that letters are
enclosed regarding the duty neglected by him, from the deceased
Chancellor's son (" Brianus filius Alani ") ; and, continues the
King, " We strictly enjoin and command that you cause to be
made out, in due form, as soon as you receive these our letters concerning the commission of the Chancellorship, in the name of the
aforesaid William, as formerly directed. Commanding also in our
letters the aforesaid Brian, that taking with him our only fellow-
guardian of the same kingdom who may happen to be present, you
are directed to make him deliver at once, in the presence of him
his associate, the deputy-seal of Scotland to the aforesaid William,
to be kept by him as our deceased Chancellor of the same kingdom used to keep it, without at all waiting for the arrival of the
other fellow-guardians. And, although you may perhaps have
had the letters patent made out before receipt of the present, yet
you are not on this account to omit to cause letters the same as
these to be made out anew, and sealed with our Great Seal ; nor
are you to omit to cause that these, together with the letters
directed to the aforesaid Brian, be delivered with the utmost despatch to the bearer of the present ; and endeavour to be anxious
and expeditious in making out those formerly sent. Given under
our private seal, at Farndone, on the 27th of February, in the
twentieth year of our reign."* Here Edward appears as the
supreme ruler of Scotland, paying but scant regard to the pussil-

* See Stevenson's Historical Documents. vol. i., p. 276, in which a transcript of
King Edward's letter appears copied from the Latin original in the Public Record
Office.

lanimous Guardians, and making no reference to the Crown rights which they had in charge.

Early in 1292, William de Boyville lost his governorship of the Castles of Dumfries, Kirkcudbright, and Wigtown ; for a while afterwards Richard Siward held the office ; then a few months later Walter de Curry again became their custodier : neither of these two barons making any acknowledgment, as de Boyville did, of the Lord Paramount's authority, when acknowledging the payment of their salaries. But if "the most illustrious Lord Edward" winked at these mutinous forewarnings, he kept a watchful eye, and laid a harassing hand upon Baliol, till the unhappy vassal-king writhed under the treatment, and at length broke out into open revolt. In the course of one brief year he had been compelled to plead six times before an English Parliament in answer to trifling complaints made against him, chiefly by his own subjects ; but when another similar demand was made upon him, conjoined with divers other indignities, he, by the advice of many Scottish nobles, disobeyed the summons, and prepared for war—first receiving the Pope's absolution from his oath of homage, and entering into a treaty offensive and defensive with the King of France. A considerable army was raised by the patriots, Dumfriesshire furnishing a portion of the force ; and Edward, not knowing whether to be more enraged than gratified by the news, heard that his viceroy for ruling the subjugated kingdom had set up as a sovereign on his own account. "Since the foolish traitor will not come to us, we shall go to him," he muttered, in a tone of mingled exaltation and menace. Though the English king was irritated at what he conceived to be Baliol's treachery, his aspirations were agreeably whetted by the tempting opportunity which the revolt of his vassal gave him to place Scotland under martial law, and to snatch its sceptre from the weak hand to which he had consigned it—results not difficult to effect, he thought, as he had an immense army at his disposal, and could not dread much opposition from a country whose strength had been undermined and spirit broken.

The events which ensued justified his anticipations : Berwick taken by assault, and thousands of its occupants put pitilessly to the sword ; Dunbar, the key of the eastern marches, capitulating after losing 10,000 defenders ; the Castles of Roxburgh, Dumbarton, Edinburgh, and Stirling, one after another garrisoned by the irresistible Southrons ; and their proud monarch celebrating on the same auspicious day the Feast of St. John the Baptist and the acquisition of a kingdom, in the Fair City of Perth, which opened its gates at his approach. From a record of the royal progress, written in Norman-French, that has just been brought to light,* we learn that when at Montrose, on the 8th of July, 1296, his triumph was intensified, and his pride further flattered, by the

* MSS. of the fourteenth century, in the Paris Library.

appearance before him of a humble suppliant—poor John Baliol, come to acknowledge himself a guilty rebel, and to crave forgiveness from his injured lord and master, which favour was graciously granted, only that he had to purchase it at the expense of his regal crown, and a sojourn with his son in the Tower of London. "Le Roy Johan d'Escose," says the courtly chronicler, "came to the King's mercy, surrendering to him entirely the realm of Scotland, as one who had done amiss ;" the Earl of Mar, the Earl of Buchan, Sir John Comyn of Badenoch, and many others doing likewise ; "and he (Edward) conquered the realm of Scotland, and searched it (et le sercha), as is above written, in not more than twenty-one weeks." Leaving the Earl of Warrene to act as Guardian, Sir Hugh de Cressingham as Treasurer, and Sir Walter de Agmondesham as Chancellor, the victorious King returned to England.

Among the nobles connected with Dumfries who took part in this disastrous outbreak, or gave it some degree of countenance, were the two Comyns, Alexander de Baliol, Gilbert de Carlyle, Herbert de Maccuswel, William de Douglas (the brave defender of Berwick Castle), and Brian, son of Alan of Dumfries, usually styled Brian Fitz Alan, who was one of the Guardians during the interregnum, and held various offices under the ex-King. All these, on making their submission to Edward, were pardoned, except Douglas, who, because he could not fall submissively at the feet of the victor, was detained in prison. Walter de Curry did not place the Castle of Dumfries at the disposal of the patriots ; but, suspected of complicity with them, he for a while lost favour at the English Court.* Some other leading men in the Burgh seem to have cast in their lot with Baliol, as the following names, with the words " Vice Comiti de Dumfres " attached to each, (a) appear in the roll of "certain Scottishmen" whose lands were forfeited at this time, and restored to them after being received "into the King's peace," namely, " Makerathe Molgan, Thomas de Kyrkecovande, Walterus de Wynham, Willelmus Polmadoc ;" the name of a heroic

* We draw this inference from the terms of two edicts—one dated the 16th of October, 1295, in which King Edward ordered his sheriffs to put an arrest on the lands, goods, and chattels held by John Baliol and certain other Scots in England ; and the other, dated 27th April, 1296, ordering all Scots residing on such lands to be removed. Of course it was only those Scottish proprietors who had proved disloyal to him that were thus severely dealt with. Walterus de Corry is mentioned among them as having an estate in Kirkandrews, Cumberland, worth 20s yearly. Gilbert de Karlilio is represented as having lands in Le Dale, Cumberland, valued at 15s a year ; David de Thorald (Torthorwald), as having lands in Gunrow (probably Greenrow), Cumberland, worth £6 a year ; Edmundi Comyn appears as a landholder in Newham, Northumberland, to the extent of £21 5s 11d ; Johannis Comyn de Badenaghe and those who follow are named as proprietors in the same county—his lands of Tyrsete bringing £200 1s 6d ; Johannis Comyn, junioris, lands of Thorntone, £19 6s 4d ; Riccardi Sywarde, lands of Espleywode, £11 16s 5d ; Willelmi Douglas, lands in Faudone (no return); and Johannis de Balliolo, the ex-King himself, appears as a landholder to the extent of £48 8s 7d, at Werke, in Tynedale, of £37 5s 1d in Bedford and Bucks, of £23 13s 11d in Cambridge and Huntindoon, and also as having lands in Cornwall, the value of which are not specified.

(a) Instead of " with the words Vice Comiti de Dumfres " attached to each, read— (ou behalf of each of which a letter is addressed Vicecomiti de Dumfres).—See Stevenson's Historical Documents.

lady also appearing in the list—Euphemia, wife of " Willelmi de Thorndone."

What were the Bruces about all this time ?   One of them— the luckless competitor, who had experienced much trouble in his day—was lying " where the weary are at rest :" Carrick, his son, now head of the house, kept moving steadily round the royal luminary of England.   Why should he go out of his course to follow the comet Baliol on the road to ruin ?   With calculating prudence he kept aloof from a movement, which, if it had terminated well, might have set Scotland free, but would have glorified his rival ; and when the revolt did end disastrously, Bruce, fondly dreaming that a favourable chance for his own claims had opened up, laid them humbly before his liege lord, who at once annihilated them with the sneering question : " Have we no other work on hand but to conquer kingdoms for you ?" Edward reserved the crown of Scotland for himself : with the view of keeping it more firmly on his head, he gave Bruce and his son something to do on his own account, sending the former to pacify the malcontents of Annandale, and the latter to perform a similar service in Carrick.* Shortly afterwards, however, Bruce withdrew from public life, to reside on his English estates, leaving the earldom of Carrick, which he had acquired by marriage, and also the administration of his Annandale patrimony, to his son, the future deliverer of Scotland.

* Rymer's Fœdera, vol. i., p. 839.

CHAPTER VI.

NITHSDALE and Galloway were for the most part devoted to Baliol, owing greatly to the circumstance that he was related to many of their ruling families ; and when the sands of his public life ran out, these districts favoured the pretensions of his nephew, John Comyn of Badenoch, as opposed to those of Bruce. King Edward, as we have seen, recognised no claims to the Scottish sceptre except his own, based upon conquest, and which he proceeded to maintain with characteristic energy and method. No half measures were now to be thought of. During the transition period ending with the revolt of his vassal these might answer well enough ; but now, when that "foolish traitor" was out of the way, and the regal fief he had forfeited was in the grasp of his superior, arrangements must be made to keep it there, and fore-close, if possible, a second insurrection. In accordance with this policy, the conqueror made it to be seen everywhere, throughout the Lowlands at least, that he was king indeed.

Dumfries and neighbourhood were assigned to Henry de Percy —the wardenship of Galloway and Ayrshire being also, at a subse-quent period, placed in his hands.* His rule was harsh : wishing to be faithful to his royal master, he could not deal very gently with the people who looked upon him as the minion of a despot to whom they only paid a forced homage. He appears to have done his work thoroughly. Some of Edward's officials in Scotland had

* Redpath's Border History, p. 201 ; and Rotuli Scotiæ, p. 30.

acted feebly, or played him false; but of the Northumbrian knight he had no cause to complain. Nithsdale and its chief town had, since the light of history was cast upon them, experienced many changes ; but never till this period had they been placed under the foot of an oppressive conqueror. The Selgovæ, as we have seen, were not tyrannised over by the Romans ; and the succeeding races who took root in the district fraternised with, and did not trample upon, the resident population. It was a new as well as a painful thing, therefore, for the inhabitants to know and feel that they were in a state of thraldom. Their native rulers were displaced ; foreign lords occupied their lands and castles ; and the "crown of the causeway" was usurped by an insolent soldiery, who paid no respect to gentle or simple, but were the rude enforcers of the English usurpation—and, as such, bent on breaking down the spirit of the people, and impoverishing them both in mind and body.

To Sir Robert de Clifford the congenial duty was assigned of assisting Percy, by traversing the dangerous Border district with a hundred and forty mounted men at-arms and five hundred footmen. Clifford was required by Edward, in terms of a regular military indenture, to scour the country with his troop, taking "hostages of the Forest of Selkirk, the Moor of Cavers, Liddisdale, Eskdale, Ewisdale, Annandale, Moffatdale, Nithsdale, and Galloway," and the other lands round about "that had come to the peace of our Lord the King." If any suspected persons were fallen in with, they were to be "made to give hostages in like manner." With the view of stimulating the zeal of Clifford, he was promised arrears of pay (the balance of £800 owing to him for his residence in the Marches and other parts of Scotland) ; and it was stipulated further that he would be repaid for any horses which he might lose, according to the price at which they were entered in the royal wardrobe. This commission took the form of a bargain between two parties, rather than of an order from a master to a servant, the document closing with these words : " In witness whereof, the seal of our Lord the King is affixed to one part of the said indenture, remaining with the said Sir Robert ; and to the other part, remaining with our Lord the King in his wardrobe, is placed the seal of the said Sir Robert."*

Scotland seemed at this season to be beyond hope of help from any of her own sons. Could not France, then, interpose to aid an old, faithful ally in time of need ? Possibly she might have done so, if the winds which swept across the Channel could have borne the wail of the conquered country to the opposite coast. King Edward took pains to prevent this being effected through any ordinary medium. No trading or friendly intercourse would he allow between Scotland and the Continent, except from a few

* Historical Documents, vol. ii., p. 36.

I

selected ports, of which Kirkcudbright was one—and the privilege in their case was guarded with such jealousy that any person wishing to leave the country with sealed letters, or who was suspected of a design to carry messages abroad, was ordered to be kept in prison till the King's pleasure should be ascertained regarding him.*

On all classes of men save ecclesiastics the English yoke fell heavily. Nearly the whole of the Scottish prelates submitted readily to Edward ; and he, appreciating their friendly behaviour, and having perhaps also the fear of Pope Boniface before his eyes, took the Church under his special protection. His soldiers were allowed a great amount of license, but they were enjoined to respect the persons of the priesthood, and to do no harm to their property. The King also sent letters to men of influence, enjoining them to protect abbeys, priories, monasteries, and other religious houses. Communications of this nature were addressed to the "Earls of Strevelyn, Dunfres, Edinburgh, and Berwick,"† (a) in favour of the Abbot "de Sancta Cruce ;" and to the Governor of Dumfries, on behalf of the Prioress of Lincluden, "Dungallus,‡ Abbot de Sacro Nemore (Holywood), Andreas, Vicar of Dalgarnock, Henricus, Vicar of Lochrutton, and Robertus filius Rodulphi, Parson of the Church of St. Cuthbert de Ewytesdale."

"Remain quiet at your peril," was the language used by Percy and Clifford to the men of Nithsdale, Annandale, and the Western Border ; "Be loyal subjects to our sovereign Lord the King," was the exhortation of Walter of Dundrennan, Dunegal of Holywood, William of Canonby, and the other prelates who bore spiritual rule over them. It was the same elsewhere ; but the temporal sword and the homilies of the Church failed to make the subjugated people quiet and resigned. King Edward, deluded by an opposite belief, had gone to Flanders for the purpose of prosecuting his designs against France ; and, before he was many months away, the Earl of Warrene sent pressing despatches urging him to return. The King thus learned, to his surprise and regret, that rebel bands (as they were termed) had risen up in numerous directions, who were galling the English with guerilla attacks ; and that if they were allowed to concentrate their efforts, and were not summarily put down, they might possibly undo all that it had cost so much blood and treasure to accomplish. One Walays, or Wallace, figured prominently in these urgent letters to King Edward.

That patriot, afterwards so famous, while only yet a stripling sorely bewailed his country's fate :

* Appendix D.
† Rymer's Fœdera, vol. ii., p. 844.
(a) Rotuli Scotiæ 1, 24. For " Earl " and " Governor " read "Sheriff."
‡ Dungallus was possibly one of the family of Dunegal of Stranid.

"Willyham Wallace, or he was man of armys,
Gret pitté thocht that Scotland tuk sic harmys ;
Mekill dolour it did hym in hys mynde,
For he was wyss, rycht worthy, wicht, and kynd."*

Soon he began to speak out on the subject, and when first rising into notice he was looked upon by his enemies as a bold, daring malcontent, who was always ready against any odds to assert his own personal independence, and proclaim his country's rights by word and deed. He would doubtless be deemed by them a mere foolhardy bravo, till his more private scuffles with the insolent soldiery at Ayr and Dundee gave place to skirmishes on a wider scale ; in which, sallying forth with a handful of followers as recklessly defiant as himself, he encountered large bands of English with unvarying success. Wallace in this way gradually became a felt power in the land ; his name, long before Edward returned from Flanders, had become the watchword of freedom ; and had been heard sounding as such not merely in the east and west, but in Nithsdale and Annandale ; where, notwithstanding the special precaution taken by the Government, a spirit of revolt was also beginning to show itself ; and that, too, encouraged by the young Earl of Carrick, on whom the King had placed much reliance. So recently as the 15th of October, 1296, we find Edward graciously remitting certain Exchequer debts due to him by the Annandale chief, in a letter commencing thus : " Whereas we have great trust in our faithful and loyal Robert de Bruce, for the good service which he has done ;"† and yet we find him early next year co-operating with Wallace against the common enemy.

For the purpose of checking the insurrectionary movement a new levy of troops was made, chiefly in Cumberland, Northumberland, Westmoreland, and Durham. It is a curious circumstance, and illustrative of the feeble tie by which the first-named county was bound to England, that Percy and Clifford asked its inhabitants to recruit the expedition, as a matter not of right but of favour, and guaranteed to them letters patent from the King that their freewill assistance to him on this occasion should not be made a plea or precedent for yielding to him compulsory service in future.‡ In the Public Record Office, London, there are to be seen "notes of letters" ordered to be written at this time "for providing troops for the Scottish war." A closed despatch to the Earl of Carrick is among the number, ordering him to join the English standard with as many men-at-arms as he can muster ; also that he bring with him " a thousand foot soldiers of the chosen men of Kyle, Cunningham, and Cumnock ;" and, " according to his discretion," another thousand men from Carrick and Galloway. Another of these notes requires Gibon Fitz Kan and Duncan

* Henry the Minstrel, Book i.
† Historical Documents, vol. ii., p. 114.   ‡ Ibid, vol. ii., p. 186.

Macdowel to raise a thousand choice foot soldiers in Galloway ;
and there is a third letter, demanding from Sir Richard Siward a
Nithsdale contingent of three hundred chosen men.   Whether
these letters were actually despatched or not it is impossible to say :
at the period of their supposed date—the summer of 1297 (a)—Bruce
was away in the West with "Wallace wight ;" and it is almost
certain that few Dumfriesshire men took part in the terrible foray
with which Sir Robert Clifford, starting from Carlisle, devastated
their hearths and homesteads.   He seems to have treated Annandale with particular severity : its chief was acting as the King's
rebel—"Since he is out of reach, let our ministry of fire and sword
show what retributive vengeance is in store for all the enemies of
our Lord the King !"   Clifford sacked the town of Annan, and then
burnt it and the half-castellated church which formed one of the
main defences of the burgh ; and he treated in a similar way no
fewer than ten villages in the vicinity—most of which never again
rose out of their ashes.*   These merciless proceedings exercised a
certain amount of present influence ; but when a reaction came,
as come it did, it was rendered more decisive and overwhelming.
Already, indeed, preparations for it were rapidly going on ; for
Wallace himself, leaving Ayrshire, appeared in the vicinity of
Dumfries, calling the people to arms, and sounding there as elsewhere the knell of Edward's hated dominion.

Under what particular circumstances the hero was led to leave
his native shore, the scene of his earlier efforts, and proceed southward, we cannot say.   Tradition and history combine to show
that late in 1296, or early in the following year, he had several
affrays with the enemy in the neighbourhood of Lochmaben.†   On
one occasion, it is said, some of Clifford's troopers maltreated the
horses of his party by cutting off their tails—for which he took
ample vengeance.   Sir Hugh Moreland, hearing of what had
occurred, hurried after the Scots, being able to trace them to
Knockwood, in the adjoining parish of Kirkmichael, by the blood
which streamed from their wounded horses.   Wallace, reinforced
by sixteen friends who had been lurking in the wood, turned upon
his pursuers and put them to the rout.   Several large stones may
still be seen in Knockwood, at a place called "The Six Corses,"
which are supposed to mark the spot where Sir Hugh Moreland
and five of his followers fell ; and near by there are slight remains
of fortifications visible, one of which is said to have been occupied
by Wallace, in order to protect himself from another English force
which hastened from Lochmaben Castle on being apprised of the
conflict that had occurred.

(a) It was not in summer that the Annan raid was made, but shortly before Christmas
          Hemingburgh 1, 146.
     * Knighton, p. 2522 ; Hailes's Annals of Scotland, p. 263 ; and Redpath's Border
History, p. 212.
                    † Henry the Minstrel, Book v.

This body, consisting of three hundred horsemen, commanded by an officer named Graystock, surrounded the fortlet; but its occupants managed to effect their escape, and it was not till a day or two afterwards that the latter were overtaken. Then ensued a stoutly-contested engagement. The Scots, whilst on their retreat, had been joined by Sir John Graham and Sir Roger Kirkpatrick, each bringing with him a few retainers; and, but for this circumstance, even the military genius of Wallace might have been of little avail against the enemy's superior force. During the thick of the fight the English leader fell mortally wounded; and his surviving followers forthwith fled, seeking refuge in the shades of Knockwood, from which the Scots had previously withdrawn. Wallace did not follow far in pursuit; but, collecting his men together, turned in the direction of Lochmaben Castle, fired with the ambition of seizing that important fortress, once a bulwark of Scottish independence, but now, owing to the pusillanimity of Bruce, converted into an English stronghold for keeping his native Annandale in check.

Fortunately for the designs of the Scottish chief, it was not in a condition to offer a formidable resistance : most of its usual defenders were lying still in death, or weary fugitives in the neighbouring woodlands; and those who remained were easily overpowered. Scarcely had the castle received its new garrison, when bands of broken men, footsore and wounded, from Knockwood, asked for admission at the gates, which they received—only however, to share the fate of their comrades who had been encountered in the field on the previous day. The stern exigencies of the situation combined with other circumstances to steel the heart of the usually generous Wallace, and the unsuspecting refugees were indiscriminately put to the sword. Leaving as many men as he could spare in the fortress, he returned to Clydesdale—from whence, however, he was soon recalled to Dumfriesshire.

The early exploits of Wallace, as recorded in the old chronicles,* seem very discursive and unsystematic. They had

---

* Wyntoun, Fordun, Knighton, Hemingburgh, and Henry the Minstrel (the latter not always to be implicitly trusted), are the chief authorities relied upon by modern writers for these and other early incidents in the career of the Scottish hero. The hardihood and courage of Wallace are well illustrated in the strains of another ancient minstrel, name unknown, who represents the hero, disguised as an old beggar, going to a hostelrie near Lochmaben to claim a reward for his own betrayal, that had been offered by the English captain. The sum was "fifty pounds of white monie," to be given for a sight of the "traitor." "Tell down the money," said the seeming mendicant, as he supported himself on a trusty staff, torn from Westmuir Wood :

" ' Tell doun your monie, if it be guid,
    And let us see if it be fine ;
For I'm sure I hae it in my power
    To bring the traitor Wallace in.'

The monie was told doun on the table,
    Silver white of pounds fiftie ;
' Now here I stand,' said Willie Wallace,
    ' And what hae ye got to say to me?' "

probably more of method in them than is generally supposed ;
and at all events they made his name well known, and originated
a pretty general belief among his countrymen that the hero of
these seemingly random efforts was ripening for greater achievements, should occasion offer.   They also brought to his standard
some of the bravest spirits in the land, who were ready to follow
wherever he led, and who closely emulated his own strong love of
country, as well as his indomitable courage.

Among the chief of these was Sir William de Douglas, who
was Governor of Berwick when it surrendered to the English in
1296.   The allegiance then extorted from him was soon cast aside,
and on the 12th of June, 1297, letters under the Great Seal were
received by the Sheriffs of Essex and Northumberland to seize
"the lands and tenements, the goods and chattels" belonging to
him within their baillywicks ;* his own patrimony of Douglasdale
having been previously confiscated to the King.   Whilst Wallace
was putting the English garrisons of Ayrshire to trouble, Douglas
was making those stationed near his own barony to feel that they
had no easy sinecure.   Watching a favourable opportunity, he
attacked the small Castle of Durrisdeer, in Nithsdale ; and had
the gratification of soon seeing the flag of Scottish independence
unfurled on its walls—this success only stimulating him to undertake a more difficult enterprise.   The neighbouring Castle of
Sanquhar was a place of considerable strength, and defended by a
powerful garrison, under the command of an officer named Beau-
fort.   If the patriots could only get possession of this fortress, it
would enable them to dispute the supremacy of the English in the
Upper Ward of Nithsdale ; but to besiege it in due form was
beyond their resources, and there was no chance of surprising it,
as the loss of Durrisdeer had doubled the vigilance of the enemy.
The idea of using force having been abandoned, an ingenious
stratagem was resorted to.

Douglas knew that the inmates were regularly supplied with
wood for fuel by a rustic named Anderson ; and he thought it
would be no impossible thing for one of his own trusty followers to
personate the wood-cutter, and thus gain entrance into the castle
for himself and others.   Anderson was easily induced to lend his

Scant time was given for any response to the question :
> " He fell'd the captain where he stood,
> Wi' a dounright straik, upon the floor ;
> He slew the rest around the room,
> And speir'd gin there were any more."

The balladist goes on to state that another party of Southrons who had been waiting at
a distance hurried in to learn the fate of their companions ; and that Wallace, aided by
the landlord of the house, served them in the same way.   The sequel is thus given :

> " Full five and twenty men he slew,
> And five he hang'd upon a grain ;
> In the morn he sat with his merry men a',
> Within Lochmaben toun at dine."

* Memoranda Roll, 24-25 Edw. I.

assistance ; and, when he pocketed the golden pieces by which his honesty was corrupted, he probably soothed his conscience by the reflection that the men he sought to betray were the enemies of his country, and a curse to the neighbourhood. Thus far the preliminary arrangements proceeded favourably ; and to Thomas Dickson, a shrewd, fearless soldier, of humble rank, the chief duty was assigned of developing the succeeding incidents of the plot. Having attired himself in Anderson's clothes, he hied to the castle gate, leading his timber-laden waggon, and was readily admitted. The unsuspecting porter who gave him entrance was stabbed by him, and stripped of his keys ; and the intrepid Dickson sounding his horn as a signal, Douglas and his men, who lay ambushed at a short distance, rushed in. As they passed to the inner court a desperate attempt was made by the startled garrison to stop the impetuous intruders : "Down with the drawbridge ! lower the portcullis !" cried many a voice ; but even if the dying porter's ear had not been adder-deaf, and his hand had not been powerless, the requests could not have been obeyed. The waggon had been intentionally driven forward in such a way that the iron door could not be lowered ; and the assailants had already crossed the drawbridge. They appeared in such numbers, and the garrison was taken at such a disadvantage, that only a feeble resistance was offered. All the defenders, together with their captain, were put to death—a doom which they had provoked by their cruel treatment of the inhabitants of the district.

In this ingenious and daring way the strong Castle of San-quhar was won.* (a) The news of its capture spread like wild-fire far and wide. Henry de Percy and Sir Robert de Clifford, the latter of whom was residing in Lochmaben Castle at the time, saw at once that the English occupation would soon be gone in the district unless an effectual check were put upon Douglas ; and they resolved, if possible, to make the fortress where he had triumphed his dungeon, if not his grave. In a trice, armed com-panies were seen trooping from the Castles of Morton and Tibbers, in Upper Nithsdale, and from those of Dalswinton and Dumfries further down, all proceeding in the direction of Sanquhar ; and before the intrepid Scot had fairly settled down in his new abode, he found himself closely blockaded, and was saluted with the summons "Surrender or die !" He was scant of provisions, and had really to consider the alternative of being starved outright, or of placing himself, his gallant followers, and his castellated prison at the disposal of the enemy.

* Hume of Godscroft's History of the House of Douglas, pp. 22-23.

(a) There is so much of romance in Blind Harry that it is not safe to rely upon him for history. He has been accepted too freely in his references to this locality. The tale of the capture of Sanquhar, written about 1480, is evidently modelled on Barbour's account of the capture of Linlithgow Peel. It was a cart of hay that stopped the gate at Linlithgow ; at Sanquhar a load of wood on a cart.

The English did not attempt to storm the stronghold, as they knew the desperate risk of so doing ; but quietly surrounded it, in the full expectation that time would fight more effectually for them than the sword. Whilst the beleaguering force were thus occupied, Wallace, then in the Lothians, was apprised of their proceedings, and of the deadly straits to which his faithful friend was reduced. The trusty Dickson had managed to run the blockade (if we may use a modern phrase). Escaping by a private postern gate, he hied away northward, and carried the tidings to Wallace, who, with a large body of followers, set out by way of Peebles and Crawford, for the purpose of raising the siege.

Just as he had reached the latter place, the English, hearing of his designs, struck their tents and hurried away from Sanquhar, not daring to await his approach. He thereupon altered his line of march, and, with a chosen band of light horsemen, dashed through the Pass of Durrisdeer, got a glimpse of the fugitives when in the vicinity of Morton, and reached their rear near the Castle of Closeburn. Not a few were there cut down : the woods of Dalswinton received the main body of the retreating English, but yielded them little protection. Partially sheltered by the trees, which must also have impeded their movements considerably, they faced round, in the attitude of stags at bay, boldly confronting their pursuers. Resistance was vain : the fall of five hundred proved how bravely, yet ineffectually, the English strove to beat back their impetuous foeman. Nothing for it but retreat. For many miles the flight had been well conducted ; now it became disorderly in the extreme. As the remnant of the great besieging force entered Dumfries, it must have presented a woeful aspect. Thoroughly disorganised and panic-stricken, the fugitives, still closely pursued, passed the town : the Castle did not open its gates to succour them, Henry de Percy having more than enough to do on his own account ; no party of their countrymen interfered for their defence ; and the last baleful drop was thrown into their cup when a body of Dumfriesians, made up of Kirkpatricks, Corries, Johnstones, Hallidays, and Maxwells, joined in the hot chase against them. The pursuit was kept up as far as Cockpool,* upon the Solway. Even as the bowers of Dalswinton gave them but deceitful shelter at an earlier stage, so the waters of the Frith received many into its fatal embrace. Some were slaughtered on the shore, some were drowned in the deep, and only a few escaped to the opposite side with life.†

Wallace rested from the fatigues of this memorable day in the Castle of Carlaverock, which was still possessed by Herbert de Maccuswel, though he had, by his devotedness to Baliol, incurred the displeasure of the English monarch. Next day the hero passed

* Near Comlongan, the ancient seat of the Murrays.
† Godscroft's House of Douglas, p. 24.

through Dumfries, proceeding thence to Sanquhar, where he had a cordial meeting with the grateful Douglas, now relieved from all anxiety, and undisputed lord of Upper Nithsdale—the few English left there remaining close in garrison, and exercising no rule over the district. After this we find no traces of the hero in Dumfriesshire. His various missions to it had been of essential service in fostering a spirit of independence among the people, and in humbling their oppressors ; and these good results obtained, he proceeded westward to carry on his patriotic propaganda—first, however, rewarding the bravery of Douglas by making him governor of the territory which stretches from Drumlanrig to Ayr.

Edward was still abroad, detained in an endeavour to recover Guienne : while so engaged, his Treasurer for Scotland, Hugh de Cressingham, kept him conversant with the affairs of that country. Cressingham, at the King's request, entered into negotiations with the patriotic party at Irvine, by which means nearly all its leading members were divorced from the side of Sir William Wallace. Bruce laid down his arms, so even did Douglas; and of all the patricians who had flocked to the standard of Wallace, Sir Andrew Murray of Bothwell alone remained, "among the faithless, faithful only he." For these desertions the patriot-chief was in some degree consoled by the continued adherence of the common people, who enabled him to maintain the national cause in a hopeful condition. How Douglas should have wavered at this critical time we are at a loss to conceive ; but it soon became evident that the English could not rely upon him. Cressingham, writing to the King on the 24th of July, 1297, says that Douglas having failed to keep the covenants made with Sir Henry de Percy (summoned from Nithsdale to assist in the negotiations at Irvine), had been imprisoned in the Castle of Berwick, where " he is still very savage and very abusive ; but I will keep him in such wise, that if it please God he shall not get out." (a) Next month we find Edward proposing to make Brian Fitz Alan Guardian of Scotland in lieu of Warrene, who seems to have been anxious to get away from the exactive office. The son of " Alan de Dunfres " was acting at that time as governor of Northumberland, which easy post he preferred to the more ambitious one placed at his disposal. Replying to his "Lord sire Edward," he declared that he had not sufficient skill and ability " to venture on such a high matter ;" though he broadly hinted, with, shall we say truly Caledonian shrewdness, that if the remuneration were made more tempting, he might accept the preferment. " The goods which I have," he wrote, " would be too small, as far as I can stretch them, to keep well that land to your honour (for they do not extend beyond £1000), and to keep fifty

(a) Stevenson's Historical Documents, ii., 204. The letter is not Cressingham's own, but an agent of his.

K

armed horses ; and, moreover, I do not think that I, in my poverty,
can be able either well or honourably to keep the land in peace, to
your profit and honour, when such a captain as the Earl cannot
well keep it in peace for what he receives from you; nor do I
know, sire, that I shall do it for less than he receives, so as to save
your honour and profit." Fitz Alan closed his epistle with the
devout petition, "May the Lord be your keeper, and give us good
news of you." The result of the correspondence was that, on the
24th of September, Clifford and Fitz Alan were appointed to assist
Warrene ; but meanwhile the English Guardianship itself had
gone—had vanished before the might of the man who at Stirling
vindicated his right above all others to be called the Guardian of
the Scottish nation. "Your enemies are dispersed and discouraged," wrote Cressingham to King Edward, when the nobles
deserted Wallace at Irvine ; but, after the lapse of a few weeks,
the Treasurer had to communicate different tidings to his royal
master—news which must have been doleful to him indeed—to the
effect that the Scots had, on the 11th of September, gained a great
victory at Stirling Bridge, and had with marvellous audacity
followed it up by making a destructive raid into Northumberland.
Thus Scotland was lost to Edward much more rapidly than it had
been won.

Hastily returning from Flanders, the King, at the head of an
immense host, encountered the Scottish army, on the 22nd of
July, 1298, at Falkirk, which he succeeded in defeating, greatly
owing, it is said, to a feud among the leaders—Sir John Stewart
and Sir John Comyn, who had previously joined Wallace, disputing the right of the latter to take the chief command. A heavy
blow was thus inflicted on the patriotic cause, and if the victors
had followed up their advantage, Scotland would have been once
more reduced to a state of vassalage. Wallace effected a masterly
retreat, carrying off the remains of his army in safety ; and, whilst
the English were resting on their way to Stirling, they were
startled, at dead of night, by a party of the fugitives, who broke
into their camp, slaughtered many of its occupants, and rejoined
their companions without the loss of a single soldier. The English
on reaching Stirling found that it had been laid in ashes, and
could afford them neither shelter nor food. They then passed
down into Ayrshire, Edward intending to chastise Bruce, who,
though he appeared in a submissive attitude at Irvine, had been
playing fast and loose with him of late. The Castle of Ayr in
flames was all the welcome given by the Scottish baron to his liege
lord ; and as the former, after firing the fortress, retreated into
the fastnesses of Galloway, the latter did not care about following
him thither, particularly as he was short of provisions. Indeed,
had the conquerors at Falkirk continued much longer in Scotland,
they would have suffered from famine, the country being laid waste

on their entire line of march.   Nominally victorious, but in reality
foiled in their purpose, they retired into England by Dumfries ;
some of the strongholds of the district surrendering as they passed
along, and the Castle of Lochmaben, which had been won by
Wallace, being retaken by them after a brief siege.* The Castle of
Dumfries was still held on their behalf, and there the King himself
remained for some time, adding to its defences during the period
of his stay, as is shewn by the following message which he sent,
in August, to the governors of Roxburgh, Jedburgh, and Berwick :
—" Henry de Empingeham and John de Karletone, clerks, shall
say to Richard de Bremesgrave this message, which the same
Richard shall tell, as from the King to Sir Robert Hastings and
his brother, and the other men-at-arms who are in their company
at Roxburgh and Jedburgh.   And also he shall tell the same
message to Sir William Latimer and to the rest of the garrison at
Berwick ; namely, that our Lord the King has gone to Dumfries
to raise his peel and to reinforce the castle.   And his son has gone
with him, and many other good men-at-arms ; and he has sent Sir
John de Saint John towards Galloway, to bring to a good end his
affairs in those parts.   Wherefore the said Richard shall pray
them that they, on their part, shall make some good expeditions
upon the Forest of Selkirk, and elsewhere where they shall perceive that it will be good, and that they exert themselves to do
this so well that the King may hereof have good news, and that
they be always occupied and busy with what the King has charged
them to do, and as far as they are able that they employ themselves herein until they have another order from the King.   And
let this message be said to them so well and so openly that they
may have good heart and courage to do well, and that they may
know that the King has this matter at heart."† (a)

* Hemingford, vol. i., p. 166.
† From the original, in the Public Record Office, as quoted in Historical Documents, vol. ii., pp. 296-297.
(a) Mr Neilson has shewn that a " peel " originally meant " a palisaded or stock-
aded close, forming an outer rampart extending the bounds and increasing the accommodation of the castle."   In the autumn of 1300 carpenters were busy at Inglewood
forest, Cumberland, making the peel that was to be sent to Dumfries.   King Edward
visited them one day ; the Queen another.   Then we hear of the King proceeding to
Dumfries, probably when workmen and materials were being escorted there.   On 18th
October he was at Annan.   On the 20th the erection of the peel was being pushed
vigorously forward by all hands at Dumfries.   Ditchers, carpenters, and smiths toiled
hard at digging, planting. and rearing beams and palisades.   " The wages account
shews that from first to last the carpenters (on an average to the number of over 60,
but sometimes over 100 being employed) laboured for eleven weeks.   The ditchers,
numbering about 250, worked for a fortnight only.   There were about two dozen
smiths. . . .   We are told very precisely what was done by the ditchers (fossatores),
but one entry makes express what otherwise would have gone without saying, that it
was a fosse (fossatum) they were making.   That entry shews that women were employed to clean out the ditch which the men had dug.   By the 30th October all was
virtually complete. . . .   From these particulars it is easy to infer the character of
King Edward's peel.   A very odd entry shews that an axe was borrowed to cut trees
near Dumfries, ' for pales there.'   The pales cut by that axe (which by the way was
never returned to its owner) doubtless went, with hundreds of others, to the making
of the peel.   The castle appears to have had thrown round it, some little distance from
the walls, a strong stockade, beyond which again a large fosse was dug.   This palisaded and moated enceinte constituted the peel.   Within it buildings might be erected,

An indenture was drawn up, dated the 20th of the following
November, having for its object the maintenance of this important
Border stronghold in an efficient state. The document is in these
terms :—" Be it remembered that the King has appointed that in
the Castle of Dumfries there should remain twelve men with
armed horses, who shall have among them all twenty-four foot
soldiers by the appointment of Sir Robert de Clifford. Also, the
twenty cross-bow men who were at Berwick, who were appointed
to the said Sir Robert at Durham, and the six crossbow men
whom the said Sir Robert de Clifford shall place there, whom he
took from the Castle of Loghmaban, and four footmen of his own,
whom he also shall provide. Also, a master engineer and four
carpenters. Also, one smith and his lad ; one engineer and two
masons, whereof the amount shall be seventy-six persons. For
whose support the provisions underwritten are appointed, from
20th November next coming at the beginning of the twenty-
seventh year of the reign of our Lord the King aforesaid, until the
last day of the month of June (the first day and the last being
reckoned), for two hundred and twenty-three days (that is to say,
for thirty-two weeks)—by the day, three bushels of wheat—one
hundred and twenty quarters of wheat ; of wine, ten tuns ; of malt,
or of barley to make malt, for beer, one hundred and sixty
quarters ; of beans and peas, twenty quarters ; of oats, for provender for the horses, one hundred quarters ; of oxen, 50 carcases ;
of herrings, ten thousand ; of dried fish, five hundred ; of salt,
twenty quarters ; of iron and steel, as much as shall be necessary ;
of cords and hides for engines . . . . ; of money, ten marks,
which should be delivered to the constable of the said castle for
small necessaries. And be it remembered, that Master Richard de
Abingdon (to whom the King by his letters has given directions
concerning these things) shall see that all these things above
written shall arrive by land in the company of the said Sir Robert,
or by sea, at the said castle ; as he more fully is directed in the
aforesaid letters of the King. Also, the said Sir Robert shall place
in the said castle two engines, two springalds, two crossbows with
winches, and two crossbows for two feet. Also, of the Bishop of
Carlisle, one crossbow with a winch, two crossbows for two feet,
and as many quarrels as possible."*

such as barracks, or store rooms, or stables. The existence of houses in the peel at
Lochmaben has been noticed. At Dumfries the same must have been the case, for
there are three consecutive entries in the wages accounts—1, for the cavalry in the
castle *(infra municionem castri)* ; 2, for the cavalry in the peel *(infra municionem peli
de Dumfres post constructionem ejusdem peli)* ; and 3, for the engineers and others in
the castle *(infra municionem ejusdem castri),* shewing by the clearest contrast that
the peel had a garrison of its own after 2d November." See "Peel : Its Meaning and
Derivation."

    * The indenture is in French : we are indebted for it to Historical Documents, vol.
ii., pp. 333-334. The liquor and provisions, &c., as given in the original in the Public
Record Office, are thus specified :—" De vyn, x toneaux ; de brees, ou de ble pur fere
brees pur beyure, clx quarters ; de feyves e de poys, xx quarters ; de aveynes a prendre
pur cheveaux, c quarters ; de boefs, l carcoys ; de haranges, x mil. ; de peisson dure, d ;
de seel, xx quarters ; de fer e dascer, tant come mester serra ; de cordes e de quyrs
pour engyns."

But for such precautionary measures Nithsdale would soon have been again lost to the King. He had learned from long experience that it was a nursery of "rebels," whom he could only keep in check with the strong hand. By a commission, dated on the 24th of November, 1298, at Novum Castrum super Tynam (Newcastle), he gave orders to receive the people of the "Valle de Nithe" into his favour ; but the exceptions to the amnesty were so numerous as to show how much the dale had been identified with the recent outbreak, and how little confidence he placed upon its loyalty. Whether in Dumfriesshire or the country at large, the English invasion bore scanty fruits, compared with the blood and treasure spent in securing them : for many months afterwards forays on a considerable scale had to be made in order to keep up the semblance of a conquest ; and, as we shall soon see, within two years from the victory at Falkirk, King Edward was under the necessity of making another hostile march across the Border, so obstinately did the Scots refuse to believe in their defeats, or in his supremacy over them.

In studying this portion of the history of Scotland, we cannot fail to be struck with the ignoble course pursued by its principal barons, and to see in their pliancy the chief source of the country's weakness and of Edward's strength. It was the aim of that potentate to separate them from the cause of their country, and to attach them to himself by appeals to their own self-interest. He played one of them off against another—Baliol against Bruce, Bruce against Comyn, all against Wallace—in order that he might weaken them, and secure his own ends at last. The position in which some of the nobles stood to Edward before his interference with Scottish affairs enabled him all the more easily to carry on this politic game, as they held lands under him, and were therefore English barons as well as Scottish subjects. All the three northern patricians named above, and many others, as we have seen, paid feudal homage to him for their estates south of the Border; and it is easy to perceive that the King had thus an opportunity of gaining a moral influence over them, which, with the lure of material rewards, contributed to their subserviency.

Baliol, the competitor for the Crown, gained and lost "the golden round of sovereignty" because he was first obedient and then rebellious; the heads of the Brucian family were rendered for a while submissive by arguments addressed to their hopes and fears ; and when, by the banishment of the Baliols, the Lord of Badenoch fancied his claims were advanced, he found that they were more likely to be so by plotting against Bruce, and otherwise pleasing King Edward. How Bruce, grandson of the competitor, tried at first, like his father, to remain neutral, taking part neither with the invaders nor the patriots—how the wardens of the Western Marches, dreading that he would one day throw his vast influence into the scale against England, summoned him to Carlisle, and, on the consecrated host and sword of Thomas-à-Becket made him renew his oath of fealty to Edward—how he shortly afterwards repented of his oath, and joined the Scottish army, as already mentioned, yet never, till a later period, took boldly and persistently the proud position to which he was called, alike by enlightened self-love and his country's cry of anguish—are facts so familiar to all readers of our national history that they only require to be noticed here as links in the general narrative. Both father and son ingloriously vacillated between sordid interest and sacred duty ; but at length, as we shall find, the logic of events made the son see that he must either be king of independent Scotland, or sink into dishonourable insignificance : fortunate it was for his country and himself that he did not submit to the latter alternative.

CHAPTER VII.

HENRY DE PERCY was rewarded for his services in Nithsdale and
Ayrshire with the lands of Ingelram de Baliol, "a rebel" relative
of the ex-King, after which he was recalled to England, and John
de Saint John put in his place ; Clifford continuing as before to
exercise a sort of roving commission over the south-western part
of Dumfriesshire. In the summer of 1299 a foray was made upon
the Western Border which appears to have produced no very
important results ;* and the turbulence of the Annandale men
had risen to such a pitch by the following autumn that the English
garrison of Lochmaben Castle had to obtain assistance from
Richard Siward and Richard de Abingdon, but for which the
fortress might have again changed owners. That its position was
critical, and that its possession was deemed of great importance by
the English monarch, are further shewn by a memorandum which
he issued on the 2d of January, 1300, of which the following is a
translation :—"The King has appointed that Sir Robert de Clifford
shall abide in the company of Sir John de Saint John at Loch-

* "William le Latimer, chief, and the lieutenant of our Lord the King in the
Marches of Scotland, to Master Richard de Abingdon, the Clerk of our Lord the King,
greeting. We command you, on the part of our Lord the King, to deliver to Sir John
de Lancaster, Banneret, with two knights, coming and tarrying at Carlisle, on 16th July
and the two following days, to take part in a foray upon the enemies of Scotland, with
ten armed horses, for the wages of the said three days, as it is usual to pay to such personages. And deliver to Sir John de Hodelstone, Banneret, with six knights with
twenty-three esquires in his company, and one hundred and twenty-two foot soldiers,
residing at Carlisle for the same cause, their usual wages, as is fitting for the said three
days. Deliver to Sir John Sprynge and his two esquires, coming and residing in the
same place, for the same reason, from Monday, 13th July, until the 18th of the same
month, viz., for six days, the first and the last days being reckoned, their usual wages
for the said six days. Deliver to two hundred foot soldiers of the lordship of Egremont,
coming in the company of Sir John de Hodelstone, and residing in the same place for
the above-said cause, their usual wages for one of the said days. And if it happens
that the whole or part of those said payments be not allowed to you, we will and grant
that we are bound to you to keep you from damage, and to repay you if aught be disallowed. In witness of which things we have put our seal to these letters patent."—
Historical Documents, vol. ii., pp. 387-388.

maben, with thirty armed horses, until the Feast of Saint John,
receiving five hundred marks of good sterling money for his abode
there: whereof he shall receive two hundred marks on the morrow
of Saint Hillary, and two hundred marks on the day after Ash
Wednesday, and one hundred marks on the morrow of the Trinity.
And the horses of the said Robert and of his men shall be valued,
and the value repaid upon the death of the horses ; and the said
Robert may go away in order to attend to his own private affairs,
if he have any pressing business ; but that this be by permission
of the chieftain, and that he leave his number of men-at-arms, and
a sufficient man with them, who shall be attentive and obedient to
the regulations and commands of the chieftain. And that the
houses which he has made in the peel of Lochmaben shall remain
for him and his men, without being disputed by any one. And if
it happen that the said Robert cannot maintain his number of
men-at-arms until the term aforesaid, that the said Robert (when
he shall discover his inability, and it shall be certified by the
chieftain) may freely depart thence, or diminish his number, provided a corresponding deduction be made from his payment, pro-
portionate to the time when he shall leave or diminish his men-at-
arms."*

As it became evident that whenever the King withdrew from
Scotland his power over it began to wane, he resolved to visit it
once more, with the view of giving his rebellious subjects such a
punishment as would keep them well-behaved in time to come. Of
all his expeditions against the Scots the one he now undertook was
the most formidable and costly : arranged on a magnificent scale,
it was designed to be final and conclusive. His campaign in 1296
was recorded by a prosaic chronicler ; but a poet or minstrel,
named Walter of Exeter, was attached to the royal retinue for the
purpose of celebrating the triumphs of the new war in congenial
strains ; and as the historical poem (written in Norman-French)
which he composed on the subject is still extant, we get from it a
familiar glance at the expedition and its progress.† (a)

Edward having summoned all who owed him military service,
in England and elsewhere, to meet him at Carlisle on the Feast of
the Nativity of John the Baptist, 24th June, and about the
1st of July the march commenced. That day, says the poet,
"the whole host was ready, and the good King, with his
household, then set forward against the Scots, not in coats or sur-
coats, but on powerful and costly chargers ; and that they might
not be taken by surprise, securely armed. There were many rich

* Historical Documents, vol. ii., pp. 407-408.

† The famous "Roll of Carlaverock," a poem, in old Norman-French, rehearses the
names and armorial designs of all the various knights, &c., who attended Edward at
the siege of Carlaverock, A. D. 1300. Heraldry is therein, for the first time, presented
to us as a science.—Debrett's Peerage of the United Kingdom, p. 513.

(a) The poet was probably a Herald : he was not Walter of Exeter, as now admitted. See " The Roll of Carlaverock," edited by Thomas Wright, 1864, preface.

caparisons embroidered on silks and satins, many a beautiful pennon fixed to a lance, and many a banner displayed ; and afar off was the noise heard of the neighing of horses—mountains and valleys were everywhere covered with sumpter-horses and waggons with provisions, and sacks of tents and pavilions : and the days were fine and long. They proceeded by easy journeys, arranged in four squadrons."

The first squadron was led by Henry de Lacey, Earl of Lincoln ; the second by John, Earl of Warrene and Surrey ; the third by Edward himself, whose appointments and bearing are depicted by our authority in courtly style. "The King," he tells us, "brought up the rear so closely and ably that none of the others were left behind. In his banner were three leopards courant, of fine gold, set on red—fierce, haughty, and cruel : thus placed to signify that, like them, the King is dreadful, fierce, and proud to his enemies ; for his bite is slight to none who inflame his anger— not but that his kindness is soon rekindled towards such as seek his friendship or submit to his power."

The fourth squadron was under the command of Prince Edward, who was just seventeen years of age, and clad in armour for the first time. Not less complimentary is the poet's picture of the royal youth. "He was a well-proportioned and handsome person, of courteous disposition and intelligence, and desirous of finding an occasion to display his prowess. He managed his steed wonderfully well, and bore with a blue label the arms of the good King, his father." Attending on the Prince rode John de St. John, who had previously assisted in maintaining the English rule over Dumfries and Nithsdale, his duty as an experienced warrior now being to instruct the royal neophyte in his knightly duties— so that, in reality, the fourth division of the army was under John de St. John's own leadership.

Eighty-seven of the most distinguished vassals of the English Crown, with their retainers, figured in the imposing array, including lords of Bretagne and Lorraine, and Scottish renegades— Alexander Baliol (brother of the ex-king), the Earl of Dunbar, Sir Simon Fraser, Henry de Graham, and other false knights, who sunned themselves in the great King's smiles regardless of their country's tears. This splendid assemblage of armed men filled, it is said, the whole way between Newcastle and Carlisle ; and never before, not even in the old Roman times, had such a host proceeded northward.

Leaving it in the neighbourhood of Carlisle, Edward, accompanied by a small escort, proceeded to Dumfries, in order to ascertain for himself the feeling borne towards him by the district and its capital. Most probably Saint John was one of the party ; but the King did not claim the hospitality of the Castle. Passing its gates, he appeared at the door of the Monastery, and asked leave

L

to become the guest of the Mendicant Brothers, who, as a matter
of course, made his Majesty welcome, and offered him their best.
Men of peace, they had no power, even if the will had been theirs,
to bid their martial visitors, with a tall, fierce-looking king at
their head, begone ; and so, for several days in June, the latter
were boarded and lodged with the Minorite Friars in the Vennel.*
The English party seem to have got on comfortably enough in
their temporary abode, as, before leaving it, the service rendered
to them was acknowledged by a handsome largesse. The object of
the King's journey to and residence in Dumfries having been
accomplished, he returned to the "Merrie Citie," and, setting his
vast army in motion, it entered the county, marking its progress
by devastation and blood.

It was part of Edward's plan to strengthen all the fortresses
he already possessed, and increase their garrisons, and to seize all
such as had hitherto resisted his authority. By such means he
expected to retain a permanent hold of the country after he had
butchered or dispersed the "rebel" army in the field. Accordingly,
as we have seen, the breaches made in Lochmaben Castle were
filled up, the Castle of Dumfries was put in good repair and enlarged ; and siege was set to the Castle of Carlaverock, whose
garrison scornfully refused to give it up to the invaders, and prepared to keep them out of it as best they could.

This Border stronghold still exists as a majestic ruin : though
much wasted by war and time, it remains one of the finest specimens of castellated architecture to be found in Scotland. Nearly
four hundred yards to the south-west, among the stunted trees of
Bows Wood, lie the rude foundations of another building that were
long looked upon as the relics of the fortress which the grandson
of Maccus built, and which Edward of England assailed ; but excavations recently made disprove this hypothesis,† showing, as

* Wardrobe Accounts.

† It was Grose, in his "Antiquities of Scotland," we believe, who first adopted
this theory, and all, or nearly all, succeeding writers on the subject accepted it unchallenged, till, at the instance of Lord Herries, the old, hidden foundations were laid
bare, and revealed a square form and unsubstantial build of wall that could not have
belonged to the massive triangular edifice described in the text. Even before the
labourer's spade had demolished Mr Grose's theory, the late Mr Francis Maxwell, of
Breoch, who was well qualified to give a sound opinion on such subjects, entertained
the idea that the Carlaverock Castle of the present day is substantially the historical
castle which formed the key to Dumfriesshire during the thirteenth and fourteenth
centuries. Possibly the remains which have been exalted at its expense are those of
an outwork, erected to defend the dam of the fortress, and hinder the moat which it
supplied with water from being tapped by an enemy. We need scarcely say that the
new light cast upon this grand old fortress on the Solway shows that it possesses much
greater antiquarian and historical interest than was formerly assigned to it. Mr W. S.
Ross ("Saladin"), after stating the result of the excavations noticed above, says :
"The present castle, in the most minute details, answers to the description of the
monkish chronicler. Accordingly the noble ruins of Carlaverock are much older than
they have ever hitherto been supposed to be. We cannot tell whether it was from
their grim and weirdly-historic shade that the cavaliers of ancient Nithsdale de-
bouched, when
          ' The starke and hawtane Maccuswall,
              Thane o' Stranide sae grene,
          Had graithed him wi' ye Haly Crosse,
              To faire wi' Ynklonde's Kynge ;'

they do, a quadrilateral form that is quite at variance with the triangular castle that figures in the verse of the chronicler of the siege. "Its figure," says the poet, "was like that of a shield, for it had only three sides, with a tower on each angle; one of them a jumellated or double one, so high, so long, and so spacious that under it was the gate, with a drawbridge well-made and strong, with a sufficiency of other defences. It had also good walls, and ditches filled to the brim with water; and I believe there never was seen a castle more beautifully situated—for at once could be seen the Irish Sea towards the west, a charming country towards the north, encompassed by an arm of the sea; so that no creature born could approach it on two sides without putting himself in danger of the sea. Nor was it an easy matter towards the south, it being, as by the sea on the other side, surrounded by the river, woods, marshes, and trenches. Wherefore it was necessary for the host to approach it towards the east, where the hill slopes."

So far as outline and locality go no better description could be given of Carlaverock Castle as we now find it; and as the Bows Wood ruin is square, the conclusion is obvious that it is the former, not the latter, which really represents the Maxwell fortress of mediæval times, whose memorable siege in 1300 we are about to describe. (a)

Very early on the 15th of July the hostile operations began, three thousand men-at-arms forming the attacking party, arranged into three battalions, and occupying the slanting eminence of Wardlaw Hill, on the east. "As soon as we were thus drawn up," says the poet, "we were quartered by the marshal; and then might be seen houses built without carpenters or masons, of many different fashions—many a cord stretched with white and coloured cloth fastened by pins driven into the ground—many a large tree cut down to make huts; and leaves, herbs, and flowers gathered in the woods, which were strewed within: then our people took up their quarters." Our poetical historian declares "that the gleam of gold and silver, and the radiance of rich colours, emitted by the embattled host, illuminated the valley which they occupied;" and with quaint simplicity he adds, "those of the castle, seeing us arrive, might, as I well believe, deem that they were in greater peril than they could ever before remember." Not a doubt of it. The garrison did not, perhaps, number more than a hundred: their supply of food was limited; their connection with the sea was cut off; and they could mark through the loopholes such

but now we know that at least its towers re-echoed to the war-cries of the chivalry of the First Edward, and that the ditches thereof, now choked up with aquatic herbage, were once red with their fierce Norman blood. This was early in the year 1300, and from then till 1640 Carlaverock Castle played its part in the annals of the time."

(a) The castle has been much rebuilt beyond a doubt. There are gun-ports in the great towers at the gate—the work of the late 16th if not 17th century.

a multitude coming up against their castle as might blockade them into a surrender, should that slow but sure mode of aggression be resorted to.

As the fiery spirit of the English King disrelished such a tedious process, he resolved to escalade the chief defences as soon as his vessels, sailing up the Solway, supplied the means. A welcome store of provisions,* as well as engines, having been brought by the squadron, the English footmen forthwith marched against the fortress. "Then might be seen stones, arrows, and crossbow bolts flying from among them ; but so effectually did those within exchange their tokens with those without, that, in one short hour, there were many persons wounded and maimed, and I know not how many killed." To missiles thrown by hand and bow were soon added other more formidable ones, projected by catapults, and showers of blows from powerful battering-rams ; the assailants suffering much loss when planting down the engines. (a) As the footmen made little impression on the massive building, the men-at-arms, ironed from top to toe, hurried to their assistance. The latter could better resist the interminable salutes of stone which were rained down by the gallant little garrison, and on which they mainly relied for defence. So fast and heavily fell these mischievous boulders that, we are told, they "beat hats and helmets to powder, and broke shields and helmets in pieces ;" and ever as a brave knight was thus done to death a shout of exultation was heard rising above the din of battle from within the beleaguered stronghold.

Some of the assailants who signalised themselves are thus depicted, and their feats described, in the curious work so frequently quoted from :—"First of all," says the poet, "I saw the good Baron Bertram de Montbouchier, on whose shining silver shield were three red pitchers, with besants, in a black border. With him Gerard de Gondronville, an active and handsome bachelor. He had a shield neither more nor less than vaire. These were not resting idle, for they threw up many a stone, and suffered many a heavy blow. The first body was composed of Bretons, and the second were of Lorraine, of which none found the other tardy ; so that they afforded encouragement and emulation

---

* It was chiefly from Ireland that Edward I. obtained supplies of food for the armies he sent into Scotland by the Western Border ; and Skinburness, near Silloth, on the Solway, then a flourishing market town, but now reduced to a few houses only, was the magazine where the provisions were stored up. In a Latin letter still extant, written at the close of 1298, the King orders a vast stock of beeves, pork, and fish to be provided, " in partibus Hiberniæ, " "et ea usque ad portum de Skinburneyse, juxta Karliolum, destinari."—Historical Documents, vol. ii , p. 356 ; and Hutchinson's History of Cumberland, vol. ii., p. 340.

(a) The English army numbered upwards of 6000. It passed up Annandale to Dumfries, and thence to Carlaverock Castle. On refusal to surrender projectile engines had to be sent for. Friar Robert of Ulm was the King's engineer. Two engines, if not more—one of them called a robinet—was it named after the Friar?—were brought from Lochmaben. Others, on 10th July, were conveyed from Skinburness to Carlaverock on board the St. George of Dartmouth and another vessel. Besides those engines the Friar Robert of Ulm constructed three others.

to others to resemble them. Then came to assail the castle Fitz-Marmaduke, with a banner and a great troop of good and select bachelors." Robert de Willoughby, Robert de Hamsart, and Henry de Graham are next noticed as joining in the assault ; and Thomas de Richmont, who, in red armour, led on a second time some lances. "These," it is stated, "did not act like discreet people, nor as persons enlightened by understanding, but as if they had been inflamed and blinded with pride and despair ; for they made their way right forward to the brink of the very ditch ;" nay, they passed, in view of the poetical reporter, "quite to the bridge, and demanded entry," receiving for reply, " ponderous stones and cornices." Willoughby also pressed forward, till a stone, alighting on "the middle of his breast," arrested his career ; though, we are told, the blow might have been warded off by his shield, " if he had deigned to use it." Fitz-Marmaduke long occupied the post of danger, his banner receiving " many stains, and many a rent difficult to mend ;" while Hamsart " bore himself so nobly that from his shield fragments might often be seen to fly in the air," he and Richmont driving the descending stones upwards, " as if they were harmless shuttlecocks." Graham's retainers suffered severely, not above two returning unhurt or bringing back their shields entire.

Hitherto, it seems, notwithstanding the intrepidity of the assailants, the defenders had the best of the fray. After a breathing time a second attack was made : the din waxed louder, and the struggle became more desperate. " Then you might hear the tumult begin ;" and the poet despairs of being able to recount all the " brave actions " that ensued, as " the labour would be too heavy ;" but he gives a few specimens :—" Ralph de Gorges, a newly-dubbed knight," with harness and attire "mascally of gold, azure," fell more than once, struck by stones or jostled by the crowd ; yet, " being of a haughty spirit, he would not deign to retire." Then Robert de Tony and Richard de Rokeley plied those upon the wall so severely that they were frequently forced to retreat ; while Adam de la Forde mined away at the walls, "though the stones flew in and out as thick as rain." " The good Baron of Wigton received such blows that it was the astonishment of all that he was not stunned."

Meanwhile an engine called the robinet was in full play. Footmen, men-at-arms, and cavalry might be beat back, and were ; but the irresistible robinet threw such large fragments of rock inside without intermission as to greatly thin the ranks of the defenders. So destructively did it operate that a stout warrior, not previously noticed, the " Knight of Kirkbride," was able to win his way to the castle gate. Many a heavy and crushing stone greeted him, which, " with white shield, having a green cross engrailed," he swept aside, and, swinging aloft his ponderous battle-axe, assailed the gate, dealing such blows upon it as "never did smith with hammer on iron."* Some of his followers plied it in similar fashion, till a party of the besieged returning, in defiance of the deadly robinet, to the overlooking wall, showered upon Kirkbride and his men "such huge stones, arrows, and so forth, that with wounds and bruises they were so hurt and exhausted that it was with great difficulty they were able to retire."

No pause in the assault—no rest for the besieged. A relay of fresh warriors, including Bartholomew de Badlesmere and John Cromwell,† followed the banner of Lord Clifford,‡ when sent by him to the gate—it being the ravager of Annandale who directed this part of the siege ; "but the people of the castle would not permit them to remain there long ;" and, as they retreated, Cromwell's shield of blue, bearing a white lion rampant, came back battered and defaced—the marvel being that its bearer, "so brave and handsome, who went gliding between the stones," got off unscathed. The attack was renewed by La Warde and De Gray ; after which a more general assault was recommenced by "the followers of my Lord of Bretagne, fierce and daring as lions of the mountain, and every day improving in both the art and practice of arms." "Their party soon covered the entrance of the castle, for none could have attacked it more furiously ; not, however, that it was so subdued that those who came after them would not have a share in their labours, as they left more than enough for them also." The followers of Lord Hastings and John Deincourt are specified as doing their duty nobly ; and "it was also a fine sight," we are informed, "to see the good brothers of Berkeley receiving numerous blows."

Throughout the entire day, the defenders, though sorely plied, continued their resistance ; and full justice is done by the poet to their bravery. "Those within," he says, "continually relieved one another ; for always as one became fatigued, another returned fresh and stout, and notwithstanding such assaults were made upon them, they would not surrender." Night came without bringing to them any repose, as the season, being midsummer,

---

* It is believed that Scott's heart-thrilling description of the storming of Torquil-stone Castle was in some degree inspired by "The Roll of Carlaverock." The action of the Knight of Kirkbride will remind the reader of what is said respecting the Black Knight. He "approaches the postern with his huge axe—the thundering blows which he deals, you may hear them above all the din and shouts of the battle—stones and beams are hurled down on the bold champion—he regards them no more than if they were thistle-down or feathers."—*Vide* "Ivanhoe." The personality of this white shielded warrior is veiled in mystery, like that which surrounded the Black Knight himself ; but we think he must have been near of kin to his colleague, the "good Baron of Wigton," and that he was most probably Richard de Kirkbride, grandson of Ada, who received the manor of Kirkbride, in Cumberland, from his ancestor, the second Lord of Wigton.

† This is perhaps the first historical appearance of the name Cromwell on record in connection with Scotland. Carlyle mentions a Lord Cromwell as having been summoned by Edward II. There is a place called Cromwell on the Trent, Notts.

‡ Sir Robert de Clifford had been previously elevated to the Peerage, as a reward, we presume, for his services in Dumfriesshire.

allowed light sufficient for the assailants to continue their labours without cessation ; and if their personal attacks relaxed for a moment, the terrible engine tore away untiringly during the twilight as it had done in the flush of day ; and as the second day dawned, the besieged counted with dismay one, two, three more robinets casting their shadows on the hill, and preparing, like so many Titans, to bury them under a mountainous pile of stones. We can readily imagine them holding a council of war, and considering what was best to be done in view of such a fresh array of destructive force. If any proposed that the castle should be given up without further resistance, such pacific suggestion was overruled ; and the clangour of battle, which had only partially died away during the night, again rose high, resounding through the embowering woods, and echoing along the Solway shore.

In vain, however, did the remnant of the garrison maintain the unequal conflict : they could have overcome mere manual assaults—they could only for a limited time bid defiance to the engines, which, says our authority, " were very large, of great power, and very destructive—cutting down and cleaving whatever they strike. Fortified town, citadel, barrier, nothing is protected from their strokes. Yet those within did not flinch until some more of them were slain, when each began to repent of his obstinacy, and to be dismayed. The pieces fell in such a manner wherever the stones entered, that when they struck any of them, neither iron cap nor wooden target could save him from a wound." At tierce, on the second day of the siege, when they saw that they could hold out no longer, they " begged for peace," making an overture to that effect in the usual manner. From a loophole of the jumellated tower in front, a small white pennon was thrust ; and ere the English marshal had time to stay proceedings in answer to the signal, an arrow from an English bow passed through the hand of him who held the olive branch, into his face, thus pinning both together. The unfortunate flag-bearer " then begged that they would do no more to him ; for they would give up the castle to the king, and throw themselves on his mercy." Upon which the assault was stopped, and the castle surrendered.

The defenders, on passing out, were reviewed before Edward, and found to number only sixty. "They were," says the poet, " beheld with astonishment ;" and it was natural that the besieging army should wonder that a handful of men should be able to resist their mighty host for such a lengthened period. The ultimate fate of this gallant few is left in doubt. Their lives, according to the poet, were spared by order of the king, and they were each presented with a new garment ; whereas, in the chronicle of Lanercost, it is stated that many of them were hanged from the trees around the castle—a treatment, if true, that

accords with the usual merciless policy of the English monarch. (a)
As the name of Sir Herbert de Maccuswel, or Maxwell, is not
mentioned by the Exeter historian, the likelihood is that he was
not present at the defence of his patrimonial towers.

Previously to the siege, or on the first day of its progress,
Edward visited the churches of Applegarth, Tinwald, and Dumfries, to offer oblations on their altars, with a view of securing a
blessing upon his efforts. Now that they were crowned with
success, he caused the castle to be repaired, and consigning it to
the keeping of Lord Clifford, proceeded to Dumfries, crossed with
his army Devorgilla's Bridge over the Nith, and entered Galloway,
where he continued about six weeks prosecuting the objects of his
expedition.* (b)

(a) It is certain, however, that the constable and eleven other Scots were sent
prisoners to Newcastle.—Bain's Col. ii., 1162.

* Rymer's Fœdera, vol. i., p. 921 ; and Wardrobe Accounts, p. 215.

(b) In midsummer it would not be necessary to rely entirely on any bridge when
crossing the Nith. There were several fords, and the river would be shallow.

CHAPTER VIII.

THE ROMAN PONTIFF INTERFERES ON BEHALF OF SCOTLAND, AND CLAIMS IT
FROM EDWARD AS A FIEF OF THE HOLY SEE—HE SENDS A MISSIVE TO
THAT EFFECT BY THE HANDS OF THE ARCHBISHOP OF CANTERBURY—
INTERVIEW OF THE ARCHBISHOP WITH THE KING IN CARLAVEROCK CASTLE
—EDWARD HOLDS A COURT AT DUMFRIES, AND, IN ACCORDANCE WITH
THE POPE'S REQUEST, GRANTS AN ARMISTICE TO THE SCOTS—HE AFTER-
WARDS, AT THE INSTANCE OF THE KING OF FRANCE, SIGNS A TREATY OF
PEACE WITH THEM FOR A SHORT PERIOD—RENEWAL OF THE WAR—
LOCHMABEN CASTLE ATTACKED—SCOTLAND AGAIN INVADED, AND TEM-
PORARILY SUBDUED—BETRAYAL AND EXECUTION OF WALLACE.

I⊤ is necessary that we should now glance at some of the leading
national events that occurred immediately prior to the memorable
siege just described, and those that followed that enterprise.
Wallace, on being defeated at Falkirk, resigned the office of
Guardian, to which he had been elevated by his grateful countrymen ; and, strange to say, it then devolved upon Robert Bruce,
John Comyn, and William Lamberton, Bishop of St. Andrews ;
Bruce and Comyn merging their rivalries, and agreeing for the
first time to act in concert : during a brief period these triumvirs,
as they may be called, ruled the country in the name of Baliol,
though that luckless sovereign was an exile in France, and politically dead.   Several times had the Scots tried to obtain assistance
from Philip of France, the brother-in-law of their oppressor ; but
as Philip allowed the claims of his ancient allies to be overborne
by those of a personal nature, they resolved to invoke the aid of
the Roman Pontiff.*

Accordingly, a deputation from Bruce and his colleagues
waited upon Pope Boniface, depicted the woes under which Scotland groaned, and prayed him to take action against the tyrant
author of them all.   "We shall interfere for the relief of your
country," said his Holiness in effect ; "but we shall claim the
kingdom that we mean to wrest from Edward as the immemorial
fief of the Holy See."   Whether the Guardians were more displeased than gratified with this intimation we cannot say : if they
desired to see an end put to the English domination, it was not
that it might be succeeded by the supremacy of Rome—his
country independent of any foreign potentate whatever, was what
Bruce at least sought to secure.   We know that this preposterous

* Fordun, p. 983 ; and Wyntoun, vol. ii., p. 105.

claim of the Pope enraged King Edward. It was set forth in a bull directed to that monarch, bearing date July 5th, 1299 ; and he was warned by it that if he resisted or demurred, Jerusalem would not fail to protect her sons, and Mount Zion her worshippers. This spirited Papal rescript was forwarded to Winchelsea, Archbishop of Canterbury, who was ordered to deliver it to the King ; and the prelate set out on his mission with a retinue of officials, incurring no small risk when in Nithsdale from numerous marauding bands, that would gladly have plundered him, and called the deed patriotic. Unacquainted with Edward's movements, he had to make a long, circuitous journey. Following the royal route into Galloway, he missed the King at Kirkcudbright : then, returning eastward, he crossed the Solway with his chariots ; and at length finding his Majesty in Carlaverock Castle soon after its capture, he there delivered to him the Pontifical missive. (a)

Many strange and momentous incidents have occurred within the walls and under the shadow of the old British fortress and its feudal successor ; and this interview between Edward I. and the Primate of England is entitled to rank high among the number, whether we look to the dignity of these personages or the subject which they discussed. Edward read the bull, his wrath gathering all the time, and eventually boiling over, as, bit by bit, the bold assumptions of the Pope broke upon him, and the document went on to lay his own proud claims in the dust. It needed not the prelate's appended admonition on the duty of obedience to Mother Church to inflame his Majesty's rage. Rising into a paroxysm of passion, he stormed and swore, declaring that he would not be silent at the bidding of the Holy See ; and that, despite of Mount Zion or Jerusalem, he would, whilst there was breath in his nostrils, claim and retain what all the world knew to be his rights. The King cooled down after this explosion. He saw that it would be impolitic to quarrel outright with the Pope, and, lowering his tone, told Winchelsea that before giving a conclusive answer to the missive of his Holiness, he would require to take the advice of his counsellers on the subject.*

(a) The Archbishop of Canterbury, the first and last of that dignity, doubtless, to ford the Solway, writes in his narrative as follows : "At length, having by diligent inquiry heard that the King in returning with his army towards the Castle of Carlaverock in Scotland, had pitched his tents near the new abbey of Sweetheart (Duzquer) in Galloway, and being willing to expose myself, my men, and my goods to danger rather than thus to dally in such remote, and in a manner desert, parts beyond my diocese and province, I kept myself concealed in certain secret places near the sea which separates England and Galloway, and took advantage of an opportunity at ebb tide. Guided by some men who were bound not to be ignorant of the direction of the crossing, I passed with my horses and harness through four streams of water in the sea, not more dangerous because of the depth of water than because of the ins and outs of the shore and the quicksands. Thus almost beyond expectation, on Friday [26th August] next after the feast of St. Bartholomew the Apostle now last past, I came to the King, then amidst his army and at dinner. And because he had not time, as he said, that day, he sent word to me that evening by two of his chief earls who were then aiding him that on the morrow, viz., Saturday, he would graciously hear me."— See "Annals of the Solway."

* Walsingham, p. 78 ; and Prynne, p. 883.

The Archbishop thereupon withdrew ; and, shortly after this remarkable audience, a court was held by the King at Dumfries, at which the Papal bull, and the propriety of granting a peace to the Scots, in terms of its recommendation, were discussed. Reserving the question of his claims, he agreed to grant a brief armistice ; and, on returning to England, he summoned a Parliament to meet him at Lincoln, by which body the assumptions of the Pope over Scotland were condemned, and the English monarch was declared to be, as regards temporal matters, entirely independent of the Holy See. A written reply to this effect was forwarded to Boniface, attested by a hundred and four seals of the nobility, and having attached to it the emphatic intimation that the barons of England would not permit their sovereign to subordinate his claims to those of his Holiness, even were he so inclined.*

The King spent a considerable portion of the summer and autumn of 1300 in Dumfries and its neighbourhood. After taking Carlaverock, he went, as has been already stated, into Kirkcudbrightshire, for the purpose of overawing the Gallovidians. He appears to have been at Lochrutton on the 17th of July, and at the capital of the shire a few days afterwards, taking up his quarters, it is supposed, in the Castle of Kirkcudbright.† Proceeding further into Galloway, Edward granted an interview to the bishop of that diocese, who—prompted by the Pope, in all probability—tried to mediate a peace, but without success. Then the Earl of Buchan and John Comyn (one of the regents) ventured into the royal presence, and had the hardihood to demand that Baliol, their lawful king, should be permitted to reign over the country, and that the estates which had been given to English nobles should be restored to their proper owners. We can fancy the mingled surprise and scorn with which the haughty Edward would receive these requests, coming, as they did, from men whom he looked upon as rebels. The wonder is, not that his answer was in the negative, but that he did not seize and send them, as he had done with Baliol, to the Tower.

On the 9th of August the King was at the town of Flete (now Gatehouse), whence he sent an armed force against some skirmishing parties, who were easily dispersed ; and afterwards he secured the adherence of the M'Dowalls, though they were disposed at first to resent his behaviour towards Baliol, their kinsman. To Sweetheart Abbey, where lay buried the mother of the unfortunate ex-king, Edward went on the 24th of August, surveying with mingled feelings, we may suppose, the tomb of his illus-

---

* Rymer's Fœdera, vol. i., p. 923 ; and Tyrrel, vol. iii., p. 146.

† This building stood on the eastern side of the Dee, near the town, overlooking the entrance to the river, the tide of which flowed into the fosse. It was erected by the old Lords of Galloway, and was inherited by Devorgilla on the death of her father Alan. When at Kirkcudbright, Edward made an oblation to the Priory Church of the burgh, which occupied a site now covered by the existing Castle of Kirkcudbright.

trious subject Devorgilla, and laying his oblations on the altar by which it was overlooked.

Returning at the close of the month to Carlaverock, where the provoking Papal bull greeted him, he, after temporarily disposing of it, went to Holmcultram Abbey—a large body of his soldiers following him through Dumfriesshire to Carlisle, and laying the country waste along their line of march. (a) Edward once more retraced his steps from Carlisle, reaching Dumfries on the 16th of October, where he continued with his Queen and court till the beginning of the following month. The inhabitants of the burgh would thus be but too familiar with the features and figure of the usurper. Often would he be seen by them, noticeable by his length of stature and majestic mein, riding with his retinue up (b) High Street to the Castle ; and, doubtless, many a muttered curse would follow the cavalcade ; for the Dumfriesians detested the English yoke, and though partially kept in check by the garrison, were always ready, as we have seen, to take part against the invaders when an opportunity offered. It is in vain for us to inquire as to the style kept up by the conqueror's court at Dumfries. His beautiful queen, sister of the King of France, would, of course, be its ruling star and attraction ; but whether the royal lady held levees and other fashionable assemblies in the Castle during her three weeks' sojourn, and tried her blandishments for a political purpose on the daughters of the town and district, is not on record. Probably on Sundays the King (for he was very pious after a sort) would repair for worship, accompanied by his queen, to the Greyfriars' Church in the Vennel ; or proceed for that purpose to Lincluden Abbey,* on the opposite bank of the Nith, which, as we have seen, had some half century before been built and endowed by Uchtred, Lord of Galloway. When Edward first visited Dumfries on the 18th of June, 1300, he became, as already stated, the guest of the Grey Friars ; but as there are no

(a) When Edward stormed Carlaverock there was a strong English fleet in the Solway, under the command of Gervase Alard of Winchelsea. "He bore the title of 'Admiral of the Fleet'—'Admiral,' a name borrowed from the East, and still quite new in England ; indeed, not used there before 1295. The strength of the fleet lay in thirty ships furnished by the Cinque Ports. . . The Admiral's pay was 2s per day. Under him were four captains at 1s. Each of the thirty ships had a master, paid 6d. Most of them carried two constables, ranking below the master, but receiving the same pay. The ordinary seaman had 3d. Of the thirty ships, sixteen had each (besides master and two constables) 39 seamen, the respective numbers of these last in the remaining fourteen ships varying from 37 to 19. The whole sea force contributed by the Cinque Ports amounted to 1099 men. Of the other vessels some were less distinctly naval in their function, and most of them were much smaller than the men-of-war." They brought up the total number of ships to fifty-eight, having on board one admiral, four captains, 58 masters, 57 constables, and 1337 sailors. A list of them, with the name and port of each, is given, from the Wardrobe Accounts, in "Annals of the Solway." The fleet, he says, "remained in the estuary until 20th Sept., when it set sail for home. Singularly enough the admiral did not sail, but rode home to Winchelsea. The King gave him a black horse for the purpose."

(b) This on the assumption that the Castle was beside the Monastery at the top of High Street. It was, on the contrary, at the other end of the town.

* We learn from Prynne that the Abbess of Lincluden about this period was named Alienore.

entries of payment to them in the Wardrobe Accounts on the occasion of his second visit, we may conclude that in October he and his court were indebted for board and lodgings to his own keeper of the Castle, John de St. John. The likelihood also is, considering the feelings of the inhabitants towards him, and the weak tenure by which he held the town and its vicinity, that he would live rather in the style of a fighting captain than of a great king, and that his consort, however bent on a queenly life in Scotland, would conform to the circumstances of their position.

Though Philip of France declined at first to act as mediator for the Scots, he eventually interceded with Edward on their behalf. Towards the end of October two French commissioners, Sir John de Barres, and Pierre de Mouncey, Canon of Angiers, visited the English monarch at Dumfries, and succeeded in negotiating a truce—Edward making it to be clearly understood that he granted the concession to Philip as his wife's brother, and not to the King of France as an ally of the "Scots people with whom he was at war." It was quite a little family compact that was entered into between the brothers-in-law. "We have acceded to a truce," said the gracious Edward ; "granting it as to a friend and loving intercessor, who is no ally of the Scots, and who holds himself as nothing to them"—the aforesaid Monsieur Pierre and Sir John having testified to that effect—"and for this said truce we have given promise to hold and protect these Scots people, their persons, their auxiliaries, their allies, their goods, and their lands, from us, our auxiliaries, and our allies, until the day of Pentecost [19th of May] next to come."* In accordance with the treaty, letters were despatched from Dumfries " by the very noble and mighty Prince Edward," to John de St. John, "established, placed, and ordained in the March of Scotland towards Galloway ;

* The document quoted from is given, with the accompanying letters, in the Fœdera, vol. 1., pp. 925-926. Some of our historians incorrectly represent the Dumfries Treaty of October, 1300, as having been brought about by the Pope ; whereas it was solely due to the intervention of the French King. We translate from the original Norman-French the conditions of the truce :—" And for this said truce we have given and promise sufferance, both to hold and protect these Scotch people, their persons, their auxiliaries, their allies, their goods, and their property, from us, our auxiliaries, and our allies, until the day of Pentecost next to come, in the following manner : That each one shall retain what he possesses, and will be able to build, to work, to labour, to sail by the coast, and to do that which he pleases or thinks during the said truce ; and that each one, on the one part and on the other, will be able to go and come, and securely trade by sea and by land from the one country to the other, here or there as he pleases, according to the laws and customs of the country ; declaring always, that they will not put nor carry money into England, nor into Ireland, nor any other part in our realm, except such as is in circulation there, if that be not our coin, or if they only wish to place it there, and not to employ it in our realm ; and that they will not carry out of our realm the money which is in circulation there, nor good silver, under the forfeiture of what is before decreed : and that neither misapprehend nor does any injury the one towards the other, until the said day of Pentecost. And this truce and this sufferance, in the manner which is before related, we promise both well and faithfully to protect and firmly to hold, by us and by ours, and for us and for ours, both by sea and by land, till the said Day of Pentecost ; and for the firmly protecting and keeping these things we have sworn before Monsieur Gautier de Beauchamp, our seneschal. In testimony of the faithfully protecting, upholding, and accomplishing all these things, we have caused these letters, sealed with our seal, to be made public. Given at Dumfries, the 30th day of October, in the 28th year of our reign."

and to Sir Adam Gordon, established, placed, and ordained in the
March of Galloway towards Scotland, by order of the rulers of the
kingdom of Scotland," enjoining them to carry out the truce, and
requesting all others who should see or hear the royal orders to
promote the observance of the same.

Acting upon the provisions of the treaty, Edward left Dumfries, and returned with his army into England, retaining, however, all the places of strength that had come into his possession.
Thus the magnificent host described by the heraldic poet in glowing terms, and from which so much was anticipated and feared,
accomplished little after all. It was essentially the same army,
however, by which the war was renewed on a great scale in 1302.

While the armistice was running its course, preparations for
war went on in Dumfriesshire. Robert de Tilliol, who, with
William de Heriz* assisting him, held Lochmaben Castle for the
English, was sore pressed soon after Whitsuntide. By the beginning of September he learned that the Earl of Buchan and Sir
John de Soulis were marching with a considerable force from
Ayrshire towards Annandale, and that another body of Scots had
occupied Stenhouses, in his immediate neighbourhood. In a
pressing letter Tilliol prayed the King to send him assistance, as
the country round about was rising, he having no troopers to
keep it in order, and as rebel bands were pouring in from every
side. Before the warden of Lochmaben received any reply to his
epistle, Sir John de Soulis, with Sir Ingram de Umphraville, hove
in sight, heading a formidable array composed of twelve score
men-at-arms and about seven thousand foot-soldiers. Hastening
to the little burgh, they set fire to it, Tilliol being unable to do
anything for its defence. More need had he for help to keep his
own towers in safety, as Soulis, after using the torch upon the
town, proceeded against the castle by storm. Its strength of wall,
however, supplemented by its fosse and the wide stretch of water
with which it was fed, foiled the Scottish chief ; and withdrawing
disappointed to the vicinity of Annan, he made his presence felt
there by fire and pillage. On the following day Bruce's burgh
again rang with the clang of arms, Soulis making another bold
dash upon the fortress, and being again beaten back with some
loss in killed and wounded. Several fierce hand-to-hand encoun-
ters seem to have taken place, and William de Heriz, the leader of
a sallying party, venturing too far out was captured—the only
success of which the assailants were able to boast. The latter
withdrew to Dalswinton, and after resting there awhile proceeded
towards Galloway. Thus Robert de Tilliol, though unable to
dominate over the district, succeeded in keeping hold of its chief

* William de Herris, or Heriz, descended from the Norman knight, Nigel de Heriz,
was head of the Galloway Herrises, and swore fealty to Edward for lands held by him
in that province.—See Ante, p. 30.

castle till the arrival of a reinforcement lessened the dangers of his position.*

The year ensuing 1302, and the following one, saw Scotland ravaged, desolated, and brought to the very verge of ruin. On the expiry of the truce, Edward sent into the country twenty thousand soldiers, chiefly horsemen, under the command of Sir John de Segrave. When encamped near Roslin in three divisions, lying wide apart, they were encountered one after the other by the Scots under Comyn and Sir Simon Fraser, and thoroughly put to the rout, only a few straggling fugitives reaching their own land in safety. The English chroniclers of the time tell us that the news of this triple defeat was very trying to the temper of King Edward—that his wrath found vent as usual in terrible oaths and maledictions. Just before receiving the unwelcome tidings he had induced his brother-in-law, Philip, to abandon the interests of the Scots, and, by bribes and artful representations, had so brought Boniface over that the Scottish bishops were enjoined by a Papal bull to submit to Edward of England, our " dearest son in Christ," on peril of themselves and country being put under ban. France had disowned the rebels, the Church had threatened them with spiritual thunder—a very serious menace in those times—yet here they were, audaciously self-reliant, snapping their fingers at the Pope, and scattering the forces of England as chaff before the wind.

What a long list of heartaches and perplexities, what an immense amount of treasure, what rivers of blood, this conquest of Scotland business had cost the King. Should he give it up in despair ? Such a question never occurred to him ; or, if it did for a moment, " to be once in doubt was once to be resolved." The Pope had given over the rebellious country to his tender mercies, backing his temporal might and authority by spiritual power ; and thus doubly armed, he would reduce the Scots to utter serfdom, even if to carry out his resolution he had to turn their country into a howling wilderness. So resolving, he crossed the Border with an army much larger than the one whose exploits are

* Tilliol's despatch on the subject runs thus :—" A son tres honurable seingnur par la graz Deu rey de Engleterre, le seon lyge bachelere Robert de Tilliol, gardeyn de Lougchmaban, honurs e reverenz.   Sachez, sire, qe le Judy la viele Nostre Dame [Sept. 7] wyndrent dewaunt nous a Lougchmaban, sire Johane de Soules, sire Ingram de Humframville, e ovekes eus quatorz banerettes, duz winz homes de armes, sete mile homes de pee, ou plus, e nous ardyrent nostre vile et assalyrent nostre pele demyway prime dekes a houre de noune, e puis sen partirent de nous e halerent logere pres de Annand et ardyrent e preyerent le pays la entore.   E lendemayne revendrent e nous asalyrent de houre de prime dekes a mirleue ; a quel assaut fu naffre sire Davy de Brechin e sire Johan de Waus, e plusures au¹r· s de lures mors et naffrees.   E devers le wesper halyrent logere de cote Dalswynton, e si wunte devers le vale de Nith e deweres Garway, e funt relevere dewers eus ceus qe furent wenuz a la pese, e recoylirent plus de poer a wenere vers nos marches, a co qe nous espayrum ; mes a le hayde de Deu nous ne avums ward de eus.   Un nostre compaynon Sir Gillam de Heriz fu prise a une issu, et un home de Wintayn mors in lasaut.   Sire, Deu wous cresce in honure.   Vostre volunte nous mandez com a vostre.   Escrit a Lougchmaban, le Dimanche procheyn apres la Nativite of Nostre Dame [Sept. 10, 1301]."—Historical Documents, vol. ii., pp. 432-433.

celebrated in the verse of the herald. It was divided into two—one
division led by himself, the other by his eldest son. Its progress
was like that of a great fire on an American prairie—consuming
everything before it.

Dumfriesshire was not subjected to the destructive visitation,
its chiefs having purchased immunity by prompt submission.
Bruce was no longer seen directing the affairs of Scotland, or
fighting on her side. Despairing of success, he gave up the
Guardianship and retired. Into private life? Not so; that would
have been a respectable, though not a very dignified course. Withdrawing from the patriotic cause, he made his peace with its relentless enemy ; and in the spring of 1304 we find him ingloriously
co-operating with Edward for the purpose of wresting Stirling
Castle from its Scottish defenders. "We are much obliged to
you," wrote the King to his cousin of Carrick, "for having arranged
to cause our engines to be carried to Stirling." Bruce had apprised his Majesty by letter that he could not find a waggon in
the country able to carry the frame of a huge catapult from Inverkip to the place of siege, and had asked to be supplied with the
means of transporting it. He was told in reply that what he
needed would be sent forthwith ; "but," proceeded the King, in
his own imperious style, "we charge you especially ('nous vous
chargeons especialement') that on no account do you desist from
using all the pains and deliberation possible to cause the said
frame to be carried to us, with stones, and all the other things
appertaining to this engine, and to the other engines, as far as
you can procure them ; and for want of lead do not on any account
desist from expediting the despatch of the said frame and the
timber, and the stones belonging to the said engine, and to the
others, together with all the lead you can procure."* But the
Inverkip engine was not required, England's sword of might doing
effectually the work for which the catapult was designed.

The invading torrent swept through the middle districts, northwards by Roxburgh and Linlithgow, no place offering resistance
but the Castle of Brechin, which succumbed after a three weeks'
siege. Stirling Castle might possibly have defied it had Comyn,
mindful of Wallace's strategy seven years before, given battle to

---

* We give a transcript of the original, which is in the Public Record Office and is
copied in Historical Documents, vol. ii., pp. 482-483 :—" R. au Conte de Carrike, saluz.
Nous avoms bien entendu par voz lettres, que vous nous [eue] enveastes par le portour
de cestes, coment vous avez ordinez de faire carier noz engyns devers Estrivelyn ; de
quoi nous vous savoms bon gre. Et de ce que vous nous avez mande que vous ne trovez
char en pais que peusse porter la verge [de lengyn] del grant engyn que est devers vous,
par quoi vous voudriez que nous enveissions a vous aucun hom qui savriot deviser
coment [il] cele verge purreit estre cariee par terre ; sachez, que nous enverrons a vous
aucun homme pour vous aider a ce faire a plus tost que nous porrens en bone manere.
Mais nous vous chargeons especialement que pour ce ne leissez mie que vous ne mettez
tote la peine et le consail que vous purrez, de faire carier avant vers nous le dite verge,
et peeres, et totes les autres choses que [vous] a cel engyn, et a les autres engyns,
appendent, si avant come vous les purrez purchacier. E [nous] pour defaute de plum
ne lassez mie qe vous ne facez venir avant la dite verge, et meryn, et peres apurtenantz
a cel engyn et les autres ensemblement, ove tot le plum que vous purrez purchacer.
Inverkethyn, xvj Aprilis."

the enemy when crossing the wooden bridge over the Forth. Vainly thinking to arrest his march, Comyn destroyed the bridge, and ere long the irresistible host, passing by a ford, overtook the Scots. A brief struggle—a total rout—a terrible massacre. Then open resistance was at an end ; and Edward, more truly than he had ever been before, was master of Scotland. With sullen reluctance the Scottish chiefs submitted to the conquerer. Some he pardoned, others he reserved for vengeance ; all acknowledged his sway save one—Sir William Wallace—name ever dear to his country and to freedom, and never more proudly, yet tearfully, remembered than at the time when, betrayed to the English soon after the defeat at Stirling, he was cruelly put to death, crowning his long fight on behalf of Scotland by dying for her sake. *

Edward, in order to secure his conquest, set about abrogating all the old laws and customs of the country, and substituting those of England in their stead. Provisional arrangements for these ends seem to have been made by him at Dunfermline, and to have been afterwards consolidated by a Commission at London, composed of thirty members, twenty of whom were English and ten Scottish. Among other regulations, it was provided that Scotland should be ruled in the King's name by a Lieutenant appointed by him; that new sheriffs should be named for the different counties : that, for the administration of justice, the country should be divided into four quarters, with two justices for each—the divisions being, first, Dumfriesshire and Galloway; secondly, the Lothians; thirdly, the land between the Forth and the mountains ; and, fourthly, the district between the latter and the sea. The judges went on circuit as they do at the present day, the principal residence of those for the southern district being Dumfries ; and there also the sheriff of the two shires had his seat and held his court.† Armed resistance rooted out—the traces of Scotland's nationality obliterated—the dead Wallace "hewn into four quarters," as Langtoft says, "which were hung up in four towns as a warning to all who, like him, raised their arms against their lord"‡ --surely if ever the English monarch was justified in supposing that the great object of his ambition had been attained, it was under circumstances such as these.

But the fond idea was a mere delusion. German philosophers speak of an impalpable emanation, which, proceeding from the human body under certain conditions, influences more or less all who come within its reach ; and the gory fragments of the mutilated martyr seem to have exercised a somewhat similar power

---

* Wallace was executed on the 23rd of August, 1305.

† Redpath's Border History, p. 225.

‡ Note of expenses for the carriage of the body of Willelmi le Walays : " xv s. quos liberarunt Johanni de Segrave, mense Augusti anno xxxiij., pro cariagio corporis Willelmi le Walays ad partes Scotiæ per breve regis et litteras ipsius Johannis de receptione. Postea allocantur in rotulo, x s."—Memoranda Roll, 33 and 34 Edw. I.

when set up near the eastern border at Newcastle, at Berwick, at Perth, and at Aberdeen. Those trophies of the usurper's triumph did not inspire terror, but mingled sorrow and admiration. All who tearfully surveyed them felt their love of country and their hatred of its enemies inflamed by the sight. They were seen and read as stirring epistles in favour of patriotism—as so many eloquent, though inarticulate, protests against tyranny, and incentives to insurrection and revenge. And the English monarch found such to be the case whilst yet in the full flush of his exultation, and before the first acclaim of his courtiers, hailing him conqueror and undisputed King of Scotland, had fairly died away. In what manner the feeling of the people, thus kept alive, was turned to practical account by one who proved to be a fit successor to the heroic Wallace, we now proceed to relate. (a)

(a) Sir Herbert Maxwell says that Bruce was " probably a witness of the trial and execution of Wallace." (See " Robert the Bruce," p. 122.) Professor Murison, echoing Sir Herbert, says :—" It is hardly any stretch of probability to believe that he (Bruce) . . . was at the trial and execution of the illustrious Wallace." (See "King Robert the Bruce.") Professor M'Millan (" Mainly about Robert Bruce ") shows that this ungenerous statement is without any evidence, and asks, " Could anything be more monstrously incredible ? "

CHAPTER IX.

WHEN the elder Bruce died, in 1304,* his son Robert was allowed
to enter upon the occupancy of both his English and Scottish
estates, just as if he had never taken up arms against King
Edward. The Earl of Carrick thus became one of the richest
noblemen in Scotland ; but he did not cherish a particle of gratitude towards the King who might have reduced him to beggary.
Bruce wished to be something more than a wealthy magnate : he
claimed the crown as a matter of right, and had no heart-thanks
for the monarch who had swept his claim aside, and showered
upon him only secondary favours. Bent on playing a politic
game, he had often subordinated duty to prudence, and taken care
not to commit himself too fully to a perilous cause, lest by doing
so he should lose all. He had already reached his thirtieth year
without manifesting the chivalrous courage which laughs at
danger, or the high-souled love of country which lays ignoble ease,
worldly goods, power, rank, life itself, if need be, on the altar of
patriotism. It would be a mistake, however, were we to suppose
that young Bruce was at any time satisfied with the solution of
the succession difficulty which placed a foreign prince on the
throne of his ancestors ; nor do we suppose that he would ever
have stooped so low as to become, like Baliol, a mere puppet-king.
Not even when acting with the English in 1304 had he been more
than their nominal ally ; and when, shortly afterwards, demean-
ing himself in the courtly ring at Westminster as nothing better
than " some vain carpet knight," he was trying to overreach his

---

* The death of Robert Bruce, fifth Lord of Annandale, son of the competitor, took
place in March, 1304. He was buried in Holmcultram Abbey, but the great central
tower of that house fell into the graveyard in 1600, and the *debris* has in its turn buried
the tomb of Bruce, and the tombs of other notable persons who were interred beside
him.

royal patron ; no easy task, but one which Bruce deemed quite
allowable, nay, right and proper—for why should he keep faith
with the man who had duped him, and had in all his dealings with
Scotland been perfidy itself ? John Comyn, surnamed the Red,
ex-Regent and Lord of Badenoch, had, after his defeat at Stirling,
also submitted to King Edward ; but he, not less than Robert
Bruce, had a desire to escape from thraldom, and still cherished a
hope that by some lucky turn of fortune's wheel he would be lifted
to the summit of his ambition—the sovereignty of Scotland—
which he claimed as descended from King Duncan by the daughter
of his son, Donald Bane, and also in right of his mother, Marjory,
sister of Baliol, the ex-king.

The two noblemen still stood awkwardly in each other's way :
they could not both win ; and at length, for their mutual advantage, they entered into a secret compact, in virtue of which Comyn
agreed to waive his own pretensions to the crown, and support
those of Bruce, on receiving from the latter the earldom and
estates of Carrick.* It appears also that about the same time
Wallace, still uncaptured, was busy organising a new revolt, of
which Bruce was to be the leader ; and that evidence of the projected movement fell somehow into the possession of the Lord of
Badenoch. There is a traditional proverb still current in Lochaber, that " while there are trees in a wood there will be deceit in
a Comyn"—a characteristic of the race which Bruce's rival
exhibited in an aggravated form. Personal antipathy between
the two men intensified their family feud, and no doubt helped to
shape the course pursued by Comyn. He had proof that the Earl
of Carrick, though acting the part of a courtier in London, still
aspired to the Scottish crown—witness the sealed instrument
surrendering his estates in order to secure that coveted object.
He had also reason to believe that Bruce was about to conspire
with the proscribed traitor, Wallace, for the purpose of securing
the same result. To betray Bruce's rebellious schemes would,
Comyn fancied, be a sure and speedy device for ruining his detested rival ; and, Bruce once out of the way, the road to Edward's
favour—perhaps also to the crown of Scotland—would stand open
to the house of Badenoch.

Comyn, by a dispatch, revealed all to the King.† " To the
Tower with Bruce !" roared the enraged monarch, on reading the
epistle. Yes—when he is caught. Warned by his kinsman, the
Earl of Gloucester, that there was a storm at hand, Bruce, accompanied by a small retinue, hurried on horseback from London,
never drawing bridle till he had crossed the Border. Whilst thus
fleeing in hot haste, he was not aware of Comyn's treachery till

---

* Ayloffe's Calendar of Ancient Charters, p. 295 ; Wyntoun, vol. iv., p. 992, and
vol. ii., p. 122.

† Wyntoun, vol. ii., p. 123.

that was revealed to him in a singular way. On the travellers approaching Lochmaben, they observed a youth coming from an opposite direction ; and, as he appeared desirous of avoiding them, Bruce caused him to be seized, when it was ascertained that he had lately left Dalswinton Castle with letters from its lord, the Red Comyn, to King Edward. When such was found to be the case, Bruce, without any delicacy, broke the seals, and his worst suspicions were realised. It was Comyn that had brought him into danger at the English Court ; and in these new dispatches the King was further informed of Bruce's designs, and urged to get rid of him. Burning with indignation, and at the same time faint with fatigue, Bruce, at the close of a seven days' journey, reached Lochmaben, where he found his brother Edward, and a devoted friend of the family, Robert Fleming, with whom and others he took counsel as to his future conduct.*

All lamented that the schemes of the patriotic party had been disclosed prematurely ; and all agreed that it would be extremely rash, in their unprepared state, to precipitate a collision with the King. To temporize awhile, and wait the issue of events, seemed to be the wisest course ; and, accordingly, Bruce did not blazon abroad the perfidy of Comyn, or his own danger in consequence, but proceeded quietly to Dumfries as if nothing had occurred.

The occasion of his headlong flight from England was as yet unknown in the burgh, and his presence there occasioned no surprise. The two justiciars whose jurisdiction extended over Dumfriesshire and Galloway were preparing, with all due formality, to hold their first court in the Castle of Dumfries ; and it was only in accordance with custom and duty that the Earl of Carrick should appear, with other barons and freeholders, to do suit and service to the representatives of the King.† According to the generality of our historians, Comyn proceeded to Dumfries for this purpose of his own accord, never for once supposing that he would there meet with the man he had so deeply injured, far less suspecting that that man knew full well by what false friend he had been betrayed. One old chronicler, however, states that Bruce " trysted " Comyn to meet him in Dumfries ; that the latter, as if dreading the result, demurred, but made his appearance at length, after Nigel Bruce had gone for him to the Castle of Dalswinton. At all events, the two noblemen did meet in the town ; and their interview was a most eventful one, altering, as it

---

* Several historians have concluded that because Bruce proceeded to Lochmaben the castle of that place must have been occupied at the time by his brother ; but it was still, we think, held by Robert de Tilliol, or some other English chief, as we have been unable to find any evidence of its having changed owners since the unsuccessful attacks made upon it by Soulis in 1301. Besides, both Barbour and Blind Harry simply say that Bruce arrived at Lochmaben, without making any reference to the castle.— *Vide* Sir James Balfour's Annals of Scotland, vol. i., p. 88 ; and Wyntoun, vol. ii., p. 127.

† Hailes's Annals, vol. i., p. 294 ; and Carruthers's Lectures on Scottish History, delivered in Edinburgh, 1859.

did, the current of history, and affecting the inhabitants of this island throughout all time. (a)

On this ever-memorable day, Thursday, the 10th of February, 1306, the streets of Dumfries are full of people. As the feeble sun rises above Criffel top, (b) its rays fall slantingly upon many a bold baron, Scottish and English, marching, with their vassal bands, through the Lochmabengate, across Devorgilla's Bridge, and along High Street—all tending towards the seat of justice, and viewed with admiring interest, or sometimes with ill-concealed dislike, by the burghers of the town and the country folks of the neighbourhood. When the glimmering sun is further southward, the streets are half deserted ; for the court has been opened, and the grave justiciars, in the hearing of a glittering throng, are trying some trembling defaulter on a charge, it may be, of stouthrief, homicide, or treason against his high mightiness King Edward.

Two barons, for some reason or other, though within the burgh, have hitherto withheld the homage of their presence from the court. They encounter each other near the Port of the Vennel; and if any curious residents in that ancient thoroughfare are looking from their casements, they may see the two patricians embracing each other, and conclude that they are loving brothers in heart, if not by blood. Fraternally affectionate they seem ; but their appearance presents such a contrast that they cannot long be looked upon as near kinsmen. Both are tall and powerful men ; but one is in the flush of early manhood, with a noble set of features and dark complexion,* whilst the other is a little past meridian, and wears a somewhat sinister visage, the expression of which is not enhanced by its hue of flaming red. The latter would perhaps be recognised by some of the spectators as John Comyn, Earl of Badenoch and Lochaber, seeing that he often resides in the town, and his complexion is peculiar ; but scarcely any would

(a) Hemingburgh, a contemporary, says that Bruce sent his brothers Thomas and Nigel to Dalswinton to invite Comyn to meet him at Dumfries. They met in the church and embraced. Bruce then accused Comyn of betraying him. Comyn returned a soft answer. But Bruce stabbed him at the altar, and *stole his horse!* Mr Andrew Lang puts these words in italics.
Sir Thomas Gray, whose father was severely wounded at the siege of Stirling, says that Bruce's brothers were instructed to kill Comyn on the way from Dalswinton ; but his graciousness disarmed them of their purpose. "He gave us such kind greeting, and such fair gifts, and shewed so open countenance, that in no manner could we do him injury." "Let me meet him !" said Bruce. At their interview Bruce advanced this offer—"Support me, and take my estates ; or give me your estates, and I will support you." Comyn replied that he must keep his oath to Edward, and Bruce stabbed him.
The ignoble suggestion that Bruce was a sort of horse-stealer as well as a sacrilegious homicide of set purpose, which Mr Lang favours, is in keeping with the opinion, advanced at second-hand, though with evident distrust, by Mr Lang, that William Wallys, pot-house thief, accused of stealing beer at Perth, was none other than William Wallace, patriot!

(b) It is noon when the sun is above Criffel.

* Scott, in describing Bruce at a later period, says :—
    "His locks upon his forehead twine
    Jet black, save where some touch of grey
    Has ta'en the youthful hue away."   *Lord of the Isles.*

identify his youthful companion as Robert Bruce, Lord of Annandale and Carrick! If the orb of day, as poets fancy, evinces sympathy with the mundane scenes it looks upon, it ought, as these two men passed from the street and entered the precincts of the neighbouring church, to have withdrawn momentarily behind a murky cloud, since " a deed of dreadful note " was about to be done, leaving as evidence an altar dappled and desecrated by human blood ; and then it ought to have shone forth with re doubled effulgence—emblematical of the way in which Scotland, as a result of the sacrilegious homicide, was to rise from bondage and darkness into liberty and light.

Angry words fall from both the barons ere they enter by the southern gate into the sanctuary of the Grey Friars ; and it is Comyn, we may be sure, who initiates their walk in that direction, from a belief that the rising rage of Bruce would be calmed down by the sacredness of the place. Instead of this being so, it waxes higher and higher. Bruce by-and-by charges Comyn with having tried to compass his death, and with having, to promote his own selfish ends, sacrificed his country. Comyn prevaricates ; and, as the accusations are emphatically repeated, meets them with a broad denial: the words, " It is a lie !" break from his lips ; and the next moment the dagger of Bruce is at his heart. Comyn falls—never, alas, so " red " before, now that the crimson tide of life is flowing over his prostrate frame. Under the influence of overmastering passion, Bruce had thus perpetrated the fatal deed ; and his demeanour and speech betray regret—remorse, as he hurries out of the sacred edifice.

To two friends—Roger de Kirkpatrick (great-grandson of Ivon) and Sir John de Lindsay—who had gone in search of him, and make inquiries, suggested by his hasteful strides and troubled look, he says, " I must be gone, for I doubt I have slain Comyn "—a statement which does not fill them with dismay, as he perhaps anticipated. Kirkpatrick, on the contrary, seems rather elated by the intelligence, and savagely rejoins : " You doubt ? then I'll mak siccar !"* Rushing in with his companion, he finds the bleeding, unconscious Comyn behind the high altar, whither he had been borne by the horror-stricken monks, and stabs him repeatedly— old Sir Robert Comyn, who had at the first alarm hurried to the spot, making a bootless effort to defend his brother's son, only to share his fate.

The clash of the weapons and the wail of the friars brought a crowd of people to the church and its environs ; and as soon as it was generally known that the Red Comyn and his aged relative had been slain, their friends cried out for vengeance. Bruce and his friends were thus put upon their defence. Swords were drawn by both sides, the burial-ground of the Monastery becoming the

* Appendix E.

theatre of battle. The struggle was sanguinary, though brief, and ended with the thorough defeat of the Badenoch party, and of the few English soldiers who assisted them.

The Earl of Carrick was thus, step by step, led to abandon a policy of compromise and procrastination for one of decision and vigour. His flight for life from London—his affray with Comyn —its fatal issue, which he had not premeditated—the encounter that ensued, bringing him into direct collision with the English— their overthrow, and that of the Comynites : all these incidents, like so many links in the chain of destiny, bound him over to a bold line of action. He entered Dumfries without any fixed resolve—ready, perhaps, if others led the way, and favourable circumstances ripened their projects, to join them in striking a blow for Scotland's freedom and the crown ; but the events of the last few hours, culminating on those that immediately preceded them, so mixed up his country's interests with his own that they became henceforth inseparable ; and instant war, open and undisguised, was alike the dictate of self-defence and of patriotism.

If Bruce, after the conflict at the Monastery, had time for thought at all, we may well suppose that some such reflections as are here expressed passed across his mind. We find him instantly afterwards acting in accordance with them. The sacred fane built by the pious Devorgilla was the scene of the first incident in this day's drama of death—its chief victim her own near relative ; the " still and peaceful " churchyard attached to it became tumultuous with the second act ; and the third and crowning one changed a quiet court of justice into a place of blood and strife. The conquering party of Bruce surged onwards to the Castle, in which the judges were still sitting ; but some of the discomfited fugitives had gone there before them, carrying the astounding news of the revolt, and preparing the court and garrison in some degree for what was to occur. To close the gates, and man the walls with such few soldiers as remained, were all the defensive steps that could be taken. "Since the gates are closed, and we have no engines to beat them open, let us try fire !" "Fire ! fire !" was shouted by some of the assailants, and the words were taken up by all. The potent element—better key to the rusty locks than any smith of the burgh could have forged—was soon brought to bear upon the huge oaken gates ; and as these began to crackle with the heat, and their utter destruction was seen to be only a question of time, the men of war and of law, who constituted the garrison, agreed to surrender at discretion, and did so before much blood was spilt.* Whilst that day's sun, which had looked upon many extraordinary scenes in Dumfries, hung above the Nick (or Pass) of Benerick, before finally sinking behind the neighbouring ridge to rest, its ruddy gleam irradiated the free standard of

* Hemingford, vol. i., p. 220.

Bruce, as it floated proudly and defiantly from the turrets of the fortress. (a) When it rose on the following day, not an Englishman was to be seen, except such as had fallen into the hands of Bruce : all out of "durance vile" had evacuated the town, taking with them across the Border the tidings of Comyn's death and of Scotland's resurrection.

For about twelve years the Castle of Dumfries had almost continuously been occupied by a foreign force, and the inhabitants of the town, though not subdued, been held in thraldom ; and it must have been with a sense of relief and a feeling of exultation that the people found themselves once more tasting the sweets of liberty—realising the sentiments so beautifully expressed seventy years afterwards by the poet historian of the hero-king :

> " Ah, freedom is a noble thing,
> And can to life a relish bring ;
> Freedom all solace to man gives—
> He lives at ease that freely lives.
> A noble heart may have no ease,
> Nor aught besides that may it please,
> If freedom fail—for 'tis the choice,
> More than the chosen, man enjoys.
> Ah ! he that ne'er yet lived in thrall
> Knows not the weary pains that gall
> The limbs, the soul, of him who 'plains
> In slavery's foul and festering chains :
> If these he knew, I ween right soon
> He would seek back the precious boon
> Of freedom, which he then would prize
> More than all wealth beneath the skies."*

Were we writing a romance instead of a history, we might here introduce a notice of the civic parliament's first meeting after the ever-memorable 10th of February, or report the gossip of the good burghers when they met in the market-place, showing how congratulations were exchanged on account of the expulsion of the common enemy, and the prospects of their country acquiring its independence.   Language of this nature would be freely indulged in by men of all ranks ; the misery of the usurpation— the successful manner in which it had been assailed—the boldness of the young baron, on whom the mantle of Wallace appeared to have fallen—the peril in which he was placed by arraying against himself not only the might of the English monarch and the revengeful fury of Comyn's friends but the thunderbolts of the Pope—the chances of the town being again plundered and taken by the Southrons, and also of being anathematized wholesale because of the bloody deed which had defiled its altars : all these topics would doubtless be discussed at the council board and in the streets ; but as no record exists of the language used on the

(a) In February the sun sets very much lower down than Benerick, as seen from Dumfries.

* Modernised from Barbour's Bruce, Book i.

occasion, that must just be left to the fancy of the reader. Forebodings of coming disaster would, we may suppose, mingle with
and check the existing joy ; and full surely dark clouds were to
obscure the firmament, and blot out for a time the sun of freedom
that was now brightly shining.

We pause not to analyse the act by which the Scottish hero
was so suddenly thrown upon his own resources. Some have
called it murder ; but even in modern times, when human life
wears a sacredness of which our ancestors knew little, such a deed
would be reckoned justifiable homicide. It is clear, we think, that
it was unpremeditated ; if Bruce had deliberately resolved to slay
Comyn, he would certainly never have followed him into the
church, but would have escaped the guilt of sacrilege—then
deemed of a deeper dye than murder itself—by stabbing his victim
in the street, or after decoying him to some private place in the
neighbourhood. Apart altogether from the grand results with
which it is intimately associated, the slaughter of Comyn was an
act that may be palliated, if not defended, by a reference to the
base treachery which provoked the affray in which he fell. If
Comyn had been an honourable rival whom Bruce "with malice
aforethought" had despatched with his dagger, the memory of his
assassin would have been loaded with eternal infamy. But it was
at worst only the "wild justice of revenge," inflicted on the spur
of the moment, under strong provocation. Though these con-
siderations lead us to palliate Bruce's conduct, we cannot without
an emotion of pity call up the figure of the slain ex-Regent, who
had in his day done the State some service, lying beside the Greyfriars' altar all disfigured and gory :—

> " Cut off even in the blossoms of his sin,
> Unhousel'd, disappointed, unanel'd,
> With all his imperfections on his head."

From that bloody scene to the glorious seizure of the Castle of
Dumfries was a bold and rapid transition ; greater still was the
change to the chief actor in both, when, a few weeks afterwards,
he was crowned King of Scotland in the royal palace of Scone—
though he had to battle bravely, and pass through many vicissi-
tudes, eight years longer, before the emblem of sovereignty was
firmly secured upon his brow. But from that hour of doom at
Dumfries, with its baptism of blood, Robert Bruce, amid all other
changes, remained true to the patriotic cause he then for the first
time heartily espoused. Through what trials he was henceforth
fated to pass, let Fordun tell : " His frequent perils ; his retreats ;
the care and weariness by which he was beset ; the hunger and
thirst he had to suffer ; the cold and nakedness to which he was
exposed ; the exile into which he was driven ; the snares and
ambushes from which he escaped ; the seizure, the imprisonment,
and the execution of his nearest and dearest." And then, after

emerging from the furnace, what a king he made— the greatest by
far that ever occupied the Scottish throne ! In view of all the
transcendent events which flowed out of this tragical occurrence
in the Friary, we do not wonder that a Scottish poet, while many
years afterwards surveying the scene, should have given vent to
his feelings in the following impassioned " Ode to Dumfries :"

" A shepherd, who beheld afar the pastures of Dumfries,
Preferred them to Thessalian hills, the fairest lawns of Greece.
Full many a sleek and seemly steer enjoys the flowery fields ;
Fully many an herb, in genial spring, the soil ungrudging yields.
To distant lands her fruitful farms their produce oft convey,
And load the board in England's halls on many a festal day.
Still nobler wealth her valleys give, that wave with golden grain,
Her river bears the gliding sail, mild breezes haunt her main.
Within there stands an ancient pile, which more renown may claim
Than Dian's fanes, or aught that Greece exalts to sacred fame.
Here Comyn false, who sold the realm, and came to share the spoil,
Fell by the sword of valiant Bruce, to stain the hallowed soil.
Scotland ! of all thy famous shrines, let one be dear to thee—
Dumfries, which bore that priceless fruit, the deed that made thee free."* (a)

* The Latin original of this ode is given in Appendix F. It was written by Dr
Arthur Johnston ; and for the above felicitous translation of it we are indebted to the
Rev. William Bennet, Moffat.

(a) Dr Arthur Johnston was of Aberdeenshire. He studied medicine on the
Continent, and obtained his degree at Padua, 1610. After travelling through Germany,
Denmark, and Holland, he settled in France, where he remained for about twenty
years. He wrote elegies on King James and other patrons ; translated the Song of
Solomon into Latin verse ; and published a new version of the Psalms, to rival
Buchanan's. Died at Oxford, aged 54.

CHAPTER X.

THE ENGLISH AGAIN INVADE SCOTLAND—DEFEAT OF BRUCE, AND DISPER-
SION OF THE PATRIOTS—EXECUTION OF HIS BROTHER-IN-LAW, SIR
CHRISTOPHER SETON, AT DUMFRIES—HIS WIDOW ERECTS A CHAPEL ON
THE SITE OF THE EXECUTION—CHARTER OF SIR CHRISTOPHER'S CHAPEL
—BRUCE RENEWS THE WAR OF INDEPENDENCE—HIS TRIUMPHS IN
CARRICK, AND SUBSEQUENT REVERSES—DEATH OF EDWARD I.—CROWN-
ING VICTORY OF THE SCOTS AT BANNOCKBURN—KING ROBERT REWARDS
HIS DUMFRIESSHIRE FRIENDS—SUFFERINGS OF THE COUNTY AND ITS
CHIEF TOWN DURING THE WARS OF THE SUCCESSION—BENEFICIAL
INFLUENCE OF THE FOLLOWING FIFTEEN YEARS OF PEACE.

WHEN King Edward heard of the revolution thus initiated at
Dumfries he was filled with astonishment and rage. He was now
" stricken in years ;" and, instead of enjoying the rest that he had
anticipated, he must resume active warfare against the people he
had often beaten but never thoroughly subdued, or see the fruit
of all his past efforts perish. Resolving at once on adopting the
former of those alternatives, he held a solemn, chivalrous festival in
Westminster Hall, at which the Prince of Wales and three hundred squires of high degree received the honour of knighthood—
as if to fit them better for the coming enterprise ; and at the
banquet that ensued, after two swans covered with golden net-
work had been placed upon the board, the King, standing with
uplifted hand, vowed to God and to the sacred birds that he would
forthwith avenge the murder of Comyn, and visit all the rebel
Scots with condign punishment ; that, to propitiate Heaven, he
would afterwards spend his latest days following the standard of
the Cross in Palestine.* All who heard the King approved of his
decision ; and liberal contributions from the clergy and the merchants supplied means for carrying on the new campaign. Aymer
de Valance, Earl of Pembroke, an experienced warrior, was chosen
as the instrument of meditated vengeance. He was appointed
Guardian of Scotland, and at the head of an immense army set
out upon his mission. Perth was his first prize ; and Bruce,
appearing before that town with a comparatively small force,
challenged De Valance to meet him in the open field. On the
following day the English commander intimated his readiness to act
upon this cartel of defiance, that had been given in accordance
with the chivalrous customs of the period. Relying on his promise

to that effect, Bruce drew off his men to the woods of Methven, distant about six miles from Perth: there, in the evening twilight,* they were treacherously attacked by Pembroke at the head of a more numerous force, and put to the rout—Bruce, who was thrice unhorsed in the conflict, escaping with difficulty into the wilds of Athole with the remnant of his army, not more than five hundred men.†

Driven thence by the want of provisions, they passed into the low country of Aberdeenshire, where Bruce was joined by his Queen and other ladies resolved on sharing the adverse fortunes of their lords. There, but momentary rest awaited them. The band of fugitives who formed the forlorn hope of Scottish patriotism had to retire, menaced by a large body of the enemy. We next find them on the bleak mountains of Breadalbane, fishing and hunting for a subsistence, and at times cheating hunger with such wild berries as the woods afforded : then on the borders of Argyleshire, where the Red Comyn's relative, M'Dougal of Lorn,‡ desirous of revenging his kinsman, repulsed the party, after a sanguinary conflict : then the small island of Rachrin, on the Irish coast, gave welcome refuge in winter to the unfortunate King of Scots and a few of his adherents—his Queen and his daughter Marjory obtaining an asylum in the Chapel of St Duthus, at Tain,§ and their female companions shelter in the Castle of Kildrummie, then held by the King's brother, Nigel Bruce.

But no fortress was strong enough, no religious structure holy enough, to stand between these illustrious refugees and the vindictive rage of the English monarch. Kildrummie was stormed by his troops. The Earl of Ross, having neither reverence for St Duthus nor regard for his Queen, tore her and the Princess Marjory from their violated sanctuary, and placed them in the keeping of Pembroke. A long course of close confinement in England was assigned to the royal captives. The Countess of Buchan, who had placed Bruce upon the coronation chair at Scone, was immured in a cage set on an outer turret of Berwick Castle ; and one of Bruce's sisters was similarly treated at the Castle of Roxburgh. In this barbarous way were the Scottish heroines treated who fell into the hands of the English ; and it need scarcely be added that the captive patriots of the sterner sex had no mercy shown to them. Young Nigel Bruce, Sir Simon Fraser, the veteran companion of Wallace, and the brave Earl of Atholle, then in the prime of manhood, are only a few of the dis-

---

* Chronicles of Abingdon, quoted by Tyrrel, vol. iii., p. 172.

† Barbour, Book ii.

‡ M'Dougal, as we learn from Barbour, was married to Comyn's aunt.

§ " The Chapel of St Duthus enjoyed the privilege of sanctuary during the middle ages. Though roofless and neglected for four centuries, it is so strongly cemented in its masonry as to remain in a surprising degree of preservation."—Fullarton's Gazetteer of Scotland, vol. ii., p. 778.

tinguished victims of Edward's cruelty who perished on the scaffold at Berwick, Dumfries, Newcastle, and London.*

It was at the close of 1306, less than a year after the slaughter of Comyn, that some of the executions referred to took place in Dumfries. During the interval, the Castle and other strengths in the vicinity won by the Scots had been retaken by their enemies ; and at the time when Bruce was struggling for bare life in the North Nithsdale lay once more beneath "the proud foot of the conqueror." We read of no tumult occurring on that account in the town—of no attempt at rescue being made when three illustrious patriots were led forth to their doom. The dread apparatus of death was erected on the Gallows Hill, a high natural eminence situated beyond the walls on the north-east of the burgh, so that the inhabitants might have an opportunity of seeing how the usurper rewarded what his judges called rebellion, and of profiting by the spectacle. The Dumfriesians of that day were, unfortunately, too much accustomed to such sights. They would, nevertheless, be dreadfully shocked by these executions—one of the sufferers being none other than Sir Christopher Seton, the brother-in-law of their King ; a most valiant warrior, who at the battle of Methven had rescued Bruce by felling his captor, Sir Philip de Mowbray, to the ground.† He was accused of treason in general, and more especially of having been present at the slaughter of Comyn. On being sought for by the English, he took refuge in the strong Castle of Loch Doon,‡ situated on the frontier between Galloway and Ayrshire, and which belonged to Bruce, as Lord of Carrick. Here he might have remained safe, had not Sir Gilbert de Corrie, hereditary keeper of the fortress, given him up to his enemies, by whom he was placed in fetters, hurried to Dumfries,

---

* Rymer, vol. i., p. 996 ; and Prynne, p. 1156.

† " The King him selff alsua,
    Wes set in till full hard assay,
    Throw Schyr Philip the Mowbray,
    That raid till him full hardyly,
    And hynt [seized] his rengye, and syne 'gan cry,
    ' Help ! help ! I have the new maid King !'
    With that come gyrdand in a lyng,
    Crystall of Seytoun, quhen he sua
    Saw the King sesyt with his fa ;
    And to Philip sic rout he raucht,
    That tho he wes of mekill maucht,
    He gert him galay disyly ;
    And hard till erd gan fullyly,
    Ne war he hynt him by his sted,
    Then off his hand the brydill yhed."
                         Barbour's Bruce, Book ii.

‡ Evidence in a remission under the Great Seal.—Vide Tytler's History of Scotland, vol. i., p. 42. Loch Doon is a beautiful sheet of clear water, about eleven miles in length and one mile in breadth, possessing a gravelly bottom and beach, bounded nearly half its length on the east by the parish of Carsphairn, and the remaining part on the west of the parishes of Dalmellington and Straiton. About half-way betwixt the Galloway and Carrick sides are the remains of an old castle, built in the octagonal form, and situated upon a rock which is surrounded by the deep waters of the lake. This ruin is the remnant of a strong fort, which, from its situation, must have been impregnable before the use of gunpowder.—Nicholson's History of Galloway, Appendix vol. i., p. 17.

and there tried, condemned, and sentenced to be hanged and then beheaded.* Seton, with his two companions, suffered accordingly ; and, no doubt, in compliance with the usual custom, their severed heads would be held up by the officiating executioner as a warning to the onlookers, who would, however, be more horror-stricken than terrified by the spectacle, and eagerly long for the day when the blood of the martyred patriots, crying for vengeance, would not cry in vain. When the period of retribution came round, and its demands were satisfied and peace was restored, Sir Christopher Seton's widow, Christiana Bruce, erected a chapel on the site of his execution, "in honorum crucis Dominici ;" and in which, by her brother's liberality, provision was made for celebrating mass for the soul of her departed husband.

The charter endowing the chapel was granted by Bruce on the 31st of November, 1323, when he was reigning as undisputed King of Scotland. It sets forth, that Christopher de Seton, our beloved soldier, having been put to death in our service, and our dear sister Christiana, his spouse, having, on the place where he suffered death, near Dumfries, founded a certain chapel in honour of the Holy Rood, be it known unto her, that for the favour and affection borne by us to the said Christopher, in his life, we have given and confirmed to a chaplain, in the same chapel, to celebrate mass for ever for the soul of the said Christopher, one hundred shillings sterling (centum solidos striviling) of annual value ; the same to be payable by the hands of our Sheriff of Dumfries and his bailies, from the rents of the barony of Carlaverock, at Whitsunday and Martinmas, in equal proportions. Wherefore we command our said Sheriff and his bailies to pay in full, and for ever, one hundred shillings out of the said annual rents for the aforesaid purpose, and to enter the same in their accounts with us and our heirs.†

Sir Christopher's Chapel, originated under such mournfully-interesting circumstances, is said to have been a beautiful little Gothic building of oblong shape, cornered by pointed buttresses, and having a richly-decorated oriel window. It was further endowed with a small portion of the surrounding land, in order that the object of its erection might be fully carried into effect.‡

As Comyn's kinsmen had (more out of hatred to Bruce than from any other motive) given material assistance in crushing the patriotic movement, they rose into high favour with King Edward : in recognition of their services, they received from him a portion of the royal fugitive's forfeited estates ; while the Earl of Hereford was rewarded with the lordship of Annandale, and Henry de Percy

---

* Barbour, p. 52.
† A copy of the original document, of which the outline is given above, is printed in the Appendix G.
‡ As is noticed more particularly in a subsequent chapter, a modern church, St. Mary's, occupies the site of the old chapel on the Crystal Mount.

with the earldom of Carrick. The English and recreant Scots, to
whom the conquered country was parcelled out, held but a feeble
and temporary tenure of it. Bruce, though an exile, and without
an army, still hoped for better times, and waited for a favourable
opportunity to re-assert his country's rights. While under shelter
at Rachrin, he lived so obscurely that a rumour of his death was
current. When it reached Edward, who was suffering from ill-
health at Carlisle, the news would have a reviving effect upon the
inexorable monarch ; and he might then flatter himself into the
belief that, though he had not turned Scotland into a wilderness,
he had done what was better—had completely subdued it, since, if
there were any " rebels " left in the country, they had now neither
head nor hope.

The winter of 1306 was indeed a cheerless season for Scotland.
One dark night in the following February, a beacon-fire was seen
blazing from a height near the Castle of Turnberry, in Carrick : it
was viewed with apprehension by the English garrison of that
fortress, and with joyful solicitude by the illustrious fugitive, now
in the Isle of Arran, to whom it was a signal that he might venture across, and renew the war of independence on his own
ancestral territory. He had only about one hundred and eighty
followers, including, however, his brother Edward, Lennox,
Lindsay, Kirkpatrick of Closeburn, the "Good" Sir James
Douglas (whose father, William, had died some years previously
in an English prison), and a few other trusty barons.

" With such small force did Bruce at last
The die for death or empire cast."*

Crossing over the intermediate sea in boats, they made a sudden
onslaught on the English soldiers quartered in the hamlet of
Turnberry, and, after putting most of them to the sword, retired
with rich booty to the neighbouring mountains, in order to recruit
their strength. Percy found his position in Turnberry Castle so
critical that he soon afterwards evacuated it ; Douglas recovered
from the enemy his hereditary barony of Douglasdale, in the
neighbourhood ; and Bruce defeated the forces of Pembroke at
Louden Hill. Thus Carrick was freed from the English : the die
cast by Bruce turned up favourably ; the beacon-light which led
him to the coast of Ayrshire proving the harbinger of Scotland's
deliverance. Two months afterwards, an event occurred which
inflicted a greater blow on the English usurpation than could
have been given to it by a series of defeats in the field. When
Edward heard that the audacious chief, who was said to have died
in exile, had re-appeared as a successful leader of the rebellious
Scots, the King resolved, though emaciated by disease and premature old age, to lead personally an overwhelming army against
him. A great military host having at his summons mustered in

* Scott's " Lord of the Isles."

Carlisle, he left the litter on which he had for previous days been carried, mounted his war-steed, reviewed his troops, and, as the trump of battle sounded in his ear, visions of fame and conquest—of the rebel Scots trodden under foot, crushed, exterminated—came up before his heated fancy.   These were the convulsive efforts, the feverish dreams of a dying man.   A weary march of six miles with his army brought him to the village of Burgh-upon-Sands ; and there, in sight of the land across the Solway which he he had deluged with blood, and vainly devoted to a new host of horrors, the unhappy King expired—his disappointments and hopes alike at an end : no more wars after this closing struggle—no more victories, now that all-conquering Death was turning him into dust.

But not into dust in the ordinary vulgar fashion. His last request to his son and barons was, that his body should not be buried, but boiled in a cauldron till the flesh fell from the bones ; and that the skeleton should be borne with them into Scotland, and kept above ground till the country was wholly subdued.   A more striking illustration of the King's implacable temper could not have been given.   His ruling passion was not only "strong in death," but he wished to make it overleap the grave.   Edward II. soon found out that the hideous legacy of his father's relics was likely to be troublesome, and associated with a difficult, if not an impracticable condition ; and before the conquest of the Scots had been a step advanced, all that remained of their relentless enemy was mingling with kindred dust in the royal sepulchre at West-minster.   On his tomb were placed the words : "Here lies the Hammer of the Scottish nation ;" but the blows he struck re-bounded as from an anvil—the recoil proving in the end deadly to himself.

When Edward I. expired, Bruce and Scotland began to breathe more freely.   His death was like the removal of an incubus from the breast of the prostrate nation—or rather of a vampire that had for twenty years been draining its heart's blood.

The new King of England was vain, weak, and vacillating. He made a sort of royal progress through Nithsdale, marching to Cumnock, then returning to Carlisle, without doing anything towards the accomplishment of his father's darling wish. When at Dumfries, in August, 1307, he granted the earldom of Cornwall to his favourite, Piers de Gaveston, as is shown by the address of the patent.   At Tynwald, on the 30th of the same month, he issued a new commission to Aymer de Valance, whereby all the King's bishops, abbots, priors, earls, barons, knights, bailies, and faithful subjects were informed that his dear cousin, the noble Earl of Pembroke, had been appointed Viceroy, "nostrum locum tenens," of Scotland during the royal pleasure, and been authorised to extend mercy to all rebel Scots who offered to submit, excepting

those who had been concerned in the death of "Johan Comyn," or
were "counsellors or assenters in occasioning the late daring
war."* Quite in accordance with the monarch's fickle character,
we find him, on the 13th of September next, superseding Pembroke
by John de Bretagne, Earl of Richmond.

The capricious weakness of the young King made Bruce
stronger by comparison : it alienated from the former many of his
own subjects, and rendered the war distasteful to them ; and not
a few Scottish barons, who had been overawed by the mental as
well as military power of the father, were led to despise the son,
and throw off his feeble yoke. At this period the Castle of Dumfries was held by the English, Bruce having long before been
forced to give it up ; and, for about the seventh time since the
date of the first invasion, the town and neighbouring territory
changed masters. But the period for their ultimate deliverance
was drawing near. Since the victory at Louden Hill, in May,
1307, Bruce's career, in spite of a few temporary checks, had been
"upwards and onwards." A great step was made towards the
liberation of the South by the success of an expedition led by his
brother Edward into Galloway ; which province was subject to
the English, not in virtue of any conquest, but because its chiefs
had given a qualified submission to the usurping King, owing in a
great degree to their hatred of Bruce.

Twice the gallant Prince defeated the Gallovidians, with their
English ally, John St John. He then, with characteristic impetuosity, stormed the Castle of Buittle, seized several other
fortlets, expelled their garrisons, native or foreign, and did not
sheathe his successful sword till the whole of Galloway had submitted to his brother, Robert I. The province thus annexed to
the Crown was given in feu to its conqueror ; and in this way
another heavy blow was inflicted on the Baliols and Comyns, who
owned extensive estates in that part of the kingdom.

Six years after the time when King Robert opened up a passage by fire into the Castle of Dumfries (on the fateful 10th of
February, 1306), the ring of his battle-axe on its gates again
demanded admission, in language which the Southron garrison,
under Henry de Bello Monte,† could neither misunderstand nor
refuse.‡ In reply to a similar summons, the fortress of Dalswinton also surrendered ; and in due time the Castles of Lochmaben
and Tibbers were wrested from the enemy.§ Carlaverock held
out against the patriot King till the following year (1313) ; and,
curious to relate, its lord, Sir Eustace de Maxwell, seems to have

---

* Rymer's Fœdera, vol. ii., p. 4.

† Henri de Bello Monte, Constabul Castri sui de Dumfres, vel ejus locum tenenti
ibidem saltim.—Rotuli Scotiæ, 1311.

‡ Fordun, vol. iv., p. 1606.

§ Dalrymple's Annals, p. 36.   Redpath's Border History, p. 240.

been subsidised by Edward II., as existing records show that, on the 30th of April, 1312, the English sovereign agreed to grant him £22 yearly for keeping the stronghold.* Sir Eustace, however, saw reason to repent of the bargain that had been made ; and the grant, if paid once, was not paid a second time. In about a year after the above date, he gave up the castle to his rightful King ; and with its tenure the last remaining tie that bound Nithsdale to the tyrannical invaders was broken The district became free ; Annandale also received full deliverance ; and on the 24th of June, 1314, the rest of Scotland was liberated, and the independ· ence of the kingdom was triumphantly secured, by the glorious victory of Bannockburn.

After a brief rest from the protracted toils of war, the King proceeded to regulate the internal affairs of the country. In doing so, he proved as wise in the cabinet as he was heroic in the field. So many forfeitures had taken place during the struggle with England, that he found himself in the position of one who has conquered a foreign territory, and is free to recognise the bravery of his followers by dividing it amongst them. With the extensive lands that reverted to the Crown, Bruce had the means of amply rewarding the chiefs who had been true to him and their country during the contest.

Throughout Dumfriesshire nearly a total change was made in the ownership of property. The Comyns were thoroughly dispossessed. Dalswinton Castle and manor were given to Walter Stewart, third son of Sir John Stewart of Bonkill, who fell at the battle of Falkirk. To two distinguished chiefs the King was particularly bountiful—Sir James Douglas and Sir Thomas Randolph : they had shared in many of his toils, they had suffered much in his service, the final defeat of the enemy was greatly owing to their valour ; and, since they had experienced with him " the iron scourge, the torturing hour " of adversity, he freely shared with them the honours of the triumph. Douglasdale was restored to its rightful owner—the "gude Lord James," as Barbour fondly calls him, getting also the whole of Eskdale, besides other lands in Dumfriesshire. Randolph was the lineal descendant of the Celtic thane who ruled Dumfries in the preceding century. He was also nephew to the King—endeared to him by blood relationship, but still more by his lovable character and his martial prowess. He shines in the verse of Barbour as a paragon knight —bold, liberal, witty, social, amorous, maintaining "rychtwysness," detesting " falset, tresoun, and felony ;"

> " With visage braid, pleasant, and fayr,
> Curtaiss at point, and debonayr."

How much the King appreciated this " noble of Nature " may be inferred from the favours lavished upon him. He had been some

* Dalrymple, p. 96.

108 HISTORY OF DUMFRIES.

years before created Earl of Moray ; he was now made Lord of
Man and Annandale,* Keeper of Lochmaben Castle, and, as heir of
Dunegal, Lord of Stranith, he received back the barony of
Morton ;† while, for his further enrichment, he was presented
with the half of the barony of Urr, which Henry de Percy had
held for a time by the " right of might." Several minor changes
were made : a charter, dated in the sixteenth year of the King's
reign, conferred the lands of Kilnorduff, Torthorwald, and Roucan
on Humphrey Kirkpatrick ; another of the same date gave the
estate of Penersax to Stephen Kirkpatrick ; and by one dated
Lochmaben, 4th June, 1320, Thomas, the son of Sir Roger, received
the manor of Bridburgh, in recognition of his own and his father's
services. Wherever, in other cases, there was fidelity to acknowledge, or little fault to find, the old families regained their former
position. Even Sir Eustace Maxwell, though he had long remained in the interest of England, was liberally dealt with. He
had, as we have seen, joined the patriots some time before their
closing victory ; and Bruce, taking this circumstance into account,
gave him back his lands and Castle of Carlaverock.

From the date of Bannockburn till the King's death, a period
of fully fifteen years, the nation enjoyed almost unbroken repose,
and a prosperity that reminded the old inhabitants of the golden
days of Alexander III. To no part of the country was this season
of peace more acceptable than to Dumfriesshire. Some counties
of Scotland suffered comparatively little from the English usurpation, on account of being remote from the enemy's usual route of
march ; but, owing to their frontier position, the districts watered
by the Esk, the Annan, and the Nith became the highway of the
invading armies, and a debatable territory, on which for fully
twenty years the destructive controversy of the sword went on
with little intermission. No industrial employment could be
attended to. The fields were left untilled—few herds or flocks,
and little produce of the soil, would be left after the Southron
hordes had repeatedly harried the country ; and how the inhabitants managed to ward off the attacks of famine remains to us a
mystery. The produce of the woods and rivers would be their
chief dependence ; and the license which war gives to plunder
would be used by many, in the absence of more legitimate means,
for procuring a livelihood. As episodes in the war, there would
be numerous freebooting forays into Cumberland, leading to re-

* " Robert I. being now king, all the lands that remained in his own natural possession were thought to have merged in the sovereigns of Scotland as Crown property.
The King himself seems to have entertained this opinion ; for in one of his latest
charters, granted by him in favour of ' Thomas le Clerk de Carruthers,' of the lands of
Moffat, the 'reddendum' (a pair of spurs) is appointed to be made 'apud manorum
nostrum,' or at our manor (of Lochmaben), thus speaking of it as royal property. But
as this, in strict law, might be questionable, Acts of Parliament were passed, in
November, 1357, annexing the lands to the Crown ; whereby they became unalienable,
unless with the consent of Parliament."—Graham's Lochmaben Five Hundred Years
Ago, p. 79.

† Caledonia, vol. iii., p. 64.

taliatory expeditions, all combining, with the war itself, to reduce society on both sides of the Border to a chaotic state. It was part of the invaders' atrocious policy to terrify the people by burning or otherwise destroying such goods as they could not carry off with them ; and by this procedure they sometimes over-reached themselves.

When the predatory forces of the English were at times reduced to a state of privation, the people whom they ravaged must have suffered still more severely. Municipal government in Dumfries would, in those fighting days, dwindle down to a dead letter ; the town would be ruled by martial law, administered now by John St John, after the English fashion—then by Wallace, Bruce, or other Scottish baron, in a milder form—then once more by the rough-handed invaders : so that the Provost, and his colleagues of the Council, if such officials were chosen at all, in the terms of King William's charters, would have little say in the management of town affairs. Dumfries, in fact, would be turned into a camp ; her craftsmen, during two-thirds of a generation, would be unable, except by fits and starts, to pursue the occupations which flourished in the "piping times of peace"—her merchants would have to close their premises for want of customers, or to keep out those unwelcome ones who took goods on trust, never intending to pay for them. Of all the industrial orders, the smiths alone—whose proud boast it was, that

> " By hammer in hand
> All arts do stand "—

would drive a prosperous trade ; the others fretting in idleness, or doing military service—many of them for, and some of them against, the interests of their country.

During the auspicious reign which preceded these times of trouble Dumfries was a growing town. But the English usurpation checked its progress. With many houses reduced to ruin—with lines of streets partially burned down—with its Castle half dismantled, its other external defences sadly perforated—it must, at the close of the war, have looked like the ghost of the town which the good King Alexander is said to have viewed with admiration when directing from it his enterprise against the Isle of Man. As sleep "knits up the ravelled sleeve of care," so peace filled up the broken walls of the burgh, and rebuilt its shattered tenements : and if ever Robert Bruce, after reigning in glory for a few years, had the curiosity to visit his native district, and the place where the first blow for freedom was struck, he would rejoice in the verdant aspect of the country, and in the revived prosperity of the town when free from the presence of "grim-visaged war." Happy were those fifteen years of repose for Scotland at large. Scarcely, however, had the body of the illustrious Bruce turned cold when the wasting fires of war were lighted up anew.

CHAPTER XI.

As guarantees for continued peace, a solemn treaty had been
signed by the belligerents at Northampton. David, the young
son and heir of Bruce, had been betrothed to Joan, sister of the
English sovereign, Edward III. ; and an unqualified recognition of
the independence of Scotland had been given by that monarch.
Whence, then, the new conflagration that swept over the northern
kingdom in 1332 ? The ostensible object of the invasion was to
set up a rival to David Bruce in the person of another youth,
Edward, son of the deceased John Baliol ; but its chief motive
power was the ambition of the English King, and its chief promoters the Lords Beaumont and De Wake, whom the late King
Robert had deprived of their lands in Scotland, on the plea that
as English subjects they were likely to prove disloyal to his
authority. De Wake claimed as his rightful inheritance a piece
of territory in the south-east of Dumfriesshire, which soon afterwards became famous as " The Debatable Land." That it originally formed part of Scotland is unquestionable ;* and, indeed, a
large portion of Cumberland was for several centuries prior to the
reign of Alexander II. attached to that kingdom, except for a
short period, when William the Conqueror took it from the Scots,
and divided it among his Norman followers, granting the barony
of Lydall, or Liddel, to a knight named De Estuteville, from whom

---

* In a treaty between the kingdoms, of date 1249, it was stipulated that when an
inhabitant of the one charged an inhabitant of the other with the theft of cattle, the
person accused was either to vindicate his character by single combat with his accuser,
or bring the stolen animals to the frontier streams of Tweed or Esk, and drive them
into the waters—a clear proof that England at that time had no claim to the Debatable
Land. See T. J. Carlyle's " Debatable Land " (Dumfries Antiquarian Society's Transactions, 1865-66).

it descended by marriage to the De Wakes. This barony comprised the lands of Esk, Arthuret, Stubhill, Carwindlow, Speirike, Randolph, Livington, Easton, North Easton, and Breconhill, all on the eastern or Cumberland side of the Esk. According to the Treaty of Northampton, signed by the English and Scottish Commissioners on the 4th of May, 1328, it was stipulated that De Beaumont should receive the lands and earldom of Buchan, claimed by him in right of his wife ; and that De Wake should be re-established in his barony of Liddel. Randolph, however, who had been made Regent on the death of Bruce, shrunk from giving effect to the agreement :* nor is it surprising that he hesitated, since both of these barons were avowedly opposed to the independence of the kingdom—had leagued themselves against it with Baliol ; and if Buchan fell into the hands of one English lord, it would afford an easy landing-place for an invading enemy ; while if another were allowed to settle down on the Scottish side of the Esk, the Western frontier would be deprived of its chief natural defence.

Strange to say, though the leaders of the inroad had only a small force, numbering at first barely five hundred men, they succeeded in temporarily overturning the fabric of Scottish independence, which had been built up at such a vast outlay of blood and treasure. Landing at Kinghorn, on the Frith of Forth, they defeated the Earl of Fife, who vainly endeavoured to drive them back to their ships or into the sea. They then, after being strongly reinforced, routed a much larger body, under the Earl of Mar, on Dupplin Moor ; and, as a consequence of these and other triumphs, young Baliol was crowned Deputy-King of Scots at Scone on the 24th of September, 1332. (a) The reader may well wonder at this result, brought about by such slender means, and that, too, in the short space of three weeks ; but it would have been impossible had not the invaders been greatly strengthened by the native Baliol party, still powerful in Scotland, and had not the best of Bruce's generals been, like himself, mouldering in the grave. Sir James Douglas had fallen a year before in an encounter with the Saracens, when bearing his royal master's heart to the Holy Sepulchre (b) ; the gallant Regent, too, was gone ; and vainly, in view of the aggressive hosts, might the Scottish cavalier exclaim,

> " Oh ! Douglas, for thy leading wand,
>   Fierce Randolph, for thy speed ;
> Oh ! for one hour of Wallace wight,
>   Or well-skilled Bruce, to rule the fight,
> And cry, ' Saint Andrew and our right !' "†

* Rymer's Fœdera, vol. iv., p. 461.
(a) Not Deputy-King, but King.
(b) Not so. Against the " enemies of God " were the terms of the commission entrusted to him.
† Scott's Marmion."

After a brief, inglorious pause, men actuated by the spirit of these heroes appeared upon the scene, to give a new current to public events ; and once more the tide of battle, surging in Dumfriesshire, turned again in favour of freedom.   Baliol, at his coronation, came under an obligation to rule the country in the name of his patron and liege lord, Edward III.;(a) and, when passing southward for the purpose of extending his influence, he solemnly ratified this engagement at Roxburgh.   He knew that he had no chance of retaining the crown many months except by support from England : that having been assured to him, as the price of his country's independence, his mind was set at ease ; and, when lying encamped on the Burgh Moor, at Annan, lapped in fancied security, he indulged in lofty aspirations, unconscious that an agency was at work that would cause them to topple over like a castle of cards.   Sir Andrew Murray, of Bothwell,* who married Christopher Seton's widow, and was therefore the brother-in-law of King Robert, having been chosen Regent by the supporters of the Brucian family, proved worthy of his position at this crisis of the national cause.

A thousand horsemen under Archibald Douglas, Lord of Galloway, third brother of Sir James Douglas, John Randolph, Earl of Moray, son of the deceased Regent, and Sir Simon Fraser, the tried friend of Bruce, were sent by Murray into Annandale, in order to watch the movements of Baliol.   On arriving in the neighbourhood of Moffat, they were apprised by scouts that the puppet-king had turned his camp into a court, and that military discipline had given way to revelry and mirth.   This was welcome news to the patriots.   That very afternoon, the 16th of December they were hurrying down the dale as fast as their fleet steeds could bear them ; and, as they drew near Annan, were guided to their destination by the glimmering lights, and also, perhaps, by the bacchanalian sounds that emanated from the encampment. Stealthily crossing " Annan water, wide and deep," they fell upon the enemy about midnight with the force of an avalanche.   King Baliol was in bed, literally dreaming over again, it may be, the visions that had delighted him in his waking hours.   Shouts of defiance, screams of terror, shrieks of agony, mad cries for mercy —could these sounds be the discordant medley of a hideous dream, following in horrible contrast upon the pleasant fancies that had preceded them ?   The royal sleeper awoke to find his camp assailed by a merciless foe, and his followers, who had on the previous day vowed to him everlasting fidelity, making but a feeble resistance —able, indeed, to offer scarcely any, as they were only half awake,

---

(a) It was not a condition of the coronation that Baliol should rule Scotland in the name of the English king.

* The Regent, like the Murrays of Cockpool and of Murraythwaite, was descended from Freskin, a Flemish gentleman who settled in Linlithgowshire during the twelfth century.

and many of them naked, with neither sword nor buckler. Short and fearful was the fight ; long and more terrible the slaughter. With scarcely the rag of a royal robe to cover him from the cold, the miserable mimic of a king threw himself upon a cart-horse, unfurnished with either saddle or bridle, and in this fashion galloped for bare life fifteen miles, stopping not till he reached Carlisle.* His brother Henry, Lord Walter Comyn, and many other persons of rank, were slain in the fray or during the flight, with many hundreds of common soldiers—the assailants losing very few of their number.†

This visitation would have finished Baliol had not the English monarch set him up anew. Next March he was again at the head of an English army, invading Scotland, and laying siege to the Castle of Berwick. While thus engaged Sir Archibald Douglas, with three thousand men, made a diversion on the south side of the Border, and returned laden with booty, after ravaging the whole district to the extent of thirty miles. With the view of paying him back in kind, Sir Anthony de Lucy, of Cockermouth, led a considerable force into Dumfriesshire. They plundered the country far and wide, till the stout Castle of Lochmaben, that had often before done good service, stopped their desolating march. Pity that its keeper, the gallant " Flower of Chivalry," Sir William Douglas of Liddesdale, did not remain under its shelter, instead of sallying forth as he did, and giving the invaders battle in the open plain. He was taken prisoner in the engagement that ensued, together with a hundred men of rank ; and upwards of a hundred and sixty of his soldiers were left dead on the disastrous field.‡ Among the slain were Sir Humphrey de Bois, of Dryfesdale (supposed by Dalrymple to be the ancestor of Hector Boece, the historian), (a) Sir Humphry Jardine, and Sir William Carlyle, of Torthorwald. Lucy, satisfied with his success, proceeded with his captives and spoil to Carlisle §—the city where the goods stolen from Dumfriesshire in those days were generally resetted. The prisoned " Flower," loaded with fetters, pined in Carlisle

---

* Wyntoun, vol. ii., p. 159 ; Hume's House of Douglas, p. 80 ; and Redpath's Border History, p. 302.

† About a mile from Moffat, on the side of the Beattock Road, may be seen an antique triple memorial, termed " the Three Stan'in' Stanes," which some authorities consider were raised on the site of this battle, to commemorate the officers slain there on the English side. Such an idea is quite untenable. While Buchanan states that the patriot army rendezvoused " prope Mophetam," near Moffat, he does not say that the conflict took place in the vicinity of that village ; and the Chronicle of Lanercost distinctly fixes the locality thus—"Usque ad villam Annandiæ, que est in marchia inter regna," the town of Annan, which is on the march between the kingdoms. Besides, it is assumed in the idea that the nobles who fell were buried on the field, whereas Baliol obtained the bodies, and would doubtless cause them to be interred in consecrated ground. " The Three Stan'in' Stanes " are probably of Druidical origin.

‡ Redpath, p. 302.

(a) Boece, in his Historia, edition of 1574, fo. 323, claims descent from Hugo Boetius, cujus pater ad Duplyn occubuerat Baro Drisdaliæ. This battle was fought at Dornock or Sandywath, not at Lochmaben. See paper by Mr G. Neilson in Transactions Dumfries and Galloway Antiquarian Society, 1895-6.

§ Walsingham, p. 132.

Q

Castle more than two years, but, unweakened by confinement, proved to be of the genuine thistle kind in many a subsequent encounter with the English.

The patriot cause suffered another serious blow when the Regent, Sir Andrew Murray, was made prisoner, in an abortive attempt to surprise the Castle of Roxburgh ; and it was almost entirely crushed when Sir Archibald Douglas, his successor in the Regency, after a wasting raid into England, recrossed the Tweed, for the purpose of relieving Berwick, attacked an intervening army, strongly posted on Halidon Hill, and was thoroughly de feated with great slaughter—Douglas himself being mortally wounded, and the Earls of Lennox, Ross, Sutherland, Carrick Monteith, and Athole being numbered among the slain. Baliol's first failure was in these ways redeemed—his disgraceful escapade at Annan was revenged—and his aspirations once more mounted to the zenith.*

At the head of an immense force—twenty-six thousand men in number, it is said—he overran the greater part of Scotland, meeting with little opposition, and subjecting the whole of it, excepting the spots on which stood the Castles of Urquhart, Loch Doon, Lochleven, Kildrummie, and Dumbarton. Even when this was accomplished, he remained but a nominal king. The Scots paid him an unwilling homage : remembering Bannockburn, they never supposed for a moment but that his puppet part would soon be played out. The English, conscious of his indebtedness to them, became voracious in their demands. They had made him a king, and he must show his gratitude for their services, or he might find himself a crownless fugitive some day soon. He gave Lord Henry de Percy Annandale and Moffatdale ; and to enable him to keep them with the strong hand, if need be, the Castle of Lochmaben was added to the grant.† In this way Randolph's lands were disposed of ; and the estates belonging to other Brucian nobles were handed over to other English lords, or those recreant patricians who were base enough to accept a reward for assisting to destroy their nation, and to feast on the honey which the lion's carcase yielded. " More ! we must have more !" was the language of the exorbitant Southrons and their king. Baliol was placed in the position of a necromancer, who, after doing many marvellous feats, and acquiring much wealth, is required, by unceasing sacri- fices, to propitiate the remorseless demon to whom he was indebted for success.

It was not enough that Baliol had become the sworn vassal of Edward III., and had curtailed his own revenue by enriching that monarch's subjects ; he must, over and above that deep humiliation, and these liberal largesses, give over in fee to his liege lord a goodly portion of Scottish land for annexation to

---

* Wyntoun, vol. ii., p. 170.   † Redpath, p. 310.

England, and henceforth to be completely Anglicised. However
mean-spirited Baliol was, he must have been disgusted by these
exactive demands. Though loath to comply with them, he durst
not hazard a refusal. In a Parliament held at Newcastle on the
12th of June, 1334, he, by a solemn legal instrument, invested his
royal master with the ownership of the castle, town, and county
of Berwick ; of the castle, town, and county of Roxburgh ; of the
forts, towns, and forests of Jedburgh, Selkirk, and Ettrick ; of the
city, castle, and county of Edinburgh ; of the constabularies of
Haddington and Linlithgow ; of the town and county of Peebles ;
and, lastly, of the town, castle, and county of Dumfries.* This
most abject and disgraceful partition of the ancient kingdom of
Scotland could not actually be carried out. The "departed spirits
of the mighty dead" vetoed the arrangement : Wallace and Bruce,
though mouldering in the dust, lived in the hearts of their
countrymen, and dictated the nation's protest against the perfidy
of Baliol and the cupidity of the English King.

Edward III. supposed he had succeeded where an abler man
(Edward I.) had failed. Having been invested in his new posses-
sions, he made arrangements for their government—appointing
sheriffs for each district, with Robert de Laudre as Chief Justice,
and assigning to John de Bourdon the important office of General
Chamberlain. One Peter Tilliol—a relative, probably, of the de
Tilliol who ruled over Lochmaben in 1301—was made Sheriff of
Dumfriesshire, and Keeper of the Castle of Dumfries.† To Edward
de Bohun were given Moffatdale, Annandale, and the Castle of
Lochmaben—Percy, their previous English possessor, receiving for
them an equivalent ; and they continued to be held by one or
other of the Bohun family till the expulsion of the Southrons from
the district. Scarcely had these police arrangements been effected
when Sir Andrew Murray, escaping from prison, unfurled the
patriotic flag with such effect that Baliol took to flight from the
country he had betrayed ; and Edward III., dreading that his own
tenure of it might be snapped asunder, passed with an army
through Dumfries towards Glasgow, at the close of 1334—returning, however, in a hurry ; for, though he encountered no military
force, hunger, and the rigour of the season, drove him back over
the Border. Next year he repeated the invasion, carrying desolation into the country as far as Morayshire, and being forced to
retire a second time by the famine he had himself created. For
fully three years longer the war continued, the Scots adopting the
policy, recommended by Bruce, of avoiding pitched battles, and
depending chiefly on guerilla attacks, by which they risked little
and severely harassed the enemy.

* Ibid.

† Fœdera, vol. iv., p. 615 ; also, Rotuli Scotiæ, vol. i., p. 271, in which the following
entry occurs :—" Petrus Tilliol, de officio vice comitatus de Dumfries, et custodia
castri R. ibidem."

In the summer of 1338 Sir Andrew Murray died. He had for some time shared the Regency with Robert Stewart, who, on his death, became sole Regent. Murray had done much to keep alive the flame of Scottish patriotism ; and when the management of affairs devolved entirely upon Stewart they did not suffer at his hands. The Castles of Edinburgh, Stirling, Perth, and many smaller fortresses, were, one after another, wrested by him from the invaders ; and the national cause looked so promising that, in May, 1341, the young King David, now eighteen years of age, ventured to return from France, where he had lived an exile nine long years. On landing at Inverbervie, in Kincardineshire, with his Queen, he was received with enthusiasm by the people, glad once more to have a sovereign amongst them, and that sovereign the son of the Bruce under whom they had fought and conquered. David, however, proved unworthy of his sire. His reign was dis-creditable to himself and disadvantageous to Scotland—the country being often humiliated, and suffering great depression, during its course.

Shortly after the King's arrival, abortive efforts were made by Randolph, Earl of Moray, to rid Dumfriesshire of the English. On laying seige to Lochmaben Castle he was repulsed, with serious loss, by Selby the governor.* A truce ensued between the Scots and English, to last till Michaelmas, 1346, during which Nithsdale and the greater portion of Annandale remained in the possession of the enemy. When the war was resumed, King David proceeded, at the head of a large army, on an ill-starred expedition into Nor-thumberland, gaining for it on the way a delusive gleam of success, by capturing the powerful fortress which had, five years before, resisted the arms of Randolph. Its defender, Selby, was beheaded ; a doom richly merited by him, as during his governorship he had been the terror of the dale. But the recovery of Lochmaben Castle, however important in itself, weighed but as a feather in the scale against the thorough defeat which awaited the Scots at Neville's Cross, near Durham. Their main centre was commanded by David himself ; near him fought Thomas Carlyle of Torthorwald, who fell slain while gallantly defending the person of the King. The victory of the English was immensely enhanced by the capture of the Scottish monarch ; and when, nine years afterwards, he acquired his liberty, it was on condition that he should pay the heavy ransom of a hundred thousand merks. David, on being restored to his throne, showed that he cherished a grateful recol-lection of Carlyle's services : a charter signed by him, bearing date 18th October, 1362, conveyed the lands of " Coulyn and Rowcan to our beloved cousin, Susannah Carlyle, heir of Thomas de Torthor wald, who was killed defending our person at the battle of Durham

* Redpath, p. 355.

and to Robert Corrie, her spouse, belonging formerly to our cousin, William de Carlyle."*

Thus in 1346 Edward Baliol, who held a leading command on the side of the victors at Neville's Cross, co-operated with them in overrunning Tweeddale, the Merse, Ettrick, Annandale, and Galloway.† Subsequently, at the head of twenty thousand men, he entered Dumfriesshire by the Western Border, and, taking up his abode in Carlaverock Castle, wasted Nithsdale and Carrick; while Adomar (or Aymer) de Atheles assumed the governorship of Dumfries, and strengthened his position by occupying the neighbouring stronghold of Dalswinton.‡ Baliol proceeded on his destructive mission as far as Perth, where he was stopped by a messenger, announcing that the King of France had, on his own behalf and that of his Scottish allies, ratified an eight years' truce with England; and before the armistice expired Baliol, despairing of realising the object he had aimed at, resigned his pretensions, for a money consideration, into the hands of Edward III., and vanished from public life, regretted by no one, scorned or contemned by most.

With the view of making good the transfer, Edward III. in February, 1356, led an immense army into Scotland by the Eastern Marches. The Scots, still acting upon the dying counsel of Bruce, did not attempt to meet the invaders in the open field, but wasted the country round about, confidently expecting that more havoc would be committed by hunger than by the sword in the ranks of the enemy. It was even so. The English found the farm-yards empty; and as their foraging parties roamed the country they met with neither herds nor flocks. No food could be obtained for men or horses; and the Southron fleet, which was to have brought provisions seaward to Berwick, suffered from a storm, which prevented it from reaching that port. Frantic with vexation and rage, Edward, more like a bandit chief than a royal commander, took insane revenge for the famine by resorting to the torch. He set fire to towns and villages, woods and towers, causing such a terrific conflagration that the season was long after spoken of by the common people as "The Burnt Candlemas." He then, from the blackened ruins of Haddington, beat a precipitate retreat; his forlorn host being galled and decimated on its homeward way by bands of Scots that sprung up on every side.

Relieved from the presence of the invaders, the patriot forces assumed the offensive. They succeeded in capturing many of the strongholds by which the English had long kept a precarious tenure of the country. Sir Roger Kirkpatrick stormed the Castles of Carlaverock, Dalswinton, and Durrisdeer. He afterwards paid a visit to Dumfries; but the friends of Edward there seem to have

---

* Barjarg Manuscripts.   † Wyntoun, vol. ii., p. 265.

‡ It appears from an entry dated 26th February, 1348, in the Rotuli Scotiæ, vol. i., p. 713, that Atheles at this time put the Castle of Dalswinton, which had suffered much during the war, in good repair.

decamped unceremoniously before he reached the town*—at all
events, he established in it without difficulty the undisputed rule
of David II., prisoner though that monarch still was, and made the
rest of Nithsdale too hot for its foreign occupants ; while John
Stewart, eldest son of the Regent, performed a similar service towards the English in Annandale—Lochmaben Castle, however,
which had once more fallen into their hands, resisting his attempts
to capture it.

Edward III., mortified by the failure of his expedition, and
actively engaged in hostilities with France, eagerly sought for and
obtained a truce with the Scots ; and the year 1357 found the
latter free, ruled by their rightful sovereign, returned from his
captivity, and beginning to taste the sweets of tranquillity, and
experience the protection of a settled government. Lawlessness,
the offspring of protracted war, had long cursed the country ; but,
as a proof that the sword of justice was not at this time quite
rusted, even in the district where the sword of war had borne
sway for ages, the following domestic episode may be narrated ;†
and the illustration will perhaps be all the more acceptable, seeing
that it is associated with a great historical event—the slaughter of
Comyn in Dumfries.

It has already been stated that Sir Roger Kirkpatrick took
the Castle of Carlaverock from the English in 1356. He was the
son of the baron who, in company with Lindsay, hurried into the
Greyfriars' Monastery, and made "siccar" the fell stroke inflicted
by Bruce on the treacherous Lord of Badenoch ; and, curiously
enough, the son of this same Lindsay was an invited guest at
Carlaverock in 1357, soon after its new keeper had begun to
occupy it. Superstition traces their meeting on this occasion to
no accidental circumstance. Bowmaker tells us, in his "Chronicle,'
that whilst the body of Comyn was being watched at the midnight
hour by the Minorites, according to the rites of the Church, the
officiating friars fell into a dead sleep, with the exception of one
aged father, who heard, with wonder and alarm, a voice, like that
of a wailing child, exclaim, "How long, O Lord, shall vengeance
be deferred ?" The answer, pronounced in an awful tone, made
the listener's ear to tingle, and his heart to thrill, as it sounded
like a voice from heaven : "Endure with patience until the anniversary of this day shall return for the fifty-second time !" This
is not history, but a priestly legend : the tragical incident, however, which ensued at Carlaverock fifty-two years after the
slaughter of Comyn, is recorded by the Prior of Lochleven and
other contemporary annalists, and is entitled to credence.

The two sons of Bruce's colleagues met in the old Border
fortress, as entertainer and guest, on or about the 24th of June,

* Hume's House of Douglas.
† Taken chiefly from Fordun and Dalrymple.

1357.(a) They were both promoters of the patriotic cause—they were seemingly on most friendly terms ; but, all the time, Lindsay, envying and hating his host, cherished towards him a spirit of revenge. Kirkpatrick had wooed and married a beautiful lady, whom Lindsay had loved in vain ; and the latter, after the festivities were over, and "all men bowne to bed," rose from his couch, stole on tiptoe to the chamber where his unsuspecting victim lay in the arms of his wife, stabbed him to the heart, took horse hurriedly, and, plying whip and spur, fled precipitately over moss and moor, through the midnight gloom.* He had thus glutted his vengeance on his successful rival ; but, bewildered by the darkness, and probably tormented by remorse, he in vain tried to secure his own safety by speeding to a far distance from the scene of the murder. After riding all night, the blood-stained criminal was captured at break of day within three miles from the castle. His rank and position, his services to the national cause the intercession of his powerful relatives, were insufficient to save him from the consequences of his guilt. The widowed Lady Kirkpatrick, hearing that the King was in the neighbourhood, went to him, and prayed for justice on the assassin of her husband. Forthwith the monarch formed a tribunal at Dumfries, by which Lindsay was regularly tried and condemned, as is recorded, in pithy, metrical terms, by the Prior of Lochleven :—

> " His wife passyd till the King Davy,
> And prayed him of his realte,
> Of lawche that scho might servyd be.
> The King Davy then also fast
> Til Dumfris with his curt he past,
> At lawcha wald. Quhat was thare mare ?
> This Lyndessay to deth he gart do there."†

How delightful it must have been for the Dumfriesians to breathe their native air in peace and security, after the long storms of war, from which they had suffered more than the rest of

---

(a) There is good reason to believe this date to be wrong, as public documents show that both Kirkpatrick and Lindsay attended Parliament in September, 1357, Acts of Parliament, Scot. i., 519. Probably 24th June, 1358, was therefore the real date.

* On this tragical incident a spirited ballad was written by the late Charles Kirkpatrick Sharpe, a descendant of the murdered knight. The following quotation from it, describing the climax, is highly poetical :—

> " Sleep on, sleep on, ye luvers dear !
> The dame may wake to weep ;
> But that day's sun maun shine fu' clear
> That breaks this warrior's sleep.
>
> He louted down –her lips he press'd—
> O kiss foreboding woe !
> Then struck in young Kirkpatrick's breast
> A deep and deadly blow.
>
> Sair, sair, and meikle did he bleed !
> His lady slept till day ;
> She dreamed the Frith flowed o'er her head,
> In bride-bed as she lay."

† Cronykil, Book viii., c. 44.

their countrymen, had subsided! Though the years between the
accession of David and his restoration were full of trouble, his
reign, after the latter event, was comparatively serene ; and the
country got time to recover in a great degree from the fearful
ravages of war, by which its trade and husbandry had been nearly
ruined.   If hostilities had been prolonged for another generation,
Scotland would have been turned into the desert which Edward I.
vowed to make it, and its people been reduced by battle and
famine to a mere handful.   At the middle of the fourteenth century, the whole population of the country, owing to the long
operation of repressing influences, would probably not exceed
eight hundred thousand ; and we can see reason for thinking that
the town of Dumfries could not have had more than eighteen
hundred inhabitants.   The likelihood is that its population was
nearly double that number in the reign of Alexander III., and
during the early years of the War of Independence.   Thirteen
blessed years of peace followed King David's release from captivity ; Nithsdale would blossom and rejoice, and its ancient
capital flourish—increasing alike in size and prosperity.

Those happy changes were certainly not due to the sovereign.
It was not by his wisdom and valour that the land was brought
out of its wilderness condition.   So far as Dumfriesshire is concerned, he was more than suspected of having secretly agreed with
the English to keep it weak and dependent, by demolishing some
of its main sources of strength and freedom—the Castles of Dumfries, Dalswinton, Morton, and Durrisdeer.*   Had this nefarious
arrangement been carried into effect, the county would have been
converted into a great hunting-field by the English Borderers, and
perhaps been eventually annexed to the English kingdom.   But
the evils which the King's perfidy or incapacity planned or made
probable were foreclosed by the firmness and patriotism of his
people—favoured as their efforts were by the inability of Edward
III., on account of his war with France, to prosecute his designs
against Scotland.

Robert Stewart, ex-Regent, in terms of the settlement made
by his illustrious grandfather, Robert Bruce, succeeded to the
throne on the death of David, in 1370.   The peace between Scotland and England remained unbroken.   It continued other seven
years, extending the repose of the northern kingdom to a period
of fully twenty years.   Edward III. died in 1377, without realising
any of his ambitious dreams ; and the English crown devolved on
his grandson, Richard II., a boy of tender age, whose " baby-brow '
was ill-fitted to wear the " golden round of sovereignty," which
proves often a diadem of thorns to full-grown men.   Soon after
his accession, negotiations for a continuation of the truce were
entered into ; but whilst these were pending Alexander Ramsay,

* Fordun, i., xiv., c. 18.

with only two score of Scots, surprised and took the strong Castle of Berwick, which the English had held for many years.

The embryo treaty was therefore cast to the winds. Berwick was recaptured by Henry de Percy ; and William, Earl of Douglas, who had vainly tried to relieve the fortress, paid a hostile visit to Penrith, at a time when one of its great fairs was being held, plundered the husbandmen and burghers, set fire to the town itself, and returned into Dumfriesshire laden with booty.* These aggressive forays proved that the Scots had increased in strength and boldness during the long suspension of hostilities ; and perhaps they were all the more ready to undertake them, now that their powerful enemy was in his grave, and the feeble hand of an inexperienced youth held the English sceptre. His subjects, however, were quite ready to take up the cartel of defiance thrown down by their northern neighbours ; and it seemed as if the war were about to take an extensive sweep, and become once more national in its character. The valour and good fortune of the Scots prevented this calamity, by restricting hostilities to the Border district, and rendering them of brief duration. For the purpose of revenging the raid against Penrith, Lord Talbot, at the head of 15,000 men, crossed the Esk. Had this formidable force succeeded in its original design, it is more than probable the victor would have been tempted to risk the hazard of a more ambitious die.

All along, during the wars with England, the ford near the influx of the Esk into the Solway was the principal passage to and from Scotland by the Western Marches, the territory further eastward being protected by Carlisle Castle, and other places of strength planted irregularly along the Border.† It was by this ford, after the tidal waters had retired, that the English army entered Scotland, and once more wakened with its war-notes the echoes of Solway shore. The invaders ravaged the lower district of Dumfriesshire, rifling granges and towns at pleasure ; and, mightily pleased with their work, halted at nightfall in a narrow mountain-gorge or valley, for the purpose of taking rest, apportioning the spoil, and deciding on their future plans. Presumptuous and reckless, they courted the dolorous fate that awaited them. A band of five hundred Scots, composed chiefly of common serfs or varlets, suddenly and secretly assembled, fell with the force of a thunderbolt on Lord Talbot's camp ; making their descent upon it more dismally appalling by wild shouts, and the ringing of rattles used by them in scaring wild beasts from their

---

* Buchanan's History of Scotland, Book ix., ch. xliii.

† The guarding of this passage was made an object of great consideration by the English Government. The duty of doing so was assigned by Richard II. to Richard Burgh ; and when he resigned the office, in 1396, it was conferred on Geoffrey Tilliol and Galfrid Louther.—Rotuli Scotiæ, vol. ii., p. 152.

flocks. (a)   The surprise was like that of Edward Baliol's army at
Annan fifty years before, only on a larger scale, and with more
destructive results.   The English, startled, appalled, paralysed,
were taken and slain in great numbers.   Many not cut down
perished in the Esk, whose tide had returned, all untimely for the
poor fugitives.   Two hundred and forty were made prisoners, and
only a remnant of the aggressive host escaped.*   The exulting
victors recovered the whole of the plunder, carrying off besides
the valuable arms and stores which belonged to the invaders.   It
is not surprising that, as a sequel to this overwhelming discomfiture, the English were glad to sign a truce for three years, on
terms favourable to the Scots.

(a) In 1380 a raid by 15,000 men-at-arms of Cumberland was in this very manner
defeated by 500 Dumfriesshire "gentill men," who were in ambush : 30 ʼ prisoners were
taken, and many were drowned, but there was no Talbot, and the rattles belong to
another story altogether.   There is evidently some confusion in the text.   See Wyntoun,
Book ix., lines 201-225 ; also, Tytler, v. i., p. 332.   Wyntoun has this passage, the occurrence referred to being about 1379 :—

> And on the West Marchis fell
> Gret jupertyis as I herd tell
> For at the wattyr off Sulway
> Schyr Jhon off Johnystown on a day
> Off Inglismen vencust a gret delle
> He bare hym at that tyme sa welle
> That he and the Lord of Gordowne
> Had a soverane gud renown
> Off ony that war off thare degre,
> For full thai war off gret bownte.

ˣ Fordun a Goodal, vol. i., p. 385 ; Wyntoun, vol. i., p. 309

CHAPTER XII.

TURN we now from the narration of events, to glance at the social
and material aspect of Dumfriesshire and its capital during the
middle ages, up till the period at which we have arrived ; and for
much of the view we must be indebted to the learned and industrious author of " Caledonia." In the thousand years which
elapsed after the invasion of Agricolo, no perceptible impression
seems to have been made on the original woodlands of the county.
When the Scoto-Saxons settled within its vales, they found clumps
of forest in all directions ; and hence the frequent occurrence,
throughout the district, of the Saxon term "weald," which signifies "a woody place." Familiar instances are found in the names
Ruthwald, Mouswald, Torthorwald, and Tinwald ; and in the
following, where the word appears in its modern form : Locharwood, Priestwood, Kelwood, Netherwood, Meiklewood, Norwood,
Blackwood, Kinmountwood, Dunskellywood, Woodhall, Woodlands ; and in others, such as Hazelshaw, Blackshaw, Cowshaw,
Laneshaw, and Bonshaw, in which a synonymous word for "wood"
is introduced. The oaks, firs, and birches embedded in the mosses
of Nithsdale and Annandale afford abundant evidence of the same
fact ; and fine natural wood, the progeny of primitive forests, still
fringes many of the rivers and streams. The parishes of Holywood, Morton, Durisdeer, and others further north, were also in
ancient times covered with trees; and through all these forests
roamed the wild boar, the wolf, the stag, the bison, and other
animals of the chase, to hunt which was the favourite pastime of
our ancestors. We read in the beautiful ballad, "Johnnie of
Breadislee," how

> " Johnnie busk't up his guid bend bow,
>   His arrows ane by ane ;
> And he has gane to Durrisdeer
>   To hunt the dun deer down."

Of a far-stretching forest in Moffatdale, another fine old lyrical
effusion, " The Lads of Wamphray," makes mention as follows :—

> " 'Twixt Girthhead and the Langwood en'
> Lived the Galliard and the Galliard's men ;
> But and the lads of Leverhay,
> That drove the Crichtons' gear away."

Sometimes, as is hinted in this verse, these old woodlands were the resort of outlawed bands, or men " put to the horn," who, by dint of archery and plunder, had no difficulty in gaining a subsistence —experiencing, like Robin Hood, how merry it is to live in the green forest,

" When shaws are sheen and shrads full fair,
And leaves both large and long ;"

for then " a strong bow, a long arrow, and a skilful hand, could furnish a plentiful table." Often, too, during the wars with England did the sylvan bowers of the Border district form a natural defence to the neighbouring dalesmen, when driven from walled town or moated grange, or when defeated in the field. Knighton states that when the Duke of Lancaster led an aggressive force into Scotland, during the reign of Richard II., he had to employ so many men in opening up a line of march, that the stroke of eighty thousand hatchets might have been heard ; while, at the same time, the heavens were made red above with the fires by which the impeding trees were burned down.*

An ancient manuscript informs us that near to the old Castle of Morton, which figured so much in the early history of Dumfriesshire, "there was a park built by Sir Thomas Randolph, on the face of a very great and high hill, so artificially that, by the advantage of the hill, all wild beasts, such as deers, harts, roes, and hares, did easily leap in, but could not get out again."(a) The writer quaintly adds : "And if any other cattle, such as cows, sheep, or goats, did voluntarily leap in, or were forced to do it, it is doubted if their owners were permitted to get them out again."†

On the 3d of March, 1333, Edward III., appointed John de la Forest Bailiff of the Park or Forest of Woodcockayr, in Annandale, an office which the Maxwells acquired afterwards, and were in the enjoyment of in the reign of James VI. Dalton Forest, on the west bank of the Annan, Loganwoodhead Forest, between the Sark and the Kirtle, Blackberrywood Forest, in Upper Eskdale, are mentioned in official records ; and we read of Robert I. and David II. granting lands in " free forest " in Dumfriesshire.

The manner in which the abounding woods of the county were tenanted may be inferred from such names as Wolfstane, Wolfhope, Wolfcleugh, Raeburn, Raehills, Hartfell, Harthope, Deerburn, Hareshaw, Todshaw, and Todhillwood. As the Scoto-Irish, like the British aborigines whom they succeeded, delighted in woods, they were sparing in the use of the axe. The forests furnished them with shelter, food, and the means of recreation ;

(a) Such deer-leaps were a regular feature of the forest craft of this period.

† MS. Account of the Presbytery of Penpont, drawn up and transmitted to Sir Robert Sibbald, the well-known antiquarian writer, by the Rev. Mr Black minister of Closeburn.

and their rural economy was in keeping with their tastes in this respect, seeing that it consisted rather in the feeding of herds and flocks than in the cultivation of the soil.

When another race—the Saxons--began to mingle on the banks of the Nith with the Scoto-Irish natives, they did not materially change the husbandry of the district, though after their appearance the plough was brought into greater request : vast herds of cattle were still seen browsing under the woodland shade ; multitudes of swine battened on the mast which fell plentifully from oaken boughs ; and countless "woolly people" continued bleating and nibbling in the glades. These and other domestic animals abounded greatly in the county ; and no stronger proof of the prevalence of pasturage could be desired than is furnished by the fact, that when Malcolm Canmore and David I. reigned, the Crown dues in Dumfriesshire were paid in swine, cows, and cheese. (a) The latter monarch granted to the monks of Kelso a share of the cattle and pigs he thus received from Nithsdale ; but as such payments were found to be inconvenient, Alexander II. allowed the same fraternity a hundred shillings instead of the "vaccarum et porcorum et coriorum" which they were wont to receive from the " Valle de Nyth." Hunting, more than farming, was the occupation of the land-owners ; but the latter business was pursued with considerable success by the monks ; "and as they," says Chalmers, "were the most skilful cultivators, as well as the most beneficial landlords, during the twelfth, thirteenth, and fourteenth centuries, it is to be lamented that they did not possess in those times more extensive districts in Dumfriesshire."

There was no great religious house within its bounds ; but the monks of Holywood owned lands in Nithsdale, the Priory of Canonby drew rents from estates in Lower Eskdale, and the monasteries of Melrose and Kelso were enriched by revenues drawn from the shire, the former having extensive property in Dunscore and Upper Eskdale, and the latter lands in other districts, which were tilled by bondsmen belonging to the brethren. From the rental of these ecclesiastical farmers we may form a pretty accurate idea of the land-rent paid at a time when acres were relatively more plentiful than gold pieces. During the thirteenth century, the monks of Kelso gave to Adam de Culenhat(b) a lease of the tithes of the parish of Closeburn, for the yearly rent of fifty-three merks and a half ; the tenant, however, being obliged, in addition to this money payment, to supply the Abbot, on his visits to the parish, with fuel, litter, hay, and grass. In the

---

(a) It is noteworthy that the characteristic tenure of Cumberland, the "cornage," "horngeld," or "noutgeld," is never found in Dumfriesshire. The only institution resembling it is the "lardner marts," levied as a perquisite of the Constable of Lochmaben.

(b) This was Conheath.

beginning of the fourteenth century, the same body of monks had forty acres of land, with a brew-house and other appendages, in Closeburn, which rented for two merks yearly ; and about the same time they had for tenant of their whole lands in the parish of Dumfries one Henry Whitewell, a burgess of the town, who paid them twelve shillings sterling annually for the same.*

The monks, in some instances, as has been stated, rented their lands to freemen ; "and they had thereby," says Chalmers, "the honour of beginning the modern policy of a free tenantry in Dum-friesshire ;" but the great body of cultivators were bondmen attached to the glebe.   The free tenants frequently enjoyed long leases, by which they were encouraged to apply greater skill and labour on their farms.   During the twelfth and thirteenth cen-turies, the land divisions of the shire were the same as in England, giving rise to the carrucate, the bovate, the husbandland, and the acre.   In the charters of Robert I. and David II. we read of pound-lands, merk-lands, shilling-lands, penny-lands, halfpenny-lands, and farthing-lands, from which valuations many farms derived names that some of them still retain.   As artificial drainage was unknown, much of the low, marshy country lay untilled ; but often towering summits, which modern agriculture leaves untouched, were scaled by the Scoto-Saxon plough, with its team of oxen—traces of the ancient furrows remaining till the present day.   Horses at that time were of far more relative value than cows :† the former were in so much demand for warlike purposes that they could not be spared for husbandry ; and there would have been less economy in using one pair of horses for a plough than four yoke of oxen.   On women of the peasant class much of the rural labour was thrown—this being the case even in the vicinity of towns, as the male population everywhere had to be drawn upon extensively for military service.

The author whom we have repeatedly quoted, and been guided by in this inquiry, sums up his account of ancient agri-culture in the shire, by saying—" The barons, the monks, and the tenants had inclosed fields ; they had hay ; they had mills of every sort ; they had brew-houses ; they had fish-ponds ; they had the usual appendage of orchards‡ from the prior Britons ; they had

* The value and the denomination of money, down till the reign of Robert I., continued the same in Scotland and England ; and the Scottish money was not much depreciated for a century or more afterwards.   The silver merk was value 13s 4d.— Tytler's Scotland, vol ii., p. 325.

† A number of horses were killed at the siege of Roxburgh, in 1298, the value put upon which by the English commander may be inferred from the following quotations : "A bay horse, which belonged to the Sheriff, price £10 ; Simon de Haudene lost a grey horse, price 100s ; Peres de Mountz lost a white horse, valued at 100s ; Robert of New-castle lost a white horse, price 12 merks."   Other horses are spoken of as respectively worth from 6 merks to 10.—Historical Documents, vol. ii., pp. 266-268.

‡ The Britons along the Annan, the Nith, and the Clyde delighted in apple trees ; while they loved the cider, as we know from the elegant writer of the "Avellenau." We may learn, indeed, from the names of places, how early they had orchards in Annandale.   The hamlet and church of Applegarth had its name, in the twelfth

salt-works on the Solway ;* (a) and they had wheel-carriages, with artificial roads : all during the early part of the thirteenth century."

Throughout the entire Scoto-Saxon period, till the doleful succession war began in 1296, the people of Dumfriesshire con-

century, from an orchard. A few miles above this, a farm has long been called Orchyard. Appletreethwaite, signifying "a small inclosure of apple trees," Appledene, or Applevale, and Appletree, are all mentioned in charters of Robert I. There were in former times several orchards at Dumfries. The monks of Holywood had a fine orchard at that monastery. There was also an orchard at the Priory of Canonby.—Caledonia, Note on p. 122, vol. iii. Thwaite is a term of Norse origin for a clearing.

* There were salt-works at various places on the shores of the Solway at this period. The monks of Melrose had one at Renpatrick, or Redkirk, which they let in 1294 to the monks of Holmcultram, who had several of their own on the Galloway side of the Solway. In the parish of Ruthwell there were many salt-works ; and there was one in Carlaverock parish at a place which obtained, on that account, the name of Saltcot-knowes.—Inquisit Special, p. 16.

(a) "In the Book of Melrose there is entered a charter executed by Richard Fleming, chamberlain of William de Brus, Lord of Annandale, in favour of the monks of Melrose. A witness to it was Roland of Galloway, so that the latest possible date is 1210. It conveyed a saltwork on the side of the great way (magna via) at the Church of Rainpatrick. The ground included was bounded on the east by a great ditch, on the south by the sea, and on the west by another saltwork already conveyed to the monks by William de Brus . . . Rainpatrick, once an independent parish, is now merged in the parish of Graitney. The church sat close to the sea, but even the spot it once hallowed has been washed away. Its prominent situation as a headland, a mile west of the Lochmabenstane, made it so much of a typical border site that the Red Kirk has in a sense passed into history. Its whereabouts is still indicated by the name of Redkirk Point, applied to what remains of the headland. In 1294 the monks of Melrose made a bargain with the monks of Holm Cultram, under which the latter acquired from the former their saltworks at Rainpatrick, subject to an annual payment of half a mark of silver. The Cistercians of Melrose and of Holm Cultram appear to have approved of the salters' motto, Sal sapit omnia, and almost divided the saltworks on the Solway between themselves and the Benedictines of Wetheral . . . . Roland, Lord of Galloway, just mentioned, son of that Uchtred whose brutal murder by his brother forms so revolting a chapter in Galwegian annals, gave saltworks to both houses. That granted to Melrose was at Preston, in Kirkbean. . . . Roland gave also, but for a rent of £10 a year, to the house of Holm Cultrum, a saltwork at Lochendello." Lochendello can be none other than Lochkindeloch, Lochkindelo, Lochkindelow, or Lochinnedeloche, a barony which at that time gave its name to Newabbey parish, and is thought to be the modern Loch Kinder. Roland made to the monks of Holm Cultram a grant of another saltwork, "where the descending slope of Criffell protracts itself into a flat promontory. It was called the saltwork of Salternes, a name attesting that before the monks got their charter the promontory had its saltworks. The word denoting simply the salters' point, naturally and regularly got worn down to Satterness : but Salterness continued to be the recognised name even at the end of the eighteenth century."—See Annals of Solway.

"It was reserved," says Mr Neilson, in that admirable study of his, "for some over-wise person, within the last hundred years, giving way, perhaps, to baseless anterior philological fancies, to improve it into Southerness ; and authorities on place-names, who ought to have known better, are accessories after the fact. Yet Satterness still lives vigorously in local pronunciation, especially amongst the older inhabitants of the district, within which it is a household word. It is an invincible witness for the self-explanatory, historical Salterness against the unwarranted upstart at present enthroned in our maps and topographies. Southerness, with its meaningless meaning of southern point—for it is not the southern point even of its own county—threatens to descend to remote posterity in the face of antiquarian protest, and in the very teeth of the parallels of latitude. Is it too late for geographers to entertain an appeal ? "

In 1656 Cromwell imposed a tax upon the salters. At the Restoration the salters of Annandale made strong protest against the impost of "the late Usurper." In the seventeenth century Solway salt, famed for its whiteness and purity, was known as "Ruthwell salt," where the manufacture had its headquarters then. The petition was complied with by Parliament : and "when a salt tax was imposed at a later time this Parliamentary proceeding kept the Annandale salters exempt. The exemption did not extend to Nithsdale, but stopped on the eastern bank of the Lochar, the very boundary of the territories of the first Robert of Brus, Lord of Annandale, in the twelfth century." The Annandale salt industry did not die out until after the first decade of the present century, when the salt tax was abolished all over the country. Holes that may still be seen along the merse near to Priestside are the pits once used in the salt manufacture : "the sterile influence of the salt still filtered there a century ago remains yet, and there is no growth or vegetation in these lifeless holes."

tinued to improve in all that could make them more affluent, civilized, and comfortable. That war not only stopped further progress, but made everything retrograde ; and the family feuds which followed ruined much that the foreign enemy had spared— each of these adverse influences operating for ages. It need scarcely be remarked, that the manners of the people were rendered ruder by the perpetual collisions of battle and the broils of faction ; and that the refinement that was beginning to spring up suffered a sad blight when the atmosphere of the district breathed constantly of war. While the inhabitants were involved in all the national quarrels with England, and generally had to bear the first brunt of the fray, their proximity to "The Debatable Land" of the Border, and the turbulent ambition of their local magnates, kept them in a chronic state of warfare, even when a truce existed between the kingdoms.

Other counties of Scotland enjoyed at times lengthened periods of repose ; but Dumfriesshire, for several reigns prior to that of James I., had only brief, fitful seasons of rest. How, under such circumstances, could the tillage of the soil, the operations of trade and commerce, and the arts, which civilize and refine, get a chance of success ? Here, as in other parts of the kingdom, a considerable foreign trade existed in the prosperous and peaceful reigns of Malcolm Canmore and Alexander III. ; but little traces of it remained, and it must have been, in fact, all but annihilated, till Bruce ascended the throne, about which time many adventurous Flemish merchants settled in the country, and gave a powerful stimulus to its commerce, which the wasting wars that succeeded weakened very much, but did not altogether destroy. Whatever aspect the vale of Nith may have presented in the Arcadian times of Alexander III., much of it must have worn a bleak and wasted look, only partially relieved by large stretches of luxuriant woodland verdure, and patches of yellow grain, during the succession war, and for at least a century afterwards.

In 1300, the neighbouring province of Galloway grew vast breadths of wheat, that help to sustain the English army of invasion, as well as its own inhabitants ; (a) but very little wheat was sown in Nithsdale or Annandale at that unsettled period. The cereals chiefly cultivated were oats and bere, or barley—the latter for furnishing the national beverage, ale ; but often before the peasantry could make meal of the one crop and malt of the other both were burned up. Edward I., however, usually interdicted, for his own sake, such acts of incendiarism ; and there is an instance on record in which he gave compensation for loss of grain caused by his troops. A cavalry regiment, in returning

(a) The Wardrobe Accounts, the entries on which this is based, do not mean what is here supposed. The grain was not bought in Galloway by Edward, but had been carried thither amongst Edward's stores.

from Galloway, on the 31st of August, 1300, having destroyed eighty acres of oats, the King compensated their owner, William de Carlyle, by a present of two hogsheads of wine,* value about £3 sterling. To the oaten diet of the common people was, however, added a goodly proportion of animal food : the humbler classes of Dumfriesians having been in this latter respect better supplied, perhaps, than their descendants of the present day. It was more easy then to breed cattle and sheep profitably than to grow corn, as, on the approach of an enemy, the herds and flocks could be driven off to the woods for safety, or penned within the lower storey of a baronial keep. Fish, too, were plentiful in the rivers that ran into the Solway : the red deer which roamed the neighbouring forests furnished venison without stint for the tables of the rich ; and not seldom, through favour or by stealth, that dainty article of diet found its way to the cottages of the poor ; though the picture drawn by Scott, so suggestive of domestic comfort, was only applicable to the houses of a much higher grade, or to the better class of hostelries :—

> " The rafters of the sooty roof
> Bore wealth of winter cheer—
> Of sea-fowls dried, and solands store,
> And gammons of the dusky boar,
> And savoury haunch of deer."

Altogether, in spite of the chronic infliction of war, the phrase of "the good old times" is by no means inapplicable, we think, to the mediæval period in Nithsdale and Annandale. This opinion is strengthened by what is known as to the low market value of food. The wardrobe accounts of Edward I. show the current rates of cattle and produce in Dumfriesshire and Galloway at the period of his visits (1300-1308). (a) An ox of large size could be purchased for 6s 6d ; a fat hog for 2s 2d to 3s 9d ; a pig for 10d ; a quarter of wheat for 7s ; a quarter of barley for 4s 4d ; a quarter of rye for 4s ; a quarter of oats for 2s to 3s 6d ; a quarter of beans for 7s 6d. These prices are relatively much lower, as compared with the value of labour, than prices in the present day. A labourer then could earn as much money in seven days as would buy a quarter of oats ; but he would have to give now more than his wages for three weeks, in exchange for the same quantity of grain. Liquors were equally cheap—ale selling at 12s to 18s a butt (108 gallons) ; good wine, £1 10s per hogshead (54 gallons) ; while there was a commoner kind—having in it, we dare say, only a small modicum of grape-juice—that was retailed at less than a penny per gallon.

Skins made into leather, or, as was sometimes the case, kept untanned, supplied a ready material for the dress of the common people ; but, even so early as the twelfth century, a coarse woollen

---

* The Wardrobe Accounts, p. 126.
(a) Previous note as to prices applies here also.

cloth of native manufacture had become an ordinary article of wear, while fabrics of silk, or other rich material, brought chiefly from Flanders, formed the raiment of the barons and better class of merchants. The villeins, or vassals, went often barefooted, like Gurth, though a pair of shoes, which cost only 3d, could not be beyond the reach of the free labourer, who was paid at the rate of 4d to 6d per day.

All the houses in town or country, except those occupied by barons, were built of wood or clay, roofed with straw or heather. " Generally," says Tytler, " we connect the ideas of poverty, privation, and discomfort, with a mansion constructed of such a material [as timber] ; but the idea is a modern error. At this day (1829), the mansion which Bernadotte occupied as his palace when he was crowned at Drontheim—a building of noble proportions, and containing very splendid apartments—is wholly built of wood, like all the houses in Norway ; and, from the opulence of the Scottish burghers and merchants during the reigns of Alexander III. and David II., there seems good reason to believe that their mansions were not destitute either of the comforts, or what were then termed the elegancies, of life."* For ages afterwards this perishable material continued to be put to the same use. Streets so formed could easily be destroyed by an enemy ; but then they could be restored at a much less expenditure of time and labour than if stone had been employed. The Dumfries of Bruce's day was a town of timber. The freestone quarries at Castledykes and Locharbriggs had been partially drawn upon, but only for building the Castle, the bridge, and the few ecclesiastical structures of which the burgh could boast ; and stone tenements for any but the middle and upper classes were rare till the reign of James III. About that time houses began to be erected with the ground storey of stone, and a projecting upper one of wood—a style which continued long in favour with the burgesses.

The Dumfriesshire strengths were of three classes : the large, massive fortresses of Carlaverock and Lochmaben occupying the first rank ; the smaller, but still powerful castles of Dumfries, Morton, Lochwood, Torthorwald,† Sanquhar, Durrisdeer, Dalswinton, Tibbers, and Closeburn, being included in the second rank ; a numerous array of keeps or fortalices forming the third, of which

---

* History of Scotland, vol. ii., p. 391.

† Torthorwald is placed in the second rank, not because of its size, for that was small, but on account of its strength and accessory defences, in which respects it was not excelled by some of the first-class fortresses. " The building," says Grose (vol. i., p. 149), " seems to have consisted solely of a tower or keep of a quadrilateral figure, 51 feet by 28, the largest sides facing the east and west. The walls were of an enormous thickness ; the ceiling vaulted. In the north-east angle was a circular staircase. It is supposed to have been last repaired about 1630 ; a stone taken from it, and fixed up against the out-offices of the manse, having that date cut upon it. An ancient man now (1789) living at Lochmaben remembers the roof of this building on it." The castle was anciently surrounded by a double ditch. The appearance of the ruin at present differs little from the picture of it given by Grose, the lapse of eighty-two years having made scarcely any impression upon it.

Amisfield and Comlongan may be deemed fair representatives. Even the humblest of these strongholds had walls varying in thickness from seven to twelve feet. Lime made of burnt shells, slightly intermixed with sand, was generally used in their erection ; and the fluid mortar, poured in hot among loose pebbles, placed between the outer and inner blocks, bound all together, so as to make a wall of adamantine strength.* The fortlets of the commoner class consisted of a square tower, with subterranean vaults for stores and prisoners ; a ground floor for a guard-room ; an upper storey, where the family resided ; the whole surmounted by battlements, within which warlike operations were mainly carried on in a time of siege. A series of similar towers, with surrounding walls, moat, and ditch, went to make up a leading baronial castle. Nowhere in Scotland was there a more perfect specimen of castellated architecture to be seen, in the thirteenth and fourteenth centuries, than that of the Maxwells, with its triangular, shield-like shape—its narrow, curtained front — its gateways, protected by a portcullis—its immense, machicolated towers on each angle—its deep fosse ; the Solway sweeping past, at no great distance, on one side—the impenetrable swamps of Lochar helping to protect it on the other. (a)

In Eskdale, Liddesdale, and Ewisdale, which formed the outside fringe of the Western Border, there were no strong castles. To their inhabitants, as Scott observes, the woods and hills of their country were pointed out by the great Bruce as their safest bulwarks ; and the maxim of the Douglases, that "it was better to hear the lark sing than the mouse cheep," was adopted by every resident chief. A rude, square, battlemented keep or peel sufficed for them, if placed on the brow of a precipice, or on the banks of a brawling stream ; and, when the nature of the ground permitted, protected also by a moat—the situation of these houses, "surrounded by woods, and rendered almost inaccessible by rocks or morasses, sufficiently indicating the pursuits and apprehensions of their inhabitants." Previous to the succession war, the men of this frontier part of the country had little to distinguish them from their more inland brethren ; but when the incursions of the English turned it into a perpetual battle-field, they became warriors by trade, and freebooters from necessity or choice ; giving

* The walls of Lochmaben Castle, as shewn by its crumbling ruins, must have been from ten to twelve feet thick, and built with run shell-lime. The place where it was prepared is still known as Limekilns. Both the outside and inside courses were of polished freestone, evidently brought from Corncockle Quarry, regularly squared.—Graham's Lochmaben, p. 73. The Castle of Sanquhar was surrounded by a double fosse. The walls are of great thickness ; and masses of them have fallen from the top without being separated into pieces. This shows the immense strongth of the mason work.—Dr Simpson's History of Sanquhar, p. 23.

(a) Sir Eustace Maxwell had received £22 a year from Edward for keeping the castle for the English. When he submitted to Bruce the building was dismantled at the latter's instance, and Maxwell was indemnified for making this sacrifice. Robertson's Index of Missing Charters contains entry of a Carta by Robert I. to Eustachius Maxwell of a discharge of "32l. sterling addebted furth of his own lands for demolishing of Carlaverock."

their territorial lords, and the King himself sometimes, scanty allegiance ; but devotedly loyal to their own clan-chiefs, whose word was their only law—unless when, by bonds of manrent, they gave vassal service to, and received protection from, some powerful baron of the neighbourhood. In Bruce's time, and during the subsequent Regency, the Western Borderers were, however, stanch and true to the patriotic side. It was mainly with them that Randolph and Douglas carried on those victorious raids into the South, which made the English weary of the war they had themselves provoked.

In Froissart's picture of them, drawn from the life, (a) we see quite a primitive set of troopers : well mounted, cumbered by no baggage, carrying no provisions except a small bag of oatmeal, roasting the flesh of the Southron cattle which they captured on wooden spits, or boiling it in the animals' own skins, and having no cooking utensil, save a small "girdle," on which they baked oaten cakes for an accompaniment to their savoury mutton or beef. Let Scott himself complete the delineation :

> " The Borderer—bred to war,
> He knew the battle's din afar,
>   And joyed to hear it swell ;
> His peaceful day was slothful ease ;
> Nor harp nor pipe his ear could please
>   Like the loud slogan yell.
> On active steed, with lance and blade,
> The light-armed pricker plied his trade—
>   Let nobles fight for fame ;
> Let vassals follow where they lead ;
> Burghers, to guard their townships, bleed ;
>   But war's the Borderer's game.
> Their gain, their glory, their delight
> To sleep the day, maraud the night,
>   O'er mountain, moss, and moor."*

*" Marmion."

(a) But not by Froissart : it was copied by him *verbatim* from Jehan le Bel's " Vrayes Chroniques," ch. 10.

CHAPTER XIII.

THE original charters granted by William the Lion to the burgh
have been lost sight of for centuries, and not even a copy of any
of them has been preserved. In the subjoined memoranda a list is
given of the principal writs belonging to Dumfries in 1633. It is
dated on the 8th May of that year. "The said day thair is taking
from out of the Towns's box the perticular wryts under wrytting
to be sent to Edinburgh, viz. :—Ane charter of the Friar's lands,
and annual rents granted be King James to the town, daited the
fourt January, 1591. Item : excerpt of sesine relating to the
above, 2d February, 1591. Item : extract of the town's original
charter of this Burghe grantit be King Robert, 28th Apryll, 1395.
Item : a Commission for halding of tua fairs, 30 Nov., 1592. Item :
the original charter of the Brig Custome grantit be James, Erle of
Dowglas, to the Freirs Minories of Dumfries, 4 January, 1452.
Item: ane charter of the said custome, and of lands therein,
grantit be King James to John Johnstoun in College of Lynclow-
den, datit 8th July, 1591." We subjoin the text of King Robert's
charter :—

"Robertus, Dei gratia Rex Scotorum, omnibus probis homini-
bus totius terræ suæ clericis et laicis, salutem :—Sciatis quod
assedavimus et ad firmam dimisimus Præposito, Ballivis, Burgen-
sibus, et Communitati Burgi nostri de Drumfreiss dictum Burgum
nostrum eis et eorum successoribus de nobis et hæredibus nostris,
in feodo et hereditate in perpetuum tenendum et habendum cum
omnibus et singulis libertatibus commoditatibus aisiamentis et
justis pertinenciis suis quibuscunque ad dictum burgum spectanti-
bus, seu juste spectare valentibus quoquo modo in futurum, cum
firmis nostris et annuis redditibus dicti Burgi, cum suis custumis
et tolloniis cum curiis et curiarum exitibus ac terris dominicis
ejusdem Burgi, cum molendinis multuris et suis sequelis ; unacum
piscariis aquæ de Nith ad nos pertinentibus (piscariis tamen datis
et concessis per predecessores nostros reges Fratribus Minoribus
ejusdem loci Divini caritatis intuitu duntaxat exceptis) ac cum

omnibus aliis privilegiis tam citra Burgum quam infra quibuscunque quæ iidem Burgenses nostri et Communitas temporibus
nostris et antecessorum nostrorum regum Scotiæ aliquo tempore
hactenus habuerunt et possederunt, adeo libere et quiete plenarie
integre et honorifice bene et in pace sicut aliquis Burgus infra
regnum nostrum Scotiæ libere et quiete de nobis tenetur seu
possidetur per omnes rectas metas suas antiquas et divisas suas ;
Solvendo inde nobis et heredibus nostris, dicti Prepositus, Ballivi,
Burgenses, et Communitas qui pro tempore fuerint ac eorum
successores annuatim pro perpetuo in cameram nostram viginti
libras usualis monetæ regni nostri, ad Festa Pentecostes et Sancti
Martini in hieme per portiones equales.   In cujus rei testimonium
præsenti cartæ nostræ sigillum nostrum precepimus apponi ;
testibus Venerabilibus in Christo Patribus Waltero et Matheo,
Sancti Andreæ et Glasguæ Ecclesiarum Episcopis ; Comite de
Fyffe et de Menteith, fratre nostro charissimo ; Archibaldo,
Comite de Dowglass, Domino Galwidiæ ; Jacobo de Dowglass,
Domino de Dalkeith, Thoma de Erskyn consanguineis nostris
dilectis militibus ; et Alexandro de Cockburne de Langtoun,
custode magni nostri Sigilli, Apud Glasgow, vicesimo octavo
die Aprillis, anno gratiæ millesimo ccc. nonagesimo quinto, et
regni nostri anno sexto."

[TRANSLATION.]

" Robert, by the grace of God King of Scots, unto all trusty
men of his whole realm, clergy and laity, greeting :—

"Know ye that we have granted to the Provost, Bailies,
Burgesses, and Community of our Burgh of Dumfries, our said
Burgh, to be held by them and their successors, of us and our
heirs, in fee and heritage for ever ; With all and every the liberties
and privileges, easements, and just pertinents whatsoever, appertaining to the said burgh, or which may afterwards in any way
rightly belong to it ; Together with our fermes and annual rents
in the said burgh, with its customs, tolls, courts and issues of
courts, revenues, and the demesne lands of the said burgh ; As
also the mills and multures, and their pertinents ; Together with
the fishings in the Water of Nith belonging to us, excepting only
the fishing granted by our royal predecessors for the love of God
to the Minorite Friars of the same place ; and with all other
privileges both without and within the said burgh which our
said Burgesses and Communities have at any time formerly held
or possessed in our reign or that of our royal ancestors in Scotland ; and that as freely, quietly, fully, wholly, and honourably
well and in peace, as any burgh within our realm of Scotland is
held or possessed of us freely and peaceably by all its old and
righteous boundaries and marches ;   Upon condition that the said
Provost, Bailies, Burgesses, and Community for the time, and
their successors for ever, shall pay into our exchequer twenty

pounds of the usual money of our realm yearly, in equal shares, at Whitsunday and Martinmas.

" In testimony whereof, we have caused our seal to be affixed to this charter before these witnesses :—The Venerable Father in Christ, Walter, Bishop of St Andrews ; Matthew, Bishop of Glasgow ; Robert, Earl of Fife and Menteith ; our most beloved brother, Archibald, Earl of Douglas, Lord of Galloway ; James de Douglas, Lord of Dalkeith, Thomas de Erskyn, our trusty cousins and knights ; and Alexander de Cockburn, of Langtoun, Keeper of our Great Seal. At Glasgow, the 28th day of April, year of grace one thousand three hundred and ninety-five years, and the sixth year of our reign."

A grant more comprehensive than is here conveyed can scarcely be imagined. In the first instance, the burghal authorities get a present of the burgh itself. It once belonged to the King—was as much his own property as any other portion of the royal dominions —but now he surrenders it to its magistrates and the community whom they represent, giving along with it the revenue derivable from its land and trade, its multures and fishings ; the only condition attached to the munificent grant being that its recipients shall pay a nominal sum per annum.

Not only so : " all other privileges without and within the burgh," previously conferred upon it, are ratified by this charter. These words have an extensive meaning, covering, among other things, the fundamental right of the royal burgh, as such, to monopolise all trade, foreign and domestic, within its jurisdiction, And as the charter does not specify in detail the exclusive privileges given to the community, so neither does it enumerate all the valuable equivalents exacted by the King. It says nothing of the liability of the parties to be called upon to serve in the royal host like other military tenants of the Crown—of their being obliged to maintain an effective police—of their being subject to direct taxation on special occasions—and of their having always to pay into the State exchequer the "great custom," an impost levied by means of his Majesty's own *custumarii* on all staple commodities of foreign trade. Yet we know from other documents that such conditions were imposed on the towns that were royally chartered : so that the privileges conferred by Robert III. on Dumfries were paid for at a much higher rate than £20 a year. It is right to remark, however, that the burgh could not be taxed for Government purposes till after it came to be represented in Parliament, which would be many years prior to 1395—the claim of all the King's burghs to form a distinct estate in the senate of the nation having been recognised in the days of Bruce. *(a)*

(a) The charter is enrolled in the Register of the Great Seal (1424-1513), No. 635. Its effect is somewhat exaggerated by Mr M'Dowall. It is a general ratification of existing burghal rights, but it does not add to them, and its main purpose is to settle the amount of burghal ferme or Crown rent that the burgh had to pay.

While the Great Chamberlain received the customs on foreign trade, for behoof of the Crown, he left what were called the "petty customs" unmeddled with : these, imposed upon articles of domestic consumption, were collected by the burgh chamberlain, and, with ground-rents, fishing rents, market dues, and court fines (exitus curiæ), made up the municipal income, as specified in the charter.

At an earlier period, as we have seen, the rulers of royal burghs were elected by the inhabitants at large ; but long before the days of Robert III. the suffrage was restricted to owners of property ; and doubtless the provost and bailies spoken of in the charter granted by him to Dumfries were chosen by the wealthier class of burgesses—acting, however, in the name of the general community. Within the course of another century even this qualified form of popular election was taken away by a statute of James III.,* which, on the plea of silencing the clamour of common simple persons at the yearly choosing of new officers, pro-vided "that the auld Counsail of the toune sall cheise the new Counsail, in sic nowmyr as accordis to the toune ; and the new Counsail, and the auld of the yeir before, sall cheise all officiaris pertenying to the toune. . . . And that ilka craft sall cheise a persone of the samyn craft, that sall have voce in the said electioune of the officiaris for that tyme; in like wise yeir be yeir.'

The charter of 1395 recognises the existence of privileges con-ferred on the burgh by preceding sovereigns. Some of these would probably include nearly all the rights and immunities specified in that document. Indeed, the charter of erection by which William I. raised Dumfries from humble villagedom to be one of the King's own burghs must necessarily have conferred upon it rights so extensive as to render future charters rather confirmative of old grants than donative of new privileges. No reference is made in King Robert's charter to any distinction between merchants and craftsmen because as yet the artisans had not acquired a political position in the realm. In some places they were beginning to form guilds, which incipient organisations provoked the jealous opposi-tion of the merchants, who did not relish the idea of having their exclusive rule in the burghs endangered by a rival class. The smiths, the tailors, the tanners, and the cordwainers of Dumfries would probably be longing, like their brethren elsewhere, to obtain a share of royal favour and of municipal privilege ; but as yet they were few in number, disunited, without a head, without a seat at the council board ; and the "blue blanket"—grand banner of the incorporated trades—had not even been seen in vision by the artisans of the burgh. But when in course of years the tradesmen came to be numbered by hundreds instead of tens, and each craft was systematically organised under its own deacon, no power in

*Acts of the Scottish Parliament, 1469, vol. ii., p. 95.

the land could long keep them unrepresented in the local parliament. Conscious of their own strength, they then determined that their officers, besides looking after the apprentices, and seeing that all fabrics operated upon were of good stuff, should try their hand at burgh-craft, and not allow the vendors of their wares, and the holders of the soil, to do everything according to their own will and pleasure. The deacons occupied their position in virtue of an Act passed in 1424, which authorised them to "assay and govern all werkis made be the wurkmen, sud that the Kingis lieges be nocht defrauded and scathyt in time to cum, as thai have bene in tyme bygane, through untreu men of craftis."* They wished to get justice done to their own body, not less than to the general community ; and for somewhat rudely seeking to bring about that result they were looked upon as unsafe demagogues by the Crown. An Act of Parliament set them up ; but a second Act, passed two years afterwards, to put them down, failed of its object.† The Trades were too powerful for the mercantile interest —could even sometimes overawe the King : their deacons, therefore, continued in office, waxing stronger and bolder, till eventually in Dumfries, as in the other royal burghs, they took their place at the council board, along with the merchants, as rulers of the town. But for a long series of years afterwards, the "merchant estate" in Dumfries managed to exercise a controlling influence over municipal affairs, retaining a voting power of at least two to one, and monopolising the office of chief magistrate, which was never till modern times allowed to be held by a craftsman.‡ At first only the principal trades acquired a right of incorporation, including self-government. This privilege was conferred upon them by the Town Council granting what were called " Sigillum ad Causas," letters under the burgh seal, which protected the recipients from all rivalry, prescribed the mode of admitting members, of electing office-bearers, and of enacting bye-laws.§ At one time there were at least eleven different crafts incorporated in Dumfries, namely : the smiths, the wrights, and masons, the websters, the tailors, the shoemakers or cordwainers, the skinners, and gauntlers or glovers, the fleshers, the lorimers or armourers, the pewterers or tinsmiths, the bonnetmakers, and the litsters or dyers ; the latter four of which became defunct, or were absorbed by some of the other trades. These acquired a monopoly within the burgh, not in virtue of any charter, but solely, as we have said, by the burgh's

---

* Acts of Scottish Parliament, vol. ii., p. 8.   † Ibid, vol. ii., p. 14.

‡ As illustrative of the text, we quote the following curious extract from the Records of the Convention of Royal Burghs (p. 31), Stirling, 20th October, 1574 :— "John Douglas, alledgit Provost of Haddingtoun, being ane cordinar [shoemaker] of his occupatioun, presented ane comissioun ; . . . . but the saidis comissionaris all in one voice fyndis and delyveris that na craftisman has ever had, nolder aucht or suld haif, voit or comissioun amangis thame." And they ordered the said John Douglas to withdraw, and admitted "John Seyttoun bailie thereof" in his stead.

§ Royal Commissioners' Report on Municipal Corporations, p. 79.

T

own seals of cause. Probably, however, when the trades, while still maintaining their individuality, joined in one aggregate corporation, which they did before the end of the sixteenth century, they obtained the requisite authority to do so from the Crown—no longer jealous of its loyal, though independent, craftsmen.

In accordance with a practice that sprang up at an early period of the middle ages, Dumfries was placed under the guardianship of a spiritual patron. No saint of the Romish calendar was fixed upon for this purpose : soaring ambitiously above all canonised mortals, the rulers of the burgh selected as their special protector the chief of the heavenly hierarchy. Till this day the figure of St. Michael remains the heraldic symbol of the burgh, and is to be seen on its official seal, and carved in low relief on the Provost's chair ; also, in a bolder form, on the south front of the Midsteeple, with wings outspread, armed with a pastoral staff, treading on a writhing serpent, yet calmly surveying his tutelary charge, as if the overthrow of the foul fiend below his feet were but an ordinary affair.* (a) The proper arms of the town were a chevron and three *fleurs de lis* on a shield argent, which device was visible about eighty years ago above the gate of the old prison that stood nearly opposite the Midsteeple ; and the stone bearing it was said to have been taken from a preceding jail that was built as far back as the beginning of the fifteenth century.† (b) This escutcheon has been long out of use, Michael the archangel doing duty in its stead. At a very early date, as we have seen, the name of the patron saint was given to the parish church. The armorial shield above noticed bore the word " Aloreburn ;" and the motto is engraved on the ivory head of a very ancient

* Though the patron of Dumfries is not exclusively a Romish saint, he has always been held in the highest reverence by the Church of Rome. He is described as follows, in a document of our own day, by the Cardinal Vicar of the Pope :—" The Invincible St. Michael, Archangel, the Captain of the Celestial Phalanxes, the first Support of Divine Justice, the glorious Conqueror of the earliest revolt—that of the rebel angels— the Defender of the Church of God under the Old and the New Testament dispensations, the Patron of privileged souls at the tribunal of the inexorable Judge of the living and the dead ; he, moreover, who is destined to confound and enchain Lucifer, in the consummation of the ages, for the eternal triumph of Jesus Christ, of his immaculate mother Mary, and his immortal Church."

(a) It is much preferable to regard St Michael in the light of Anglo-Norman history. The period of the settlement of this race was one in which dedications to Michael are frequently found clearly associated with the actual settlement. To talk of the rulers of the burgh⎮selecting their patron is unwarranted. St. Michael became patron of the burgh because probably some early Norman lord's church was dedicated to that saint.

† Burnside's MS. History.

(b) " The old prison that stood nearly opposite the Midsteeple," forming the north side of Union Street, the then Council Chambers forming the south side of said street, was demolished in the year 1808. Mr James Barbour says the stone is preserved among other sculptured memorials in the wall of a summer-house at Knockhill. (See Transactions Dumfries and Galloway Antiquarian Society, session 1895-6.) The coat-of-arms, with motto *A Lorburn*, is figured in Riddell's collections in the library of the Society of Antiquaries of Scotland under the title of "The Armorial Bearing of the Burgh of Dumfries and the Slughorn which belongs to that Burgh " (vol. iv., page 190). It is noteworthy that the same device was used by Robert Brown of Newabbey in 1588. (Riddell as above, ii., 166).

ebon staff put into the provost's hand at the time of his election. A memorable term it is, full of high significance, suggestive of forays and broils, of invasions and sieges. Often, from the reign of Robert III. till the Rebellion of 1715—a period of three hundred years—did this ominous word, shouted from street to street, shake the echoes of the town, calling all its male lieges between the ages of sixteen and sixty to arms; their familiar place of meeting being the margin of a sluggish little stream west of Sir Christopher's Chapel, anciently named the Lordburn—a term which, when slightly altered, furnished a slogan to the burgh.* Much of the ground which lay between this rivulet and the castle (a) was as swampy as if it had been a continuation of Lochar Moss. This marsh, especially in rainy weather, would be felt as an unpleasant neighbour by the inhabitants; but, unhealthy as it was, it helped to guard the castle, especially at a time when the burgh had no mural defences. Early in the fourteenth century, however, a wall was built around it, which afforded more security than the swamps, mosses, and trenches previously relied upon. Stone was chiefly employed in its erection, the height being generally eight feet. Where the nature of the ground allowed stone was dispensed with, and a deep ditch, having an earthen bank on its townward side, formed an excellent link in the defences; while at other intervals both wall and ditch gave place to horizontal piles of wood, formed in breastwork fashion, between the natural loopholes of which the townspeople could securely reconnoitre the enemy, and salute him with their feathered shafts, their cross-bow bolts, or the culverin balls of a later period. The wall, starting from the Moat overlooking the Nith at the Townhead, stretched almost in a straight line to Sir Christopher's Chapel, forming an acute angle on the townward side of that building; it then took an oval sweep, coming round the north side of the Parish Church, and terminating at the river a little to the south of what is now called Swan's Vennel. Three huge gates strengthened the wall, and allowed communication with the country lying north and east: one, called the North Port, stood near the Moat; the second, called the East Port, adjoined the Chapel; and the third, called the South Port, rose near the Church. The bridge was also fortified by means of a port; and in course of time a series of inner ports –the Vennel Port, the Lochmaben Gate, and the Southern Gate—were added to the defences of the town.

* We have repeatedly met with the word "Lordburn," as applied to the little brook in question, in old records. Mr Bennet, in his History (Dumfries Magazine, vol. iii., p. 11), takes a different view of the origin of the term :—"The place of rendez-vous was appointed," he says, "near a low, swampy piece of ground to the eastward, where, in rainy weather, a considerable quantity of water is collected, which discharges itself into the Nith by two small rivulets, or rather ditches, the one running north-ward, the other towards the south. These two rivulets, which, connected as they are by their common source, form to appearance only one, are known by the name of Lowerburn, or rather, according to the popular elision which they have undergone, Lorburn."

(a) We have seen that the locating of the castle at the top of the town is an error.

Lochar Moss, which is now felt to be a noxious blot on the face of the county, was then of profitable service to Dumfries. Stretching from the shores of the Solway to the base of Tinwald hills, it formed a natural protection which no force or artifice of an enemy could neutralise or overcome. Then it was more marshy, as well as more extensive, than it is at the present day ; and woe to the rash marauders who, for the purpose of avoiding the forts which defended the more accessible way to Dumfries, tried to cross its treacherous expanse. It was rarely, indeed, that invaders from the South made such a hazardous attempt ; the road usually taken by them being an indirect one, round the western extremity of Tinwald hills, which was indifferently guarded by the towers of Torthorwald and Amisfield, or a more direct, but dangerous one, that lay between the castles of Carlaverock and Comlongan, and between the western fringe of the morass and the Solway. By means of this vast wilderness of peat, intersected by bogs and ditches innumerable, and fringed by an array of strongholds, beginning at the shore seven miles south of Dumfries, and ending at Dalswinton, five miles to the north-west, a regular line of defence retarded, though it often failed to repel, the English visitors to Nithsdale, on foraying or fighting bent, and quite prepared to engage in both.

When an invading force, though signalled by blazing balefires, challenged by angry garrisons, and, it may be, confronted by opposing bands, succeeded in reaching the gates of Dumfries, and evinced an unmistakable desire to get inside, the wall would stand inconveniently in their way. When the mural impediment was at length breached or scaled- a degradation to which it was often doomed—and the assailants had fairly entered the town, its defenders had other resources left, which they were in the habit of exhausting before they yielded to the enemy. They could, and often did, resist the advance of the intruders, by disputing with them every inch of the ground ; but their common practice was to retire into certain strong peels, or fortified town houses, belonging to the neighbouring gentry, where their wives and children, goods and gear, had been previously placed, and there remain, whilst the enemy, perhaps, was employed in appropriating moveables that lay unprotected elsewhere, or in setting the defenceless parts of the burgh in a blaze.

Besides these peel-houses, small and great, some of which rose into existence at a very early period, many of the humbler houses were turned into places of defence in times of need ; and some of the closes connected with the High Street were furnished with iron gates, and turrets overhead, capable of giving a stout resistance to the foe. One side of a gate of this description was visible at the head of Assembly Street so recently as 1826 ; and only a few years before a part of the superincumbent arch was also standing. In prosecuting this domestic warfare, if it may be so termed, the females of the period are said to have exhibited amazonian strength and courage, so that they not unfrequently rivalled the actions of their parents, husbands, or lovers ;* and, if we are to place full reliance on what is said respecting their achievements, the glowing picture given of the heroine of Saragossa will correctly represent the warlike damsels of Dumfries when defending their household shrines :—

> " Her lover sinks—she sheds no ill-timed tear ;
> Her chief is slain—she fills his fatal post ;
> Her fellows flee—she checks their base career ;
> The foe retires—she heads the sallying host."†

To this mode of defence the narrowness of the streets and the numerous high houses gave peculiar facility. With brands of fire, boiling water, stones, and other weapons of promiscuous warfare, showered from doors, windows, and gate-surmounting turrets on the heads of the invaders, they were often compelled to decamp altogether, or commence operations at some more vulnerable portions of the burgh.

A picture is extant, which professes to represent Dumfries as it appeared a century or so after the date to which the preceding remarks chiefly refer. The town wall has the range already assigned to it ; the castle at the head of the burgh,(a) St Michael's Church at the foot, and "Christy's" Chapel at the east, forming an angle with them, are the only objects that have a prominent bulk—no tall spire having as yet risen above the other buildings. The castle looks large and massive—quite a Titan, as compared with the wooden fortalice of Celtic times : a series of battlemented turrets, extending to the verge of the river, is crowned by a tall square tower, looking down High Street—the whole built in the Norman style, and suggestive of colossal strength. St Michael's Church is seen occupying a site a little eastward of the present building, the only imposing feature abut it being a square turret above the main entrance ; the Chapel, with its pointed buttresses, fine east window, two side windows, and stepped gables, presenting a more ornate appearance.‡

---

* Their females caught the warlike spirit of the country, and appear often to have mingled in battle. Hollinshed records that, at the conflict fought near Naworth (1570) between Leonard Dacres and Lord Nunsden, the former had in his company many desperate women., who there gave the adventure of their lives, and fought right stoutly.—Border Antiquities, p. 81.

† Byron's " Childe Harold."

(a) Not *the* castle, but Maxwell's town-house.

‡ We have heard it vaguely reported that the original painting was sold at Drumlanrig Castle about fifty-five years ago. A sketch of it from memory, as supplied by the late Mr John M'Cormick, Dumfries, an intelligent and enthusiastic local antiquarian, has been lithographed.

CHAPTER XIV.

AT this period the Douglasses begin so to occupy the canvas that
Nithsdale and Galloway are scarcely seen except associated with
some of them. Archibald, younger brother of Bruce's companion-
in-arms, married Dornagilla, daughter of the Red Comyn, thus
acquiring, as he thought, a claim to the lordship of Galloway ;
which the Crown gave partial effect to by granting to him all the
land lying between the Nith and the Cree as a reward for the
patriotic services rendered by his family. When slain at Halidon
Hill, as already noticed, he left two sons—William, who heired the
Douglas estates on the death of his uncle Hugh, and was created
Earl of Douglas ; and Archibald the Grim, (a) who became Lord of
Galloway. William was succeeded in the earldom by his son
James, the favourite hero of the old balladists— the " dead Douglas
who won the field," and who ever lives in the pages of Froissart,
and in the ballads of " Otterbourne " and " Chevy Chase." Dying
without issue, he was succeeded by the Galloway chief, who in this
manner effected a junction between the two branches of the
family. Before this period he had, by an enforced purchase, added
to his other possessions the lands of Thomas Fleming, Lord of
Wigtown ; so that the third Earl of Douglas had become also the
undisputed Lord of Galloway. Alan de Dunfres, the hereditary
ruler of that province, was called by Buchanan " Scotorum longe
potentissimus ;" and now, after the lapse of a hundred and forty
years, the same expression might have been truly applied to Alan's
successor. Archibald Douglas, the Grim, became the most powerful subject in Scotland ; having a giant's strength, he used it like

(a) A bastard son of the good Lord James.

a giant—the huge Castle of Threave, rebuilt by him on an island
in the Dee, being the chief seat of his power, and the centre of a
grinding despotism that stretched over the whole district.(a) Yet he
partly made up for his cruelty and rapacity at home by his valour
in the field.　On the termination of the truce which followed Lord
Talbot's defeat, the Lord of Galloway, with other nobles, laid siege
to Lochmaben Castle.　It surrendered after a siege of eleven days,
on the 4th of February, 1384 ; the English thus losing the solitary
hold in Dumfriesshire of all their sanguinary conquests.　When
some time afterwards Richard of England penetrated to Edinburgh,
with the view of foreclosing a threatened attack upon himself, and
was so galled by guerilla bands that he had to hurry home again,
Archibald Douglas, at the head of one of these, entered England
by the Esk before Richard had time to return, devastated the
country as far as Newcastle, demolishing in his route the formidable Border fortresses of Wark, Ford, and Cornhill.

　　William, surnamed the Black Douglas, a natural son of this
mighty autocrat, became first Lord of Nithsdale.　His bodily
strength is said to have been prodigious.　According to Hume of
Godscroft, a single blow of his was sufficient to prostrate any one,
however stout and well-accoutred.　So fearless was he in the field
that the exploits attributed to him by reliable historians wear an
aspect of romance.　He was distinguished also for his wit, sagacity,
and benevolence.　This illustrious knight was not less fortunate
than good and brave.　The Black Douglas obtained in marriage
Egidia, King Robert's daughter, the fairest woman of her age ;*
getting with her Nithsdale as a dowry, also the sheriffship of
Dumfries, the wardenship of the Western Marches, the offices of
justice and chamberlain, besides an annual pension of £300
sterling, paid from the customs of certain burghs — Dumfries
among the rest.

　　Another truce having been entered into between England and
Scotland after Otterburn, William Douglas of Nithsdale, tired of
inactivity, took farewell of the beautiful Egidia and joined the
Teutonic knights of Prussia in a crusade against the Pagan natives
of the country.　Fortune still smiled on the adventurous Dumfriesshire baron.　Many victories, due chiefly to his valour, were

　　(a) This about grinding despotism is not proved at all.　Archibald was a
judge (justiciar) quite as much as a soldier, and his Galloway charter was his
reward as judge—so it expressly states.

　　* She was (says Hume, vol. i., p. 202) a mirrour of rare and singular
beauty ; so that wherever she went, she drew the eyes of all men towards her
with admiration.　The chief noble youths of the land did suit her in marriage,
but the King preferred our William of Nithisdale for his worth before them
all.　Boetius writes that the King of France, having heard of the fame of her
beauty, sent a painter into Scotland privately, who having drawn her portrait-
ure truly and showed it to the King, he was so enamoured thereof that he
despatched ambassadors to desire her in marriage ; but all too late, for she was
married to Nithsdale before their coming."

munificently rewarded. He was made Admiral of the Prussian
fleet, Duke of Prussia, and Prince of Dantzic. But his heart was
in Nithsdale, with its fair lady, who waited long and wistfully for
his return. He never saw her nor home again. While Egidia was
counting the hours that would intervene before his return, he—
woefully unfortunate at the last—was lying stiff and gory, basely
murdered on the Bridge of Dantzic by a band of assassins in the
pay of Lord de Clifford, with whom he had had a quarrel, arising
out of "an old emulation," and an envious grudge borne by the
English nobleman against the Scottish chief.* The memory of
William Douglas was long preserved in Prussia by his family
escutcheon being sculptured on a gateway near the spot where his
blood was shed. A brother-in-arms of the hero, Mareschal
Boucicant, went repeatedly from France to Prussia for the purpose
of avenging the assassination of his friend, but was told in answer
to his challenge "That vengeance belonged only to the Scots."†
The sorrowing widow of the Black Douglas did not long survive
him. Their only child, inheriting her personal charms, came to be
known as the Fair Maid of Nithsdale. This lady was married to
Henry Sinclair, Earl of Orkney, a descendant of the Norman
knight St Clair, who followed David I. into Scotland. The fruit
of their union, William, acquired the lordship of Nithsdale and the
sheriffship of Dumfries.

Archibald the Grim, dying in 1400, was succeeded by his son
Archibald, surnamed Tyneman, because his headlong valour in the
field often got the better of his prudence, so that he "tined," or
lost, battles that he might otherwise have won (a). At Linton, in
1401, he defeated Hotspur and his Scottish ally, the Earl of March,
who was exasperated against King David because his daughter,
the Princess Margaret, after being betrothed to March, had been
given by her father to Douglas. Next year, however, the allied
chiefs exacted a dread revenge at Homildon, where Douglas lost
the day and his personal liberty—the unlucky Tyneman losing
also an eye and being wounded in five places whilst the battle
raged. Between the prisoner and his English captor such a
fellowship sprang up that they were soon afterwards seen fighting
side by side against Henry IV. of England. So Shakespeare makes
Henry say to his son when speaking of young Percy's achievement :—

> " What never-dying honour hath he got
> Against renownéd Douglas, whose high deeds,
> Whose hot incursions, and great name in arms
> Holds from all soldiers chief majority,
> And military title capital,

* Hume, vol. i., p. 206.
† Note by Aikman in Buchanan's History of Scotland.
(a) Others think tineman is *tiny man*, and suppose him to have been of
small stature.

> Through all the kingdoms that acknowledge Christ,
> Thrice hath this Hotspur, Mars in swathing-clothes,
> This infant warrior, in his enterprises
> Discomfitted great Douglas ; ta'en him once—
> Enlargéd him, and made a friend of him,
> To fill the mouth of deep defiance up,
> And shake the peace and safety of the throne."*

When King Henry defeated the rebels at Shrewsbury, Douglas, after performing prodigies of valour, by which the fortunes of the field were nearly redeemed, was again made captive ; and on paying a heavy ransom he regained his freedom.

Peace prevailed between England and Scotland for a long while prior to 1415, in which year Douglas made a foray into Cumberland—Penrith suffering severely, as usual on such occasions. On his return a large English force retaliated by a raid across the Esk into Dumfriesshire. The capital of the county had for more than a generation been exempt from the penalties of war ; but this year it was doomed to suffer from both fire and sword. It appears that no effort was made to stay the march of the invaders, as they approached menacingly from the south ; and soon the waters of the Nith reflected the gleams of a fire which raged in various parts of Dumfries, and attested the triumph of the enemy.† Doubtless the town would be plundered before the torch was resorted to ; and, at all events, the unwelcome visitors returned unharmed to their own land, laden with booty. What Tyneman, Lord Maxwell, and other local chiefs were about at the time is not explained by the historians of the period. Douglas received from his royal father-in-law the lordship of Annandale when it was forfeited by the rebellious Earl of March—which gift helped to make up for his many losses and crosses. No paladin of the olden time had a more romantic career than this "capital chief" of Christendom. Tired of idleness at home, he joined the Scottish Legion in France—won great victories, in spite of his uncomplementary surname—received from the grateful Charles VII. the duchy of Touraine—but "tined" all his well-won honours, and life itself, a few years afterwards, at the battle of Verneuil, in 1424.

The superiority of Galloway then devolved upon his widow. In the following year she received from her royal brother a confirmation of the lordship ; and, taking up her residence at Threave, dispensed her rule with such benignity and wisdom as made her highly popular throughout the province. On the death of this amiable lady, about 1440, her remains were brought from Threave to the College of Lincluden, and there interred in a magnificent tomb that had been built into the north wall of the choir near the altar when that part of the edifice was erected by Archibald the Grim. The recess formed to receive the body was canopied by a

---

* " King Henry IV.," part i.
† Hume's House of Douglas, vol. i, p. 134.

spacious, richly-ornamented arch, having at its apex a heart—
which became the leading symbol of the house of Douglas after Sir
James was slain when carrying the heart of Bruce to the Holy
Sepulchre—with three chalices, and a mullet or star accompanying
each. On the back wall of the recess the words " A l'aide de
Dieu !" were cut, and further down was engraved the epitaph,
" Hic jacet Dna. Margareta, Regis Scotiæ filia, quondam Comtissa
de Douglas, Dna. Gallovidiæ et Vallis Annandiæ "- -" Here lies
Lady Margaret, daughter of the King of Scotland, Countess of
Douglas, and Lady of Galloway and Annandale." Sculptured on
the front of the tomb were nine shields, two of them blank, one
bearing a St. Andrew's cross, one with three stars—the original
coat of the house—one having a heart added to these symbols, the
others being emblazoned with the arms of the family as Lords of
Douglas, Galloway, Annandale, and Eskdale. Finally, over the
stone cover of the recess was placed a full-length sculptured figure
of Lady Margaret, recumbent, the head resting on two cushions.
A truly magnificent tomb it was, worthy of its royal occupant ;
and, though now sadly defaced, it still forms the finest feature in
the beautiful remains of the College.*

When James II., a child of less than seven years of age,
ascended the throne after the murder of his father in the Blackfriars' Monastery at Perth, the administration of affairs devolved
on Sir Alexander Livingstone, as Regent, and Sir William Crichton, as Chancellor—the latter a direct descendant of William de
Crichton, who acquired half of the barony of Sanquhar in the
thirteenth century. These two ministers, instead of faithfully
discharging the onerous duties assigned to them, began a protracted duel, each seeking to circumvent the other, till their
respective factions brought the country to the verge of a civil
war.

There was one potentate who cared for neither Regent nor
Chancellor—William, who had succeeded his father, Archibald
Tyneman, as Earl of Douglas and Lord of Galloway ; and who,
had he possessed as much patriotism as influence, might have
saved his country from a host of evils. Scotland at this crisis
needed a man like the Good Sir James Douglas : unhappily, his
present successor had none of his disinterested virtue, but, like the
Grim Baron, his grandfather, was boundless in his arrogance and
ambition.

When Earl William rode out his customary following was a
thousand horse. His household was conducted with regal magnfi-
cence. He affected royalty in other respects—conferring knight-

* Pennant, who visited the ruins in 1772, states that the figure at that
time was still to be seen, though mutilated ; and he adds, the bones of the
deceased " were scattered about in an indecent manner, by some wretches who
broke open the repository in search of treasure."

hood, and doing many things which right or usage restricts to the sovereign. It was no rare incident for this puissant and audacious nobleman to appear with a little army of mounted adherents before the gates of Edinburgh, as if for the purpose of letting the young King see that there was a power in the land that laughed at the sovereign's will, and looked with contempt on the representatives of royalty. And this was no empty display on the part of Douglas; it was full of significance : as he not only wished to look like a king, but strove to act as unlike a subject as possible. He did not convert his strong fortress on the Dee into a palace, nor style himself William, King of the Southern Scots ; but he kept up princely state in Threave, and publicly proclaimed that no man within Douglasdale, Galloway, Annandale, and his other Dumfriesshire estates, should pay any heed to the authority of the Government, but take law from himself alone. Though he held no office in Dumfries, the influence of his family was paramount in the town, and its burghers must have felt themselves placed in a bewildering predicament when this ukase appeared. Their loyalty looked to Edinburgh—their fears were operated upon by Threave.

Crichton and Livingstone, finding at length that their feuds made them weak in the presence of the mighty Douglas, became friends ; and a plan to get rid of him was the first fruit of their reconciliation. "All the King's horses and all the King's men" would have been insufficient to effect their object. Fraud must be resorted to, since force would be of no avail. Accordingly, the Regent and Chancellor suddenly discovered that the Earl of Douglas was King James's best friend, and the chief prop of the monarchy. Why was such a mirror of patriotism and chivalry a stranger to the Court which he was so well fitted to adorn? Let our good cousin by all means pay a visit to Edinburgh, that the King may have an opportunity of thanking him personally for his public services, and of cultivating his friendship.

Such glozing language told on the heart of Douglas. It flattered his vanity, fostered his self-esteem, set his fancy a castle-building. Impetuous in all his thoughts and movements, he in an unhappy hour resolved to accept the invitation sent to him in the name of the sovereign, and set out for Edinburgh, accompanied by his brother David and a few personal friends. He was courteously received by the Regent, and introduced to the King, who soon formed a genuine attachment to his gallant and distinguished guest. A few days elapsed, and the infamous plans of Livingstone and Crichton were fully matured. Whilst the brothers were seated with them at a banquet, several ill-favoured men, in no festal guise, presented themselves. The arms which they bore were in perfect keeping with the murderous glances directed by them against the Douglases. "Spare them ! spare them !" cried the King, as the ruffians seized the Earl and his brother. The young monarch pleaded for their lives in vain ; he even, Lindsay of Pitscottie tells us, "grat verie sore," without effect, when he saw his guests bound with cords and hurried out of the hall.

Never had merry feast a more mournful interruption and sequel. The next minute the sullen sounds of the headsman's axe told all within hearing that the great, proud chief of the house of Douglas was lying a mangled corpse alongside that of his brother. The youths, whatever may have been their faults, were lovely and affectionate towards each other ; and in "death they were not divided." The rapaciousness and inordinate ambition of the unfortunate Earl were forgotten by the public, in contemplation of his fate ; and the popular indignation was forcibly expressed by a contemporary minstrel in the dread imprecation :

> " Edinburgh Castle, town, and tower,
>   God grant thou sink for sin !
>   And that even for the black dinner
>   Earl Douglas gat therein."

James, uncle of the murdered youths, succeeded to the earldom ; many of the estates, however, in Nithsdale and Annandale, passing to Beatrice, sister of the previous Earl, on account of their being unentailed. The new chief was a Douglas in name only. Of a heavy, corpulent body, he was surnamed the Gross ; of an indolent turn of mind, he manifested no resentment towards the men who had treacherously put his nephews to death. His successor, William, a thorough Douglas, threatened them openly, and used all his power and artifice to effect their overthrow.

In William were concentrated much of the talent and all the characteristic pride and ambition of his family. He began well— restoring it to its territorial opulence by marrying his cousin Beatrice. He did not, however, like his former namesake, aim at an independent sovereignty, but sought to obtain the chief direction of affairs, whilst remaining nominally subject to the King. Into the twelve years during which he flourished as the chief magnate of the kingdom many important incidents associated with Dumfriesshire and the country at large were crowded. His secret intrigues against and public opposition to the Regent and the Chancellor— his dexterous attempts to ingratiate himself with and become the chief minister of King James—and the league he formed with the Earl of Crawford and the Lord of the Isles for the purpose of gaining supreme authority by force when other means failed—are themes which occupy a prominent place in the histories of the period. The lawlessness which prevailed on the Scottish Border in consequence of its chief ruler being absorbed by these ambitious projects, the misery thus entailed on the inhabitants, the wasting English incursions provoked, and his energetic endeavours to remove these evils, and prevent their recurrence, are matters which must have made a deep impression at the time, and have exercised no inconsiderable influence on the condition of Dumfries-shire.

We learn from Hume that immediately on the accession of William to the earldom he convened the whole of his friends and retainers at Dumfries, choosing from among them "a number of councillors, besides officers for collecting his rents and casualties, and made such other arrangements as he deemed necessary for the administration of his affairs." It has been supposed, with good reason, that, besides these ostensible objects, the crafty chief secured from the meeting a concurrence in the aspiring political schemes which he had thus early already formed : at all events, the influence of himself and followers was, throughout his career, employed in the prosecution of these unpatriotic measures, more than in furthering the well-being of the district in which, for good or evil, the Douglases exercised an unrestricted sway for nearly a hundred and fifty years.

Whilst Earl William was away in the north, playing out his perilous game of chess in real life for the possession of the king, the English (to continue the figure) captured some of the pawns which he should have done his best to defend. A truce concluded between the kingdoms had still some years to run when, in 1448, the Earl of Northumberland entered Scotland by the Western Marches, and the Earl of Salisbury by the Eastern Marches, each leading a large army. The insults and injuries received from the Scottish Borderers were alleged by the invaders as an excuse for their hostile movements ; but the probability is that they were prompted in a great degree by a knowledge that the country was ill-defended owing to the absence of Douglas. Northumberland advanced to Dunbar, pillaged that town, and then set fire to it, returning unmolested, burdened with spoil.

Dumfries was once more destined to pass through the fiery ordeal to which it was subjected only thirty-three years before, and from which it had several times previously suffered. Crossing the little stream that may be looked upon in some respects as the Border Rubicon, Salisbury swept along the Solway shore, pounced down on Dumfries, entering without resistance, took possession of the Castle, and began to act the part of conqueror in the old English manner. Seated in the fortress, he issued orders to his men to sack the town. Forth they went, nothing loath, visiting all the principal houses, and carrying off what property they could find. This done, they set fire to the burgh, and then, greatly enriched by their foray, recrossed the Esk into Cumberland.*

House building in Dumfries must, once in every generation or so, have received a powerful stimulus from these periodical visits. It was fortunate that huge oaks abounded in the forests of Niths-dale, so that materials were always at hand with which to restore

* Hume, vol. i., p. 254 ; and Pitscottie's Chronicle.

the streets destroyed by the English incendiaries. Very likely some of the fire-raisers of 1415 reapplied the torch at the bidding of Salisbury in 1448 : if so, they must have been surprised to see the town that they had half reduced to ashes larger than ever, as if the new streets had literally grown like the timber of which they were formed. The Earl of Salisbury and his men probably thought that this time at any rate they had ruined Dumfries ; but it possessed a wonderful vitality ; and before many years more elapsed the charred embers left by the devouring element had disappeared, and the burgh was itself again. (a)

Neither the Earl of Douglas nor any of the other barons in the district lifted a finger to save Dumfries on this occasion. James Douglas, however, brother of the Earl, soon afterwards put Alnwick into similar plight—as if the stripes inflicted on that town could have mollified the wounds received by Dumfries. But of this unreasoning retaliatory course of procedure the wars of the time were in a great degree made up ; and it is, need we say, a leading characteristic of all wars, ancient and modern.

The turbulent conduct of his own retainers, and the wasteful incursions of the English, drew Douglas home for a season, and constrained him to pay attention to his duties as Warden of the Western Marches. His predecessor, Archibald the Grim, whose power extended over all the Marches, had drawn up a code of rules for his regulation ; and the present Earl, who liked to do things on a large and imposing scale, resolved, with the assistance of all parties concerned, to revive and improve these laws so far as they related to his own territory. He accordingly called a meeting of the whole lords, freeholders, and heads of Border families within his wardency.

In ordinary circumstances, perhaps, this gathering would have taken place in the Castle of Dumfries ; but on account, we suppose, of that building being left in a dilapidated condition by its last English occupant, the Earl of Salisbury, the little parliament was held in the religious house of Lincluden, which had become the property of the Douglases, as Lords of Galloway. (b)

(a) Boece says " the town of Dumfries was shamefully plundered by the Earl of Salisbury and consumed with flame." This, he states, occurred in June, 1449, and Mr Neilson inclines to the opinion that that, not 1448, is the correct date. The municipal records do not mention the burning. The burgh's annual ferme to the Crown, fixed under feu charter at £20 1s, was duly accounted for during all the years from 1445 until 1451 without any deduction for waste or disturbances. So that, says Mr Neilson (Transactions D. & G. Antiquarian Society, 1896-97), " in the one quarter where assistance might have been expected [on the question of date] we appeal in vain."

(b) This is wrong. The religious house of Lincluden had not become the property of the Douglases ; and it is an extreme statement in next paragraph for which there is no sufficient warrant that Archibald the Grim had turned Lincluden into an ecclesiastical college " for the benefit of his own family."

Since its erection by Lord Uchtred Lincluden had experienced important changes. It was no longer a nunnery—Archibald the Grim having, about fifty years before, expelled its inmates, enlarged the building, and then converted it into an ecclesiastical college for the benefit of his own family.* The chroniclers of the change seem rather at a loss to give a good reason for it. The Grim, in spite of his gross misdeeds, kept on good terms with the Church ; and with all his hardihood and cupidity, he would scarcely have ventured to suppress the convent if its character had been irreproachable. One author affirms vaguely that the "insolence" of the female devotees provoked their dismissal ; † while Major boldly assumes that they must have been conspicuous for their incontinence, or "the good Earl" would never have expelled them ; and improving on this hint, Hume declares that Douglas had solely in view "an eye for religion, and a special care for the pure and sincere worship of God"—though the suspicious admission is made by the same historian that the Earl did thereby "greatly increase his revenues and enlarge his dominions." ‡ (a)

From whatever cause, the Sisters of St Benedict were forced to vacate the Abbey, to make way for a brotherhood of twelve bedesmen and a provost, for whose maintenance its opulent revenues were assigned. A magnificent church was added to the original fabric, also a domicile for the provost : so that the building in 1448 differed essentially from the original edifice, with

> " Its massive arches, broad and round,
> That rose alternate row on row,
> On ponderous columns, short and low,
>   Built ere the art was known ;
> By pointed aisle, and shafted stalk,
> The arcades of an alley'd walk,
>   To emulate in stone." §

All the additions made to the Abbey of the twelfth century by Earl Douglas were in the florid Gothic of the fourteenth century ; and as, later still, some other portions were added in the Scotch baronial style, the picturesque ruin, which still overlooks the "meeting of the waters" a mile above Dumfries, combines three orders of architecture, though the distinctive features of the primitive Saxon are overlaid or lost.

---

* The term " college " did not at this period mean a place of learning, but simply a religious establishment in which masses were said for the souls of its patrons or their friends.

† Extracta e Chronicis, p. 207.

‡ House of Douglas, p. 114.

(a) The word "thereby" is not in the text quoted from, and there is no proof for the aspersions on Douglas in this connection. No lands of the abbey were, so far as has been shewn, ever appropriated by Douglas.

§ Scott's " Marmion."

Lincluden College was made up of buildings that enclosed a spacious court, the east side of which was occupied by the Provost's residence, looking down upon the river Cluden, and by a tall octagon tower ;* the south side comprised a choir, with transepts, nave, and side aisles ; the north, a refectory and dormitory ; the western boundary being formed by a high wall, with a general entrance-gate to the interior. At the date of Earl William's visit, the choir especially must have presented a beautiful aspect. Though of small dimensions, the large size of its details, as in the case of Michael Angelo's statues, gave it a colossal effect—a peculiarity shown in the massive corbels and capitals of the vaulting shafts from which the groined arches sprang, in the moulding round the priest's door, in the still bolder crocketing of the public entrance, and in the flamboyant tracery of the windows, all fashioned on strictly geometrical principles.† Much of the inner ornamentation ministered to the pride of the family, speaking as it did, in heraldic language, of their rank and achievements ; and a gorgeous tomb, with a sculptured effigy in its recess formed a meet monument for a countess of Galloway, the wife of a Douglas, and the daughter of a king, who, as already noticed, had been laid there not long before, to neighbour in "the narrow house" the dust of Uchtred, the lord of that ancient province.

Here, then, at Lincluden, in the closing month of 1448, Earl William held his court, and took counsel of his brother nobles—all "lesser lights," compared with him as the central luminary—and of the freeholders and others who had responded to his summons How the proud lord demeaned himself when presiding at the meeting is not recorded ; but we can easily conceive that his habitual haughtiness gave place to a courtesy not unknown to the members of his house when mingling with those who readily bowed to their supremacy. The Harleian Collection bears unmistakable witness to the ability and wisdom which signalized the deliberations under his guidance, embodying as it does " the ordinances of war sett doune at Lincludan College, by all the lords, freeholders, and eldest borderers of Scotland, on the 18th of December, 1448, by the commandment of Earl William of Douglasse."

We learn from the document in question, that old statutes were revised, and a number of new rules drawn up, and that the code thus completed prohibited intercommuning with the enemy ; enjoined that all men were to keep by their own respective com-

* The octagon tower, which formed a very prominent and interesting portion of the edifice—the more so, as the royal arms of Scotland were sculptured on its front—suddenly fell, with a tremendous crash, on Sabbath, the 16th of February, 1851 ; and thus one fine feature of the ruins was utterly destroyed.

† Billings's Antiquities of Scotland, vol. iv.; in which valuable work views are given of the windows as restored.

panies ; that they were to answer to their names when the host
was arrayed ; that all were to fight on foot, except such as got
special leave from their chief to be on horseback ; that it regulated
the conditions of ransom, and prescribed the penalties incurred by
desertion and other offences. The eleventh clause runs thus :
"Whatever he be that brings a traytor to the warden or his
deputy, he shall have his reward, a hundred shillings ; and he that
puts him away fraudfully shall underlie the pain of death, like as
the traitor should have done." The thirteenth clause is in the
following terms : "Whoever he be—an host of Englishmen arriving
in the country, the bales being burned—that follows not the host,
on horse or on foot, ever till the Englishmen be passed off Scotland,
and that they have sufficient witnesses thereof, all their goods
shall be escheat, and their bodies at the warden's will, unless they
have lawful excuse for them." Before departing, the presiding
Earl, we are told, made all present swear upon the Gospels that
they would, within their respective jurisdictions, observe, and
cause to be obeyed, all these ordinances, and assist him in carrying
them into effect.

At this important conference, also, the system of signalling
the approach of an enemy by balefires was brought to a perfection
unknown before.   It was enacted that nine beacons should be
erected in Nithsdale, on the following eminences, and fired in time
of need : Wardlaw, Rachochtoun, Barloch, Pantwa, Malow, Corsincon, Crufel, Dowlwerk, and Watchfell ; and that other eleven
should be kept ready in Annandale—on Gallowhill, Kinnelknock,
Bleis, Browanhill, Burane-Skenton (Dryfesdale), Quitwewin, Cowdens, Balehill, Penchathill, and Trailtrow.   It was also arranged
that on the Sheriff of Nithsdale, and the Stewards of Annandale
and Kirkcudbright, should devolve the responsibility of employing
proper persons to erect, maintain, and fire the beacons.* (a)   When

---

* Introduction to Nicholson and Burns's History of Westmoreland and
Cumberland, p. 59. The names are incorrectly given in the book from which
we have quoted. We should probably read Tynron Doon for Rachochtoun ;
Brownmuirhill and Barr (in Hoddam) for Browanhill and Barrow ; Quhytwind
or Whitewoollen (at Lockerbie) for Quitwollin ; and Pendiclehill (in Tinwald)
for Penchathill.

(a) Rachouchton is Trohoughton, two miles to the south-east of Dumfries.   Mr Neilson quotes the full text of the Beacon Act in his " Repentance
Tower and its Traditions " :
" Acts, Parl. Scot., i., 716—The full text of the passage is as follows :—
' Item it is fundin statut and usit in tyme of werfar anentis bailis birning and
keping for cuming of ane Inglis oist in Scotland, ther sal ane baill be brynt on
Trailtrow hill ; and ane uther on the Panchnat hill ; ane on the Bailze hill,
abone the Holmendis ; ane on the Coldanis, abone Castelmylk ; ane on Quhitwewin, in Drivisdaill ; ane on the Burane Skentoun, in Apilgarth parochin ;
ane on the Browane hill ; and ane on the Bleise, in the tenement of Wam-
fray ; ane on Kyndilknok, in the tenement of Johnestoune ; ane on the Gallowhill, in Moffet parochin : and syne in Nyddisdaill, ane on the Wardlaw : ane

the whole of them, in a winter's night, threw their ruddy glare on
high the effect must have been grand as well as startling ; and
hundreds of households must have been protected from pillage,
and thousands of lives been saved, by the timely alarm thus communicated.   No doubt Dumfries sometimes owed its safety to the

on Rahothtoun ; ane on Barlouch ; ane on the Pantua hill ; ane on the Malow
hill ; ane on Corswintoun ; ane on Crwfell ; ane on the fell abone the Dowlwerk ; and ane on the Watchfell.   And to ger ther balis be kepit and maid
the Shiref of Nyddisdaill and the stewart of Ananderdaill, and the stewart of
Kirkcudbricht, in Gallowai, salbe dettouris, and quhasa kepis nocht the balis
ordinance and statut beand maid in tym of werfar sal pay for ilk defalt a
merk.   Item quhatever he be, and ane oist of Inglismen cum in the cuntre
the balis beand brynt that followis nocht on the oist on hors or on fut ever
quhill the Inglismen be passit of Scotland, and at thai have sufficient witnessing thairof all their gudis salbe escheit and ther bodyis at the wardanis will
bot gif thai have lauchfull excuse for thaim.' "
      " These various beacon stations are," adds Mr Neilson, " with two or three
exceptions, easily identified.   (1) Trailtrow is 350 feet above sea level.   (2)
Panchnat, a copyist's mistake for Panthuat, now Pantath (400 feet), on the
confines of Mouswald and Ruthwell.   (3) The ' Bailze hill abone the Holmendis ' is, I think, that called the Bailie hill (797 feet) in Crawford's Map of
Dumfriesshire, in Dalton Parish near the ruins of Holmains Tower.   (4)
Coldanis is Cowdens (603 feet) in St Mungo Parish.   (5) Quhitwewin is Whit-
wollin (733 feet), a green conical hill near Lockerbie.   (6) Burane Skentoun I
have failed to identify.   (7) Browane Hill is Brown Hill (871 feet), on northern
boundary of Applegarth parish.   (8) The Bleise, in Wamphray parish, is still
well known by that name : it was called Bleize hill in Crawford's Map ; the
Ordnance Survey spells it Blaze hill (846 feet).   (9) Kyndilknok is Kinnelknock (552 feet) in Johnstone parish.   (10) The Gallowhill, at Moffat (832
feet), is a favourite walk of the visitors to that spa.   A glance at the relative
position of these places on the map shows how well devised the beacon system
of Annandale was—how well the framers of the Lincluden Ordnance were
versed in their topography.   The Nithsdale beacon stations are not so easily
identifiable as those of Annandale—at least I have failed with nearly half of
them.   (11) The Wardlaw (313 feet) is the wood-crowned hill above Carlaverock Castle.   (12) ' Rahothtoun ' was long an unsolved puzzle.   One day,
however, struck by the nobly extensive view from the hill at Trohoughton
(312 feet), not far from Dumfries on the road to Carlaverock, I bethought me
that Rahothtoun was a very natural misreading of Trohoughton in some early
spelling.   From its commanding position and its mention next in order to
Wardlaw, I am quite satisfied that this identification is correct.   (13) Barlouch
is now the Beacon hill (803 feet) of Barlouth, on the eastern confines of Torthorwald parish, and overlooking Lochmaben.   (14) Pantua hill I take to be
the same height as No. 2 supra, viz., Pantath hill, which being as it were the
junction point of Nithsdale and Annandale, fell naturally enough into both
lists.   (15) Malowhill I have not identified.   (16) Corswintoun (read Corswin-
coun) is Corsincon or Corsancone (1547 feet), in New Cumnock parish, on the
border line of Ayrshire and Dumfriesshire.   (17) Crwfell is Crufell (1828 feet),
in Sanquhar parish.   (18) ' The fell abone the Dowlwerk ' I am not quite sure
of, though I suspect it to have been a hill near Dowlarg in Troqueer parish, in
the Stewartry of Kirkcudbright.   Dowlarg (see Reg. Mag. Sig., iii., 989)
approximates Dowlwerk in pronunciation.   (19) The Watchfell I cannot even
guess at."
      After the appearance of Mr Neilson's book Colonel Rogerson of Gillesbie
wrote that Burane Skentoun must be Burram Skelton, on Sibbaldbie estate.
It is so styled on an estate plan of about 1828.

arousing flame seen streaming up from Wardlaw Hill, on the Solway, and responded to by the friendly light on Corsincon.

It is whilst thus employed, as a local legislator, that we like best to look upon the eighth Earl of Douglas. Pity it is that we can rarely view him so beneficially employed. Had he attended more to such matters, and less to the promptings of lawless ambition, he would not have provoked the violent and premature death that awaited him, and his memory would have been held in more honour by his countrymen.

CHAPTER XV.

AFTER the burning of Alnwick, a truce for seven years was agreed
upon between the two kingdoms ; but, owing to the commotions
in both, resulting from the weakness of their respective Govern-
ments, it was soon broken, the English in this instance being the
aggressors. A large body of them, under the command of the
younger Percy, son of the Earl of Northumberland, made an
incursion into Annandale, burning several villages, and carrying
off all the goods they could lay hands upon. Luckily, Douglas
was not far distant from the post of duty and danger. Falling
upon the retiring Southrons, he made them accelerate their retreat,
and yield up all the spoil with which they were burdened. So far,
so well ; but Douglas, for reasons of his own, wished to widen the
area of the war-field, in order to counteract the coalition formed
against him by King James (now aged 17), the questionable
Crichton, and Kennedy, the patriotic Bishop of St Andrews. He
therefore mustered a large army, and, under the plea of revenging
a wrong for which he had already exacted a heavy penalty, entered
Cumberland. Not content with imposing upon it an ordinary
amount of punishment, he acted with such merciless severity that
it was reduced to the condition of a desert. Not only the barons
on the English side of the Border, but the whole nation felt
aggrieved and indignant on account of this ferocious Douglas raid :
forgetting how often Dumfriesshire had been gratuitously pillaged

by them, and that for one complaint against the Scots, the latter could have preferred fifty against those who were loudly crying for vengeance, and busy preparing to exact it with all their might.

Early in 1449 (a) an army that has been variously estimated at from 14,000 to 40,000 entered the county by the ordinary way, and encamped on the banks of the Sark, the little stream that, after forming the boundary line between the kingdoms for a few miles, flows into the Solway. The force, which probably did not exceed 20,000 in number, was commanded by the Earl of Northumberland and his son—the latter anxious to wipe out the disgrace of his defeat in the preceding year. Not encountering any opposition, the invaders began forthwith to pillage and destroy. Whilst so employed news was brought by their scouts that a Scottish army was advancing as if for the purpose of giving them battle—information which proved strictly correct, the force from the north being about 12,000 strong, under the leadership of Douglas's brother, George, Earl of Ormond. The conflict that ensued was, says Chalmers, one of the greatest fought between two spirited nations from the engagement at Homildon, in 1402, till the battle of Flodden, in 1513 ;* and it certainly was the most important battle fought in Dumfriesshire since the formation of the Scottish monarchy.

As the Scots drew near, the English recalled their marauding parties and prepared for the threatened encounter. They had the advantage of choosing their own ground ; and having selected what seemed to be a favourable spot, adjoining their tents, they calmly waited the coming onset. The centre was commanded by the two Percys ; the right by one whose valour, bodily strength, and implacable hatred of the Scots, gained for him that distinction —a warrior whom the chroniclers of the time call Magnus Redbeard ; while the left, composed chiefly of Welshmen, was entrusted to Sir John Pennington. The centre of Ormond's force was directed by himself ; Herbert, the first Lord Maxwell of Carlaverock,† and Sir Adam Johnstone of Lochwood, led the right wing,

(a) Mr Neilson's chronology, in his paper on the battle of Sark, has these entries : "1449, June—Salisbury burns Dumfries. June 3—Douglas burns Alnwick. July 10—Truce concluded at Winchester, to begin on 10th August and endure till 20th Sept. July 18—Douglas burns Warkworth. Aug, 10— Truce begins. Sept. 18—Truce renewed till 19th November. [This must have been interrupted by hostilities.] Oct. 23—Battle of Sark. Nov. 3— James II. appoints Commissioners to negotiate a truce. Nov. 5—Truce concluded at Durham."

* Caledonia, vol. iii., p. 89.

† He was twice married : first to a daughter of Sir Herbert Herries of Terregles, by whom he had two sons, Robert, second Lord Maxwell, and Sir Edward Maxwell—from the latter of whom are descended the Maxwells of Tinwald and Monreith ; and, secondly, to a daughter of Sir William Seton of Seton, by whom he had, with other issue, George, ancestor of the Maxwells of Carnsalloch, and Adam, of the Maxwells of Southbar.

in opposition to Sir John Pennington ; while Wallace of Craigie, a lineal descendant of the great patriot "who rescued Scotland thrice," conducted the left against the redoubtable Magnus.

Ormond, we are told, delivered a spirited address to his countrymen, based chiefly on the idea that "thrice is he armed who hath his quarrel just." He prudently said nothing about his brother's excesses, but dwelt strongly on the fact that the guilt of first breaking the truce lay with their old enemies the English. Justice was on the side of his countrymen ; and they might there-fore, he said, expect victory to smile upon their efforts. They had their homes to protect, their country's honour to maintain—con-siderations which ought to stimulate their valour ; and then, if success crowned their bravery, they would cover themselves with glory, and purchase a lengthened peace for the district and the nation. If the leader of the invaders said anything to them, the burden of it would doubtless be revenge for the cruel Douglas raid ; but he either was silent, wishing to speak by deeds and not by words, or there was no reporter in the camp to take down his eloquent address, or chronicler to put one into his mouth worthy of the occasion.

As usual, most of the Scots were armed with the national weapon—a pike or spear—the length of which was fixed by Parlia-ment at six ells, or eighteen feet six inches. A phalanx so armed was all but invincible. "Standing at defence," says the author of the "Journal of Somerset's Expedition," "they thrust shoulders likewise so nigh together, the fore ranks well-nigh kneeling stoop low before, their fellows behind holding their pikes with both hands, and therewith in their left their bucklers, the one end of their pike against their right foot, and the other against the enemy, breast high, their followers crossing their pike's point with them forward ; and thus each with other so nigh as space and place will suffer, through the whole ward, so thick, that as easily shall a bare finger pierce through the skin of an angry hedgehog as any encounter the front of their pikes."

Had the Scots at Sark been on the defensive, and attacked hand-to hand by the enemy, the pikes would have vindicated the truth of the national motto, as they had often done on former fields ; but when Wallace of Craigie marshalled his spearmen, there was no foe within reach ; and a shower of missiles was rained down upon them from a distant eminence with irresistible effect. In this ominous way the battle was initiated, and seemed almost on the point of being decided against the Scots. Great gaps were formed in their left wing, which wavered in consequence, and appeared on the verge of being thrown into inextricable con-fusion—the sure prelude of a general panic and flight.

It is at a crisis such as this that generalship is invaluable. Wallace possessed military genius worthy of his ancestor ; he apprehended at once the full import of the danger in which, not only his own division, but the whole army was placed ; and he was not slow in devising relief. Addressing his soldiers, he said, " Why do we stand thus, to be wounded afar off ? Follow me, and let us join in hand-strokes, where true valour is only to be seen !" His men were re-animated by this appeal. They had not the passive endurance to enable them to stand much longer the arrow-flights that were drinking their hearts' blood, but they had courage sufficient to assail a host, however numerous or strongly posted.

The leader's words were followed by corresponding action. What avail bow and arrow to the gallant English archers, who had so nearly decided the day, now that two thousand Scottish spear-men have crossed the intervening ground, and are grappling in close quarters with their assailants ! Magnus the Redbearded stands aghast as he sees his ranks thinned and reeling. Why, when the right wing is decimated and threatened with total ruin, does no supporting force come to it from the centre ? Whether it was that the nature of the ground forbade such a movement, or that Northumberland was so engaged in baffling Ormond that he had no men to spare, certain it is the leader of the English right found, to his dismay, that it was doomed to fight and suffer unaided. If the prowess of an individual could have redeemed the fortunes of the field, the superhuman exertions made by Magnus would have accomplished that result. He could not revive the courage of his followers, nor arrest the merciless march of their assailants ; but he could die in harness like a dauntless warrior as he was. Surrounded by a few personal adherents, he kept his ground, nay, actually advanced in face of that bristling forest of spears, anxious, it is supposed, to engage in a personal combat with the Scottish chief—a fate which was not vouchsafed to him, as he fell by some unknown hand among heaps of slain.

The overthrow of the right division of the English might not in itself have led to their entire defeat ; but when that disaster was followed by the death of Magnus, and both events became known over the entire army, a sore discouragement was the result, It would seem that the fighting on other parts of the field was mere child's play, as compared with that in which the divisions led by Magnus and Wallace were engaged. The English fully anticipated that their archers would decide the battle in their favour ; and being disappointed in this respect, they appear to have lost heart. At all events, they made no adequate effort, in the centre and left, to atone for the loss of the right division and its leader. They fought on doggedly, however, for a while—hope-less of success, yet loath to retire—till, pressed on all sides by the impetuous and exulting enemy, they at length gave way along their whole line. When the general retreat took place the

slaughter in their ranks was terrific.   Three thousand of their
number fell whilst the battle raged, and more than that number
perished by the sword of the pursuer, or in the blood-dyed waters
of the Sark, on whose banks they had the day before indulged in
merry wassail.   The Sark, as has been mentioned, is only a small
river, but the retreating English found it swollen by the tide, and
rushing fierce, like the conquering Scots, as if the latter had been
in league with the Solway against the enemies of their nation.

Many men of rank, including the younger Percy and Sir John
Pennington, were made prisoners, together with hundreds of
gentlemen and common soldiers.   According to Buchanan, the
spoil in money, arms, and equipments that rewarded the victors
" was greater than ever had been known in any former battle ;"
and a tradition, still current in the locality, tells of fabulous heaps
of gold pieces being found by fortunate rustics on the banks of
the Sark generations after their luckless owners perished by flood
or field.   In this memorable battle the Scots lost only six hundred
men, in addition to the wounded, who may be estimated at three
times that number.   There was, however, one sad drawback to
their triumph.   The brave Wallace of Craigie, to whose skill it
was chiefly due, died three months afterwards of wounds received
in the heat of the fight.*

A truce was concluded, which lasted for several years ; but
Dumfriesshire, though freed for a lengthened period from the
presence of a foreign enemy, continued to be distracted by its own
barons—and Douglas was still the chief offender.   Actuated by a
variety of motives, the chief of which was probably a love of
display, the proud Lord, with a most imposing retinue, visited the
city of Rome, proceeding through Flanders and France into Italy.
Sir John Douglas, Lord Balveny, was left to act as his procurator
or representative,† a post which was no sinecure ; and its difficulties were aggravated by the increased licentiousness shewn by
many retainers during the absence of their chief, he being the
only one able to restrain them, when he chose so to act.   Complaints of their tyranny and oppression were daily poured into
the King's ear ; and Balveny himself was murmured against, as
one who encouraged rather than checked the offenders.   On the
procurator being summoned to appear in Edinburgh, and plead to
the charges brought against him, he, imitating his haughty master,
despised the citation till he was taken thither by force.   He underwent a regular trial ; and it having been proved to the satisfaction
of his judges that certain acts of extortion had been committed by
him and others in the name of Earl Douglas, heavy fines in money
were imposed as a penalty—the same to be paid out of the Earl's

* The authorities relied on for the account given of this battle are chiefly
Pitscottie and Buchanan.
† Pitscottie, folio edition, p. 34.

rents. Balveny, protesting that he durst not interfere with the revenue of his chief, prayed that the fines might be allowed to stand over till the Earl's arrival, who was expected home in the course of a few months. This evasive proposal did not satisfy King James, who, though wishing to be lenient, was resolved not to be trifled with ; and he commissioned Sinclair, Earl of Orkney, to take means for collecting such an amount from the rents of the Douglas estates as should discharge the damages adjudged by law.

Easier said than done. A king gave the order ; but barons who acted in the name and according to the spirit of one who was mightier in Galloway and Dumfriesshire than himself treated it with scorn. The very idea of the thing was laughed at by the relatives and dependents of Douglas. To be mulcted in their own district by a royal commissioner—and that as a punishment for deeds they gloried in—was totally out of the question ; and when Sinclair, "accompanied with a small number of folks," made his appearance in Nithsdale as a penal rent collector, he was received with such a storm of ridicule that he was fain to hurry northward without obtaining a plack of the damages. James, enraged by the contempt thus poured on his authority, summoned "by a herald all men whatsoever, of high or low degree, pertaining or favouring a Douglas to underly the law," and declaring all disobeyers to be rebels and traitors.*

No response having been made to this comprehensive summons, the King found there was no alternative left but to give up his sovereignty over a great part of the south of Scotland or enforce it by the sword. He resolved to adopt the latter course ; and putting himself at the head of a considerable army he marched into Galloway to break the power which had defied him—"to beard the lion in his den—the Douglas in his hold." He encountered no opposition in the open field, the enemy he came to punish having prudently retired to their places of strength, which they defended with such valour that those who followed to assail were "very contumeliously repulsed."† When a portion of the royalists entered Annandale, they were dealt with in a similar fashion. The fortresses of Threave and Lochmaben, and other lesser strongholds, displayed each a rebel flag ; and the King, unable to capture them by storm, had to subject them to a regular siege, which proved in most instances successful : after which result, the royal authority was—nominally at least—re-established in the district.

Even in his hour of triumph the King tempered justice with mercy. No frowning gibbet, with its human tassel, rose to glut judicial vengeance : all he required was submission, and the money penalty originally imposed. The former was no longer refused, and the latter was promised in full, and partially paid.

* Pitscottie, p. 34. † Ibid, p. 35.

Y

Well content with having humbled the haughty Douglases, and, as he thought, taught them a lesson in loyalty, the King broke up his army and returned to Edinburgh.

It may readily be conceived that when the news of what had occurred in Nithsdale reached Douglas at Rome he was over-whelmed by rage and shame. Whilst basking in the sunbeams of the Papal Court, "the observed of all observers," to have his ancestral domains despoiled and his family degraded was indeed mortifying to his proud mind ; and as he hastened homeward schemes of "vaulting ambition," rife with vengeance against his sovereign, would doubtless occupy his thoughts and give a colour to his dreams. But as he passed through England on his way he learned that King James had so consolidated his royal authority that it could not be any longer safely defied, even by a Douglas. Smothering his resentment, on reaching the Border he sent his brother James in advance to sound the disposition of the King towards him, which was found to be conciliatory.

On presenting himself at Court he was received not as an enemy but as a friend—a treatment he did not look for, which soothed his wounded spirit, and made him, for the time being, one of his Majesty's most loyal subjects. The King, indeed, acted towards Douglas with an excess of tenderness, as if desirous of melting him with kindness rather than of crushing him with the rigour he had provoked. The incensed monarch and the turbulent baron became like sworn brothers to each other. "The Earl," says Pitscottie, " was received right heartfully by the King, and was remitted of all things bygone : wherefore he promised faithfully to rule all things within his bounds at the King's command and pleasure ; and then he received all fortalices and strengths again out of the hands of the King's men of war ; and thereafter was holden in such great estimation and favour by the King that he was made lieutenant-general of the kingdom." *

How sad to find the Earl of Douglas, a few months afterwards, intriguing personally with the King of England, and justly exciting the suspicions of the sovereign from whom he was receiving so many favours. James was naturally indignant at such conduct on the part of Douglas ; but the placable monarch once more ex-tended his forgiveness to the offending noble, though he removed him from the lord lieutenacy, and entrusted the administration of affairs to Sir William Crichton and the Earl of Orkney.   Douglas was more offended by what he had lost than gratified by what he had regained.   There was an old feud between him and Crichton, which the elevation of the latter caused to flame up afresh. Douglas hated his successful rival, and no love was lost between them ; Crichton, enjoying the royal sunshine, being in no ways disposed to help his enemy out of the shade.

* Pitscotttie, p. 35.

The ambitious and infatuated Earl had been more than suspected, half a year before, of treasonable tamperings with England : he now openly entered into a league with the Earls of Crawford, Ross, and Murray, to overthrow the King's ministers— ay, and if need be for that end, to dethrone the King himself. Whilst his Majesty was highly exasperated at this combination, fresh causes of offence were given by Douglas, which called aloud for punishment ; the chief of these being his treatment of Sir John Herries, younger of Terregles, and M'Lellan, tutor of Bombie, whom he put to death—hanging the former, and beheading the latter—because they were not sufficiently submissive to his rule.

James II., now aged twenty-one, had acquired increased energy with his years. Fully prepared for the pending emergency, he resolved once more to try fair means with his contumacious subject ; and should these fail, to crush him, and be truly king. The result is well known. Douglas, placated by a conciliatory letter from his sovereign, visited the Court at Stirling, where, after being luxuriously banqueted, he was summoned to a private chamber by his royal master, and required to break the covenant entered into between him and other nobles. The Earl gave an evasive answer ; but the King was not to be trifled with, and pressed the question : upon which Douglas, after saying he must first consult his associates, emphatically refused to comply with the King's demand. James, losing all self-control, then exclaimed, " If thou wilt not break the bond, this shall !" and plunged a dagger into the heart of Douglas. Some of the royal attendants rushed in and completed the deed of slaughter.* Thus perished, in his prime and pride, William, the eighth Earl of Douglas. Rebellious and tyrannical though he was, his assassination by the King is utterly indefensible, and is a dark blot on the reputation of that prince. The atrocious deed was no more premeditated by him than the slaughter of Comyn at Dumfries by his royal ancestor ; but that he should have allowed himself to be betrayed by passion into the perpetration of such a crime, aggravated by the breach of his word, and of the sacred rights of hospitality, is truly deplorable.

Though the eighth Earl of Douglas involved Dumfriesshire in a " sea of troubles," his death did not purchase tranquillity. James, brother of the slaughtered nobleman, and ninth Earl of Douglas, took up arms to avenge his death, the strife which

* In an Edinburgh newspaper of 14th October, 1797, there is the subjoined paragraph :—" On Thursday se'nnight, as some masons were digging a foundation in Stirling Castle, in a garden adjacent to the magazine, they struck upon a human skeleton, about eight yards from the window where the Earl of Douglas was thrown after he was stabbed by King James II. It is thought, and there is little doubt but what it is his remains, as it is certain that he was buried in that garden, and but a little distance from the closet window."

ensued involving not the district merely, but the kingdom. It continued for upwards of two years ; and it was at times uncertain whether the Stewarts or the Douglases should reign in Scotland. The general current of the contest need not be traced. Confining our attention chiefly to its course in Dumfriesshire, let us state that the King, about eleven months after the outbreak of the rebellion, led a large army into the country, in order to punish Douglas in the chief seat of his power and pride. Being winter, however, he could not carry out his design effectually. " He burnt the corns and houses, herried the countries, and slew some spies ;" * and, in spring, sent his troops back to renew the destructive warfare. Annandale became the chief theatre of hostilities. In that district Douglas, notwithstanding numerous reverses, was still lord and king : but other parts of Dumfriesshire boldly disavowed his rule ; for which act of independence and loyalty they were much harassed by his three brothers, Archibald, Earl of Murray, Hugh, Earl of Ormond, and John, Lord Balveny. Highly imprudent it was for these noblemen to inflame still further in this way the resentment of barons who would rather have served both Douglas and King James, had the conduct of the former not rendered that impossible. It was a bad day for this domineering family when they arrayed against them the chiefs of a county over which they had long exercised an unrivalled sway, and many of whom were of their own kith and kin. " A house divided against itself cannot stand."

On the 1st of May, 1455, the ground now occupied by the town of Langholm, in Eskdale, was the scene of an engagement which sealed the doom of the house of Douglas. The three noblemen named above led one party of the belligerants, who were confronted by the men of the county, headed by Maxwell, Johnstone, Scott, Carlyle,†*(a)* and other chiefs. A brief sanguinary battle resulted in the utter rout of the Douglases. The Earl of Murray was slain, and his head sent as a trophy to King James ; the Earl of Ormond was taken prisoner, tried for treason, and executed ; and Lord Balveny fled to the Earl, his brother, in England. Those who were chiefly instrumental in freeing Dumfriesshire from the rule of this imperious family were liberally rewarded for

---

* Pitscottie, p. 35.

† This was William, Lord of Torthorwald. He presented a bell to the Parish Church of Dumfries, inscribed thus : " Wilhelmus de Carleil, Dom. de Torthorwalde, me fecit fieri in honore Sancti Michaelis : Ann. Dom. MCCCCXXXXIII." " William de Carlyle, Lord of Torthorwald, caused me to be made in honour of St. Michael. The year of our Lord, 1443." This bell still survives. It hangs on the bartizan of the Mid Steeple, and was, down till about fifteen years ago, employed in the secular duty of warning the lieges when fires broke out in the Burgh.

(a) The bell has now, for many years, been deposited in the Observatory Museum.

their services. Johnstone and Carlyle obtained a grant of the forty-pound land of Pittenain, in Clydesdale ; Sir Walter Scott acquired the lands of Abington, Phareholm, and Glengonar, in the same district—thus making broader and deeper the basis of the noble house of Buccleuch ; and the Maxwells and Beatties were not overlooked.(*a*)

In the following year an act of Parliament completed what the sword at Arkinholm had begun. It attainted the Douglases —deprived them of their rank and estates by one fell swoop— their lordships of Eskdale and Galloway becoming the property of the Crown, and Annandale, with its appendant Castle of Loch- maben, being granted by King James to his second son, Alexander, whom he created Earl of March, Lord of Annandale, and Duke of Albany. It was not, however, till the King marched with an army into Galloway that that province acknowledged the royal authority, and the Castle of Threave submitted to receive a royal garrison. Another fortress of the family, Lochrutton Castle, was placed in the keeping of Herries of Terregles, near kinsman to the loyal chief whom the eighth Earl of Douglas hanged like a felon for the crime of being loyal to his sovereign. The exiled and dis- inherited Earl made repeated attempts to redeem his fortunes. In 1456 we find him undertaking a foray into Berwickshire, where he was encountered and defeated by one of his own blood, George, Earl of Angus, descended from William, first Earl of Douglas, by his third wife, Margaret, Countess of Angus. This overthrow gave rise to a popular saying, founded on the different complexions of the two branches of the family, that " the Red Douglas had put down the Black." *

Before the rebellious Earl comes again prominently on the scene, James II. is killed by the bursting of a cannon employed in the siege of Roxburgh Castle, which had been held by the English since the battle of Durham ; and his son James, a boy who had just seen seven summers, ascends the throne. It is not till July, 1484, twenty-four years after the latter event, that James, ninth and last Earl of Douglas, is seen engaged in another enterprise, with the view of blotting out the sentence written against him in the records of Parliament and the book of Fate. Alexander, Duke of Albany, the late King's second son, had long been inflamed by

---

(*a*) The Exchequer Rolls for the period shew a number of remissions of Crown debts made to loyal subjects. For instance, John Murdoch, fined for salmon poaching, was let off because he had fought at Arkinholm.

* This defeat was also made the subject of a Latin epigram, which has been thus Anglicised :

> " Pompey by Cæsar only was o'ercome,
> None but a Roman soldier conquered Rome ;
> A Douglas could not have been brought so low,
> Had not a Douglas wrought the overthrow."

guilty aspirations ; and fancying that with the help of Douglas and the King of England he might make a successful stroke for the throne, he entered into a negotiation with the expatriated noble-man, the result of which was their joint invasion of Dumfriesshire with a small English army. The arrangement was of this nature : in the event of success, Albany to become King of Scotland, acknowledging Henry of England as his superior ; Douglas to receive back his rank and estates. Once more the smaller proprie-tors of the county saved it and the nation from ruinous disaster. Dreading the restoration of a family whom they had good reason to dislike, and devotedly loyal to the throne, they turned out in great force when summoned by the signal fires which announced the approach of an enemy. The Master of Maxwell, Johnstone of of Johnstone, Murray of Cockpool, Crichton of Sanquhar, Carru-thers of Holmains, and Charteris of Amisfield, were the principal leaders of the Dumfriesians as they proceeded in the direction of Lochmaben, again to cope with their old enemies the English, and their old oppressor the Earl of Douglas. Though King James sent no troops to their assistance, he yet, by way of promoting their undertaking, issued a proclamation offering a hundred-pound land to any one who should kill or capture his rebellious subject.

The invaders had only a small force, numbering less than a thousand men ; but they supposed that when pushing up the country many of the inhabitants, lured by hopes of pillage, would join them. They reached the parish of Hoddam unopposed, and according to Hume, a body of English footmen, under Musgrave, occupied the old Roman encampment of Burnswark, while the main body proceeded towards Lochmaben—the leaders announcing that they desired to deposit offerings on the high altar of Bruce's burgh, whereas their real intention was to make a ravenous descent on the wares exposed for sale in its streets during the fair held on the 22d of July, St Magdalene's Day. The patriotic men of the county were there before them, to defend things small and great--the movables of the market—the permanent institutions of the kingdom ; and had they not, by fighting heroically, rolled back the aggressive tide, the deluge of a destructive revolution would have swept over the land, engulfing, perhaps, the monarchy in its waters. An obstinate conflict took place. It commenced early in the forenoon ; when the summer's sun sank, victory still hung in the balance ; and if at any time Musgrave had struck in with his auxiliary force, he could have easily turned the scale ; but, says Hume, " they fled at the first sight of the enemy, so that the rest behoved either to do or die, and therefore they fought it out manfully." Even the clouds of night failed to separate the combatants ; but long before the early dawn of another day, Albany, thoroughly beaten, was on the south side of the Border, with his back to Scotland, the remnant of his routed followers accompanying him ; and Douglas was a captive.

Though somewhat enfeebled by age, the Earl fought with characteristic bravery. Late in the day he was struck from his horse, and while wandering about the field, careless of life, if not "a-weary of the sun," he was met by one who had in happier times served him as a squire—Kirkpatrick of Ross, brother to the Laird of Closeburn*—and to whom he at once surrendered, saying "I have foughten long enough against my fortune, and since I must die, I will rather that ye (who have been my own servant, and faithful to me as long as I did anything likely for myself) have the benefit thereby, than any other. Therefore, take me and deliver me to the King, according to his proclamation ; but see thou be sure beforehand that he keep his word." Much affected, the young man offered to flee with his former chief to England. "Nay, nay," said the Earl, "that may not be." Wearied with endless troubles—impressed, too, with the feeling that his game of guilty ambition had been fully played out and irretrievably lost, he despairingly declined the offer ; and, after being secreted in a neighbouring cottage for some days, he was delivered to the King.† When the distinguished captive was carried before his Majesty—actuated by shame, perhaps by pride, or a mixture of both—he turned his back upon the sovereign ; and when, instead of being sent to the scaffold, as his crimes merited, he was sentenced to confinement for life in the Monastery of Lindores, he muttered despondingly, "He who may no better, must needs turn monk."‡

The victors in this contest were duly rewarded by their grateful sovereign—one of them, Sir Robert Crichton, being created a peer, under the title of Lord Sanquhar ; while to Kirkpatrick was given the fifty-pound land of Kirkmichael ; "which," says Hume, "is possessed by his heirs unto this day."§ (a)

---

* The barony of Ross, in Mid-Annandale, was held by a branch of the Kirkpatricks at a very early period. On 27th April, 1372, William Kirkpatrick of Ross granted a charter to John of Garroch of the two-merk land of Glengys (on the west side of the water of Wamphray) and Galvilgil.—Writs of the Carlyle family.

† Hume, vol. i., pp. 378-9.

‡ Hawthornden, Hist., p. 150 ; and Hume, vol. i., p. 381.

§ The historian does not explain why, when the King had offered a hundred-pound land for Douglas, dead or alive, he only recompensed his captor with land of half that value. The term "fifty-pound land" means that the land was entered in the Government cess book at that amount of yearly value.

(a) Kirkpatrick received apparently his full stipulated £100 land. At anyrate £90 land is included in the charter of 2nd Oct., 1484, in Registrum Magni Sigilli, ii., 1603. A share of his reward was claimed by Charteris of Amisfield (Acta Dominorum Concilii, p.* 95).

More important from the Dumfries standpoint than these, however, was an incident of the Exchequer audit of 1484. The town was £20 in arrear with its burgage rent due to the Crown ; but on 30th July, 1484, the auditors received letters from the King that these arrears were remitted, and the claim

In the inglorious manner just described, the proud earldom
which had existed for ninety-eight years (an average of barely eleven
years to each possessor of the title), and the noblest branch of the
lofty line of Douglas, became extinct. Some few of its members
were, as we have seen, virtuous as well as brave. Its chiefs, with
perhaps one exception, were intellectually great ; and several of
them were highly accomplished, considering the age in which they
lived. Ambition, " the last infirmity of noble minds," was, however,
the besetting sin of the family. Dumfriesshire for a century was
so mixed up with their fortunes that the history of the one during
that period is almost the history of the other. Had the talents and
influence of the Douglases been always wisely directed, what a
blessing they would have been to their native district and to the
kingdom ! We like to dwell on their indomitable valour, their
military genius, their magnificent hospitality ; but the tendency
to yield them hero-worship is kept in check when we reflect upon
the wicked uses to which their natural gifts and power were often
turned. None of them, except the stainless warrior, who, though
dead, conquered at Otterburn—and perhaps also the fourth Earl,
who fell in France—was worthy of the epithet " good," which their
progenitor, Sir James, acquired. Speaking of them generally, they
were mighty men of war ; but most of them were indifferent landlords, and bad subjects. Heavy penalties were paid ; but punishment brought no reformation. The lessons taught by adversity
were despised ; and now we see the haughty house, that would not
be curbed or counselled, utterly overthrown.

discharged " to the community of said burgh for their faithful services rendered by said community in times past, and specially now in resistance of
rebels and traitors and English enemies."--(Exchequer Rolls, ix., 297.)
      In consequence of this episode no doubt it was that at this time San-
quhar as a burgh of Barony had conferred upon it the coveted rights of cross,
market and fairs.—(Reg. Mag. Sig., ii., 1606.)

CHAPTER XVI.

Scarcely had the reign of James III. commenced, than Warwick (known in England as the " King-maker ") is said to have come to Dumfries, and obtained an interview there (in 1462) with Mary of Gueldres, for the purpose of soliciting her consent to a marriage with his royal master, Edward IV. So it is stated by Wyrcestre, a contemporary annalist. The match, if ever projected, did not take place ; and the very next year Warwick appeared in the county, not as a peaceful matrimonial agent, but as a destructive soldier—the venerable town of Lochmaben suffering especially from his visit. Hostilities were not long continued ; and on the 1st of June, 1464, they were followed by a truce, the terms of which were arranged by Warwick and the Scottish Commissioners, at Lochmaben Stane—which frequently figured in these times as a place of rendezvous and treaty.* (a)

---

* Lochmaben Stane stands on the farm of Old Gretna, in the parish of Gretna. It measures eight feet in height, and twenty-one in circumference. It was formerly neighboured by a number of smaller stones, enclosing, in oval form, half an acre of ground—the remains, probably, of a Druidical temple. The "Stane," which still remains, is specifically referred to in many old charters and other deeds, and doubtless derived its name from the circumstance that it was situated within the barony of Lochmaben. The following are extracts from Pitcairn's Criminal Trials, vol. i., part i., p. 398 :—" May 12, 1557. —Roger Kirkpatrick of Closeburn, William Kirkpatrick of Kirkmichaell, and Thomas Kirkpatrick of Frierkerse, got remission from the Queen for abiding from the army ordained to convene at Lochmaben Stane on February 16 last, to meet the Warden before sunrise, to push forwardt with him to the day of trew, for meeting of the Wardone of England." " May 14.—Alexander Stewart of Garleise, John Dunbar of Mochrame, John Gordoune of Barskeoche, John M'Culloch of Torhouse, John Jardine of Apilgerth, Robert Moffet (senior and junior) of Grantoune, Thomas Moffet of Knok, Robert Johnnestoune of Coittis, and John Creychtoune, tutour of Sanchare, found caution to underly the law at the next aire of Dumfries, for abiding from the Queen's army ordained to convene at Lochmaben Stane."

(a) " The character of Solway as a Border meeting-point is seen to be maintained in the fourteenth century by the record of prisoners being ransomed,

The Angus branch of the Douglases now began to flourish. When the turbulent nobles of the kingdom rebelled against their weak sovereign, Archibald, fifth Earl of Angus, agreed, in the words of the well-known parable of the rats and mice, propounded by his confederate, Lord Grey, to " bell the cat ;" that is, seize the King's powerful favourite, Cochrane, who, from being an architect, had been created Earl of Mar. How the cat's prototype was entrapped and hanged, and the King himself was for a while imprisoned by the rebel chiefs, we need not describe in detail. Other six years filled up the measure of the King's reign, which "treason, malice domestic, foreign levy " continued to embitter. When the final crisis came, and the barons, in open rebellion against their sovereign, gave him battle at Sauchieburn, a large proportion of their force was furnished by Galloway, Liddisdale, and Annandale ; (b) and when the royal army broke up, utterly undone, its defeat was chiefly due to the long spears from the Western Border. Thrown from his horse as he galloped off the field, the monarch,

---

and of a kind of market being held there. . . . There are unfortunately no documents on the administration of March law on the western border until 1398, when the first of a long series of allusions is made to the Clochmabenstane, afterwards oftener styled Lochmabenstane, as the specific forum of the West March. From 1398 onward the Lochmabenstane plays a large part in Border litigation and negotiation. The Warden courts were held there, and generally, it may be said, that exactly the functions of that sort assigned to the Sulwath in the end of the thirteenth century have at the end of the fourteenth century come to belong to the Lochmabenstane. . . It is close to the junction of the Sark and Kirtle with the Esk. Geographically, functionally, and historically, it answers at the end of the fourteenth century closely to the characteristics of the 'place called Sulwat, at the marches of the realms,' a hundred years before. Hence the belief that this is no chance coincidence, but that in very truth the Lochmabenstane marks the Scottish terminus of the great historic ford. This conclusion, if well founded, must add a new interest to that old grey stone. Dropped from some iceberg in an earlier geological period, it lay, when the land emerged from the sea, an unheeded block until the barbaric piety of some ancient race installed it as the presiding stone of an oval group—the chief stone of the cluster, as its original Celtic name of Lochmaben possibly means. Or it may mark the grave, or be otherwise associated with Maponus, a heathen deity equalled with Apollo, worshipped in Cumberland and Northumberland during the Roman occupation ; or with the memory of Mabon, that vague Arthurian heroic adumbration. Whatever its original connotation, we can see that in after centuries the solemnity inherited from a forgotten purpose clung to it like the mossy verdure around its base, and it became a fit adjunct of the courts of Border justice and the transaction of grave international business. And if the while, besides all this, it pointed out the great track across the Solway, one must perceive in it a landmark of extraordinary interest, past which, in alternate flux and reflux, like the sea beside it, there swept for centuries successive invasions. In 1296 it saw advance the first battalion in the War of Independence. In 1449 it gave its name to the battle of Sark, called by contemporaries 'the battell of Lochmaban Stane.' In any view its geography requires scrutiny."—See " Annals of Solway."

(b) Bot at the last the theiffis of Annerdaill come in schotting and crying and feirit the king sa that he had no praticke in weir, that he tuike purpois and raid his way.—Pitscottie (ed. Scottish Text Society), i., 208.

maimed and bleeding, was borne into a neighbouring cottage. On being asked his name by its female tenant, he answered incautiously, "I was your king this morning!" adding, "let me have a priest." The woman went out, calling wildly for a priest to shrive the suffering King. "I am a priest; lead me to him," said a straggler who presented himself. Whether he was so or not has never been properly determined. According to Buchanan, the stranger was actually a priest named Borthwick, who had joined the rebel army; and certainly not one of the vengeful barons arrayed against the sovereign could have acted towards him with more felonious hate. The ruffian, on finding that the illustrious sufferer's bruises were not likely to prove fatal, exclaimed, in reply to his request for absolution, "This shall presently absolve thee!" and plunged a poinard repeatedly into the King's heart.

The dreadful dagger scene in which the royal victim's father was the actor, and William, Earl of Douglas, the sufferer, twenty-six years before, in the same neighbourhood, rises up to memory as we read, horror-stricken, of this parallel atrocity. The murderer of King James III. never came forward to ask from the rebellious lords a reward for his black deed : he slunk away into the congenial shadows, as if overcome by remorse—his identity and motive remaining an unravelled mystery.

It must not be supposed, because many Annandale and Liddisdale men fought against the king at the battle of Sauchie, that the county generally sympathised with the rebels.(a) John, fourth Lord Maxwell, who was rapidly becoming the leading nobleman in Nithsdale, supported his sovereign on that fatal field; yet, after the death of James, he managed to make good terms with the victorious barons, in virtue of which he was appointed to rule Dumfriesshire jointly with the Earl of Angus, till the young king, James IV., now aged fifteen years and seven months, should reach his majority in 1494. This arrangement was made by Act of Parliament. It was a tribute to the rising influence of Lord Maxwell ; and, as further proof of consideration shown to him by the Government, we learn from the royal treasurer's accounts that being in arrear, as Steward of Annandale, the sum of £3745, he obtained, in 1508, a full discharge from the king on paying £1000.

As James increased in years he exhibited a rare combination of energy and prudence, which, together with his captivating manners, enabled him to control in some degree, without irritating, the powerful and jealous nobles who had placed him upon the throne. Scotland began to feel that the sceptre was swayed by a real, not a nominal, king ; and as, through his marriage, in 1503

(a) The lairds of Amisfield and Cockpool were both summoned on charges of treason because of their adherence to the royal side as against the victorious faction headed by the Prince.—Acts Parl. Scotland, ii., 201. Lord Treasurer's Accounts, i., 92.

with Margaret, daughter of Henry VII. of England, the country was blessed with peace for a series of years, it enjoyed for the time being a measure of prosperity to which it had been long a stranger. In the year after this seemingly happy nuptial alliance the young sovereign paid a visit to Dumfries for the purpose of holding an "ayre," or criminal court, in accordance with an act passed by his first Parliament, which bore this striking preamble : " It is avisit and concludit, anent the furthputting of justice, throw all the Realme, that our Soverane Lord sal ride in proper persoune about to all his aieris."* Though the king came on a grave mission, it was not in the nature of the man to be morose or stern, even at such a period. In his train were harpers and pipers, as well as a dempster and an executioner ; and music, feasting, and revelry ruled the hours which the serious duties of the court left free. During his stay, the old burgh would luxuriate in the radiant atmosphere of the royal presence—dreading neither Border banditti nor Southron marauders so long as it remained. If ever "the divinity that doth hedge a king" is enhanced by mental grace and manly beauty, it must have been so in the case of our Fourth James, the most lovable, and, spite of his faults, the best of all the Stewart line.

> " The monarch's form was middle size ;
> For feat of strength or exercise
> Shaped in proportion fair ;
> And hazel was his eagle eye,
> And auburn of the darkest dye
> His short curled beard and hair.
> Light was his footstep in the dance,
> And firm his stirrup in the lists ;
> And, oh ! he had that merry glance
> That seldom lady's heart resists."†

It was in early autumn that King James arrived. On the 13th of August there was paid from the royal purse, xiij.s. [13s] to the " pyparis of Dumfrise ;" his Majesty employing "local talent" in the musical line as well as his own staff of minstrels. After remaining in the town a day or two, making arrangements for the assize, he passed on a justiciary tour to the Western Border, taking with him an armed escort, and his customary retinue of bards, singers, and bagpipers, including a reverend personage who figures in the books of the treasury as "the cruikit Vicar of Dumfreis," he having received a largesse of "xiiij.s." (14s) for singing to the King in Lochmaben town. James's passion for music and sport is illustrated by other entries in these accounts ; and they also show that he and his father-in-law stood at that time on the best of terms. The Prior of Carlisle sent a butt of Malvoisie to the Scottish monarch, the two men who carried the welcome present getting a gratuity of "lvj.s. ;" "twa wiffis brought aill to the King

---

fra Sir Johne Musgrave," for which they were duly rewarded ; and the same English knight sent his own huntsmen to beat cover and blow the horn when James indulged in the pleasures of the chase. On the 23d of August the King played at cards in Bruce's burgh ; and who should be his opponent but Lord Dacre, the doughty English Warden—both well content to enjoy for once a bloodless, friendly contest. James seems to have been worsted in the game, as there is charged against him, in connection with it, the sum of " xlvj.s viij.d." (46s 8d). Happy would it have been for Scotland and himself had he never played with English warrior in a less peaceful arena for a heavier stake. That his Majesty did not spend all his time on trifles when in Annandale and Eskdale is sufficiently shewn by such dread entries as the following :—" Aug. 17.—To the men hangit the theves at Hullirbus, xiij.s. [13s] ; for ain raip to hang thaim in, viij.d." [8d]. " Aug. 21.—To the man that hangit the theves in Canonby, be the Kingis command, xiij.s." [13s].

On the 24th of the same month James returned "furth of Eskdale" to the county town, remaining there twenty-three days, during the continuance of the court. He lodged with the Cunningham family ; and the likelihood is that he occupied a spacious chamber belonging to them, of which we get an inkling afterwards, under the designation of the Painted Hall. The court, sitting in the Castle, presided over by " Andrea Domino Gray ' as justiciar, and, doubtless often graced by the presence of the King, disposed of the following, among other cases, from the town or district : " Robert Grersoune, in Drumfreis, produced a remission for art and part of the cruel slaughter of Sir John M'Briar, chaplain in the town of Drumfreis." Under what circumstances M'Briar, who belonged to a family of distinction, was put to death, is not stated, nor is the result of the trial recorded. " Gilbert Thomesone, convicted of the theftuous taking of merchandise from the merchants of Drumfreis, at the time of the Burning thereof : Item, for art and part of theftuous taking and concealing xlv. sheep furth of Schellop : Item, of common Theft and common Reset of Theft—Hanged." Whether the burning here referred to, of which Thomesone took advantage was accidental or the work of incendiaries, does not appear. " Adam Baty [or Beattie], convicted of art and part with the King's rebels in Eskdale—Hanged." " James Monse,* near Lochmabane, came in the King's will for destroying the woods of Lochmabane, Bukrig, Heichrig, Rammerskalls, and Rowekellpark.

---

* This name appears to be the same with that now known as Mounsey. It is a singular coincidence that Dr Mounsey, who sprang from the lowest origin in the vicinity of Lochmaben, lived to become the proprietor of the estate of Rammerscales, &c., here described.—Note in Kincaid's Criminal Trials, vol. i., part i., p. 40.

Gavin Murray, brother of the Laird of Cockpule, became surety to
the King." "John Pattersoun, in Tasseholme, convicted of fishing
salmon in the water of Annand during the prohibited time, was
amerciated in v.l." (£5). "William Jarding, called Braid-suerd to
the King ; Robert Dunwedy, son of the Laird of Dunwedy ; and
Gavin Johnestoune, were admitted to our sovereign lord the King's
composition, for art and part of the stouthrief of four horses, price
xl.l. [£40], two candlesticks, one goblet, with sundry other goods,
worth xx.l., from Bartholomew Glendumvyne, in company with
the Laird of Johnestoune and his accomplices.—Sir Thomas Kirkpatrick of Closeburne, knight, became surety for the said Robert,
and Adam Johnestoune of that Ilk became surety for the said
Gavin, to satisfy parties." Other minutes disclose two bloody
deeds, such as were of no rare occurrence in those days of violence
—the murder of the Laird of Dunwedy or Dinwoodie, and of the
Laird of Mouswald, by neighbours of their own rank. The Dinwoodies, who had been for a long time previously settled on lands
called after them in Applegarth, were at feud with the Jardines
the chief proprietors of that parish. Some time in 1503, a band of
armed men made sudden entrance into Dinwoodie Tower, slew
Thomas, the chief of the clan, and then disappeared. The
mysterious outrage was, naturally enough, attributed to the
Jardines, but was never fairly brought home to them. John
Jardine, in Sibbaldbesyde, and Robert Brig, residing with
Alexander Jardine of Applegarth, were specially charged with the
crime. As, however, they presented "a remission from the King,"
when brought before Lord Gray, at Dumfries, they were set at
liberty—their chief engaging to reproduce them if called upon.*
Justice seems to have been also baffled in the other murder case.
Thomas Bell, of Curre, or Currie and Stephen Johnstoune,
arraigned for the crime, kept out of the way ; as also did their
sureties, the Laird of Castlemilk, and William Purdum, portioner
in Middlebie ; and all that the judge could do in the matter was to
"denounce" the accused at the horn, as rebels, and to "amerciate"
their sureties. During the sittings of the court the judge was
paid forty shillings per day—in all, forty-six pounds. It broke up
about the middle of September. On the 13th of that month
James cleared off scores with his landlady, as recorded in the
following quaint note of payment :—" To William Cunnyngham's
wif in Drumfreise, for the Kingis bele chere [good cheer], x.l.'
(£10). A few days before, his Majesty gave a dole to the Minorite
brethren in the Vennel, which is thus entered :—"Sept. 8.—To the

* "Only nine years afterwards," says Anderson, in his Manuscript History, Advocate's Library, "the Laird Dinwiddie was slayne in Edinburgh by
two persons, who escaped, by taking the Sanctuarie of Holyrood House." Sir
James Balfour (Annales, vol. 1., p. 235) says that this second act of assassination was committed by the Jardines.

Freris of Drumfreis, xiiij.s." (14s). The King's sojourn, so curiously made up of work and play, being now over, he bade farewell to his loyal burgesses of Dumfries, all sorry, we doubt not, that such a sunny episode in their annals had come so soon to an end.* (a)

Truly, a gay, genial, pleasure-loving monarch was James IV. ; yet, with all his habitual mirthfulness, he was subject to fits of gloom, that usually came upon him in midsummer, and under the influence of which even his outward man sometimes underwent a strange alteration.

> " In offices as strict as Lent
> King James's June was ever spent."†

He had, as a boy, taken part with the barons when they joined in warlike array against his father. Though scarcely a voluntary agent at that time, he yet wore a macerating iron belt round his waist by way of penance, to which some ounces were added annually ; and every recurring anniversary of Sauchieburn found him in a bitterly penitential mood. It was on one of those occasions that the King came to the gates of Our Lady's Chapel in Dumfries,‡ habited as a lowly Franciscan—the royal devotee, in his gown of coarse grey serge, appearing as unlike as possible to

---

* For the proceedings at this justice ayre, and the extracts from the Accounts of the Lord High Treasurer in the reign of James IV., we are indebted to the first volume of that most valuable work to the historian, Pitcairn's Criminal Trials. Subjoined are a few more entries :—" Aug. 2.— For twa hidis to be jakkis to Thomas Boswell and Watte Trumbull, minstrals, agane the raid of Eskdale, lvj.s. To James Hog, tale-teller, to fee twa hors in Eskdale, with kingis harnes, in part payment, xxxiij.s. For foure corse bowis and ane hundreth canyais [arrows], agane the raid of Eskdale, xij.li. [£12]. Aug. 8.—Payit for v. pair spurs to the King, twa pair stirrup irnis, xij. riding girthis, xij. housing girthis, iiij. hors collaris, x. hors houses, and for hors schoing, v.li. x.d. To ane man of Sir Alexander Jardinis, that come to the King with thingis [tidings] of the taking of Gib Lindesay and his complices, xiii.js. Aug. 13.—In Drumfrese, to minstrales to fee thaim horsis to Eskdale, and syne again to Drumfrese, xlij.s. To twa Inglise women that sang in the Kingis pailzeoune [pavilion], xxiij.s. Aug. 31.—Be the Kingis command, to Sir A. Jardine and his men for the taking of Gib Lindsay and uther twa with him, xxxli."

(a) William Cunnynghame, whose wife provided the " bele chere " for the King, is probably, says Sir Herbert Maxwell (" Dumfries and Galloway "), the same merchant to whom £42 had been paid in June previous for six tuns of wine sent by his Majesty as a present to Lord Dacre.

† " Marmion."

‡ This chapel was situated on the west side of what is now Irish Street, and northward of Bank Street, formerly called Calvert's Vennel. The locality is indicated by an old sazine, for the following extract from which we are indebted to Dr Dickson, Edinburgh, who is sprung from a Dumfriesshire family of note, and who takes much interest in the ancient history and muniments of the county :—" H. Aikin, Convener of Trades, his yard, near the Lady Chapel, lately purchased by me from Harley, betwixt Irishgait on the east, the chapel yards of John Rigg on the west, the way to the Nith on the south, and the lands sometime belonging to John Dickson on the north."

the jovial, care-defying prince who, a short while before, held court in Dame Cunningham's Painted Hall. After making his offerings at the altar, he proceeded staff in hand to pay his devotions before the shrine of St Ninian at Whithorn, whether he often went to bewail his fancied parricidal guilt, and the unlawful indulgences for which, unlike it, he was truly responsible.*

Four years after King James held his justice ayre at Dumfries, Lord Maxwell, to whom he had been so considerate, showed extreme disrespect to the royal authority, as represented by Robert, second Lord Sanquhar, Sheriff of Nithsdale. The Crichtons, like the Maxwells, had grown greatly in favour since the fall of the Douglases. There had been long a deadly feud between the two houses, which was at this time intensified by the circumstance that Lord Sanquhar seemed to be extending his influence over Lower Nithsdale, at the expense of Lord Maxwell, who, though Steward of Annandale, did not like to see the neighbouring sheriffdom possessed by his rival. The idea that a district occupied by many of his own adherents should be legally presided over by any other than a Maxwell was the reverse of pleasant to Lord John ; that it should be placed under the sway of a Crichton was deemed by him intolerable. "We must teach this aspiring chief a lesson—let him see who is the real master of Dumfries !" muttered the wrathful Steward. Probably Maxwell gave a readier

---

* There are some vague traditions in Dumfries regarding the visits paid to it by James IV., and his son, James V. ; one of these being that King James (which of them is not specified) slept all night under a huge tree that grew a little to the north-east of the town, near the present English road. The following inscription, taken from a tombstone in St Michael's Churchyard, is adduced in corroboration of the tale :—" In memory of John M'Neil, of Royal Oak, near this town, who departed this life, April 30th, 1836 ; aged 101 years." The epitaph is curious in itself, as being, we believe, the only one in the same cemetery in memory of a centenarian. That any of the Jameses should have spent a night in the open air, in the vicinity of Dumfries, cannot be credited ; but James IV. might, by resting himself, when on his barefooted pilgrimage, below an umbrageous oak, have originated this tradition. The Rev. Joseph Duncan (now of Torthorwald), who drew up the notice of Dumfries Parish, dated 1833, for the Statistical Account, says (p. 12) : " A curious relic of antiquity was some time ago discovered by Mr Affleck, ironfounder, while employed in selecting some pieces of old metal to throw into the crucible. It is circular, fully two inches in diameter, and about the thickness of a penny. Upon being struck with a hammer, a crust of verdigris came off, and on one side of it was discovered, engraved, a lion rampant, in the midst of a shield bordered with fleur de lis, and surrounded, in reversed characters, by the legend, ' Jacobus Dei Gra. Rex Scotorum ;' after which is a figure nearly similar to the letter ' S,' which we conclude must have been intended to represent the buckle of the belt on which the inscription is engraved. The seal, for such it is supposed to be, is formed of a compound of copper with some other metals, and is, with some plausibility, supposed to have been the privy seal of one of the kings of Scotland." Very likely this relic belonged either to Mrs Cunningham's royal lodger or his son, James V. ; and if the latter, may have been dropped by him when out on some of his nocturnal revels.

effect to this menace because he knew that the Sheriff of Nithsdale
had a charge of disloyalty hanging over his head.

Lord Sanquhar held a court in the county town towards the
close of July, 1508. On the 30th of that month no trials were proceeded with—the "dittays" having been deserted—the hall of
justice abandoned for the Lower Sandbeds that skirt the burgh,
where the warlike vassals of the noble Sheriff stood drawn up in
battle array, prepared in some degree for the threatened onset, of
which he had received timely notice. Lord Maxwell, at the head
of a considerable force, and accompanied by William Douglas of
Drumlanrig, entered the town by the Annandale road, from the
south, and attacked the Crichton party with a fury that proved
irresistible. How long the engagement continued is unknown.
Sir James Balfour speaks of it as "a grate feight"*—that it was a
sanguinary one is beyond any doubt. The same annalist records
that "Lord Sanquhar was overthrowen, and many of his frindes
killed."† Bishop Lesley, describing the issue of the affray, says:
"Lord Creychton was chaissit with his company frae Drumfries,
and the Laird of Dalyell and the young Laird of Cranchlay slain,
with divers uthers, quhairof thair appeared greit deidly feid and
bludshed." Thoroughly routed, Lord Sanquhar was chased from
the town over which he professed to hold rule in the King's name
—driven for refuge to his castle among the hills; leaving his
exulting rival, if not Sheriff of Nithsdale, undisputed chief of its
principal burgh.

Maxwell, however strange it may appear, was allowed to go
unpunished. Whether it was that extenuating circumstances were
brought forward to palliate the grossness of the outrage, or that
its perpetrator was too powerful to be meddled with, he was not
proceeded against judicially. "Partley be justice, and partley be
agreement, the whole cause [against him] was suddenly quyeted
and stanched;" but his chief colleagues in the affray, William
Douglas of Drumlanrig, John Fergusson of Craigdarroch, with his
son Thomas, and their accomplices, went through the form of a
trial on the 30th of September, 1512, at Edinburgh, for the murder
of Robert Crichton of Kirkpatrick (one of the Sheriff's party, and
probably a near relative), and were acquitted, on the ground that
the deceased Robert Crichton was "our soveraine lordis rebell, and
at his horne," when the conflict occurred.‡ The still unsettled and

‡ The Magna Assisa, or Great Assize, consisting of twenty-one lords and
gentlemen, presided over by Archibald, Earl of Angus, in giving a verdict in
the case, counselled the King's Highness "That the said allegit crimes be na
ditty; and that Lettres be written of Discharge; and Inhibitioun be gevin
and direct to Justice and Justice-Clerk, be our Soverane Lorde, and till all
utheris officiaris, that nane of them tak in Dittay, attache, arrest, or accuse
the said William Douglas, or his complices foresaide, for the said actioun, and
na crime be imput to thairapon, because it was funde obefore be the said

unsatisfactory state of Dumfriesshire may be inferred from the circumstance that the steward of one portion of it could in this flagitious way commit a murderous outrage on the sheriff of another with impunity.

If peace had continued, however, and length of days been vouchsafed to the King, he would, there is no doubt, have done much more to strengthen the power of the Crown, and extend the influence of the law, than he was privileged to accomplish. Henry VIII. of England having proclaimed war against France, Scotland, as the ally of the latter, after years of comparative tranquillity, again rang with the sound of hostile preparations—James, actuated by knightly devotion to the French Queen, as well as by friendship to her consort, having resolved to cross the Border with an invading army. Her Majesty, as the poet tells us,

> " Sent him a turquoise ring and glove,
> And charged him, as her knight and love,
>   For her to break a lance ;
> And strike three strokes with Scottish brand,
> And march three miles on Southern land,
> And bid the banners of his band
>   In English breezes dance." *

Many Dumfriesshire chiefs, including Lord Maxwell, joined the King's unfortunate expedition. It is not necessary that we should follow its fortunes by telling again " red Flodden's dismal tale," with which every reader of British history is familiar. Flodden was indeed a

> " Fatal field,
> Where shivered was fair Scotland's spear,
> And broken was her shield." †

James fell fighting desperately, and reckless of life, on seeing the ruin he had provoked. Among the " chiefs, knights, and nobles many a one " slain alongst with him in the disastrous battle were John, Lord Maxwell,‡ with his four brothers ; Robert, Lord Herries, with Andrew, his brother ; the two sons of the Earl of Angus ; two hundred gentlemen of the Douglas name, and numerous other men of note connected with Dumfriesshire and Galloway. In all the Border district, among high and low, there

---

Lordis that the said umquhile Robert, the time when he was slane, was our Souverane Lordis rebell, and at his horne, and for uthir resonable cause, moving the said Lordis ; except Fergy Fergussoun and Robin Fergussoun, to wham this declaratioun and counsall sall nocht extende, and thaim to be punist, as is contenit in the decret and deliverance be certane of the said Lordis thairapoune.—Pitcairn, vol. i., part i., p. 79.

* " Marmion."   † Ibid.

‡ In the Terregles Papers there is a brief of succession, dated 16th October, 1513, of Robert, son of John, Lord Maxwell, who fell " in Campo Bellico, in Northumberland."

was great lamentation for friends or relatives left lifeless on the field.(*a*)

This memorable battle was fought on the 9th of September, 1513. Stunning and terrible was the blow which it inflicted upon the Scots ; but, though thus deprived of their king and chief nobility, they rapidly recovered from its effects. Surrey, the victorious leader of the English, suffered so severely in the conflict that he was unable to enter Scotland and gather in the full harvest of his triumph. At first Margaret, the widowed Queen, was made Regent ; but, as she was mistrusted on account of being the sister of the English monarch (Henry VIII.), and of having hurriedly contracted a marriage with Archibald, sixth Earl of Angus, she was soon deprived of the office, which was then conferred on John, Duke of Albany. As his accession was opposed by Angus, one of the new Regent's first acts was to banish the Queen and her husband out of the country.

Though no general invasion of Scotland took place, in conse-quence of the late defeat, the English King let loose large bands of armed men upon the devoted Border territory, which they wasted with fire and sword. One of these marauding parties, headed by Lord Dacre, entered Dumfriesshire in the spring of 1514, his motive being very different from that which drew him to Lochmaben, ten years before, to encounter, in a card-playing tour-ney, Scotland's chivalrous King. The leading men of the country, with hundreds of their followers, had been "wede away" in the carnage of the preceding autumn, so that the invaders met with little resistance ; and they ravaged the district nearest them in a style of wanton barbarity. Dacre, in writing, on the 17th of May, an account of his destructive achievements to the English Council, says that he had laid waste Ewisdale, in which there were one hundred and forty ploughs (plough-lands) ; that he had almost depopulated Lower Annandale and Eskdale, in which there were more than four hundred ploughs ; that he had wholly destroyed the town of Annan, and thirty-three other townships. He boasts that all these ploughs and townships "are now clearly wasted, and no man dwelling in any of them at this day, save only in the towns of Annan, Stepel, and Wauchope." The sanguinary and remorse-less Warden concludes his report by intimating that he meant to continue his service " with diligence, from time to time, to the utmost annoyance of the Scots." Had not the Steward of Annan-

---

(*a*) Among the slain, besides those named above, were Sir William Douglas of Drumlanrig, Irving of Bonshaw, and from Galloway the Earl of Cassilis, Sir Alexander Gordon of Lochinvar, Sir Alexander Stewart of Garlies, the MacDoualls of Garthland, Logan, and French, M'Culloch of Myrtoun, Adair of Kilhit, and Sir William Maclellan of Bomby. A valuable list of the slain, made up from the records, has been printed by Mr J. H. Stevenson in his article, " The Flodden Death Roll," published in *Scottish Antiquary* for January and April, 1899.

dale been mouldering in his grave, and had not his son Robert, Lord Maxwell, been young, inexperienced, and with few retainers left on his muster-roll, Dacre would not have been in a condition to make such a report.

CHAPTER XVII.

JAMES V. VISITS DUMFRIESSHIRE, TO OVERAWE AND PUNISH THE TURBULENT
BORDERERS—JOHNNIE ARMSTRONG ENTERS INTO A BOND OF MANRENT
WITH LORD MAXWELL AT DUMFRIES—VISIT OF THE "GUDEMAN OF BAL-
LENGEICH" TO AMISFIELD TOWER—THE KING PROCEEDS TO ESKDALE—
TRAGICAL FATE OF JOHNNIE ARMSTRONG—CONDITION OF THE DEBATABLE
LAND—BEGINNING OF THE REFORMATION—OPPOSITION GIVEN TO IT BY
JAMES—ABORTIVE ATTEMPT OF ANGUS TO REGAIN HIS INFLUENCE BY
ENGLISH AID—HENRY OF ENGLAND REVIVES THE CLAIM OF HIS PREDE-
CESSORS TO THE SOVEREIGNTY OF SCOTLAND—VILLAINOUS SCHEME OF
LORD WHARTON TO CAPTURE THE KING OF SCOTS—BATTLE OF SOLWAY
MOSS—ROUT OF THE SCOTS, AND CAPTURE OF LORD MAXWELL AND OTHER
CHIEFS BY THE VICTORS—KING JAMES DIES OF A BROKEN HEART.

DURING the new King's minority, the Earl of Angus kept him
almost as a prisoner, and ruled the country at his pleasure ; but
the youthful monarch having acquired his freedom by an ingenious
stratagem, banished his autocratic keeper, and began to administer
public affairs with extraordinary vigour. Turbulent chiefs and
predatory bands kept the Border districts in perpetual " broiley,"
to use an expressive old term. "These disturbers," said the King,
"must be subdued, and rendered loyal and peaceable, at all hazards."
For this purpose he entered Dumfriesshire at the head of a large
army, letting it be known beforehand that he meant to "make the
rasch bush keep the cow ;" in other words, that he would put down
cattle-stealing—the chronic offence of the Borders—and render all
ranks, high as well as low, amenable to his rule.

At this period the predatory clan of the Armstrongs occupied
a large portion of the Debatable Land and its vicinity—their chief,
the Laird of Mangerton, having become a feudatory of the Earl of
Bothwell when he acquired the lordship of Liddisdale in 1491.
When Lord Dacre wasted Eskdale and Lower Annandale in 1514
there is reason to suppose that he received a helping hand from the
Armstrongs. The following extract from the records of the
Justiciary Court shows, at all events, that a few years afterwards
they had been legally proceeded against on some serious charge :—
"15th May, 1517.—Respite to the Armstrongs, Tailyors, and all
their kinsmen, friends, servants, and other dependants on them of
the clan Liddisdale, now dwelling in the Debatable Land and
Woods, that will deliver to the Governor sufficient pledges to
remain for good rule where they sall be assigned." This act of
grace was not appreciated by the lawless tribe. "Elliots and

Armstrongs ride thieves all," was still a true proverb so far as they were concerned ; and the King's representative in the district, Robert the fourth Lord Maxwell, finding the Armstrongs irrepressible by force, endeavoured to keep them in check by means of a treaty obligation. That nobleman had a special interest in the matter. He was next-door neighbour to the turbulent reivers of the Debatable Land : all around that den of doughty thieves lay rich possessions inherited by his family ; and the corn and oxen upon them were not a bit more secure than others in the district because they happened to belong to the Lord Warden of the Marches.

William, surnamed of Mangerton, seems to have been too tamely respectable for his position as a bandit chief ; and on his brother, the renowned Johnnie Armstrong, devolved the virtual leadership of the clan, All Maxwell's overtures were therefore made to Johnnie, who, with all his love for fighting and foray, was willing, if tempting terms were offered, to turn over a new leaf. Late in the autumn of 1525, in obedience to a request from Lord Maxwell, he left his Tower of Gilnockie, on the Esk, and, in company with his son Christie, met his lordship at Dumfries.* What transpired at the interview is not recorded, but the result is known : a bond of manrent signed for Johnnie on the 3rd of November, 1525, "with his hand at the pen, as he could not subscribe his name ;"† in which document the bold marauder swore submission to the Lord Warden, on condition of receiving his protection, and obtaining a grant of the lands of Langholm, with other pendicles in the same locality. Christie Armstrong entered into a similar bond on his own behalf—the material consideration in his case being a ten-pound land in Eskdale. These bonds were not very strictly interpreted by the Armstrongs. Perhaps they thought that all that was meant by them was immunity to the Warden's cattle from their ravages ; but if they spared these, they continued their raids elsewhere ; and when news on the subject reached King James it was accompanied by the aggravating report that his own representative, whose special duty it was to keep the peace of the Border, was protecting the lawless and living hand and glove with " broken men."

The first act of the young monarch on entering Dumfriesshire was a bold one. The Maxwells had all along maintained his cause against the Douglases, and their influence was paramount in the county ; but neither the memory of past favours nor the apprehension of converting a friend into an enemy prevented him from doing what he felt to be his duty. Maxwell was thrown into prison ; Lord Holme, the Lairds of Buccleuch, Polwart, and Kerr were also placed in ward : which chiefs, says Pitscottie, deserved punishment, since, instead of restraining the thievish Border clans, as in

---

* The Terregles Papers.   † Ibid ; and Barjarg MSS.

duty bound, they had "winked at their villainies, and given them way."

The King had also, if tradition is to be relied upon, a score to settle with the Laird of Amisfield, who occupied an official position as custodier of Castlemilk, Bellstower, and other fortresses on the Border. Before setting out from Stirling a poor widow, it is said, who had travelled all the way from the neighbourhood of Lochmaben, laid before him a tale of cruel hardship, and claimed redress. A party of Englishmen had penetrated to her little toft, carried off her only son, and whole stock of cattle—two cows; and when Sir John Charteris was told of the outrage, instead of capturing the marauders, as he could easily have done, he treated the complaining widow with rudeness and contempt, protesting that he had something else to do than look after her paltry concerns. The gracious monarch dismissed the petitioner with the assurance that her case would be attended to.

On arriving in Nithsdale he proceeded in disguise to Amisfield Tower, and "tirling at the pin" apprised the porter who answered the summons that he was the bearer of an important message to his lord. "Sir John is at dinner, and cannot be disturbed." "But, my good fellow," rejoined the King, "the English have crossed the Border in great force, and the Captain of Castlemilk must cause the beacons to be fired;" and the porter, propitiated by a few silver groats, broke in upon his master's revels with the tidings—only, however, to receive a curse for his intrusion. When another servant, pale with emotion, bore to Sir John a second message from the King, to the effect that the Gudeman of Ballengeich* had been long waiting at the gate seeking admittance but in vain, the terrified knight changed his tune, and knowing rather too late that his visitor was King James himself, he craved pardon on bended knee for his misconduct. The humbled Laird was then told in angry tones that he had something else to be sorry for and to atone—his gross neglect of the Annandale widow. "Her loss you must repay tenfold," said the indignant monarch; and, as for the poor woman's son, unless he is ransomed within ten days you shall die for it on the gallows.' As a further punishment a large portion of the royal troops was billeted on the offending officer during his Majesty's sojourn in the district.

After this characteristic episode James proceeded at the head of several thousand men on his justiciary excursion through the worst parts of the country. During his progress many men of substance submitted quietly to the King's will, giving security that they would appear if called upon to underlie the law for all crimes laid to their charge. Other offenders, whom he deemed

---

* The name usually assumed by James V., when roaming, according to his wont, through the country in disguise.

incorrigible, were relentlessly dealt with. Over a hill situated on the north side of St Mary's Loch runs a track (now barely visible) that is still termed the King's Road, as by it James passed from the Braes of Yarrow into Ettrick.* An old song embodies a tradition to this effect, and a reference to the roving gallantry of his disposition, which " The Jolly Beggar " and other ballads of his own commemorate :

> " The King rade round the Merecleuch head,
>   Booted and spurred, as we a' did see ;
> Syne dined wi' a lass at Mossfennan yett,
>   A little below the Logan Lee."

Be the amour here hinted at true or false, there can be no doubt as to James's tragical dealings with a gentleman-reiver who lived hard by—William Cockburne of Henderland. Cockburne was seized by James's orders, sent forthwith to Edinburgh, where he was tried, condemned, and executed—the charges against him, besides the general ones of high treason and common theft, being that he had, in company with certain Englishmen, plundered Archibald Sommerville and the lands of Glenquhome. There is a prevalent tradition that the unfortunate Laird of Henderland was hanged over his own castle gate, and that his widow Marjory buried him at a spot which is still shown as his grave in Meggat-dale ; but the facts are that he was regularly tried as above, on the 16th of May in the following year (1530), and beheaded in Edinburgh.† Adam Scott of Tuschelaw was taken at the same time as Cockburne, tried by the same tribunal two days after-wards, and was also convicted and beheaded : the charges against him were that he had theftuously taken " black maill " from certain parties, among others the tenants of Elsieshiels and the poor tenants of Hopcailyow.

To the luckless Laird of Gilnockie, Johnnie Armstrong, James determined to show as little mercy. If the bandit chief had

---

* Chambers's Picture of Scotland, p. 163.

† Both Sir Walter Scott and Robert Chambers, accepting the tradition, considered that the tragedy was embalmed in the beautiful ballad of " The Border Widow's Lament," which tells how the King " broke into her bower," " slew her knight," and " left her in extremitie ;" and then the mourner is made to say, with touching pathos :—

> " I sewed his sheet, making my maen ;
> I watched the corpse myself alane ;
> I watched his body, night and day—
> No living creature came that way.
>
> I took his body on my back,
> And whiles I gaed, and whiles I sate ;
> I digg'd a grave, and laid him in,
> And happ'd him wi' the sod sae green."

Pitcairn's matter-of-fact minute (vol. i., part i., p. 145) shews that the ballad was not inspired by the fate of Cockburne.

resolved on eluding the King he could easily have done so by crossing into Cumberland ; or, if he had been bent on a boldly defiant course, he might, by entrenching himself in one of his strong keeps on the Liddel, or by retiring to the fastness of Tarras Moss, have held out for a long period against the royal army. None of these steps was taken. Was Johnnie mad or infatuated when, with thirty-six of his followers, he rode within the infuriated monarch's reach ? or is the tale of the old ballad true, that "the King had written a loving letter, with his ain hand sae tenderlie," promising pardon to the freebooter if he would only submit to ask for it ? "He came before the King," says Pitscottie, "with his foresaid number, richly apparelled, trusting that in respect of the free offer of his person he should obtain the King's favour. But the King, seeing him and his men so gorgeous in their apparel, with so many brave men under a tyrant's command-ment, frowardly turning him about, bade take the tyrant out of his sight, saying, 'What wants that knave that a King should have ?' But John Armstrong made great offers to the King—that he would sustain himself with forty gentlemen ever ready at his service on their own cost, without wronging any Scottishman ; secondly, that there was not a subject in England—duke, earl, or baron—but within a certain day he should bring him to his Majesty, either quick or dead." * To all such tempting offers the King's ear was deaf, and to every entreaty of the outlaw the King's heart was sealed :—

> " Away, away, thou traitor strang !
>   Out o' my sicht soon may'st thou be !
> I granted never a traitor's life,
>   And now I'll not begin with thee !"

At length Johnnie, seeing when it was too late that his doom was irrevocable, retorted proudly, "It is folly to seek grace at a grace-less face !(a) But had I known this, I should have lived on the Borders in despite of King Harry and you both ; for I know that King Harry would downweigh my best horse with gold to know that I were condemned to die this day !" "God grant our men weel back again !" cried the ladies of Gilnockie and Tarras, as they looked from the turret windows when the gay cavalcade rode off to meet King James ; and the words of another ancient ballad well express the sad fidelity of their forebodings :

> " O lang, lang may their ladies sit,
>   Wi' their gowd kaims in their hair
> A' waiting for their ain dear lords,
>   For them they'll see nae mair."

* Pitscottie, p. 146.

(a) There is reason to believe that this phrase is an allusion to an ancient usage that the sight of the king's face entitled even a condemned prisoner to pardon. The usage is mentioned in "Pier's Plowman" (ed. Skeat).

Neither Johnnie nor one of his goodly company was allowed to revisit the glades of Eskdale ; they were led forth to instant execution, by command of the Rhadamanthine King, and hanged on growing trees at a place called Carlenrig Chapel, about ten miles above Hawick, on the high road to Langholm.

Of Gilnockie, long the outlaw's principal hold, no trace is left, the last relics of the tower having been removed to make room for a bridge over the Esk. On the opposite bank of that river, a little further up, still stand the ruins of Hallas, or Hollas, where, according to Sir Walter Scott, Johnnie Armstrong usually resided ; but that is more than doubtful. Hollas Tower was held in fee or wardenry by Lord Maxwell ; and though he granted lands in Eskdale to the outlaw it is nowhere mentioned that Hollas was included in the gift.*

After the King had by these tragical proceedings done his utmost to break up the system of robbery and terrorism that prevailed on the Borders, he relented so far as to set Lord Maxwell and the other chiefs whom he had imprisoned at liberty. He then returned with his army to Edinburgh. There is every reason to suppose that his Majesty soon came to see that no very heinous crime had been committed by the Lord Warden. On the 22d of June, 1526, Maxwell received from the King confirmation of his rights as Steward of Annandale and Kirkcudbrightshire ; not long afterwards he obtained an appointment in the royal household as " Chief Carver ;" and on the 5th of July, 1530, the escheated estates of Johnnie Armstrong were assigned to him as an additional proof that he had regained his sovereign's favour.†

Christie Armstrong, luckily for himself, escaped his father's fate by avoiding an interview with royalty. On learning what had occurred he took refuge in Cumberland, and became henceforth the sworn enemy of the Scottish monarch, and the enthusiastic ally of the English in their raids across the Border. The ballad from which we have already quoted states with some truth that Johnnie Armstrong performed patriotic service in defending the frontier line between the kingdoms—being such a terror to the Southrons "that nane of them durst come near his hauld." On this account, perhaps, it would have been politic had the King

---

* Pamphlet on the Debatable Land, by Mr Thomas Carlyle of Waterbeck ; a valuable little work, manifesting much research on the part of the author.

† Terregles Papers. We learn from the same source that some time after the latter date a feud broke out between the Maxwells and Dalzells, during which the head of the latter family was slain by Lord Maxwell. In a paper, entitled " The Forgevance of the Laird of Dawzeill," Alexander Beg, notary, of the diocese of Glasgow, certifies that on this day, 5th February [on or about 1534], Robert, Lord Maxwell, did " on his knees, before the altar of the Blessed Virgin, in the Church of St. Giles's, Edinburgh, seek and obtain forgeiness " from Robert Dalzell of that Ilk, for the slaying of his grandfather. Witnesses, James Douglas of Drumlanrig, and others.

come to terms with him : the hanging of the outlaw was, at all events, bitterly remembered by his clansmen, and for many a day cost the country dear. The readers will learn afterwards how fearfully, when fighting under the invading banners of Dacre and Wharton, they avenged the fate of their lamented chief.

In 1579, the Master of Maxwell (afterwards the celebrated Lord Herries), while acting as Deputy Warden during his father's captivity in England, drew up a report on the Debatable Land for the King, in which he states that after Gilnockie's execution the inhabitants were reduced to twenty or thirty, but that they now numbered from 300 to 400 men-at-arms, and had during the interval built eight or nine peel-houses, so strong as to be "impregnable to any power at the disposal of the Warden." The names of these strengths are not given ; but they were probably Morton or Sark, Woodhouseleys, Barngleis, Hollas, Stakeheugh or Auchenriffoch, Mumbyhirst, Hallgreen, and Harelaw ; all of which rose up in the district during the sixteenth century, though none now remains but Hollas,* hoar and roofless—" a brotherless hermit, the last of its race." The Armstrongs at that period, and for some time afterwards, were still the principal occupiers of the Debatable Land, residing in their houses of Sark, Hollas, Hallgreen, and Harelaw, all in the parish of Canonby ; the Grahams, though less numerous, mustered strongly in Kirkandrews parish, the other portion of the disputed district. These septs usually kept on friendly terms, intermarrying frequently, and foraying together. The Grahams had also settled down on the land lying between the Lyne—then called the Levyn—and the Liddel, a notorious spot of ground, where formerly hordes of self-expatriated Armstrongs, Elliots, Scotts, and other "broken" men, outlaws, rendezvoused, and were known in their day as "the traitors of the Levyn." Surrounding the Debatable Land were the Armstrongs in Liddisdale and Canonby, the Bells in Middlebie, the Irvings on Kirtle-Water, and the smaller clans of Rome and Little in Gretna.

In his fondness for adventure, and in some other respects, James V. resembled his father very much. Under the influence of a romantic sentiment he projected a "love chase" among the fair ladies of France—not in "the Gudeman of Ballengeich" style, but with a view to marriage. The royal "Cœlebs in search of a wife," disguised as a private gentleman, and accompanied by Lord Maxwell (for whom he entertained a fraternal affection), embarked in a ship freighted for the purpose ; but a storm arising, the vessel had to sail back, landing the disappointed King at Whithorn. Next year, however, he realised the object of this singular expedition in a regular way by proceeding with a magnificent retinue to France, and marrying Magdalene, the eldest daughter of its King. The young Queen—she had only seen sixteen summers

* Mr T. Carlyle's Pamphlet.

—was as delicate as she was beautiful. Within forty days after the arrival of the royal pair at Leith, on the 19th of May, 1537, the "Lily of Scotland" pined away, and died, leaving James and the country plunged in grief.

James V. paid another visit to Dumfriesshire in 1538, but under very altered circumstances, as during the twelve years elapsed since his justiciary tour events of vast importance had occurred to himself and to the nation. It might have been supposed that a prince of his disposition, who curbed the nobles, and took pride in being called "King of the Commons," would have encouraged the Reformation from Popery. That great revolutionary movement was already progressing rapidly throughout the kingdom;(a) and if James had placed himself at its head, how much happier might have been his fate, and from what trials and conflicts would he have saved his country ! At one time he seemed to be on the point of dismissing his priestly councillors, when he rated them as "a pack of jugglers," and bade them reform their own lives, instead of urging him to punish heretics;* but, unhappily, he succumbed to their views, wedded Mary of Guise, a Roman Catholic princess, instead of his cousin, the daughter of Henry VIII., whom he had half promised to espouse—Lord Maxwell being in this instance the negotiator and proxy of the marriage†—sanctioned the persecution of the Reformers, and eventually placed an impassable gulf betwixt himself and them. Patrick Hamilton, the protomartyr of Scottish Protestantism, perished at the stake in 1525 ; soon after three "godly men who professed the evangel of Christ were called before the bishops and kirkmen, and condemned

(a) In this district there seems to have been a clash of ecclesiastical authorities about this time. On 22nd November, 1535, the archbishop of St Andrew's publicly carried his cross and gave his benediction to the populace in the town of Dumfries, whereupon the official of the archbishop of Glasgow made formal protest against the invasion of his archiepiscopal privileges —Registrum Episcopalus Glasguensis, 550. The same acts were done and protest made again on 27th November, 1539.—Reg. Episc. Glasg., 553.

* William Eure, a correspondent of the English Government in Scotland, writing to Lord Cromwell on the 26th January, 1540, says he learns from one of King James's Privy Councillors that he favours the Reformation, and that he is "fully mynded to expell all spirituall men [priests] from having any authoritie within the realme."—State Papers, vol. v., p. 176.

† A Manuscript Account of the Family of Maxwell (quoted in History of Galloway, vol. i., p. 452) says that King James, in reward of Lord Maxwell's services on this and other occasions, confirmed to him the lands of Ewisdale, Eskdale, and Wauchope, by a charter under the Great Seal. " He was," it is added, "possessed of an immense estate, and had no less than fourteen charters from the King of different lands and baronies—inter 1530 et 1540." In one charter there are confirmed to him the lands of Maxwell, in Roxburghshire ; Carlaverock, in Dumfriesshire ; Springkell, in Annandale, with the office of Steward thereof, and of Kirkcudbright ; the lands of Garnselloch, Dursguhen, and Balmacruth, in Perthshire; Gordonston and Grenan, in Kirkcudbright; with the lands and baronies of Mearns and Nether Pollock, in Renfrewshire, &c., &c.

and burnt by the King's commission."* These were the Vicar of
Dollar, Norman Galloway, and David Straiton. Others shared
their fate ; but all the rigour which James and his ecclesiastical
advisers could put forth failed to avert the downfall of Popery,
Meanwhile the monarch's own end was rapidly approaching. For
several years, though there was no settled peace, there had been no
decided hostility with the English ; but in 1541 the latter made a
predatory foray into Scotland, and when restitution was applied
for King Henry, who was now eager to hasten a rupture with his
nephew, returned an unsatisfactory answer. James, in anticipation of such a result, levied an army of 10,000 men, which was
placed under the command of the Earl of Huntly, that nobleman
being at the same time commissioned to act as Lieutenant-General
of the Borders.

King James sometimes went southward for the purpose of
inspecting the troops ; and it was on one of these occasions, and
while war between the realms was still undeclared, that Sir Thomas
Wharton, the English Warden, laid an important project before his
royal master. He represented to King Henry that his youthful
nephew was in the habit of visiting Dumfries and its vicinity with
a small retinue ; and that it would be no very difficult matter to
seize him during some unsuspecting moment, carry him across the
Border, and acquire the dictatorship of Scotland through the capture of its King.

This scandalous proposal found great favour with the English
monarch.† Wishing, above all things, to get the King of Scots in
his power, he was perfectly indifferent about the means that might
be employed for that purpose. He had a complete confidence, also,
in Wharton—knew him to be a bold, crafty, unscrupulous soldier—
the very man, in short, for carrying his own vile scheme into effect.
Henry commended it to the careful consideration of his "right
trustie and well-beloved Counsailours," enjoining them to report
upon it with all due speed.

The Privy Council read and re-read the letter from Wharton in
which his audacious scheme was developed ; and the more they
perused it, it pleased them the less. Nor did they mince matters
with his Majesty—they had the honesty and courage to say that
they disapproved of the base stratagem laid by the Warden for
capturing the King of Scots, and to counsel its abandonment. They
told Henry that they "wold have been afrayed to have thought on
suche a matier touching a Kinges persone," had they not been enjoined by him to consider it ; and after pointing out the discredit-

---

* Pitscottie, p. 150.

† The plot seems to have escaped the vigilance of Tytler, though, in writ-
ing his excellent History of Scotland, he drew extensively upon the State
Papers of the period. Our account of it is taken from a letter of the Privy
Council to King Henry, in vol. v. of the State Papers, p. 204.

able character of the device, they affirmed that it was full of diffi-culty and danger. Using the language of remonstrance, they said: "But, Sir, we have also wayed that matier aftre our symple wittes and judgementes, and we fynde in it many difficulties. First, we considre that the Castle [Carlaverock] whereunto He [King James] resortethe is [   ] myles within the grounde of Scotlande. We con-sidre also that the cuntrey betwene that and Englande is so well inhabited, that it should be very difficile to conveye any such num-ber of men to the place where he shuld be intercepted, but the same wold be discovered. We considre again that Doonfrese, oon of the best towns in Scotlande, is in that part where the entreprize shuld be doon; and the cuntrey so inhabited at their backes, that if it were doon, it wold be harde to bring Him thens, specially alyve." Then, in the event of discovery and failure, what "slaunder" would grow out of it! what "deidlie feud" would ensue! And should King James be taken, would there not be a rescue, or such tumult and deray as would put the royal life in peril? For all these reasons, expressed or implied, the Council declared that they durst not advise the adoption of the enterprise, "but rather thinke it mete that Wharton (who hath, we thinke, had a good meanyng in it) shuld nevertheless surcease, and make no living creature privye to any suche matier." Henry bowed reluctantly to the decision of his ministers, and sought to realise his object by tardier and less dishonourable means.*

In the summer of 1542 an English force, 10,000 strong, crossed the Eastern Marches in the direction of Jedburgh and Kelso; and who should be the leaders of it but the banished Earl of Angus and his brother George—to such debasement were they willing to stoop in order to wreak their vengeance on King James, and recover their influence in Scotland. Huntly, hearing of their movements, inter-posed in time to save the threatened towns; and at Hadden-Rig he encountered and defeated the enemy, taking prisoner many men of note, Angus himself only escaping a similar fate by de-spatching his captor with a dagger. On receiving the news of this disaster, Henry proclaimed war in due form, revived the obsolete claim of his predecessors to the superiority of Scotland, and sent the Surrey of Flodden (now Duke of Norfolk) across the Border at the head of a large army. A Scottish force encamped on Fala Muir checked the progress of the invaders, who, after doing some mis-chief, withdrew comparatively unmolested.

To follow them was the first impulse of the impetuous King. He longed to meet the slayer of his father face to face in the battle-field; but the chiefs whom he had with him doggedly refused to cross the Border, averring that their military service only extended to the defence of their own country, while some of them did not scruple to say, "The King is king of the priests; let him ask

* State Papers, vol. v., pp. 204-5.

followers from those whose counsel he has acted upon, and not from the nobles whom he has humiliated and despised, and who have no heart to fight his battles." James could do nothing with such a contumacious host but disband it; which having done, he returned to Edinburgh, vowing that he should on an early day cause another force to be raised for the invasion of England, and that if the barons opposed his resolution Scotland would no longer hold both him and them.

Before many more months elapsed a second army was formed, chiefly through the exertions of the clergy, who sent rescripts for a military muster to all over whom they had any influence. Some of our historians allege that Robert, the fifth Lord Maxwell (who had succeeded his father some time previously), was appointed general of this new force; and that Oliver Sinclair, one of the King's household servants, was only nominally associated with him in the command. Others, again with more credibility, state that Sinclair (who was a tool of the priesthood, as well as a royal favourite) received secret letters from the King appointing him sole leader of the invading army, but enjoining him to keep his commission secret till the time of action arrived. According to Buchanan, Maxwell, with the view of mollifying the King's rage against his nobles, had engaged to cross the Esk with 10,000 men, and retaliate upon the English; but his Majesty could not accept the offer, having previously committed himself to another course.

James accompanied the army, and perhaps by his presence encouraged the idea that he would himself assume the command. He had no such intention, however, and remained at Carlaverock Castle, there to wait the result of the enterprize, as if he feared that it would prove a failure.

It would have been extremely marvellous had it prospered, as it wanted nearly every element of success. The soldiers had no great relish for the expedition on which they were sent; they had no acknowledged leader; some of those barons whose retainers swelled the ranks had a standing grudge against the sovereign; and when the Esk was crossed, and a cry arose, "Who is to lead us against the enemy?" and it was answered by Oliver Sinclair being raised shoulder high, and proclaimed General with sound of trumpet, secret discontent merged into open mutiny. Many scenes of tumult and disaster have been witnessed on the banks of the little Border stream, but none so wild and strange as that which now ensued. In vain the Popish Lords who had approved of the invasion sought to calm the storm: discipline was gone—rank mingled with rank—hoarse cries of disapproval, interspersed with curses on the low-born caitiff insultingly thrust upon them as commander, rose like thunder from a thousand voices, till the mighty host became nothing better than a riotous mob.*

* In the Diurnal of Occurrents, p. 25, the disaster to the Scots at Solway Moss is expressively spoken of as "ane unhappie raid, begylit be thair awne gyding."

Its confusion did not pass unseen by the English, a party of whom, fourteen hundred strong, led by Sir Thomas Wharton and Sir William Musgrave, sallied forth on horseback, and observing how matters stood, dashed headlong upon the disordered throng. Only a faint show of resistance was made by the Scots. A few of them fought single-handed under the instinct of self-defence ; but there was not even the semblance of a general engagement. To surrender without a struggle or escape by flight were the alternatives which the great mass adopted. To fight might have saved themselves ; but it might also have secured a victory for the King's detested favourite ; and, rather than bring glory to him, they covered themselves with disgrace. Upwards of a thousand yielded without striking a blow ; and the rest, numbering nearly nine thousand, turned their faces homeward, throwing away the weapons which they did not use, and which only encumbered their flight. Night came down upon the fugitives, adding much to their bewilderment. They recrossed the Esk with little loss, though the tide had flooded it four fathoms deep. "We are safe now," they fancied, "our own land has been reached, and there is a dark rolling sea between us and the enemy." But it is not land they have stumbled on ; it is a treacherous morass ; and down—down—perishing ignobly in the dismal swamp—go many stout warriors, and are seen no more, till, centuries afterwards, some are accidentally disentombed !

Whilst the retreating Scots were doing their utmost to cross this appalling quagmire, a party of their pursuers approached, and by raising hideous shouts increased their confusion. At this stage of the deplorable rout numerous additional prisoners were taken ; and it is stated by Buchanan that not a few Scots were captured by the predatory bands of the neighbourhood, and sold to the English. What proportion of the force arrived at home in safety is not recorded : the likelihood is that the loss in killed and prisoners was nearly one-third of its whole array. Comparatively few fell by the sword; though Pitscottie must, we think, greatly understate the number when he says there were only twenty-five persons slain—ten Scots and fifteen English. How many were swallowed up by the morass was never known. Among the prisoners of rank were the Earl of Cassilis, the Lords Maxwell, Fleming, Sommerville, Oliphant, and Grey, and Oliver Sinclair, the officer of an hour, and the main cause of the disaster.*

Wharton's report of this triumph to King Henry is still extant. It is a plain, soldierly document, containing no boasting, and attri-

---

* In the State Paper Office, London, there is a paper showing the resources of the prisoners. It includes the following entries :—"The Lorde Maxwell, in landes per annum, 4000 merkes Scottishe, which is sterling 1000 merkes ; and in goodes, 2000£ Scottishe, which is sterling 500£. Henry Maxwell, brodyr to the Lorde Maxwell, in landes per annum, nothinge ; and in goodes, nothinge."— State Papers, vol. v., p. 233.

buting the result to good fortune and Divine favour. "It may please your Majesty," says Wharton, "to be advertised that herewith I do send into your highness the names of the noblemen and gentlemen prisoners which I delivered at Darnton to my Lord Scroop, and the names of their takers in the same. I do send also to your Majesty the order of that fortunate service done by the power of Almighty God to your highness against your highness's enemies ; and the names of such gentlemen and the numbers [of followers] with them in that your Majesty's service ; together with such communication in effect as I have had with the Lord Maxwell and Oliver Synclere. I shall attend your Majesty's most noble commandment for all the other prisoners, according to my most bounden duty . . . . ; and shall daily pray to Almighty God that your Majesty may most long in prosperous health reign over us. At Carlisle, the 10th of December."

The capture of the Warden is thus entered in the list : "The Lord Maxwell, Admiral of Scotland, Warden of the West Marches of the same, and one of the King of Scots' Privy Council. Edward Aglionby, or George Foster, his taker." Batill Routledge is represented as having captured the Earl of Cassilis, only "John Musgrave claimeth a part for the loan of his horse to the said Routledge ;" and poor "Oliver Synkeler" is stated to have been borne off and claimed by one "Willie Bell."

Such was the rout of Solway Moss,*(a) with some of its results. It constitutes one of the most remarkable and disreputable incidents of Scottish history. Its evils are not all summed up in the disloyal mutiny, the mockery of a resistance, the tame surrender, the panic-flight, and the devouring bog ; it crazed the brain and broke the heart of the obstinate, yet in many respects noble-minded King of Scots. The news of the inglorious discomfiture of his army reached him late in the day at Carlaverock Castle,(b) and the royal halls echoed all night long with the lamenta-

---

* Solway Moss is about seven miles in circumference, and lies in the English portion of the Debatable Land ; the Sark flowing along its western side, and the Esk forming its boundary on the east. The battle, such as it was, must have taken place in the neighbourhood of Longtown, on the left bank of the Esk. Gilpin describes the moss as covered with grass and rushes, presenting a dry crust and fair appearance, but shaking under the least pressure—the bottom being unsound and semi-fluid. He states that the adventurous passenger who sometimes in dry seasons passes this perilous waste, to save a few miles of travel, picks his cautious way over the rushy tussocks as they appear before him —for on these the soil is comparatively firm ; but if his foot slip, or if he venture to desert this mark of security, it is possible he may never more be heard of.

(a) Solway Moss derives its name not from the Solway but from the long extinct village of Salome. The battle is by contemporaries usually styled that of Sollom-moss.

(b) Historical authorities are divided as to whether he was at Lochmaben or Carlaverock. A curious report from an English source, dating from the very time of the affair, states that James from the summit of Burnswark watched the southward march of his army.

tions which it wrung from him. He was thoroughly unmanned—prostrated, wrecked—by the terrible tidings; and the image of his favourite, a fugitive and a prisoner, figured prominently among the tormenting phantoms that crowded round his couch. "Fie! fie! is Oliver fled? is Oliver taken?" shrieked the poor King, ever and anon, in an agony that no one could minister to, far less remove. He retired to his palace of Falkland only to die. When the tide of life was ebbing rapidly, the intelligence was brought to him of the Queen's safe delivery of a child. "Is it male or female?" he asked. "A daughter," replied the messenger—an intimation that aggravated his sufferings and hurried on the end, by calling to his remembrance how the Stewart race had succeeded to the Crown. "It came with a lass," said the dying monarch bitterly, "and it will go with a lass." Then the engrossing woe of Solway Moss came back upon his mind, eliciting the old wail: "Is Oliver fled? Is Oliver a prisoner?" Speaking little from that time henceforth, but commending himself to the mercy of Almighty God, he "turned his back unto the lords, and his face unto the wall,"* till his spirit passed away.

The death of James V., at the early age of thirty years, added to the woes of Scotland. His daughter Mary was but a few days old when the melancholy event occurred, so that the country was again doomed to a long interregnum, during which angry factions contended for supremacy; and Henry VIII. and his successor strove to take advantage of the weakness thus produced—Dumfriesshire, as usual, suffering much from the machinations of its Southern neighbours. A new element of strife was also introduced by the Reformation; the conflict it originated becoming in the end so engrossing as to swallow up, or at least to subordinate, all other rivalries and matters of debate. Both Nithsdale and Annandale clung with some tenacity to the old creed after other districts had flung it aside; but, as we shall see, before Mary Stewart came from France to enter upon the government of her kingdom, in 1561, the cause of Protestantism prevailed extensively over the county, though a few of its leading chiefs continued to oppose it.

---

* Pitscottie, p. 177.

CHAPTER XVIII.

WHEN the news of King James's death reached his royal uncle,
that scheming potentate hit upon a new device for extending his
rule over Scotland. This was to unite in marriage his only son,
Prince Edward (then little more than five years old), to the infant
Queen of Scots. Henry gained over to his views the Scottish lords
taken at Solway Moss. To them the prospect of a long captivity in
England was the reverse of pleasant ; and in order to avoid it
they came under a written obligation, not simply to promote his
matrimonial project, but his desire through that means to become
the virtual master of Scotland.* They were liberated on these
degrading conditions, engaging at the same time upon oath to
return to their prisons if they failed in their object, or if required to
do so by the King. The terms imposed on Lord Maxwell seem to have
been peculiarly harsh. Henry, knowing that he could obtain no
permanent hold of southern Scotland unless the castles of Carlaverock and Lochmaben were garrisoned by English soldiers, pressed
their prisoned owner to give them up—plied him alternately with
threats and entreaties, but at first without effect ; and Maxwell,
without submitting to these superadded obligations, was set at
liberty. He proceeded to the court of the Regent Arran, remaining there for some months, and forming at least a nominal member
of the English party, whose objects were to promote the ascendancy

* Sadler's State Papers, vol. i., pp. 69, 74, 75.

of Henry, and help on the Reformation, as opposed to the Catholic
party under Cardinal Beaton, who aimed at maintaining the old
corrupt faith and the old French alliance.

When this new conspiracy against the independence of Scotland became generally known throughout the kingdom all classes
were filled with alarm, and the popular movement towards
Protestantism which had previously set in received a check. So
great was the ferment that Sir George Douglas (brother of Angus)
told Sir Ralph Sadler, the English agent with whom he co-
operated, that for Henry to become ruler of the Scots at such a
juncture was simply impossible; "for," said he, "there is not so
little a boy but he will hurl stones against it; and the wives will
handle their distaffs; and the commons universally will rather
die; yea, and many of the noblemen, and all the clergy be fully
against it." Heedless of such representations, Henry proceeded
with his scheme, scrupling at no means for its furtherance, however cruel or dishonourable.

The State Paper correspondence of the period supplies a
revelation of the compulsory influences brought to bear upon
Maxwell when in England—of his anxiety to escape from the life-
long captivity held above his head without sacrificing his loyalty
and patriotism—and of the finesse with which he tried to foil the
machinations of his regal inquisitor. One of the papers, entitled
"Confeschyon of Lord Maxfyld," brings out the curious fact that
Maxwell was allowed to pass into Scotland in the interests of the
King on giving his word of honour to return; that when there
Arran and his Council strove to induce him and the Earl of Angus
to take part against the English army that had crossed the Border;
and that the Nithsdale chief, resisting the tempting offers made
to him, remained true to his plighted word. They offered, we are
told, a thousand pounds in spiritual benefices, and a pension of
three thousand francs from the French King, to Angus; and a
thousand merks of benefices, and the money named for his ransom
(a thousand merks sterling), to Maxwell. Whereupon the latter
answered, "I am the Kingis Majestyis prisoner, trustyng ye wyll
not have me disyonneryd. But if I do go, what are you the wekar?
But here my frendis do tarry: ye may command them to do seche
servys as ye wyll have them; for they be under youer powyr." *

False to his blood and country—the paid agent of a foreign
prince—Angus declined to be patriotic on such terms; and both
of the noblemen were placed in ward, but liberated after the lapse
of five weeks—Maxwell, in spite of a request made to him by
the Regent, declaring that he would return to England, and
reasoning thus: "Ar you not Governer? Do I not leve behynd
me all my servauntes, all my tenauntes, my landes, and my

* State Papers, vol. v., p. 428.

goodes : what nede you fere, whethur I go or tary ?" *   He appears
to have advocated the marriage scheme, and in other respects to
have fulfilled his promise ; but Henry rated his services at little
value, and gave him no credit for good faith.

There was another scheme of lasting interest which Maxwell
seems to have done his utmost to promote—the diffusion of the
Scriptures in the vulgar tongue.   During his enforced sojourn in
England he acquired a decided bias towards Protestantism ; and
if on his temporary return to Scotland he had had full liberty of
action, the likelihood is that he would have fairly cast in his lot
with the Reformation party ; and the house of Maxwell would
have been divorced from the old creed, to which in after times it
so persistently clung.   The period of his return was a critical one,
the spring of 1543, when the ecclesiastical edifice was beginning to
totter, and men of all ranks to determine whether they would aid
in trying to keep it up, or lend their influence to pull it down
Lord Robert Maxwell was ranked with the most reckless of the
latter class when, on the 15th of March, he submitted to the
Estates a revolutionary proposal making it lawful for all " Our
Soverane Ladyis lieges to possess and read copies of the Bible in
Scotch or English." † Arran, the Regent, approved of the measure,
so did the Lords of the Articles.   Beaton would have opposed it to
the uttermost had he been outside the prison to which Arran had
consigned him ; and in his absence Gavin Dunbar, Archbishop of
Glasgow, cried it down as a pernicious device.   A reference was
made to Tyndale's English version, with the view of showing that
it, at all events, was free from any poisonous ingredient ; and all
the answer made by the Most Reverend Father was that Tyndale
had corrupted the text by using the word "love" instead of the
canonical term "charity" in the well-known passage, "Now
abideth faith, hope, and love."   With feeble argument, but bitter
hatred, the prelates opposed Lord Maxwell's bill.   It was sanctioned by Parliament in spite of them ; and soon a Government
proclamation read at the Market Cross of Edinburgh announced
that it had become law.   By this act the fountain of truth was
unsealed, and its refreshing waters were made free, for a time at
least, to all.   "This was no small victory of Jesus Christ," says
Knox, "fighting against the common enemies of his verity ; no
small comfort to such as before were holden in such bondage
that they durst not have read the Lord's Prayer, the Ten Com-
mandments, nor the articles of the faith, in the vulgar tongue, but
they should have been accused of heresy.   Then might have been
seen the Bible lying almost upon every gentleman's table.   The
New Testament was borne about in many men's hands.   We grant
that some, alas, profaned that blessed Word ; for," adds the

* Ibid, pp. 429-430.   † Appendix H.

historian, with a flash of the peculiar humour that sometimes lights
up his page, "some that perchance had never read ten sentences
in it, had it most common in their hand : they would chap their
familiars on the cheek with it, and say, 'This hath lien under my
bed-feet these ten years !' Others would glory, 'O how oft have I
been in danger for this book ! how secretly have I stolen from my
wife at midnight to read upon it !' And this was done, we say, of
many to make court and curry favours thereby : for all men
esteemed the Governor to have been one of the most fervent
Protestants that was in Europe. Albeit we say that many abused
that liberty granted of God miraculously ; yet thereby did the
knowledge of God wonderfully increase, and God gave His Holy
Spirit to simple men in great abundance : then were set forth
works in our own tongue, besides those that came from England,
that did disclose the pride, the tyranny, and the abuses of that
Roman Antichrist." *

Though the Earl of Arran took certain steps for promoting the
success of Lord Maxwell's wise measure, he could not summon up
sufficient courage to identify himself thoroughly with the leaders
of the Protestant movement—the Lords of the Congregation.†
Soon afterwards he fairly deserted them—"turning his tippet" (to
use a phrase then in vogue), and appearing as a flaming Romanist.

From Lord Maxwell as the enlightened advocate of religious
freedom to the same nobleman as the pining captive of a tyrant
king, there is a painful transition. Before the year ended Maxwell was again in durance, experiencing the exactive demands of
the English monarch. The correspondence already specified
shows that he resisted them resolutely for a lengthened period, till
a threat of sending him to the Tower was tried, under which he
fairly broke down. The Earl of Hertford, writing to Secretary
Paget, on the 29th of July, 1545, states that the harassed prisoner
was reduced to so great "a perplexitie and hevynes that he coulde
neyther eate, drynke, nor sleepe"—that he was ready to serve as a
red-cross English soldier, if required, rather than be sent southward, from which, if once there, "he knewe well he suld never
returne on lyve." ‡ The threat was not enforced, as its mere emission served the purpose for which it was designed.

It was arranged that Lord Maxwell's second son, John, who
held Lochmaben Castle, should at once give it up to the English ;
and that on a future day that was fixed the liberation of Lord
Maxwell and the surrender of his other fortress, Carlaverock,
should take place simultaneously ; the eldest son, Robert, giving
personal security for his father's good faith. But Robert Maxwell,
instead of fulfilling the bargain, made a raid across the Border
accompanied by his uncle, John Maxwell of Cowhill ; and both

---

* History, p. 77.   † Keith, p. 37.
            ‡ State Papers, vol. v., p. 479.

had the ill-luck to be captured by the enemy. The next step was to despatch Cowhill with letters from Lord Maxwell to his second son, John (better known afterwards as Lord Herries), soliciting the latter to repair to Carlisle and lie in pledge for his father, and enjoining him to deliver the house of Lochmaben into his uncle's hands.

The result is narrated by the Earl of Hertford, in a letter to Sir William Paget, dated Newcastle, 5th October, 1545. He refers the Secretary to an enclosure from Wharton, conveying the unpalatable information that Lord Maxwell's practices for the surrender of his houses "cometh to nothing"—his second son declining to give them up, or become hostage for his father. Not only so ; Cowhill, safe on the Scottish side, a willing captive among his countrymen, refuses to come back. "So," says the wrathful Hertford, " can I judge non otherwise of the same but that yt is a mere practise and devise of the said John Maxwell of Cowhill, whereby, being a prysoner, and appoynted to retorne agayne into England furthwith, in case John Maxwell, sonne to the Lorde Maxwell, wold not accomplishe the tenour of his letter, he may nowe excuse his entree, and saye that he ys taken and holden against his wille." The noble Earl proceeds to express his belief that the Scottish Lord himself is privy to all this deceit, and is selfishly bent on acquiring his liberty and at the same time keeping his castles.

In a second letter, dated a few days afterwards, addressed by Hertford to the Privy Council, he expresses more confidence in Lord Maxwell, and repeats a statement made by him to the effect that the House of Carlaverock, being his own inheritance, and in the keeping of a priest, his kinsman, he doubteth not, with the help of Lord Wharton, so to handle the matter that the said priest shall deliver the place to any one duly authorised to receive it for the King's Majesty's use ; and that, this being done, should his highness send him home, he feels assured that he will be able to put him in possession of Lochmaben Castle also, and reduce the whole country to his obedience.

Hertford consulted with Wharton on this important business ; and his report of their interview is so interesting that we must introduce its principal passages. "To the first he [Wharton] saithe, that upon the West Marches of Scotlande, the countrey of ytsilf being a wylde and waste grounde, there is no exployte to be don uppon that frontier nearer than Drunfreys, whiche is twentie miles within Scotlande ; excepte that he shuld make a rode yn to overthrowe and caste downe a certen chirch and steple, called the Steple of Annande, which is a thinge of litle importaunce and lesse annoyaunce to the enemye. And to go to Drunefreyes, he sayeth the countrey is so stronge of nature, and the passages thither so straight and narrowe, that he thinketh yt over harde and dangerous to be attempted with a Warden's roode. So that, by his saynge, the West Marches of Scotlande being so bareyn a countrey, and alredy wasted by the conteynenance of the warres, there is non exployte to be done there other then aforesaide. To the seconde poynt : for Carlaverok we have also devised with the said Lord Wharton and the Lord Maxwell howe that matier be accomplished. And after some reasonyng and communication therof, wherin outwardly the said Lord Maxwell showeth himsilf very ernest, he hath taken uppon him that, yf he might have lycence to go to Carlisle with the saide Lorde Wharton, that in case the priest that kepith the house for him woll at his sendyng comme to him to Carlisle (whereof he putteth no doubte), that then he will so handell the matier, as he doubteth not but the house shal be delyvered into the Kinges Majestes handes."

Accordingly, Maxwell and Wharton proceeded to the Border city, and Hertford goes on to say, " Because the said priest had the charge of the said house of Carlaverok commytted unto him by Robert Maxwell, and for that yt may be that he woll do as moche or more for Robert Maxwell then for his father, as the Lord Maxwell himself doth also suppose, the said Robert was therefore called to this matier ; and showing himself no less desirous to serve the Kinges Majeste, both in this matier and all other wayes to his power, then his father, he hath by the devise of me wrytton to the said priest one letter, requyryng him furthwith to make his entree to Carlisle for the discharge of his band, because he is a prysoner, and the said Robert Maxwell bound for his entree whensoever he shall be called ; and an other letter he hath also writton to be delyvered by his father to the priest at his commyng to Carlisle, whereby the priest shall perceyve that the said Robert ys bothe willing, prevye, and consenting to do in all things as his father woll devise for the delyvere of the said house of Carlaverok to the Kinges Majestie. And nowe, because you shall knowe what ys thought emonges us here to be the best waye to come by the said house, yt is devised, that ymediatly uppon the commyng of the said priest to Carlisle, there shall be a convenyent nombre appoynted to go with him furthwith to Carlaverok in the night tyme, to receyve the house ; and the priest shall never be out of theyr handes till the house be delyvered, wherein yff he shall make any staye or difficultie, he shall be sure to dye for it—which is also a pece of the Lorde Maxwell's own devise."

On the 28th of October * the banner of England once more floated above the turrets of Carlaverock ; an adventurous soldier

---

* In the Diurnal of Occurrents, a manuscript of the 16th century, in possession of the late Sir J. Maxwell of Pollok, Bart., and printed by the Bannatyne Club, the following entry occurs, under date 28th October, 1545 :— " The Lord Maxwell delyvert Carlaverok to the Englishmen, quhilk was great discomfurt to the cuntrie."

Thomas Carleton, of whom we shall afterwards hear much, being entrusted with its defence. His office was no sinecure, as we learn from a report sent by Wharton to the King, dated on the 28th, apprising his Majesty that the Lairds of Johnstone, Drumlanrig, and Lochinvar had, with the countrymen of Nithsdale, Annandale, and Galloway, beleaguered the fortress, which he had in vain tried to relieve. Wharton, in a second letter, dated on the following day, furnished his royal master with a curious, but not very correct, topographical sketch of this Border stronghold and its vicinity." " It may please your Highness to understande," he says, " that the Castle of Carlaverok standithe from your Highness citie of Carlisle 28 myllis, as the same must be passid with a powre [army], wherin er many strait passagies, amongst which one is called Lokermosse, thorowe whiche mose is maid a way with earthe, wherupon ther may pase foure men in renk, and not above ; and, within fyve houres, no gret nombre of folkes may cut the same earthe and dam the passage ; and if that may be dammyd, then the powre must be carried 8 myles about. The same mosse standdithe 4 mylles on this sidde Dumfreis. The powre must pase within a mylle of the town of Dumfreis ; sa that, albeit the Castle of Carlaverok standithe nerer Carlisle than Dumfreis, yet the passaig of the wayes, having noon other by lande thene is aforsaid, makithe the same furder from Carlisle then Dumfreis is. And if the weyther chaunce so contagious [stormy].as at this present it is in these parties, ther can no watters be passid for a day or twoo, having dyvers great rivers between Carlisle and Carlaverok.' Wharton further informs the King that he had engaged a number of boats, capable of holding from four to six men each, or three hundred in all ; but that they " can not cume nere the lande at Carlaverok by more than a mylle, except at a hie springe and a full sea ;" and the owners of the little craft did not care to venture on the troubled waters of the Solway at that time of the year.

In a third communication, dated the last day of the same month, Wharton tells his Majesty that a spy from Carlaverock had informed him that the Laird of Johnstone and his colleagues had received a letter from the Scottish Regent thanking them for their services against the defenders of the castle, and exhorting them to continue in good cheer, as he meant to join and reward them on the following Tuesday. Wharton also intimates that he intended, at the head of two hundred horsemen, " within three or foure nightes, to prove ane enterprise for the comfort and relief of Thomas Carleton, and the others that servythe your Majestie in that holde."

We know rather by inference than from any direct statement the result of all these machinations on the part of King Henry, and of the operations to which they gave rise. Wharton succeeded in reinforcing the garrison of Carlaverock : the castle was held by

the English during the whole winter and spring ; it surrendered
to the Regent in May, 1546, and was eventually restored to Maxwell.   That unfortunate lord did not long survive the harsh treatment given to him by Henry, and the torturing abasement to
which he had been brought. When set at liberty with his friends a
written instrument of protection was furnished to them, available
"so long as they should serve the King truly ;" and the next
glimpse we get of him is in the "Diurnal," * which states that
about the close of October the Regent held a council with Cardinal
Beaton, the bishops, and abbots, where it was resolved "That all
maner of men should meet the Governour at Carlaverok, with ten
days' victuall," on the 2d of November ; that on the army going
thither it was found to have been vacated by the English ; that on
the 21st of November the Scottish force captured Lochmaben
(which had, like Carlaverock, been given up to the enemy), and set
siege to Threave, which latter hold "was in my Lord Maxwellis
handis," and "was gevin over tua or thrie dayes after, be appointment ;" that Lord Maxwell was had to Dumfries, with certain
Englishmen, as a traitor ; and that the Laird of Garlies had been
made Captain of Threave, and the Laird of Lochinvar Captain of
Lochmaben.

    Traitor undoubtedly Lord Maxwell was ; but his new captors,
knowing the trying circumstances in which he had been placed,
showed him great forbearance. He executed an instrument of
protest, dated at Dumfries on the 28th of November, 1545, declaring that his surrender of his castles, and that all his other degrading engagements with the English had been wrung from him under
terror of his life ; that he was truly loyal at heart ; and that he
would live and die a faithful subject of Queen Mary.† All his
faults were freely forgiven ; and, as a proof of the renewed confidence placed in him by the Scottish Government, he was soon after
appointed Chief Justice of Nithsdale, Annandale, Kirkcudbright,
and Wigtown, and received commission again as Warden of the
Western Marches, on the 3d of June, 1546.‡

    What availed the honours thus heaped upon him ? His lease
of life, shortened by the sufferings he had undergone, was about to
close. On the 9th of the following month Robert, the fifth Lord
Maxwell, was numbered with the dead. The elements of his nature
were "antithetically mixed," and his life was full of inconsistencies ;
but his services to Protestantism must be accepted as a set-off

---

* Diurnal, p. 41.

† Terregles Papers. The deed bears to have been signed in the "new
house Dumfries."   Notary, "John Turnour." (a)

    (a) He was no doubt rector of the church of Annan, who appears as
notary executing notarial acts at Dumfries in 1535 and 1539.—Registrum
Episcopatus Glasguensis, pp. 550, 553.

‡ Ibid.

against his political faults. As the first of Scottish statesmen to recognise the right of his countrymen to read God's revealed Word in their own language, he occupies an honoured place in history. The Scottish army at Solway Moss was emphatically a Papal host ; but the conquerors there did less harm to Romanism than the captives taken by them after their return to Scotland. From this point of view, the rout, which in the long run promoted the cause of the Reformation, was the reverse of disastrous ; though in other respects, as we have seen, it was ruinous and disgraceful.

CHAPTER XIX.

THE scheme of Henry VIII. for uniting the two kingdoms under
the Prince of Wales by marrying him to the young Queen of Scots
fared no better than his former attempt to effect a matrimonial
alliance between his daughter and James V. Beaton and the
Catholic party still in power preferred wedding Mary to a French
prince rather than to the son of the Pope-abjuring King of England. She was accordingly married in Paris on the 14th of April,
1558, to the Dauphin, who soon afterwards became King of
France ; but his early death left her a widow at the age of
eighteen ; and on the invitation of the Scottish Parliament she
returned to her native country in the autumn of 1561. During
Mary's absence of twelve years the Romish Church in Scotland
had been completely overthrown, the celebration of mass forbidden
under heavy penalties, the Protestant Confession of Faith ratified,
and the Presbyterian system of ecclesiastical polity established by
Parliament, though the Queen viewed these proceedings with
aversion, and had steadily refused to sanction them.

Before noticing the collision between the reformers and the
sovereign, thus provoked, we must glance at the way in which
Dumfriesshire was affected by the rejection of the English alliance. During the three years in which Henry was cruelly operating upon Maxwell and the other captive lords, as already related,
he was trying to accomplish his ends in Scotland by other agents
and influences ; and whether he should gain or lose, he was resolved at all events to make the inhabitants of the Border dis-

trict mourn with him that his matrimonial project had proved a failure.

On the 28th of September, 1543, a council of war was held by his command at Darlington, to consider what should be done "to Scotlande this wynter by the Westmarchers of Englande." Wharton, as a matter of course, took part in the deliberations. The proposals made by him, and concurred in by three other chiefs, Lowther, Leigh, and Aglionby, which are still extant, illustrate strikingly the savagery of Border warfare.* The style in which they proposed to "annoy" their neighbours of the North was thus explained by themselves after a devout prelude expressing their trust in God to assist them—which sounds rather incongruously. They "trust," in the first instance, to "burne, distroye, and maik waist" all the land watered by the Annan and the Milk ; then to enter Eskdale, Ewisdale, Wauchopedale, and the Debatable Land, sparing none of them ; taking special note of the "towne of Anande, which is the chief towne in all Anerdaill except Dumfreis,† and all the townes, steids, beuldinges, and corne" within the whole parishes of the same, and those of "Dronoke, Reidkyrk, Gretnoo, Kyrkpatrik, Eglefleghan, Penersarkes, and Carudders ; and in Wawcopdaill, the parishing of Wacoppe ; in Eskdaill, the parishinges of Stablegorton and Watsyrkett ; and in Ewsdaill the Over Parishing and the Nether Parishing, with all the townes, steids, beuldinges, and corne, within every of the said peryshings :" no one to receive immunity unless by agreeing to serve the King's Majesty of England. Detailed plans for the devastation of the Middle Marches were also submitted ; and though the Darlington programme was not carried out to the letter, it was acted upon in spirit.

The winter that was to see an immense tract of Dumfriesshire and Selkirkshire turned into a howling desert passed harmlessly away ; and the wild-flowers of the next spring were just beginning to decorate the waysides and fields of Nithsdale when Wharton's armed host, going northwards, trampled them into nothingness, while hurrying on to treat human beings in the same manner with as little remorse. Encountering no opposition, they were encouraged to advance further than was at first designed ; and the people of Dumfries, who had suffered much at Solway Moss, saw, to their dismay, the Southron army approaching, as they were conscious of possessing no adequate means of resistance or defence. The burgh was entered and occupied by the invaders, who seem once again to have had their own wild wasting way. No more deadly visitation had Dumfries ever before experienced.

* State Papers, vol. v., pp. 344-5.

† Occasionally, in very old documents, the modern spelling of the town is anticipated, or nearly so, as in this instance.

They came for the purpose of leaving tokens of their vengeful presence in the county town, and obtained their wish—no one appearing with voice and look of authority to bid the ravagers begone. Entire streets were burned or demolished ; and when the barbarous enemy disappeared a large portion of the burgh looked (to use the expressive Eastern term) as if it had been "sown with salt," so desolate was its aspect.* Bearing with them the valuable movables they could seize, and driving before them many herds and flocks "lifted" from the fields around, the plunderers withdrew to carry on their depredations in other parts of the county. Wharton, as may have been inferred, was the chief agent in these ruthless incursions ; and that he might prosecute them with less molestation and more fatal effect, he enlisted some of the lawless tribes of Eskdale and Liddisdale, the Armstrongs, Beattisons or Beatties, Thomsons, Littles, and other "broken men," under his brigand banner, giving them an unrestricted commission to ravage and slay.

With the same base ends in view the English chief fomented a quarrel between the Maxwells and Johnstones, who, had they co-operated in defending the county, might have made him pay dearly for his visits. His perfidy in this respect is depicted in a letter written by himself to the Earl of Shrewsbury, on the 10th of February, 1545, in which, after mentioning that he had placed in Langholm Tower a considerable body of foot and a troop of fifty horse, he said he had long used a follower of Johnstone as an emissary to fan the flame of discord between the chief of the Johnstones and Lord Maxwell's son (Maxwell himself being a prisoner with the English), and that a feud between them had broken out in consequence, which the Scottish Council in vain tried to allay ; that he had offered Johnstone three hundred crowns for himself, one hundred for his brother, the Abbot of Soulseat, and one hundred for his followers, on condition of the Master of Maxwell being put into his power ; that Johnstone had entered into the plot, but, unfortunately, he and his friends "were all so false" that the writer "knew not what to say"—was not sure of trusting them ; but he added that he would be "glad to annoy and entrap the Master of Maxwell, or the Laird of Johnstone, to the King's Majestie's honour and his own poor honesty." Yet the knight who could thus coolly write himself down a knave was about this time ennobled under the title of Lord Wharton by his royal master, Henry of England ! He could not trust Johnstone ; and we suppose the latter felt no remorse when, though pocketing the proffered bribe, he resolved to shew his antipathy towards the Maxwells in some less dishonourable way than by betraying the heir of their house into the hands of the English.

* Haynes, in whose work Wharton's reports of his expedition are embodied, pp. 43-51.

While Wharton was thus engaged in the Western Marches Sir
Ralph Evre and Sir Brian Latoun emulated his destructiveness, if
not his artifice, in the Eastern Marches ; for which service the
former received, by deed of gift from Henry, the rich counties of
Merse and Teviotdale— the King forgetting that he would thereby
be sure to incense the Earl of Angus, some of whose estates were
included in the donation.   Angus, since the period of his disgrace,
had, as already hinted, favoured Henry's designs ; and his marriage
with Margaret, that monarch's sister, together with a sum of
money settled upon him by his royal brother-in-law, rendered him
additionally devoted to the English party in Scotland.   When,
however, the proud old Earl—whose attainder had been removed
soon after the death of James V.—saw his patrimony ravaged, and
then conferred upon an English chief, his blood boiled within him :
and his services having been accepted by the Regent Arran, he
rushed to arms.   With five hundred men he encountered and utterly
routed the invaders on Ancrum Moor, though they numbered five
to one.   Pitscottie gives the chief credit of this extraordinary
triumph to the Laird of Buccleuch, at whose suggestion the small
Scottish force withdrew into a hollow, making the enemy suppose
that they had taken flight.   As was anticipated, the English
advanced tumultuously, eager to annihilate the fancied fugitives ;
but they, "lighting on the ambush of the Scots all wearied and
out of breath," met with a fierce reception, which soon issued in a
disastrous repulse.   The Douglas party were favoured by having
the sun and wind on their side—the former darting its beams, and
the latter blowing the canons' smoke in the eyes of their opponents :
"besides, the Scottish men's spears were an ell longer than the
English " ones.   The assailants' first line was driven back upon the
second, the second upon the third, till inextricable confusion was
produced, and something like a parallel to the Solway Moss
catastrophe ensued, only that the slaughter of the defeated party
was more extensive, and the success of the victors more due to real
valour, than on that memorable occasion.   Evre and Latoun, the
two English leaders, with about five hundred of their followers,
including many gentlemen, were slain, and the prisoners taken
numbered one thousand ; the Scots, as a small set-off to these gains,
losing only two men—killed by the recklessness of their own
artillery.*   After the battle, "the Governor, calling for the Earl
of Angus, highly commended his valour, resolution, and wisdom,

* When Henry received news of this defeat he accused Angus of black
ingratitude, and threatened him with his deepest resentment ; to which the
Earl characteristically replied, "What !" said he, "is my brother-in-law offended
because, like a good Scotchman, I have avenged upon Ralph Evre the defaced
tombs of my ancestors ?   They were better men than he, and I ought to have
done no less ; and will the King take my life for that?   Little knows King
Henry the skirts of Kernetable : I can keep myself there against all his English
host."—Hume's House of Douglas, vol. ii., p. 123.

and thanked Sir George Douglas, his brother, for his valiant
service, assuring them that that day's service had cleared them of
all aspersions of disloyalty and love to England, laid upon them by
their enemies."*

In the following year we find Johnstone and the Master of
Maxwell friends once more, and, in company with Gordon of
Lochinvar, leading a successful expedition across the Western
Border ; while, with the view of protecting the Scottish side, its
two principal fortresses, Carlaverock and Lochmaben, were
strengthened by the direction of the Government. But neither
the victory in Teviotdale nor the retaliatory raids made by the
chiefs of Dumfriesshire, nor yet the increased attention paid to its
defences, served to keep the English in check ; for early in 1547
they succeeded in overrunning a large portion of the county.

Sir Thomas Carleton, of Carleton Hall, Cumberland, who commanded the invading force under the orders of Lord Wharton (and
with whose name, as captain of Carlaverock in 1545, the reader is
already familiar), has left a manuscript account of his predatory
mission, from which we gather many particulars of it, interesting
in themselves, and richly illustrative of the fighting times on the
Border, and from which, therefore, we borrow extensively in the
following narrative.

Carleton tells us that in February, 1547, he made "a road into
Teviotdale, and got a great booty of goods." Lacking proper
shelter in the sore weather for both men and horses, they pushed
into Canonby ; and, after lying there "a good space," proceeded to
Dumfries—the lieges of which town submitted themselves to him,
and "became the King's Majesty's subjects of England." "The
morrow after coming to Dumfries," he goes on to say, "I went into
the Moot Hale [Moat Hill, probably on the north side of the town],
and making a proclamation in the King of England's name that all
manner of men should come in and make oath to the King's
Majesty, every man at his peril, they all came and swore; whereof
I made a book [list of names], and sent it to the Lord Wharton.
And so I continued about ten days ; and so making proclamation
that whoso should come in and make oath and lay in pledges to
serve the King's Majesty of England, he should have our aid and
maintenance, and who would not, we should be on him with fire and
sword, many of the lairds of Nithsdale and Galloway came in and
laid in pledges."

"The town of Kirkcobree," to its credit be it mentioned, set
the proclamation at naught, so that Carleton was moved by Lord
Wharton to give it a "prieffe [proof, threat] to burn it." "And so
we rode thither one night, and coming a little after sun-rising, they
who saw us coming barred their gates and kept their dykes; for
the town is dyked on both sides, with a gate to the water-ward,

* Pitscottie, p. 186.

and a gate to the over end of the fell-ward.* There we lighted on foot and gave the town a sharp onset and assault, and slew [wounded] one honest man in the town with an arrow, in so much that one wife came to the ditch and called for one that would take her husband and save his life. Anthon Armstrong, being ready, said, 'Fetch him to me and I'll warrant his life.' The woman ran into the town and fetched her husband, and brought him through the dyke, and delivered him to the said Anthon, who brought him into England and ransomed him." The invaders, however, did not get all their own way. M'Lellan, the tutor of Bombie, coming to relieve the town, "impeached them with a company of men ;" "and so," continues the English reiver, "we drew from the town, and gave Bombye the onset ; where was slain of our part Clement Taylor, of theirs three, and divers taken, and the rest fled."

Though the outside defenders of "Kircobree" seem to have been scattered, its assailants did not persevere with the siege. In retiring they "seized about two thousand sheep, two hundred kye and oxen, and forty or fifty horses, mares, and colts, and brought the same towards Dumfries." Whilst thus employed, a force of "Galloway folks, from beyond the water of Dee," came in sight, bent on recovering the booty, and prepared to cross the interposing river at Forehead Ford. "So," says Carleton, "we left our sheep, and put our worst horsemen before the nowte and nags, and sent thirty of the best horse to preake at the Scots, if they should come over the water, and to abide with the standard in their relief ; which the Scots perceiving, stayed, and came not over. So that we passed quietly that night to Dumfries, leaving the goods in safety with a good watch."

Next morning a curious scene occurred. The party repaired to the place where the plunder had been stored, a mile beyond Dumfries, in order to divide it ; "and some claimed this cow, and some that nagg," while, "above all, one man of the Laird of Empsfielde came amongst the goods, and would needs take one cow

---

* The town of Kirkcudbright was anciently encompassed by a wall, with a fosse or ditch on the outside of it, into which the tide flowed. The fosse is still traceable in many places. It commenced at the river, in the present dock, and having passed between the gardens belonging to Castle Street and the west side of the park in which the new church is built, it proceeded in a straight line, nearly south, and crossed the street at Mr William Johnstone's house, where there was a gate called the "Meikle Yett," which was taken down about seventy-six years ago. After the fosse and wall had extended a little on the other side of the street in the same direction, they formed a right angle, and proceeding towards the west, enclosed the gardens on the south side of the town. Much of this portion of the fosse is still open. At the end of the field belonging to the Academy, which is occupied as play ground, the ditch and wall turned towards the north, and having enclosed the gardens on the west side of the town, the ditch entered the river : this part of it is entirely open. The wall continued along the edge of the river, and had another gate at the harbour or old ferry. The space included was almost a square, each side being upwards of 300 yards long.—History of Galloway, vol. i., pp. 472-3.

saying that he would be stopped by no man, insomuch that one
Thomas Taylor, called Tom-with-the-Bow, being charged with the
keeping of the goods, struck the said Scotsman on the head with
his bow, so that the blood ran down over his shoulders. Going to
his master there, and crying out, his master went with him to the
Master Maxwell. The Master Maxwell came, with a great rout
after him, and brought the man with the bloody head to me, saying, with an earnest countenance, 'Is this, think ye, well ; both to
take our goods and thus to shed our blood ?' I, considering the
Master at that present to be two for one, thought best to use him
and the rest of the Scots with good words, and gentle and fair
speeches, for they were determined, even there, to have given us
an onset, and to have taken the goods from us, and to have made
that their quarrel. So that I persuaded him and the rest to stay
themselves ; and for the man that hurt the other man, he should
be punished, to the example of all others to commit the like,
giving him that gave the stroke sharp words before them ; and
[commanding that] the goods should all be stayed, and none dealt
till the next morrow, and then every man to come that had any
claim, and, upon proof, that it should be redressed ; and thus
willed every man quietly, for that time, to depart."

It seems to us marvellous in the extreme that the Master of
Maxwell, instead of being cozened in this fashion by the pawkie
Southron leader, did not at once try to settle the question at issue
between them by sword and spear. The English influence must
have been indeed overpoweringly great in the district to have
made its chiefs and their retainers so spiritless and submissive.

Carleton, fearing that the Scots might be ashamed of their
own apathy, and try to catch him at a disadvantage, made ready
for war. On returning to Dumfries, "about one of the clock in
the afternoon," he gave "every one of the garrison secret warning
to put on their jacks, and bridle and saddle their horses," and
ordered them to join him immediately at the Bridgend. They
having obeyed his commands, he sent forty-two men for the goods,
with instructions to meet him at a ford a mile above the town.
At that point the booty was conveyed across the river, and taken
forthwith to Lochmaben, where it was quietly divided that night.
The party then returned to Canonby, Carleton concluding this
part of his narrative by complacently remarking, "And thus with
wiles we beguiled the Scots." He has evidently been a smart,
clever, unscrupulous moss-trooping chief, not overstocked with
modesty, and prone to swagger in his speech. The way in which
he won Lochwood Tower is so graphically recorded by him that
we must give the history of the achievement in nearly his own
words. The ruins of this old castle, once the chief seat of the
Johnstone family, are still to be seen in the north end of the
parish of Johnstone. It was built in the fourteenth century, and

from the thickness of its walls, its insulated situation, surrounded by almost impassable marshes, and by an inner circle of defence composed of huge trees, some of which still survive,* it must have been difficult to take by storm or siege.

Carleton, before telling how he captured it by stratagem, says : " Considering Canonby to be far from the enemy (for even at that time all Annerdale, Liddesdale, and a great part both of Nidsdale and Galway, were willing to serve the King's Majesty of England, saving the Laird of Drumlanricke, who never came in, nor submitted himself, and with him continued Alexander Carlel, Laird of Bridekirk, and his son, the young laird), I thought it good to practise some way we might get some hold or castle, where we might lie near the enemy. . . . . Thus practising, Sander Armstrong, son to Ill Will Armstrong, came to me and told me he had a man called John Lynton, who was born in the head of Annerdale, near to the Loughwood (being the Laird Johnstone's chief house), and the said laird and his brother (being the Abbot of Salside) were taken prisoners not long before, and were remaining in England. It was a fair large tower, able to lodge all our company safely, with a barnekin, hall, kitchen, and stables, all within the barnekin, and was but kept with two or three fellows and as many wenches."

Lynton's opinion was that the fortress might be captured ; and with this end in view the whole English troop set off, arriving in the vicinity of it an hour before sunrise. Most of the men lurked outside the wall ; while, according to previous arrangement, about a dozen climbed over it, " stole close into the house within the barnekin, and took the wenches, and kept them secure in the house till daylight." So far the plot had proved successful ; and now for its full development. " Two men and a wench " were in the tower, and, at dawn, one of the former, rising in his shirt, went to the tower-head, and seeing no one astir, he bade the woman who lay in the tower to get up and open the tower door, and call up them that lay beneath. " She so doing, and opening the iron door and a wooden door without it, our men within the barnekin brake a little too soon to the door ; for the wench, per-

---

* One of our own poets gives the following fine picture of these forest patriarchs :—

" The reverend Oak takes back
The heart to older days of holy awe.
Such oaks are they, the hoariest of their race,
Round Lochwood Tower, the Johnstones' ancient seat ;
Bowed down with very age, and rough all o'er
With scurfy moss, and parasitic hair,
They look as if no lively little bird
Durst hop upon their spirit-awing heads ;
But solemn visions swarm on every bough
Of Druid doings in the days of old."

Aird's " A Summer Day."

ceiving them, leaped back into the tower, and had gotten almost the wood door to, but we got hold of it, that she could not get it close to. So the skirmish rose ; and we over the barnekin, and broke open the wood door, and she being troubled with the wood door, left the iron one open : and so we entered and wan the Logh-wood." A most valuable capture it proved, as the castle was well stocked with salted beef, malt, butter, and cheese.

Leaving Armstrong in charge, Carleton rode off to Carlisle, and reported his success to Lord Wharton, who constituted him keeper of Lochwood. At his lordship's instance, he then proceeded to Moffat, and made a proclamation there similar to the one issued at Dumfries ; intimating also, that "whoso did others wrong, either by theft, oppression, or otherwise, he should order it amongst them, and refer all weighty causes to his Lordship and his council." "So," proceeds the writer, "I continued there for some time, in the service of his Majesty, as captain of that house, and governor and steward of Annerdale, under the Lord Wharton. In which time we rode daily and nightly upon the King's Majesty's enemies ; and amongst others, soon after our coming and remain-ing there, I called certain of the best horsed men of the garrison, declaring to them I had a purpose offered by a Scotsman, which would be our guide, and that was to burn Làmington, which we did wholly, took prisoners, and won much goods, both malt, sheep, horse, and insight, and brought the same to me in the head of Annerdale, and there distributed it, giving every man an oath to bring in all his winnings of that journey ; wherein, truly, the men offended so much their own conscience, every man layning [concealing] things, which afterwards I spiered out, that, after that time, my conscience would never suffer me to minister an oath for this, but that which should be speired or known to be brought, and every man to have share accordingly."

This miniature Cæsar, the congenial chronicler of his own doughty deeds, closes his record in the following terms : "After that I made a road in by Crawfurth Castle and the head of Clyde, where we seigèd a great vastil [bastile] house of James Douglas : which they held till the men and cattle were all devoured with smoke and fire ; and so we returned to the Loughwood, at which place we remained very quietly, and, in a manner, in as civil order for hunting and pastime as if we had been at home in our own houses. For every man within Annerdale being within twelve or sixteen miles of the Loughwood would have resorted to me to seek reformation for any injury committed or done within the said compass ; which I omitted not, but immediately after the plaint either rode myself, and took the party complained of, or sent for him, and punished or redressed as the cause deserved. And the country was then in good quietness : Annerdale, Nids-dale, and a great part of Galloway, all to the Water of Dee, were come in and entered pledges ;" and "Kircobree," vanquished at last, "came in and entered pledges also."

In the summer of this year [1547]—a disastrous one to Dumfriesshire—Robert, the sixth Lord Maxwell,* son of the chief who was captured at Solway Moss, proceeded to the Court of the Regent Arran at Edinburgh, to ask for aid against the enemy. He stated that the fields of Nithsdale and Annandale were as so many wildernesses ; that the fortresses of the district were in the hands of the English ; that the cultivators of the soil, expelled from their paternal roofs, had been reduced to beggary—all which miseries they endured rather than renounce their allegiance ; but that if no steps were taken for their relief they would be forced to swear fealty to the King of England, and that others, fearing similar misfortunes, would be in danger of doing the same.

The Regent, moved by these representations, led a small force into Dumfriesshire, and captured the Tower of Langholm, which the Armstrongs had three years before treacherously taken when its owner, Lord Maxwell, was a prisoner in England, and had delivered it to Lord Dacre. Arran was preparing to attack other garrisons, when he was under the necessity of returning with his troops to join a French auxiliary force that had landed in the Forth, for the purpose of besieging the Castle of St Andrews— then held by the conspirators who in the preceding year had assassinated the tyrannical Cardinal Beaton. Scarcely had the foreign allies departed, after accomplishing their task, than the Duke of Somerset, who had been appointed Protector on the death of Henry VIII., entered Scotland by the Eastern Marches at the head of fourteen thousand soldiers, gave battle to the Scots under Arran on the field of Pinkie, and routed them with great slaughter.

A few days prior to this defeat, Lord Wharton and the Earl of Lennox appeared in Dumfriesshire at the head of five thousand foot soldiers and eight hundred light cavalry, for the purpose of preventing the inhabitants from sending aid to the main army, and also for completing the work of subjugation which Carleton had begun. Crossing the River Esk, they spent all night upon its

---

* Sasine of R. L. M., as heir returned to R. L. M., in the barony of Maxwell, comprising the following lands, &c. : The £40 lands of Maxwell, in Roxburgh ; the barony of Carlaverock and Lochirwood, in Dumfries ; the lands of Springkell, Newtoun, and Logan, in Annandale : the office of Steward of the Stewartries of Annandale and Kirkcudbright ; the lands of Cansallauch and Durisquen ; the superiority of the £5 lands in the burgh of Dumfries ; the barony of Balmacreuthy, in Perth ; the lands of Gordonstown and the barony of Grenane, in Kirkcudbright ; the lands of Spottes, also in said Stewartrie ; the barony of Mernis, Drippis, and Nether Pollok, in Renfrew ; all incorporated with the barony of Maxwell, sasine to be taken for the whole. Dated at Carlaverock, 6th November, 1551.—Terregles Papers. A few days afterwards tha same lord obtained sasine of the family estates in Eskdale— "Brumeholm, Arkinholme, Quhitschetis," &c.

banks, and next morning they made a destructive raid through Lower Annandale, obtained an easy entrance into Castlemilk, and then pushing down to the town of Annan, called upon it to surrender. It so happened, however, that the Master of Maxwell had come to Annan beforehand, with the view of assisting the Laird of Cockpool and other local chiefs to stop the progress of the enemy. To the English summons they returned a defiant answer ; and, considering that their resources were small, they made a noble defence. Driven from the outer barriers, they withdrew to the strong church, which, with its turretted spire had been subjected to many fierce assaults in days gone by ; and hurriedly throwing up protecting earthworks around the building, they prepared to offer a desperate resistance. It might have been a hopeful one had not the assailants possessed some pieces of ordnance, with which they made the citadel-church too hot for its brave occupants, who at last, while it was filled with fire and smoke, and the roof was falling in upon them with deadly results, and the undermined floor was giving way beneath their feet, took refuge in the steeple, and prolonged for a time the unequal conflict. At this stage the Earl of Lennox offered to spare their lives if they abandoned all further resistance. The condition was accepted, and the heroic garrison, now reduced to sixty-two persons—including, we presume, the Master of Maxwell—were allowed to march out "with the honours of war." In a few minutes afterwards the church and steeple were blown up with the powder stored below, and all that remained of them were levelled with the ground. The burgh itself, after being pillaged, was set fire to, and left a miserable wreck. (a) Influenced by these severities, many land-holders in Annandale and Nithsdale swore allegiance to Edward VI., and gave hostages for their fidelity. The Master of Maxwell appears to have been among the number.*

(a) The siege of Annan is dealt with on some counts differently in Mr Neilson's " Old Annan" essay.—(Dumfriesshire Antiquarian Society's Transactions, 10th May, 1895.)

* A record has been preserved of the chiefs of Dumfriesshire, with their followers, who swore fealty to England at this dismal period. It is here subjoined :—William Johnstone, the Laird's brother, with 110 followers ; Johnstone of Coites, with 162 ; Johnstone of Lochmaben, with 67 ; Johnstone of Malinshaw, 65 ; Johnstone of Crackburns, 64 ; the Johnstones of Dryfesdale, 46 ; the Johnstones of Craigyland, 37 ; Gavin Johnstone, with 31 ; Jardine of Applegarth, 242 ; the Laird of Kirkmichael, 222 ; Patrick Murray, 203 ; the Laird of Ross, 165 ; the Laird of Amisfield, 163 ; the Laird of Holmains, 162 ; the Laird of Wamphray, 102 ; the Laird of Tinwald, 102 ; the Laird of Dunwoodie, 44 ; the Lord Carlyle, 101 ; Irving of Coveshaw, 102 ; Jeffray Irving, 93 ; the Irvings of Pennersacs, 40 ; Irving of Robgill, 34 ; Wat Irving, 20 ; the Lairds of Newby and Gretna, 122 ; the Laird of Gillenby, 30 ; Sir John Lawson, 32 ; the Bells of Tintells, 222 ; the Bells of Toftints, 142 ; the Romes of Torduff, 32 ; the Moffats, 24 ; the town of Annan, 33. The chiefs of Nithsdale mentioned in the catalogue were the Master of Maxwell, 1000 and more ; Edward Maxwell of Brackenside (afterwards of Hills), and the Vicar of Car-

The oaths of homage exacted by terror were not kept. When Wharton and Lennox withdrew their forces from Dumfriesshire a mutinous spirit began to manifest itself in both Nithsdale and Annandale, the chiefs encouraging it, but at the same time professing devoted allegiance to the Crown of England. Doubting their sincerity, the Earl of Lennox, who was son-in-law to Angus, and who had become the servile agent of Edward VI., summoned his Scottish allies to meet him at Dumfries ; but when he entered the burgh, with about two hundred light horsemen, instead of finding an extensive muster of two thousand men, as he had been led to expect, there were scarcely three hundred in attendance. William, Earl of Glencairn, was the only nobleman who was waiting to welcome him, and Lennox saw good reason to suspect that he came rather as a spy than a friend. "Here be letters from the Laird of Drumlanrig," said Glencairn, "in which he maketh it known that if the Lord Lennox will come, accompanied by Scotishmen onlie, he will both serve and honour him ; but if he brings those Englishmen with him he will not onlie refuse to aid him, but raise all the power he can and proffer him a repulse." Lennox saw the snare laid for him at once ; and, meeting deceit with craft, he professed to see no danger in trusting himself to a troop of Scots ; but after leaving his artful adviser, he resolved on making an example of Drumlanrig, who he knew "was the chief instrument to stay all the Scotishmen in these parts from entering friendship with the Englishmen."[*]

At deep midnight, "by torch and trumpet sound arrayed," six hundred chosen horsemen marched away from Dumfries, under the leadership of Lord Wharton's second son, Henry, in order to punish Douglas. By dawn of morn they came within sight of his hold—which, however, they did not assail, resting satisfied with raising a red line of fire along two miles of country, "even hard to the gates of Drumlanrig," spoiling all the homesteads within reach to the value of 2000 merks, and driving off 2000 head of cattle, 3000 sheep, and nine score of horses. Never before had that part of Nithsdale suffered from a more destructive visitation. "The Annandalers," as Hollinshed calls them, who made up the chief portion of Wharton's force, hurried homewards with their prey, leaving him with only a hundred and twenty horsemen. Just as the latter had leisurely crossed to the left bank of the Nith, the Laird of Drumlanrig, who had lain in ambush with seven hundred men, entered the water in pursuit ; but he was soon himself, with his host, in the position of a beaten fugitive. Taken at advantage

laverock, 310 ; Kirkpatrick of Closeburn, 403 ; Grierson of Lag, 202 ; the Laird of Cowhill, 91 ; the Laird of Cransfield, 27 ; Edward Crichton, 10 ; the town of Dumfries, 201. In Eskdale, the Beattisons and Thomsons, 166 ; and in Eskdale and Liddisdale, the Armstrongs, 300.

* Hollinshed's Scottish Chronicle, p. 243.   •

by the returning foe, before they could emerge from the river, they were thoroughly repulsed, Douglas making a narrow escape, as several spears were broken on his armour ; and but for his fleet-limbed steed he would have been slain or taken captive. Many of his followers fell, and many others were carried off prisoners to Dumfries.* The submission of Galloway to the English was one of the results of this victorious raid ; several of its leading men, together with the Master of Maxwell, proceeding to Carlisle and delivering hostages for their fidelity.

"Fidelity !" Neither they nor the other chiefs who acted in the same manner meant to give Edward more than lip-service—

> " Mouth-honour, breath,
> Which the poor heart would fain deny,
> But dared not "—

till the compulsory influence was withdrawn. The old story of dissimulation and revolt was repeated in Nithsdale next spring. Hence the reappearance in the county town of the twin destroyers Lords Howard and Lennox with a greater host than ever. Angus still doubtful, Drumlanrig dissembling, the Master of Maxwell and the Earl of Glencairn repeating their false assurances of friendship ; and the English Earls, doubting the whole pack, but believing devoutly in the truth of blazing torches and devouring swords, hastened towards the hilly district of Durrisdeer, nearly captured Angus—who had, under the mask of friendship, invited his son-in-law to meet him in Drumlanrig Castle—and, failing to secure the person of that wily chief, they set the village of Durrisdeer in a blaze. While retracing their steps, and just as the far-away van of the footmen approached Dalswinton, the Scottish auxiliaries, according to previous arrangement, hoisted a black pennon, at which signal they were joined by numerous countrymen who had been secreted on the hills around, and the whole, headed by Maxwell and Drumlanrig, stepped in between the English horsemen and infantry, expecting to divide and conquer. The division was but temporary, and the triumph went all the other way, as the separated cavalry soon "fetched a compass," by which movement they were enabled to join their comrades further down the valley, just as the unfounded rumour had reached them that their horsemen had been cut to pieces, and that they themselves had been doomed to a similar fate. Plied by the reunited forces, the Scots were put to flight ; Drumlanrig was taken, but his keepers, probably ignorant of his rank, liberated him on receiving a few gold pieces ; and the Master of Maxwell had a perilous passage of escape through a clump of spears. About four hundred prisoners

---

* Hollinshed says the prisoners numbered a hundred and twenty ; but that is scarcely credible, as the English party were exactly of that number before the engagement.

were captured, including the Abbot of Sweetheart, Christie Irving of Bonshaw, and a brother of the Laird of Amisfield. On the victors arriving at Dumfries they rifled the town ; and named a court-martial to mete out justice against the hostages whose lives had been forfeited—meanwhile asking instructions regarding them from the English Government.* Let Hollinshed tell the rest. "Therewith," he says, "were letters directed down from the Council to the Lord Wharton for the execution of certain pledges —that is to say, the Maister of Maxwell's pledge, being one of his nearest kinsmen of the house of the Herries ; also, the Warden of the Greie-friars in Dumfries ; the Vicar of Carlaverocke ; and divers others [all of whom] were executed at Carlill."(a)

* For the account of these forays in 1547 and 1548 we have had to rely chiefly on the brief contemporary reports by Wharton to the Duke of Somerset, as preserved in the State Paper Office, London, and in Hollinshed—the latter of whom is sometimes rather careless about his dates, and usually writes with a strong English bias.

(a) Though success was with the English, they were so severely handled that they were obliged to retreat. There is a strange wild story of romance connected with the hanging of the hostages. Repentance Tower, on Trailtrow Hill, in Cummertrees, "has a tradition which has given it renown as a veritable ballad-makers' joy." According to one version a Lord Herries, out of remorse for having taken the stones of Trailtrow Chapel to build his Castle of Hoddom, set up the Tower. Another is that John the Reif, by which name the Lord Herries was known, while returning across the Solway with booty and prisoners, was overtaken by a storm, cut the throats of the men, and threw them overboard. Repentance Tower he afterwards erected for the welfare of his soul. The truth about the Tower, which Mr George Neilson has traced out, is more romantic than the tradition. William, Lord of Herries, proprietor of Hoddom, died about 1543 leaving three daughters, Agnes, Catherine, and Janet. For the hand of Agnes, a peeress in her own right, there were two competitors. One was Lord John Hamilton, son of the Earl of Arran, who, as Regent, had the heiresses in ward and was anxious to foster the suit of his son. The other was John, second son of the fifth Lord Maxwell. According to a Kirkconnell MS., which was transcribed for the *Dumfries Standard*, and printed in three instalments in 1889, " It hapened that in anno 1547 the haill inhabitants of Annandale, Eskdaill, Wauchopedall, Galloway beneath Cree, and Nithsdaill to Drumlanrig, in absence of the Lords of Maxwell, being overcomed be the (h)oast of Ingland, was compelled to hold and be at the oppinione of the King of Ingland, and have delyvered for obedience the pledges to my Lord Ouhartoune, Wardane for Ingland. The said Lord comeine forward to Duresdear with ane great oast minding to persew furder in Scotland, the said Sir John Maxwell and Sir James Douglas of Drumlanrig, who aboid still at the oppinione of Ingland, sett creully upon the Inglish army, and swa drave the Inglish Wardane and his army back again to Dumfreis and from thence home again to Carlyle, making the weter of Sullway the march and Esk as it was before. In recompence of the whilk good service the said Sir John gott the heretrix of the Lordship of Herries to wife from James, Earl of Arran, then Governor of Scotland, and swa was the Lord of Teregells ; altho it was dear to the pledges of Scotland, who were all executtied in Ingland for break of Scotland's promise." On the eve of the affair at Durisdeer Drumlanrig had, it is said, an interview in the Kirk of Keir with his nephew, John, Master of Maxwell, and promised to secure for him from the Regent the hand of the heiress if ou a given signal he should cross over from the English ranks with his followers when the battle

Truly a dismal supplement to the fierce foraying of the preceding years. But the Scoto-English Border warfare, with its
bloody engagements, its lawless executions, its wasting conflagrations, its riotous excesses, and its courageous enterprises, round all
which genius has thrown a halo of romance, was drawing rapidly
to an end, after enduring with but brief intervals for nearly three
hundred years. If the Duke of Somerset had followed up his
victory at Pinkie he might have imperilled the independence of
Scotland. Pressing business, involving his own influence at
Court, having recalled him to London, the country he had half
subdued gradually recovered its courage and freedom. Dumfriesshire remained but outwardly submissive for a year or so after it
had been overrun by Lord Wharton ; and while his rule was being
disputed by some of the county chiefs, favourable influences were
at work which enabled them to get rid of his unwelcome presence
for ever, and which eventually made the Western Border what it
had never been before, a great moral bulwark to the nationality
of the North.

On the 24th of March, 1550, the English, when entering into
friendly relations with France, agreed, at the instance of the
latter, to terminate hostilities with Scotland. A treaty of peace
was accordingly signed at Norham, in June, 1551,* which continued
unbroken for nearly ten years, and formed the prelude of a perpetual peace between the two kingdoms. It comprehended in its
provisions the settlement of the famous Debatable Land, which,
as already explained, formed part of Scotland originally,† but had,

was on and join the Scots. Maxwell succumbed to the temptation ; and fourteen of the fifteen hostages at Carlisle, all of them kinsmen of his own, were
hanged for this act of treachery, the only one reprieved being Maxwell of
Terraughty, who was too much of a child to be so cruelly treated. John felt
most bitterly his responsibility for this horrid massacre, and sent a challenge
to Wharton, who scornfully declined to "answer you who is perjured, and
hath broken your faith, whereby you consentyd the death of your pledges
delyvered by you." Maxwell, however, acquired not only the estates of
Hoddom and Terregles, but the title of Lord Herries by his wife, and held the
office of Warden in the long minority of his nephew of Carlaverock. It was
his business to maintain the beacon on Trailtrow Hill ; and it was he who
built the tower there, to have a fire on the top of it. "It was," says Mr
Neilson, "the monument of that proud man's bitterest regret. Carving above
the lintel the word ' Repentence,' did he not own his broken faith and confess
his tragic error ? . . Did he not also thus seek to appease the unquiet spirits
of those hostages whose young and innocent blood rose to heaven, accusing
not less terribly than if he had strangled with his own hand the victims who
for his dishonoured promise were hanged by Wharton on Haribee ?" In point
of fact they were hanged within the Castle grounds—not at Haribee, which
is on the outside of the town.

* Rymer's Fœdera, p. 265.

† "The tract," says Chalmers (vol. iii., p. 98), "certainly belonged to
Scotland, as many charters of the twelfth, thirteenth, and fourteenth centuries evince with full conviction." He refers to Rymer, pp. 245, 289, and
337, in corroboration of the statement.

in the course of the Border warfare, been often occupied by England, and had at length become a sort of neutral territory, claimed by both kingdoms, really possessed by neither, and ruled by laws of its own : that is to say, when these were not set aside by the sword.   In times of peace the subjects of both countries pastured their herds on its untilled fields during the day, but were required to remove them before sunset at their own peril ; and when they did foolishly run the risk of leaving their cattle exposed in the night, the likelihood is they would be carried off by reivers like Clym of the Cleuch, Hobbie Noble, or Jock o' the Side, in which case no redress was obtainable by the owners.

The tract lay along the Scottish side of the Esk and Liddell, was bounded on the west by the Sark, and was eight miles long and four broad.   After several conferences between the commissioners of both nations, assisted by an envoy from France, a division of the Debatable Land was resolved upon ; according to which, it was intersected by a line drawn from the Sark on the west to the Esk on the east—the northern portion, or parish of Canonby, being assigned to Scotland ; the southern, or parish of Kirkandrews, to England : " and lest the stones, by evil practice or length of time should be destroyed or moved," the places where they were to be set were specified, namely, " the stone upon Esk where the course of the river bends on the western banks of a field called Dymmisdale, where Dymmisdale Syke comes in ; and the stone upon Sark to be at a red cliff in Kirkrigg, where also the water of Sark makes a turn."*

By this arrangement a tract of country that was fruitful of violence and strife, but in other respects little better than a waste, was brought under culture ; and the little stone pillars put up to form the line of partition looked like the literal pale of civilisation, within which the territory and its turbulent population had at length been brought.† While the treaty of Norham exercised a most beneficial influence on both England and Scotland, it conferred an especial boon on Cumberland and Dumfriesshire, both of which had often reason to regret their indissoluble connection with the Debatable Land.

---

* Hutchinson's History of Cumberland, vol. ii., p. 531.

† Robert Maxwell of Cowhill sent the news of the settlement to Sir John Maxwell of Pollok, in these terms :—" Ye sall understand that the Baithepland is devydit, and the merches set between Ingland and Scotland ; and Lytill Thomas the Grame [his] howis is fallin to Ingland, and Sande Armistrangis howis to Scotland ; and the tua Vardanis suld met at Lowmabane Stane this Thryday, and radres to be maid sin the peiss."—Maxwells of Pollok, Preface, p. 179.

CHAPTER XX.

Up till this period Dumfries retained possession of all, or nearly
all, its ancient landed patrimony, extending over a large portion
of the parish. The income arising from it, and the tolls and customs levied by the Council, must have been quite sufficient to keep
the burghal machinery in operation without, except on rare occasions, resorting to a personal impost on the lieges. There is too
much reason to suppose that before the death of James IV. practices were introduced which destroyed this happy equilibrium
between income and outlay, and eventually left to the burgh only
a small portion of its territorial inheritance. The lands granted
at various periods by the Crown were to be held for all time
coming ; they were, in point of law, strictly inalienable ; it was
only, at all events, when the King, as overlord, sanctioned the sale
or perpetual lease of any of these lands that such proceedings
were allowable. So wisely jealous was the Government lest the
" res universitatis " (the " common good " arising to royal burghs
from rents and customs) should be tampered with, that the Great
Chamberlain of the nation was required to make periodical in-
quests into their management. Once a year at least that official,
or his deputy, held a sort of exchequer court at Dumfries, at which
the magistrates made count and reckoning with him of all their
intromissions.

A salutary check to mal-administration was thus supplied ;
but in the reign of James I. the office of the Great Chamberlain
was superseded by that of the High Treasurer, who seems never
to have exercised any efficient supervision over the revenue of
burghs-royal. Even before this change Parliament deemed it
necessary to " statute and ordaine that the common gud of all our
Soverane Lordis burrowis be observit and kepit to the common
gude of the toun, and to be spendit in commoun and necessare
thingis of the burgh, be the avise of the Consale of the town for
the tyme, and dekkynis of crafts quare thai ar, and attour that the

rentis of burrowis, as landis, fishingis, fermis, myllis, and utheris yerely revenuis be nocht set bot for thrie yeris allenerly."* Freed from a strict Government inspection, the magistrates of burghs become in some instances careless or culpable stewards of the trusts committed to them ; and when in 1503 Parliament passed an Act permitting the King to give permanent tenures of Crown property in lieu of short leases, and barons and freeholders to do the same thing, a vicious precedent was introduced which the rulers' of towns were eager to follow ; and they were soon allowed to do so—Edinburgh, Aberdeen, and several other royal burghs obtaining in the first instance special licenses from the sovereign for converting their common property into heritable estates, given in feu-farm in return for what ere long became little more than a nominal quit-rent. From this period "may be dated the commencement of that system of mal-administration which, with greater or less rapidity, ultimately tended to the destruction of the far greater portion of the common good of burghs-royal."†

When James IV. was in Dumfries, however, the deteriorating process had scarcely, if at all, begun ; and this circumstance, in conjunction with others of a favourable kind, leads us to the inference that during his reign the burgh reached its feudal meridian. In after times it acquired increased municipal privileges, more trade, more population ; but it never was so richly endowed with territorial wealth. Under the same sovereign, also, the trades, who had hitherto been subordinated to the merchants, took high social rank in the town, and, it may be safely inferred, acquired a direct representation in the Council, though the precise period at which the deacons became members of that body cannot be ascertained.

When the reign of James V. is reached we can speak in more precise terms than hitherto regarding the constituents of society in Dumfries. Seven different grades are distinctly visible :—1. The patrician class, possessing land in the neighbourhood, obtaining for payment or by favour the freedom of the burgh, in order that they may share the honour and patronage that arise from the direction of its affairs. 2. The merchant burgesses, consisting of men actually engaged in business, who may, or may not, be also landed proprietors. 3. The master craftsmen, trying, not without success, to hold their heads as high, and wear their furred gowns as jauntily as the merchants. 4. The ecclesiastics, consisting of the dean and his clergy, the vicar, the parish priest, the Minorite friars, and other churchmen, regular or secular, making altogether a numerous body. 5. The artisans and mechanics, who work for wages. 6. The yeomen, or free farmers. And, 7, the cottars—

* Acts of Scottish Parliament, 1491, vol. ii., p. 227.
† Report of Municipal Commissioners, p. 23.

"hewers of wood and drawers of water"—rapidly casting away
their serfdom, though some of them still in a state of absolute
slavery.*
The earliest provosts of the burgh were, in all likelihood,
cadets of the Douglases, Maxwells, Kirkpatricks, Carlyles, Johnstones, and other families who owned land and held rule in the
district. In the early half of the sixteenth century, when the
burgh was becoming increasingly independent, some of its own
sons—merchants as well as lairds—took a leading part in the
management of its affairs. Among the first of these were the
M'Brairs. Of Celtic origin, we find them at an early period settled
in Dalton, Mid-Annandale ; and it is as the M'Brairs of Almagill,
in that parish, that they first appear in the records of the burgh.
A "retour," dated 19th December, 1573, warrants the supposition
that they occupied Almagill at least a hundred years before that
date,† as in it Archibald M'Brair, Provost of Dumfries, is entered
as heir "to his great-grandfather, William M'Brayre of Almagill,
in the 100s. land of Almagill, in Meikle Dalton, and the three
husbandlands in the town of Little Dalton, called Hallidayhill."‡(a)
When the Convention of Royal Burghs met at Edinburgh, on the
4th of April, 1552, John M'Brair, Provost of Dumfries (probably
the father of Archibald), appeared as Commissioner for the town·
Provost Archibald M'Brair and Bailie James Rig were its representatives in the Convention of 1570. On the 5th of January,
1561, John M'Brair, by obtaining a charter of the Mains, which
constituted a portion of the church lands of Dumfries, acquired a
still stronger footing for his family in the town ; though they do
not appear to have given to it any chief magistrates after 1577.

* These were termed " villeins " at an antecedent period ; but even when
the bondage system was at its worst, and the villeins could be given away,
bequeathed, or sold, these expressions, which seem so inconsistent with any
degree of personal liberty, bore a different meaning to that which we would
now assign to them. " In no instance," says Sir F. Palgrave, " can we find
the ceorl or villein separate from his land. He was always a " villein appur-
tenant ;" and, notwithstanding the language employed, the gift, bequest, or
sale was the disposition of the land and his services."

† We find the following minute in Pitcairn (vol. i., p. 39) of a case tried
at Dumfries, August 15th, 1504 :—" Robert Grersoune, in Dumfreis, produced a precept of remission for art and part of the cruel slaughter of Sir John
M'Brair, chaplain, in the town of Drumfreis. William Douglas of Drumlanrig
became surety to satisfy parties." (See ante p. 163.)

‡ The parish of Dalton, prior to the Reformation, was divided into Meikle
Dalton and Little Dalton ; but, since their union in 1633, the Church of Meikle
Dalton is used by the parishioners of the united parishes as their place of
worship.—Statistical Account of Dumfriesshire, p. 371.

(a) In 1506 Thomas Makbraire appears as a chaplain in Dumfries witnessing a deed touching property in le Myd-raw, le New-werk, and le Perissoun
Herbare (the Parson's harbery or herbergage). (Registrum Magni Sigilli,
1424-1513, No. 3010.) Herbert Makbraire appears as an owner of lands in
Dumfries on 10th October, 1510.

How, before the lapse of another hundred years, this family had increased in opulence, may be inferred from the following list of the lands belonging to Robert M'Brair, on the 10th of January, 1666 :—The five-pound land of Over and Nether Almagill, with the two husbandland of Hallidayhill ; the one-merk land of Cluserd ; the five-merk land of Little and Meikle Cloaks ; two merks of the four-merk land of Corsenloch (parishes of Urr and Colvend) ; the five-pound land of Nether Rickhorne ; the half-merk land of Glen-shalloch ; the twenty-shilling land of Auchrinnies ; the two-merk land of Little Rickhorne ; the forty-pound land of Over and Nether Wood, and Long Holm, holding of the Crown ; part of the twenty-pound land of Rigside, with mill and salmon fishing ; the lands of Spitalfield, with the salmon fishing formerly belonging to the Friars Minors of Dumfries, holding of the Crown ; the lands of Castledykes, holding of the Crown ; four acres of land lying between the Doocot (or Dovecot) of Castledykes, on the south of the burgh of Dumfries—Sinclair's tenement on the north, King's High Street on the east, and the river Nith on the west ; and two merks of the fifteen merks of the Kirkland of Drumfries, feu of the King.*

We find Herbert Raining Commissioner for Dumfries in the Convention of 1578, Matthew Dickson and John Marschell its Commissioners in 1582, and Simon Johnnestown its Commissioner in 1584—all these being familiar household names at this early period.† In the Convention of 1585 Dumfries was represented by no fewer than four members—"Alexander Maxwell‡ of Newlaw, Provost, Maister Homer Maxwell and Herbert Ranyng, tua of the Bailies, James Rig their Conburges." Bailie Homer Maxwell was also Commissary of Dumfries, and held the lands of Speddoch, which originally belonged to the Monastery of Holywood.

The Corsanes, or Corsons, a more ancient family than the M'Brairs, emulated them as municipal rulers. They claim to be descended from the patrician Corsini, and say their first ancestor in Scotland came from Italy to superintend the erection of Sweet-heart Abbey and Devorgilla's Bridge over the Nith, though it is right we should state that frequently in old writs the name appears with the prefix "A" or "Ap," indicating a British or Celtic origin ; and even so recently as 1469 we read of the marriage of Janet, daughter of Sir Robert Acorsane of Glen, to Edward

---

* Appendix I.

† At this session of the Convention of Burghs four of the members (one of whom was the Commissioner for Dumfries) were unable to write, and had to sign the minutes "with our handis at the pen led be the notaris under-written at our commandis, because we can nocht wryte ourselves."—Records of the Convention.

‡ We give the entry as it appears ; but we learn from a more trustworthy source that Provost Maxwell's Christian name was John : he was an illegiti-mate son of John, Lord Herries.

Maxwell of Lochrutton and Hills. (a)   Some time before 1400 Sir
Alexander Corsane was witness to a charter granted by Archibald
the Grim, Earl of Douglas, to Sir John Stewart, of the lands of
Calie.   In 1408 Dominus Thomas Corsanus, perpetual Vicar of
Dumfries, granted a charter for certain church lands within the
royalty.   The Corsanes took the designation of Glen till, in the
reign of James IV., the barony so called passed with Marion,
another daughter of the above Sir Robert Corsane, or Acorsane,
to her husband, Sir Robert Gordon, who thereupon styled himself
of Glen, but afterwards of Lochinvar, on the death of his elder
brother at the battle of Flodden.   From Gordon of Lochinvar and
his wife Marion sprung the barons of that ilk and the Viscounts
of Kenmure.

Sir John Corsane, next heir male of Glen, settled at Dumfries,
the head of a far-descending line, which for eighteen generations
presented an unbroken array of heirs male, all bearing the name
of John—pedigree occurrences that are perhaps without a parallel·
John Corsane, the 12th in descent from Sir John, was Provost of
Dumfries, and its Parliamentary representative in the critical year
1621.   He married Janet, daughter of the seventh Lord Maxwell
(slain at Dryfe Sands), by whom he had several children, one of
whom was wedded to Stephen Laurie of Maxwelton.   This Provost
Corsane was one of the richest commoners in Scotland.   Besides
his country estates, the chief of which was Meikleknox, he is said
to have owned a third part of his native town ; and at one time,
not very far back, many of its old houses bore the family arms—
the head of a pagan pierced by three darts, with warriors as supporters, and the motto, " Præmium virtutis gloria." His life seems
to have been inspired by that noble sentiment.   He died in 1629,
in his seventy-sixth year, and was buried near the entrance-gate
of St Michael's Cemetery, at a place where eleven of his ancestors
had been laid before him.   His eldest son, John Corsane of Meikleknox, by whom he was succeeded, married Margaret, daughter
and co-heiress of Robert Maxwell of Dinwoody, obtaining with
her the lands of Barndennoch.   He was also Provost of the Burgh,
and, as we shall see, took an active part in the popular struggle
against the aggressions of Charles I.   The ruins of a once magnificent monument erected by him over his father's dust remain
to attest his filial love, and the lines upon it were meant to inform
the meditative stranger that an honoured Dumfries worthy sleeps
below.   In addition to a brief, simple inscription, " In memoriam

(a) Its prevailing form is ACARS\N, to be compared with *Amulligane*, the
stock form of Milligan.   We actually have *Ap Molegan* on record in Ragman
Roll in the time of Edward I., viz.—*Macrath ap Molegan del counte de Dunfres.*
(Bain's Calendar II., p. 198.)   Accordingly, there can be no doubt the Corsini
are (says a correspondent) imaginary, and *Ap Corsan* is the prouder ancestry
of the two.

viri optimi hujus urbis consulis," there is trace of another longer
one, so defaced by time that it is quite illegible; but we may
assume that it was the following epitaph, as preserved in Nisbet's
Heraldry :

> " Ter tria fatales et bis tria lustra sorores,
> Dimidiumque Ævo contribuere tuo,
> Ter tria civiles humerum circumdare Fasces
> Lustra dedit Sophiæ gratia digna tuæ
> Ter tribus ac binus tandem prognatus eodem,
> Et lare Corsanis contumularis Avis."*

These lines may be thus translated :—" The fateful sisters assigned
thrice three and twice three lustres and a half [year] to thy lifetime [*i.e.*, seventy-five and a half years]. Regard due to thy
wisdom caused thy shoulders to wear the badges of civic authority
for thrice three lustres [forty-five years]. Sprung at length from
thrice three and two [eleven] progenitors of [the] Corsane [family],
thou also art buried with them in the same place."†

John Corsane of Meikleknox, who died in 1777, was the last of
the male line. Agnes, a daughter, was married to Mr Peter Rae,
minister of Kirkconnell, in Upper Nithsdale. They had twelve
children ; the eldest of whom, Robert, was, at his mother's request,
to assume the name and arms of Corsane of Meikleknox when he
came of age, but all the children died minors. In this way the
stem of this ancient house was unexpectedly broken. The Corsans
of Dalwhat, parish of Glencairn, were a branch of the family. The
name Corson, often written Carson, is still common in Dumfries ;
and about a hundred and sixty-five years after the death of

---

* Vol. ii., p. 113. In the Appendix to Nisbet (not written by that eminent genealogist) a lengthened account is given of the Corsane family, some
portions of which are far from being correct. The writer, misinterpreting the
above inscription, says of Provost Corsane : " Having in his younger years
executed the inferior offices of the magistracy in Dumfries, he was provost of
the said burgh *forty-five years.*" This is incredible. No single individual
could ever have enjoyed such a monopoly of the Provostship ; and the list of
the Dumfries Provosts given in the Appendix, and other indubitable evidence,
prove that other gentlemen besides Mr Corsane occupied the civic chair at
various periods during the forty-five years which ended in 1629, the date of
his death. The continuator of Nisbet also speaks of a coat of arms, and quotes
several Latin inscriptions, which he says were put upon the monument, but of
which there is no trace ; and the general appearance of the monument at
present is such as to force us into the belief that, though they might have
been prepared for the purpose in question, they were never actually engraved
upon the monument. A long Latin eulogium appears in Lockhart's Life of
Burns, which professes to be a copy of the epitaph inscribed upon the mausoleum erected over the poet's remains, but the said epitaph never was put upon
the mausoleum ; and in the same way we think some of the " many excellent
inscriptions " spoken of in Nisbet had never any existence except on paper.

† We are indebted for the English version of the epitaph to an accomplished scholar—Rector Cairns of the Dumfries Academy, now deceased.

Provost Corsane of Meikleknox [in 1671), James Corson, a probable descendant, was Provost of the Burgh * (a)

The genealogical tree of Coel Godhebog, already noticed, gives, as one of its goodly branches in the fifth century, the prolific Annandale family of Irving. Another account transplants them from Orkney to Eskdale, in the middle of the eleventh century. There were two gentlemen of the name in Bruce's royal household, with whom he had become acquainted, probably when ruling his hereditary lordship on the banks of the Annan—one of them, William de Irwyn, who acted as the King's secretary ; and the other, Roger de Irwyn, who seems to have officiated as his chamberlain.† An Irving, possibly the former of these two, received from the same gracious monarch the lands of Drum, in Aberdeenshire.‡ His descendant, Sir Alexander Iruinge, of Drum, was among the slain warriors for whom

* Mr W. R. Corson, architect, Manchester, writing to a Dumfries newspaper, says . "I have a drawing (a copy from one in the possession of my preceptor, the late Walter Newall) of the town residence of the Corsanes—a quaint design, with crow-stepped gables, and with five dormer windows in front, having plain gables, on the centre one of which is cut the following :

```
|   ᴗ  1622.   |
| Iᴍ C M M     |
| FEIR GOD.    |
```

The crescent also crowns this gable. I apprehend that the second line should be " Iɴ. C. M. K.," for " John Corsane, Meikle Knox," and that either the original or my copy is in fault, This house was pulled down in 183—(?) The crescent forms no part of the arms of the family, as given in Burke's General Armoury, but is a bearing of the Carsons. Query, Are these two families from one stock ? For the information of the antiquary I may add that the Carson shield, surmounted by a mitre, may be seen upon a stone erst belonging to the Priory of Tongland, built into the wall of a cottage in the clachan of that name, near Kirkcudbright.

(a) Sir Robert Threshie Reid, K.C., G.C.M.G., member of Parliament for the Dumfries Burghs, and late Attorney-General, is a distinguished scion of the family.

† The Accounts of the Chamberlain of Scotland, for 1329-1331, include several entries in which their names occur, e.g., " Et clerico Rotulorum pro feodo suo, viz., Willielmo de Irwyn, quamdiu fuerit in dicto officio capienti per annum viginti libras de terminis Pontecostes et Sancta Martini hujus compoti £20." " Idem onerat se de 348 ulnis tele linel et 3 quarteriis recept, superius per emptionem. De quibus Rogero de Irwyn, 311 ulnis de quibus respondebit."

‡ Dr C. Irving, in a MS. account of the family, says that Bruce, flying one stormy night from the English, came to Bonshaw Tower, where he was hospitably entertained. He took a younger son of the family, Sir William, of Woodhouse, to be his secretary and companion. As a reward for his services the King, when settled on the throne, conferred upon him the lands and the forest of Drum, and the pricking bay tree, or holly, for his armorial bearings, with the motto, " Sub sola, suo umbra virescens." (See a valuable little work, " Walks in Annandale," originally published in the *Annan Observer*.)

" The coronach was cried on Benachie,
    And doun the Don an' a',
When Hieland and Lawland mournfu' were
    For the sair field of Harlaw."*

The representative of the family in the reign of Charles I.
espoused the cause of that sovereign, and when lying under
sentence of death by the Covenanters was opportunely rescued
by Montrose.†

In Bonshaw Tower, on the classic banks of the Kirtle, resided
the acknowledged head of this great Border clan--other offshoots
of the family having as their domiciles Cove, Robgill, Woodhouse,
and Stapleton, the ruins of which give a romantic interest to a
district that is dowered with rich natural beauty, and ever vernal
in the minstrel's magic verse of Kirkconnel Lee.‡ The Irvings of
Bonshaw signalised themselves on many occasions by their valour
and patriotism. Like most Scottish families they suffered at
Flodden—Christopher, their chief, with his son, falling on that
dismal field ; while his grandson, " Black Christie" of Robgill and
Annan, perished in the pitiful catastrophe—for battle it cannot

---

* Balfour's Annals, vol. i., p. 147. The battle was fought on the 25th of
July, 1411. Irving was buried on the field ; and a heap of stones raised over
the spot was long known by the name of " Drum's Cairn."—Kennedy's Annals
of Aberdeen, vol. i., p. 51.

† This cavalier is the hero of the favourite old ballad, " The Laird of
Drum," written on his marrying, as his second wife, a damsel of humble birth,
named Margaret Coutts, an alliance which gave sore offence to some of his
kindred. The taunt of one of them, and the Laird's rejoinder, are well worth
quoting from the ballad : —

" Then up bespak his brother John,
    Says, ' Ye've done us meikle wrang, O ;
Ye've married ane far below our degree,
    A mock to a' our kin, O !'

' Now haud your tongue, my brother John,
    What needs it thee offend, O ?
I've married a wife to work and win,
    And ye've married ane to spend, O !' "

‡ The reference here made, it need scarcely be explained, is to the old
ballad of " Fair Helen of Kirkconnel," supposed to have been an Irving, and
who, in attempting to save her lover, Adam Fleming, was inadvertently shot
dead by his envious rival. The entire ballad is exquisite, and poetry has
produced scarcely anything more pathetic than the closing verses, in which
Fleming wails forth his sorrow :—

" O Helen fair ! O Helen chaste !
If I were with thee, I were blest,
Where thou lies low and takes thy rest,
    On fair Kirkconnel Lee.

I wish I were where Helen lies !
Night and day on me she cries ;
And I am weary of the skies,
    For her sake that died for me."

be called—of Solway Moss. A grandson of the latter, also named Christopher, became closely connected with two other distinguished Border houses, by marrying, in 1566, Margaret, sister of Sir James Johnstone, the victor of Dryfe Sands, whose mother was one of the Scotts of Buccleuch.

Soon after that period the Irvings began to be noticeable in Nithsdale ; and we must now somewhat abruptly leave the chief stem to see how one of the branches fared in Dumfries. It flourished exceedingly. Francis Irving, on returning to the burgh from France, where he was educated, married the daughter of Provost Herbert Raining, already mentioned as Commissioner for Dumfries in the Convention of 1578, acquiring with her a rich fortune of lands and houses. We find him sitting as member for the burgh in the Parliament of 1617, and high in favour at Court, receiving from King James VI. bailiary jurisdiction over some Crown property in the county ; still, however, carrying on his business, that of a merchant, in which capacity he was the first to form a trade connection with Bordeaux, for the purpose of importing French wines into the burgh.* This merchant prince of the olden time frequently occupied the chief magistrate's chair ; and when, in the early autumn of an honoured life, he breathed his last, his remains were laid close by the mouldering dust of the Corsanes— an imposing monument like theirs being raised in due time to commemorate his worth.† The tomb, which was renovated about thirty-five years ago, has several Latin inscriptions, the chief of which may be freely rendered as follows :—" A grateful spouse and pious children have dedicated to Francis Irving, Provost, a very dear husband and a prudent father, this monument which is far inferior to his worth. He died 6th November, 1633, aged 68." The back of the monument, which fronts the street, bears a Latinised "sermon in stone," illustrated by the emblematic cross-bones and sand-glass, which, freely translated, reads as follows : —" Be mindful of death, O traveller ! Life is a tale, a bubble, a cloud, vanity. What have we been but a flower, a shadow, a dream. Therefore, behold in a sand-glass the flow of our existence: certain and near is the hour of death. So live that thou mayest learn how to die." "Ane epitaphe," in the vernacular tongue, on the lower part of the structure, is in these terms :

> " King James at first me balive named.
> Dumfreis oft since me provost clamed,
> God hast for me ane crowne reserved ;
> For king and country have I served."

For more than a century afterwards municipal honours flowed upon the Dumfries branch of the Irvings ; some of them being also

---

* Family Tree of the Irvings, compiled by Mr J. C. Gracie.

† Like the Corsane monument it is built into the churchyard wall, and forms the fifth monument from the entrance-gate.

called, like their founder, to represent the burgh in Parliament. John, his eldest son, did so in 1630 and 1639, and was repeatedly elected Provost. He left two sons, John and Thomas, both of whom filled the latter office ; and Thomas also sat in Parliament for the burgh.

According to the same doubtful pedigree which traces the descent of the Irving family from a Cumbrian prince, Lywarch-Hen, another of the race was the progenitor of the Lauries, one of whom, Stephen, was a flourishing Dumfries merchant before James VI. became king. Prior to 1611 he espoused Marion, daughter of Provost Corsane, proprietor of Meikleknox, getting with her a handsome marriage portion. About the same time he obtained a charter from John, Lord Herries, of the ten-merk land and barony of Redcastle, parish of Urr. His wealth enabled him afterwards to purchase, from Sir Robert Gordon of Lochinvar, Bithbought, Shancastle, and Maxwelton ; for which estates he received a royal charter, dated 3rd November, 1611. Stephen Laurie, now a man of many acres, took the designation of Max-welton, leaving at his death the lands and title to his eldest son, John, married in 1630 to Agnes, daughter of Sir Robert Grierson of Lag. The next head of the house, Robert, was created a baronet on the 27th of March, 1685. He was twice married, and had by his second wife three sons and four daughters. The birth of one of the latter is thus entered in the family register by her father :— "At the pleasure of the Almighty God, my daughter, Anna Laurie, was borne upon the 16th day of December, 1682 years, about six o'clock in the morning, and was baptized by Mr Geo." [Hunter, minister of Glencairn.]* The minute is worth quoting here, seeing that the little stranger, whose entry into life it announces, grew up to be the most beautiful Dumfriesian lady of the day, and the heroine of a song which has rendered her charms immortal :—

> " Her brow is like the snaw-drift,
>   Her neck is like the swan,
>   Her face it is the fairest
>   That e'er the sun shone on—
>   That e'er the sun shone on,
>   And dark blue is her e'e ;
>   And for bonnie Annie Laurie
>   I'd lay me down and dee." (a)

* Barjarg Manuscripts.

(a) The song was altered to its present form and the music to which it is sung was composed for it by the Lady John Scott, who died March, 1900, at the advanced age of ninety years. She was the elder daughter of John Spottiswoode of Spottiswoode and Helen Wauchope, second daughter of Andrew Wauchope of Niddrie. In 1836 she became the wife of Lord John Douglas Montagu Scott, younger son of Charles William Henry, 4th Duke of Buccleuch and 6th of Queensberry. She was predeceased by her husband, who died Jan., 1860. Lady Scott was a fine type of the Scottish lady of the olden time, and was the author of a volume of lyrics, with music. She was deeply affected by

The well-known lyric, of which these lines form a part, was composed by Mr Douglas of Fingland, an ardent admirer of "Bonnie
Annie." She did not reciprocate his affection, however, but preferred his rival, Alexander Fergusson of Craigdarroch, to whom
she was eventually united in marriage.*

While the Irvings held rule on Kirtle Water and the western
fringe of the Debatable Land, they were neighboured in Gretna by
the small clan of the Romes, some of whom settled in the county
town during Archibald M'Brair's burghal reign, if not before,
acquiring a good position in it, as is proved by the frequent appearance of their names in the sederunts of the Council. We find traces

the death of her husband ; and to the end of her long life she acted as if he
were still alive. " She had his chair set for him at every meal "—we quote
from a newspaper notice of her at the time of her death ; " his luggage continued to go with her own when she travelled ; and many were the letters
she wrote to him, as if absent on a journey, and by and by to be expected
home." But well she knew that " returning is none from the grave ;" for in
one of her plaintive lyrics she sings not of him, but with a curiously prophetic
forecast of what his death would really mean to her :—

> " The yellow broom is waving abune the sunny brae,
>   And the rowan berries dancing where the sparkling waters play ;
>   Though a' is bricht and bonnie, it's an eerie place to me,
>   For we'll meet nae mair, my dearest, either by burn or tree.
>
> Far up into the wild hills there's a kirkyaird auld and still,
>   Where the frosts lie ilka morning, and the mists hang low and chill ;
>   And there ye sleep in silence while I wander here my lane,
>   Till we meet ance mair in heaven, never to part again."

In the beginning of 1890 a question having arisen as to the authorship of the
air to which " Annie Laurie " is now invariably sung, the present editor of the
Dumfries Standard addressed a note of inquiry to Lady Scott, and received
the following reply, dated from Spottiswoode, Lauder, February 4 :—

" Lady John Scott, in answer to the editor of the *Dumfries Standard*,
begs to say that she did compose the tune to ' Annie Laurie,' and altered the
words a little to what she thought would sound better in singing. The tune
of ' Annie Laurie ' she had before made for the words of an old ballad,
' Kempye Kaye,' but being at Marchmont, Sir Hugh Campbell's, whose wife
was her sister, she one day met with Allan Cunningham's poetry in the library
there, and was much taken with the words of ' Annie Laurie.' She adapted
the music she had composed to ' Kempye Kaye ' to them. The second verse
of Allan Cunningham's words begins—' She's backit like a peacock ; She's
breasted like a swan,' &c., which Lady John did not like. She therefore
altered it. The third verse she made entirely. She sang the song to Sir
Hugh and Lady Campbell to see whether they liked it, and they did like it.
Lady John long afterwards published it, with some others, for the benefit of
the widows and children of the soldiers killed in the Crimea. The time she
put the tune to ' Annie Laurie,' at Marchmont, was about the year 1834 or 5."

* One of the Fergussons of Isle married a sister of Annie Laurie. He was
buried in the family vault in Dunscore Churchyard ; and probably the old
tombstone there having upon it the inscription, " Here lyes entombit ane
honest and verteous mane, Alexander Fergussone," was placed above his
remains. His wife would doubtless be laid in the same grave. We have not
been able to ascertain where " Bonnie Annie " was buried.

of them soon afterwards as landed proprietors. A "retour" of 1638 represents John, son of John Rome of Dalswinton Holm, as enjoying the multures of the thirty-six pound land of Dalgonar, including the lands of Milliganton. In a general inquest in 1674 Robert appears as heir to his father, John Rome of Dalswinton ; so that the estate which the Red Comyn owned had, after a lapse of four hundred years, fallen into the hands of this Annandale family. The lands of Cluden were acquired by them at a later period ; and the second Provost of Dumfries chosen after the Revolution belonged to the family.

Long before Flodden was fought the Cunninghams (of whose origin something was said in a preceding chapter) ranked among the Corinthian pillars of the burgh. The lucrative office of town-clerk was frequently held by members of the family ; and the "retours" of property, in 1506 and 1510, show that one of them, William, must have been in the receipt of considerable house-rents. The family mansion, situated on part of what is now Queensberry Square, was the wonder of the town, on account of its " Painted Hall," a spacious chamber which seems to have been lent by them for public purposes ; and which acquired historic interest, as in it Protestantism was first preached to a Dumfries audience, and James VI. gave to it, as we shall see, the prestige of the royal presence on a memorable occasion ; while there is good ground for supposing that that king's grandfather, the Fourth James, lodged in it during his memorable visit to the burgh in 1504.

A few more prominent names require to be mentioned. Amongst the merchant burgesses of Dumfries at the opening of the seventeenth century were Ebenezer Gilchrist, of Celtic origin (the name signifying in that language a " servant of Christ ") ; John Coupland, belonging to a family who claim descent from the Yorkshire warrior by whom David II. was captured at Neville's Cross ; George Grierson, and Bailie William Carlyle, both members of old local houses—the latter, by marrying Isabella Kirkpatrick, about 1630, adding another nuptial alliance to the many ties of that kind by which their forbears were made one. Other marriage contracts of which a record lies before us furnish forth both old names and new :—Thomas M'Burnie, merchant, on wedding Isabel, eldest daughter of Bailie Edward Edgar and Agnes Carlyle, his spouse, got with her a tocher of 1000 merks. This was on the 2nd of January, 1663 ; and on the 24th of August, 1697, Agnes, the first fruit of the union, gave her hand to James Grierson of Dalgonar, the tocher given with her being simply the remission of 2000 merks out of 5500 owing by the bridegroom to the father of the bride. On the 21st of September, 1667, John, son of George Sharp, also a merchant in the burgh, espoused Elizabeth, eldest daughter of John Hairstens of Craigs. The happy swain in this instance was commissary clerk of Dumfries, which office was held a short time before by James,

son of John Halliday, advocate, cadets of an Annandale clan, who
gloried in recognising as their founder the chief of whom Wallace
spoke so fondly : "Tom Halliday, my sister's son so dear !"

At least four other families from the same district had at this
time representatives among the lairds and merchants of Dumfries :
the Dinwoodies, long settled in the parish of Applegarth, descended,
it is supposed, from Alleyn Dinwithie, whose name appears in the
Ragman Roll ; the Corries, or Curries, who took their name from
the old parish of Corrie (a Celtic compound, meaning a narrow
glen), where they first appeared as vassals of Robert Bruce, and
one of whom, Walter, as already noticed, was governor of Dumfries
Castle in 1291-2 ; the Flemings, sons of enterprising traders from
Flanders, who gave their name to a Dumfriesshire parish, Kirkpatrick-Fleming, where, on the left bank of the Kirtle, rose Redhall,
their ancient baronial hold ; and the Bells, whose chief occupied
Blacket House, on the right bank of the same stream, and who at
one time mustered so strongly in the neighbouring parish that
"the Bells of Middlebie" became a proverbial expression throughout the district.*

A few Grahams from the east bank of the Esk, descendants, it
is thought, of a brave knight, Sir John Graham, named "Bright
Sword," were to be found in Dumfries at this period ; also, some
members of a celebrated Celtic family, the Kennedys, who look
upon Roland de Carrick as their founder, and whose great grandson, Sir John Kennedy of Dunure, was the first to assume that
name instead of Carrick.†

---

* These two last-named families are both intimately associated with the
tragical story of "Fair Helen of Kirkconnel Lea," already referred to. Two
neighbours, one named Adam Fleming, and the other supposed to have been a
Bell of Blacket House, having sought her hand, she gave the preference to
Fleming. The disappointed suitor, meditating vengeance on his favoured
rival, traced the lovers to their usual nocturnal tryst on the banks of the
Kirtle, and, by the light of the moon, aimed his carabine at Fleming, and fired.
Fair Helen threw herself before her lover, in order to save him, received in her
breast the fatal bullet, and died in his arms. A desperate combat followed
between the two men, in which Bell was "hacked in pieces sma'." Poor
Fleming fled to foreign lands, seeking in vain for the peace of mind he had
lost for ever ; and then, following the impulse of his heart—

> "O that I were where Helen lies !
> Night and day on me she cries"—

returned home and died upon her tomb ; and now the ashes of the lovers
mingle together in the churchyard of Kirkconnel.

† Nisbet (System of Heraldry, vol. i., p. 161) considers that the old Celtic
thanes of Carrick, which was originally a part of Galloway, were ancestors of
the Kennedys. So far back as the eighth century, Kennedy, father of Brian
Boru, was Prince of Connaught ; and, in 850, Kennethe was Thane of Carrick.
The earldom of Cassillis (now Ailsa), in Ayrshire, is held by this family. The
Rev. Alexander Kennedy, minister of Straiton, Ayrshire, born in 1663, acquired
the estate of Knockgray, in the Stewartry of Kirkcudbright. His great-great-
granddaughter, Anne, married, 10th September, 1781, John Clark, Esq. of

It appears from these details that Annandale and the Western Border contributed much more to the population of Dumfries than Nithsdale ; and it is interesting to observe that all the household names we have enumerated, except M'Brair* and Rome, are still more or less common in the burgh—a remark which also applies to those of Turner, Lawson, Stewart, Mundell, Blacklock, Carruthers, Waugh, Clark, Paterson, Nicholson, Scott, Beck, Welsh, Thomson, Henrison or Henderson, Menzies, Dickson, Anderson, Lindsay, Gordon, Affleck, Ramsay, Forsyth, Goldie, Moffat, Simpson, Farish, Gibson, Crosbie, Pagan, Tait, Muirhead, Dalyell, Neilson, Gass, Weir, Glover, Coltart, Black, Reid, Wilson, Craik, Lorimer, Short-ridge, Newall, Rigg, Barbour, Spense, Martin, Milligan, M'Kie, M'George, and M'Kinnel—which names, like the others, frequently appear in the ancient burgess rolls, showing that their owners have had "a local habitation" in the capital of Nithsdale for at least three hundred years.†

These statements will enable the reader to see by whom the town was ruled and its public opinion guided during the Reformation period, and for a century afterwards. Let us now explain what part the old leading county families took in the conflict of creeds which had long been raging. Many of them remained neutral, or kept the Romanist side ; yet a considerable number cast in their lot with the Reforming party. Lord Maxwell's two sons, as well as himself, the Earls of Angus and Glencairn, the Laird of John-

Nunland, also in the Stewartry of Kirkcudbright ; and their eldest son, Colonel Alexander Clark Kennedy, succeeded in 1835 to the estate of Knockgray. An honourable augmentation was granted to his arms, in commemoration of his having, when in command of the centre squadron of the Royal Dragoons at Waterloo, captured the eagle and colours of the 105th Regiment of French Infantry with his own hand. (Scottish Nation, vol. ii., p. 609.) His son, the late Colonel John Clark Kennedy of Knockgray, born in Dumfries, also a distinguished officer, unsuccessfully contested the representation of the Dumfries Burghs with Mr William Ewart in 1865.

* The name Robert M'Brair appears in the list of burgesses for 1708, after which we lose trace of the family.

† Most of the local names mentioned in this chapter occur in the " retours," or Town Council minutes, at dates extending from 1506 downwards, till the middle of the following century. The reader will recognise modern localities in the old names of places in the second of the two extracts that we subjoin :— " 1506. Wm. Cunynham, 9 merk land 20s, et 12 do.; 3 tenements in burgo de Dumfries, val. 4s, de terr de Lordburn, ac itiam 4s ; di orto infra territorium dicti burgi." To this valuation return the following are witnesses :—" Dom. Fergusis Barbour, vic de Trawere [Troqueer], Hug Rig, Gul. Maxwell, David Welsche, John Lorymare, John Rig, Thomas Cunyngham, Thos. Stewart, Herb. Patrickson, burgos de Drumf." Also, " Dom. Tho. Makbraire, Gilbert Bek, et John Turnour, capillanus apud Drumf. 1510. William Cunyngham and his wyfe, de tenementis dict burg [in the said burgh of Dumfries], 12s ; de tenementi in dict. burg. in le Sewtergait, 10s ; de tenementi in capiti dict burg, 6s 8d ; de tenementi in Lochmabingait, 8s ; de alio tenementi, 4s ; de orrio et orto prope le Mildam, et le Clerkhill, 10s." Testified to, among others, by " Dom. Jon Walker."

stone, the Laird of Closeburn, the Laird of Amisfield (son of the knight whose memorable visit from the "Gudeman of Ballangeich" is narrated in a previous chapter), and James, chief of the Drumlanrig Douglases, promoted the Protestant movement from motives of policy or religion, or a mixture of both—the last-named nobleman manifesting special zeal on its behalf. He was descended from William, son of James, second Earl of Douglas, and on receiving the barony of Drumlanrig, in the parish of Durisdeer, from his father, he acquired the designation of Dominus de Drumlanrig. In 1740 his direct descendant, James, married the eldest daughter of Sir David Scott of Branxholm, ancestor of the Dukes of Buccleuch and Queensberry. William fell at Flodden, leaving two sons, the younger of whom, Robert, was Provost of Lincluden College—the last who held that lucrative appointment; the elder, James, being the nobleman under notice, and who signalised himself in endeavouring, with Sir Walter Scott of Buccleuch, to rescue King James V. from the grasp of Angus in 1526. James Douglas of Drumlanrig was knighted by the Regent Arran, and subscribed the Presbyterian Book of Discipline in 1561, remaining ever afterwards true to his profession. Sir Cuthbert Murray of Cockpool was also a decided Reformer; his mother's family, the Jardines of Applegarth, adopted the Reformed doctrines; so did the Griersons of Lag; and all these houses were matrimonially united to the Protestant Douglases—the eldest surviving son of Cockpool having wedded one of Drumlanrig's daughters, and their daughter having been married to the Laird of Lag.*

---

* Many of the leading families of the county were allied by intermarriage in this and succeeding centuries; and it not unfrequently happened that those families who were thus united took opposite sides in the wars that sprang up. The mother of Stewart of Garlies, who, as is afterwards shown, initiated the Reformation in Dumfries, belonged to the Catholic house of Herries. The marriage contract, dated 12th February, 1550, sets forth that "James Hamilton, Duke of Chatelherault, taking burden on him for John, his second son, as his tutor and administrator, on the one part, and Katherine Herries, with consent of James Kennedy of Blairquhan, her guidsire, on the other, hath contracted her to be married to Alexander Stewart, son and heir apparent of Alexander Stewart of Garlies, and is bound to pay 2300 merks of tocher with her; and grants to her, in conjunct fee with the said spouse, the £20 land of Dalswinton, and the £30 land of Bishoptown and Ballaghuyre." After the lapse of another generation, Barbara Stewart, the fruit of this marriage, was wedded by a Kirkpatrick, in terms of the following nuptial contract, dated 3rd May, 1581 :—" Contract of marriage between John, heir apparent to Thomas Kirkpatrick of Alisland, and Barbara Stewart, wherein Alexander Stewart of Garlies [the Reformer], her brother, and Dame Catherine Herries, her mother, burden themselves with her tocher, 7000 merks from Alexander and 400 from her mother, on the one part; and on the other part, Thomas, the bridegroom's father, engages to maintain them in his house, and to give them 100 merks yearly to buy clothes."

CHAPTER XXI.

TILL 1543, the date of Lord Robert Maxwell's Act, no one throughout the kingdom could read an English or Scottish version of the
Scriptures without serious risk. Long before that year, however,
the old wood of Airds, in Kirkcudbrightshire, was often rendered
vocal by the Word of Life, read, in the vulgar tongue, to a secret,
sympathising audience, by Alexander Gordon of Airds, a man of
rare excellence, who may be fairly reckoned the pioneer of the
Reformation in Galloway and Dumfriesshire. He was the third son
of Sir Alexander Gordon of Auchenreoch. Having gone across the
Border on matters of business, he happened to fall in with some of
Wickliffe's followers ; and he became so attached to one of them
that he engaged him as tutor to his family. Returning, thoroughly
embued with Reformation principles, accompanied by a Wickliffite,
and possessing a copy of Wickliffe's Testament, he became forthwith a zealous missionary of Protestantism.

Gordon was of gigantic size and strength, and was the father
of an immense family ; and on these accounts, as well as from the
pious supervision held by him over his household and numerous
dependants, the epithet of "The Patriarch," by which he was
popularly known, was exceedingly appropriate. When, after the
Regent Arran's apostacy, the Beaton party got the upper hand,
and enacted stringent laws for the observance of holidays, the
stalwart Laird of Airds set them and their laws at defiance.
According to one of those statutes every beast of burden made to
labour at such seasons was liable to forfeiture. By way of practical protest against it the Patriarch, who had a spice of humour in
his composition, gave a large festive entertainment on Christmas
Day ; and yoking ten strapping sons in a plough, he held it him-

self, whilst his youngest boy acted as caller ; and thus, in the presence of his astonished friends, and not a few emissaries of the Church, he tilled a ridge of the land of Airds, daring either layman or shaveling to distrain his team.*

His woodland congregations for studying the New Testament were held in a less open and defiant style. Among those who frequented them was Gordon's near kinsman, Alexander Stewart, younger of Garlies, the lineal descendant of the patriotic Sir Thomas Stewart whom Bruce rewarded with the barony of Dalswinton. Young Stewart spent some time in England as pledge for his father, the Laird of Garlies, one of the prisoners taken at Solway Moss ; and probably when there adopted those religious views which the teachings of the Patriarch confirmed. Soon the pupil emulated his master in the ardour with which he disseminated the doctrines of the Reformation. The estate of Dalswinton still belonged to the family ; and being thus territorially associated with Dumfries, he resolved to make that town the scene of his proselytising labours. The inhabitants were by no means ignorant of, or unconcerned about, the great revolution that was going on in the ecclesiastical world. Some of the leading men had been induced by the preaching of the Lollards in Kyle, a neighbouring district, to embrace Protestantism ; the secret converts to it numbering among others several members of the Cunningham family, in accordance with the example set by their noble relative the Earl of Glencairn. The burgh was therefore to some extent ripe for Stewart's evangelising experiment. That it might have a greater chance of success he invited William Harlow, a lay preacher belonging to Edinburgh (who had been forced to flee from that city by the priests), to visit Dumfries. Knox, writing many years afterwards, characterised him as " a simple man, whose condition, although it excel not, yet, for his whole and diligent plainness in doctrine, is he, to this day, worthy of praise, and remains a fruitful member within the Church of Scotland."† Harlow accepted the invitation, and, humble tailor though he was, became the burgh's first Protestant missionary.

A document is in existence ‡ which enables us to record the precise hour in which Harlow first denounced the Mass as rank idolatry, proclaimed salvation through simple faith in the crucified Redeemer, and sounded the knell of Popery in one of its strongest citadels. This took place at early morning watch, "nine houris afore noon," on the 23d of October, 1558—the light of the coming day symbolising, as it were, the dawn of the pure faith which the

* Sir Andrew Agnew's Hereditary Sheriffs of Galloway, p. 154.

† History of the Reformation, p. 117.

‡ Niem. Glasg. in Colleg. Scot., Paris, F 159. See Keith's History of the Affairs of Church and State in Scotland, vol. i., Appendix, p. 90.

speaker heralded.   Harlow, passing to the manor-house of Garlies, began his mission there ; and then, at three o'clock in the morning of the above day, "preached in the fore-hall of Robert Cunninghame, within the burgh of Dunfrese," one of his hearers being his patron and coadjutor, Mr Stewart.   What unpardonable audacity ! for a mere layman—a poor, vulgar maker of material garments—a heretic proscribed and vile—thus to lift up his testimony against "Holy Mother Church," and speak of her penances, pilgrimages, and peculiar dogmas as no better than filthy rags.

But the "pestilent rebel" was watched by indignant officials, sacred and secular : the Dean of Nithsdale invoked the intervention of the civil authorities ; and one Archibald Menzies, a legal emissary, with a good scent for heresy, and anxious for a job, hearing of what had occurred, "past incontinent to the presence of the said Alexander Stewart of Garlies, and the said Harlo, within the said burgh of Dunfrese, and required him of quhais authoritie, and quha gaif him commissioun to preach, he beand ane laittman [layman], and the Quenis rebel, and excommunicate, and wes repelled furth of other partis for the said causis."

The answer given was bold, and to the point : "I will avow him," said Garlies, "and will maintain and defend him against you and all other kirkmen that will put at him."   Whereupon the officer, through the agency of "David Makgee, *notarius publicus*," protested by a written deed, "quhilk instrument," we are told, "wes tain in the lodging place of the said Laird of Garlies, before thir witnesses : Schir* Patrick Wallace, curat of Dumfres ; Schir Jhone Ireland, parson of Rewll [Ruthwell] ; Schir Herbert Paterson, Schir Oles Wilson, chaplains ; Robert Maxwell, Williame Maxwell, Herbert Maxwell, Jhone Frude, John Menzies, Mark Rewll, and utheris."

With the view of obliterating the impression made by Harlow, 'Schir" Patrick Wallace preached a sermon in St. Michael's "for the weill and instruction of his parishioners ;" and then the pertinacious "Maister Archibald Menzies," anxious to do his part in the matter effectually, "past to the presence of David Cunninghame and James Rig, baillies of the burgh of Dumfres," and representing that Harlow had been put to the horn at the instance of the Queen's Grace, "for sic enormities and contemptions" as he had committed in divers parts "against the privilege of Haly Kirk and Acts of Parliament," he required them, in the sovereign's name, to seize the offender, and "putt him in sure hold."   To their

* This courtesy title of "Sir" was formerly prefixed to the name of all curates and such priests as had taken the academic degree of Bachelor of Arts. Justice Shallow, in the "Merry Wives of Windsor," when addressing Hugh Evans, a churchman, says : "Sir Hugh, persuade m e not, I will make a Star Chamber matter of it : if he were twenty Sir John Falstaffs, he shall not abuse Robert Shallow, esquire, master parson."

credit be it recorded, the magistrates said nay to the solicitation.
One of them, it may be inferred from his name, was related to the
owner of the hall in which Harlow preached—a noted historical
hall, let us not forget to say—the very Painted Chamber in which
the Sixth James was afterwards entertained ; and whether it was
that they decidedly favoured Protestantism, or simply wished to
remain neutral, they declined to interfere, even when the man of
law threatened them with pains and penalties, and "asked instruments," which were "maid and ta'en in the parioch-kirk," to that
effect.   Harlow, therefore, in spite of the enraged Dean of Nithsdale, his curate, "Schir" Patrick, and the mortified "Maister"
Menzies, and encouraged by the bountiful heir of Garlies, continued his services in Dumfries undisturbed, preparing the field
for other labourers, who soon sprang up.*

In the catastrophe that ensued down went the deaneries of
Nithsdale and Annandale ; the religious houses of the county, great
and small, were suppressed ; the ritual of Rome vanished from
public view ; the revolution which these words suggest being
effected with little violence and no bloodshed.

The oldest monastic establishment in Dumfriesshire was that
of Holywood.   The Abbey, which occupied the south-east corner
of the present churchyard of that parish, was in the form of a
cross, a spacious arch supporting its oaken roof.   The upper part
of the edifice was used as the parish church till 1779, when the
remains were absorbed in the existing place of worship ; and, hung
up in it, the old Abbey bells (though consecrated more than seven
hundred years ago) still ring in with dulcet peal the seasons of
religious service.†   To the Abbey were attached many lands in
Nithsdale and East Galloway, its monks enjoying a jurisdiction
over the whole.   Its rental in 1544 amounted to £700 Scots ; nineteen chalders, fourteen bolls, and three firlots of meal ; nine bolls
and three firlots of bere ; and one chalder of malt.‡   At the
Reformation its revenue was reduced to less than £400 Scots ; and
in 1587 the remains of the property were vested in the Crown.

* In the following spring Harlow prosecuted his evangelising labours in
Perthshire, for which he was prosecuted by the Government, as the following
extract from Pitcairn's Criminal Trials (vol. i., p. 407) will show :—"May 10,
1559.—Freir John Christesoune and William Harlow denounced rebels, as
fugitive, &c.; and their cautioners, John Erskine of Dune and Patrick Murray
of Tibbermuir, were amerciated, for their not entering to underly the law for
their usurping the authority of the Church, in taking at their own hands the
ministry thereof, as above, within the burgh of Perth, and other places adjoining, within the shire of Perth."

† The Statistical Account (p. 559) bears testimony to the excellent tone of
these venerable bells, and states that an inscription on one of them gives as the
date of consecration, by John Wrick, the year 1154.   A late incumbent of the
parish, the Rev. R. Kirkwood, who wrote the account in 1837, states that the
charter seal of the Abbot, dated 1264, was at that time in his possession.

‡ Keith, vol. i., Appendix, p. 185.

Thirty years afterwards an Act of Parliament was passed annulling this arrangement as to the temporalities of the Abbey and its spiritual jurisdiction (extending over the parish churches of Holywood, Dunscore, Penpont, Tynron, and Kirkconnel, with their parsonages, vicarages, tithes, and glebes), in order that King James VI. might grant the whole to John Murray of Lochmaben as a free barony, to be called the barony of Holywood, for a nominal yearly rent of £20 Scots, he, moreover, engaging to pay the stipends, to uphold the churches, and supply "the elements of breade and wyne for the celebratioun of the communioune" within the same.* Murray was a great favourite of the King, and had previously acquired from him the barony of Lochmaben, with other property in Dumfriesshire. Thomas Campbell, the last Abbot of Holywood, faithful to the fortunes of Queen Mary, furnished her with assistance after she had escaped from Lochleven Castle, for which he suffered forfeiture in 1568.†

At a very early date the parish church of Dunscore belonged to the Abbey of Holywood—gifted to the brethren, it is supposed, by Edgar, grandson of Dunegal, the Lord of Stranith. A portion of land in the parish was conferred by Edgar's daughter, Affrica, on another fraternity, the Monks of Melrose, who in course of time claimed the church also.‡ The Abbot of Darcongal, resenting this assumption, appealed to William, Bishop of Glasgow, and received a decision in his favour ; that prelate, when at Kirkmahoe in June 1257, ruling that Melrose had no business with the church, and could only of right tithe its own lands in Dunscore.§ These lands, however, were at one time very extensive, and included the classical soil of Friars' Carse, held, too, by a direct descendant of the renowned Sir Roger Kirkpatrick, and who took his title from the

---

* Acts of Scot. Parl., vol. iv., pp. 575-6.

† One of the greatest mathematicians of the middle ages, Joannes a Sacro Bosco, threw a lustre over this monastic establishment, he having been an inmate of it in his early years. "He was born," says Dr George Mackenzie, "in Nithsdale. Having finished the course of his studies, he entered into holy orders, and was made a canon regular of the order of St. Augustine, in the famous Monastery of Holywood, from whence he has his name of Joannes a Sacro Bosco. After he had stayed for some years in this monastery, he went over to Paris, where he was admitted a member of that University on the 5th of June, 1221. He was in a few years made Professor of Mathematics, which he taught for several years with great applause."—Lives and Character of the Most Eminent Writers of the Scots Nation (Edin., 1708), vol. i., p. 167. The same author sums up his notice of Joannes by saying :—" He is acknowledged by all not only to have been the most learned mathematician of his age, but the noble restorer of those sciences, then sunk into desuetude ; and his works have been ever since, and still will be, esteemed by all learned men ; and some of the most eminent mathematicians of the last age, as Gemmas Frisius, Petrus Ramus, Elias Venetus, and Christophorus Clavius, have thought their labour not ill bestowed in illustrating them with their commentaries." (Vol. i., p. 168.) Joannes died in 1256.

‡ Chartulary of Melrose, Nos. 103, 104, 105. § Ibid, No. 107.

farm in Dunscore long afterwards tenanted by Robert Burns. A commission given by Cardinal Antonius, dated at Rome on the 13th of September, 1465, confirmed a charter from the Monastery of Melrose to John Kirkpatrick of Allisland of the thirty-six pound land of Dalgonar, including " Killieligs, Bessiewalla, Over and Nether Bairdwell, Dunpaterstoun, Over and Nether Laggan, Over and Nether Dunscoir, Ryddingins, Edgarstoune, Mulliganstoun, Culroy, and Ferdin, together with the lands of Friars' Kars." This commission, addressed to certain dignitaries of the Scottish Church, proceeded on the curious narrative that Andrew the Abbot, and the brethren of Melrose, in augmentation of their rental, and for certain sums of money paid to them by the said John, had granted to him and his lawful heirs male, bearing the name of Kirkpatrick, whom failing, to his nearest heirs female, without division, the said lands to be holden in feu farm of the said convent of Melrose, he paying 46 merks, 6½ lib. sterling, or 110 ounces of pure silver, at least eleven pence fine, and doubling the same the first year of his entry thereto ; the said John and his heirs becoming bound to entertain each year the abbot, convent, and company with their horses— once in summer during three days and three nights, and once in winter for the same space—in their dwelling of Friars' Kars, furnishing them with meat and drink, and all other necessaries. As Kirkpatrick's landlords were proverbial for their jollity, the expense of these periodical visits would amount to a heavy rent in itself.

> " The monks of Melrose made gude kale
> On Fridays when they fasted ;
> And wanted neither beef nor ale
> As lang's their neighbours' lasted."

But, lest their bargain with him should seem a stingy one, they threw into it the baillery of the thirty-six pound land of Dalgonar, with all the privileges and profits thereof, including power to hold bailie courts ; he paying for the office the nominal sum annually of one penny Scots.* For a while after the Reformation, the property in Dunscore that belonged to Melrose was still administered by the commendator of the Abbey, Michael Balfour by name—that officer having, in August, 1565, granted a charter to Thomas Kirkpatrick of Allisland and Friars' Carse of a 24s 6d land ; also, the tack of the teinds or tithes in the over part of the parish, the latter for twenty pounds Scots a year.

Next in importance, though not quite so ancient as the Abbey of Holywood, was the Priory of Canonby, in Eskdale, erected, as we have seen, by Turgot de Rosindale, and granted by him, with adjacent territory, to the monks of Jedburgh.† In Bagimont's

---

* No. 824, Ant. Soc., Edin.

† The Revenue of Jedburgh Abbey, including the Priories of Canonby and Restennent, Angusshire, was £1274 10s Scots, besides meal and bere.—Keith, p. 185.

Roll* Canonby was taxed £6 13s 4d Scots. Its prior sat in the great parliament held at Brigham in March, 1290 ; and, together with his canons, swore fealty to Edward I. at Berwick, in August, 1296. In 1341 the brotherhood received from Edward III. a writ of protection. But that did not hinder them from being frequently harassed, and their possessions plundered, in the Border wars ; and both the priory and church are said to have been demolished after the rout of the Scottish army at Solway Moss, in 1542.† The establishment was vested in the King by the Annexation Act of 1587 ; and it and the Abbey of Jedburgh, with which it was associated, were in 1606 granted by the legislature to Alexander, Earl of Home, he obtaining as pertinents of the priory the patronage, teinds, and tithes of the churches of Canonby and Wauchope. Eventually the priory, with its property, passed from the family of Home to that of Buccleuch.‡

We have already seen how Lincluden Abbey was converted into a collegiate church by Archibald, Earl of Douglas. Its revenue was much increased by the liberality of his son's wife, Margaret, Duchess of Touraine, who founded in it a chaplainry, and endowed it with the lands of Eastwood, Barsculie, Carberland, Dumnuck, and the domains of Southwick and Barns.§ Many of the Provosts of the College, soaring beyond its sphere, held high positions in the State. Elese, the first Provost, was succeeded by Alexander Cairns, who became Chancellor to the Duke of Touraine ; the next was John Cameron, a great favourite at Court, who died in 1446, previously to which the provostry had devolved on John M'Gilhauck, rector of Partoun. The next name on the roll is that of Halyburton, whose arms, carved on the south wall of the church, bespeak his high rank. Winchester, who was made Bishop of Moray in 1436 ; Methven, who became a Secretary of State and a diplomatic agent ; and Lindsay, who was keeper of the Privy Seal and Ambassador to England, came next in order ; these in their turn being followed, says Chalmers, " by other respectable men, who evinced by their acceptance the importance and perhaps the profit which were then annexed to the office of Provost of Lincluden."‖

At the period of the Reformation this lucrative provostry was held by Robert Douglas, second son of Sir William Douglas of Drumlanrig. He was appointed to it in September, 1547 ; and, on

* A roll showing the value of all benefices, named after a Papal Legate who caused it to be made, that the revenue might yield its due amount of taxation to the Court of Rome.

† Some vestiges of the convent are still (1836) to be seen at Halgreen, about half a mile to the east of the parish church.—Statistical Account, p. 490.

‡ Inquisit. Speciales, pp. 212, 242.

§ Caledonia, vol. iii., p. 308.　　　　　　　Ibid, vol. iii., pp. 308-9.

11

his death, after enjoying the benefice for more than fifty years, he
was succeeded in it by his elder brother, James Douglas, who obtained, however, only a portion of the collegiate property, including "all and haill the salmond fischeing in the water of Nethe."*
The major part was granted, in 1617, to Sir Robert Gordon of
Lochinvar, and to Sir John Murray of Lochmaben, the lucky
knight who, as groom of the royal bedchamber, had gained the
love and favour of King James ; they becoming bound to pay the
feu mails to Douglas during his life, and afterwards to the Crown·
How rich the College of Lincluden was may be inferred from the
enumeration of its estates in the Act conferring them in equal
shares on Gordon and Murray.   In that document they are designated as "all and haill the five-merk land of Little Dryburgh ;
the five-merk land of Drumjarg ; the five-merk land of Ernephil-
lane ; the five-merk land of Ernecraig ; the five-merk land of
Blairony ; the five-merk land of Chapmantoun ; the five-merk
land of Blankerne ; the five-merk land of Ernmingzie ; the
five-merk land of Crocemichell ; the five-merk land of Garran-
toun ; the two-and-a-half merk land of Blackpark ; the fifteen-
shilling land of Staikfurd [now Nithside]; the forty-shilling
land of Newtoun ; the one-merk land of Clunye and Skelling-
holme ; the six-merk land of Terrauchtie ; the six-merk land
of Drumganis ; the five-merk land of Troqueer ; the one-merk
land of Stotholme ; the five-merk land of Nuneland ; the five-
merk land of Cruxtanis [Curriestanes]; the six-merk land of
Holme [now Goldielea]; the twenty-shilling land of Marieholme ;
and the four-merk land of Nuneholme :"† these comprising some
of the most fertile arable farms, meadows, and grazing grounds
that are to be found in the vicinity of Dumfries.

At a very early period the Church Establishment in Dumfries
was intimately associated with the Abbey of Kelso.   In the thirteenth century, the Abbot of that great house entered into an
agreement with the Dean of Nithsdale, in virtue of which he
received certain charters respecting the benefice, and gave to the
Dean all the places of worship in the burgh, on condition that that
dignitary should pay twenty merks of silver yearly to the Abbey.‡
A rectory, dependent on Kelso, was established with this sum, but
served by a vicar, who was allowed for his maintenance only the
tithes of a few acres attached to the vicarage—the tax on which
was fixed at four pounds in Bagimont's Roll.   As already noticed,
a tuneful churchman, who possessed a merry soul, though physically deformed, held the office in 1504—"the crukit Vicar of Dumfreise, that sang to the King in Lochmabane be the Kingis command."   The last vicar was Thomas Maxwell, who dying in 1602

---

* Acts of Scot. Parl , vol. iv., p. 570.

† Acts of Scot. Parl., vol. iv., pp. 571-4.   ‡ Chart Kelso, No. 322.

the tithes and lands were inherited by his daughter, Elizabeth—their annual value being £10 6s 8d.

The Greyfriars' brotherhood in the Vennel* shared the common fate of all such fraternities—the recent execution of their Warden at Carlisle proving but the prelude of their own suppression. To the revenue of the bridge customs, granted them by Devorgilla, some of the Scottish monarchs had added a right to fish for salmon in the Nith ; and at least two of her successors in the superiority of Galloway showed a considerate regard for the order she had housed. Margaret, Duchess of Touraine, who bore in some points a resemblance to that illustrious lady, granted to the Minorite Friars a charter, dated at " Le Trief," her castle on the Dee, 16th of January, 1425, conveying to them the bridge dues anew ; her motive being, it is stated, to benefit the souls of her deceased husband Archibald, of herself, of their son James, of their ancestors and descendants, and of all who had died in the faith ; and in the quaint yet reverent style of the times she dedicated the dues to the Almighty (Deo Omnipotenti) in the first instance, then to the Blessed Virgin Mary, then to St. Francis, and, last of all, to the real recipients of the charter, " ac Gordiano et Fratribus Minoribus de Drumfres," who were required on that account to serve the Lord there for ever, and to give to the testatrix the suffrages of their prayers. Her brother-in-law James, who, on the barbarous execution of her son William, succeeded to the earldom, granted another charter to the brethren, very similar in its import, which is dated at Dumfries, the 4th of January, 1452.†

For years before the Reformation was effected many of the ecclesiastical bodies, seeing what was about to happen, feued out or made over their possessions to secular friends. This prudential course was followed by the Minorites of Dumfries in 1557, as is shown by a charter dated on the 10th of July that year, which is still extant. It is granted by Friar Charles Home, the Superior

---

* The name of John Scot of Duns, usually termed Duns Scotus, is, according to Mackenzie, the learned author already quoted, closely associated with this religious house. He was born at the town of Dunse in 1274 ; and " having learned his grammar, our historians say that two Franciscan Friars falling acquainted with him, and finding him to be a youth of wonderful parts, took him alongst with them to Dumfries, where they induced him to enter into their order." (Vol. i., p. 215.) Spottiswoode gives a similar statement ; but some English writers are of opinion that it was not at Dumfries, but Newcastle, where Scotus became a Franciscan Friar. He afterwards studied at Oxford, went to Paris in 1301, where, as President of the Theological College, he soon became the greatest scholastic luminary of his age, acquiring the title of " The Subtle Doctor," on account of his marvellous powers of disputation, and drawing crowds of students to the University (30,000 it is said, but that must be an exaggeration) by the depth and brilliancy of his intellect He died at Cologne in 1308, at the early age of forty-three

† Appendix J.

or Warden of the body, and by the whole brethren assembled in their chapter-house, with consent of the reverend father John Fergusson, the Provincial Master of the whole Order of the Minor or Grey Friars within Scotland. By this deed the bridge dues were feued out to John Johnston in Nunholm, son of Edward Johnston, burgess of Dumfries, for a feu duty or perpetual annual payment to the Friars or their successors of ten merks and forty pence Scots, being 11s 4⅔d sterling. The deed narrates, as the motive for its being executed, that John Johnston had been of service to the Monastery in several ways, and that the feu duty was forty pence more than the dues had ever yielded to it. As appears from the charter, the dues had at the time been held by John Johnston as tacksman, under a tack from the Friary to his father which had some years to run, and the rent on which was ten merks Scots, or 11s 1½d sterling. The charter is signed by Charles Home, Herbert Stewart, Christopher Walker, and Richard Harlaw, who, it may be inferred from its terms, were all the Friars then resident in the house. Under this deed John Johnston became proprietor of the dues as vassal of the brethren, whose right became a right of superiority, with the above-mentioned feu duty attached to it.

At the Reformation this superiority and feu duty, with the whole other possessions of the Friars, fell to the Crown, as being subjects that had no owner, the purpose for which they had been originally given to the fraternity having been declared illegal. By a charter dated 23rd April, 1569, James VI. gave all these possessions to the burgh of Dumfries, in order that the burgh might support an hospital and maintain Devorgilla's Bridge. This charter narrates that his Majesty considered it his duty to provide that an hospital should be kept up within the burgh for poor people who were maimed or sick, and for orphans; and also to provide for the safety of his subjects whose business made it necessary for them to cross the river, and whose lives would be endangered if the bridge were not kept in repair. It accordingly conveys to the Provost, Bailies, Council, and community of the burgh, and their successors for ever, all the property and rights whatever which had belonged to the Grey Friars; but in order that the brethren and other religious persons who had been thereby supported before the Reformation might not come to want, the charter reserved to them during their lives the full enjoyment of their income from the subjects conveyed. It erected and incorporated these subjects into one fund or estate, which was to be called "The Royal Foundation of the Hospital of Dumfries," and provided that, so far as the revenues therefrom went, the burgh should be bound to keep up the bridge and to support the orphans and poor people in the hospital. Owing to some cause or other, however, no charitable institution under this charter was ever founded in the burgh. Amongst the rights conveyed by King James's charter there is specially mentioned the half of the bridge customs falling to the Friars. This would seem to have been merely the 11s 4⅔d of feu duty which had remained with them after they had feued out the customs to John Johnston. The right of superiority itself, to which the feu duty was annexed, appears to have remained with or to have been resumed by the Crown ; and in 1591 King James renewed the rights to the bridge dues in favour of John Johnston—a descendant, probably, of the original feuar.

When, about the middle of the sixteenth century, the Castle of Dumfries needed repair, materials for that purpose were quarried out of the Greyfriars' Monastery. The church portion of it was, however, left untouched, as appears from the ode addressed to it by Dr Arthur Johnstone, about 1640, already noticed.* Part of the south wall of the building, including two dilapidated arched windows, was still standing, about sixty-five years ago, in front of Comyn's Court, at the Port of the Vennel ; but now no relic remains of a house which superstition looked upon as accursed, and patriotism viewed with worshipful reverence, except the huge fireplace of the refectory where the food of the friars was cooked, which once turned out dinners for a king, and which is now doing service in the kitchen of a tavern† (a)—remaining a tough piece of masonry after passing through six centuries of smoke and flame.‡

By the slaughter of Comyn, the Greyfriars' Monastery lost its previous high repute ; it was believed to have been desecrated by the blood shed before its high altar, and to have shared in the awful curse pronounced by Pope John on the perpetrator of the murderous deed ; yet, as we have seen, the Warden and chapter continued to occupy it till the middle of the sixteenth century. Charters to houses in its neighbourhood, given by them in 1497, are said to have been seen and read at a comparatively recent period.§ Many of the inhabitants of the town worshipped within

* See ante p. 99. Dr Arthur Johnstone's ancestor, Stiven de Johnston, who lived in the reign of David II., is said to have been the eldest brother of the Laird of Johnstone, in Annandale. Being addicted to learning, he withdrew from the troubles of his own district to Aberdeenshire, where he found congenial employment as secretary to the Earl of Mar. By his marriage with Margaret, daughter and heiress of Sir Andrew Garioch, he got the lands of Caskieben, &c., also those of Kinburn, which he called after his own name ; and from him are descended all the Johnstones of the North.—Scottish Nation, vol. ii., p. 575.

† The " Grey Horse " public-house, Friars' Vennel.

(a) About a hundred years now since the window disappeared. The tavern was demolished in or about 1875, when new premises were erected on the site by Mr Hume, clothier.

‡ An old house which, down till 1863, formed the west corner of Irish Street, had a fragment of the original gate built into its gable.

§ Burnside's MS. History.

the church of the Monastery, till, scared from it by Bruce's outrage, they were led to frequent the undefiled sanctuary of St.
Michael's Wark—the old parish church, situated at the southern
extremity of the burgh.　Soon the little edifice became over-
crowded, and an addition was made to it : for defraying the expense of which every person admitted a burgess or freeman of
Dumfries was required to pay five merks ; and when a sufficient
fund for the building was thus realised the rest of the money was
spent in purchasing wine and spice for performing, with congenial
hilarity, the festival plays of Robin Hood and Little John—a
custom that was kept up for a century afterwards.*　By an Act
of Parliament passed in 1555, the obligation to devote the burgess
money to such purposes was discharged.

　　Long after the desertion of the Greyfriars' Church, the missal
service was continued in Sir Christopher's Chapel.　Sir Richard
Maitland states, in his account of the Seton family, that he had
heard mass in the building, and that it was standing undecayed in
1552.　After the lapse of a few subsequent years, its doors would
be closed and its endowment be secularised.　For more than a
century the little chapel, when falling into ruin, looked forlorn yet
picturesque, till nearly all that remained of it was carried away for
defensive purposes during the Jacobite Rebellion of 1715.　It has
already been stated that the eminence on which it was built was
the scene of Seton's judicial murder, and the Tyburn of the burgh.
When, in 1837, the foundation was excavated of the edifice that
now crowns the " Crystal Mount "—St. Mary's Church—upwards
of seventy human skulls were dug up.　Were any of these deserted
" domes of thought " tenanted by the doughty warrior who, by
saving Bruce at Methven, saved his country ; and proved his
patriotism in the more terrible ordeal of the scaffold ?　Or were
they only the " chambers desolate " of ordinary malefactors, or
miserable suicides—for it was long the custom to bury here, also,
those who violated the canon against self-slaughter ?†　The questions must remain unanswered.　Undoubted relics of the sacred
building by which Seton's memory was enshrined were, however,
picked up whilst the present church was being founded ; and these
have been tastefully set up within an inclosure on the south-west
side of the church.　They constituted part of the beautiful east
window noticed in a former chapter, and bear the following inscription :—" These stones, the relics of the ancient chapel, dedicated to the Virgin Mary, erected by King Robert Bruce, in

---

* Ibid.

† In a paper by Mr James Starke, on Sir Christopher's Chapel, he says :
" There is no reason to doubt but that the patriot Seton suffered at the common place of execution at that day. . . . It was the Tyburn of Dumfries ;
and here also, as tainted and polluted ground, all suicides were buried."
—Transactions of Dumfriesshire and Galloway Natural History and Antiquarian Society, vol. ii., p. 44.

memory of Sir Christopher or Chrystal Seatoun, are here placed
by Major James Adair, 1840."*

Newabbey, the greatest religious establishment founded in the
district by Devorgilla, still remains, half ruined, but supremely
beautiful in decay.   Of the tomb where,

> " In Dulcicorde Abbey she taketh her rest,
> With the heart of her husband embalmed on her breast,"†

there is no certain trace left ;‡ but the mighty fane itself is her
own best monument—lying, as it does,

> " Lonely and low,
> Where the pines of the mountain descend to the vale ;
> Where the rivulet lingers, reluctant to flow
> From its haven of rest, to the grasp of the gale
> That rides the sea-horses of Solway in foam
> O'er the long level strand and the desolate holm ;"§

all the surrounding locality, and even the little village adjacent,
being in harmony with the ruin by which they are enriched.|| (a)
What remains of the building—a nave, with aisles, choir, and
transepts ; an aisle on the east side ; and a central square tower,
rising ninety-two feet high, over the intersection of the nave with

---

* This inscription is erroneous. The chapel, as we have seen, was built
by Lady Seton, and only endowed by her royal brother ; and it was not dedicated to the Virgin, but, as the charter distinctly states, was " erected in honour
of the Holy Rood." Major Adair, who was a member of the kirk-session of
St. Mary's, merits thanks for collecting and authenticating these relics of this
interesting historical edifice. Time is making havoc with the inscription, as
some of the words are already obliterated.

† " The Briar of Threave," by Henry Inglis.

‡ Below the central tower there is an oblong slab, now serving as the cover
of a table-shaped tomb, the upper surface of which has been smoothed, re-
lettered, and sculptured, at a recent date, but having a very florid edging, old
enough seemingly to have been cut in the thirteenth century. This sculptured
fringe abounds with ornamental work, such as might have been appropriately
placed upon the tomb of Devorgilla. A thistle and rose supported by a fleur
de lis and crown ; and a pair of hearts, with an intermediate thistle, are repeatedly introduced. Another slab, which leans against one of the pillars of
the tower, bears the same kind of heart and thistle tracery. Not a few antiquaries are of opinion that both of these slabs are relics of the Devorgilla
monument.

§ " The Briar of Threave."

|| Except, perhaps, the mean-looking modern parish church, the north wall
of which is part of the Abbey ; but arrangements have been made for the
reconstruction of the church according to a plan that will bring it into better
keeping with its venerable neighbour.

(a) The "mean-looking modern church" no longer exists. A handsome
new parish church was erected on a new site some way off in 1876—opened
21st Jan., 1877 ; the old church was demolished soon after—the stones being
used to build the present United Free Church ; and, thanks to the intelligent
interest of the Rev. Dr Wilson, the whole aspect of the Abbey has been
greatly improved.

the aisles—furnishes to the contemplative onlooker a vivid idea of Sweetheart Abbey in the olden time.

In its palmy days the Abbey enjoyed a liberal endowment : the churches of Newabbey, Kirkpatrick-Durham, Crossmichael, Buittle, and Kirkcolm belonged to it, together with the baronies of Lochkinderloch and Lochpatrick, and other landed property ; all of which lapsed to the Crown in 1587. On the 31st of August, 1503, Robert, the last of its abbots who bore an undisputed crozier, executed a deed of resignation of the bailierie of Sweetheart and lands of Lochrutton in favour of John, Lord Maxwell.* Following him came Gilbert Brown, the prototype of Scott's Abbot of St. Marie's, whose rule was disturbed, and eventually overturned, by the shock of the Reformation.† In 1624 all that remained of its endowments, value £212 10s 10½d sterling yearly, was given as a temporal barony to Sir Robert Spottiswood—the barony being afterwards burdened with a mortification payable from the lands of Drum, as a stipend to the second minister of Dumfries, amounting, with several decreets of locality, to £141 4s 8½d per annum.

In addition to the monastic brotherhoods already noticed, two orders of religious knights acquired a settlement in Dumfriesshire —the Templars or Red Friars‡ and the Knights of St. John. The

---

* Terregles papers.

† The ground below the central tower has long been used as a place of sepulture. On the oldest tombstone that we see there is the inscription, "Joani Brown de Londensis," with the date MDCXIII. Built into a comparatively modern wall that half fills up an adjoining arch to the north there are two tablets—one with the initials, "R. D.," the other with the words, "Heir lyes Gauvine Browne, of Bishoptone, 1683." The lintel of a venerable house within the village bears the inscription, "Z. R. B., 1615." These mural remains of the past all relate to members of the Brown family, who at one time exercised great influence in the district. We pass into the modern parish church(a) through an arched gateway, that is in itself quite a study. You see in it patches of ornamental stone picked up from the ruins ; a dog-tooth moulding, telling of Norman architecture prior to Devorgilla's day ; a niche which once held an effigy of that lady ; beneath it, fading away into the undecipherable, a carved representation of our Saviour and the woman of Samaria at the well ; while over all hangs the original vesper bell, which has long been mute as the harp of Tara.

(a) As already explained, the "modern parish church" no longer exists.

‡ When the Templars were formed into an order the Abbé de Verlot, in his "History of the Knights of St. John," states that "St. Bernard ordered them, instead of prayers and offices, to say every day a certain number of paternosters, which would make one imagine that those warriors at that time knew not how to read." One of the statutes required that the knights should not eat flesh above three times a week. The holy abbot, with regard to their military service, declared that each Templar might have an esquire or serving brother-at-arms, and three saddle horses ; but he forbade all gilding and superfluous ornaments in their equipage. He ordered that their habits should be white ; and, as a mark of their profession, Pope Eugene III. added afterwards a red cross placed over the heart. (Vol. i., pp. 56-7.) De Verlot records that the idea of making the monastic inmates of St. John's Hospital into a military order was first mooted by Raymond Dupuy, and characterises it as "the most

former, instituted by Baldwin II., King of Jerusalem, took their
name from a residence he gave to them near the Temple of that
city ; the founders of the latter were certain devout Neapolitan
merchants, who, trading to the Holy Land, obtained leave to build
a church and monastery in Jerusalem for the reception of pilgrims,
to which buildings were added, in 1104, a larger church, with an
hospital for the sick, dedicated to St. John : hence the name of the
order, and the designation of Knights Hospitallers, by which they
are also well known.

Portions of the property that belonged to the Templars in the
county bore their name long after they fell into other hands at or
before the date of the Reformation.   Thus we read in old records
of the temple-lands of Ingleston in Glencairn ; the temple-land in
Durrisdeer ; the five-pound temple-land of Carnsalloch ; the temple-
land lying beside the Glen of Lag ; the temple-lands of Dalgarno ;
the temple-lands, two in number, near Lochmaben ; the temple-
lands, also two, beside Lincluden College ; the temple-land of Torthorwald ; the temple-land of Carruthers, in the old parish so
named ; the temple-land of Muirfad, near Moffat ; and there is a
village in the vicinity of Lochmaben called Templand, built on
ground that was once owned by this opulent fraternity.   In the
particular register of sasines kept at Dumfries sasine was registered on the 6th of April, 1636, in favour of Adam Johnstone,
brother of Archibald Johnstone of Elsieshields, in the temple-land
of Reidhall, and the forty-shilling land called Templands, both in
the Stewartry of Annandale.   The same register contains an entry
of sasine, dated 21st May, 1636, in favour of John Johnstone of
Vicarland and Adam, his son, of the temple-land termed the
Chapel of Kirkbride, in Kirkpatrick ; and an instrument is recorded whereby the five-pound Carnsalloch temple-land already
mentioned, which belonged to William Maxwell of Carnsalloch,
was conveyed to Adam Shortrig, eldest son of John Shortrig, the
precept being dated at " The End of the Bridge,"* 21st of December, 1619.   At Bectoun, Dryfesdale, may still be seen the vestiges
of a small religious house that belonged to the order, together with
the Chapel-lands, by which it was endowed.†

The Hospitallers had not so much property in the shire as
their fellow-knights ; but they seem to have possessed a greater

noble, and withal extraordinary, design that ever entered into the mind of a
monk, tied down by his profession to the service of the poor and sick." They
were divided into three classes—1. Gentlemen used to arms.   2. Priests and
chaplains.   3. Men neither of noble families nor ecclesiastics, who were termed
frères servans (serving brethren).   The habit consisted of a black robe, with a
pointed mantle of the same colour (called a *manteau à bec*), upon which was
sewn a pointed cowl, and the left side of which displayed an eight-pointed cross
of white linen.   (Vol. i., pp. 43, 44, 45.)

* Or Bridge End, the name borne by Maxwelltown before it was erected
into a burgh of barony.

† Inquisit. Speciales, p. 291.

number of foundations.   One of their principal houses was a pre-
ceptory at Kirkstyle, about ten miles from Dumfries, in the parish
of Ruthwell, the ancient burial ground of which exhibited, up till
a recent period, several memorials of their presence in the shape of
sculptured stones, each containing an ornamented cross, having a
sword on the right, a figure resembling the coulter and sock of a
plough on the left ; but no names of the knights " long gone to
dust, and whose swords are rust," over whom the stones were originally laid.*   One of their establishments stood rather more
than a mile south-east of Dumfries, on an estate which bore in
consequence the name of Spitalfield, till it was bought by the late
Mr John Brown, merchant, Liverpool, who called it Brownhall.
On the opposite side of the Kelton Road lies Ladyfield, with its
ancient orchard and well, which may have been a pendicle of the
hospital.   Above the town of Annan, on the west bank of the river,
there was another hospital belonging to the Knights of St. John,
from which two adjacent hamlets, Howspital and Spitalridding,
acquired their designation ; and they had a second one in Annandale, at Trailtrow, the cure of which was granted by James VI. to
Edward Maxwell, with the land revenues of the same, vacant by
the decease of Robert M'Gilhance, the last master of the hospital.†
Their largest hospital in the county, however, grew up under the
shadow of Sanquhar Castle, on the northern bank of the Nith.
Many ages after all traces of it had disappeared the plough turned
up numerous relics of its inmates, the mouldering memorials of a
brotherhood who were men of note in their day, though they are
now all but forgotten throughout the district—a fate which they
share in common with their more distinguished fraters the military monks of the Temple.

    Both orders fell into decay long before the Papal establish-
ment, of which they formed a singular feature, ceased to flourish ;
and when abolished at the Reformation their remaining property
was secularised : Ross of Rosile obtaining a considerable share of
it ; Murray of Cockpool getting what belonged to the Hospitallers
in the parish of Ruthwell ; Lord Herries their house and lands at

---

* " These memorials of the dead," says Dr Henry Duncan, in his Account
of the Parish of Ruthwell, written in 1834, " were found by the present incumbent [himself] lying in the parish burying-ground, whence he removed
them ; and they now form part of the wall of a summer-house attached to the
front wall which separates the garden from the churchyard."   In the same
garden is placed the celebrated Runic Cross, for the preservation of which
memorable monument of Anglo-Saxon times we are also indebted to Dr
Duncan.(a)

    (a) By the exertions of the late Rev. Mr Macfarlane a sort of apse was
annexed to the parish church some years ago, and the Runic Cross was there
placed for better preservation.

                    † Privy Seal Register, vol. iv., p. 211.

Trailtrow ; while, as already mentioned, the Spitalfield of Dumfries was acquired before 1666 by the M'Brairs of Almagill.*

* The masters of both orders in Dumfriesshire having submitted to Edward I. in 1296, were confirmed in their possessions by precepts addressed to the Sheriff by the King.—Rymer, pp. 724-5. Inquisit. Speciales, p. 291 ; and Caledonia, vol. iii., p. 154.

CHAPTER XXII.

FOUR years after the memorable visit of Harlow to Dumfries the
intrepid Knox arrived in the burgh, in order to preside at the
election of a superintendent, or moderator, over the various congregations formed in the district. Reference to the Reformer's
mission is made in the following minute of the fifth General Assembly, as given by Calderwood :—" For the planting of kirks in the
sheriffdomes of Dumfries, Galloway, and Nithisdaill, and the rest
of the West daills : the Assemblie nominat in lites for the superin-
tendentship Mr Alexander Gordon, entituled Bishop of Galloway,
and Mr Robert Pont, minister of Dunkell ; ordained edicts to be
sett forth for the admission upon the first Lord's day of Aprile,
and appointed the superintendent of Glasgow, Mr Knox, minister
of Edinburgh, Mr Robert Hamilton, minister of Ochiltree and
Mauchlin, and other learned men, to be present at the inauguration of the person elected ; the place of admission to be the parish
kirk of Drumfries." Gordon, one of the candidates, had occupied
many different sees under the old Papal system. He was first
Bishop of Caithness, then of Glasgow, then of the Isles, then of
Galloway, and was sometimes known as Bishop of Athens, which
title he had received from the Pope on being deprived of the see of
Glasgow. He was an able man, but full of duplicity ; and in trying to curry favour with each of the two religious parties he lost
the confidence of both. Pont, on the other hand, was an earnest,

straightforward Presbyterian divine, and intellectually well fitted for the high position to which he aspired.*

A few weeks before the election Knox, as is related in his own " History,"† had an interview with Queen Mary, at which, curiously enough, she introduced this subject. Having met her Majesty by appointment, when out on a hawking expedition near West Kinross, she, after a reference to other matters, said," I understand that ye are appointed to go to Dumfries for the election of a superintendent to be established in those countries." " Yes," said the Reformer, " those quarters have great need of such a one, and some of the gentlemen there so require." " But I fear," said she, " that the Bishop of Athens would be superintendent." " He is one, madam," answered Knox, " that is put in election." " If ye knew him," said she, " as well as I do, ye would never promote him to that office, nor yet to any other within your kirk." " What he hath been, madam," said Knox, " I never knew, nor yet will I enquire ; for, in time of darkness, what could we do but grope and go wrong, even as darkness carried us ? but if he fear not God now, he deceives many more than me ; and yet, madam, I am assured God will not suffer His Church to be so far deceived, as that an unworthy man shall be elected, where free election is, and the Spirit of God is earnestly called upon to decide betwixt the two." " Well," rejoined her Majesty, " do as ye will ; but that man is a dangerous man." " And therein," adds the historian, " was not the Queen deceived ; for he had corrupted most part of the gentlemen, not only to nominate him, but also to elect him : which being perceived by the said John [Knox] he delayed the election, and left it with the Master of Maxwell. Mr Robert Pont was put in election (with the foresaid bishop), to the end that his doctrine and conversation might be the better tried of those that had not known him before, and so was this bishop frustrate of his purpose for that present ; and yet was he at that time the man that was most familiar with the said John in his house and at table."

* Robert Pont, born at Culross about 1524, was a learned and accomplished divine. In July, 1574, he was, with others, appointed by the General Assembly to revise all books that were printed and published. About the same time he drew up the Calendar, and framed the rules for understanding it, for Arbuthnot and Passandyne's edition of the Bible. He had also a considerable share in the preparation of the Second Book of Discipline. He was elected no fewer than five times Moderator of the General Assembly ; and enjoyed the rare distinction, for a clergyman, of having been appointed a Senator of the College of Justice—an office which he only accepted after receiving permission from the Assembly. Mr Pont published several works, among others " A newe Treatise of the right reckoning of Yeares and ages of the World, and men's lives, and of the estate of the past decaying age thereof, this 1600 yeare of Christ (erroneously called a yeare of jubilee), which is from the Creation the 5548 yeare. Containing sundrie singularities, worthy of observation, concerning courses of times, and revolutions of the Heaven and reformations of Kalendars, and prognostications, &c., &c. Edin., 1599, 4to. Latine, 1619, 4to."

† Knox's History, p. 282.

The election of the superintendent devolved upon the min - sters settled in the district. They, after hearing the two candidates preach, and testing them in other respects—and doubtless giving due weight to the counsel of Knox and Lord Herries— chose Mr Pont, who in virtue of his office bore a rule slightly resembling that of a bishop over Galloway and Carrick, as well as Dumfriesshire. He resided in Dumfries, but was seldom long at home, as he had to devote most of his time to the visitation of his diocese—building up new congregations, supplying them with pastors (or, when these could not be obtained, with readers) ; trying the life, diligence, and behaviour of the ministers, the order of their churches, and the manners of their people ; seeing how the poor were provided for, how the youth were instructed ; giving admonition where called for ; and, finally, taking note of all heinous crimes, that the same might be considered by the censures of the Church.* This office, to which so many onerous duties were attached, was but of temporary duration, as when the fabric of Presbyterianism had been fairly erected it was not required. After Mr Pont had for some time done pioneering work in Dumfriesshire, the General Assembly of the Church found matters ripe enough for the erection of four Presbyteries in the county—those of Dumfries, Penpont, Lochmaben, and Annan—and for forming them into a provincial Synod. The presence and exertions of Knox in Dumfries did much to extend the congregation there which Harlow had originated, and also to consolidate its Presbytery, which, in the course of a short period, came to occupy nearly the same sphere as the abolished Deanery of Nithsdale.

That Protestantism had made little advance in Dumfries fifteen years after the Presbyterian form of it had been ratified by Parliament is shown by the following extract from the minutes of the General Assembly, dated 6th August, 1575 : " Mr Peter Watsone, Commissiouner of Nithisdale, compleaned that the toun of Dumfreis at Christmasse-day last by past, seeing that naither he nor the reader would naither teache nor read upon these days, brought a reader of their own with tabret and whissell, and caused him to read the prayers, which exercise they used all the days of Yuile. The Assemblie thought good this complaint should be intimated to my Lord Regent's grace." Thus we see that the inhabitants tenaciously adhered to the old " Yule " ceremonies, and observed them in spite of the Presbyterian Commissioner's example and remonstrance. We infer from another quotation that after the lapse of thirteen years more Popery, though losing ground, had still a powerful hold of the town.

In 1588 a General Assembly was convened for the special purpose of " repressing Jesuits and other Papists " who had come to subvert the established religion, to which Assembly the subjoined

* Spottiswoode, vol. i., p. 343.

report was given in : "In the South, about Dumfreis, Mr John Durie, Jesuit corrupting and practising too and fro under the name of Mr William Laing, who with his complices had masse within the toun of Dumfreis before Pasche and Yuile last was ; the Lord Hereis, the Laird* of Kilquhomate, the Goodman* of Dum-rushe, Mr Homer Maxwell, commissar, John Mackgie, commissar clerk, Johne Bryce, merchant, John Rig, notar, Paul Thomsone, My Ladie Hereis, elder and younger, My Ladie Morton, the Lady . . . the Lady Tweddail, Papists, apostats, interteaners, and professed favourers of Jesuits. *Item*, there is a certaine woman that doeth no less hurt in Dumfreis than the Jesuits, called Kathe-rine Hairstens.† No resorting to heare the Worde there [in Dum-fries] ; no discipline ; holie dayes keeped by [in opposition to] plain commandement and controlling of the deacons of the crafts ; all superstitious ryotousness at Yuile and Pasche, &c. ; no kirks planted there."‡

As previously stated, during the absence of Queen Mary in France the Romish Church in Scotland was overthrown, and the Protestant religion, under a Presbyterian form, set up in its stead. It was the misfortune of Mary that she did not accept the new state of matters ; it was the madness of bigotry to attempt, as she did, to unmake the Reformation. Her return, in 1561, was hailed with enthusiasm by all parties. She was the most beautiful woman of her age ; and there was at least room for hope that she would prove prudent and virtuous. "May God save that sweet face !" was the universal cry as the Queen rode in procession to the Par-liament ; but the aspirations and wishes breathed regarding her were mournfully disappointed. Ten years elapsed, bringing with them numerous important events, most of them detrimental to the Queen—some of them involving on her part gross indiscretion, if not dreadful guilt—and ending in her deathward flight to the shores of England. Her marriage with Darnley, in opposition to the wish of her Protestant lords and of Queen Elizabeth—her further alienation from them when she joined the league formed by the Emperor of Germany and the Kings of France and Spain to extirpate the Protestant religion—the murder of her husband, and her marriage soon after with Bothwell, who was more than sus-pected of having planned the horrible deed—her enforced surrender to the Lords of the Congregation—her imprisonment in Lochleven Castle—her escape—her exertions to resume the power of which she had been deprived, and their thorough failure at Langside— are the leading incidents between Mary's joyous landing at the pier of Leith and her disastrous defeat by the Regent Murray.

* The distinction formerly recognised between these two designations was this : the laird was a Crown vassal or baron, the goodman (or gudeman) was one who held land of a baron, and was often also called a feuar.

† Probably one of the Craigs family.   ‡ Wodrow's History of the Church.

How far Dumfries and the men of the town and district were associated with the fortunes of Queen Mary we have now to show. Of all the hapless Queen's adherents none was more faithful, and few were more conspicuous, than Sir John Maxwell, called of Terregles because of his marriage with Lady Agnes, eldest daughter of William, Lord Herries ; called also the Master of Maxwell because he was the nearest male heir of Sir John, son of Robert, the fifth Lord Maxwell ; but best known in history as Lord Herries. For several years prior to 1553 he was Warden of the Western Marches. At that date he resigned the office, on the ground that he had " becum under deidlie feid with divris clans " of the Border, who impaired his influence. He took part in framing the Treaty of Norham, and other treaties with the English, in 1561 and 1563 ;[*] and was, on account of his talents, not less than his position, employed in many other acts of a national character. In right of his marriage he became possessed of one-third of Terregles and Kirkgunzeon ; and he subsequently acquired the other portions of these baronies which had belonged to the sisters of his wife. Having ability, wealth, and high rank, it was of great consequence to the Queen that he should become attached to her interests.

On the 20th of August, 1563, Mary visited Dumfries for the first time. As she was accompanied by her Council, it has been thought that the peace negotiations then going on with England occasioned her journey to the south. But she felt more interest in the chief negotiator of the treaty than in the treaty itself—was less desirous of securing peace with the English than gaining the favour of the Maxwell family, whose late chief had been lost to her service, but whose present virtual head might still be won over, though he, too, had been holding dangerous dalliance with Protestantism, and disloyal communion with her foes. Before returning to Edinburgh Mary paid a complimentary visit to the Maxwells, in order, it may be conceived, to secure this object. Secretary Lethington[†] having laid before the Queen certain correspondence between himself and the English Warden on the ostensible business that had drawn her to Dumfries, she broke up the Council and proceeded to Terregles, where she spent the remainder of the day and the night, to the high gratification of her hosts,

----

[*] Keith, Appendix, p. 95.

[†] The Maitlands of Lethington and of Eccles, in Dumfriesshire, are branches of the same family, both being descended from the Norman knight Richard de Mantelent, by his wife, the heiress of Eklis. (See ante, p. 25.) Secretary Lethington was also closely related to the Seton family, his grandmother having been Martha, daughter of George, Lord Seton, the latter of whom was descended from Sir Alexander Seton, the brother of Sir Christopher, who was executed at Dumfries in 1306.(a)

(a) The late Mr Lauderdale Maitland, who was survived by an only daughter, was the last of the Maitlands in Eccles. The estate is now a possession of the Duke of Buccleuch.

pleased and flattered with having an opportunity to entertain the highest lady in the land, the most accomplished woman of her time —the queen of beauty not less than the Queen of Scots.

Five years afterwards Mary Stewart spent a second night under the roof of Terregles Tower in very different circumstances ; radiant, cheerful, buoyant, ready to believe that the few clouds that were gathering in her track would break up and usher in a golden future ; downcast, frenzied, despairing—a wandering fugitive, with but a solitary meteor to twinkle on the gloom—a false meteor, leading only to a lingering captivity and a cruel death : under such contrasted conditions did the old Nithsdale fortress on these two occasions furnish hospitality to Queen Mary of Scotland.* What impression she made on Sir John Maxwell during her first visit is not recorded. If she succeeded in shaking his resolution to join the Protestant Lords, she would look upon that as a great point gained. At first Maxwell openly favoured the Reformers. The Act of Council deposing Mary of Guise from the Regency, dated October 23d, 1559, bears his signature† as one of the Protestant Lords ; his name appears attached to the first Book of Discipline in January, 1561 ;‡ and, as we shall afterwards see, he joined Murray and his colleagues when they took up arms against the Queen in the summer of 1565 for marrying Darnley, and thus, as they said, bringing Protestantism into peril. Certain it is that Sir John Maxwell's antecedents were of such a nature as to justify Knox when he expected to find in him a powerful ally for the overthrow of Popery.

The Reformer in his "History" states that, in 1562, he passed from Ayr to Nithsdale and Galloway, and had a conference on divers matters with "the Master of Maxwell, a man of great judgment and experience."§ They soon afterwards differed, however, on the question of deference to the Queen ; and thenceforth they pursued opposite courses. In the following year the Bishop of St. Andrews, the Prior of Whithorn, and others, celebrated mass. On this account " some priests in the Westland were apprehended : intimation made unto others—as to the Abbot of Crossraquel, the parson of Sanquhair, and such—that they should neither complain to the Queen nor Council, but should execute the punishment that God hath appointed to idolators in his law, by such means as they might, wherever they should be apprehended." The Queen stormed at such freedom of speech, but she could not amend it ; and thereupon sent for Knox in the hope that he would be induced by her

* Queen Mary and her Privy Council were at Dumfries on 20th August, 1563. . . . Mary, in all likelihood, visited the town in connection with the business [the treaty of 1563] ; and, to pay a compliment to the Maxwell family, she stopt at Terregles ; and the Queen's room was lately shown there, till that part of the house was demolished.—Burnside's MS. History.

† Keith, p. 106.   ‡ Calderwood, p. 30.   § Knox's History, p. 174.

blandishments, or overawed by her power, to be less intolerant of the mass. The conference took place at Lochleven ; and there, we are told, "she dealt·with him earnestly two hours before supper that he would be the instrument to persuade the people, and principally the gentlemen of the west, not to put hand to punish any man for the using of themselves in their religions as pleased them. The other, perceiving her craft, willed her Majesty to punish malefactors according to the laws ; and he durst promise quietness upon the part of all them that professed the Lord Jesus within Scotland ; but if her Majesty thought to elude the laws, he said he feared some would let the Papists understand that without punishment they should not be suffered so manifestly to offend God's majesty."

With bold outspoken words like these Knox defended the course taken by himself and colleagues ; and the Queen, in no gentle mood, abruptly closed the interview. Next morning two messengers from her Majesty ordered him again into the royal presence ; and then took place the singular conference at the hawking expedition near West Kinross already noticed. As if the exhilarating pastime had exercised a soothing influence on the Queen, she exhibited quite a friendly temper, gossipped pleasantly with Knox on secular affairs, gave him, as we have seen, good advice regarding the settlement of a superintendent at Dumfries, and, while still bent on carrying out her own ends, seemed equally anxious to avoid an open rupture with her unconquerable subject. Mary closed this her second interview with the Reformer by saying, "And now, as touching our reasoning yesternight, I promise to do as ye required. I shall cause to summon all offenders, and ye shall know that I shall minister justice."* Soothing words, lightly said and soon broken !

In the autumn of the same year, whilst the Queen lay at Stirling, mass was celebrated with great pomp in the royal chapel at Holyrood House, Edinburgh. The ministers of the Reformed faith were scandalised by this daring violation of the law ; and two of them, Andrew Armstrong and Patrick Cranston, hurrying to the chapel, protested against the proceedings. Cranston, finding the altar covered and the priest preparing to go on with the ceremony, cried out, "The Queen's Majesty is not here ; how then dare you be so malapert as openly to do against the law ?" Nothing further was done or said ; but on the report of the ministers' interference being conveyed to the Queen, they were required by her to find surety to underlie the law "for forethought felony," by " violent invasion " of the royal palace and " spoliation of the same." Knox, in a letter dated Edinburgh, 8th October, 1563, summoned the brethren to meet him in that city on the 24th of the same month, in order to make common cause with the two ministers who were

* Knox's History, p. 282.

that day to be tried. At a Cabinet Council held afterwards the
Reformer's letter was declared to be treasonable—an announcement which pleased the Queen not a little, as she expected thereby
to get him fairly under her control.

How this matter terminated for ever the intimacy between
the Reformer and the Lord of Nithsdale is thus narrated by Knox
himself :—" The Master of Maxwell gave unto the said John, as it
were, a discharge of the familiarity which before was great betwixt
them, unless that he would satisfy the Queen at her own will.
The answer of John Knox was that he knew of no offence done by
him to the Queen's Majesty, and therefore he knew not what satisfaction to make.   ' No offence !' said he ; ' have you not written
letters desiring the brethren from all parts to convene to Andrew
Armstrong and Patrick Cranston ?' 'That I grant,' said the other;
' but therein I acknowledge no offence done by me.'   ' No offence !'
said he, ' to convocate the Queen's lieges ?'   ' Not for a just cause,'
said the other ; ' for greater things were reputed no offence within
these two years.' ' The time,' said he, ' is now otherwise ; for then
our Sovereign was absent, and now she is present.' ' It is neither
the absence nor the presence of the Queen,' said he, ' that rules my
conscience, but God plainly speaking in His Word.   What was
lawful to me last year is yet lawful ; because my God is unchange-
able.' ' Well,' said the Master, ' I have given you my counsel, do
as you list ; but I think you shall repent it if you bow not unto
the Queen.'   ' I understand not,' said Knox, ' what you mean ; I
never made myself an adverse party unto the Queen's Majesty
except in the point of religion, and thereunto I think you will not
desire me to bow.'   ' Well,' said he, ' you are wise enough, but you
will not find that men will bear with you in times to come as they
have done in times bypast.' ' If God stand my friend,' said the
other, ' as I am assured He of His mercy will, so long as I depend
upon His promise and prefer His glory to my life and worldly
profit, I little regard how men behave themselves towards me ;
neither yet know I whereinto any man hath borne with me in
times bypast unless it be that out of my mouth they have heard
the Word of God, which in time to come, if they refuse, my heart
will be perfect, and for a season I will lament ; but the incom-
modity will be their own.'   And after these words (hereunto the
Laird of Lochinvar was witness) they departed ; but unto this day,
the seventeenth day of December, 1571, yea, never in this life, met
they in such familiarity as before."*

The Queen married Lord Darnley on the 27th of July, 1565 ;
and in the following month the Duke of Hamilton, the Earls of
Argyle, Murray, Glencairn, and Rothes, Lords Boyd and Ochiltree,
and the rest of the Protestant chiefs, resolved upon a warlike
demonstration for the purpose of averting the perils which they

* Knox's History, pp. 289-90.

expected to arise from this inauspicious union. At the head of a thousand horsemen they proceeded to Edinburgh ; but meeting there with less encouragement than they looked for, they went to Lanark, and thence to Hamilton, where they were joined by the Master of Maxwell and the Laird of Drumlanrig.

Maxwell at this time appears to have had the confidence of both parties, though his devotedness to the Queen was gradually increasing at the expense of his Protestantism, and lessening his attachment to his former colleagues. After an interview with them he informed her Majesty, by letter, that, on being required by the Lords to pay them a visit he could not refuse, as being in the vicinity on his way homewards at the time ; that he had coun- selled them to disband their army ; and that they had resolved to pass to Dumfries, where they would take his advice into considera- tion and apprise her Majesty of the result. Accordingly the Lords went with their army to Dumfries, where, says Knox, " they were entertained most honourably " by the Master of Maxwell, " for he had the government of all that country."* Maxwell laboured zealously to effect a reconciliation between them and the Queen. They saw, however, that the great cause for which they had struggled was at stake—that if they winked at the Romish prac- tices of the Court, at the favour shown by their Majesties to all who promoted Popery, and the discouragement given by them to the Protestant cause, the Reformation might by such an insidious system of warfare be rooted out, even if it were not assailed by main force ; and so they would make no concessions.

"Abolish the mass, eradicate idolatry, maintain the true reli- gion as by law established, and govern the realm by the advice of its true nobility ; and we shall disperse our troops and submit our- selves for trial." Such was the burden of the manifesto issued by the Protestant Lords at Dumfries ; and it was accompanied by a remonstrance against the royal marriage, which would be viewed by their Majesties as its bitterest ingredient. Calderwood's quaint account of the matter is worthy of being quoted. "They pro- claimed," he says, " a declaration of their grievances at Drumfreisse, the nineteenth of September. In this declaration they reported that the Queen, after arrival, craved one quiet masse to her own household only ; and how they hoped that by process of time she might be converted, and therefore passed it over with silence, but to the great grief of their consciences ; for from thence it proceeded that all that resorted to her chappell royall were unpunished ; from saying it proceeded to singing, and from her chappell to all the corners of the countrey."†

Maxwell failed in his efforts to propitiate the nobles, and at the same time he incurred the displeasure of the Queen. She ima- gined that he could not be on such intimate terms with them and

* Ibid, p. 324.   † Calderwood, pp. 39, 40.

be true to her. In great wrath she summoned him, as well as the remonstrant Lords, to her presence, and when he obeyed the citation, which they despised, she commanded him "to give over the house of Lochmaben and the castle which he had in keeping for the Queen."* No one knew Mary's impulsiveness of character better than Sir John Maxwell ; he bowed to the storm, assured that it would soon blow over ; and he managed both to retain his fortresses and regain the confidence of the royal lady, who, after scolding him in the heat of passion, felt as if she had rated him too severely, and then trusted him more than ever.†

Meanwhile the Queen made preparations with the view of overcoming the Lords of the Congregation by force. On the 8th of October, accompanied by the King, she proceeded from Edinburgh in the direction of Dumfries, "the whole body of the realm" following her, says Pitscottie. In other words, an army of three thousand men, accoutred with jack and spear, and rendered additionally threatening by being supplied with "certain carted pieces" of cannon‡—war-engines that were only then beginning to come into general use. They passed the first night after leaving the capital at Lanark, the second at Crawford ; and next day Douglas of Drumlanrig and Gordon of Lochinvar§ joined the royal host. Some of the Lords clung long to the belief that Maxwell, who had not yet openly declared for the Queen, would at the last hour join their ranks ; and it may easily be imagined that, whilst waiting in mingled hope and fear at Dumfries, they would send pressing messengers to Terregles Tower, urging its lord to join them with his retainers. Disappointed of help from that direction, they evacuated the town and proceeded to Carlisle.

When Mary arrived in Dumfries on the 11th she found nothing but friends. Maxwell presented himself amongst them, and received not only forgiveness but favour at the hands of his sovereign ; and in proof of his loyalty he voluntarily placed the Castles of Dumfries and Carlaverock at her disposal. Though long a waverer, intriguing with the Protestant party, as if irresolute whether to swim with or resist the prevailing current, we find him steadfastly true to the Queen's fortunes ever after his interview at Dumfries in the autumn of 1565, and doing what he could to roll back the tide of the Reformation. From that date also Mary's doubts of him seem to have vanished ; but as he was viewed

---

* The King and Queen having reposed themselves a short space at Dumfries, and visited the Castle of Lochmaben, which had been in the keeping of Sir John Maxwell (formerly one of the rebels, but at this time on his humble submission received into favour), they returned forthwith to Edinburgh.—Keith, p. 316.

† Knox's History, p. 324.   ‡ Pitscottie, p. 217.

§ Both Douglas and Gordon were Protestants, and, though for a time gained over to the Queen's side, they eventually took an active part in promoting the Reformation.

with suspicion by some of her counsellers he was formally put upon his trial. The result was made known by the Queen and her husband on the 1st of January, 1566 *—a proclamation issued by them stating that, after an examination by the Lords of Council into all the accusations brought against Maxwell, they had granted him full pardon and exoneration, believing the things laid at his door " to be perfectly untrue, and founded upon particular malice," and " that as regards some of the charges they understood right perfectly the plain contrary." " So far from his having been a traitrous evil-doer, he has been," said the royal pair, " and is, our true servant, and our good justiciar ; and, in execution of our service, has taken great travail and pains ; bearing a weighty charge in the common service of this our realm many years by-past, and execute the laws upon many and notable offenders, de-fending our good subjects from such enormities and oppressions as is laid to his charge ; nor has received no augmentation of any reversion, as is unjustly alleged, nor no gold from England ; neither has, nor will, discover our secrets to them, nor others, to the hurt of us his sovereign, this our realm, nor subjects." Refer-ence is made in the following passage to some specific charges based on his connection with the Wharton raids :—" For that he accumpanyeit in Dumfreis of late ane number of oure subjects quhilk now ar rebellis, and past into Ingland ; for that we under-stand that he was nevir of mynd to ayd thame against us ; and also be his continowal humane labouring to us for thame ; and also that he wald on na wayis tak pairt nor assist with Ingland ; nor pass with thame into that realme ; nor as we knaw wes nevir of counsal, nor privy to no particularis we haif to lay to thair charge befoir cuming to oure toun of Dumfreis."†

Sir John Maxwell, now become quite a favourite at Court, was present at the baptism of the young Prince (afterwards James VI.), on the 15th of December, 1566 ; and it was long generally sup-posed that on this auspicious occasion he was first honoured by his royal mistress with the title of Lord Herries, his lady being heiress of that estate ; but the Committee of Peers who gave judg-ment on behalf of the present Lord Herries in 1858, found that there were no good grounds for this supposition, and favoured the opinion that the title was not assumed by Maxwell till after the whole lands of his wife's family had come into his possession.‡ Sir John was the fourth Lord Herries, and the first of his house

---

* Keith, p. 321.

† Privy Council Records, 1st January, 1565.

‡ It is worthy of being mentioned, however, that a short time before the baptism his name appears on the Sederunt of the Privy Council as " Joannes Maxwell de Terreglis, miles ;" and that five months after the ceremony it is entered on the list of jurors who tried Bothwell as " Johne Maxwell, Lord Hereis."

who bore the title. When Mary, three days after the murder of
the King, intimated her resolution to bestow her hand upon
Bothwell, Lord Herries, according to Sir James Melville, fell upon
his knees before the Queen, and entreated her not to ruin her
reputation, peace of mind, and prospects, by such a disgraceful
union.* But this is an incredible statement, seeing that his lordship, after serving on the jury that acquitted Bothwell, joined
with other noblemen in subscribing a bond approving of the
marriage, and engaging to promote the same by their "votes,
counsel, fortificatioun, and assistance in word and deid ;"† and that
he was present as one of the witnesses to the nuptial ceremony.

At the Parliament held in December, after Bothwell had been
ostracised, Mary immured in Lochleven Castle, and her natural
brother, Murray, made Regent, the critical condition of the country came to be discussed. Lord Herries took part in the debate ;
and a report of his demeanour, furnished by Sir Nicholas Throg-
morton, represents him as being wonderfully reconciled to the
new state of affairs, and making a noble harangue "to persuade
the union of the whole realm in one mind." "Wherein he did not
spare to set forth solemnly the great praise that part of this
nobility did deserve which in the beginning took means for
punishment of the Earl of Bothwell ; as also, seeing the Queen's
inordinate affection to that wicked man, and that she could not
be induced by their persuasion to leave him, that in sequestering
her person within Lochleven they did the duty of noblemen. That
their honourable doings, which had not spared to hazard their
lives and lands to avenge their native country from the slanderous
reports that were spoken of it among other nations, had well deserved that all their brethren should join with them in so good a
cause. That he, and they in whose names he did speak, would
willingly, and without any compulsion, enter themselves in the
same yoke, and put their lives and lands in the like hazard for
maintenance of our cause ; and if the Queen herself [Elizabeth]
were in Scotland, accompanied with twenty thousand men, they
will be of the same mind, and fight in our quarrel"—that is, in
behalf of Protestantism. "So plausible an oration," continues the
English Ambassador, "and more advantageous for our party, none
of ourselves could have made. He did not forget to term my Lord
Regent by the name of Regent [there was no mention at all of the
Earl of Murray], and to call him Grace at every word when his
speeches were directed to him, accompanying all his words with
low courtesies, after his manner."‡ Quite the picture of a courtier ;
true, we doubt not, in its main features, though touched up a little
te heighten the general effect and the better to please the royal

* Melville's Memoirs, p. 156.
† Keith, p. 381.   The original document is in the Cotton Library.
‡ State Paper Office.

lady for whose special behoof it was sketched.   Lord Herries was,
in spite of these artful declarations, still a partisan of the deposed
Queen, and plotting with others for her deliverance ; and much of
the antipathy shown by the people of Dumfries to the Regent
Murray may be traced to his influence in the town.

Both the inhabitants and their magistrates sympathised
strongly with Queen Mary ; and when, about the end of August, a
herald made his appearance at the Market Cross in High Street to
proclaim Murray Regent in name of the young King, he narrowly
escaped falling a victim to the indignation of the populace.
Assembling in great force, they broke through the guards and
tore the dignified official from his elevated position before he had
time to say a word.   This violent conduct on the part of the Dumfriesians called forth a rebuke from the Government, and also a
warning of what would befall the burgh in the event of the outrage being repeated.   The magistrates were enjoined to protect
the sheriff and sheriff-officers in executing the Regent's letters,
and that under the terrible penalty of " losing their freedom for
ever," the threat, bad enough in itself, being aggravated by an
injunction to elect at next Michaelmas such persons only " as
were affectionat to our sovereignis service and obedience ;" and by
an order to remove from office all factious persons entertaining
opposite sentiments.   What effect this edict had is not recorded ;
but, as we shall afterwards see, the inhabitants of the town soon
became thoroughly leavened by Protestant doctrines, and eventually gave a cordial support to the cause of the Reformation.

On the 2nd of May, 1568, Mary escaped from Lochleven.   Once
more personally free she might yet hope to reign.   With the view
of making that hope good six thousand men (all too few for its
realisation) flocked to the royal standard—Lord Herries, Lord
Maxwell, Edward Maxwell, Commendator of Dundrennan* (third
son of Lord Herries), and Gordon, Bishop of Galloway, signing a
bond, with others, to do battle to the uttermost on her behalf.
With such a force Mary resolved to risk an engagement with the
Regent Murray's army ; and on the 13th of the same month the
eventful conflict took place near Glasgow, the Queen with anxious
eye marking its varied movements from a neighbouring height.
Both Lord Herries and Lord Maxwell were present ; and it is said
hat the former, while taking an active part in the fight, wounded

* The Crown or family possessing the patronage of an abbey, often, as a
piece of lucrative preferment, placed a layman at its head, who drew the revenues, just as if he had been a churchman, and who was called Commendator.
Edward Maxwell, Commendator of Dundrennan, married the heiress-daughter
of Sir William Bailie of Lamington, representative of the patriot Wallace.   He
left four sons :—1, William, who took his father-in-law's name and designation ; 2, John Maxwell of Newlaw (from whom are descended the Maxwells of
Breoch, now represented by Mr Robert Maxwell) ; 3, James Maxwell of Bal-
mangan ; and 4, Edward Maxwell.

one of the Protestant leaders, Lord Ochiltree, in the neck. Neither individual gallantry nor the ardent bravery of the royalist rank and file proved of any avail. The Regent had a good position to begin with, and in virtue of that advantage and superior generalship he succeeded in breaking up the Queen's vanguard ; and though this disaster was more than half redeemed by her "stubborn spearmen," it was the forerunner of a universal rout — of utter ruin to her unhappy cause.

On seeing the issue of the fight Mary, accompanied by Lord Herries and a few other faithful followers, set off at full gallop, never drawing bridle till two score miles or more had been placed between her and the deadly field of Langside. Galloway had furnished a large proportion of her army, and thither fled the royal fugitive, threading the wild recesses of the Glenkens, pausing for a brief space on an eminence (since named Queenshill for that reason), and there, for the first time on her dolorous ride, partaking of refreshment—a simple crust of bread, moistened with water from the neighbouring spring.* Rest the poor lady much needs ; but with mind distraught by terror she cannot, dare not stay, even in the deep shadow of these friendly bowers. Crossing a wooden bridge that spanned the River Dee, about a mile above the village of Tongland, she tarries in a wayside cottage† till the bridge is broken down to retard the pursuing foe, whom her troubled fancy sees hard upon her track. Then away to the strong mansion of Corra : it belongs to her faithful Herries, and here she may venture to remain for the night—the dark night of a dismal day—one of the saddest in her whole sorrowful history.

Tradition tells us that Queen Mary "slept " at Corra on the night of the 13th ; but we fear that this is not true in a literal sense, and that the precious "balm of hurt minds" neither closed her wearied eyes nor calmed the throbbings of her harassed brain. To Terregles next morning ; but even in that powerful hold of her chief protector Mary Stuart cannot think of remaining long. On Scottish ground, so rife with angry rebels, she may not abide. She will not trust herself to any fortress, however strong—to any sanctuary, however sacred—within their reach. And so, hurrying from Terregles on the morning of the 15th, she proceeds to Dundrennan Abbey, of which Edward Maxwell is superior, and spends her last night in Scotland under its hallowed roof.‡ Vainly do

* The Queen's Well is still pointed out near Tongland Bridge.

† The walls of the cottage long remained on the farm of Culdoach. They were called Dun's Wa's—Dun being probably the name of the individual who tenanted the house when it was entered by the Queen.—History of Galloway, vol. ii., p. 507.

‡ There is at Terregles House a most interesting souvenir of Queen Mary —the remains of the bed occupied by her on her visits, and which the tradition of the Maxwell family especially associates with the last night spent by her under their roof. The remains consist of a wooden scroll, some eight feet long

Herries and her other steadfast friends implore her on their knees
to keep out of Queen Elizabeth's reach—to stay for a while at
Dundrennan, from which, if need be, she could take ship for
France. Frenzied, and half-despairing, she does not heed their
entreaties, but sets sail for England : there to find a worse prison
than had held her in her own country, and from which the grim
headsman was to deliver her, after the lapse of nineteen lingering
years.*

and one foot broad ; a flat cloth roof or canopy, which must originally have
been supported by a timber framework ; and a headpiece, measuring six feet
by five, which must have hung from the roof inside till it touched the pillow
which was pressed, on the sorrowful night referred to, by the head of the royal
fugitive. The stuff is of serge, padded with wool, still white and fresh, and
covered outside with satin that was once white, but is now no longer so, and
very lavishly embroidered with needlework—the design, a graceful-looking floral
one, and which, under happier circumstances, must have looked charming in
the eyes of the fair occupant of the couch. A small missal   also to be seen
at Terregles which belonged to Queen Mary.

    * Mary could have reached Terregles by a much shorter route had she
gone direct from Langside into Upper Nithsdale ; but she appears to have
been undecided at first what course to pursue. We know from a letter
written by her to Queen Elizabeth, dated Workington, 17th May, 1568, that
after the battle she " hasted first to Dumbarton ;" she then adds, " but soon
changing my course, God, of His infinite goodness, preserved me to fly into
your country."

CHAPTER XXIII.

IN a small fishing-boat, with about twenty attendants, the hapless
Queen sailed from a creek in the parish of Rerwick (since called
Port Mary) to the Cumberland coast, on the 16th of May, landing
at the place which received from her the name of Maryport :
thence she was conducted by the local authorities, with many
tokens of respect, to Carlisle. From that city Mary penned
several letters to Elizabeth, soliciting her protection and assistance. On the 5th of July she wrote to her sister sovereign : "I am
come to make my moan to you, the which being heard, I would
declare unto you mine innocency, and then require your aid." In
the same letter the Queen, sighing in heart for the presence of a
true friend, said, "In meantime, I beseech you to send to me my
Lord Herries, for I can't be without him." A few days afterwards
Mary was removed, in spite of her complaints and remonstrances
to Lord Scrope's castle at Bolton, on the borders of Yorkshire,
where she could only with difficulty maintain correspondence with
her friends in Scotland, and from which she had no chance of
making her escape.

A remarkable letter from Lord Herries, addressed by him on
the Queen's behalf to Lord Scrope and Sir Francis Knollys, is preserved in the State Paper Office, in which he inveighs strongly
against the detention of his royal mistress, and exposes the

duplicity of Elizabeth, The following characteristic passage is well worth quoting :—" Now, my Lords," he argues, " gif the Queen's Majesty of that realm [England], upon quhais promise and honour my maistress came there, as I have said, will leave all the French writings, and French phrases of writings, quhilks amongis them is over meikle on baith the sides unfit, and plainly, according to the auld true custom of England and Scotland— quherein be a word promist truth was observ'd—promise in the name of the eternal God, and upon the high honour of that nobill and princely blude of the Kings of England, quhereof she is de- scendit, and presently wears the diadem, that she will put my mistress in her awin country, and cause her as Queen thereof, in her authority and strength, to be obeyit ; and to do the same will appoint an certain day (within two months at the farthest), as we understand this to be our weil [for our welfare] sua will we, or the maist part of us, all follow upon it, leaving the Frenchmen and their evil phrases togidder. And therefore, and for the true per- petual friendship of that realm [England] will condition, and for our part, with the grace of Almighty God, keep sic heads and conditions of agreement as noble and wise men can condescend upon for the weill of this haill island." The letter concludes in these terms :—" This is plainly written, and I desire your lord- ships' plain answer ; for in truth and plainness langest continues gud friendship, quhilk in this matter, I pray God, may lang con- tinue, and have your lordships in his keeping. Off Dumfreis, the 3rd day of September, 1568. Your lordships at my power to com- mand leifully.—HERRIS."

A short time before the date of that letter the writer of it was forfeited in Parliament ; but the Regent, from motives of policy, caused the execution of the sentence to be delayed. Lord Herries continued to be a prominent character till the day of his death. Proceeding to London in the autumn of 1568, he there, with earnestness and ability, pleaded the cause of the Queen of Scots. Soon afterwards he went to advocate her interests at the French Court, and returned with Arran, Duke of Chatelherault, to assist the latter in making good his commission from the Queen to be Lieutenant-General of the kingdom, in opposition to the Regent Murray. Hostilities were averted at an interview between the rival claimants ; the Duke agreeing to acknowledge King James, on condition that the sentence of forfeiture should be removed from those who had supported Queen Mary. With the view of cementing the friendship thus somewhat hastily formed, Arran and Herries were entertained at a splendid banquet by the Regent in presence of King James ; but in the course of a few days, Murray's suspicions being aroused against them, they were both, by his order, committed to Edinburgh Castle ; from which, how- ever they were soon released, on the barbarous assassination of

Murray in January, 1570. Some months afterwards Lord Herries joined with the Duke of Chatelherault, the Earl of Hamilton, and others, in a last attempt to promote the cause of Queen Mary by force of arms. To give a show of legalitv to their proceedings, the Duke summoned a meeting of the Estates. Only a very partial response was given to this citation ; but, of six burghs which sent commissioners, Dumfries was one. This small Parliament (according to the author of the Diurnal)* sat in the Tolbooth of Edinburgh, and sustained a supplication, tabled in the Queen's name, setting forth that she still claimed the crown, her surrender of it having been extorted by force. On the failure of this movement. Herries, in the summer of 1571, laboured to effect a reconciliation between the contending parties, and with such success that a convention for this purpose was signed by the chiefs on both sides early in the following year.

Lord Herries, towards the close of life, embraced the Protestant faith, which he was so nearly doing at the outset of his public career ; and he was honoured with the confi lence of King James. He died suddenly at Edinburgh on Sabbath the 20th of January, 1582, under the following circumstances, as related by Calderwood :†—When at dinner he remarked that he found himself so weak that he durst not trust himself to go to the afternoon's preaching. He then went out, with the intent of going "to an upper chamber in William Fowler's lodging, to see the boys bicker." On the way he "fell down by little and little," exclaiming feebly to a woman that followed him, "Hold me ; for I am not weale :" after which he expired, four years before the execution of the unfortunate Queen to whose cause, so long as it was in the least degree hopeful, his services had been devoted. John, fourth Lord Herries, was one of the ablest Scotchmen of his day ; and while on some occasions he was vacillating and inconsistent, his character exhibited many points of excellence which we cannot but admire.

In 1570 Dumfriesshire, owing to the support given by some of its leading men to the cause of Mary, was ravaged by an armed force, sent by her rival Elizabeth, under Lord Scrope. John, eighth Lord Maxwell, nephew of Lord Herries, Lord Carlyle, and several other chiefs, mustered their followers, in order to resist the invaders, and were opportunely joined by a large body of burgesses from Dumfries, who, responding to their gathering cry of "A Loreburn !" appeared armed at the usual place of rendezvous, headed by the magistrates of the town. Scrope was enjoined not to injure the tenants or friends of Drumlanrig, "as he favoured the King's faction, and the Queen's Majesty of England." The allied force of military retainers and warlike merchants and tradesmen appear to have exhibited a creditable amount of prowess.

* Diurnal, p. 220.   † Appendix to octavo edition, vol. viii., p. 232.

Repeated attacks were made by them upon the enemy's cavalry with varying results ; but, inferior in number and equipments, they were eventually repulsed, with the loss of some prisoners, including the bailies of the Burgh.

Lord Scrope forwarded an account of the affair‡ to the English Government, under date Carlisle, 21st April, 1570, the substance of which we subjoin. After announcing that he had entered Scotland and encamped at "Heclefeagham" [Ecclefechan], he states that Simon Musgrave had, at his instance, "burned the towns of Hoddame, Maynes, Troltrow, Revel, Calpoole, Blackshaw, Sherrington, Bankend, Lowgher, Lougherwood, and Hecklefeugham ; that the said Simon Musgrave and his company having come to Old Cockpool, "there was the Lord Maxwell with his forces, and the inhabitants of Dumfriese assembled, who skirmished with the couriers, and compelled them to retire ; thereupon the said Simon marched into Blackshaw, where the Lord Maxwell was, and, with a hundred horsemen, did give the charge to Maxwell, and made him flee, in which flight there were a hundred prisoners taken, whereof the principal was the alderman of Dumfriese, and sixteen of the burgesses. The chase was followed within one mile of Dumfriese. After which the said Simon returned to Blackshaw, and burnt it, and seized a great number of cattle ;" and as he was proceeding to inflict a fiery visit of the same kind on "Bankend, Lowgher, and Lougherwood," Lords Maxwell and Carlyle, and the Lairds of Holmends, Closeburne, Lagg, Hempsfield, Cowhill, and Tenoll [Tinwald], at the head of four hundred horsemen and six hundred footmen, charged Musgrave's forces very sore, forcing them to alight and draw their company to a strong place, and to abide the charge of their enemies ; and so they remained till the said Simon came to them, and alighted, and put his company in order, and set his horses between his company and the sea, and so stood in order to receive the enemy ; and in this sort continued, charging and receiving their charges, the space of three hours. I being at Cembretreys [Cummertrees], sent my band of horsemen with my brother Edward, and a hundred and fifty foot with Mr Audley and Mr Herbert, to their relief." Thus reinforced, Musgrave compelled the Scots to flee, and captured a hundred of them, including some petty lairds—Maxwell, Carlyle, Johnstone, and the other chiefs only escaping "by the strengthe of the Laird of Cockpool's house, and a great wood and morass near adjoining."

The writer states in a postscript, that though, according to orders, Drumlanrig's tenants had been spared, "they were as cruel against us as any others ;" and he closes with the ominous intimation that he had applied for five hundred men, with whom to march against Dumfries, "and lie in that town and burn and spoil it ; for the open receipt of her Majesty's rebels is there manifeste."

‡ Cabala, p. 164.

Scrope, on being joined by a fresh body of soldiers, under the Earl of Sussex, executed his mission mercilessly. The sweep of his vengeance took in a wider field than was at first intended ; but it fell always with double force on the estates of Lords Maxwell and Herries, Murray of Cockpool, and such other noblemen as were noted for their attachment to Queen Mary. Dumfries suffered terribly : it had audaciously harboured the English Queen's rebels ; and did it not deserve, on that account, to be razed to its foundations ? The English leaders thought the town merited no forbearance, and they showed it none. Its desolated Castle, its flaming houses, leaving but the " blackness of ashes " to mark where the populous streets once stood, proved how well the mauraders had done their work. Similar evidences of their destructive expedition were visible in many parts of the surrounding country ; its results being summed up in the dry formal report made by Scrope to the English Government, setting forth that he had " took and cast doun the Castles of Carlaverock, Hoddam, Dumfries, Tinwald,* Cowhill,† and sundry other gentlemen's houses, dependers on the house of Maxwell, and, having burnt the toun of Dumfries, returned with great spoil into England." James Douglas, fourth Earl of Morton, became Regent in 1572 ;‡ and he having, with the aid of an English force, reduced Queen Mary's only remaining stronghold, Edinburgh Castle, the civil war was brought to a close, and Dumfriesshire was relieved from the presence of a foreign enemy.

This was the last of the great English raids across the Western Border ; but soon afterwards a deadly feud broke out between the two leading families of the county, the Maxwells and Johnstones, originated by a circumstance connected with the personal history of the eighth Lord Maxwell. In right of his mother, he was heir to one-third of the earldom of Morton :§ he had acquired right to

* The Old Place of Tinwald, situated in what was formerly a part of Lochar Moss, and a seat of a branch of the Maxwell family, seems to have been well fitted for a place of defence. Till within a few years, part of the old building remained. It is now (1834) entirely demolished, and the materials have been removed.—Statistical Account, p. 44.

† Cowhill Tower, says Grose (vol. i., p. 146), stood upon an eminence commanding a charming prospect of the Vale of Nith, from Friars' Carse to Dumfries : it had long been the seat of the Maxwells, cadets of the noble family of Nithsdale. In the year 1570, the old castle being burned by the English, this tower was built in 1579. Grose took a sketch of the second tower, and a few weeks afterwards it was taken down by George Johnstone, Esq. of Conheath, who had purchased it from the previous proprietor in order that he might erect a stately mansion on its site.

‡ He was the second son of Sir George Douglas of Pittendriech, younger brother of Archibald sixth Earl of Angus.

§ In the Scottish Nation, vol. iii., p. 208, it is stated that the title was taken from the lands of Mortoune, in the parish of East-Calder, Mid-Lothian ; but it is far more probable that it was derived from the old Castle of Morton (once the seat of Dunegal), in the parish of that name, both of which were

another third from Margaret, her elder sister, with consent of her
husband, the Duke of Chatelherault ; and he was also heir apparent
of the youngest and only other sister, who died childless. Lord
Maxwell considered, therefore, that he had the best claim to the
earldom—that certain entails executed upon the estates by Douglas,
the Regent, were illegal ; and he insisted on both the title and
property being made over to him. A contemporary historian
states that the Regent, as if conscious that he had no legal right to
call himself Earl of Morton, "pressed by all means that Lord
Maxwell should renounce his title thereto." The latter refused ;
and the Regent, instead of submitting the question at issue to
Parliament, consigned his rival to the Castle of Edinburgh, and
then to the Castle of Blackness, in the latter of which he lay for
several months, till he was liberated in March, 1578.

Next month he was charged by his Majesty to attend the
meeting of the Estates ; and a letter is extant, written by Maxwell,
asking Sir John Maxwell of Nether Pollok to appear as one of his
followers in warlike array at the Riding of Parliament. About a
year afterwards, Sir John received another epistle, addressed to
him by his chief, which ran thus :—"Traist friend, after hartlie
commendatiouns, this sal be to aduerteis you that I wes send for
be the Kingis Majestie upon schort warnying, and am disapoyntit
of silwer that suld have bene send fra hame ; quhairfor I will
desyre you effectuuslie to send me with this berar fourtie poundis
at the leist, to ane gud compt of your dewitees by gane, as ye wald
do me plesour at this tyme. This hoiping ye will do with all
deligence, I commit you to God. Off Streveling, the viij. of Apryle,
1579.—MORTOUN."*

His visit to the Court brought about no good results. The

conferred on the Black Douglas when he married the Princess Egidia. The
writer of the article " Morton," in the Statistical Account, says :—" Douglas,
Earl of Morton, was proprietor of the whole parish, with the exception of the
Mains of Morton, lying north-west of the castle, which belonged to James
Douglas, Laird of Morton. The last of this family was Captain James Douglas,
who died at Baitford, Penpont, about the beginning of last century. The Earl
of Morton sold his whole property and interest in this parish to Sir William
Douglas of Cashoggle, who erected a house a little south of Thornhill, where
he sometimes resided ; but the Earl of Queensberry having obtained from
Cashoggle all his lands, as well as the lands of Morton Mains from the other
family, and being lord of the regality of Hawick, he obtained authority to
translate that regality to Thornhill in 1610, and called it New Dalgarnock."
(Page 95.)

* In the original letter the " y " used appears as " z ;" but when used in
this and contemporary writs, it was, we have reason to think, pronounced as
" y," and we have so printed the letter. It may be as well here to state that,
just as the " z " appears to have been the old Saxon " y," so the Saxon " th "
was usually written " y " like the " h " in modern German. For this reason
whenever " ye," " yat," occur in any old manuscript we have occasion to quote
throughout the volume, we have printed the words as " the " and " that," instead of adopting the vicious form that is in vogue.

Regent had some of the worst characteristics of the Douglas family.
Like Haman of old, he could tell his friends of the things wherein
the King had promoted him, and how he had advanced him above
the "princes and servants of the King;" but Mordecai sitting at
the King's gate was no greater object of envy to the grasping
Amalekite than the Nithsdale chief wearing the Morton coronet
was to the envious soul of Douglas.   Proud and haughty, though
poor enough at times to be straightened for forty pounds, Maxwell refused to relinquish his claim, and was further punished for
his pertinacity by being deprived of the wardenship of the Western
Marches : an office, we need scarcely say, of great trust and profit,
which for ages had been held by members of the Maxwell family.*
This degrading blow fell with double effect, as the office when taken
from Maxwell was conferred upon the head of a rival house—the
Laird of Johnstone.

Douglas as Regent had but a short career : undermined by
the influence of James Stewart, captain of the Royal Guard, he
fell suddenly from power, and was put to death on a charge of
having been concerned, " art and part," in the murder of Darnley
for which there was no adequate proof.   The wardenship of the
Western Border was thereupon restored to Maxwell ; and, now
that the rival claimant was out of the way, he obtained a charter
of the coveted earldom.   Thus raised in rank he rose at the same
time rapidly into favour at Court, till, as a result of the treasonable Raid of Ruthven, he had to flee with the Duke of Lennox,
against whose influence it was directed.   Towards the close of
1581 we find him accompanying the Duke in an aggressive movement against the capital, which, however, was not persevered in.
Eventually the attainder passed on the deceased Regent was rescinded by royal letter, under the Great Seal, and the heir of
entail, Archibald Earl of Angus (grandson of Bell-the-Cat), suc
ceeded to the *old* title of Earl of Morton ; and thus the Scottish
peerage exhibited the curious anomaly of having two noblemen
possessing the same title : for, though Maxwell had been concerned
in treasonable proceedings, he was Earl of Morton still in virtue
of the royal patent that had been granted to him.

Soon a new embroglio arose, in which Lord Maxwell was
involved, through the cupidity of Captain Stewart, who, upon the
downfall of the Regent, received a grant of his estates, was created
Earl of Arran, and obtained the chief direction of affairs—all

* The Scottish Wardens were allowed by the Crown forage and provisions
for their retinue, which consisted of a guard of horsemen, by which they were
constantly attended.   These were levied from the royal domains on the Border.
They had also a portion of the "unlaws," or fines and forfeits imposed in the
Warden Courts ; and no doubt had other modes of converting their authority
to their own advantage, besides the opportunities their situation afforded them
of extending their power and influence.—Border Antiquities, Introduction by
Sir Walter Scott, p. 90.

through the unmerited favour of the King. The lands of Upper Pollok and Maxwellhaugh, in Lanarkshire, which had descended from Maccus to his lineal representative the Nithsdale baron, lay temptingly near those just acquired by the lucky adventurer, who on that account took a fancy for them, which he hastily assumed their owner would be ready to indulge. But Maxwell would not part with his patrimony, even when offered an equivalent for it : a decision which offended Arran's pride, as well as disappointed his acquisitiveness. In revengeful mood, therefore, he resolved to break the power of Maxwell, since he could not bend him to his wishes. Naturally enough, about this time, Maxwell was particularly anxious to draw strength from his family connections. On the 2nd of September, 1583, we find him again writing to his "traist cousing" of Pollok, announcing his arrival at Falkland, stating that he would remain there with his Majesty till the Parliament was prorogued, requesting Pollok to show himself to be friendly to his chief, and glad at his return, by coming to St. Johnston " honestly accompanied," that they might thence proceed homewards together.* Another letter from the same to the same was written from " off Drumfres " on the 22nd of April, 1584, in these terms : " Ye sal witt that the Kingis Majestie hes written to me to be at his Heiness with all possible dilligence, accompanied with my haill freyndis and forces, aisweel on hors as on fute, quhilk I am abill to mak or procuir, in their best array."† It was at this time, while Maxwell was doing courtly service and attending to his Parliamentary duties, that he was marked out for vengeance by the unappeasable Regent.

As one step towards this result the Regent endeavoured to weaken the Maxwell interest in Dumfries. The provostship was held by a cousin of the Nithsdale chief, Maxwell of Newlaw ;‡ and with the intent of getting it taken out of his hands the Laird of Johnstone was brought forward as a rival claimant for the office ; he being selected not simply on account of his local connection with the burgh, but also because Lady Johnstone had great influence at Court ; she being " verie familiar and favoured with and of " the Earl of Arran.§ Accordingly the whole machinery of the Government short of absolute force was set in operation to secure the return of Arran's *protégé* at the Michaelmas election of 1584. In due time a royal rescript was received by the merchant councillors and deacons of incorporations, who formed the electoral body, exhorting them to discard Maxwell and choose Johnstone as their municipal chief. What effect this arbitrary edict would have

* The Maxwells of Pollok, p. 155.
† The Maxwells of Pollok.
‡ Not Maxwell of Newbie, as stated by Chalmers and some other historians.
§ Botville's Continuation of Hollinshed, p. 430 ; also Spottiswoode, vol. ii., p. 325.

exercised upon the Town Council had it been left to influence them it is impossible to say, as the Provost of the burgh took effectual means to render it a dead letter, and secure his re-election in defiance of the Laird of Lochwood, the Earl of Arran, and the Government. When Johnstone, with a few retainers, appeared on the day of election in the vicinity of the town, he was kept from entering it by a powerful body of the Maxwells, drawn up in battle array under the leadership of their lord ; and after the crestfallen Annandale laird had departed, without the " blushing honours " he had aspired to, Newlaw was once more chosen Provost of Dumfries.*

Arran was not slow to support the complaints made by John-stone regarding the conduct of his rival ; and between them a new charge was trumped up against the Laird of Nithsdale, the nature of which he learned by a precept issued in the King's name accusing him of intromitting with and protecting the predatory Armstrongs. By way of sequel a sentence of outlawry was pronounced upon Lord Maxwell ; and a commission was given to the Laird of John-stone to pursue him with fire and sword as a contumacious rebel who deserved no mercy—to assist in which congenial work a band of mercenaries under Captain Lammie was sent into Dumfriesshire by the Earl of Arran. Maxwell was composed of sterner stuff than to be daunted by these preparations. Mustering his followers, he made ready to return at least blow for blow. A detachment of them, under his natural brother, Robert Maxwell of Castlemilk, encountered the Government soldiers at the head of Nithsdale, and thoroughly defeated them—killing Lammie, and taking Cranston, another officer, prisoner.† The war thus initiated raged for months over the county. It seemed as if it would only end in the ruin of one or both of the great families thus relentlessly pitted against each other. When the Regent Morton tossed the wardenship, like a tennis ball, from Maxwell to Johnstone, he little knew what a bone of contention it would prove ; but the Earl of Arran seems to have been quite conscious, when he introduced new elements of discord between them, that a fearful collision would be the conse-quence ; and he undoubtedly expected that it would prove fatal to the man against whom he had formed an inveterate dislike,

Botville tells us that Johnstone made prodigious efforts to revenge the defeat of his mercenary allies ; " for that cause assem-bling such power as he had, he used the strength of one element against another, of the highest against the lowest, of the heaven against the earth, of the fire against metall, and of burning against fighting "‡—the plain English of these high-sounding words being set forth in the next sentence : "for with all speed he hastened to

*Spottiswoode, vol. ii., p. 326.

† Spottiswoode, vol. ii., p. 326.   ‡ Botville, p. 430.

the lands of the Earl Morton, which he cruellie spoiled, and in the same did burn certain houses and other places belonging to the Earl, as Comerstrees, Duncoll [Duncow], and such like."* Maxwell, however, had not the worst of it in this the first stage of the deadly struggle. Many of his houses were burned, and some of his estates were devastated by the Johnstone party ; but "with the like furie and more hurt" did he burn and slay. "We shall give Dame Johnstone light to set her hood by !" he cried, with savage humour, as the devouring torch was applied to Lochwood.† Lochhouse, another seat of the Annandale magnate, was similarly dealt with ; and during the assault several of his near relatives were killed, including "the two brothers of Lockerbie, a brother of the Laird Wanefraie, and some of the sons of John Johnstone of Polgill."‡

Burned out of hold and home the Laird of Johnstone hied away to Bonshaw Tower ; but scarcely had he received a greeting of welcome from its owner, Edward Irving, when siege was laid to it by Maxwell, who at the head of a large party had hurried off in pursuit. Through the opportune mediation of the English Warden, Lord Scrope, the two wrathful barons were brought to "chap hands"—which pledge of peace, however, was badly kept ; "the coles of inward griefe being covered with cold ashes of outward reconciliation, did not long lie covered, but in the end began afresh to show their fire."§ Johnstone, hearing that Robert Maxwell of Castlemilk had set out with a small retinue from Dumfries to Langholm, on a mission from his brother of Morton, lay in wait for him beside the Warden Ditches, on the verge of Lochar. But the attack of the ambushed party was anticipated by Carruthers of Holmains. Aware of their hostile designs against Castlemilk, he pounced suddenly upon them—their slogan of "Ready, aye ready," proving for once untrue—and succeeded in capturing their chief, who was forthwith consigned to prison. The Regent Arran, finding that all his endeavours to crush Maxwell had been baffled, resolved to gain his ends if possible by a more direct way. He succeeded in obtaining from the Estates a vote of £20,000 for the sole purpose of levying war against Maxwell. A proclamation

---

* Ibid.

† The immense strength of this castle, and its position among impassable bogs and marshes, have already been noticed. A remark has been attributed to James VI. respecting Lochwood, to the effect that the man who built it, though he might have the outward appearance of an honest man, "must have been a knave at heart." We can scarcely think that our British Solomon ever uttered such a foolish saying. Lochwood was erected in a warlike and turbulent age ; and if made impregnable, it was on that account an evidence of the wisdom, and not the knavery, of the builder. Soon after being burned by Maxwell, it was repaired ; and it was inhabited till three years after the death of the first Marquis of Annandale, in 1721, when it was deserted by the family and allowed to fall into decay.

‡ Botville, p. 431.   § Botville, p. 431.

was then issued requiring all the King's loyal subjects on the southern side of the Forth to meet him in fighting array, and march into Nithsdale. A deadly pestilence, which broke out at Edinburgh, decimated the royal army and saved Maxwell and Dumfriesshire from the threatened attack.*

Seeing that the Nithsdale chief was marked out for ruin by Arran, it was not surprising when a league was formed by Angus and other fugitives against the King's minion that it was joined by Maxwell. The associated Lords aimed at nothing less than the expulsion of the royal favourite by force. With this object in view they raised a large body of men, to meet whom there was a new muster of Government troops, who, however, were prevented from proceeding southward by the representations of the English Ambassador, whose policy it was to keep Arran in check. Maxwell and his allies, however, boldly took the initiative. They made a hurried march to Stirling, with two thousand followers, beset the castle, in which the Court at that time resided, before daybreak on the 2nd of November, 1585, and took the fortress after a two days' siege. This act, not less patriotic than daring, was accomplished chiefly by the men of Nithsdale. It was productive of important results. Though Arran secured his personal safety by flight, he was deprived of his title and estates, and his pernicious domination was thoroughly overthrown. At a Parliament held a few days afterwards an Act was passed granting to Lord Maxwell, his servants and friends, entire indemnity for all their irregular or unlawful doings in the realm since April, 1569 ; and through his means special provision was made for giving the town of Dumfries the full benefits of the pacification. Of the men named in the amnesty about six hundred were from Maxwell's estates in Nithsdale and Galloway ; about the same number from his estates in Eskdale, Ewisdale, and Wauchopedale—mostly Beatties, Littles, and Armstrongs ; three hundred and forty from Lower Annandale —chiefly Bells, Carrutherses, and Irvings ; and about three hundred and fifty better organised soldiers, in three companies of infantry and two troops of cavalry—one being furnished by Nithsdale and Galloway, under John Maxwell of Newlaw, Provost of Dumfries ; the other by Annandale, under George Carruthers of Holmains, and Charles Carruthers, his son.

The act referred to "in favour of the towne of Dumfreis" sets forth "that the King's Majesty, with the advice of the Three Estates of the present Parliament, understanding that his trustie cousin and counsellor John Earl of Morton, Lord Maxwell, with his haile kin, friends, and servants, during the time of the feid and trubles betwixit him and Sir John Johnstone of Dunskellie, knight,†

---

* Spottiswoode, vol. ii., p. 326.

† It appears from this designation that Johnstone had received the honour of knighthood some time before the Act quoted from was passed.

maid their special repair into the towne of Drumfreis, stuffit and
garnissit with men of armes, victual, and all other furnitor neidfull
for thair defense, quherento the inhabitants of the said burgh
might not oppose thameselffis in consideratioun of the said noble
Lordis frendis dwelling round about, and within the said burgh."
This wordy preamble is followed by a provision absolving the
armed intruders and their successors from the legal consequences
of any blame that might be thrown upon them by the burgh ; and
also extending pardon to such of the inhabitants as had resetted,
intercommuned with, or otherwise assisted them.   Intimation is
then made that the King, out of his " special favour and clemencie,"
extends to " his lovittes, the Provest and Bailleis, Counsal, and
Comonitie of the said burgh, the lyk benefite, favour, and guid-
will " that are contained in the Acts of abolition and general pacification granted to Angus, Morton, and their colleagues ; the Act
closing thus :—" And furder declairis the electioun of Johnne
Maxwell, of Newlaw, Provest of the said burgh, to be guid and
sufficient in itis selff, and to stand for him, and his successors, sua
long as the saide Johnne Maxwell sal be authoriset be common
election or consent of the inhabitants thairof ; discharging quhm-
sumiver utheris rychtis, and securitie maid at any time bypast, or
to be maid to any other persoun of the samyne to the contrair."*
Maxwell, thoroughly placated by these enactments, set the Laird
of Johnstone at liberty, the unfortunate chief soon afterwards
getting release from all his troubles in the grave.

Stewart, no longer either earl or captain, took refuge in the
wilds of Western Ayrshire, where he lived secretly for many years,
till, in 1596, lured by the delusive hope of regaining the King's
favour, he passed to the neighbourhood of Dumfries on his way to
Court. He was, it is said, encouraged to take this rash step by a
" spaewife " whom he consulted. " Low as ye are now, and high
as ye aince were, ye're head will be raised higher yet," was the
oracular response on which he acted ; but he was warned by some
one, who did not affect the possession of supernatural wisdom, to
beware of the Douglases—whose leader, Morton, he had brought
to the block—and more especially to avoid the dead Regent's
nephew James Douglas, who had a short time previously acquired the
barony of Torthorwald. To this warning Stewart returned a reply
that would have been foolish anywhere, and became the very
essence of folly when uttered as it was almost beneath the shadow
of the old keep occupied by Morton's kinsman : " Fear the Douglases who may, I shall not go out of my road for any of their
blood and name." Yes ; but Torthorwald will go out of his way in
order that he may take revenge on the man who could thus add
impotent contempt to foul wrong. Accompanied by three retainers

* Acts of Scot. Parl., vol. iii., pp. 398-9.

Douglas, hurrying after the discarded favourite, slew him with a spear ; and the weird woman's promise was " kept to the ear, but broken to the hope," when soon afterwards Stewart's gory head, elevated on a lance, was displayed, like a grisly ensign of death, from the battlements of Torthorwald. The chief actor in this tragedy suffered for it after the lapse of twelve years. Captain William Stewart, encountering Douglas on the High Street of Edinburgh, in 1608, ran him through the body, in revenge for the slaughter of his uncle, the ex-Regent.*

As has already been mentioned, the progress of the Reformation in Dumfries was impeded by the Maxwells. They still clung to the old faith ; and in 1584 the fifth Lord Herries was accused of openly defying the law by causing mass to be publicly celebrated in the town, and compelling the Protestant ministers to leave its bounds.†

His kinsman Lord Morton, or Maxwell, as we prefer calling him, on the Christmas which followed the receipt of the royal amnesty, also signified his adherence to Romanism in the same illegal way. About this time the Castle of Dumfries was beginning to rise anew, by his order, out of the ruins in which it had been left by Lord Scrope fifteen years before ; and it was probably at the chapel attached to it that Maxwell summoned a meeting of followers and ecclesiastics for the purpose of making a defiant display of his religion. A gathering of this kind, at all events, was held in Dumfries on the 25th of December, 1585 ; and, after those composing it had been arranged as a procession, they marched to the neighbouring College of Lincluden, going, doubtless, by the Causeway Ford over the Nith, nearly opposite to the Castle.‡(a) On arriving at the College mass was performed in the ancient fane with unusual splendour and effect. For six hundred years Lincluden, first as an abbey and next as a collegiate institution, had been the scene of such religious rites ; but the choral swell with which the venerable walls rang on this occasion was as the dying requiem of the ancient faith—mass never having been since said or sung in the house of Uchtred. It threatened at first to cost

* Wood's Peerage, vol i., p. 123.   † Spottiswoode, vol. ii., p. 381.

‡ Naturally, the river is still shallow at this place—a bed of sand stretching from the right, or Nithside, bank, till within a few yards of the Dumfries side. When, early in the spring of 1867, the Caul below the Old Bridge was ruptured by the breaking up of ice, the water was reduced to such a small volume that the track of the ford was distinctly traceable. In ancient times the ford led to the Castle, and also along the left shore or Upper Sandbeds to the foot of the Vennel, and to the bridge. The ford was made passable on foot when the river was of moderate size, and was fenced from assailing floods by stakes of wood. Hence the name Stakeford. It is called Chapel-rack Ford in some documents of last century's date.

(a) This castle was probably Maxwell's town house, a place of strength at the head of High Street.

Lord Maxwell a heavy price. He was summoned to appear before the King in Council, to answer for the daring offence of celebrating mass contrary to the statute ; and on his proceeding to Edinburgh he was consigned to the Castle, where he lay for several months ; but he was set at liberty on condition of going abroad for a season, without being subjected to any formal trial—the King probably not wishing to press with severity on one who had done the State some service, and from whom he expected future favours.*

* Calderwood's version of the matter (page 225) is in the following terms : —"The Lord Maxwell was committed to ward in the beginning of the year 1586 for having masse openly in the Kirk of Glencluden at the Christmas before."

CHAPTER XXIV.

WHEN James heard of his mother's execution, early in 1587, he
consulted with Lord Maxwell and other Border chiefs as to the
propriety of avenging her death by a destructive raid against the
Southrons. But his wrath very soon evaporated, and the only
foray undertaken by him into England was a pacific one, in
1603, when he went southwards to receive the English Crown as
Queen Elizabeth's heir. Prior to that event James laboured diligently to secure the tranquillity of Dumfriesshire : for this
purpose he caused its " Capulets and Montagues " to enter into
assurances of peace with each other, and to promise to submit
their disputes to the consideration of his Council, instead of
bringing them to "the dread arbitrament of the sword." The death
of Johnstone in 1586 greatly promoted the success of these pacific
measures, and the civil war in the county was suspended for
about a year ; but only to be renewed on a larger scale, and with
more disastrous consequences.

The origin of the Johnstone family has already been taken
notice of.* John de Johnstone, who submitted to Edward I. in
1296, is supposed to have been the father of a chief of the same
name who witnessed a charter of the barony of Comlongan and

*Vide p. 31.

other contiguous lands, bequeathed in 1332 by Thomas Randolph, Earl of Moray, to his nephew William. Prior to the latter date the family had acquired large possessions in the county, and were beginning to acquire more than a local repute by their prowess in the field. Gilbert, the next chief, was succeeded by his son, Sir John de Johnstone, who made a distinguished figure in the reign of Robert II.: he was one of the guardians of the Western Marches in 1371, and often exerted himself with good effect against the English Borderers, especially in 1378, as is recorded by Wyntoun in the following passage :—

> " When at the wattyr of Sulway
> Schyr Jhon of Jhohnystown, on a day
> Of Inglis men wen cust a gret dele :
> He bare him at that tyme sa welle,
> That he and the Lord of Gordowne,
> Had a sowerane guid renown,
> Of ony that was of thar degre,
> For full thai war of gret bownte."

The grandson of this valorous knight, Sir Adam Johnstone, contributed by his gallantry to the Scottish triumph at Sark ; and the latter was succeeded by Sir John Johnstone, who, by marrying Mary, eldest daughter of John, the fourth Lord Maxwell, effected an alliance between the two houses that were shortly afterwards to be arrayed against each other in deadly hate. We find James, the fruit of this marriage, and next chief of the clan, actively engaged in repelling the invasion of Scotland by the Earl of Douglas and the Duke of Albany in 1484. His heir, Adam Johnstone, died in 1508, and was succeeded by James, whose eldest son and heir John signalised himself at the battle of Pinkie. Two or three additional links of the genealogical chain—John, James, John, son, grandson, and great grandson of the Pinkie warrior—bring us to the immediate progenitor of the doughty chief who received the wardenship in 1579, contested the provostship of Dumfries in 1584, and, after long warring with the Maxwells, was " gathered to his fathers " in 1586, leaving his lands, and also the heritage of an implacable feud, to his eldest son James, born to him by his wife Margaret, daughter of Sir Walter Scott of Buccleuch.

In 1580 the young chief of the Johnstones obtained a letter of provision under the Great Seal assigning to him the revenues of the suppressed Abbey of Holywood ; he was served heir to his deceased father in 1588 ; and when two years afterwards the newly-married consort of the King, Anne of Denmark, was crowned, he received the honour of knighthood—a coveted distinction that had been enjoyed by several of his ancestors—the style assigned to him being Sir James Johnstone of Dunskellie, now called Cove, where he had a castle, which he occasionally occupied.

By the middle of the fourteenth century an immense number of families bearing the Johnstone name were to be found in Annandale, all counting kinship with the Lord of "Lochwood's lofty towers": their relation towards him being in every respect more like that borne by Highland clansmen to their chief than the feudal vassalage of Norman origin that generally prevailed throughout the Lowlands. As illustrative at once of the numerical extent of this great Border sept, and of the close relationship in which its members stood to each other, we quote, in an abridged form, an agreement entered into by them on the 14th of November, 1555 :—" Bond by Gavin Johnstone ; Ninian Johnstone in Fingland ; David Johnstone in Stagwood ; John Johnstone in Langside ; David Johnstone in Banks ; John Johnstone in Vilehol ; Adam Johnstone, son to Vilehol ; David Johnstone in Rayhills ; Adam Johnstone his brother ; Matthew Johnstone of the Thrid ; William Johnstone in Kirkhill ; William Johnstone in Brumewell ; John Johnstone his brother ; John Johnstone in Banks ; George Graym ; Fergus the Graym ; James Grahame in Grahame of Badoch ; James Graham of Bordland ; Andrew Johnstone in Fuldoun ; David Johnstone his brother ; Edward Johnstone ; Thomas Johnstone ; John Johnstone ; Mark Johnstone of Fairholm ; Herbert Johnstone in Castlehill ; and Robert Johnstone ; obliging them by the faith and troth of their bodies, if it happened any Johnstone pertaining to them, when they are pledged for man-tenant or servant, to comit stouthreif, fire, slaughter, oppression, or any crime, to seik the person that committed the crime and deliver him up to the Laird of Johnstone to be punished for his demerits ; and if they cannot apprehend him they obliged them to herry and put them [out] of the country, and to satisfy and redress the complainers with their own goods and gier."*

Among the branches of the family a distinguished position was occupied by the Johnstones of Dryfesdale or Lockerbie, whose head resided in a fortalice at the town of that name (now used as a police station), which was well defended by deep lochs on three sides. " Their lands (which up till the beginning of last century extended to Annan Water, taking in Roberthill, Shillahill, and Tarmuir) had been always chiefly occupied by people of their own name and kindred : the 'Johnstones of Driesdale' being enrolled about 1550 to bring to the field forty-six fighting men."†

* Annandale Papers.

† Mr Charles Stewart of Hillside, who, in a little work entitled " Rides, Drives, and Walks about Moffat," and in various communications to the local newspapers, has supplied much valuable information regarding the Johnstones, and Annandale in ancient times. " Lockerbie," says Mr Stewart, " seems to have been one of the Saxon towns, clustering round the dwelling of the laird, which are still numerous in England, though there are scarcely any in this country now to be seen, excepting Torthorwald. It would seem to have been,

In April 1587 Dumfries was visited by King James at the head of a considerable force, his inducements for doing so being complaints by the General Assembly regarding the attempts made in 1584 by Lord Herries to revive Romanism, and renewed disturbances on the Border, which were laid at the door of Lord Maxwell.* Herries, on hearing of these proceedings, repaired to Edinburgh and offered himself for trial. The charges against him could not be substantiated ; but he was found to have proved remiss in his office of Warden, to which he had been appointed on the death of the Laird of Johnstone. On promising amendment in this latter respect, and engaging to obey any summons that might be sent to him by the Assembly, he was allowed to return to Terregles.†

Lord Maxwell's followers were so reduced in number by the recent feuds that he durst not face the royal troops as his combative nature prompted. He was unable even to stand out for terms ; and withdrawing from the neighbourhood, he left these to be made for him by Lord Herries, Sir John Gordon, and other friends, who gave bonds on his behalf that he would leave the realm beyond seas in a month, that in the meantime he should not trouble the country, that when abroad he should do nothing to injure the Protestantism or the peace of Scotland, and lastly that he should not return without his Majesty's license to that effect.

Behold, then, the unruly Border baron bidding adieu to his native Nithsdale, and seeking refuge in a distant land. It would have been better for him and Dumfriesshire if he had continued an exile, and closed life's discordant day by a twilight of peace, even though his dust had been left sleeping in a foreign soil. To Spain he directed his course, but found no rest there. Perhaps he did not seek repose, "for quiet to quick bosoms is a hell." The Spaniards were busy fitting out their "Invincible Armada," by which they had already, in imagination, conquered Britain, the chief bulwark of Protestantism, and annihilated the Reformation ; and the expatriated Scottish lord, influenced by aspirations which so accorded with his own devotedness to Popery, resolved to assist the meditated expedition by returning to his native country and making a diversion in its favour.

in 1617, in nearly the same form of street as it is now. The houses were chiefly occupied by little farmers, who possessed among them, in runrigg, 300 or 400 acres of surrounding arable land—their cattle grazing on the extensive common of 1500 acres of moor to the westwards. Most of them had also avocations as the handicraftsmen and little traders of the district. The town was, as now, the central resort of the adjacent valleys and dales ; and, being on the high road to the English border, the fairs had been long established by royal charter."

* Spottiswoode, vol. ii., p. 381.

† Spottiswoode, vol. ii., p. 381.

With this evil end in view Maxwell landed at Kirkcudbright in April, 1588, where he was joined by several of the nobility, and a large body of his own retainers. Lord Herries, disapproving of this rash and unpatriotic movement on the part of his kinsman, took council with the King regarding the course to be pursued in such an untoward crisis. "Summon the traitor to appear before us," said his sapient Majesty. A royal precept to that effect was issued forthwith, which Maxwell treated with contempt ; and in a trice afterwards Dumfriesshire was in the throes of a rebellion. The Castles of Dumfries, Carlaverock, Lochmaben, and others in the Maxwell interest were garrisoned—the flags from their turrets fluttering a defiance to the King, which their booming guns proclaimed in a fiercer tone. Their resistance was merely nominal, however, except that which was given by Lochmaben. So serious did matters seem that King James once more proceeded to Dumfries, in order to encourage by his presence the royal troops commissioned to cope with the insurrection. When about to enter the burgh they were resisted at the gates by a large party of burgesses ; and Maxwell, who was in the Castle at the time, and had concluded that it would be unable to sustain a siege, withdrew from it, whilst his friendly townsmen kept the assailants in check.*

Hurrying on horseback to Kirkcudbright, he there embarked on board a vessel in the Dee. Soon another ship hove in sight, freighted from the port of Ayr by Sir William Stewart, and which the fugitive lord learned, when too late, had come to capture him. After a rapid chase from Kirkcudbright along the Carrick shore to Crossraguel, Maxwell's vessel was run down and himself put under arrest.

Meanwhile, though the Castles of Dumfries and Carlaverock no longer frowned rebelliously upon the royal troops, the fortress of Lochmaben, which was commanded by David Maxwell, brother of the Laird of Cowhill, held out against them bravely. They laid regular siege to it, but the walls were so stout and well defended that it made no progress. The King had only small pieces of ordnance, which made little impression on the stubborn stronghold. Heavier cannon, however, having been borrowed by him from the English Warden, a hot bombardment was proceeded with, which, after continuing two days, caused the garrison to capitulate. Its valiant commander and five of his leading men were hanged before the castle gate—an act of severity which contrasts strangely with the forbearance shown towards the chief rebel and originator of all the mischief, who, after being brought

* Spottiswoode accounts for the resistance given to the royal forces by saying that the burgesses were not aware that the King was personally present. (Vol. ii., p. 283.)

by his captor Stewart to Dumfries, was sent to Edinburgh Castle, where he suffered but a brief and lenient imprisonment.

According to Calderwood, the plot thus crushed was first made known to the King by Queen Elizabeth, some of whose officers had intercepted letters sent by the Earl of Huntly, Lord Maxwell, and Lord Claude Hamilton to King Ferdinand of Spain, in which their plans were divulged. Even after Lord Maxwell was put in ward a written intercourse was kept up by his party with Ferdinand and the Duke of Parma by means of a priest named Bruce, belonging to the household of that nobleman. Bruce, in a letter to the Duke, makes the following reference to the imprisoned conspirator :—" The Earl of Mortoun, alias Lord Maxwell, to whom I have given consolation by writ in prison, hath instantly prayed me also to writ, to remember his most affectioned service to your Highness, finding himself greatly honoured with the care it pleased you to have of him. By the grace of God he is no more in danger of his life by way of justice, it not being possible for his enemies to prove against him anything which they had supposed in his accusation ; as also the King's affection not so far alienated from him as it hath been heretofore ; and in case they would annoy him, or that it were presently requisite for the weel of our cause to deliver him, we have ever moyen to get him out of prison, and abide nought in the meane time but the King's will towards his libertie, only to avoid all persute that they would make if we delivered him extraordinarlie. When they offered him in the King's name his libertie if he would subscribe the Confession of the Heretick's Faith, he answered he would not do it for the King's crown, nor for an hundreth thousand lives, if he had them to lose ; and hath offered to confound the ministers by publick disputation. I shall solicit the lords his friends to procure of the King his libertie very soon ; for he importeth the well of our cause more than any of the rest, by reason of his forces, which are neer England, and the principal town of Scotland, and the ordinar residence of our King ; as also he is the lord most resolute, constant, and of greatest execution of any of the Catholicks."*

King James, having re-established his authority, returned in triumph to Dumfries, the inhabitants of which gave him but a cold welcome—relishing his visit all the less because he summarily dismissed from the provostship Maxwell of Newlaw, brother of Lord Herries, who had incurred his displeasure by opposing the entrance of the royal troops. The subsequent fate of the ex-Provost was tragical in the extreme : he having been waylaid and slain by a party of Johnstones and Grahams, because his father, the late Lord Herries, had treated them with rigour when Warden of the Marches. Whilst his Majesty was at Dumfries he also presided over a justiciary court held for the trial of Lord Maxwell's

* Calderwood, pp. 236-37.

followers, and other offenders. After making an imposing royal progress through part of the Border district, and in token of his ire against treason, and other forms of lawlessness, burning the Towers of Langholm,* Castlemilk,† (a), and Morton, the King proceeded to Edinburgh, leaving John, Lord Hamilton, to act as his lieutenant over the whole Borders, with the assistance of Lord Herries and other Dumfriesshire barons.

It was now Johnstone's turn to exhibit disloyalty. When Francis Stewart, Earl of Bothwell,‡ with the view of obtaining pre-eminent power in the State, made a bold attempt to seize the King's person, he had for one of his accomplices the Annandale chief—for which disloyal deed the latter, like Lord Maxwell, was imprisoned in Edinburgh Castle. Maxwell was liberated by an act of grace on the day of the royal marriage, 12th September, 1589 ; and Johnstone managed to break out of his prison, and, with the stigma of rebel still attached to his name, returned to Lochwood. Again the King visited Dumfriesshire, for the purpose of overawing such of the Border clans as had given assistance to Bothwell, or had in other respects poured contempt on his authority. James did not find the gates of the shire town barred against him on this occasion. The burgesses opened them readily to his Majesty, giving him a hearty welcome ; for their friend Maxwell was now a favourite at court, and had renounced his rebellious designs, and nominally at least his Romanist opinions. James issued a proclamation from Dumfries offering pardon to all who would repudiate Bothwell and engage to keep the peace. These merciful conditions were accepted by many, though not by Sir James Johnstone ; and when his Majesty left the county it was still far from being thoroughly tranquillised. Whether from motives of policy or conviction, Lord Maxwell subscribed the Confession of Faith on the 26th of January, 1593, before the Presbytery of Edinburgh, the signature used by him being that of " Morton," the earldom of which he still claimed. There is good reason to suppose that he continued a Romanist at heart ; at all

* The Tower of Langholm, which still survives as a ruin, was a small square keep that belonged to Johnnie Armstrong, and was, after his execution, acquired by the Maxwells.

† Castlemilk, in the parish of St. Mungo, was built by one of the Bruces, and came into the family of Stewart by the marriage of Walter, the High Steward, with one of King Robert's daughters. The Maxwells eventually acquired it by marriage. A house of the same name, built in 1796, occupies its site ; and a stately new mansion has just been erected near it, by the proprietor of the estate. It belongs, with the estate, to Robert Jardine, Esq., M.P. (a) Created a baronet in 1885.

‡ He was the eldest son of John Stewart, Prior of Coldingham, natural son of James V.; his mother being Lady Jane Hepburn, sister of the infamous Earl of Bothwell who was charged with the murder of Darnley, and afterwards married his widow, the Queen of Scots. Francis Stewart received the title from James IV. in 1576.

events his profession of Protestantism and his practice in after
life were often broadly at variance.

When in 1601 the General Assembly saw reason to bewail a
great defection from the zeal and purity of the true religion, they
attributed it in some measure to the want of a sufficient number
of pastors "in places that are of chiefest importance, as the town of
Drumfries,"* near to which Lord Herries resided. Arrangements
were made by the Assembly to settle additional ministers in the
most destitute localities ; also to bring their influence to bear
upon the Popish lords by means of personal visitation—Mr David
Lindsey and Mr John Hall being the clergymen appointed to
operate on Lord Herries.† In the Assembly of the following year
these two visiting commissioners reported that they had been
unable to hold a conference with his lordship on account of the
shortness of his stay in Edinburgh. The whole question was then
entered upon anew ; and it was resolved by the Assembly that
certain noblemen's houses and families should be temporarily supplied with pastors or chaplains, able not only to instruct and confirm them in the Protestant faith, "but also to procure that their
families be not corrupted with the companie and resorting of professed Papists, Jesuits, and other seminarie priests."‡ For these
purposes Mr Robert Wallace was appointed to wait upon Lord
Herries, and Mr Henry Blyth on Lord Maxwell.§ It is curious to
note the instructions given to these clerical visitors.

The Assembly, bent on subduing the nobles who stood in the
way of their good work, enjoined their representatives to use an
amount of moral pressure which is inconsistent with modern ideas
on the subject, and the nature of which may be inferred from the
subjoined quotation :—" Ye shall addresse your selves with all
convenient diligence, and necessarie furniture, to enter into their
companie and families, there to remain with them for the space of
three moneths continuallie ; during which time your principal
care shall be, by public doctrine, by reading and interpretation of
the Scriptures ordinarily at their tables, and by conference at all
meet occasions, to instruct them in the whole grounds of true
religion and godliness ; specially in the heeds controverted ; and
confirme them therein. Take pains to catechise their families
ordinarily every day once or twice at the least, or so often as may
bring them to some reasonable measure of knowledge, and feeling
of religion, before the expiring of the time prescribed for your
remaining there, and let this action begin and end with prayer."‖

At the same Assembly visitors were set apart for inquiring
into the " life, doctrine, qualification, and conversation " of all the
ministers ; and in this capacity John Knox¶ proceeded to Niths-

---

* Calderwood, p. 453.   † Ibid.   ‡ Ibid, p. 459.   § Ibid.

‖ Calderwood, p. 460.   ¶ Ibid, p. 461.

dale and Annandale, taking with him Mr Patrick Shaw and Mr John Smith as colleagues. No report from the visitors has fallen under our notice ; and we are left to conjecture the way in which Mr Wallace fared when he went on his proselytising mission to Lord Herries, and whether or not Mr Blyth succeeded in re-establishing the Protestantism of Lord Maxwell. We suspect that in both instances failure was the result. The King had begun to look coldly on Presbyterianism. He was preparing to graft on it a strange Prelatic shoot, and to hamper in many respects the action of the Assembly—thus retarding the Reformed cause, and encouraging both its avowed and secret enemies. It was scarcely to be expected that the nobles who had opposed it all along, or had only nominally embraced it, would under such circumstances change their creed or their policy.

On the 2nd of February, 1593, Lord Maxwell and Angus, the new Earl of Morton, came to an unseemly issue on the question of precedency in St. Giles's Church, Edinburgh ; and just as they were about to draw swords within the sacred edifice the Lord Provost interfered, and caused the combative barons to be sent guarded to their lodgings in the city.

Soon after this bloodless incident Maxwell returned to Dum-friesshire, never more to leave it in life. Sir James Johnstone having by his recent rebellious acts forfeited the wardenry of the Western Marches, that office was again given to the Lord of Niths-dale ; and thus armed, he proceeded to the Border for the purpose of allaying its turbulence. Probably the King meant him to adopt stringent measures towards the Johnstones ; but when it seemed as if the strife between the families was about to be renewed, a peace was patched up between them through the mediation of mutual friends. The rival chiefs were thereby induced not only to give up their antagonism but to enter into an alliance offensive and defensive with relation to the wily chief of Drumlanrig, who was, for sufficient reasons, distrusted by both. This agreement, duly signed by the contracting parties, is still preserved among the Annandale papers. In accordance with it, John, Earl of Morton, Lord Maxwell, and Sir James Johnstone of Dunskellie, agreeing for themselves, and taking burden upon them for their next kin, friends, tenants, and servants, " oblige them by the faith and troth of their bodies that they nor their foresaids intromit or agree with Sir James Douglas of Drumlanrig, nor his kin, friends, tenants, and servants, without the special advice and consent of the other had thereto ; and that both their [own] assurance and assurance with the said Sir James Douglas should be done in one day ; and in case any of them had an action of law against him, to concur, fortifie, and assist [each] other to the intensist of their power ; and should take a true, upright, and aefold part with others while the feid were agreid or reconciled."

This contract is dated the 13th of March, 1592, only twenty-one
months previous to the battle of Dryfe Sands ; and there is another
more general one of a still later date—April 1st of that year—in
which Maxwell and Johnstone come under a solemn obligation for
themselves and friends to "freely remit and forgive all rancours
of mind, grudge, malice, and feids that had passed or fallen furth
between them in any time bygone."* A noble resolution, truly !
which, if faithfully carried out, would have had a happy effect on
the rival houses, and given a slight foretaste of the millenium to
the county. Unfortunately their bond of union was feeble as a
thread of flax, their friendship transitory as a wintry sunbeam on
snow-clad hills, their interchange of kindly words delusive—

> " The torrent's smoothness ere it dash below."

The Johnstones had become hand and glove with the Lord
Warden. They would therefore be able, so far as he was concerned, to enter upon predatory pursuits with impunity, if they
only left unharmed the dependants of the house of Maxwell. So
thinking, a party of the Annandale men, headed by William Johnstone of Wamphray, surnamed the Galliard, sweeping into Upper
Nithsdale, ravaged the lands of Lord Sanquhar ; but all the rich
"hereship" acquired by them was no equivalent for the loss they
sustained—as their trusty leader, taken by the Crichtons, was
without remorse converted by his captors into a "tassel" for the
gallows tree, though the poor fellow, in view of such an ignomini
ous doom, prayed hard for mercy, and tried to win by bribe what
he could not gain from pity. "O ! Simmy, Simmy !"—so he
pleaded to his chief captor, Simon of the Side—

> " O ! Simmy, Simmy, now let me gang,
> And I'll ne'er mair a Crichton wrang ;
> O ! Simmy, Simmy, now let me be,
> And a peck o' gowd I'll gie to thee."

William Johnstone of Kirkhill, on whom the leadership of the
"lads of Wamphray" now devolved, mustered them in great force,
in order to levy more spoil, and exact what was even sweeter to a
Borderer than any amount of stouthrief—revenge.

> " Back tae Nithsdale they hae gane,
> And awa the Crichton's nowt hae ta'en ;
> And when they came to the Wellpath-head,
> The Crichtons bade them ' 'Light and lead.' "

That is to say, dismount and give battle—the very thing that
Kirkhill Willie wanted, and which he promised to supply the
Crichtons with to their hearts' content.

> " Then out spoke Willie of the Kirkhill,
> ' Of fighting, lads, ye'se hae your fill ;'
> And from his horse Willie he lap,
> And a burnished brand in his hand he gat.

* Annandale Papers.

> Out through the Crichtons Willie he ran,
> And dang them down, baith horse and man.
> O but the Johnstones were wondrous rude,
> When the Biddes Burn* ran three days blude."

In returning homewards the exulting victors left other unpleasant
memories of their foray on the lands of Drumlanrig, Closeburn,
and Lag ; and if the ballad from which we have quoted is to be
relied upon, they—quite in character—wound up their saturnalia
by a jovial carouse in a tavern at the head of Evan Water :—

> " As they cam in at Evan head,
> At Ricklaw Holm they spread abread.
> ' Drive on, my lads, it will be late ;
> We'll hae a pint at Wamphray Gate.' "

And there Willie of Kirkhill, proud, exultant, elated with success,
and (shall we say ?) "glorious" with the "barley bree," thus complimented his gallant followers :—

> " Where'er I gang, or where'er I ride,
> The lads of Wamphray are on my side ;
> And of a' the lads that I do ken,
> The Wamphray lad's the king of men."†

---

* Biddes Burn, a brook which waters a mountainous tract lying between
Nithsdale and Annandale, near the head of the Evan.

† Sir Walter Scott seems to have attached no small amount of historical
value to the ballad from which these verses are taken—"The Lads of Wamphray ;" and we have quoted from it because it is true to the spirit, if not to
the letter, and the incidents tend to illustrate the character of the Border
raids.

CHAPTER XXV.

THE sufferers from this rapacious incursion naturally complained
of it to the Warden, and asked for redress at his hands—a request
which placed him in an awkward dilemma. He did not wish to
revive his old feud with the Johnstones; and perhaps he also
believed that they had some right to reckon on his forbearance,
though there was no express compact to that effect between them.
Two influences, however, combined to make him resolve on warlike
measures, though he was personally inclined to peace. The proprietors who had been pillaged, and were impatient for revenge,
offered to enter into bonds of manrent with him to maintain his
quarrels against all and sundry, provided he would exercise his
authority as Warden to punish the Johnstones; and the King
about the same time issued a special commission to him, by which
he was enjoined to execute justice on the guilty clan. James had
been induced to take this step by a singular deputation from
Nithsdale, consisting, says Calderwood, of "certain poor women,
with fifteen bloody shirts," who presented themselves in the
streets of Edinburgh on Monday, the 23rd of July, and in presence
of the Court prayed for justice on those who, at the instance of
the Laird of Johnstone, had cruelly murdered their husbands,
sons, and servants. As their petition did not receive that prompt
attention which they expected, a procession of the bloody shirts
was resolved on; and these were carried through the streets "by
pioneers," whilst a sympathising crowd cried out for vengeance

upon the King and Council,* till they at length paid attention to the widows' prayer.

Lord Maxwell saw in the offer of the Nithsdale gentlemen a means of increasing his following and strengthening the power of his family ; and when to this temptation was added the positive command of his sovereign, he hesitated no longer, but forthwith took the field against his hereditary enemy. Perhaps we do the noble lord no injustice when we suspect that the prospect of wreaking vengeance on the ancient foes of his house had some influence also in determining his conduct.

Johnstone on his part was not idle. On seeing sure indications of a pending storm,† he prepared to meet it by an alliance with his maternal relatives the Scotts of Eskdale and Teviotdale, five hundred of whom came to his aid under the leadership of Sir Gideon Murray of Elibank, who bore the banner of the Buccleuch in the temporary absence of that chieftain abroad. The Elliots of Liddesdale, the Grahams of the Debatable Land, and other Border tribes, also allied themselves to Johnstone ; and, as we learn from the Privy Council Records, "divers Englishmen, tressounablie brocht within this realme," swelled his ranks.

Maxwell, as a matter of form, summoned Johnstone to surrender in the King's name, and submit to be tried on the charges brought against him. The citation being treated with scorn, war was inevitable ; and, considering that it was a county conflict, the forces brought into the field were numerous on both sides. No fewer than two thousand men followed the royal banner, as displayed by the Lord Warden, into Annandale ; and nearly as many of the Johnstone party went forth to meet them. Sometimes the fate of kingdoms has been decided by smaller armies than those marshalled against each other by these rival chiefs.

The Nithsdale men would probably assemble at the usual place of wappenschaw—the meadow watered by the Lordburn, eastward of Dumfries—and be thence led round the head of Lochar Moss towards Lochmaben. A popular modern ballad‡ written on the battle that ensued gives what is at best a doubtful list of the different companies that made up Lord Maxwell's army. Two churchmen—the Abbot of Newabbey and the Vicar of Carlaverock—are represented as leading a hundred men each into the field ; but some years prior to the date of the conflict they had

* Calderwood.

† According to Spottiswoode, the bond of agreement between Maxwell and the Nithsdale gentlemen, " being negligently kept, fell into the hands of one Johnstone of Cummertrees, and was by him carried to the Laird of Johnstone," who thus got timely notice of the combination entered into against him. (Vol. ii., p. 446.)

‡ The Battle of Dryfe Sands, by William M'Vitie, of which a neat edition, with notes, was recently published by Mr Halliday, bookseller, Lockerbie.

both been forfeited, and the days of fighting ecclesiastics had been brought to an end. The other contingents are given as follows : Crichton, Drumlanrig, and Dalzell, fivescore each ; Dalswinton and Cowhill, eighty-nine each ; Kirkpatrick, Carnsalloch, and Breckenside, " full fourscore" each ; Charteris, sixty ; Lag, fifty-four ; while, we are told,

> " The town Dumfries two hundred sent,
>   All picked and chosen every one ;
> With them their Provost, Maxwell, went,
>   A bold, intrepid, daring man.*
>
> Lord Maxwell's own dependants rose,
>   Eight hundred warriors truly bred ;
> Kirkconnell doth the reckoning close,
>   An hundred valiant youths he led."

It was in the dead of the year, when " dark December glooms the day," that this goodly-bannered host moved from the county town—its leader, as a matter of precaution, sending a recon-noitring company on before under the command of Captain Oliphant. The ill-fated troop went to watch the enemy's move-ments, but was too rash and regardless of its own. When in the neighbourhood of Bruce's ancient burgh, a numerous body of the Johnstones, led by James Johnstone of Kirkton, rushed suddenly upon Oliphant's men, and put many of them to the sword, the Captain himself falling in the fray. The rest fled for safety to the parish church ;† but it afforded them no protection. Fire was ruthlessly applied to the sacred building. As the roof was formed of straw, which fed the destructive flames, the edifice soon became literally too hot to hold the refugees, and they were forced to sur-render. Thus the war opened in a manner that foreboded evil to the men of Nithsdale. Maxwell, however, on hearing of the disaster, hurried forward, hoping soon to eclipse it by a brilliant victory.

Late on the 6th of December, 1593, he crossed the Lochmaben hills with his army, encamping for the night on the Skipmyre heights, below which, at a considerable distance, flowed the Dryfe —so called from the driving rush of its waters when swelled by rain. Crossing this river next forenoon, the Maxwells found themselves faced by the Johnstones, the latter of whom were strongly posted on an elevated piece of ground, which now forms part of the parish glebe. This ridge is about forty feet high at its north end, and slopes gradually away southward : the Dryfe

---

* Whether the Provost was present at the battle or not, the name is correctly given, Homer Maxwell of Speddoch having been chief magistrate of the burgh in 1593.

† This church was a Gothic building, and dedicated to Mary Magdalene. After standing in a ruinous condition for some years, it was taken down in 1818. During the process the key of the old fabric was found, and after-wards sent to the Antiquarian Society of Edinburgh.

flowing at that time much further westward than at present, and
leaving room on its left bank for the evolutions of the combatants.
Sir James Johnstone possessed no small amount of military skill ;
and by disposing his men on this acclivity he was able to force
the Maxwells into an engagement on ground which the latter
would never of their own choice have taken up. Their position
was quite exposed, and they must either fight under serious disadvantages or commence a humiliating retreat—an alternative
which they never thought of resorting to. Johnstone further
strengthened himself and encouraged his men by some adroit
preliminary manœuvring, which Maxwell, relying mainly on sheer
force, failed to counteract. Had the hostile ranks closed on equal
terms, and in a trial of strength alone, the likelihood is that
Maxwell's high hopes would have been realised ; but from the
manner in which he was situated, and the mode of warfare chosen
by the opposing army, he was never able to bring above the half
of his men into action. Johnstone initiated the fighting by
" sending forth some prickers to ride and make provocation." On
went the horsemen thus commissioned, flaunting their pennons in
the faces of their foemen, hurling at them stinging epithets, if not
material missiles, challenging them to come on if they dared,
shouting the Johnstones' war-cry, "Ready, aye ready !" as if to
reproach the unreadiness of their opponents, and then riding back
unharmed to their own ranks.

To be bearded in this fashion was more than flesh and blood
of the Maxwell stamp could bear ; and when the tormentors
returned, repeated their exasperating conduct, and then exultingly
retired, the Warden—enraged at a time when coolness was
specially needed—sent a large detachment after them, who rushed
forth impetuously, crying, "Wardlaw ! Wardlaw !" varied by " I
bid you bide, Wardlaw !"*—the well-known slogan of the Nithsdale chief. This was the very movement which Johnstone had
wished to provoke. The retreating horsemen never thought of
turning rein in a vain attempt to stem the torrent let loose upon
them. Getting out of the way as rapidly as possible, they allowed
it to be met by those who were standing ready to roll it back, and
who did so. The Nithsdale detachment was received by a much
larger body, and broken up ; and its fragments, falling back, communicated to the main body of the Maxwells a share of its own
confusion. This was the crisis of the battle. As yet there had
been nothing but skirmishing, and little bloodshed ; and if the
Warden's army had stood firm when the Johnstones, in full force,
charged down upon them, the fortunes of the day might still have
been redeemed. As soon as the Annandale men left the heights

* Wardlaw is the name of a hill in the immediate vicinity of Carlaverock
Castle.

they gave up all the advantages of their position—only, however, to improve the advantage given by the panic into which the Maxwells were thrown. The latter never recovered from the disorder caused by the repulse of their assailing troops ; and when, consequent upon that mishap, they were visited with a general assault, they, after a brief but desperate resistance, gave way on all sides. The Lairds of Lag, Closeburn, and Drumlanrig escaped by the fleetness of their steeds ; but there is no historical evidence that the charge represented as brought against them by Lord Maxwell's son in the old ballad was well founded :—

> " Adieu ! Drumlanrig, false wert aye,
>   And Closeburn in a band !
> The Laird of Lag frae my father that fled,
>   When the Johnstone struck off his hand.
>
> They were three brethren in a band—
>   Joy may they never see !
> Their treacherous art and cowardly heart
>   Has twined my love and me."

Lord Maxwell was less fortunate than his brother barons. When resistance was useless he retreated with the relics of his army from the field—each of the fugitives going his own separate way, but most of them proceeding in the direction of Lockerbie, the victors following hard upon their track, and ruthlessly slaying all whom they overtook. On the Holm of Dryfe, about half a mile below the old churchyard of the parish, were to be seen till recently two large bushes called " Maxwell's Thorns," which commemorated this sanguinary battle and its sorrowful episode—the death of the defeated nobleman. To the spot where these venerable trees " scented the dewy air" came the Lord of Nithsdale when the fight was over and hope was gone, no way eager to survive his disgrace, and easily overtaken by a young Annandale trooper—the sanguinary hero of Biddes Burn—who had resolved to capture, maim, or kill the enemy of his clan. Some days before the battle Maxwell, it is said, had offered a ten-pound land to any one who should bring him the head or hand of Johnstone ; which caused his antagonist to retaliate by announcing that, though he had not a ten-pound land to give, he would bestow a farm of half that value on the man who should bring him the head or hand of Maxwell. Stimulated by this tempting offer, and also perhaps by hatred towards the Nithsdale men, which all the blood shed at Biddes Burn had failed to slake, William Johnstone of Kirkhill hurried after the fugitive lord and struck him from his horse.*
According to a report mentioned by Spottiswoode, the unfortunate baron held out his hand and claimed to be taken prisoner, even as he had in similar circumstances spared the life of the Laird of Johnstone ; but, instead of his plea being heeded, the

---

* Spottiswoode, vol. ii., p. 446.

supplicating hand was cut off, and then he was slain outright. Tradition, on the contrary, states that Willie of Kirkhill, after obtaining the ghastly sign-manual which attested his claim to receive a five-pound land from his chief, rode away, and the wife of James Johnstone of Kirkton, discovering Maxwell lying wounded, beat him to death—a story which we reproduce, though it seems to us highly improbable.

Soon after the battle, it is said, Dame Johnstone issued forth from Kirkton Tower, with a female attendant, for the purpose of seeking her husband, and also of giving relief to those who might have been left wounded on the field. Locking the gates with her own hand, and having the heavy keys suspended to her girdle, she soon reached the precincts of the fatal spot, and there, in the dim gloaming, discovered the hapless warrior lying bleeding and faint under an old fir tree. On her bending down to inquire his name and condition, the sufferer gasped out, "I am the Lord Maxwell ; succour me, or I die !" and caught his visitor convulsively by her garment. Thus appealed to, the Dame, cruelly dour, as if she had not had a drop of "weeping blood" in her bosom, swung the ponderous keys by the cord which fastened them, and brought them down sheer on the head of the prostrate suppliant. Blow after blow of this kind, until the chieftain's brains were knocked out, formed the sole answer given by this fiend in lady's likeness to his cry for mercy ; and she strode away from the mangled carcase mightily satisfied with her evening's work. But this Annandale monster is, we believe, a mere creation of the fancy ; and we notice the legend only to say that it is unworthy of credit. The likelihood is that Willie of Kirkhill, taking a lesson from the Kirkpatrick motto, made sure of his reward by cutting off the head as well as the hand of the prostrate warrior. Slain he was at all events ; and the body of the brave lord, lying gory and mutilated on the banks of Dryfe, was a pitiful sight, had it been seen by eyes susceptible of pity ; a chief of high descent, the head of a noble house, the representative of royalty, and in spite of his turbulent temper possessing many personal claims to respect and affection—being, as Spottiswoode says,[*] "of great spirit, humane, courteous, and learned"—to be thus ruthlessly mutilated and slaughtered in his manhood's prime, was indeed tragical, and strikingly illustrative of the fury too often engendered by the Border feuds.[†]

His followers suffered to a fearful extent. Never before had

---

[*] Spottiswoode, vol. ii., p. 447.

[†] Sir Walter Scott, in "Tales of a Grandfather" (p. 153, royal octavo edition), speaks of Maxwell as being an elderly, grey-haired man—agreeing in this respect with most other historians ; but Maxwell, as we learn from the family pedigree at Terregles, was born in 1553, and was consequently only forty years of age at the time of his death.

the Johnstones obtained such an opportunity of smiting their hereditary foes. Comparatively few of the Maxwells fell in the battle, but hundreds of them were cut off in the flight ; and many who escaped with life were cruelly wounded, especially by slashes in the face—called proverbially " Lockerbie licks "—marks of which they bore till their dying day. The fugitives were pursued as far as the Gotterby ford of the river Annan, in which numbers sank, and swelled the roll of victims. Altogether not fewer than seven hundred of the Maxwell party perished in the disastrous battle of Dryfe Sands, the bloodiest of an internecine kind ever fought on the Border fells.

When visiting the scene of this conflict on a late occasion, we in fancy summoned forth the opposing squadrons, and watched them closing in deadly combat. Johnstone, skilled in strategy, coolly keeping his vantage ground ; the Maxwells, provoked to advance when their sole chance of safety lay in remaining still, advancing, climbing the ridge under the bewildering dazzle of a meridian sun ; the terrific counter-charge, as the men of Annandale, rolling down like an avalanche, broke the enemy's battalions, and turned their confusion into a ruinous panic-rout ; the luckless Lord of Nithsdale, hurrying from the field, overtaken, and mercilessly slaughtered ; the other fugitives, not caring to climb the hills over which they had travelled on the previous day in hope and joy, wending their darkling, dolorous way to the south-west, and thus, as it were, rushing into the heart of the enemy's land, to be mutilated or perish : all these scenes and incidents crowded vividly on our mental vision, till we forgot the glory of the natural scenery watered by the Dryfe, in the exciting reminiscences of a struggle which made its stream run red. We sought unsuccessfully for the Maxwell Thorns—those interesting memorials of the chief's violent death, and of the bloody field. Not a trace of them is now to be seen, they having been swept away by the river when in flood upwards of twenty years ago. A fragment of one of them was transplanted to a place not far distant, beyond the water's sweep ; but this vestige of the monumental bushes has also disappeared.*

The oldest funeral letter we have seen is one sent by William Lord Herries to Sir John Maxwell of Pollok, asking him to attend the obsequies of his kinsman. It is in these terms :—" Ye have hard of the unfortunat slauchter of your chieff, my Loird Erle of Mortoun. I, with advyis of his frendis here, hes thocht meit that the buriall of his body salbe upon Soneday, the penult of December

---

* Another arboreal memorial of the conflict may still be seen in the neighbouring parish of Applegarth—" The Albie Thorn," planted about half a mile distant from the locality of the battle, to denote the place where Bell of Albie, a follower of the Johnstones, fell while in pursuit of the discomfited fugitives.—Statistical Account, p. 183.

instant ; and [your attendance is desired] becaus ye are ane of
his speciall friendis quhais presence is most requisite, baith for
the furthset of the burriall, and for youir counsell to be had anent
the taking ordour with his Loirdshippe's bayrnis leving and
friendis.—Dumfries, xi. Dec., 1593."* Soon after the funeral of
her husband the sorrowing Countess of Morton left the district
which was so full of bitter memories, seeking for repose in the
Castle of Mearns, Clydesdale, the barony of which had been
acquired by the Maxwells in the thirteenth century.

When news was brought to King James of the despite done to
his authority by the defeat and slaughter of his representative in
Dumfriesshire he was much incensed ; and had he not been
detained in the north by engrossing State affairs, he would have
taken active measures personally to chastise the Annandale chief.
Johnstone was forthwith "put to the horn," and proscribed as a
rebel ; and it was announced that those who intercommuned with
or harboured him would be deemed traitors to the King's majesty.
But Johnstone had discomfited the royal host, had abased and
slain his proud rival, the King's lieutenant, and did not care a
pin's fee for the King's proclamation. James might be monarch
of Scotland, and obeyed as such by barons who had not coped
with him ; but the head of the Johnstones was king in his native
dale, and to think of outlawing him there, or isolating him from
his kinsfolk, was simply ridiculous.

Nevertheless for nearly two years after the conflict at Dryfe
Sands Dumfriesshire enjoyed a considerable amount of repose ;
and it was not till an attempt was made, in the autumn of 1595,
to seize some of the refractory Johnstones that the peace of the
county was again broken. On the death of Maxwell Lord Herries
was appointed Warden of the Western Marches. He was enjoined
by the King to meet with other barons in Dumfries for the purpose
of restoring quiet ; and but for the steps taken by them the banks
of Nith would, in all probability, have suffered from an Annandale
raid. Having maintained order in Nithsdale for many months,
the new Lord Warden thought he would endeavour to tranquillise
the district over which Sir James Johnstone held lawless sway.
With this good object in view Herries summoned a meeting of
Maxwells in the shire town ; and as the fighting men of the clan
had been much reduced by the late defeat, the Nether Pollok
branch of the family furnished a welcome contingent for the
meditated expedition. At the head of three hundred followers
Herries proceeded from Dumfries to Lockerbie, and daringly laid
hold of several offenders belonging to the dominant clan. Other
Johnstones—true to their family motto—mustered in great force,

* Maxwells of Pollok, p. 170.

rushed to the rescue of their friends, and after a sanguinary engagement drove the invaders from the dale.

What to do with Sir James Johnstone now was a perplexing question, which the King tried to solve by the singular expedient of constituting him Warden in room of Lord Herries. When the turbulent baron found himself, in April, 1596, invested with that high office he must have been filled with wonder. It was indeed strange that he should have been made keeper of the King's peace who had broken it so often ; but it was in noways strange that he felt awkward in his new office, and gained no credit for the way in which he discharged its duties.

The gossiping chronicler Birrel records in his diary,* under date July 13, 1597, "an feight or combat betuix the Laird of Drumlanrick and the Laird of Johnestoun, and their assisters ;" and afterwards the latter fell into such disgrace that, we are told, on May 27, 1598, "the Laird of Johnestoun his pictor [was] hung at the Crosse [of Edinburgh], with his heid dounwart, and declarit ane mansworne man ; and upon the 5 of Junij he and his complices wer put to the horne, and pronuncit rebellis at the Crosse be opin proclamation." According to the same authority Johnstone soon recovered from his fall, he having been, on the 2nd of July, 1600, "restorit to hes honours, at the Crosse of Edinburgh, be the proclamatione of a herald and four trumpettis." We may infer that the wardenship was again conferred upon him. For a year or more previous to the latter date that perilous office was held by Sir John Carmichael, who was cruelly murdered by a party of "broken men" whilst going to open a court at Lochmaben—his death affording another instance of Border lawlessness at this period.

In November, 1597, James found himself under the necessity of going down to the Western Border to act as his own warden. Early in the month he arrived at Dumfries firmly bent on repressing the turbulence of the district. "A resolution," says Moysie,† "not to return therefra till that turn was effectuale, as indeed his Majesty did meikle to it." In order to secure this object the King established a Court of Redress in the burgh, made up of "aucht special honest gentlemen of the county, least suspect, maist neutral and indifferent, and the best inclined to justice," with "twa or three of his Majesty's Council appointit to be present with them." A large military force attended upon the sovereign, without which his judicial efforts would have been unavailing ; the individuals he had to cope with caring nothing about the majesty of the law, and being totally unconscious of the "divinity that doth hedge a king." The court and its royal president had a busy four weeks

* Diary of Robert Birrel, burgess of Edinburgh.
† Memoirs of the Affairs of Scotland, by David Moysie (MS.), as quoted in Chambers's Domestic Annals.

of it. During that time they, after trial, "hangit fourteen or fifteen limmers and notorious thieves ; whilst from every branch of the offending septs they seized one or two leaders as hostages "that the haill stouths and reifs committed by them, or any of their particular branch, should be redressed, and that they and all theirs should abstene from sic insolency in time coming, under pain of hanging." These live pledges were not, it appears, put into the ordinary pledge-house, but distributed, to the number of thirty-six, over houses rented for the purpose, where they were required to pay rather less than twopence sterling [each] for their maintenance daily. In this way the King to some extent redressed the wrongs which Johnstone had overlooked ; and on returning to Edinburgh he carried with him the hostages, as a security that the Johnstones, Armstrongs, Bells, Irvings, and others whom they represented, should continue at peace. He also constituted Lord Ochiltree his lieutenant ; and that nobleman remained at Dumfries several months, doing his best, by a judicious distribution of rewards and punishments, to pacify the shire. "In the course of that period," says Moysie, "he hangit and slew three score of the most notable thieves, and kept the country in great quietness and guid order."

But the young Lord of Nithsdale had no desire to live at amity with the Johnstones so long as his father's death remained unavenged. He cherished a feeling of vindictive hatred against their chief, which the King (who had, as we have said, again taken the latter into favour) tried in vain by threats and entreaties to allay. In order to keep the incipient strife in check his Majesty commanded Lord Maxwell to withdraw to the Castle of Mearns, in Clydesdale. After remaining there a year or more he returned, towards the close of 1601, without the royal permission, for the avowed purpose of compassing the ruin of his rival ; and, as an earnest of his purpose, he made a destructive incursion into Annandale. Proceeding to Dalfibble with his friends, they set fire to the place, slew William Johnstone, brother to the Laird of Elsieshields, and burned down the house of Briggs—its owner, James Johnstone, perishing in the flames. The disorders thus created brought the King again into Dumfriesshire. Probably, if he had banished both Johnstone and Maxwell, and taken security that they would remain "furth of the realm," he might have secured the repose of the county.

James adopted no such resolute measures. In his usual feeble way he ordered Lord Maxwell to betake himself again to the banks of Clyde, and before doing so to grant "letters of slanes," dated 11th June, 1605, on behalf of his hated rival ; according to which Maxwell "for himself, and taking burden for all others concerned, in favour of Sir James Johnstone of Dunskellie, knight, his kin, friends, servants, and dependents, remits and forgives all hatred, rancour, mutual grudge, and quarrel which he had against him for the slaughter of John, Lord Maxwell, his father, and all other slaughters, mutilations, and insolencies which followed thereon."* The "mutilations" here specified refer, doubtless, to the "Lockerbie licks" received by the men of Nithsdale after their defeat at Dryfe Sands. So soon as his Majesty's back was turned, and in spite of the meek, forgiving spirit breathed in this document, the obdurate young nobleman reappeared in Dumfries to concoct new plots and stir up fresh broils.

Edinburgh Castle, to which Maxwell was next consigned as a sort of reformatory prison, wrought no improvement upon him, and indeed could not cage him long. Escaping in January, 1603, he was proclaimed an outlaw. For some time neither the Government officers nor the chroniclers of the period could trace his whereabouts, till at length the latter discovered him, near the close of 1607, suddenly restored, like the hero of a pantomime, to the free enjoyment of his rank and estates; and we do not learn from them that he was ever called upon to underlie the law for his numerous offences. At the above period, says Chalmers,† "a contest arose between Lord Maxwell and the Earl of Morton [Angus] about their several jurisdictions in Eskdale ; and both parties called out their people to decide their pretensions—not in the forum, but the field. The Privy Council, which in some measure now governed Scotland, commanded the contending parties to dismiss their forces, and not approach the scene of their controversy ; but Maxwell contemned the order [as might have been looked for], and challenged his antagonist to single combat. For these contempts Maxwell was submitted to Edinburgh Castle, which seems never to have been a safe State-prison, and from which Maxwell again effected his escape. But he only escaped to engage in a more fatal outrage." This last sentence introduces us to a new act in the dreadful Border tragedy, which, originating mainly in the capricious disposal of the Western wardenship, culminated at Dryfe Sands, and did not terminate till the two principal remaining actors in it, the chiefs of the rival clans, fell dead upon the stage ; one treacherously shot by the other, and the assassin publicly executed for his crime.

It was by a combination of violence and stratagem that the noble prisoner effected his escape. On the 4th of December, in accordance with arrangements made between himself and his fellow-captives, Sir James M'Connell and Robert Maxwell of Dinwoodie, or the Four, he gave an entertainment to them and the keepers of the castle ; which the latter, who must have been a set of jolly, easy-minded varlets, patronised to such an extent that they became intoxicated. Lord Maxwell, artfully pandering to

---

* Annandale papers.   † Caledonia, vol. iii., p. 113.

the vanity of the inebriates, requested to see which of them wore
the best weapon. Their swords being produced, he handed one to
each of his friends, and took one himself : but instead of comparing the arms, they hurried off with them ; and when the astonished
wardens reeled to the door to seize the fugitives, they found it
locked. A few minutes before Maxwell had sent his servant to
Struthers, the porter, to facilitate their passage through the inner
gate. The servant easily enough obtained leave to pass, but when
Struthers wished to close the gate again the former put his back
to the wicket, upon which the three men coming up glided out,
the porter receiving a cut in the hand from Lord Maxwell as he
tried to arrest their progress. M'Connell having his irons on was
unable on that account to surmount the outer wall, which the
other two prisoners readily scaled, and secured their freedom.
How wroth King James was on account of Maxwell's forcible
breach of ward is shown by a letter which his Majesty addressed
to his Privy Council, on the 14th of December, 1607, the substance
of which we subjoin :—" The leatt escheap of the Lord Maxwell,
furth of our Castell of Edinburghe," says his Majesty, "haveing
gevein to us moir nor just caus of discontentment at his foly, we
have thocht meitt heirby to direct you how to proceid aganes him.
And first, we will this Proclamatioun, herewith sent, to be pub-
leissed at all placeis neidfull ; and that you hairefter tak ordour
fore tryale of all reseattares and suppleares, and caus the extream-
etie of the law to be prosequit aganes thame. And also you sall,
upon ressait heirof, presentlie send chairges of tressoune for the
rendering of his castellis and houssis, and you sall put garesounes
and keipars in everie one of the same to be interteined upon the
rentis belonging to the houssis, unto such time as we doctak
farder orders thairwith. And als our will is that you give particular directioune to suche as sall ressave the Castell of Lochmabene
that they mak delyverie of the same to our rycht trustie coising
and counsallovr the Erll of Dunbar, or to ony other quhome the
said Erll of Dunbar sall direct, with our uther warrand for ressave-
ing thairof. Furthermore, you sall cause chairge the principallis
of the said Lord Maxwell, his name and followairis, being ony way
men of mark, to find cautione and suertie, under gritt pecuniall
panes, that they sall noway resailt, supplie, nor intercommune
with him. You sall in lyk maner geve speciall ordour to our
garisoune under the Lord of Scone's command, and als to that
uther under Sir Wm. Cranstoune's chairge, that they mak specialle
searche for the said Lord Maxwell, his taking and apprehending.
And heiroff, willing you to be cairfull, and to omit nothing that
may haisten ane exempler puneishment upon him, for his prowd
contempt."

In the course of a short time after the receipt of this letter one
of the Privy Councillors, Sir Thomas Hamilton, in name of the

whole, addressed a letter to the King setting forth that it had been represented to them that unless the crimes for which Lord Maxwell and Sir James M'Connell had been imprisoned were treasonable their breach of ward could not import treason. "As to the Lord Maxwell," he said, "I have heard of his raising of fyre at Dalfibbill, when he slew Willie Johnestoun, callit of Eschieschielles, and ane uther Johnestoun;" but he added circumspectly, "because he has sensyne had the honour to be admitted to your royall presence I wald not presume to summond him for that fact while first I sould knaw your Majestei's mynde thairanent; the knaulege whairof sall lead me to proceid or desist."

The royal reply to this request for instructions has not been preserved. That it was of an unrelenting nature may be fairly inferred from the letter subsequently sent to the Council by the King, dated at the Palace of Whitehall, 2nd February, 1608, and which (omitting some unimportant passages) runs thus :—" We ar informed that, notwithstanding of the treassonable fact committit be the Lord Maxwell in eschaiping fourth of our Castell of Edinburghe, and in forceing and hurting of the keipares and portaris of the same, and of our speciall commandis and proclamatiounes, send doune for his taking and apprehending, that nevertheles in plane contempt of our authoritie, that he oppinley travellis throuche the countrie accompanied with no fewer than twentie horse, and hes mead his repaire at syndrie tymes to our burgh of Drumfreis ; quhiche insolence is no way tolerabill, and skairse excussabill on your pairtis, that ony of our declarit tratouris sould assume to themeselffis so mutche libertie without controlment. And thairfoir our pleasour and will is, that upon ressait heiroff, you direct that our Gaird, under the command of the Lord of Scoone, to repair to the burghe of Dumfreis, and thare, with that Gaird under Sir William Cranstoune's chairge, to make a present diligent searche for the said Lord Maxwell, and either to apprehend him or put him out of thoise boundis. Thairwith also the Baillies of Drumfreis wold be chairgit to compeir befoir you, and if you can try any thing of their knawledge of the said Lord Maxwellis being in thair toune, We ar to will you to inflict ane exemplare puneishment upone thame, baith by fynning and wairding. And als, you are to proceid in rigoure, according to the warrant of our lawis, aganes all reseattares and accompaniaris of the said Lord, that so others may be affrayed from coming within the compass of the lyk contempte."

CHAPTER XXVI.

IT was when Lord Maxwell was in the harassing and perilous circumstances indicated by the correspondence given in the preceding chapter that a memorable meeting was brought about between him and the man who had occasioned the slaughter of his father at Dryfe Sands. An opinion prevails that Maxwell made the overtures that led to it, and that he planned the interview to secure an opportunity of gratifying his desire for vengeance. While it appears to us very evident that he cherished this murderous intent, and longed for a chance of carrying it into effect, it seems not the less true that Johnstone of his own accord, and for objects of his own, took steps to secure a meeting with Maxwell.

Sir Robert Maxwell of Spottes, or Orchardtoun, declared in his deposition on the subject before the Privy Council that " the Laird of Johnstoun desyrit the deponar (being in his house of Lochwood for the tyme) to speik the Lord Maxwell quhen he fand the opportunitie, to sie iff the deponar could mak a [all] good in the materis betuix them." Sir Robert, however, declined the mission, assigning as his reasons that the matter was too weighty for him to take in hand : " that the Lord was a perellous man to haif ado with," and that Maxwell " haid evir a mislyking of him because he (the deponar) maryed Johnstone's sister."

Accordingly Maxwell of Spottes did not in the name of his brother-in-law bring the subject before Lord Maxwell ; but he stated further in his deposition that at the instance of Maxwell he met with the latter, who besought his advice and influence with the view of securing a pardon from the King ; upon which "the deponar" told Maxwell "that he sould keipe him quiet, and do no thing quhilk micht offend the Kingis Majestie farder nor he had done ; and that he (the deponar) wald move the noblemen, who were his friendis at Court and Counsell, to report the best of him

R1

to his Majestie and Counsell." A question from Sir Robert
Maxwell as to the relations in which his lordship stood towards
his neighbouring barons turned the conversation on the Laird of
Johnstone—Lord Maxwell asking "quhat he micht look for att
his handis in tyme comeing?" Sir Robert appears to have evaded
this question, and ultimately it was arranged that his lordship
should write out the heads of an agreement between himself and
Johnstone. At parting, the deponar said to my Lord : 'If this be
a mater that your lordship thinks in your hairte ye can tak up
and remett to the Laird, I will very willinglie travell in the
mater, and do the best I can ; otherwise, I desire nocht to mell
[meddle] in it.'"

Honest-looking and plausible was Maxwell's reply, to the
effect that "if he saw ony willingnes in the Laird to do dewtie to
him he wald willinglie pas it over, and if he resavit ane ressonn-
able answer of the Laird he wald be content to meete with him at
ony convenient place ; and promest that he sould keepe honnestlie,
for his pairt, and these that were with him, providing it war
keepit quiet for boith their weillis."

We learn from the rest of the deposition that the articles of
agreement drawn up by Lord Maxwell had a suspicious mistiness
about them ; that at a second audience given by him to the Laird
of Spottes the latter inquired as to their true meaning, and was
answered by his lordship that he was "not a good wreater,"* and
would not again put his wishes upon paper, but that all he
required was that Sir James Johnstone should show he had "not
bene a dealer aganis him in tyme bigane," and "what he micht
look for at his handis in tyme comeing ;" that Sir Robert, bearing
his relative's written answer to this verbal message, met Maxwell
a third time in the forest bowers beside the Abbey of Holywood ;
that the latter read the reply, and was "weill content thairwith ;"
and that then "the deponar" arranged for an interview, as agreed
to by Johnstone, the same to take place upon the following
Wednesday afternoon between three and four o'clock near the
House of Beal, his lordship to be accompanied only by one attendant—Robert Maxwell of the Tower ; Johnstone also to have but
one companion ; and "the deponar" to be present as a sort of
umpire between the principals. Finally, Sir Robert states that,
as a security that this "tryst" should be truly kept, and that
neither Maxwell nor his man should be guilty of foul play, he
received "my Lordis faithfull promeis, with my Lordis hand
strekit in the deponaris hands," that all their proceedings in the

---

* Scott makes Douglas, Earl of Angus, say—

    "Thanks to Saint Bothan, son of mine,
     Save Gawain, ne'er could pen a line."

But the ability to write was by no means a rare accomplishment among the
Dumfriesshire nobles and gentry so early as the sixteenth century.

matter should be faithful and honest, even should his projected agreement with Johnstone prove a failure.

If this "deponar" is to be received as a trustworthy witness, the Annandale chief was desirous of being reconciled to the son of the nobleman whose death he had occasioned, and was willing to secure that end by pleading for him with the King ; while, on the other hand, the son seemed ready to forgive the slaughter of his sire, provided he should through his good offices regain the royal favour. If, however, they mutually desired to meet with each other there is room for suspecting that the motives of one of the parties— Maxwell—were very different from those he professed to entertain. The result we think proves clearly that under the guise of peace and forgiveness he cherished implacable hatred ; that he intended the interview to have a fatal issue to the enemy of his house ; and that the circumstances associated with it were artfully contrived beforehand, for the purpose of making the foul murder look like an untoward accident, or at worst an unpremeditated case of manslaughter. So much by way of prologue : let us now endeavour to reproduce the scene itself.

On the afternoon of April 6, 1608, William Johnstone of Lockerbie visited his chief at Lochwood, by whom he was cordially welcomed. "Cousin," said the Laird, "ye must this day do a greater turn for me than ever I asked at your hands before. I am to meet with the Lord Maxwell, and ye shall go with me : push forward then to Little Lochwood, where I will join you presentlie ; but let no one ken where ye are riding to, or on what errand ye are bound." William Johnstone does as required, and whilst on the road is overtaken by two men on horseback—one of whom proved to be Sir Robert Maxwell of Spottes, and the other Sir James Johnstone (whom he had left a few minutes before), but whom he did not at first recognise, as he was differently apparelled than usual, and, for "secrecie of the tryst," was riding upon an old nag only fit for bearing a hind of low degree. After brief converse the three went on together, and ere long descried in the far distance the Lord of Nithsdale, attended by Charles Maxwell, "hoofing" on horseback to meet them. Whereupon Maxwell of Spottes, bidding his companions bide where they are until he returns to them, or give them a sign to advance, rides forward, meets Lord Maxwell, remonstrates with him that he is accompanied by such an ill-conditioned individual as Charlie Maxwell, instead of Maxwell of the Tower, and is told by his lordship that he will be answerable for his relative's good faith ; his lordship also renewing his own promise (suspiciously protesting too much) that, so far as both are concerned, there will be nothing but fair play.

The good-natured, well meaning mediator, though only half assured, resolved to risk the interview. Tying a napkin on his riding-switch, he displays it as a signal ; and thus summoned the Laird of Johnstone and his kinsman advance. Johnstone, though informed that Maxwell has with him an unlooked-for companion, seems well content, and to be troubled with no misgivings. "Ye need have no fear of the Lord Maxwell himself, at anyrate," said Sir Robert, "for I have taken his oath and promise, upon his faith and honour, that he will meet fairlie and part fairlie, whether a paction is made between ye or not ; and," added the good knight, "I must take from you the same oath and pledge." These are freely given ; and ere five minutes more elapse, the rival chiefs meet at a place called Auchmanhill, exchange friendly greetings, ride slowly on, accompanied by their mutual friend, who with characteristic prudence keeps between them as they (both directing their speech to him) begin to talk about their long fierce feuds, and the propriety of forgetting them henceforth ; though one of the parties, while indulging in honied words, is brimful of bitter hatred, and bent on shedding blood before that pacific period shall come to pass.

Whilst the principals are thus engaged the two subordinates wait near each other, as instructed by Sir Robert Maxwell, and the following dialogue ensues between them :—"Gif I had known of this tryst," said Charles Maxwell in a querulous tone, "the Lord Maxwell naither could nor should have brought me here." To which remark his companion replies : "I hope in God, Charlie, ye do not rue of coming here for so good an object ! for thir twa noblemen have been lang at variance, and I hope now they shall agree, and be gude friends." To which the other, working himself into a rage, retorts : "Agree ! impossible ! The Laird of Johnstone is not able to mak amends for the great skaith and injury he has done to the house of Maxwell !" "But," said Johnstone, soothingly, "our chief can come in his lordship's will, and do all he is able to satisfy him and his friends." "Not so," said the other, waxing more furious, or, at all events, getting seemingly into a tempest of passion ; "and as for this tryst, it is only made for our prejudice ; and that man "—pointing to Dunskellie—"has sought his wraik, and we should never have met you ; for ye are all traitors !—all traitors !"

Most provoking language this ; but Johnstone, knowing how all-important it is to avoid a quarrel at such a critical period, patiently protests that he will not enter into any altercation that day. "But," he added, his Border blood warming at the insulting language addressed to him, "send your man to me in a day or twa, and I shall satisfy you." No answer in words is returned to this remark : Charlie replies to it with a pistol shot. Johnstone raises his pistol to return the fire, but it flashes in the pan ; and then, at the pitch of his voice, he shouts, "Murder ! treason !" Sir James Johnstone, hearing the alarming cry, turns round to ride back ; so does Lord Maxwell ; the latter at the same time drawing a pistol, and preparing to take aim at Sir James. " Fie, my Lord !" cries Sir Robert Maxwell, in terror, "mak not yourself a traitor, and me both." " Upbraid me not," answers his lordship, " I am wyteless." Yet he follows the unsuspecting Laird of Johnstone—fires—the shot takes fatal effect—for a minute or more the dying man retains his seat—then the weak old nag below him founders—its girths give way—prone to the earth falls the ill-fated chief, treacherously slain in the flower of his age—life's sands ebbing rapidly away. His faithful friend vainly endeavours to get him borne off on his own powerful steed. While thus employed Charles Maxwell with superfluous malignity fires another pistol at the bleeding victim, who, after dolefully exclaiming, " I am deceived !" and fervently praying, " Lord have mercy on me !—Christ have mercy on me !' breathes his last, and is beyond the reach of the fiendish hate that plotted his ruin, and the help of the strong human love which his kinsman manifests by ineffectual sobs and tears !

"Come away ! let us be off !" cried Lord Maxwell, when the butchery was completed. "My lord," remonstrated his demoniac emissary, " will ye ride away, and leave this bludie thief Johnstone of Lockerbie behind ?" "What reck of him," quoth his lordship, " since the other has had enough !" and with these words both rode away from the dismal scene, and soon disappeared. Such is the picture obtained of this fearful tragedy from the legal depositions made by those who witnessed it, and who had no motive for depicting it otherwise than correctly.

It may be received as perfectly authentic, and it is sufficiently horrible without the aggravations given to it by Shawfield, whose manuscript account of the murder closes as follows :—"Sir James, hearing the shott and his man's words, turning about to see what was past, immediately shot him behind his back with ane pistoll chairgit with two poysonit bullets, at which shott the said Sir James fell from his horse. Maxwell, not being content therewith, raid about him ane lang tyme, and pursued him farder, vowing to use him more cruellie and treacherouslie than he had done ; for which it is known sufficiently what followed." We have never seen any evidence to support the allegation that Maxwell used poisoned bullets in order to render his shot more deadly ; but the " dittay," or indictment, charged him with having done so—the words used being " humerum duabus glandibus plumbeis vene-tatis." Maxwell and his colleague in crime were allowed to ride away without being called to account by the two friends of the murdered nobleman, which remissness on their part may be accounted for by supposing that they were in some measure deprived of their self-possession by the suddenness of the attack, and were but indifferently armed. Sir James Johnstone, thus barbarously slaughtered, was a brave, accomplished knight—"full

of wisdom and courage," says Spottiswoode ; and his death was
"severely lamented," and the manner of it "detested by all
honest men."

The murder of Dunskellie created a most painful sensation
throughout Annandale : it excited the indignation of the Government ; and the whole machinery of the law as it then existed,
local and general, was set in operation in order to bring the
criminal to justice. The kinsmen of the deceased clamoured for
the life of Maxwell ; and it was felt by the King and his councillors that the measure of his cup was now filled, and that he
must be severely—mercilessly dealt with. He had committed a
crime of the highest magnitude (that of treasonable murder, as
slaughter under trust was then termed), and must be called to
expiate it with his life. He was sought for in Nithsdale and on
the Border without success ; a hue and cry was raised for him
throughout the realm, with the same result. He durst not stay
in any nook or corner of broad Scotland ; and, uttering his
"Good-night !" as attributed to him by the old balladist from
whose lines we have already quoted, he sought for refuge in
France. The supposed feelings of the fugitive are so beautifully
expressed by the minstrel that we make no excuse for again
borrowing from his verse :—

> "Adieu ! madame, my mother dear,
>   But and my sisters three ;
> Adieu ! fair Robert of Orchardstane ?
>   My heart is wae for thee ;
> Adieu ! the lily and the rose,
>   The primrose fair to see ;
> Adieu ! my lady and only joy !
>   For I may not stay with thee.
>
> Though I hae slain the Lord Johnstone,
>   What care I for their feid ?
> My noble mind their wrath disdains :
>   He was my father's deid.
> Both night and day I laboured oft
>   Of him avenged to be ;
> But now I've got what lang I sought,
>   And I may not stay with thee.
>
> Adieu ! Dumfries, my proper place,
>   But and Carlaverock fair ;
> Adieu ! my Castle of the Thrieve,
>   Wi' a' my buildings there :
> Adieu ! Lochmaben's gates sae fair,
>   The Langholm holm where birks there be ;
> Adieu ! my lady and only joy !
>   For I may not stay with thee.
>
> 'Lord of the land,' that ladye said,
>   'O wad ye go wi' me
> Unto my brother's stately tower,
>   Where safest ye may be !
> There Hamiltons and Douglas baith
>   Shall rise to succour thee.'
> 'Thanks for thy kindness, fair my dame,
>   But I may not stay with thee.' "

No ! Maxwell durst not trust for safety even to the princely Hamiltons (a daughter of whose house he had married), nor to the doughty Douglases, to whom he was also related ; and so—

> " The wind was fair, the ship was clear,
>   The good lord went away ;
> The most part of his friends were there
>   To give him a fair convey.
> They drank the wine, they didna spare,
>   Even in that gude lord's sight—
> Sae now he's o'er the floods sae gray,
>   And Lord Maxwell has ta'en his good-night."

Meanwhile, legal proceedings were instituted against him ; the relatives of the murdered knight pressing on the trial with pardonable eagerness. In accordance with a precept from King James, dated Greenwich, June 6th, 1609, a Parliamentary Commission sat at Edinburgh on the 24th of the same month to try the case—Sir Thomas Hamilton of Bynnie, the King's Advocate, conducting the prosecution. The indictment was in the form of a summons of treason and forfeiture, drawn up in the Latin language, which set forth the several points of "dittay" laid to his charge, and was prefaced by an announcement to the effect that the summons had been found relevant by the Lords of the Articles, and Lord Maxwell been thrice called at the Tolbooth Wynd to answer it, but that he did not "compear ;" that thereupon the Advocate had been allowed to establish his case against the said Lord ; and that for this purpose the depositions of the witnesses examined in the case before the Lords of the Articles and the Lords of the Secret Council were read over, as also the Acts of Parliament bearing on the case, and the " Lettre of Horning aganis the said Lord Maxwell, for nocht compeirance befoir the Lordis of Secret Counsaill, to ansuer befoir thame for his breking of waird furth of the Castell of Edinburcht, for the burning made be him at Dalfeble, and for slaughter of the Laird of Johnestoun ; that lykwayes the said Advocat producit in presence of the said Lord Commissionar and haill estaitts Lettres of Relaxatioun, beirand the said Johne, Lord Maxwell, to be relaxit be James Dowglas, Messinger, fra the process of all horningis at the Mercatt Crosses of Lochmaben and Dumfreise, upon the xv. day of March, 1609 years, and at the Mercatt Croce of Edinburt, be Johne Moneur, Messinger, upon the xxiii. day of Marche, the yeir of God above writtin."

It is then stated that the summons having again been read on June 24th, in presence of the Commissioner and the Estates, and Lord Maxwell having again failed to appear in answer to it, his Majesty's Advocate desired the Estates to declare if the reasons of the summons were relevant ; and they having found that they were so, and having again heard the evidence, at his instance gave a verdict, finding that—" The said Johne Lord Maxwell committit and did open and manifest Tressoun, in all the pointis, articlis, and maner, contenit in the said Summondis : and thairfoir it was given for dome, be the mouth of David Lyndsay, Dempster of Parliament, in manner and forme as followss : *Sentence*—This Court of Parliament sehawes for law, the said JOHNE LORD MAXWELL to have committit and done all the foirsaidis crymes of Treassoun and Lesemajestie, be him self and others of his causing, command, assistance, and ratihabitioun, aganis oure said Soverane Lord and his authoritie ; and that he is and wes giltie and pairtaker, airt and pairt, of the samin crymes of Treassoun ; all in maner at lenth contenit in the ressounes of the said summondis : and thairfoir Decernis and Declairis that the said Johne Lord Maxwell aucht and sould underly and suffer the paynis competent to the saidis crymes of Treassoun and Lesemajestie, to witt the tynsall and confiscatioun of his lyfe, and all his guidis, moveable and unmoveable, landis, tenementis, dignities, offices, richtis, and all utheris thingis belanging to him ; and all the saidis landis, rowmes, and all gudis moveable, and unmoveable, digniteis, offices, richtis, and all utheris belanging and pertening to the said Johne Lord Maxwell, and quhilkis may ony way belang and pertene to him, to be confiscatt, to pertene to the said Soverane Lord, and to remane with his Majestie for evir in propertie." Such are the terms of the sweeping judgment passed upon the Nithsdale chief ; the grim official who pronounced it finishing as usual with the emphatic words, " And this I give for doom !"

Years passed away. Then the expatriated lord began to cherish a hope that the lapse of time had deadened the Johnstones' desire for vengeance, and that he might venture back to Scotland, and his crime be overlooked, if not forgiven. He had bidden his native land " good-night ;" but he shrunk from the idea of con- tinuing a perpetual exile and seeing Nithsdale no more. He thought as with the emigrant in the song that though the sun shone fair in France it had not the same sweet " blink " as in his own country. Mingling with regret for his guilt and its results (remorse would perhaps be too strong a term), and dread of judicial punishment, came overpowering thoughts of home—a yearning that would not be said nay to revisit the hills and dales among which he first drew breath. Yielding to its influence, he in 1612 returned to Scotland. The news of his arrival could not be kept a secret ; and whilst lurking in the Border district he was hunted like a wild animal by his old enemies, and was making ready to embark for Sweden when George Earl of Caithness offered him an asylum in the North. Thither the wearied Lord Maxwell went, dreading no harm, as the Countess was a cousin of his own. By a singular retribution he who had slaughtered the Laird of Johnstone under trust was while under trust betrayed by his own near relative to the Government. For the purpose of

currying favour with the King, the Earl of Caithness, who had by
fair promises lured Maxwell to Castle Sinclair, basely gave him up
to the officers of the law ; and from that day forth he and death
were brought face to face.

A short time afterwards the Lords of the Privy Council
addressed a letter to his Majesty asking him how they were to
deal with their prisoner. It is dated 28th April, 1613, and is in
the following terms :—" Most Gracious Soverane,—According to
your Majestie's directioun we [did] wryte for the Laird of Johnnstoun his moder and goode dame, to understand of thame gif they
wald persest in the persute of that petitioun, exhibite unto your
Majestie in their names, whairby they craved justice to be execute
upon the forfeeted Lord Maxwell for the slauchter of the Laird of
Johnnston with his moder and tutour presentit tham selffis before
us and declairit that thay wald insist in that persute and prose-
quutioun of that mater according to tennour of thair petitioun.
The auld Lady Johnnstoun, through seiknes and inabilitie of hir
persone, being unable to compeir before us, haveing with grite
difficultie come to this burgh for this same errand, we directit and
send the Bishop of Caithness, the Lord Kildrymmie, and Lord
Prevey Seale to hir, to understand hir will and pleasoure in this
mater ; unto quhome scho declarit, that scho come heir purposeli
for that mater, and that scho wald insist according to the tennour
of the petitioun ; sua that now thair restis no farder bot youre
Majestei's will and pleasoure to be declairit, quhat farder youre
Majestie will haif to be done ; wherein, although the conclusione
of your Majestei's lettre beiris that we sould proceid to the
administratioun of justice, yitt in respect of a word cassin in the
preface of the lettre, beirin that your Majestie had not as yitt
geiven a direct ansuer to their petitioun, we haif presumed first to
acquent your Majestie afoir we proceid ony farder ; and whatevir
it sall pleis your Majestie to direct in this mater sall be immedi-
atlie and without delay execute. Thair was a petitioun gevin in
this day unto us be Robeet Maxwell, brother to the said laite
Lord, with some offeris to the pairtie ; bot because the mater con-
cernit not us, we wald not mell tharin ; alwyse, we haif heirwith
send the same to your Majestie, to be considderit of as your
Majestie sall thinke goode."

In the petition or supplication of Lord Maxwell's brother here
referred to the Lords of the Council are entreated to use their
endeavours to get certain offers made by Maxwell to the Laird of
Johnstone and his relatives laid properly before them. Some of
the ministers of Edinburgh had been solicited to undertake this
duty, but they declined ; the bishops were then applied to, with
the same result—neither presbyters nor prelates wishing to be
troubled with the case of the condemned man, unless authorised
to interfere in it by the Council : " Sa that now," his brother

S1

wrote, " thair restis no menis quhairby the offeris may cum to the
parteis handis except your lordships will athir appoint sum
persones to present the same, or otherwayis that your lordships
wald convene the pairtie before your lordships, that the same in
your lordships' audiens may [be] red and delyverit to thame.
Theirfoir I maist humbly beseik your lordships to haif consideratioun of the premisses, and that your lordships wald gif directioun
to sum of the ministrie of this burgh to present the said offeris, or
otherwayes that your lordships wald call the pairtie in your
presence to the effect foirsaid."

The " Offiers of Submission by Lord Maxwell for the settlement of all differences between him and the surviving relatives of
Sir James Johnstone of that Ilk, Knight," which no one of note
would agree to lay before the proper parties, and which never
were brought under their consideration, were set forth in the
subjoined letter :—" Thir offeris following ar maid be me, Johnne,
sumtyme Lord Maxwell, for my selff, in name of my kyn and
friendis, to . . . . . now Laird Johnstoun, and his Tutouris
and Curatouris, Dame Sara Maxwell, Ladie Johnstoun, younger
for the tyme, his mother, Dame Margarret Scott, Ladie Johnstoun,
elder, his guddame, and to thair kyn and friendes, for the unhappy
slauchter of umquhile Schir James Johnstoun of that Ilk, Knyte,
committit be me.

" In the FIRST, I humblie confes my offens to God, the Kingis
Majestie, and to the foresaidis persones, for the said unhappie
slauchter, and declairis my selff to be maist penitent thairfoir ;
craveing first mercie at the Almichty God for the same, nixt
favour and grace of the Kingis Majestie, my soverane lord, and
forgifness of the great offence done to the foresaidis persones ;
testifeing be my solemne aith, upon my salvatioun and condemp-
natioun, that the foirsaid unhappie slauchter was nawayis committit be me upone foirthocht, fellonie, or sett purpois, but upone
meir accident : Lykas for cleiring thairof I am content to purge
my selff be my greit aith in publict, quhair it pleissis the parteis
to appoint and do quhat farder homage sall be thocht expedient.

" SECONDLIE : I am content, not onlie for my selff but for my
haill kyn and friendis, to forgiff the slauchter of umquhile John,
Lord Maxwell, my father, committit be the said umquhile Laird
of Johnnestoun and his complices, and to mak all persones quha
wes ather gyltie, culpabill, or airt and pairt of the said slauchter,
in securitie thairfoir, sua that thai nor nane of thame sall nevir
be trublit for the same be me nor be nane of my kyn and friendis,
directly nor indirectly, in tyme cuming ; and for that effect sall
mak sik forme of securitie as sall agrie with reasoun.

" THIRDLIE : Becaus . . . . Johnstoun, dochter to the said
umquhile Sir James, wes by the suddant and unhappie slauchter
of hir said umquhile father left unprovydit of ane sufficient tocher,

and for the better avoyding of all inmitie that may arryse betuix the houssis of Maxwell and Johnstoun, and for mair suir establisching of friendschip amangis thame in tym cuming, I am content to marie and take to my wyffe the said . . . . . without ony tochir.*

"FOURTHLIE : I desyre that the Laird of Johnstoun may be mareit to Dame . . . .† Maxwell, eldest dochtir to Johne, Lord Hereis, and sister dochtir to me, quha is a person of lyke aige with the Laird of Johnstoun. Lykas I sall be obleist to pay to the said Laird of Johnstoun, in name of tochir, with my said sister dochtir, twentie thowsand merk Scottis ; and quhat farder shall be thocht expedient, be the sicht of friendis.

"FYFTHLIE, and last : I am content, for the farder satisfactioun of the house of Johnstoun, to be banischit his Majestei's dominions for the space of sevin yeiris, and farder at the will and pleasour of the Laird of Johnstoun.

"Thir Offeris to be augmentit at the sicht and discretioun of newtral freindis, to be chosyn to that effeet. Under protestation, alwayis, that thir offerris befoir wryttin maid unto the pairtie, be nawayis offensive to the King's Majestie, nor to his hienes Counsall."

It is to be regretted that Lord Maxwell's declaration that the death of Sir James Johnstone was accidental is not supported by a particle of evidence. Had it been so, or had his crime assumed any aspect short of deliberate murder, the Government would gladly, we doubt not, have commuted the sentence in spite of the Johnstone family. The matrimonial offers made by the doomed lord would be amusing were not the accompanying circumstances so sad. It seems clear to us that the simple references in his lordship's "Submission" under the second head to the slaughter of his father ought finally to dispose of the outrageous legend which represents Dame Johnstone of Kirkton as having beaten the suppliant's father to death with a key at Dryfe Sands. If the lady had really acted such a diabolical part it would certainly have been pleaded by Lord Maxwell as in some degree a set-off to his own "unhappie" deed.

This document must have been penned by Maxwell when in prison , and on the 18th of May—less than a fortnight afterwards —the magistrates of Edinburgh visited him there, to say that his appeal for mediation and mercy had been disregarded, and that upon the following Friday, the 21st, he must be prepared to die. Their authority to this effect was given by the Privy Council in

* Lord Maxwell was at this time a widower; Lady Maxwell—heart-broken, it may be—having died when he was in exile.

† The blanks in all these instances occur in the original ; Lord Maxwell having, it would seem, been ignorant of the Christian names of the parties he wrote about.

the subjoined minute :—" Maij 18, 1613.—Ano Warrant past and exped to the Provest and Balyies of Edinburghe, to tak the lait Lord Maxwell to thair mercat croce, upon xxj. of this instant, and thair to caus strik his head from his body. The delay of tua dayis wes thocht meit to be grantit, to the effect that he micht have leaser to be resolved ; and that the ministeris micht have tyme to confer with him for his better resolution." The prisoner received the dread announcement with composure, professed to the magistrates his willingness to abide the pleasure of God and the King, and then requested liberty for such of his friends as he named to visit him, which was readily granted. " He had," says the writer of the Donmylne MSS., " diverse conferences with sindrie of them, in presence of ane of the Balyies, but refuised to ressave ony assistance or comfort from the ministeris, professing him selff not to be of thair religioun, but ane Catholik Romane." When the fatal day arrived, we learn from the same author, that, whilst the unfortunate nobleman was being conveyed to the scaffold, he declared that as he had justly deserved to die, so he was ready patiently to meet his fate, asking mercy of God for his sins, and anxiously wishing that his Majesty might be graciously pleased to accept his life's blood as a sufficient atonement for his offences, and not punish his house further, but be pleased to restore his brother Robert to the rank and place that had been forfeited by himself. On arriving at the place of execution he prayed that he might receive forgiveness from the Laird of Johnstone, his mother, and other relatives ; acknowledging " the wrong and harm done to them, with protestatioun that it was without dishonour or infamie (for the worldlie pairt of it—for so were these his wordis reported to me)." He also craved pardon of Pollock, Calderwood, and other friends present, bewailing that, though he ought to have promoted their honour and safety, he had brought to them nothing but discredit and harm. Then, drawing near to the block, he kneeled in prayer, turned to take leave of his friends, and the officials had his eyes covered with a handkerchief ; and offering his head to the axe, the weapon fell, and all was over in a moment.*

Thus ignominiously perished the ninth Lord Maxwell. He merited his awful doom ; but it was deplored by a host of mourners, many of whom looked upon his crime as a legitimate piece of feudal revenge. In the halls of Carlaverock and Terregles, in the burghal residences of Dumfries, and throughout all the borders of Nithsdale, there was much lamentation and woe on account of his cruel and untimely end. His own kinsmen and people did not view him in the light of a malefactor brought to justice : they pitied him as one who had been more unfortunate than guilty. He was their chief, the representative of an ancient and honoured house, who,

---

* The chief authority drawn upon for the incidents of this chapter is Pitcairn's Criminal Trials.

whatever might have been his faults to others, had done nothing
to forfeit their affection ; and how could they do otherwise than
sorrow for his fate? The execution of Lord Maxwell was, however,
followed by beneficial consequences. "It put a final end," as Sir
Walter Scott remarks, "to 'the foul debate' betwixt the Maxwells
and Johnstones, in the course of which each family lost two
chieftains : one dying of a broken heart, one in the field of battle,
one by assassination, and one by the sword of the executioner."
It also tended to the pacification of Dumfriesshire. As Dryfe
Sands was the deadliest party conflict ever waged in the county,
so it was the last by which its tranquillity was disturbed. Four
years after Lord Maxwell suffered at Edinburgh the forfeiture
included in his sentence was reversed ; and as he left no issue, his
estates and honours devolved on his younger brother Robert.

But the long, weary, wasting wars and feuds in which the
family had been engaged wrecked their patrimony. The lands,
burdened by crushing mortgages, yielded a balance of rental that
was inadequate to meet necessary outlays and maintain the
dignity of the house. Abundant evidence is supplied by the Pollok
Papers to show that the social position of Robert, tenth Lord Maxwell, was anything but an enviable one. What bitterness must
have been his when penning the following epistle to the Laird of
Pollok, sometime in 1616 :—

"I being ingageit in fortie thousand poundis Scotis, and
haveing tried all the friendship and meinis I can for the reliue of
the sam, and finding no posabilitie to help my present miserie
quhairby I may follow furth the suit at his Majestie's hand for
relief of the distressit hous of Maxwell, quhairoff, prasit be God,
thar is some hoip ; I offer to Sir John Maxwell, so that he will
will hezard to ingage him self in thes soumis for me, and the weill
of the hous quhairoff we are dissendit, that I shall infeft him in all
the landis and possessionis quhich I have alredie acqueyrit, upon
reversion, and that he sall haue power to plase factoris and
chanceilairis at his plesur for resaving the rentis therof, ay and
quhile he be lafullie fred and relivit of the said fortie thousand
pundis ; as lykweyis quhatsoever landis I shall acqueyer farder at
his Majestie's handis or anie utheris, the said Sir Johne sall be
presentlie infeft thereinto ; and all lykweyis that I sall cause my
brother James ratifie quhatsoever sall be contrackit betwixt the
said Sir Johne and me. Farder, I offer, if it sall pleis God to call
me and my brother James, the said Sir Johne sall be next in tallie
preferit to the hail estat that we or other of us sall acquyer, and
that he sall be our nyxt and immediat heir to us for that luife he
shois at this tyme. Farder, I sall give him libertie to sell anie
part of the landis that I am presentlie to infeft him into—spetiallie,
the barronie of Mernis, Carluerok, and the rest of the landis resingit
be Sir Jideon Murray, he alweyis hauing the advyse of the Erle of

Abercorne, his lordship being alyve; and that if the said Sir Johne
be so stratit for the prinsipall soum that he may not zielie uther-
weyes furnish the sam . . . . .   and giue the said Sir Johne
Maxwell find nocht him selfe abill to discharge this burding, I
offer the sam self condisinus to the rycht noble Erle of Aber-
cornie,* or anie of his bairns that it sall pleis him to nominat, they
alway acsepting the name of Maxwell upon them; and in case his
lordship or they sould thynk hard to change their name, I only
crave ane reversion to my nerest airsmill for the doubill of the
soume quhich his lordship or they sall be ingageit for me."

Lord Maxwell, however, obtained some measure of relief in a
less humiliating way than by bartering his birthright. King James
may possibly have stood his friend ; and we know with certainty
that the sale to the Laird of Pollok of some of the family estates
in Clydesdale brought him comparative ease, mental and pecuniary.
In 1620 we find the once impecunious baron no longer a prey to
poverty, and acquiring a new peerage—the earldom of Nithsdale—
created for him in lieu of that of Morton, which had been given
back to the Douglases.   This royal favour was, in all likelihood,
obtained through the influence of the Duke of Buckingham, whose
mother was cousin to Elizabeth Beaumont, the wife of Maxwell.

* This was Maxwell's near relative, James Hamilton, created Earl of Abercorn, Baron Arbroath, Hamilton, Mountcastle, and Kilpatrick, in 1606.

CHAPTER XXVII.

WHEN King James VI. had been fourteen years settled in the
southern portion of his dominions he, according to his own statement, felt "a salmon-like instinct" attracting him to the land of
his birth ; but, as events proved, there was something of a shark-
like design against Presbyterianism that drew him thither—the
chief object of his journey being, says Miss Aitken, "the establishment of the ecclesiastical system of England on the ruins of that
haughty Presbytery which continued to hold out an example of
such encouragement to the pretensions of the English Puritans."[*]
Wishing to dazzle the eyes of his Caledonian subjects, he set out
for the North, accompanied by a splendid train of courtiers,
headed by Buckingham, the dashing and handsome duke whom he
doated on and used to address familiarly as "Steenie." Afterwards,
however, a large proportion of the King's lavish expenses had
to be defrayed by a tax of 200,000 pounds Scots, levied in equal
proportion on "the Spiritual Estates, the Barons, and the Burghs"
of his poor ancient kingdom.[†]

James travelled by the east coast to Edinburgh, reaching it on
the 18th of May, 1617. In returning by the west he passed down
Nithsdale with his retinue in the closing week of July. His
"Sovrane Grace" reached Sanquhar on the 31st of that month,
the rulers of the royal burgh presenting him with a eulogistic
address, in which he was likened to Solomon and Lycurgus, to
Numa Pompilius and Julias Cæsar. Passing on to the old Tower
of Drumlanrig, he remained for a day under its roof as the guest of

---

[*] Memoirs of the Court of King James the First (of England), by Lucy
Aitken, vol. ii., p. 59.
[†] Acts of the Scot. Parl., vol. iv., p. 558.

William Douglas, first Earl of Queensberry*—the nobleman, who, some years afterwards, built the present magnificent Castle of Drumlanrig. In a grand Latin poem, of which specimens in English† are subjoined, Douglas sounded the praise of his own house, and gave cordial welcome to his royal guest :—

> " Divinely favoured, led by lucky star,
> Not for the first time sparkling from afar,
> Come to Drumlanrig Castle, gracious King—
> Rest thee beneath its broad palatial wing ;
> A banquet rich enjoy, and grateful sleep,
> For here the weary have no cause to weep.
>
> Why ranks this mansion high in storied fame ?
> 'Tis gilded by the glorious Douglas name ;
> And now new lustre o'er its turrets falls
> Since Sovereign Majesty has graced its halls.
> This kingly visit leaves a brilliant trace
> Which Time's destroying hand shall ne'er efface.
>
> If records of the past can thee invite,
> And deeds of other days thy soul delight,
> Among the Douglases of royal race
> There's one to whom attaches no disgrace—
> A James, who valiantly did fight for Bruce,
> Giving his foes no resting-place nor truce,
> Alumnus of the Muses and of Mars,
> Who won the symbol-heart with deadly scars.
>
> King Bruce had vowed if ever, when in life,
> He should be free from toil of mortal strife,
> He would repair unto the Holy Land,
> Which lay sore trodden by a Syrian Band.
> But leisure came not, and his vigour failed,
> By sickness, age, and public cares assailed,
> And as his wish could near be gratified,
> He gave this strange command before he died :
> ' My heart out of my body, Douglas, take,
> And for its shrine a silver casket make,
> Then bury it in the soil of Palestine,
> And thus accomplish that old vow of mine.' "

The poem goes on to recount the valorous mission of Douglas to the Holy Land, with the heart of his royal master, and his slaughter by a band of Saracens, whom he encountered on the way. Then it is said—

> " At death to his descendants he bequeathed
> The qualities with which they are enwreathed,
> Those virtues rare, which to this very day
> The house of Douglas ne'er has thrown away."

From this episode a return is made to the King's Majesty, who is

---

* This nobleman was the eldest son of Sir James Douglas of Drumlanrig, grandson of the baron of the same name who actively promoted the cause of the Reformation. He had three brothers : Sir James Douglas of Mouswald ; David Douglas of Airdoch ; and George Douglas of Penziere.

† Kindly supplied by Mr James M'Donald of the Dumfries Academy.

again cordially greeted, and on whom the favour of Heaven is (in classical style) invoked :—

> "And now to mighty Jove the prayer ascends—
> To Jove, who o'er the guests benignant bends—
> That he may will this famous day to be
> To Scots and British friends a jubilee ;
> Upon thy Highness may this day of days
> Pour pleasant memories, fraught with joy and praise.
> May Jove preserve thee long, our prayer is now,
> Till flowing grey hairs grace thy honoured brow ;
> Nay, more ; when thou, alas, art laid in dust,
> May Britons aye be bound by love and trust,
> And have the fortune on their throne to see
> A noble branch spring from the good old tree."

Bidding adieu to the Earl of Queensberry, King James continued his journey, making a call, it is said, on John, sixth Lord Herries, the grandson of his mother's friend, at the house which gave her temporary shelter after her flight from Langside. According to tradition, his Majesty spent the night of the 2nd of August in Lincluden College. Next day, Monday the 3rd, the joyful cry "Oor gude King's come !" rang through his loyal town of Dumfries—

> "Carle, noo the King's come !
> Carle, noo the King's come !
> Ye shall dance and I shall sing,
> Carle, noo the King's come !"

He was attended thither by the gentry of the district ; the probability being also that Duke "Steenie"—"the glass of fashion and the mould of form"—gave a crowning lustre to the royal train. On James's last previous visit to the county it was distracted by civil war : he now found it at peace, occupied with the pursuits of industry. Then he appeared in the shire town brandishing the sword of Justice—figuratively, we mean, for his Majesty shrank instinctively from the sight of bare steel ;* now he had no controversy to settle with its leading men, and he wore the gracious smiles of a paternal monarch. So recently as 1608 he had complained to his Privy Council of the audacious way in which the proscribed traitor Lord Maxwell had been countenanced in the burgh, and he had ordered its bailies to be taken to task on that account ; but in 1617 he has no faults to find with, and nothing but favours to confer upon, the magistrates and people.

How to give a fitting reception to the grand party must have been rather perplexing to the local authorities. The gentleman then at the head of the burgh, Provost John Corsane,† conferred

---

* In the "Fortunes of Nigel," chapter fifth, James is made to say of himself : "I am accounted as brave as maist folks, and yet I profess to ye I could never look on a bare blade without blinking and winking."

† In the first edition of this work it was mentioned as a tradition that Weir was the name of the Provost at this period. We have ascertained, however, that Herbert Cunningham was chief magistrate in 1616, and that

on the subject not only with his council and the town-clerk,
Cuthbert Cunningham, but also with the burgh's Parliamentary
representative, Francis Irving, and the Commissary, James Halliday of Pitlochie, advocate, all of whom, after "laying their heads
together," adopted a programme for the occasion, which included
a presentation from the ladies of the district, the delivery of an
address from the inhabitants generally, and a festive entertainment from the authorities of the town.

The first part of the proceedings must have made an effective
scene, performed as it was in the open air. King James, though
now venerable with age, and though rather odd-looking in his
bulky dagger-proof coat of green velvet and scarlet braguette to
match, would, of course, be the principal figure ; but the Duke
of Buckingham, stately and graceful in the picturesque attire that
will ever live on the canvas of Vandyke, would receive a large
share of notice, and be beyond the reach of rivalry from any of
the local magnates that were present. So popular, however, was
the member for the burgh that he would be sure on making his
appearance to receive an ovation from the assembled crowd ; and
when, following him and introduced by him, a bevy of fair matrons
graced the scene, hooded, ruffed, and farthingaled, as became ladies
of their condition, the excitement would reach its highest pitch,
and be expressed in such cheers as might sound rather boisterously
in the sensitive ears of the King.   The preliminary greetings over,
out stepped Dame Irving (the fair daughter of ex-Provost Raining,
and wife of the member) to perform the leading part assigned to
her in the ceremony. Making due obeisance to his Majesty, she
prayed him to accept a broad, massive gold coin, from an Italian
mint, as a token of love and welcome from his leal subjects, the
ladies of the burgh.* How James demeaned himself is not
recorded ; but it may easily be supposed that with all his natural
warmth, and all the awkward gallantry of which he was capable,
he would accept the offering, and tender his grateful thanks in the
expressive Doric, which—Latin perhaps excepted—came most
readily to his tongue.

During these proceedings his Majesty was still outside the
town, and when just about to enter it a deputation from the
authorities appeared, consisting of Provost Corsane, ex-Provost
Herbert Cunningham, Mr James Halliday, and others, supported
by a sympathising crowd. While making his royal progress the
King had received many eloquent addresses ; but we question if
any of them fell so delightfully on his ear as the one which the
learned Commissary of Dumfries read to welcome the arrival of his
"Sovrane Grace."   Brimful of extravagant compliments, and

John Corsane acted as such in 1618, and have been led to conclude that the
latter gentleman was also Provost in the preceding year.
        * Manuscript Account of the Irvings of Gribton.

teeming with quaint allusions, according to the fashion of the time, it yet possesses considerable merit as a piece of literary composition, and is, indeed, the best written local document of the age that has come under our notice.

"Your Royall Majesty," said Commissary Halliday, reading from a roll of parchment, "in whose sacred person the King of Kings hath miraculouslie united so many glorious kingdoms, under whose scepter the whyte and reid crocies are so proportionablie interlaced, the lion and leopord draw up one equall yok, and the most honourable ordors of the thistle and garter march togidder, is most heartelie welcome to this your Majestie's ever loyall towne, whose magistrats and people, now beholding your long-desired face, doe imitat the lizard. For no diamonts nor carbuncles by lustre can so allure the eyes as doeth the brightness of your countenance our eyes and hearts. Hence it is that the mynds of your good subjects are filled with such incomprehensible joy. And considering the innumerable comforts which this your Majestie's ancient and unconquered Scotland (*unica vicinis toties pulsata procellis, Externi immunis*) hath received under your happie government, both in Kirk and politie, what merveile it is to see the flamme of their love kyth in their faces and tongues, two infallible witnesses of their hearts? To recken all it wer impossible, to speake of none it wer ungratful: if I speake out of one, which is Peace, they who, with bleeding hearts and weeping eyes, did daylie taist of the bitter fruicites of discord, inward and outward broyles, shall acknowledge even that onlie Peace to bee all they could have wished, and more than ever they could have hoped for. For what is to be wished that wee doe not enjoy with it? *Omnia pace vigent.* Now Justice hath unsheathed her sword ; now basse assentation hath no place, and sycophants ar put to silence ; now is not sucked out the marrow of the people by odious and unjust monopolies ; now is not the husbandman his face worne with the grindstone of extortion, but sitting under his owne aple-trie, he in Peace eateth the fruictes of his labours ; Religion hath her place ; Law is in vigour ; Naboth bruketh his owne vin-yard, Achitopell his just reward ; simonie prefereth not Balaam ; nor doeth corrupting gold set up a judge in Israel; but everie place is provided with some one fitting and suttable for the same.

"If silent in these things (continued the Commissary), should wee not be convinced of ingratitude to Almightie God, by whose grace wee have this oure Solomon, by whose providence, under God, these good things are procured unto us, and at the fountaine of whose wisdome so many kingdoms and states get daylie refreshments? Who wold essey to speake worthelie of your worthie, rare, royall, and heroicall vertues, should have eloquence for his tongue ; and let any speake what hee can, what can he speake but which everie man doeth know? For there is no corner of the

earth which hath not heard of your Majestie, that yee are not only
a mirour but a master of kings ; not only a patterne to their lyfe,
but also a patrone of their cause.   Doeth not your royall practise
and penning prove all these? and knoweth hee any thing to whom
your *Basilikon Doron*, and your learned writings against the supporters of the Antichristian Heirarchie, is not knowne ? O, Sir,
your Majestie oweth much unto your King, that King of Kings by
whome so much unto you is bestowed.   That wee see the face of
him whome God hath anoynted so above his fellowes is the ground
of all these joyes which we enjoy this day.   In the fulnesse of
which joyes this one thing breeds us anguish, that this your
Majestie's ever loyall towne (whose people ever were, are, and shall
be, resolved to sacrifice their lyves in their Prince's service, and of
which God made choice that it shud be the place where your
Majestie's most royal ancestor, the waliant Bruce, killed the
Comyn, extirped the Baliol blood, and re-established the royal race
of our native Princes), now should bee the last period of your
Majestie's progresse within this your most ancient kingdome.
Wold God it could bee circular, as that of our other sunne, that all
your Majestie's subjects might enjoy the comfort of your presence
be vicissitude !   But let God's will and your Majestie's weel be the
measure of our desires.

"And (said Mr Halliday, in conclusion), since we perceive the
force of our load-stone failing, so that it hath no more power of
retention ; seeing your Majestie will southward, wee would wish
your course more meridionall, even trans-Alpine, that the Romish
idol, the whore of Babel, might repent of her too presumptuous
sitting in the Kirk of God, in God's owne chaire, above the crownes
of Kings.   Let her feel the furie of your sword, let her knowe the
sharpnes of your pike, as weel as of your pen ; in that expedition
shall not be last, *mavoritia pectora Scoti.*   For may wee not now,
by God's assistance, in like courage and magnanimitie, levell with
the ground their walls there, as wee did heere of these monstrous
heapes of stones and rampires reared be their Emperour Severus
and Hadrian ? Especiallie now, having the concurrence of that
bellicose and resolute natione which God hath made to come under
your standard with us, how can wee but have hope to cause all
them who will fight against God for Babylon, like as many herds
of animals scattered on Mount Aventine and Appenine will make
jacks of old dyks ?   But, remitting this and all other your
Majestie's deseignes to God's gratious dispensation and your worthie
disposition, wee close up our speach, praying Almightie God that
you and your Highnesses' Royol progenie may sit upon the thrones
of your dominions with incresse of all heavenlie and earthlie blessings, so long as the sunne and moone shall have place in the
firmament of Heaven. —Amen."*

* The Sanquhar, Drumlanrig, and Dumfries addresses to King James are

In reply to such a document, what could its royal recipient say, except to belaud the deputation in the same high-flown style : surely it was sufficient to sate even his appetite for flattery ; and one may fairly assume that it elicited from him a most cordial response.   After the out-of-door demonstration, the King was banquetted in great style.   The dinner given to him by the Council and the Trades took place, as our readers already know, in the Painted Chamber of the town-clerk's mansion—the only room, probably in the burgh adapted for it, the halls of the Castle being still in bad repair.   The Provost would, of course, preside ; and if he had the good-natured but exactive King on his right, and the fastidious royal favourite on his left, his social powers, whatever they were, would be severely taxed ; but the jovial cheer on the table would by-and-by soften the starch of etiquette, harmonise all ranks, and make the convener of the Incorporated Seven feel that he was somebody, even when sacred majesty was present, and keep the dean and the deacons from being quite annihilated by Buckingham the magnificent.   Indeed, the men of the Trades had good reason to be proud that day.   It had been whispered beforehand that his Majesty meant to bestow upon them a tangible mark of his regard.   They were to be presented with a miniature piece of cannon, all made of silver—a metal far more relatively precious in those times than it is now, seeing that three ounces of it were equal in value to one ounce of gold ; and the token, besides its intrinsic worth, would let the civilised world see how the puissant King of the British Isles delighted to honour his faithful craftsmen of Dumfries.   If there were present at the banquet any true-blue Presbyterians, who detested the system of chants and surplices, of liturgies and genuflexions, which his Majesty had thrust upon the Kirk, they would be prudently silent on the subject, and allow the praise of royalty to flow round as freely as the wines in which the King's health was toasted.

It is said, on what authority we know not, that the harmony of the party was sadly broken in upon by James himself.   Some strange little fishes—vendaces, from Lochmaben*—were set before him, with the intimation that they were a delicacy peculiar to the neighbourhood, which it was hoped would prove acceptable to the royal palate.   James, thinking they emitted a peculiar smell, and that they had a suspicious appearance, viewed them with as much horror almost as was felt by his ancestor Macbeth when the ghost

printed in a very rare volume, entitled "The Muses' Welcome," Edinburgh, 1618.

* The vendace is a beautiful fish, slightly resembling the parr.   It is usually five or six inches in length, and when taken out of the water it has a bright, silvery appearance, with a faint shade of blue along the back and part of the sides.   It is nowhere found in Scotland except in the Castle Loch of Lochmaben.

of Banquo glided in to disturb the feast at Glammis. Starting to
his feet, he shouted "Treason !" and it was not till the offending
dish was removed that he resumed his seat and his equanimity.
The story is an improbable one ; and we must conclude in spite of
it, that the Dumfries dinner to King James passed off not only
without disturbance, but with complete success.

That greater effect might be given to the presentation of the
gun, the ceremony was performed on the outside stair or balcony
of the hall, in sight of the general community. The crowd below
would, we may be sure, include all the journeymen and apprentices specially interested in the proceedings, as well as such of the
freemen as were not at the feast ; making altogether, perhaps, not
fewer than four hundred persons connected with the crafts. We
wonder if worthy Mr Thomas Ramsay, minister of St. Michael's,
was there to invoke a blessing on the ceremony. He was, we
suspect, too little of a courtier, and too fierce an anti-Prelatist, to
be honoured with a commission to that effect ; and it is more
likely that time-serving William Cowper, Bishop of Galloway,
would officiate. We can easily fancy the sort of oration made by
our British Solomon before handing his gift—the now far-famed
SILVER GUN—to the convener. In a speech rich with pithy, vernacular sentences, racy of the Scottish soil—which would be
relished by the populace, and elicit from them ringing acclamations—and well garnished with Latin phrases to astonish the
burgesses with his learning, he would express his regard for the
good burgh, and his interest in its industrial welfare. He would
descant upon the Trades as the bone and sinew of the State, speak
of the Dumfries incorporations as a portion of the body politic
which well merited his paternal favour ; and ask them to accept
his present as a proof that they were highly prized by the King ;
he telling them at the same time, that whilst pursuing the arts of
peace, it was necessary that they should be prepared for war ; and
that for this purpose he desired them to keep up their wappen-
schaws, and to improve their skill as marksmen by shooting for
the token at a target yearly with harquebuss or culverin. Alas !
that the precise words of the royal oration, and those of the
eloquent or any other speeches made by the chief of the Trades
and the Provost of the burgh in acknowledging the gift, have
proved as transitory as the cheers that greeted them. It is to be
regretted, also, that another address of which tradition speaks—a
doggerel effusion in which the common people sung the wisdom,
virtue, and liberality of King James, and expressed their own
devotedness to his sacred person—has likewise perished, all save
a small scrap which makes us wish for more, the symphonious
chorus of the poem :—

> " Leal and true subjects we ever will be,
> Hal-il-lu-ah ! hal-il-lu-ee !"

King James spent part of two days in the burgh. Before
bidding a final farewell to it he attended religious services in St.
Michael's Church on the 4th of August, which were conducted in
the piebald transition form which then prevailed. No liturgy was
used ; but Bishop Cowper, who had recently received consecration
at the hands of an English prelate, officiated as the preacher ; and,
says Spottiswoode, his discourse was so full of melting allusions to
the King's departure that it " made the hearers burst into tears."
His Majesty arrived at Carlisle on the same day, and thence proceeded by easy stages to the English metropolis.

The little " war engine " presented by King James to the
Trades was about ten inches in length, and mounted on a wheeled
carriage, also of silver. In some unaccountable way the accompaniments of the tube disappeared at a remote period ; and about
fifty-five years since a butt was added to the tube, which altered
the piece from a cannon to a musket—a change which improved
its appearance, but lessened its archæological value.* Parliament
had some years before enacted " that wappenschawings be kepit
throw all the realme at twa tymes in the yeir—that is to say, the
xx. of July and the tent of October ;"* and the gift of the Silver
Gun was accompanied by the condition that it was to be competed
for in connection with or as a sequel to these military musters.

A piece of meadow land skirted by the river, situated about
half a mile below the town, called Kingholm, was the customary
arena for the competition.† (a) Could the scene when the shooting

* On the gun is engraved the following modern inscription : " Presented
by King James VI. of Scotland to the Seven Incorporated Trades of Dumfries,
MDXCVII." It was not till long after that period that James entertained a
friendly feeling towards the Burgh or the Trades. The date is evidently
incorrect. James would rather have bombarded Dumfries with real cannon
than have presented it with a mimic one in 1598. There is every reason to
suppose that Dr. Burnside and other chroniclers whom we have followed were
right in giving 1617 as the date of the presentation.

* Acts of Scot. Parl., vol. iii., p. 91.

† It has been supposed that King James gave not only the Silver Gun,
but the ground on which it was to be competed for ; but we have seen no
evidence to that effect. The Holm was probably granted to the town by one
of his ancestors, and took its name of Kingholm from that circumstance.

(a) Like some other burgh properties the Kingholm passed into private
hands. On the death of the late Mrs Wood intestate, the estate of Hannahfield, of which Kingholm forms a part, reverted to the Crown as *ultima hæres*.
Representations were made to the Government by the then Provost (Mr T. F.
Smith) that it was the intention of Mrs Wood's husband to leave Hannahfield
to the town for the benefit of the Academy, and, so far as Kingholm
was concerned, the recreation of the public. Mr Alexander Young (afterwards Lord Young, judge of the Court of Session) was Solicitor-General
for Scotland, and as an old Academy pupil he took up the matter sympa-
thetically. A scheme was prepared and received the Queen's sanction by
which the whole of Hannahfield was gifted to the town for the purpose of
a public park. There was great rejoicing when the good news came to Dum-

was first inaugurated—probably on the 20th of July, 1618—be reproduced, it would be richly illustrative of a time when the usages of war and peace were strangely intermingled. The little trinket was an emblem of both, having been presented to men who lived by the labour of their hands, in order that they might become more qualified to defend their homes and country, if endangered by foreign enemy or internecine assailant. Each fair banner displayed by the freemen—as, numbering two hundred or more, and officered by their deacons and convener, they marched down to the verdant arena—spoke, in plain or heraldic terms, of peaceful industry ; but the craftsmen wore weapons of war, offensive and defensive, according to an act which required that all persons not noble, and having less than three hundred merks yearly, should be provided with brigandines, jacks, steel bonnets, sleeves of plate, pikes six ells long, culverins, halberds, or two-handed swords : provosts and bailies within burghs to see the act carried into effect. On this occasion that most primitive of fire-arms—the clumsy culverin—would, to the exclusion of all other weapons, be shouldered by the freemen ; but following them, like so many feudal retainers, would come " a clump of spears," consisting of their journeymen, partially harnessed, but wearing only pikes or swords, none but members of the master class being permitted to compete with guns for the trophy. The Provost, bailies, and merchant burgesses would take a prominent but still only secondary part in the procession, as the Trades were rather jealous of them, and especially careful that their convener should reign unrivalled "cock of the walk," whenever it was graced by the

fries—a cake and wine banquet, clanging of bells, and crackers in the streets at night. But a provision relative to the Academy, diverting the free funds to the creation of bursaries open to pupils in public schools over the three southern counties, when its terms were ascertained, provoked criticism, and the Provost sought to have the whole scheme reconsidered in order to obtain more money for the formation and maintenance of a park. There was consequent delay ; and a change of Government occurring, Conservatives succeeding Liberals, the Militia interest at the War Office was brought into competition with the Municipal in conditions which left the latter no chance. As a result the educational provision remained practically unaltered, but the Hannahfield estate was conveyed to the War Office, with a stipulation that when not required for military purposes the Kingholm should be available to the public. The Hannahfield bursaries, for school and college, are valuable educational foundations instituted by a body of trustees created under a deed of gift granted by Queen Victoria, dated 26th July, 1879. By this deed her Majesty as *ultima hæres* vests the sum of £9500 of Hannahfield estate in the three parish ministers of Dumfries, the Provost, the Sheriff, and three Sheriff-Substitutes in Dumfries and Galloway, and the successors in office of all of them, "for the improvement of education in the counties of Dumfries and Wigtown and in the Stewartry of Kirkcudbright," by means of "bursaries, scholarships, or prizes open to competition " by " persons educated in primary schools within the said counties and stewartry." In 1880 a "tentative scheme for the Hannahfield bursaries " was prepared by the trustees, and approved by the Scotch Education Department,

Silver Gun, or when the blue banner of the United Incorporations led the way.

The locality of the contest and its surroundings were sufficiently picturesque. The Nith took a bolder sweep westward at Kingholm than it does now ; and, overlooking the broad meadow, there rose from its rocky basement " a stern old tower of other days "—Comyn's Castle *(a)*—confronting which stood, as it yet stands, a still more ancient object, the Mote of Troqueer. Both of them would probably be occupied by spectators of the competition ; and we may be sure that it would attract to the Holm itself crowds of people from town and country. The Stewartry hills curving from the west, with huge Criffel on the south, would form a fitting framework for the pleasant low-ground picture ; and if the sun shone auspiciously from an azure sky during that notable summer day, and if, at the same time, the " white horses of the Solway "— as the crested tide from the Frith is poetically termed—hurried past Kingholm, their cool breath would refresh the rival marksmen, and they would give additional animation and beauty to the scene. Refreshing influences of a more substantial kind would be drawn upon. Many a bicker of ale and cup of claret would be drained, both by competitors and onlookers, in order to fortify the inner man, and to toast the royal donor of the prize, and the champion shot who bore it away for the first time. A proud man he would be ; but his name remains unrecorded, just the same as the names of the awkward rank and file who never so much as hit the target.

A truce to such vague conceptions. Instead of pursuing them further let us pass over an intermediate period of a hundred and sixty years, and obtain from an eye-witness of the martial pastime all its salient features, as depicted in expressive verse.[*] At the comparatively modern date of 1776, the shooting for the Silver Gun had become less warlike and utilitarian, and more thoroughly recreative in its character. Those engaged in it knew about defensive armour only by tradition, and the fire-arms they bore had never figured in actual warfare. The contest, divested of all its sterner features, had become a festive carnival, that was enjoyed by people of every rank ; the period of its occurrence being therefore a red-letter day in the Dumfriesian calendar. Here is the arousing opening stanza of the poem :—

> " For loyal feats and trophies won,
> Dumfries shall live till time be done,
> Ae simmer's morning, wi' the sun,
>   The Seven Trades there
> Forgathered, for their Siller Gun
>   To shoot ance mair."

(a) The Castle of Dumfries.

[*] " The Siller Gun," a poem by John Mayne.

The smiths or hammermen headed the procession ; then came the
squaremen, the weavers, the tailors, the cordwainers or sons of
Crispin, and the tanners ; the fleshers or butchers bringing up the
rear.   After the muster,

> " The different bands
> File off in parties to the Sands,"

where they are reviewed ; and then we are humorously told—

> " But, ne'er for uniform or air
> Were sic a group reviewed elsewhere !
> The short, the tall ; fat gouk and spare :
> Syde coats and dockit ;
> Wigs, queues, and clubs, and curly hair :
> Round hats and cockit !"

And, as the aspect of the men is grotesquely diversified, so is that
of their arms, which are of all sorts and sizes, while

> " Maist feck, though oiled to mak them glimmer,
> Hadna been shot for mony a simmer ;
> And Fame, the story-telling kimmer,
> Jocosely hints
> That some of them had bits o' timmer
> Instead o' flints !"

As the motley but imposing army moves on,

> " Frae the Friars' Vennel, through and through,
> Care seemed to have bid Dumfries adieu."

And

> " As through the town the banners fly,
> Frae windows low, frae windows high,
> A' that could find a neuk to spy
> Were leaning o'er ;
> The streets, stair-heads, and carts forbye
> Were a' uproar !
>
> Frae rank to rank, while thousands hustle,
> In front, like waving corn, they rustle ;
> Where, dangling like a baby's whistle,
> The Siller Gun,
> The royal cause o' a' this bustle,
> Gleamed in the sun !"

The place of meeting is, on this occasion, not Kingholm, but a field
overlooked by the Maidenbower Craigs, situated about a mile
southward of Dumfries, where the competition was occasionally
held.   Here a gay scene is presented—tents tastefully bedecked
occupying a portion of the ground, and merry groups standing
around waiting the appearance of the procession, whose approach
is announced long before by the music of its band, and the cheers
of the accompanying populace :

> "'Out owre the hills and far awa',
> The pipers played ;
> And, roaring like a waterfa'
> The crowd huzzaed.'"

Soon the sports of the day begin, and then,

> " Wi' mony a dunder,
> Auld guns were brattling aff like thunder.
>
> Wide o' the mark, as if to scare us,
> The bullets ripped the swaird like harrows;
> And, frightening a' the craws and sparrows
> About the place,
> Ramrods were fleeing thick as arrows
> At Chevy Chase!
>
> Yet still, as through the tents we steer,
> Unmoved the festive groups appear;
> Lads oxter lasses without fear,
> Or dance like wud;
> Blythe, when the guns gaed aff sae queer,
> To hear the thud!"

The poet, after noticing the crowd of charmed spectators, and signalising the men of mark amongst them, thus proceeds:—

> " Hail! kindred spirits, ane and a'
> Men of account, without a flaw,
> Pushing your fortunes far awa,
> Or, fu' o glee,
> Rejoicing at our wappenschaw,
> Dumfries, with thee!
>
> How beautiful, on yonder green,
> The tents, wi' dancing pairs between!
> In front, though banners intervene,
> And guns are rattling,
> There's nought but happiness, I ween,
> In a' this battling!
>
> For miles, by people overrun,
> The air resounds wi' mirth and fun,
> Frae grave to gay, frae sire to son,
> And great to sma',
> The shooting for the Siller Gun
> Delights them a'.

At length one of the competitors—"a tailor slee"—puts a bullet through the centre of the target, gains the prize, and soon,

> "Wi' loud applause frae men and women,
> His fame spread like a spate wide foamin'."

The homeward march is then made:

> " And as the troops drew near the town,
> With a' the ensigns o' renown,
> The magistrates paraded down,
> And a' the gentry;
> And love and friendship vied to crown
> Their joyous entry!
>
> Like roses on a castle wa',
> The leddies smiled upon them a';
> Frae the Auld Kirk to the Trades Ha',
> And New Kirk Steeple,
> Ye might have walked a mile or twa,
> On heads o' people!"

As darkness comes on, the indoor festivities are proceeded with, and the streets sparkle with fire-works :—

> " Ding, ding, ding-dong, the bells ring in ;
> The minstrels screw their merriest pin ;
> The magistrates, wi' loyal din,
> Tak aff their caukers ;
> And boys their annual pranks begin
> Wi' squibs and crackers !"

The toasts in the Trades Hall almost trip each other, they follow so rapidly in honour of the King,

> " And names of whilk the country boasts,
> And may be proud :
> The Johnstones, Lords of Annandale ;
> The Douglases, and Murrays hale ;
> The Maxwells, famed through Nith's sweet vale ;
> Kirkpatricks too ;
> And him of a' that's guid the wale,
> The great Buccleuch !"

We take leave of the "Siller Gun," and its laureate, John Mayne, by quoting and echoing part of his concluding address : —

> " Our closing strain shall be :
> May Scotland, happy, brave, and free,
> Aye flourish like the green bay tree !
> And may Dumfries,
> In a' her revelry and glee,
> Blend love and peace !"*

This was the chief pastime of the Dumfriesians after the suppression of the Robin Hood pageant on saints' day at the Reformation, which was "the darling May-game both in England and Scotland" for centuries ; and for keeping up of which, as we

---

* Before taking leave for the present of the Silver Gun festivity, it is proper we should state that the neighbouring Burgh of Kirkcudbright possesses a similar trinket, the gift of the same sovereign ; but under what circumstances it was presented we are unable to say. In Nicholson's History of Galloway, vol. i., p. 529, the annexed information is given regarding it :—"The year 1587 is graven on the barrel of this miniature fusee, and also the capital letters, T. M. C., supposed to be the initials of Thomas M'Clellan of Bombie (ancestor of the Lords of Kirkcudbright), who was at that time alderman of the Burgh. The trinket ('like a penny whistle,' seven inches in length,) has been shot for only three times in the memory of the oldest person now living [1841]. In the summer of 1781, the Incorporated Trades applied by petition to the Magistrates to have the gun placed in the hands of their convener, 'that they might shoot for it at a target as formerly, and as is still practised by the Trades of Dumfries for the Silver Gun of that Burgh,' which petition was of course granted. The next time it was shot for was on the 22nd of April, 1830, the day on which the present Earl of Selkirk attained his majority. On this occasion the great wassail bowl of the Burgh, which had been presented by Hamilton of Bargeny, M.P., soon after the Union, was used for the first time in the memory of the oldest inhabitant. It was placed at the Market Cross, and after the Trades had contended for the Silver Gun, it was filled and refilled with potent liquor. The last time it was shot for was on the occasion of the Queen's coronation. on the 28th of June, 1838."

have already noticed, every person, when made a burgess or freeman of Dumfries, was required to pay a trifling sum.

In the seventeenth century, the custom of Riding the Marches ranked next to the Silver Gun contest as a popular recreation. Every first of October the Magistrates, Town Council, Incorporated Trades, and other burgesses, assembled at the Market Cross or White Sands, and, having been duly marshalled, proceeded with banners and music along the far-stretching line which enclosed the property of the burgh. Their course was first to the Castle, then down Friars' Vennel, and along the Green Sands to the Moat at the head of the town. As a matter of course, the cavalcade was accompanied by a crowd of juveniles, who at this stage were treated to a scramble for apples, the town-officers throwing among them the tempting fruit.* The marchers then passed through the grounds of Langlands and Lochend to the north side of St. Christopher's chapel, and thence to the village of Stoop, at the race-ground near which a race was engaged in for a saddle and pair of spurs. Thence they went eastwards and southwards, betwixt the town's property and the estates of Craigs and Netherwood, stopping at Kelton-well, at which point the superiority of the burgh terminates. Here, after being refreshed with something stronger than the produce of the said well, the officials heard the roll of heritors read over by the town-clerk, a note being taken of all absentees, who were liable to a fine for not being present at the ceremony. This over, the procession returned to town. The Riding of the Marches is a usage of the past, though it has been performed several times during the present century. (a)

Horse-racing was an established sport at Dumfries from a remote period. When Regent Morton, towards the close of 1575, held a criminal court in the burgh, for the trial of some offending Borderers, he, according to an old chronicle,† judiciously relieved

---

* In the accounts for 1641 the following entries occur :—" To Patrick Crawford and Jon Jonstown, for paper and wryting the Town-roll at the mertches ryding, 12s ; for ane pek of apples that day, £1 4s."

(a) There was a picturesque revival of the "riding," or, more correctly, "redding"—that is, clearing up—of the Marches, carried out by the burgh authorities, on Rood Fair Thursday, 1901—the year of King Edward VII.'s accession—when a speech was delivered by Provost Glover at Douievale, and the charter read by Mr John Grierson, the Town Clerk. In the following year, and in association with the Coronation festivities, there was also a revival of the Siller Gun competition, under new conditions. The shooting, which was in classes, military and civil, took place at the Conhuith of Troqueer range. It was almost exclusively in the hands of Volunteers, and the various stages occupied several days. Medals bearing on the face an affixed copy of the gun were awarded to the best marksmen ; the first prize, with gold medal and gun in silver upon it, being won by Mr Joseph White, Volunteer, a cabinetmaker to trade. When this revival was resolved upon it was understood that the names of first prizemen in each year of competition should be engraved upon a plate and placed beside the Siller Gun itself in the Town Hall.

† Historie of King James the Sext, quoted in Chambers's Domestic Annals.

his grave duties by lighter pursuits. "Many gentlemen of England," we are told, "came thither to behold the Regent's Court,
where there was great provocation made for the running of horses.
By chance my Lord Hamilton had there a horse sae weel bridled,
and sae speedy, that, although he was of meaner stature than other
horses that essayit their speed, he overran them all a great way
upon Solway Sands, whereby he obtained praise both of England
and Scotland at that time."

In a Town Council minute dated the 15th of April, 1662,
the treasurer is ordered by the magistrates to provide a silver bell
four ounces in weight as a prize to be run for every second
Tuesday of May by the work-horses of the burgh, "according to
the auncient custome ;" the regulations being that whenever the
bell was borne away by one rider and one horse three consecutive
years it was "to appertain unto the wooner theerof for evir.
About two years afterwards the Council offered a "Silver Cup of
ffourty unce weght or therby," to be run for at the ordinary course
within the burgh by the horses of such noblemen and gentlemen
in the county as were duly entered for the race. Then it was the
custom, every first Monday in May, for the day-labourers and
servants of heritors to parade the town on horseback, armed with
swords and dirks, and bedizened with sashes and ribbons ; next to
proceed to Dalskairth, or other neighbouring wood ; and, each
furnished with boughs of the sacred birch, to return to the race-
ground and run for a silver "muck-bell" belonging to the burgh,
the winner receiving five merks by way of substantial reward in
addition to the honour of being the nominal owner of the prize for
a year.

Even as the Trades had their convener and the Councillors
their provost, so this more humble fraternity had a chief entitled
the Lord of the Muckmen, who was annually appointed to that
dignity by popular suffrage. In 1688, John Maxwell, the person
who then occupied that high office, conceiving himself ill supported
by his vassals, complained to the Council on the subject. "It is
verie weel knoun unto your honours," said his *lordship*, "that it is
the ancient custome for your petitioner, or any being in the office
for the tyme, to ryde with his men accompanying him with their
best apparel everie fyrst Monday of May yeirlie, and that the
Council grant them power and warrand to poynd such of the
inhabitants who meanlie refuse, and are found to be deficient, at
that solemnitie." After this pompous prologue, *Lord* Maxwell
descends to absolute bathos when he reminds the authorities
"that it is the use and custome to grant percept upon their treasurer for as much money as will drink their honours' good health."
The prayer of his petition is a sweeping one, as he asks that each
defaulter shall be "poynded to the value of six shillings Scots,"
and that a trifle for the indispensable toast may be duly forth-

coming. The Council, with mingled liberality and prudence, ordained the treasurer to give the supplicant half-a-crown, and to redeem the muck-bell for five merks, that it might be run for that year, but declined to punish offenders in the mode proposed by the petitioner. Even at that early date the pageant was beginning to lose its hold on the populace; and in May, 1716, the Council passed an act to abolish it altogether. The preamble states that the sport had been accompanied by "severall irregularities and misdemeanours, to the scandal of the place and dishonour of God." They therefore, "by a plurality of votes, prohibit the riding of the muckmen in all time coming; and, in order to the entire extinguishing of this custom, they appoint the treasurer to sell the muck-bell for the best advantage." Horse-racing has fallen into disrepute, there having been none in the town or neighbourhood—that is to say, on a large scale—during the last thirty years; and though the work-horse competition, which was old two hundred years ago, was brought down by the burgh carters till our own day, it too has disappeared.

CHAPTER XXVIII.

FOUR years after King James's visit the burgh received from him
a precept for a new charter. Among other favours it authorised
the erection of a merchant guildry. But, owing probably to the
civil strife which ere long arose, the document was lost sight of,
and infeftment was never passed upon it. For fully two hundred
years it lay unnoticed and unknown, till it was discovered in 1826,
when the burgh records were being removed from one depository
to another.* This embryo charter is not of parchment, as it would
have been if it had acquired full legal authority, but of paper,
which, frail with age, has suffered seriously from wear and tear.
It appears to be superscribed by " our Sovrane Lord, James :" the
King's name, however, we suspect, is not holograph, but printed
from a wooden block, a practice that was not uncommon when, in
his Majesty's absence, the Scottish Privy Council issued the first
draft of any document to which he had given his sanction. It
required an expenditure of fully six thousand words on the part
of our British Solomon to recount the privileges already possessed
by his ancient burgh, to confirm the same, and to shower upon it
new immunities ; but a brief summary of his loquacious yet
gracious charter must here suffice.

" Our Sovrane Lord " states, as a reason for his benefactions,
that the Provost and Bailies of Dumfries had always given to him
dutiful service, and had so administered the law that, by " the
help of Almightie God, common robberis and thieves are not
amaist at all to be fund in their pairts." The rights and immunities already possessed by Dumfries as a burgh-royal are then set
forth in general terms ; among others its power to " use and
exerceese the tred and traffic of merchandise, and to by and sell
all kynde merchandise, as weill hamewart gudes as of uther
natiounes, not onlie within the said burgh, landis, tenements, and
liberties thereof, but also within all uther boundis and landis of
the sheriffdome of Drumfries, as weil in regalitie as royaltie, in

the length and breid thairoff." These the burgh is still to retain
and that " for ever ;" over and above which the King now authorises it to "use and possess ane Merchant Gildrie, with Gild
Courtis, consulting members," and necessary officers, the same in
all things as had been granted by his Majesty's predecessors and
himself " to the town of Edinburgh, or any other royal burgh
within the realme."

" Further," the King grants to the " Magistrates and Council "
authority " to have and use within the said burgh, upon ilk Mononday and Friday, ane publick mercat day, togiddir with tua
fairis in the year, the ane theroif to begin upon the [blank] day of
Apryle, and the uther upon the fourtene day of September yearlie,
and aither of thaim to continue for the space of aucht days their-
efter." It is then explained that the trading privileges are to be
used by burgesses—those who are not being debarred from usurping the same on penalty of having their goods escheated and their
persons imprisoned. The bridge and river privileges are next
mentioned, as follows : " all and haill the said Brig of Drumfries,
and haill wayis, roadis, and passages to and fra the samen at
aither of the endis thairof, with the haill customes of the said brig,
as weil in that end thairof lyin nearest the said burgh, and free-
dome thairof, and the uther end of the samen that lies towardes
the country of Gallowey, with full powers to thame, thair factors
and servitors in thair names, to mell, intromitt, uplyft, and receive
all customes and dewties of the samen, at aither the ends of the
said brig . . . . and in lykmaner, all and haill the said Water
of Nyth, haill boundis, ysles, and bayes thairof, fra the brig of the
burgh to the ysle callit Haisten, haill privileges and commodities
thairof, with libertie and power of anchorage on aither of the
sydes of the said water, and to tow and laden their schyppes,
barkes, bottis, and uther veschellis as weill within the fend mark
as without the samin ;" power being also given to construct all
necessary ways, passages, and docks on both banks of the river,
and for behoof of the said " port and pearin."

Next, with an appropriate flourish, his Majesty gives new
power and dignity to the burghal rulers, that they may be an
increasing terror to evil-doers, if not a praise and protection to
them that do well : " Furder, the said Soverane Lord, in remembrance of the cair and pains taken be the said Provest and Baillies
for repressing and abandoning of all kinds of stouthrief, oppression, and uther crymes quhilk used to fall out in their quarteris,
hes given, grantit, and disponit, and be the terms heirof gives,
grants, and dispones to the said Provest, Baillies, burgesses, and
inhabitants of the said burgh, and their successors, for ever, the
heritabeill offices of sheriffship and commissioners within the said
burgh," the provost for the time being to act as sheriff, and the
bailies as sheriffs-deputes, and their jurisdiction to extend over the

X1

entire burgh, its liberties, water, and port on both sides of the
river, with power, moreover, to try all criminal cases whatever
occurring within their bounds, the same as had been granted to
Edinburgh, Perth, Dundee, Aberdeen, or any other burgh-royal
throughout the kingdom.

All the property, customs, duties, and powers enumerated in
the document are then specified anew, with a circumlocution which
bears a striking contrast to the terse and simple terms of King
Robert's charter. But, apart from verbal repetitions, Dumfries
had increased vastly in size and importance during the two centuries and a quarter which intervened between the two royal
deeds, and hence in some degree the complexity and extensive
range manifested by King James's writ. The latter, before finishing, provides "that ane sazine of this his Majestie's charter be
taken with the Provest and with the Baillies of the said burgh, at
the Mercat Croce thereof, be deliverance of ane golden penney
with eird and stonne,* which shall be ane sufficient sazine for the
saidis Provest, Baillies, Counsal, communitie, and inhabitants of
the said burgh, and their successors," the whole closing with the
"pepper-corn" conditions required by the charter of 1395—namely,
that the burgh should requite the Crown by paying to it "twentie
punds usuale money of this realme" yearly, ane half payable at
Whitsunday, the other at Martinmas, throughout all time coming.

From "the brig of the burgh to the ysle callit Haisten" was
an extensive water jurisdiction, the Isle of Hesten lying across the
mouth of Auchencairn Bay, ten miles further down the Solway
than the rule of the Nith Commissioners extends to at present.
Very likely the power of the Dumfries Magistrates over such a
large portion of the Kirkcudbrightshire coast and waters arose out
of the circumstance that at one time the whole of eastern Galloway was comprehended in the sheriffdom of Dumfriesshire. King
James proposed by his charter to erect Dumfries into an independent sheriffdom—which, however, we know was acquired (or one
of regality equivalent to it) by the burgh about this time,
though the guildry scheme unfortunately miscarried.

At the period of King James's visit the town was in a prosperous state. It had grown considerably in size, and its trade
had greatly increased since the Union of the Crowns and the
settlement of the Debatable Land. The existence in it of so many
crafts, each of sufficient importance to be made a corporate body,
intrusted with peculiar privileges, is of itself an evidence of the
burgh's advancement. Not only were there settled in it such
indispensable trades as smiths, masons, wrights, weavers, tailors,
shoemakers, and butchers, but others suggestive of luxury and

---

* This old symbolical infeftment, by which a superior gave to a vassal
possession of property by the delivery of earth and stone, was but recently
abolished by the Acts 8 and 9 Vict., c. 35.

refinement—glovers, furriers, and dyers. All these, as has already been explained, were combined into one aggregate corporation before the close of the sixteenth century ; and early in the seventeenth they occupied such a good position as to merit special recognition by the King.

Long before the latter period Dumfries had become the seat of a flourishing cloth manufacture, which gave employment to innumerable distaffs throughout the district.* Spinning wool into yarn was at that time, and ages afterwards, the chief indoor occupation of females in town and country ; and the highest ladies in the land, like the Roman matrons of old, took delight in the labours of the wheel. From the home-spun article thus produced the websters of the burgh wove a substantial cloth, which, as "hoddin-gray,"† garmented common folks ; or, when of a finer sort, and dyed a patrician blue by the litsters, became a fit attire for the lairdly and mercantile classes, or others of high degree. This fabric was the chief staple of the burgh, and much money must have been turned over yearly by the regular shopkeepers who dealt in it—not to speak of what was done by pedlars, who carried it on their own backs, or by pack-horses, to all the country round ; and who, when crossing the Sark with their burdens, became the forerunners of the famous "Scotch travellers" in the South of a later day.

The exclusive system on which the very existence of burghs-royal was believed to hang had now acquired its full development All the merchants authorised to "pack and pell" within the burgh had first obtained a ticket of burgess-ship, without which they would have been deemed rebellious interlopers, and liable as such to lose their goods and suffer imprisonment ; and under similar penalties no person was allowed to carry on any mechanical occupation unless he had served an apprenticeship to it, and had afterwards acquired the freedom of the town by purchase, by marriage with a freeman's daughter, or through special favour. The Trade Incorporations were at this period in their full glory, each governed by its deacon, and all ruled over by a deacon-convener ; while the mercantile classes, who had received political privileges earlier than the craftsmen, were striving to emulate them in organisation by being constituted into a guild. Two days each week, Monday

---

* Galloway was one of the principal wool districts of Scotland ; and [in 1600] much of its produce was sent to the burgh of Dumfries, to be made into broadcloth, in the manufacture of which this town had obtained much celebrity.—History of Galloway, vol. ii., p. 6.

† Hoddin, "homely," a corruption of home-done : (a)

"What though on hamely fare we dine,
    Wear hoddin-gray, an' a' that ?"—Burns.

(a) Jamieson defines Hoddin-grey thus : "Cloth worn by the peasantry which has the natural colour of the wool ;" and he quotes Ramsay's definition of "hoiden"—namely, "rustic, clownish."

and Friday, were especially set apart for business, which, as
regards handiwork products, was carried on chiefly in booths or
covered stalls, planted along the leading thoroughfares—the privileged makers of the wares being also the favoured sellers of the
same ; their customers, the inhabitants generally, and the people
of the country round about ; and besides these market days, two
great chartered fairs, dating long prior to 1621, were held annually, as at present, in the spring and autumn.

There was less of timber and more of stone in the domestic
tenements than formerly. As a rule, the houses had a narrow
frontage, with their gables to the street. In many cases there was
a basement story, half sunk below the street level, which formed
the kitchen, over which rose an apartment used as a shop ; then a
third storey, where the family resided ; the attics, over all, being
used as a dormitory. All apprentices, whether artisan or mercantile, lodged with their masters, and often also their unmarried
journeymen got meat as well as fee in recompense for their
labours. Outside the town, beyond its walls and its liberties
clusters of inferior cabins gave refuge stated or occasional to
" outland folks," to " gangrel bodies," and to " broken men " from
the Border side, these parasite and unprivileged classes forming
the Pariahs, and sometimes also the Ishmaelites, of the burgh.
On the opposite bank of the Nith stood the village of Bridge-end,
originated probably by the erection of a few houses soon after
Dumfries and Galloway were linked together by Devorgilla's
fabric ; not a few of the freemen of the burgh carrying on their
trade in the village, and, though living " outland," still retaining
all their privileges.

Something is learned about the shoemakers so far back as the
time when Flodden was fought, from a Seal of Cause granted to
them by the Town Council on the 1st of December, 1513. That
document tells us that the market for leather and made work was
held in "the Cowgate, fra the New Well to the Greyfriars ;"* that
the goods were to be exposed from seven o'clock in summer, and
nine in winter, till twelve at noon ; that searchers were authorised
to overhaul the goods, and to bring any found insufficient to the
magistrates for confiscation ; that no unfreemen were allowed to
purchase leather in the market till eleven o'clock ; nor to sell boots
or shoes of their own make except at the market on Mondays, the
freemen being, of course, permitted to dispose of their wares on
any day of the week, in their own booths, " when gude," Sundays
excepted.

These and other such like regulations were, it seems, but

* Probably Friars' Vennel was at this time called Cowgate, and that the
site of the market was from the gate of the Monastery to the foot of the street
—a part of the town that continued to be much occupied by " cordwainers "
down till our own day.

indifferently observed ; and on the 20th of October, 1595, Patrick Aiken, deacon of the shoemakers, and several of the other masters, made a complaint to the Council on the subject, which led to the re-enactment of the code with additional clauses. The minutes of the proceedings give some more curious particulars respecting these primitive Crispinites. In the interval their place of tryst had been changed from the Cowgate to the Kirkhaugh, and they had become increasingly rigorous towards piratical dealers, and such of their own incorporated body as had any commercial intercourse with fremmit outland folk. Penalties were enacted against all and sundry who forestalled the market, or who brought any " barkit [tanned] lether " to the market that was not of their own manufacture. Outsiders who came within the walls with rough hides except on " Mononday " were warned to expect rough treatment, and were sure to get it. All booths were to be searched " weeklie, or sa often as need be "—this inquisitorial duty devolving on the deacon and six freemen. No work was to be done on Sabbath, though the booths were allowed to be open on that day till nine o'clock in the morning. " Item, that no able young men be suffered to keep ane cobler's booth, but only the same be permitted to them that ar thirty year old past, that the freimen may hev servands to serve them ; and that the said coblers sel their old wark to the lieges on the Monondays, and not at the Cross, nor on the Hie Street, to the dishonour of the gude town :" penalty, escheat of goods. " Item, that na freiman of the said craft being burgess, pake or pell, nor be pairtner with unfriemen, nor make conditiouns with them :" penalty, £10, or " tinsell of his friedom." Freemen were debarred from residing or working beyond the royalty, lest by the undue multiplication of apprentices the craft should become less select. Rules were prescribed which savour much of modern trade-unionism. No master was allowed to receive a new apprentice till the one previously taken on had served three years : the entire period of service was five years ; and when the young son of Crispan was " out of his time " he had to serve other three years for meat and fee as a journeyman before he could aspire to freemanship, unless he got rid of this additional servitude by wedding a master's daughter, and thus placing himself under a more alluring sort of bondage.

These irrepressible outland folk ! How they did pester the weavers, and not less other privileged craftsmen, and put the burghal authorities to their wit's end. Early in 1608 James Aiken, deacon-convener of the websters, forwarded an appeal to the King himself, praying his Majesty to order the better enforcement of acts made on their behalf by the Town Council on the 31st of May, 1542, and other statutes to the same effect passed by the Conven tion of Burghs in 1584. The petition of these " wabsters gude ' embodied a long list of grievances, and they respectfully asked, among other things, "that na manner of persones, burgesses, and indwellers of burrows, be themselves, their servants, or uthers in their naime, in tyme coming, suld tak upon hand to carrie, send, or delyver ther yairne, claithe or uther stuff, to be wrocht, maid, or dressit by onie webster unfrieman dwelland in the suburbs, or within half ane mile of the town wallis." King James, by a missive, "given under our signet, at Edinburgh, the tent day of August, 1608, and of our reign the 46 yeir," commanded the Provost and Bailies of the burgh to give "dew execution in all poynts" of the "acts and statutes set down for preserving the liberties of the said craft "within thrie dayis next after they be chargit" to that effect, "under the paine of rebellioun, and of putting of them to our horne."

It was the custom of the glover fraternity to prepare the material used by them in the way of trade; and certain audacious fleshers having in 1651 been detected "limeing and puttyng of sheip skynes," forth went Mr James Newlands, deacon of the glovers, to the Council, complaining of the great prejudice thus done to their craft. As a result the offending parties were enjoined to mind their own business, and not encroach on that of their neighbours for the time to come.

In virtue of acts passed by the Council on the 9th of October, 1594, the incorporated fleshers got a monopoly of the meat trade, except on market days (Monday and Saturday), when unfreemen were allowed to bring beef and mutton in bulk, or large pieces, to the "Sand Mercat." The same statutes prohibited the inhabitants from buying any "flesches beyond the brig," and landward men from bringing any "muttoun or beef deid to the towne, except it be of thair awn grouth," and fed within a distance of four miles; and provided that "sic flesches as sall be slaine at the Bridge-end sall not be sauld at the said mercat of Dumfries," under the pain of confiscation. To pass such restrictive edicts might be easy enough, but to carry them into effect was scarcely possible. Hence we read of frequent complaints, such as the following, dated sometime in 1643: that "pairties who have never been frie daylie bring their nolt and scheip within the burgh, and sell the same in bak houses and closses where they best pleis, both skin and bouk, in as small portions as they think expedient; opening booths as if they were frie, and bringing little or nane thairof to the mercat," as required by law.

From a representation to the Town Council about similar encroachments made on the tailors' vested rights, we obtain an instructive glance at the protective system under which these "knights of the thimble" plied needle and thread. On the 2nd of August, 1639, whilst Provost Corsane and Bailies Richardson and M'Burnie were holding a court in the Tolbooth, there "compeirit Richard Herries, deykone of the Tailyours, Jon M'Burnie, Jon

Clerk, Thomas M'Kynnell, William Martin, Hew Fergusone, and Jon Padzean," members of the said craft, "quha for themselves, and in name of the remanent brether" masters, reminded the authorities that, on the 31st of March, 1547, their predecessors had authorised the trade to make statutes for its protection; that they had, on the 1st of March, 1586, confirmed these enactments; and that notwithstanding of this, the lawful craftsmen had of late been "heavily hurt and dampnified be ane great number of unfreimen, wha lives licentiouslie, working all manner of work in privie houses, lofts, and chalmeris, and taking payment thairfore as if they were admitted to the freidome, and thereby hinders and prejudges the frie brethers of the said craft." Further, the deputation complained that certain traitorous tailors had admitted unfreemen to work within their booths, falsely calling them servants and apprentices; and that the neighbours round about had been giving employment to the same unchartered libertines, instead of confining their favours to the free craftsmen of the burgh. For the freemen to throw the measuring-tape over the "outland folk" in this exclusive way was a far stretch; but, lest the latter should be incommoded by the law "debarring of the unfreimen to mak or mend their claithes in ther housis," the deacon and brethren, it appears, had agreed to "mak the said neighbours as guid and readie service within or without their housis as they were wont to have be the said unfriemen," and at the following terms: Any master, on receiving twenty-four hours' warning, was bound "to appoynt ane of his servands, for whom he sall answer, to pass to the neighbour's dwelling-hous, for mending and repairing of sic ornaments and claithing as are to be mendit, of all sorts—the said servand to enter to wark at five houris in the morning," continuing till "nyne houris at evene; and to have thairfoir ilk day twelffe pennys and his meit give he be ane prenteis, and give he be ane journeyman, to have two shillings and his meit daylie." In case of any difference as to the quality or price between a freeman and neighbour the disputants were required "to abyde and underly the trial and judgement of ane baillie, the deacon, two of the Council, the ane a merchant and the uther a craftsman, named by the baillie." The money obtained for country work went into the purse of the master, and the proportion allowed to the journeyman out of twopence sterling (the equivalent of two shillings Scots) would be but a small daily wage, even when accompanied with food. The necessaries of life, however, were correspondingly cheap, clothing included; but dearer, perhaps, than in the "days when gude King Robert rang;" though the old balladist tells us that his Majesty, on being charged only half-a-crown for his trews, declared

"They were a groat owre dear,
And ca'ed the tailor thief and loon."*

* From the ballad of "Tak' yere Auld Cloak about ye," which must have been written long before the Silver Gun was presented, as Shakespeare quotes verse of it in *Othello*,

Deacon Herries and the other deputies having laid bare all their grievances, were bowed out of the Tolbooth with an assurance that the burghal authorities would duly enforce the law on their behalf.*

For a long period the incorporations had no building of their own, so that their annual meetings to choose office-bearers were held in the open air, at Kingholm, on the Upper Sandbeds, in "Adam Anderson's orchard neuk," or under such shelter as the ruined Castle, or St. Christopher's Chapel, could afford. The oldest Trade minute extant, except one, records an election by the weavers, in the following terms :—"At Dumfreis, the twenty-nynt day of September, the year of God 1655 years, the whilk day conveint at the back of the Castell-yeard, James Fergusone, deacon ; Thomas Patterson, tresserer; Robert Gibson, William Mackburny, Richard Dun, John Kennan, William Grier, Thomas Gibson, masters ; Roger Wardloa, officer—with the consent of the haill traid were ellectit for ane year to come."†

The minutes of the shoemakers go back to the 23d of October, 1657; and as an entry of that date gives the list of the entire free-men then belonging to the trade, it is worthy of being subjoined. It runs thus :—"The whilk day the whole body of the shoemaker trade of the Burgh of Drumfreis and Bridge-end having convenid with the deacons, masters, and box-master of the said trade, at the Chrystall Chapple, having finished their former buik, have fund it expedient that the names of all the freimen be insert in this buik, viz.:—John Maxwell, deacon ; John Scott, lait deacon ; Robert Neilson, treasurer ; William Paterson, Thomas Hayning, Andro Grierson, John Dickson at Goatheid, and John Dickson at Porthole, masters ; James Wright, officer ; Thomas Kirkpatrick, Henry Grierson, John Freemont (elder), John Wright, Thomas Dickson, James Heron, James Smith, James Hayning, John Braid-foot, John Freemont (younger), William Swan, James Mason, John Batie, Archibald Edingtoun, Adam Newall, William Henrison, Robert Urie, and William M'Kinnell, freimen in Drumfreis, and indwellers there ; and thereupon the said deacon, masters, and haill body of the said trade have received articles.—R. Bartane, clerk. And further, the same day they thocht it expedient to insert in this buik the names of their freimen dwelling at Bridge-end, viz.:—Edam Kirkpatrick, Robert M'Kill, John Welsh, David

---

* The MSS. from which the foregoing particulars relating to the Trades were obtained consist of old copies in the possession of Dr Dickson, Edinburgh, of Town Council minutes more ancient in date than any now in the Burgh Record Room. The MSS. were obligingly put at our disposal for the present edition of the History of Dumfries.

† The oldest records the measurement by the Deacon of the weavers, and other office-bearers, of some webs, in the course of their official duty—date, "the twalt day of Agust, 1654." The Minute-book of the Weavers, from which we have quoted, is in the possession of Mr David Dunbar, Dumfries.

Welsh, William Crosbie, John Denholm, James Wilson, John Lewis, William Irving, Thomas Williamson (elder), Thomas Williamson (younger), and Thomas Lewis.—R. Bartane, clerk."*

Such is the roll of these primitive "cordwainers," thirty-nine in all, the fathers of the craft in Dumfries and Maxwelltown. By 1790 the freemen shoemakers had increased to a hundred and ten; and in 1833, when the corporation was about to break up, they numbered a hundred. No such list has been preserved of any of the other trades. In 1703 the master weavers were twenty in number; in 1790 they had increased to forty-two, and in 1833 had diminished to thirty.

All the internal affairs of each craft were regulated by fixed rules, some of which were very stringent. Before an apprentice could be articled or a journeyman engaged by a master leave had to be obtained from the office-bearers of his corporation. On the 2nd of February, 1668, the rules as to shoemakers' apprentices were made more precise at a Trades' meeting in the "Orchard Neuk," where it was enacted, that after liberty had been given by the deacons, box-masters, and masters, to any freeman to take an apprentice, the name of the latter was to be entered in the Trades' books, and that the term of service should be fixed at five years, besides "a yeare for meat and fie, as use is." At a meeting of office-bearers, held on the 19th of September, 1673, for regulating the affairs of the same craft, it was enacted, "with consent from the whole traid," that a master's son on being apprenticed was to treat the freemen to a dinner instead of making a money payment; "uthers, not freemen's sons, to pay the traid fourtie punds Scots; apprentices in Bridg-end, not being freimen's sons, to pay thirty punds." We subjoin the substance of two other illustrative minutes, as furnished by the books of the same corporation: "18th July, 1667.—Jon and Robert Lewars, cordinars, accused befoir the deacon, box-master, and masters, of using loose and idle speiches, and other scandelous language against the traid;" and they being anxious to give satisfaction, agreed to forfeit their freedom if ever they did the like again. On the 17th of December, 1674, the shoemakers at a general meeting resolved, on account of "the great skaith that the traid sustains by staying ovir lang on the gait on the mercat day, doe thairfore enact that every man of the traid that comes to sell on the mercat day that he enter precisely at ten hours, and stay till one afternoon, and nae langer"— penalty, twelve shillings. Interesting muniments of the craft are specified in a list of articles consigned to the box-master's custody in October, 1666; these including two Seals of Cause on parchment, with papers relating to the same, and King's letters; also the old books and flag. These would have supplied valuable

---

* Minute-book of the Shoemakers, in the possession of a surviving freeman, Mr Williamson, Dumfries.

information regarding the erection of the Trades : deep but vain
is our regret that no trace of the venerable relics is left, except
the minute from which we have quoted.

When the Trades acquired a right to be specially represented
in the Town Council seven members were assigned to them, consisting of the deacons, one of whom was also convener of the
united incorporation : as such, he was reckoned the third in
municipal rank, the provost and the oldest bailie alone taking
precedence of the deacon-convener. The entire Council, down till
the passing of the Burgh Reform Act in 1833, consisted of these
seven deacons, twelve merchant councillors, and the members of
the bench—a provost, three bailies, a dean, and a treasurer. As
recorded in their charters or seals of cause at the period of the
Union, in 1707, the Trades ranked thus :—(1) The gows or smiths ;
(2) the wrights and masons, generally termed squaremen, with
whom were also associated cabinetmakers, painters, glaziers,
coopers, and slaters ; (3) the websters, or weavers ; (4) the tailors ;
(5) the shoemakers, or cordwainers ; (6) the skinners and gauntlers
or glovers, and furriers ; and (7) the fleshers. The deacons were
freely chosen by their respective freemen ; but the other members of the burghal parliament, though once chosen by their
constituents, were self-elected at the time we have now reached ;
or, more strictly speaking, the annual vacancies that occurred in
the merchant part of the body were filled up by the remaining
councillors, so that the inhabitants at large had no direct voice in
the election. The Trades appointed their deacons annually ; but
the legitimate usage was to continue them in office two years,* so
that the latter were also biennial members of Council. A week
before the annual election of magistrates four new merchant
councillors were chosen, who, with four additional votes, called
"led votes, or voices," exercised by the trade members, swelled
the number of voters at an election to thirty-three.

At one time, as already explained, there were four other
trades incorporated in the burgh—the lorimers or armourers, the
pewterers or tinsmiths, the bonnet-makers, and the litsters or
dyers—all of which became defunct, or were merged into the
remaining seven ; the dead, vanished corporations, however, still
speaking in virtue of these "led voices," uttered on their behalf.
When the provost, bailies, dean, and treasurer were chosen, these
supplementary votes lay dormant for another year ; and as a
week after the annual election the Council was purged by the

---

* Towards the close of the seventeenth century, however, the practice
crept in of re-electing the deacons much more frequently. In 1684 John
Dickson was chosen deacon of the shoemakers for the ninth time consecutively. An act was passed on the 7th December, 1685, prohibiting deacons
from continuing in office more than three years at a time.

ejection of four merchant members, it was thereby reduced to its legal numerical strength of twenty-five.*

In 1627 a prison was erected on the site of the old Deanery, an apartment of which was occupied as the Burgh Court and Council Chamber. This "Tolbooth" stood on the east side of High Street, a little more southerly than the present Mid Steeple. In two important respects the Merchants differed from, and were inferior to, the Trades : they had no head or chief, and were not properly incorporated. Edinburgh, Glasgow, Aberdeen, and Perth possessed merchant guilds, presided over by a dean ; but though Dumfries numbered an official of the same name in its list of magistrates he had no more authority over the merchants than was exercised by the other occupants of the bench. To the Dean of Dumfries was entrusted the duty of regulating weights and measures, and taking other securities for fair dealing between buyers and sellers ; but he acted in this and other respects simply as a magistrate, and not as having any special connection with the mercantile community.

At the close of 1660 the merchants endeavoured to overcome the disadvantages under which they laboured for want of organisation. Less than forty years before, King James had expressed his resolution to grant them a guildry ; but seemingly ignorant of this fact, and knowing nothing of the incipient charter already quoted from, they applied to the Town Council for an act of incorporation. Their movement aroused the jealousy of the deacons, who supposed that what was meant for a gain to the shopkeeping interest would prove a loss to the sons of labour. No sooner was the obnoxious bill introduced, on the 30th of December, than up rose the chief of the deacons, and the convener of the Trades, William M'Kinnell by name, and stoutly protested against the measure. After doing so, he and his brother craftsmen in the Council rose in wrath to leave the meeting ; whereupon Provost Irving bade the officer keep the door "steekit," and let no one out till the close of the proceedings. Deacon John Taylor, however, exclaimed defiantly, "Wha daur keep us in ?" and the uncompromising Seven rushed out of the chamber, Bailie James Muirhead "taking instruments," and setting forth that "the haill merchants of the Counsall hes thought fitt, and hes voted that this burgh be a gild burgh, if they can get it conveniently and honourably done." At the next meeting of Council Convener M'Kinnell followed up the opposition by protesting, in name of his constituents, that all the business done by the Council,

---

* Some irregularities as regards the purging of the Council appear to have taken place, so as to render necessary an act, dated 14th September, 1724, which fixed the 22nd September as the day for electing four merchant councillors, and the 2nd of October as the day for putting off four old merchant councillors ; and the 29th of September as the day for electing the magistrates.

between the last day of December, 1660, and the 5th of January, 1661, was "null and of nane effect, and sall have no binding power." In the course of a month or so, however, the irate men of the Trades became more placable, and the merchants having made some concessions a resolution in favour of the Guild bill was adopted unanimously, the deacons stipulating that the guild be formed on the Edinburgh and Glasgow pattern, "and that the gildrie may not prejudge them of the benefit of a former act of Counsall granted in their favour in the year 1648 ;" the merchants, on the other hand, requiring that both the constitution and rules of the projected body shall be referred to the Convention of Burghs.* From some cause or other, however, the guild movement, as we have seen, did not prosper ; and till this day the Dumfries merchant burgesses have never been incorporated. (a)

Like the Trades, however, they possessed valuable rights conferred by the Council and the Convention, and ratified by the Crown. Over all articles embraced under the general term merchandise they had exclusive sway—bringing to the Nith in their own ships such foreign goods as were allowed to be imported, and selling these, with home products, in the booths, or other places of business. Their far-extending monopoly, as may easily be conceived, was sometimes encroached upon : wine occasionally found its way into the burgh through illegitimate channels, and was vended by stealth in obscure howfs or cabins—the shebeens of that early period ; and trusses of tobacco that had never paid custom or been sold by regular traders helped to make the lieges familiar with the " weed " which King James IV. abhorred, and that too pretty soon after he had fulminated against it his famous " Counterblast." Of " sundrie persons unfreimen dwelling outwith the burgh, in suburbs, landwart kirks, villages, and other places," the merchant burgesses had but too frequently to complain ; " forasmeikle " as these undesirable neighbours were every now and then making " licentious " encroachments, by " opening buiths and stands, frequenting fairs and mercats, buying and selling in great and haill sale, wines, wax, spicenes, wad, and sicklike stuff, and staple goodes, packing and pelling, outwith the said burgh, and other wayes using the privileges and liberties of free burgesses in manifest defraud of the custome, and to the great hurt and prejudice " of the town. A representation to this effect having been made on one occasion to Charles I. by the magistrates, he gave them special authority to exact caution from the culprits that they would not misbehave again ; and failing their appearance, the authorities were enjoined by him to " de-

* Town Council Minutes.

(a) The Dean of Guild Court was created by the Burgh Police (Scotland) Act, 1892, and received extensive powers.

nounce the disobeyers as rebells, and inbring their haill moveable gudes and geir to the King's use for their contempt "—the Crown receiving one half of the merchandise found in their booths or houses, and the other half being left at the disposal of the magistrates.*

* Dr Dickson's Manuscripts.

CHAPTER XXIX.

THE Town Council, as shewn in the preceding chapter, was a
self-chosen body, all the remaining vestiges of popular election
having been swept away by Acts of Parliament passed in 1469
and 1474. When on Michaelmas day yearly new dignitaries had
to be appointed, it was quite well known beforehand who the
favoured individuals were ; but the form of preparing "leets," or
lists of candidates, was observed, care being taken that no trades-
man should be entered, as the high places of authority were
reserved for the patrician merchants. Matters were usually so
arranged, also, as to give the mercantile interest a majority of not
less than two-thirds at the Council board.

At a meeting of the Corporation held on the 18th of March,
1623, a resolution was adopted, "that the merchant estate shall
have two votes both in Council and election, and the craftsmen
one ;" with this further provision, that if any councillor happened
to be absent at the annual elections, "in that case there shall ay
be chosen ane merchant to have vote for the merchant that is
absent, and ane craftsman to have vote for the craftsman that is
absent." This is, we believe, the oldest minute of Council in
existence ; and the closing portion—curious in itself—is therefore
all the more worthy of being copied. After the record of the
resolutions, it is said :—"In witnessing whereof, the Provost,
Baillies, Dean of Gild, Treasurer, Counsell, and Deacons of Crafts,
so many of them as can write, have subscribed these presents, and
the Common Clerk of this Burgh has subscribed for them that
cannot write ; and they caused Master Thomas Ramsay, minister
at Dumfries, and Robert Hislop, procurator for the common weill
thereof, to subscribe the same." Eleven signatures are appended
—being those of Provost Roger Kirkpatrick, two bailies, five
merchant members, and three deacons ; and then it is said to be
subscribed by—"We, Gilbert M'George, convener ; John Richardson, Thomas M'Millan, John Raining, John Blacklock, James

Corsane, William Williamson, Thomas Glencross, John M'Kie, George Rome, James Maxwell, Peter Forsyth, and Thomas Aiken, with our hands at the pen, led by our notaries at our command, because we cannot write our selves."*

Constituted in the manner we have described, the Council possessed an extraordinary amount of power in ancient times. The regular minute-books of their proceedings, which go back about two hundred and twenty years, illustrate at once the manners of the people and the policy of their rulers—both of which in the seventeenth century differed materially from what they are at the present day. Dumfries, let us repeat, possessed exclusive privileges, on the enforcement of which it was thought its very existence depended. Maintain these, and the town would prosper ; relax them, and beggary, ruin, would be the result. No stranger could settle within the burgh unless leave was asked and obtained ; and no one, even after being allowed this liberty, could open a shop for the sale of wares or work as a tradesman, till he had become a burgess in the one case, or both a burgess and a freeman in the other. The Council was the chief fountain of all this power and honour ; and after the merchants and opera-tives, native or "fremmit," had safely passed through these pre-liminary ordeals, and had begun to practise their respective callings, they were tantalised by a set of inquisitorial rules and orders, all, however distasteful, being reckoned advantageous to the trade and general interests of the town. Our forefathers must have often winced under the lash of such over-legislation ; but they comforted themselves with the thought that the system under which they bought, and sold, and laboured, protected them from being swamped by a flood of rivals, and was a very good thing in spite of its defects.

How far protection and monopoly prevailed, and how little of anything like freedom in trade or merchandise was permitted, we have already seen. It mattered not whether the article fabri cated or sold was food or drink, light or fuel, raw clothing material or finished garment, each and all had to be vended or fashioned under certain specified conditions, the breach of which was punished by fine, imprisonment, and, in extreme cases, by for feiture of burgess-ship, or banishment from the burgh. Some times the Council would speculate largely in meal or fish. Thus on the 22nd of May, 1660, they accepted of "ane bargain of 40 bolles meill, maid to them be William Craik, at 20s 6d [Scots] a peck ;" and about the same period they fined a cooper from Glasgow in ten merks because he had the hardihood to sell her-rings within the burgh to private individuals before first offering them to the honourable the Corporation. Forestalling the market

* Dr Dickson's Manuscripts,

and selling goods in private houses were deemed serious offences, and as such severely punished. A delinquent who disposed of his salmon anywhere save at the Fish Cross was liable to a fine of ten merks, and to the loss of his fish. So recently as November, 1717, we find the Dean seizing a daring Annandale man, because he "pactioned for the pryce" of several bundles of lint with private people—dragging him before the Council, and getting him amerced in five shillings sterling ; and in the following year an act was passed discharging the inhabitants "from buying up any fowls or eggs till first the same be brought by the owners thereof to the mercat-place, viz., the Fisherow ;" the penalty for infringement being forty shillings Scots and the confiscation of the articles. Then it was a common thing to fix arbitrarily the market value of goods ; our ancestors knowing nothing, apparently, respecting the laws of supply and demand. Cloth had to be measured in a certain specified way, as well as sold at a stated price. On the 12th of November, 1658, the Council "ordained" that all Scotch and English candles within the burgh "shall be sold at ffour shilling six pennies Scotts ilk pund Scotts weight, and the half pund at eight-and-twentie pennies," under a penalty of five merks ; and at the same sitting it was decreed that no person should sell tallow outside the town, "nor transport it furth thereof," under a fine to the same amount and the confiscation of the tallow.

To bring grist to their own mills exclusively was a ruling object of the Council. On the 24th of January, 1645, a person was fined in five merks for getting his malt or bere ground elsewhere, and had to give besides double multure* to the miller ; and on the following 25th of June an edict was issued confiscating all malt that should be brought ready ground into the town.

Ale was the national liquor of the humbler classes during the seventeenth century, whisky being then unknown. None were allowed to brew or sell liquor unless they were burgesses, and had received a license (for which only a nominal sum was charged) from the magistrates ; and, by an Act passed in 1689, innkeepers were also required to possess accommodation for quartering "four footmen and two horsemen in meat, drink, and bedding." Those who brewed the drink sold it also, in what were sometimes called change-houses. Then, as now, we need scarcely say, "the barley-bree" was the cause of much mischief, though we see no reason to suppose that the Dumfriesians of two hundred years ago were addicted to intemperance : we are disposed to conclude that they were the reverse, as few names of bacchanalians are noticeable in the criminal records of the burgh. The public-houses at that time were subjected to a rigorous inspection, two councillors being

---

* Multure. " 1 Nov., 1687.—The tacksman of the mills allowed to take half a peck of ilk ten pecks of malt as multure."—Town Council Minutes.

appointed to do this duty in each of the four wards—the Town-head quarter, the Cross quarter, the Lochmabengate quarter, and the Kirkgate quarter ; and, however wonderful it may seem, it is nevertheless true, that our burghal legislators (who, with all their ignorance of free trade, did many wise things) actually anticipated and outrivalled Mr Forbes Mackenzie by limiting the hours in which it was lawful to sell intoxicating liquors in Dumfries. In accordance with this legislation the brewers, before obtaining leave to brew and sell liquor, were required to make a declaration as follows :—" That no vitious or scandelous personnes shall be harboured or resett in our houses, and that we nor any of our families sall be found drunk, and that we sall resett no drunken personnes whatsoever, and that we sall not sell drink to any per-sone or personnes within our houses on the Sabbath, and sell nor resett nor give drink to any personnes after nine o'clock at nyght ; and that if we sall be at any tyme found contravenors of these presents, we sall pay for the first fault five merks, for the second ten merks, and for the third fault to be depryvit of the libertie of brewing."

Wine, chiefly brought from France, was then, as at present, the favourite beverage of the upper classes. In 1661 it appears the supply had become very short ; and the Council, according to their stereotyped notions in matters of trade, ordered all vintners within the burgh " to sell their French wyne for fyve groats a pynt, under the penaltie of ten marks Scots money." A resolu-tion to this effect was carried, but not till "Thomas Irving, eldest baillye "—who lived in advance of his colleagues—had protested against the folly of " setting pryce upon any forraine wair."

The treasurer's accounts relating to the middle of the seven-teenth century show that the burgh authorities were often very liberal in their " spendings " for liquor at the public cost.* At one time—and probably the practice was long maintained—they had a tavern of their own, kept by Dame Agnes M'Kill, who ran up a regular score against them, which amounted annually to a good round sum. It was customary, too, for the Provost to keep a well-stored wine cellar and a hospitable board—the " little bill " due for which by the town amounted to £797 Scots, from the 29th of March, 1670, till the 6th October, 1673. Not content with treating themselves and others on great public occasions, the magistrates and councillors fortified themselves for their routine duties by frequent potations. On the anniversary of the King's birth-day,

---

* It may be useful here to state that since the close of the fourteenth century Scots money had become so depreciated that its value, as compared with sterling or English, was as one to twelve. One shilling Scots, after that period, was just equal to one penny sterling ; and one pound Scots to one shilling and eightpence sterling. One merk Scots was equivalent to 13⅓d sterling.

at the yearly elections, at the letting of the burgh revenues, at the allotment of the pastures, and when any notable person was made a burgess, they "pushed about the jorum" in no stinted style ; but then, in addition to such allowable libations, we find in the books such entries as the following :—" 10 Jan., 1669.—Item : Before the magistrates went to church, a gill of brandie and a choppin of ale, the Provest and Bailie Cowpland being present, 2s 10d. 11 Jan.—Item : Due by them, a choppin of seck and a pynt of aill, befoir they went to the Counsell, the Proveist, Baillie Cowpland, Bailie Newall, and the tua Deacon M'Kinnels being present, £1 1s 8d." Again :—" 12 Feb., 1672.—Two pynts of aill befoir the magistrates went to the kirk, 3s 4d. 13 Feb.—Mair ane choppin of wyne and ane qwart of aill before the magistrates went to the Counsell. 28 Feb.—Mair three pynts of aill befoir the baillies went to the court, 5s."

"Leeze me on drink !" was the favourite congratulatory motto of these burghal magnates ; and how they did act upon it to propitiate their lordly patrons, as well as to " moistify their own leather," is seen in such charges as these :— " 23 July, 1672.—With William of Terregles and Springkell when they came from my Lord Maxwell anent the Bridge-end Mercat, seven pynts of wine, and 4 shillings for tobacco and pypes, £7 4s. 30th July.—Sent for to the Castle by the Provest, Bailie Stephan [Irving], Bailie Cowpland, and the Conveiner, with my Lord Maxwell, four pynts of wyne, and a glasse, is £4 6s. Nov. 11.—The Pro., B. Steph., B. Coupland, the Conveiner, Deacon Crosbie, and Deacon Herron, with William of Terregles, Maeby, Carnsallock, Newlaw, and the gentlemen of the pairty, when they were made burgesses, fyftein pynts of wyne, tua pynts of ale, and one gill of brandy, £15 5s 10d. Ap. 5, 1669.—Drunken in companie with the Erll of Nithsdaill, my Lord and Master of Maxwell, the Lairds of Mabie and Cowhill, younger, and severall uther gentlemen, the Proveist and thrie Bailies being present, £7 4s. Item, in that same companie for fyve pynts of aill, and for tobacco and pipes, 10s 4d. 10 May, 1672. —Ane pynt of wyne sent for by Bailie Stephan to the Castle, with my Lord Nithsdale, £1 ; that day sent for by the Provest to the Castle, with the Earl of Nithsdale and Lord Maxwell, ane pynt of wine, £1. May 25.—With the Earl of Nithsdale, Lord Maxwell, Gribton, and other gentlemen, when Capt. Wachope was made burgess, the Provest and Bailie Stephan present, ten pynts wine, and vi. sh. for aill, tobacco, and pypes, £10 12s."

These bacchanalian jottings may be fittingly followed up with an entry or two about the magisterial feasts. When the fires of persecution were raging over the district in 1664, the rulers of the burgh, heedless of the sufferers outside, dined luxuriously, like Dives, on the election day. They spent £6 2s for "six pynts of wyn, four pynts of ail, and tobacco and pypes" on the preceding

evening, the charges for the banquet itself being as subjoined :—
" October 3, the day of the election.—Threttie-two pynts and one
chopin of wyne, £28 16s ; three muchkins of seck, £1 16s ; six
quarts of extraordinar ail, £1 ; tobacco and pypes, £1 16s ; ordinary, forty-thrie men at two tables, at 12 sh. ilk man, £25 16s ;
after tables, threttie at 6 shs., £3 18s"—the whole account amounting to £69 4s. The charge for the dinner in 1667 is less extravagant :—" 46 men dinner is £27 12s ; 15 later meat men, £4 10s ; 14
pynts of wyne, £14 ; brandie, £1 5s ; aill extraordinar, £1 10s ;
tobacco and pypes, 18s :" in all, £49 15s.

A case of assault, which occurred towards the close of 1670,
and made a great noise at the time, arose, probably, out of one of
these convivial gatherings. No wonder that it occasioned much
excitement. The sufferer was the greatest official personage in
the burgh : his assailant a scion of the house of Douglas. Under
what precise circumstance the Laird of Kilhead "laid violent
hands" upon Provost John Irving cannot be ascertained ; but it
is recorded that on the 9th of December in the above year the
Council, all in one voice, reprobated the outrage committed on
their chief, and ordered letters to be sent to the Earl of Annandale
and the offender's father, Lord Drumlanrig, craving redress, with
the intimation that if it were withheld they would "pursue for a
legal reparation before the Lords of his Majesty's Privie Counseil."
Well advised by his friends, Sir James Douglas of Kilhead, accom
panied by Robert, Lord Maxwell, presented himself at Provost
Irving's house, where, in expectation of his visit, were assembled
the Provost, the three bailies, Stephen Irving, Martin Irving, and
Francis Irving, the late bailies, John Cowpland, John Corbet,
and James Kennan, the deacon-convener, Thomas Anderson, the
treasurer, Thomas Richardson, and the deacon of the smiths,
William M'Kinnell. In the presence of this representative meeting Kilhead, going—figuratively—down on his knees, before the
offended majesty of the burgh, "acknowledged his late inscuradge
towards the said John Irving, Provost, and humbly craved the
said Provost, and the haill incorporation, pardon therefor ; and
declared that quhat he did was not of any prejudice against him
or the town, but that, on the contrair, he loved and respectit him
and the hail toun ; and faithfully promised that he should be so
far from wronging of any inhabitant of this burgh quhsoevir,
heirefter, that he should be a friend to them, in all tyme comeing,
to the utmost of his power." A most handsome apology, which,
we need scarcely say, the Council at their next meeting accepted ;
and thus a difficulty which might, if mismanaged at the beginning,
have ruptured the friendly connection that existed between the
burgh and the Drumlanrig family, was amicably disposed of.

When Mrs M'Kill, at whose house these burghal entertainments were held, furnished her quarterly bill against the Council,

she also supplied the treasurer with a note of her own expenses,
some items of which are curious and instructive. When the
websters came to warp her sheets of home-spun she treated them
to three pints of ale, charge 3s 8d. The landlady had a little
farm, which grew not only barley and oats, but wheat ; and when
the wheat was reaped an extra dinner, including "ane leg of
mutton," at 10s (tenpence sterling), was provided for the occasion.
Then for "aill at the shearing of the wheat" there was a charge
of 13s 6d ; "for the sheirers for sheiring the wheat, 11s ;" "the
man that mowed the beir" received 4s ; and among the other
entries at the harvest season we find charges "for aine sheip's heid
and ane leg of mutton, 8s 8d ;" for three chickens, 5s [rather more
than three half-pence farthing sterling each] ; and for herring at
the inning of the wheat on the 10th day of September [old style]
9d." We learn from other charges that in those days a peck of
meal cost 1s 2d sterling, a pound of butter 4½d sterling, and a
dozen of eggs fully a penny farthing. Mrs M'Kill's daughter or
maid-servant, Marion, was supplied with a pair of shoes, the cost
of which is set down at £1 2s Scots : that is to say, 1s 10d sterling
—no inconsiderable sum, being equivalent to the third part of a
labourer's weekly hire two centuries ago.

So multifarious and heavy were the duties of the Council that
meetings were held every Monday ; and the member who was a
quarter of an hour late was fined 12s Scots ; while if he did not
shew face at all the fine was increased to 20s, unless protected by
"an excuse intimated to and accepted by a magistrate." A small
annual allowance, called a "pension," was enjoyed by the chief
office-bearers. In 1639, there was paid to John Corsane, Provost,
£66 13s 4d ; £40 to each of the three bailies, and to the dean and
treasurer. Much of the business done at the table was deemed
sacred ; and woe to the reckless representative who dared to make
it patent to the vulgar public—an act, dated 3rd December, 1674,
providing that "any councillor divulging any secrets moved or
spoken in council shall be fined in 40 lib., and put out of the
Council with disgrace."

One of the Council's wise enactments was passed on the 10th
of June, 1667, when they resolved to give effect to a permissive law
adopted by the Convention of Burghs, in favour of making uniform all the weights and measures used in the town—the weights
to be according to the Lanark standard ; the firlot according to
the Linlithgow standard : the ell-wand, rule, and foot measure to
be furnished by the Edinburgh Dean of Guild ; and a measure
called a gauge, or jug, to be made after the Stirling model.
Another act, of a more recent date, prohibits butchers from
"blowing and scoreing meat," and from offering for sale "dead
kids, lambs, or spoyled meat," under pain of forfeiting two pounds
Scots, and the meat besides. If at harvest season any poor people

desired to earn a "penny fee" in reaping corn at a distance, they might be hindered by such an edict as the following, which bears date 29th July, 1661 :—" It is ordaint that no persone or persones, residenters within this burghe, goe to Lowthian to shear, under the payne of [blank], as also that they nevir be resett within this burghe ; and that the peats and turves now in their howses sall be takine out and put in the tolbooth for the use of prisoners ; and that all resetters of them at their home-comeing pay ten punds Scots." Sometimes the Council interfered with the Trades in a manner that must have been peculiarly repugnant to the craftsmen. Thus, on the 10th of September, 1662, a bailie was appointed to attend the election of the deacons, to tender the oath of allegiance to each freeman, to debar from voting those who refused to be sworn, and to imprison all who, in defiance of his interdict, exercised their suffrage.

Not only did the Council exercise a despotic oversight of secular affairs, but they co-operated with the Church courts in efforts to enforce morality, and at least an outward observance of religious ordinances. Thus, on the 14th March, 1664, they passed an act intended to check the practices indulged in by many of going abroad, walking idly from house to house, and gossipping out of doors on the Sabbath day—the penalty imposed for each of such offences being a fine of twelve shillings Scots, to be paid to the kirk treasurer for the use of the poor ; and on the same day the Council, understanding that there were "many idle persones quho habitually curse and sweir, both publicly in the oppin markittis and streitts, and in aill-houses and inns," resolved to amerce each offender six shillings Scots— such fines to be also applied for the benefit of the poor.

The ubiquitous power of the burghal parliament was specially felt in social matters : it was manifested at births and marriages, and only terminated with the grave. If a young couple wished their wedding to be signalised by imposing festivities they had first to consider whether they might not have to pay too dearly for the indulgence. At one time, it would seem, it was customary in Dumfries to have large, costly, and protracted marriage enter-tainments. which provoked the Council to launch forth an edict, on the 6th of July, 1657, restricting the attendance at and expense of such convivial meetings—the former being limited to twenty-four persons, the latter to eight pounds Scots, "and that under the payne of twenty pounds, whereof the one half is to be payt by the bridegroom, and the other half by the inkeiper quher the brydle is kept." Then, if the same or any other married pair desired to make a hospitable or ostentatious display at the baptism of their first-born, they had to bear in mind a ukase, also passed at the above sitting, restricting the attendance at the sacred rite to twelve individuals, under a penalty of ten merks, *toties quoties*.

The reader, after these statements, will be quite prepared to learn that the subject of education did not escape the Argus eyes of the Council. Honour to them that they patronised the grammar school that had been set up in pre-Reformation times in the burgh ; but that they should have sought to maintain it, and crush all rival seminaries, by the means revealed in their minutes of March 14th, 1660, is not at all to their credit. The record of that date states, in effect, that the Council, considering the prejudice the town sustains by the inhabitants detaining their children from the burgh school, and sending them to other "pettie schooles" in the town or neighbourhood, ordain "that all the inhabitants put their children, especially lads, to the High School," between the present time and the 21st of May next, "and that under the penalty of ffyve merkss, to be payit by ilk persoun faillyen, for ilk manchyld they sall abstract frae the said schoole" —the same penalty to be paid by those who have children come of due age, with means to educate them, who do not put them to the burgh school ; while, further to secure a monopoly to that favoured establishment, the "pettie" dominies who attempted to break it down by teaching any of the pupils reserved for it were also made liable to a fine of five merks for each offence.

These false views in political economy were not by any means peculiar to Dumfries or to Scotland—they were characteristic of the age ; and when the magistrates of the town undertook the censorship of morals they only carried into effect principles that were pretty generally recognised at the time, though the influence of Calvin on Scotland, through her great reformer Knox, gave them more prominence there than in other States—Geneva perhaps excepted. Calvin's ideal was that of a Christian commonwealth : "Christian in the details as well as in the general spirit of its laws, and considering itself responsible before God for all the actions of the citizens." He wished faith to occupy in the State the place which we in modern days assign to it in the individual ; and consequently he wished the State "to force the individual to do, in virtue of the common faith, all that the same individual, supposing him to be a true Christian, would do in virtue of his individual faith."* It was because views of this kind,

* Bungener's Calvin, p. 108. The same writer, in describing the influence of Geneva on Scotland, through Knox, says :—" Knox, on leaving Geneva, felt as a new man ; and Scotland, on seeing Knox again, felt as if she had been breathed upon by a new breath of doctrine and of life. Let us leave to abler men to study how the genius of Scotland, personified by Knox, entered into communion so intimate with the genius of Calvin. Let us simply state what was, and what is. For three centuries Scotland has manifested it with noonday clearness. She has been proud and happy to be connected, through Knox, with a greater than Knox ; and this gratitude, deeper now, perhaps, than at any other period, is not less glorious to Scotland than to Calvin." (Pp. 279-80.)

communicated from Geneva, where they were practically realised, pervaded the Scottish mind that the magistrates, great and small, felt themselves bound to take cognisance of sins against the Decalogue as well as transgressions of the civil law. Then while our town councils seemed sometimes to be encroaching upon clerical rights and duties, presbyteries and kirk sessions often invaded the magisterial domain by exacting pecuniary penalties for spiritual offences. But on this topic, and others allied to it, we shall have more to say in a subsequent chapter.

Other functions exercised by the Council remain still to be noticed—those of a judicial kind. They shared with the magistrates the right to try all cases, civil or criminal, brought before the burgh court. We never read in the old minute-books of the Provost and Bailies administering the law : it was the Council, inclusive of them, who dealt out justice on all persons charged with intemperance, slander, theft, assault, forgery, or other crimes which did not involve a capital sentence or transportation. The burgh was itself a sheriffdom, and very jealous its authorities were lest their jurisdiction should be invaded by the county officials. On the 11th of July, 1662, the Council sentenced Thomas Johnstone, the turnkey of the Tolbooth, and William Douglas, a town's officer, to be imprisoned eight days each, "for taking a country man to the Shirref-depute to be judged who committit a batterie" in the burgh. The same feeling is still more forcibly shewn in the following minute, dated 5th September, 1663 :— "The Council, considering the great abuse of their authoritie by Elizabeth Gibson, relict of Thomas Crawford, by writing an address to the Sheriff-deput of Nithsdaill for repairing a wrong done by one of our burgesses to her, whereby she has endeavoured to move the Shereff-depute to encrotch upon the privileges of this burgh, contraire to the bound fidelitie of a burgess's wife ; therefore the Magistrates and Counsel discharges hir of aney privilege or libertie she can pretend to of freedom of trade within this burgh."

Sometimes, on the other hand, the burgh authorities encroached upon the baronial rights of their neighbours. In the same year (1663) two "cronies" from the country having met at Dumfries, one of them, Roger Safely, laughingly told the other, James Gilkers or Gilchrist, that he was sorely in want of a wife, adding, "could ye wish me to yin, it wad be a great obligement." "I'm the very man for that,' was the ready response ; "providing I can get quat of my wyfe, I shall be weil content to let ye have her for a groat." A "chappin'" of hands clenched the bargain. News of the scandalous transaction was carried to Stephen Irving, commissary-depute and bailie, who caused buyer and seller to be brought before him ; and, though they pleaded that the whole affair was a joke, he sentenced them to pay a fine of £100 Scots, and to stand in the " juggs " for an hour.   On another plea—that the offenders were vassals to Lords Nithsdale and Herries, and living as such beyond the jurisdiction of the burgh magistrates— the sentence against them was quashed by the Privy Council.*

Minor offences were punished in the burgh court by slight fines, or exposure on the pillory or in the stocks, and those of a more serious nature by heavy fines,† lengthened imprisonments, scourgings, or banishment from the town ; and often two or more of these punishments were conjoined in the sentences passed upon incorrigible delinquents.‡   A few illustrative instances will suffice :—On the 29th of January, 1668, a woman, whose " raucle tongue " had been too roughly used against a neighbour, was ordained to be " put upon the trone with great letters of 'Scandall' on her heid."   On the 9th of July, 1670, a " servitor " to Yorstoun having, when " most scandalously drunk," abused the magistrates by " scandalous speitches," was sobered by being " set upon the Mercat Cross " for four hours, and afterwards " cast into the Thieves' Hole " for eight-and-forty hours.   A man who had counterfeited " the subscription and hand-wryte of Major Thomas Carruthers " in a letter purporting to have been sent by that gentleman to George Maxwell of Munches, was, on the 4th of August, 1662, condemned to be imprisoned till the following Wednesday, then to be placed on the pillory, with the forged letter and a label " making mention of his trespasse " pinned to his breast ; and finally to be conveyed beyond the burgh roods by the common executioner, with the intimation that there would be

* Privy Council Records.

† In 1666 the Council fixed the fine for a simple assault at £5 Scots, and for assault to the effusion of blood at £25.   In 1676 it was enacted that " the first that votes in the Council to give doun [reduce] a fine, was to pay the fine himself."—Town Council Minutes.

‡ The old Scottish pillory, known in history by the title of the " Collistriguum," or neck stretcher, is utterly forgot.   By this instrument a very savage punishment was inflicted.   The culprit being placed on a low scaffold, in a standing position, his neck was encased in a wooden collar or board, not so closely as to provoke suffocation ; but, being elevated to such a height as just to allow the tip of the toes to barely touch the ground, the weight of the body on the chin and back of the head produced a painful sensation.   The thumbikens, or small iron vice, which squeezed the thumb to extort confession, and the iron boot and wedge, were principally used in the reign of Charles II.   Nailing the " luggs " to the trone (a post at the market place at which goods were weighed) was a very common punishment in Scotland prior to the eighteenth century.   It was latterly only applied to gipses or tinkers ; who could be so used merely for being habit and repute " Egyptians." Another very usual punishment at one period was the chaining of evil-doers to the gateways of the parish churches by an iron collar fastened with a padlock.   Sometimes the culprits were dressed in sackcloth, and passengers had a liberty of spitting upon individuals so unfortunately condemned to this species of pillory.   The collars used on these occasions were called the " jougs " (from *jugum*, a yoke), and answered the same purpose as the stocks in England.—Chambers's Book of Scotland, pp. 328-9.

a rod in pickle for him should he venture to return. We close with the following curious case of red-handed justice, administered in accordance with the well-known principle of Scottish law, by which summary punishment might be inflicted on criminals "taken in the act." On the 12th of June, 1663, an individual was ordained " to be convoyed out of the town be the hand of the hangman, and nevir to return therein, and a bauk [drum] to be bait at his heills ; nane to resett him in their howses under the pain of ten merks, he being taken reid-hand steiling malt out of the sack standing in the mylne."

In the early part of the seventeenth century periodical justiciary courts were held at Dumfries which exercised a very extensive jurisdiction—cases involving a death penalty coming before them from the sheriffdoms of Berwick, Roxburgh, Selkirk, Peebles, and Nithsdale, and the stewartries of Annandale and Kirkcudbright. A glance at the proceedings during part of a single session will shew the kind of crimes most prevalent at that time in these districts, and how they were dealt with by the court. On the 21st of May, 1622, the justiciary court was opened in the burgh by " Walter, Erle of Buccleuche ; Lord Scott of Whitchesters and Eskdaill ; Sir Andrew Ker of Oxnam, knight, Master of Jebrut ; Sir William Setoune of Killismure, knyt. ; and Sir John Murray of Philiphaugh, kt., commissioners appoyntit by our Souvrane Lord, under his Majesties Greit Seale for that effect ; Gilbert Watt, notar-public, clark ; Wm. Cornwath ; Robert Scott ; Messrs Steven Young, officer, and John Douglas, dempster." A good deal of time is taken up with the fencing of the court, and other preliminary forms, after which sundry men of substance step forward and give bond for the good behaviour of certain lawbreakers or their surrender for trial if called upon. For example, John Jardine of Applegarth becomes surety for William Carruthers, brother of Holmends, that " he, his wyf, bairnes, their tennents, nor servands," shall not trouble, molest, nor injure John Gask, in Kirkstyle of Rewell, "his wyf, bairnes, servands, men tennents, cornes, cattle, guidis, nor geir uther wayes," and that he shall keep the peace, under the pain of five hundred merks ; while, on the other hand, Lancelot Murray, in Arbigland, bailie to the Laird of Cockpule, gives security to the same amount that Carruthers, his family and property, will receive no harm at the hands of Gask.

Next day the serious business begins—George Riddick, in Dumfries, as Procurator-Fiscal, bringing before the court no fewer than seventeen panels or prisoners, " remitted to the trial of ane assyze," consisting of the following gentlemen :—" John Lindsay of Auchinskeoche ; Gawine Johnstoune in Midlegill ; Robert Herris of Killilour ; Thomas Dunbar, brother to Harbart Huntar in Halywood ; John Thomsoune in Kirkland of Tarregillis ; Thomas Wricht in Carruquhane ; William Glendinning of Lagnane ; David

Neilsoune of Barncaillie ; William Veitch of Skar ; Robert Scott,
laitt baillie of Hawick ; Robert Scott, Westport in Hawick ; John
Dickiesoune, provest of Peiblis ; William Eliott, late provest of
Peiblis ; James Keine, laitt bailie of Selkirk ; and William Scott,
callit of the Pillaris, laitt bailie ther." This jury, it will be
observed, is composed in equal proportions of landed proprietors,
tenant farmers, and burghal gentry ; and, curiously enough, as
shewing the prevalence of cattle-lifting, the chronic offence of the
period, nearly all the cases brought before them are of that
character. The stealing of "ane kow" from Blacketrig ; of "twa
fat scheip fra Andro Little in Rig ;" of "twa yows from Newland ;"
of "four rouch unclippit scheip fra Jon Makgill in Kirkconnell ;"
of "fyftein wedderis pertaining to Bailie Nicholsoune in Park-
burne ;" of "ane meir of four yeir auld furth of the lands of
Hershaw ;" of "seven ky and oxen furth of Yarrow-heid ;" of
"threttene cheises, ilk ane ten pounds wecht ;" of "ane sack of
fustiane fra James Lyndsay and his brother, pedleris and mer-
chands, furth of their packs ;" of "certaine claithes perteneing to
Jon Lytle, callit the King, furth of his house in Annane :" such
are the kind of cases that come up. In each instance the accused
are "clengit," or cleansed—that is to say, acquitted—by the jury ;
and a similar verdict is returned in the subjoined case, which is
given in greater detail, as a fair specimen of the rest. George
Colthart, servitor of Jaffray Irwing, "is accusit for airt and pairt
of the steilling of ane stott of thrie yeir auld, perteneing to Jon
Bell, in Butter-daillis ; and for airt and pairt of the steilling of
six ky and oxen fra Robert Mundell, in Tinwald, and William
Makmorrane, the first therof, in October, 1620 years ; and for the
steilling of twa ky perteneing to umqule Adam Corsane, merchant,
burgess of Dumfreis, furth of the lands of Cocklekis ; and for the
receting, manteneing, and intercommuning with Ritchie Irwine,
in Wodhous, and Jaffray Irwine of Rabgill, fugitives and out-
lawes." Witnesses are examined ; the evidence is considered by
the assize ; the chancellor, Mr John Lindsay, pronounces words
pleasant to the ear of the panel—"Clengit and acquite of the
haill ;" and away he goes out of court rejoicing. A small proportion of the trials terminate differently. Two brothers, named
Irwing, acquitted on one of the preceding charges, are again
brought to the bar, accused of having, so far back as 1616, stolen
forty pounds Scots from a chest belonging to David Irwin, at
Stapleton. One of them, Gilbert, gets "clean" off ; the other,
George, is "fylitt"—stained, convicted ; and the dempster begins
to realise the fact—pleasant or otherwise—that he will yet have
something to do ; something very serious he sees it will be, when
the same two criminals, again indicted for the "stouthrief" of
twelve sheep belonging to James Irwing of Wyseby, are "fylitt
thairof."

Other capital convictions follow, providing work, not simply for the dempster, but for the executioner :—Adam Henrie, who had made too free with the cattle of Yarrow-heid ; Walter Lytle, who had harried a hirsel at Elven Water " perteneing to the Lady Johnstoune," and " burned Andro Lytle his house in Bombie ;" " Bauld Jok Armstrang," who had tithed the flocks of Hairlaw-mill ; and Thomas Moffat, in Hightae, who had borrowed without leave four hundred merks from the coffers of Bailie Wilsonne, Lochmaben—are all found guilty ; and, together with the two Irwings, are " ilk of thame adjudgit and condampnit to be taken to the place of execution in Dumfreis, and ther to be hangit be the heid, ay and quhill thay be deid, as was pronouncit in judge-ment be the mouth of the said Jon Douglas, dempstar "—all except " Bauld Jok," who, as his offence (stealing five sheep) was of a lighter hue than the crimes of his fellow-convicts, is sentenced to the less ignominious doom of drowning till " he be deid in the wattir of Nith."*

* The record of these cases was first published in a supplement to the Annals of Hawick, in which work it is stated that the original manuscript had " slumbered apparently unnoticed for more than two centuries amongst the archives of the burgh of Hawick," having probably found its way thither " in consequence of Mr Gilbert Watt, town-clerk of Hawick for at least twenty years prior to 1658, having also been clerk of circuit." It is further explained " that no similar record of so early a date has been preserved in the General Register House at Edinburgh."

CHAPTER XXX.

REFERENCE has already been made to King James's treatment of
the Church of Scotland by which its Presbyterian character was
subverted ; and on this subject it is necessary that we should give
a few more details.   He was made to believe by the Anglican
clergy that if the Scottish Establishment were assimilated to
theirs the process would help on his own favourite scheme for the
legislative union of the two kingdoms.   That he might with more
safety carry out his plans he refused to summon a General
Assembly ; but the representatives of nine Presbyteries met at
Aberdeen in 1605, and constituted themselves into an Assembly in
the name of the great Head of the Church.   The leader of this
contumacious movement was the celebrated John Welsh, whose
father, of the same name, was Laird of Colliston, and other estates
in Dunscore and Holywood.*   Being of a romantic, adventurous
disposition, Welsh, when a mere boy, left his father's house, and
lived for a while a vagrant, lawless life with a band of Border
robbers.   His wild oats were soon sown out ; and the repentant
prodigal, presenting himself at the door of his aunt, Mrs Forsyth,

---

* The Welshes were settled at a very early period in Nithsdale.   Nicholas
Welsh was Abbot of Holywood in 1488 ; Dean William Welsh was Vicar of
Tynron in 1530 : soon after the latter date, Dean Robert Welsh was vicar of
the same parish ; and John Welsh was Vicar of Dunscore, and he took office
in the Reformed Church in 1560.—Young's "Life of John Welsh."

who resided in Dumfries. He was received by her with motherly tenderness, and through her good offices was reconciled to his father. He is said to have attended the grammar school of the burgh—the teacher of which, Ninian Dalyell, was eventually deposed by the General Assembly for having read the Roman Catechism to his scholars. In 1592 we find young Welsh (he was just twenty-two) settled down as a devoted Christian minister in the parish of Kirkcudbright ; and in 1598 we see him entering the controversial lists against Gilbert Brown, Commendator of Sweetheart Abbey, and that with such success as to elicit a hearty eulogium from the King, who, besides praising Welsh's defence of Protestantism, rated Brown as "a foolish reasoner." If James could only bring over to his views this profound and brilliant Nithsdale divine, the battle he had with Presbytery would be more than half gained. Welsh scorned to accept the high preferment with which his Majesty sought to bribe him : he paid more regard to his own integrity than to royal favour—preferred the perilous wilderness of Presbyterianism to all the treasures of the Prelatical Egypt ; and so we find him, in 1605, bearding Majesty, and courting persecution, if not death, at Aberdeen. Welsh and five of his colleagues were actually convicted of a capital crime, their offence being treated as treason by the Crown officers ; but the sentence was commuted to transportation.*

James, having got rid of these and other obstructives, proceeded to augment the power and influence of the Scottish bishops. Invested by him with paramount authority over the ministers, they superintended settlements and fixed stipends as they pleased. Gavin Hamilton was made Bishop of Galloway in 1606. Since the see was occupied by a Romish prelate, thirty years before, its revenues had been reduced by alienations, annuities, and pensions, to a beggarly pittance ; but the considerate King dowered it with the neighbouring Abbacies of Dundrennan and Tongland, the Priory of Whithorn, and the Monastery of Glenluce, with all their churches, lands, and rents, so that Bishop Hamilton became no mean dignitary of the new Episcopal Kirk. A jovial, indolent, pleasure-loving, care-defying prelate he was. "When," says Calderwood, "Mr Gilbert Power, a brother of the ministry in

* Welsh spent about sixteen years of exile in France, where he gained the favour of Louis XIII., who allowed him to exercise his vocation as a preacher. On his health failing, he was permitted to return to England in 1622 ; but King James would on no account allow hi 1 to cross the Border when he wished to get the benefit of his native air—his Majesty declaring that he would never be able to establish Prelacy in Scotland if Mr Welsh revisited that country. James even debarred him from preaching in London, till informed that he could not long survive ; and when the preacher at length obtained access to a pulpit, he discoursed with his wonted fire and eloquence, but, on retiring to his house, expired within two hours afterwards ; "and so," says Calderwood, "endit his dayes with the deserved name of an holy man, a painfull and powerfull preachour, and a constant sufferer for the trueth."

Galloway, modestly refused a carouse offered by him, he abused him in presence of other ministers, plucking his hat from his head in his furie, and casting it upon the ground. He dispensed with the marriage of a gentleman in Galloway, named Niven Agnew of Mais, having his first wife alive ; notwithstanding that the brethren of the ministry in open synod opponed unto it, as a perillous preparative, tending to the overthrow of discipline in that rude diocie, and to open a door to adulterers."* Upon Hamilton's death, in 1616, William Cowper, minister of Perth, who had in other days denounced the Episcopal system, was promoted to the bishopric, after which, says the author we have just quoted, he ceased to reside in Galloway, but dwelt " in the foot of the Cannongate, that he might be near to the Chapell Royal, where he preached as dean, neglecting his diocie, where he ought to have preached as a bishop, if his office had been lawful."† Calderwood, it ought to be noticed, is especially cynical and severe when handling the bishops ; and if his picture of the Galloway ones be not overdrawn, it is little wonder that Prelacy made slow progress in the diocese. Besides their jurisdiction in the Stewartry and Wigtownshire, they bore rule over the ministers of Dumfries, Closeburn, Trailflat annexed to Tinwald, Drumgree annexed to Johnstone, Staplegordon annexed to Langholm, all in Dumfries-shire. When Episcopacy was abolished at the Revolution, the net revenue of the see amounted to £5634 15s Scots, a larger income than that of any other Scottish bishopric, and only exceeded by the two primacies of St Andrews and Glasgow.

In 1610 the royal plot against Presbyterianism was further developed, by the erection of the prelates into two courts of High Commission, with well-nigh absolute powers over the ministers and members of the Church. They were invested with authority to try all persons accused of heretical opinions or immoral practices, and to punish them, on conviction, by fines, imprisonment, and excommunication—a power which they usually exercised in a most inquisitorial spirit, and so as, on mere pretences, to harass unmercifully the anti-Episcopal pastors of the Church. The Earls of Cassilis and Wigtown, the Bishop of Galloway, James Halliday, Commissary of Dumfries, and Thomas Ramsay, minister there, officiated as members of the Commission for the southern division of Scotland ;‡ but from what is known of Mr Ramsay, we may be sure he had no relish for the work assigned to him. Calderwood truly says :—" This Commission put the King in possession of that which he had long hunted for—to wit, absolute power to use the bodies and goods of his subjects at pleasure, without form or processe of the common law. So our bishops were fit instruments to overthrow the liberties both of kirk and countrey." The King

* Calderwood, p. 648.   † Ibid.   ‡ Ibid, p. 617.

ventured to summon an Assembly in the same year, confidently anticipating that it would give full effect to his new device. It met at Glasgow on the 8th of June ; the Presbytery of Dumfries being represented in it by Messrs Thomas Ramsay, Robert Hunter, Robert Henrison, and Simeon Johnston ; and that of Kirkcudbright by Bishop Hamilton, and Messrs William Hamilton, Robert Glendinning, and James Donaldson. His Majesty was correct in supposing that the Assembly would prove subservient to his devices. Resolutions were passed by it, declaring the Assembly at Aberdeen to be null, establishing the courts of High Commission, and adopting other disgraceful measures—there being but seven dissentients, of whom the minister of Dumfries was one.*

Chiefly for the purpose of completing his victory over Presbyterianism, King James, as we have seen, visited Edinburgh in 1617. To the General Assembly, then sitting, he bluntly declared : " The bishops must rule the ministers, and I rule both ;" and the Assembly of the following summer was sufficiently obsequious to adopt, with forty-five dissentients, the Five Articles of Faith, which enforced—(1) Kneeling at the communion ; (2) private communion ; (3) private baptism ; (4) confirmation of children ; and (5) observance of festivals.

When James died, in 1625, he was succeeded by his son Charles I., who had imbibed all his father's extravagant ideas of the royal prerogative, and who proceeded to act upon them with a recklessness which soon evoked the opposition of his subjects in both kingdoms. Scottish Presbyterianism was so diametrically at variance with that passive obedience which Charles deemed his birthright, and with that ecclesiastical system of which he was a bigoted votary, that he resolved, if possible, to render Prelacy paramount in his northern dominions, and thus complete the fabric begun by his predecessor. After a few preliminary steps he commissioned the Earl of Nithsdale to hold a Convention of Estates, in order to obtain from them an act restoring to the Crown all the tithes and Church lands that had been shared among the nobility, or been otherwise disposed of during the two preceding reigns—the infatuated monarch desiring by means of this wealth to build up the Scottish hierarchy in a style of imposing magnificence. In vain, however, did Nithsdale press this self-sacrificing project on the assembled barons. They resisted it with such firmness that it was hopelessly abandoned.

Though baffled in this endeavour, Charles continued to prosecute his darling scheme ; and with Laud, Archbishop of Canterbury, as his willing instrument, he resolved to impose a liturgy on the Church—the hazardous experiment to be tried first in Edinburgh, it being supposed that, as many of the citizens were depen-

* Calderwood, p. 632.

dent upon the Court, it would have the best chance of success among them ; and that if it really succeeded the country at large would follow the example of the capital.   How the fine-laid scheme of the King and Prelate was thwarted, annihilated, by a humble Presbyterian matron—the immortal Jenny Geddes—is known to everyone.   " Villain ! dost thou say mass at my lug !" were the words, and a " cutty stool " was the weapon, with which the audacious innovation was indignantly challenged and repelled. The violent opposition given in Edinburgh to the Service-book met with general approval, and elicited a kindred feeling in all quarters.   In order to direct it with concentrated force against the King's obnoxious measures a meeting was held in the metropolis, comprising influential men from all parts of Scotland ; a petition of redress, emanating from it, was replied to by a royal letter, arrogantly commanding the petitioners to leave the city within twenty-four hours ; and the latter, finding that they need look for no concessions, formed a national committee, or provisional government, to protect their rights, consisting of members elected from the various classes of noblemen, gentlemen, clergymen, and burgesses.   Thus the far-famed Four Tables were originated, after which their constituents returned to their own homes.

The signing of the National Covenant, on the 28th of February, 1638, was the next great stage of the patriotic movement.   Such a burst of enthusiasm was thereby elicited as had not been witnessed in the land for centuries.   The monarch must have been infatuated when he saw but heeded not the warning lesson which it gave.   The prelates looked on in terror and dismay ; one of them, the Archbishop of St. Andrews, expressing their sentiments when he exclaimed despairingly, " All that we have been doing for thirty years is now scattered to the winds !"

The King, with the view of averting the threatened storm, sent the Marquis of Hamilton to Scotland, authorising him to make some important concessions.   These had no effect upon the Covenanters, who continued to pursue their schemes with unrelaxing vigour.   They invited their friends employed in military service abroad to return home and assist them in the struggle that was full surely approaching ; and they instituted extensive measures for procuring the munitions of war.   Provision for the extension and better maintenance of the Presbyterian Church as opposed to the Prelatical Establishment was also made.   Among the ministers settled at this time were Mr James Hamilton, over the Dumfries congregation, and Mr John M'Lellan, over that of Kirkcudbright ; whilst the distinguished Samuel Rutherford, who had been deposed and banished from Anwoth at the instance of Sydserff, Bishop of Galloway, for preaching against the Five Articles, returned to his old parishioners, by whom he was welcomed with gratitude and joy.   Hamilton was sent back to Scotland, armed with new instructions of a conciliatory kind ; and thinking by one crowning act to satisfy the malcontents, he summoned a General Assembly, which met, according to appointment, at Glasgow on the 21st of November, 1638. No more impolitic step could have been taken by the Royal Commissioner, as the Assembly supplied the Tables with the legal machinery for carrying out their schemes ; and the members who composed that venerable body proved willing agents in the work.

The Dumfries Presbytery was represented at this ever-memorable Assembly by Mr William M'George, of Carlaverock, Mr Alexander Train, of Lochrutton, ministers ; and by Mr John Irving, ex-Provost of Dumfries, and Mr John Charteris, younger of Amisfield, elders. The burgh also sent its own members to the special Parliament of the Tables : these were, William Farish and John Copland, whose instructions, dated the 7th of July, 1638, ran thus :—" You are constituted our comissionaris to attend at Edinburgh, or whatsumevir other place shall be fund expedient, until the several dyattis do ces, for receiving such answer or answeris as shall cum from his Majesty, the Lordis of Privie Counsell, or any uther his Majestie's Comissionaris, of our former supplicationis and complents against the Service Buik, Buik of Canons, the Comissione, and other innovations and grivancis, particularlie expresit and generally conteint in our former supplications ; and the Prelatis, our pairties [enemies], as the authoris and contryveris thereoff ; and to give in new remonstrances, and to prefer new petitions to his Majestie, conform to the laitt Covenant sworne and subscryved be us ; and to treat, resolve, and consult upon such offerturis and expedienteis as may conduce for furthering the contentis of the said supplicationis and Covenant ; and for eschewing any prejudiciall to the same ; and to concurre be all laufull means with the Comissionaris of the nobilitie, barones, ministeris, and remanent burrowis, in all laufull means fund be comon consent to conduce to such good issues."* These thoroughgoing instructions were signed by Provost John Corsane and ten councillors, who promised, in the name of the community, to " abyde, fulfill and underly " whatever " the said Comissionaris shall laufully doe " in the business assigned to them.

The Tables and the General Assembly vied with each other in giving effect to the declared will of the country against the King. So sweeping were the measures mooted in the Assembly that the Royal Commissioner stood aghast, and then in his sovereign's name ordered the sittings to terminate. He dissolved the Assembly with all due form, but the refractory members declined to separate. After he left the court they coolly proceeded with the business before them ; and by a succession of acts

* Burgh Records.

excommunicated the two archbishops and six bishops, annulled the Five Articles and the Service-book, and raised Presbyterianism up anew on the ruins of the Episcopal Establishment. Against Bishop Sydserff a special charge was brought of being but a half-disguised Papist. The Provost of Dumfries, in giving evidence against the accused prelate, deponed :—" That when he was in their towne on the Sabbath day, they expected his comeing to the kirk, and layd cushions for him ; yet he came not, but went to an excommunicat Papist's house, and stayed all day." None of the dignitaries were present—no one had a word to say in their defence ; and their downfall was the theme of general congratulation out of doors. The Assembly which had been so destructive to the Episcopate made many important arrangements for the better development of the resuscitated Presbyterian system, and was altogether an extraordinary one—the reflex and exponent of the Scottish ecclesiastical mind at a most critical time. Much ingenuity and labour had for years been expended in building up the Prelatical Establishment ; but it was inveterately disliked by the people over whom it was set, and it needed nothing more than the breath of their representatives to blow it down. At the close of the solemn proceedings, Alexander Henderson, the moderator, was well entitled to exclaim, as he did, " We have now cast down the walls of Jericho : let him that rebuildeth beware of the curse of Thiel the Bethelite."

Charles, unhappily, sought to reconstruct the shattered ecclesiastical edifice, and to lay stone after stone on the arbitrary political structure he wished to build up : both schemes signally failed, and involved his own ruin. War—with the Scots first, then with the English, terminating at last with the entire defeat of the royal troops at Naseby, by Cromwell, on the 12th of June, 1645—brought matters to an issue ; for a while the military genius of Montrose cast a halo of splendour and success over the desperate fortunes of the King, and when that disappeared they were left in utter darkness.

Among the myriads who flocked to the Greyfriars' Churchyard, Edinburgh, to subscribe the National Covenant were many persons of all ranks from Nithsdale ; and soon copies of the document sent down to the district were signed there so unanimously and heartily that its inhabitants became inseparably mixed up with the terrible fifty years' struggle which Scottish Presbyterianism underwent before its rights were won. The subscribers of the Covenant expressed by their so doing their resolution " to adhere to and defend the true religion ;" " to labour by all means lawful to recover the purity and liberty of the gospel as it was established and possessed " before the late innovations were made ; " to resist all these contrary errors and corruptions " to the utmost of the power that God had put into their hands, while life continued : "to support the King's person and authority" in the defence and maintenance "of the foresaid true religion, liberties, and laws of the kingdom ;" and, finally, that they would never, directly or indirectly, suffer themselves to be divided or withdrawn, "by whatsoever suggestion, combination, allurement, or terror," from this " blessed and loyal conjunction."

Within a few months after the memorable day when the Earl of Sutherland affixed his name, the first upon the roll of this famous bond, the people, as a whole, had signed it—the Covenant had become thoroughly nationalised ; and forthwith the War Committee of the Tables commenced to levy an army for its defence, which, on being formed, was placed under the command of Alexander Leslie, afterwards Earl of Leven, who had seen much hard service in Holland and Sweden, and risen from obscurity to be the favourite field-marshal of Gustavus Adolphus A large force was needed ; and eventually thirty thousand men were enrolled, ready to follow the Covenanting flag to victory or death. Immense difficulties had to be encountered before such a body of soldiers could be secured, disciplined, and placed on a permanent footing ; and of these we obtain a striking idea from a work recently published—the Minute Book kept by the War Committee of the Covenanters in the Stewartry of Kirkcudbright,"* the original of which has been carefully preserved in the charter-chest of Cardoness. As this Committee exercised jurisdiction over a part of Nithsdale, as it sometimes held meetings in Dumfries, and as the principal member of it, Thomas, second Lord Kirkcudbright, was appointed Colonel of the South Regiment, which was raised on both sides of the Nith, it will be proper for us to take special notice of its proceedings.

The Committee usually sat at the village of Lauriston, then called Cullenoch. Their first minute, dated 27th June, 1640, embodies a resolution that a troop of eighty horsemen demanded from Galloway should be drawn in due proportion from each parish : "and that ilk horseman have for arms at the leist ane steill cape and sworde, ane paire of pistolles, and ane lance :" for furnishing of which each trooper was to be allowed twenty rixdollars. At another sederunt ten days afterwards the captains of the regiment were assigned their different quota of soldiers, and various arrangements were made for their maintenance by rates on land and voluntary contributions in money and goods. Gradually the free-will offerings became exhausted, and forced loans, as well as fines on non-Covenanters, were resorted to. The Committee, taking their instructions from and acting in the spirit of the Four Tables, relied in the first instance on the patriotism and religious zeal of friends, and then on exactions drawn from

* Published by J. Nicholson, Kirkcudbright, 1855.

doubtful, apathetic, or niggardly individuals, or from those who were the declared opponents of the Covenant. The two latter classes were stringently dealt with. Friends and foes were required to give of their substance to support the national cause ; and those who from any motive desired to remain aloof from the movement were soon made to feel that no neutrality would be allowed—that they who were not for the Covenant would be treated as enemies to it, and forced to uphold it, if not by personal service, at least by their money and their goods. A great crisis had come, and the men who ventured their all in trying to bring out of it a new state of things were sometimes not too particular as to the means they employed for accomplishing their object. They were terribly in earnest ; they realised the tremendous issues bound up in the conflict on which they had entered ; they saw that failure would be ruin, not simply to themselves, but to their country and the sacred cause of which they were the champions—that success would secure political freedom, and the full recognition of the rights of conscience : and so feeling and thinking, they could not be expected to deal very tenderly with wavering adherents, much less with those "malignants" who either openly opposed them or covertly endeavoured to thwart their plans and bring back the deluge of prelatic and regal despotism from which they had been so recently delivered.

By the arbitrary measures of the King and his advisers Scotland had been turned into a camp, and its occupants could not, in the nature of things, be expected to regulate their proceedings by the rules of ordinary life. Since peace and its amenities were gone the Covenanters were shut up to the necessity of adopting means that were in themselves harsh but which the exigencies of their attitude rendered just. They would have been very well content if his Majesty had permitted them to worship God in their own way ; but since he insisted on their doing it in a way which they detested and deemed unscriptural he was responsible for the evils which arose out of their resistance to his tyranny. We learn from the Stewartry minute-book that in each of the midland and southern counties a war committee, composed of influential men, was formed, which, in subordination to the Committee of Estates in Edinburgh, held military occupation of their respective localities. The chief duty of these committees was to prepare armed levies for the pending struggle ; but in doing so they had to assume and exercise a dictatorship over secular and ecclesiastical matters, and even occasionally to act as judicial tribunals.

On the 2nd of December, 1640, the Kirkcudbright Committee found, from a warrant sent from the metropolis, that they were empowered " to sit upon civil affairs ;" and they accordingly resolved that all parties " having controversies betwixt thame shall upon laufull pursute have justice"—a determination which they sought to carry into effect by giving judgment in divers cases recorded in their minutes ; though they never thought of superseding any of the ordinary magistrates who were willing to officiate. "Treulie," say the Committee of Estates, in giving instructions on this subject to their representatives at Kirkcudbright, "it were incumbent to you, in respect to the generall calamitie throw want of justice, to advert particularlie that justice be administrate, and necessar and trew debtes satisfied ; and gif your ordinar judges be deficient, being desyrit be you to doe justice, it is your pairt, in caicess of necessitie, to bring the pairties befoir you, and sie order and credit keepit within your boundes sae far as you are able."

All other matters, however, were, as we have hinted, subordinated to those of war. "Give us recruits—men to fight our country's battles, and means with which to maintain them !" was the constant cry from Edinburgh. How urgently and eloquently it is enforced in the following message, dated the 30th of June :— " Because barrones and gentilmen of good soirt are the greatest and maist pouerful pairt of the kingdome, by quhas valure the kingdom hath ever been defendit, we do maist earnestly requyre and expect that everie barron and gentilman of good soirt shall come to the armie in thair own persones, or at leist thair ablest sone, brother, or freind. And that all noblemen, gentlemen, and uthers may be encouraged to come out as volunteires in sua good ane cawse, for mantainance of religione and preservatioun of the libertie of this antient and never conqueirit kingdome, which we are all sworne to maintain, it is earnestlie desyrit that all brave cavalieres will tak the business to hart, and considder that now or never is the tyme to gaine honour and eternal reputatioun, and to saive or lose thair countrie." Following up this spirited exhortation, the Committee at Cullenoch, on the 13th of July, expressed an opinion that one or more commissioners should be appointed for each parish in the Stewartry "to uplift the sogers, both the foote and horss, mantainance and armes ;" and they ordained " the said commissioners to plunder any persone that shall happen no to mak thankfull peyment of the sogers pey, and that the parochinares assist the commissioners for doeing thairof."

Some of these officials, after being nominated, either refused to act or performed their work carelessly, which insubordination and neglect the Committee could not tolerate. On the 1st of September, William Lindsay, commissioner for Colvend and Southwick ; John Charteris (of the Amisfield family), commissioner for Terregles ; the Laird of Dalskairth and John Brown, commissioners for Troqueer ; Hugh Maxwell, in Torrorie, commissioner for Kirkbean ; and David Cannan, commissioner for Buittle, were cited " to compeir befoir the Committee of Estaites, at Edinburgh,

the viij. day of September instant; thair to answer for thair
neglect for not out-putting of the troupe and baggage horss." At
this very time, as we shall afterwards see, the Earl of Nithsdale
was in arms against the Covenanters, and maintaining the King's
cause in his castles of Carlaverock and Thrieve. He was looked
upon by Charles as the leader of the royalist party in the district;
and in vindication of this opinion Nithsdale not only called out
his followers but exercised his influence, which was still strong,
over many families in the district, to secure their active support,
and failing that their neutrality. It was he chiefly who set
agoing the strong undercurrent which the War Committee in
Kirkcudbright and Dumfries encountered in various quarters, and
of which the contumacy of the above-named commissioners was
an illustrative display.

It was further manifested by refusals to sign the Covenant,
by evasions of the rate levied to support the army, and by desertions from its ranks. On the 30th of September John Halliday
of Fauldbey, David Halliday of Marguillian, John M'Ghie in
Barnbord, and James M'Connel of Creoch, threw themselves upon
the pleasure of the Committee, "for not subscribing to the General
Bond;" and the Committee at the same sitting ordained "David
M'Mollan, in St. John's Clauchan, for his contempt to his captaine,
minister, and elderes, in not going forth to the armie, being
enrolled, to pey presentlie fourtie punds, and to stay in ward in
the tollbuithe of Kirkcudbryt until the day of the rendevouez at
Milnetown of Urr, and then to march with the rest of the runawayes; and gif the said fyne of fourtie punds be not peyit befoir
he march, in that caice he shall pey ane hundred merks of fyne."
The Committee sat at Dumfries on the 29th of December and
determined the cases of several deserters, some of whom were
excused on account of sickness. The following minute records
part of the business :—"The quhilk day the Committee, finding
that severall of the captaines of the parochess have been negligent
of the charge committed to thame, and in especiall that of the
inbringing of the runawayes, Thairfore ordains John Reddick of
Dalbeattie, captaine of the parochen of Urr; John M'Cellane
of Auchengule, and John Cutlar of Orrdand, captaines of the
parochen of Rerrick, betwixt and the last of this instant, to
inbring thair runawayes, and delyver thame to the captaines here
at Drumfries; and for ilk man they failzie to produce to pey xl.
merks money attour the production."

We subjoin another suggestive minute of the Committee's
proceedings, when sitting at Kirkcudbright on the 1st of January,
1641 :—"The whilk day, anent the supplicatione presented be
Johne Murray of Broughtone, in the name of Robert Maxwell of
Culnachtrie and Mary Lindsay of Rascattell, schawing that they
bothe, to the dishonour of God and evil example of uthers, did

kythe thamesellffes enemies to the gude caus in hand, *in verbo et facto*, which did proceed from ane oath raschlie given be thame to thair maister the Erle of Nithisdaill ; are now maist willing to give obedience to the law of God and man, and has beene supplicating the presbiterie to reseve thame in to the bosom of Christe's Kirk againe ; desyering, in the meantyme, that the said Committee would caus thair Commissar-Depute desist in proceeding against thame, or with intromissione with thair goodes and geir, as the said supplicatione beirs. The quhilk being heard, sein, and considderit, doeth ordain the said Laird of Broughtone cautioner that thair haile gudes and geir shall be furthcummane for the use of the publict, and the said commissar to desist with anie intromissione thairwith."

In spite of numerous hindrances the Kirkcudbright Committee managed to raise something like their full complement of soldiers. When reports to that effect were sent to Edinburgh down came pressing demands for money, articles of silver, and clothing. " You have, as faitful servants of the Kirk, provided the men, but your duty is only half done till you provide for their maintenance also ; you must collect 'the haile tenth and twentieth penny' of the lands valuation ; 'the rentes and gudes of all Papists, anti-Covenanters, pretendit bischops, recusants, and uther unfreindes ;' you must in addition borrow money, silver plate, and jewels ; and furnish uniforms and boots and shoes for your own division of the national army." Messages of this purport were ever and anon received by the little junto sitting at Cullenoch, Kirkcudbright, or Dumfries ; and dutiful attention was paid to the same. Whilst the people in general co-operated cheerfully with the Committee, paying their rates, and lending their money and goods for the support of a cause which was dear to them as life itself, there were, as we have said, a considerable proportion of recusants, from whom contributions had to be wrung, as if, instead of being required to draw their purses, they had been asked to part with their teeth.

Every day, Sabbath excepted, might be seen sitting in the Tolbooth or Town Hall of Dumfries or Kirkcudbright, from ten o'clock till two, half-a-dozen " substanteious " burgesses, appointed by the Presbytery and sanctioned by the Committee " to ressaive any lent monie, or silver or gold worke quhilk shall be delyverit to thame "—the lenders receiving tickets of acknowledgment, entitling them to obtain security from the Estates that after the troubles were over, if not sooner, they would be paid at the rate of three pounds per ounce of Scots silver work, three pounds two shillings per ounce of English silver work, and twenty-eight pounds per ounce for articles of gold. If individuals known to be wealthy come with their goods or gear of their own accord, all the better ; if not, a list is made out of such and they are cited to appear before the Committee and explain why they have not responded to the call made upon their liberality. When the defaulters "compeir" they perhaps plead poverty or debt, or promise to be speedily forthcoming with the sums required of them. Thus we find such statements as the following made upon oath :—"Johne Greggane, eldir in Newabbay, hes only jc. [one hundred] merks monie of the realm ;" "Johne Broune, eldir at Bridgend of Dumfries, about xjxx [eleven score] merks ;" "Johne Broune, younger thair, has iijc. [three hundred] merks, which he is awand to creditors ;" "Johne M'Dowall in Kirkmabreck, nihil ; and John Cutlar in Dundrennan, nihil." Then, as showing how productive the demand for wares made of the precious metals proved, we have such articles as these dropped into the Covenant-ing treasury :—"Twa silver piecess, ane paire long wyres, nyne silver spoones, broken and haile," weighing over twenty ounces, and containing three ounces of "evill silver," which were rejected ; "four silver spoones, ane pair belt heides, ane pair silver weires, and foure uther litle piecess of silver, broken and haille," weight eleven ounces, fifteen drops ; "ane gilt coupe, Inglis worke," weight five ounces, fourteen drops ; "ane silver peice, Scots worke, ane gilt silver saltfat, with xiiij. silver spoones," weight two pounds nine ounces ; "delyverit by John Charters of Barnecleuche [formerly a stout recusant] sex silver spoones, Scots work," ten ounces in weight ; "delyverit by the Lady Cardyness, in name of her husband, ane silver coupe, ane stak of ane fann and sax silver spoones," weight fifteen ounces, fifteen drops. On the first of September, 1640, James Gordon of Lochinkit was taken to task "for conceiling of the monie in prejudice of the publict, and lend-ing of the sameyn to ane uther partie ;" Grissell Gordone, spouse to the deceased minister of Urr, was ordained "to present her silver worke, viz. :—The twa piecess that was bought by the paroche of Urr for the use of the kirk, and sex silver spoones pertaining to the aires of said minister ;" and a widow, whose name is mentioned, is required "to present her bairnes silver worke, and that notwithstanding" any reasons adduced to the contrary. If moneyed men failed to appear before the Committee or collectors when summoned they were heavily fined ; and if repeated warnings and penalties proved ineffectual a portion of their property was poinded and sold for the public service.

When the South Regiment was fairly raised in Nithsdale and Galloway, it was billeted on the burgh of Dumfries : its presence, we suppose, being required there to keep the Maxwell influence in check. But the inhabitants, though good Covenanters, considered, reasonably enough, that the burden of providing quarters for the troops should be divided ; and they having represented their grievance to the Committee of Estates, that body, in a letter dated the 10th of December, 1640, enjoined Lord Kirkcudbright to make three divisions of the army, placing one at Dumfries, one at Kirkcudbright, and one within Lord Johnstone's division (probably Annandale), unless he could manage to pay the town of Dumfries "tymelie satisfactione" for the undue draught made upon its resources. "But," said the Committee in continuation, "if the regiment could be keipit togither, we wold rather wish it, quhilk cannot be unless your lordship caus hasten the uplifting and peyment of all that is dew within your divisione, such as the tenth and twentieth penny, anti-Covenanters' and Papists' rentes, and uther dews to the publict, conforme to the generall instructiones, and caus the samen to be delyverit to the commissar at Dumfries, for the use of the said regiment." It is peremptorily stated in a postscript that "if money cum not into the commissar for the use of the regiment beforre the xxth of this instant, they cannot indure longer delay, and they have orders to devyde, efter that tyme, in caice betwixt and that they get not a supplie."

CHAPTER XXXI.

BETWEEN John Lord Maxwell, who perished on the scaffold, and
his brother, the first Earl of Nithsdale, there was a striking contrast—the former having been a fierce, uncultured savage, the
latter a student of science and a lover of literature, and pervaded
at the same time with knightly heroism :

> " A baron stout and bold, as ever wore sword on thigh –
> A brave old Scottish cavalier, all of the olden time."

Charles knew that if his cause in the south of Scotland could be
maintained at all it must be consigned to the guardianship of
Nithsdale. Accordingly, in January, 1639, the Earl received a
royal letter exhorting him to disregard the doings of the Glasgow
Assembly, and to make arrangements with his friends for protecting the interests of the Crown. Immediately afterwards Nithsdale entered into a compact for that purpose with his cousin Lord
Herries, with the Lairds of Cowhill, Gribton, Orchardton, Carnsalloch, Killielung, Portrack, and other relatives. Thenceforth
they were all recognised as " malignants" by the Cullenoch Committee ; and some of them were made to feel the significance of
that epithet, when, before war was declared, a body of about two
thousand Covenanters swept into the district, under Captains
Munro and Pitscottie. Both Nithsdale and Herries withdrew to
Carlisle ; and Terregles Tower, being left undefended, was occupied by the invaders. In another letter from King Charles to the
Earl, dated in February, 1640, " Nithisdaille " was required to
look to himself, for that longer than the 13th of the next month,
" I will not warrant you that ye heare of a breache betwixt me
and my Covenanting rebelles.* Preparations for the crisis had

* The original letter is preserved at Terregles House.

been carried on quietly at the castles of Carlaverock and Thrieve ; but Lord Nithsdale could do nothing for the royal cause in Dumfries, as the inhabitants were opposed to it ; and its places of strength, even if they had been held by him, were of little value in a military sense. The Castle, though partially repaired, still bore evidence of the rough handling given to it by Lord Scrope in 1570. Thirteen years after that date a second fortress on a small scale was built eastward of the ancient Market Cross, and north of the present Queensberry Monument. In contrast to the old decayed Castle it was called the New Wark. It was a dull, heavy pile, composed of two stories above the street level, with a bartizan running along the top to protect the garrison, and strong vaults underground, in which the movable property of the inhabitants was stowed away in periods of danger. The New Wark was often of good service when raiding mosstroopers from the Border paid hostile visits to the burgh ; but a party of Covenanters armed with cannon would have made short work with its defences.

Carlaverock and Thrieve, however, were still strong ; and each was furnished with provisions for a year, with a sufficiency of warlike stores, and with a considerable garrison—the Solway fortress having two hundred men, and the Galloway one half that number. When Camden saw Carlaverock in 1607, it was, he tells us, "a weak house of the Maxwells," Lords Sussex and Scrope having done it much harm. Within twenty years afterwards it rose to a state of greater magnificence than ever ; the Earl of Nithsdale employing the best architectural and engineering skill to make it at once a palatial residence and a first-class fortress. The jumellated double tower forming the north front, which had frowned on the assailing chivalry of England in 1300, was still extant, though weakened by the influences of war and time ; the turrets on the east and west corners had suffered more seriously ; and a large portion of the interior was scarcely habitable. Partly rebuilt and partly repaired, rendered florid by new architectural decorations, and the moats so deepened as to make the waters of the Solway more available for defence, this storied Border stronghold presented an imposing appearance when the Covenanting army went up against it in 1640. The massive gateway, pierced by a narrow curtain, and having a tower on each side, formed a colossal front. Over the arch of the gate was sculptured the Nithsdale crest—a stag attired proper, lodged before a holly bush, with a shield resting on its fore legs, bearing the Maxwell saltier, and the motto below "I bid ye fair." This escutcheon was surrounded by other heraldic decorations ; the well-known double-headed eagle of the Maxwells occupied the sinister chief corner ; in the dexter corner was displayed the royal arms of Scotland ; a band between six crosslets in the dexter corner of the base

marked the relationship which subsisted between the Maxwells
and Douglas, Earl of Mar ; and the sinister corner of the base told
their connection with the Stewarts of Dalswinton, a daughter of
whose house was mother of the first Lord Maxwell.

Entered by the gateway was a spacious triangular court, the
east side of which, three stories high, constituted the family residence ; it is designated in some contemporary documents as the
" daintie fabric of Nithisdaile's new lodgings," and so florid was
its outside, and so rich its furnishings, that it might have become
the abode of royalty. On the pediments of the lower storey were
engraved the Nithsdale arms, with the initials of Robert, the first
Earl, and his wife Elizabeth. A heart-shaped shield, with the
plain Maxwell saltier, was carved above the first window ; a
shield, with the two-headed eagle, charged with a smaller shield
and saltier, surmounted by a coronet, rose above the second staircase window ; the third window was similarly adorned, excepting
that it wanted the supporters ; and the fourth bore the familiar
holly bush, with its usual occupant the stag. Above the first
court door a huge eagle, defensive like, spread its wings, having
below it a shield, and on each side a rose. Two guardian cherubs
supported a shield over the first window of the second storey, the
shield displaying a double-headed eagle, charged as before, and
having under it the mask of a human head, with hands drawing
the jaws apart in such a way as to give a grotesque expression to
the face. A tree, carved above the right-hand side of the second
window of the second storey, bore as emblematic fruit a tiny
shield with the Maxwell saltier and coronet, their owner being
indicated by the initials " R. E. N." cut below. From a second
tree, on the other side of the window, hung similar fruitage, only
that the initials were E. C. N., those of the noble Countess of
Nithsdale. The lavish ornamentation of this part of the castle
was crowned by a series of classical groups placed over the three
third-storey windows, the subjects of which were taken from
Ovid's " Metamorphoses."

Such was the strong and beautiful house which constituted
the forlorn hope of royalty in Nithsdale : not strong enough to
resist the war-engines which were soon arrayed against it ; too
beautiful to be marred by the baptism of their relentless fire.

Thrieve, as has already been shewn, was the chief castle of
the Douglases in Galloway. On their downfall it became the
property of the Crown ; and by a royal grant, dated the 9th of
September, 1524, this fortress and that of Lochmaben, with their
appendages– the King's lands at Duncow, Dumfriesshire, and the
office of Steward of Kirkcudbright—were given to Robert Lord
Maxwell, whose family continued to be possessors of Thrieve till
the forfeiture of the last Earl of Nithsdale, in 1715. At the period
now reached it was still in its primeval strength. Situated in an

islet of the river Dee, it consisted of a massive square building, buttressed by round turrets at each corner, the whole walled in by a stout envelope having numerous curtains bristling with cannon.

The Estates in Edinburgh were duly apprised of Maxwell's hostile preparations; and as the South Regiment, under Lord Kirkcudbright, was yet in an undisciplined condition, they sent down a large body of hardy troops, under the command of an experienced officer, Lieutenant-Colonel John Home, to invest Carlaverock and Thrieve, so as to keep them from becoming rallying points for the Royalists. Colonel Home's contingent formed a portion of the Scottish army sent southward under General Leslie in the autumn of 1640; and while Leslie led his "blue bonnets over the Border," to co-operate with the English Parliamentarians, Home laid siege to the Maxwell fortresses, and thus took one of the initiatory steps of the great civil war which convulsed the country for eleven years.

Early in August the defenders of Carlaverock descried the van of the besieging force, and proceeded to man the ramparts. They were in no immediate danger, however, as Colonel Home had no cannon of sufficient size to make any impression on the walls, and he saw that they were too strong to be taken by assault. The Estates had plenty of powerful war engines; but in these days there were few good roads, and how to get heavy ordnance brought all the way from Edinburgh to Dumfries was a difficult problem to solve. By an opportune beat of the "drum ecclesiastic" the requisite motive power was soon forthcoming. On Sabbath, the 11th of August, proclamation was made from the pulpits of all the parishes round about that Lord Nithsdale had garrisoned Carlaverock in the interests of the tyrant King—that he was setting the hosts of the Covenant at defiance; and the faithful were urged to assist the good cause in every way, more especially by sending four draught horses from each parish to convey to the beleaguering force certain pieces of ordnance that were lying between Edinburgh and Biggar, and with which the trusty Home meant, if need were, to demolish the house of the malignant chief as thoroughly as the son of Nun overthrew the walls of Jericho.

The cannon having been obtained after a repose of several weeks, their heavy shot told severely upon the south curtain between the towers, and the "daintie new lodgings," against which it was also directed.* Probably a platform of some kind

---

* Last summer (1872) the moat was cleaned out by order of Lord Herries, so as to allow the water that flows into it to have a freer sweep than it had obtained for a long while previously, During the process six cannon balls, all thirty-six pounders, were found embedded in the mud of the fosse, near the Dungeon Tower at the front of the castle; relics, probably, of the Covenanters' cannonade.

would be raised to support the ordnance, as the ground southward was marshy. The ground in front of the castle was of a rocky hardness; but we suspect that Colonel Home planted no ordnance in that quarter, as the double tower was made of less vulnerable stuff than the turrets on the other side. Lord Nithsdale saw that unless assistance reached him he would be compelled to surrender. He parleyed ingeniously with the enemy, tried also to wile away the time by other devices, thinking that the King would in the end send him the long-looked-for relief. But it never came; and meanwhile as week after week passed away, the breaches made by the remorseless cannon waxed wider, till the defence became increasingly difficult, and the brave lord was beginning to consider whether it might not be better for him to die, pike or pistol in hand, rather than be taken alive—feeling, as he did, that his worldly fortunes were ruined still more than was his castle.* While his heart was "sick with hope deferred," Colonel Home, ignorant perhaps of the extreme straits to which he was reduced, offered him honourable terms of capitulation. These Nithsdale accepted, after asking for and receiving permission from his Majesty. The King's letter, suitably addressed, is in these terms: —" CHARLES R.—Right trusty and well-beloved cousen and councellor, we greet you well. Whereas you have represented unto us by your letter of the 12th of September, that those who have besieged you so long in the Castle of Carlaverock have now offered you honourable conditions to come out; and forasmuch as our affairs permit not to relieve you so soon as we had determined, and as seems your necessities require, and being withal most willing to free your person from further danger, and to ease you of the trouble and toyle you have sustained by so long a siege, we do hereby (graciously condescending unto your humble request) give you leave to embrace and accept the aforesaid conditions, for the safety and preservation of your person and estate, having withal a regard to our honour, so far as the necessity of your present condition will permit; and we shall still, as we have done hitherto, continue our gracious esteem of you. Given at our Court at York, this 15th day of September, in the sixteenth year of our reign, 1640."

This royal epistle was followed by another, addressed as before, and written later on the same day, in these terms:—" CHARLES R.—Right trusty and well-beloved cousen and counsellor, we greet you well. Understanding by this bearer, that altho you were agreed with those that have beleaguered you in Carlaverock upon honourable terms, for your coming forth, and rendering thereof, yet that those conditions are not valid until such time that they be ratified by those that have made

---

* Terregles Papers.

themselves members of the great Committee in Edinburgh, and
fearing that your enemies there will not give way to your coming
forth in such good terms, we are therefore graciously pleased, and
by these presents do permit and give you leave to take such conditions as you can get, whereby the lives and liberties of yourself,
your family, and those that are with you, may be preserved ; and
in case they should urge the surrendering of our Castle of Thrieve,
which hitherto you have so well defended (and we wish you were
able to do so still), our gracious pleasure is that you do rather quit
the same unto them ; which, if so the necessity require you, to do
so on the best and most honourable terms you can, rather than
hazard the safety of your own person, and those with you ; and in
such case this shall be your warrant and discharge. Given at our
Court at York, the 15th day of September, in the sixteenth year
of our reign, 1640."

In accordance with the permission thus granted, both
fortresses were surrendered to the Covenanting general, after the
annexed form of capitulation had been signed by him and
Nithsdale :—

"At Dumfries, the 21st day of September, 1640 : The quhilk
day pns. of the Committee of Nithsdale, residing at Dumfries,
compeared Lieutenant-Colonel Home, and gave in and produced
the articles of capitulation past betwixt Robert Earl of Nithsdale
and the said Lieutenant-Colonel, at the Castle of Carlaverock, the
26th day of September last bypast, and desired the said articles to
be insert and registrate in the buiks of the said Committee, and
that the extract thereof might be patent to any party havand
interest, and the principal articles redelivered to him, quhilk the
said Committee thought reasonable ; of the quhilk articles the
tenor follows, viz. :—Articles condescended upon betwixt the Earl
of Nithsdale and Lieutenant-Colonel Home, the 26th day of September, 1640, at the Castle of Carlaverock. For the first article,
it is condescended on that for my Lord, his friend and followers,
that there shall no other course be taken with him and them in
their religions than with others of his or their professions.
Whereas it is desired be my Lord that he, his friends and followers,
be no farther troubled in their persons, houses, and estates, house-
guids therein, then according to the common course of the
kingdom ; it is agreed unto, that no other course shall be taken
with him and his foresaids, then with others of his and their professions. Whereas it is desired he and they may sorte out with
bag and baggage, trunks, household stuff belonging, on their
honour and credit, to his Lordship and them, with safe conduct to
the Langholm, or any other place within Nithsdale, is granted.
Whereas it is desired be my Lord that guids intromitt with
belonging to his Lordship's friends and followers, restitution
thereof be made; it is agreed to what course shall be taken with

others of his and their condition shall be taken with him and them. It is condescended upon be my Lord, takend the burden on him for himself, his friends and followers, that he nor they sall not, in anytime coming, tack arms in prejudice of this kingdom, nor shall have any intelligence with any prejudice thereof, upon their honour and credit. It is condescended on be my Lord and his friends and followers, that they sall contribute and do everything lying incumbent on them, according to the general course of the kingdom. Lastly, it is condescended on be my Lord, his friends and followers, that he and they sall deliver up the house and fortalice of Carlaverock to Lieutenant-Colonel Home, with the cannon, superplus of ammunition, and other provisions ; and that he shall remove himself, officers, and whole garrison and followers, out of the said castle and fortalice ; and this his Lordship obleist himself and his to perform, upon his honour and credit, betwixt this and the 29th day of September instant, 1640. *Sic subscribitur :* Nithisdale.—JON HOME."

The "bag and baggage, trunks and household stuff," "left in the house of Carlaverock at my Lord's departure," were worth bargaining about. Fortunately the list of them made at the time, and duly attested by witnesses, has been preserved, and it affords us a singularly interesting peep into a seventeenth-century nobleman's household. The Earl of Nithsdale was, as we have seen, addicted to literary and scientific pursuits, and that a large stock of books should therefore figure in the catalogue is not surprising. There were lavish furnishings for the mind, as well as sumptuous upholstery, luxurious apparel, and rich dainties for the palate. The library is stated to have "stood my Lord two hundred pound sterling," an immense sum (equal perhaps to six hundred pounds of our present money) to be spent on books at that period. In one cellar were four barrels of the wine which Falstaff favoured ; in another three hogsheads of claret. We read that in my Lord's chamber there was "a bed furnished with damask, and laid over with gold lace ;" and that there was in my lady's chamber "a burd and a falling bed." Musical instruments and pictures enter into the list ; but all else of a material kind is eclipsed by the number and magnificence of the household "plenishings," which include five beds, two of silk and three of cloth, every bed supplied with five coverings, massive silk fringes of half-a-quarter deep, "and ane counterpoint of the same stuff, all laid with braid silk lace and a small fringe about, with chairs and stools answerable, laid with lace and fringe, with feather bed and bolster, blankets and rug, pillars and bedsteads of timber answerable ; every bed estimate to be worth an hundred and ten pounds sterling. Then we read of ten smaller beds, value fifteen pounds sterling; of "seventy other beds for servants, consisting of feather bed, bolster, rug, blankets, and estimate to be seven pound sterling a-piece ;" of two open trunks, "full of Hollond shirts and phillabers, damask table-cloths, and gallons of towels;" forty pair of sheets or thereby, and "seventy stand of neprey"—every pair of sheets consisting of seven ells of cloth, at six shillings per ell, and amounting to five pounds two shillings sterling per pair. Among the weapons mentioned were twenty-two pikes, thirteen lances, twenty-eight muskets, twenty-eight bandoliers, and a pair of two-handed swords.*

Nithsdale became bound, as we have seen, that neither he nor his friends and followers should for the time to come take up arms "in prejudice of this kingdom," which phraseology, though loose, was doubtless designed to prevent them from fighting against the Covenant in future. But it had no such effect. He had left the castle with his followers, accompanied by an escort of musketeers; not going to Langholm, however, but crossing the Border; and soon after the Committee of Estates learned that he, his officers, and adherents were carrying arms on behalf of the King. The Committee retaliated by causing Colonel Home to "intromit," in rough military fashion, with the costly furniture left under his charge, and to "spoil" the castle that had already suffered severely during the siege. From the injury thus done to the ancient fabric by cannon, pickaxe, and crowbar, it never recovered; yet, though unrepaired and desolate, it still appears, after the lapse of more than two additional centuries, as the choicest specimen of castellated architecture to be found in Scotland.†

"The howse of the Thrieve,' as it is termed in the documents of the period, was similarly dealt with. At a meeting of the Stewartry War Committee, held within its ancient walls on the

---

* The complete list is given by Grose.

† The siege and dismantlement of Carlaverock at this time are popularly attributed to Cromwell; but neither he nor a Puritan force ever attacked the castle; and it was not till some years after 1640 that the future Lord Protector took a prominent part in public affairs. There are among the Terregles Papers several interesting documents relating to the capitulation, and subsequent treatment of the castle by the Covenanters. These documents have very properly been reserved for a work now going through the press, under the editorship of Mr Fraser, in which will be embodied all the muniments of the Nithsdale Maxwells, and which will constitute a companion work to "The Maxwells of Pollok," of which he was also the editor. In one of these papers, as we are permitted to state, the Earl of Nithsdale pleads that it was Home who first violated the terms of the capitulation, by his failing to deliver to the Earl the houses of Kirkconnell and Langholm, and the Earl, being thus left without a home, went to England. Further, that his lordship never did, and never would, appear in arms against his native country; but that, as he had not got possession of his two houses aforesaid, as he expected, his soldiers like himself were thrown destitute, and would not stay behind, but accompanied him across the Border. The Earl, it appears, neither expressly admitted nor denied that he and his men had joined the royal army; but the inference deducible from his statement is that his breach of the terms made with Home was more nominal than real, and only forced upon him by the exigencies of his position.

D2

19th of October, 1640, it was resolved, in accordance with a warrant from Edinburgh, "that the sklate roofe of the hows and battlement thairof be taken downe, with the lofting thairof, dores and windowes of the samen, and to stop the vault of the said hows." This destructive duty was assigned to the Laird of Balmaghie, who was also empowered to dispose of the timber, stones, and iron work removed from the fortress for the use of the public; "his necessar charges and expenses" being deducted from the proceeds of the sale.* On this subject, the captor of the castle addressed the following note to Ensign Gibb, whom he had left in charge of it :—"I did heir, at the Committie at Edinburgh, that they had written to the Committie of Galloway, answering to their letter, that they had fund the Thrieve to be unprofeitable, giving orderes that they should flight [dismantle] the samen. If they have deseyerit you to cum out that they might flight the samen, seing the warrand, and taking the coppie thairof, signed under thrie or foure of thair hands. In doing heirof, cum out with your gareson. Thir presents shall be to you sufficient warrand.—HOME. At Dumfries, the 17 October, 1640." And so the castle was given up to the Committee, and "flighted" by their orders; William M'Clellan, of Barscoib, who had "use for certaine friestane for building," being, it seems, the chief purchaser of the spoils. A few days after the date of the above letter, orders were received by Home from the Estates "to march up with the South Raigement to the army with all convenient dilligence."

John Corsane of Meikleknox was Provost of Dumfries at this period. On the 3rd of December, 1640, he appeared before the Kirkcudbright War Committee, and presented a commission from Colonel Home to the following effect :—"These are to give full power, commissione, and warrand to Mr John Corsane, provest of Dumfries, to resaive from the commissares or collectores of the tenth and twentieth pennies and rentes of our friends and bischopes within Galloway, all such soumes of money as they have in readiness for the use of the South Regiment ; with power to him to give acceptances and discharges of his receipt thairof, quhilk shall be as valid and sufficient to the foresaid collectores as I had given thame discharges myself ; and whereanent I obleis me to renew thame discharges myselfe, upon sight of the Provest's discharge, be thir presents, wrytten by me, Mr Cuthbert Cunynghame, and subscribed with my hand at Dumfries, the last November, J VIᶜ and fourtie yeires, befoir thir witnesses, Roger Kirkpatrick, bailie of Dumfries, and the said Mr Cuthbert Cunynghame.—HOME." Provost Corsane did much to promote the popular movement. He was a decided Covenanter, but anxious at the same time to get a reconciliation effected between

---

* Minute Book of the War Committee, p. 67.

the contending parties. The nephew of Lord Nithsdale, and allied by marriage with another branch of the Maxwell family,* he was naturally averse to the prolongation of the war; and, on account of some pacific overtures made by him, and other acts disapproved of by the uncompromising Parliament which sat in 1644, he was fined in ten thousand merks.

The burgh was represented in this Parliament by George Johnstone, and the county by Sir Robert Grierson of Lag and James Douglas of Mouswald. On the 2nd of July (to quote from the proceedings), "the House ordained commissions and letters of intercommuning to be directed against them that are fugitives, and were cited to the Committee of Drumfreis in the rebellione of the South." On the 22nd of July the House took up the case of "Robert Earl of Nidisdaill, and his deputies, who are Steuarts of Kirkcudbright;" and inasmuch as the Earl was found to have been guilty of "rebellione," he was deprived of his stewardship, and the office was conferred on Lord Kirkcudbright.

The Scottish Covenanters were now in full alliance with the English Puritans under Cromwell. A bond of civil as well as of religious union between the three kingdoms—the Solemn League and Covenant—was signed on the 26th of September, 1643, in St. Margaret's Church, Westminster. As a result of this alliance, Leslie, Earl of Leven, entered England and joined his forces to the Parliamentary army at York. The organisation effected by means of the War Committee was extended, in order to meet the increased demands made upon Scotland by the widening battle-field. As illustrative of the extent to which the landed interest of Dumfriesshire was identified with the Covenanting cause, we may quote the list of the Committee for Nithsdale and Annandale in 1644:—"The Earl of Queensberry; the Earl of Annandale; the Earl of Hartfell; Lord Dalyell; the Laird of Lag; the Laird of Closeburn; the Laird of Amisfield; Maister John Douglas of Penziere; James Douglas of Morton; Thomas Fergusone of Caitloch; John Crichton of Crawfurdston; John Laurie of Maxwellton; John Wilson of Craigleme; John Hunter of Ballagan; John Douglas of Stanehouse; James Grierson of Dalgonar; Archibald Johnstone of Clochrie; the Laird of Tindell; John Dalrymple of Waterside; the Laird of Applegirth; the Laird of Mouswald; James Johnstone of Corheid; Andrew Johnstone of Lockerbie; Archibald Douglas of Dornok; the Laird of Wamfra; Francis Scot of Cairtertown; Mathew Wilson in Greenhill; John Kennedy of Halleithis; Robert Johnstone of Newtoun; the Laird of Drumcrieffe [Murray]; George Johnstone of Poldean; and John Johnstone, called Viccarland." In the preceding year Corsane of Meikleknox was not only on the Committee for the

burgh, but he was the convener or chairman of the whole body ;
but his name, for an obvious reason, does not appear in the list in
1644, the burgh members being given in it as follows :—"John
Irwin, late Provost of Dumfries ; Roger Kirkpatrick, bailie there ;
John Johnstone, bailie there ; Robert Richardson, there ; John
Maccleane, there "—Bailie Johnstone, convener.*

At the period now reached, James Graham, fifth Earl and first
Marquis of Montrose, comes prominently upon the stage. He is
seen first as a devoted champion of the Covenant. When Leslie's
troops entered England, Montrose was the first man to cross the
Tweed ; and encountering the vanguard of the English army, he
put it to the rout at Newburn on the Tyne. Soon afterwards, his
jealousy of Argyle extinguished his devotedness to the Covenant ;
and the outbreak of the civil war found him opposed to his old
colleagues, and fighting in defence of the monarchy. The Marquis
of Hamilton, the King's minister for Scotland, having fallen into
disgrace, Graham was called to occupy his place as lieutenant-
general of the kingdom. In an interview with his Majesty at
Oxford he divulged a daring scheme that he had planned on
behalf of the royal cause : it was to do battle against the Leaguers
in Scotland, with the view of crushing the Covenant in the land
of its birth, leaving Rupert and his cavaliers to cope with Cromwell in England. In this manner, he argued, the force of the
Covenanting arms would be drawn away from the King upon
himself. " But the garrisons and passes of Scotland were in the
possession of the Covenanters. He requested, therefore, an order
upon the Marquis of Newcastle—now opposed to Leslie in the
north of England—for a detachment of his troops, or at least a
sufficient escort force to enable him to cross the Borders. Even
with these slender resources, he undertook to reach the Highlands
of Scotland, and to make such head there as would ere long
encourage the loyalists of that kingdom to rally round the standard."† Charles having sanctioned the bold design, Montrose
proceeded northwards, bearing instructions from his royal master
by which he hoped to obtain the nucleus of an army.

He was accompanied by the Earl of Nithsdale, and also, however strange it may appear, by James Johnstone, Earl of Hartfell
(son of the knight slaughtered by Nithsdale's brother), and by
James Murray, Earl of Annandale, both of whom were at the very
period members of the Dumfriesshire War Committee ; and afterwards another recreant, Sir John Charteris of Amisfield, joined
the royal army with a contingent of followers.

Montrose obtained only a small ill-disciplined force from the
Marquis of Newcastle ; but, putting himself at its head, he pushed

* Acts of Scot. Parl., vol. vi., p. 132.

† Napier's Life and Times of Montrose, vol. ii., p. 386.

into Cumberland, crossed the Western Border, and on the 14th of
April, 1644, startled the Covenanting lieges of Dumfries by entering it with the royal banner displayed—no one attempting to
arrest his progress. When the South Regiment left the district
Dumfries was comparatively undefended, and the War Committee
had been weakened by defections ; but for which circumstances
the champion of despotic rule could not have found such a ready
entrance into the burgh. As the inhabitants generally were still
steadfast in their adherence to the Covenant, they received the
King's troops coldly, and, indeed, so discouragingly, that Montrose
profited nothing by his march across the Border.

Rightly or wrongly, he attributed his failure to bad faith on
the part of professed friends, rather than to the opposition of open
enemies. If he had received the support that he anticipated he
would have made Dumfries a starting point for his meditated
expedition into the Highlands ; but in a disappointed mood he
resolved on retiring to Carlisle—a determination which he carried
into effect all the more hurriedly on learning that the Earl of
Callendar, from whom he expected assistance, had gone over to
the other side, and was advancing against him at the head of
seven thousand men. Before Montrose was many miles out of
Dumfries the blue banner of the Covenant took the place lately
occupied by the royal flag, and was doubtless hailed with
enthusiasm by the inhabitants. Callendar's troops continued for
some time in the town, whilst those of Montrose ravaged Northumberland and Durham, and eventually captured Morpeth
Castle, in spite of a stout resistance offered by its garrison under
Captain M'Culloch.

That officer, in afterwards giving an account of the affair to a
Parliamentary committee in Edinburgh, repeated the views expressed to him by Montrose as to the double-dealing of Lord
Hartfell. When parleying with Montrose, before submitting to
him, M'Culloch inquired "the reason of his incoming to Dumfries,
and invasion of this kingdom :" upon which the Marquis "declared
to the deponer that he had assurance from the Earl of Hartfell of
his assistance, and raising of the country in his favour ; but the
said Hartfell deceived him, having promised from day to day to
draw up his men, and yet did nothing but proved the traitor ; and
further he said he thought to have betrayed him by drawing him
to his house." When, some time afterwards, Lord Ogilvie was
captured by the Covenanters, certain documents were found upon
him which he had received from Montrose for presentation to the
King. In one of these he used the following strong language with
reference to his treatment by the Border barons :—" You are to
inform his Majesty," he says, " of all the particulars that stumbled
his service—as of the carriage of Hartfell, Annandale, Roxburgh,
and Traquair, who refused his Majesty's commission, and de-

bauched our officers, doing all that in them lay to discountenance the service, and all who were engaged in it. Your Lordship is seriously to represent the notable miscarriage of the Earls of Crawford and Nithsdale ; how often they crossed the business, and went about to abuse us who had undertaken it, to the great scandal and prejudice of the service." A curious game would seem to have been played by Hartfell and Annandale, identifying themselves with the Leaguers, and at the same time professing loyalty to the Crown. They appear to have been false to both ; but Nithsdale had given such evidence of his devotedness to the King as should have placed him above suspicion.

Montrose, after reducing Morpeth Castle, was required to unite his forces with those of Prince Rupert. Before he could do so, however, the battle of Marston Moor was won by the valour of Cromwell and the skill of Leslie. The royal cause was thus over-thrown in England, and the plans formed by Montrose on its behalf were hopelessly shattered. Disguised as a groom, and accompanied by only two friends, the hero, brooding over new schemes, hastened to the Highlands, there to give them birth and development. By sheer military genius, he, before many weeks elapsed, raised the fortunes of his royal master from the dust of abasement to the summit of a splendid but short-lived success. But at the very period when he was vanquishing the Covenanters at Tippermuir and the Bridge of Dee, the anti-Royalists were carrying all before them in the north of England. Callendar, now that the enemy he had been sent to waylay was out of the road, left Dumfries, effecting a junction with the Earl of Leven ; and to their united forces Newcastle capitulated in October. Among the prisoners were the Earl of Crawford, its commander, and Lord Maxwell, the Earl of Nithsdale's eldest son, who were carried to Edinburgh, and incarcerated in its Tolbooth, where they and other captives lay till they were liberated by the irresistible Montrose, who, following up five previous victories, routed the Covenanters at Kilsyth, and became not only master of the capital, but virtually dictator of the kingdom. The dictatorship, however, was so brief that it must have seemed to Montrose him-self in retrospect but a dazzling dream. On the 12th of September he experienced the stern reality of a defeat, at Philiphaugh, by General David Leslie, which all but annihilated his followers, and destroyed the vision of a restored monarchy which he had built up on the basis of his six great triumphs. Not a few Nithsdale and Galloway men fought under Leslie on this famous field, and, among others, a regiment of infantry raised at his own expense by Lord Kirkcudbright, and headed by that zealous anti-Royalist. Some Dumfriesians were also present on the other side, under the Earl of Hartfell, who, though at first mistrusted by Montrose, proved his devotedness to Charles at Philiphaugh. When the royal troops were dispersed the Earl, in company with other fugitives, lost his way, was seized by the country people of the neighbourhood, sent to Edinburgh, and sentenced to death by the Scottish Parliament, but had his life spared through the interposition of the Marquis of Argyle.

Montrose himself escaped to the Highlands, then took refuge in Hamburg ; and returning to Scotland in 1650, for the purpose of renewing the war, he fell into an ambuscade, was captured, and executed in Edinburgh on the 21st of May, about sixteen months after the beheading of the King, whom he had served with incomparable gallantry and devotedness. The Earl of Nithsdale, who had been forfeited for treason by the Scottish Parliament, also went abroad when the royal cause became hopeless, and died in exile, a loyal cavalier to the last.*

In 1649 an ineffectual attempt was made by the late King's son, Charles II., to restore the monarchy which Cromwell had set aside. The Scots, aggrieved by its abrogation, and deeply resenting the execution of the King, though he had treated them shamefully, proclaimed Charles a few days after that dread event ; and he having subscribed the National Covenant and the Solemn League and Covenant, a Scottish army, under David Leslie, prepared to do battle for his cause. Its defeat at Dunbar, and again at Worcester, left Cromwell "master of the situation," and the Commonwealth without an open enemy. On the death of the Protector, in 1658, he was succeeded by his son Richard, whose feeble rule only continued for a few months ; and in 1660 Charles was recalled from his exile—he having first, with his usual facility for promise-making, made the " Declaration of Breda," in which he offered indemnity for the past, and liberty of conscience for the future.

* After the restoration of the monarchy, the second Earl of Nithsdale applied to the Crown for compensation for the losses incurred by his family during the civil war, estimating them at £39,000 sterling, exclusive of interest ; the injury done to Carlaverock Castle, and the expense of its defence, being computed at £10,000. The burgh of Dumfries also put in claims for damages to the extent of £2280, alleged to be due on account of the " frie quarters " taken up in the town by the Covenanting troops, at various periods, chiefly in 1650-51. (See Appendix K.) We believe that neither Nithsdale nor the burgh ever received so much as a farthing of compensation.

CHAPTER XXXII.

IT has been repeatedly observed that the Reformation made at
first slow progress in Dumfries. By the beginning of the seventeenth century, however, Protestantism was greatly in the ascen-
dant, nearly all the inhabitants professing it, and only a few,
chiefly of the upper ranks, adhering to the proscribed faith. Not
only had the Dumfriesians become Protestant, but, as we have
seen, intensely Presbyterian, and, as such, hating Episcopalianism
nearly as much as Popery. Detesting the Prelatical measures
which Charles I. tried to thrust upon the country, they rejoiced
when the public voice and the General Assembly put the Service-
book and its accompaniments under ban. After the Presbyterian
form of religion had been established, the old Roman Catholic
place of worship—St. Michael's—was constituted the parish church
of Dumfries.

Ninian Dalyell was a licentiate of the Church as well as
teacher of the burgh school ; but if he ever possessed a clerical
charge in the town, it must have been for only a short period. In
1574 Peter Watson, formerly of Markinch, Fife, became minister of
St. Michael's ; and after officiating for about six years, he accepted
a call to Flisk. The next successor of whom we read is Alexander
Forsyth, appointed in 1585, and translated to Craigie in the
following year. He was succeeded, in 1586, by Hew Fullerton,
A.M., formerly of Maybole. Fullerton was translated to Kilwinning in 1605. In the same year Thomas Ramsay entered upon a
lengthened ministerial career in Dumfries. He had the honour of
being made perpetual moderator of the Presbytery by the General
Assembly of 1606. To him succeeded, in 1638, James Hamilton,

nephew of Viscount Claneboy, ordained as an Episcopalian minister by the Bishop of Down : probably enough he would have continued as such if the Prelatic establishment set up in Scotland by King James had not been overthrown. After acting as Presbyterian minister of St. Michael's for nine years, he accepted a call from an Edinburgh congregation ; and was succeeded, in 1648, by Hugh Henryson or Henderson, A.M., translated from Dalry, who, as is shewn afterwards, suffered much for conscience sake during the troublous times of his ministry.* It was not till 1657 that the officiating minister had a colleague appointed to him, so that for nearly a hundred years after the Reformation the spiritual oversight of the parish devolved upon one incumbent ; but he was supported by a large and active staff of laymen.

In the year above named the Town Council consulted the inhabitants on the propriety of obtaining the services of a second minister ; and at a meeting on the 26th of September they "having before thair eyes the glorie of God, the propagatioune of the gospell, and the putting downe of sin and iniquitie in this place, and considering that it is impossible for ony ane minyster to dyscharge all the dewties of the ministrie to this populous and numerous congreggatioune," they "with consent of the hail comunalitie," and the requirements of the Presbytery and Synod, "resolvit unanimouslie with all diligens to set about the calling of ane helper and colleigue" to the incumbent, Mr Henderson. At the same sitting the Council granted a thousand merks Scots as annual stipends to the assistant, and by their signatures to the minute gave legal effect to the agreement it embodied.

An entry in the Session record, dated 19th July, 1646, shows that on that day several elders and deacons were ordained ; and about this period there appear to have been twenty-one elders and eighteen deacons officiating in the burghal, and ten of both in the landward part of the parish. These lay office-bearers were specially entrusted with the exercise of church discipline. For this purpose they took strict cognisance of Sabbath-breakers, profane swearers, drunkards, and transgressors of the seventh commandment ; and so many cases occurred that meetings of Session were held every Monday and Friday afternoon, at which they were disposed of. We may think that the ministers and the under office-bearers often over-stretched their authority, and interfered with matters which they ought not to have meddled with. Undoubtedly, they were at times guilty of intolerance ; but there is abundant evidence to show that they honestly acted out their convictions, and according to the light given to them endeavoured to restrain iniquity and render the people of the

* For some of these details we are indebted to a very learned and valuable work—Fasti Ecclesiæ Scoticanæ, by Dr H. Scott.

parish God-fearing and moral. In this work, as we have said, the church courts were actively assisted by the civil magistrates ; and, between both, the inhabitants were in danger of suffering from too much law—though we must not overlook the circumstance that the long wars which roughened society and the laxity pre-vailing in the pre-Reformation period had left their traces upon the people, so that a severity approaching to despotism was perhaps needed to keep them in check. At all events the rulers, clerical and municipal, felt themselves called upon to put down vice with a high hand ; and the means they adopted for this purpose are strikingly illustrative of the spirit of the times.

Some specimens of the actings of the Town Council in matters religious as well as secular have already been given. Let us now look at the Session and Presbytery in the mirror of their own minutes. At a meeting of the Session on the 19th of October, 1654, elders were ordered "to attend the four parts of the burgh ilka Wednesday, from twa till sax," bailies being elders excepted, "in respect of the great affairs that occur to them on market days ;" and these ecclesiastical constables, when going their rounds, were enjoined to take note of all persons "found drunk or scan-dalous," and, "if they have ane officer with them," to take such offenders into custody, "there to remain during the bailie's pleasure." The power to impose civil penalties was possessed and exercised by the Session. They could fine and imprison as well as excommunicate. Anyone brought before the Session found guilty of swearing or blaspheming in the streets might be mulcted in two shillings or sent to jail for twenty-four hours. Adultery was sometimes punished by the forfeiture of two or more dollars ; but two persons who had sinned in this way were, on the 15th of October, 1635, ordained "to sit seven Sundays in sackcloth, and to stand the first and last Sabbath at the church door bare-footed :" and a third, on another occasion, for a similar offence, was adjudged to pay one dollar, and wear the gorgets on Sabbath, between the second and latter bell, with "ane paper upon her head" announcing the nature of her guilt. On the 2nd of February, 1654, a man caught playing at cards on a Saturday was required to pay twelve shillings to the Session treasurer. Persons guilty of slander were made to stand at the kirk-stile on Sabbath with the branks upon their mouths muzzling the unruly member ; callers of bad names were put on the pillory at the Cross ; a termagant lady was liable to be imprisoned in the Bell-house, and carted through the town to boot ; and, strangest of all, we read that the magistrates were requested by the Session to do justice on an inveterate purveyor of malicious scandal by causing her to be docked or shaven at the Market Cross.

On another occasion we find the elders calling on the bailies to visit with "civil and corporal punishment" an obstreperous miller from Troqueer accused of cursing and swearing ; and the burghal authorities sometimes evinced a feeling of reciprocity by taking security that those whom they punished should also present themselves before the tribunals of the Church. Thus, the Council, on the 5th of March, 1660, took bail from Adam Dickson, that a friend of his who had been fined for assault in absence should, on his first return from Ireland to Dumfries, appear before the Kirk Session, under the penalty of twenty pounds, and " satisflie the Sessioune for thrie dollors of penalties imposit upon him be the Sessioune, in cais the Sessioune think it expedient."

The Session and Presbytery were zealous enforcers of Sabbath observance. One curious instance is recorded in a minute dated 25th February, 1685, which sets forth that a brace of apprentices, whose names are given, " being lookit upon by the Session as twa of the perversest knaves in all the burgh for Sabbath-breaking," the magistrates had caused them to be soundly whipped before the Session, and then sent to the Bell-house ; the clerical court taking the opportunity which the case afforded of admonishing their masters, " and all within the burgh, that they shall be countable for their sons and apprentices on the Sabbath day." On the 27th of September, 1638, a man and wife from Palmerland were found guilty by the Session of drinking on the Sabbath " in Joan Edgar's house," and ordained " to confess thair fault publickly out of their seat on Sunday, and withal to pay twenty-four shillings to the poor." Total abstinence was by no means insisted upon by the Session, but they earnestly strove to prevent the immoderate use of intoxicating drinks, and to abolish or check all social practices which encouraged rioting and carousing.

On New-Year's Day, 1649, the following resolution was minuted :—" The Sessioune, resenting the great dishonour done to the Lord by sundry persons in the burgh not only abusing the creatures to excess of riot thro' drinking healths, but likewise in the height of their cups do calle for the drummer to beat the drum to them at every health, as they sinistrously term it, do henceforth discharge the drummer to answer any persone whatever in such ungodlie demands, under the paine of inflicting upon him the sharpest measure of kirk discipline, and extruding him from his place withal." Three years afterwards, when the Commonwealth was set up, and some of Cromwell's soldiers were in the town, a professional musician named John Laurie craved leave from the Session " to exercise his calling of piping and playing ;" but, though he coupled his prayer with the patriotic condition that he would undertake never to play a spring to any of the interloping English, he found the court to be mercilessly unmusical. Conceiving " his former way of living to be useless and unnecessary," the elders " discharged him from henceforth to use the same," and required that he " should betake himself to some honest and lawful way of living."

Here is a curious illustration at once of the state of society at the period and of the stringent discipline exercised by the Session in a case which was more fitted to awake a smile than provoke a frown. Three young buxom brides on their way to be wedded started off from the sides of their intended husbands, each anxious "to obtain the foregait of ane anither"--thinking, we suppose, that the first marriage would be the luckiest. For this bridal race the Amazons were, on the 23rd of July, 1657, ordered to be rebuked before the congregation on the following Sabbath, and to be handed over to the magistrates for civil punishment. Quite in accordance with a salutary edict of the Town Council previously quoted, the Session, on the 23rd of December, 1649, appointed the minister to intimate publicly that no person whatever was to be found drinking in tavern or ale-house after ten o'clock at night, under the pain of ecclesiastical censure.

In those times a regular attendance on the ordinances of religion was required by the Kirk Session : a demand that was right enough in itself, only that it was enforced not merely by admonition and rebuke but by fine. By an edict passed on the 28th of January, 1641, every gentleman absent from church was made liable to a fine of thirty shillings for each day's absence : a burgess committing the same offence had to pay twelve shillings, a farmer ten shillings, and a servant five. All the Incorporated Trades had seats assigned to them in the gallery of the parish church ; and three years before the above resolution was adopted the Session, taking into account the absenteeism of which many were guilty, "especially wrights and masons," intimated that they must be more punctual in their attendance on peril of losing their sittings. About the same time the inhabitants of Kelton, a village near Dumfries, then more populous than now, were, at the request of the Session, warned from the pulpit to be present in St. Michael's more regularly ; the Session, moreover, desiring the minister "to publicly read the names of the indwellers in Kelton every Sabbath ; and if these be found to be out of the kirk, they, and every ane of them, shall pay for every day they are absent six shillings."

Against Roman Catholics and breakers of the Covenant the church courts at this period took stringent proceedings. "Young Protestantism," it has well been said, "at first partook largely of the intolerance of old Romanism ;" but if the Covenanters are to be blamed for intolerance, remember their fault was the blindness of their times, in which their opponents, and other sects and parties, were as much, if not more, involved than themselves. And Presbyterianism was at least self-curing ; it carried in its bosom the antidote as well as the bane. "Unlike the dark, close, unventilated hierarchies, Presbyterianism, by its institutions and opinions, threw itself open to lay influences—to the voice of the eldership, to the election of the people, to the full breeze of public opinion ; and public opinion, as it became more enlightened, was sure, in the end, to blow away and dissipate the fumes of intolerance."* When we add that the clergy looked upon the Solemn League as the palladium of their civil liberties as well as of their religious rights, and recognised Romanism as the insatiable foe of both, we shall wonder less at the steps taken by them to uphold the League, and to check, and if possible root out from their midst, the adherents of Popery. With these general explanations we shall now adduce some illustrations of the way in which professors of the old faith and contemners of the Covenant were dealt with two hundred years ago by the Government in Edinburgh, and by the church courts of the district.

The Presbytery of Dumfries fully realised the fact that within their bounds more than in other parts of Scotland it would be requisite to maintain a merciless warfare against Popery. If they did not do so their own faith would be gradually undermined and eventually undone ; and if there was one member of the Presbytery who felt a need for this uncompromising antagonism more than another it was Mr Thomas Ramsay, minister of St. Michael's. One instance of his zeal may be noticed here, and others will be given at a later period. Whilst he, with several co-presbyters, was one day in September, 1626, passing along Devorgilla's bridge, a suspicious-looking person on horseback rode up. "A mass priest !" Not a doubt of it—a pestilent emissary of the Pope, notorious for having converted many country folks, "not only in their religion, but in their allegiance to the King's Majesty."† He was at once recognised and challenged by Mr Ramsay ; but the man of the mass, instead of surrendering to the summons, slipped off his steed, and, favoured by some sympathisers who followed him, effected his escape—leaving behind, however, his horse and a capacious cloak-bag, which proved to be as full of perilous chattels as Pandora's box, containing as it did "a number of oisties, superstitious pictures, priests' vestments, altar, chalice-plate, boxes with oils and ointments, with such other trash as priests carry about with them for Popish uses."‡ Forthwith Mr Ramsay, accompanied by several of his friends, proceeded to Edinburgh, and reported the occurrence to the Privy Council ; who commended their diligence, and ordered them to burn the captured articles at the Market Cross of Dumfries, excepting the silver plate, which was to be melted down for behoof of the poor.

At a subsequent period, when the Reformed faith had become firmly rooted in the town and district, one of Mr Ramsay's suc-

* Dodds's Fifty Years' Struggle of the Scottish Covenanters, pp. 51-2.

† Privy Council Records.   ‡ Ibid.

cessors, Mr Hugh Henderson, manifested no less hatred towards all that savoured of " Papistry." In March, 1658, he addressed a petition " to the Honorable the Comissioneirs for the adminystration of justice to the people of Scotland in caises criminall " in the following terms :—" Whairas thair ar severall preistis vestmentis, chalices, alteris, and uther idolatrous and superstitious monumentis and habitis laitlie fund within and neir to this burgh of Drumfreis—the priest where they were himselle fled—which the petitioner concevis were fitt to be abolished and putt away : thairfore humbly desires your honoris to give orders that these vestmentis, chalices, alter-books, and utheris, be exemplarlie put away, destroyed, and abolished, conforme to the lawis and practice of this natioun." The answer given to Mr Henderson was according to his heart's desire :—" 10th Apryll, 1658.—The Comissioneirs ordaines the plates to be broken and bestowed on the poore, and the vestmentis, books, and utheris, to be burnt and destroyed be the hand of the hangman at the place of execution, the first Wedinsday of May, 1658."* So that again, as in 1626, there would be a bonfire of " Popish trash " at the Market Cross of the burgh.

Though the Lord Herries of Queen Mary's day and the Lord Maxwell slain at Dryfe-Sands conformed to Presbyterianism before they died, their successors adhered to the Papal Church, as did also several other influential families in the district. Do what the Privy Council and the local Presbytery might, these incorrigibles persisted in their " obdured and Popish opinions and errors ;" and, to the sore scandal of their lordships, demeaned themselves like "free and lawful subjects," and were "reset, supplied, and furnished with all things necessar and comfortable unto them," though they had been previously subjected to excommunication and horning. As a last resort, the Council in 1628 issued a commission for the apprehension and trial of all persons " who are suspect guilty of the reset and supply of the said excommunicat rebels ;" the list of the latter including Herbert Maxwell of Kirkconnell ; Gilbert Brown, formerly Abbot of Newabbey ; Charles Brown, Newabbey (his brother) ; Barbara Maxwell ; Lady Mabie ; John Little, master of Lord Nithsdale's household ; John Allan in Kirkgunzeon ; and John Williamson in Lochrutton. Two of the Commissioners, Sir William Grierson of Lagg (father of the persecutor) and Sir John Charteris of Amisfield, succeeded in apprehending the ex-abbot and his brother in the parish of Newabbey. This act occasioned a serious outbreak among the females of the parish. Headed by the wife of Charles Brown, they mobbed the minister and schoolmaster, who were suspected of having been concerned in the capture of the prisoners,

* Burgh Records.

and subjected their wives and servants to rough usage, "pursuing them with rungs, and casting of stones." The Council looking upon this riot as nothing short of sheer rebellion, caused those concerned in it to be cited before the Commissioners at Dumfries, that they might be tried and punished.*

A few years later we find the Privy Council flying at higher game. On the 17th of November, 1631, their lordships, considering that the Earl of Nithsdale "is vehemently suspected in his religion, and that the remaining of Lord Maxwell, his son, in his company, may prove very dangerous to the youth, and now in his tender years infect and poison him with opinions wherefra it will be difficult thereafter to reclaim him," ordered his lordship to "exhibit" his son, that "direction may be given for his breeding and education in the true religion." "When we remember," says Robert Chambers, "that the Earl of Nithsdale was then the most powerful man in the southern part of the kingdom, and had, so lately as 1626, acted as the royal commissioner to Parliament, and since conducted a large auxiliary for the service of the King's brother-in-law in Germany, the character of this interference with his domestic arrangements becomes all the more noticeable."† About the same period "ane busy and trafficking Papist," named Andrew Anderson, was consigned to a place of durance in Dumfries known as the Pledge-house, on a charge of making arrangements for conducting gentlemen's sons beyond sea that they might be educated as Roman Catholics. The Lords of the Council ordered that he should be sent to Edinburgh for examination ; but the unfortunate emissary, summoned before a higher tribunal, died in the tolbooth ; and they could do no more in the matter than command the magistrates to inquire into the "form, manner, and cause of his death."

In June, 1634, the Privy Council had on hand the cases of numerous other Dumfries delinquents ; one of whom, Robert Rig, a Brigend resident, was accused of having been united in matrimonial bonds to "ane excommunicat Papist named Elspeth Maxwell, for which offence he had been previously dealt with by the Presbytery. The terrified Benedict exhibited a tearful mood when examined by the lordly inquisitors. He ruefully acknowledged his fault, craving pardon for the same. From his statement it appeared that "he was married by a Popish priest upon the 17th of November last (being Sunday), at night, with candle-light, above the bridge of Cluden, in the fields, and that four were present at the marriage beside the priest, whereof some were men and some were women, whom he knew not, because they had their faces covered." The Lords having heard the prisoner's confession, and the evidence of Mr Ramsay, parish minister of Dumfries, as

* Privy Council Records.   † Domestic Annals, vol. ii., p. 59.

to what had been done by the Presbytery in the matter, found
that "Robert Rig has violat and contravened the laws of this
kingdom in marrying ane excommunicat woman by a priest, who
has no power to exerce any function within this kingdom ;" and
they adjudged him to be incarcerated in Edinburgh jail during
their pleasure, with instructions that no one from his wife should
have access to him " by word or write."

Meanwhile the woman herself was enduring involuntary
penance in the Dumfries tolbooth, from which she was only
liberated that she too might be taken before the Lords of Council.
With her went other fourteen females, chiefly wives of tradesmen in the burgh, who had been her companions in prison, "for
hearing of mass, and being present thereat sundry times within
thir twelvemonth bygane, as their confessions bears," all being
"exhibited" before the Council by Mr Ramsay and Bailie Williamson, "to the intent such order may be taen with them as may give
terror to others to commit the like." Eight of the accused
"declared that they were heartily sorrowful for the scandal they
had given to the kirk by hearing of mass, and craved parden for
the same ;" adding a solemn promise, "in all time coming to obey
the laws, and for that effect to resort to the kirk, hear preachings,
and to communicate, and that they should not hear mass nor reset
Jesuits." These penitents were ordered to remain in their Edinburgh lodgings till further notice ; but seven other women
obstinately "refused to conform to the religion presently professed within the kingdom ; in respect whereof the Lords ordain
them to be committed to ward within the tolbooth of Edinburgh,
therein to remain upon their own expenses, till they be freed and
relieved by the said Lords." Shortly afterwards, the seven
recusants were remitted to the Archbishop of Glasgow, "to be
dealt with as he might think fit."*

On the 22nd of April, 1647, the Synod of Dumfries ordered
intimation to be made from all the pulpits within the bounds,
that a sentence of excommunication had been passed upon John,
Lord Herries, Dame Elizabeth Beaumont, Countess of Nithsdale,
Dame Elizabeth Maxwell, Lady Herries, Dame Elizabeth Maxwell,
elder of Kirkconnell, and about thirty other persons of a humbler
degree. What this sentence implied we can scarcely say, though
it was not, certainly, of such a serious nature as its name used to
import when Popery was predominant.† All persons were for-

* Privy Council Records, as quoted in Chambers's Domestic Annals.

† "I conceive," says Samuel Rutherford, "that excommunication hath
neither election nor reprobation, regeneration nor non-regeneration, for its
object or terminus ; but only it cutteth a contumacious person from the
visible Church on earth, and from the Head Christ in heaven, not in regard
of his state of regeneration, as if Christ, ratifying the sentence in heaven, did
so much as cut him off conditionally from being a member of His body. No,

bidden "to reset or resort to" those mentioned under ban, "without licence of Presbytery or the kirk judicatories, upon evidence asked and given, under peril of ecclesiastical censures;"* but we do not suppose that this decree of isolation would tell very terribly on the parties concerned. A week after it was fulminated we read that the Session gave liberty to two individuals "to speak with Lord Herries, notwithstanding he be excommunicat, in respect that both of them have sundry business of good concernment with his lordship."

At a meeting of Presbytery on April 5th, 1647, Mr George Gladstanes reported that John Herries of Croghmore had "begun his obedience;" that is to say, had submitted to certain terms imposed upon him for the purpose of being relieved from a sentence of excommunication he had incurred. It was also intimated to the court that "whereas Elspet Herries, his mother, having been excommunicat for recusancy, had departed this life, and had by divers gentlemen and others been accompanyied to her burial," and "the brethren for purging of that scandal, thocht fitt that such as were thaire should be inquired for, and cited for the first day." In obedience to the summons thus resolved upon, John Herries appeared penitentially before the brethren, on the following 18th of May; but he was punished no further than by being "ordained to acknowledge his fault before the congregation at Lochrutton," in which parish Croghmore is situated.† In 1648 the Presbytery brought a more serious charge against Lord Herries than the profession of Popery. When Montrose was at Dumfries in 1644 Herries went from Terregles to bid him welcome,‡ and allowed his son to follow him into the Highlands. On account of these misdeeds he was cited to appear before the court; and not being in a position to contemn its authority, he presented himself for trial. He appears to have fenced a little with his clerical inquisitors. When, however, he was questioned as to the furnishing of his son with troops, he "admitted that, being put upon by the Duke of Hamilton, he did what he could for his son's furtherance." Thereupon, it is stated, the Presbytery agreed "to dismiss his lordship till they be certified by the commissioners of the kirk anent his censure." Everything considered Lord Herries was tenderly handled by the brethren; but they

---

but in regard of the second acts of the life of God, and the sweet efficacy and operation of the Spirit, by which the ordinances are less living, less operative, and less vigorous—the man being, as Mr Cotton says, as a palsied member, in which life remaineth but a little withered and blunted, and he in Satan's power to vex his spirit : and therefore I grant all to imply that excommunication is not a real separating of a man from Christ's body—only unbelief does that—but it follows not—therefore it is a separation only from the external society of the Church."

* Synod Records.
† Presbytery Records.   ‡ Terregles Papers.

were at this time negotiating with him regarding a stipend to the
parish minister of Terregles—which was eventually fixed at two
chalders of corn, five hundred merks, with the tiend of the
fishings in the College water—and, perhaps on this account, they
did not wish to press matters to an extremity with his lordship.*
We find the following entry in the Session record, dated 3rd
February, 1659 :—" Capt. Ed. Maxwell delate for dishaunting the
ordinances and that he is suspect of Popery—instance his inviting
Lady Nithsdale and Lady Semple, both excommunicat for Popery,
to a publick feast. Confesses that he invited the Lady Semple,
but knew not that she was excommunicat ; and that Lady Nithsdale came to visit his wife in her seickness. He was ordained to
consider the Confession of Faith, and be ready to declair what
profesioun he was of."

* Burnside's MS. History.

CHAPTER XXXIII.

In the Presbytery minutes for 1647 and 1648 numerous cases are entered of individuals being called upon to satisfy the Church for "Covenant-breaking," "malignity and hostility," accompanying the enemy towards Philiphaugh, for taking part in "James Graham's invasion," and the "lait sinful engagement under the Duke of Hamilton." One of the chief delinquents was Sir John Charteris of Amisfield. Though a member of the Dumfriesshire War Committee, and under a double bond to the cause of the Covenant, he proved false to his vows by following Montrose to the field, when that great captain made a daring but fruitless effort to redeem the fortunes of Charles the First. For so doing the knight of Amisfield was called before the General Assembly, where he appeared in a submissive attitude, professing his readiness to endure any amount of punishment rather than remain unreconciled to the Church. He acknowledged his heinous offence in violating "the great oath of God taken by him in the National Covenant and Mutual League and Covenant, and in his joining in the late rebellioune, and his being accessory to the shedding of the bloode of the people of God : which his confessioune, being made in all humilitie before the Assembly, so far as men could discerne, and lykwise *genibus flexis* [on bended knees], he signed and subscribed, as his autographe, ordained to be preserved, will testifie." Charteris's case was an aggravated one ; but he too seems to have been leniently dealt with. The reverend fathers might, according to the views prevalent at the time, have fined him heavily. They did not so much as amerce him in a single plack, or even force him to undergo a lengthened period of probation before being received back into the fold. Probably, however, the proud knight would feel the penance imposed upon him worse to endure than the loss of world's gear ; the Assembly having

"ordained him to satisfie, for his scandalous offence, in the kirk of
Dumfries, in a seat before the pulpit, and that there, *genibus flexis*,
he should make the former declairatiounes, and such like, in his
own parish kirk of Tinwal ; and that at Tinwal, the minister, Mr
Humphrey Wood, receive him accordinge to the fore-mentioned
order and ordinance." All these proceedings in the Amisfield case
were duly reported to the Dumfries Presbytery on the 29th of
April, 1647 ; and the brethren, after considering it, ordained that
the contrite baron be "advertised to expede his satisfactioune," in
order that he might gratify his desire of being restored to the
Church.

About this time a temporary breach was caused among the
Scottish Presbyteries by what is called "The Engagement,"
which was a treaty entered into by the more moderate party with
Charles, in virtue of which he was to receive their support on
condition of his confirming the Solemn League and Covenant,
and re-establishing Presbyterianism. The treaty was repudiated
by the inflexible Covenanters of the Dumfries Presbytery, and by
all "true blue" Scots everywhere, because they felt that the King
who had so often broken his promises before was unworthy of
their trust. Yet many recruits were obtained in the district by
the Duke of Hamilton, the leader of the Engagers ; and at the
head of about fifteen thousand ill-disciplined soldiers he passed
southward ; only, however, to have his force scattered, and him-
himself taken prisoner, near Warrington, by Cromwell. Very
indignant were the Dumfries Presbytery against all within the
bounds who had been seduced into this defection.* An order
having been received by that body from the General Assembly for

---

* Mr John Semple, minister of Carsphairn, a noted man in his day,
preached against "the Engagement" at Dumfries, and that too in presence of
officers and men who were about to take part in it. He exposed its sinful-
ness and predicted its failure. "Go ye up," said the bold divine—"Go ye up
to Ramoth Gilead and prosper ; but if ye prosper in the way that ye are
going, God never spoke by me ; for I have beheaded your Duke like a sybow ;
if ye were once in England, his head shall as sure go off as if I had it in my
gown lap ; for God is not with you, and he will break you in his wrath.
Many of you shall never see your native land again ; and those of you that
escape, however brave ye are now in your fine clothes, ye shall come home
bare and naked, swarming with lice, for God shall smite you with one of the
plagues of Egypt."—*Biographia Presbyteriana*, vol. i., pp. 192-3. Peter
Walker, the reporter of this discourse, adds : "An old man who was one of
them told me that he was sure this threatening was made out upon them, for
they were like to be eaten up with a swarm of them. After sermon a colonel,
being his hearer, challenged him upon the street for speaking against what
was their duty and good design, to fight for King and country ; and gave him
ill names, calling him a varlet and an old greeting carle. To whom he
answered, he was no more a varlet than he (the officer) had the saving grace
of God, and that he was as free of as the birk is of leaves at Yule-even ; and
as to my preaching, I have told you the truth, which you will find to your
sad experience, and many will see to be no falsehood : for ye are neither for
the good of the King nor country, but against God."

renewing the Solemn League and Covenant, they, on the 7th of December, 1648, proscribed certain parties from signing it, as being manifestly unworthy ; among others, all who had in any way promoted " the lait unlawful engagement under the Duke of Hamilton," special mention being made of those who voluntarily countenanced the Duke's rendezvous at Annan Moor ; of all captains of parishes who took part in the rebellious movement ; of the heritors who contributed troops, or rations to sustain them ; of all soldiers who, of their own accord, were "out" on the occasion ; and of "all women malignantly disposed."[*] It is obvious from these and similar intimations, that though the Covenanters were dominant over Dumfries and the district, not a few persons from the vicinity took part with the Crown against the League.

During the seventeenth century witchcraft was an article of almost universal belief in Scotland, and many Acts of Parliament were passed in the reigns of Mary and James VI., as well as in those of preceding sovereigns, for the punishment of such as gave "thame selfis furth to haif onie sic craft or knowlege," or who consulted these professors of the Satanic art. Numerous instances occur in the criminal records of old women having been tried, convicted, and strangled, or burned to ashes, on such a charge After the Reformation, as well as before, the so-called crime was taken cognisance of both by the municipal and spiritual authorities, the latter deeming themselves specially called upon to interpose for its restriction and punishment. Colonel Cleland, the laureate of the Covenanters, and one of their military leaders, in celebrating the characteristics of the district, thus notices its supernatural visitors :—

> " There's as much virtue, sonce, and pith,
> In Annan, or the Water of Nith,
> Which quietly slips bv Dumfries,
> As in the rivers of old Greece.
> For here, we're told, in sundry places,
> Beside mill-dams and green brae-faces,
> The elves and eldrich brownies strayed,
> And green-gowned fairies danced and played."

The poet might have added that other professors of *diablerie* abounded on the banks of Nith. Of reputed witches there were, at all events, more than enough ; and, according to tradition, Locharbridge Hill, long used as a warlike rendezvous, was the favourite trysting place of the weird women of Dumfries. Thither, it is said, they trooped to confer together when they had any extraordinary business on hand, encouraging each other by chanting a gathering hymn, of which the following rather apocryphal snatch has been preserved :—

> " When the gray howlet has three times hooed ;
> When the grimy cat has three times mewed ;

[*] Presbytery Records.

When the tod has yowled three times in the wud,
At the red moon cowering ahin the clud ;
When the stars hae cruppen deep i' the drift,
Lest cantrips had pyked them out o' the lift ;
Up horses a', but mair adowe !
Ryde, ryde for Lochar-brigg Knowe !"*

" Roused by this infernal summons," says Allan Cunningham, " the
earth and the air groaned with the unusual load. It was a grand
though daring attempt for man or aught of mortal frame to view
this diabolical hurry. The wisest part barred their doors, and
left the world to its own misrule."

In Dumfries the church courts seem to have had a monopoly
of the business—so far, at least, as the initiatory proceedings
against witches went—the only notice of the Council's interference
with any of " those close contrivers of all harms," being contained
in the following minute, dated 14th November, 1664 :– " The
Counsall being informed that Janet Burnes, commonly reputed a
witche, and quho hath bein banished out of severall other burghis,
and put out of this burgh in the month of August last, for cheating
the people upon pretence of knowledge of all things done by them
in tym past, or that may fall out in tym cuming, with certification to be scurgit if ever she was sein within the burgh thaireafter ;
and being well informed that she was sein within the town on
Saturday, they have ordaint that intimation be maid by touk of
drum, that non of the inhabitants resset or give meit or drink
unto the said Janet Burnes." Whatever belief the honourable
councillors had in witchcraft, abstractly considered, they had no
faith in this professor of it, and came to the sensible conclusion
that she was simply an impostor, and ought to be treated as such.

The following is an extract from the Presbytery records, dated
22nd April, 1656 :—" John M'Quhan in Urr, compeared, confessing
that he went to Dundrennan, to a witch-wife, for medicine for his
sick wife, and that he got a salve for her, and that the wife said to
him, ' If the salve went in his wife would live, if not she would die.'
Janet Thomson in Urr, compearing, confessed that she went to the
said witch, and got a salve to her mother, and that the witch bade
her take her mother, and lay her furth twenty-four hours ; and
said that her mother got her sickness between the mill and her ain
house, and bade her tak her to the place where she took it, and
wash her with [elder] leaves. She also confessed that the deceased
Thomas M'Minn and his friends sent her at another time to the
same witch, whose name is Janet Miller. They were both rebuked
[by the Presbytery], and referred to their own Session to be
rebuked from the pillar in sackloth."

About this time the Kirk Session of Dumfries, after solemn
deliberation on the subject, required the minister to announce

* Cromek's Remains of Nithsdale and Galloway Song, pp. 276-7.

from the pulpit that all persons having evidence to give against such as were under suspicion of "the heinous and abominable sin of witchcraft," should be ready to furnish the same to the Session without delay ; and at their next meeting the elders wisely qualified the order, by resolving that any one who charged another with being guilty of " sic divilisch practises," without due reason, should be visited with the severest discipline of the Kirk. In the summer of 1658, we find the members of Presbytery girding up their loins for a wholesale razzia against all users and practisers of witchcraft, sorcery, charming, and soothsaying. Public intimation was made to that effect, and the brethren were each required to take notice of suspected persons, and to urge their congregations to collect evidence against them, in order to enable sessions to bring the cases in a matured form before the Presbytery.

This was no idle resolution, as the following dread entry will show, dated 5th April, 1659 :—" The Presbytery have appoynted Mr Hugh Henrison, Mr Wm. M'Gore, Mr George Campbell, Mr John Brown, Mr Jo. Welsh, Mr George Johnston, Mr Wm. Hay, and Mr Gabriel Semple, *to attend the nine witches,* and that they tak thair own convenient opportunity to confer with them ; also, that they be assisting to the brethren of Dumfries and Galloway *the day of the* EXECUTION." Dr. Burnside states that he examined all the records of the town and neighbourhood that appeared likely to throw further light upon this horrible judicial tragedy, but without success.

The books of the High Court of Justiciary,* however, supply the requisite information regarding it. We there learn that the court was opened at Dumfries on the 2nd of April, in the above year, by the " Commissioners in Criminal Cases to the people in Scotland," Judge Mosley and Judge Lawrence ; and that ten women, each charged with divers acts of witchcraft, were brought before them for trial. The proceedings appear to have lasted till the 5th. One of the accused, Helen Tait, had a rather narrow escape—the jury finding by a plurality of voices that the " dittay " in her case was " not cleirly proven." Nevertheless, before being dismissed from the bar, she was required to find security to the extent of £50 sterling for her good behaviour, and that she would banish herself from the parish. The nine other unfortunates were all convicted, as is shown by the subjoined minute, giving the finding of the jury and the deliverance of the judge, as pronounced by the official dempster, " F. Goyyen."

" Drumfreis, the 5th of Apryle, 1659.—The Commissioners adjudges Agnes Comenes, Janet M'Gowane, Jean Tomson, Margt. Clerk, Janet M'Kendrig, Agnes Clerk, Janet Corsane, Helen Moorhead, and Janet Callon, as found guilty of the severall articles of

---

* Kept at the Register House, Edinburgh.

witchcraft mentioned in the dittayes, to be tane upon Wednesday
come eight days to the ordinar place of execution for the burghe of
Drumfreis, and ther, betuing 2 and 4 hours of the afternoon, to be
strangled at staikes till they be dead, and therefter ther bodyes to
be burned to ashes, and all ther moveable goods to be esheite.
Further, it is ordained that Helen Moorhead's moveables be intromitted with by the Shereff of Nithsdaile, to seize upon and herrie
the samin for the king's use."

Nine women given to the flames in one day ! The scene at the
execution must have been so inexpressibly shocking that we dare
not examine it too closely. The planting of the stakes, and building up about them vast heaps of peats, straw, and other combus-
tibles ; the executioners with their ropes and torches ; the venerable victims, frail with age, trembling with terror or palsy, crazed
by a natural visitation, or the dread of a cruel death—whom the
horrid functionaries bind till they shake no more ; the attendant
ministers striving to benefit their souls before their bodies are
charred into blackened clay ; the curious onlookers, who would be
pitiful, perhaps, were their hearts not annealed by the belief that
the miserable women, being witches, are alike beyond the pale of
sympathy or forgiveness ; the first stage of torture, by which they
are kept literally hanging between life and death ; the second
which shortly finishes by fire what the suffocating noose and
smoke had only half accomplished ; the lurid blaze, which, bursting forth, dispels the vapour that for awhile in pity veiled the
shrivelling forms from sight ; the wild leaping—the loud crackling
of the fire as it gains full mastery ; its subsidence when its
consuming work is done ; the awful close of all, when, as the clock
strikes four, the crowd, which had " supped full of horrors," can
see nothing where the nine poor martyrs to superstition stood,
save a morsel of blackened bones and a heap of bloody dust, while
the grimy hangmen, like so many scavengers of death, are sweeping up and preparing to carry out of sight.

Just two years before the date of this fearful *auto-da-fé* the
Council were required to carry out a sentence of the same kind
against two other females, as we learn from the following strange
items of charge entered in the burgh treasurer's books :—27th May,
1657.—For 38 load of peitts to burn the two women, £3 12s.
[Scots.] Mair, given to William Edgar for ane tar barrell, 12s ; for
ane herring barrell, 14s. Given to John Shotrick, for carrying the
twa barrells to the pledge [house], 6s. Mair, given to the four
officers that day that the whiches was brunt, at the provest and
bayillis command, 24s. Given to Thomas Anderson for the two
stoups and two steaves [to which the women were tied], 30s."

At an assize held in the burgh in 1671, eight or more females
were charged with witchcraft ; five of them, whose fate we cannot
trace, were eventually sent for trial to Kirkcudbright. An official

document, signed by two judges, which lies before us, thus announces the doom of the other three :—"Magistrates of Drumfreis,—Forasmuch as in ane Court of Justiciarie, holden be us within the Tolbuthe of Drumfreis, upon the fyftein day of May instant, Janet M'Muldritche, and Elspeth Thomsone, now found guiltie be ane assyze of the severall articles of witchcraft specified in the verdict given against them thereanent, were decerned and adjudged be us, the Lords Commissioners of Justiciary, to be tane upon Thursday next, the eighteen day of May instant, betwixt two and four houres in the afternoune, to [the] ordinare place of executione, for the toune of Drumfreis, and there to be worried* at ane stake till they be dead : and theirafter their bodies to be brunt to ashes, and all their moveable goods and geir to be escheit. You shall thairfoir cause put the said sentence to due executione, whereanent thir presents shall be your warrand. Given at Drumfreis the sixteen day of May, 1671."†

For a long season the parishes lying in the southern part of the Presbytery were kept in terror by a horde of reputed witches. These were Marion Dickson in Blackshaw, Isobel Dickson in Locharwoods, her daughter Agnes, and Marion Herbertson in Mousewaldbank. "Many grievous malefices, committed upon their neighbours and others," were laid at their door ; and the Presbytery, horror-struck and indignant at the reports laid before them regarding these dangerous sybils, declared it to be "damnifying to all good men and women living in the country thereabouts, who cannot assure themselves of safety of their lives by such frequent malefices as they commit." Encouraged by the Presbytery, a party of country people made bold to lay hands upon the women, and carry them to be imprisoned at Dumfries by the sheriff, who sent them to jail on their captors consenting to appear as witnesses in the case. He then, fortified by a certificate of the witches' dread doings from the Presbytery, brought the matter by petition before the Privy Council, who ordered the delinquents to be sent to Edinburgh for trial.‡ The district was thus delivered from their presence ; how they fared afterwards is not recorded.

On the 15th of February, 1697, the following curious case of alleged divination was brought before the reverend court, at the instance of the Session of Carlaverock. About a month before, John Fergusson in Woodbarns, Cummertrees, and William Richardson, Cummertreestown, on coming from Dumfries, went into the tavern of William Nairns, Bankend of Carlaverock, for the pur-

---

* *Worried*, " strangled." The word sometimes means " smothered."
　　　　" Oh, mother dear, gie up the house,
　　　　For the reik it worries me."
　　　　　　　　　　　　　　Ballad of " Edom o' Gordon."
　† Burgh Records.　‡ Privy Council Records.

pose of enjoying a social dram ; Richardson leaving his horse,
which carried a sack with cheese and herrings in it, tied at the
door. The latter, after the lapse of a considerable time, on going
out to see about his steed, perceived to his dismay that its burden
of provender had vanished. Returning to the interior, he affirmed
that some one had stolen his property ; whereupon his fellow-
traveller and boon companion, Fergusson, called for two Bibles,
declaring that if the pilferer were anywhere in the whole "town
of Bankend" he would find him out. Mine host, with a salutary
regard for the reputation of his house, declared that he would
allow no charming with Bibles to go on within it. The diviner
swore that if they refused his request he "would make bloody
work among them ;" and, under dread of this threat, "some
brought two Bibles to the said John Fergusson, who brought a
key out of his pocket, and put the one end of it within one Bible
and the bowl end out, clasping the Bible upon it, and two holding
the bowl of the key upon their fingers. The said John then read
three verses of the fiftieth Psalm out of the second Bible, beginning always at the eighteenth verse, always naming a person
before he began to read, till they came to William M'Kinnell in
the same town ; and when they named him, and were reading the
said Scriptures, the key and the Bible turned about and fell on
the table. This was done three times, as attested by James Tait,
mason, who is quartered in Townhead ; James Fergusson, servitor
to George Maxwell of Isle ; George Fergusson, in Bankend ; and
William Nairns, in whose house it was done."

Evidence to this effect having been given, the moderator was
instructed to write to Mr Gilbert Ramsay, minister of Cummertrees, to "cause summon the said John to next meeting of Presbytery," the minute of which meeting reveals the upshot of the case.
"22nd March, 1697.— Compeared John Fergusson in Woodbarns,
who acknowledged his scandalous carriage in charming and
turning the key at Bankend, conform to the accusation, but says
he knew not there was any evil in it. The Presbytery appoint
him to stand on the pillar in the church of Carlaverock, and be
sharply rebuked for his scandalous practice, and recommends him
to the magistrates to be secured till he give bail to answer and
satisfy, conform to this act."*

Before the next century was far advanced enlightened views
on the subject of witchcraft began to prevail ; and exactly fifty
years after the ninefold execution previously noted, the last trial
for witchcraft by the Court of Justiciary in Scotland took place
at Dumfries. The accused was named Elspeth Rule ; the indictment against her being that she was habit and repute a witch,
and had used threatening expressions towards persons at enmity

* Presbytery Records.

with her, who, in consequence of such menace, suffered from the death of friends or the loss of cattle, while one of them became mad. The jury, by a majority of votes, found the charges proved ; and the judge condemned the prisoner to be burned on the cheek with a hot iron, and banished for life—the first part of which barbarous sentence was carried out with such merciless effect that persons living in 1790 had been told by their parents that the smoke caused by the torturing process was seen issuing out of the mouth of the unhappy woman.*

* Burnside's MS. History.

CHAPTER XXXIV.

THE Parish Register of Dumfries goes back to the 6th of October,
1605, as regards baptisms ; in the following year the names of
sixty infants, "bairns lawfullie begotten," are entered in the list ;
and it is not till the 12th of May, 1616, that marriages, and not till
the 11th of May, 1617, that burials begin to be inserted in the
record. In 1618 the total baptisms were 111, marriages 19, and
deaths 51 ; though, in all probability, the latter figures considerably underrate the mortality for the year. In 1660 there were,
according to the register, 116 baptisms, 31 marriages, and 122
burials ; but we may very safely add a fourth to the first two of
these entries, and a third to the other, to make up for omissions,
which would bring up the returns to 145 births, 39 marriages, and
139 deaths. These bear the proportion of less than one to four of
the registrar-general's figures for the parish in 1860 ; and supposing the population to have been in the same ratio to the returns
in both years, the inhabitants of the parish, burghal as well as
landward, must have numbered barely 4000 two hundred years
ago.* This is a rough mode of calculation, and can only be
regarded as approximately correct. There is every reason to
believe that the long desolating wars, and the cruel persecution,
to which the town and district were subjected seriously thinned
their population, and otherwise checked their prosperity. Other
agencies, the chief of which were famine and pestilence, produced
like results.

---

* Nearly the same result is arrived at by taking the number of the Trades
as a basis of calculation.

As we learn from the "Chronicle of Perth," the wheat, in 1598, was "blasted" over all Scotland, and oatmeal was so scarce that it sold for 6s the peck ; "ane great deid amang the people" being occasioned by the dearth. A virulent plague followed—Dumfries suffering much from both visitations ; while, to add to its distress, it was cut off from all intercourse with neighbouring towns. A minute of the Kirkcudbright Town Council shows that that body, on the 20th of April, 1599, took alarm on account of "the pest being verie ill in Drumfries," and prohibited the inhabitants, "under the paine of xi. s. ilk fault, and tinsall of their freidome," to enter the infected burgh, or even to venture below the Water of Urr, or hold intercourse with any one from the east side of that river. As a consequence the trade of the town was utterly paralysed ; the cattle of the burgesses disappeared, and none came from a distance to supply their places.

In such sad circumstances two men, James Sharpe and John Martin, were sent into the western parts of Galloway on a cattle-buying mission. On reaching the burgh of Wigtown they were well received by its magistrates, and allowed to bargain for as many beeves as they needed, on condition of paying the market dues as well as the price of the stock. Whilst the men were driving their purchase—thirty-eight head of nolt—homewards, they were encountered at Minnigaff by a large armed party, commanded by the Wigtown authorities, Provost Hannay and Bailies Edgar and Tailfer, who, by dint of main force, brought both cattle and drovers back to their burgh ; the reason assigned being, it is supposed, that the latter had not paid the full amount of custom. When at Wigtown the cattle were detained eight days on scanty fare, so that they were reduced to the condition of Pharaoh's lean kine. In the end their purchasers, after laying down a hundred additional merks, were allowed to depart with the animals, which, by cropping the wayside pasture as they went along, would probably reach their journey's end in tolerable "fettle." This pitiable affair, which reads so strangely of Dumfries, now the scene of considerable markets for the transfer of cattle, came under the notice of the Privy Council, and was remitted to the ordinary judges, to be settled by them as they might think best.*

Again the two fell destroyers visited the country in 1623. At midsummer that year, Calderwood tells us, the famine was so sore that "many, both in burgh and land, died of hunger ;" numerous poor folks, who flocked into Edinburgh in a vain search for succour, falling down lifeless in the streets of the city. For several months prior to Michaelmas the mortality in Perth was at the rate of ten or twelve deaths per day :† some other towns suffered in the same proportion ; and Dumfries, perhaps, in a greater

* Chambers's Domestic Annals, vol. i., p. 305.   † The Perth Chronicle.

degree than any. Fearful must have been the condition of the burgh in that fatal year : many of the people pining for want— many more perishing under the "arrows of the pestilence "—some suffering from both the famine and the plague. To the names of a hundred persons who died during the year the words " puir," " extreme puir," or " pauper," are annexed in the register of the parish. During the first ten months there were no fewer than 492 deaths (those for the rest of the year not being recorded) ; so that the parish must have lost about a ninth of its inhabitants by this terrible scourge.

We cannot wonder that the Dumfries Town Council, after such sad experiences of the plague, should, in the summer of 1665, when it was raging in London, have taken special precautions with the view of keeping the burgh unvisited by the destroyer. The importation of English merchandise was strictly forbidden ; and it was duly certified that any inhabitant who should receive such goods would be liable to a penalty of five hundred merks, to have his house closed up, and himself and " haill family seques- trate without the town for the space of 40 days thereafter." Then, as some of the Dumfries pedlars were away south, hawking the linen and woollen cloths manufactured in the burgh, they were debarred from returning to it under a similar penalty, unless fur- nished with " a bill of health ;" and, finally, lest strangers should enter the ports, bringing more mischief in their wake than even the English Borderers of old, twenty-four men kept watch and ward over the town by night and day.*

When the Revolution brought peace and rest to the country, Dumfries began once more to thrive : the population of the town rapidly increased, till it rose to about 5000 in the beginning of the eighteenth century ; and in 1790 it numbered nearly 6000, besides 1400 in the rural portion of the parish ; the annual births in the parish being then 200, marriages 50, and deaths 150.

In the first half of the seventeenth century, full of trouble though it was, the town acquired some new elements of material progress. Its great annual trysts, in February and September, at which horses, cattle, agricultural produce, and merchandise were disposed of, became increasingly important, and did much to promote the trade of the town. How Dumfries acquired what has come to be called " the backbone " of its revenue—the right to levy tolls and customs at the bridge—has already been ex- plained ; and we have now to tell of an incident which, calamitous in itself, helped in the end to secure to the burgh the continued possession of this somewhat lucrative source of income. One day in 1620 the Nith, which had tolerated the bridge for more than three centuries, swelled by tributary streams and the rains of

* Town Council Minutes and Burnside's MS.

heaven, came down with such tremendous force that Devorgilla's useful structure was turned into a wreck, "to the great hurt of the burgh and countrey, and discouragement not only of the haill inhabitants thereof, and countrie people thereabout, but also of all his Majestie's subjects of all his Majestie's three kingdoms of Scotland, England, and Ireland, it being the onlie passage" by which they can traverse the said kingdoms to and fro. In such dolorous language as this the disaster was described, in a royal document dated 16th July, 1621.

Though the value of the bridge was thus highly rated by his Majesty, the burgh was left to build it up anew from its own resources. When Government aid for the work was solicited by the magistrates, they were told to appeal for voluntary contributions to "his Majestie's good subjects in burgh and land throughout the whole kingdome ;" and this having been done without eliciting a favourable response, the burgh single-handed and bravely proceeded with and completed the structure—nearly ruining itself by the exhaustive effort. In a second appeal to "the most gracious and sacred Sovrane," the rulers of the town spoke of their enterprise in the following terms :--"So being left to ourselffs without all hope of help, we resolved to interpoise and begin the work ourselffs ; wherein, after long stryving, and in end over-riding all difficulties, with continual turmoyl, trouble, and labour both day and night, wherefra none within the said burgh was exemit, neither in their persones nor purses, we brought the work to a gude and happy conclusion ; and in one yeare we performed and accomplished the samyn in a more substantionire and stately manner nor it was befoir ; and now may trewlie affirm, without ostentation, or ydle or vane show, that it was the greatest work that ever was done in Scotland in so short a space be ane handful of puir persones, without the help or assistance of uthers." The weakening results were thus set forth :—"For doing whereof we have exhausted the whole common rent and patrimony of the burgh, and hes not left so much as one penny therof frie ; and by continuall and daylie contributiones, most frelie and willinglie advanced among ourselves, our purses are so emptied, and we sae disabilled from undertaking any uther, ether for the weill of the said town or comon weil of the kingdom, that we are forced to yield to necessitie, and to sink under the heavie burdens which we have so long supported, and which now indeid hes ourmaisterit us." The petitioners become more pathetic and eloquent as they proceed :—"The estate of the town is no longer yable to subsist in that positione wherein it formerlie stood amonge the burrowes, bot as ane decayit and faillit member, will fall of from the rest of the bodie, unless your Majestie, out of your accustomat princlie comiseratioun of the distresit of everie particular member of the common weill, put to your helping hand, the consideratioun whereof hes moved us in most submissive and humble attitude to prostrate us befoir your Majestie's feet, and to lay open befoir your Highnes (as the soveraine fountaine and livelie spring wherewith the politique body of the estate, and everie particular member thereof, is cherished and nourished) these our wants and necessities : besieching your Majestie to consider the necessitie whereunto we are driven be this occasioun of the bridge, and accordingly to extend such proportion of your benevolence and favour towards us as your Majestie shall think fit for redemptioun and relief of our comon rentis engagit by us for the performing of the said work." The petitioners conclude by expressing a hope that his Majesty will send "ane favourable and gracious answer to their request."

This well-written and interesting document,* drawn up by the town-clerk, Mr Cunningham, is signed by Provost Coupland, two bailies, and by the clerk, in name of the other councillors. A most considerate reply was given to it by the King. "Inasmuch," he said, "as the burgh of Dumfries had re-edefeit and biggit up the brig of new agane," and put it in a better condition than before, being a work "maist incrediblie to have been performit be thame without his Majestie's help," he, by way of recognition and recompense, grants and dispones to the magistrates, Council, and community of the said burgh a right to levy the tolls and customs at the bridge as hitherto, for ever.† It must not be supposed that the bridge of the thirteenth century was thoroughly destroyed by the flood of 1620, and that what we see of the fabric just now is but the remains of what was "re-edified." In so far as we have been able to learn, five entire arches were rebuilt in this year—the old piers of these arches, or some of them, having been still retained. In other words, about a half of Devorgilla's structure was rebuilt, and the remaining portion repaired.

The burgh soon after this period claimed and exercised the authority to levy custom on articles crossing the Nith at any point twelve miles above and twelve miles below the bridge. In 1681 this claim was disputed by the noblemen and gentlemen of the district, who, in petitioning Parliament against it, went the extreme length of questioning the right of the burgh to levy any bridge custom at all.‡ On the 6th of September in the same year

---

* The petition, a copy of which is among the Burgh Records, has, we believe, never been previously published.—*Note to the First Edition.* The style of the composition very much resembles that of the address presented by the burgh to King James VI. in 1617 ; and both, we doubt not, emanated from the same pen.

† Report of Robert Kemp, town-clerk of Dumfries, upon the Bridge Custom : a little tract containing much valuable information on the subject, and drawn up, we believe, by the present town-clerk, Mr Martin, when acting as Mr Kemp's assistant.

‡ Burgh Records.

the case for the town was laid before the Estates, and was so well maintained that its right to exact custom at the bridge, and beyond it, within certain restricted limits, received legal confirmation, in terms of the subjoined agreement :—" It is agreed betwixt the Shyre and Town of Dumfries, anent the customs of the water of Nith, anent which there is a bill depending before the Parliament, That in tyme comeing the same shall be regulat as follows, viz. :—That the custumes and imposition of all goods and bestiall, as the same has been in use to be exacted by the burgh of Dumfries, shall be uplifted be them hereafter, from Portractfoord exclusive, downward to the water mouth of Nith, whereunto they are declared to have right, for maintaining the bridge of Dumfries and Portractfoord, and all upwards to the march of Kyleshall, in all tyme coming, be uplifted be such as shall be appointed be the Earle of Queensberry and the Commissioners of the Shyre, for repairing and maintaining the Bridge of Drumlangrig, qherunto the said burgh are to have no interest ; and that ane Act of Parliament be extended in favour of both parties, giving them right to the said Custome and Imposition, as the same has been in use to be uplifted, according to the division above written. In witness qhereof, the Earl of Queensberry and Commissioners for the Shyre, and the Provost of Dunfries for the burgh, has subscribit thir presents at Edinburgh, the 15th Sepr., 1681. *Sic subr.*, QUEENSBERRY. W. CRAIK, for the Burgh."*

This agreement, with other documents bearing on the question, having been laid before the Duke of Athole, as Lord High Commissioner, and the Lords of the Articles, they recommended Parliament to sanction the same. The result appears in the following minute : —" Edinburgh, 17th Septr., 1681.—His Royal Highness, His Majestie's High Commissioner, and Estates of Parliament, haveing considered the within written petition and report foresaid, doe approve of the said report, and appoint ane act to be extended conforme thereto. *Sic subr.*, ATHOLE, Jpd. par."†

An Act of Parliament, in accordance with this recommendation, was forthwith passed, which, whilst it put a veto upon an unauthorised assumption on the part of the burgh, placed its rightful claims to the bridge custom on an unassailable basis.‡

The houses, at the period we speak of, were rude and poorly furnished ; but stone had in a greater degree than ever taken the place of timber for their construction, and it was chiefly obtained from a quarry belonging to the town, situated in what is now a beautiful garden at Castledykes, and from which the burgesses were at liberty to take, for a trifling charge, as much material as

---

* Burgh Records.   † Ibid.   ‡ Appendix K.

they required. (*a*) There must have been few masons settled in the
burgh in 1665, since the Town Council, that year, were under the
necessity of sending for a quarrier to Carlaverock to " wyn "
stones for them before they could erect a new meal market*
which they had resolved to build, and which in due time arose on
a site north of the Tolbooth. There would, however, be no difficulty in getting any smaller public structures or private houses
erected by resident workmen. A fish cross, which cost just
£39 17s 2d Scots, was built, in or about 1640, by Herbert Anderson
—a native mason, we infer from his name. His charge amounted
to £13 6s 8d ; and among other items in the account there are
£3 10s to Henry Logan, quarrier, for " 70 draught of stanes, some
of them great lang stanes ;" and £5 5s to Thomas Crocket and
George Blunt, carters, for leading the same from the quarry to
the Cross. Glass for windows was a rare luxury, restricted to
ecclesiastical houses and the mansions of the affluent. The
Council in 1666 contracted with a Glasgow glazier to supply glass
for St Michael's Church at the rate of six shillings Scots per foot ;
and inasmuch as there was " no glassier in this countrie," they
encouraged him to commence business amongst them by making
him a freeman of the burgh. †

Postal communication of a regular kind was begun in the
district in 1642. That year a rebellion raged in Ireland ; and the
English Parliament, wishing to keep up a closer intercourse with
the troops sent to cope with it, arranged with commissioners
from Scotland to establish a line of posts between Edinburgh and
Portpatrick, and between Portpatrick and Carlisle. To Robert
Glencorse, merchant in Dumfries, was assigned the duty of
making the necessary arrangements—Robert himself having the
good luck to be installed as the first postmaster of the burgh, his
charge extending twelve Scots miles to the town of Annan. The
other appointments were : " Mark Loch, betwix Carlisle and
Annan, twelve mile ; Andrew M'Min, betwix Dumfries and Steps
of Orr, twelve mile ; Ninian Mure, betwix the Steps of Orr and
Gatehouse of Fleet, twelf mile ; George Bell, from thence to the
Pethhouse, eleven mile ; John Baillie, from thence to the Kirk of
Glenluce, thirteen mile ; and John M'Kaig, from that to the Port,
ten mile." These persons were looked upon as " the only ones fit

(*a*) Castledykes was purchased by the Town Council in 1901 for a site
for the purification of sewage, and the " beautiful garden " has given place to
bacterial beds.

    * On the 20th of June, 1662, the Town Council ordained that the Com-
missioner to Parliament should be reimbursed for the expenses incurred by
him " in getting a warrand from the Parliament to build ane meal mercat ;"
and they resolved to impose " four lib. Scots on everie sack of meal " sent
into it for sale.

            † Town Council Minutes.

for that employment, as being innkeepers and of approved honesty."*

Up till 1664, however, there was no direct postal connection between Dumfries and the capital ; the inconvenience arising from which being much felt, a committee of the magistrates was appointed, in December of that year, "to establish a constant foot-poast to go weikly betwixt this and Edinburgh, to appoynt his selarie, and consider quhat sall be payit for the post of lettres.† We thus see that even in the stormy period of the Persecution the material interests of the town were not altogether retrogressive— a circumstance that may partly be attributed to the favourable harvest seasons which marked the reign of Charles II., and to which the Jacobites afterwards made a boastful reference :—

> " When I see the corn growin' green on the rigs,
> And a gallows set up to hang the Whigs."

* Privy Council Records.   † Town Council Minutes

CHAPTER XXXV.

CHARLES II. OVERTHROWS THE PRESBYTERIAN CHURCH, RE-ESTABLISHES
EPISCOPACY, AND PROSCRIBES THE COVENANTS — DOINGS OF THE DRUNKEN
PARLIAMENT—ADDRESS OF THE DUMFRIES PRESBYTERY ON THE KING'S
RESTORATION—THE COVENANTING ELEMENT PURGED FROM THE COUNCIL
—CASE OF JOHN BLACKADER OF TROQUEER—HE AND HIS CO-PRESBYTERS
APPREHENDED AND TAKEN TO EDINBURGH—EXODUS OF FOUR HUNDRED
MINISTERS FROM THE CHURCH—MR BLACKADER BIDS FAREWELL TO
HIS FLOCK—HUGH HENDERSON, MINISTER OF DUMFRIES, RESIGNS HIS
CHARGE—GEORGE CHALMERS SUCCEEDS HIM—HIS MINISTRY HATED BY
THE COMMON PEOPLE—HEAVY PENALTIES FOR NON-ATTENDANCE AT
CHURCH—THE TOWN COUNCIL CELEBRATES THE ANNIVERSARY OF THE
RESTORATION—RIOT IN IRONGRAY AT THE SETTLEMENT OF A CURATE—
RISE OF ARMED CONVENTICLES—DUMFRIESSHIRE AND OTHER DISAFFECTED
DISTRICTS PLACED UNDER THE RULE OF SIR JAMES TURNER.

BEFORE the monarchy had been many months restored, both
England and Scotland began to see that the event which they had
hailed with enthusiasm ought rather to have been mourned over
and deplored. Charles had learned no wisdom from adversity : he
returned from exile hardened in his selfishness, debauched in his
morals—resolved, in the teeth of his promises, to set up an absolute
political sovereignty, and to claim unqualified supremacy in
spiritual affairs. The Scottish Presbyterians had done him good
service, for which he owed them gratitude and support ; but he
hated the views they held in regard to the royal power and the
rights of the Church ; and he could not brook their doctrines so
sternly exactive, and which were a standing remonstrance against
the immoralities which his personal example and encouragement
had brought in like a flood.

His agents for enforcing passive obedience and overturning
Presbyterianism were the Earl of Middleton, whom he appointed
King's Commissioner, and James Sharpe, who was made Archbishop of St. Andrews—the chief dignitary of the Episcopate
which was introduced as soon as the old system was subverted. A
packed Parliament, opened at Edinburgh in January, 1661, accomplished what Charles I. had for years attempted without success.
In a series of sweeping decrees they annulled and overthrew those
venerable institutions and wholesome enactments which their
royal master and most of themselves had sworn to maintain
inviolate. They conferred on the King the right of nominating to
all civil offices ; of summoning conventions, parliaments, and

public assemblies ; and of putting a veto on the renewal of the
National Covenants. They passed an Act which, in its preamble,
states that " the ordering and disposal of the external government
and policy of the Church doth properly belong unto his Majesty
as an inherent right of the Crown, in virtue of his royal prerogative and supremacy in causes ecclesiastical ;" and the measure
itself restored the " state of bishops " to " their ancient places and
undoubted privileges in Parliament, and to all their other
accustomed dignities, privileges, and jurisdictions." They next
condemned and rescinded " all Acts of Parliament or Council
which might be interpreted to have given any church power,
jurisdiction, or government, to the office-bearers of the Church,
other than that which acknowledgeth a dependence upon and
subordination to the sovereign power of the King as supreme ;"
and, by way of corollary to these tyrannical decrees, the
Covenanted Reformation, and all that was done for its accomplishment from 1638 to 1650, were declared to be treasonable and
rebellious, the Covenants were cancelled "as in themselves unlawful oaths," and all such leagues or bonds were denounced as
illegal.

This Convention of the Estates has come to be known as the
Drunken Parliament : a fitting name for it, whether we look to
the personal conduct of its members—not a few of whom,
Middleton included, caroused and legislated at the same time—or
to their measures, which were wild with the frenzy of intemperance. And these bacchanalian senators—sad to say !—shed blood
as well as wine. Lest the murmurs that arose against their
iniquitous proceedings should find vent in open mutiny, the
supporters of the Covenant were fined, imprisoned, and some of its
chiefs put to death—the great Argyle being the principal victim.

Dumfries rejoiced, with all Scotland, " when the King came
back to his own again." The Town Council voted congratulatory
addresses ; and the Kirk Session set apart a day of thanksgiving,
in that " the Lord hath restored the King to his throne," and
"taken power out of the hand of the sectary," and that the Word
of God " is yet standing, in defiance of all the opposition it hath
met with." On the 31st of October, 1660, the Presbytery of
Dumfries took into consideration a letter sent by Charles to the
metropolitan Presbytery, professing the most devoted affection for
the Scottish Church, and his resolution to maintain and defend it.
Regarding this royal epistle the Presbytery sent a communication
as follows :—" We cannot but count our selves obleged to glorify
the Lord our God, who hath put such pious resolutions in the
heart of our King, as to discountenance and suppress profanity,
and maintain Presbyterial government in this kingdom, as it is
established by law, without violation, and to protect and encourage
the ministers of the gospel in the due and faithful exercise of their

ministry.   As for our pairts, we resolve, by the grace of God, to
watch in our stations, with Christian sobriety and faithfulness,
and to promote his Majestie's just authority and greatness within
our bounds, being strictly bound thereto by our constant engagement, and shall make conscience, privately and publicly, to pray
for the preservation of his Majestie's person ; and, as his Majestie's
letter bears, we do also resolve to protect and preserve the government of this Church of Scotland, as it is settled by law, without
violation, and government of his kingdom, that his heart may be
enlarged as the sand of the sea shore, and filled with all royal
endowments and graces for the advancement of religion and
righteousness, that we may live a peaceable and quiet life, in all
godliness and honesty.—WM. HAY, Moderator."*
     So wrote the reverend fathers, in the simplicity of their
hearts. Soon afterwards the ukase of the sovereign, in whose good
faith they had placed firm reliance, destroyed their legal status as
a spiritual court, and made them personally liable to persecution
unless they abjured the principles which he, in common with
themselves, had sworn to uphold.
     The Town Council records bear ample evidence at this time of
the terrible reaction brought about by a bad king and his
myrmidons. What a change is thus revealed ! Dumfries was
emphatically an independent and covenanted burgh ; but now we
begin to find in the minutes uncouth signatures endorsing a
slavish oath of allegiance, and an entire repudiation of the
National Covenant, the Solemn League, and all treaties or bonds
of a similar import.
     On the 2d of October, 1660, according to the annual custom
four merchants were elected councillors, in room of the same
number who retired ; and seven tradesmen, deacons of their
respective crafts, were also added to the Corporation, in place of
the deacons who had gone out of office. Thus partially made up
anew, the Council elected magistrates for the ensuing year ; and,
significant of the revolution at headquarters, Robert Graham, who
had acted as provost during nearly the whole of the Protectorate,
was passed over, though anxious for a new lease of power, and
John Irving,† treasurer, who was considered to be more acceptable
to Middleton, was placed in the civic chair.   But not only was it
necessary that the chief magistrate should be of the Government
pattern—the members of Council must also be made conformable
to it. Accordingly, on the 16th of April, the Council took into
consideration a letter they had received from the subservient
Convention of Burghs, intended to instruct them in the mode of

* Presbytery Records.

† The Irvings of Bonshaw and Drum took the Royalist and anti-Presby-
terian side in the reigns of Charles I. and II. ; and their relatives in Dumfries
did the same.

purging their membership, so that it should come to be made up exclusively of ultra-Royalists. It is gratifying to find that the people of the town had some true and staunch representatives in the local parliament who refused to take the oath and to subscribe the declaration. Out, however, they had to go ; and no very great difficulty seems to have been experienced in supplying the place of these doughty Whigs by pliant burgesses, who, like the Vicar of Bray, were ready to make any concessions for the sake of office.

Next day (17th April) the clerk was instructed to answer the letter from the Convention ; and in so doing he set forth the steps that had been taken to obey the requirements of that body. We thus learn that, at the first meeting of the Council on the subject, " the said oath and acknowledgment being read, was by some few accepted, and by the most part refused ;" that at a second meeting, held next day, some of the refusers did then, upon better consideration, give obedience ; that at a third meeting, on the third day, " some few more did take the oath and sign the acknowledgment foresaid," but that two bailies and divers councillors continued contumacious, the former of whom had since been superseded, and the vacancies filled up ; and that eventually the Council had been completed in a satisfactory way, all the members " having asserted his Majestie's prerogative under their hand," and complied with the other conditions of office.* The men of the Trades, too, who loved the Covenant, and detested the new order of things, murmured loudly, and threatened to be troublesome. Foremost among the malcontents were certain smiths or hammermen, and glovers,† who, when others of their number chose Conformist deacons, held meetings, and elected chiefs of their own stamp ; and it seemed as if the latter would at one time have taken their places in the Town Council by force. Forthwith Stephen Irving, one of the new bailies, and another magistrate, were despatched to Edinburgh, to apprise the Privy Council of this audacious procedure. Armed with instructions, the nature of which may be guessed at, the bailies returned ; and in the course of a few weeks afterwards three of the clamorous hammermen publicly confessed that they had sinned in ignorance, and that they were sorry for their fault, prayed for forgiveness, and engaged to be more circumspect in future.‡ We hear no more of the smiths' opposition ; and we suppose that both they and their fellow craftsmen, the glovers, were subdued if not converted.

---

* Town Council Minutes.

† It will be seen that a member of this corporation—James Callum—took a leading part in the armed outbreak which soon afterwards occurred against the Government.

‡ Town Council Minutes.

As illustrative of the way in which the faithful ministers of the Church were now dealt with, the case of Mr John Blackader may be noticed in detail. Descended from an ancient but decayed family, the Blackaders of Tullialan, he was a man of cultured mind as well as of gentle birth. By his marriage with the daughter of Mr Homer Haining,* a wealthy Dumfries merchant, in 1646, he became connected with the district, and in 1652 he accepted a call to Troqueer, the parish church of which looks over upon that of St. Michael's from the opposite side of the Nith. A proclamation of the Parliament enjoining all loyal subjects to celebrate the anniversary of the Restoration having been disregarded by the Dumfries Presbytery, a troop of fifty horse was despatched by Middleton to bring the refractory court to Edinburgh. Mr Henderson, and his colleague, Mr George Campbell, ordained as such in 1657, had already gone to the capital for the purpose of consulting privately with their friends regarding the crisis that had arisen, Mr Blackader agreeing to preach in St. Michael's for the two ministers till their return. Meanwhile the troopers arrived, and the Town Council, fearing that the minister of Troqueer "might come to hazard by his free speaking," judged it advisable to dispense with his services on the following day, the Sabbath. He, however, preached in his own church, with his usual fearlessness and fervency ; though the "gentlemen of the guard" who had come to apprehend him formed a portion of his audience. Taking his text from Hosea ix., 10-12, he discoursed pathetically on the declensions and sorrows of Scotland's Zion, once sweet as "the first ripe on the fig tree," now sour as the grapes in the wilderness ; and he did not spare those in high places who had brought her to grief, likening them to Ephraim, whose root should be dried up, and whose glory should fly away like a bird. As if disarmed by the spell of the preacher's eloquence, the soldiers listened attentively ; and the Sabbath was allowed to pass by before they acted upon their orders to seize Mr Blackader and his co-presbyters. When taken to Edinburgh they were at first allowed to choose their own lodging, and there they were joined by the two Dumfries ministers. At a conference held by them it was unanimously resolved that they could not in conscience observe the statute which set apart the 29th of May "as a holiday to the Lord for ever." Several times they were taken before the Privy Council, Middleton threatening to lay them in irons, or transport them to the American plantations ; but they remained firm, and, thanks to the interposition of some of Blackader's relatives, they were all eventually set free, with a caution to be careful of what they said and did in future.

* His father was Mr Thomas Haining of Nether Gribton, in Holywood, and he had possessed the lands of Overtown, on the estate of Tullialan, Perthshire.

But Mr Blackader and his brethren were about to pass into a more fiery furnace. At a Privy Council meeting held in Glasgow on the 1st of October, 1662, a blow was struck which destroyed all the few faint remaining vestiges of religious liberty in Scotland That body, by way of supplementing the deeds of the Drunken Parliament, passed a resolution requiring all the ministers who had been ordained from the year 1649 to take out a presentation from the patrons, and receive collation from the bishops ; in other words, to renounce Presbyterianism and accept Episcopacy—extrusion from their parishes to be the penalty of non-compliance. Four hundred—fully one-third of the entire clergy of the Church of Scotland—gave up their churches, manses, and stipends, rather than submit to this outrageous mandate : braved the winter's blast, the prospects of want, of persecution—which many of them, alas ! had to endure to the death—rather than purchase immunity and ease by sacrificing their Christian rights. The lapse of less than twenty years had brought with it a state of affairs that contrasted sadly with the time when the Covenant had its potent war committees and its triumphant armies. After the defeat at Dunbar, the latter never recovered their prestige ; and Presbytery, long robustly militant, now appears as a hunted wanderer, weak and weaponless, sorrowful and forlorn. "By the 1st of November, 1662, in the five western counties, through Mid-Lothian and Fife, in the dales of the Nith, and Annan, and Esk ; in the uplands of the Tweed and the Teviot ; in short, through all the Lowlands, wherever there was religious feeling, the darkness of night and the silence of death fell upon the churches."*

Restricting the reader's attention for a while longer to the case of Mr Blackader, let us state that his farewell sermon to his sorrowing flock was preached on the last Sabbath of October. "The audience," we are told, "was not numerous, but every feature appeared settled with a deep and earnest concern. Most of them were dissolved in tears, and at many parts of the discourse there were loud and involuntary bursts of sorrow. Towards the middle of the sermon an alarm was given that a party of soldiers from Dumfries were on their march to seize him, and had crossed the bridge. Upon this he closed hastily, pronounced the blessing, and retired to his chamber. The military surrounded the churchyard, and, as the people departed, they took down the names of all those who belonged to Dumfries, or any of the other parishes, as the law had affixed a penalty of twenty shillings Scots on every person absent from his own church. They offered violence to none, and went away without entering the manse, being assured that no strangers were there. When they were gone the minister assembled the remains of the

* Dodds's Fifty Years' Struggle, p. 125.

congregation in his own house, and finished the sermon, standing
on the stairhead, both the upper and lower flat being crowded to
the full. The people seemed very loath to depart, lingering in
suspense about the door, expressing their concern for his safety,
and their willingness to shed their blood in his defence. Mr
Blackader conjured them to have regard to the peace of the
country, and give no handle to their adversaries by any disturbance. ' Go,' said he, ' and fend [provide] for yourselves : the hour
is come when the shepherd is smitten, and the flock shall be
scattered. Many are this day mourning for the desolations of
Israel, and weeping, like the prophet, between the porch and the
altar. God's heritage has become the prey of the spoiler ; the
mountain of the house of the Lord as the high places of the forest.
When the faithful pastors are removed, hirelings shall intrude,
whom the Great Shepherd never sent, who will devour the flock,
and tread down the residue with their feet. As for me I have
done my duty, and now there is no time to evade. I recommend
you to Him who is able to keep you from falling, and am ready,
through grace, to be disposed of as the Lord pleases.' "

Mr Blackader spent the closing week of his incumbency at
Troqueer in visiting his parishioners ; and he had resolved in his
own mind to deliver to them a few more last words from the
pulpit, but, learning that parties of the military were on the
look-out for him, he rode to Caitloch, in Glencairn, for the purpose
of securing a safe residence for himself and family beyond the
bounds of the Presbytery. Next day (Sabbath) a party of soldiers
crossed the bridge, and, proceeding to Troqueer Manse, behaved
with characteristic insolence to Mrs Blackader and her children.
One of them, a boy,* told the story of the troopers' unwelcome
visit in the following simple words :—" A party of the King's Life
Guard of horse, called ' Blew-benders,' came from Dumfries to
Troqueer to search for and apprehend my father, but found him
not : for what occasion I know not—whether he stayed beyond
the set day for transporting himself and numerous family of small
children ten miles from his parish church, or because he was of
the number of those who refused to observe the 29th of May. So
soon as the above party entered the close, and came into the
house, with cursing, swearing, and damning, we that were the
children were frightened out of our little wits, and ran upstairs,
and I among them ; who, when I heard them all roaring in the
room, like so many breathing devils, I had the childish curiosity
to get down upon my belly and peep through a hole in the floor
above them, to see what monsters of creatures they were ; and it
seems they were monsters indeed for cruelty, for one of them
perceiving what I was doing, immediately drew his sword, and

* Afterwards Dr Blackader, a distinguished physician.

forced it up with all his force where I was peeping, so that the
mark of the point was scarce an inch from the hole, though no
thanks to the murdering ruffian who designed to run it through
my eye. Immediately after we were forced to pack up bag and
baggatch, and to remove to Glencairn, ten miles from Troqueer.
We who were the children were put into cadgers' creels, where
one of us cried out, coming throw the Bridgend of Dumfries, ' I'm
banisht ! I'm banisht !' One happened to ask, 'Who has banisht
ye, my bairn ?' He answered ' Byte-the-sheep has banisht me.' "
Even when removed from his parish, the outed clergyman got no
rest for the sole of his foot. The troopers tracked Blackader
with the stealthiness of ravening wolves ; but on entering the
family fold at Glencairn they again missed the object of their
search, the minister having gone that very day to seek a place of
securer refuge elsewhere. He remained about the district for
some time, taking, as we shall see, an active part in conventicle
preaching, and never resting in his labours till he was sent to the
Bass.* (a)

Mr Hugh Henderson was still the parish minister of Dumfries. He had laboured faithfully in the town and district fourteen years, and was deservedly beloved by the people of his
charge. What of that ? He was a devoted, uncompromising
Presbyterian ; it was morally impossible for him to renounce his
convictions and accept a system which he loathed. No alternative remained to him, therefore, but to bid a tearful farewell to his
flock. There is a trace of rough pathos in the reference made to
this subject in the Town Council books. That body, though submissive to the Government, were attached to the minister, who
had in happier times been the people's devoted spiritual guide ;
and the affection they bore to him is breathed in the record—the
usual dry, conventional style o˙ the minutes being in this instance
departed from. We subjoin the entry, very slightly modernised :—
" 11th October, 1662.—The Council consideering that the Erll of
Middletoun, his Matie's [Majesty's] Commissioner for the part of
this kingdom, hath dischargit Mr Hugh Henderson from preaching within this Brugh, thairfoir they have enacted that thai
presentlie at their removing from the tolbooth, all in one body,
and with one hart and desyre, to goe deall with and earnestly to
beseatch the said Mr Hugh Henderson, that he would give satisfactioune unto the said Lord Commissioner in his grace's desyres,

* The information given about Mr Blackader is derived from the Memoirs
of him by Andrew Crichton, and from Wodrow.

(a) A mural brass to the memory of Blackader was unveiled in Troqueer
Church on Sabbath, 17th August, 1902, when the service was conducted and
the ceremony performed by the Rev. Professor Cooper. Dr Cooper, notorious
for his High Churchism, did not conceal his lack of sympathy with the cause
of the Covenanters ; and his sermon provoked a vigorous platform reply from
the Rev. Dr Ker, Glasgow.

that they be not frustrat of his ministrie ; and to declare their grief and sorrow for the loss of a minister to quhom they are so affectionatt, in cais of his refuisall." The entreaties of the Council were of no avail : Mr Henderson left Dumfries,* and was succeeded in his ministerial office by Mr George Chalmers, M.A., formerly of Cullen, who proved anything but acceptable to the inhabitants.

Mr Henderson had made himself so obnoxious to the Privy Council that they levelled a special act against him, which would have taken effect even if he had not been included within the sweep of the more general measure. According to Wodrow, the ministers of the Dumfries Presbytery extruded alongst with him, or soon afterwards, for non-compliance with the Glasgow Act, were George Campbell of Dumfries,† John Campbell of Torthorwald, William Shaw of Garran, William Hay of Holywood, Robert Archibald of Dunscore, John Welsh of Irongray, Robert Paton of Terregles, John Blackader of Troqueer, Anthony Murray of Kirkbean, William Mein of Lochrutton, Alexander Smith of Colvend, and Gabriel Semple of Kirkpatrick-Durham. A few ministers— William M'George of Carlaverock, Francis Irving of Kirkmahoe, George Gladstones of Urr, and James Maxwell of Kirkgunzeon— received the modified punishment of being restricted to their respective parishes ; and we only read of two belonging to the Presbytery who absolutely conformed, namely, Ninian Paterson, whose charge is not given, and John Brown of Tinwald.‡

---

* At this time there was no manse for the parish minister ; but a house was rented by the burgh for his use, as shown by the following document :— " Accompt with Mr Hew Henderson for the yeirly rent of his house from the tearme of Martinmas, 1648, which was his entrie to Dumfrise, untill this ensewing tearme of Whitsunday, 1658, being in all the space of nine years and ane half, in which yeirs he possessed ane house belonging to Mr John Corsan, for the space of foure yeirs and an half, 100 marks yeirly, the rent will be for that space 450 marks. Also, he possessed an house belonginge to John Newall for fyve yearis come Whitsunday of the said space, at 80 marks yeirly —400 marks. Suma for the said space of nine yearis, 850 marks. Paid him as follows : — Be William Walls, treasurer, for ane year, 100 marks ; out of the tythe (1648), 100 marks ; be Patrick Younge, be order of the Counsell, 100 marks ; be Baillie Cunninghame (be John Newall), be order of the Counsell, 100 marks ; bond granted to Mr Hew, 276 marks :" in all, 676 merks, leaving a balance of 174 merks, which was paid to the minister, he signing the discharge.—*Burgh Records.*

† Among the burgh records there is the following letter from Mr Campbell —who was son-in-law as well as colleague of the senior minister—about the last receipt he wrote for his stipends in Dumfries :—" I, Mr George Campbell, minister of Drumfrise, grants me to have received fra James Kennan, merchant burgess of the said burgh, in name of the magistrats, Toune Counsell, and communitie, the sum of five hundredth and fourtie merks Scots money for my proportion of stipend and manse money, for the terme of Martinmas fiftie-nine ; and I doe by these presents discharge the saide magistrats. Toune Counsell, and communitie of the said sum, &c. In witness quhereof I have subscribed these presents with my hand, at Drumfrise the 20 of April 1660 years.—GEO. CAMPBELL.

‡ Wodrow, vol. i., p. 326.

In due course Mr George Chalmers commenced his ministry in St. Michael's : though when he introduced the Service-book no wrathful Jenny Geddes started up to oppose the innovation ; the pews—chairs rather, there being nothing but movable seats in the church at that time—were half deserted ; and one Bessie Harper expressed a pretty general feeling when she reproached two individuals whom she saw going to the preaching, by saying, "It seems the word of God which they have heard formerlie had taken little ruit in their hearts, seeing they were going to heir one that preaches against the trew word of God." Rash words these, though possibly very truthful ; and the same outspoken dame was heard to declare defiantly, "That though the magistrats of Drumfreis would hurle her upon a cairt, she should nevir heir one sermone of this present minister." For these treasonable statements the poor woman was tried by the Town Council on the 10th of November, and, on conviction, fined in twenty pounds Scots, with the alternative of lying in prison till the money was paid, or of banishing herself perpetually from the burgh.*

Next day the town drummer startled the lieges by announcing in the streets that inasmuch as divers persons continued to despise the order of the Council to attend service on the Lord's Day, "to the great skandell of the gospell and breache of the Sabbath," it is now enacted that every master and mistress of a family within the burgh, being in health, who shall wilfully absent themselves from the kirk on Sabbath shall be fined for each day's absence in forty shillings Scots, and each servant who shall go out of the town on that day shall be fined in six shillings Scots.† There is a good deal of the Pharisee as well as of the persecutor in this intimation : the burgh authorities, at the bidding of Middleton, supersede the popular Presbyterian preacher by a time-serving Prelatist, and yet hypocritically profess to be actuated by a holy zeal for Sabbath observance, and a jealous regard for the honour of the Gospel, when they threaten those with vengeance who refrain from hearing a minister who is repugnant to them, and from taking part in a service which they utterly, and from conscientious motives, detest.

In another more telling way still some of the good Covenanters of the burgh testified against the tyranny of the times. Parents who had children to be baptised carried them to "the secret places of the hills," or the solitary glens, where the outed ministers were hiding, that the sacred ceremony might be performed in Nature's own temple, and according to the simple ritual of the Presbyterian Church. Such conduct being deemed intolerable by Provost Irving and his colleagues, they resolved, if possible, to put it down. Again the town-crier lifted up his voice

* Town Council Minutes.   † Ibid.

in the market-place to announce that the inhabitants must not
only attend the curate's ministry, but that he, and he alone, was
the recognised administrator of the sacraments, and that those
who poured contempt upon him by getting their infants baptised
in the country would be subject to a heavy penalty, varying from
ten pounds Scots on such as were worth less than five hundred
merks yearly, to one hundred merks payable by rich offenders.*

In the year 1662 the fines levied for nonconformity in the
county amounted to £164,200 Scots,† John Laurie of Maxwelton
suffering to the extent of £3600 ; from James Muirhead, merchant
Dumfries, was exacted no less a sum than £1000 ; Robert Wallace,
merchant there, had to pay £600 ; James Moffat, merchant there,
£300 ; John Ewart, John Gilchrist, and John Copland, all burgesses, £360 each ; James Callum, glover, £300 ; and John Short
and John Maitland, also members of this uncompromising craft,
were mulcted in £240 each, for (figuratively) throwing down the
glove to Middleton the Dictator.

The imposition of Prelacy in this high-handed fashion, as a
result of King Charles's recall, was a bitter draught to the Dumfriesians ; and, to give it a greater infusion of gall, they were
forced to go through the farce of rendering public thanks for the
altered state of affairs. On the 25th of May, 1663, the Council
met, brimming with loyalty, and on sanctimonious deeds intent.
The minute informs us that they called to mind that the 29th day
of May was approaching, the eventful day which Parliament had
ordered to be set apart for thanks and praise, " in commemora-
tioune of his Majestie's wonderfull restoratione, by God's blyssing,
to his crown and kingdomes ;" and that therefore, not simply in
obedience to the Act, " but from their awin trew sense of God's
mercie therein, they do ordain and command all the inhabitants
of this burgh " to attend the magistrates, at eight o'clock on the
morning of the 29th, on the Upper Sandbed, " and thereafter
accompany the said magistrats unto the kirk of this burgh, and
ther to heir sermone ; with certificatioune to all such as sall not
give punctuall obegience to this Act, they sall pay ten merkes of
fyne unforgevin."‡ This kirk-going ceremony and service over,
some wild revelry, called "rejoicings," followed, in course of which,
it is said, Chalmers the curate went to the market-place, " and,
having sung a psalm, danced about the bonfires, and got so drunk
that he could not go to his own house."§

Soon after the soldiers' raid upon Troqueer Manse the settle-

---

* Town Council Minutes.   † Wodrow, vol. i., p. 273.
‡ Town Council Minutes.

§ Answer to Scotch Presbyterian Eloquence. In the same document
it is stated that " Nisbet, curate of Kirkgunzeon, did usually fuddle himself
when he went to Dumfries; and having divers times fallen off his horse into a
kennel, was dragged out like a beast."

ment of Mr Bernard Sanderson as curate of Irongray caused a great deal of commotion in the latter parish. The people could not bear the idea of seeing their devoted pastor, Mr Welsh,* superseded by one of whom they knew nothing, except that he was the nominee of the arbitrary Privy Council, and a Prelatist. To Mr John Wishart was assigned the duty of introducing the new minister, but the parishioners refused to receive either of them ; and on Sanderson again applying for admission, he brought with him a retinue of soldiers, thinking thereby to overawe any opposition that might be offered. When the party drew near the church they received a rough greeting from a shower of stones thrown over the churchyard wall by a crowd of women, led on to the crusade by a humble heroine, named Margaret Smith. They had laid in beforehand a large store of missiles, and used them with such effect that the minister and his men, armed though the latter were, faltered in their resolution to force an entrance ; and fairly gave up the attempt when they saw other irate parishioners of the rougher sex flourishing swords, and heard one of them, as he set his back to the door of the sacred edifice, daring them for their lives to settle a curate in Irongray that day.

The occurrence of this popular tumult, and of a similar one at Kirkcudbright about the same time, so enraged the Privy Council that they appointed a commission, consisting of the Earls of Linlithgow, Galloway, and Annandale, Lord Drumlanrig, and Sir John Wauchope of Niddry, to proceed to the south, and take the requisite steps for bringing the offenders to justice. The commissioners sat at Dumfries when inquiring into the Irongray case and on the 30th of May, 1663, reported upon it in these terms :— "In pursuance of the commission as to the trial of the abuse lately at Irongray, we caused cite before us William Arnot of Littlepark, George Rome of Beoch, and several other persons said to be concerned therein ; and after we had examined witnesses, we

* The departure of Mr Welsh from Irongray is recorded in a very affecting manner by Mr Blackader, who appears to have been an eye-witness :— " He was accused for having, in his sermon, called the Parliament a ' drunken Parliament.' An order was sent to Maxwell of Munches, Steward-Depute of Galloway, to apprehend him,—who came on Sabbath night to his house at Irongray. But as he was to preach on Monday at Holywood communion, he begged to stay, which liberty Maxwell (though a Papist) civilly granted. Most of the parish was convened, and many others about, with some ministers who waited to convoy him a little on his way. There was great sorrowing and outcrying of the poor multitude beside the Water of Cluden, where he was to take horse. It was with great difficulty he got from among them, who were almost distracted, and cried most ruefully, with tears. But he being resolute, would not be detained ; and after two or three of the ministers had knelt down and prayed, he got to horse, the people still holding him. The ministers and he rode quickly through the water, to win from among them. Many, both men and women, brak in on foot after him, and followed on the road a good space, with bitter weeping and lamentation."—*Blackader's MSS.*, in the Advocates' Library.

found that there had been several unlawful convocations of the
people of that place, for the opposing of the admission of Mr
Bernard Sanderson to be preacher at the said parish, especially
against the serving of his edict, and thereby hindering Mr John
Wisheart to preach, who was to have admitted the said Mr
Bernard. By the said depositions, we find that the said William
Arnot did keep several meetings before the tumult; and that
when he was desired and required by the messengers who went to
serve the edict to assist to hold the women of them, he declared
he neither could nor would do it, that he drew his sword, and set
his back to the kirk door, and said, 'Let me see who will place a
minister here this day!' Therefore we find him guilty of the said
tumult, and ordain him to be sent into Edinburgh under a guard
We find George Rome of Beoch accessory, as being present upon
the place, and not concurring for compescing of the tumult, and
ordain him to go to prison until he find caution under five
thousand merks to appear before the Council when called. And
as to the rest of the persons, we find there hath been a great
convocation and tumult of women; but by reason there is no
special probation of any persons particularly miscarrying, more
than these being there present at the tumult, we thought fit to
ordain the whole party of horse and foot to be quartered upon the
said parish of Irongray, upon free quarters, until Monday next;
and that the whole heritors of the said parish give bond, upon the
penalty of one hundred pounds sterling, for their future loyal
good behaviour. And recommended to the Sheriff of Nidsdale to
apprehend and try some who had not compeared, and report to
the Parliament or Council betwixt and the 28th of June."

The Council found no difficulty in convicting Arnot; he was
fined in the sum of five thousand merks, and commanded,
"betwixt and the 25th of October next to come, to make public
acknowledgment of his offences two several Sabbaths, at the Kirk
of Irongray, before that congregation." Arnot, it appears, was
but a small farmer of limited means, who would have been ruined
by the exaction of such a sum; and on his making a representation
to that effect to the Lords, and declaring that he was a loyal
subject, and had previously suffered loss under the Commonwealth,
they mitigated the fine one thousand merks. There is no reference
in the above report to the Irongray heroine. Blackader tells us,
however, that "the said Margaret was brought prisoner to Edinburgh, and banished to Barbadoes. But when before the
managers, she told her tale so innocently that they saw not fit to
execute the sentence."*

About this period it would seem as if the Dumfries authorities,
afraid of disturbances, had taken special means to have such

* Blackader's MS.

burgesses as they could trust better armed than usual. A partial list has been preserved of "the guns and partizans belonging to the town" on the 22nd of September, 1662, which contains the names of seventy-three persons, with the figure 1 attached to each, the document closing thus :—" The Counsell ordaines Thomas Irving, bailie, to goe along with Jon Mertine, treasurer, to the houses of all the persons of the list above written, who dwell betwixt the Kirkgaitt port and Castlegaitt, on the west syde of the towne, and to delyver to each person, or leave at their houses, ane firelock gun; and appoynt Stephan Irving, bailie [the indefatigable Stephen], to goe throw with the said treasurer the rest of the town, and to leave one of the said pieces at every one of the houses according to the said list, and to intimate unto them they are to pay 8 lib. 10 sh. to the treasurer for ilk piece of them, to be payit within fyfetein days under the pein of imprisonment."*

It may be inferred from subsequent events that, in spite of the edicts against nonconformity, not a few influential burgesses of the town, and farmers in the landward part of the parish, systematically absented themselves from St. Michael's Church, and were subjected to fines and imprisonment on that account. Passive resistance of a similar kind was extensively practised throughout the south and west of Scotland; and the stringent measures taken by the Government to overcome it increased the disaffection, till the country seemed to be on the brink of insurrection. Armed conventicles now began to spring up; and, for the purpose of crushing them, and enforcing implicit submission on the people, the standing army— raised to 3000 infantry and eight troops of cavalry—was sent into the insubordinate districts, with orders to maintain itself by fines, and free quarters exacted from the Nonconformists. To Sir Thomas Dalziel of Binns—a fierce, unscrupulous savage—was assigned the chief command of this coercive host; and he found a congenial subordinate in Sir James Turner, an unprincipled soldier of fortune, who had once professed zeal for the Covenant, and now readily placed his sword at the disposal of the Government.† As time rolled on it brought new rigours; and by 1666 the reign of terror instituted by the Privy Council reached a stage of refinement and perfection not previously attained. The Earl of Lauderdale had succeeded Middleton as King's Commissioner. His chief colleague in the administration was Archbishop Sharpe; the one was the complement of the other; and between both a despotism in all civil and

---

* Burgh Records.

† His approaching visit to Dumfries was intimated to the Town Council on the 6th of June, 1666, on which day the Provost produced a letter " fra Sir James Turnor for provyding quarter for himself and his officers and souldiers, quho are to be heir about the first of July nixt;" upon which the Council appointed a committee " to draw and lift of the brewars and others fitting for their quarters."

religious matters was set up, such as Scotland had never suffered from before. A secret irresponsible tribunal, called the Court of High Commission, was instituted by them and their minions on the model of the Spanish Inquisition, which set aside all forms of justice; acted independently of accusers, witnesses, and defenders; impoverished rich offenders by merciless exactions; filled the prisons with poorer recusants; whilst its armed emissaries scoured the country for the double purpose of keeping the court in work, and of foreclosing, if possible, the threatened outbreak of popular vengeance.

Ayrshire, Dumfriesshire, and Galloway formed the district assigned to Sir James Turner, in which to carry out the measures of the Privy Council. No arbitrary junto could have had a fitter or more faithful servant. To do him justice, he does not seem to have been gratuitously cruel. If suspected persons quietly conformed, he did not punish them to excess; but woe to the wilful, obstinate deserters from the parish churches and frequenters of conventicles! In such cases he was utterly ruthless—his plea being that as a soldier he was bound in duty to obey orders. He found the intruded curates useful assistants, they supplying him with the names of non-attenders on their ministry, who, when arrested, were fined forthwith; and if they could not pay the money they were sent to jail; or if they would not, some of his soldiers were quartered upon them till their contumacy was overcome. The following minute of a somewhat later date shows the part taken by the town authorities in this coercive work :—" The Counsall being informed that there is a company of foot and a partie of hors appoynted to quarter in this burgh, which is occasioned by several inhabitants who doe not frequent the ordinances, it is therefoir enacted that such as are able and have never as yitt come to the church of this burgh to hear the service of the minister, shall have sex foot soldiers quartered upon them, or two hors."

CHAPTER XXXVI.

WHEN such explosive materials as these existed it required but a trifling incident to fire the train. In November, 1666, the flames of insurrection broke forth in Galloway under such unpremeditated circumstances as we are about to describe. On the 13th of that month a party of Turner's soldiers stationed at St. John's Clachan of Dalry, in the hilly region of Glenkens, confiscated a patch of corn belonging to a poor old man named Grier, and threatened him with personal maltreatment unless he paid the balance of church fines with which he was charged. At this juncture four Covenanting refugees entered the village in search of food—one of them, Mr M'Lellan of Barscobe, who had been subjected to much persecution for conscience sake. They felt keen sympathy for their fellow-sufferer, but smothering their feelings, withdrew to a small change-house,* where soon after tidings reached them that the soldiers carrying their menaces into effect, had stripped Grier naked in his own house, with the intention of subjecting him to torture by setting him upon a red-hot gridiron.

The four wanderers could remain patient no longer ; hurrying to the old man's house, they remonstrated with the soldiers, who told them to mind their own business, and not to interfere, or it

---

* The house in which they sat is still standing, but was partially rebuilt a few years ago : it was called Midtown. John Gordon then occupied it as a kind of tavern. Mr Train says : " My friend, Mr John M'Culloch, of New Galloway, kindly procured from the proprietor for me one of the old rafters, of which I intend to make some articles of vertu."—*History of Galloway*, vol. ii., p. 158.

might be worse for them. After a brief altercation, several
country people entered and began to remove the bandages with
which Grier's arms were fastened. The soldiers then drew their
swords and wounded two of them; upon which one of the latter
retaliated by firing a pistol, loaded with a piece of tobacco pipe
for bullet. A general fight of short duration ensued terminating
in the defeat of the troopers, who were all made prisoners and
disarmed. What to do next became a matter for serious consideration. There was another party of ten or twelve soldiers
at the neighbouring village of Balmaclellan; and, lest they should
resort to reprisals, some of the country people set off early next
morning, and made the whole of the soldiers captive, except one
man, who offered resistance, and was killed. The outbreak was
carried to its second stage for the purpose of securing the safety
of those accidentally led to engage in it; but if they now dispersed they would certainly be pursued by the merciless soldiery
belonging to the rest of Turner's force; and if they should succeed
in escaping the district would be subjected to such vengeful
devastation as was fearful to contemplate. These reflections
induced M'Lellan and his comrades to unfurl boldly the flag of
insurrection. They were joined by another gentleman of the
district, Mr Neilson of Corsock, by Mr Alexander Robertson,
son of an outed minister, by Mr Andrew Gray, an Edinburgh
merchant, who happened to be in the district at the time; and
these, the leaders of the movement, easily succeeded in raising
a considerable force, the rural population all around being ripe
for insurrection.

A council of war was held, at which a march on Dumfries, for
the purpose of surprising Sir James Turner, was resolved upon;
the place of rendezvous being fixed at Irongray Church, about
six miles distant from the town. With wonderful secrecy and
despatch due notices were given and acted upon; and on the day
after the casual skirmish at Dalry a force of two hundred infantry and fifty horsemen mustered at the appointed place; the
Blue Banner of the Covenant, the ensign of rebellion against the
Government—rather, we should say, of righteous resistance to
a tyrannical faction—flying above their small but resolute ranks.
Gray—who seems to have been a fussy, pretentious gentleman,
without any real regard for the cause with which he was
prominently mixed up—was appointed leader of the little host.
Starting from Irongray Church soon after sunrise on the 15th,
they marched quietly on their appointed way, reaching the
Bridgend of Dumfries about eight o'clock in the morning. Sir
James Turner has sometimes been spoken of as a model soldier;
yet though rumours of the insurrection had reached him, he
appears to have made no preparations for meeting it, even when
it was rolling to his very door; and, strange to say, though in the

midst of a warlike people, who bore him no goodwill, he had not, on this critical occasion, a solitary sentinel posted at the entrance of the town from Galloway.

Accordingly, when Captain Gray and his men reached the place where the populous burgh of Maxwelltown now stands, they were agreeably surprised at finding the bridge u; ;darded, and the road to the headquarters of the renegade "malignant" open before them. Matters being in such a favourable train, it was thought best to allow the foot soldiers to remain outside, while a party of the horse rode across to pay the compliments of the morning to Sir James. Corsock and Robertson were entrusted with this delicate and perilous duty. Followed by several others, they, at about half-past eight o'clock, crossed the bridge, passed up Friars' Vennel, and then down to Turner's lodgings, in Bailie Finnie's house, High Street. Aroused too late by the ring of the horses' hoofs upon the pavement, he rose in great alarm, ran in his night-dress* to the window, and, seeing an armed band below, exclaimed, "Quarters! gentlemen, quarters! and there shall be no resistance!" "Quarters you shall have," said Corsock, "on the word of a gentleman, if you surrender at once without resistance." "Quarters he shall have none!" said Gray, who now came up; and, suiting the action to the words, he presented a carbine at Turner; and had not Corsock, who was the real leader of the enterprise, interposed, the unscrupulous agent of the Government would have been instantly sent to his account. One soldier only, as at Balmaclellan, resisted, and died of the wounds he received; all the others giving themselves quietly up, according to the example and orders of their commander.

According to Turner's own statement, no more than thirteen of his men were in town at the time, the rest being quartered in the country on persons who "refused to give obedience to church ordinances." "Some few of my sogers," he adds, "were taken in their lodgings. They [the insurgents] looked for Master Chalmers, the parson of Dumfries, but found him not, yet did they bring away his horse."†

There was great rejoicing in Dumfries on account of this over-throw of the tyrant captain and his troop. "He had," says Gabriel Semple, "been reigning [there] like a king, and, lifted up in pride, with insolence and cruelty over the poor people;" and it is no wonder that, to signalise his degradation, they, as the same authority informs us, "set him on a low beast, without his vest-raiment, and carried him through the town in a despicable manner." It says much for the forbearance of the insurgents and the people of the burgh that Sir James Turner received no worse treatment than was involved in this pardonable exhibition

---

* Sir James Turner's Memoirs, p. 148.   † Ibid, p. 149,

of him in his new character. They then held a meeting at the
Cross, where the leaders explained and vindicated their conduct ;
and to show that it was not the monarchy, nor the King, but his
despotic ministers against whom they had taken up arms, they
expressed aloud their devoted attachment to his Majesty's person
—a sentiment that was readily responded to with cheers by the
listening crowd.

The Town Council of Dumfries had seen with horror the capture of the Government troops and the occupation of the burgh by
an insurgent band ; and they too convened a meeting, differing very
much in character, however, from the exuberant one outside. To
think that their loyal town had been the scene of such a scandalous
insult to the dominant powers, and that their sycophantic selves
might be implicated in the disgrace and its consequences ! The
very idea of such an affront upon the State, and such a stain upon
their own escutcheon, was intolerable. Dismal faces and troubled
shakings of the head were seen, lugubrious regrets and sad misgivings were expressed, at this conclave of the burgh magnates ;
and before it broke up it was resolved to send Bailie Stephen
Irving to Edinburgh* for the double purpose of acquainting the
Privy Council with what had occurred and putting the best
possible face on their own connection with it. Late on the
following evening (the 16th), the magistrates announced to
Lauderdale and his colleagues that a Covenanting rebellion
had broken out, headed by Neilson of Corsock, M'Lellan of
Barscobe, M'Cartney of Blaiket, Alexander Robertson, son of
a conventicle preacher, and the notorious Nonconformist, James
Callum, glover in Dumfries ; that Dumfries was in the hands of
the triumphant insurgents, greatly to the sorrow of its loyal
lieges and their rulers ; and that, in order to crush the audacious
traitors, decisive measures would have to be promptly resolved
upon. This was astounding intelligence indeed : alarm was the
first emotion that prevailed among the Privy Councillors ; rage
followed ; then uncontrollable fury, that found vent in a resolution which was speedily put in force, to exact a fearful measure
of revenge.

Meanwhile the insurgents, now numbering three hundred,
marched from Dumfries to the Church of Glencairn, situated at a
distance of fifteen miles, on the west bank of the Nith ; and on
the 16th they re-entered Dalry, still carrying with them their
prisoners. Here, as we learn from Turner himself, Hugh
Henderson, the outed minister of Dumfries, in the spirit of
genuine Christian charity, returned good for evil to the man
by whom he had been harshly maltreated. Mr Henderson had
taken refuge among his old parishioners in the neighbourhood,

* Town Council Minutes ; and Wodrow, vol. ii., p. 19.

and, hearing of what had occurred, got permission from Gray to entertain Sir James at dinner, and even pleaded, though without success, that he should be set at liberty. "Though he and I," says Turner, "be of different persuasions, yet I will say that he entertained me with very reall kindnes."* A beautiful trait of character is thus presented, which those who take delight in disparaging the Nonconformist clergy of this period would do well to study. At Dalry, we also learn from Turner, Captain Gray, the "By-ends" of the movement, gave his men the slip: "for the day before he had sent away the money and other baggage, which he had got from me ; and thinking he had sped well enough, resolved to retire himself before the fire grew hotter."

When the Edinburgh Covenanters heard of the rising at Dalry many deemed it premature ; but the general opinion was that since it had occurred it ought to be supported. Not a few of them accordingly made common cause with their insurgent brethren ; and among other men of note who joined them in the West country were Lieutenant-Colonel Wallace, who had earned distinction in the civil wars ; Maxwell, the young Laird of Monreith, in Galloway ; John Welsh, the outed minister of Irongray ; and two other preachers, also well known—William Veitch, afterwards minister of Dumfries, and Hugh M'Kail of Ochiltree. The somewhat irregular host was properly organised : Colonel Wallace was appointed commander ; and a resolution was adopted to march towards the capital, with the view of calling out their friends there in greater force, and, if possible, of making a powerful demonstration against the Government. Continuing their journey during a protracted storm, they passed through Cumnock and Muirkirk, arriving at Douglas on the 24th of November, where a council was held, at which it was conclusively resolved to proceed with the enterprise at all hazards.

At Douglas another question was debated : whether the persecuting chief, delivered by Providence into their hands, should not be put to death. The propriety and duty of thus dealing with Turner were vehemently insisted upon by the more violent of the leaders ; whilst Corsock and others contended as stoutly that his life ought to be spared. Sir James, as we learn from his own account of the matter, had a narrow escape. "That night," he says, "a councell or committee was keepd, where it was concluded that nixt morning the Covenant should be renewed and sworne. And the question was, whether immediately after they should put me to death ; they who were for it pretended ane article of the Covenant obliged them to bring all malignants to condigne punishment. Bot it was resolved that I sould not dy so soone,

* Memoirs, p. 152.

bot endeavours sould be used to gaine me. All this was told me
by one of my intelligencers before two of the clocke nixt morning.
Yet I have heard since that it was formallie put to the vote
whether I sould die presently, or be delayed, and that delay was
carried in the councell by one vote onlie."

Even after the insurgent army had been pelted by the elements, it made a creditable appearance in the eyes of Turner,
military martinet though he was, and by no means anxious to
present a flattering picture of his captors. "The horsemen," he
tells us, " were armed for most part with suord and pistoll, some
onlie with suords ; the foot with musket, pike, sith, forke, and
suord ; and some with staves, great and long. There [at Douglas]
I saw two of their troops skirmish against other two (for in foure
troopes their cavallerie was divided), which I confess they did
handsomelie to my great admiration. I wondered at the agilitie
of both horse and rider, and to see them keepe troope so well, and
how they had comd to that great perfection in so short a time.'
He closes his verdict by saying : " I never saw lustier fellows than
these foot were, or better marchers ; for, though I was appointed
to stay in the car, and notwithstanding these inconveniences [of
darkness and tempest], yet I saw few or none of them straggle."*

It is not necessary that we should follow the various steps of
these bold, devoted men. Their enterprise was one of the most
daring of that adventurous day. Forlorn and desperate it proved ;
but had they received even a moderate degree of support from
their suffering fellow-countrymen, the issue might have been more
favourable, and "from Fate's dark book a leaf been torn." For
their unpremeditated outbreak the country was not prepared.
Arrived at Lanark, numerous recruits joined them, swelling their
ranks to two thousand men or more ; but when the vicinity of
Edinburgh was reached they had to lament numerous desertions :
and, what was worse, they found the gates of the city barred
against them, and no friends hurrying from it to hail their
approach. In this dilemma they learned that General Dalziel
was following rapidly on their track ; and in the dead of night,
faint with hunger and fatigue, heart-sore with disappointment,
the wandering host, retreating to the Pentland Hills, encamped
on the elevated table-land of Rullion Green, there to " dree " what
fortune had in store for them. Defeat, death by the sword and
on the scaffold, were in the cup. The insurgents did not now
amount to more than nine hundred, and they had suffered much
in condition as well as in number, being, as a contemporary
described them, " pitifully bad appointed—neither saddle nor
bridle, pistol or sword, amongst the ten men of them ; baggage-
horses, some whereof not worth forty shillings. They are mighty

* Memoirs, p. 167.

weary with marching."* They were encountered on the 28th of November by Dalziel, at the head of three thousand soldiers, and, after a gallant resistance, in which they thoroughly repelled several headlong charges, were put to the rout, fifty of them falling on the unequal field, and about one hundred and thirty surrendering as prisoners, on receiving a promise that their lives would be spared. But the scaffold was set up, and Sharpe resolved that it should not be cheated out of its anticipated victims.

The insurgents who spared Sir James Turner's life had no such mercy meted out to them. Twenty were adjudged to death at Edinburgh : "and all of them," says Mein, "died adhering to the Covenant, declaring that they never intended in the least any rebellion ; and all of them prayed most fervently for his Majesty's interest, and against his enemies." Amongst the sufferers were the heroic Mr Neilson of Corsock, and the pious and accomplished Hugh M'Kail, who died on the scaffold in the true spirit of martyrs ; and their constancy and devotedness were emulated by a "cloud of witnesses," executed on account of their being connected—some of them very remotely—with the Pentland rising. No fewer than thirty-five were hanged or shot in various parts of the country, in addition to those executed in Edinburgh ; a large proportion of them being natives of Nithsdale or Galloway, as many rude memorials, scattered over our moorlands, hillsides, and churchyards still attest.

On the 30th of December, 1666, the obsequious Town Council of Dumfries met for the purpose of receiving orders for the disposal of two poor fugitives from Pentland, who, on returning to their native district, had been tracked, caught, and tried at the instance of the Government. It need scarcely be added that they were convicted and doomed to death. A justiciary court —or rather a military tribunal, presided over by Lieutenant-General Drummond —had been held at Ayr, where these two prisoners, with ten others, were capitally sentenced ;† and, as they had been captured within the jurisdiction of the Dumfries magistrates, to them was assigned the duty of carrying the sentence into effect. The orders from the court enjoined the authorities " to sie their sentence for hanging the persounes, and affixing of the heides and right armes of Jon Grier in Ffourmerkland, and William Welsch in Carsfairne, upon the eminenest pairts of this burgh ;" which mandate having been communicated by the magistrates to the Council, the latter " condescendit that the Bridge-port is the fittest place quhereupon that the heids and armes should be affixed ; and therfoir appoynted them to be affixed on that place.‡ Martyred the two men were, as

* Robert Mein's (postmaster of Edinburgh) report to Government, quoted in the Fifty Years' Struggle, p. 166.

† Town Council Minutes ; also, Wodrow, vol. ii., p. 53.

‡ Town Council Minutes.

a matter of course ; and we can find no trace of the Dumfries
authorities being troubled with any " compunctious visitings " on
the subject, though we doubt not the inhabitants generally pitied
and honoured these poor victims of oppression. And when, in pursuance of their sentence, their heads and right arms were pilloried
on the bridge, the gory spectacle would be viewed by many a tearful eye, and elicit many a burst of indignation.

After the severed relics of the sufferers had wasted for several
weeks in the wintry air, a rumour reached the authorities that a
design had been formed for removing them.   How the honourable
gentlemen must have been shocked by this report ! They intended
the bridge-port exhibition to tell with salutary terror on the
people far and near, to teach them that the exercise of free
thought, and resistance to the powers that be, were treasons
rightly involving death, and that there was no safety for the
subject except in entire submission to the decrees of the Privy
Council : and yet, in daring contempt of these lessons, the silent
teachers of their truthfulness were threatened with removal !
Lest the menace should be carried into effect, the Town Council
directed application to be made to the Earl of Lauderdale, to allow
the martyrs' heads and arms to be transferred to the top of the
tolbooth, for their better security, and thus to disappoint the
" disloyall persounes," who, it was feared, would " take them away
under cloudes of night, to the prejudice of this burgh."* Prejudice
of the burgh, indeed ! Alas for the time when the honour or
credit of the town was thought to be bound up in the safe retention
of those ghastly mementoes of the tyrant's persecuting rage !

When other and happier days came round the real feeling of
the townspeople towards the two sufferers expressed itself in the
erection of memorial stones over their honoured remains in St.
Michael's Churchyard ; and till this day an interest is felt in the
humble tombs of Welsh and Grier (or Grierson) which vies in
depth with that awakened by the proud mausoleum reared beside
them above the dust of the national poet—the poet who, in one of
his best moods, after reading a narrative of the persecution in
Galloway, penned the well-known lines :—

> " The Solemn League and Covenant
>   Cost Scotland blood, cost Scotland tears ;
> But it sealed Freedom's sacred cause :
>   If thou'rt a slave, indulge thy sneers !"

On the 9th of May, 1668, a royal proclamation was issued for
the apprehension of about one hundred outstanding " rebels,'
sixteen of whom belonged to Dumfriesshire.   The name of Mr
James Callum, glover, appears upon the list.   He seems to have
been a devoted, consistent, and courageous Covenanter. How

---

* Town Council Minutes.

terribly he suffered for conscience sake is shown in the following affecting extract from Wodrow's History :—"James Callum, in Dumfries, was forfeited some time after Pentland, but his being there was never proven : he was indeed present, being dwelling in the town, at the taking of Sir James Turner ; but no other guilt was ever made out against him but mere nonconformity. In the years 1662 and 1663, for refusing to hear the curates, he paid for a year's space forty pence every Monday for himself and wife. He underwent much trouble and several imprisonments for his Parliament fine—five hundred merks—and paid the half of it, and fifteen pounds sterling riding money, and more by far than the other half in expenses and clerk's fees, to get his discharge. Sir James Turner, before Pentland, exacted considerable sums of money from him. When he was declared rebel, most unjustly, after Pentland, he left the kingdom, and was seven years in the East Indies. At his return he was taken by Claverhouse, and imprisoned at Dumfries fourteen months, and at Edinburgh a year and a half ; after which he was banished to Carolina, where he died. When the accounts of this came home, his wife and daughters at Dumfries were attacked for nonconformity, and spoiled of anything they had, and forced to wander up and down in the hills and mountains for three years and a half."[*]

At the close of the same disastrous year (1668) the inhabitants of the burgh were required by the Council to subscribe a statement declaring that they " deteste and abhor the rebellioune laitly broken out in Galloway, and in other places in the West ;" that they will not, in any way whatever, assist or intercommune with those concerned in it ; and that they were ready to venture their " lives and fortounes against thes traitors, for suppressing their horrid traysone and rebellioune." Everyone was required to sign this declaration, it being intimated that refusers would be looked upon as sympathisers with the insurrection, and as such be proceeded against according to law.[†]

When the insurrectionary outbreak had been thoroughly suppressed, and the vengeance of the Government been sated, Lauderdale, under the influence of what seemed to be a conciliatory whim, cashiered Sir James Turner,[‡] Sir William Bannatyne, and other

---

[*] Wodrow, vol. ii., p. 79.   [†] Town Council Minutes.

[‡] A committee, consisting of Lord Kenmure, the Earl of Nithsdale, and the Laird of Craigdarroch, was appointed to investigate Turner's "haill carriage in Dumfriesshire and Stewartry of Kirkcudbright." As a result, he was found guilty, among other illegal acts, of exacting for more soldiers than were under his command ; of imposing fines without citation or hearing parties ; fining for causes for which he had no warrant from Parliament or Council ; of fining people who lived orderly ; of fining fathers for their children ; of fining for whole years previous to coming to that part of Scotland, and without proportioning the sum to the fault. Turner, however, urged in his own defence that he had the Privy Council orders and letters from Sharpe, which

military tools, who had become odious to the common people, and
sought to propitiate the Presbyterian ministers by getting the
Privy Council to pass an Indulgence, in virtue of which those who
still refused to receive collation from the bishops might be
reinstated in their manses and glebes, with a royal annuity instead
of stipend, on condition that they would restrict their preaching
to their own parishes, and submit to State control in other
ecclesiastical matters.   There is every reason to believe that these
proposals were devised for the purpose of dividing the Covenanters, and thus weakening them, and for forming part of a plan
by which Scotland was to be kept quiet, whilst preparations were
being made by the Duke of York, Charles's brother and heir, to
re-establish Roman Catholicism in both kingdoms, should a
favourable opportunity for doing so arise.   Many ministers
accepted the Indulgence : between those who scorned it and the
Government a wider gulf than ever was formed ; and Lauderdale
found, in their rejection of the measure, a motive and a pretext
for increased severity towards the frequenters of conventicles.
During the lull produced by his temporary moderation, he
hastened on the formation of a militia in Scotland, in order that
he might foreclose other rebellious outbreaks, and be ready in
time of need to give the despotic Romanising party of England a
helping-hand.

We find numerous traces in the Dumfries County Records of
the steps taken at this period to raise the quota of men required
from the shire and its various towns, and otherwise provide for the
maintenance of the military despotism wielded by Lauderdale and
his colleagues.   The chief agents in the business were the Commissioners of Excise, as county gentlemen when acting in their
corporate capacity were then styled.   A meeting of the Dumfriesshire Commissioners was held at Thornhill on January 28th, 1668,
at which two Acts of the Privy Council were read and adopted,
regulating the way the parishes twelve miles round the county
town were to provide hay and straw for a troop of fifty horse
stationed there.   The supply for each horse was fixed at sixteen
pounds of hay or eighteen pounds of straw in the twenty-four
hours ; and it was provided that in case the country people will
not sell the same, the Commissioners were to constrain * them."
At another meeting, held in Dumfries on the 24th of September
following, the Earl of Annandale read his Majesty's instruction
regarding the establishment of a militia regiment in the county,
consisting of eight hundred foot and eighty-eight horse (afterwards reduced to seven hundred foot and seventy-seven horse), of
which he had been appointed colonel, and Drumlanrig lieutenant-

warranted much greater oppressing than he had ever been guilty of.— *Wodrow*,
vol. i., pp. 283-5 ; and *Burnet's History*, vol. i., p. 246.
* Minutes of the Commissioners.

colonel. These instructions were chiefly as follows :—All the commissioned officers were to be nominated by the colonel and lieutenant-colonel, and were to sign the declaration against the Covenants ; the colours, drums, and trumpets were to be provided at the expense of the shire ; the foot were to be armed with muskets having a bore for sixteen balls to the pound, "which may be had of Alex. and Robt. Mills, merchants in Lithgow, at eight merks apiece," and with pikes fifteen feet long, "which may be had in the country, good and cheap, made by Alex. Hay, the king's bow-maker, in the Cannon-gate ;" two-thirds of the men in each company were to be musketeers, the rest pikemen ; the horsemen were to be sufficiently mounted and armed with swords and pistols at the expense of the heritors ; and those soldiers who removed from their parishes without leave of their officers were to be fined or imprisoned, or both. Much difficulty was experienced in getting some of the parishes to co-operate. Though each minister, with "three discreet men" to assist him, was ordered to make up a roll of all the fencible men in his parish, and though afterwards a committee of Commissioners was appointed for a like purpose in each Presbytery, the lists produced were mani-festly defective : till at length, on the 30th of December, the baffled Commissioners resolved to apply for assistance to the Privy Council ; which having been given, the rolls were rendered more complete. To determine the proportion of men to be raised by the burghs was the next duty of the Commissioners. They met for this purpose on the 22nd of April, 1669, and resolved that Dumfries should be required to provide forty men, Sanquhar and Annan four each, and Lochmaben three ; leaving the rest to be raised in the rural districts, at the rate of one man for each three hundred merks of rent.*

By the Parliament of 1672 increased measures of repression were directed against conventicles. More soldiers were therefore needed ; and accordingly, on the 20th of March of that year, the Dumfriesshire Commissioners of Excise received a letter from the Privy Council enjoining the heritors of the County and the magistrates of its burghs to raise forty-one men, as their propor-tion of one thousand required to be levied in the kingdom for his Majesty's service. A committee, with Robert, Lord Maxwell, as preses, was appointed to put the matter into shape ; who reported next day that the burgh of Dumfries would have to "outreik" and provide two men, also "the twentieth part of a third man," for assisting the burghs of Annan, Sanquhar, and Lochmaben, who were to raise said third man on receiving such fractional support ; and that the remaining thirty-eight soldiers were to be provided by the county at the rate of fifty merks for each. The

* Ibid.

report was approved of ; and at a subsequent meeting the Commissioners resolved that there should be expended on each man £24 Scots, to furnish him with a good blue cloth coat, well lined with sufficient white stuff or serge, a pair of double-soled shoes, a pair of stockings, a black hat, two shirts, two cravats, an "honest" pair of breeches, and an inner coat : a goodly outfit, certainly, for forty shillings sterling—money going a far way at this period of our history. It was also arranged that the men were to meet on the 21st of April at Locharbridge Hill, a common place for military gatherings, and then march to the town of Leith.* As time rolled slowly on the hills around Dumfries became more than ever the haunt of the persecuted Covenanters ; and the Government, instead of sending away troops from it, felt the necessity of placing a large force in the town.

The Commissioners, on the 5th of August, 1675, were honoured with a visit from the Earl of Queensberry, Lord Chancellor of Scotland, who, being also one of themselves, attended to assist in the discussion of the following letter, subscribed by him and fourteen other members of the Privy Council :—" We have emitted an act appointing garrisones to be in divers places, particularly at the Castle of Dumfries, in which there is to be fifty foot and twelve horsemen, who are ordered against the 6th of August to be at the said place. We have ordered you to convene any three or four of the Commissioners of Excise of the Shire of Drumfreis, and have appoynted you and your depute, with the said Commissioners, and Captain Dalziel, who has the command of said garrisone, to sight the said Castle of Drumfreis, and see the same be made ready to receive the garrisone against the said day ; also that you and the said Commissioners cause furnish the said garrison with bedding, potts, pans, coal, and candle, as is ordinar ; and sett prices upon the hay, straw, and corne for the horse ; and cause carry in and delyver to the soldiers and to the garrisone such quantities as shall be necessary for the horses, upon payment of the said prices. We expect your ready obedience, and ordain you to return an account of your diligence between and the 10th of August next."†

The order thus given to "sight" the old Castle enables us to get a slight glimpse of its condition in the middle of the seventeenth century. It was all but demolished, as we have seen, by the Earl of Sussex and Lord Scrope in 1570. The Maxwells, in whose keeping it was placed, put considerable repairs upon it ; and it would appear to have suffered some injury from the Covenanters in 1640, as a claim on that account helped to swell the list of losses for which the second Earl of Nithsdale asked compensation from Charles II. Some of the apartments continued to

---

be occupied as a town house by the Nithsdale family ; though
their chief residence was at Terregles after their " daintie new
lodging at Carlaverock had been laid waste by Colonel Home.
The County Commissioners found the venerable fortress at the
head of High Street much dilapidated in its upper works—with
the consolatory qualifications, however, that the defective storeys
contained " dales lying there to repair them," and that the vaults
and first storey over them would supply ample accommodation for
a greater garrison than the one for which quarters were required.
A misunderstanding arose as to the sources from which the
soldiers were to be maintained, whereby the preparations for
their reception were delayed ; and the Privy Council, losing temper, sent letters of horning to the tantalised Commissioners,
ordering them to proceed at once, and draw upon the revenue of
the Excise for the support of the troops.   Thereupon the Commissioners, on the 14th of September, ordered their collector to
supply, for the garrison, 499 ells of plaiding for thirty-one beds,
at 5s Scots per ell ; coverlets uniform, at £82 19s ; " harden " uniform, at £84 ; for every eight soldiers a five-quart pot, at £4 each ;
six pans, two quarts each ; three quart stoups, and six cups ;
thirty load of peats weekly, at 2s per load ; and seven lbs. of
candle weekly, at 5s per lb.   A report was received at the same
meeting to the effect that £80 Scots would make the roof water-
tight ; and the business was finished by a resolution "advising
the collector, with the magistrates of Dumfries," to see the horsemen sufficiently provided with corn, hay, and straw, at the ordinary rates.   In all these warlike preparations the gentlemen of
the shire were well assisted by the burgh authorities ; the latter
of whom, in June, 1667, gave directions to store up " pouder and
leid" in the Castle ; to place "all the gunes and partizanes" there ;
" that thair be twenty-foure men and a captaine upon the gairde
every night thair, according to the order and row sett doun be the
provest and baillies ; as also that the toun ports be with all expe-
ditioun put up ; and that thair be foir scoir or a hundredth pykes
maid for the tonne's uyseis."

CHAPTER XXXVII.

GREAT CONVENTICLE ON SKEOCH HILL—THE COMMUNION STONES OF IRON-GRAY—INCREASING SEVERITY OF THE PRIVY COUNCIL—GRAHAM OF CLAVERHOUSE: SKETCH OF HIS PERSONAL APPEARANCE AND CHARACTER; HE IS SENT INTO DUMFRIESSHIRE; HIS ACTIVITY IN SEIZING COVENANTERS, AND IN SUPPRESSING CONVENTICLES—GRIERSON OF LAG—DOINGS OF CLAVERHOUSE IN DUMFRIES AND NEIGHBOURHOOD, AS REPORTED BY HIMSELF—HE COMPLAINS TO HIS SUPERIOR OFFICER THAT THE PRISON OF DUMFRIES HAS BEEN TURNED INTO A CONVENTICLE—BOON COMPANIONSHIP OF THE BURGH RULERS WITH THE PERSECUTORS—CAROUSING OF THE BAILIES WITH NISBETT, WINDRAM, STRAUCHAN, LAUDER, AND LIVINGSTONE—KING'S BIRTH-DAY REJOICINGS IN THE TOWN—ROUT OF CLAVERHOUSE AT DRUMCLOG—DEFEAT OF THE COVENANTERS AT BOTHWELL BRIDGE—THE SANQUHAR DECLARATION—CLAVERHOUSE PAYS A SECOND VISIT TO THE DISTRICT.

THE Indulgence was meant by its projectors to be a bone of contention and a snare to the Presbyterians. It proved to be so, inasmuch as it separated the clergy into two antagonistic parties—the indulged and the non-indulged. The people for the most part adhered, and that with more steadfastness than ever, to those ministers who declined to purchase ease and comparative comfort by sacrificing an iota of what they deemed to be the imprescriptible rights of the Church. Conventicles, in house and field, as a consequence, increased; and to crush them, and punish their frequenters, the whole machinery of a merciless Government was set in operation. Among the many other means adopted for these ends landlords were required to enter into bonds pledging themselves that neither their families, domestic tenants, nor the servants of their tenants, nor any one residing on their land, should attend the ministry of the proscribed preachers, or in any way give them countenance. "We cannot possibly come under such stipulations," pleaded a body of the proprietors before the Privy Council. "By the Lord Jehovah! you must and shall!" retorted Lauderdale, as the savage significantly bared his arms above the elbows; and, to assist him in making his threat good, eight thousand armed Highlanders were let loose upon the fertile districts of the South and West. This locust-like host ravaged the country for three months; and on being recalled, the other soldiers raised by the Government took their places, emulating them in rapacity, surpassing them in the art of hunting down the wandering occupants of the hills and glens.

With the honoured name of John Blackader conventicle preaching is closely associated ; it may be said, indeed, to have originated by him, by Gabriel Semple, and by John Welsh. On the 25th of January, 1666, letters of Council were issued against these and other two worthies—Alexander Peden and Samuel Arnot—for presuming to exercise their ministerial functions ; Blackader being especially charged with having " oft times convened great numbers of the parish of Glencairn and neighbouring parishes, sometimes to the number of a thousand and upwards, and continuing so to do every Lord's Day : at which meetings he baptises the children of all disaffected persons." On being cited at the Market Cross of Dumfries to appear in Edinburgh to answer these charges, he disobeyed the summons ; and " Byte-the-sheep ' Turner was ordered to apprehend him. Favoured by another " singular cast of Providence," to use his own words, he had just left home with Mrs Blackader for the North, when an armed party entered ; and, finding him gone, they acted with the same rude violence as at Troqueer Manse, rifling the apartments and abusing the children. We find him in the summer of 1678 still officiating as a field preacher. When returning from a conventicle held near Culross, Perthshire, he was met by James Kirk of Sundaywell—the same poor fellow who seven years afterwards was buried in a martyr's grave at Dumfries—by whom the preacher was invited, " in the name of the country," to assist John Welsh in holding a great communion service in the parish of Irongray on the following Sabbath.

Cordially responding to the request, Mr Blackader set out on horseback from Edinburgh, accompanied by his wife and son Robert, who wished to see their relatives in Nithsdale, and to share with him in any danger that might arise. Intimations of the intended gathering had been mysteriously circulated among the faithful, and as the little party proceeded by way of Leadhills down Enterkin pass, they fell in with numerous persons pursuing the same route—" farmers gash in riding graith," village operatives, peasants of both sexes ; while about fourscore gentlemen from Clydesdale, " reasonably well accoutred," acted as a sort of vanguard to the promiscuous host.* Attendance at the service on the upland wilds of Irongray was what they had all in view ; and multitudes flocked thither also from the neighbouring parishes, where it had been " noised abroad " that Mr Welsh and other favourite preachers were to be assisted by Mr Blackader, and that the celebration was likely to be the greatest of the kind ever held throughout the district. A preliminary meeting took place at Meiklewood Cross, in Holywood, on Saturday, at which the nature and design of the Lord's Supper were expounded by Mr

* Memoirs of Blackader, pp. 214-5,

Blackader. Mr Welsh, who preached afterwards, intimated that the hallowed ordinance would be celebrated next day on a hill-side about four miles distant ; but, mindful of the many enemies they had to deal with, he forebore to name the precise place of rendezvous.

His hearers had no difficulty in finding its whereabouts—a platform on Skeoch Hill, a hundred and fifty feet or so below the summit. A dreary, secluded spot it was ; in modern times agricul-tural enterprise has done much to soften its aspect, making the skirts of this solitary place "to blossom as the rose ;" but even yet the mountain looks bleak and lonely, and still

> " The heather climbs its barrenness,
> And purples half its throne."

To the men and women who toiled up its rugged sides on the morning of that memorable Sabbath day its loneliness was a powerful charm. In its remoteness lay their chief earthly security ; and with their strong trust in Heaven they felt that the hollow of the hill was to them as the hollow of Jehovah's hand. Few better places, indeed, could have been found anywhere for such a gathering ; it was so spacious as well as so secluded, so hidden from ordinary observation, and yet afforded such a commanding prospect from the heights above. No one could approach this "cleft of the rock" without being reconnoitred by the sentinels posted on Skeoch top, and on the higher and neighbouring sum-mits of Cornlee and Forest. Portions of twenty parishes or more are embraced in the view ; it sweeps south-east over the winding Nith, across the Solway to Skiddaw and the Isle of Man ; north-ward and westward it traverses a fine undulating country till it touches the crests of Screel and Bengairn, and is only stopped by the bolder masses that curve over the vale of Ken ; while a softer scene, spreading out eastward, sparkles with the stream of Cluden, blooms with the woodland bowers of Holywood, and fades gradually away along the gentle acclivities of Kirkmahoe and Tinwald.

The vast congregation numbered, we should say, not fewer than six thousand persons, about one-half of whom were, on appli-cation, admitted to the communion. The hill-sides supplied ample sitting accommodation, but for partakers of the rite a little flat, central piece of ground was set apart as a sanctuary whereon were laid four parallel rows of large whinstones, with a higher pile at the south-west end ; the former being used as seats by the com-municants, and the latter as a table for the emblematical bread and wine. At the present day the rows extend about sixty feet in length ; allowing for occasional gaps that are now visible, the stones must have numbered nearly two hundred ; and, according to tradition, there were many other stones which continued the sittings up the brae-face at the north-east end—but of these latter no trace is left. Making ample allowance for missing stones, the communicants at each service or table may have numbered three hundred; and allowing for each service only half-an-hour, and three hours for the opening and closing exercises, eight hours at least must have been occupied by this grand Eucharistic festival of the Covenanters, if Wodrow's statement be correct, that it was partaken of by three thousand persons.

Summer tide though it was, the sky wore a troubled aspect, as if in sympathy with the worshippers; but they soon lost sight for a time of their earthly sorrows, when realising by faith the glories of the land unseen. To these the preachers pointed; and of Him who had promised to watch over his suffering people the congregation sang, not in tones of timid unbelief, but in those of boldness and triumph :

> " I to the hills will lift mine eyes,
> From whence doth come mine aid;
> My safety cometh from the Lord,
> Who heaven and earth hath made :
> Thy foot he'll not let slide, nor will
> He slumber that thee keeps;
> Behold He that keeps Israel,
> He slumbers not nor sleeps." *

Mr Samuel Arnot, the outed minister of Tongland, gave the opening lecture; Mr Welsh followed with the action sermon; and on Mr Blackader and the only other minister present, Mr John Dickson, of Rutherglen, the duty of exhorting the communicants chiefly devolved. A heavy rainfall was all day threatened, though happily not a drop bedewed the heather; but towards the close an alarm of a more serious disturbance was signalled by the sentinels: "The soldiers are coming; make ready for an attack !" Mr Blackader, who was speaking when this cry arose, paused for a few minutes, and no doubt a feeling of anxiety crept over the women and children present, but none of the worshippers offered to leave the scene of danger, and prompt arrangements were made for, if need were, repelling force by force. The Clydesdale men took to horse and formed; Alexander Gordon of Earlston,† who had served as a captain in the civil war, drew up a large cavalry troop; and another, from the holms of Dalswinton, was set in array by a Nithsdale gentleman whose name is not recorded. A resort to arms was fortunately not required. No troopers appeared; no enemy more formidable than some domestic followers of Lord Nithsdale ‡ and Sir Robert Dalzell of Glenæ—numerous enough to

---

* The Psalm from which this stanza is taken was emphatically the song of the persecuted Covenanters, and admirably adapted it was for their hill-side gatherings.

† Descended from Gordon of Airds, the pioneer of the Reformation in Dumfriesshire and Galloway.

‡ This was John, seventh Lord Herries, who, upon the death of Robert, Earl of Nithsdale, without issue, succeeded to the earldom in 1678.

warrant the alarm, prudent enough to slip away quietly after showing themselves. Mr Blackader then resumed, and the extra-ordinary services were closed comfortably before the gloaming; but "ere the people got to their houses and quarters, there fell a great rain, which that night waxed the waters, and most of them had to pass through both the Cairn and the Cluden," which were flooded to the brim. A monument commemorative of the services has recently been set up on Skeoch Hill ;* and the rude, unhewn Communion stones remain in part, bearing their own more eloquent testimony to the inflexible faith and fortitude of our persecuted forefathers; hallowed memorials of a heroic time—meet monuments of Welsh, Blackader, and its other worthies tried and true.

An additional pretext for violence was unhappily supplied by the assassination of Sharpe, on the 3rd of May, 1679—the deed of a few zealots, for which the Covenanters generally ought not to have been held responsible. The blame of it was, however, thrown upon the whole party, and a testing question was based upon it, which increased the inquisitorial resources of the military. If when a suspected individual was asked "Do you consider the killing of Archbishop Sharpe murder?" a negative answer was given, or no answer at all, he was dragged to prison, or summarily despatched. At length the patience of the persecuted sufferers gave way, and they resolved once more to offer armed resistance to their rulers. On the 29th of May in the same year—the anniversary of the Restoration—a band of eighty armed Covenanters entered Rutherglen, extinguished the bonfires lighted in honour of royalty, burned the Acts of Council by which Episcopacy was established, and finished their demonstration by affixing to the Market Cross of the town a written document repudiating and condemning all the tyrannical doings of the Government in Scotland during the existing King's reign.

These daring acts were correctly looked upon by the Privy Council as a declaration of war; and they, nothing loath, commis-

---

* This monument is of light-coloured granite, and pyramid form. It bears inscriptions as follows :—(1) "Erected by voluntary contributions, in 1870." (2) "To mark the spot where a large number of Covenanters met, in 1678, to worship God; and where about three thousand communicants on the occasion celebrated the sacrament of the Lord's Supper." (3) "The following ejected ministers officiated: John Welsh, of Irongray; John Blackader, of Troqueer; John Dickson, of Rutherglen; and Samuel Arnot, of Tongland, the adjacent stones being used as the communion tables." (4) "These stones are significant memorials of those troublous times in which our fathers, at the peril of their lives, contended for the great principles of civil and religious freedom." The last of these inscriptions dissatisfied many of the subscribers to the monument fund, they complaining that it did not set forth in terms sufficiently explicit the principles for which the Covenanters struggled and suffered; and certainly in this respect it is susceptible of improvement. (a)

(a) The proprietor of the land objected to any more adequate inscription.

sioned John Graham of Claverhouse to take up the gauntlet on
their behalf, feeling assured that he would make short work with
the rebels. Claverhouse had already proved his fitness for such a
task. After serving some time with distinction in the Dutch
army, he returned to his native country, at the age of thirty-five,
to become policeman-general over the disaffected districts, and
gain transitory rewards and deathless infamy by punishing the
bodies of his poor fellow-countrymen when he failed by threat and
fine to enslave their souls. The Council soon saw that he was
admirably adapted for their purposes; he was so cool, self-reliant,
unscrupulous, and cruel. An impression to the same effect is conveyed by the two authentic portraits that have been preserved of
the notorious cavalier; one representing him when quite a youth,
and comparatively unknown; the other when in the prime of
manhood, and raised to the peerage of Viscount Dundee. An unmistakable "dourness" is visible in the first of these likenesses;
the curl of the upper lip—the mouth compressed—the nostrils
distended—the troubled, anxious, almost sorrowful, expression
thrown over the face—impress the beholder unfavourably, in
spite of the regularity and graceful outline of the features. This
portrait gives us the idea that he must have been cold, reserved,
proud, and pitiless before the age of puberty was reached. The
youth is "Bonnie Dundee" in embryo—handsome, yet sinister and
unattractive; and the impression conveyed by the other picture,
though in some degree different, is of the same general kind. The
countenance is rather softer, if anything, and is equally sad and
haughty; the lower part of the face, however, having become
heavy, without any trace of that effeminacy of which Sir Walter
Scott speaks, except in the mouth, which is small as compared
with the colossal nose, indicative of the possessor's energy and
power. Scott's sketch of the man may be fittingly inserted
here :—"Profound in politics, and imbued, of course, with that
disregard for individual rights which its intrigues usually gene-
rate, this leader was cool and collected in danger, fierce and ardent
in pursuing success, careless of facing death himself, and ruthless
in inflicting it upon others."* This is, on the whole, a fair outline
of Graham's character, as indicated by his portraits, and as
exemplified during his ten years of military misrule over the West
and South of Scotland.

In a letter dated Moffat, December 28th, 1678, Claverhouse
thus announced his arrival in Dumfriesshire to his commander-in-
chief, the Earl of Linlithgow :—"My Lord, I came here last night
with the troop, and am just going to march for Dumfries, where I
resolve to quarter the whole troop. I have not heard anything of
the dragoons, though it is now about nine o'clock, and they should

* Old Mortality, chap. xii.

have been here last night, according to your lordship's orders. I suppose they must have taken some other route. I am informed since I came that this county has been very loose. On Tuesday was eight days, and Sunday, there were great field conventicles just by here, with great contempt of the regular clergy; who complain extremely that I have *no orders* to apprehend anybody for *past* demeanours. And besides that, all the particular orders I have being contained in that order of quartering, every place where we quarter must see them, which makes them fear the less. I am informed that the most convenient posts for quartering the dragoons will be Moffat, Lochmaben, and Annan; whereby the whole county will be kept in awe. Besides that, my lord, they tell me that the end of the bridge of Dumfries is in Galloway, and that they may hold conventicles at our nose, [and] we dare not dissipate them, seeing our orders confine us to Dumfries and Annandale. Such an insult as that would not please me; and, on the other hand, I am unwilling to exceed orders, so that I expect from your lordship orders *how to carry* in such cases."

The impatient trooper, as we learn from another of his letters, was soon at work. Before his arrival, some of the Dumfries Covenanters and others occasionally met for worship during winter in a large building on the Galloway side of the Nith; and he having received ample licence to act in the Stewartry as well as in Dumfriesshire, arranged with the Steward for the demolition of the meeting house; with what success, is reported by him in the following terms:—"I must acknowledge," he says, by way of prelude, "that till now, in any service that I have been in, I never inquired farther in the laws than the orders of my superior officers. After (he proceeds to say) I had sent the Council's orders to the Stewart-Depute, he appointed Friday last the 3rd of January, for the demolishing the meeting-house, and that I should bring with me only one squad of my troop. He brought with him four score of countrymen, all fanatics, for they would not lay to their hands till we forced them. Everybody gave out that house for a byre; but when they saw that there was no quarter for it, and that we were come on the place, nobody had the impudence to deny it to have been built a-purpose for meeting, and that upon the expense of the common purse of the disaffected. It was a good large house, about sixty foot of length, and betwixt twenty and thirty broad. It had only one door, two windows on every side, and one in every end. They had put up stakes alongst every side, and a hek and manger in one of the ends, to make it pass for a byre; but that was done lately, after that they had heard that it was taken notice of for a meeting-house. The Stewart-Depute performed his part punctually enough. The walls were thrown down, and timber burnt. So perished the charity of many ladies."

The Steward who co-operated with Claverhouse in this mighty achievement was none other than Sir Robert Grierson of Lag, who held the office during the minority of the Earl of Nithsdale, the hereditary Steward of Kirkcudbrightshire. This was the first occasion of their meeting with each other, and they henceforth became fast friends, united by a community of tastes and pursuits; though, to do Claverhouse justice, he was in his personal habits far above the sensual and besotted Laird of Lag. Sir Robert succeeded to the family estates on the death of his cousin, in 1667; he was created a Nova Scotia baronet in 1685, and was united in marriage to Lady Henrietta Douglas, sister of William, first Duke of Queensberry. His participation in the overthrow of the conventicle house, just noticed, was but the prelude to a long series of outrageous measures taken by him against the proscribed Presbyterians, and for which his name has been branded with infamy scarcely less foul than that which attaches to "The Bloody Claver'se."

In another letter, dated Dumfries, February 7th, 1679, Claverhouse reported to his commander his diligence in "seizing" disaffected persons, and otherwise carrying out his mission. He had forwarded a list of them to his lordship; had ridden to Annan to instruct his emissary, Captain Inglis, in the business; had then hurried to Moffat, where he "gave Lieutenant Cleland orders to seize on three;" sent an express to Inglis, "that he might seize on other three;" appointed them "Wednesday, at six o'clock at night, to march;" returned to Dumfries, found twenty dragoons going on relief, but "sent them to seize on Holmains, Dormont, and Denby" (all Nonconformists of the Annandale family of Carruthers). They got only Dormont, the other two having, it is reported, "gone to Edinburgh to give satisfaction to the Council," but if they remained in the country he should endeavour to find them; sent a corporal for the two Welshes, who found them both; sent another to seize on Dalskairth, but found him not in his own house—made search for him in Dumfries without success; sent the third brigadier to "seek the wabster," who brought his brother instead, and "though he maybe cannot preach like his brother, thought it would be no great fault to give him the trouble to go with the rest;" and, finally, "have sent the prisoners away this day with a guard of twenty," commanded by Corporal Crawford.

This comprehensive communication, in which the hustling, energetic, indefatigable character of the writer is well illustrated, concludes with an expression of his wish that Lord Linlithgow would forward instructions regarding the fining of certain parties on the rolls who had not yet been disposed of. Thus "Seize! seize! seize!" was, morning, noon, and night, the cry of this predatory captain; the objects of his seizures being the

God-fearing burgesses, yeomen, and peasantry of Scotland, as if they had been noxious vermin whom it was a duty to extirpate.

More tokens of his wolfish desire to seize victims are shown in a fourth letter, written by him from Dumfries on the 24th of February :—" I obeyed the order," he says, " about seizing persons in Galloway, that very night I received it, as far as it was possible ; that is to say, all that was within forty miles, which is most that can be ridden in one night ; and of six made search for, I found only two, which are John Livingstone, bailie of Kirkcudbright, and John Black, treasurer there.   The other two bailies were fled, and their wives lying above the clothes in the bed, and great candles lighted, waiting for the coming of the party ; and told them they knew of their coming, and had as good intelligence as they themselves ; and that if the other two were seized on, it was their own faults, that would not contribute for intelligence.   .   .   .   The names of the other two I made search for were Cassincarry and the Lady Lauriston, but found them not.   There is almost nobody lays in their bed that knows themselves anyways guilty within forty miles of us ; and within a few days I shall be upon them, threescore of miles at one bout, for seizing on the others contained in the order."

Had Claverhouse been in Dumfries when the gigantic Irongray conventicle was held he would scarcely have shrunk from attacking it ; and he would at all events have done his best to seize some of the "fellows," "rogues," and "villains"—as he was accustomed to call the Covenanters—who frequented such assemblies.   Yet, in spite of his sleepless vigilance and his merciless system of repression, the hill-side congregations were never entirely put down ; and, wonderful to relate, after he had been about four months in Dumfries, the very prison of the town was turned into a treasonable Presbyterian meeting-house, "under his very nose."   This "great abuse" was attributed by Captain Graham to the laxity of the magistrates, to whom he pays an ironical compliment, which they could not have merited had they not been of a different stamp than their predecessors in the time of Sir James Turner.   Claverhouse thus complained to his superior officer on the subject :—" There is here in prison a minister who was taken above a year ago by my Lord Nithsdale and by the *well-affected* magistrates of this [town] has had the liberty of an open prison ; and more conventicles have been kept by him there than has been in any one house in the kingdom. This is a great abuse ; and if the magistrates be not punished, at least the man ought not to be suffered any longer here, for that prison is more frequented than the kirk.   If your lordship think fit, he may be sent in with the rest."

It will be recollected that John Irving was chosen chief magistrate in 1660.   For thirteen years afterwards, he and another member of the Irving family had a monopoly of the provostship ; but in 1674, William Craik of Duchrae, a Moderate Presbyterian, was called to that office, and continued in it till 1678, when David Bishop, a gentleman of similar views, succeeded him for a short period, Mr Craik again becoming provost in 1679, when Claverhouse visited the town.   From such a man as Duchrae the Covenanters would receive something more than toleration : hence the remonstrance of Claverhouse against the indulgence shewn to them by the "well-affected" magistrates of Dumfries.

Though the burgh authorities in 1679 were suspected of disloyalty by Claverhouse, some of their predecessors kept on good terms with his persecuting colleagues and subordinates. The Provost, bailies, and convener had frequent convivial meetings with the officers, who with whetted swords and fleet-limbed steeds scoured the neighbouring district ; and it is most melancholy to reflect that sometimes the very men who were one day boozing merrily over the blood-red wine in Dumfries with its burghal rulers were the next busily employed in slaughtering their innocent countrymen on the hills and moors around. In the treasurer's accounts, under date 9th January, 1669, when John Irving was still provost, the following entry occurs :—" Dew by the magistrates, in company with Sir Robert Dalzell, Patrick Nisbett, Robert Moorhead, and Birkhill, with severall uther gentlemen, the haill magistrats being present, with severall of the counseil, at the admitting of the said Patrick Nisbett, burges, twelf pynts of seck, quhereoff there was 4 unce of suygar to ilk pynt of eleven of the said pyntes, and the uther but [without] suygar, with twa shortbreid, and 3 sh. for tobacco and pypes, £28 15."* This Nisbett, thus feasted and honoured, became soon after a notorious persecutor, as the gravestones erected at Fenwick and elsewhere, over his martyred victims, still attest.†

We quote one other illustrative entry from the same record. Mistress Rome, who kept the town's tavern in 1687, charged the subjoined account against the Council that year :—" Spent with Lieutenant Colonell Windram, Captaine Strauchane, Captain Bruce, Leivetenant Lauder, Leivetenant Livingstone, six pynts of wine, with tobacco and pypes, £6 9s 4d." Here is a pretty batch of blood-stained Bacchanalians — convened, perhaps, to arrange over their cups for some fresh raid against the children of the Covenant. Of many cruel deeds Livingstone and Lauder were guilty ; and the above tavern score contrasts curiously with the rude elegy in St. Michael's churchyard over the remains of James Kirk, who was shot dead on the Dumfries Sands, in June, 1685, at the bidding of one of the convivialists :—

* Burgh Treasurer's Accounts.   † Cloud of Witnesses, p. 527.

" By bloody Bruce and wretched Wright
I lost my life, in great despite ;
Shot dead without due time to try
And fit me for eternity :
A witness of Prelatic rage
As ever was in any age."

The remaining two of the same party, Windram and Strauchan, met just two years before, under very different circumstances : the scene was not a cosy Dumfries change-house, but the wild beach of Blednoch Bay ; their object was not to quaff the flowing bowl, but to drown two feeble women, a hoary matron and a girl of tender years, beneath the ravenous ocean tide, Lag and David Graham assisting them in their murderous work.* Had magistrates of the Craik and Corsane stamp ruled the burgh at this period, they would have scorned to sit at the same board with such infamous men as these.

During all these troublous times, too, the anniversary of the tyrant King's birth and restoration (both of which fell on the 29th of May) was celebrated in jovial style by the very loyal magnates of the burgh. Fancy can catch the echo of their fulsome toasts, and the flash of their festal fires, in such prosaic business entries as the following :—29th May, 1672.—At the bonfyre at the Croce, nyne quarts of wyne, £18 ; item at the bonfyre before the provest's gate, three quarts, £6 : it., at the treasurer's direction to the peit leaders, and spent in his company, 9s. ; the night after the bonfyres, with Carnselloch, Alexander Dowglas of Penzerie, Mr Jon Crichton, and the clerk, three chopins of wine ; and that night, with Mr Cairncross [the curate], Mr Mair and his wife, thrie chopins of wyne ; and 1s. 8d. for tobacco and pypes, is together £3 1s. 8d.† 29th May, 1678.— Payed for 2 duzen and a half of glassis broken at the crosse, at 6 pence a piec, £9 ; paid to the offichers that day, 4s. ; for ringing the bell, 12s."

Claverhouse, as has been stated, was summoned by the Privy Council to take action against the Covenanters of Lanarkshire, when, on the 29th of May, 1679, they published their defiant Declaration at Rutherglen. In that very month, a measure that had been carried by Sharpe in the Council a few days before his death received the royal assent, which gave power not only to judges, but to the officers of the forces " to proceed against all such who go with any arms to those field meetings, as traitors"— in other words, to put them to death without further warrant. Possessed of such ample powers, and placed at the head of a strong military force, Graham entered the revolted districts of

---

* The reader will at once see that the reference here is to the martyrdom of Margaret Maclachlan and Margaret Wilson, in the water of Blednoch, near Wigtown, on the 11th of May, 1685.

† Tavern and other charges, as given in the Town Treasurer's books.

the West, and had just begun his destructive work when he
learned that preparations had been made for holding a conventicle
on a great scale in the neighbourhood of Loudon Hill. Hurrying
forward from Glasgow with a troop of horse, and two companies
of dragoons, he found the male worshippers of the assembly, to
the number of a hundred and fifty foot, armed with halberds,
forks, and such-like rude weapons, fifty musketeers, and fifty
horse, all drawn up in battle array, ready to repel force by force.
Claverhouse, eager for the fray, and confident that he would
scatter the insurgents like chaff, attacked them with characteristic
impetuosity. How he must have been chafed, when the "fanatics"
he had despised, after steadily returning the fire of his troops,
crossed an intervening swamp, and fell with such resistless force
upon them, that they reeled, broke, and fled !

This Covenanting victory was won on Sabbath, the 1st of
June ; but a fortnight afterwards, the Royalists, at Bothwell
Bridge, under the Duke of Monmouth,* far more than made up
for their defeat at Drumclog. In the one instance proof was
given of what a few brave men firmly united can do ; in the
other numbers, courage, and enthusiasm availed nothing in ranks
already divided by jealousy and dissension. The chief bone of
contention with the Covenanters in the latter case was the
Indulgence—that artfully concocted measure, which proved of
more service to the Royalist commander than a reinforcement of
five thousand men. Welsh was the chief of the Moderate party ;
and among others at the battle belonging to the district were
M'Lellan of Barscobe, Gabriel Semple, Alexander Gordon, younger
of Earlston,† Dr William Blackader, son of the Troqueer minister,
and Mr Ferguson of Caitloch.‡ The last-named gentleman es

* He was the King's natural son, and had previously married the heiress
of Buccleuch.

† The house of Earlston stands on the banks of the Ken, at a short distance above the village of Dalry, with the wood of Airds in its immediate
vicinity.

‡ Ferguson of Caitloch, in Glencairn, was a pious and brave man ; and
his wife was as much devoted to the cause of the Covenant as himself. She
was cousin to Mr Blackader ; and it was to Caitloch, as already noticed, that
he fled for refuge in 1662. After the fight at Bothwell Bridge, Mr Ferguson
was forfeited, and his house converted into a garrison. Mrs Ferguson and
her children, says Wodrow, " were turned out when her husband had fled,
and wandered in the fields, without any habitation except occasionally the
shelter of a barn. At length she found means to escape with them out of the
kingdom, and died abroad."—vol. i., p. 286. The part taken by Caitloch at
Bothwell Bridge seems to have resembled that assigned by the novelist to
Henry Morton :—" Morton, who beheld the columns of the enemy beginning
to appear on the right bank, and directing their march upon the bridge, raised
his voice to its utmost pitch, and pointing at the same time with his hand,
exclaimed—'Silence your senseless clamours ! Yonder is the enemy : on the
maintaining the bridge against him depends our lives, as well as our hope to
reclaim our laws and liberties. There shall at least one Scottishman die in

pecially distinguished himself in the crisis of the engagement. Heading a party from Nithsdale and Galloway, he assisted Balfour of Burley in keeping the pass—the long narrow bridge, the loss of which at last was the sure forerunner of utter defeat. Earlston the elder, ignorant of the rout of his friends, was hastening to join them when he was seized by a party of Royalist dragoons, and by them put to death. In all, four hundred Covenanters fell on the field ; twelve hundred were made prisoners, of whom only a few, thanks to Monmouth's clemency, were sent to the scaffold, and the rest were banished to the Barbadoes. Terrible and crushing though the fight was, its remote results were perhaps even more disastrous—it being made ever afterwards, till the Revolution, an ensnaring test and a new pretext for spoliation and violence.

Hitherto the suffering Presbyterians had made no open war against King Charles ; but in the summer of 1680 the famous "Queensferry Paper," prepared by Donald Cargill, was extensively signed ; the subscribers thereby declaring their rejection of the King, and those associated with him, because they had "altered and destroyed the Lord's established religion, overturned the fundamental laws of the kingdom, and changed the civil government of this land, which was by a king and free parliament, into tyranny." They further, in conclusion, entered into a bond for the [mutual defence of their natural, civil, and religious rights—a bond never to be broken "till," they declared heroically and hopefully, "we shall overcome, or send them down under debate to posterity, that they may begin where we end." Cargill, enfeebled by age, was unfitted to embody this bold manifesto in deeds ; that was done by the young Joshua of the movement, Richard Cameron, when, on the following 22nd of June (anniversary of the defeat at Bothwell), the remarkable Declaration penned by him was published by his brother and a few adherents in the burgh of Sanquhar—meet place for such testimony against the tyrant King, since it was, says Dr Simpson, the "centre of a spacious martyr field, every parish around it except one having been the scene of a Christian martyrdom."

On the morning of that day a band of twenty armed horsemen descended from their haunt among the neighbouring hills, rode leisurely down the principal street of the town ; and having reached the Market Cross, they there, in the hearing of the inhabitants, solemnly pronounced the doom of dethronement

their defence. Let any one who loves his country follow me.' Burley being about to act upon the advice, Ephraim Macbriar [the Hugh M'Kail of history] sought to dissuade him from joining Morton. ' Hinder me not,' replied Burley, ' he hath well said that all is lost if the enemy win the bridge, therefore let me not. Array yourselves under your leaders—let us not lack supplies of men and ammunition ; and accursed be he who turneth back from the work on this great day.' "—*Old Mortality*, chap. xxxi.

on Charles Stuart. With all due formality, and the utmost deliberation, they performed an act which made them amenable to torture and death. It was the deed of a daring—we shall not say a desperate—body of men, impelled by conscience to proclaim openly, on the house-tops as it were, what they thought of the despotic monarch and his deeds. They saw wickedness rampant in the high places of the land—the representative of Scotland's royal house proving a recreant to the trust reposed in him, trampling on the spiritual rights of the people, and in matters civil setting the very *leges regnandi* at nought. On account of these things, they said, the land mourned ; and they deemed it part of God's controversy with them that they had not disowned the perjured King long ago. But, though meriting such treatment, his power was still unbroken : he was surrounded by a strong army which protected him, by a clique of crafty statesmen who confirmed him in his course, and by a mob of servile courtiers who regaled the royal nostrils with the incense of adulation.

"Come what may, and hold silent who list, we must and will publish the truth of this cruel King, protest against his misdeeds, and proclaim in the face of heaven that he has forfeited his claim to the throne and to our allegiance." So saying, and under the influence of such sentiments, the little Cameronian band issued their manifesto, declaring that Charles Stuart, who had " been reigning, or rather tyrannising, on the throne of Britain these years bygone," had forfeited " all right, title to, or interest in, the crown of Scotland," and proclaiming war " against the tyrant and usurper, and all the men of his practices, and against all such as have strengthened him, sided with, or anywise acknowledged any other in like usurpation and tyranny." There was high moral sublimity in the uttering of this document. Brimful of treason it might be deemed by the upholders of the Government ; but a few years afterwards the sentiments it embodied became the gospel of a new political dispensation, and were transformed into fact when, in 1688, William, Prince of Orange, acted out the bold, true words of his forerunner, Richard Cameron.

The men who had thus bravely spoken at the Market Cross of Sanquhar knew well also how bravely to do and die. Returning to the hills once more, they rejoined their comrades ; and the party, learning that soon after Bruce of Earlshall, with a troop of horse, was searching for them, resolved to make what resistance they could. The Cameronian force, numbering some sixty-three men, was attacked by Bruce at Ayrsmoss, near Cumnock, overpowered by superior numbers, and killed or scattered, the heroic founder of the sect, and author of the Declaration, falling among the slain.

During the occurrence of these aggravated troubles the resources of the country were exhaustively drawn upon to uphold the military instruments of the dragonnade. Dumfriesshire, as one of the chief seats of the disaffected, had to bear a heavy share of the burden. Extracts have already been given from the minutes of the County Commissioners, showing that the task imposed upon them, at an earlier stage of the Persecution, was both difficult and exorbitant ; we subjoin a few additional notices to the same effect dated after Bothwell Bridge. On the 26th of October, 1679, the Commissioners gave force to an Act of the Privy Council, ordaining the Sheriffdom of Wigtown and Stewartry of Kirkcudbright to pay locality to the forces under the command of the Earl of Linlithgow, conform to their valuation with Dumfriesshire ; and they found, from a list given in by the Laird of Earlshall, lieutenant to Claverhouse, and Mr Dalmahoy, quartermaster to the King's guard of horse, that they had to provide locality for seven score and ten horse, whereof the one-half was the King's guard aforesaid. On the 25th of June in the following year, the Commissioners ordained " forty-eight horses to be provided out of the parish of Dumfries and Stewartry of Kirkcudbright, with graith for the carriage of the baggage, etc., of his Majesty's force through this country." On the 3rd of January, 1681, a letter from the Privy Council was considered, ordering a garrison of thirty horse to be furnished with all due requisites at the Castle of Dumfries. The magistrates of the burgh were accordingly recommended to "sight the stables, and assist in provyding what may be useful, and to furnish the hie rooms of the Castle with beds and dales, and cause the windows to be fitted up with divots." A few weeks afterwards the collector and clerk were appointed to proportion upon the several parishes in the Sheriffdom of Nithsdale, Stewartry of Annandale, and Five Kirks of Eskdale, " ane month's locality for sixty horse, more or fewer, as shall happen to be in the garrison."

On the 27th of January Claverhouse was again sent by the Privy Council with a troop of guards "to punish all disorders, disturbance of the peace, and church irregularities in Kirkcudbright, Annandale, Wigtown, and Dumfries." That he might carry on his murderous work under some colour of law, he was made Sheriff of Wigtownshire in room of Sir Andrew Agnew of Lochnaw, a devoted Covenanter, who had been deprived of his office because he refused to subscribe the subservient oath called the Test, which had been framed by the Parliament of the preceding year. The letters written by Sheriff Graham to the Marquis of Queensberry, the King's Commissioner in Scotland, breathe relentless hostility towards the scattered Presbyterians and show his determination to put them down as a party at all risks, and without a scruple of remorse ; though, of course, it would be absurd to expect to find in them minute particulars regarding his modes of action, or a list of those who perished through his means by weariness, hunger, exposure to the elements, or by the bullets of his dragoons. Of that black catalogue there is no transcript in the letters of the persecutor, or full copy in the books of the Privy Council; though doubtless the Recording Angel has taken a note of their sufferings, and history, aided by tradition, has to some extent embalmed their names, and given them to imperishable honour.

Claverhouse wrote as follows from New Galloway a few weeks after the beginning of his raid :—"The country hereabouts is in great dread. Upon our march yesterday most men were fled, not knowing against whom we designed. . . . My humble opinion is, that it should be unlawful for the donators to compound with anybody for behoof of the rebel till once he have made his peace. For I would have all footing in this country taken from them that will stand out. And for securing the rents to the donators and the Crown, it is absolutely necessary that there be a fixed garrison in Kenmure, instead of Dumfries; for without it, I am now fully convinced, we can never secure the peace of this country, nor hunt these rogues from their haunts. . . . I sent yesterday two parties in search of those men your lordship gave me a list of—one of them to a burial in the Glencairn, the other to the fair at Thornhill. Neither of them are yet returned; but Stenhouse tells me that the party at the burial miscarried; that he pointed out to them one of the men, and they took another for him, though I had chosen a man to command the party that was born thereabout. They shall not stay in this country but I shall have them."

At first Claverhouse occupied the mansion belonging to Sir John Dalrymple of Stair, and a humbler dwelling in Kirkcudbright possessed by Sir Robert Maxwell; he afterwards, as is indicated by the above letter, made Kenmure Castle his headquarters. "My Lady [Kenmure] told me," he said, in reporting to Queensberry on the subject, "if the King would bestow two or three hundred pounds to repair the house, she would be very well pleased his soldiers came to live in it." Accordingly, on the 1st of November, after Claverhouse had warned the noble owner of the castle to "make it raid and void," he took up his residence there, and it became thenceforth the chief citadel of the infamous sheriffship exercised by him in Galloway and Nithsdale.

His principal colleagues were Colonel James Douglas, brother of the Duke of Queensberry, Sir Robert Grierson of Lag, Sir Robert Dalziel, Sir Robert Laurie of Maxwelton, Sir James Johnstone of Westerhall, Captain Inglis, and Captain Bruce; all of whom, by their activity and zeal against the Covenanters, proved that they were worthy of the persecuting commissions entrusted to them. It is right to add, however, that Colonel Douglas afterwards forsook his party, and served with distinction under William III.; and that he is said to have bitterly lamented the cruelties of which he had been the agent.

CHAPTER XXXVIII.

BEFORE giving any further particulars of the Persecution we must
notice briefly the career of one against whom much of its fury
was directed, and who about this time came prominently forward
as the leader of the Cameronians—James Renwick.   Since the
slaughter of Cameron in 1680, and the martyrdom of Cargill in
the following year, the extreme party among the Presbyterians
had been without a head—had no stated ministers, indeed, and
were very imperfectly organised.   Renwick, whilst quite a youth,
adopted their views, and identified himself with their fortunes.
When nineteen years of age he witnessed the martyrdom of
Cargill, which so stirred his whole moral nature that he devoted
himself heart and soul to the cause for which the aged martyr
suffered.   The Cameronian party, appreciating his fervour, piety,
and talent, offered to send him to the University of Groningen, in
Holland, to complete his training for the ministry—a proposal
which he cheerfully accepted.   Leaving his native village of
Minnyhive, in Nithsdale, he proceeded to the university, and,
after a six months' course of theological study, and being presby-
terially ordained, he returned to the south of Scotland the
accepted pastor, the recognised chief, of the wandering Covenanters.   In a paper called the "Informatory Vindication," he
explained the views and position of the United Societies; and in
1683 followed this up by the emission of a boldly defiant document
styled "An Apologetical Declaration," in which they, after the

manner of Richard Cameron's Sanquhar manifesto, abjured Charles Stuart as a cruel tyrant, and intimated their resolution to continue in the exercise of their Christian rights, and, if attacked, to repel force by force.

Whilst the publication of this paper nerved the courage of the Covenanters, it at the same time intensified the fury of their enemies. Before it was many weeks old the Privy Council passed an Act ordaining that any person who owned, or would not disown it, was to be immediately put to death, though unarmed; the only qualifications to this exterminating edict being that it was to be enforced by the military in presence of two witnesses. On the 30th of December, 1684, a Government proclamation was issued having a still wider sweep—commanding as it did all the inhabitants of the country to swear that they abhorred, renounced, and disowned the Apologetical Declaration. The Abjuration Oath thus first prescribed soon acquired an infamous notoriety, and gave rise to much suffering in the west and south of Scotland, where it was ensnaringly tendered as the touchstone of loyalty to people of all ranks.

Under Renwick's leadership the witnesses for "God's covenanted work of Reformation" had their courage renewed and their faithfulness confirmed; field-preaching, which had been for a season given up, was revived; and though no conventicles were held on a very large scale as in former years, the hills and valleys of Upper Nithsdale and Galloway became at times once more vocal with the song of praise ascending from bands of worshippers, who thus foiled in these solitudes remote "a tyrant's and a bigot's bloody laws," and prepared sword in hand if need be to act upon the bold menace expressed in their Declaration.

A few illustrative details of the Persecution that set in against them with redoubled fury may now be given, the dates being chiefly 1684 and 1685, "wherein," says Patrick Walker, "eighty-two of the Lord's suffering people were suddenly and cruelly murdered in desert places;" so that these two years came to be called emphatically "the killing time." First let us record a few more of Sheriff Graham's own achievements :—"His commission at this time," says Dr Simpson, "was to scour Nithsdale, from New Cumnock to Sanquhar, in quest of all disaffected persons, and to search every nook and ravine, and hunt unsparingly on both sides of the Nith. . . . As it regarded the populace no exemptions were to be made—the peasantry, man, woman, and children, were to be driven like a flock of sheep before the soldiers to a given place, and there to be interrogated, and treated every one as the commander should dictate." When Claverhouse, by such means as these, ferreted out his victims, he usually made short work with them. Take the Test, abjure the Covenants, agree to all the other conditions of abject mental slavery prescribed by the Privy Council, and safety, except in the case of old opposers of the Government, was secured; but let the dastardly terms be rejected, then Heaven might have mercy on such as heroically repudiated them, but Claverhouse and his troopers had none.

On the 18th of December, 1684, he surprised six refugees wandering destitute on the banks of Dee, at Auchinday, in the parish of Girthon. Four of them, Robert Fergusson, John M'Michan, Robert Stewart (son to Major Stewart of Ardoch), and John Grierson, were, after brief warning, left lifeless on the sward. Three of the bodies were carried away by their friends and buried at Dalry, which so irritated Claverhouse, that the gory remains were disinterred by his orders, and lay exposed for several days, after which they were recommitted to the grave. The two other captives, William Hunter and Robert Smith, were carried to Kirkcudbright, condemned after the semblance of a trial, hanged, and then beheaded. In the same year, whilst three of the wanderers were returning from a conventicle held in the parish of Carsphairn, they were encountered by Graham and his men, and shot without ceremony. The martyrs—Joseph Wilson, John Jamieson, and John Humphrey—were buried in the neighbouring moorland of Crossgellioch, and about eighteen years ago, when the foundation of a monument, erected over the resting-place of the sufferers was being excavated, their bodies, says Dr Simpson, were found embalmed in the moss, "shrouded in their hosen, in their coats, and in their bonnets, exactly as they fell."

In the same year Claverhouse apprehended Thomas Harkness of Mitchelslacks; Andrew Clark, Leadhills; and Samuel M'Ewan, Glencairn. Not only were these men staunch Nonconformists, but they were charged with having assisted in rescuing a party of Covenanters when being conveyed to Edinburgh by the military through Enterkin Pass. Harkness and his companions, exhausted by protracted wanderings, were caught sleeping on a hillside in the parish of Closeburn, and "brought into Edinburgh," says Wodrow, "about one of the clock, and the same day they were sentenced and executed about five." Before suffering martyrdom they emitted a joint testimony, declaring that they owned all authority that is allowed by the written Word of God, sealed by Christ's blood, and disowned Popery and all other false doctrine; adding, that they blessed the Lord, who enabled them to bear witness on His behalf, being content to lay down their lives with "cheerfulness, boldness, and courage," and that if they had had a hundred lives "they would willingly quit them all for the truth of Christ." James Harkness, brother to Thomas, and of the same heroic spirit, was also taken by Claverhouse, and capitally sentenced; but he succeeded, with twenty-five fellow-prisoners, in escaping from Canongate Jail, Edinburgh, and lived to a good old age, enjoying the sweets of the Revolution Settlement at his farm-house of Locherben.*

Among the barbarous acts chargeable against Colonel James Douglas are the following, perpetrated in 1685 :—Five Cove-nanters, named respectively John Gibson, Robert Grierson, Robert Mitchell, James Bennoch, and John Edgar, having taken refuge in a cave at Ingleston, in the parish of Glencairn, Niths-dale, were betrayed to Douglas by one Andrew Watson, dragged forth, and, without being left a breathing time for prayer, shot dead. In the same summary style he treated John Hunter at Corehead, Moffatdale ; Thomas Richard, a veteran of seventy years, at Cumnock ; and Andrew Macquhan, who was seized in bed when sick of a fever, and despatched at New Galloway.

Of Lag's persecuting achievements Wodrow and the author of the " Cloud of Witnesses " preserve numerous instances. In 1685 he captured and shot, under cover of night, George Short and David Halliday of Glenap, in the parish of Balmaghie. In the same year, when scouring the parish of Tongland with a party of dragoons, he surprised another David Halliday, portioner of Mayfield, Andrew M'Crabit, James Clement, Robert Lennox of Irlintown, and John Bell of Whiteside, all of whom he put to death. When the last-named prisoner pleaded for a moment's respite, in order that he might commend himself and fellow-sufferers to God, Lag, it is said, exclaimed, in his usual irreverent way, " What the devil have you been doing so many years in these hills ? Have you not prayed enough already ?" and so saying, gave the fatal order which laid them lifeless at his feet.

The records of the time show that Captain Bruce was as ruth-less a tool of the Privy Council as any member of it could have wished. In the same sanguinary year he surprised at Lochenkit,

---

* He was interred beside not a few of his kindred in the romantic churchyard of Dalgarno. Over his remains was placed a tombstone, thus inscribed :—" Here lyes the body of James Harkness, in Locherben, who died 6th Dec., 1723, aged 72 years :—

Belo this stone this dust doth ly,
Who endured 28 years persecuted by tyranny ;
Did him pursue echo and cry
Through many a lonesome place.
At last by Clavers he was tane, and sentenced for to die,
(But God who for his soul took care did him from prison bring)
Because no other cause they had but that he would not give up
With Christ his glorious King,
And swear allegiance to that beast—the Duke of York, I mean :
In spite of all their hottest rage a natural death did die,
In full assurance of his rest with Christ eternally."

Provost Christopher Harkness of Dumfries is a lineal descendant of the Harknesses of Mitchelslacks. His nephew, Mr Thomas Harkness, is tenant of that farm ; and it has been possessed by the family of Harkness for upwards of two centuries.

parish of Kirkpatrick-Durham, six men, and instantly killed four
of them, viz., John Gordon, William Stewart, John Wallace, and
William Heron ; the other two, Edward Gordon and Alexander
M'Cubbin, after being allowed a day's grace, were, at the instance
of Lag, hanged upon a growing tree near Irongray Church, and
buried at the place of execution.   About the same time James
Kirk, of Sundaywell, Dunscore,* while lurking in the parish of
Keir, was betrayed by one James Wright into the hands of Bruce ;
who, as has been already incidentally noticed, carried his prisoner
to Dumfries, detained him there one night, brought him forth
next morning to the Whitesands, and added one more to the list
of martyred victims whose dust lies in St. Michael's churchyard
waiting the resurrection day.

Many Nonconformists died in captivity or in exile who
were as truly martyrs as if they had perished at the stake.   A
refusal to attend the curate or take the Test was, in countless
instances, followed by an imprisonment which terminated only
with life itself.   For such " crimes " as these Bailie Muirhead of
Dumfries was consigned to the prison at Leith, fell ill there, and
died ; James Glover, while skulking among the woods of Tinwald,
was shot at, wounded, and carried to Dumfries in a dying state,
and breathed his last in the Edinburgh tolbooth ; Andrew Hunter,
a burgess of Dumfries, old and decrepit, was immured in the town
prison, and experienced the same fate—the poor sufferer praying
in vain that he might get home, where he would be better
attended to : a home of another kind awaited him.   More pitiful
still was the fate of those Nonconformists who perished in the
vile, noisome pit at Dunnottar Castle, which is still known as the
Whigs' Vault.   Among the hundreds of both sexes there confined
during the sweltering summer months of 1685 were twenty-nine
men and women, who had previously been lodged in the Dumfries
jail ; two of the latter having first been scourged through the
town by the common hangman, " merely because they would
swear no oaths, and refused to engage to hear the curate of their
parish."†   A devout matron of Dumfries, Euphraim Threipland
by name, was also of the number.   She was the widow of George
Macbirnie, a merchant of the burgh, who, after he had been
tossed since Middleton's Parliament with finings, confinings,
wanderings, and imprisonments, contracted a sickness whereof

---

* There are two old square towers still standing in the upper part of
Glenesslin, and on opposite sides of the glen, at a point where it contracts to
a narrow pass.   The names of these towers are Bogrie and Sundaywell, and
both of them anciently belonged to district families of the name of Kirk, or
Kirko.   That of Sundaywell is still inhabited as a farm-house.   There is a
stone over the door bearing the initials " I. K.," and opposite " S. W.," meaning John [James ?] Kirk of Sundaywell.   Under the initials is the date 1651.
—Statistical Account, pp. 341-2.

† Wodrow, vol. iv., p. 289.

he died in 1681.* Because Mrs Macbirnie would not specify the conventicles she attended, name the officiating preachers, and promise to hear the curates, she was fined in a very heavy sum, and, being unable to pay it, was sent to "the thief's hole" at Dumfries, from which, though too sick to leave her pallet, she was dragged, with her fellow-prisoners, and despatched to Dunnottar, where she lay for three months. She was fortunate enough to escape transportation, "by a mistake of her name in the clerk;" and, after an additional imprisonment of six months at Leith, she was liberated on giving bond to appear when called upon. "However," says Wodrow, "the Sheriff-depute kept possession of her goods, and threatened her person if she returned to Dumfries." The tragedy of the Whigs' Vault at Dunnottar has, not without good cause, been compared to that of the Black Hole of Calcutta. John Stock, a burgess of Dumfries, perished in the vault, and several others who were suffocated by its noxious atmosphere drew their first breath in the same town, before the air of Nithsdale had become morally contaminated by a tyrant king and his minions. James Carran, John Renwick, and Andrew M'Lellan, all householders in Dumfries, were, among a multitude of other Covenanters, the flower of the country in every sense, cast out of it as if they had been vile human weeds, and died prematurely in exile.†

Whilst the sword of persecution was being wielded with increasing fury, the wretched King who had allowed it to be unsheathed died in the midst of his revels, not without suspicion of having been poisoned. In his closing moments he received the last rites of the Romish Church—thus avowing a faith which he had long secretly cherished. He was succeeded by his brother the Duke of York as James the Seventh; who was not only an avowed and bigoted member of the Papal Church, but had never concealed his wish to establish it, and undo the Reformation throughout the British dominions. For a brief space after his accession the Covenanters enjoyed a breathing time : anon the butcheries were renewed ; and when the punishment of death was commuted for transportation to the American colonies the sufferers were savagely marked to prevent their returning—the men having their ears lopped off, and the women being branded on the cheek. On the 30th of June, 1685, the Earl of Argyle was beheaded at Edinburgh, after the failure of an attempt made by him to defeat by force the despotic and Romanising policy of the

* Ibid, p. 326.

† It must not be supposed that we accept as beyond challenge all the instances of persecution recorded by Wodrow ; he seems at times to have been too credulous ; but, after making every reasonable deduction on this account, there still remain a vast number of well authenticated cases, of which those specified by us are merely a sample.

King—the martyred nobleman testifying on the scaffold that he
died a Protestant, and "not only a Protestant, but with a heart-
hatred of Popery, Prelacy, and all superstition whatever." Other
victims followed ; and their blood was not altogether shed in vain
—proving as it did "the seed of Freedom's tree," that still had its
roots fixed in the British soil, and was destined, ere many more
years elapsed, to flourish in unprecedented vigour.

James, encouraged by the overthrow of Argyle's attempt, and
the suppression of a similar movement made in England by
Monmouth, developed his measures with increasing boldness.
That he might advance his Roman Catholic subjects to offices
of power, he, under the colour of a universal act of clemency, set
aside certain political disqualifications, the repeal of which incidentally benefited the Covenanters. Afterwards, early in 1687,
he by direct means endeavoured to conciliate them : first by a
permission to assemble for worship in private houses during the
royal pleasure ; then by allowing all Presbyterians to worship in
their own churches, by repealing all the laws against them,
leaving only those that prohibited* field preaching in full force
Many ministers accepted this toleration ; and favoured by it,
the Synod of Glasgow and Ayr met in August of the same year,
after a long interval, to resume their deliberations.

The young Nithsdale hero Renwick, with many of his brethren,
rejected these indulgences, because they emanated from an impure
source, were clogged with dishonourable conditions, and were
meant as part of the price with which the sovereign sought to
purchase the establishment of Popery. He protested against
them as a mockery and a snare : the Government retaliated by
offering a large reward to any one who would seize him, dead or
alive. Bearing still unflinchingly the Banner of the Covenant,
his conscience would not permit him to make any compromise
that might stain its unspotted blue ; and thus, defending the
ensign of the Church, separating himself from its pliant friends,
defying its implacable enemies, bearding the power of the
deceitful King, he became exposed to perils innumerable. "Thirteen times during the one year (1687) had the troops made the
strictest search for him throughout the whole country, prying
into every cellar, and tearing off the thatch and pulling down
the ceilings of the houses. He had to travel in disguise by the
most unfrequented paths, chased like a partridge on the mountains ; and to him the mist was a protecting garment, and the
dead hour of midnight the guardian of his footsteps. He lived in
rude and remote cottages, in shepherds' huts on the top of the
hills, in bosky forests, in caves and in rocks. Wherever he was,
he had watchers stationed all round to give the alarm. He
preached with a fleet horse standing beside him, saddled and

bridled, on which he could mount in a moment, and leave far behind him all the troopers in Scotland."*

Renwick eluded their vigilance, whilst he continued preaching and testifying in his native district; but when visiting Edinburgh, in January, 1688, on business connected with a protest against the indulgences, which he had forwarded to the General Assembly, then sitting, he was apprehended in the house of a Cameronian friend, where he lodged, tried on charges of disowning the King, refusing to pay the cess, condemning the toleration, maintaining the right of self-defence, and holding conventicles; and having been found guilty on his own confession, he was adjudged to death. Before his execution, whilst he lay in prison bands, strenuous efforts were made to induce him to recant—he was even tempted with the offer of life if he would only renounce the principles for which he had been condemned; but he resisted the insidious tempters who visited his cell with the same courage that enabled him to tread the hills of Closeburn, or the moors of Kyle, with the step of a freeman, when to do so was counted treason.

On the day fixed for his execution (the 17th of February) the Privy Council, fearing, if he made a speech from the scaffold, that it would dangerously excite the populace, enjoined him by a messenger to refrain from so doing, and intimating that if he offered to speak the drums would be set abeating. With characteristic resolution he repudiated this last attempt at dictation by his persecutors; and though, when he delivered his farewell address, the roll of the drums rose harsh and high, a few broken sentences of it were caught by the eager ears of his followers, " and treasured up as the precious fragments of a distinguished martyr's dying testimony." " I leave my testimony," he said, "approving the preaching of the Gospel in the fields, and the defending of the same by arms. I adjoin my testimony to all that hath been sealed by blood, shed either on scaffolds, fields, or seas, for the cause of Christ. I leave my testimony against Popery, Prelacy, Erastianism; against all profanity, and everything contrary to sound doctrine; particularly against all usurpations made in Christ's right, who is the Prince of the Kings of the earth, who alone must bear the glory of ruling His own kingdom, the Church; and, in particular, against the absolute power usurped by this usurper, that belongs to no mortal, but is the incommunicable prerogative of Jehovah; and against this toleration flowing from that absolute power."

Under such circumstances died the pious, gifted, and heroic James Renwick, just as he had completed his twenty-sixth year. Nine months afterwards he would, if alive, have been hailed as a noble champion of national freedom. Pity that William of

* Dodds's Fifty Years' Struggle, p. 371.

Orange did not arrive in February instead of November, for
then the scaffold would have been cheated of its last Covenanted
victim. But the illustrious sufferer laid down his life cheerfully,
and, as he himself declared, was ready to give ten hundred lives
if he had possessed them, in the maintenance of the glorious
cause.

In order that the King's scheme for subverting Protestantism
might be promoted, the oath by which officials professed their
adherence to it was set aside ; and thus the door was opened for
the admission of Roman Catholics to places of trust and power.
By means of this device, Dumfries—Presbyterian and Covenanting
though most of its inhabitants were—came to be furnished with
a Romanist chief magistrate. Mr John Coupland was Provost of
the burgh for the three years ending Michaelmas, 1683 ; at which
term, James, Lord Drumlanrig, was chosen as his successor, and
continued in office three years, though he was never present at
the deliberations of the Council, and seems to have been little
more than the nominal ruler of the town.   In 1686 no new
magistrates were appointed.   Before the preliminary steps for
the annual election could be taken a prohibitory letter was
received by the authorities from the Lord Chancellor of Scotland.*
It was addressed on the back, "For the Provost and Baylies of
the Brugh of Dumfreise, or any of them to whom this shall be
first addressed, to be communicat to the Town Council—in heast ;"
and ran thus :—" Affectionat freinds, Whereas his sacred Majestie
hes by his royell Letter daited at the Court of Windsor, the
twenty day of September instant, signified that all elections in
royall burrows be suspendit untill his royall pleasure be known
theranent : you are ther for in pursuance therof heirby expresslie
prohibited and discharged, as you will answear at youre perill, to
elect any new magistrats or counsell within your burgh for this
yeir : and you and the present counsell are by his Majestie's
authoritie heir by authorised to continew and exist as magistrats
and counsell until his Majestie shall signifie his further pleasure
Signed at command and in name of his Majestie's Privie Counsell
—By—Your affectionat freind,

Edinburgh, the 16th   PERTH, cancell.,
   September, 1686.   I. P. D.

In accordance with this arbitrary exercise of the royal
prerogative Lord Drumlanrig and the other syndics of the town
continued at the head of affairs for another year ; and when 1687
arrived his Majesty thought he might safely venture to stretch
it a great way further, by nominating as Provost a distant
relative of the powerful Nithsdale family, and who, like its head,
was devoted to his interests and a decided Romanist. The
Council having met on the 6th of January in the above year,

* Burgh Records.

John Maxwell of Barncleugh, Irongray,* appeared, and presented two acts of the Privy Council, dated the 16th of December, 1686, in one of which he was nominated by them as Provost of Dumfries, and the existing bailies, dean, treasurer, and councillors were authorised to continue officiating as such for the ensuing year. The other Act was in the following terms :—" Whereas the Lords of his Majestie's Privy Counsell have, by their act of the date heirof, pursueant to a letter direct to them from the King's most excellent Majestie, nominat and appointed the magistrats and other counsellors therein mentioned for the Brugh of Drumfreis, and particularly John Maxwell of Barncleugh to be proveist theirof, with the dispensatione after mentioned ; therefore the

---

* So many families of distinction in Galloway and Dumfriesshire are connected by blood or marriage with the Maxwells of Barncleugh, that the following genealogical note may be deemed interesting. Thomas Maxwell, merchant burgess in Dumfries at the end of the sixteenth century, was a younger son of Maxwell of Kirkconnell   Thomas married Agnes Rig, whose father was a notary in Dumfries. John, their son and heir, married in 1637 Agnes Irving, daughter of John Irving. On the 7th of July, 1638, he obtained from George Rome of Irongray a wadsett right of the lands of Barncleugh and others. Agnes Irving survived her husband, and married secondly Robert Maxwell of Carnsalloch ; and it was their only son who became Provost of Dumfries under the curious circumstances described in the text. Provost Maxwell married Margaret, daughter of John Irving (Provost of Dumfries in 1661-2-3-4 and 5, and again in 1668-9-70-1-2 and 3), by Elizabeth Crichton, his wife, who was daughter of Sir Robert Crichton of Ryehill, a brother of the Earl of Dumfries. James Maxwell, eldest son of the Provost, married Janet Carruthers, a widow, whose first husband was Alexander Johnstone. He married secondly, Mary, daughter of Dr James Wellwood, a distinguished member of the College of Physicians, London, and whose father, of the same name, was parish minister of Tundergarth. By his second wife, James had Barbara Maxwell, who married James Johnstone, brother of Thomas Johnstone of Clauchrie, a cadet of the Westerhall family, Annandale. Wellwood Johnstone, born in 1747, youngest and only surviving son of James Johnstone and Barbara Wellwood, succeeded in 1776 as Wellwood Maxwell of Barncleugh, on the death of James Maxwell of Barncleugh, son of Wellwood's grandfather by the first marriage. Wellwood Maxwell (or Johnstone) married Catherine, daughter of John Maxwell of Terraughtie. He died in 1833, leaving five sons, John, Wellwood, Alexander, William, and George, and three daughters, Agnes, Mary, and Catherine. John, the eldest, born in 1784, married in 1815 his cousin, Clementina Herries Maxwell, heiress of Munches, and died in 1843, leaving a son, Wellwood Herries Maxwell, born in 1817, now of Munches, and member of Parliament for the Stewartry of Kirkcudbright. He married, in 1844, Jane Home, eldest daughter of Sir William Jardine, Bart., the eminent naturalist, and chief of the ancient family of Applegarth. (a) Wellwood, Alexander, and George carried on business together as merchants in Liverpool. The latter, who was the proprietor of Glenlee, and unsuccessfully contested the representation of the Stewartry in 1857, died in 1858. The two other brothers, Wellwood Maxwell of The Grove, and Alexander Maxwell of Glengaber, after amassing a fortune, spent the autumn of their honourable and useful lives together at The Grove, and died within a few months of each other, in 1867. William, a Liverpool merchant, and Catherine, now Mrs Davis, still survive.

(a) Died 13th August, 1900, aged 82, and succeeded by his son William Jardine Herries Maxwell, M.P. for Dumfriesshire.

said Lords doe heirby require and command the said John Maxwell to be entered and admitted proveist of the said brugh without taking the test, or any other oath, prescribed by law, except the oath *de fideli administratione*, conforme to his Majestie's said letter."

Mr Maxwell had for some time previously to this appointment been town-clerk of Dumfries, and appears to have occupied a highly respectable position in both burgh and county. It need scarcely be said that the commands of the Privy Council respecting his appointment were implicitly obeyed. Barncleugh, as he was usually called, remained Provost for the current year; and soon after it expired, another edict came down from Edinburgh authorising his re-appointment, and embodying such other orders as rendered the whole members of the burghal senate nominees of the Romanising Court. This tyrannical missive is so richly illustrative of King James's general policy at this time, as well as so interesting locally, that we must introduce it *verbatim*. The Town Council having met on the 22nd of February, 1688, received and resolved to give effect to the following letter, dated the 9th of that month :—" The Lords of his Majestie's Privie Counsell, in pursuance of his Majestie's royall commands, signified to them in a letter dated at Court of Whitehall, the tenth day of November last, heirby nominate and appoynt the persones underwrit to be Magistrats and Counsell of the Brugh of Drumfreis during this current year, they being such whom his Majestie judges most loyall and ready to promote his service, and most forward to support the good and interest of the said brugh, viz. :—John Maxwell of Barncleugh, to be proveist thereof ; John Irving (son to the deceast John Irving, late proveist), Walter Newall, and John Rome, bailies ; Andrew Coupland, dean of gild, and James Dalzell to continue treasurer ; and Gavin Carlyle, merchant ; Richarde Gibsone, merchant: John Leith, merchant ; and John Shillingtoune, merchant, to be new counsellors ; and the deacons of crafts to be John Corsbie, present deacon of the squairemen, and deaconconvener ; John Dicksone, deacon of the shoemakers, John Mairtine, deacon of the ffleshers, Thomas Dicksone, deacon of the weavers, William Blacklock, deacon of taylers, Walter Newall, deacon of the smiths, and James Lawsone, deacon of the glovers— all which persones are heirby authorized to continue in their respective offices untill Michaelmas next to come, in the year 1688 ; and appoynts the twentie-twa day of Ffebruary instant ffor their entrance and admittance. And recommends to the Shereff-Principal of Drumfreis, or his depute, or any of them, to be present and to sie his Majestie's pleasoure afoiresaid regularly and effectually put in execution."

Before " Michaelmas next " had come and gone, however, the King's fortunes had reached a perilous stage. When, in the summer of this eventful year, he caused six bishops of the Church of England to be sent to the Tower because they refused to allow a crowning Act of Indulgence to Papists to be read in their churches, the storm that had been long gathering reached a crisis. The nation was still Protestant at heart; and now, thoroughly aroused by the infatuated conduct of the bigoted King, turned for relief to his nephew and son-in-law, William Prince of Orange, already distinguished as the protector of the Reformed faith against Louis XIV. of France. Responding to the expressed wish of the country, William landed at Torbay on the 5th of November, with about 14,000 men; and, as has been well said, "his march through the English counties was more like a military promenade or triumphal procession, than an invasion in which the crown of three kingdoms was to be won."

King James, after leaving London in dismay, departed in a fishing-smack from the land that had literally cast him out, and to which he never returned. Renwick denounced his reign as a usurpation; and it was now so regarded by all save the sect he had pampered, and the minions he had promoted. Many of the latter, sharing his alarm, followed him in his flight. His Commissioner in Scotland, the Earl of Perth, never for once thought of making a bold stroke on behalf of his royal master, but fled, like his officials in London, when startled from their propriety by the hurried tramp of the troops from Holland. To the honour of the populace, no bloody saturnalia were indulged in when the power of the detested Privy Council was broken, and they and their satellites, the Episcopal clergy, were left defenceless. The people of Scotland, who had suffered from a cruel oppression for twenty-eight years, rejoiced when the day of deliverance came, but resorted to no violent acts of retaliation or vengeance, well content when they saw the last of their persecutors—when the Test and the Abjuration Oath, the thumb-screw and the bootikin, the hangman's rope and the headsman's axe, and all the vile system of mental and physical torture from which they had suffered, vanished with the men who had planned and carried them mercilessly into effect.

The great lords of the Court decamped like the King, and so did the smaller magnates whom, in his zeal for Romanism, he had invested with civic rule. Before Michaelmas day, 1688, came round, in Dumfries the cry arose, "Where is the Provost?" He had disappeared suddenly, and no one could tell his whereabouts. Little did he imagine at midsummer of that year that before many months elapsed he would be degraded from office, a fugitive and an exile. It seemed really at one time as if the Papal Church had acquired its old predominance in the town; its chief magistrate, and some of his subordinates, were devoted members of it, and basking under the radiance of the house of Nithsdale, as well as of the royal favour, they thought "their bow would long abide in its strength;" and that, by and by, mass would be said in St. Michael's, and Protestantism be fairly sent to the wall.

The better to consolidate his power, Provost Maxwell had left his residence in the country, and commenced housekeeping in Dumfries on a grand scale—lavish hospitality then, even more than now, being deemed a valuable auxiliary to municipal government. The members of the Corporation appreciated his liberality so much that on the 5th of April, 1688, when the political sky was yet untroubled, they adopted a grateful resolution on the subject, as embodied in the following minute :—" The Counsell taking to their consideratione the expense and trouble of John Maxwell of Barncleugh, their present proveist, in comeing with his family from the country to dwell in this brugh, not only in taking of a lodgeing, and other incident charges, bot in taking in of wines to his house, to sustaine the inevitable charge of his office ; and it being customary in other burrowes of note to lay in provisione of wynes yearly to their proveist out of their common good ; thairfore, and for his incuradgment to dwell within this brugh, the Counsell have thought fitt to allow, and doe heirby allow to him of cellarie for this present yeir, and yierly in tyme comeing, during his Majestie's will to continue him in the said office,·the sum of ffyve hundred merks Scotts money, with ane tierce of Ffrench wyne yearly, provydeing alwayes the common good of the brugh be so manadged be him that it shall not be burdened with any accompt of incident charges, or accompts of spending be him within brugh, except at extraordinar occasiones, to be approven or not by the Counsell."*

Jovial doings are indicated by this extract from the minutes of Council ; but brief though merry was the burghal reign of Barncleugh. News of Prince William's landing having reached the town, a sympathising crowd of the inhabitants gathered in the market place on the evening of the 17th of December, and proceeded noisily through some of the streets. We cannot tell whether or not they threatened the magistrates, or passed revolutionary resolutions : they must, however, in some highly significant way have shown their antipathy to the ruling powers, and their sympathy with the Prince's movement, since Provost Maxwell no more ventured to appear at the Council Board, and the Bailies had to organise an armed force for the purpose of preserving tbe peace of the town. Again, on the 25th of December (Christmas Day), the populace made a fierce anti-Romanist demonstration. " They collected," says Burnside, " from the religious houses in the neighbourhood all the remains of Popish vestments and imagery they could lay their hands upon ; they

* Town Council Minutes.

tore down the carved work from the upper storey of the Castle of Dumfries, wherein mass had been celebrated, and burnt all together, with effigies of the Pope, at the Market Cross."* Before the month closed, the Revolution was received by the nation as an accomplished fact ; and Dumfries, like other parts of Scotland, was once more in the enjoyment of religious and municipal freedom—exempt alike from the scourge of the Persecution and the Papal incubus.

The first evidence of this happy change is supplied by a minute of the Town Council, dated 26th December, from which we learn that on that day a letter was received by the civic body from Lord Athole, President of the reconstructed Privy Council, restoring to the burghal representatives of Dumfries the right to elect their own magistrates. We subjoin the substance of this important communication :—" Gentlemen, his Majestie's Privy Council understanding that, in the late nominatione of Magistrats and Counsell for your brugh, Papists have been imployed in offices of power and trust among you, which may occasion fears and jealousies, to the indangering of the peace and quiet, and the Counsell being willing to remove any ground of such fears, have thought fitt heirby to authorise the Magistrats and Town Counsell who were in before any such nominatione, and were legally chosen by your predecessors, to meit and choose Magistrats and Counsell for the ensuing year, conforme to the custome and constitution of your brugh : for doeing whereof this shall be to you, and all who may be herein concerned, a sufficient warrant."† In accordance with these instructions the Council, on the following day, by " a plurality of votes," chose the Presbyterian Laird of Duchrae,‡ Mr

---

* The New Church of Dumfries was built upon the site of the Castle, and partly out of its remains. In 1866 the church was taken down to make room for a more imposing ecclesiastical structure—named Greyfriars' Church —and during this process some relics were picked up, the most interesting of which was a bronze image of the Saviour, four and a half inches in length, very artistically executed. The position of the figure, with the expression of the face, shows that it must have been attached to a cross, and have formed, with its wooden appendage, such a crucifix as is used by Roman Catholic worshippers. The arms were wanting, and they were probably fractured by the forcible removal of the image from the cross. The likelihood is that it formed part of the furnishings of an upper chamber of the Castle that was used as a chapel, dedicated to St. Bride, when the fortress belonged to the Maxwell family, and that it was torn down during the wrecking of the chapel as described above.

† Town Council Minutes.

‡ RATIFICATION OF WILLIAM CRAIK OF ARBIGLAND, 1681.—" Our Sovereign Lord affirmes and confirms the charter made and granted by his Majestie under the Great Seale, at Whitehall, the eight day of June, 1666, in favour of his Majestie's lovit William Craik, Provost of Dumfries. . . . . all and haill the lands of Duchraw, extending to ane ten-pound land of old extent, containing and comprehending the particular lands underwritten, viz. :—the lands of Tornorroch, Rone, Drumglass, the two Duchraws, Clone, Barbech, Uroch, Uliack, The Maines, the two Craigs, Drumbreck, with the

William Craik, who had ruled over the burgh before as Provost,
and they superseded six members by appointing other six in
whom they had more confidence. The radical change thus effected
in the government of the town caused considerable commotion
amongst the Romanist party. For the " care and diligence shewn
by the authorities in preventing threatened disturbances," they
received a letter of thanks from the Privy Council, which com
munication closed in these terms :—" We doe aprove of your
procedure in this affair, and look upon it as good and acceptable
service at such a dangerous juncture as this, and alowes you to
detain as prisoners in your tolbuith thos persons apprehended be
you on this account, except the Laird of Barncleugh, your late
proveist, who is to be sent hither prisoner by the gentry of your
shire, by order of the Laird of Lag,* and others who have the
Counsell's former commands anent him ; and the Counsell doe
heirby give order and warrant to Lag and Closeburn, or any two
of your Toune Counsell, to sight what is in the said Barncleugh's
cloak-bag, found with him, for his disguise, and to delyver to him
such papers therein as properly belong to himselfe ; and such as
pertaine to your toune, to you ; and such as belong to the public
to be sent, under your sealls, to the Clerke of Counsell. Your cair
and diligence for the future, to prevent troubles and to keip peace
amongst yourselves, and keiping your toune in a conditione of
defence for the Protestant religion and security of the kingdom, is
expected, ther being ane frie electione allowed you by the Counsell, in whose name this is signified to you by your humble
servant, ATHOLE."†
    We thus see that the missing ex-Provost, who was objected to
solely on account of his religion, was found at last ; and the records show that after being for a while imprisoned in Dumfries he
was sent to Edinburgh—where, we doubt not, he was leniently
dealt with, like other great offenders. On the 9th of January,
1689, the new Town Council met under the presidency of Provost
Craik, and gave orders that the Prince of Orange should be proclaimed King at the Market Cross. This coremony, however, was
not performed till the 24th of April, in order, probably, that due
time might be given for rendering it imposing. A minute of the
preceding day states that the Council had fixed " the morrow,

---

milne of Duchraw, milne lands, multure, &c., togither with the fishing in the
water of Die, belonging to the said lands, all lying within the parochis of
Balmaghie and Stewartrie of Kirkcudbright and Sheriffdome of Dumfries."—
Acts of Scot. Parl., vol. viii., p. 393.

    * It thus appears that Sir Robert Grierson managed, in spite of his past
misdeeds, to gain favour from the Revolution Government, which may be
accounted for by the circumstance that he was brother-in-law to the abler but
almost equally pliant Queensberry, as well as by the necessities of the new
Administration.
                        † Town Council Minutes.

betwixt thrie and four o'clock in the afternoon, for proclaiming
King William and Queen Mary, King and Queen of Scotland, with
all solemnities used in such caises, conforme and in obedience to
the meiting of the Estates, their proclamatione published thereanent; and appoynts intimatione to be made throu the toune be
touk of drum to the effect the inhabitants may appear in the
Sandbeds at the bating of the drum, in their best arms." The
treasurer's accounts show that "10 pound 6 unce of powder," value
£8 6s Scots, was burnt on the joyous occasion; that whilst the
cannons fired salutes, a bonfire made of "9 gritt loads of peitts,"
costing £1 16s, sent forth a ruddy blaze; and that the health of
the new sovereigns was toasted at the Cross in six "pynts of
ale," ordered by Bailie Irving;* indoors, doubtless, the same toast
would be honoured in more patrician liquor.

Whilst these events were transpiring, Graham of Claverhouse,
no longer hunting Covenanting game on the hills of Dumfriesshire
and Galloway, hurried to the Highlands with the view of upholding the desperate fortunes of King James. Complimented with a
coronet by the royal fugitive, who had really ceased to be the
"fountain of honour," Claverhouse entered upon his chivalrous
enterprise, and for the first time in his career appeared as a hero.

> " He waved his proud arm, and the trumpets were blown,
>   The kettle-drums clashed, and the horsemen rode on ;
>   Till on Ravelstone crags, and on Clermiston lea,
>   Died away the wild war-note of Bonnie Dundee."

But the cause he sought to maintain was rotten at the core.
King James was doomed; and the days of the doughty cavalier on
whom he placed his chief reliance were numbered. Though
victory smiled on the royal flag at Killiecrankie, it was with a
faint, dismal, deceptive smile, in view of the dead Dundee—all
gory and cold as ever lay John Brown on the sward of Muirkirk,
or any of the persecutor's other victims in the glens of Nithsdale.
The fall of Viscount Dundee, on the 17th of June, 1689, the failure
of his followers before Dunkeld, and the decisive defeat of James
at the battle of Boyne in the following year, destroyed all the
remaining hopes of the Stuart dynasty; and the dis-crowned
monarch, deeply mortified by the failure of his schemes and the
overthrow of his house and throne, retired to France.

Mr Richard Brown, the prelatical curate of St. Michael's, who
succeeded Mr Alexander Cairncroce † in 1684, disappeared about
the same time as the papistical Provost; and on the 15th of
August, a month after the battle of Killiecrankie, the Presbyterian

---

* Burgh Treasurer's Accounts.

† Mr Cairncroce, who was seventeen years parson of Dumfries, was, on
the recommendation of the Duke of Queensberry, promoted to the see of
Brechin in August, 1684, and to the bishopric of Glasgow at the close of the
same year.

form of church government was once more, after an interval of
twenty-six years, brought into full operation in Dumfries.   A
meeting of Session was held that day, attended by Mr George
Campbell, reponed as minister of the parish, John Irving of Drum-
coltran (afterwards Provost of the burgh), and John Shortridge
(formerly deacon of the glovers), elders; assisted by Mr Robert
Paton, minister of Terregles, who had that day preached in St.
Michael's Church.   The Session having been duly constituted by
prayer, proceeded to consider what could be done in the way of
constituting ruling elders and deacons, so as to fill up the blanks
created during the persecuting times.   A lamentation was made
" that hitherto there was little access by reason of many letts and
impediments in the way, and that difficulties not a few did continue."   "Nevertheless," continues the record, "seeing endeavours
should be essayed, there was ane list offered of persons fit for these
employs; and, forasmuch as some of these had been in the time of
the late violent trials and troubles, hurried into a sad compliance
with illicit engagements, who in the judgment of charity are
looked upon as much grieved for, and dissatisfied with themselves
for that, and judged to be no less fit, but more than many others,
it was enquired what was fit to be done for such."*   This question
having been fully debated, it was unanimously agreed that the
persons referred to should be desired to signify before the minister
and one or two elders their sorrowful sense of their conduct, and
that other likely individuals not similarly involved should be
requested to attend next meeting of the court.   Accordingly on
the following day several elders and deacons, after professing
penitence for having taken the Test, were received into the
Session.   Others were afterwards admitted, so that by the 30th of
the month the elders numbered thirteen, and the deacons twelve.

For some time before the Revolution Mr Campbell, Mr Paton,
and Mr Francis Irving, the faithful remnant of the Dumfries
Presbytery, met occasionally to exercise a stealthy jurisdiction
over the district; and when King James, for his own purposes,
put a grain or two of toleration into his government, these
ministers, officiating more openly and systematically, supplied
pastors not only to several parishes within the bounds, but to
Canonby, Borgue, Glencairn, and others, Mr Campbell at the
same time preaching occasionally to the faithful remnant of his
flock in a small meeting-house situated in the East Barnraw, now
called Loreburn Street.†   Before 1690 commenced, not only the
Session, but the Presbytery and Synod of Dumfries, were re-con-
structed, and the parish and county were placed once more, by the

---

* Session Records.

† " Raw," or " row," was synonymous with street.   The High Street
was the " Midraw," Chapel Street was "Rattenraw," and now Loreburn
Street was " East Barnraw."

authority of Parliament, under that ecclesiastical system which
the greater portion of their inhabitants had openly or secretly
adhered to during all the protracted troubles of the Persecution.

The delight of the Dumfriesians in getting back their old
minister, Mr Campbell, must have been very great; but his
venerable father-in-law and colleague, Mr Henderson, never
preached to them again, after parting from them in 1662, and he
died an exile from the parish before Presbyterianism was restored.
In October, 1690, Mr Campbell again took farewell of his flock,
but this time under different circumstances, the General Assembly
having appointed him Professor of Divinity in the University of
Edinburgh—"a situation," says M'Crie, "which he was extremely
averse to, but for which he was eminently qualified by the learning and modesty ascribed to him, even by the avowed detractors
of the Presbyterian ministers of that period." Considerable difficulty was experienced in finding a suitable successor at Dumfries
for this good man and gifted preacher, and it was not till nearly
four years afterwards that one was obtained, in the person of the
celebrated Mr William Veitch.

When only twenty-six years of age Veitch, as stated in his
memoirs, was "prevailed with, by Mr John Welsh, minister of
Irongray, and others, who came to his house at the Westhills of
Dunsyre, to join with that party who were so oppressed by the
inhuman cruelties and excessive robberies of Sir James Turner
and the forces he commanded, lying at Dumfries, for their non-
compliance with abjured Prelacy, so that they were necessitated
to endeavour their own relief if possible."* Though not present
when the persecutor was captured, he thoroughly identified himself with the insurgents, took part in the battle of Pentlands, and
narrowly escaped from that disastrous field. When, towards
nightfall, the Covenanting ranks were broken, he "fell in," to use
his own words, "with a whole troop of the enemy, who turned his
horse violently in the dark, and carried him along with them, not
knowing but that he was one of their own." "But," he goes on to
say, "as they fell down the hill in pursuit of the enemy, he held
upward till he got to the outside of them, and the moon rising
clear, which made him fear he would presently be discovered, he
saw no other way of escape but to venture up the hill, which he
did, being well mounted; which, when the enemy perceived, they
cried out, 'Ho! this is one of the rogues that has commanded
them?' Several pursued him up the hill a little, and shot at him
sundry times, but their horses sunk, and were not able to ascend
the hill, so that he escaped, and came that night to a laird's house
in Dunsyre Common, within a mile of his own dwelling."†

Mr Veitch, after continuing in hiding for several days, fled to
the North of England, where he resided many years, ministering

* M'Crie's Memoirs of William Veitch, pp. 23-4.　　　† Ibid, p. 44.

to various attached congregations, when such a liberty was allowed him. In 1678, when Prelacy was rampant, he was apprehended at Stanton, near Morpeth, on a magistrate's warrant, charged with being "a preacher or teacher to the Nonconformists in the Church of England," and with being an outlawed rebel fugitive from Scotland. Dragged before the Scottish Privy Council, he was subjected to a searching interrogation by Archbishop Sharpe; and, as the Council failed to make him criminate himself, and they had no evidence of his having been engaged in the Pentland rising, he was sent back to prison. "The next news was a letter from the King to turn him over to the criminal court, and there to intimate an old illegal sentence of death unto him;" but, owing to an opportune change in his Majesty's counsellors, and much influence being used in his behalf, the sentence was commuted to the lenient one of banishment from Scotland for life, in virtue of which he was left at liberty to rejoin his old friends in Northumberland.

At the Revolution this uncompromising champion of the Covenant, who had suffered so much for his principles, obtained welcome repose. Several calls from vacant parishes having been addressed to him, he accepted one from Peebles, where he remained for four years, though, strangely enough, objections to his settlement there were made at the instigation of the Duke of Queensberry, on account of his being compromised in the Pentland affair; and before these were finally disposed of he received competing calls from Edinburgh and Dumfries, the latter of which, in accordance with the decision of the Assembly, he accepted in September, 1694. Mr Veitch, as he himself narrates, was at first disinclined to accept the charge demitted by Mr Campbell, and only did so after preaching repeatedly at Dumfries, and "acquainting himself with the people;" and, he adds, "this was a great encouragement, that after several conferences with some leading persons in the town, wherein he told them, among other differences needless here to be mentioned, that except they would free him of the drawing of the tithes (with which he had got on the finger-ends at Peebles, and 'burnt bairns fire dread') and take tack thereof from him as long as he should continue minister of the place, he could not settle among them. They at length, consulting among themselves, complied with this, and so he set them a tack of them so long as he was to continue their minister, at the rate that they had often told him the tithes were worth, viz., twenty-two hundred merks per annum, out of which he is obliged, by charter from the King, to pay the second minister four hundred merks per annum."*

In the following year Mr Veitch concurred with his Session and the magistrates in giving a call to Mr Robert Paton, minister of Carlaverock, who was admitted as his colleague in February, 1696. It is pleasant to contemplate the venerable man, after all

* Memoirs, p. 191,

his troubles and trials, ministering in comfort to his Dumfries congregation, and looked up to with respect throughout the parish. He had been of some service to Mr Gilbert Elliot, afterwards Lord Minto, when that young lawyer was in a humble condition, for which favour his lordship had afterwards an opportunity of shewing his gratitude ; and when the old friends met in Dumfries, which they often did, their conversation was sure to turn on the perils of the Persecution, contrasted with the peace of the present times. On one of these occasions Lord Minto facetiously remarked, " Ah ! Willie, Willie ! had it not been for me, the pyets wad hae been pyking your pate on the Netherbow Port !" and Mr Veitch's happy response was, "Ah ! Gibbie, Gibbie ! had it no been for me, ye would have been writing papers for a plack the page !" In 1709 his constitution, though vigorous, gave way, so that he had to obtain successive assistants ; one of whom, Mr Patrick Lynn, was ordained on the 19th of May, 1715, as the second minister of Dumfries, Mr Paton being recognised as occupying the first charge. Mr Veitch demitted his charge on the same day, on account of his increasing infirmities, though he still retained a right to preach occasionally. His faithful partner, to whom he had been married fifty-eight years, died in May, 1722 ; and next day he breathed his last, at the ripe age of eighty-two.

CHAPTER XXXIX.

FROM a very early period, down till the Union with England, the
burgh, or rather its Council, as an electoral college, sent a Commissioner to the Estates, or Parliament, the Provost being often
appointed as such. The name of the burgh usually appears as
the fifteenth on the Parliamentary roll, a place that indicated the
period of its erection rather than its rank. An Act passed in
1701 in favour of Dumbarton, reserves the right of the members
of Ayr, Irvine, Renfrew, Dumfries, and several other burghs, to
ride, sit, and vote, and take precedence in all national meetings
before the representative of the said burgh. In the reigns of the
Jameses, and for a century afterwards, Dumfries had a much
higher relative position than that which it now occupies.
Chalmers, writing in 1823, observes that "Dumfries has gradually
changed its place of precedence, as it has increased in people and
prosperity. According to the tax roll of 1771, it stood the seventh
on the scale of assessment of sixty-six royal burghs, there being
only six higher, and no fewer than fifty-nine lower." By a reference to the tax roll of earlier years we find that the town occupied
a still higher grade than the author of " Caledonia" assigns to it.
In the roll of 1695 Edinburgh stands first, and is rated at £35
Scots ; Glasgow follows far behind, at a rating of £15, which,
however, rose ten years afterwards to £20 ; Aberdeen ranks next,
at £6 10s ; Dundee follows, at £5 6s 8d ; then comes Montrose, at
£2 8s ; and next Dumfries, at £1 18s 4d. In 1705 the tax on
Montrose had fallen to £1 13s 8d, and that of Dumfries remained
stationary, making it, in the last-mentioned year, the *fifth* of the
royal burghs, as tested by taxable wealth. The rate on Lochmaben in 1695 was 3s, on Annan 2s, and on Sanquhar 1s. The
oldest tax roll extant, dated 21st February, 1578, makes Dumfries
the eighth royal burgh : at that period its proportion of the
general assessment was £1 7s 6d.

A high degree of prosperity was enjoyed by the burgh during the reign of James IV. ; and though it was more populous at the date of the Revolution, it was relatively poorer, the various troubles through which it passed in the interval having operated discouragingly on its trade and commerce ; while its landed patrimony had become much reduced through improvidence or neglect, and its fishings on the Nith, conferred by royal grant after the Reformation, had passed into private hands. We have no means of knowing what amount of revenue the burgh derived from feus and leases before its common good began to be tampered with, about the beginning of the sixteenth century ; but it must have been considerable as compared with the expenditure, and we know that before the lapse of another hundred years it had become very much reduced. Had that not been the case the " re-edification " of the bridge in 1629 would not have been a very exhaustive effort ; and a more favourable report could have been given of the public finances than the authorities were able to furnish to certain representatives from the Convention of Royal Burghs who in 1692 visited the town to obtain information upon the subject. Provost Rome, Bailie Johnston, Bailie Irving, and Mr Menzies, town-clerk, gave in a statement to the deputies which was the reverse of cheering. " To the best of their knowledge " the common good was worth yearly " 2,666 lib. 13s. 4d., or thereby "—that is to say, about £222 sterling ; and their debts "twentie thousand merks," or nearly £2,100 sterling. We learn from other sources that the bridge custom that year amounted to £122 sterling ; the dues levied at the tron and three ports to about £27 sterling ; and the rent for the meal market to about £22 sterling ; which sums make up within £9 of the whole reported revenue, leaving only that trifling balance to be received for rent of the mills, feus, and other small miscellaneous items not specified.

The inland trade, annually, is said to consist of "thretie packs of linen cloath at twentie pounds sterline the pack, in neat twelve hundred pounds sterline, and other goodes of that nature, to the value of four hundredth and eighty pounds sterline ; five thousand sheep skins, at fyftie pound sterline the thousand, in neat two hundreth and fyftie pound sterline ; sex thousand lamb skins, worth seventeen pounds sterline, which they sell yearly to merchants in Edinburgh and others." It may be inferred, from the silence observed respecting the manufacture of woollen cloth, that that branch of industry, once so flourishing in the burgh, had little or no existence at the date of the report. In retail business, it is stated, there are " ten or twelve merchants' shops,' whose staples are iron, tar, and lint ; " two that sells cloath and London goodes ;" three that deal in drugs ; " some other shops of little accompt, that sell brandy, pipes, tobacco, candle and such

like wares ; " and "there is vented within the burgh about three
tunns of wyne yeirly ; " but "they cannot condescend upon what
malt they consume yeirly, in regard their milns are rouped with
the rest of their common good." As respects liabilities, it is stated
that the minister draws the tiends of the burgh acres for their
share of his stipend, the rest being paid by the landward part of
the parish ; that he is allowed 30 lib. for half the rent of his manse ;
"as also they pay to their schoolmaster, doctors, precentor, and
other their public servants, 970 lib. Scots yeirly ; " all which,
with the interest on the debt of 20,000 merks, is drawn from the
common good. But this is not all : they have out of it to
maintain the fabric of the church, "also the bridge, consisting of
nine large arches, tolbooth, prison houses, milns, miln-dams,
cluses, and school houses," the expense of which is estimated at
£500 Scots annually ; " whereby, and by the expenses of their
Commissioners to the Parliament, Convention, and other publict
charges, their patrimonie is exhausted, and will necessarily end-
gage them to contract debts ; and by reason of the inconvenience
of the river, and the chairges of lighters, it's feared that trade will
totally decay, even tho' there were peace."

Equally doleful is the account given by the reporters regarding two of the chief thoroughfares :—" About twentie tenements
in the High Street ruinous, besides some houses in closses ; and
the wholl north syde of Lochmabanegate totally destroyed by
fire about a twelvemonth since or thereby, a great deal whereof
is as yet unbuilt." Dumfries in 1692 must have been in a woefully
depressed condition to have warranted such statements as these :
though, as the magistrates at the close claimed "to be relieved of
the fyve shilling they were heighted with in the tax roll "* a year

---

* The Convention of Royal Burghs, at their annual meetings in July,
fixed the quotas of land-tax to be paid to the Crown by each burgh, according
to its wealth ; and had power to vary the proportion payable by them according to their prosperity or decay. Use and wont, rather than Acts of Parliament, authorised the Convention to exercise an almost inquisitorial oversight
of the burghs in matters of finance. We quote the following illustrative
minute from the Records of the Convention (vol. i., p. 191), dated at Linlithgow, 15th July, 1584 :—" The samyn day Symon Johnstoun, commissioner for
the burgh of Dumfreis, made offer of the thrid penny mair to the customes of
the said burgh, nor presentlie is payit be James Geddes, customer thairof,
quhilk Commissioners, respecting his gude and profitabill offer, ordanis the
said James to be chargit to compeir in Edinburgh, upon the xviij. day of
October nixt, thair to mak his compte to the burrowis to be appoynted to the
hering and allowing thairof, discharging him of any further using or exercing
of the said office from the said day of Oct. ; and that at the said day of his
comptis he delyver to the additouris of the samyn, the half seill or stamp
being in his possession, and that the magistrates of the said burgh of Dumfreis,
then present in Edinburgh, are sufficient customer and comptroller, for quhame
they [the auditors] sal be answerabill for the dew executioun of thair office to
the burrowis foirsaidis, the said auchtene of Oct. nixtt : quhairunto the said
Symon consented." Rather sharp practice this on the part of the Convention

previously, they perhaps deepened the shadows of the picture for the sake of giving effect to their request. We know that in several preceding years a much more cheerful report was given in by their own treasurer, showing a revenue varying from £300 sterling annually to £320 ; and that in 1699 some separate items of revenue that have been preserved warrant the supposition that the whole would amount to the latter mentioned sum at least In 1699 the bridge customs yielded £118 12s 2d sterling ; the dues at the other three entrances, £24 3s 1d ; Mildamhead Park, £22 4s 5d. If we add for other land rents and feus, say £50 ; for mills, £50 ; for burgess fees, £15 ; for meal market, £20 ; and for miscellaneous branches, £20 ; the aggregate will be nearly £320 which may be accepted as the annual worth of the common good in the closing decade of the seventeenth century.

As regards the commerce of the port, an unfavourable account was also given in 1692 ; but before quoting from it, a few preliminary remarks are called for respecting the river and its estuary. The Solway, into which the Nith flows, has peculiar characteristics, that render it quite a topographical study. Numerous currents meeting near its mouth keep up a perpetual conflict ; and twice in every twenty-four hours the tidal flow, suddenly raised above its ordinary level, and rendered fierce by the tumult, seeks an outvent at the estuary, through which it rushes with a speed that is nowhere rivalled in the United Kingdom, or perhaps in the world. It hurries on, carrying a head four to six feet high, filling up the tortuous channels, and sweeping over the broad level beds of the frith with a rapidity that has earned for its foam-crested billows the title of the white steeds of the Solway.* Gradually, as the tide approaches Dumfries, its pace moderates, and its head is absorbed ; and only on very rare occasions does the briny current surmount the Caul, though before that barrier was erected it must have frequently swept through and far beyond the arches of the bridge. The entire domain of the Solway, except the narrow channel of the Nith, and the waters that enter near its eastern extremity is "alternately a surgy brown sea—now misty with sand and now tinctured with silt, oscillating with the rebound of the tide ; and a naked, flat, unrelieved expanse of sand interposing its dreary projection between the blooming slopes of Cumberland and the finely-outlined and warmly-tinted lands of Scotland. Much of its beach, or rather of its bed, even its broader and more sea-ward parts, is of the same character ; so very much, indeed, that were

—Cashiering the "said James," in his absence, and appointing a new "customer" for Dumfries, because he had offered a trifle more for the customs than the old one.

* Appendix L.

the frith estimated or measured only by the space it covers at low water, it would figure in extremely limited proportions."*

The singularities of the Solway, whether at high or low water, though very interesting as natural phenomena, are rather adverse to the prosaic purposes of trade ; and the red sandstone which stretches athwart the southern shore of the frith forms a rocky bar over the Nith at Kingholmbank, which has always operated discouragingly on the interests of the port and river.

For some time before the end of the sixteenth century Dumfries was the seat of a considerable trade, which soon afterwards suffered a serious reduction. Mr Tucker, a revenue officer appointed by Government to draw up an account of the Scottish ports in 1656, concludes his notice of those in the South as follows :—"Last of all (he says) Dumfreese, a pretty mercat town, but of little trade—that they have being most part by land, either for Leith or Newcastle, the badness of coming into the river upon which it lies hindering their commerce by sea ; soe that whatever they have come that way is comonly and usually landed at Kirkcudbright. This town of Dumfreese was formerly the head port of these parts, the town of Ayre being then within the district of Glasgow ; but there being nothing to doe, the Commissioners thought fit to remove the collector to Ayre."† From the same authority we learn that "the accomt of the beere, ale, acque vitæ lett to farme" in the several shires of Scotland during the year 1655 amounted to £35,054 8s 8d, and that the proportion yielded by the port of Dumfries was £694.

In 1692, as we learn from the report to the Convention, the town owned one large vessel of 140 tons, named the "Elizabeth ;" three of a smaller size—the "Adventure," thirty-six tons ; the "Concord," twenty tons ; the "Providence," also twenty tons ; a boat of three tons and a yawl. The estimated value of the whole fleet was about £300 sterling ; but owing to the want of trade the ships were laid up in port, and out of repair. The commerce with other countries, once considerable, had fallen off to such an extent that during the five preceding years it could be summed up in this narrow compass : "Ane smale ship from France with eighteen tunns of wyne and sex tunns of brandie or thereby ; item, ane other vestell from Noraway with fyve thousand daills ; item, a small vestell from Stockholm, loaded with iron ; item ane other small vestell from Bristoll, of the burden of twentie tunns, loadened with cydar, botles, hopes," and some other small goods of inconsiderable value. At that period there was no quay or harbour on the river or port, and "there being but a small water and very shallow, and sand-banks all down the water twenty

* Sketch of the Solway, in the *Builder*.
† Tucker's Report upon the Settlement of the Revenues of Excise and Customs in Scotland.

miles from the town," the use of lighters from Kirkcudbright and
Isle of Heston was rendered necessary : the outlay for which
"consumed the profit of their trade."*

Gradually the commerce of the port increased, so as to require
a large staff of officers for its supervision ; and though the Union
with England was, as we shall see, viewed with marked displeasure by the burgh, the measure exercised a beneficial influence
on all its business concerns. Consequent on that event, a large
legitimate trade sprung up with the American colonies, which,
added to that already carried on with the north of Europe, contributed much to the prosperity of the port.

The poor of the parish were maintained from the weekly
church door collections ; a small allowance—the interest of £600
sterling — left for that purpose by a benevolent burgess (Dr
Johnston,†) in 1639, for which the rent of the mills was chargeable ;‡ and an occasional tribute levied from the richer class of
burgesses. A glimpse of its pauperism at the close of the
seventeenth century is given in a minute of proceedings taken
by a committee appointed to raise a special fund for indigent
persons in the winter of 1698. After visiting the various quarters
of the town, the committee gave in a list of thirty-eight
individuals, constituting the "most creditable and honest sort of
poor, fallen back burgesses," whom they recommended to be paid
nine pounds sterling quarterly out of Dr Johnston's mortification ;
while, for the sustenance of ninety-four persons in a destitute
condition, the committee proposed to exact from the well-to-do
inhabitants such a sum as would amount to thirty-five pounds
Scots weekly for the half-year ending the following 1st of June—
all which allowances were over and above the "collections at the
kirk door and other church causualities." These figures do not
suggest the existence of any overwhelming amount of pauperism :
it seems, indeed, to have been lighter than the depressing influences, long previously at work, prepared us to expect.

When the magistrates reported on the state of the burgh in

* General Report on Municipal Corporations in Scotland, Appendix, p. 43.

† Dr Robert Johnston was a gentleman of varied accomplishments and
great professional skill. He was brother-in-law to George Heriot, and was
at one time physician to James VI. By his will, dated in the parish of St.
Ann, Blackfriars', London (where he died), he left benefactions to Glasgow,
Dundee, Montrose, Kirkcudbright, and Moffat, as well as to Dumfries. A
bursary connected with Moffat, and an endowment for the usher of the school
there, are still in existence ; but it is supposed that some of his injunctions
were neglected by his executor, Lord Johnston, during the turmoil of the civil
wars.

‡ "1st June, 1678.—I, James Richardson, kirk-treasurer, grants me to
have received fra John Mairtin, town thesaurer, the soume of nine pund
sterling for the hav quarter ; and that off the rent of the mylls, being for the
use of the poor thereof. I grant the resait, and discharges the above-named
John of the foirsaid soume."—Treasurer's Accounts.

1692, they complained that staple commodities were sold to its
prejudice in " several regalities, baronies, kirk-towns," and other
country villages in the vicinity ; one of these was the hamlet of
Bridgend, which has been repeatedly mentioned in our pages.
Soon after Devorgilla's bridge was built a few houses, as has
been already surmised, would probably be planted down at its
terminus on the right bank of the Nith ; and we know that at
a very early date the village, with the ground it occupied,
belonged to the Abbey and College of Lincluden. In 1621 James
VI. annulled the annexation of Bridgend to the Crown, that he
might confer it and other heritages upon his favourite Murray ;
the property being thus designated in the Act passed for that
purpose :—" The tenementis, housses, and yairdis lyand besyid
the Brigend of Dumfreis, quhilk perteinit of auld to the sacris-
tenes and prebendaries of the Colledge Kirk of Lincluden, and
all and haill the fyve-pund land of Truqueir."

A contract of wadsett, dated 9th May, 1635, bears to have
been signed at "Bridgend of Dumfreis ;" and we have seen that
the freemen of the burgh recognised it as a suburb before the
middle of the seventeenth century, and that in 1658 no fewer than
twelve master shoemakers, belonging to the cordwainer's corporation, resided in the village—a proof that then it must have had a
considerable population, amounting perhaps to four hundred at
least. Its growth was fostered by the Maxwells, its feudal
superiors ; but all the strenuous efforts put forth by them to
make it a market town were foiled by the Dumfries Town Council,
who could not bear the idea of having markets to rival theirs set
up on the opposite bank of the river.*

Its oldest surviving house (occupied till lately as an inn) sits
so near the bridge as to receive support from it. In a precept
charter † granted by the Dumfries Council to the owner of the
tenement, James Birkmyre, cooper, dated the 3rd of October,
1660, it is described as " that new house builded upon the far end
of the bridge, on the south syde," which was to be held by him
and his successors in feu farm and heritage for ever, " on payment
theirfor yeirly the soome of ten merks Scots," and on condition of
giving his attendance at the bridge to see that no draughts of
timber be taken across it till the magistrates grant permission.
The charter is signed by Robert Graham, provist ; John Cunyne-
ham, bailie ; Thos. Irvyne, bailie ; Ja. Thomesone, bailie ; Wm.
Craike, deane ; John Irving, thesarer ; Jo. Coupland, counsellor ;

* On the 16th of March, 1663, a minute was drawn up by the Council
showing that " the tacksman of the bridge and town officers were empowered
by antient custom to go to the crofts in Bridgend holding of the town, and
drive all cattle therefrom presented there to sale, and bring them to the Sands,
the ordinary mercat."

† Now in the hands of Mr J. H. M'Gowan, solicitor, Dumfries.

Edward Edgar, counsellor." Bridgend, as we shall afterwards see, was erected into a burgh of barony, under the name of Maxwelltown, in 1810.

Numerous other burghs of barony existed in Dumfriesshire before the seventeenth century was far advanced—Langholm, in Eskdale, Lockerbie and Ecclefechan, in Annandale, Thornhill and Minnyhive, in Nithsdale, all of which remain in vigour ; and the two first-named have grown into populous and flourishing seats of trade. Other baronial burghs that were once prosperous—Torthorwald, (a) Ruthwell, and Amisfield—have fallen into decay ; while Dalgarno, or Dalgarnock, whose merry market tryst lives in Burns's well-known lyric, "Last May a braw wooer,"* has disappeared, leaving no memorial save its romantic burial-ground, where "the rude forefathers of the hamlet sleep." Traces more or less distinct of other deserted villages are visible in various portions of the county. Near Dumfries that of Lincluden, which rose up under shelter of the College, left some remains up till a recent period ; and the site of one on the farm of Terreglestown can be pointed out, though every vestige of it has long since passed away.

When agriculture was neither known as a science nor practised systematically, almost every substantial householder in the burgh was his own grazier; and the wealth of some of them lay, like that of the Bible patriarchs, in herds and flocks. The large extent of the "commonty," or town lands, gave full scope for this pastoral occupation. Even after the territorial patrimony was of small extent, as compared with the ground apparently laid claim to at the Riding of the Marches, it included Castledykes, Kingholm, Milldamhead, Barkerland, a large share of Lochar Moss, and several tofts on the Galloway side of the Nith. A large proportion of the whole was unfenced and used as a common, on which all who paid scot and lot had a right, for a trifling sum, to pasture their cattle.

Early every summer a tuck-of-drum proclamation informed

(a) Item ane charter grantlt be his Majestie under the great seal to Jon. Lord Torthorwald, erecting the town of Torthorwald, in all tyme comeing to be callit the town of Cairleill, in ane free burgh of barronie ; give and power to the inhabitants therein to buy and sell in the said burgh of Cairleill all merchandice pertaining to ane burgh of barronie, with power to have baxters, brousters, fleshers ; and workmen of all airts and trades, pertaining to the libertie of ane burgh of barronie, and to have ane cross and mercat day ilk week, and oppen fairs ilk year, daitit 3 December, 1473." [Old Inventory of Torthorwald and Carlyle Writs, 1686, at Drumlanrig.]—Historical Manuscripts Commission.

* " But a' the neist week, as I fretted wi' care,
  I gaed to the tryst o' Dalgarnock ;
  And wha but my fine fickle lover was there !
  I glowr'd as I'd seen a warlock, a warlock ;
  I glowr'd as I'd seen a warlock ! "

the lieges that the time for grazing had arrived, and that (to borrow from a Council minute, dated 30th May, 1709) "the whole inhabitants of this burgh who have bestiall intended for the Kingholm and Barkerland grass," were to enter them on the following Friday, "conform to their interests in the stent and land rent-rolls, and at this entry to make payment of half ane crown to the treasurer for each soum.* And the treasurer is to attend at the Kirkgate port, at seven of clock in the morning, to receive the same at the entry of the said bestiall;" and appointing those who have beasts for pasture "to repair to the Tolbooth the morrow, to give in notes of their stents and fractions to the magistrates," declaring at the same time, "that no person who is not on the stent-rolls is to have liberty to procure fractions or any privleedge in the grass."

In 1642 the "soumes" of cattle pastured at Kingholm numbered fifty-nine—"Jon Corsane, Proveist," leading the list with an allotment of three; and those of Barkerland amounted to twenty-four. The list of "such of the bestial pertaining to the burgh of Dumfries as were entered to Barkerland the 2nd of June, 1688," apprises us that a small charge was levied on each animal. Thus, John Allan pays 10s Scots money for a cow; James Ritchie 14s for "a naig;"† the whole entrants numbering ninety-three, and paying for the season's grass £61 6s, which sum was probably spent in maintaining the fences of the pasture ground, in feeding a herd, and defraying other incidental expenses. A salaried keeper was regularly appointed to take charge of these burghal quadrupeds when cropping the grass and chewing the cud, and a bovine superior was provided for them, which was sold by public auction at the close of the season. The town lands not let out for grass were granted in feu for the benefit of the revenue; and it is more than suspected that in some instances the feuars conveniently forgot their obligations, and, becoming free squatters on the soil attached to them, were transformed from "puir tenant bodies, scant o' cash," to petty lairds.

The lapse of half a century brought little change in the style

---

* A "soum" was as much ground as would pasture one cow or five sheep.

† For the privilege much higher sums were charged in 1664, as is shown by the appended minute, dated 18th May of that year. "The Counsal, taking into consideration that many of the inhabitants who bear little or no public burthing, nor have not any grass nor land of their awin quherupon to feid their cattle, nor evir payit for any soumes grasse either in the Kingholm or Barkerland, though on pretence of the common pasture [they] have eatin up the Barkerland grass; thairfore for preventing such abuis it is enacted that besyd those horse and nolt quich sall be this yeir meyted for the Kingholm and Barkerland, for quich threttie shilling Scots is to be paid for ilk soume, all other hors and old nolt that sall be keipit within this burgh after Witsonday nixt, and pretendit to be fed upon the common pasture therof, sall pay twentie shilling Scots; and all other stirkis within two years old and above one, ten shilling Scots."

of burghal government: the rulers in 1690-1700 being as prone as their grandfathers to the vice of over-legislation, and as ignorant as they of the natural laws which regulate supply and demand. We find them still guarding with unslumbering vigilance the chartered rights of the burgesses and freemen; endeavouring with laudable but often unavailing zeal to enforce morality, and at least the semblance of religion, by Acts of Council, and inter-meddling with a multitude of petty concerns which had better have been left alone.

On the 22nd of September, 1680, pestered by the children of the Grammar School petitioning for the vacation to begin sooner than usual, they actually passed a resolution rendering such refractory juveniles, and all who absented themselves from the classes before the 5th of September each year, liable to imprison-ment. When the burghal senate could stoop to such trivialities it is less strange to see them causing habitual drunkards and swearers to sign an obligation enforcing their perpetual banish-ment from the burgh; or carrying out several stringent Acts of Parliament directed against intemperance and profanity, in accordance with which "persons convicted of drunkenness, and haunting of taverns and ale-houses after ten of the clock at night, or any tyme of the day except the time of travell or for refresh-ments," were liable to be put in the jugs or jail six hours; and "all persons whatsoever within this burgh or suburbs thereof" were enjoined "not to brew, or to work any other handiework or labour on the Lord's Day, or to be found on the streets standing or walk-ing, or to go in company, or vage [roam] to the Moat, Chappell [St. Christopher's], Dock, or Grein Sands, or any other plaice whatsoever on that day, at any tyme thereof," under a penalty of £10 Scots; and all the inhabitants were "discharged from going to ale-houses or taverns, for eating or drinking the tyme of sermon, or unseasonably or unnecessarily, at any tyme on the Lord's Day." For the administration of these edicts, eight unpaid special constables, consisting of influential burgesses, were ap-pointed each year, with power to command the services of the burgh officers, town guard, and the inhabitants generally, and to enter houses when requisite in the execution of their duty.

Nominally the magistrates were elected for one year; but as some of the provosts, preferring the sweets of office to the insipi-dities of private life, managed to occupy the burghal chair for five or more consecutive years,[*] a popular cry was raised against this monopolising practice, and it was put a stop to in 1676. At the

---

* Robert Graham, elected provost at Michaelmas, 1655, remained in office till 1660; John Irving, elected as his successor, continued provost till 1665; and the latter afterwards obtained a longer lease of the provostship, dating from 1668 till 1673; William Craik was chief magistrate from 1674 till 1678, and it was under his rule that the above arrangement was put in force.

annual elections held that year, and at every succeeding Michaelmas down till the Burgh Reform Bill was passed, the Councillors
were required to sign an obligation which rendered any of them
who held the office of provost, bailie, dean, or treasurer, "more
than one year, or two at the most," liable to a penalty of £1000
Scots. By the same agreement all persons who manufactured or
sold intoxicating liquors of any kind were prohibited, under a
similar penalty, from officiating as provost.

Just as the seventeenth century was drawing near a close, a
great trading scheme, which promised to enrich the whole country,
was sanctioned by the Scottish Parliament. This was the colonisation of Darien, to be effected by an incorporate body named "The
Indian and African Company of Scotland." Dumfries heartily
encouraged the project; and it could scarcely do otherwise, seeing
that its distinguished originator, William Paterson, was born in
the farmhouse of Skipmyre,* within seven miles of the town, and
was, there is every reason to conclude, numbered among its freemen. It has often been stated that Paterson was so closely
associated with Dumfries that he represented it in Parliament;
but this is certainly a mistake. There is an inherent improba-
bility in the idea that the son of a humble farmer should, before
he rose to fame, and without wealth or aristocratic patronage,
have acquired such a position; and it is sufficiently clear that after
he became distinguished as a great financier and projector he did
not sit as the member for Dumfries or any other place in Parliament. Had he really at any time officiated as the representative
of the burgh, his name as such would have appeared in the records
of the period; and as it is not to be found there among the names
of other members this circumstance, in the absence of positive
evidence to the contrary, ought to negative the statement.

The burgh, however, and the district round about, looked
with all the more favour upon the Darien scheme because of its
being launched by a Dumfriesshire man. They showed their full
faith in it by a liberal purchase of shares; the town itself, though
its strength had been so recently overtasked by an exhaustive
outlay on the bridge, taking stock to the extent of £5000 sterling.
This fact we learn from a curious document † relating to the
equivalent money granted by Government, after the failure of the
undertaking, and which may be quoted entire, as follows :—

"I, John Inglis, writer to the signet, clerk-depute to Sir
James Murray of Philiphaugh, Lord Register, and specially constitute by him to the effect underwritten, do hereby certifie that the
town of Dumfreis, as a proprietar in the Indian and African Com-

---

* This point was, up till lately, a matter of some doubt; but it has been
conclusively established in Mr William Pagan's valuable little work, "The
Birthplace and Parentage of William Paterson," published in 1865.

† Burgh Records.

pany of Scotland, their joint stock, for the sum of five hundred pounds sterling subscription, hath due unto them for the several payments made thereon, and the annual rents of the same to the first of May last, in whole the sum of three hundered and two pound and one ninth part of a pennie sterling money, conform to their account, No. 173 in Folio 9 of the subscrived lists or accompt of the Proprietars of the Joynt Stock of the said Company, given in to the Lord Register and signed by five of the Directors of the said Company, conform to the Act of Parliament, without any diligence affecting the same, the fourteenth day of June, 1707 This subsrived upon the nineteenth day of August, 1707.

To the honourable the Commissioners of the Equivalent.

(Signed)   Jo : INGLIS."

Then mark how munificently individual inhabitants—though the population was a generation before self-represented "as ane handful of pure personis"—patronised the enterprise.   Robert Paterson, merchant, Dumfries, subscribed for it the substantial sum of £400 sterling ; John Crosbie and James Coulter, merchants, took shares jointly to the extent of £500 ; Robert Johnston and John Reid subscribed between them £400.   Our old acquaintance Barncleugh, the Romanist ex-provost, now settled doucely down as a loyal subject of the new dynasty, bought £200 worth of Darien stock ; so did John Irving, son of Provost Irving, and Thomas Irving, merchant ; John Lanrick, writer, Robert Corbet, merchant, and John Crosbie, severally subscribing £100.   Some of the neighbouring lairds and noblemen also purchased largely, according to their means ; the burgh's patron, Charles, Duke of Queensberry, becoming a shareholder to the extent of £5000. The entire capital raised for Paterson's scheme was £400,000 sterling, of which no less than £11,600, or fully a thirty-fifth part, was contributed by the district of his birth.

The auspicious commencement of the colony in 1698, and its disastrous failure, brought about mainly by the mean jealousy of the English and Dutch, more particularly the former, need not here be dwelt upon.   It merited success, and with fair play it would have succeeded, and its proprietors been enriched : "New Caledonia, which remains to this day a wilderness, might have become the emporium of half the commerce of the world,"* and the poor mother-country, Scotland, have been made one of the wealthiest kingdoms of Europe.   As we shall afterwards see, the people and rulers of Dumfries strenuously opposed the Union with England—the shameful treatment given to their favourite colonisation scheme by the English having re-awakened against them all their old resentment ; and but for a promise that Scotland would be allowed to share in the commercial privileges of

* R. Chambers's Scottish Biographical Dictionary.

the sister kingdom, and receive from the English Exchequer re-
payment of the money lost by the Darien scheme, the Union
could scarcely have been consummated.

A supplementary Act passed by the United Parliament in
1715 granted £18,241 10s 10⅜d of compensation to the great projector himself, on account of the losses he had sustained in
connection with the scheme ; but he died without receiving a
farthing of that amount.   By his will, written in his sixtieth year,
and dated Westminster, 1st July, 1718, Mr Paterson left to Elizabeth, his step-daughter, only child of his first wife, Mrs Elizabeth
Turner, widow of a New England clergyman, £500 ; to his eldest
step-daughter, Anne, by his second wife, Mrs Hannah Kemp,
£600 ; to his second step-daughter, Mary Kemp, £600 ; to his two
other step-daughters, Hannah and Elizabeth, £800 each ; to Jane
Kemp, relict of Mr James Kemp, his step-son, £300 ; to William
Mounsey of Skipmyre, eldest son of his late sister Janet, £200 ; to
the two daughters of the said sister, Elizabeth and Janet, £200
each ; to John Mounsey, younger son of his said sister, £400 ; to
his only sister, Elizabeth, married to John Paterson, younger of
Kinharvey, in the Stewartry of Kirkcudbright, £800.   The surplus
of the estate, if any, was to be equally divided among the above-
mentioned persons, in proportion to their specified legacies.   Mr
Paul Daranda, of London, merchant, whom the testator calls " his
good friend," and one to whom his family and himself had been
under great obligations, was appointed sole executor of the trust,
with £1000 " for his care therein, over his expenses with relation
hereto."

" It was," says Mr Pagan, " from the fund provided or secured
to him by the Act of 1715, that Paterson, as may be supposed, was
enabled to leave the several legacies specified in his will.   The
executor, Paul Daranda, stands high in the estimation of Mr
Bannister.*   But in that opinion the Scottish relations would not
concur—at least the present survivors are under the distinct
impression that the legacies never were paid ; and probably for
this reason, that the executor had not been able to recover from
the Treasury the full compensation money ordered by the Act of
Parliament to be paid to Paterson or his heirs.   At sundry times
the Scotch relations made searching investigations, but entirely
without effect.   Mr Stewart of Hillside has obliged us with the
perusal of notes of a case drawn up for them in 1853, with a view
to further inquiry.   That document leaves little doubt that the
compensation money so justly due to Paterson had not been
realised—certainly that the Scotch relatives never received the
legacies designed for them."   We may add to this statement, that
the numerous Patersons in Dumfries and the neighbouring dis-

* Author of a Life of Paterson.

trict who claim connection with the projector through his sister Elizabeth, or otherwise, have a traditional idea amongst them that a large proportion of the compensation money was actually paid to Daranda, but never accounted for by him. This is a mere vague supposition, to which we attach no credit : rather would we believe that Paterson's "good friend" vindicated his title to be so called when the testator was dead and gone ; and that if there was any wrong-doing in the matter the blame of it rests with the Government of the day.

CHAPTER XL.

Soon after the beginning of the next century a great building
scheme absorbed the attention of the Dumfries public, the money
available for which was obtained in a very singular way. In the
year 1697 the tack or lease of the Customs and Foreign Excise of
Scotland was exposed by public auction, and taken by a committee of the Convention of Royal Burghs for £33,300 sterling.
Each burgh having been offered a share of the lease in proportion
to the amount of the tax paid by it, the Town Council of Dumfries engaged in the speculation, and then sold their share to Sir
Robert Dickson of Inveresk and Mr John Sharpe of Hoddam. At
this transaction the inhabitants were indignant. They held a
public meeting, at which it was thoroughly repudiated ; and with
the view of getting it annulled legal proceedings were instituted
by them against the civic authorities. An internecine war, involving the loss of much money and temper, seemed about to be
declared, when, at the instance of Mr Sharpe, a truce was agreed
to, and the question at issue was wisely left to arbitrators, who
decided that the tacksmen should be permitted to retain their
bargain on condition of paying 20,000 merks into the burgh purse.

Here was a windfall great and unexpected ; and what to do
with it became an interesting question. The burgesses and
"burden bearers" who had taken a lead in arraying the commonalty against the magnates of the Tolbooth wished the compensation money to be spent on something that would be both useful
and ornamental— which idea was, as may be conceived, highly
acceptable to the latter body ; and, as the result of several public
meetings, it was unanimously resolved that a new town-house

overtopped by an imposing steeple, should be erected to benefit
and adorn the burgh. It was on the 30th of April, 1703, that a
definite arrangement was made to this effect, at a meeting of the
"magistrates, members of Council, the most eminent and considerable heritors, burden-bearers, burgesses, and haill community,"
and that after receiving an overture subscribed by ninety-three
influential persons, the principal passages of which we subjoin :—
" We doe hereby propose and offer to the magistrates and Council
. . . . that whereas the toun is not at present provided with
sufficient prisones, whereby several malefactors guilty of great
crimes, and others for debt, have made their escape, to the dishonour and iminent perill of the burgh ; as also that there is not
ane steeple in the whole toun, nor ane suitable council-house and
clerk's chamber for keeping the charter chist and records of the
burgh, nor ane magazine house, nor room for the sure keeping of
the toun's arms and ammunition thereto belonging ; therefore it
is our opinion and unanimous advice . . . . that the said sum
of twenty thousand merks be disposed of and employed for the
uses foresaid, which we judge may be conveniently done for the
money ; and that the same be built on the waist ground at the
back of the Cross, being in the middle of the toun and highest
place thereof."*

A committee was appointed to carry the wish of the meeting
into effect, consisting of John Sharpe of Hoddam ; Thomas Rome,
ex-Provost ; William Craik of Duchrae : John Irving of Drumcol-
tran ; John Irving, younger of Logan ; Alexander M'Gowan,
writer, Edinburgh ; and Walter Newall, late Convener of the
Trades : to whom were added by the Council, John Coupland of
Colliston, Provost ; Bailies Crosbie and Barclay : Captain Robert
Johnston of Kelton, ex-Provost; John Irving of Logan, ex-
Provost ; James Milligan, dean ; John Gilchrist, merchant ; John
Brown, ex-treasurer ; John Irving, deacon-convener ; and Robert
Newall, deacon of the wrights. John Moffat, a Liverpool architect, was employed by the committee to come to Dumfries and
"furnish a modall" for the proposed fabric. He arrived in due
time ; and, that he might obtain the requisite architectural
inspiration, he proceeded to the city of St Mungo, as is shown by
an item in the Treasurer's account :—" To Mr Moffat, architect,
and Dean Johnston, 24 lbs. [Scots] to bear their expenses in their
journey to visit Glasgow steeple." According to another entry in
the same account, dated 10th April, 1704, Mr Moffat was paid
£104 Scots "for drawing the steeple scheme, and in name of
gratification for his coming to Dumfries." For some reason or
other he backed out of his engagement with the committee ; and
they, in January, 1705, "considering how long the designed

* Town Council Minutes.

building is retarded for want of an architect," resolved "to send for one Tobias Bachup, a master builder now at Abercorn,* who is said to be of good skill."† What Moffat left at an incipient stage Bachup cordially agreed to complete—he coming to the burgh for that purpose in the following month.

Whilst the committee were put to some little trouble in this matter, they had many other difficulties to surmount. There was no adequate timber, as in ancient times, in the vicinity of the town ; and the first impulse of the committee was to freight a vessel and send it for material to "Noroway o'er the faem." Then there was no available lime lying nearer than Annandale ; and though there were plenty of stones in the town's quarry at the foot of the Dock, men able to excavate and use them were exceedingly scarce in the district. The erection of a fabric that was to cost 19,000 merks (£1041 13s 4d sterling) was such an extraordinary enterprise for a small town of that day that the committee were often at their wits' end ; and they must have spent a vast amount of time and energy, and lost many a night's sleep, whilst engaged with their herculean task. At one of their sederunts Provost Coupland reported "that he and Bailie Corbet, when they were at Edinburgh, had made search for a free Danish or Swedish bottom for fraughting for timber to Norway, and after diligent search they found that there can be none gotten at a easy rate."‡ A resolution to search for the article in this country was therefore come to ; and after an exploratory raid trees of sufficient size were discovered at Garlieswood, in the Stewartry, which the proprietor was willing to dispose of. How to bring the Galloway oaks to the banks of the Nith—"Birnam Wood to Dunsinane"— was the next difficulty. The forest was some miles inland ; so that the trees after being felled had to be transported by horses over wretched roads to the Dee, and then conveyed in a flat boat or gabbart, and in rafts, down Kirkcudbright Bay into the Solway, and thence up the Nith to Kelton or the Dock, where horse-power was again needed to take them to Dumfries.

These processes were extremely perplexing, laborious, and expensive to our ancestors ; and when the committee had by means of them laid in a considerable stock of timber, they were very glad to come to such terms with the new architect as rolled upon him a very large share of their burden—he agreeing, at their urgent request, to supply all the remaining materials as well as to erect the building. A sub-committee having met with Mr Bachup

---

* Bachup was then engaged in building a house at Abercorn House ; but he resided in Alloa, his native town.

† Minute Book of the Steeple Committee. This book, consisting of nearly sixty pages of beautiful manuscript, is preserved in the Record Room of the Town Hall.

‡ Steeple Committee's Minutes.

on the 14th of February, 1705, reported to the "Grand Committee" the result of their interview as follows:—"That with great difficulty they had brought him to offer to furnish all materialls necessar for the said fabrick, and to construct the same conform to the scheme drawn, and the alterations of the dimensions which the committee had made, so as the same may be complete both in mason and wright work, and in the doors, windows, roof, and other parts thereof, against Martinmas, 1707, and to carry the work on as followes, viz. : to build the first stories to the jests in the first year (the work being to be begun in May nixt), and to cover the roof of the Council-house, and carry up the steeple as high the nixt year, and to complete the steeple, and all the other work, and ridd the ground betwixt and Martinmas, 1707 years, and then to deliver the keys at that term, to the toun ; and that for the sum of nineteen thousand merks Scots, with a complement to his wife, and another to himself, by and attour five hundred merks, which he refers to the toun's will whither they will give it to him at perfecting the work or not."* All the terms being duly settled and signed, the foundation-stone of the steeple buildings was laid on the 30th of May ; and Mr Bachup having brought a large body of masons from a distance, and vanquished all remaining obstacles as to the supply of materials, he finished his undertaking at the appointed time, and to the satisfaction of his employers.

It was at first intended that the stair at the south end of the Council-house should be fenced with a stone wall ; but, instead of that, it was supplied with a rail of wrought iron, forged by an Edinburgh artificer, the existing remains of which prove it to have been a magnificent piece of workmanship.

In order that the lieges might be duly apprised of the time of day, a clock for the spire was commissioned from Mr John Bancroft, Stockport, which cost £21 sterling, the four dial-plates for the same having been painted by Mr John Chandley, Cheedle, at an expense of £11 ; these sums being exclusive of the personal charges incurred by the contractors in visiting the town. Then by way of furnishing a voice to the burgh in seasons of festivity and triumph, and to announce the time for church-going, three bells were cast for the steeple by Mr George Barclay of Edinburgh, one eight hundred pounds weight, another of five hundred pounds, and the third of three hundred pounds ; the whole costing £1,698 14s 6d Scots, including the expense of tagging, tongueing, transporting, and hanging of the said three bells."† (a)

---

* Steeple Committee's Minutes.　　† Ibid.

(a) The ten o'clock bell, which had lost its rich tone by fracture and wear, was recast in 1903. It bore, in raised letters, the following inscription : —"This of 800 lib. weight, with other two bells, viz., one of 500 and another

When all these items are taken into account, it appears very obvious that the cost of the Tron Steeple (as it was first called), the Council Chamber, and the rest of the buildings, with their furnishings, would much more than exhaust the original fund of 20,000 merks ; and the probability is that the entire expense was not less than £1,500 sterling.

To Inigo Jones the credit of designing the Mid-Steeple is usually attributed ; but that, it now appears, must be shared between Mr John Moffat and Mr Tobias Bachup, the former having supplied the first sketch, the latter modifying it less or more before translating it into stone, lime, and timber. That Bachup had much more to do with the building than mason-work and superintendence is evident from the terms in which he is spoken of by the Committee ; these being, " Mr Tobias Bachup, our architect," "builder and architect of the fabric and desyned steeple," "architect and builder of the steeple and Council-house."*

Some other works of considerable importance were carried on contemporaneously with the steeple. When the century commenced the banks and braes on both sides of the river appeared very much as Nature had formed them. In Bridgend there was not a house further down than the one belonging to James Birkmyre ; there were no mills nor road in that direction, the only regular roads from the village being those leading to the parish church of Troqueer, Terregles House, and Lincluden College. Dumfries terminated a little below St Michael's Church : and, save the excavations at the Castledykes quarry, and the road which swept round the west of Lochar Moss to England, there were few traces of man's handiwork in the southern vicinity of the burgh. The Dock, the lands of Castledykes and Kingholm, all lay in pasture—their virgin soil unpierced by plow or spade, and unprovided with either road or fence. A portion of Castledykes at the period to which we refer was private property ; but it having been acquired by the burgh about 1707, a road was constructed from the foot of St. Michael Street to Kingholm, for the special use of carters doing business at the quarry or with the shipping ; and at the same time an enclosure was formed on the

of 300 lib., were founded for the Burgh of Dumfries, Edr., 1708, upon the Town's charges. William Copland of Colliestoun, Provost."

    * We have been favoured by an Alloa gentleman with the following note :—" It appears that the architect's father, Thomas Bachup, was mason to the Earl of Mar, in the end of the seventeenth century. John Crawford, our local antiquary, has a curious document in his possession, a contract between John, Earl of Mar, and Thomas Bachup, 'masone in Alloway, for building a new arch at the Bridge of Tullibody, mending the pier and the calsie,' 18th January, 1697. The deed is signed by Tobias Bachup as a witness. There is an old house in Kirkgate here, which was built by Tobias. It has a sculptured stone on the front dated 1695, with the initials of himself and wife, ' T. B.' and ' M. L.' His wife, to whom he was married in 1684, was named Margaret Lindsay."

east and south sides of the burgh roods, the river itself being deemed a sufficient boundary on the west. A farther innovation was made when, in 1712, forty-two acres of Kingholm Merse were converted by the plough into arable land, the same being let to John M'Nish, deacon of the weavers, for three years, at rather more than 10s sterling an acre. Two horses and eight oxen bought by the Council for this "clod-compelling" duty were resold —one horse for £3, the other for £3 10s, the cattle for £2 10s each. More than double this rent was obtained in 1749, when the enclosed land at Kingholm was let on a nineteen years' lease. In the same year the braes of Castledykes were also let for nineteen years to one Robert Anderson, gardener. He became bound by the conditions of his tack to turn one-half of the ground into a garden, the other half into an orchard, and to enclose the whole with a feal dyke and ditch at his own expense. As the ground was just about an acre in extent, it must have been reckoned of good quality, since the stipulated annual rent was £1 5s sterling, a high rate for land at the period in question.

The Dock and "land belonging thereto and inclosed therewith," was let on a seven years' lease, at £23 sterling annually, in 1756. Their appearance then, so different from what it now is, is partly indicated by the articles of the lease. The tacksman was required to apply a sufficiency of manure or sea-sleitch to the high ground, to free it from brambles and thistles ; to lay it down with bere or barley ; to sow it with white clover and ryegrass during the fifth year of his lease, or soon after ; to abstain from ploughing up the ground afterwards, and to keep all the dykes and ditches in good repair ; the magistrates reserving to themselves the right of improving the bank of the Dock next the water, by sloping and planting it with willows ; to keep clean the sewer from the poundfold along the back of the Dock into the water, and reserving also a passage from the houses at Cats' Strand to the river, for the use of the tenants.

When Dumfries was still but a very insignificant place, it possessed a grain mill, that being an indispensable adjunct of all towns great and small in ancient times. We read of Stakeford Mill, opposite the Castle, on the Galloway side, which belonged to the barony of Drumsleet ; of a mill on the Upper Sandbeds ; of two horse mills in the same locality ; and of a mill south of the burgh, the water-motive power of which gave its name to the property of Milldamhead. From 1685 till 1707, the main dependance of the burgh seems to have been on the horse mills ; but these having gone out of gear, the Council were led in the following way to erect others on quite a new site. For the purpose of correcting the tendency of the Nith to encroach on the Dumfries side a small supplementary bed was cut in the opposite bank, through which a large flow of water was diverted. Thus a division was made in the

river, a little below the bridge ; one stream, the main one,
continuing with an eastward bias to pursue nearly the old path,
and the other narrow one passing over the newly-formed channel
for a hundred yards or more, and then mingling with the larger
body.

As by this operation a water-course suitable for a mill was
incidentally supplied, the Council, with the consent of a public
meeting of the community, held on the 2nd of March, 1705,
resolved to utilise it for that purpose. Accordingly, a contract
was signed with Mr Matthew Frew, who agreed, for three thousand
merks and an adequate supply of stone, to build "on the other
syde of the water, ane sufficient miln, capable of grinding malt,
meall, flour, and all other sorts of grain, with a sufficient caul and
other pertinents." Ground for a road through the fields, or rather
brae-side, lying between the bridge and the new building, was
purchased by the Council ; and in a short time kilns were erected,
and a few dwelling-houses for millers and others sprang up in the
neighbourhood—Bridgend thus obtaining an addition to its size,
and new elements of progress, from which it received a lasting
benefit. On the 27th of October, 1707, the new water-mill was let,
in a completed form, for the first time, alongst with the existing
one at Mill-hole, and two smaller branches of revenue, the whole
bringing a rent of two thousand four hundred and fifty merks. A
barley mill and a wheat mill were afterwards added, the latter in
1742. Such is the origin of the town mills, which, three in number,
still yield a considerable amount of revenue to the burgh—the rent
in 1865-6 being £300, with an addition of £35 for a waulk mill,
built some time prior to 1790, and £19 for granaries.* (a)

The construction of the caul was opposed by Mr Maxwell of
Carnsalloch, and other fishery proprietors in the higher reaches of
the Nith ; they contending that it would prevent salmon from

* A return, prepared by the Town Chamberlain, Mr James H. M'Gowan,
of the rents and profits of the mills and granaries, and the cost of maintaining
the same and the caul for twenty years, ending 15th September, 1866, shows
the following results :—A total annual revenue, varying from £343 11s, which
it was in 1848-49 (the year of the second cholera visitation) to £499 3s, which
it was in 1859-60 ; and a net yearly profit, rising from £119 11s 1d to £446
13s 4d. An explanatory note is appended in these terms :—" In addition to
the mills and granaries, the [contiguous] property at Williesdale, belonging to
the burgh, includes the Millgreen, with the house thereon, and three gardens,
the rents of which are not included in the above return. The public burdens
cannot be easily divided, and the amount given above (an annual average of
£35), is chargeable on the whole property. I estimate the proportion of those
chargeable on the Millgreen and gardens at £4, which being added to the
surplus each year, will make the total profits on the mills, granaries, and caul,
during the last twenty years, £6000, or an average of £300 per annum." All
these sums are, of course, in English money.

(a) The revenue from the mill subjects has much diminished. In 1903 it
was £183 for all the above properties. The estimated value of the heritable
properties belonging to the common good was £43,429.

running up the river as formerly, and that it was clearly at variance with the existing law regarding cruives and similar obstructions. These objections were pleaded without effect in the Supreme Court. It was represented on the part of the magistrates that the town had formerly a mill a little above the bridge, the dam for which was on the opposite or Galloway side, and so easily sanded up that it was of little service ; wherefore the magistrates, taking advantage of the cutting already referred to, built a new mill on the Galloway side, and placed the dam dyke in such a position that it could not be sanded up by floods. This, it was argued, the magistrates had a perfect right to do. They were heritors on both sides of the river ; the *alveus* of the water was therefore their property, though others claimed the fishing ; and they could not be stopped from building their own dam dyke through their own water, upon the pretext of the erection being prejudicial to those who claimed the fishings above. The pleas in law for the town were : (1) Because mill-dam dykes are no prejudice to fishes going over, they being "not a foot and a half above the ebbest water." (2) The water being theirs, they may build as they please, though some accidental prejudice to a neighbour may arise ; such as the building of a house may stop a neighbour's lights, and yet will not hinder the building. And (3) in the present case " the town had the like dam dyke formerly, and this shall be of the same height ; and as the former dyke had a mid-stream open nightly by the space of six foot, so shall this, though no law requires the same, that being only in cruives and wears, which are of a huge height and thickness. And the town does not understand what argument can be brought from cruives and wears applicable to the mill-dam dyke, wherein there is no cruive made or designed, nor any *novum opus*, but only the former, which was failing, renewed, and with a greater ease to the fishing.' It was urged, on behalf of the town, also, that the caul being pitched in much deeper water than the former dyke, and having a mid-sluice kept open nightly, shoals of fish would pass through with the utmost freedom.

A curious supplementary statement was made, as follows :— "The great drought which hinders the going of burn-mills, and the stop put to the building of this mill, puts the town and inhabitants to a great hardship for want of the grinding of meal and malt; and besides this, Dr. Johnston having doled to the poor of the town 600 lib. sterl., which poor are infeft in thir milns for payment of their annual rent, which, if stopped, their provision fails, and the town must sustain the burden of them, which they cannot otherwise defray, and the inhabitants above measure straitned through their not getting their corn and malt grinded, they being thirled to the miln; and besides, there is no going miln near to the town, they being all standing by reason of the drought."

The objectors failed to do more than stop the works for a short time ; and when they were all finished they gave a picturesqueness to the river which it did not formerly possess. It used to flow rather tamely past the town; but now, partially separated, a verdant peninsula—the Mill-green—rising up be tween the divisions, and a miniature cascade formed by the Caul crossing it diagonally below the venerable bridge, it presents a view that is ever varying and never otherwise than attractive ; and the sound of the broken water, whether murmuring softly or swelled to tempest-pitch, is like music in the ear of all the genuine sons and daughters of St. Michael.*

The papers from which we have quoted bring out a fact which must be new to most of our readers, that the Sandbeds mill was kept in motion by means of a caul erected above Devorgilla's bridge. There is a prevailing belief in Dumfries that the town mills, prior to the erection of those built on the opposite bank, stood below the bridge, near the head of the Whitesands ; but in the preceding pleas put forth for the Burgh (a copy of which lies oefore us in a printed form) the explicit statement is made that the town of Dumfries had "formerly a miln *a little above their bridge,* whereof the dam dyke or water-caul was upon the other side ;" and we have been unable to find in any document the faintest trace of a mill having ever existed below the old bridge on the Dumfries side † *(a)*.

* " The Caul," says a writer in the *Dumfriesshire Monthly Magazine,* " is generally recollected very forcibly by the wandering natives of our good town, and often forms an important subject of conversation when two or three of them chance to meet. Perhaps an infusion of our national predilection for the romantic in sound as well as show may mingle with the home recollections of the Dumfriesian. We remember meeting, in a little town near London, with a woman, 'bred and born in the Back Barnraws,' who, after some general conversation about Dumfries, turned of a sudden to the Caul. ' I never sit doun mysel', said she, 'especially o' an afternoon, when the bairns are out, but I hear the sough o' the Caul as plain in my ears as when I was bleachin' claes on the island.' "

† In the action that arose out of the erection of the mills and caul, it was stated that "the stoups for the dam dyke were fixed in an rock that goes throw the water, being the very same rock whereupon the bridge is founded ;" but for all that, it has on at least four occasions been partially swept away, as if it had been built upon sand. An account of the first catastrophe of this kind, and how it was dealt with, is given in the subjoined Council minutes. 24th December, 1742.—" The magistrats and Council finding that there is a great breach in the caall of the miln-dam, in the Water of Nith, and that it will be necessary to have the same repaired as soon as possible, they appoint a committee of the magistrats, dean, and treasurer," with others, " to provide materials and employ workmen to repair and make up the said breach." 27th December, 1742.—The magistrats, in name of the commitee, report "that they had viewed the breach, and had considered several proposals for repairing thereof ; and, as the most probable, had taken in a proposal from John Baxter, wright, whereby he proposes to take up all the stones washen off from the caall that can be recovered, and to make up the said breach lately made

During the period in which these public works were being constructed, the Commissioners appointed by England and Scotland to frame a treaty of incorporation between the countries were holding their deliberations; and the object of them was viewed with dislike by many persons in Dumfries, as well as by the people of North Britain generally. Queen Anne, who succeeded to the throne on the death of William in 1702, appointed James, second Duke of Queensberry,* the leading nobleman in

---

therein by the frost and ice sufficiently, so as to continue in good order till Lambas next; and to make and put in a sufficient frame of timber, fourteen feet long, for the gullett door to open and shutt upon, within fourteen days after this day inclusive, for ten pounds sterling —the town furnishing and laying down on the Sands what more stones shall be needful from the quarry, and furnishing timber for the frame ; which being considered by the Council," they unanimously accepted the proposal. In 1800, in 1820, and lastly on the morning of the 24th of January, 1867, portions of the Caul gave way; the destructive agent having been each time the same, namely, huge masses of ice pressing against the dyke after being loosened by a thaw.

(a) In 1884 certain decayed buildings on the south side of the narrow opening between Bridge Street and Brewery Street, exactly opposite to the Old Bridge, were removed, and excavations disclosed below the surface substantial masonry, which Mr J. Barbour examined and reported upon to the Antiquarian Society. In his opinion it had formed part of the east abutment of the Old Bridge, which must thus have extended to at least 457 feet, and consisted of nine arches. The remains also shewed a culvert 4 feet 3 inches wide, the floor of which was 9 inches below the surface of the water in the river. This proved to Mr Barbour that provision had been made in the east abutment for a mill lade in connection with the old Sandbed Mill. It would thus appear that the "prevailing belief" was well founded in fact; and that before the Maxwelltown side of the river was occupied by a mill there was one on the Dumfries Sandbed. The present fish pass on the east end of the Caul was constructed by the Town Council on the requirement of the fishery proprietors and the Scottish Fishery Board. An offer had been made by the fishery proprietors to do the work at their own expense. They were willing to come under an obligation so far as they were themselves concerned to maintain it ; but they declined, as being beyond their power, to bind their successors. In consequence of this refusal, the offer was rejected by the Council on a vote ; and the result was that ultimately, after much delay and negotiation, the Council had to comply with the requirements of the fishing interest, at considerable cost to the town, and without getting rid of the future upkeep A gullet at the west end of the Caul had a strong door which was opened by lever and chain worked from the Mill Road. This gullet has been built up.

* This distinguished nobleman was born in 1662 at Sanquhar Castle, which, with the barony of Sanquhar, was purchased from the Crichtons by Sir W. Douglas of Drumlanrig in 1630. For his services in carrying the Union movement to a successful issue he received a pension of £3000 a year, the entire patronage of Scotland was conferred upon him, and he was created a British peer, with the titles of Duke of Dover, Marquis of Beverley, and Earl of Ripon. The Duke died in his forty-ninth year, just four years after he had realised the great object of his ambition. His wife, Mary, fourth daughter of Charles Boyle, Lord Clifford, predeceased him in 1709. They were buried in the family vault in Durisdeer churchyard, and a magnificent mausoleum, containing marble figures of the deceased, was raised over their remains. The contents of the vault, when examined in 1836, were, in addition to the dust of the Duke and Duchess, that of Isabella Douglas, wife of William, the first

Dumfriesshire, to be her High Commissioner in Scotland for promoting the Union; but all his influence in the county and its
chief town failed to make them pronounce on its behalf.

The Presbyterian ministers there, and generally, were afraid
that the Union would be the means of advancing Prelacy, if not of
endangering the very existence of the Established Church; and
on patriotic as well as religious grounds it was vehemently
opposed by a majority of the nation. On the 3rd of October,
1706, the Scottish Parliament sat down to discuss the articles of
the projected Union, as previously agreed to in London; and the
General Assembly, as representing the Church, and the Convention of Royal Burghs in name of the general community, sent in
petitions against the measure—the petition in the latter case
having been carried by a large majority, with whom voted the
Burgh's Commissioner. The representative of the Presbytery in
the Supreme Ecclesiastical Court took a similar course, as instructed to this effect :—" That in a calm and regular way ye move
that the Commission [of Assembly] use what method they think
fit for them in the capacity of Church judicature, for the preventing the passing of that article of the giving up of our Parliament :
That ye do nothing in the Commission that may be accounted a
compliance with the passing such an Act. If any such thing be
likely to be conducted by the Commission that may be accounted
such a compliance, or any other way endanger the present Church
Establishment to the Claim of Right, and all Acts of Parliament
made thereanent, ye shall in our name protest against it."

These instructions were given by the Presbytery on the 29th
of October; and on the 20th of next month a more emphatic testimony on behalf of the independence of the nation was uttered at
the Market Cross of the burgh. The demonstration originated
with the followers of Cameron, the remnant of the extreme Covenanting party, the successors of those who, in the same month
exactly forty years before, captured the persecutor Turner, and
celebrated their triumph over him at the Cross.* Matters were

Duke; that of Lord George Douglas, son of the latter nobleman; of Charles,
the third Duke; of his wife, Catherine Hyde, daughter of Henry, Earl of
Clarendon, celebrated for her beauty and wit by Pope and Swift, and who was
the bountiful patroness of Gay, who said of her,

" Yonder I see the cheerful Duchess stand,
For friendship, zeal, and blithesome humours known;"

of Charles, Earl of Drumlanrig, younger son of the third Duke; of Elizabeth
Hope, Dowager Countess of Drumlanrig; of Henry, Lord Drumlanrig; and of
Elizabeth, daughter of the Union Duke. All these remains are in lead coffins.
There is one also in which the bones of the early chiefs of the house are stated
to have been placed; and there are also several other coffins without any
inscriptions to indicate their contents.

* After the Revolution the party was divided; a portion rendering substantial services to the Government; others, like Sir R. Hamilton, maintaining
a kind of passive resistance.

moving quietly within the town. There was a powerful feeling of
discontent against the incorporating alliance with England; but it
had not been openly, or at all events violently, expressed. The
merchants were selling their wares as usual, the workmen following their ordinary avocations; and whilst the masons of Mr
Bachup were busy at the bartizan of the Mid-Steeple, they would,
from their elevated position, be among the first to notice the incoming, at twelve o'clock, of a somewhat tumultuous crowd,
including a force of nearly three hundred armed men. The latter
had assembled in the neighbourhood of the town to arrange their
mode of procedure ; and as they entered within its precincts,
numbers of the populace, aware of their object, joined heartily in
the movement. Near noonday this formidable band—made up
partly of resolute, high-minded, well-organised men, and partly of
the burgh mob—appeared menacingly in High Street, and, making
their way to the Cross unopposed by the authorities, many of
whom sympathised with them, they, in a calm, deliberate manner,
proceeded with their task ; and so exciting was it, that every other
sort of work was abandoned in the town, even the great enterprise of the Steeple making no further progress on that eventful
day.

    "We must have a fire kindled !" said the leaders; and forth-
with plenty of materials were supplied—the workmen at the
adjoining building contributing, we may be sure, odd bits of the
Garlieswood timber to swell the rising blaze. In order to foreclose
any attempt at interruption, a double guard of horse and foot was
placed in martial order round the anti-Union ring, outside of
which stood the applauding populace. As the flames rose bright
and high from —shall we say ?—the altar of the Market Cross, one
of the men stepped forward—the officiating priest of the ceremony
—and, producing a copy of the detested Articles of the Union,
announced to all present that he was about to commit them to the
devouring element, in token that the measure to which they
referred merited destruction. The paper was accordingly tossed
into the angry fire, all the people by their acclamations saying
"Amen !" to the deed, and cheering to the echo when the charred
document was exhibited for a moment on the point of a pike and
returned to the flames. Scarcely had it been consumed when
another leader of the party, holding up a roll, intimated that there
were inscribed on it the names of those Commissioners who, by
signing the Treaty, had sold their country ; "and thus," added
he, throwing it amongst the ashes of the other document, "may all
the traitors perish !" Something still remained to be done in
order to make the demonstration complete; and this was the
uttering of a declaration explaining and vindicating the conduct
of the party. It was boldly and eloquently drawn. After a
recital of some of the evils supposed to be involved in the measure

the protesters against it went on to say—"But if the subscribers of the foresaid Treaty and Union, with their associates in Parliament, shall presume to carry on the said Union by a supream power, over the belly of the generality of this nation, then and in that case, as we judge that the consent of the generality of the same can only divest them of their sacred and civil liberties, purchased and maintained by our ancestors with their blood, so we protest, whatever ratification of the foresaid Union may pass in Parliament, contrar to our fundamental laws, liberties, and privileges concerning Church and State, may not be binding upon the nation, now nor at any time to come: And particularly we protest against the approbation of the first article of the said Union, before the privileges of this nation, contained in the other articles, had been adjusted and secured ; and so we earnestly require that the representatives in Parliament, who are for our nation's privileges, would give timeous warning to all the corners of the kingdom that we and our posterity become not tributary and bond-slaves to our neighbours, without acquitting ourselves as becomes men and Christians ; and we are confident that the soldiers now in martial power have so much of the spirit of Scotsmen that they are not ambitious to be disposed of at the pleasure of another nation." Truly a spirited protest, appealing in powerful terms to the patriotism of the audience.* The originators of the movement having in this way fulfilled their mission, withdrew, and soon disappeared. They came mysteriously, unexpectedly; and till this day the names of even the leaders among them remain unknown. Highly exaggerated accounts of their doings reached Edinburgh. It was reported that the 5000 armed men had entered Dumfries ; that 7000 others had assembled on the neighbouring hills to support them ; and that unless strong measures were promptly taken, there might soon be a dangerous anti-Union outbreak in the south of Scotland. The subject was brought before Parliament by the Duke of Queensberry on the 29th of November, in connection with other disturbances of a similar kind. His Grace, according to the minutes of the sederunt, stated that the Secret Council, at their last meeting, had under their consideration several accounts of

---

* A broadsheet printed copy of the protest lies before us, with which we were favoured by Mr David Laing, and which bears intrinsic evidence of having been printed at the time. It is headed thus :—" An Account of the Burning of the Articles of the Union at Dumfries. These are to notify to all concerned what are our reasons for and designs in the burning of the printed articles of the proposed Union with England, with the names of the Scots Commissioners subscribers thereof ; together with the minuts of the whole treaty betwixt them and the English Commissioners thereanent." A note at the end says :—" A copy hereof was left affixed on the Cross, as the testimony of the South part of this nation against the proposed Union as moulded in the printed articles thereof. This we desire to be printed and kept in record *ad futuram rei memoriam.*"

irregular and tumultary meetings, by some people of the common and meanest degree, in arms, and of abuses committed by them at Glasgow, Stewartry of Kirkcudbright, and Dumfries, and several places of Lanarkshire; and that there were papers dropt, inviting people to take up arms, and to provide ammunition and provisions, in order to their marching to disturb the Parliament; all which he was directed by the Right Honourable the Lords of her Majesty's Secret Council to lay before the Parliament, to the effect proper methods might be resolved for preventing the evil consequences of such practices.* His Grace then presented a letter from the magistrates of Dumfries to her Majesty's advocate "bearing an account of the abuses and tumultuary meetings in that place, with a declaration emitted by those who met, which was affixt on the mercat cross of Dumfries :" both of which were read. Whereupon a draft of a proclamation to be emitted by the Parliament, "against all tumultuary and irregular meetings and convocations of the lieges," was presented and read : and after some discussion, it was objected "that it did not appear that there was a particular information of any tumultuary meetings or irregular convocations in any other part of the shire of Lanark than at Glasgow." Her Majesty's High Commissioner was thereupon pleased to notify "that he had information not only from Glasgow and Dumfries, but also from several places in Lanarkshire, of tumultuary and irregular meetings of men under arms, and of their giving out and publishing their design of marching to disturb the Parliament." Eventually, the draft of the proclamation, on being verbally amended, was carried by a majority.†

Defoe, commenting upon this minute, says :—"It is observable that even in the House there appeared some who were very loth to have these rabbles discouraged and discountenanced ; and though I could give more particular instances of it, yet this of objecting against the certainty of the accounts is a clear proof of it : whereas the matter of fact was that the Lord Commissioner had real and direct information of this affair of Dumfries and of private emissaries gone abroad to excite the people to take arms ; and the respective meetings of these agents or emissaries in the county of Lanark, and elsewhere, are more than sufficient to justify the precautions mentioned in the minute."‡

The proclamation thus passed by Parliament was issued in name of the Queen. The various statutes against the raising of tumults and the holding of disorderly meetings having been recited in the preamble, her Majesty proceeded to say :—"Yet, nevertheless, We and our Estates of Parliament are certainly

* Defoe's History of the Union, p. 98.
† Defoe's History of the Union, p. 99; and Acts of Scot. Parl., vol. **xi.**, p. 343.
‡ Defoe's History of the Union, p. 384.

informed that in several corners of the realm, and particularly
in our burgh of Glasgow, and other places within the sheriffdom
of Lanark, and in our burgh of Dumfries, and other places adjacent,
people have presumed, in manifest contempt of the foresaid laws,
to assemble themselves in open defiance of our Government, and
with manifest design to overturn the same, by insulting the
magistrates, attacking and assaulting the houses of our peaceable
subjects, continuing openly in arms, and marching in formed
bodies through the country, and into our burghs, and insolently
burning, in the face of the sun and presence of the magistrates,
the articles of treaty betwixt our two kingdoms, entered into by
the authority of Parliament ; and such crimes and insolencies
being no ways to be tolerated in any well-governed nation, but,
on the contrary, ought to be condignly punished conform to the
laws above mentioned." Orders are then given in the proclamation to all persons so assembling to disperse ; and certification is
made that all who should henceforth "be guilty, actors, abettors
or assistants, in convocating or assembling in arms, or those who
shall convocate and commit these practices above-mentioned, shall
be treated and pursued as open traitors." "Finally, our Lyon
King-at-Arms," and his brother heralds, with the Sheriffs of
counties, were charged to pass "to the mercat-cross of Edinburgh,
and the mercat-crosses of Dumfries, Lanark, and Glasgow, and
other places needful, and there make publication hereof, by open
proclamation of the premises, that none pretend ignorance."

This document reflects, as in a mirror, the alarm created by
exaggerated reports of the anti-Union movements. No wonder
that a powerful minority in Parliament opposed its adoption ; mis-
representing, as it does, the design of the protestors, and accusing
them of attacking private property as if they had been a band of
highwaymen, instead of being enthusiastic patriots whose only
error was that they adopted a somewhat boisterous and tumultuous mode of discharging what they believed to be a national
and religious duty. Mr Robert Johnston of Kelton, Provost of
Dumfries in 1692-3-4-6, who sat for the burgh in this Parliament,
might have stated—and possibly did so—that the men who entered
the town on the 20th November, and his constituents who joined
them, had no wish whatever to overturn the Throne, and that
they neither pillaged the peaceable inhabitants nor insulted the
magistrates. According to Defoe, the proclamation provoked the
Glasgow populace and "made them more furious than before ;"
but "generally it had a very good effect." The subject was again
brought under the notice of Parliament on the 30th November,
a printed paper having been then given in, entitled "An Account
of the Burning of the Articles of Union at Dumfries," as read and
affixt at the mercat-cross thereof, by the tumult assembled on
that occasion." It was then moved, "That inquiry shall be made

who has been the printer and ingiver of the said scurrulous paper, and that the print be burnt by the hand of the hangman."* This motion was carried, and, in accordance with it, the Union-denouncing manifesto was publicly burned at the Market Cross of Edinburgh ; but the daring printer of the document—luckily for him—managed to elude the vigilance of the Government.

The opposers of the Union out of doors were represented by a resolute minority in Parliament, led by the Duke of Athole and Lord Belhaven ; and when a motion was brought forward affirm-ing the principle of the measure, it was, after much opposition, carried by a majority of thirty-three votes. It need scarcely be explained that, in this the last Scottish Parliament, Lords and Commons deliberated as usual together ; so that by one testing division the opinion of both Estates was at any time readily ascertained. On this occasion there voted for the Union forty-six lords, including the Duke of Queensberry, the Earls of Galloway and Stair ; thirty-seven barons, including William Maxwell of Cardoness ; and thirty-three burgh members. Twenty-one lords, among whom were the Marquis of Annandale and the Earls of Wigtown and Selkirk, voted on the other side ; also thirty-three barons, including Alexander Ferguson of Isle and John Sharpe of Hoddam, and twenty-nine burgesses, of whom Provost Johnston of Dumfries was one. When the die was cast, and turned up in favour of the measure, the Duke of Athole tabled a spirited protest against it, which was signed by the minority. The con-stitutional opposition given by Lords and Commoners, and the tumultuous displays which manifested the feelings of the populace proved equally unavailing to stay the progress of the measure. Its passage through the House, too, was facilitated by bribery ; several peers and burgesses who stoutly opposed it at first having been bought over or silenced by English gold. Provost Johnston was not one of these recreants : what influence he possessed was given against the Act all along ; and in accordance with his wish it was inscribed on his tombstone that as the Parliamentary representative of Dumfries he asserted the liberties of Scotland and opposed the Union. — "Scotiæ libertatis assertor, Unioni fortiter opposuit." †

It was probably by a local press that the proclamation pub-lished at the Cross against that measure was printed. We know that, at all events, a few years later a " History of the Rebellion of 1715 " was printed at Dumfries by Robert Rae ; the book, a small quarto, forming a very good specimen of the typography of the period. There was no newspaper in Scotland till the *Cale-*

* Acts of Scot. Parl., vol. xi., p. 344.

† The monument is in St. Michael's churchyard. It is of a tabular form, with an upright slab or headpiece (the latter comparatively modern) screwed on to it.

donian Mercury started in 1660 ; and previously to that date
letters containing the current news and town gossip of the day
were written in Edinburgh, copies of them finding their way to
the leading provincial towns, and thus keeping their inhabitants
conversant with public affairs.   So early as 1696 the people of
Dumfries enjoyed the luxuary of a newspaper ; but then it was
only at the rate of one copy weekly, which the Town Council
with laudable enterprise commissioned for the edification of the
lieges, the cost of each tiny sheet being no less than 4s 2½d
sterling.   In the year above named a complaint was made to the
authorities that the weekly news-letter received from Edinburgh
was frequently borrowed by neighbouring gentlemen, so that
those for whom it was purchased lost the use of it ; whereupon
the Council ordered that " it should not be sent abroad out of the
town, in all tyme coming," but that the same was " to ly in the
clerk's office, there to be kept by him for the use and benefite
of this burgh ;" it being, however, politely intimated that if any
country gentleman desired to take duplicates of the letters
they were to be allowed to do so.   Some years later the Council
acquired a news-room or coffee-house of their own—in the same
building, we understand, that is similarly occupied at the present
time.   The range of which this edifice formed a part was planted
down on the east side of High Street, encroaching upon it—just
as the Mid-Steeple farther up encroached upon the west side.
The ground floors of the news-room, which are now occupied as
shops, were at one time used as an Exchange, having been built
with open piazzas for that purpose.*   By 1755, however, the
Council, under the pressure of monetary difficulties, had given up
this news-room luxury.   The house itself was sold by them to
Mr George Lowthian (son of Prince Charles's landlord) ; and he
was informed that they had discontinued the newspapers, so that
he might, if he thought fit, provide others for the room at his
own charge. (*a*)

Though the Union was viewed with marked displeasure, it
soon exercised a stimulating influence on the commerce of Scotland ; and of this benefit the port of Dumfries obtained its due
share.   A large legitimate trade sprung up with the American
colonies, which, added to that already carried on with the north
of Europe, contributed much to the prosperity of the town.   A

* Manuscript Guide to Dumfries, by the late Mr John Anderson, bookseller.   A well-written production, upon which we might have drawn more
largely had not the M.S. been unfortunately lost sight of, and only turned up
when it was too late to be made available by us to any great extent.

(*a*) The old Town Chambers were at the north end of this range, and the
building they occupied, which still exists, is burgh preperty.   The range
indeed consists only of the two buildings—the old Chambers and the Coffee
House.   In those days the prison was on the other side of the " Neuks "—the
opening from High Street to Queensberry Street between this range and the
range to the north of it.

considerable addition was made to the officers of Excise and Customs ; this being needed, however, not simply for the regulation of the lawful traffic, but to check smuggling, which, owing to the heavy duties imposed on various articles, had become a flourishing occupation along the coast of the. Solway. The Custom-house officers of the port, with their regular quota of tide-waiters and boatmen, numbered fifteen in 1710 : too few for the duties imposed upon them, as a large portion of the Galloway coast, including the port of Kirkcudbright, was now under their care. At this time Dumfries owned only two or three vessels ; but the craft engaged in the contraband trade—yawls, luggers, and wherries—which the Government officers had to cope with, were numerous, active, and defiant. The Isle of Man was their chief home or place of rendezvous ; tobacco, brandy, rum, and wine were their principal cargo—to run which, under cover of night, or even in the glare of day, into some familiar creek, for their expectant customers, was their constant aim.

To purchase a truss of the Virginian weed, or a keg of stimulating liquor, at a cheap rate, from these adventurous Manxmen, was looked upon as a light offence by the country people ; nay, many of them were active partners in the business, ready to reset or carry the cargo into the interior, and to withstand the King's officers when the latter audaciously stepped in to seize the prize. Collisions of this kind are frequently noticed in the reports sent by the collector at Dumfries, M'Dowall of Logan, to his superiors in Edinburgh. Writing on the 16th of April, 1711, he relates that two small boats having been seen hovering on the coast, all the officers were ordered to be on the look-out ; that tracks on the sands at Ruthwell led to a search in that parish, resulting in the seizure of a secreted cask of brandy, which the tide-waiters, five in number, were ordered to bring to the Custom-house next morning ; and that, when they were ready to set out with it, upwards of a hundred women broke the doors and windows of the place where it was kept, and carried off the liquor. " We humbly lay before your honours," continues the collector, " the necessity of prosecuting such abuses, as well for the security of the revenue as the protection of the officers, who are so discouraged that they dare not, without the hazard of their lives, go about their duty ;" and he adds, that the Ruthwell folks are " such friends to the running " that they will not, for any money, give lodgings amongst them to a revenue officer.*

A still more serious smuggling affray occurred in the following month, a few miles further down the coast. A tide-waiter named Young, hearing of some suspicious circumstances, hurried early in the morning to Glenhowan. There he learned from a fisherman that a notorious native smuggler, Morrow of Hidwood, had "come

* Custom-house Records.

home " from the Isle of Man. Accompanied by the parish constable, he proceeded to Morrow's house, found in it a large pack,
and two trusses of leaf tobacco, and was just preparing to return
with the precious spoil, when a "multitude of women" pounced,
vulture-like, upon the captors. The wrathful amazons first dispossessed the constable of the pack which he carried ; and whilst
they were running away with it, Young, leaving the trusses to the
care of his companion, foolishly set off in pursuit. The consequences may be readily guessed at. He might as well have sought
to make a troop of wolves give up their prey as these Glenhowan
termagants surrender theirs. The bold rash man of the revenue
was soundly beaten by them, and lodged as a captive in the
smuggler's stronghold, Hidwood House, till they had secured the
whole of the tobacco ; after which, sore in mind as well as in
body, he was set at liberty. On reporting himself at headquarters, he was sent back to the scene with a force of ten men.
They searched all the houses, fields, and gardens—discovered at
length a pack of tobacco in a dry ditch near "the town of
Bankend"—were hieing homewards with it, when, lo ! another
"monstrous *regiment* of women," armed with clubs and pitchforks,
waylaid the party. Young, thinking to terrify his assailants,
shouted out that they would be punished with the utmost rigour
for resisting the Queen's officers. "Punish us with those who
deforced you at Arbigland and Rival !" (Ruthwell), was the scorn-
ful reply. After a smart conflict, the women were put to the
rout, and the men carried their capture to Dumfries without
further disturbance.*

In the report of this affair forwarded to Edinburgh much
emphasis was laid on the impunity with which the law was defied,
and its representatives maltreated ; and an urgent request was
made for the prosecution of the offenders, and for a troop of
dragoons to assist the revenue officers in the execution of their
duty. Some of the women were tried at the Circuit Court of
Justiciary in Dumfries on a charge of rioting and deforcing the
officers ; but the witnesses in the case intentionally neutralised
their own testimony, by professing to entertain malice against the
prisoners, and so the latter escaped punishment.† Occasionally
the Customs' warehouses were broken into by marauding parties
and their contents carried off. A gang of this kind, towards the
close of 1711, assaulted the officer in charge at Kirkcudbright and
rifled his premises ; another, about the same time, effected an
entrance into the warehouse at Dumfries by means of false keys,
and made away with five hundredweight of tobacco ; whilst some
years later a crowd composed of smugglers and their friends
mobbed the magistrates and collector there, in order that they

* Custom-house Records.   † Ibid.

might intercept four confiscated casks of brandy that had been forwarded from Annan.

If the legal commerce in tobacco and brandy bore anything like a due proportion to the contraband trade in these articles, the importations of them must have been immense. The seizures alone might have gone far to supply the wants of the district, unless our forefathers' propensities for smoking and drinking were inordinate. We read of the collector getting hold of thirty-four rolls of leaf tobacco and a rundlet of brandy in one house, and of a hundred-weight of the former commodity in another ; of five hundredweight rewarding the officer's search in a third locality ; of five tuns of brandy being pounced upon at Heston ; of a hundred quarter-hogsheads of the same liquor being seized in Balcary Bay, and of four big casks of it and twelve hogsheads of wine being captured at Annan—such seizures as these being matters of weekly occurrence, and strikingly illustrative of the extent to which the "running" business was carried on. (a)

Mr Crosbie, Provost of Dumfries, and one of its leading merchants, owned in 1712 a vessel named the "James," which brought regular cargoes of tobacco from Virginia and Maryland, and sometimes tar, timber, or other products from the Baltic ; and we find him in the summer of 1719 importing nearly 5700 hundred-weight of tobacco in another ship, the "Kirkconnell." There is every reason to believe that about this latter period, and for long afterwards, from 1000 to 1200 hundredweight of this, the great staple of the Dumfries trade, paid duty in the port every year. The monthly return of the Customs' revenue dated 21st November, 1717—the earliest we have been able to discover—amounts to £116 6s 10d on all articles. In that year the staff of officers was composed of a collector, Walter Murray, at an annual salary of £50 ; a deputy-collector, at £25 ; a comptroller, at £40 ; a deputy-comptroller, at £20 ; a land surveyor, at £40 ; a land waiter and searcher, at £25 ; an overseer of boatmen, at £30; ten tidesmen and four boatmen, at £15 each ; the whole numbering twenty-one, and maintained at a yearly expense of £440.*

(a) The gentry who resided in sea-board parishes, and some of the clergy too, were in active sympathy with an illicit traffic which enabled them to re-plenish their cellars on easy terms. There is a trap-door in the floor of the dining-room of the manse of Colvend opening upon a secret chamber, where contraband spirits were stored.

* Custom-house Records.

CHAPTER XLI.

WE have now reached that eventful period of British history when the first attempt was made by the exiled royal family to recover the throne from which James VII. was driven, under the circumstances described in a previous chapter. The Earl of Mar, resenting his dismissal from office by George I., readily undertook the leadership of a movement designed to "bring the auld Stuarts back again ;" and, having retired to his estates, he convened a meeting of such Highland chiefs and Lowland lords as were supposed to be favourable to the undertaking.

To this gathering, held on the 26th of August, 1715, under the pretext of a great hunting match, the chivalrous house of Maxwell sent its chief ; there repaired to it also "the bonniest lord that ever Galloway saw ;" and, in presence of the assembled thanes, the standard of the Pretender—the flag of insurrection—was planted "on the braes of Mar." Some time before this daring step was taken, several provincial meetings of Jacobites had been held, for the purpose of manifesting their views, and ascertaining the state of public feeling regarding them. One of these is thus described by Rae, in his "History of the Rebellion ;"*—"Upon Saturday, the 29th of May, 1714 [the anniversary of the Restoration], there was a great confluence of gentlemen and country people at Lochmaben, on the occasion of a horse-race there. Two plates which were the prizes had peculiar devices : the one had a woman

---

* "The History of the late Rebellion ; Rais'd against his Majesty King George by the Friends of the Popish Pretender. Drumfries : Printed by Robert Rae, and sold by him, and by Mr John Martin, in the Parliament Closs, Edinburgh, &c., MDCCXVIII." The author, the Rev. Peter Rae, was minister of Kirkconnell, in Upper Nithsdale. He published several treatises in divinity, and was deemed a good scholar and philosopher, as well as an able divine. His brother, who printed the volume, was at that time the only typographer in the south of Scotland.

with balances in her hand, the emblem of justice, and over the
head was *Justitia*, and at a little distance *Suum cuique.* The other
had several men, with their heads downwards, in a tumbling
posture ; and one eminent person, erected above the rest, with
that Scripture, Ezek. xxi. 27, ' I will overturn, overturn, overturn
it : and it shall be no more, until he come whose right it is ; and I
will give it him.' After the race, the Popish and Jacobite gentry,
such as Frances Maxwell of Tinwald, John Maxwell, his brother,
Robert Johnston of Wamphray, Robert Carruthers of Rammerscales, the Master of Burleigh (who is under sentence of death for
murder, and made his escape out of the tolbooth of Edinburgh a
little before he was to have been execute), with several others I
could name, went to the Cross, where, in a very solemn manner,
before hundreds of witnesses, with drum beating and colours
display'd, they did upon their knees drink their King's health," the
Master of Burleigh prefacing the toast by invoking perdition on
the heads of those who refused to drink it.* The same historian
states that, in the year before, there was a similar demonstration,
though less defiant, in the same burgh ; and laments that these
warning presages were left unheeded by the Government.†

---

* Rae's History, pp. 49-50.

† The gathering at Lochmaben was celebrated by a Jacobite minstrel in
the following spirited strains :—

> " As I came by Lochmaben-gate,
>   It's there I saw the Johnstones riding ;
> Away they go, and they feared no foe,
>   With their drums a-beating, colours flying.
> All the lads of Annandale
>   Came there, their gallant chiefs to follow :
> Brave Burleigh, Ford, and Rammerscales,
>   With Winton and the gallant Rollo.
>
> " I asked a man what meant the fray :
>   ' Good sir,' said he, ' you seem a stranger ;
> This is the twenty-ninth of May—
>   Far better had you shun the danger.
> These are rebels to the Throne—
>   Reason have we all to know it ;
> Popish knaves and dogs each one !—
>   Pray pass on or you shall rue it.'
>
> " I looked the traitor in the face,
>   Drew out my sword and ettled at him :
> ' Deil send a' the Whiggish race
>   Downward to the dad that gat 'em !'
> Right sair he gloomed but naething said,
>   While my heart was like to scunner :
> Cowards are they born and bred,
>   Ilka whingeing, praying sinner.
>
> " My bonnet on my sword I bare,
>   And fast I spurred by knight and lady ;
> And thrice I waved it in the air
>   Where a' our lads stood ranked and ready.

On the other hand, several noblemen and gentlemen in the
south and west, fearing that the success of the Pretender—who
was, like his father, a Roman Catholic—would, among other evils,
lead to the re-establishment of Popery, and an arbitrary form of
government, adopted various precautionary measures in view of
the threatened outbreak. They met at Dalmellington on the 18th
of March, 1714, and passed resolutions to the effect that a general
correspondence be entered into among the well-affected nobility,
gentry, and citizens "within the shires of Clydesdale, Renfrew,
Ayr, Galloway, Nithsdale, and the Stewartries and bailiaries
thereof ;" that meeting be held in each of these districts, for
furtherance of the common object ; that each district shall be
invited to send representatives to general quarterly meetings, the
first of which was fixed to be held at Dalmellington ; that
intercourse by letter or otherwise be kept up with their friends in
Great Britain and Ireland ; and that "it be earnestly recommended
to each of the said particular meetings to fall upon such prudent
and expeditious methods to put their people in a defensive posture,
in such a manner as they shall see most proper and conform to
law."* Sir Thomas Kirkpatrick of Closeburn (descended from a
long line of heroes), Mr Alexander Fergusson of Craigdarroch
(whose father fell fighting against Claverhouse at Killiekrankie),
and other influential men in Nithsdale, took an active part in this
defensive movement ; the magistrates of Dumfries and the
ministers of the Presbytery gave to it their cordial co-operation ;
money for the purchase of arms and ammunition was liberally
contributed in the district ; and the people of each parish were
placed under military drill, and accustomed to the use of fire-
arms : so that, when the rebellion actually broke out, the

> 'Long live King James !' aloud I cried,
>   ' Our nation's King, our nation's glory !'
> ' Long live King James !' they all replied—
>   ' Welcome, welcome, gallant Tory !' "
>
> " Then I shook hands wi' lord and knight,
>   And mony a braw and buskined lady ;
>   But lang I'll mind Lochmaben gate,
>   And a' our lads for battle ready.
>   And when I gang by Locharbriggs,
>   And o'er the moor at e'en or morrow,
>   I'll send a curse into the Whigs
>   That wrought us a' this dool and sorrow."

Hogg, after quoting Rae's account of the demonstrations at Lochmaben,
says :—" Mr Rae does not mention that the Lords Winton and Rollo were
present there at either of the meetings. I find, however, from another part of
his history, that they were both in Annandale that year first mentioned, else
the elated balladmonger would not have included them."—*Jacobite Relics*, vol.
i., p. 294.

* Rae's History, p. 42.

Dumfriesians and their neighbours were in a fit condition to cope with it.

We have seen how resolutely the inhabitants of the burgh and their rulers opposed the Union ; and if their sentiments on that subject had not been kept in check by a counter feeling, they would perhaps have encouraged rather than opposed the pretensions of Prince James. But their antipathy to the Union was feeble as compared with their sense of the wrongs done towards them by the Stuart race, and their zeal for Protestantism· Claverhouse and Lag foreclosed the success of any attempt that might be made in Nithsdale or Galloway to restore the exiled family ; and it is not too much to say, that the bloody Persecution instituted by Charles II. foredoomed the Rebellion raised by his nephew to a hopeless failure. Had it not been for that circumstance the descendant of Scotland's ancient kings would have met with a better reception from its inhabitants generally when he claimed their allegiance, and his enterprise would have had a greater chance of success.

The magistrates of Dumfries having, on the 23rd of July, 1715, been apprised, by letters from London, of the Pretender's design to land in Scotland, communicated this intelligence to the Council, and forthwith means were taken to mature the defences of the burgh. It was deemed probable that the debarkation would take place on the shores of Lochryan, or nearer still, at the harbour of Kirkcudbright ; and that afterwards an attempt would be made to seize Dumfries, as the chief town of the district. Hence the necessity for proceeding promptly with protective measures on a large scale. The various trained bands were drawn out; strong guards were posted at the four ports ; and seven companies, corresponding in number to the Incorporated Trades, were formed, composed of sixty effective men each, the Provost officiating as commander-in-chief of this municipal force. It was carefully trained almost daily; "and," says Rae, "for the more effectual training of the younger sort, a company of bachelors was formed out of the rest, who assumed the title of the Company of Loyal Bachelors."*

Stimulated by the example of Dumfries, and the sense of a common danger, many county gentlemen, ministers of the district, and others, made extensive arrangements to protect themselves, and defeat the machinations of the enemy. Towards the end of July Major James Aikman arrived in the district from Edinburgh, commissioned to superintend and promote the military preparations. On the 10th of August, in company with Sir Thomas Kirkpatrick of Closeburn, Mr Gordon of Earlston, and others, he reviewed the fencible men of Upper Nithsdale, at a general

* Rae's History, pp. 182-3.

rendezvous on Marjorymuir. Proceeding to Closeburn, he assisted at a meeting held there representing some parishes in Lower Nithsdale, at which it was resolved that a volunteer company should be formed in each parish; and that, when the period for action arrived, Sanquhar should be the place of rendezvous for the western shires.

In accordance with a resolution come to at the Braemar gathering, on the 26th of August, the Jacobite chiefs held a second meeting at the same place, on the 6th of September, with about two thousand followers, and proclaimed the Pretender King of Scotland, England, France, and Ireland. On marching to Dunkeld they were largely reinforced by the people of the district, by two thousand clansmen under the Marquis of Tullibardine, by fourteen hundred from the braes of Athole, and by five hundred sent by the Earl of Breadalbane. Mar himself mustered no fewer than three thousand additional followers; and the insurgent army, thus swelled to about eight thousand men, boldly pushed down to Perth, which city they occupied without resistance, the Earl of Rothes not finding himself able to offer them any effectual opposition. Whilst the Prince's friends in the north were thus employed, William, fifth Earl of Nithsdale,* and William, sixth Viscount of Kenmure, raised his standard in the Border counties to co-operate with the Jacobite forces under Forster and Derwentwater in England. Maxwell, on account of his great local influence, and the services rendered by his family to the Stuarts, would have been placed at the head of the rebel movement in the South had it not been that he was a devoted Romanist, whom it would have been imprudent to appoint to that office.

And, in truth, if we may judge from the portrait of Earl William at Terregles House, as painted by Sir Godfrey Kneller, he was not designed by nature for such a warlike enterprise. The armour in which the figure is attired is out of keeping with the face, which is that of a peace-loving, ardent, warm-hearted man. There is no trace of wile or craft in the countenance; the brow is well-developed; the nose of such size and breadth as betoken mental strength, but it has no lines of combativeness; and when the noble lord was led into the rebellious fray, it must have been from no love of fighting, but from chivalrous enthusiasm, mingling with a sober sense of duty. The eyes are so prominent that he must have been a fluent speaker; and wit—perhaps poetry—is visible in the full rounded lips. Altogether, if our inferences be correct, he would have been more in his element at home, or in the

---

* On the death of the second Earl of Nithsdale, in 1667, without issue, his title and estates devolved upon John, seventh Lord Herries. The son of the latter was the fourth earl, and had, by Lady Lucy Douglas, his wife, William, the fifth earl, and a daughter, Lady Mary Maxwell, Countess of Traquair.

social circle, or shining at the court of his sovereign, than in the camp or battle-field.

The Protestant Lord Kenmure, who was raised to the chief command, was of a more warlike temperament. He was, however, but indifferently conversant with military affairs—had, indeed, received no soldierly training—a sad want for one in his position ; but he had all the indomitable bravery of his race—

> " There ne'er was a coward of Kenmure's blood,
> Nor yet of Gordon's line !"

was prudent withal, and possessed sufficient intellectual capacity for the perilous and onerous trust assigned to him. When, after bidding a last adieu to his lady, he endeavoured to mount his favourite charger, the horse, usually docile, repeatedly baffled his efforts. Disconcerted by this inauspicious omen, a gentle voice reassured him with the words, "Go on, my lord ! go on ! you are in a good cause ! Remember, faint heart never won fair lady !" Having at length leaped into the saddle, the noble Viscount rode off, never to return—never to hear again the voice which, with more than trumpet's power, stirred his blood—as he hastened to encounter the enemies of his Prince, and alas ! meet with "dusty death," in its most repulsive form, upon the scaffold.

Mar expected to receive a supply of both men and arms from France. But in this he was disappointed ; and it soon became obvious that if James VIII. was ever to be more than a nominal king, he would owe his success solely to "native swords and native ranks." With the view of preventing Mar from marching into the Lowlands, and also, if possible, of extinguishing the Rebellion at its birth-place, the Duke of Argyle, the Royalist commander-in-chief, formed a camp at Stirling, and summoned the friends of King George throughout the country to meet him there.

Letters to this effect were sent by his grace to the well-affected burghs, including Dumfries ; and also to particular individuals on whose services he thought he could depend. The zealous and influential Laird of Craigdarroch, who was looked upon as the leading loyalist in Nithsdale, received from Argyle a communication dated Edinburgh, 16th September, 1715, announcing the outbreak of the insurrection, and stating that the writer recognised the necessity of raising volunteer forces to assist the King's army in coping with it :—"Your Lord-Lieutenant not being yet come down," proceeds the Duke, "to give orders for drawing out such other of the well-affected people as should be thought necessary, and I being convinced of your zeal and good inclinations to serve our King and country, and looking upon you as my particular friend, I apply to you on this occasion, and desire you would forthwith come to Stirling, with what number of well-arm'd men you can get together to join the King's regular forces. This will be of infinite service to his Majesty, and will not fail to be acknowledged as such."*

If Argyle had suspected the existence of serious danger in the South he would not have summoned Mr Fergusson to Stirling; and that gentleman not thinking that his services would soon be pressingly required at home, proceeded to Keir-moss, Penpont, with about sixty well-armed recruits, raised in the parishes of Glencairn and Tynron. At that place he met with many from neighbouring parishes, assembled in arms under Sir Thomas Kirkpatrick, James Grierson of Capenoch, John Dalrymple of Waterside, Thomas Hunter of Bateford, Provost Crosbie (a) of Dumfries, and other gentlemen, including several ministers. After patriotic addresses from Mr Fergusson and Sir Thomas Kirkpatrick, many more volunteers were obtained for the King's army; and Mr Crosbie (a) announced that Dumfries was enlisting a hundred men, who would be ready to set out with him in a few days for Stirling, Next day Craigdarroch, accompanied by Mr Hunter of Bateford, Mr M'Gachan of Dalquhat, and by Mr Simon Riddell, Mr John Pollock, and Mr James Hunter, ministers of Tynron, Glencairn, and Dornock respectively, marched with his men towards the royal camp. The company he brought to Stirling proved a valuable acquisition to Argyle; but hearing soon afterwards of the Jacobite movement in Dumfriesshire, Mr Fergusson, at the Duke's instance, retraced his steps, that he might defend the King's interests in his native county.

By the beginning of October matters began to wear a very serious aspect. Mar had put his army in motion; and the rebels under Kenmure, after being reinforced from England, were hovering menacingly in Cumberland, as if they intended to attack Dumfries. As yet there had been no serious fighting—nothing approaching to a trial of strength; but that, to all appearance, could not be long deferred, as Argyle was fully alive to the necessity of confronting the rebel chief before he could effect a junction with his friends in the South. In view of the pending struggle, the militia of several shires were called out, and formed with the volunteers a large force, apart altogether from the regular army at Stirling. At this time the lord-lieutenancy of Dumfriesshire was held by the head of an old Border house—William Johnstone, first Marquis of Annandale;† and he had as deputies, to act with

* Rae's History, pp. 230-31.

(a) Provost Corbet, not Crosbie. John Crosbie of Holm was Provost 1708-10; Corbet, 1710-12; Crosbie, 1712-14; Corbet, 1714-16; Crosbie, 1716-18.

† When, by the death, in 1685, of James Murray, Earl of Annandale, that title became extinct, it was revived for the purpose of being conferred on James Johnstone of Lochwood, the second Earl of Hartfell (who, as we have seen, fought under Montrose). His son William was the second Johnstone who bore the title of Earl of Annandale. In 1701 he was created Marquis of

him during the crisis, the representatives of other ancient families
—Kirkpatrick of Closeburn, Fergusson of Craigdarroch, Johnstone
of Corehead, Grierson of Capenoch, Maxwell of Dalswinton, and
Johnstone of Broadholm.   The first decisive step taken by the
Marquis was to call a meeting of the "fencible men" of the
county, which accordingly took place on Locharbridge-hill : a
great wappenschaw it was, numerically large, and pervaded by
the utmost enthusiasm.

On Saturday, the 8th of October, when the people of the
burgh were at worship in St. Michael's Church—it being the
preparation day for the communion Sabbath—they were somewhat disturbed by seeing a messenger entering and handing a
packet to Mr Gilchrist, one of the bailies, which induced the latter
to withdraw.   The communication was well fitted to excite the
alarm of the congregation, had they known its nature ; as it
informed the magistrate of a Jacobite plot to seize the town next
day, during the celebration of the sacrament.   Bailie Gilchrist
consulted with the Provost on the subject ; and they, concluding
that the letter—which was dated from Locharbridge, and professed to be written by a loyal countryman—was a forgery, and
that its author wished to create a false alarm, took no action upon
it, except to double the guards.   The writer was perfectly honest,
however, in so far as he indicated the approach of danger ; and
on Monday (the 10th) another warning communication was received by the magistrates from certain parishioners of Tinwald
and Torthorwald, who had assembled at Locharbridge with arms,
and who offered their instant services to defend the town.
Provost Crosbie, unwilling to cause any undue excitement among
the inhabitants, stated in answer that the parties might retire
home for the night, though they might hold themselves in readiness to come to Dumfries when called upon.

Annandale. By his wife Sophia, heiress of John Fairholm, of Craigiehall,
Linlithgowshire, he had James, second Marquis of Annandale, two other sons,
who died unmarried, and two daughters, the eldest of whom married Charles
Hope, afterwards created Earl of Hopetoun. William, the first Marquis, had,
by Charlotte van Lore, only child of John Vanden Bempde, of Pall Mall,
London, his second wife, George, third Marquis of Annandale, and John, who
died young. "James, the second Marquis of Annandale," says .the "Scottish
Nation, "resided much abroad, and dying unmarried at Naples, 21st February,
1730, was buried in Westminster Abbey. The estate of Craigiehall went to
his nephew, the Honourable Charles Hope ; and his titles and the other
estates to his half brother, George, third Marquis of Annandale, born 29th
May, 1720. The loss of his brother, Lord John, in 1742, occasioned a depression of spirits which finally deranged his mind. He died 24th April, 1792,
when the title of Marquis of Annandale became dormant—claimed by Sir
Frederic John William Johnstone of Westerhall, Baronet, and by Mr Goodinge
Johnstone. It is understood that the titles of Earl of Annandale and Hartfell devolved upon James, third Earl of Hopetoun, who, however, did not
assume them, but took the name of Johnstone in addition to that of Hope."
The earldom was also claimed by Mr Hope-Johnstone of Annandale.

A third warning was received on the following day—one which could not be disregarded, coming, as it did, in the form of the following letter from the Lord Justice-Clerk addressed to the Provost :—" Edinburgh, October 8th, 1715.—Sir,—Having good information that there is a design framed of rising in rebellion in the southern part against his Majesty and the Government, I send this express to advise you thereof, that you may be upon your guard : For by what I can rely upon, their first attempt is to be suddenly upon your town. I heartily wish you may escape their intended visite.—I am, sir, your well-wisher and humble servant,—AD : COCKBURN."

Most fortunate it was that the Provost never had been able to go, as he intended, with a hundred men to Stirling, seeing that there was now so much need for his directing head and their stout arms at home. Though slow to apprehend peril, he had all along zealously promoted defensive measures ; and he acted with un-hesitating promptitude when the real juncture arrived. He forthwith called a meeting of the Town Council and other influential burgesses, laid before them the letter he had received, and pointed out the imminency of the danger with which they were menaced, and the necessity of obtaining aid from a distance to enable them to ward it off. The Provost's representations received unanimous approval ; and as a general meeting of the fencible men of the Stewartry was being held that very day at Leaths-moor, a deputation, consisting of Bailie Gilchrist, William Craik of Duchrae, John Neilson of Chappel, and James Gordon writer, was forthwith sent to it from Dumfries soliciting assist-ance. Before the application was made the gathering was partially dispersed ; but the deputy lieutenants and other gentle-men, about fifty in all, proceeded to the town that night, and expresses were dispatched to various quarters, which had the effect of bringing to it next day numerous volunteers from both Nithsdale and Galloway. As showing the promptitude with which the appeal of the Dumfriesians was responded to, it is worthy of notice that Captain Hugh Fullerton, Provost of Kirk-cudbright, Mr Samuel Ewart, and Sergeant Currie, set out from thence with a company of foot on the morning of the 12th of October, and arrived at their destination that night, though twenty-eight miles of bad road lay between the two towns ; whilst Abrahm Creighton of Gareland, Provost of Sanquhar—who was later in receiving a notice of how matters stood—hearing a vague rumour on the 14th that the enemy had invested Dumfries, called out a company of foot, mounted them on country horses, and arrived at their head without drawing bridle—the distance in this case being also twenty-eight miles.

Among others who appeared at the Locharbridge rendezvous was Sir James Johnstone of Westerhall, with a body of militia.

He had provided a large supply of arms, seventeen stand of which, temporarily left by him at Broadchapel, near Lochmaben, were seized and carried off by a party of rebels, headed by none other than Viscount Kenmure himself so that it was no unfounded report which represented the Jacobite chief as being in the district bent on mischief.   The exulting captors of this unlooked-for and most welcome prize, after being reinforced by some friends at Mid-Annandale, hurried northward to Moffat, which they made their headquarters for a short while; and where they were that same night joined by the Earl of Winton with a party of gentlemen and their followers from the Lothians.

On the 11th of this memorable month, when all strangers appearing in the town were viewed with suspicion, the notorious Simon, Lord Lovat, who had been out of the kingdom for several years, arrived with a few friends, and was immediately apprehended.   He declared that the Marquis of Annandale would be ready to assure them of his loyalty ; and one of the magistrates, Bailie Currie, having gone to Lochwood to consult the Marquis in the matter, returned with the request that Lord Lovat should be detained till he saw him at Dumfries.   Mr Currie also bore an order from the Lord-Lieutenant requiring the magistrates to repair with an escort to his residence next day and conduct him to the burgh ; as his lordship had been put to peril by Winton's party, and had also narrowly escaped being intercepted by the rebels under Kenmure when on their way through Upper Annandale.

Mr Currie having delivered his message, the town-crier proceeded through the principal streets at eleven o'clock that night, and in the usual way warned such burgesses and residents as possessed horses to appear mounted and with their best arms at next beat of drum.   All that night through great excitement prevailed ; few of the inhabitants closed their eyes ; the windows looking into the leading thoroughfares were illuminated, for the double purpose of supplying light for the warlike muster, and affording a greater sense of security ;* and when, about an hour after midnight, the roll of the drum again reverberated through the town, followed by the neighing of steeds, by the ring of their hoofs upon the pavement, as they hastened to the Market Cross, by the jangling of arms, and the less discordant calls of the bugle, those of the lieges who did not know precisely how matters stood might well be excused for believing that the dreaded enemy, favoured by the darkness, had really stolen a hurried march upon the town : and, sure enough, the rebels had moved from Moffat soon after that terrible midnight hour, for the purpose of attacking Dumfries, and would have carried their resolution into effect had not discretion got the better of their valour.

* Rae's History, p. 251.

The magistrates, putting themselves at the head of the troop summoned under such exciting circumstances, proceeded to Loch-wood, returning next forenoon with the Lord-Lieutenant, who allowed Lord Lovat to depart for the North on being satisfied of his steady loyalty to King George. They came back in good time to have received the rebels under Kenmure, if the latter had carried their designs into execution. By two o'clock the enemy were within a mile and a half of the town, exulting in the idea that they would soon be masters of it. They just numbered one hundred and fifty-three—all horsemen; and must have been kept in complete ignorance of the Dumfries preparations, or they would never have moved out of Moffat with so slender a force on such an undertaking. Hastening along, they would certainly have fallen into the snare they were preparing for others, had they not learned from a sure source that the burgh, half full of armed men, was ready to give any assailant, however powerful, a hot recep-tion. With this unwelcome news they were furnished in the following way. One afternoon a half-witted rustic named James Robson presented himself at the rebel camp with the curious intimation that he had come to make a present of his broad blue bonnet to Lord Kenmure. Another similar head-piece is celebrated in song as acquiring renown on account of its wearer :—

> " It was na the bonnet, but the head that was in it,
> Made the hail warld talk o' Rab Roryson's bonnet."

But in this case it was really the bonnet, and not its owner—" Daft Jamie "—that was of any consequence to Kenmure ; and the noble Viscount surmising as much, at once dissected the homely present made to him, and found within its lining a letter from Lord Nithsdale urging him to be off, as Dumfries was armed to the teeth. The bearer of the warning note, unconscious of the service he was performing, had been bribed to perform it by the Terregles people. How provoking the intelligence he brought to the Jacobite leader and his friends, dissipating, as it did, their dream of conquest like a column of mist ! So far from their being on the point of seizing the chief town of the South, they were in deadly danger of being captured themselves.

Some of the more adventurous of the party were for making a stand, in the expectation that many friends would flock to their aid, and that, when thus reinforced, they might after all make a bold dash at Dumfries with some likelihood of success. Viscount Kenmure, however, who best knew the feeling of the town, and fully realized the consequences of failure, paid no heed to such foolish counsels ; and declared emphatically that he feared too truly the place was defended by gallant gentlemen, and that he would therefore defer his intended visit to it. Thereupon he ordered his force to wheel about and retire to Lochmaben. Whilst going to that burgh they captured Bailie Paterson, Mr Johnston, postmaster, and Mr Hunter, surgeon, who had been sent from Dumfries to reconnoitre them. The prisoners were civilly treated and set at liberty on the burgh agreeing to liberate three of their friends who had been seized as suspected Jacobites.

When it was known in Dumfries that the rebels were so near at hand, the entrances were barricaded, earth-work entrenchments were formed, the guards were strengthened, and the trained bands were called out ; and had the enemy numbered thousands instead of scores they would have encountered a stout resistance. Just when the inhabitants expected that the threatened onset would be made, word was brought that the rebels had called a halt, and then that they had beat a retreat. "Let us follow and give them battle !" was the general cry. "Not so," said the wary Lord-Lieutenant ; and so excessively cautious was he, that when a party of gentlemen, headed by Lord Lovat, asked leave to set out and surprise the enemy next day at Lochmaben, he refused his consent, declaring that under existing circumstances a defensive policy was the best.

Fearing that the people's anxiety for aggressive measures might prompt them to some rash movement, he summoned to his residence the ministers, who had much influence with them, and there pointed out the hazards that would be run if in a premature encounter the rebels should be victorious. "They would then," he said, "readily get possession of Dumfries, and might justly give out that they were masters of the south of Scotland—an announcement that would encourage their friends all around to join them, and a force would be raised that might endanger the Government ; besides, great effusion of blood might thereby be occasioned, for which he would not be able to answer either to God or the King If," continued his lordship, speaking in a style worthy of his ancestry, " the people will only be patient till things are in proper order, I shall go forth at their head, and venture my life and lands in assisting them to defend our religion, our country, and our King." He closed by intreating his clerical hearers to impress these sentiments on the inhabitants. He had an opportunity of doing so himself when reviewing them at the Moat a few days afterwards ; and so effective was his address, that it was greeted with a round of hearty cheers.* Probably the Lord-Lieutenant was not aware at the time of the numerical weakness of the rebels, or he would really have attempted to capture them in their retreat- no very rash venture : failure would not, as he fancied, have involved the loss of the town ; and success would have been a death-blow to the Pretender's cause in Dumfriesshire.

Though the Earl of Nithsdale was fully committed to it, comparatively few of his dependants took part in the Rebellion,

* Rae's History, pp. 233-4.

and many of them enrolled themselves as loyal volunteers. Soon
after the arrival of the Lord Lieutenant, he took steps to overawe
the Maxwell tenantry in Carlaverock parish—a large proportion of
whom were Roman Catholics, and therefore deemed more likely to
favour Prince James. Mr John Somerville, minister of the
parish, was ordered to remove the Back-bridge of the Isle, in order
to cut off the communication between the tenants and the rebels
in Galloway and the Western Border ; and Mr Patrick Linn, one
of the Dumfries ministers, was empowered to co-operate with his
brother clergymen in maintaining a guard at Bankend, near to
where Carlaverock parish joins that of Dumfries. "As my Lord
Nithsdale's tenants in Carlaverock," says Rae, "so likewise his
other tenants in Troqueer, Terregles, and Kirkgunzeon, with those
of the Viscount of Kenmure and Earl of Carnwath, were in arms at
Dumfries, and manifested a great deal of zeal against the Rebellion ;
nor were there any with these noblemen in the Rebellion but two
or three domestic servants with each. And this I thought just to
make known to the candid reader, to wipe off a calumny cast upon
these people by a late historian [Mr Patten] who was also a rebel,
who speaking of the chiefs in Scotland, and what men they could
raise, says :—'The Earl of Nithsdale, 300 men, with their chief,
against the Government ; the Earl of Carnwath, 300 men, most
with their chief, against the Government, and in the Rebellion ;'
and the same he affirms of the Viscount Kenmure."*

     When Lord Kenmure, with his small party of followers, reached
Lochmaben, on the evening of Thursday, the 13th, he caused the
Pretender to be proclaimed at the Market Cross of the burgh.
On the approach of the unwelcome visitors, the inhabitants placed
their cattle in a fold to make room for the horses, which arrangement led to a ludicrous episode. The cattle, not liking their
unwonted quarters, broke through the enclosure, and some of them
strayed into a townsman's yard during the dusk of the following
morning. " Help !" cried the owner of the invaded territory, at
the top of his voice, "Help ! Help ! ! Help !" This was simply a
summons to his dog, which bore that name ; but the terrified
sentries, interpreting the word differently, sounded an alarm—their
belief being that the Dumfries loyalists had entered Lochmaben.
In the utmost consternation, the rebels--many of them only half-
dressed—prepared to evacute the town ; and it was some time
before the mistake was discovered, and order restored. Rae, who
had probably exaggerated this incident, seems to have relished it
vastly. Some of the terrified troopers, he tells us, "cut up their
boots in haste to get them on ;" others, who could not get their
horses in an instant, left them that they might flee on foot ; and
some, who managed to mount their chargers, "almost dropped off
for fear."† Next day, at Ecclefechan, the rebels were nearly thrown

* History, pp. 256-7.   † Ibid., p. 254

into another panic, by the sudden arrival of a party of fifteen horsemen. These, however, proved to be friends, not assailants; their leader, Sir Patrick Maxwell of Springkell,* having brought them to prove his devoted attachment to the interests of the Prince.

The Jacobites, continuing their march, entered Langholm on the 15th, Hawick on the 16th, Jedburgh on the 17th; obtaining considerable reinforcements as they went along, and proclaiming the Pretender at all these towns. On the 18th they crossed the Border; on the 19th they joined their north of England friends at Rothbury, the united forces proceeding next day to Wooler. Here they waited two nights, and having re-entered Scotland, effected a junction with a body of Highlanders, under Brigadier M'Intosh, on the 22nd, at Kelso,† by which means their strength was raised to two thousand men.

* The Maxwells of Springkell are a branch of the Auldhouse family, of which Maxwell of Pollock is the senior representative. George Maxwell of Auldhouse had by his first wife one son, whose son succeeded to the Pollock estates. By his second wife, Jane, daughter of William Muir of Glanderstone, he had, among other issue, a son, William, who acquired in 1609 the barony of Kirkconnel (scene of Fair Helen's tragical fate), and Springkell, in Annandale. His son, Patrick, it was who joined the rebel army in 1715. Patrick was created a Nova Scotia baronet in 1683. Lieutenant-General Sir John Maxwell, the fourth baronet in direct descent from him, married Mary, only surviving child and heiress of Patrick Heron of Heron, in the Stewartry; and on the death of his father-in-law, he added the surname and arms of Heron to his own. His eldest son, Sir Patrick Heron Maxwell, who succeeded him, died unmarried in 1844, and was succeeded by the present baronet, Sir John Heron Maxwell, born in 1808. (a)

(a) Sir John was brother to Sir Patrick. He was married to Caroline, seventh daughter of the Earl of Galloway, by whom he had four sons and five daughters. Died, 1885. Succeeded by his son, Sir John Robert Heron Maxwell. Subsequently the estate of Springkell was acquired by Mrs Johnson-Ferguson.

† Next day, being Sunday, the 23rd of October, the Lord Kenmure ordered Mr Robert Patten, a Northumberland minister, and one of their chaplains, to preach in the great church of Kelso, at the same time commanding the men to attend divine service. Hereupon Mr Buxton read prayers, and Mr Patten preached on these words, Duet. xxi. 17—The right of the first-born is his; where, 'tis plain, his scope was to assert and maintain the Pretender's hereditary right. He was succeeded in the afternoon by Mr William Irvine, a Scots Episcopal clergyman, and chaplain to the Earl of Carnwath, who read prayers and preached a sermon full of exhortation to his hearers to be zealous and steady in the cause in which they were now engaged.—Rae, p. 628

CHAPTER XLII.

LORD KENMURE, finding himself at the head of a considerable army, resolved on making some decisive movement. His thoughts again turned towards Dumfries; his idea being that he was now in a condition to attack it with success. The inhabitants, antici-pating a second and more serious visit from his lordship, renewed their defensive preparations, which had been partially put a stop to. The Marquis of Annandale, having granted commissions to the officers of militia, and made arrangements for calling out the force if necessary, left Dumfries for Edinburgh on the 20th of October; and no immediate danger being apprehended, the country people returned home, leaving the town to the care of its own inhabitants. When, however, news of the ominous rebel conjunction at Kelso reached the magistrates, they despatched ex-presses to their friends throughout Nithsdale and Galloway; and in a short time, in answer to their urgent requests, two thousand well-armed men volunteered their services for the protection of the burgh. A few of the inhabitants favoured the Jacobites; one of whom went bustling about, assuring the country folks that Kenmure would be down upon them with irresistible force; that the town would have to give in; and that they would all be massacred wholesale. The tongue of this tattling busy-body might have occasioned mischief, had he not been promptly con-signed to durance vile. Next morning (the 28th) the Town Coun-cil met; and, in order to dissipate the impression made by such treasonable gossip, they issued a proclamation setting forth:

"That whereas some person or persons, disaffected to his Majesty's person and Government, have raised and spread a false and groundless report that the town would surrender, we do therefore certify all concerned that we have no such design; but that we are firmly resolved to make a vigorous resistance if attacked by the rebels; and we hope none will credit the malicious stories to the contrair that have been contrived by the enemy."[*]

It was not traitorous tale-bearers merely that the authorities had to deal with: there were Achans in the camp of a more dangerous kind—plotting incendiaries, who repeatedly endeavoured to fire portions of the town. One notable attempt of this nature was made on the night of the 26th. A train of gunpowder, nine yards long, was laid at the foot of a close of thatched houses near the centre of the burgh, which, on being ignited, set one of the tenements in a blaze. Fortunately two of the magistrates were near at hand, by whose assistance the fire was extinguished before much damage or alarm was occasioned. A reward of a hundred merks was offered for the discovery of the guilty parties; and the authorities, fearing that on the approach of the rebels their friends inside would perpetrate similar acts of incendiarism in order to withdraw the loyal inhabitants from their posts, and otherwise create confusion, adopted all possible precautions to prevent or mitigate the threatened evil. The militia of the county was not yet raised—why, it is difficult to say; so that Dumfries had to depend for its defence on volunteer soldiers alone.

These, as has been mentioned, were forthcoming to a large extent. In the last week of October the burgh wappenschaw could boast, we should say, of fully three thousand men; (a) one half of whom were well trained and armed, the other half raw recruits, including five score of such inhabitants as had little skill in firearms, who were furnished with scythes, and set to do duty at the barricades and in the trenches. The magistrates, with prudent forethought, resolved that Mr Currie, one of their number, should be sent on a mission to General Carpenter, who had arrived at Jedburgh in search of the Jacobites under Kenmure. On learning the condition of affairs at Dumfries, the General assured Bailie Currie that if the town were attacked, and held out for six hours against the rebels, he would at the close of that time be ready to fall upon them in the rear. Fully aware of the importance of retaining Dumfries, the Duke of Argyle sent Major Campbell, Captain William Graham, Lieutenant Francis Scott, Lieutenant Anthony Smith, Lieutenant David Reid, Lieutenant John Kay, and Ensign Robert M'Arthur, all half-pay officers, to superintend its defence.

* Rae's History, p. 227.
(a) This is by much too large an estimate.

On the 24th, soon after their arrival, the work of thoroughly fortifying the town was proceeded with. In earlier times, as we have seen, it was surrounded, except where the Nith formed a natural defence, by walls, ditches, and earthen banks. Pursuing a somewhat similar plan, the loyal inhabitants, under skilful military direction, soon rendered the fortifications tolerably complete —quite able to resist the enemy's assaults for ten times the six hours that General Carpenter had bargained for. All the gates and avenues were built up with stone, except the bridge and Lochmaben-gate. A line of wall was raised from the river to the churchyard, and thence through the adjoining meadow to the high road beyond Lochmaben-gate; it then ran towards the east, curved towards the north-west, then to the south-east corner of Sir Christopher's Chapel; the whole constituting a covered way in the form of a half-moon. From the south-west corner of the chapel another line was drawn nearly parallel to the former, for the safety and convenience of the defenders, in the event of the rebels forming on the fields betwixt that locality and the Loreburn, which streamlet was also intrenched; and the meadow beyond it was protected by a deep ditch, dug behind a thick thorn hedge that separated it from the highway leading to the Townhead. Here also the gate was walled up, and a trench of bastion shape gave protection to the Moat on the other side. It took fully a week to complete these works; for though hundreds of hands were employed, suitable materials were not easily obtained; and in the pressing emergency, the stones of the east gable of the sacred edifice erected by Christiana Bruce in memory of her patriotic husband, were appropriated by the workmen. Little did the royal lady think when she erected the chapel, or Robert Bruce when he endowed it, that its walls would be thrown down for the purpose of resisting the march of one of their descendants to his ancestral throne. What piety and widowed love fondly built up, patriotism unreluctantly cast down. But curious cross-purposes such as this are frequently met with by the historian.

The 30th and 31st of October formed the crisis of this extraordinary passage in the annals of Dumfries. As the former of these days was Sabbath, those who laboured at the defences expected to enjoy a short season of rest. At half-past nine o'clock in the morning, however, a proclamation was made by tuck of drum that they were all to repair to the works as usual; the Provost and deputy-lieutenants having received an express announcing that the enemy had arrived at Hawick, on their route by Langholm to Dumfries. Accordingly the din of preparation was redoubled on the sacred day; trenches were extended or deepened; several trees growing in the churchyard were cut down—the ringing sounds made by the axe-men rising simultaneously with the song of the worshippers—and stakes formed

of the timber with which to dam up the Mill-burn, so as to cause
the waters of that brook to fill the trenches, and prevent the
mounted rebels crossing the meadows. It was on the 30th, too,
that the remains of the ancient chapel, consisting chiefly of a fine
arch and back wall, were put to use. With the stones of the arch
a redoubt was built to cover the entry of the highway near at
hand ; and the wall was lowered to serve as a rest for firelocks.

Langholm was reached by the rebels that evening ; and long
before sunrise next morning a detachment of them, numbering
about four hundred horse, commanded by the Earl of Carnwath,
arrived at Ecclefechan, with orders to blockade Dumfries till the
main body arrived to attack the town. Carnwath and his men
rested in their saddles at Ecclefechan, for further instructions ;
which having been brought by Mr Burnet of Carlops, they took
quarters for a brief space in the village, and then remounted, with
the design of being at Dumfries by break of day.

On the lieges there learning from a special messenger that
the rebels were within eight miles of them, the preconcerted
alarm was given by beating of drums and ringing of bells ; a
muster of all the able-bodied men was made at the Moat ; after
which they were marshalled into companies, and took their posts
at the trenches, "marching thither," says Rae, "with an un-
daunted courage," the ministers going with them, prepared to
fight as well as their people, and surgeons attending in case of
need.* From the 13th of October (with the exception of a short
period, when it was erroneously supposed that the Jacobites had
abandoned their intention to attack the town), meetings for
prayer and exhortation were held daily in the church, and the
windows looking into the principal streets were lighted all night.
What a season of excitement it must have been ! and the night of
the 31st, when it reached a climax, must prove the most painfully
anxious experienced by that generation of Dumfriesians, and be
referred to by them ever afterwards with mixed emotions of
terror, thankfulness, and pride.

A Town Council minute of an after date, in noticing the
recompense given to "the countrymen come in for defence of this
place, and that particularly on the 31st of October last and 1st of
November instant, when the rebels were within a little space of
this burgh, in order to the attack thereof," states that "people
were obliged to be fourty-eight hours in the trenches made round
this town, during which time they could not be removed from
duty for refreshing themselves, and therefore the magistrates
caused give them bread and provisions for refreshing themselves
in the fields." It was felt that if the least relaxation were made
the enemy might take ruinous advantage of it, and therefore the

* History, p. 275.

watch was unremitting. With the clouds of night came pelting showers of rain, and the air waxed piercingly cold ; but every man continued at his allotted post in the trenches, at the barricades, or with a chosen body of reserve in High Street, two hundred in number, with three pieces of cannon, whose orders were to reinforce those defenders against whom the main assault of the enemy should be delivered.

They had friends outside, too, ready on certain conditions to give them a helping-hand, if necessary. These consisted of about three hundred and twenty Cameronians, under their minister, Mr John Hepburn of Urr, who having some military knowledge had exercised it in training them for the express purpose of coping with the *Pretender.* These men belonged to that section of Richard Cameron's followers who could not accept the Revolution Settlement, and who yet were loath to separate altogether from the national Church, which they viewed with affectionate interest, though it was to them only what "the second Temple was to the old men who had seen and remembered the glorious structure of King Solomon."† On the 31st of October Hepburn's men were in the parish of Kirkmahoe, a few miles distant from Dumfries ; and Bailie Gilchrist, accompanied by the Laird of Bargaly, was sent thither to solicit their assistance. Marching towards the town, they yet, operated upon by their religious scruples, declined to enter ; then crossing the river, they took up a position on Corbelly Hill, at the west end of the bridge, to watch the current of events from that commanding eminence. There they were visited by the Provost and other gentlemen, who offered them any post they might choose within the town ; upon which they presented an unsigned paper to the deputation, asserting "that they had no freedom in their consciences to fight in defence of the constitution of Church and State, as established since the sinful Union." They mentioned the conditions on which they would enter the burgh to join in its defence ; but as many of these were of a political and general nature such as the King or Parliament only could grant, no arrangement was effected ; and the party

---

* The Rev. John Hepburn, a native of Forfarshire, began his ministerial labours in Urr about the year 1680. He was a devoted Cameronian ; and his opinions as such made him a resolute opponent of the Jacobites. He employed his soldierly skill in drilling his parishioners on Halmyre Hill, near his church, that they might be the more able to resist the Pretender. The late Dr. Mundell, rector of Wallace Hall Academy, who was great-grandson to Mr Hepburn, had in his possession the claymore and drum that were used by his martial ancestor. Dr. Walker, in his "Theology and Theologians of Scotland," says (p. 110) "Mr Hepburn was a man of spiritual power, who bore witness for God, not merely in ecclesiastical deeds but in human consciences ; and with him " the protesting party "kept up for many years their negative separation, forming a sort of distinct community within the Church."

† Theology and Theologians of Scotland, p. 109.

continued on Corbelly Hill, where they were supplied with necessaries by the inhabitants, whom they would no doubt have helped had their services been required.

The night of the 31st, with its pitiless showers and inclement winds—ill to bear by the wearied watchers, but of no moment compared to the racking thoughts that troubled them—passed slowly on. " Would that it were day, even though the enemy should appear with it !" was, we may suppose, the anxious wish of many, as the leaden hours crept lazily along. At brief intervals the officers visited their men, to see that they were prepared for the expected emergency ; and about four o'clock in the morning the news went round that the attack might be looked for at seven, and the men were told to mind their arms and to keep their powder dry—precautions all the more requisite as it still rained heavily. At five o'clock an express arrived from the hamlet of Roucan, affirming that the rebels had passed the old castle of Torthorwald, and were within three miles of the town. This was found out to be erroneous, friendly scouts having been mistaken for the enemy, but not till the false alarm had caused a great flutter of excitement. Seven o'clock arrived, and still the enemy remained unseen—eight o'clock—nine !—without bringing a single rebel in view. Was it possible that the bold Jacobites, after all their threats and boastings, had resolved to leave Dumfries unharmed in its loyalty ; without so much as striking a blow for a town the possession of which they at one time deemed essential to their success in the south of Scotland ?

It was even so. Good news to this effect reached its defenders by ten o'clock. The intelligence was rapidly circulated that the rebels, afraid to attack a place so well defended, were preparing for a retrograde march ; and the inhabitants, so long stretched upon the rack, began to feel at ease and breathe freely. Soon after Carnwath's party left Ecclefechan, on their way to Dumfries, an express from their friends in the burgh informed them of its condition—bristling with arms, strongly fortified, bravely defiant —and beseeching them " not to try their teeth on so obdurate a morsel." This discouraging letter was forwarded to the main body of the army, then lying about two miles west from Langholm, and formed the subject of a keen debate.

A proposal, made by Lord Kenmure, to continue moving on Dumfries, though favoured by the Lowland horse and foot, was resolutely opposed by the English gentlemen, who desired to carry on the war in their own country. Kenmure, reluctantly giving way to the opinion of the latter, ordered a march into England. About five hundred Highlanders, who did not relish the idea of crossing the Border, set out for the North, proceeding through the moors by Lockerbie—near which town ten were taken by the country people, and sent prisoners to Dumfries ;

some were seized at Sanquhar ; a great many about the head of
Clydesdale ; scarcely a tithe of the poor Celts reaching their own
mountain land in safety. All dread of a rebel attack being now
over at Dumfries, the country friends who had helped to stave it
off withdrew, promising to return within twenty-four hours, if
called upon.

Ere another month had passed away the rebel cause was
crushed in England and beginning to wear a forlorn aspect in the
Highlands. It would, in all human probability, have fared much
better if its adherents had succeeded in becoming masters of
Dumfries. Kenmure's plan of operations, after the Scottish and
English forces united at Kelso, was to move westward along the
Border, occupying first Dumfries, next Ayr, and eventually
Glasgow. He proposed then to open the passes, held chiefly by
militia and volunteers, in order to allow the Argyleshire clans,
under General Gordon, to rally round the Prince's standard. This
movement effected, it was reasonably supposed that the Duke of
Argyle, when he found himself confronted by a superior army
under the Earl of Mar, and with the forces of Kenmure, Forster,
and Macintosh upon his left flank and in his rear, would be
compelled to evacuate his strong post at Stirling ; and in that
case King George would have had but a frail tenure left of his
northern dominions. Once possessed of Dumfries, the Jacobites
would readily have obtained reinforcements and supplies by sea
from France and Ireland ; the gentlemen of the district who
sympathised with them would have been encouraged to join their
ranks ; and the first great step of a promising campaign would
have been taken. But the unexpected opposition given by the
burgh altered the whole character of the rebel movement ; and by
enforcing the separation of its promoters, contributed materially
to its failure.

When the Pretender's forces entered England Forster, in
virtue of a commission from the Earl of Mar, assumed the chief
command ; Kenmure still continuing to act as leader of the
Scottish soldiers, who by the desertion of the Highlanders were
reduced to about a thousand in number. The Earl of Nithsdale,
who had joined the movement personally at Langholm, was
amongst them ; also William Grierson of Lag, Gilbert Grierson,
his brother, John Maxwell of Steilston, Edmund Maxwell of
Carnsalloch, Robert Maclellan of Barscobe, William Maxwell of
Munches, George Maxwell, his brother, Charles Maxwell of Cowhill, Andrew Cassie of Kirkhouse, Basil Hamilton of Baldoon,
lieutenant of Kenmure's troop of horse, and other gentlemen of
the district. It was on the 1st of November that the rebels
turned their backs to Dumfries. On the 12th of that month we
find them, after gathering considerable strength in the town of
Preston, preparing to resist a large Royalist army under General

Wilks. On the 14th they are seen, after making an unavailing defence, in the attitude of hopeless captives--"the white rose of loyalty" vanished from their grasp, leaving nothing to them but its rankling thorns.

The prisoners, nearly fifteen hundred in number, were cruelly treated : six were shot, according to martial law, as holding commissions under the Government against which they had borne arms ; and many were banished to the plantations in America. Those of most note were sent up to London, and after being led through some of its streets in triumph, were consigned to prison. Crushed in the north of England, the Rebellion was at the same time, as we have said, faring badly in the ancient kingdom, on which the Chevalier chiefly relied. Mar half gained a victory at Sheriffmuir ; but, under the peculiar circumstances of his position, his partial triumph was tantamount to a defeat. If in any way an early junction could have been effected between his army and the one led by Kenmure and Forster, the insurgent movement would have become more hopeful ; and when the latter force withdrew to England, Mar ought to have boldly crossed the Forth, seized Edinburgh, which could have offered little opposition, and swept into the South. Instead of adopting, or trying to adopt, such an energetic line of policy, he allowed the Royalists time to muster powerfully in his front, was forced to fight a testing battle, which resulted in his retreat to Perth, and lost a chance of success that never again presented itself. On the 22nd of December, nine days after the disastrous no-victory at Sheriffmuir, and eight after the inglorious and woeful surrender of Preston, the Prince arrived at Peterhead, all too late to revive the bloom of his blighted fortunes. The Northern army melted gradually away, " without even the *éclat* of a defeat ;" and in the following February the unfortunate Pretender and his faithful Lieutenant-General, the Earl of Mar, were forlorn fugitives in France.

Trial and condemnation followed rapidly to the leaders of the collapsed Rebellion. On the 9th of February Lords Derwentwater, Kenmure, Nithsdale, Wintoun, Carnwath, Nairn, and Widdrington were brought to the bar of the House of Commons, and, having pleaded guilty to the articles of impeachment previously served upon them, were adjudged to death. The four first named peers were ordered for execution, in spite of great intercessions made on their behalf ; the other three were eventually pardoned.

When Winifred, Countess of Nithsdale, first heard of her good lord's capture at Preston, his imprisonment in the Tower, and— sad climax of all !—his dread death-sentence, she was overcome with sorrow.

"Our ladie did nocht noo but wipe aye her een !
  Her heart's like to loup the gowd lace o' her goun,
But she's busked on her gay cleeding, an's aff for Lunnon toun—"*

resolved to risk everything in an attempt to cheat the gibbet of
its victim. With true wifely devotedness—only the less wonderful when we think of the loveable nature of her husband—she
travelled night and day, in tempestuous weather, that she might
solace him in his dark hour of need, appeal to the clemency of the
King on his behalf, or in some other way not yet apparent obtain
a reversal of his sentence. His Majesty rudely repulsed the noble
suppliant, rejected her petition, and she relapsed into despair ;
which, however, soon gave way to a hopeful resolution to win by
love and wile what harsh royalty had denied.

The Countess was fifth and youngest daughter of William,
Marquis of Powis, and must at this time have been in the bloom
of early womanhood. Her picture is at Terregles House, forming
one of its chief art-treasures : it bespeaks a heroine from whom
we might expect such a daring and ingenious enterprise as that
upon which she entered with full heart and mind. Rarely do we
meet with a finer face : it is full of intellectual beauty. It manifests great force of character and intellectual strength, softened
by womanly sweetness—no Amazonian roughness being noticeable
in any of the lineaments. The brow is broad and high ; the face
oval, with a rare blending of the Roman with the Grecian features ;
and the general expression is extremely captivating. When the
vision of such a radiant countenance as this lighted up the room
where her imprisoned husband lay, he might well believe that a
bright celestial apparition had come to cheer him in his passage
through the valley of death ; and what must have been his rapture
when he saw that it was the wife of his bosom come to give him
hope, liberty, life itself !

His sentence was fixed to take place on the 24th of February ;
and two days before, the Countess, whose plans were nearly
matured, visited her husband, as she had previously been allowed
to do on several occasions. Affecting an air of cheerfulness, she
assured the guards that she was the bearer of joyful news for the
prisoners : their petition praying the House of Lords to intercede
for them had been passed, she said, and their early liberation might
be looked for. By such representations, and a pretty liberal
distribution of money, the guards were led to relax their vigilance,
and inadvertently to favour her designs. Having prepared Lord
Nithsdale for their being carried into effect, she took her leave,
returning on the eve of the following day, when he must be
delivered from the dungeon and the scaffold, if at all. Her
faithful attendant Evans, an acquaintance of the latter, named

* Allan Cunningham's Remains of Nithsdale and Galloway Song.

Mrs Morgan, and her own landlady, Mrs Mills, were her accomplices in the projected stratagem. On the arrival of the fair conspirators at the Tower, the Countess, who was only allowed one companion at a time, introduced Mrs Morgan in the first instance ; and she having purposely left a superfluous riding hood in the prison, was sent out to request the attendance of another servant, Mrs Mills. The latter, a stout, portly woman, appeared accordingly, holding a handkerchief to her face, as if overcome with grief. To her was assigned the difficult duty of personating the imprisoned Earl ; but though sufficiently masculine for the purpose, her eyebrows and hair were ruddy, Lord Nithsdale's dark. His lady— fertile in forethought and resources—by means of paint, chalk, artificial headgear, the clothes left by Mrs Morgan, and other articles of her own, so disguised the captive that, when viewed superficially, he seemed the veritable Mrs Mills, though that lady had already, in her ordinary attire, slipped out unchallenged. Accompanied by his Countess he safely passed the sentinels, whose suspicions had been lulled asleep by her plausible statements and liberality.

" When "—to quote from her own account, drawn up many years afterwards in a letter to her sister, Lady Lucy Herbert— " When I had almost finished dressing my lord in all my petticoats excepting one, I perceived that it was growing dark, and was afraid that the light of the candles might betray us ; so I resolved to set off. I went out leading him by the hand ; and he held his handkerchief to his eyes. I spoke to him in the most piteous and afflicted tone of voice, bewailing bitterly the negligence of Evans, who had ruined me by her delay. ' Then,' said I, ' my dear Mrs Betty, for the love of God run quickly and bring her with you ! You know my lodgings ; and if ever you made despatch in your life, do it at present : I am almost distracted with this disappointment !' The guards opened the doors, and I went down stairs with him, still conjuring him to make all possible despatch. As soon as he had cleared the door, I made him walk before me, for fear the sentinel should take notice of his walk ; but I still continued to press him to make all the despatch he possibly could. At the bottom of the stairs I met my dear Evans [who had only been blamed for delay as a pretence for hastening the disguised lord's departure], into whose hands I confided him. I had before engaged Mr Mills to be in readiness before the Tower, to conduct him to some place of safety in case we succeeded. He looked upon the affair as so very improbable to succeed, that his astonishment, when he saw us, threw him into such consternation that he was almost out of himself ; which Evans perceiving, with the greatest presence of mind, without telling him any thing, lest he should mistrust them, conducted him to some of her own friends on whom she could rely, and so secured him, without which we should have been undone."

So far matters had progressed in a manner that seemed almost miraculous ; but the heroine of the escape had still some delicate work on hand to prevent detection and pursuit. She had pretended to send Mrs Mills on a pressing message for another attendant, and had therefore to return to the cell on the further pretence of waiting her arrival. When there, she says, "I talked to him as if he had been really present, and answered my own questions in my lord's voice as nearly as I could imitate it. I walked up and down as if we were conversing together, till I thought they had time enough thoroughly to clear themselves of the guards. I then thought proper to make off also. I opened the door, and stood half in it, that those in the outer chamber might hear what I said, but held it so close that they could not look in. I bade my lord a formal farewell for that night ; and added, that something more than usual must have happened to make Evans negligent on this important occasion, who had always been so punctual in the smallest trifles ; that I saw no other remedy than to go in person ; that if the Tower were still open when I finished my business, I would return that night ; but that he might be assured I would be with him as early in the morning as I could gain admittance into the Tower ; and I flattered myself I should bring favourable news. Then, before I shut the door. I pulled through the string of the latch, so that it could only be opened in the inside. I then shut it with some degree of force, that I might be sure of its being well shut. I said to the servant, as I passed by—who was ignorant of the whole transaction—that he need not carry in candles to his master till my lord sent for him, as he desired to finish some prayers first. I went down stairs and called a coach, as there were several on the stand. I drove home to my lodgings, where poor Mr Mackenzie had been waiting to carry the petition, in case my attempt had failed. I told him there was no need of any petition, as my lord was safe out of the Tower, and out of the hands of his enemies." After lying in concealment for several days, Lord Nithsdale, disguised as a livery servant to the Venetian ambassador, proceeded in that gentleman's coach and six to Dover—where it was going on other business—and then took ship for Calais. Lady Winifred, after the lapse of several weeks, succeeded in getting an interview with King George, when she presented a petition, praying that the forfeited Nithsdale peerage and estates might be conferred upon her son ; but his Majesty, resenting her conduct, not only disregarded her petition, but treated her with rudeness. She had the gratification of knowing, however, that her husband was beyond the King's reach. Lord Nithsdale lived twenty-nine years after the date of his extraordinary deliverance, and died at Rome in 1744, on the very eve of another great rebellion in favour of the House of Stuart. Lord Derwentwater and Viscount Kenmure were beheaded on the 24th February ; both of them continuing firm Jacobites to the last.

The estates of the convicted insurgents were forfeited to the Crown; and though the property belonged to nearly forty individuals, its annual revenue was comparatively small—only £30,000. A Government surveyor, appointed for the purpose, estimated the rental of the Earl of Nithsdale, from depositions made by the tenants, at £803 2s 8d, of which fully £749 was payable in money ; the rest in goods, including such items as forty-four bolls of barley, at 10s 5d per boll; about the same quantity of oatmeal, at the same price; three hundred and forty-seven hens, at 5d each ; and 13s 6d for peats, at 1d per dozen loads. The forfeited estates were purchased from the Crown by a London company; but as this speculative investment was badly managed, they were afterwards exposed for sale, and for the most part bought at moderate rates for the late proprietors by their friends. The Nithsdale peerage was never restored, though the estates continue to be possessed by the Maxwell family. Lady Kenmure survived her chivalrous and unfortunate husband sixty-one years, and so managed the property that when her son Robert reached majority it was delivered to him free of debt. She died at Terregles House in 1776 ; and in 1824 the attainted title was given back to her grandson, John, the sixth Viscount of Kenmure.

We complete our account of the Rebellion by a local episode that ought not to be overlooked. Whilst the Marquis of Annandale was busy superintending the defences of Dumfries, his brother, Lord John Johnstone, who had served James the Seventh in Ireland, was doing his best to promote the pretensions of that monarch's son. His design was to assist in the meditated attack upon the town at the head of some of his brother's retainers ; but before he could marshal them he was seized at the instance of the magistrates, and kept in the Tolbooth till the whole affair was over.* According to a tradition in his lordship's family, the authorities honoured his exit from prison with a procession, and expressed a hope, in parting with him, that they had not acted improperly.

What the liberated Jacobite said in reply is not recorded ; but when, fifteen years afterwards, a deputation from the magistrates waited upon him at his house, to compliment him on his birthday, he presented the town with two valuable pictures, accompanied by the following note, addressed to the Provost :—"Sir,—The

---

* Though thus placed in durance, Lord John was hospitably treated, the magistrates appointing "M'Noe, the town drummer, at that time the best valet in the place, to wait on him sedulously, and supply his table with the best the principal inn afforded."—M'Diarmid's *Picture of Dumfries*, p. **73**.

great civilities the good town of Dumfries has been pleased to show my brother and his family makes me earnestly wish for an opportunity to show them my sense of the obligation this lays upon both of us. King William and Queen Mary is so well, that I have chosen to send their pictures as a present to the Corporation ; and I hope, as I value those great deliverers, on public as well as private considerations, they will receive them as a pledge of my disposition to do all the good in my power to this county and burgh ; and beg you would take the trouble to make these, and my compliments, acceptable to the Corporation, which tie me to be still more, sir, your most humble servant,—JOHN JOHNSTONE. Dumfries, 30th August, 1730."

Though a slight vein of irony is visible in this letter, the writer of it had reason to be truly thankful to the magistrates for keeping him out of an embroilment by which he might have lost his head ; and the beautiful portraits presented by him remain in the Town Hall—the mementoes of his gratitude, and the best pictorial treasures possessed by the burgh. (a)

(a) Important correspondence relating to this period appears in the Fifteenth Report, Appendix, Part IX., of the Historical Manuscripts' Commission, compiled from the Raehills Muniments by Sir William Fraser.

On Oct. 12, 1715, Provost Corbett, Dumfries, writes to William, Marquis of Annandale, who was Lord-Lieutenant not only of Dumfriesshire but of the Stewartry of Kirkcudbright and the county of Peebles. He states that he sends Bailie Corrie to acquaint the Marquis of an express from the Lord Justice Clerk intimating " that a considerable number of disaffected persons, both on the Scots and English borders, were to have mett, Munday last, in the west of Teviotdale, and then if they receaved no contrair orders from their own faction yesterday they were there to display the Pretendar's standart under the command of the Viscount of Kenmuir, and one of their main designs is to seize this burgh." The Provost goes on to say that he had sent expresses for aid, and most well-affected gentlemen from Tinwald, Torthorwald, and Kirkmahoe parishes were come in to help. He thus explains that the burgesses cannot attend the general rendezvous of the shire to be held at Locharbriggs, and he begs the Marquis to assent thereto. " There is," he adds, " likewise come with the bearer one Mr Frazer, who calls himself brother to the Lord Lovit, who with his said brother, ane aged man of about 60 years, and about six servants come to this place yesternight. Whom being challenged to give account of themselves, Mr Frazer produced a pass said to be from Secretary Stanhope. But his brother producing no pass, by the advice of the deputy livetennants of Galloway, who are here, we have caused sett a sentury upon them till we hear your lordship's orders annent them."

[In the Calendar of the Stuart Papers, of the Historical Manuscript Commission, published 1902, there is this entry under heading William, Marquis of Annandale : " 1715, Oct. 13 [-24]. Dumfries.—Pass for Lord Lovat and his brother John Frazer, and his cousins James and Hugh Frazer, with their servants, to go to the camp at Stirling or to join Lord Hay in the Highlands.]

The Marquis, writing from Dumfries, 14th Oct., 1715, to Brigadier-General Thomas Stanwix, at Carlisle, reports that a party of rebels, headed by the Earls of Nithsdale, Wintoun, and Carnwath, Viscount Kenmure, and others, numbering 200 horse well mounted, have got together about Dumfries. They have tried to capture him (the writer), but failed, and now design to attack the town. He therefore asks for arms, ammunition, and officers, to command the country people. There is a letter of same date from General

Stanwix, to which the other is probably a reply, that he will do all he can to support the Marquis and his friends against the rebels.

On 15th Oct. Sir W. Maxwell (of Westerhall) writes from Glasgow to the Marquis that he is glad to learn of the safety of his lordship, and of the town of Dumfries, as it had been reported that the Marquis had been surprised by the rebels.

On the 16th October the Marquis writes from Dumfries to General Stanwix that the party of rebels who had appeared there had increased by others joining them in their march from Lochmaben to Ecclefechan on Friday and this day (Sunday) to the English border. They are not, he says, rebels from Northumberland, but " our owne people about this countrey ;" and he adds that they evidently expect assistance from England, as 1000 Highlanders had possessed themselves of Haddington, &c. Stanwix replies on 17th that the party referred to had formerly been with Derwentwater, and "they are now gon, I suppose, to meet that lord, who came last Friday night again to Hexham, left his wholl partie in that town, except thirty, which with several gentlemen he took to his own house, where they stayed all Saturday, and I believe are there still." It " looked to me," he adds, " as if he was going to drop those poor people he'd drawn in."

The Marquis writes to Stanwix, October 19, that he must leave Dumfries the next day for Edinburgh. He has, he says, left orders as to the care of the district with his deputy-lieutenants ; and he asks Stanwix to write to Sir William Johnstone if necessary.

Sir William Johnstone on 20th October writes from Dumfries to the Marquis that several of Kenmure's party have come back, particularly Niths-dale, Glenriddell, and Wamphray ; and Lag, younger, has sent a message that he is willing to come in and find bail. He desires commands as to this. The Galloway gentlemen are, he says, entirely marched off with their men. Their own country people have come in, but want arms. With the advice of Craig-darroch he has answered an enclosed letter from Viscount Stormont to the Marquis. He tells the Viscount that if he would come in he should be " civilly dealt by and only keepit by centries at his doors and windows " till the mind of the Marquis was known. Stormont's letter informs the Marquis that " I was surprised to understand that my house was searched for me yesterday (19th Oct.) and garisoned. . . . I have given no offence to the Government except in not obeying a citation which nothing hindered me from but the fear of a prison, considering the present bad circumstances of my health. But such is the entire trust I putt in your lordship that ill as I am I resolve to wait upon your lordship to-morrow at Dumfreise and surrender myself." To this the Marquis replies that if he had known the Viscount's design he would have stayed at Dumfries to make him as " cosy " as he could. As it is he will endeavour so effectually to recommend his early submission to the King as to entitle the Viscount to his favour.

The duplicity of Sir Patrick Maxwell of Springkell is exhibited by two letters. Writing to Viscount Kenmure, Oct. 31, he regrets that his lordship had not advertised him so that he might have afforded him a complement of men. " Pray," he says, " let me know what I shall do to raise them or not, to be with you or to keep the Borders. . . . If, please God, you gaine Dumfries, put out a proclamatione that you are for defence of your countrie's property and libertie, and order sermons in the church by your own ministers, and lett them preach the same, and order that all who do not go to hear sermon be seized upon, that the commons may hear and beleave the reasons of your taking arms." Four days after this, November 4, Sir Patrick, writing to Sir William Johnstone from Kirkconnell, makes excuse for not having complied with a demand for men, and proceeds as follows : " You talk of my being absent from my house, when I went to visite sick people and my friends. I think it was more charity then to stay for your guards. I wish with all my heart, Sir William, that you had skill in physick, then you would be more happy in the blessings of the poor then in your imployments or worldly concerns. Pray let me know if I can live without trouble at home, for I would not go alongst with Kenmure, nor give him a man. But I am in the conditions of those whom the ministers, in the 1642, preached against most severely who were guilty of the damnable sin of newtrality. You are not in that sin. I love to live quiet if I can. Tell me what you would have me to do, if possible, for I cannot observe impossibilities." Rather a bold bit of mockery, and it was taken as such.

On the 4th November Sir William Johnstone writes to the Marquis of Annandale that on Monday he went with Major Campbell through the works to be done, and that night got to Lochmaben, on his journey home, "to look after our militia." On Tuesday, by nine in the morning he met one of his servants with letters "of the rebells designed march to attack Dumfreis." Knowing this he returned, and that night despatched expresses to every deputy-lieutenant and minister, "and the result is that we have this day 1300 verry hearty but bad armes in Dumfries. Our works (he goes on to say) are so weell done that we wold have stood our ground against thrice the number was against us, and not run for it, as Kelso, for which I hope they have payed. Major Campbell has been very active, and all the half-pay officers most dilligent." As to Stormonth, Sir William believes he will join him, but he dare not trust him on the road ; and "Nithsdale is gone with the rebells." John Johnstone, Sir William's son, has been chosen captain of the Volunteers. "They are gone to the Borders to catch stragglers, and to bring up from the Langholme a cannon and one other piece of ordinance from the Langholme which the rebells left." Sir William further reports that Stanwix had sent him a copy of Sir Patrick Maxwell's letter to Kenmure and a line from Sir Patrick about the militia. "Contradictorry in every poynt and shufling his duty in raiseing the militia." He suggests Sir Patrick's arrest.

On the same sheet of paper with an unimportant letter from General Stanwix is written : "Copie of the instructions given to the Magistrats of Drumfries by the deputy-lovetennants of the shyre of Drumfries, stewartries of Annandaill and Kirkcudbright. Imprimus. That the magistrats of Drum-fries be provyded with ammunition necessar, and that the bullets be cassen in several caums, both for muskets and cannons, and that cartarages be made. 2nd. That ane express be sent to Whytehaven to know what arms can be had ther for money. 3dly. That orders be given for making of bagonets. 4thly. That Bailly Corrie and two or three to attend him be sent to waite upon the rebells motion, and to send expresses dailly of the enimies motion, and to take notice of the enimies passage by Kysock road. 5thly. To write to Bailly Melvill to secuir all expresses goeing to or from the rebells. 6thly. That the pryces of hay and corne be regulate within the toun of Drumfries. 7thly. That no expresses or posts go off without acqwanting of the deputy love-tennants."

This Bailie Currie was a Dumfries merchant, who was also proprietor of Speddoch. His father, who died 1709, had filled a bailieship, and he himself became Provost in 1718, holding the position till 1736. His brother Joseph was Town-clerk ; and after Joseph, Joseph's son James. Their term of office covered the Prince Charlie period.

CHAPTER XLIII.

EXTENSIVE BUILDING SCHEMES ENTERED INTO — IMPROVEMENTS IN
DWELLING-HOUSES—A ROAD FORMED THROUGH LOCHAR MOSS—THE
GRAMMAR SCHOOL OF THE BURGH—SINGULAR REGULATIONS FOR ITS
MANAGEMENT—COCK-FIGHTING IN THE SCHOOL A FAVOURITE PASTIME
OF THE PUPILS—ENDOWMENT OF SEWING AND MUSIC SCHOOLS—
LIBERAL EDUCATIONAL BEQUESTS BY BAILIE PATERSON—CHARITABLE
BEQUESTS BY THE REV. JOHN RAINING—-PROGRESS OF THE PORT—
CONTINUANCE OF SMUGGLING — FRESH ILLUSTRATIONS OF THE
"RUNNING" TRADE—GIPSY LIFE IN THE DISTRICT : NOTICES OF BIG
WILL BAILLIE AND JOCK JOHNSTONE—FEARFUL SCENE AT THE
EXECUTION OF JOHNSTONE.

WHEN the excitement caused by the Rebellion had fairly subsided,
a spirit of improvement sprang up in Dumfries which produced
valuable results ; and before the first half of the eighteenth
century had passed away, the sky-line of the town—to use an
artist's term—did not differ very materially from what it is at
present. At the date of the Union, the Mid Steeple rose up in
the centre of the burgh ; a spire-surmounted church soon afterwards was erected at its northern extremity, which was ere long
followed by another in the south ; whilst, in the meantime, many
houses were rebuilt, several roads were formed to connect the
town with the neighbouring district, new schools were instituted
or endowed, and several springs of charity began to flow for
behoof of the poor. Leaving the building of the churches to be
noticed afterwards at greater length, we shall briefly glance at
some of the other operations and occurrences belonging to the
period

For many years after 1715, the Town Council books contain
numerous references to the removal of ruinous tenements, and
their replacement by new erections ; as if in the course of a
generation or so a considerable proportion of the burgh had been
rebuilt. And the new houses were, it may be inferred, much
better than the old ones had ever been. The latter for the most
part were roofed with straw or other vegetable substance, and
many of them were of wood or clay. As a consequence fires were
of frequent occurrence : a most destructive one nearly ruined
Lochmaben-gate in 1691, and another of less extensive sweep did
much damage to Friars' Vennel in 1701. Not till 1724 did the
town possess a " water engine " for use on such occasions. On the

15th of July, 1723, the Council, after taking into account the great
loss caused by fires, ordained that henceforth all heritors and
others, in re-constructing or re-roofing houses joining with or
fronting into High Street, should cause the roofs to be made of
slates or tiles, and not of straw, heather, broom, breckans or
other combustible matter, under the penalty of one hundred
pounds Scots.

In the old fighting times, as has been repeatedly noticed,
Lochar Moss was prized by the inhabitants as a natural barrier of
defence. Now, however, they had no need to dread hostile
incursions from the South ; and, in order to open up a closer
communication with Lower Annandale and Cumberland, the
Council, assisted by neighbouring proprietors, projected a passage
through the moss. In terms of the contract, it was to extend from
" Hannay's Thorn to the syde of the Lake of Lochare, in the place
where the bridge went over to Colin ;" was to cost a hundred and
fifty pounds sterling ; and to be completed by Michaelmas, 1724,
about which time it was duly opened for public use.*

Education in the burgh received a new impulse. The germ of
the Dumfries Academy existed in pre-Reformation times.
" Master John Turnbull, rector of the school of Drumfreis," and
Robert M'Briar, provost, are witnesses to the sazine of Robert
Lord Maxwell, in a tenement in the town, so far back as 1481.
At first the masters of the burgh school taught English as well as
the classical languages ; and up till nearly the close of the seventeenth century there seems to have been only one authorised
teacher in the whole town. When, in 1663, Mr Matthew Richmond
was appointed to succeed Mr M'George as rector of the grammar
school, he was spoken of in comprehensive terms as " schoolmaster
of this burgh." The duties assigned to him were multifarious, he
being required to precent in the church, to officiate as parish clerk,
as well as to give instructions in Greek, Latin, and English, all
for £100 Scots a year, " with the benefit of quarter-days " (free-
will offerings from the pupils), and fees for marriage proclamations, baptisms, and burials. Mr John Fraser was schoolmaster
in 1673, with a salary of £40 Scots per quarter.

In June, 1724, the Council were fortunate enough to secure
the services as rector of the Rev. Robert Trotter, M.A., who by his
learning threw a bright lustre over the burgh school. He was son

----

* Pennant, writing in 1770, says :—"Over Lochar Moss is a road
remarkable for its origin. A stranger, a great number of years ago, sold some
goods to certain merchants in Dumfries upon credit ; he disappeared, and
neither he nor his heirs ever claimed the money. The merchants, in expectation of the demand, very honestly put out the sum to interest ; and after
the lapse of more than fifty years, the town of Dumfries obtained a gift of it,
and applied the same to the making of this useful road. Another is now in
erection for the military, to facilitate the communication between North Britain
and Ireland by way of Portpatrick."—Tour in Scotland, vol. ii., p. 95.

of the Laird of Prentonnan, parish of Eccles, Berwickshire, head
of the old Border clan of the Trotters, who boast of a Norman
lineage, and who fought gallantly at Flodden under the Earl of
Home. Rector Trotter published a valuable Latin grammar, that
was long popular as a school-book.* On his induction he had to
subscribe twenty conditions, some of which were in effect as
follows. During the summer half-year, beginning on the 1st of
April, the teacher, under teacher, and children were to enter the
school at seven o'clock each morning, and continue there till nine ;
the rest of the hours being from ten till twelve, and from two till
six, forming altogether eight hours daily, except on Saturdays,
when the school was closed at noon. In winter the morning
classes were omitted, the course of study remaining in other
respects the same. After such lengthened hours during the week,
the children might have been permitted to remain away from
drill, and out of harness, on the Lord's Day. But no : it was
anything save a day of rest to them. Rule number four required
that the teacher, his usher, and the pupils should be present at
the school each Sabbath morning by nine o'clock, and should at
the ringing of the steeple bells repair to the church, the master
going before, his assistant bringing up the rear ; that they should
return to the school at one o'clock, proceed to the church again, go
back to the school after worship, and there be catechised on the

---

* "Grammaticæ Latinæ Compendium ad Puerorum captum summa ope
concinnatum. In usum Scholæ Drumfriesiensis, Auctore Roberto Trottero,
A. M., Scholarcha ibidem. Edinburgi : Typis, Thomæ Lumisden and Joannis
Robertson. Anno Dom., 1732." In a presentation copy to him of Johnston's
Latin " Psalms of David," from the editor, Guleilmus Landerus, he is styled
" Doctissimo Viro Roberto Trottero, A.M., Scholæ Drumfriesiensis Proefecto
meritissimo, 1740." The year of his death is not certain ; but he was alive in
1760, in the winter of which year he went to place his grandson Robert at
College in Edinburgh, and travelled with him on foot from Dumfries in one
day to Morton Hall, the seat of Mr Trotter, a relation of his. A "thruch "
stone, with a Latin inscription written by himself, was erected to his memory
in St. Michael's churchyard, but has unaccountably disappeared, and
when searched for about forty-five years ago it could not be found ; but
the late Mr Crombie said he had seen the stone some years previously. He is
mentioned in "Heron's Tour " as an eminent Latin scholar, in the "Scottish
Nation," also in a note to Anderson's " Lives of the Poets," and by other
authors ; and he could converse with learned men in Greek, Latin, and Hebrew.
When at church he always used a Greek Testament.   It is also related of him
that when engaged in prayer during the great storm known as " Windy Saturday," the window was violently blown in on his sick grandson, then in bed,
hurting him severely.   This grandson was afterwards an eminent physician
for fifty-five years in the Glenkens, Galloway, where the family have long
maintained a respectable position in society. In Douglas's " Baronage " the
family is said to have born originally the Norman name of Gifford ; and in the
" Ulster Journal of Archæology " it is stated that the first of the name in
Scotland was a Celtic chief, who saved the life of King Fergus when his galley
was wrecked on the shore of Skye ; who, taking hold of the King, cried out
" Trouthard ! " viz., " Come here to this rock !"   The place where this
occurred was called Troutharness, now Trotternish, in Skye, and the Celtic
chief and his descendants took the name of Trouthar, now Trotter.

lectures or sermons they had listened to ; and then, supplementary
to all this, two scholars were selected each Sabbath to repeat or
read the Larger or Shorter Catechism in the church, during the
intermission, to such of the congregation as chose to remain
between the services.   In accordance with the seventh rule, the
under teacher was enjoined to put fresh rushes on the schoolhouse
floor once a month, " for preventing the spoiling of the children's
cloaths."

We learn from other regulations, that on Candlemas Day
literal candles, as well as other gifts, were brought as offerings by
the children to their teachers ; and that the Latin scholars were
required, in their converse with each other, in and out of school,
to speak exclusively in that tongue.   But the strangest rule of all
was one relating to the mode in which the rough pastimes of an
annual festival were to be conducted by the pupils.   Fastern's
E'en * had for ages been associated with fighting cocks; and
always, when the season came round, young and old, rich and
poor, shared eagerly in the cruel but exciting sport.   It must have
been looked upon as something like a national institution, when
" the most potent, grave, and reverend signiors " of the Dumfries
Town Council made the following arrangements for its observance
in their Burgh School :—" That at Fastern's Even, upon the day
appointed for the cocks fighting in the schoolhouse, the under
teacher cause keep the door, and exact no more than twelve
pennies Scots for each scholar for the benefit of bringing in a cock
to fight in the schoolhouse ; and that none be suffered to enter that
day to the schoolhouse but the scholars, except gentlemen and
persons of note, from whom nothing is to be demanded ; and what
money is to be given in by the scholars the under teacher is to
receive and apply to his own use for his pains and trouble ; and
that no scholars except who pleases shall furnish cocks, but all the
scholars, whether they have cocks or not, are to get into the
school "— such children as have none paying two shillings Scots
by way of compensation.   What a ludicrous mixture does this
academic code display of piety and pedantry, of hard mental
labour and boisterous relaxation !   The scholars of a former generation, and probably those of this one also, were allowed play-
acting by way of pastime, as appears from a charge made against
the Council in 1693 of £7 5s Scots "for 10 pr. deals at 14s 6d each,
for a stage to the scholars when they acted ' Bellum Gramatical.' "

Rector Trotter retired in 1760 on a yearly allowance of £30
from the burgh.   His assistant and successor was Dr George
Chapman, who also earned literary distinction as the author of an
excellent treatise on education.

So early as 1719 the Town Council instituted and endowed a

---

* The English Shrove Tuesday, held on the 6th of April.

school in which girls were to be taught "shaping and sewing all sorts of white and colloured seims, embroydering and paistry." We are apt to think that such an institution as this is a thing of modern growth; and it says much for the wisdom of our ancestors that they in this manner made provision for the industrial upbringing of their female children. Dame Glendinning, the first teacher of the school, was allowed five pounds sterling of annual salary, besides a fee of half-a-crown per quarter from each pupil, burdened with the condition of instructing six children of poor burgesses free of charge.

In further illustration of the growing refinement of the times, it may be stated that, about twenty years afterwards, the Town Council voted an annual salary of £100 Scots to a teacher of "the tuneful art." They were led to do so from a belief "that it will be of considerable advantage to the youth of the burgh and others that a music school be erected." The school, when opened, was made free to all--the usual distinctions between burgesses and other inhabitants having been set aside; and that the music-master might have plenty to do for his money, he was required to give lessons daily in the burgh school, Sundays excepted, from twelve till one o'clock, and from six till eight o'clock in the evening."* We find early traces also of a spinning school, the numerous wheels in which had for their chief motive power a money grant from the Town Council. It was superintended in 1751 by Elizabeth Hill. Her scholars that year numbered forty, for teaching whom she received a salary of £2 10s sterling per annum.

To Bailie John Paterson, who died in 1722, the High School and the cause of education generally in Dumfries were deeply indebted. He bequeathed eight thousand merks as a fund from which to maintain a schoolmaster "for teaching children in ane free schooll in this burgh the Latin rudiments and grammar, rhetorick, classick authors, and Greek New Testament;" also seven thousand merks in payment of a second preceptor "for teaching of children of burgesses, who shall be indwellers and burthin bearers within the burgh, and of eight children of the poorer sort of merchant burgesses and burthin bearers, in the arts of writing, arithmetic, book-keeping, and navigation." The moneys, amounting to £835 6s 8d sterling, were secured partly over the twenty-four merk land of Preston, with the merse and fell of Criffel in the parish of Kirkbean, the eight-merk land of Kirkbean, and the eight-merk land of Nimbellie and Fallowend in the same parish; and partly over the seven-merk land of Meikle Culloch, in the parish of Urr. The mortifications or deeds of the

* Education in other useful occupations was also promoted by the Council. On the 24th of December, 1753, Thomas Hiddleston, cook and confectioner, was admitted a freeman and burgess, on condition that he should teach three poor girls "the arts of cookery and confectinery or paistry."

intelligent and benevolent testator were laid before the magistrates and Town Council on the 5th of February, 1722 ; and they, with the ministers of the parish, being named administrators of the trust, took steps for giving it effect with the least possible delay.

Bailie Paterson was born in the parish of Newabbey, in Kirkcudbrightshire. In early life he commenced business as a merchant in Dumfries, and for many years took an active part in its public affairs. In his benefactions he remembered the place of his birth, as well as the town of his adoption. The bridge at the entrance to the picturesque village of Newabbey bears an inscription that it was built by him in 1715 ; and the poor of that parish have reason to bless the name of Bailie John Paterson, he having left a large sum for their behoof—£156—which, invested in land, and slightly added to from other sources, yields a handsome rental of £190 to the parochial funds of Newabbey. A humble tombstone in St. Michael's churchyard, just at the entrance on the right hand side, bears the simple inscription :—" Here lies John Paterson, merchant, late Bailie of Dumfries, who died 17th January, 1722, aged 65 years."* With all truth there might have been added—" Bailie Paterson was a large benefactor to the public, having left considerable sums for the endowment of Dumfries schools, and built a bridge at Newabbey, and provided for the poor of Newabbey, his native parish."†

In the following year Mr John Raining, a Dumfriesian long resident in the city of Norwich, "devised liberal things" for the benefit of his native burgh. An extract from his last will and testament was produced at a Council meeting held on the 24th of October, in which he bequeathed £500 sterling to be laid out to interest or in the purchase of lands or tenements for behoof of six poor old widows, sixty years of age or more, belonging to the town —the overplus, after so doing, to be applied in paying a schoolmaster for teaching destitute fatherless boys in English, Latin, and arithmetic. Mr Raining also left ten pounds to be distributed among the poor of Troqueer parish, a similar sum for the poor of Holywood parish, and many additional sums for charitable and religious purposes in other parts of Scotland and in Norwich.

* An adjoining stone, erected in memory of Bailie Paterson's son, who died in his seventeenth year, bears upon it the following epitaph :—
" When parents, friends, and neighbours hoped to see
This early bud of learning, piety,
And temper good, produce some fruit,
Behold, Death plucks the plant up by the root."

† Birth-place and Parentage of William Paterson, by William Pagan of Cupar. Mr Pagan shews pretty conclusively, in this work, that Bailie Paterson was not, as is popularly believed, brother to the projector of the Darien scheme, and that it is probable they were not in any way related to each other.

As results of these benefactions, two seminaries apart from the grammar school were opened; one for arithmetic, mathematics, and writing, the first master of which was Mr Charles Mercer; the other for English, which was first taught as a separate branch by Mr James Turnbull. Mr Alexander Shand, who succeeded the latter in 1755, had an annual salary of £11; £6 of it being taken direct from the burgh revenue, and £5 from Raining's mortification. He was also provided with a schoolhouse and residence; and his income was eked out by the quarterly wages, whose amount was left to the generosity of the inhabitants," and by £4 paid to him yearly for precenting in the New Church. If Young Dumfries was not well tutored a hundred years ago, in Latin, Greek, English, mathematics, writing, and music, it was certainly not for the want of teachers.

The importance of the Nith, as a means of trading intercourse, was now more than ever recognised. We find the Council, in the summer of 1772, causing sundry huge rolling stones to be removed that impeded the channel at Kingholm, and taking other steps to make the river more navigable. For a series of years after the Rebellion had been suppressed, the legitimate commerce of the port steadily increased; and the lapse of time brought no diminution of the "running trade;" though, after a party of soldiers had been stationed at the town, in 1720, the smugglers conducted their proceedings with greater caution.

In this respect the annals of Dumfries from 1715 till the second Jacobite insurrection are characterised by the same incidents as those that occurred during the earlier part of the century: the systematic landing of contraband goods, extensive seizures of them by the Government officials, frequent conflicts between the daring free traders of the Dirk Hatteraick * type, and the not less courageous guardians of the law; and all the other features of the long war waged for and against the revenue duties. A few details will suffice. In order that the Custom-house officers might be able more effectually to cope with the enemy, they procured two fast-sailing skiffs from Whitehaven, "built as near as possible to the shape of an Isle of Man boat," the dimensions being sixteen and a half feet keel, six feet two inches beam, twenty feet from stem to stern, and costing with full outrig about £12 each. By means of these cutters in the Solway, and numerous riders, runners, and waiters, on shore, a good look-out was kept, and many a smuggling enterprise was checked or rendered fruitless; though hundreds more, in spite of all that could be done, were carried to a successful issue every year.

"On the 10th of September, 1722," the collector writes, "we went to a place called Kirkbride, about seven miles from Dumfries,

---

* Yawkins, the prototype of Dirk Hatteraick, plied his vocation for many years in the waters of the Solway.

in pursuance of an information of some brandy lying there. Accordingly we found five small casks of brandy in and about the house of one Andrew Hewitson ; and after we had got it upon horseback, and brought it a small way from the house, the said Hewitson raised the whole country about upon us, who came with stones, clubs, and fire-arms, and violently deforced us of the said seizure."* "This is to inform you," the collector writes again, under date 2nd May, 1726, "that upon the 28th ult. the King's warehouse here was broken open betwixt one and two of the clock that morning, and five casks of brandy taken out thereof ; to our great surprise, considering the strength of the warehouse, for it had a strong double door," with a big lock, and padlock affixed by a chain, which everybody thought impregnable ; but it appears the door has been forced open by a crow iron, and the great chain been broken by the same instrument. As soon as we were informed of the same, we immediately got a warrant to search for the stolen brandy, and were informed that it was lodged in the Bridgend of Dumfries, where we found it in a house belonging to Robert Newal, wright there, and brought the same back to the warehouse."† It is then stated by the writer that, after great exertions, two of the "authors of the villainy" had been apprehended, and that he expected all the others would be secured. "We persuade our-selves," he goes on to say, getting virtuously indignant, "that a vigorous prosecution of the guilty now will effectually secure the warehouse from ever being broken again ; for altho' the warehouse has been broken open in this place before, yet the offenders were not discovered, which has given those fellows the assurance at this time to commit such a villainy."

A Leith merchant, named Briceson, figures in the next narrative as a smuggler bold. He is described as "one of the greatest runners upon the coast,"‡ for the apprehension of whom both the Excise and Customs' officers held warrants, which they had vainly tried to enforce. It was his practice, we infer, to run tobacco and brandy from the Isle of Man to the Solway coast ; sell as much of them as he could to the people of the district, and send the rest overland to his establishment at Leith. On the 12th of August, 1726, whilst a boatman named Affleck was proceeding to Dumfries with three casks of brandy which he had seized at Glenluffing Moss, Briceson appeared upon the scene. He had brought the liquor across the sea to a friend ; and not liking the idea of its being diverted into another channel, he, assisted by the son of his confederate, set ruthlessly upon the revenue officer, who had to relinquish his prize, and was glad to escape with bare life from his assailants.§ Whether this notable smuggler-merchant, who acted

---

* Custom-house Records.　　　　† Ibid.
‡ Custom-house Records.　　　　§ Ibid.

so much in the style of a modern filibuster, was ever brought to justice, is not mentioned ; but we may be sure that his premises in Leith would not be allowed to remain long open after this outrage was reported.

Often, it is said, the smugglers obtained a wonderful amount of co-operation from the well-trained horses which they either had in their employ, or which were placed at their services by the people of the district. Individuals, according to a writer in the *Dumfries-shire Magazine*, then alive (1821), or only recently dead, had frequently seen one famous troop of these quadrupeds, heavily laden, at day-dawn, with contraband goods, unattended by any human being, and preceded by a white horse of surpassing sagacity, scouring along the Old Bridge, down the White Sands, and through the streets of Dumfries, without any one daring to interrupt their progress. Indeed, in those days, such an attempt was not likely to be often made ; for it was notorious that the inhabitants themselves were too deeply implicated in similar transactions to induce them to restrain others. "It is related, however, that on one or two occasions, when some individual more officious than the rest rashly attempted to intercept the leader of the troop, the wily animal either suddenly reared and struck its opposer to the ground, or by a peculiar motion swung the kegs with which it was loaded with so much violence that no one durst approach within its reach."

It was found in course of time that the boats from Whitehaven, though built according to the Manx model, were easily distanced by the free-trading craft ; that the aid given to the revenue officers by soldiers was irregular, and of little value ; that the export of prohibited articles, as well as the import of contraband goods, went on increasing ; and that, therefore, a reform of the protective system of the Solway was urgently required. Actuated by this conviction, representatives from the ports of Dumfries, White-haven, Carlisle, and Workington, held a conference at Wigtown, Cumberland, on the 20th of November, 1724, and agreed to lay before the Customs' authorities certain remedial proposals. They recommended that two well-armed, well-manned sloops should be procured, fitted for both sailing and rowing, and that one of them should be stationed at Silloth, on the English side, the other at Annan Waterfoot, so as to command the open channel, whilst the smaller boats in the service should be employed along the shore. The Dumfries collector, in urging the adoption of this scheme says :—" The charge of each of these sloops would amount in the first year to £180, and afterwards to £130 yearly, which, indeed, will be an additional charge upon the revenue ; but I am convinced your honours will find it very sufficiently made up, either by the increase of the King's moiety of seizures, or the advance of the duty at the foresaid ports, and particularly the duty on tobacco ; for, notwithstanding of the great quantity of tobacco made use of in this country, there is but a small consumption of what is legally imported and fairly pays duty, which makes it plain that there are vast quantities of that commodity run from the Isle of Man." He expresses his belief that were one of these sloops placed on each side of the Frith, the passage betwixt them is so narrow that it would be difficult for any boat to pass undetected ; though at the same time the little revenue yawls would be needed to cruise after such contraband craft among the sandbanks and up the creeks, as succeeded in eluding the guardians of the channel.

These proposals were partially acted upon ; yet the profits of the running trade were so much greater than its risks, that it continued to flourish. Thi first notice of tea being brought into the county occurs in September, 1724, in which month "one small cask of Bohea" was seized near the Border. In the same year we begin to read of malt and wool as articles of export—quantities of the latter being carried from farm-houses down to the Colvend coast, and smuggled from Glenstocken to that rendezvous of all lawlessness, the Isle of Man."*

So rigid were the revenue regulations at this period that when some charitable people in Dumfries. commissioned two shiploads of oatmeal from Ireland that the poor might obtain it cheap when it was hardly to be had of home growth for love or money, the collector durst not permit the meal to be landed till he was specially authorised to do so by his official superiors. The officers were also scandalised by a daring innovation which had sprung up, especially at Kirkcudbright, of importing Irish cattle, and they sorely bewailed the connivance given to it by the county gentlemen and their tenants. Long before other districts of Scotland knew anything of tea save the name it was a familiar beverage on the banks of the Nith and along the shores of the Solway. Unfortunately "the cup which cheers but not inebriates" was for the most part obtained by the Dumfriesians in an illicit way, the

---

* In a valuable manuscript account of the burgh of Annan, prepared by the late Mr John M'Lellan, writer there, he says :—"Annan Waterfoot, Newbie, Seafield, Battle Hill, and Port Stormont, were all noted landing-places for contraband goods. There is a vaulted subterranean cellar standing till this day at Waterfoot, which was used in these times as a depot for smuggled brandy, etcetera. At Kenziol and the other places named there were also depot cellars ; and frequently ankers of liquor were secreted in fields and gardens along the shore. Having been checked by legislation, another system of smuggling sprang up, viz., the carrying of whisky across the Border in skins and tin casks, which has also now ceased, owing to the alteration of the revenue laws, by a wise equalisation of the duty in Scotland with that of England. Large casks of whisky were brought from Leith by carriers to supply the spirit merchants of Annan. Several puncheons would often be disposed of in a night, to gangs who proceeded across the Frith, the difference of duty (4s or 5s a gallon) being the gain for the risk of detection by the revenue officers."

same smuggling boats that brought them casks of rum, wine, and brandy, or rolls of tobacco, supplying them with chests of tea; and so common had it become in 1744 that magistrates and moralists lamented its use by the lower classes as a pernicious luxury.

At a meeting of the burgh and county authorities, held in the summer of that year, presided over by Sir William Maxwell of Springkell, with Provost Ewart of Dumfries taking a part in the proceedings, a solemn manifesto was launched against smuggling, which was decried on four grounds—because of its illegality, the thriftlessness to which it led, the luxurious habits it engendered, and the encouragement it gave to the King's enemies in France, from which many of the "run" goods were derived. Mark the weighty words, the serious tone, of the opening statement. "We, the Justices of the Peace, Commissioners of the Land Tax, and Heritors of the shire, comprehending the Stewartry of Annandale, the Five Kirks of Eskdale, and the Magistrates and burgesses of the burgh of Dumfries hereafter subscribing, under a just concern for the welfare of our country, in a special manner for this part of it, observe with regret that much idleness and luxury prevail, and being in a particular manner highly sensible of the pernicious consequences of unlawful smuggling, equally notorious and disgraceful, and that the people of all ranks have been for many years past so infatuated that, disdaining the produce of our own grain, out of an affected delicacy have wantonly indulged themselves in the excessive use of French wines and brandies, and of late years run teas have been purchased at so low a rate that the use thereof is become universall, even among artificers, to the impoverishment of this country, and the ruin of the usefull and industrial husbandman."

This grave preamble is followed by a lamentation "that to such a scandalous height is this hurtful practice arrived, that in some parishes upon the sea-coast even servants of both sexes have no sooner earned their wages than the same are laid out in carrying on this unlawful business, whereby the smugglers secure their assistance, so that many attempts of the proper officers to seize run goods have been audaciously defeated, and they themselves beat and abused." All this would have been bad at any time, but at present it is doubly criminal, "now that this nation is engaged in a just but dangerous and expensive war against France," when "it would be a kind of treason against our country to use goods which are the produce of France, whereby money, which is the sinews of war, would be impressed into our enemies' hands, to our own destruction." For these reasons, morally and patriotic, the subscribers of the document covenanted "to discourage and bear down this infamous trade," by refraining from the use of French liquors during the continuance of the war, by discouraging all public-houses in which they were sold, by moderating and dis-

couraging the drinking of tea in their several families, and suffering none knowingly to be used in them which was not bought in
the way of lawful trade, and by dismissing all servants who took
part in or patronized the running traffic.

One portion of this curious agreement breathes the very spirit
of Burns's lines :—

> " Wae worth that brandy, burnin' trash !—
> Fell source o' mony a pain and brash—
> Twines mony a poor, doylt, drucken hash
> O' half his days !
> And sends, besides, auld Scotland's cash
> To her warst faes !''

And the closing part of it looks almost like a prose version of
other stanzas in the poem from which we have just quoted, so re-
commendatory is it of "guid auld Scotch drink, in glass or jug."
"And, moreover," say the subscribers, "we resolve and promise
that we encourage the brewing and retailing of strong ale, the
distilling and retailing of spirits made from our own malt or other
grain ; and we will not countenance any public-houses who do not
retail our own strong ale and spirits, and will discourage all who
retail French winess and spirits." Right cordially could the reso-
lutionists have sung the lines, had they been penned, in which
their own sentiment is so forcibly expressed :—

> " Let husky wheat the haughs adorn,
> An' aits set up their awnie horn,
> An' pease and beans, at e'en or morn,
> Perfume the plain ;
> Leeze me on thee, John Barleycorn,
> Thou king o' grain !
>
> On thee aft Scotland chows her cood,
> In souple scones —the wale o' food !—
> Or tumblin' in the boilin' flood,
> Wi' kail and beef ;
> But when thou pours thy strong heart's bluid,
> There thou shines chief."

Three hundred copies of this document were printed and circulated, and its originators were at great pains otherwise to get its
sentiments generally adopted and acted upon in the district.
Considerable success attended their efforts ; but neither this well-
meant movement nor the whole local machinery of the Custom-
house backed by military power sufficed to stop the adventurous
Manxmen, who continued to prosecute their trade, till, in 1784,
Pitt cut it up effectually by his celebrated commutation measure,
which reduced the duties on exciseable articles so that the lawful
dealer was enabled to compete with the smuggler. By those who
had thriven upon the illicit traffic, this statute of the "heaven-
born minister" was denounced as "the burning and starving Act."

With the smugglers were often conjoined another lawless
class, the gipsies—the latter of whom swarmed in some parishes of

Dumfriesshire during the early half of the eighteenth century, and long afterwards. Among these strange people "of the wandering foot" were the Kennedys, who made Mid-Annandale their chief haunt; the Gordons, whose tents were chiefly set up in Dryfesdale and on the Galloway side of the Nith; and the Baillies, who roamed about in all directions, and were ranked as the "upper ten" of the tinkler tribes. And truly, to see a band of the Bailies mounted on horseback, attired in coats of scarlet or Lincoln green, ruffled in front and at the wrist, booted and spurred, with cocked hats for head-gear, armed with swords and pistols, and followed by hunting dogs, was an imposing spectacle, that went far to vindicate their claim to high descent and gentle blood. With showy, fantastic cavalcades such as this our Dumfries forefathers a hundred and forty years ago were not unfamiliar; but they were much more conversant with the shady side of gipsy life—with the plebeian vagrants who vended or mended small tin wares, who robbed the hen-roost or the fold, and who with nimble finger did a large stroke of business in the High Street or on the Whitesands at every Candlemas Fair. Even the haughty Bailies, who held their heads so high, and cut such a dash as they rode through Nithsdale, lived, like the mosstroopers of old, whom they otherwise resembled, by plunder alone. If labour was irksome to the sons of little Egypt generally, it was doubly odious to those of them who bore the name of, and counted cousinship with, the royally-descended Laird of Lamington.

Of their predatory doings tradition has preserved numerous illustrations; but we shall only adduce one, of rather an agreeable nature, the hero of which was none other than "Big Will Baillie," the chief of the clan, who, though "a rank reiver," almost rivalled Robin Hood himself in acts of generosity. A stalwart farmer from Hutton, in Annandale, having had his pocket picked at a crowded Dumfries fair of a large sum in gold, with which he was on his way to buy cattle, bethought him of a plan for recovering his lost purse, or at all events of getting some trace of it. Filling another purse with small stones, he mingled in the crowd, and soon after he felt the bait nibbled at. A young spare fellow, whose tawny face betrayed his origin, having stealthily clutched the fancied prize, he was seized in turn by the farmer, who, taking the pickpocket aside, laid before him the alternative of bringing back the purse of gold, or being treated to free lodgings in the Tolbooth. The gipsy lad, having due regard for his own neck, took the farmer, by whom he was still held fast, to a low house down one of the closes leading from the Vennel, and there introduced him to a tall, portly individual, dressed like a gentleman. The latter, on being whispered to by the youth, told his rural visitor to describe the purse he had lost, and the nature of its contents. "A purse of green worsted, with forty gowden guineas in it," was the prompt reply. "There it is," returned the stranger, giving back to the delighted farmer his own veritable purse, with its full tale of "jingling Geordies." Need we add that it was the gentle gipsy *riah*, or chief of the Bailies, who acted this congenial part. Will had his headquarters for many years in this same house whenever he visited Dumfries, which was usually twice a year at least, during the great horse fairs in February and September; and, by means of numerous light-fingered emissaries belonging to his tribe, he managed to make more money on such occasions than any dozen of honest dealers. No wonder that he and his boon confederates, male and female, "lived like lords and ladies gay." But never after the incident we have just narrated did he make the little house in the Vennel his place of rendezvous. The Annandale farmer returned to it in the evening, in order, as he told the occupier, a poor widow, to give Mr Baillie a treat for restoring his purse; but the gipsy chief, knowing that he had been identified, and his retreat revealed, had, to the great grief of his hostess, who knew him only as Mr Stewart, bidden her a long adieu. For many years afterwards, however, a stranger called every six months with money for her rent—in recognition, it was understood, of the former attention which she had paid to her mysterious lodger.*

So much for the Bailies and their chief; let us turn for a minute to notice a humbler gang, and illustrate by a more tragical incident the darker features of gipsy life. On the 7th of March, 1732, John (or, as he was usually termed, "Jock") Johnstone, was, with several other "tinklers," found guilty by the Kirkcudbright justices of being "an Egyptian vagrant and sorner;" and for such negative crimes he was whipped through Bridgend, and then burned on the cheek. This was not the first or last time in which Jock suffered punishment; but all the stripes, scorchings, and imprisonments he was subjected to did no more to cure his wandering and thievish disposition than to take the tan from his visage. When Jock was roaming about he was invariably accompanied by quite a seraglio of women; and on one occasion—ever memorable to him—he withdrew with some of them to a small ale-house, kept by an old widow named Margaret Farish, at Parkgate, eight miles from Dumfries, on the Edinburgh road. A quarrel between one of his concubines and the hostess, about the price of the liquor, provoked the interference of Jock. Heated with drink and rage, he repeatedly struck the poor old woman on her head with the heavy pint stoup in which the ale was served, killing her on the spot.

He was apprehended at Lockerbie next day, and forthwith

---

* This story forms one of M'Vittie's Tales, and is also related in Simson's History of the Gipsies, pp. 197-8.

lodged in the Dumfries Tolbooth. During the dreary interval before his trial he was allowed the companionship of a pet jackdaw, which had travelled the district with him in happier days for them both. But just as the judges passed the prison, on their way to court, the heralds of the procession blew a flourish with their trumpets, and that moment the gipsy's feathered favourite dashed convulsively against the iron bars of the window, and dropped down dead. "Lord ha'e mercy on me! for I am gane!" cried Jock, naturally enough considering that the fate of the poor daw was ominous of his own; and so it turned out. He was condemned to die; but life was sweet, and he resolved to keep it, or sell it dearly, while deceitful hope buoyed him up with the idea that the men of his tribe would yet enable him to elude the gallows. Jock doggedly refused to leave his cell; and as he was one of the strongest men in all Dumfriesshire, it was with the utmost difficulty that he was dragged out and carried to the upper storey, from the front of which the fatal noose hung dangling, waiting for its human tassel. The convict wanted the thumbs of both hands, and was often called "Thoomie Johnstone" on that account; but this defect no way unfitted him for maintaining a tremendous resistance. Apprehensive of a rescue, the authorities placed a hundred stout burgesses, armed with Lochaber axes, as a guard around the Tolbooth. Eventually, long after the appointed hour, the figure of Johnstone appeared upon the scaffold, enclosed by six town officers; and we must leave the scene that ensued to be described by the Rev. Dr Carlyle of Inveresk,[*] who, when a boy, viewed it from the neighbourhood of his uncle Provost Bell's house, which was situated opposite the prison.

"When Jock first issued from the door," says Carlyle, " he

---

[*] Autobiography of the Rev. Dr Alexander Carlyle, minister of Inveresk. W. Blackwood & Sons, 1860. In this work there are numerous references to Dumfries, Dr Carlyle having at various periods paid visits to it, as he had several relatives residing in the town. "The first journey I made," he says, " was to Dumfriesshire, in the summer of 1733, when I was eleven years of age. There I not only became well acquainted with my grandfather, Mr A. Robison [minister of Tinwald], a very respectable clergyman, and with my grandmother, Mrs Jean Graham, and their then unmarried daughters, but I became well acquainted with the town of Dumfries, where I resided for several weeks at Provost Bell's, whose wife was one of my mother's sisters, two more of whom were settled in that town—one of them the wife of the clergyman, Mr Wight, and the other of the sheriff-clerk. I was soon very intimate with a few boys of this town about my own age, and became a favourite by teaching them some of our sports and plays in the vicinity of the capital that they had never heard." Again he says : " I passed most of the summer of this year [1739] in Dumfriesshire, where my grandfather kept me pretty close to my studies ; though I frequently walked in the afternoons to Dumfries, and brought him the newspapers from Provost Bell, his son-in-law. . . . During the period when I so much frequented Dumfries, there was a very agreeable society in that town. They were not numerous, but the few were better informed and more agreeable in society than any to be met with in so small a town."

looked a little astonished; but looking round a while, he proceeded
with a bold step. Psalms and prayers being over, the rope was
fastened about his neck, and he was prompted to ascend a short
ladder fastened to the gallows, to be thrown off. Here his
resistance and my terror began. Jock was curly-haired and fierce
looking, and very strong of his size--about five feet eight inches.
The moment they asked him to go up the ladder he took hold of
the rope round his neck, which was fastened to the gallows, and
with repeated violent pulls attempted to pull it down, and his
efforts were so strong that it was feared he would have succeeded.
The crowd in the meantime felt much emotion, and the fear of the
magistrates increased. I wished myself on the top of Criffel, or
anywhere but there. But the attempt to go through the crowd
appeared more dangerous than to stay where I was. I returned to
my station again, resolving manfully to abide the worst extremity.
Jock struggled and roared, for he became like a furious wild beast,
and all that six men could do they could not bind him; and
having with wrestling hard forced up the pinions on his arms, they
were afraid, and he became more formidable; when one of the
magistrates recollecting that there was a master mason or
carpenter of the name of Baxter who was by far the strongest
man in Dumfries, they with difficulty prevailed with him, for the
honour of the town, to come on the scaffold. He came, and
putting aside the six men who were keeping him down, he seized
him, and made no more difficulty than a nurse does in handling
her child; he bound him hand and foot in a few minutes, and laid
him quietly down on his face near the edge of the scaffold, and
retired. Jock, the moment he felt his grasp, found himself
subdued, and became calm, and resigned himself to his fate."
Carlyle closes his graphic narrative by saying: "The dreadful
scene cost me many nights' sleep"—a circumstance not to be
wondered at. If a rescuing party of Jock's friends had appeared
in his time of need, they would very likely have succeeded in
carrying him away in triumph.*

* We are partly indebted to Mr W. F. Johnstone, bookseller, Dumfries,
for our reminiscences of Jock Johnstone. He had them from his father, the
late Mr Walter Johnstone, who possessed a rare store of Annandale traditions,
many of which he committed to paper; but unfortunately the manuscript has
been lost sight of. An account of the gipsy chief is also given by Simson,
pp. 200-1. (a)

(a) Mr William Todd, joiner, supplies us with another version of the
Jock Johnstone affair. It came through Mr Wallace, formerly in Corriehall,
Goldielea, whose father, then at Hightown, had taken part in the arrest.
The place where the murder occurred was at the point where the Dumfries
road and the old Roman road from Burnswarck crossed, 200 or 300 yards
above South Lanegate. The smithy was there, with the smith's dwelling
beside it, which was also an alehouse. Johnstone's party consisted of women.
They had reached the house before him, had obtained some liquor, became
noisy, and were refused more. For this they abused the blacksmith's wife;

CHAPTER XLIV.

LONG before the outbreak of the Rebellion the want of adequate
church accommodation was fully recognised by the authorities ;
and when peace was restored they adopted measures for obtaining
a second place of worship, A difficulty having been experienced
in compensating the inhabitants for their sacrifices when the town
was threatened by the Jacobites, the device was hit upon of applying to Parliament for authority to levy such a duty on malt liquor
as would discharge these patriotic claims as well as build the
church. The initiative in this ingenious scheme was taken by the
Council on the 9th of April, 1716 ; and when the bill took shape,
the Legislature was asked to impose a duty of two pennies Scots
on every pint of ale or beer brewed and sold within the burgh, the
proceeds to be applied for the above purposes—the preamble
stating as regards one of them, " that the present church doth
not accommodat more than the half of the congregation." In due
time the bill was passed, Government being very willing in this

---

and when Johnstone arrived the poor woman was more like death than life.
Surveying the situation, he exclaimed, " Ah well, it canna be helped noo ; but
there's nae use keepin' a wee finger waggin'." And thereupon he lifted a pint-
stoup and completed the slaughter of the landlady. Then they set her upon
a chair and fled. They went by the old Edinburgh road through Kirkmichael
and Applegarth. When the smith, who was also a farrier, came home, it was
this ghastly spectacle that met his horrified gaze. The whole district was
immediately roused. A man came to Hightown and asked Wallace to go out
on the search. Wallace returned to his house for a gun, and then followed
after the pursuers. He overtook them at Dinwoodie Green, where they were
engaged with Johnstone, who was overmastering them as they rushed in upon
him. Wallace called out " Stand back, boys ; if we canna tak' him leevin'
we'll tak' him deed." " Dinna shoot," cried Johnstone, " I'll rather gie in
than be shot." He was pinioned and brought into Dumfries.

way to acknowledge the loyal services rendered by the Dumfriesians. In October of the following year they were required by the
Council to " give in upon oath the accounts of horse meat and
man's meat furnished by them, by the Marquis of Annandale's
order, to the country people in defence of the town, the time of
the late rebellion, and how much is resting to them unpayd, to the
effect ane account thereof may be laid before the overseer named
in the Act of Parliament, anent the duty lately granted to the
burgh."*

It was a comparatively easy thing for Provost Crosbie and his
colleagues to acquire a right to tax the national beverage, but to
enforce the duty was a different matter. Whilst they were preparing to give it effect, an adverse storm was brewing among the
brewers. What ! Punish the beer-drinking lieges, and ruin our
trade, by your kirk-building schemes ? Not, by St. Michael, if we
can help it ! Actuated by such a spirit, the malting interest petitioned against the bill ; and when that was of no avail, resolved
doggedly and defiantly to look upon it as a dead letter. At this
time there were no fewer than ninety-one brewers and retailers of
ale in the burgh : some of them had large establishments ; others
little shebeens that could not boast of more than a couple of
barrels each. The rating on the whole of the stock, numbering
255¼ barrels, amounted to £14 for six weeks, which would realise
£112 per annum. About one-third of the trade quietly paid the
impost ; the rest offered a sullen, passive resistance ; and when a
determined effort was made to overcome their obstinacy, they rose
with the occasion, forcibly encountered his Majesty's representatives and made the streets ring with the voice of tumult. A
warrant having been granted to distrain the " goods and cattels "
of the recusants to the extent of their liability, varying from £1
sterling down to 8d, the burgh officers issued forth on the 8th of
April, 1718, to carry it into effect. But the publicans, banded
together, easily beat off the legal emissaries ; whereupon the
magistrates personally, accompanied by several burgesses, undertook the perilous task of poinding the defaulters. Meanwhile a
mob of beer-loving sympathisers had rallied round the victuallers,
and joined in their cry of " Free trade in ale and confusion to the
exciseman !" The Provost and bailies, nothing daunted, pushed
forward in the belief that their dread presence would disperse the
clamorous rabble. Vain delusion ! Before the august authorities
could with official finger touch a plack's worth of furniture they
were hustled by the crowd and driven violently from the streets.

* The outlay incurred must have been very heavy a minute of Council
dated 5th November, 1715, states that, owing to the extraordinary and
inevitable expenses " entailed on the town, the treasurer is entirely exhausted
of any effects ;" and that he was authorised to borrow £80 sterling on that
account.

The magistrates and their supporters took shelter from the popular storm in the town clerk's chamber ; but as it had not been made to resist a siege, they were soon joined in their retreat by the ringleaders of the populace ; and though the Riot Act was read, and the friends of law and order offered a stout resistance, King Mob became for the time being master of the town and of its rulers, the latter of whom received no mercy. The rioters first broke the office windows, next threw stones and softer unsavoury missiles on the inmates ; and, having succeeded in forcing the door, they—how shall we tell it !—literally beat with their irreverent fists the magistrates of the burgh. After perpetrating this crowning indignity, the rabble retired triumphant but appeased ; and doubtless would be treated to a supply of "reaming swats that drank divinely" by those in whose behalf they had fought and conquered.

This serious émeute having been brought under the consideration of the Council at their next meeting, a resolution was adopted to transmit a report to the Government regarding it, and to prosecute the rioters at the town's expense. The brewers, on their part, continued their opposition to the duty, transferring the war against it from the streets to the Court of Session ; but an amicable interview having been brought about between them and the magistrates, mutual concessions were made, according to which the litigation was abandoned, and the obnoxious duty on beer was modified so as to amount only to " thirteen shillings four pennies Scots upon each barrel, consisting of twelve gallons, and soe proportionally for greater or lesser quantities, after deduction of the seventeenth pairt made by wrong valuation, and of two and ane half of each twentie-three shillings." Though this arrangement does not seem very intelligible to us, it was deemed satisfactory by the publicans, who agreed henceforth to pay the duty in peace ; and the mollified magistrates, overlooking the insulting treatment given to them, dropped the criminal process they had raised against the rioters,* and proceeded with the scheme that had been the innocent cause of all these disturbances.

In October, 1722, a committee of the Council, appointed to select a site for the proposed ecclesiastical edifice, reported that " John M'Dowall, younger of Logan, had been communed with anent selling ane part of the Castle closs and Castle garden pertaining to him, for that purpose ; and that Logan declared

---

* A curious compromise was effected. " The brewers engaged in the late riot agreed to come under the judgment of the magistrates, while the magistrates engaged to endeavour to get the diet deserted against them in the Court of Justiciary—each party to pay the half of the fees to the King's advocate and the clerks of Justiciary for deserting the diet." The Provost went to Edinburgh, and succeeded in his mission of getting the diet deserted at an outlay of £8 12s. — Pamphlet by Mr W. R. M'Diarmid on the *Established Churches of Dumfries*, pp. 21-2.

himself willing to sell to the town such an part of the said closs and garden, with the stones of the old castle and old houses adjacent, as the burgh should have use for." The ruined edifice had remained in the possession of the Maxwells till after the commencement of the eighteenth century, and been purchased from Lord Nithsdale by Mr M'Dowall some time prior to 1715. No better site than the one it occupied could have been found for the new building in all the burgh : it was purchased on the recommendation of the committee, and early in the following year a bargain was made with Logan, in virtue of which the ground at the head of High Street, and what it still bore of the venerable baronial residence, became the property of the town for £85 sterling. It was not till the beginning of 1724 that the building was actually proceeded with. The contractors for the mason work were James Waddell, William and Andrew Mein, and William White, who agreed to supply materials, and erect the church and steeple, after a design furnished by Mr Alexander M'Gill, architect, for £730 sterling. The joiners engaged were : William Copland, Matthew Frew, James Johnston, and John Swan, who were to receive £820 for their materials and labour. No difficulty was experienced by the Council as regards a supply of stone and wood, and men to use them, such as they encountered when the Mid-Steeple was contracted for ; but the undertaking, for all that, did not progress smoothly, and was not completed satisfactorily.

The masons were accused by the Council of violating their agreement ; and at a meeting held in May, 1726, the latter resolved to send the contract to their Edinburgh agent, "that horning might be raised on the same," so that the undertakers and their cautioners might be compelled to implement their obligations. On the 5th of the following July, a petition on the subject was presented to the Convention of Royal Burghs by the commissioners from Dumfries, setting forth that the burgh had contracted with sundry of its own inhabitants for building a new church at a cost of £1550 ; that though the town had advanced nearly the whole of that money, yet the work was far from being finished ; that " by a modest computation " it would cost above £400 additional to complete the church ; and that it appeared to the Council the contractors had erroneously estimated sundry of the articles. On these grounds the Convention were asked to appoint a committee of their number to view the works, examine the accounts, "assist with the best advice, and grant such releefe to the undertakers as was necessary for finishing" the same. In accordance with this prayer a committee was appointed consisting of the commissioners from Sanquhar, Annan, and Lochmaben.

To these gentlemen was also entrusted the duty of "answering the ends" of another petition from Dumfries, which represented " the very great burthens of debts" the town was suffering from, with the probability of their being increased, "especially by the apparent danger of three arches of our bridge that were likely to fall ;" that several portions of the commons lay unimproved, and, by reason of their remoteness, were very liable to be trespassed upon by neighbouring heritors and tenants ; and prayed that the Convention would allow the burgh to feu or let long leases of the land at the sight of a committee of their number, in order that a fund might be raised towards liquidating the debts of the town.

Through the agency of this committee the matters at issue between the Council and the contractors were adjusted. Some slight deductions were made from the sum originally bargained for, on account of deficient work ; new charges were allowed for additional work ; and when the balance was struck, the town had to pay a supplementary account of £335, which brought the entire cost of the church, including site, up to £1970, or about £470 more than the cost of the Mid-Steeple, with its accompanying buildings. After all, the original design was never fully carried out. The spire was scrimped of its fair proportions, and had a squat, stunted appearance, that contrasted badly with the handsome square tower on which it was placed. The New Church, as the building was named, was opened for worship on the 5th of September, 1727 ; arrangements for the settlement in it of Mr Robert Paton, the colleague of Mr Patrick Linn in St. Michael's Church, having first been completed between the Council and the Presbytery.

That reverend body met at Torthorwald Manse, and came to a deliverance on the subject, the principal points of which were as follows :—The Presbytery find, from many years' experience, that the Old Church of Dumfries is not large enough to accommodate the whole parish ; that the town has now built a New Church for the greater and better accommodation of the inhabitants, and that they at this time are not in a condition to make suitable provision for a third minister ; that the Presbytery therefore judge, in present circumstances, " it will be for the glory of God, the greater interest of the Gospel in the place and corner, and to the further usefullness as well as comfort and satisfaction of their reverend bretherine the ministers of Dumfries, that each of them preach and dispence all other Gospell ordinances in a separate church ;" and seeing that this whole affair has been remitted to the Presbytery, they therefore, from a sincere desire to promote the foresaid ends, hereby ordain that the Reverend Robert Paton, and his successors in office, shall preach and dispense ordinances in the New Church, and have pastoral care over that part of the town that lies "from the Bridge to Hoddam's stone house, including that and the whole closs adjoining on the one side, and from the Townhead to the end of Lochmaben-gate, including the west part of that street, on the other side with the Mid-raw, containing about one thousand three hundred and thirty-four examinable persons, from ten years old and upwards." They likewise appoint the Rev. Patrick Linn, and his successors in office, to preach and dispense ordinances in the Old Church, and have under his pastoral superintendence "the whole country parish, with that part of the town which lyes next to the said church, extending to the end of Lochmaben-gate on the east side, and to Hoddam's lodging on the other side, containing about six hundred and ninety-five examinable persons, from ten years old and upwards, in that part of the town beside the landward parish." For purposes of discipline the Presbytery judge it expedient that there be only one session ; that the same shall meet every Thursday, or any other day on which the weekly sermon is preached, and which is required to be in the two churches alternately.

The Presbytery also proposed "that the town shall pay or give bond to Mr Paton for the sum of one hundred pounds sterling yearly, in regard that he has in his old age undertaken a separate charge, reserving to him also what he already possesses in teinds, glebe, and manse ;* and that the town shall become bound to allow Mr Linn also the sum of one hundred pounds per annum." These and other conditions were agreed to by the Council, who, in their minute of approval, pointed out in more detail the sources from which the stipends for St. Michael's Church were derived ; it being there stated that Mr Linn was to receive six hundred merks over and above his previous income of one thousand two hundred merks, derived from the teinds payable to the Crown out of the parish, and the rents formerly payable to the bishop out of the parish of Newabbey ; the whole amounting to eighteen hundred merks, or fully one hundred pounds sterling. Thus the town obtained the additional church that it needed so much ; and in the course of a few years afterwards, as we shall see, chapels or meeting-houses for other religious communities than the Established Church began to rise up. Many of the stones in the new structure had rather a singular fortune : at first they formed part of the Friary ; then of the old fortress ; and last of all, they were re-transferred for a religious purpose, by being embodied in the walls of the new place of worship.†

---

* A curious little document lying before us furnishes an "Inventory of Household Plenishing pertaining to the Town of Drumfries, and left in the Manse thereof, for the use of Mr Robert Paton, Minister of the Gospell of the said Burgh, to be made forthcoming to the said Burgh be him, his airs and executors." It is drawn up by Mr Paton himself, as follows :— "Imprimis, ane old Dutch cupboard in the high hall ; Item, four bedsteads ; it., four graits ; it., ane large cupboard in the kitchen ; it., ane kitchen table there, and shelfs for peuthery." The minister acknowledges his obligation to produce the articles, if called upon, by appending his signature to the list.

† When, in 1866, the New Church was taken down, to be replaced by Greyfriars Church, many stones were discovered that had evidently belonged

Mr Paton, who died in 1738, was succeeded by Mr John Scott of Holywood ; and he, at his death, in 1770, was succeeded by Dr. Andrew Hunter. The latter was appointed professor of divinity in the University of Edinburgh in 1780 ; and the vacancy thus occasioned was filled up by Dr William Burnside, whose manuscript history of Dumfries has been frequently quoted from in these pages ; and of whom Dr Hew Scott says truly :—" His elegant taste, cultivated talents, extensive information, and impressive manner, rendered him highly useful, while his warmth of heart endeared him to society."* Dr Burnside was made first minister of the parish, by his translation to St. Michael's, in 1794. His successor to the New Church was Dr Alexander Scot, who also, ten years afterwards, succeeded him in St. Michael's. In 1806, Dr Thomas T. Duncan of Applegarth became minister of the New Church, continuing so till his death, in 1858. Mr Andrew Gray (now of St. John's, Glasgow), Mr Malcolm C. Taylor (now of Crathie), Mr Donald M'Leod (now of Dundee), have since successively occupied this charge, and it is now held by Mr Robert W. Weir, settled in 1868. The stipend is £231 13s 4d (*a*).

A few years after the remains of the Castle had been absorbed

to the Castle, and some which, it is supposed, had formed part of the Monastery. From an interesting paper regarding them, read to the Dumfries and Galloway Natural History and Antiquarian Society by Mr Barbour, architect, we borrow the following notice of the Castle stones :—" A number of rope mouldings ; two curved and moulded stones that have formed part of the corbelling of a corner turret ; portions of steps of a wheeling stair ; several pieces of a fine string-course corbelling, consisting of three cavettoes, one over the other, and having ovolo dentils in each cavetto. There is a part of a very beautiful tapering pinnacle, probably from the top of a door-piece ; the stone has a rope bead on each corner, a semicircular hollow on each side, and fillets between the hollows and beads. There is one large block corbel, such as is usually found under the parapets. There are portions of two stones that seem to have formed part of a coat-of-arms ; on one of them is a naked figure, with the head broken off, and there is a broken line extending from the hand across the shoulder, which seems to indicate a club. From the boldness and richness of the few details of the Castle that have come down to us, I think it may be safely inferred that, grand as the remaining baronial buildings of Scotland are, the Castle of Dumfries has not been below the average in its imposing appearance and ornamental character. The upper parts of the walls have been corbelled out so as to overhang the lower portions, and the corbellings have been enriched with mouldings and dentils. The corbellings, after running horizontally, have suddenly taken a perpendicular course for a short distance, and then returned again to the horizontal. Large rope mouldings have been interwoven with the building, and probably followed horizontal and perpendicular courses like the corbellings ; and circular turrets have projected from the corners, resting on corbellings and projecting their cone-shaped roofs above the main building, thereby giving an irregularity and picturesqueness to the outline in harmony with the broken line of the mouldings."

* Fast ecclesiæ.

(*a*) Mr Weir's faithful ministry was closed by his resignation in 1904 owing to ill-health. He was the recipient of various farewell gifts from his congregation and the Presbytery.

in the building of the New Church, the more modern stronghold, that stood north-east of the Market Cross—the New Wark—was partially demolished, on account of its dangerously ruinous condition. In 1737 it was, for the same reason, still further reduced ; what remained of the roof, the entire gables, and other portions, having been taken down at that date by the order of the Town Council. Only about one half of the edifice was left after these repeated assaults ; and much of that, incorporated with a range of dwelling-houses, remained till 1846, when it was removed with them, in order that Queensberry Square might be rendered more spacious and salubrious.

The Committee appointed by the Convention of Burghs, in 1726, did little to help the town out of its financial difficulties. These increased, till absolute bankruptcy stared its rulers in the face. Year after year the expenditure had gone on increasing ; the new buildings erected, and the general improvements made, being far too costly for the resources of the burgh. In 1731, the desperate device was resorted to of selling a portion of the burgh lands ; but even after that had been done, a committee of the Council reported, in 1735, that the debts amounted to £3,807 11s sterling, the interest of which was £120 7s 6½d ; that the yearly salaries, ministers' stipends, and other annual disbursements, with the interest on the debt, amounted to £770 10s 6½d ; that the revenue arising from grass maill rents, customs, multures, seats in the New Church, feu duties, and miscellaneous sources, with a sum of £112 11s 6d due by the deceased Robert Johnston of Kelton, amounted to only £552 12s 4d yearly ; so that there was an annual balance on the wrong side of £217 18s 2½d, and no provision made for liquidating the debt. Still further, the Committee reported that the public school-house was in a very ruinous condition ; that sundry arches of the bridge were very much decayed ; that the navigation of the river was in a miserable state ; and that heavy annual charges would have to be incurred for repairing the churches, mill, caul, pavements, and other public works.*

Truly a disheartening report. The Committee did not give way to despondency, however, but unfolded another scheme for relieving the town from its embarrassment. They proposed that Parliament should be asked to allow the Council to continue the duty on ale—which had been granted for only nineteen years— and to impose certain other duties and customs, so as to bring the income to something like an equality with the outlay. This proposal was adopted and carried into effect. A bill in accordance with it was prepared, and Provost Corrie and Mr John Goldie of Craigmuie, who were commissioned to watch over the

---

* Town Council Minutes.

measure in London, had the satisfaction of being able to report to the Council in May, 1737, that it had been sanctioned by the Legislature.* Their report may be quoted from, as it is instructive and curious. They set out on horseback for the English metropolis—a momentous journey at that period—on the 21st of February, arrived on the 4th of March, and remained there five weeks, facilitating as best they could the passage of the bill. Mr William Kirkpatrick, member for the Dumfries Burghs, "did exert himself in a most active manner, not only in obtaining dispatch in the Houses, but also in getting it done at the most frugal charge, in which he was exposed to charges out of his own pocket." All the members of this neighbourhood cheerfully assisted him, as did Mr Erskine, the Solicitor-General, the latter gentleman having been especially of service "in prevailing with my Lord Findlater to take on him the management" of the bill in the House of Peers. The deputies left London on the 8th of May, and reached home on the 16th ; bringing with them, as the best proof of their success, a copy of the bill, now clothed with the authority of law.†

The Act, which took effect on the 24th of June, 1737, was to remain in operation for twenty-five years, and until the end of the next session of Parliament. Though needed to extricate the burgh from difficulties, its influence upon trade must have been discouraging. It imposed a duty of eightpence sterling on every ton of " goods, wares, merchandise, or other commodities," brought into the port or exported from it, with the exception of coals, lime, and limestone ; and a duty of 3d per ton on every vessel from foreign parts, and of three-halfpence per ton on every vessel from Great Britain and Ireland, entering the port. It also renewed the duty on ale for the same period. The latter impost proved much more productive than the one on general goods and shipping. During the first year the entire dues levied under the new Act, after deducting the charge for collection, amounted to about £214 sterling, four-fifths of which were yielded by the ale duty ; and by this welcome addition, increasing with the trade of the port, the financial difficulties of the burgh were considerably reduced.

It appears that the burgh's application to the Convention, for

---

* Town Council Minutes.

† The entire expense of their mission was £215 18s 6d, which sum was made up of the following, among other items :—Retaining fee paid to William Murray, Esq., councillor-at-law, £2 2s ; paid to John Crawford for the fees of Parliament, and his own fees " soliciting the affair," £143 14s 4d ; to the clerk of the committees, £11 2s 2d ; expense of their journey to London with a servant, £6 12s 11½d ; expense of their horses, five weeks in London, £8 13s 6d ; expense of barbers there, 18s ; charges for their lodgings, fire, and candles, £2 13s ; for their spendings, £28 19s 10d ; expense of their journey home, £7 1s 6d.

liberty to feu out a portion of its landed patrimony, was granted. A beginning was made with Barkerland—a fertile tract comprising about a hundred and fifty acres, lying south-east of the town, and which had belonged to it from time immemorial. On the 11th of February, 1731, two sections of this estate were disposed of—one to Bailies Bell and Ewart, for £150 premium, or grassum, and an annual feu of £5 10s ; and the other to Bailie John Johnstone for £50 premium and a feu of £1 10s. The money thus acquired and the ordinary revenue were insufficient to meet the requirements of the Council ; and their language was still like that of the thriftless Lord of Linne :—

> " My gold is gone – my money is spent ;
>   My land now take it unto thee ;
> Give me the gold, good John o' Scales,
>   And thine for aye my land shall be."

Acquisitive men like John o' Scales were standing by ready to take advantage of the straits of the town to enrich themselves ; and as regards the further slices of Barkerland obtained by each, the words of the same ballad were still applicable :—

> " Then John he did to record draw,
>   And John he gave him a god's pennie ;
> But for every pound that John agreed,
>   The land, I wis, was weel worth three."

Again the disinheriting sales were proceeded with. Commissary Goldie and Mr Hynd purchased, on the 10th of January, 1738, a lot for £60 premium and an annual feu of £2, with 8s of teind or tithe ; on the same day Mr Thomas Kirkpatrick acquired another for £74 premium, an annual feu of £2 3s 4d, and 8s 8d teind ; and a third lot became the property of Mr George Gordon for £32 premium, feu duty 25s, and teind 5s. There was still a goodly fragment of the estate left. " Shall we keep it, or let it go with the rest ?" " We cannot afford to keep it. Who bids for the last lots of Barkerland ?" Bailie Francis Johnstone did, on the following 6th of February, he paying for his portion £84 premium, feu duty £2 5s, teind 6s—the feu including the house occupied by the herd,* who in happier days looked after the cattle of the burgesses as they grazed on the surrounding meadow ; Mr Thomas Kirkpatrick acquired a second section for £31, feu £2 6s 8d, teind 7s ; and Mr Robert Corsane of Meikleknox had a third section knocked down to him for £35 premium, feu £2 13s 4d, teind 8s. All the lots that we have specified were sold by public auction—clogged with this condition, however, that none but resident burgesses or heritors were allowed to make an offer. A few good patches—cuttings and carvings left over when the large lots were squared off—still remained ; which, with several roods that did not form part of Barkerland, were acquired privately by Bailie Francis

---

* The present mansion of Frankfield occupies the site of the herd's house.

Johnstone, price £56, feu £1 10s, teind 4s ; by Mr Robert Corsane, price £3 13s 10d, feu 5s 8d, teind 10½d ; and by Mr George Gordon, price £25, feu £1 5s, teind 2s 6d. The amount received for the whole of Barkerland was £590 13s 10d of premium, £22 14s of feu duty, and £2 10s 0½d of teind—a small sum indeed, when the feus are capitalised, at thirty years' purchase, and added to the premiums, the aggregate is less than £8 10s per acre.* By these sacrifices the Council obtained at least temporary relief. Upwards of a thousand acres still remained to the burgh, a great proportion of which lay in moss and pasture.

With the view, we suppose, of putting St. Michael's Church on a footing of equality with its younger sister fabric, its patrons resolved, in 1740, to place a spire on the tower attached to it ; and on its being ascertained that the walls of the tower were too weak to bear the proposed superstructure, the bolder and better proposal for an entirely new steeple was eventually adopted. At first a contract for the erection of a tower eighteen feet square on the site of the old one was entered into ; and that having been finished, an agreement was made, in 1742, with Alexander Affleck and Thomas Tweddle, masons in the burgh, to build upon the tower, for £100, " a stone spire fifty feet high, with an iron spire of nine feet, surmounted by a weathercock, the cock and other ornaments on the top of the spire to be exactly such as on the New Church." The cost of these erections appears to have been exclusively defrayed by public subscriptions, Lord John Johnstone, the repentant Jacobite, generously contributing £31 10s, or, as nearly as we can learn, about a sixth part of the whole.

When the steeple, which is a very handsome and stately one, was completed, it made the little building below look more insignificant than it had ever done : it was, besides, getting rather debilitated ; and so, after sundry ineffectual attempts to put it in a decent state of repair, the Council determined to rebuild the Church. On the 3rd of September, 1744, Provost Ewart, in name of a committee appointed to contract with tradesmen for the purpose, reported that they had entered into a contract with the two craftsmen aforesaid, Alexander Affleck, deacon-convener of the Trades, and Thomas Tweddle, mason, as principals, and William Reid, blacksmith, as cautioner for them, "to take down the old walls of the Church to the foundation, and twa eastmost pillars thereof to the floor, dig a new foundation for the out walls, four feet deep from the surface of the earth, and four feet wide, and to erect and build the whole stone and mason work of the said Church of new, sixty feet wide and sixty-seven feet long, betwixt and the first day of July next to come," according to the plan produced—the contractors providing all materials necessary for

*All these records of the sales appear in the Town Council Minutes.

the said work, except centres and scaffolding ; " for which the
committee, in name of, and having full power and commission
from, the Council, and taking burden on them for the heritors of
the country parish," became bound to pay to the said contractors
the sum of £185 3s 10d sterling.   As also, that the committee had
agreed with James Harley, wright, as principal, and Thomas
Tweddle, Alexander Affleck, and William Wood, wrights, as his
cautioners, " for the whole carpenter work of the roofs and
windows of the said Church, to be finished after the walls and
arches are built—the contractor to provide all timber and rails
that are required, and deals for scaffolding to the masons, for
which the committee become obliged to pay to him the sum of
£186 sterling." This report was approved of by the Council ; and
they recommended the committee to provide lead for the gutters
and spouts, slates for the roofs, glass for the windows, locks, bolts,
and bands for the doors, as these articles were not included in the
previous contracts.   At the same meeting the Council took into
consideration an Act of the Presbytery, in which the cost of the
Church was estimated at £402 3s 11½d ; and the country heritors
were required to pay, as their proportion of that sum, £130, on
being assigned a fifth part of the area for their accommodation.
The Council agreeing to this arrangement, passed a resolution
requesting the Presbytery to assess the heritors, according to their
valued rents, in the foresaid amount ; and the Council, in the
event of all the conditions being complied with, bound themselves,
their successors in office, and the community, " to keep up the
fabrick of the said Church, when rebuilt, in sufficient repair, for
all time coming, upon the town's expense, except in the case of
rebuilding the same, if by decay or otherwise it shall become
necessary to be rebuilt."* A portion of the gallery, amounting to
two-thirds of its whole extent, was assigned to the Seven
Incorporated Trades, on their agreeing to fit up the same, and
contribute £80 towards the erection of the Church.†

Whilst the operations were being proceeded with in the
following year, the town was taken possession of by the Highland
army under Prince Charles ; and there is a tradition that the
building was placed in serious peril by a party of the rebel clansmen.   Whilst wandering up and down in search of plunder, or to
gratify curiosity, they passed unceremoniously within the

---

* Some external improvements were made upon the church, and the
lower part of the interior was re-seated in 1869.   Before this latter alteration
was effected, a pew in the south-west was shewn which had been occupied by
Burns and his family during their residence in Dumfries.   " All visitors (says
the Visitor's Guide, p. 34, 2nd ed.) must deeply regret the vandalism by
which this fine memorial of the poet was removed, on the miserable plea that,
if allowed to remain, it would have been out of keeping with the new timber-
work of the interior."

† Town Council Minutes.

precincts of the sacred edifice ; and on being challenged by the workmen, they snapped their pistols among some straw, by which the wood-work was set on fire, and then decamped. Fortunately the flames were extinguished before much damage had been done ; though, it is said, the mischievous Celts withdrew in the belief that they had ruined the fabric. As the old materials were extensively used, and as no site had to be purchased, the modern St. Michael Church cost much less than the New Church, though it proved to be a more imposing structure ; and its steeple—a Gothic spire on a Romanesque tower--has a beauty which the stunted steeple of the other building could never boast of.

On the death of Mr Linn, in 1731, Mr Robert Wight became minister of St. Michael's Church. He was succeeded by Dr Thomas Mutter in 1764 ; and the latter was succeeded by Dr William Burnside in 1794. Dr Alexander Scot was the next pastor of the Church, his induction taking place in 1806. He had as successor Dr Robert Wallace, who died in 1864. Early in the following year Mr John Duncan of Abbotshall was appointed to the charge ; and on his translation to Scoonie, Dr James Fraser, formerly of Glasgow, became his successor, but for a brief season only, as he died six months afterwards. The vacancy thus created was filled up by Mr Alexander Bryson, of Paisley, translated to Alloa in 1870 ; and the present minister is Mr James Barclay, who had laboured for some time before at Dalbeattie. It thus appears that while there have been four changes in this incumbency during the last eight years, there were just the same number of changes during the long period of a hundred years, ending in 1864. St. Michael's, we ought to add, yields a stipend of £332 1s 11d, with a glebe of fully £25 annual value (a).

(a) Mr Barclay, now Dr Barclay, of Montreal, Canada, was succeeded by the Rev. John Paton, now Dr Paton, who was inducted 17th September, 1874. Dr Paton is the author of a sumptuous volume, published 1904, entitled "The Book of St. Michael's." The stipend still stands at £332 1s 11½d ; and from this there falls to be deducted £22 4s 5⁴⁄₁₂d in respect of the New (or Greyfriars) Church stipend. But during Dr Paton's incumbency a stately and spacious manse has been built—not without considerable curmur in consequence of the charge having been devolved by the old heritors upon the whole community of small proprietors ; and the glebe land has been so successfully feued for residential building that the minister's stipend has thereby been supplemented by about £200. The income is returned at £537, and manse.

CHAPTER XLV.

THE year 1745 is a memorable one in the history of Scotland, on account of the attempt then made by Charles Edward, son of the Chevalier de St. George, to recover the crown of his ancestors. In the flush of youth, in the glow of ardent hope—spurred by ambition, and sustained by an idea that the claims of his family were sanctioned by heaven, and must eventually be admitted by the nation—Charles, who had vainly waited for assistance from France, landed at Moidart, Inverness-shire, on the 25th of July, relying for success on his own resources and the pecuniary assistance of some private friends. He was attended by the Marquis of Tullibardine (outlawed for his share in the insurrection of 1715); Sir Thomas Sheridan, the Prince's tutor; Sir John MacDonald, an officer in the Spanish service; Francis Strictland, an English gentleman; Æneas MacDonald, a banker in Paris; Kelly, who had been implicated in what was called the Bishop of Rochester's plot; and Buchanan, who had been intrusted with the duty of summoning Charles to proceed from Rome to Paris when the movement was resolved upon. These "Seven Men of Moidart" did not constitute a very influential company; and if their chief had been a common-place individual, the enterprise would, at its very first start, have proved a failure. But Charles Edward had a graceful appearance and engaging manners. With a fine oval face, the individual features of which indicated a rare combination of martial energy, lofty enthusiasm, and courtly polish, he exercised a personal influence which few, on whom the charm fell, were able to resist. No wonder that the Jacobites likened him to Bruce, and fancied they saw the figure and countenance of the hero-king reproduced in "the young Chevalier." But for this marvellous power of impressment possessed by the Prince, he could

never have invested his desperate undertaking with the rosy hue
of success; and when it did end ruinously, he could never have
come to be mirrored in that beautiful minstrelsy of his country,
which "breathes and burns" with "Bonnie Prince Charlie," and
is the best evidence of the interest he awakened amongst his
followers. Abstract Jacobitism doubtless did much for him; but
it was chiefly because that principle was so attractively represented in its youthful champion that the Rebellion of 1745 was
not nipped in the bud.

A few clansmen joined Charles soon after his arrival at
Moidart; but many who fully sympathised with his movement
waited to see what the leading man in all the Highlands, Cameron
of Lochiel, intended to do. He went to Charles, for the purpose
of counselling him to abandon his rash undertaking. "If such is
your purpose," said his brother, Cameron of Fassefern, "write to
the Prince your opinion; but do not trust yourself within the
fascination of his presence." Lochiel, however, ventured on an
interview with the Prince, and left him with the resolution to
take part in his fortunes, even though ruin should be the result.
His decision to that effect aroused the North; "for," says Scott,
"it was generally understood at the time that there was not a
chief in the Highlands who would have risen if Lochiel had
maintained his pacific purpose."* On the 19th of August the
Jacobite flag was unfurled in the lone vale of Glenfinnan. Before
a month elapsed, it was waving in triumph over the proud towers
of Holyrood Palace—the Government commander, Sir John Cope,
having hurried off to Inverness, in an erratic search for the
rebels, at the time when they marched southward and took unmolested possession of the capital. Cope, transporting his force
by sea from Aberdeen to Dunbar, marched towards the city, and
the Highland troops having gone out to meet him, a battle ensued
on the 20th September, at Prestonpans, which terminated in the
utter rout of the whole army. By this victory Charles became
virtual master of the whole of Scotland, except the Castles of
Edinburgh and Stirling, and a few unimportant Highland forts.
"To England! in the flush of our triumph, and before the enemy
has time to recover from the stunning blow we have struck!'
was the bold resolution of the Prince. "Not so, your Royal Highness," remonstrated his Council; stay here and keep court and
revel for a while in the halls of your ancestors;" and Charles,
holding "silken dalliance" for upwards of a month in old Holyrood, instead of at once hurrying forward, as his first impulse
prompted, did not start on his sadly-romantic expedition to South
Britain till the 31st of October, by which time the friends of the
Government had recovered in some degree from their alarm, and
had made ample arrangements to counteract the invaders,

* Tales of a Grandfather, royal octavo, ed., p. 383,

Early in September, messengers were sent by the magistrates of Dumfries to Edinburgh and Glasgow, for the purpose of obtaining reliable information regarding the rebel movement; and about the same period, Mr John Goldie,* Commissary and Sheriff-Depute of Dumfriesshire, entered into a correspondence on the subject with Dr John Waugh, chancellor of the diocese of Carlisle, the latter of whom communicated the reports he thus received of the insurrection to a clerical dignitary in London, and also, it is believed, to the Government. By means of their own expresses, and copies of the *Edinburgh Evening Courant*, which had superseded the manuscript news-letters, the magistrates obtained intelligence from the North three or four times a week; and it appears that the *Courant* had a correspondent in the Burgh or neighbourhood who sent to it despatches from the South. The following paragraph appeared in its impression of 10th September:—"There are letters from Dumfries yesterday morning, dated the 7th instant, advising that there is not the least stir, but everything is as quiet and peaceable as usual; that the Erskinites (friends of the Earl of Mar) have been stocking themselves with arms, and got a standard made for them; and as these letters mention nothing of any cannonading being heard on the coast there, 'tis believed the story told with respect thereto must be groundless." Mr Goldie, writing to Dr Waugh on the 12th of September, gives the origin of the above alarming report. "The firing mentioned," he says, "was heard on our coast on Sunday was se'enight; but, upon the most diligent enquiry, it came from a West India ship belonging to the sugar-house at Whitehaven, which that day came into port. However, from this letter and others, it was firmly believed at Edinburgh that an engagement had happened on the coast of Galloway, and it was given out that General Keith was landed with an army at Wigtown: so easy is it to alarm at such a conjuncture."†

The Government naturally fancied that the rising in the Highlands would be followed by a corresponding movement among the Jacobite families of Nithsdale and Galloway; but though vague rumours to that effect, like the one just quoted, reached Edinburgh and London, they were groundless. Charles received few recruits from the district, owing in a great measure to the sad impressions left upon it by the former insurrection; and the only gentleman of note belonging to it who espoused his

* The first of the Goldies, or Gowdies, who settled in Scotland, were carpet manufacturers from Flanders. The Goldies of Marbrack and of Stenhouse, their descendants, became allied to some of the leading gentry of Dumfriesshire,

† Carlisle in 1745, by George Gill Mounsey. A highly interesting work, embodying, among other curious matter about the Rebellion, the correspondence of Mr Goldie and Dr Waugh regarding it.

cause was James Maxwell of Kirkconnell, a lineal descendant of Aymer, second son of Sir Herbert Maxwell, brother of the first Lord Maxwell, who in the middle of the fifteenth century married the heiress of Kirkconnell.* What rank Maxwell bore in the rebel army is not known; but he was reckoned one of the best swordsmen of his day, and had all the bravery of his distinguished race. He was, besides, an accomplished man of letters, wielding the pen with nearly as much ease and power as the sword. A tangible proof of his literary acquirements lies in the charter chest at Kirkconnell—a manuscript account of the Prince's expedition, drawn up by the author in France, to which country he fled after the battle of Culloden.†

The inaction manifested by the Pretender's friends in Niths-

---

* See *ante*, p. 20.

† He was son of William Maxwell of Kirkconnell, who died in 1746. When the old man heard that his son was out with Prince Charles, he said he was glad to hear of it, and that if his life was sacrificed it would be in a good cause. This work was printed by the Maitland Club in 1841, under the title of a "Narrative of Charles, Prince of Wales's, Expedition to Scotland in the year 1745, by James Maxwell of Kirkconnell, edited by Walter Buchanan." The editor says truly that "the narrative is composed with a remarkable degree of precision and taste—insomuch as rather to appear the production of a practised *litterateur* than the work of a private gentleman." (Preface, pp. 5, 6.) In 1750, James Maxwell left the Court of St. Germain's, where he resided for several years, and returned to Kirkconnell. The modern part of that mansion (as we learn from Mr Maxwell Witham) was built by him in 1750 and the following year. He sold the estate of Carnsalloch, a few miles above Dumfries, on the left bank of the Nith, which he had acquired by his mother, to Mr Alexander Johnston, and then purchased the estate of Mabie. He married, in 1758, Mary, youngest daughter of Thomas Riddell of Swinbourne Castle, and died four years afterwards, aged fifty-four; leaving three sons, the second of whom, William, settled in Dumfries, and became one of the ablest physicians of his day : he was on intimate terms with Burns, and attended him on his death-bed. James, the eldest son of the Jacobite officer, was served heir to his father in 1764. By his second wife, Dorothy, daughter of William Witham, Esq., solicitor, London, grandson of William Witham of Cliffe, Yorkshire, he left one child, Dorothy Mary Maxwell, who married, in 1844, her cousin, Robert Maxwell Witham, the present proprietor of Kirkconnell. (*a*)

(*a*) Mr R. Maxwell-Witham died 21st May, 1893. His widow survived him till 31st December, 1903. He was succeeded by his eldest son, Lieut.-Colonel James Kirkconnell Maxwell, who commanded the Scottish Borderers Militia in South Africa during the war with the Dutch republics, and received the order of C.M.G. for that service.

Burns's friend, Dr Maxwell, was educated at the Jesuit College at Dinant, and afterwards studied medicine at Paris. There he imbibed revolutionary ideas, and in 1792 he started a subscription in London for the French Jacobins. In December of the same year Burke in one of his speeches accused him of having ordered three thousand daggers at Birmingham, As a member of the French National Guard he was present, 21st January, 1793, at the execution of Louis, and it used to be alleged that he dipped his handkerchief in the King's blood. But of this, as of the daggers that flashed in the imagination of Burke, there was neither evidence nor likelihood. Dr Maxwell was a humane man and a skilful physician, and long outlived the rancour he had incurred because of his Liberal opinions.

dale imparted to his enemies in Dumfries a careless sense of
security, of which they had soon reason to repent. A considerable
display of energy, however, was at first manifested by the burgh
authorities. Having met in the Council-house on the 2nd of
September, Provost George Bell presiding, they discussed the
alarming news received from Edinburgh, and adopted certain
resolutions on the subject, as set forth in the following minute :--
" The said day the Magistrates and Council being informed that
there is a considerable insurrection in the North and Highlands
of Scotland against the present Government and our happy
constitution, and considering the defenceless condition of this
burgh and adjacent country, in case any attempt should be made
to disturb the peace and quiet thereof, and that the town's arms
are not only reduced to a small number, but many of them much
decayed and insufficient, they appoint a committee of the Magistrates (Provost Crosbie, Provost Ewart, Mr Clark, Bailie James
Gilchrist, Mr Carruthers, Mr Fergusson, the Dean and Treasurer,
and two deacons, whereof five a quorum) to examine the arms of
the town's magazine, and cause mend and repair such of them as
are decayed and insufficient ; and to make search through the
burgh, and take an account of what arms are in the hands of any
of the inhabitants, see what condition the same are in, and to have
such as are decayed or out of order repaired and made fit for
service ; and to cause the clerk keep an account of such arms as
are found amongst the inhabitants, and of the names of the
persons who hath them, and the condition they are in ; and also
to concur with the well-affected gentlemen of the county in all
proper measures for the defence of the Government and our happy
constitution in Church and State, and to take all proper measures
that can contribute to the safety and preservation thereof."*

It was unfortunate that these resolutions were not acted
upon, as the Council knew by their own messengers that the
rebels were preparing to march southward. " By our best
accounts they will go by Dumfries, which I'll be extremely sorry
for," wrote the Provost of Glasgow, on the 14th, to Provost Bell ;
yet little or nothing was done to prepare for the threatened
visitation—the blame of this neglect, however, resting as much on
the Government as on the local authorities.

About the close of the same month (September), one of the
magistrates sent to the *Gentleman's Magazine* an interesting statement regarding the condition of the town as affected by the rebel
movement " at Dumfries and in this County." We took (he says)
an exact account of the effective men and arms, that they might
be in readiness to rise upon the first warning ; and writing to
Edinburgh, were answered by the people in power there, that they

* Town Council Minutes.

were glad to hear of the steadiness and loyalty of the people, but had received no instructions from the Government : which when they did, we should be acquainted with. So far as I can judge, the same spirit which you took notice of in 1715 was, with proper encouragement and support, ready to have been exerted at this time ; numbers being still alive, in all the places you mention, who ventured themselves and their all in the same cause. But would you know the truth of the matter ? This unhappy affair was represented still as a trifle ; and the rebels as a contemptible mob that would soon be subdued. Everybody was so over prudent, that nobody would take upon him to head us without a warrant from the King or Regency."

The writer, after describing the Royalist defeat at Preston, went on to say :—"The rebels were now absolutely masters of Scotland : our hands were, at the beginning, tied up ; and they might, when they pleased, have cut all our throats. All this country is now enraged and discouraged ; and the more so, as they must remain idle spectators of their country's ruin, without having it in their power to prevent it, or help themselves. All our towns are laid under heavy contributions. There is no law, no trade, no money ; and we are now at the mercy of those who measure all right by the length of their sword. And yet the people remain unmoved, and are no way determined by this rash adventurer ; regarding as nothing all his successes, promises, threatenings, and boastings."

The picture here drawn of Dumfries contrasts unfavourably with the condition of the town in 1715, when its bold, warlike attitude did much to foil the schemes of the first Pretender. A new generation had risen up, less conversant with the art of war —having a diminished sense also, perhaps, of the evils of arbitrary rule ; and the Duke of Perth, when within half a day's march of the burgh, was certainly viewed with far less apprehension than Viscount Kenmure when he menaced it thirty years before. Hence the comparatively feeble exertions made in 1745 to put the town into a proper state of defence, and to give the rebels a hot reception, should they come that way. The mural defences had fallen into neglect, and no adequate steps were taken to repair them ; there was no mustering of the able-bodied inhabitants—no influx of volunteers from the vicinity ; the militia was not called out : the town was therefore left an easy prey to the enemy, who but for this circumstance would scarcely have been tempted to seize or plunder it. Under such circumstances, it evinced no audacity on the part of the insurgents that they, when yet at a far distance from the town, demanded from it a money contribution.

Immediately after the battle of Prestonpans, Provost Bell received an unwelcome message to that effect from Prince Charles.

The letter embodying it (dated Holyrood House, 26th September, 1745, and written by the Prince's secretary) ran thus : —" Sir,— You are hereby ordered, upon the receipt of this, to repair to the secretary's office in the Palace of Holyrood House, there to have the contribution to be paid by the town of Dumfries for his Highness's use ascertained, which shall be done according and in proportion to the duties of excise arising out of the said town of Dumfries ; for the payment of which said contribution the said duty shall be assigned: This you are ordered upon pain of rebellion forthwith to obey.   By his Highness's command—J. C. MURRAY."

Mr Goldie, writing on the 1st of October to Dr Waugh, says :—" Letters are sent by common Edinburgh cadys from the new Secretary of State to all the provosts of burghs in this corner of Scotland, requiring them to repair to the Secretary's office immediately, to settle the contributions to be paid by the several burghs, under the pain of rebellion. This is carrying matters with a very high hand. But what can be done ? To comply or refuse are equally hazardous. Are the mighty promises of making us a free and happy people to be thus fulfilled ? I believe the demand will not be complied with till it be renewed with an armed force. How will the English like our Scotts way of levying money ? You got once a king from us, will you long for such another ? If a party [of the rebels] come here, your humble servant must retire. They know us all by head-mark ; and it is not unlikely but, on second thoughts, two or three of us may come your way."*

The Dumfries Town Council, in hopes that " something might turn up" for their protection, treated the rebel missive with neglect, till a second summons from Holyrood compelled them to meet for its consideration—with what result is shown in the following minute :—" The said day (October 21) the magistrates and Council considering the present commotions and confusions in this kingdom, and that it is incumbent on them to take the best and prudentest measure for the honour, safety, and benefit of this place, with respect to a contribution demanded from this burgh, they appoint a committee of the magistrates—Dean and Treasurer, Provost Crosbie, Provost Ewart, Bailie James Gilchrist, Mr Fergusson, Mr Corson, the convener, and two deacons, whereof five a quorum—to concert and devise with the most considerable inhabitants of the place the properest measures to be taken by the town in the present circumstance of affairs, and to report their opinion from time to time to the Council when they shall see it necessary."† A marginal note, afterwards written in the record,

---

* Carlisle in 1745, p. 30.   Dr Waugh had previously invited Mr Goldie to take refuge in Carlisle in the event of the rebels visiting Dumfries.

† Town Council Minutes.

explains what the minute only hints at, that it was "the rebels" who called for this tribute—the obnoxious term being probably omitted at the time in accordance with the very prudent policy adopted by the authorities. The "honour" of the old Whig burgh, which they professed to have in view, should have led them to send a cartel of defiance in reply to the Jacobite demand for money ; though, every thing considered, they best secured the "safety" of the place by returning a compliant answer. A refusal to pay the contribution might have provoked a vengeful visit from the Prince, which they had no sufficient means to ward off ; and the vain bravado of the Council might have had for its sequel the town laid waste.

When the rebel army reached Duddingston, on its way to the South, it was separated into two divisions. One, commanded by the Prince in person, proceeded towards the eastern border, and on the 8th of November occupied the village of Brampton, in order to check Marshall Wade, in the event of that officer advancing from Newcastle to protect Carlisle. The other division, under the Duke of Perth, took the western route to the latter city.

The enemy's progress was carefully watched by the agents of the magistrates and Mr Goldie, and faithfully reported to Dr Waugh. The latter, addressing his London friend on the 2nd of November, says :—" The Provost of Dumfries writes last night ' that a gentleman of that town was just arrived from Edinburgh, who came out last Thursday about twelve o'clock at noon, and brings advices that the baggage, artillery, ammunition, &c., were upon waggons and carts going to Dalkeith, and that the whole army were in motion and preparing to march southward ; that they gave out they were to go by Kelso, and were resolved to meet Marshall Wade and give him battle.'" Two days afterwards, Dr Waugh received a note from Provost Bell, inclosing a communication from a Dumfries merchant, to the following effect :—" Two gentlemen who can be depended on, in riding between Moffat and the Crook, on Saturday, 2nd November, after five at night, met a countryman about three miles from the Crook, who said he was going to Annandale. Upon asking the news of him, he told them he had come from Peebles, and that before he came away the Provost had got a message sent him by the rebels to prepare meat, drink, and lodging for 1,800 men. . . . The other returned to Dumfries, who relates that on Sabbath the 3rd, at ten o'clock forenoon, he was overtaken at Moffat by another man riding express from Peebles, of whom his friend had taken the opportunity of writing a letter that he might call upon him at Moffat ; and there that express told him he left Peebles about two o'clock, Sabbath morning, and that the above-mentioned 1,800 men, with 150 carts with baggage, ammunition, &c., were come there on Saturday night, and a little before he left the town a larger body came up, which he was informed were to the number of 4,000 men, and of this an express was immediately sent to General Wade from Moffat." We close our obligations to this interesting correspondence by copying the subjoined note :—

"*The Provost of Dumfries to Dr Waugh.*

"DUMFRIES, 5th November, 1745, 8 at night.—This moment I have advice by an express from Moffat that a quartermaster belonging to the Highlanders came there about one of the clock this day, to secure quarters for 4000 foot and 600 horse, and the messenger says he saw them within half a mile of the town before he came away. We expect them, or part of them, this way to-morrow. I beg you will despatch expresses to Penrith, Kendal, Lancaster, and Whitehaven ; and am most respectfully your most obedient servant."

The rebels, however, did not pass from Moffat to Dumfries—the doom of the burgh was delayed. Carlisle was the game they had in view ; and that city, strongly walled and thoroughly warned though it was, fell into their hands like a bird into the net of the fowler. The Duke of Perth's division marched down the vale of Annan towards the Border city. So bad were the roads that the baggage waggons could scarcely keep up with the men, and a portion of the stores were on this account left by them at the village of Ecclefechan. Intelligence to this effect having reached Dumfries, a party of the loyal inhabitants resolved upon an anti-rebel raid. Hurrying to the village—a distance of sixteen miles—they surprised the soldiers left in charge of the baggage, seized the articles of which it was composed, and returned with them in triumph. Among the spoils were numerous pikes and scythe-blades used by the Highlanders at Prestonpans, some of which—rusty relics of the time—are still preserved within the Mid-Steeple of the burgh.

On Saturday, the 9th of November, the insurgents passed through the Border parish of Graitney. Anticipating their arrival, the minister, Mr James Galt, withdrew on the preceding day to Bowness, so that no service was held in the church on the following Sabbath. By the 15th the dreaded visitors were on the southern side of the Esk, and Mr Galt ventured to return ; yet the alarm on their account was so great that when he resumed his pulpit duties on Sabbath the 17th, the church bell was not rung, lest the far-away Highlanders should hear the sound, and construe it into a loyal Presbyterian protest against themselves.*

Carlisle Castle, utterly neglected by the Government, and garrisoned chiefly by the Cumberland and Westmoreland militia —which had "a leaning towards the Stuarts, or at least an in-

---

* Graitney Session Records. For the privilege of inspecting of which we are indebted to the Rev. William Bell, minister of the parish.

difference towards the House of Hanover"*—made no defence. It surrendered with the city to the Duke of Perth on the 15th of November ; who, on entering to take possession of his prize next day, solemnly proclaimed King James– the mayor and other officers, in their robes, and bearing the city sword and mace, giving their attendance. The keys of Carlisle were presented to the Prince at Brampton by the mayor and corporatiou on bended knee ; and on the 18th Charles Edward made his entry into the city, mounted on a white charger, and preceded by not fewer than a hundred pipers.

Stimulated by so many triumphs, Prince Charles set out on the 21st at the head of his army in the direction of London, fully impressed with the idea that he would have little difficulty in becoming master of the English metropolis. After the lapse of a fortnight, the bright dream of Charles Edward had well-nigh vanished. The Highland host reached Derby, and then, like the waters of an ebbing tide, retired northward—no auxiliary streams having flowed in to carry it on to the seat of Government.† The Prince confidently expected that his ranks would be greatly swelled on his southward journey, and that succours would also reach him from France, He was disappointed as regards both ; and with three armies marching to oppose him, and his own officers unwilling under such adverse conditions to proceed, he was constrained to retrace his steps, and to admit that the crown which beckoned him onward was but a delusive phantom, like the air-drawn dagger of Macbeth.

There is still extant a journal, kept by the Rev. George Duncan, at this time minister of Lochrutton, near Dumfries, which contains several curious references to the Rebellion. The following entry is given, dated Monday, 16th December :—" News came to Dumfries that the rebels were flying before the Duke of Cumberland ; and orders were sent by him to the northern counties to arm, in order to catch the fugitives. On this the several parishes of the Presbytery were ordered to arm." In obedience to this command the parishioners of Lochrutton tendered their services to the magistrates of Dumfries ; and twelve of them, it is stated, " went with other volunteers to guar l Annan bridge," the patriotic minister going with them to animate their zeal ; but, being induced to return to his pastoral duties by the authorities of the town, the retreating rebels reached Carlisle on the 19th of December ; and, with the view of withstanding them at the various passes into Scotland, and giving time for the Government troops to overtake them, armed parties were sent out

* Carlisle in 1745, p. 98.

† The army, according to Maxwell (Narrative, p. 73), was never in better spirits than at Derby : it was only the urgent representations of Lord George Murray that induced the Prince to order a retreat,

from several parishes. These volunteers proved quite incompetent for the perilous task assigned to them, which could only have been done, with any chance of success, by veteran soldiers. A large party from Annandale took up a position on the Scotch side of the Esk, big with the ambition of pitching the Highlanders headlong into that river as they attempted to cross it. But when the plaided warriors appeared on the opposite bank, and the battle-notes of the pibroch rose loud and defiant, the raw volunteers wheeled round and vanished : only one officer, afterwards minister of Middlebie, remaining to fire a solitary random shot by way of testimony against the rebels. The dozen doughty defenders of Annan bridge evinced the same discretion, as, on learning the flight of their brethren, they hurried home to Lochrutton—the minister's own man being one of the first to flee ; and no sooner did he reach his master's kitchen than he dropped down on a long settle, and fainted away.

The Highlanders crossed the Esk at Longtown, one hundred men abreast. There were at once two thousand of them in the river ; and so swollen was it at the time that nothing of them was visible but their bonneted heads and shoulders. Holding each other by their coat necks, they stemmed the impetuous current, losing not a man in the passage ; and as soon as the opposite bank was reached, the pipes struck merrily up, and they danced till they were dry again. Some of the party, we are told, in passing Graitney Manse, threatened Mr Galt ; while several of his parishioners suffered by them considerably—"particularly John Gass of Flushead."[*] After a muster had been made, about 2000 of the force, under Lord George Murray, the Marquis of Tullibardine, Lord Ogilvie, and Lord Nairn, proceeded northwards by Ecclefechan ; and the main body, 4000 strong, with the Prince, the Duke of Perth, Lord Elcho, Lord Pitsligo, Lochiel, and Keppoch, marched towards Dumfries by a more westerly route. On Friday (the 20th) Lord Elcho rode forward, along the old Annan road, at the head of 500 men— "all plaided and plumed in their tartan array"—but wearied with their protracted travel. When, towards dusk, they entered Dumfries by St. Michael's Street, they met with neither check nor challenge, though a partial muster of the county militia had been made whilst the rebels were in England. The rest of the division, commanded by Prince Charles, halted midway at Annan all night, joining their comrades early on the following day. Such house accommodation as could be obtained was taken advantage of by the strangers ; but most of them, winter though it was, camped down in the fields to the south of what is now called Shakespeare Street.

---

[*] Graitney Session Records.

CHAPTER XLVI.

BEHOLD, then, the ancient burgh once more under a military despotism ! It proved of brief duration, but it was grinding and oppressive ; and doubtless many of those who suffered from it regretted, when too late, that more had not been done to prevent the calamity. On the evening of Saturday, the 21st of December, the rulers and other leading men of the town met in the Presbytery house attached to the New Church, for the purpose of considering a renewed demand upon them for money. They could not assemble in the Council Chamber, for that was occupied by a band of Highlanders. Provost Bell -was not present to preside over them, he having been seized as a hostage that the burgh would keep good faith with its captors. A sad meeting it must have been ; which conviction is deepened as we read the following record of its proceedings :—" The said day Bailie Graham and Bailie Carruthers represented to the Council and community of this burgh called to attend the meeting, that Mr John Hay represented he had commission from his Royal Highness Prince Charles, called by him Regent of Scotland, now in this burgh with a powerful army, to demand of the said burgh a contribution of two thousand pounds sterling, to be paid to-morrow against eight o'clock at night, and to deliver to him, for the use of their army, one thousand pair of shoes, together with all their arms, public and private, that are to be found in town, against the same time, and that as they would redeem their houses and families from destruction and ruin ; which certification was by the said Mr Hay frequently repeated to the said magistrates, and who would not allow them any longer time for paying in the said contribution, and delivering the said shoes and arms, than as above ; Which being considered by the said magistrates and Council, with advice and consent of the community called to attend this meeting, they, the said magistrates and Council, with advice and consent foresaid, unanimously grant warrant to, and appoint the bailies and the convener, the dean, and treasurer, or any one or two of them, to borrow the said sum of two thousand pounds sterling, in whole or in parcils, wherever it can be had, to be lodged in the treasurer's hands for paying the said two thousand pounds sterling : and also to purchase and procure the said number of shoes, and to take up the foresaid arms, for answering the foresaid demand ; and to grant bills and bonds for the said money and shoes to any person or persons who shall lend and provide the same, bearing interest from the time of borrowing and until payment. And the magistrates and Council hereby bind and oblige them and the other magistrates of this burgh, and their successors in office, and the community of the said burgh for the time being, to free and relieve the said obligants, and every of them, and their heirs, executors, and successors, of the said bills and securities so to be granted to them : the which sums are to be assessed and proportioned upon and amongst the merchants, heritors, craftsmen, and other inhabitants of and in this burgh as shall afterwards be judged proper."

Charles, on entering Dumfries, accompanied by the Duke of Perth, Lord Elcho, Lord Pitsligo, the French ambassador, and the chiefs of Lochiel, Clanranald, Glengarry, and Keppoch, forthwith assumed the absolute sovereignty of the place. In the Lochrutton journal, under the date of Sabbath, December 22nd, occurs the following entry :—" A melancholy day—the rebels in Dumfries— about 4,000—with the Pretender's son at their head—in great rage at the town for carrying off their baggage from Annandale, and for raising volunteers, and calling out the militia of the country in defence of the Government— demanded £2,000 sterling of contributions, . . . and that they convey their carts, with their carriages after them, to their headquarters. They were most rude in the town—pillaged some shops—pulled shoes off gentlemen's feet in the street. In most of the churches for some miles about Dumfries, no sermon. God be blessed ! we had public worship. I lectured 1 Sam iv. ; Mr John Scott, minister of Dumfries (there being no sermon there), preached. Much confusion in all the neighbouring parishes—rebels robbing people's stables—pillaging some houses. They came to the border of our parish, but, God be thanked ! came no further, and we suffered no loose usage."

At that time the Blue Bell Inn—a house still standing near the foot of High Street, on the west side—was the chief place of public entertainment in the Burgh ; and the tenement now occupied as the Commercial Hotel* was one of its principal

* Prince Charlie's room is No. 6. Two new stories were added to the house about ten years ago.

mansions. Charles took possession of both for his own special use, residing chiefly in the former, and holding high state in the latter on one or two particular occasions. The apartment in which he held his levees, and indulged in other courtly ceremonies, was not unworthy of such distinction. Preserved as much as possible in its original condition, its ample dimensions (twenty feet square), and its walls enriched with gilded mouldings and grooved pilasters, still give to it something of a palatial aspect. What a striking picture that hall must have presented when occupied by the leaders of the rebel movement—the dauntless Clanranald, the lofty Lochiel, the impetuous Lord Elcho, the prudent Duke of Perth ; the other chiefs with less distinctive features, but all men of mark ;·and the central figure, easily recognised as a prince even in such a patrician circle, but wearing a pensive air, all unlike the sunny radiance which lighted up his handsome face when he commenced his journey to the South. In the two months that have elapsed he has become visibly graver and older, less buoyant, more exactive and imperious. He has learned during the interval that the "right divine" on which he leaned is but a feeble reed—that his race has no hold of the English heart—that many of the Scots who once cried "God bless him !" deserted his cause as soon as he left their country—that on his return to it his foes have multiplied—and that before he can be much more than the nominal Regent of Scotland, he will have to enter upon a fiery conflict, which may after all fail miserably. It need not be wondered at that Charles Edward looks sad—gloomy, even, at times—as, sitting in council with his friends at Dumfries during these memorable days in December, 1745, he receives despatches announcing dangerous Hanoverian movements in the North, or messengers who tell him that Wade or Cumberland is following rapidly on his track. We feel persuaded that much of the Prince's ill-treatment of Dumfries is due to the morbid influence of his own mishaps. He stood in great want, too, of money and stores ; so that necessity combined with other causes to render his temporary rule over the Burgh exactive and severe. Not only was a heavy pecuniary contribution levied on the inhabitants, and a large supply of foot-gear called for, but much horse furniture, many stands of arms, nine casks of gunpowder, and the funds possessed by the Government officials, were appropriated by the rebels.

Private property did not altogether escape their vindictiveness or cupidity, though there is every reason to believe that the Prince desired it to be respected by his followers. "The provost of Dumfries," says Sir Walter Scott, in his "Tales of a Grandfather," "a gentleman of family named Corsane,* who had shewn

* This is a mistake. The chief magistrate, as already mentioned, was Mr George Bell.

himself a staunch adherent of the Government, was menaced with the destruction of his house and property. It is not very long since the late Mrs M'Culloch of Ardwell, daughter of Provost Corsane, told your grandfather that she remembered well, when a child of six years old, being taken out of her father's house, as if it was to be instantly burned. Too young to be sensible of the danger, she asked the Highland officer who held her in his arms to show her the Pretender ; which the good-natured Gael did, under condition that little Miss Corsane was in future to call him the Prince. Neither did they carry their threats into execution against the Provost or his mansion."

Mr Robert Chalmers furnishes some pleasant gossip regarding the Jacobite occupation of the burgh. "Within the last three years," he says, "an aged female lived in Edinburgh who recollected the occupation of Dumfries by the Highland army, being then seventeen years of age. She lived opposite to the Prince's lodgings, and frequently saw him. In her father's house several of the men were quartered ; and it was her recollection that they greatly lamented the course which they had taken, and feared the issue of the expedition. The proprietor of the house occupied by the Prince was a Mr Richard Lowthian, a Nonjuror, and proprietor of Stafford Hall, in Cumberland. Though well affected to the Prince's cause, he judged it prudent not to appear in his company ; and yet neither did he wish to offend him by the appearance of deliberately going out of his way. The expedient he adopted in this dilemma was one highly characteristic of the time. He got himself filled so exceedingly drunk that his being kept back from the company of the guest was only a matter of decency. His wife, who could not well be taxed with treason, did the honours of the house without scruple ; and some other Jacobite ladies, particulary those of the attainted house of Carnwath, came forward to grace his Court. When the writer was at Dumfries in 1838, he saw in the possession of a private family one of a set of table napkins of the most beautiful damask, resembling the finest satin, which the ladies Dalzell had taken to grace the table of the Prince, and which they had kept ever after, with a care due to the most precious relics."*

* There is a set of similar articles—perhaps the very same—in the museum of the Crichton Institution, Dumfries. A plate with a red floral design which formed part of a dinner service used by the Prince at the Blue Bell Inn, is now in the possession of Mr Robert Gillies, engraver, Dumfries. It belonged to his father-in-law, the late Mr John M'Cormick, a great enthusiast in local antiquities. We know of a third genuine relic of Prince Charlie. After leaving Dumfries for Upper Nithsdale, the Prince, with two Highland officers, entered the house of Dr John Trotter, Burnfoot, Tynron, and called for refreshments. A bottle of brandy was produced, and Charles, without waiting for glasses, poured part of the liquor into a china bowl, and drank ; after which he handed it to his officers, who did the same. The bowl —a handsome one, of real Oriental manufacture—is preserved in the family as a prized memento of the Prince's visit.

As noticed by the minister of Lochrutton, there was no public religious services in Dumfries on the Sunday of the occupation. Instead of worship and rest, there was the turbulent license of military rule ; the stirring bugle call, the harsh notes of the bagpipe, for the music of the Sabbath bells.   The douce burgesses, instead of proceeding churchward as usual, sat within their dwellings in fear and trembling ; few of them caring to encounter the tartaned strangers, who, scattered in parties here and there, made the streets look singularly foreign yet picturesque.   Not a few unwelcome domiciliary visits were paid by the unceremonious mountaineers.   Some of them prowled stealthily about, enriching themselves at the expense of the Lowland Whigs, whom they deemed fair game ; but we have no means of knowing to what precise extent this pillaging system was carried on.   Less unwelcome, though far from agreeable, were the calls made that day on the inhabitants by the committee appointed to borrow the heavy sum exacted by the rebels.   Bailies Carruthers and Graham, with their colleagues, to whom this business was assigned, must have spent a wearisome Sabbath in carrying it through.   Landed proprietors, professional gentlemen, merchants, and tradesmen, were appealed to by the committee ; and, lest the townspeople should not contribute liberally enough to the forced loan, applications were made to rich persons at a distance for aid to the burgh in this perplexing juncture of its affairs.

Many large subscriptions were obtained.   Thus, we read in the list that William Gordon of Campbeltown contributed £356 7s 9d ; Joseph Corrie, town clerk, Dumfries, £218 ; John Johnstone, provost of Annan, £100 ; James Hoggan, in Comlongan, £100 12s ; William M'William, in Greenhead, Carlaverock, £80 ; John Milligan, merchant, Kirkcudbright, £80 ; and Sir Robert Laurie of Maxwelton, £40.   But the aggregate was in a great measure made up of smaller sums—Charles Kirkpatrick & Sons, merchants, giving £17 10s ; John Ewart, late provost of Dumfries, giving £8 2s ; James Aitken, convener of the Trades, £2 2s ; Adam Marchbank, deacon of the weavers, £1 ; Charles Mercer, mathematician, £1 ; William Reid, deacon of the smiths, 10s 6d : down to 5s, the mite of a poor widow, named Agnes Lewars.*   Of the £2,000 demanded, £1,195 was obtained by the appointed time—eight o'clock at night—in hard cash, for which bills were granted to the lenders by the burgh authorities, and other men of substance.   The rest of the money was not subscribed for, or at least remained unpaid till after the lapse of several days.   It was no easy task to borrow such a large sum, on a short notice, in a town that could boast of little wealth, even though the district around was also drawn upon ; and to supply a thousand pairs of shoes in twenty-four hours was found to be

* For a full list of the contributors, see Appendix M.

impossible. We know that, forty-five years afterwards, there
were in Dumfries exactly 236 men and boys engaged in King
Crispin's craft ; and probably they numbered about 200 in 1745,
of whom not more than a fourth would have establishments of
their own.   All these were visited by the collecting committee ;
and after having emptied them, and added to the new articles all
the old shoes that could otherwise be obtained, it was found that
the entire stock at the hour of call numbered only 255 pairs, or
little more than a quarter of the supply demanded by the rebels.
Late at night the committee reported to the Prince, through the
medium of his secretary, the measure of success that had attended
their exertions, and received orders to complete the contribution
of money and shoes with the utmost speed.

Still later the miniature Court at Mr Lowthian's was convulsed by the receipt of startling intelligence. Towards midnight,
and whilst Charles and his counsellors were still busily engaged
in State affairs, a messenger called in breathless haste, and insisted
on seeing the Prince. As he was known to be a friend, he was
admitted to an interview with the Pretender in a separate room.*
When Charles soon afterwards rejoined his chiefs he was observed
to be more than usually dejected. It was evident to them that
he had received unpleasant news of some kind ; and their worst
apprehensions were realised when he announced that the son of
the Elector of Hanover was hurrying down upon them at the
head of a great army, and might reach Dumfries before daybreak.
There was no rest in the rebel Court or camp that night. Long
ere the sun rose on the following morning, the drum beat to arms ;
and whether the Highlanders or the townspeople were most
terrified by the discordant summons, it would be difficult to say ;
but when the cause became known, the alarm of the latter gave
way to exultation. They had suffered much from the Pretender's
visit—were delighted at the idea of being relieved from it soon ;
and when he did disappear, they never thought of singing the
Jacobite strain, "Will ye no come back again ?" Off next day
went the Prince and his entire army, carrying with them, as
hostages for the balance of the contribution, Mr Andrew Crosbie
of Holm, formerly provost of the burgh, and Mr Walter Riddel
of Glenriddel, one of its merchant councillors.

The alarm which hastened their departure was quite unfounded. A devoted Dumfries Jacobite, named M'Ghie, a painter
by trade, hearing that the Duke of Cumberland had laid siege to
Carlisle, went, with the approval of some sympathising friends,
towards that city, in order to watch the movements of the royal
army. He set off for that purpose on the morning of the memorable Sabbath to which frequent reference has been made ; and,
wearied with hovering all day on the road, he had just sat down

* This is No. 7 of the Commercial Hotel.

to supper in a public-house at Annan—which stands nearly mid-way between Dumfries and Carlisle—when a practical humourist, who guessed the nature of his secret mission, announced with rueful visage that the Whig Duke had captured Carlisle, crossed the Esk, and was in full march after the rebels. Big with the burden of this fictitious tale, Mr M'Ghie galloped to Dumfries, a distance, by the circuitous road then in use, of about seventeen miles, never resting for a moment till he had communicated the alarming tidings to the Prince, as already stated.

The Highland host proceeded up Nithsdale towards the west country ; the Pretender and his principal officers resting on the night of Monday, the 23rd, in Drumlanrig Castle. Three full length portraits—those of King William, Queen Mary, and Queen Anne—that still adorn the staircase of that ducal mansion, bear disfiguring tokens of the visit ; some of the party, in order to manifest their hatred to the royal family, having stabbed their dirks through the pictures. The two gentlemen carried away captive by them from Dumfries did not effect their escape when a short distance from the town, as has been frequently stated. On the contrary, they were taken to Glasgow, and only set at liberty after they had paid down in full tale £815, the balance that remained of the £2000 levied upon the burgh.

Once more the Town Council assembled in peace and freedom in their own hall, under the presidency of Provost Bell, all well pleased to get rid of the rapacious strangers ; though sorry at the same time that a disagreeable duty had devolved upon them in consequence of the rebel visit—namely, to devise means for paying back the sums that had been borrowed. The first business meet-ing after the precipitate flight of the Jacobite army was held on the 27th of January, 1746 ; at which the Provost, after reporting the steps taken to raise the money, explained " that the foresaid sum of £2000 sterling had been paid at Glasgow by Andrew Crosbie, late provost, and Walter Riddel, merchant, who were taken hostages for the same, conform to a discharge thereof, under the hand and seal of John Murray, secretary, dated the first day of January, just now produced." The Provost also tabled a receipt, signed "Andrew Lumsden," acknowledging the delivery to the latter of the 255 pairs of shoes exacted from the town ;* and he gave information also regarding the arms that had been delivered up, and the forage that had been furnished, at the call of the insurgents.

These statements having been duly considered by the meeting, it was resolved that an assessment should be levied to pay off the debt that been incurred. The stentmasters appointed to under-take this laborious duty gave in to a subsequent meeting a valuable return, which supplies us with reliable information

* Town Council Minutes.

regarding the wealth of the town at this period of its history. According to the instructions given to them, they "took up an account of the rents of the tenements and buildings in the burgh, the yearly value of such parts as are possessed by the heritors themselves, also the value of all goods, household plenishings, corns, wares, merchandise, and other perishable effects in the possession of the inhabitants," bodily clothing excepted : and they reported the value of the houses and public buildings to be £34,483 4s ; of the goods to be £28,130 19s 9d—in all, £62,514 3s 9d : so that the latter sum represents the pecuniary worth of Dumfries at the date of the Rebellion. For the purpose of letting the burden fall with diminished weight on the poorer classes, some of the wealthy heritors generously volunteered to pay an extra rate amounting to £11,134 13s 4d, which raised the aggregate to £73,748 17s 1d—the amount on which the assessment was to be levied. The stentmasters found that, after allowing £159 11s 1d for the shoes and forage and the expense of the collection, a rate of three per cent. would cover £2,159 11s 1d, the entire sum due ; and accordingly, a cess was imposed of three pounds on every hundred—a grievous exaction, which many of the people did not submit to without grumbling, and which was not finally paid without great difficulty and till after the lapse of nearly two years. It has been computed that the loss incurred by the town on account of Charles Edward's visit amounted to not less than £4,000.

A claim for reimbursement made by the town was favourably entertained through the exertions of the Duke of Queensberry and of Sir James Johnstone, member for the Dumfries district of burghs. His Grace, in a letter to the Provost, dated London, April 14th, 1750, intimated that the Government had agreed to allow the sum of £2,848 5s 11d to cover the money tribute and the other exactions. "Not thinking it advisable," he says, "to trust the warrant to the common post, I propose to put it into Sir James Johnstone's hands, who will set out from hence in a day or two, and I daresay will take care to deliver it safe, as I can vouch for his having been all along extremely anxious for the procuring of it." The royal warrant here referred to was duly received. It was addressed to the Barons of the Exchequer, the preamble being as follows :—"George R.—Trusty and well-beloved, we greet you well. Whereas, the Commissioners of our Treasury have laid before us a petition of the Provost, Bailies, Dean of Guild, and Treasurer of Dumfries, on behalf of themselves and the community of the said town, representing unto us that during the late Rebellion they were at great expense in providing arms and raising and subsisting men for the said town, as also in raising recruits for the marching regiments who served in the battles of Falkirk and Culloden, and were also obliged upon the return of the

rebel army from England to pay a contribution of two thousand
pounds sterling, and to deliver to the rebels two hundred and
fifty-five pair of shoes ; which said contribution money, with the
other expenses before-mentioned, do amount in the whole to the
sum of two thousand eight hundred and forty-eight pounds five
and eleven pence (after deducting one hundred and thirty-three
pounds six shillings and eight pence for interest money which we
have disallowed) : and therefore the said magistrates and community have most humbly besought us to take their case into our
royal consideration, and grant them such relief as we shall think
proper."* His Majesty, after stating that he considers it just and
reasonable that the claim should be conceded, authorises the
Barons to pay the specified sum out of "the monies arising from
the estates of the late Lord Elcho," forfeited to the Crown by his
having been guilty of high treason.

The Duke of Queensberry, in acknowledging a letter of
thanks sent to him by the Provost for his good service on this
occasion, disclaimed all merit on account of it ; expressed his
satisfaction with the result, and added : "I shall always rejoice at
every event tending to the prosperity of Dumfries, and will never
fail to use my endeavours, upon all occasions, to promote it"—a
profession that was no hollow one on the part of "the good Duke,"
as he was deservedly called by the people of the burgh. The
compensation money thus obtained was in due course distributed
among those of the inhabitants on whom the three per cent.
assessment had been levied ; the chief duty of doing so devolving
on the town clerk, Mr Malcolm.†

After occupying Glasgow, the rebels retired into Stirlingshire,
beat the Royalists on Falkirk moor, and then retreated, even in
their hour of triumph. Whatever glimpses of good fortune might
at times smile upon their flag, the gloom of irretrievable defeat
was "casting its shadow before ;" and, like the wounded stag,
they retired to their Highland coverts only to die. A cruel
Nemesis, in the person of the Duke of Cumberland, was at hand,‡

---

* Town Council Minutes.

† Mr Malcolm built, at the foot of High Street, a house that was at the
time perhaps the best mansion in the burgh. (a) Extract from Council minute,
23rd July, 1753 : "A petition was received from Mr Archibald Malcolm,
setting forth that he wished to remove several old thatched houses at the
foot of Southgate-brae, of which he was proprietor, in order to build upon
it a double house for his own residence."

(a) The tradition is that some of the Prince Charlie money unclaimed
went to pay for the building.

‡ On the 3rd of March the Town Council of Dumfries, having learned
that the Duke had entered North Britain "to command his Majesty's forces,"
appointed a committee of their number to repair to Edinburgh and "con-
gratulate his Royal Highness upon his arrival in Scotland, and at the same
time to express the loyalty and affection of this burgh to his Majesty's person
and Government, and our present happy establishment."

commissioned to pour out the vials of wrath on the forlorn Prince and his Highland followers, because the tyranny of his fathers had alienated the nation from the House of Stuart. The rebels could vanquish the incompetent Hawley at Falkirk, but they could not expect to cope successfully with the royal Duke, at the head of a force which nearly quadrupled their own ; and so they hastened northward, depressed though resolute, as if conscious of their approaching doom. On Drummossie Moor, near Culloden, they were brought to bay and utterly defeated.

One body of Highlanders retired in good order, their pipes playing, and carrying with them the Stuart standard : the rest were broken up with fearful carnage ; and the Prince, only when all hope was gone, withdrew from the fatal field. Well might the Celtic minstrel tune his harp to a doleful air, and lament the catastrophe in congenial strains like these :—

" There was no lack of bravery there—no spare of blood or breath ;
For one to two our foes we dared, for freedom or for death.
The bitterness of grief is past, of terror and dismay ;
The die was risked and foully cast, upon Culloden day."

No fewer than 1,200 rebels were slain or wounded on the field and in the pursuit ; the Royalists behaving with a wanton brutality that sullied the glory of their triumph. Charles Edward was accompanied from the scene of his thorough overthrow by the Duke of Perth, Lord Elcho, and a few horsemen. Crossing the water of Nairn, he retired to the house of a gentleman in Stratharick, where, after a conference with Simon, Lord Lovat, he bade a final adieu to the wreck of his brave army, and then took refuge from his merciless pursuers in the Western Islands and among the mountains of the mainland. For five months the unfortunate Prince roamed about a hunted fugitive— the price of £30,000 set upon his head—incurring innumerable dangers and hardships, and bearing all his adverse fortune with a fortitude and even good humour that were truly heroic. The tale of his sufferings is pathetic in the extreme ; and the effect it produces on all readers finds fit expression in the wail of the lyrical " wee birdie," " Waes me for Prince Charlie !" On the 20th September he succeeded in effecting his escape to France ; but he was never in a position to attempt the revival of the Stuart cause. Prostrated on Drummossie Moor, it experienced no resurrection ; and, however much we may admire the young Pretender's gallantry, and feel pity for his fate, it was doubtless well for the country that his enterprise failed, and that, as a consequence, the House of Hanover was fixed more securely on the throne than before.

CHAPTER XLVII.

THOUGH Dumfries was greatly put about, and severely dealt with by the rebels, it soon recovered its equanimity. Except for the difficulty experienced in connection with their exactions, we find no impress of their visit in the records of the following year. How to improve the navigation, and thereby foster the rising trade of the port, was a question that engaged much of the Council's attention in 1746. About the beginning of the century buoys had been placed in the lower reaches of the river, and something was done to remove obstructions from its channel; but it had no harbour worthy of the name. In order to supply this felt want, a committee was appointed in March, who presented a report in the following month, from which it appeared that the chief merchants and shipmasters had, at a conference held with them, expressed their opinion that the best site for the proposed harbour was at Glencaple Burnfoot, in the parish of Carlaverock; also that ground, measuring six acres, "for building warehouses upon, and other conveniences," had been laid out there by Mr Mercer, mathematician, according to a plan produced; and that, on the committee offering to purchase the land from its proprietor, William Maxwell of Nithsdale, that gentleman "had frankly agreed to make a compliment of it" to the burgh. A second committee were named to carry this proposal into effect, the instructions given to them being that they should cause a search to be made for a stone quarry near Glencaple, in order that building materials might be conveniently obtained, should make other requisite provisions for constructing the harbour, and should confer with the merchants in town who were not members of Council as to the best mode of defraying the cost of the operations.

The quay appears to have been completed in the course of the following year. Soon afterwards houses began to rise up on the hill side overlooking it, and originating the pretty little village of

Glencaple, which contains at present about six hundred inhabitants. In the summer of 1749 a beacon, to direct the course of vessels passing from the Solway into the Nith, was erected on Southerness Point ; its dimensions being fourteen feet square at the base, two and a half feet thick in the shaft, and thirty feet high. As the Nithsdale family had shown their continued interest in the welfare of the burgh by the free grant to it of land for the harbour, and also by allowing a search to be made for building-stones in the neighbourhood, the Council reciprocated this kindly feeling by enacting that all goods passing the bridge for the use of Mr Maxwell and his successors should be exempt from duty, a regulation that is still in force.

Another smaller quay was commenced at Kingholm, about a mile below the town, before Glencaple Quay was finished. Both were appointed as places of discharge towards the close of 1746 ; and on the 15th May, 1747, Glencaple quay was first turned to practical account by having a cargo of Maryland tobacco landed there by the good ship " Success," the property of ex-Provost Crosbie, merchant.

With greater facilities for trade, the exports as well as the imports increased : salt, made from sea-sleich, on the Ruthwell shore, had long figured as an article of commerce ; and freights of wood, linen cloth, and of leather, from tanneries established in the town, were subsequently added. Smuggling grew in a ratio with the legitimate traffic of the port. It seems to have reached its climax in 1752. During that year it became so systematic and audacious that the revenue authorities in London were led to make special inquiries regarding it ; and the statement returned in answer revealed a very unsatisfactory condition of affairs. " We have reason to believe," said the Dumfries collector, " that the representation [made by the Board] is so far true, that considerable quantities of foreign spirits, wine, tea, and other goods, have been run in our district for many years past, in open boats, from the Isle of Man ; that the smugglers run these goods in fleets of boats, ten or twelve at a time, each of which carries twenty-seven or twenty-eight small casks ; that they come in upon the coast at spring-tides, in the night-time, and disperse to different places ; that their carriers and assistants are attending upon the shore to receive their cargoes ; that they have slings of ropes fitted for the carriage of two casks upon each horse, and in a few minutes after the boats land, receive their carriage and ride off, and before daylight hide the goods many miles distant from the shore, and no doubt convey the greatest part of them into England." Busy rumour represented to the London Board that the contraband articles were transmitted South from the Solway coast by " great gangs of smugglers armed and disguised ;" but the local officer, whilst admitting that the lawless deeds above

detailed were of habitual occurrence, doubted the existence of these
disguised desperadoes ; so that they may be looked upon as somewhat mythical ; and, indeed, the "running" fraternity were so
favoured by the country folks that they scarcely required either
to mask themselves or their operations.

Whilst increased attention was being paid to the river, its
"braes" opposite the Castledykes quarry were partially embanked, and the Dock acquired a heritage of sylvan beauty with
which it is still enriched. The Town Council having, for the
"good and ornament" of the meadow, wisely resolved to plant a
portion of it with trees, were supplied with a number of choice
young limes for this purpose from their ducal patron's grounds at
Drumlanrig—his Grace sending down his own gardener, John
Clark, to see the precious saplings properly rooted in their new
home. This important æsthetic operation was performed in the
autumn of 1748. The trees numbered at first eighty or more ;
and, though now reduced to thirty-five, they constitute a double
woodland row of imposing aspect, for which the inhabitants
entertain a feeling of reverence bordering on that cherished by
our Druidical ancestors for their groves of oak. About ninety
years afterwards upwards of a hundred young trees were planted,
by which the lime-shaded walk was gracefully continued in single
file to the foot of the Dock.

Scarcely had the trees from Drumlanrig got accustomed to
their fresh soil, than the walls of a new public building began to
peer down upon them from the adjoining Kirkgate, and to form
an interesting feature of that ancient thoroughfare. This was
Moorheads' Hospital, designed as a domestic retreat for decayed
burgesses and destitute orphans, natives of the town. On the
27th of November, 1739, James Moorhead, tenant of Castledykes,
and merchant in Dumfries, executed a deed of mortification, by
which he bequeathed £150 for this object. By a second deed,
of the same date, he joined with his brother-german, William
Moorhead, merchant in Carlisle, in mortifying for it £400—the
proportion of this sum contributed by the latter being £100 ; and,
according to the terms of the settlement, the £400 was not
payable till the first term of Whitsunday or Martinmas after the
decease of the longest liver of the two. William, the survivor,
having died towards the close of 1745, the sum (with interest, £79
0s 3d) became due at Whitsunday, 1747. The other smaller sum
was not available till the 18th of June, 1752, by which time the
interest on it had swelled the amount to £232 10s. These figures
brought the bequests for the Hospital up to the handsome sum of
£711 10s 3d ; and with it the administrators of the trust, consisting of the Town Council, the two parish ministers, Mr Robert
Wight, Mr John Scott, and the Kirk Session, were enabled to
carry it into full effect. Some old tenements opposite St. Michael's

Church were purchased and cleared away, in order that a suitable site might be obtained. A contract was entered into with Mr James Harley, "late deacon of the squaremen in Dumfries," according to which he agreed to erect the building for £564, and it was duly completed and opened in the summer of 1753. A small balance of £52 remained after all expenses had been paid. The funds of the charity were enriched by a donation of £300 from the "good Duke," and it was further endowed by the legitimate application of various sums mortified for behoof of the Dumfries poor, so that an annual revenue sufficient to maintain from forty to fifty inmates was secured.

The benevolent brothers to whom the town was indebted for this excellent institution intended that it should to some extent be a workhouse in the modern sense of that term. Accordingly, the third rule drawn up by the directors, "relating to the behaviour of the poor," required "that all who shall be employed in any labour shall repair to such rooms in the house as are appointed for that purpose ; and such poor as are capable of working out of the house " shall be permitted by the master to do so, he allowing them in each case a penny for every shilling of their earnings ; and by a resolution of the directors of the Hospital in 1756, the sum of £60 was drawn from its funds, to be laid out in buying lint for improving the poorer sort of people in the town and parish of Dumfries to spin into yarn.

For a long period the house has been exclusively a charitable asylum for old people who had seen better days, and for orphan children who receive in it maintenance, education, and guardianship. Its directors have long since ceased to take oversight of the ordinary poor ; but by means of legacies left by Mr Hunter, Mr Raining, and Mrs Archibald, they allow small out-door pensions to some twenty-six elderly widows, whose dwellings have been left comfortless—perhaps desolate—by the death of their natural protectors. The annual expenditure of the Hospital has sometimes exceeded £600 ; latterly, including the annuities, it has been limited to £400. Moorheads' Hospital is a plain, homely building ; the interest attached to it arises from the unobtrusive benefactions of which it is the source, and which give to it in our eyes more than architectural beauty. Honoured in the burgh through all time be the memory of its liberal-hearted founders ! (a)

Soon after the second Rebellion, increased attention was paid to tillage by the farmers of Nithsdale. Fields were enclosed— waste lands were reclaimed ; shell-marl and lime lent their fertilising influence to the soil—the culture of the potato was

(a) In 1874 a legacy of £1000 was obtained from the estate of Mr George M'Lellan, baker, and a considerable addition for the sick was made at the rear of the building. Numerous other legacies and donations have gone to enlarge the capital fund.

commenced, and afterwards of the turnip ; the former supplying a cheap article of diet for all classes, and rendering dearths less frequent ; the latter furnishing food for stock, and permitting the cattle trade of the locality to be developed. On the Ayr bank being opened, in 1760, not a few landed proprietors around Dumfries were enabled by its aid to carry out extensive improvements. When intelligence, enterprise, and capital are jointly devoted to a given purpose they are not easily baffled. Employed upon the husbandry of the district, great results were accomplished, which added to its productive value and scenic beauty. In the year just named the great military road was formed from the county town through Galloway to Portpatrick ; and about twelve years later another leading artery of traffic was opened up—the road from Gretna, by Ecclefechan, Lockerbie, and Moffat, into Peebleshire. Thus, whilst Dumfries was being improved externally, the valley in which it rises was growing in rural wealth, and new channels were constructed for its increasing trade.

During the reign of Cromwell the rents of Dumfriesshire were computed at 238,031 merks, or £13,223 18s 4d. A hundred years afterwards the annual value of the land was threefold that amount at least ; in 1795 it had risen 800 per cent. since 1656 ; in 1808 this augmented sum was doubled, and the lands of the county were yielding sixteen times the rent drawn from them at the time of the Protectorate.* A small property in Dunscore, that was purchased in 1756 for £142, yielded a rent of £160 fifty years afterwards ; the large estate of Netherwood, which brought only £4000 in 1740, was sold for £30,000 in 1790 ; and, generally speaking, the rents of other land around Dumfries experienced a nearly corresponding advance during the half century which followed the introduction of the improvements that have been referred to.†

* Forty-two Scotch acres of "ploughable land" belonging to Dumfries at Kingholm were let at an annual rent of £22 sterling in 1712 ; sixty acres of the same estate brought a rent of £150 in 1817, and were sold in 1827 for £6300.

† The Tax Roll of Nithsdale in 1554, a copy of which is still extant, represents the annual value of land there on the eve of the Reformation to have been only £116 sterling, or £1400 3s 4d Scots. We suspect, however, that these figures do not represent the real yearly worth of the estates, but the low-rated value put upon them by their owners. The Roll of Nithsdale in 1671 shows an advance to £3676 10s. According to these returns, the whole of Dumfriesshire was valued at only £225 in 1613, and at £9429 in 1671. Dr Ramage, writing in *Notes and Queries* of 4th November, 1871, on this subject, says :—" It is curious to observe how few ratable properties in Nithsdale there were in 1554. There were only fifty names, as follows : Caerlaverock, £53 6s 8d ; Garnsalloch and Dursquens, £15 13s 4d ; Tynwall, £20 ; Duncow, £20 ; Milnhead within Kirkmaho. £2 ; Lord Maxwell's Lands within the territory of Dumfries, £5 ; Barony of Halywood, £120 ; Terreglis, £66 13s 4d ; Kirkunzean, £40 ; Torthorwall, £53 6s 8d ; Dalswintoun, £41 : Keltoun Maxwell, £8 ; Kelwoodie, Charteris, and Lowrie Lands, £10 ; Glen-

Though the Maxwells suffered severely for their loyalty to the House of Stuart, they still continued to be the leading proprietors of Lower Nithsdale. John, Lord Maxwell, came into possession of the family estate on the death of his father, the expatriated Jacobite chief, in 1744. He died in 1776, and his sole surviving child, Lady Winifred, having married William Haggerston Constable of Everingham, an English stem was grafted on the stock of this ancient and honoured Scottish house. The Johnstones, Douglases, Murrays, Jardines, Kirkpatricks, Griersons, and Herrieses, were still, as in the old fighting times, large landholders in the county. Its principal proprietor at this period was Charles, third Duke of Queensberry. In 1706 his father, "the Union Duke," resigned into the hands of the Queen his titles of Duke of Queensberry, Marquis of Dumfriesshire, Earl of Drumlanrig and Sanquhar, Viscount of Nith, Torthorwald, and Ross, and Lord Douglas of Kinmount, Middlebie, and Dornock, for a new patent, granting those titles to him and his heirs of entail, male, or female, succeeding to the estate of Queensberry, with this proviso, that such heirs of entail should be descended from William, the first Earl. In this resignation the titles of Marquis, and Earl of Queensberry, Viscount of Drumlanrig, Lord Douglas of Hawick and Tibbers, were not included, so that their descent to his heirs male was not affected by the change.

His third son, Charles, who succeeded him in 1711, died, after a long life of active benevolence, on the 22nd of October, 1778, in his eightieth year. He possessed the largest and the most valuable estate in Dumfriesshire, extending to above 150,000 acres, lying chiefly in the upper part of Nithsdale, and, as we have seen, did much to promote the interests of the county town, where he was exceedingly popular. At the request of the magistrates he sat for his portrait in 1769 ; and the picture, which represents a mild, pleasant, portly face, in keeping with his character of goodness, graces the Town Hall in company with the portraits of William and Mary. A neat Doric pillar, erected in Queensberry Square, commemorates the virtues of this nobleman, and testifies to the merited respect in which his character was held by the inhabitants of the county.

crosh, £2 10s ; Auldgirth, £2 ; Kelwoodie Craigs, £10 ; Barony of Sanquhar, £120 ; Crawfordstoun, £28 ; Kirkpatrick of the Gait, £6 13s 4d ; Barony of Glencairn, £120 ; Auldgirth Dunduff, £3 6s 8d ; Monkland, £40 ; Cloisburne, £48 ; Brogburgh, £10 ; Aleisland, £2 ; Affleck, Sindrim, and Leyne, £9 6s 8d ; Kirkland of Dalgarno, £5 ; The Ross, £48 ; Drumlangrig, £120 ; Tibberis, £93 6s 8d ; Dalgarnock, £6 13s 4d ; Over Glencrosh, £2 ; Mortoun, £40 ; Halydayhill, £2 ; Enock, £20 ; Carzeille and Kirktoune, £10 ; Windiehillteris and Charteris, £2 ; John M'Brair's Land, £2 ; Conheath Rig, £3 6s 8d ; Laag, £4 13s 4d ; Aird, £14 ; Dalgarno Holm, £13 ; Windyhills Grierson, £5 ; Tibbers, called Messengers' Lands, £6 13s 4d ; Dunreggan and Barbouy, £5 ; Laird of Kirkmichael's Lands, £30 ; Durisdeir, £31 13s 4d ; Hempsfield, £40 ; Snaid, £20 ; Ecclis, £20—£1400 3s 4d (all in Scots money).

As he lost his sons—two in number—during his lifetime, certain British titles conferred upon him, and his Scottish earldom of Solway, became extinct; whilst the dukedom of Queensberry, with very large estates, both in England and Scotland, devolved on his cousin William, Earl of March, who died unmarried so recently as 1810.* In him terminated the male line of William, first Duke of Queensberry; and in virtue of the patent issued in 1706, and of an entail executed by the second Duke, the titles of Duke of Queensberry, Marquis of Dumfriesshire, Earl of Drumlanrig and Sanquhar, Viscount of Nith, Torthorwald, and Ross, Lord Douglas of Kinmount, Middlebie, and Dornock, with the barony of Drumlanrig, and other extensive property in the county, devolved on Henry, third Duke of Buccleuch, the heir of line of the Queensberry family, who was thenceforward designated Duke of Buccleuch and Queensberry.† In this way the famous

* This nobleman was, in his "hot youth," a great patron of the turf. In 1756 he rode a match in person, dressed in his own running stable livery, and won the stakes. In maturer life he abandoned horse-racing, and betook himself to recreations in literature, natural history, and the fine arts. A collection of shells made by him was the finest at the time in Britain.

† This nobleman, who died in 1811, was succeeded by his eldest son Charles William Henry. He died in 1814, leaving, by his Duchess, Harriet Katherine Townshead, youngest daughter of Viscount Sydney, two sons, Walter Francis, Earl of Dalkeith, who succeeded him, Lord John Douglas Scott, who died in 1860, and six daughters. Walter Francis Montague Douglas Scott, the nobleman who now worthily wears the united dukedoms of Buccleuch and Queensberry, with numerous other titles, was born on the 25th November, 1806; married, 13th August, 1829, Lady Charlotte Thynne, youngest daughter of the second Marquis of Bath, and has issue, William Henry Walter, Earl of Dalkeith, Lord Lieutenant of Dumfriesshire; Lord Henry John, M.P. for Selkirkshire; Lord Walter Charles; Lord Charles Thomas; Lady Victoria Alexandrina, married to Lord Schomberg-Kerr in 1865; Lady Margaret Elizabeth, married Donald Cameron of Lochiel, 1875; and Lady Mary Charlotte, married 1877 the Hon. Walter Rudolph Trefusis. (a)

(a) Duke Walter, 5th of Buccleuch and 7th of Queensberry, died 1884, universally regretted. Animated by great public spirit and displaying much personal activity, he presented a fine example in the peerage of blameless conduct in private life. He took a keen interest in agriculture, did much to improve his immense estates, and was extremely popular with his tenantry. As illustrating the reputation he enjoyed in this district, there was a once familiar story of a farmer's salutation on whom he was calling. "I'm glad to see your Grace. They're a' dukes when you're awa'. But when you are here there's nae duke at a'."

He was succeeded by his son William Henry Walter Montague Douglas Scott, who married 1859 Lady Louisa Jane Hamilton, third daughter of the first Duke of Abercorn, and has issue—(1) Walter Henry, Earl of Dalkeith, born 1861, died 1886; (2) John Charles, Earl of Dalkeith, elected M.P. for Roxburghshire 1895, born 1864, married 1893 the Lady Margaret Alice Bridgeman, daughter of the Earl of Bradford; (3) Lord George William, born 1866, married 1903 Lady Elizabeth, younger daughter of the Duke of Rutland; (4) Lord Henry Francis, born 1868; (5) Lord Herbert Andrew, born 1872; (6) Lady Katharine Mary, born 1875, married 1899 the Hon. Thomas Brand, eldest son of Viscount Hampden; (7) Lady Constance Anne, born 1877; (8) Lord Francis George, born 1879. The Duchess was Mistress of

old Border family of the Scotts became the leading one in Dumfriesshire ; their yearly rental amounting to £88,007 19s 2d in 1872 ; while that of the original Queensberry family,* represented by the descendants of Sir Charles Douglas of Kelhead, amounted, in the same year, only to £11,724 18s.

For awhile the burghal authorities were much engaged with the erection of the Hospital, and in getting it put into good working order. Afterwards we find them busy opening up a new

the Robes to Queen Victoria, and has also served Queen Alexandra in this capacity.

* Sir Charles Douglas, who succeeded as fifth Marquis of Queensberry, was descended from Sir William Douglas of Kelhead, second son of the first Earl of Queensberry. He was succeeded by his third eldest surviving son, Sir James Douglas, who by his wife Catherine, daughter of the second Earl of Queensberry, had a son, Sir William, the third baronet. The latter was in turn succeeded by his eldest son, Sir John, who was chosen as the member for Dumfriesshire in 1741. His eldest son, Sir William, who became the fifth baronet, was at one time representative of the Dumfries burghs. By his wife, the daughter and coheir of William Johnstone of Lockerbie, he had five sons and three daughters—the eldest of whom, Sir Charles, as stated in the text, became fifth Marquis of Queensberry. He married Caroline Montague, third daughter of Henry, Duke of Buccleuch and Queensberry, by whom he had five daughters. He was succeeded by his brother John, who married Sarah, daughter of James Sholto Douglas. Their son, Archibald William, was, as Viscount Drumlanrig, elected M.P. for Dumfriesshire in 1847. He married the daughter of Major-General Sir William Robert Clayton, Baronet, and had issue four sons and two daughters. Soon after becoming seventh Marquis of Queensberry, he was killed by the accidental discharge of his gun, at Kinmount, on the 6th of August, 1858. His eldest son, John Sholto Douglas, born 20th July, 1844, succeeded him, as the eighth Marquis of Queensberry ; and married, in 1866, Sybil, second daughter of Alfred Montgomery, third son of Sir Henry Conynham Montgomery, Bart.

Archibald William, the seventh Marquis, had issue, besides (2) John Sholto, the eighth Marquis—(1) Lady Gertrude Georgiana, born 1842, died 1893 ; (3) Lord Francis William Bouverie, born 1847, killed on the Matterhorn 1865 ; (4) Lord Archibald Edward, born 1850, entered the Roman Catholic priesthood ; (5 and 6) Lord James Edward and Lady Florence Caroline, twins, born 1855. Lord James Edward died 1891. Lady Florence married Sir A. B. Churchill Dixie, Bart., and early achieved a reputation as a traveller, war correspondent, and courageous advocate of various social reforms. Her published works, including some remarkable juvenile verses, are distinguished by daring speculative thought and intense humanity.

John Sholto Douglas, the eighth Marquis, died in 1900. The Queensberry rules for boxing were his ; but he had gifts that would have fitted him to shine in the senate or in literature, and a fearless individuality, together with views so advanced that he renounced the Church and was himself renounced by the Scottish Peers. He had issue—(1) Francis Archibald Viscount Drumlanrig, born 1867, died 1894, created a Peer in his own right in 1893, under the title of Baron Kelhead ; (2) Percy Sholto, born 1868 ; (3) Lord Alfred Bruce, born 1870 ; (4) Lord Sholto George, born 1872 ; (5) Lady Edith Gertrude, born 1874.

The eighth Marquis was succeeded by his second son, who married 1893 Anna Maria, daughter of the Rev. Thomas Walters, vicar of Royton, Cornwall, and has issue—(1) Lady Dorothy Madeline, born 1894 ; (2) Francis Archibald Kelhead, Lord Douglas of Hawick, born 1896 ; (3) Lord Cecil Charles, born 1898.

line of street, leading from Lochmaben-gate to the Townhead ; widening the way at that entrance to the burgh, expanding a narrow passage—Calvert's Vennel—running from High Street to the river's edge, now called Bank Street ; building a salt market in it ; and adopting means for improving the lighting of the principal thoroughfares. These operations increased the debt upon the town ; and how to make the income cover the expenditure was a sort of chronic difficulty, which often drove the Town Council to their wits' end. In order to get rid of its pressure for a season, borrowing money at a heavy rate of interest was often resorted to ; and Mr Richard Lowthian, formerly noticed as Prince Charlie's host, was the wealthy citizen to whom the Council frequently applied in time of need. In 1752 they became his debtor in £2000 at one sweep ; and soon afterwards they had, as already noticed, to adopt the retrograde course of selling a public establishment—the coffee-house or news-room in High Street, which was bought by that gentleman's son. To aggravate matters the Act imposing a duty on ale and tonnage was about to expire. The authorities could scarcely get on with the aid thus afforded them : were it to stop, their credit would be in danger of stopping too. A resolution was therefore formed to obtain, if possible, the renewal of the Act. Entrusted with a mission of this nature, Mr Mackenzie, town clerk, proceeded in February, 1762, to London— not on horseback, like his predecessors on a similar errand a quarter of a century before, but in a chaise : and after an absence of less than six weeks, he returned, in the same kind of convey- ance, with the agreeable announcement that a bill for continuing the duties other twenty-five years had received the royal assent. The bill of 1737 cost, exclusive of personal charges, the sum of £157 : that of 1762, £270 : the latter amount including £56 as fees for the second reading in the House of Commons. In the former case the personal expenses of Provost Corrie and Mr Goldie, his colleague, were under £14, while those of Mr Mackenzie were nearly £37 ; his chaise hire and charges on the road absorbing about one-half of that sum. So well satisfied were the Town Council with that gentleman's good management in the matter, that they voted him a "gratification" of ten guineas, which, however, he declined to take ; and the Council, not to be outdone in generosity, constrained him to accept a set of silver tea-spoons. This fact, trifling in itself, is only noticed as intro- ductory to a remark that the Council books, at this period and during a rougher age, give abundant evidence that the Shylock style of driving a hard bargain, or adhering stubbornly to the letter of an exactive bond, was not the practice of our ancestors.

CHAPTER XLVIII.

FOR a period of nearly thirty years, Mr George Bell of Conheath
was a leading man in the burgh. He was elected its Provost for
the first time in 1740 ; and for three other triennial periods, ending
in 1756, he acted in that capacity. He bore his honours meekly.
If civic greatness was not literally thrust upon him, he did not
grasp at it, or seek to monopolise the civic chair. He seems to
have been popular with the inhabitants, and highly respected by
the Council ; but there was one man—Mr Robert Maxwell of
Cargen—who grudged him his official power and patronage, and
sought to get a share of these good things for himself. That sort
of ambition was quite honourable—commendable even. Mr
Maxwell, however, tried to gratify it in a very improper way.
One day in August, 1752, when the burghal authorities were
returning from the burial of Bailie M'Gowan, Mr Bell was asked
by Mr Maxwell to adjourn with him and two or three of his
companions to the King's Arms. The request was complied with,
wine was produced, and whilst it was being discussed Maxwell
proposed to Bell that they two should hold the office of chief
magistrate by turns, so as always to retain the government of the
town in their own hands. Following up this audacious proposal,
the Laird of Cargen tabled a document embodying it, cut and dry,
and urged the Provost to put his signature to the same. That of
course Mr Bell did not do and could not do : astonished and
indignant, he gave a prompt refusal, and then withdrew.*

* From a pamphlet printed in 1759, in the possession of Mr David
Halliday, printer, entitled "An Address to the Inhabitants and Landlords of
the Town."

A few months after holding office for the last time, Provost Bell died. For the game Maxwell had in view there was now a wider field, and one in which he had less chance of being bowled down. He offered himself as a candidate for provost at next election : his opponents, of whom he had many, offered the prize to Mr Andrew Crosbie and Mr Robert Cultar, neither of whom was in a condition to accept it ; and in 1756 Cargen became the municipal king. In order to maintain his rule, he must have some loyal ministers as a cabinet ready to do his will and pleasure. For this purpose, he succeeded at next election in getting his brother Edward, his brother-in-law James Corbet, and one of his partners in trade, Mr George Gordon, made merchant-councillors, those excluded to let them in belonging to the anti-Maxwell party.* When the 22nd of September again came round, the process of packing the Council was continued with the same successful results. John Dickson, another of the Provost's trade partners, and three other friends, Thomas Corbet, Robert Wright, and Thomas Creighton, were all made merchant-councillors ; though, to disarm the remonstrant trade members, the Provost, it is said, promised to accept one of their nominees, and yet got Creighton elected in his stead.†

By these proceedings of Provost Maxwell, the municipal influence of the deacons was weakened, and their crafts endangered. A rivalry between the trades and the merchants had long prevailed, and it now reached a furious height, productive of fierce litigation, and a tremendous faction fight—to the latter of which the rest of this chapter must be devoted. The Laird of Cargen durst not attempt to prolong his stay in office more than three years consecutively, as that would have been so directly at variance with the "sett" of the burgh : he retired, however, only to make way for his brother-in-law, Bailie James Corbet ; and the first symptoms of the coming storm were described when, on the 29th of September, 1758, Corbet was chosen Provost by "a plurality of votes" only. The merchant-councillors supported him as a matter of course ; whilst the minority, consisting chiefly of craftsmen, had set their affections on John Graham of Kinharvie, whom, though not ostensibly a candidate, they would fain have placed in the civic chair.

On the following 2nd of October the Council met for the purpose of voting out of their body, "according to the sett and constitution of the burgh," four merchant members in lieu of four voted in prior to the magisterial election. Before the business of the day was fairly begun, John Jardine, deacon-convener of the trades, rose, and in due form protested against the proceedings, and withdrew, followed by all the other deacons, save the deacon

---

* Address to the Inhabitants. † Ibid.

of the glovers, Nicholas Dickson. The gauntlet of defiance was thus thrown down—but the Provost's adherents, taking the matter quite coolly, went on to purge the Council, as if nothing out of the way had occurred ; the gentlemen unanimously "voted off" being Gilbert Paterson, William M'Murdo, William Burnet, late Bailies, and Alexander M'Courtie, late treasurer.

The real tug of war commenced on the 22nd of September, 1759, at which time four new councillors fell to be chosen. Each party tried eagerly to gain thereby an accession of power ; the merchants being anxious to increase, or at all events maintain, their supremacy, and the deacons to render their minority more potential—to transform it into a positive majority was scarcely hoped for, though they were warmly supported by the popular voice. After the usual preliminaries ex-Provost Crosbie protested, for himself and all others who should concur with him, that his voting at the election of new councillors that day was no homologation of the claims of any whose election at Michaelmas last remained under dispute. He thereupon took instruments in the clerk's hands—ex-Provost Graham, Convener Jardine, and Deacons Patoun, Walker, Gibson, Johnston, and Howat adhering to the protest. This interruption over, Provost Corbet proposed that the meeting should choose William Carruthers and James Bell, merchants, Gilbert Gordon, collector of excise, and Dr Alexander Gordon. Deacon Howat proposed the election of other four—William Kirkpatrick, James Clark, James Jardine, and James M'Whirter, all merchants ; but all, it is presumed, more favourable to the Trades than the nominees of the Provost. The former were elected by a majority of sixteen votes to eight.

Utterly beaten in the Council-house, the craftsmen looked for assistance out of doors. They accordingly made much of the Dumfriesian democracy, who readily joined with them against the patrician merchants and their chief. A battle of classes had begun—those in the upper ranks of life enlisting on the Provost's side, those in the lower declaring for that of John Graham and the deacons ; and at this ripe stage of the conflict the former party, by a play on their leader's name, were dubbed "Corbies,' whilst their opponents rejoiced in the name of "Pyets :" so termed, we suppose, because of the antipathy cherished by these birds—the crows and magpies- towards each other.

On the 29th, seven days after this fresh triumph of the Corbies, the streets of the ancient burgh presented an animated aspect. It was Michaelmas Day—the day of the annual election ; and in view of this event flocks of Pyets fluttered eagerly about anticipating a fray, longing to leave the impress of their claws and beaks on the rival faction, who for the most part, however, kept prudently within shelter of their household nests. The Mid-Steeple clock strikes the hour of three in the afternoon ; and, unless the election be immediately proceeded with, the legal period for it will expire, and the burgh be disfranchised. At last the Provost and some of his party are seen hurrying, as fast as the throng will permit, from the George Tavern in Southgate Brae, towards the place of meeting. Guarded by the officers, they pass on unharmed, receiving nothing worse than hootings and mock huzzas from the crowd ; but three or four recreant trades-men, who afterwards try to slip up to the Council-house, are recognised, hustled, mobbed ; whilst, on the other hard, the Pyet voters are greeted with hearty cheers. As the business proceeds, the crowd in the vicinity grows denser, and seems increasingly bent on mischief. So deafening is the din that the town-clerk Joseph Corrie, is heard with difficulty by the burghal senators as he reads the Parliamentary enactment bearing on the business, which finishes with the following stringent provision :—" It is hereby enacted and declared, that it shall not be in the power of the magistrates and Council of this burgh at any time hereafter to alter or procure any alteration hereof ; and that no person or persons shall vote for or endeavour the repealing or alteration of this present Act, directly or indirectly, in time coming, under the penalty of two hundred pounds Scots money, to be paid by each contravener *toties quoties*." This document having been read, Graham, chief of the Pyet clan, rises and protests that by their assembling, sitting, and voting in this Council, they do not homologate the rights of any voter disputed at the last election or rendered since disputable ; and he insists, therefore, that the clerks shall take notice for whom John Dickson, George Gordon, Andrew Wright, and William Bell record their votes ; to which protest ex-Provost Crosbie, ex-Bailie Lawson, Convener Jardine, and the other deacons, adhere.

The buzz of excitement caused by this combative display increases as ex-Bailie Paterson follows it up by insisting and protesting that the four merchant councillors illegally voted off on the 2nd of October, and who were there present, should have their names entered on the roll. Provost Corbet thereupon pro-tests in his turn that these gentlemen had been lawfully removed from the Council ; that they cannot be allowed to vote ; that if they will insist on going through the form of offering their suffrages their votes could be marked on a separate paper, but that on no account could they be inserted in the record. The excitement waxes warmer within—the clamour increases without ; the crowd is pressing menacingly up stairs, and it is with diffi-culty that the halberdiers keep it from surging by and swamping the Council hall. At this critical stage the Provost receives an intimation, which he reads, to the effect that Thomas Nairn, hammerman, James Harley, wright, Nicholas Dickson, glover, and Charles Edgar, weaver, whilst on their way with protests to the

meeting, had been "obstructed or prevented by a mob of common
people, assembled in a tumultuous manner." "Let the Riot Act
be read, and the rabblement be dispersed!" cry several of the
Corbie councillors. The first suggestion is acted upon. From
the Council-house window Mr Corrie reads the said Act; Bailie
Hepburn, more venturesome, performs the same duty in the
street : still the mob does not move ; the intercepted tradesmen
cannot push through. It is well for themselves that they at last
give up the vain effort and vanish. "Gentlemen, let us proceed
with the election!" cries the presiding magistrate ; and accordingly the clerks begin by calling over the names of the voters,
omitting by order the names of the four outed councillors belonging to the Pyet clan. Next the new merchant councillors and the
Trades' representatives qualify ; after which ex-Provost Crosbie,
resuming the wordy warfare, denounces the Act of Election
previously read, and gives expression to views which the conservative Corbies cannot but deem wild and revolutionary.

"By this Act," says the honourable gentleman, "a material
change has been made in the municipal constitution, at variance
with the sett of the burgh, without the consent of the community,
and that has never even received the sanction of the Convention
of Burghs. I protest against it on these grounds, and because it
contains a most arbitrary and direct infringement of the liberty
of succeeding Councils, in that clause which enacts that it shall
be unalterable, and guards against the repealing of it by penalties
upon councillors who should take steps for so doing. This clause
renders the whole Act null ; but," continues the Pyet leader,
waxing warmer as he goes on, "not only this Act, but many
particulars in the sett of the burgh, need to be corrected. In
particular, a rotation ought to be established in the merchant
part of the councillors, in order to preserve the liberty of the
place, and to establish peace amongst the people. The enormous
power of naming proxies for absent merchants, now vested in the
chief magistrate, ought to be removed, that the freedom of elections may not thereby be brought into peril. A proper method
ought also to be thought upon of naming proxies for absent
tradesmen, who, in the present working of the sett, lose their
votes ; though the sett requires that the number of tradesmen
should be eleven at all the steps of the election. Many other
matters need amendment. For all these reasons, I move that a
day be appointed for a general meeting of the community under
the authority of this Council, where all those who claim a right to
vote, as well disputed as disputable, may be present ; said meeting
to take place about the end of October next, for the purpose of
revising the sett, and ordering an application to the Convention
of Burghs for the recording either a new sett, or such an amendment of the existing one as shall be thought necessary."

All the members of the Pyet party concur in the motion ; and, as a matter of course, the Provost sets his face as a flint against it. He affirms that it has taken him by surprise ; and that, as the observations by which it was introduced were equally unexpected, he is not prepared to answer them *seriatim.* "This, however, I am prepared to say," he continues, "that the Act of Council condemned by Mr Crosbie, and which has been long in observance without being objected to, is calculated to answer very salutary purposes in the government of this burgh ; and that the sett of it, as approven by the Convention, needs no amendment." To this anti-reform declaration all the merchant councillors adhere, except Mr Graham and Bailie Lawson. The Pyets are outvoted ; and the mutinous mob, as if conscious of the defeat and yearning to avenge it, besieges the hall-door, and presses against it in battering-ram fashion, spite of the protecting spikesmen and halberdiers. "Quick ! gentlemen, or the rabble will be in upon us !" cries the Provost, now in visible terror. The Act against bribery and corruption is hurriedly read ; the Act anent magisterial elections is hurriedly signed—some of the signatures, as we now see them, wearing a tremulous aspect, as if fear-shaken hands had formed them, though that of "James Corbet" is boldly written in big characters, and that of "John Graham" looks scholarly and refined.

Whether to open the door, with the doubtful expectation of pacifying the populace, or to keep it closed, becomes a question. At the instance of the Provost, a vote is taken on the subject ; and it is carried by a plurality that the door shall remain shut during the proceedings. Remain shut ! Comparatively easy it is to pass a resolution to that effect, but how, ye sapient magistrates and merchant councillors ! is it to be enforced in defiance of such an angry multitude ? It cannot be done. The patrician Crows, with all their legal potency, are not a match for the democratic Magpies, who, swarming at the top of the stair, fiercely demand admission, and in order to enforce their own summons, disarm the sentinel-officers, by main strength break down the stout barrier that keeps them outside, and the next minute are occupants of the hall, and masters of the situation.

Then ensues a scene of indescribable confusion. The mob leaders have a method in their madness, however, and that is to foreclose the election rather than see the man of their choice defeated. "Graham for Provost !" is their war-cry, as they rush in, seize several obnoxious Corbies and send them out well guarded, and prepare to proceed with a mock election of their own. In vain the Provost and his remaining friends remonstrate with the crowd. Coaxing and threatening are alike unavailing : as well might they bid a Lammas flood not to flow over the Caul as command the intruders to withdraw and allow the lawful business to go on. The Provost, finding this to be the case, and fearing that he might be called to suffer personal violence, formally protests against the conduct of the mob, quits the chair, and retires with such of his colleagues as have not been placed in durance vile— glad to get away scathless—and leaving the place of authority in the undisturbed possession of the exulting Pyets.

Such is a faint sketch of this notable election riot, in its earlier phases, as revealed by the records.* Other outrages followed the incidents we have narrated ; and next day—Sabbath though it was—saw the conflict renewed in a fiercer and more systematic form. It must have been about five o'clock in the afternoon when Provost Corbet and his friends beat a rapid retreat from the hall, to reunite at a later hour in their favourite place of rendezvous, the George Hotel. No sooner were they gone than the rioters shut up certain electors whom they saw fit to detain ; and having thus in divers ways purged the Council, they with little ceremony, but with acclamations that shook the building and found a hearty echo outside, joined with the deacons in recognising John Graham of Kinharvie as Provost of Dumfries. Whether Mr Graham was present or not does not appear ; but that he was a party to the proceedings admits of little doubt.

Daylight faded, twilight deepened into darkness, but still the insurgents occupied the Council-house and crowded High Street ; and it was not till twelve o'clock, when Michaelmas day was done, that they liberated their captives and dispersed ; retiring to their homes big with the fond idea that if they had not legally secured a chief magistrate of their own, they had at least rendered the election of the rival candidate impracticable, seeing that the set period for doing so had now expired. Whilst the Pyets, well pleased but exhausted with their exciting work and protracted vigils, were separating at midnight, the Crows were preparing to hold a secret parliament in the George.

Thither their chief had gone, on being ejected from the Council Chamber. Such of his adherents stealthily joined him as had not been made prisoners by the mob, and the captives liberated at twelve o'clock furnished a large and welcome accession to the party. Though some of their friends, including the senior town clerk, Mr Corrie (abducted during the day), were unwillingly absent, those present—nineteen in all—conceived themselves numerous enough for going on with the election that had been so rudely interrupted. The Provost, having taken the chair, availed himself of his arbitrary privilege (sanctioned by custom) to nominate proxies for the absent merchant councillors of the Pyet feather—Graham, Crosbie, and Lawson ; the substitutes named being birds of the requisite dusky hue. Not so much

---

* The Minutes of Council supply the chief incidents narrated in this chapter.

as a solitary deacon was there to represent the Trades element in
the corporation, yet the election was pushed forward; the apologetic minute of the meeting explaining, that though the deacons
and their led votes were absent, they had been convened in the
Council-house, "and it not being safe to make any open declaration in face of the mob that the councillors were retiring to this
house, nor even to acquaint the said deacons of it, in respect it
appeared from the beginning and throughout that the same was
raised and made by the Trades," and that, moreover, as the custom
or sett of the burgh did not require votes for absent Trades'
members, to name such was unnecessary. What followed may be
fittingly told in the language of the minute just quoted from.

The preliminary steps having been gone through, "the electors now present proceeded to the election of magistrates and
office-bearers; and the Provost having proposed the persons
following to go out in the leet for provost—to wit, Provost James
Corbet and Bailie Hepburn, for both of whom he gave his own
vote—the roll was called and the votes of the other electors
marked, by which it appeared the whole electors unanimously
voted the said Provost James Corbet and Bailie Hepburn to go
out in the leet : and these gentlemen having removed, the roll of
the other electors except themselves two was called over, and the
votes marked, by which it appeared that the whole electors remaining unanimously voted the said James Corbet to be Provost;
and he and Bailie Hepburn being called in, they each of them
gave their votes for the said Provost James Corbet; and therefore
the magistrates, councillors, and electors have unanimously elected
the said James Corbet to be Provost for the year ensuing; and he
accordingly accepted of the said office, and gave his oath *de fideli
administratione officii.*" The other vacancies having been filled
up, the proceedings terminated between three and four o'clock on
the Sabbath morning.

Was ever municipal election conducted before under such
extraordinary circumstances? the voters meeting, like conspirators,
secretly in a tavern after the midnight hour, during a season that
ought, for a double reason, to have been devoted to rest. If
the rioters who stormed the Council-house during the day had
dreamed of this nocturnal gathering there would have been more
crows to pluck than one—the entire Corbie's nest at the George
would have received a rough harrying at their hands. When,
after day-dawn, the news of the conclave and its doings was
circulated through the town, much indignation was felt by the
Trades and the lower classes who sympathised with them. They
felt that they had been deceived—ont-generaled—and they made
ready to exact revenge. "John Graham is our Provost!" they
said; "and we shall complete his election by kirking him in due
form, in spite of all that has been done by the cowardly Corbies!"

In these days the churching of the new magistrates was looked upon as an indispensable sequel to the election ; and the merchant party also proposed in this way to give a sacred and public impress to their hole-and-corner proceedings. When each of the rival factions made arrangements of this nature a collision was almost sure to arise. So it turned out : the advent of the Sabbath did not hinder the merchant councillors from voting their favourite into the civic chair ; and when that day's sun reached the meridian, the business of the early morning led to an unhallowed riot. When the bells rang for worship, one party, the Corbies, marched to the New Church, with their Provost guarded by the burgh officers ; whilst the other, the Pyets, proceeded with their chief to St. Michael's, the Trades forming nearly as strong a muster as if they had been going to compete for the Siller Gun. Leaving the former to hear the discourse of Mr Wight, and the latter that of Mr Linn—both doubtless appropriate and pithy— let us look at what was meanwhile going on outside, near the heart of the town.

In front of the crumbling New Wark, and resting against its walls, stood the Cheese Cross, where on market days the damsels of the district were wont to dispose of their dairy produce. On this occasion it was occupied by many of the wives and other female friends of the burgh tradesmen, who from its elevated platform waited to see the Pyet procession returning from church. Tradition affirms that they were well supplied with whisky-punch, for the purpose of toasting the health of Provost Graham when he made his appearance, and drinking confusion to the Crows ; but this may possibly be only a bit of scandal, originated by some spiteful dame connected with the other side.

Prominent among the group on the Cheese Cross stood Judith Kerr, a stalwart randy, noticeable by her impatient gestures as much as by her Amazonian height. "I wonder if the buirdly Pyets are coming yet ?" she said, addressing a cronie as one o'clock struck. "Run a bit down the Hie Gate, woman Jean, and see if there are onie signs of the bonnie yellow pikes glistening i' the Southergate Brae ; for I'm weary o' waiting on the lads." The same gossipping report already quoted from adds to this authentic speech words designed as a stimulant to Jean's speed : "Haste ye noo, woman ; for between ourselves I'm turning unco drouthy." The messenger ran as desired, and soon returned with the tidings that the Pyets were appearing. "And so are the Corbies !" cried a voice from the crowd. The parties met opposite to the New Wark, and stood for a moment frowning defiance at each other, both "willing to wound, but yet afraid to strike." No one offered to move till the spell of inactivity was broken by James Dickson, a brewer, whose bold signature appears in the books as a supporter of Provost Corbet. As if actuated by a destructive impulse, he stepped from the ranks of his party, borrowed an axe from an officer at its head, and attacked—not the rival force, but certain articles of creature comfort, bread, cheese—shall we add bottled punch?—with which a corner of the Cross was garnished. The irate brewer with one fell swoop made a sad mess of the refreshments ; some of the women-folks shrieking wildly when they saw the produce of their aumries treated in this destructive fashion. Not so Judith Kerr. That heroic female was above such weakness ; and instead of weeping, wailing, and wringing of hands, she girded herself to carry on the war that had been so recklessly begun by the Corbie faction. Indignant at the rude assault—especially wroth at seeing the good whisky-punch spilt, says the tradition, which persistently associates the shedding of strong waters with blood on this memorable day—she seized Dickson by the nape of the neck, took the halberd from his feckless grasp, and gave him a push which made him embrace mother earth ; telling him with grim humour as he floundered downwards to drink the liquor where he had brewed it. Turning to the craftsmen, who seemed about to second her efforts, she bade them stand by and not to meddle with the Corbies, for that the women were full match for such a crew.

The Pyets, however, advanced on their opponents ; whilst the latter, inferior in both numbers and courage, and unable to get up or down the street for the surrounding mob, rushed through the portals of the New Wark, and then tried to close its oaken door upon their pursuers. Thereupon a gigantic skinner from the Millhole named William Trumell, by setting his shoulder between the door and the wall, thwarted this device, and a terrific scene ensued. The chief belligerents, cooped into a comparatively narrow space, pushed and struggled and fought with each other like the wild tenants of a menagerie ; and at the height of the hurly-burly the rotten flooring gave way, and down went Pyets and Corbies, sweating, bleeding, roaring, and raging, into the noisome vaults below. Whilst this chaotic strife, and some minor affrays outside the Wark, were going on, a sound contrasting strongly with the din of battle, and one more in accordance with the sacred day, arose from the bartizan of the building. A number of children had been placed there by their parents, under the charge of two peaceful burgesses, one of whom, Paul Russell by name, occasionally officiated as a precentor. When the fighting commenced, with the view of engaging the attention of his juvenile charge, he gave out for singing the 140th psalm—probably choosing it as embodying a pointed rebuke to the ungodly combatants ; though we dare say the respected "letter-gae of holy rhyme" did not desire to see the following apposite passage of the same in any sense fulfilled :—

" As for the head and chief of those
  About that compass me,
Ev'n by the mischief of their lips
  Let thou them cover'd be.
Let burning coals upon them fall,
  Them throw in fiery flame,
And in deep pits, that they no more
  May rise out of the same."

Such solemn verses sang the little children from the top of
the New Wark as the warring factions fought below, and, falling
into its deep pits, continued the struggle.   It at length terminated
in the utter abasement of the merchant party.   The Pyets, as has
been already stated, were more numerous than their opponents ;
and, on being strongly reinforced, they succeeded in caging nearly
the whole of the Corbies in the vaults to which they had made an
unwilling descent.   There, with aching bones and moody thoughts,
they lay till long after midnight, when their wearied guards
dropped off or relaxed their vigilance, and the captives effected
their escape.   What deeds of daring were performed during the
conflict by Judith Kerr are not recorded ; but it may be safely
inferred that she would not rest satisfied without consigning some
more councillors to the kennel.   Neither is it known precisely
what befel the rival chiefs ; though there is reason to believe that
they suffered no personal violence, but escaped homewards, whilst
their infuriated adherents fought out the fray.

Months elapsed before the town regained its composure and
magisterial government was fairly re-established.   More than one
Court of Session case arose out of the riots, entailing much expense, and keeping up the combative feeling that only waited
for a fresh opportunity to display itself again in deeds of violence.
As regards the election of Mr Corbet, the law authorities of Edinburgh held that it was valid, though irregular ; but in spite of
this decision, the craftsmen offered a passive, many of the democracy an active, resistance to his rule.   On the 2nd of October
following, the councillors were summoned to meet in the usual
place, for the purpose of purging the roll.   Once more an angry
mob interposed.   It was known beforehand that the favourite of
the populace, with his principal friends, was to be victimised by
the dominant party.   " Not if we can help it !" screamed the
indignant Pyets, who crowded the Council-house, allowed ingress
to birds of their own feather only, and dared the Corbie senators
to enter at their peril.   The latter, anxious to prevent a repetition
of the Michaelmas riot, prudently retired, and, assembling at the
house of Mr Corrie, town clerk, voted off the Council John
Graham, Andrew Crosbie, Hugh Lawson, and Andrew Wright—
an act dictated, some will say, by bitter vindictiveness, others, by
the natural instinct of self-defence.   It was not till the 9th of
January—about fourteen weeks after the secret election at the

George—that the magistrates and their merchant followers durst shew face in the Council Chamber ; and when they did convene there on that day, not a solitary deacon was present to give them countenance.

In the minute of the business occur the following significant entries :—" The Provost represented that Andrew Black, work-man, who was employed to light the lamps, was some time ago threatened by certain persons concerned in the mobs and riots which have of late prevailed, and was put in fear of his life, whereby he was obliged to desist ; and the Council, considering it is very necessary the lamps should be still lighted through the remaining part of the winter season, do therefore recommend to the magistrates to cause light the lamps accordingly." "The Provost represented that the town's officers have been stripped of the town's livery-clothes, and their halberts broke and destroyed by the mob since Michaelmas last ; which being considered by the Council, they grant warrant to the magistrates to cause buy and make new livery-clothes for the officers, and to cause make new halberts ; and to draw precepts upon the treasurer for the ex-penses thereof." Provost Corbet retired from office at the ensuing Michaelmas term. On that day the representatives of the Trades were present for the first time since his appointment, and took part with the merchant councillors in electing his successor. For going out on the leet as such Mr Corbet named his brother-in-law, Robert Maxwell of Cargen and Portrack, and Ebenezer Hepburn ; while Convener Gibson, true to the Pyet cause, proposed John Graham and Andrew Crosbie ; and when it was objected that these latter gentlemen were not members of Council, he contended that they had been voted out of it by persons who had no legal qualification so to do. The staunch convener was, however, over-ruled—Mr Maxwell was chosen Provost by a majority of eleven votes ; and with his election the protracted conflict between the Pyets and the Crows was brought to an issue, though the memory of it long rankled in the public mind. Maxwell held a lengthened tenure of the provostship, he having been re-elected at various periods afterwards, down till 1781, when his name disappears from the list ; and he seems to have made a better chief magistrate than his antecedents warranted or his opponents looked for.

The judicial issue of the strife still requires to be told. A solemn, tragical one it is ; being, unlike the affair itself, unre-lieved by any features of revelry or frolic. The scene is the High Court of Justiciary in Edinburgh, where, on the first of December, 1759, twelve men are placed at the bar, " indicted by the King's Advocate for the crimes of riot and tumult at Dumfries, with a view to obstruct the election of magistrates and councillors last Michaelmas Day, and to quash the authority of the magistrates

then chosen."* The prisoners are not of the sort usually seen in
such a humiliating position : they are for the most part decent,
respectable-looking tradesmen, who will bear a fair physiog-
nomical comparison with the fifteen jurymen on whose judgment
their fate will depend, after the witnesses for and against them
have been examined, the pleadings on both sides have been
finished, und the Lord Justice-Clerk has summed up the evidence
and laid down the law bearing upon the case. At the bar stand
John Smith, deacon of the weavers ; Thomas Gibson, deacon of
the tailors ; John Paton, deacon of the smiths ; eight other craftsmen, and one merchant, William Kirkpatrick—the latter one of
the four Pyet burgesses who on the eventful 22nd of September
were proposed to fill up the vacancies in the Council, and were
rejected by Mr Corbet's party. Three more Dumfriesians figure
on the indictment—Joseph Dyet and James Hodge, tailors, and
James Johnston, smith ; but, failing to appear when called upon,
they are fugitated—that is to say, outlawed. Before the tedious
preliminaries are over, and the case is fairly entered upon, daylight fades : candles are introduced ; and all through the night,
whose gloom they only half dispel, the fierce municipal contest is
fought over again verbally ; and the clock of St Giles' sounds the
hour of five in the morning before the judges pause and the jury
retire to consider their verdict.

At two o'clock in the afternoon they gave it in, finding all
the panels guilty except Deacon Paton, whom they unanimously
acquit. Counsel are heard on the import of the verdict, the
relevancy of which is so ingeniously questioned that the judges
adjourn the proceedings and give no decision till the Court resumes on the 15th, when all the cobwebs of casuistry spun by the
learned advocates for the defence are ruthlessly blown aside ; and
the verdict being held good, sentence is pronounced. Poor Deacon
Smith is adjudged to banishment for life ; John Gordon, tailor, is
transported for fourteen years, and William Ewart, shoemaker,
for seven—all to be kept in the tolbooth of Edinburgh till an
opportunity offer for sending them to his Majesty's plantations in
America ;" with certification that if, after being delivered over
for transportation, they return to or be found in Scotland—Smith
during life, or Gordon or Ewart within the respective periods
specified in their sentence—each of them, as often as he shall so
return, shall be whipped and re-transported ; and Gordon shall
remain abroad fourteen years, and Ewart seven years, from the
time of their being respectively last delivered over for trial."
Seven are sentenced to be carried back to the Edinburgh tolbooth,
there to remain—William Macnish, tailor, three months ; Thomas
Gibson, flesher, two months, and till he pay a fine of five hundred

* Scots Magazine, vol. xxii., pp. 667-8.

merks ; William Wood, gardener. George Bell, nailor, and John Rae, tailor, six weeks ; James Thomson, smith, and Charles Sturgeon, shoemaker, one month. A fine of nine hundred merks is imposed on William Kirkpatrick, merchant ; and all except the three persons to be banished are required to find bail for their good behaviour for two years—Kirkpatrick and Gibson in nine hundred merks each, and the rest in three hundred merks each. Kirkpatrick, finding bail in Court, is set at liberty ; the others being carried away by the officers, we see them no more ; and the curtain drops on the last sad scene of this extraordinary municipal contest.

A vague tradition, which we cannot verify, represents Deacon Smith as returning home not long after the date of the trial, and all the other convicts as having had their sentences mitigated by the Crown.

CHAPTER XLIX.

MORE rioting ! Has the quarrel between the Pyets and the
Corbies broken out afresh, that bands of angry men are gathering
in the High Street, and frantic-looking women are moving to and
fro, instead of minding their household affairs ? The groups merge
into one great turbulent throng, and, actuated by a common
impulse, and swelled by contributions from Bridgend, move at
twilight towards the mills on the Galloway side of the Nith, as if
they had serious work to do in that direction. It is no municipal
question, no party conflict, that is generating such a commotion.
A terrible dearth of food is experienced in the burgh ; meal has
been at a famine price for weeks ; the patience with which hunger
was borne for a long time has given way ; and the prevailing
maxim with the populace is now that of the freebooter—that

> "They should take who have the power,
> And they should keep who can."

Not that indiscriminate pillage is the main design of the mad
rabble : to prevent the exportation of grain and meal is what they
chiefly wish. This is why they surround the mills, and what is
expressed in hundreds of hoarse voices ; the plundering which
ensues being but the natural sequel to long suffering, and the
tempting opportunity for removing it that is now enjoyed. The
rioters are so powerful and fierce that the local authorities
scarcely attempt to cope with them ; and by the midnight of this
dreadful day the mills, granaries, and many private stores have
fallen into the undisputed possession of the mob.

At this grave juncture Provost Dickson, after consulting with
his brother magistrates, resolved on applying for aid to the chief
of the law establishment in the metropolis. A communication to
that effect was sent off, addressed to the burgh's agent, " John
Davidson, Esq., at his house in Castlehill, Edinburgh," with a note
to that gentleman as follows :* (a)—" Sir, the enclosed Letter to

---

* The original is in the hands of Mr David Laing.

(a) Probably now among the manuscripts that went to Edinburgh University Library on Mr Laing's death.

Lord Justice-Clerk contains an information of a mobb that has the happened here to prevent the exportation of meal from this part of the country to the west parts of Scotland, which the peace officers of the law have not been able to quell ; and application is made to his Lordship for a military aid, and his authority and counsel on this unhappy occasion—and as dispatch and much secresy and prudence are necessary, we have thought it best to give you the trouble of managing the matter ; and I beg you will immediately make the application to his Lordship, for which we shall gratefully acknowledge.—We are, Sir, your most obedt. servt., JNO. DICKSON, Provost. Drumfries, 23 Febry., 1771, Saturday night."

It is obvious from this application, and the legal proceedings which arose out of the riot, that it must have been of a very alarming character indeed. The indictment served upon its captured leaders charged them with holding " unlawful and tumultuous assemblies," with committing " masterful invasions, depredations, assaults, riots, batteries, and other criminal acts ;" but as they were not accused of having withstood the military when sent from Edinburgh at the request of the magistrates, it may be safely inferred that peace was restored, and the law rendered paramount without much difficulty. One William John- ston and several others were tried at the circuit court of the burgh in the following August for the above crimes, perpetrated with others their associates, " during the night between the 22nd and 23rd days of February, in or about Dumfries and the village of Bridgend." A somewhat indefinite verdict was returned by the jury, they finding the libel not proved as to several of the panels ; but as to the rest finding " it proved that there were mobs at the time and places libelled, and that certain of the panels (whose names they specified) were guilty art and part of the crimes libelled." The High Court of Justiciary, on being appealed to, were of opinion that, though the verdict was not so distinct and accurate as it should have been, yet execution should pass upon it ; and therefore they sentenced two of the prisoners to be trans- ported, and the rest to be imprisoned, some for a longer, some for a shorter term.*

A few years after this riotous outbreak some of its leading features were reproduced, with the addition of others still more tragical. Another dearth, with its train of suffering and repining, visits the burgh ; and it is again caused or aggravated by the grain dealers and farmers exporting their stuff rather than sell it to the townspeople at a lower price. The "masterful invasions and depredations " of 1771 are repeated, only they are this time

* For a report of this appeal case see Maclaurin's Arguments and Deci- sions in Remarkable Cases before the High Court of Justiciary, pp. 541-551.

directed against vessels in the river, and the yellow corn growing upon its banks. A party of the marauders, hurrying down the Dock, lay violent hands on some farmers who are sending their produce out of port. Not a single sack can be got on board; and the ships have to sail away minus their expected cargo, whilst the frightened ruralists beat a rapid retreat, leaving their precious stuff in the possession of the crowd. Another party of them openly resolve upon a plundering expedition to Laghall, a farm on the Galloway side of the Nith. Fortunately the announcement reaches the ear of one Janet Watson, "a servitrix" at the very farm that is threatened with such an unwelcome visit. Off at once she sets down the Dumfries bank, crosses the river, which was very shallow at the time opposite Mavis Grove, hurries to Laghall, near by, and raises the hue and cry with such effect that before the predaceous rioters arrive such a guard is mustered at the farm that the former, resolute though they are, never venture within fighting range, and, fairly out-generaled by the faithful Janet, beat a retreat back to the burgh—only, however, to become more unruly there.

Days elapse, and the mob becomes increasingly mischievous and threatening, till the military have to be called out; and in a moment of indiscretion the chief magistrate bids them fire. Most of the soldiers elevate their pieces when doing so; and but for this humane movement the results would have been dreadful. As it is, a stray shot takes effect on a fine young man not connected with the rioters, who falls lifeless on the street. Truly a tragical *finale* to these protracted bread riots; and the wonder is that those engaged in them did not exact summary vengeance when they saw the poor youth's blood reddening the pavement. On the day of his burial the whole trading population turned out; so that from Townhead to St. Michael's Gate nothing was seen but a mass of mourners with countenances expressive of grief and indignation. The funeral procession had to pass the offending Provost's shop—the first south of the King's Arms Hotel, in High Street* (a)—while proceeding to the churchyard; and the pall-bearers, acting according to a previous arrangement, advanced to the door of the premises, in order by way of testimony to lay the coffin for a minute or two on the counter. But before this could be done those inside closed the door with such critical haste that it struck the coffin; and the bearers, unable to gain admission, knocked solemnly with it three times on the door, and then departed.

Though sometimes interrupted by disturbances such as these, and always straitened by inadequate resources, the Town Council

---

* At present occupied by Messrs Lawson & Shaw, clothiers.

(a) Messrs Lawson & Shaw were succeeded by Mr Andrew Patterson.

kept the external improvement of the burgh steadily in view. To enable them to meet liabilities and carry on public works, they, in 1770, opened a cash account to the extent of £1000 in the Dumfries branch of Douglas, Heron, & Company's Bank. Having such a command of funds, they effected many salutary changes. One of the principal undertakings entered upon at this time was the erection of a new butcher market and slaughter-house, on a site between the back street called East Barnraws and the Loreburn ; this being associated with another scheme scarcely less important, the opening up of a market square by the removal of the existing flesh market and slaughtering place, together with part of the ruins of the New Wark ranging beside them along the east side of High Street. All that remained of that ancient structure was purchased from Mr Patrick Heron of Heron at an expense of £90, and nothing more was left standing except the north wall ; the inhabitants being, it is said, thankful to see such a memorial of the late unhallowed scenes put out of the way.

All these operations, together with the opening of a street named the Wide Entry, or King Street, leading from the new square to the new flesh market, were completed in 1770, at an expense of more than £700, about £114 of which was raised by public subscription. For the market an annual rent of from £40 to £50 was obtained, in the form of rates on the sheep and cattle slaughtered and exposed in it for sale. In the year preceding the grain mills were rebuilt, after a design by the celebrated engineer Mr Smeaton, at a cost of £633. Among the minor works effected at this busy period was the enlargement of the Council-house. It was rickety with age, as well as restricted in its accommodation ; and the authorities were spurred on to its reconstruction from a rather singular circumstance. In 1769 the portrait of their patron, the Duke of Queensberry—for which he had sat, at their request, to an artist in London—arrived in due course ; but, like the Vicar of Wakefield's grand family picture, it was so large that the low-ceilinged house could not take it in ; so that the councillors were laid under a renewed obligation to amplify their hall, which they did accordingly. As a more striking illustration than any yet given, perhaps, of their enterprise at this time, it may be mentioned that, anticipating the great sanitary enterprise of our own day, they patronised a scheme for supplying the town with water, to be distributed from a tank in pipes, by means of the new machinery at the mills—a most laudable project, which proved abortive owing to no fault of theirs.

A hospital or infirmary for the sick poor was still awanting ; and to secure that *desideratum* a committee was formed, presided over by Charles, Duke of Queensberry, and with Sir William Maxwell, Bart. of Springkell, vice-president. The Town Council cordially granted an acre of the High Dock as a site for the pro-

posed building, for an annual feu duty of £5, which the Council
allows as a yearly subscription, so that no ground-rent burdens
the establishment.   With due masonic pomp, the foundation-
stone was laid on the 11th of July, 1777, by the worthy vice-
president, who had from the beginning zealously promoted the
philanthropic undertaking.   The Infirmary, a neat, plain structure of three stories, was completed at an expense of £823, and a
score of patients or more in a temporary hospital, were, at the
close of 1778, transferred to the new house—the first of a long line
of inmates that have been ministered to within its walls.   So
many patients were there in 1789, with an increasing demand for
admission, that a wing had to be shortly afterwards added to the
building, on the north side.   In that year the subscriptions
amounted to £229, the total receipts to £387—figures which furnished proof that the institution was felt to be much needed, and
that it was heartily appreciated.   As time rolled on, bringing an
increase of population to the district, with a perpetual increase of
the sick poor, many more patients pleaded yearly for admission
into this mansion—hospitable in the truest sense ; and additional
wards were obtained by the construction of a wing on the other
side, in 1809 ; by the filling up of the interval between the main
block and the north wing, in 1828 ; lastly, by a similar change on
the other side, in 1840 ; and the reconstruction of the south wing,
so as to supply new wards above, and to allow the culinary operations of the establishment to be carried on below.*

On the 13th of May, 1807, a charter from the Crown incorporated the contributors into a body politic under the name of
the Governors of the Dumfries and Galloway Royal Infirmary—
the governors consisting of benefactors to the extent of twenty
guineas or more, paid within two years, who thereby become
governors for life ; subscribers of not less than one guinea
annually, and the two physicians, the two surgeons, and the
treasurer for the time being.   For the first fifteen years the
medical officers were paid nothing for their services, except a
small allowance of five shillings a day granted by the Government
for military patients, when troops used to be billeted in the burgh.
That allowance having ceased in 1821, a salary was given to the
staff ; the amount of which at present is £20 to each of the
physicians, and £25 to each of the surgeons.   A house surgeon,
who is termed clerk and apothecary, receives £40 a year, besides
board and lodging.

---

* From a period soon after the opening till 1839 a ward was set apart
for insane patients—an arrangement only excusable because there was no
lunatic asylum in the County. By the completion of the Crichton Institution, in that year, due provision was made for the proper treatment of
sufferers from mental disease ; and the Infirmary was freed from a class of
patients to whom it could offer little better than seclusion and restraint,
according to the old mad-house system – now, happily, exploded.

The number of patients, from the opening of the house till 1826, cannot be ascertained, but 9320 were under treatment ; and if the proportion of admissions, which each year was about a twelfth, be deducted, the result—8544—indicates the number of inmates during that period. From 1826 till 1858 the admissions were 14,739 : total of both periods, 23,283—a yearly average in the first period of 170, in the second of 460. These figures are exclusive of 1026 soldiers admitted prior to 1826, and a few militiamen since. From 1836 till 1858 the average admissions yearly ranged from 402 to 650 ; the highest of these numbers applying to 1847, the saddest year in the annals of the institution. There are, in addition, many out-patients, who visit the Infirmary for medical or surgical treatment. Prior to 1831 they sometimes numbered fully 2000 yearly ; but of late the average has not been more than 1093. From an elaborate calculation we learn that medical cases in the house last twenty-three days on an average, with a mortality of 10 per cent. ; and that the average period of the surgical cases is thirty-one days, with a mortality of $1\frac{1}{4}$ per cent. : the rate in both together averaging about 7 per cent. Down till 1837 the mortality for medical cases was only 7 per cent., and for surgical 2 per cent. For the year ending 11th November, 1865, the death-rate was only 6·2.*

The Infirmary is supported by donations, legacies, and church collections, in addition to annual subscriptions. During the first ten years the subscriptions averaged £177 ; and in the ten years ending 1826 they rose to an average of £324. Usually the expenditure has been in excess of the annual income. In the decade ending 1836 the yearly outlay (less the permanent expenditure) was £889, and the income £927 ; in the next decade the average outlay was £1037, and the income £811 ; and in the next, the average outlay was £1153, and the income £869. The balance is made good by drafts upon the fund formed from donations and legacies, which have been truly munificent ; and but for which the doors of the institution must have been long since closed, or its usefulness very seriously impaired.†

The Infirmary contains one hundred beds, which are never all occupied at a time ; and as the existing accommodation is more ample than the demand for it, no applicant for admission is rejected, provided he is recommended by one of the governors, and his complaint is not incurable. Most of the patients, as

---

* For the sake of comparison we give the mortality in the other principal infirmaries of Scotland in 1865 :—Greenock, 15·578 ; Glasgow, 11·669 ; Edinburgh, 11·35 ; Dundee, 8·97 ; Perth, 8·33 ; Paisley, 8·152 ; Aberdeen, 7·994. —*Eighty-ninth Report of the Dumfries and Galloway Royal Infirmary*, p. 7.

† For many of these facts and statistics we are indebted to a well-written M.S. History of the Infirmary, by Philip Forsyth, Esq., of Nithside, a gentleman who takes a great interest in the establishment, and who officiated for many years as chairman of its weekly committee.

might be supposed, belong to the district ; but Ireland and the
North of England furnish a large proportion ; and occasionally
some poor foreigner fallen down, far away from his birth-place,
finds a second home in the house, and, set up there anew by
kindly treatment, resumes his journey grateful and rejoicing.
The liberality of the directors in this respect is beyond all praise.
As a whole the Infirmary is excellently managed : it is a blessing
to the poor and a credit to the district.

Whilst prosecuting improvements, and raising or helping to
raise new public buildings, the Council, prudently mindful of the
old ones, caused them to be insured to the extent of £4600 in the
Sun Fire Office, London.* This prudential step was well and
speedily rewarded, as the grain mills were accidentally burned to
the ground on the night of the 31st of October, 1780 ; and the
managers of the insurance office, after a process of arbitration,
paid the town £1530, which, with the value of the blackened
materials, and such machinery as was rescued from the flames,
went far to make up the loss that had been sustained. Masons
and millwrights soon made the spectral ruins give way to a more
commodious erection ; and, before a twelvemonth passed by, the
plash of the wheels churning water into foam, and grinding husky
grain into stuff for life-sustaining bread, rose as pleasantly on the
ear as if no sad catastrophe had occurred.

But for the existence of Douglas, Heron, & Company's Bank
some of the town improvements noticed in this chapter could not
have been carried out and would scarcely have been undertaken.
The bank itself had a brief, brilliant, meteor-like course, going
down in little more than two years, and bringing to ruin not a
few families connected with the town and district. It was not
without reason that Burns characterised it as a "villainous
bubble." Originated in November, 1769, by the Honourable
Archibald Douglas and Mr Patrick Heron (the gentleman already
named as owner of the New Wark), it soon acquired popularity
and patronage, on account of its imposing list of shareholders and

* The policies, as still preserved, shew what these edifices were, and furnish an idea of their pecuniary worth. Schedule 1 consisted of the Council
Chamber, town clerk's office adjoining, and two upper rooms, occupied as a
public school, in which Dr Dinwiddie taught arithmetic and mathematics : the
buildings, which were all under one roof, were insured for £300. 2. The
grammar and writing schools, with the lodging above, occupied, among others,
by Dr George Chapman, the grammar schoolmaster—insurance, £500. 3.
The Presbytery-house, insured for £100. 4. The new salt market, and room
above the same, also insured for £100. 5. The English school, and sheriff-
clerk's office under it, insured for £200. 6. The new flesh market and
slaughter-house—insurance, £700. 7. The guard-room, weigh-house, court-
house above these, and rooms in the upper storey, all in the Mid-Steeple
buildings—insurance, £400. 8. The town's proportion—one-half—of the
minister's manse, £200. 9. The Millhole mill, then used as a snuff mill,
insured for £100. 10. The town's mills, on the Galloway side, as rebuilt in
1769, insured for £2000—the building £700, and the machinery £1300.

its accommodating mode of doing business. Long and liberal credits were given ; the directors being seemingly more anxious about the number than the commercial stability of their customers. And the former had among themselves several needy adventurers, who had neither money nor reputation to lose ; some who had both, but were destitute of knowledge and prudence : so that, between the knaves and fools of the directory, the original capital of £150,000 could not but melt away with fearful speed, and all the exhaustive calls that came to be made upon the proprietors failed to keep the concern afloat. At Ayr, its headquarters, a speculative mania sprang up, resulting in the production of several mercantile companies—airy nothings in a double sense, formed by partners of the bank out of its cash account, who thus traded with themselves, under the name of Whiteside & Co., Maclure & M'Cree, and such like. To complicate matters, these shadowy firms transacted business with each other. The Bank of England, with its millions of bullion, could not have borne up long against such gross recklessness.

When early in 1772 a storm from without gathered round Douglas, Heron, & Company's establishment, it had no resistive force, having been already exhausted from within. Their own notes came showering in upon them, representative of crushing debts which they could not meet nor stave off. The local crisis was intensified by the occurrence of a general monetary panic. Anything—everything, to save the doomed ship. The desperate device of selling redeemable annuities was tried among other measures, only to render the ruin more complete : and in June it went down. The assets of the bank, including debts and bills of exchange, amounted to £1,237,043 7s 1d, the liabilities considerably exceeding that sum ; for though there were debts due to the extent of £700,000, the larger half of this sum had been contracted in the way already explained by the directors themselves. A committee appointed to wind up the company's affairs found it necessary to make a fresh call of £1400 per share upon such partners as still remained solvent ; and, from the report given in, it appeared that after allowing for all assets the balance against the bank was £366,000, involving a loss of £2600 on each share, exclusive of interest.

How seriously Dumfries suffered from the collapse of this gigantic bubble company may be inferred from the many names of the burgesses belonging to the town, and of proprietors intimately connected with it, that appear in the share list. On consulting it we find that Ebenezer Hepburn, the Provost, is down for £500 ; that Edward Maxwell, merchant, is a subscriber to double that amount ; that Gilbert Paterson, James M'Whirter, David Forbes, William Hunter, John Wilson, John Graham, junior, all merchants, Thomas Stothart, writer, and Ebenezer Wilson,

bookseller, are in the list for £500 each.   There are four subscribers to the extent of £2000, including the burgh's patron,
Charles, Duke of Queensberry, and Archibald Douglas of Douglas.
Henry, Duke of Buccleuch, is in the list for £1000.   The ancient
family of Craigdarroch sustained a severe shock by being involved
to the amount of £1500 ; and Andrew Crosbie of Holm,* who
subscribed £1000, lost by the disaster all the fortune he had
gained by his eloquent pleadings as an advocate.   Among the
remaining Dumfriesshire partners, with their liabilities, were
Patrick Heron of Heron, one of the projectors, £1000 ; William
Douglas of Kelhead, £1000 ; Robert Maxwell of Cargen, £1000 ;
John Dickson of Conheath, £500 ; Captain William Maxwell of
Dalswinton, £500 ; Gilbert Gordon of Halleaths, £500 ; Dr William
Gordon of Mossknow, £500 ; John Carruthers of Holmains, £500 ;
William Hay of Crawfordston, £500 ; and Sir Robert Laurie of
Maxwelton, £500.   Dumfriesshire furnished nearly one-third of
the original shareholders and one-fourth of the capital ; and
when the ruinous calls that were made upon them, enforced by
diligence and hornings, are taken into account, it is not surprising
that sad memories of the Ayr Bank still linger in the district.

The first eighty years of the eighteenth century were thus, as
we have seen, fruitful of great events in Dumfries ; and during
that time the aspect of the place experienced a greater change
than in any period of corresponding length before or since.   Here,
in old St. Michael's burying-ground, among the dust of these
generations, sleep the relics of some whose lease of fourscore years
began with the century.   Before they laid them down to die, what
curious tales would they tell their grandchildren of what had
passed before their eyes in youth and age : the burning of the
articles of Union at the Market Cross ; the desperate conflicts
between the "runners" of tobacco and the enforcers of the
revenue ; the troubles of the '15, when the town was turned into
a military camp ; the unwelcome visit of Prince Charlie, with his
reiving Highlanders, in the '45 : the brewers' anti-exciseman riot ;
the other internecine feuds of the burgh, crowned by the never-
to-be-forgotten conflict between the Pyets and the Crows ; and
next the fell bank catastrophe, which ruined many families, and
broke some sufferers' hearts.   When those patriarchs were boys
the town consisted of the High Street, the East Barnraws and the
West Barnraws running parallel with it for a short way on each

* Andrew Crosbie, advocate (son of Provost Crosbie, Dumfries) was a
successful lawyer, and justly looked upon as one of the most eloquent pleaders
of his time at the Scottish bar.   As many of the incidents in "Guy Mannering"
occurred in Dumfriesshire, it was all the more natural in Scott to take the
ablest lawyer of the county as the prototype of the learned, witty, and benevolent advocate who had the Ellangowan family and Dandie Dinmont for his
clients.   In these respects the character of Mr Crosbie corresponded pretty
closely with that of Paulus Pleydell, Esq., in the romance.

side ; Kirkgate, by which the leading thoroughfare was continued southward to the gates of St. Michael's ; the Friars' Vennel, running at a right angle from it to the Nith ; and Lochmaben-gate and Townhead Street diverging from it in other directions. Then the river wandered pretty freely according to its own sweet will, there being no banks eastward to restrain its revels ; the Dock meadow, habitually visited by Lammas floods and Solway tides, lay a comparative waste, partially fringed with willows, but wearing no woodland crown. There was no harbour worthy of the name ; no place of refuge for the aged or orphan poor ; no asylum for the sick ; only one church ; and not a solitary steeple. They had seen a narrow lane widened to secure a second convenient approach to the river ; St. Michael Street prolonged far past the Church ; the commencement of Queensberry Street, an intermediate one between High Street and the East Barnraws (a); the expansion of the suburbs ; the formation of extensive roads ; the construction of a new market-place, Queensberry Square ; the arborial decoration of the Dock ; the embankment of the wayward Nith ; the erection of a caul over it below the bridge, of the grain mills on its right bank, and of Glencaple Quay on its left bank, five miles further down. They had witnessed, moreover, the building of the Mid-Steeple, always associated in their recollection with a terrific anti-Union riot ; the building of the New or Castle Church ; the rebuilding and spiring of St. Michael's place of worship, at a time redolent of tartan kilts and Gaelic gibberish—the figure of a " pretty " youth mingling in the maze— with sinister faces that long afterwards terrified them when asleep ; the erection of a home in which decayed burgesses and destitute children received the merited hospitality of the town ; the opening of a house in which pale disease put on the hue of health, and " death, which comes to all," was rendered less dismal to the poor and destitute ; and the completion of several other great undertakings, designed for purposes of utility or ornament. And if any of those octogenarians had survived another decade, they would have seen many additional town improvements projected and carried into effect.

(a) Queensberry Street must have formed a thoroughfare long before this, for on both sides of it there were some very ancient buildings, including one of some considerable pretension to architecture at the foot of the Passcolly Close.

CHAPTER L.

AT Michaelmas, 1783, a gentleman was elevated to the provostship who, for more than a generation afterwards, took a leading
part in public affairs--Mr David Staig. If, during much of that
time, any one deserved to be termed the king of the town, it was
he. It is related of a member of Council who, being rather deaf,
could not well hear the discussions, that he habitually asked
before a vote came to be taken "What does Provost Staig say?
I say the same as Provost Staig." And to many councillors
besides this openly subservient one, Mr Staig's word was law. He
had a fair share of natural abilities; was shrewd, inventive, enterprising, politic, fond of power, not insensible to flattery; was
withal warm-hearted and virtuous—using his influence so far as
his judgment went for the advancement of the public weal. For
upwards of forty years he represented the Bank of Scotland in
the burgh, and was thus a monetary potentate with a host of
most obedient subjects; and but for the electoral law that prohibited one man from being chief magistrate longer than one
year, or two at most together, under a penalty of a thousand
pounds Scots, he might have reigned as provost for life.

The first important undertaking with which his name is
closely associated was a measure to provide for the paving,
cleansing, lighting, and watching of the burgh, for which there
had long been a felt necessity. It received from Mr Staig a
hearty advocacy; and when the Council agreed to apply to
Parliament in the matter, he and Mr Aitken, town-clerk, were
sent to London for that purpose; and also to obtain, if possible,
another renewal of the duty on ale and tonnage, which was about
to expire, and which had become more than ever a necessary item
of the revenue. Thanks to the energy of the deputation, and the

valuable assistance rendered by William, Duke of Queensberry, Sir James Johnston of Westerhall, member for the burghs, and Lord Kinnaird, an Act of Parliament for the joint objects aimed at was obtained—the police portions of it taking effect from 1788.*

In the rank and file of the merchant councillors there was a man of a far higher stamp than the civic chief. His name first appears associated with town matters in the following minute :— " 29th September, 1789.—The said day, Patrick Miller, Esq., of Dalswinton, one of the four new merchant councillors, before being sworn in, was admitted a burgess in the usual manner, and accepted and gave his oath of burgess-ship in the ordinary way, and promised to keep a sufficient gun and sword for the defence of the town when called for ; and the Council, for good services done and to be done by the said Patrick Miller, remit the burgess composition payable by him." Well might the members of Council pay this compliment to their illustrious colleague " for good services done." He had already, by improving his estate of Dalswinton, a few miles from Dumfries, set a noble example to the agriculturists of the district ; and had, just a few months before, launched on a lake formed by him out of a noxious swamp the first paddle-propelled vessel ever made—the product of his mechanical genius, and the pioneer of those magnificent steamers that have revolutionised the commerce of the world.†

---

* The Act was a very costly affair. Exclusive of personal charges, the expense was £421 12s ; contrasting seriously with the outlay for the Ale Act in 1737, which was only £157, and for its renewal, £270, in 1762. Besides, Mr Aitken was paid £26 5s for drawing the bill, and for loss of time in going to London ; which, with the expenses incurred when staying there seven weeks, and for travelling, increased the entire charge against the town to £550—one-third of which was charged on the police rate to be henceforth levied, one-third on the ale-duty, and the remaining third on the tonnage.

† Attempts have been made in our own day to rob Mr Miller of his claim to be considered the originator of steam navigation ; but that he not only invented the paddle-wheel, but was the first to propose the application of steam to it as a motive power, has, we think, been proved satisfactorily. As early as February, 1787, Mr Miller published a pamphlet, in which, after describing his proposed mode of propelling ships, he said : " I have reason to believe that the power of the steam-engine may be applied to work wheels, so as to give them a quicker motion, and consequently to increase that of the ship. In the course of this summer I intend to make the experiment ; and the result, if favourable, shall be communicated to the public." During that year Mr James Taylor, for whom the credit has been claimed of suggesting the application of steam to the wheels instead of manual power, was engaged as tutor at Dalswinton ; and when Mr Miller's invention was put to a practical test in October, 1788, Mr Taylor furnished the subjoined notice of the great event to the *Dumfries Journal* :—" The following is the result of an experiment no less curious than new. On the 14th instant, a boat was put in motion by a steam-engine upon Mr Miller's (of Dalswinton) piece of water at that place. For some time past his attention has been turned to the application of the steam-engine to the purposes of navigation. He has now accomplished and evidently shown to the world the practicability of this, by executing it upon a small scale : a vessel twenty-five feet long and seven

In the spring of 1796 the burgh once again suffered from a dearth of food, and consequent disturbances. For several seasons before the harvest was deficient ; and, in consequence, oatmeal, the staple of the district, rose from about its usual price of 1s 10d a stone to 2s 6d—a large sum at a time when labourers earned barely 1s a day, and few tradesmen so much as 2s. Even in ordinary years it was customary for the Town Council to store up grain or meal when they could get a good bargain, in order to retail it at or below prime cost to the inhabitants ; and when a pinch came, or was threatened, the Council used special diligence to obtain supplies. On the 2nd of February, 1795, the Council, at the instance of Mr Staig, laid in 10,000 stones of meal, he liberally advancing the purchase-money. Before the year closed this large supply was exhausted ; the renewed scarcity was rendered less endurable by the rigour of a December day : a resolution was therefore adopted to purchase no fewer than 16,000 additional stones of meal. Mr Staig once more furnished means for so doing ; and a public subscription was opened towards the expense of selling out the meal, and paying the interest on the money advanced for its purchase. Whilst these patriotic arrangements were being made by the Council the lower classes, either ignorant or mistrustful of them, and suffering the pains of a protracted scarcity, rose to riot and pillage in almost the same manner as is described in a preceding chapter. The alarming saturnalia began on Saturday, the 12th of March, 1796, became increasingly violent on Sabbath, the 13th, and were with difficulty suppressed in the evening of the latter day. On Monday, the 14th, the Council met with the Sheriff-Substitute of the county and several justices, to devise means for allaying the prevailing excitement, and to prevent further breaches of the peace. Among other steps taken by them for these purposes, they issued a printed notice of the following tenor : " Disturbances of a very serious nature having taken place within this burgh and the neighbourhood about the want of meal, the Sheriff-Substitute of this shire, sundry justices of the peace for the county, and also the stewartry of Kirkcudbright, and the magistrates and Town Council of Dumfries, think it necessary to give this public intimation, that a very large quantity of meal is now purchased by the town for the supply of the inhabitants until a new crop comes in, and that it will be sold out as the necessities of the community require. Notice is also given, that if, after this intimation, the tumults which have

broad was, on the above date, driven with two wheels by a small engine. It answered Mr Miller's expectations fully, and afforded great pleasure to the spectators present. The engine used is Mr Symington's new patent engine." In this and other instances Mr Taylor gave Mr Miller the undivided honour of the inventions ; and it seems sufficiently clear that Mr Symington's connection with it was simply that of a practical mechanic.

already taken place are persevered in, the civil power will think it incumbent on it to call out the assistance of the military to repel such outrages ; and it is earnestly requested that all heads of families keep within doors their servants and children." The authorities on the following day issued an address to farmers, "requesting, in the most anxious manner, that such of them as have quantities of meal to spare will without loss of time send the same into the town of Dumfries, to be sold in the market place ; a word of caution being added to the inhabitants "not to impede, hinder, or molest farmers or dealers from bringing their meal to market."

At a conference which the Provost held some time previously with the members of "The Practical Farming Society of the Shire of Dumfries and Stewartry of Kirkcudbright," they had signified their readiness to supply the burgh "with meal sufficient for the consumpt thereof, at the market and selling price," only objections had been taken to the mode in which certain dues were levied at the market. No sooner were the sacks of meal, pease, beans, and potatoes set down there for sale, than in came the Calcraft (a) of the day, armed with a capacious iron ladle, which he dipped into each sack, and depositing what was drawn from them in a wallet of his own, walked off: thus in a legal but repulsive manner tithing the staff of life in part payment of his services as the dread minister of death to evil-doers. Many abortive attempts had been made by farmers and grain-dealers to get rid of these exactions ; and on one occasion, in 1781, when the executioner, Roger Wilson, was about to levy his dues, he was violently opposed by a dealer named Johnston, who refused to let the detested ladle of the detested functionary pollute his meal-bag, and was sent to jail in consequence—from which, however, he was soon liberated, as he threatened to prosecute the magistrates for wrongous imprisonment.

There being a likelihood that this opposition would be followed up by others, the Council asked advice on the whole matter from the distinguished advocate, Mr Andrew Crosbie of Holm (the Pleydell of "Guy Mannering," as we have already explained). In the memorial laid before him the following among other statements were made :—" The town have a common executioner or hangman, who executes not only the sentences pronounced by the magistrates of the burgh, and of the King's judges on their circuits, but also the sentences of the sheriff, and of the justices of the peace at their quarter-sessions. The town has been in use to pay his house rent, and a salary over and above. Roger Wilson, the present executioner, has, since he was admitted,

(a) Calcraft was public hangman in the middle of last century. He was so much employed all over the three kingdoms for so long a period that his name became synonymous with his horrid occupation.

received from the town £6 of salary, and £1 13s 4d for a house rent. Over and above this salary and rent, he and his predecessors have been in use of levying and receiving weekly— to wit, each market-day, being Wednesday—the full of an iron ladle out of each sack of meal, pease, beans, and potatoes, and the same as to flounders. . . . Nor is it known how the custom came to be introduced, whether there ever was any agreement thereanent betwixt the town and county ; but certain it is, that such custom or tax has been levied past the memory of the oldest people without quarrel or dispute till Wednesday." The resistance given by Johnston to the tax is stated, and the memorialists then proceed to say :—" As there appears a fixed resolution and conspiracy to resist and forcibly obstruct the levy of this usual custom, and as it is of some importance, being, according to the executioner's own account, worth upwards of £13 yearly, the magistrates and Council request the advice of counsel how to act in the business."

In answer to this memorial and queries annexed to it, Mr Crosbie expressed his belief that an officer of the law can acquire rights to duties "established by custom upon no other title than that of his office ;" and that therefore the Dumfries executioner had a clear right to the market dues "that have been levied by himself and predecessors in office from time immemorial." He, however, though approving of what had been done to Johnston, counselled a more formal course of procedure towards future delinquents, adding : " If the officers, when assisting the hangman in his exactions, are deforced, the deforcers may be committed to prison and tried criminally by the magistrates for the deforcement." The opinion thus obtained was acted upon with good effect ; but the question continued in an unsettled state till, at the juncture which arose in 1796, Provost Staig, with characteristic sagacity, proposed to surrender the obnoxious tribute ; and the Council concurring, it was forthwith abolished. In lieu of the dues, Joseph Tait, the then executioner and the last functionary of his kind placed on the regular staff of the burgh officials, was allowed £2 a year in addition to his former salary.*

At the close of March the meal purchased by the town was sold to labourers at 2s 6d per stone, and to the higher classes at 3s ; by midsummer it fell to 2s ; and before the season's crop was gathered in, it rose to 2s 4d and 2s 6d. But we do not read of any further food riots occurring ; and it may be fairly inferred that peace, with comparative plenty, was enjoyed by the burgh during many after years. It was acknowledged on all hands that

* The Dumfries hangman's ladle is still to be seen, we believe, among other " auld nick-nackets " at Abbotsford. It was for many years lost sight of, till, in 1818, Mr Joseph Train, the zealous antiquarian, hunted it out, and, all rusty as it was, sent it as a present to Sir Walter Scott.

Mr Staig was "the pilot who weathered the storm" at this tumultuous period. The county magistrates concurred with those of the town in thanking him for " his cool and steady conduct" whilst the tempest raged ; and a massive silver *epergne*, value £80, was voted to him by the Council as a token of their gratitude for this and other valuable services rendered by him to the burgh.

The closing years of the century were distinguished by something better than bread riots—more especially the building of a handsome bridge over the Nith. As the traffic of the town year after year increased, the old bridge, on which much of it was thrown, became the less able to bear the burden. The venerable pile had withstood the flood below, and borne its living tide of passengers, for fully five hundred years. It required and deserved rest and relief ; and the burgh and the district needed more accommodation than its narrow thoroughfare supplied. Not only the burgh of Dumfries, but the county, and the stewartry of Kirkcudbright, went heartily into the movement for a new bridge, as soon as the subject was fairly mooted, in 1790. A committee of thirteen gentlemen, made up of representatives from each, managed the undertaking. The contractors engaged by them—Mr Thomas Boyd, architect, who furnished the design, and Mr William Stewart, mason—became bound to build the bridge for £3735 ; but owing to alterations in the plan and unlooked-for difficulty in founding one of the piers, a much greater outlay was incurred. Besides, in order to make a suitable access at each end, land and houses had to be purchased at a dear rate, by which the expense was still further swelled ; so that the enterprise came to be a very serious one in a pecuniary sense. The burgh, the county, and the stewartry contributed £1000 each to the fund ; the Government, after many pressing representations, gave a similar sum : individual subscriptions being relied on to make up the rest. In presence of vast crowds stationed on both banks of the river, and on the old bridge, the foundation stone of the fabric was laid with masonic honours.*

For awhile the work went smoothly onward ; but when, at the close of 1792, preparations were made for founding the abutment nearest Dumfries it was discovered that the rock, which was easily reached on the Galloway or west side, sloped away to

---

* The stone bore a Latin inscription, of which we append a translation :— " By the will of Almighty God, in the reign of the most august prince, George III., and in a most flourishing period of the British empire, the foundation stone of the bridge over Nith, to be built for public convenience, and at the joint expense of the county and town of Dumfries and stewartry of Kirkcudbright, was laid (amidst the acclamations of a numerous concourse of spectators) by Alexander Fergusson of Craigdarroch, Esq., grand master of the Mason lodges constituted in the southern district of Scotland, accompanied by a respectable body of the order, on the 19th August, 1791, of the Christian era—from the institution of Masonry, 5791. May the undertaking be fortunate and prosperous, and merit the approbation of posterity."

such a depth on the east as to be virtually inaccessible. With the view of getting a solid resting place for the abutment, a proposal was made to place it eight or ten feet further west, at the risk of spoiling the symmetry of the bridge by contracting its three mid arches to that extent. On a day in July, 1793, when the Nith was low, a final trial was made : thirty men working at three ordinary pumps, and twelve at a chain pump, whilst the contractors drove down an iron rod in search of the coveted sandstone. The water, as if jealous of the operations, would and did rush in, spite of all the pumping, which proved as ineffectual to keep it out as were the webs of silken cloth and twine to save the Scotch king's ship from the destructive tide.* In the words of the committee's report, "the water came pouring in on all sides so fast that the workmen had much difficulty in emptying it ; and it appeared that the further they went down, the greater quantity of water came in." Though the rod was driven down nineteen feet four inches below the surface of low water, "there appeared no certainty of reaching the freestone rock, and the quantity of water that issued from the gravel on all sides continued to increase." In these perplexing circumstances, Mr Staig, at the committee's request, took means for obtaining the opinion of a skilful engineer, Mr John Richardson, Edinburgh, on an ingenious device contrived by themselves for founding the abutment. Wooden piles to support the masonry were at one time thought of. It was ascertained that the third pier eastward of the old bridge was based on timber, and why not this abutment of the new ? A timber foundation was ascertained to be as impracticable as one on stone ; and the plan proposed by the committee having been sanctioned by the engineer, was acted upon and found to answer. It was of this nature :—The pier or landstool was commenced thirteen feet and a half below the surface of low water mark, with a course of stones in the front, each six feet long, two feet broad, and fourteen inches thick, the ends projecting fully a foot from the face of the pier. Behind this row another was placed ; the stones of the same breadth and thickness, but only five feet in length. Thus a foundation was laid, eleven feet broad at the base, on which stones lessening gradually in size were built, till the requisite thickness was obtained when the masonry reached the surface. The advantage secured by this process was that the stones were laid in the gravel in such a way as to be level at the upper end with one another, whilst each kept its own quantity of water at bay ; the whole being well pointed with

* "They fetched a web o' the silken claith,
    Anither o' the twine,
And they wrapped them into the gude ship's side,
    But aye the sea came in."

                                            Sir Patrick Spens.

mortar, so as to prevent the insidious element from impairing the solidity of the mass. The pier, after about a month's labour, was successfully finished on the 3rd of August, 1793, and the whole bridge was satisfactorily completed in the autumn of the following year.

In connection with the bridge, a new street had to be formed between it and the old bridge, and an embanked roadway—the precursor of Buccleuch Street—had to be made in the direction of the New Church, so that the whole character of this part of the town was revolutionised. When the expense of these and other works was added to that of the bridge, it was found that the sum amounted to £6356 19s 6d ; the cost of the bridge itself, and of the approaches to it, being £4588 3s 6d. To meet this large outlay there was the £4000 formerly mentioned contributed in equal proportions by the burgh, the county, the stewartry, and the Government, and £2006 subscribed by sundry noblemen and gentlemen ; leaving a trifling balance, which was cleared away by additional subscriptions. By the erection of the new bridge a low, flat, unoccupied bank of the Nith was transformed into an elevated site for stately houses, and a beginning made to the most fashionable part of the burgh ; and it may safely be said that no previous undertaking since the middle ages so altered and improved the aspect of the town, not to speak of the direct advantages which it secured. (a)

Both the Infirmary and the new bridge were, as we have seen, founded with masonic pomp and display. Freemasonry was first represented in the district by the Kilwinning Lodge, Dumfries, chartered on the 7th of February, 1750—twenty-two years before the Infirmary was founded. The Journeymen Lodge, Dumfries, followed ; date of erection, 10th December, 1754. In course of time this lodge almost lost its distinctive character by the admission of members who could neither hew nor build ; and eventually the latter swarmed off to form the Operative Lodge—those who remained receiving a new charter as the Thistle Lodge, on the 7th of February, 1776. Another lodge was erected in Dumfries in April, 1775, under the name of St. Michael. So numerous did the brethren of the "mystic tie" soon become in Dumfriesshire that it was constituted into a "district" or province in 1756. Its first president or grand master was Mr Andrew Crosbie (Pleydell) ; its second, Mr Alexander Fergusson of Craigdarroch, "so famous for wit, worth, and law," and the triumphant hero of the "whistle" symposium at Friars' Carse ; its third, Mr William Campbell of Fairfield ; its fourth, Mr Francis Sharpe of Hoddam ; its fifth,

(a) In 1893 the New Bridge was widened and assumed its present imposing character at a cost of £4000, generously defrayed by Miss M'Kie of Moat House ; the plans being by Mr Barbour, architect, in consultation with Sir William Arrol.

Major William Miller, younger of Dalswinton, and son-in-law to Provost Staig; its sixth, Mr John Babington of Summerville, near Dumfries; its seventh, Mr Stewart of Nateby Hall; while its eighth and present "P.G.M." is Mr Lauderdale Maitland of Eccles, one of whose ancestors was the Norman knight Eklis, already introduced to our readers. (*a*) There are at present three masonic lodges in the burgh: the Thistle, the Operative, and what was originally called the St. Michael, but is now known by the name of St. Michael Kilwinning. The Kilwinning itself, after having been long dormant, was reponed last year, and had its charter renewed; but two other old Dumfries lodges—the St. Andrew and the Union—have been less fortunate: a decadence in membership naturally led to poverty of funds, and the utmost period of grace having expired without the requisite donations being made to the central purse, the lodges became extinct. Altogether, the Dumfries brethren in active membership number at present about a hundred—the greater proportion of these belonging to the Thistle Lodge.

(*a*) The Provincial Masters after Mr Maitland have been in succession Mr F. E. Villers, Closeburn Hall; Mr A. H. Johnstone-Douglas, Comlongon Castle; Mr W. A. Dinwiddie, manufacturer (who was presented with his portrait in oils); and Mr W. Murray of Murraythwaite.

CHAPTER LI.

TOWARDS the close of 1791 Dumfries could number among its
citizens a man who had already made some noise in the world,
and who came to be recognised as one of Scotland's most illustrious sons. His figure was remarkable ; so that even a cursory
observer must have at once seen that it was the outward frame-
work of an extraordinary individual. Five feet ten inches in
height, firmly built, symmetrical, with more of the roughness of a
rustic than the polish of a fine gentleman, there was a something
in his bearing that bespoke conscious pre-eminence ; and the
impress thus communicated was confirmed by his swarthy countenance, every lineament of which indicated mental wealth and
power : the brow broad and high ; the eyes like orbs of flame ;
the nose well formed, though a professional physiognomist would
have said that it was deficient in force ; the mouth impassioned,
majestic, tender, as if the social affections and poetic muse had
combined to take possession of it ; and the full, rounded, dimpled
chin, which made the manly face look more soft and lovable.
When this new denizen of the burgh was followed from his humble
dwelling in Bank Street to some favourite friendly circle where
the news of the day or other less fugitive topics were discussed,
his superiority became more apparent.   Then eye and tongue
exercised an irresistible sway : the one flashing with emotional
warmth and the light of genius—now scathing with its indignant
glances, anon beaming with benignity and love ; the other tipped
with the fire of natural eloquence, reasoning abstrusely, declaim-
ing finely, discoursing delightfully, satirising mercilessly, or
setting the table in a roar with verses thrown off at red heat to
annihilate an unworthy sentiment, or cover some unlucky opponent with ridicule.   Need it be said that these remarks apply to
the ex-tenant of Ellisland, Robert Burns ?
  His first appearance in Dumfries was on the 4th of June, 1787,
two months after the second edition of his poems had been pub-

lished.   He came, on invitation, to be made an honorary burgess ;
neither the givers nor the receiver of the privilege dreaming, at
that date, that he was destined to become an inhabitant of the
town.   All honour to the Council that they thus promptly recognised the genius of the poet.   Provost William Clark shaking
hands with the newly-made burgess, and wishing him joy, when
he presented himself in the veritable blue coat and yellow vest
that Nasmyth has rendered familiar, would make a good subject
for a painter able to realise the characteristics of such a scene.
The burgess ticket granted to the illustrious stranger bore the
following inscription :—" The said day, 4th June, 1787, Mr Robert
Burns, Ayrshire, was admitted burgess of this burgh, with liberty
to exercise and enjoy the whole immunities and privileges thereof
as freely as any other does, may, or can enjoy ; who, being present,
accepted the same, and gave his oath of burgess-ship to his
Majesty and the burgh in common form."

Whilst tenant of Ellisland farm, about six miles distant from
Dumfries, Burns became, by frequent visits to the town, familiarly
known to its inhabitants.   Soon after Martinmas, 1791, accompanied by Bonnie Jean, with their children, Robert, Francis, and
William, he took up a permanent residence in the burgh, and
there spent the remainder of his chequered life ; so that Dumfries
became henceforth inseparably connected with his latest years.
He had just seen thirty-one summers when he entered upon the
occupancy of three small apartments of a second floor on the
north side of Bank Street (then called the "Wee Vennel").*   After
residing there about eighteen months—or, according to another
account, two years and a half, he removed to a self-contained
house of a higher grade in Mill Street, which became the scene of
his untimely death in July, 1796.

What varying scenes of weal and woe, of social enjoyments,
of literary triumphs, of worldly misery and moral loss, were
crowded within the Dumfries experiences of the illustrious poet !
There he suffered his severest pangs, and also accomplished many
of his proudest achievements.   If the night watches heard at

---

* Robert Chambers thus describes the accommodation of the poet's Bank
Street premises :—" The small central room, about the size of a bed closet, is
the only place he has in which to seclude himself for study.   On the ground
floor immediately underneath, his friend, John Syme, has his office for the
distribution of stamps.   Overhead is an honest blacksmith, called George
Haugh, whom Burns treats on a familiar footing as a neighbour.   On the
opposite side of the street is the poet's landlord, Captain Hamilton, a gentleman of fortune and worth, who admires Burns, and often asks him to a family
Sunday dinner."   (Vol. iii., p. 266.)—Nearly all the contemporaries of Burns
in Dumfries have passed away.   Of the two or three who still remember him,
one is John Brodie, now a veteran of 96 years.   John, when a " callant," was
often about the house in Bank Street, and used to run messages for " Jean."
He distinctly recollects seeing the poet burning a " barrowful " of written
papers soon after coming from Ellisland.

times his sorrowful plaint, and the air of the place trembled for a moment with his latest sigh, it long burned and breathed with the immortal products of his lyre ; and when the striking figure we have faintly sketched lay paralysed by death, its dust was borne to old St. Michael's, and the tomb of the national bard became a priceless heritage to the town for ever.

Dr Burnside says of his parishioners, at the time when Burns became one of them :—" In their private manners they are social and polite ; and the town, together with the neighbourhood a few miles around it, furnishes a society amongst whom a person with a moderate income may spend his days with as much enjoyment, perhaps, as in any part of the kingdom whatever."* Other evidence tends to shew that the society of the burgh was more intellectual than that of most other towns of the same size in Scotland. Soon after Burns came to reside in it, various circumstances combined to make it more than at any former period, perhaps, a gay and fashionable place of resort. A new Theatre was opened, which received liberal patronage from the upper classes of the neighbourhood,† several regiments were at intervals stationed in the burgh, the officers of which helped to give an aristocratic tone to its society ; and the annual races in October always drew a concourse of nobles, squires, and ladies fair to the county town.

The Theatre was opened for the first time on the evening of Saturday, 29th of September, 1792, under the management of Mr Williamson, from the Theatre Royal, Haymarket, London, assisted by Mr Sutherland, from the theatre of Aberdeen ; when, says the *Dumfries Weekly Journal*,‡ " the united elegance and accommodation of the house reflected equal honour on the liberality and taste of the proprietors, and design and execution of the artists, and conspired with the abilities of the performers in giving universal satisfaction to a crowded and polite audience." In a word, it is allowed by persons of the first taste and opportunities, that this is the handsomest provincial theatre in Scotland." It is

---

* MS. History of Dumfries.

† Burns, writing to his friend Nicol, under date, Ellisland, Feb. 2, 1790, says :—" Our theatrical company, of which you must have heard, leave us this week. Their merit and character are indeed very great, both on the stage and in private life, not a worthless creature among them ; and their encouragement has been accordingly. Their usual run is from eighteen to twenty pounds a night ; seldom less than the one, and the house will hold no more than the other. There have been repeated instances of sending away six and eight and ten pounds a night for want of room. A new theatre is to be built by subscription ; the first stone is to be laid on Friday first to come. Three hundred guineas have been raised by thirty subscribers, and thirty more might have been got if wanted."

‡ The *Journal* was owned and edited by Provost Jackson ; and it is to his grandson, Mr Robert Comrie of Largs, that we are indebted for the passages quoted from it.

added that Mr Boyd was the architect of the building, and that the scenery was from the pencil of Nasmyth. *(a)*

How the rein was given to fashionable dissipation and animal enjoyment during the racing season, in these exuberant days, is graphically described by the *Dumfries Journal.* "The entertainments of the hunting, races, balls, and assemblies, by the Caledonian and the Dumfries and Galloway Hunts, being now over (October 30th, 1792), we embrace the earliest opportunity of informing the public that they have been conducted with the utmost propriety and regularity, and we believe have given general satisfaction. The sports of the field in the morning were equal to the wishes of the gentlemen of the chase ; the diversions of the turf through the day afforded the highest satisfaction, not only to those immediately interested, but to thousands of spectators, and the performances of the stage in the evening gave high entertainment to crowds of genteel people collected at the Theatre. Lady Hopetoun's box on Thursday evening, being the play asked by the Caledonian Hunt, exhibited an assemblage of nobility rarely to be seen in one box in the theatres of the metropolis. Besides, the noblemen and gentlemen of the Caledonian Hunt had drawn together almost all the genteel families in the three southern counties of Dumfries, Kirkcudbright, and Wigtown, and we believe it may be safely affirmed that there never was on any occasion such an assemblage of people distinguished for their rank, fortune, and elegance of manners seen in this place, or perhaps in any provincial town in Scotland. Besides the daily entertainments at the ordinaries, there was a ball and supper given by each of the Caledonian and Dumfries Hunts, which, for the number and distinguished rank of the company, the splendour of the dresses, the elegance and sumptuousness of the entertainments, the richness and variety of the wines, exceeded everything of the kind ever seen here."

Lest it should be thought that the local journalist, from a feeling of partiality, should be over-colouring the picture, let us see how it looked in the eyes of a comparative stranger. It so happened that Robert Heron, the topographical writer and historian, visited Dumfries in the very week of these festivities, and put upon record his impressions of the burgh.* "It is perhaps," he says, "a place of higher gaiety and elegance than any other town in Scotland of the same size. The proportion of the inhabitants who are descended from respectable families, and have

(a) The Theatre, one of the few "Royal" houses in Scotland, was reconstructed in order to improve and beautify it, in 1876, according to plans by Mr Phipps, the eminent London architect. The property belongs to Mr Thomas M'Kie, advocate, who has maintained it not as a source of profit but out of public spirit.

* Observations made in a Journey through the Western Counties of Scotland, by R. Heron, 1792, vol. ii., pp. 72-76.

received a liberal education, is greater here than in any other town in this part of the island. These give, by consequence, a more elevated and polished tone to the manners and general character of this city. The manner of living which prevails here is rather showy than luxurious. To be esteemed genteel, not to sit down to a board overloaded with victuals, is the first wish of every one." After sketching at greater length, in the same style, the normal condition of the burgh, he goes on to describe its holiday aspect. " Both the Dumfries and Galloway and the Caledonian Hunt," he says, " were assembled here at this time. Every inn and alehouse was crowded with guests. In the mornings the streets presented one busy scene of hairdressers, milliners' apprentices, grooms, and valets, carriages driving and bustling backwards and forwards. In the forenoon almost every soul, old and young, high and low, master and servant, hastened out to follow the hounds or view the races. At the return of the crowd they were all equally intent, with the same bustle and the same ardent animation, on the important concerns of appetite. The bottle, the song, the dance, and the card table, endeared the evening, and gave social converse power to detain and to charm till the return of morn. Dumfries itself could not afford ministers of pleasure enough for so great an occasion. There were waiters, pimps, chairmen, hairdressers, and ladies, the priests and priestesses from all those more favourite haunts where Pleasure ordinarily holds her court. Not only all the gayer part of the neighbouring gentry were on this occasion assembled in Dumfries, but the members of the Caledonian Hunt had repaired hither from Edinburgh, from England, and from the more distant counties of Scotland. The gay of the one sex naturally drew together the gay and the elegant of the other. There was such a show of female beauty and elegance as, I should suppose, few country towns, whether in Scotland or England, are likely to exhibit on any similar occasion."

A gay, refined, intellectual town enough, truly ; and quite suitable, therefore, as a place of sojourn for Burns, the sentimental bard. But inasmuch as it was fashionable, aristocratic, courtly, given up in no small measure to the idolatry of rank, and fanatically afraid of anything that could be called ungenteel or democratic, it was no congenial home for the man who dared to say—

> " Ye see yon birkie, ca'd a lord,
>   Wha struts, and stares, and a' that ;
> Though hundreds worship at his word,
>   He's but a coof for a' that :
> For a' that, and a' that,
>   His riband, star, and a' that,
> The man of independent mind,
>   He looks and laughs at a' that."

In another respect the town was but too congenial to the poet's tastes and habits. " John Barleycorn," to use his own metaphor, bore potential sway within it. "The curse of country towns," says Robert Chambers, writing in 1852, "is the partial and entire idleness of large classes of the inhabitants. There is always a cluster of men living on competencies, and a greater number of tradesmen whose shop duties do not occupy half their time. Till a very recent period, dissipation in greater or less intensity was the rule, and not the exception, amongst these men; and in Dumfries, sixty years ago, this rule held good."* Thrown into company of this kind, sought after and lionised by all casual visitors, is it at all wonderful that a man of Burns's temperament should have often indulged too deeply? It was no disgrace then for either lords or commoners to fall drunk below the Bacchanalian board. More's the pity that poor Burns, so supreme in many things, was not superior to the jovial drinking customs of his day. Had he lived in a discreeter age he would have been a better and a happier man. Whilst the burgh had its full share of jovial fellows, who habitually caroused and sang, in a doubtful attempt "to drive dull care away," and called the marvellous gauger, nothing loath, to their assistance, he had frequent opportunities, which he willingly embraced, of breathing a purer atmosphere, and enjoying a higher communion than theirs. Burns was a man of many moods; he was mirthful and gloomy by turns: the pride and paragon of a refined circle at Woodley Park,† Friar's Carse, or Mavis Grove, one day; and on some not distant night, the hero of a merry group, fuddling madly in the Globe Tavern, singing in all tipsy sincerity the challenge of his own rollicking song :—

"Wha last frae aff his chair shall fa',
He is the king amang us three."

At Ellisland he had never lost the reputation of being a sober man, though he was fond of company and sometimes drank to excess. He indulged more frequently, however, when he ceased altogether to be a tiller of the soil, "turning down no more daisies," "binding" no more "after his reapers," tied to town-life and an uncongenial occupation. More exposed to temptations, and less able to resist their influence, he too often sank deeply in

* Life and Works of Burns, vol. iii., p. 209.

† A fine old mansion, beautifully situated, four miles south-west of Dumfries, and originally called Holm. It belonged to Andrew Crosbie, the Whig ex-Provost of Dumfries, whom the Pretender carried off in 1745. Mr Crosbie's son, the prototype of Counsellor Pleydell in Guy Mannering, spent much of his leisure at the family mansion. Afterwards the house was bought by a gentleman named Goldie, who called it Goldielea, a combination of his own name and that of his wife, who was called Leigh. Mr Walter Riddel having become possessed of the house, named it Woodley Park in honour of his spouse, with whom Burns was on intimate terms. It is now, as Goldielea once more, owned and occupied by Mrs James Newall. (a)

(a) The present proprietor is Mr Balfour Browne, K.C.

the mire ; but he did not wallow in it. In spite of all that has been said to the contrary, we feel justified in stating that he never became habitually intemperate, or a lover of the bottle for its own sake. His extreme sociality often led him into excess : none can tell how often he drained the intoxicating cup in order to purchase a momentary forgetfulness of his disappointments and his cares. And when Burns sinned in these respects, how he did suffer ! the very poetry of his nature giving a keener edge to his remorse.

> " See Social Life and Glee sit down,
>   All joyous and unthinking,
> Till quite transmogrified they've grown
>   Debauchery and Drinking."

One summer morning, while Burns, after an experience of this sad kind in the King's Arms, was proceeding homeward, he met with his neighbour, Mr Haugh, who had risen to his work somewhat earlier than usual : " O, George !" said the poet, more penitent than elated, " you are a happy man ; you have risen from a refreshing sleep, and left a kind wife and children ; while I am returning like a condemned wretch to mine."

Dumfries had ceased to be the Whig town which it was during the troubles of 1745. When a cry arose in favour of Parliamentary reform, the municipal body voted addresses to the King against it, and brimful of devoted loyalty ; and when news of the French Revolution reached the town, it excited a general feeling of alarm. Provost Staig and his colleagues looked upon the British Constitution as perfection itself, and their reverence for it was only equalled by their horror at the doings of the French democracy. In the following extracts from the *Dumfries Journal* we find the loyal, anti-democratic, and orthodox condition of the town faithfully mirrored. " On Tuesday, June 4th, 1793 [King George the Third's birth-day], an unusual display of loyalty eminently manifested itself through all ranks of people in this place. In addition to what we observed last week, it is but justice to notice the ardent loyalty of the rising generation, who, having procured two effigies of Tom Paine, paraded with them through the different streets of this burgh ; and at six o'clock in the evening consigned them to the bonfires, amid the patriotic applause of the surrounding crowd." After a general description of the enthusiastic mode in which the anniversary of his Majesty's birth-day was celebrated that year, special notice is taken by this sympathising journalist of the proceedings in which the gentle men of the Loyal Native Club* manifested " their attachment to

---

* Burns's impromptu satire on this club is well known :—

> " Ye true, loyal natives attend to my song ;
> In uproar and riot rejoice the night long :
> From envy and hatred your corps is exempt,
> But where is your shield from the darts of contempt ?"

the best of sovereigns on this joyous day." This association, formed on the 18th of January, 1793, "for preserving Peace, Liberty, and Property, and for supporting the Laws and Constitution of the Country," included among its members many influential inhabitants, their president being Commissary Goldie, and their secretary Mr Francis Shortt, town-clerk. "A few ladies," we are told, "on the morning of the auspicious day, brought bandeaux of blue satin ribbon, embroidered by themselves with the words 'God save the King!' which were presented in their name by the president to the members, and worn all day by the latter round their hats. The club met at three o'clock afternoon in the King's Arms tavern, and after partaking of an elegant dinner, no less than fourteen loyal and well-adapted toasts were drunk ; and a fifteenth bumper toast of 'God bless every branch of the Royal Family!' was given by way of finale to this species of toasts. The club also drank bumpers to the loyal town of Dumfries, and to the magistrates ; and in like manner to each of the ladies who had contributed so obligingly and attentively to the decoration of the members. At six o'clock the club adjourned in a body to the Town Hall, where they joined in the loyal and distinguished rejoicings which took place there in the evening. At eight o'clock they went to the assembly, and wore their bandeaux across their breasts."

Burns, unlike most of his fellow-townsmen, did not deplore the French Revolution ; on the contrary, he heartily sympathised with it, and was not the man to conceal his sentiments on any question at the dictate of prudence. "He was (says Lockhart) the standing marvel of the place ; his toasts, his jokes, his epigrams, his songs, were the daily food of conversation and scandal ; and he, open and careless, and thinking he did no great harm in saying and singing what many of his superiors had not the least objection to hear and applaud, soon began to be considered, among the local admirers of the good old King and his minister, as the most dangerous of all the apostles of sedition, and to be shunned accordingly."* A curious and characteristic illustration of the way in which the poet gave vent to his political views may here be recorded. A public library was opened in the burgh towards the close of 1792 ; and Burns, who had assisted in establishing it, was admitted a member on the 5th of March, 1793 ; the minute of the proceedings stating that the committee had, "by a great majority, resolved to offer him a share of the library free of the usual admission money (10s 6d) out of respect and esteem for his merits as a literary man." Reciprocating this kindness, Burns, on the 30th of the same month, presented four books to the library —" Humphrey Clinker," " Julia de Roubigné," " Knox's History of the Reformation," and " De Lolme on the British Constitution."

* Life of Burns, pp. 211-212.

The last-named volume contained a frontispiece portrait of the author, the back of which displayed these words, written in the poet's bold, upright hand :—" Mr Burns presents this book to the library, and begs they will take it as a creed of British liberty till they find a better.—R. B." Very simple, innocent words in themselves ; but awfully daring at that time, and excessively imprudent when proceeding from a Government officer. Burns, on reflection, quailed before the danger he had thus rashly incurred ; and, hurrying next morning to the house of Mr Thomson (afterwards provost of the town), with whom the books had been left, he expressed an anxious desire to see De Lolme, as he was afraid he had written something upon it " which might bring him into trouble." On the volume being produced, he, before leaving, pasted the fly-leaf to the back of the engraving, in order to seal up his seditious secret ; but anyone holding the double leaf up to the light may easily find it out, the volume being still in the library, and its value immeasurably enhanced by this inscription.

In the same library, now the property of the Dumfries and Maxwelltown Mechanics' Institution, there is another book, the thirteenth volume of Sir John Sinclair's Statistical Account of Scotland, which reveals another glimpse of the poet in Dumfries. Under the head " Balmaghie," a notice is given of several martyred Covenanters belonging to that parish, and the rude yet expressive lines engraved on their tombstones are quoted at length. The pathos of the simple prose statement, and the rugged force of the versification, seem to have aroused the fervid soul of Burns ; for there appears, in his bold handwriting, the following verse pencilled on the margin by way of foot-note :—

> " The Solemn League and Covenant
> Now brings a smile, now brings a tear ;
> But sacred Freedom, too, was their's :
> If thou'rt a slave indulge thy sneer."

We had occasion in December, 1859, to consult this volume ; and on discovering the lines, which had never before been brought to light, we recognised the poet's caligraphy at once, and had no difficulty in concluding that they constituted the first rough draft of his well-known epigram in praise of the League and the Covenant, quoted in a preceding chapter. The matured lines are usually represented as an impromptu rebuke by Burns to some scoffer at the Covenant ; but this precious holograph demonstrates the real circumstances under which they were originated.

Burns identified himself by more than rash words with the democrats across the Channel. A vessel engaged in the contraband traffic from the Isle of Man having entered the Solway, was watched by a party of Excise officers, including the poet. She became fixed in the shallows, but her crew were so numerous and well-armed that the party durst not attempt her capture unaided ;

and Mr Lewars, the poet's friend and brother exciseman, was sent to Dumfries for a guard of dragoons. Burns, with a few men under his orders, was meanwhile left on the look-out in a wet salt marsh ; and as the time thus passed wearily away, Lewars was blamed by the impatient watchers for his seeming tardiness, one of them going as far as to wish that the devil had him in his keeping. Burns saw a humorous ingredient in the irreverent desire, and in a few minutes expanded it into the well-known ditty, " The Deil's awa wi' the Exciseman," with which he diverted his colleagues till Lewars arrived with the soldiers. Our poet could, when occasion required, play the part of Captain Sword as well as Captain Pen. Putting himself at the head of the force, he waded sword in hand to the vessel's side, and was the first to board her and call upon her lawless crew to surrender in the King's name. Though outnumbering the assailing party, the smugglers quietly submitted. The vessel was condemned, and, with all her arms and stores, sold at Dumfries.

Had the matter ended here, the poet's services might have secured his promotion ; but unfortunately he sinned them all away, by purchasing four of the captured carronades, and sending them, with a eulogistic epistle, as a present to the French Convention. The carronades and letter were intercepted at Dover ; and forthwith the Commissioners of Excise ordered an inquiry to be made into the conduct of their officer. Burns, in a letter to his patron, Mr Graham of Fintry, stated that he was "surprised, confounded, and distracted" on hearing of the threatened investigation. He warmly repudiated the interpretation put upon his behaviour, declared his devout attachment "to the British Constitution on Revolution principles ;" and closed with the touching appeal: "I adjure you to save me from that misery which threatens to overwhelm me, and which, with my latest breath, I will say I have not deserved."

It was long believed that the poet's official prospects were utterly blighted by the inquiry ; and that, as a consequence, he became more dissipated and reckless. Some of his biographers have gone further, and attributed his early death to the same cause ; but what says Burns's superior in the Dumfries Excise district, Mr Findlater ? In a letter on the subject that gentleman says :—" I may venture to assert that when Burns was accused of a leaning to democracy, and an inquiry into his conduct took place, he was subjected in consequence thereof to no more than perhaps a verbal or private caution to be more circumspect in future. Neither do I believe his promotion was thereby affected, as has been stated. That, had he lived, would, I have every reason to think, have gone on in the usual routine. His good and steady friend, Mr Graham, would have attended to this. What cause, therefore, was there for depression of spirits on this account?

or how should he have been hurried thereby to a premature grave? I never saw his spirit fail till he was borne down by the pressure of disease and bodily weakness ; and even then it would occasionally revive, and, like an expiring lamp, emit bright flashes to the last."

Besides, Burns, the very year before he died, actually officiated as a supervisor ; and there is every reason to conclude that he would soon have been permanently promoted to that rank had not death intervened. Whilst we think that the charge against the Excise Board, of neglecting or ill-using Burns, is undeserved, we are decidedly of opinion that the treatment he received from the superiors of the Board and the Government of the day was infamous. It was a disgrace to them, and must ever be a source of the deepest regret to all admirers of the poet, that they allowed a few random sparks of disaffection to rise up between them and the lustre of his genius ; and that, too, when it was pervaded and intensified by the purest patriotism. When the war between Britain and France broke out in 1793 Burns joined a volunteer company that was formed in Dumfries ; and, according to the testimony of his commanding officer, Colonel De Peyster, he faithfully discharged his soldierly duties, and was the pride of the corps, whom he made immortal by his verse, especially by the vigorous address beginning—

> " Does haughty Gaul invasion threat ?
>   Then let the loons beware, sir ;
> There's wooden walls upon our seas,
>   And volunteers on shore, sir.
> The Nith shall run to Corsincon,
>   And Criffel sink in Solway,
> Ere we permit a foreign foe
>   On British ground to rally !' "

Burns was the laureate of the company, " and in that capacity," says Lockhart, " did more good service to the Government of the country, at a crisis of the darkest alarm and danger, than perhaps any one person of his rank and station, with the exception of Dibdin, had the power or the inclination to render."

His " Poor and Honest Soger," says Allan Cunningham, " laid hold at once on the public feeling ; and it was everywhere sung with an enthusiasm which only began to abate when Campbell's ' Exile of Erin ' and ' Wounded Hussar ' were published. Dumfries, which sent so many of her sons to the wars, rung with it from port to port ; and the poet, wherever he went, heard it echoing from house and hall. I wish this exquisite and useful song, with ' Scots wha hae wi' Wallace bled,' the ' Song of Death,' and ' Does haughty Gaul invasion threat ?'—all lyrics which enforce a love of country, and a martial enthusiasm into men's breasts—had obtained some reward for the poet. His perishable conversation was remembered by the rich to his prejudice : his imperishable lyrics were rewarded only by the admiration and tears of his fellow peasants."

In the spring of 1793 Burns addressed the following letter " To the Hon. the Provost, Bailies, and Town Council of Dumfries." " Gentlemen,—The literary taste and liberal spirit of your good town has so ably filled the various departments of your schools as to make it a very great object for a parent to have his children educated in them. Still to me, a stranger, to give my young ones that education I wish, at the High School, fees which a stranger pays will bear hard upon me. Some years ago your good town did me the honour of making me an honorary burgess. Will you allow me to request that this mark of distinction may extend so far as to put me on the footing of a real freeman of the town in the schools? If you are so very kind as to grant my request, it will certainly be a constant incentive to me to strain every nerve where I can officially serve ; and will, if possible, increase that grateful respect with which I have the honour to be, gentlemen, &c.,—ROBERT BURNS."[*] The request was at once complied with, to the great gratification of the poet, who was devotedly attached to his children, and desirous above all things to give them a liberal education. "In the bosom of his family," says Mr Gray, one of the teachers in the Academy, "he spent many a delightful hour in directing the studies of his eldest son, a boy of uncommon talents. I have frequently found him explaining to this youth, then not more than nine years of age, the English poets from Shakespeare to Gray ; or storing his mind with examples of heroic virtue, as they live in the pages of our most celebrated English historians. I would ask any person of common candour if employments like these are consistent with habitual drunkenness."

But though not systematically intemperate, his habits were too lax and irregular for the community in which he lived, con-

---

[*] As to Burns," says Mr Carruthers of Inverness, writing to us on the 27th of January, 1866, " I have one scrap for you. You will most likely print the short letter which the poet addressed to the Provost, Bailies, and Town Council of Dumfries, respecting the education of his children. The original draft of the letter, in Burns's handwriting, is in the British Museum ; and when there lately, I copied a part of it which was omitted in publication. After the second paragraph of the printed letter, ending with the words, ' put me on the footing of a real freeman of the town ' of Dumfries, there occurs this passage :—' That I may not appear altogether unworthy of the favour, allow me to state to you some little services I have lately done a branch of your revenue, the two pennies exigible on foreign ale vended within your limits. In this rather neglected article of your income I am ready to show that within these last few weeks my exertions have secured for you of those duties nearly the sum of ten pounds ; and in this, too, I am the only one of the excise (except Mr Mitchell, whom you pay for his trouble) who took the least concern in the business.' It will be worth your while seeing," continues Mr Carruthers, " if the letter is preserved among the Town Council papers, whether Burns himself omitted the above passage (which is certainly not in good taste), or whether it was thrown out by Currie." We have been unable to discover the original, and suspect that the interesting question raised by our esteemed correspondent must continue to remain unanswered.

vivial though it was; and many who disliked him on other
grounds magnified his excesses, and made these a pretext for
"sending him to Coventry." On one well-known occasion our
errant poet received the cut direct from some of the patrician
citizens. During an autumnal evening in 1794 High Street was
gay with fashionable groups of ladies and gentlemen, all passing
down to a county ball in the Assembly Rooms.* One man, well
fitted to be the cynosure of the party, passed up on the shady side
of the thoroughfare, and soon found himself to be doubly in the
shade. It was Burns. Nearly all knew him, but none seemed
willing to recognise him; till Mr David M'Culloch of Ardwell,
noticing the circumstance, dismounted from the horse on which
he rode, politely accosted the poet, and proposed that he should
cross the street. "Nay, nay, my young friend," said the bard
pathetically, "that's all over now!" and after a slight pause he
quoted two verses of Lady Grizel Bailie's touching ballad :—

> " His bonnet stood aince fu' fair on his brow,
> His auld ane looked better than mony ane's new ;
> But now he let's wear ony way it will hing,
> And casts himsel' dowie upon the corn-bing.
>
> O ! were we young, as we aince hae been,
> We sud hae been galloping doun on yon green ;
> And linking it over the lily-white lea ;
> And werena my heart light I wad dee."

This incident has been adduced as a proof that Burns at this
period (admittedly the darkest in his career) had become an
object of "universal rejection." Never was there a greater mistake ; and it would be even wrong to suppose that the dejection
that he felt, and expressed in Lady Grizel's verse, was more than
momentary, or otherwise than semi-dramatic. One who is overcome by real heart distress does not seek to give it vent by
measured poetical quotations. Half an hour after the rencontre
Burns and Mr M'Culloch had some cheerful chit-chat over a glass
of punch in the bard's own house, the latter having thoroughly
recovered his spirits ; and so charming was his discourse, and so
sweetly did Bonnie Jean sing some of his recent effusions, that
the Laird of Ardwell left the couple with reluctance to join his
fashionable friends in Irish Street.

Mr Gray, referring to the poet about this time, states that
though malicious stories were circulated freely against him, his
early friends gave them no credit, and clung to him through good
and bad report. "To the last day of his life," he says, "his judgment, his memory, his imagination, were fresh and vigorous as
when he composed the 'Cottar's Saturday Night.' The truth is,
that Burns was seldom intoxicated. The drunkard soon becomes
besotted, and is shunned even by the convivial. Had he been so,

* At the foot of the George Inn Close, Irish Street.

he would not long have continued the idol of every party." We have the testimony of the poet's widow that her husband "never drank by himself at home," and that he still continued to attend church– two facts which, apart from other more decided evidence, tell against the stigma that he had become recklessly dissipated in his latest years.

Burns's circumstances whilst in Dumfries were humble, but not poverty-stricken. His official income was £50, extra allowances usually bringing it up to £70 ; and his share in fines averaged an additional £10. "Add to all this," says Chambers, "the solid perquisites which he derived from seizures of contraband spirits, tea, and other articles, which it was then the custom to divide among the officers, and we shall see that Burns could scarcely be considered as enjoying less than £90 a year.

If the poet would have accepted money payment for the glorious coinage of his fancy, he might easily have doubled this income or more ; but, with a magnanimity which, however mistaken, illustrates the unselfishness of his nature, he steadily refused all offers of pecuniary reward for his lyrical productions. Of George Thomson's "Musical Miscellany" Burns was the chief minstrel, but he scorned to barter his melodious contributions for worldly gear, even when "one pound one he sairly wanted." Thomson having ventured to send some cash to the bard on one occasion, drew down upon himself this rebuke, dated July, 1793 :— "I assure you, my dear Sir, that you truly hurt me with your pecuniary parcel. It degrades me in my own eyes. However, to return it would savour of affectation ; but as to any more traffic of that debtor and creditor kind, I swear by that HONOUR which crowns the upright statue of ROBERT BURNS'S INTEGRITY, on the least motion of it, I will indignantly spurn the bypast transactions, and from that moment commence entire stranger to you."

According to the testimony of the bard's eldest son, given to Mr Chambers, and amply corroborated by others, the house in Mill Street was of a good order, such as was occupied at that time by the better class of burgesses ; and his father and mother led a life that was comparatively genteel. "They always had a maid-servant, and sat in their parlour. That apartment, together with two bedrooms, was well furnished and carpeted ; and when good company assembled, which was often the case, the hospitable board which they surrounded was of a patrician mahogany. There was much rough comfort in the house, not to have been found in those of ordinary citizens ; for, besides the spoils of smugglers, as above mentioned, the poet received many presents of game and country produce from the rural gentlefolk, besides occasional barrels of oysters from Hill, Cunningham, and other friends in town ; so that he possibly was as much envied by some of his neighbours, as he has since been pitied by the general body of his countrymen."

CHAPTER LII.

AMID all Burns's changes of mood and condition the muse never long deserted him; and were he tested by his productions in Dumfries, exclusive of his previous poems, he would still be recognised as our greatest lyrical bard. Indeed, considering the time absorbed in the faithful performance of his work as an exciseman, and of his family duties, and the time spent by him in company, good, bad, or indifferent, we cannot but wonder at the teeming wealth which his mind disclosed during his latest years.

Fully a hundred songs are the fruit of this period, the list including his most humorous ditties, many of his finest amatory effusions, and all his best battle lyrics. "Willie Wastle," "Auld Rob Morris," and "Duncan Gray," are referable to it; so are "Contented wi' little and cantie wi' mair," "Cauld kail in Aberdeen," "Meikle thinks my luve o' my beauty," "Ken ye what Meg o' the Mill has gotten?" "What can a young lassie dae wi' an auld man?" and "Last May a braw wooer cam' doon the lang glen." With these mirth-moving creations mingle many pervaded by the soul of pathos, and which one can scarcely name without tearful emotion, such as "Thou hast left me ever, Jamie," "The lovely lass o' Inverness," "O mirk, mirk is this midnight hour," "My heart is sair, I daurna tell," "How lang and dreary is the night," "Here awa', there awa', wandering Willie," "Farewell! thou stream that winding flows," "Ye banks and braes o' bonnie Doon," "Canst thou leave me thus, my Katie," "Ae fond kiss, and then we sever," "O wert thou in the cauld blast, on yonder lea, on yonder lea." Then, what images of female beauty, warm heart-affection, and pictures of rural life, are suggested by the mere titles of others on the list :—" Lovely Polly Stewart," "The lassie wi' the lint-white locks," "The fairest maid on Devon's bank ;" with other heroines, to whom the poet promises, "I'll meet you on the lea rigg ;" or petitions, "Wilt thou be my dearie?" or depicts, whilst mixing up

other congenial ideas in the verse, "Sae flaxen were her ringlets,'
"O wat ye wha's in yon toun?" "Flow gently, sweet Afton,"
"'Twas na her bonnie blue een was my ruin," "My love is like a
red, red rose," "Love will venture in where it daurna weel be
seen," "Yestreen I had a pint o' wine, a place where body saw
na.'" The catalogue of soft, tender, amatory effusions is enriched
also by "The braw, braw lads on Yarrow braes," "There was a
lass and she was fair," "True-hearted was he, the sad swain of the
Yarrow ;" and others having a sprightlier air, such as "My wife's
a winsome wee thing" and "O whistle and I'll come to ye, my
lad." Sparkling with surpassing brilliancy in this galaxy of song
are the charming patriotic ballad of "The Soldier's Return ;" the
noble martial ode, "Bruce's Address ;" the lay in which love and
patriotism blend beautifully together, "Their groves o' sweet
myrtle let foreign lands reckon ;" the proud lyric of the honest
man, though poor, "A man's a man for a' that ;" and the best
exponent of what Scotsmen feel towards friends, home, and
country, "Auld Langsyne."

Such are a few of the matchless songs composed by Burns in
his little chamber in Bank Street ; in his more stylish parlour or
closet in the street since honoured with his name ; on the Dock
meadow, "adown winding Nith," along the side of the river by
Martintonford, or among the ruins of Lincluden Abbey on the
opposite bank. While thus employed he was not only fulfilling
his chief mission as a poet but performing a great moral work.
Many a line was written by Burns which "dying he might wish
to blot ;" but, let it be borne in mind to his everlasting honour,
that he blotted from the book of Scottish song many foolish and
licentious pieces ; and that, after divorcing his country's airs from
improper company, he matched them with verses that are in every
way worthy of such glorious music.

All the localities in Dumfries, as elsewhere, mentioned in the
poet's verse acquired an interest, however commonplace before—
such is the influence of genius ; and many scenes or objects in
themselves sweet look more lovely since he sang their praise. The
river that flows past the town was always picturesque ; but it
seems a finer stream since the words of Burns were penned—

> "Adown winding Nith I did wander,
> Of Phillis to muse and to sing ;"

and these other lines,

> "As on the banks o' wandering Nith,
> Ae smiling simmer morn I strayed,
> And traced the bonnie howes and haughs,
> Where linties sang and lambkins play'd ;"

and since he declared that, as compared with the proudly-swelling
Thames,

> "Sweeter far's the Nith to me,
> Where Comyns aince had high command."

The huge hill that overlooks the river's conflux with the sea appears to rear a loftier crest since he patriotically protested that before an invading foe should be allowed to desecrate our shores,

> "The Nith shall rin to Corsincon,
> And Criffel sink in Solway ;"

and Tobias Bachup's rare old spire was more than ever taken from the category of ordinary buildings when the loyal bard doomed King George's enemies to

> " Hang as high's the Steeple."

Even the King's Arms Inn was no longer quite prosaic, after one of its window panes had scratched upon it the well-known epigram of the gifted and sometimes irreverent gauger—

> " Ye men of wit and wealth, why all this sneering
> 'Gainst poor excisemen ?   Give the cause a hearing.
> What are your landlords' rent rolls ?   Taxing ledgers !
> What premiers, what ! even monarchs' mighty gaugers !
> Nay, what are priests, those seeming godly wise men—
> What are they, pray, but spiritual excisemen ?"

The Parliamentary elections for the Dumfries Burghs acquired more than a political or local interest as soon as he etherialised them, and rendered the Five Carlins classical by his famous ballad regarding a contest in 1790, when the two rival candidates* sought to curry favour with " Maggy by the banks o' Nith,"   Blinkin, Bess o' Annandale," " Whisky Jean," " Black Joan," and " Marjory o' the mony lochs," than whom

> "Five wighter carlins werena foun'
> The South countrie within."

" Yon roofless tower," the ruined Lincluden Abbey or " Auld College," seems more eerie and romantic since Burns described his nocturnal " Vision " beside its shattered walls :—

> " By heedless chance I turned mine eyes,
> And, by the moonbeam, shook to see
> A stern and stalwart ghaist arise,
> Attir'd as minstrels wont to be.
> Had I a statue been o' stane,
> His darin' look had daunted me ;
> And on his bonnet grav'd was plain,
> The sacred posy—Libertie."

---

* James Johnstone of Westerhall, the " Border Knight," and Captain Miller, younger of Dalswinton, the " Sodger Lad."   " The Laddies by the Banks o' Nith " and " Epistle to Mr Graham of Fintry " were written on the same contest ; it ended in the defeat of Johnstone, the Tory candidate. Three other Election Ballads were written by Burns after he went to Dumfries, two of them respecting a contest for the Stewartry of Kirkcudbright, in which the candidates were Mr Heron, of Heron and Kerrouchtrie, Whig, and Mr Gordon, of Balmaghie, Tory ; and a third on a contest for the same seat between Mr Heron and the Hon. Montgomery Stewart, which resulted in the return of the former, but he was unseated on petition.

And the honoured Nithsdale family get fresh lustre from the
" welcome home" which he gave them—

> " The noble Maxwells and their powers
> Are coming o'er the border,
> And they'll gae bigg Terregles towers
> An' set them a' in order.
> And they declare Terregles fair,
> For their abode they choose it ;
> There's no a heart in a' the land
> But's lighter at the news o't."*

It would have been well for the bard if he had had no
drinking "howf" like the Globe, with its siren-servant, Anna of
the "gowden locks ;"† but who without emotion can visit this
famous Dumfries tavern—once too familiar with his presence, and
often vocal with his song ; or sit in the old-fashioned chair, that
still continues in " Burns's corner," and trace his charming lines
on the window of its upper parlour ?—

> " O lovely Polly Stewart,
> O charming Polly Stewart,
> There's not a flower that blooms in May
> That's half so fair as thou art."‡

* The small poem from which this extract is taken was written when
Lady Winifred Maxwell, descended from the forfeited Earl of Nithsdale,
returned to Scotland, and rebuilt Terregles House, three miles distant from
Dumfries. Mrs Burns says, in her memoranda, that during the Ellisland
period Burns dined once or twice at Terregles House, that the family lived in
great style, and she recollects of her husband talking with wonder of the
number of wax candles he had seen lighted at supper. Lady Winifred had a
great liking for the poet, and called once at the house in Bank Street. She
presented him with a splendid snuff-box, of Oriental manufacture, on the lid
of which was a likeness of Queen Mary from an original portrait. When
William Nicol Burns went to India he took the box with him, and it was
unfortunately broken to pieces soon after he landed.

† " Annie wi' the gowden locks " was Helen Ann Park, barmaid at the
Globe, and niece to its landlady, Mrs Hyslop. Burns's admiration of her was
more than Platonic. During a visit paid by his wife to Mauchline, he contracted a discreditable *liaison* with the girl, which resulted in the birth of a
daughter. Mrs Burns adopted the child as a " neibour's bairn," and it was
rocked in the same cradle with her own infant. Elizabeth Burns, as she was
called, grew up to be one of the bonniest lasses of the town, and, when woman-
grown, was wedded to a soldier named Thomson.

‡ In some of the editions of Burns's Poems, the subjoined verse is given
as one of his inscriptions on a window of the Globe :—

> " The grey-beard, Old Wisdom, may boast of his treasures,
> Grant me with gay Folly to live.
> I grant him his calm-blooded, time-settled pleasures ;
> But Folly has raptures to give." (*a*)

(*a*) The late Mr David Dunbar, Dumfries, possessed a pane of glass on
which the following four lines of the charming lyric, " Sae flaxen were her
ringlets," were inscribed in the unmistakable caligraphy of the poet :—

> " Her's are the willing chains of love,
> By conquering beauty's sovereign law,
> But still my Chloris' dearest charm,
> She says she lo'es me best of a'."

An attestation in these terms accompanies the relic :—" The above manu-

Preserved in the amber of his imperishable verse are the names of many persons—some to honour, others to shame—most of which would have been utterly forgotten, save for their casual association with his own. When Provost Staig's daughter recovered from a fever under the care of a distinguished Dumfries physician, he canonised the lady in the following lines :—

> " Maxwell, if merit here you crave,
> That merit I deny.
> *You* save fair Jessie from the grave !
> An angel could not die."

While the same fair lady was being wooed by the swain whom she afterwards wedded—Major William Miller, younger of Dalswinton, Burns again complimented her, and commemorated the courtship in the charming lyric which begins—

> " True-hearted was he, the sad swain o' the Yarrow,
>   And fair are the maids on the banks o' the Ayr ;
> But by the sweet side o' the Nith's winding river,
>   Are lovers as faithful, and maidens as fair :
> To equal young Jessie seek Scotland all over ;
>   To equal young Jessie, you seek it in vain ;
> Grace, beauty, and elegance fetter her lover,
>   And maidenly modesty fixes the chain."

And when another Jessie (Miss Lewars) proved a "ministering angel" to him whilst suffering from his last illness, he expressed his gratitude, and performed for her a similar service, by making her the subject of some of his sweetest lyrics and of his best impromptus. Taking up a crystal goblet containing wine and water, he wrote upon it the following toast, and then presented to her the brimming chalice :—

> " Fill me with the rosy wine,
> Call a toast, a toast divine ;
> Give the poet's darling flame,
> Lovely Jessie be the name :
> Then thou mayest freely boast
> Thou hast given a peerless toast."

On Miss Lewars complaining of indisposition, Burns, with the pleasantry which rarely forsook him, said that to provide for the worst, he would furnish her with an epitaph as companion to the toast :—

> " Say, sages, what's the charm on earth
> Can turn Death's dart aside ?
> It is not purity and worth,
> Else Jessie had not died."

And when she recovered a little, the poet, saying there was "a poetic reason for it," wrote as follows :—

script, from the hand of the immortal Burns, written on a pane of glass on one of the windows of the Globe Inn, Dumfries, is presented by John Thomson, writer in Lockerbie, to Mr John Spiers, Glasgow, in token of his friendship and regard, 15th Sept., 1824."

> " But rarely seen since Nature's birth,
>   The natives of the sky ;
>   Yet still one seraph's left on earth,
>   For Jessie did not die."*

John Bushby of Tinwald Downs, who raised himself from humble circumstances to wealth and position, first as a solicitor and then as a banker in Dumfries, was long on friendly terms with Burns ; but a quarrel between them brought down upon his head some bitter diatribes, which he scarcely merited ; and it would have been better every way had " black-lippit Johnnie " never been made to figure in the poet's pages.   More creditable to Burns are the epigrams by which he has rendered John Syme of Ryedale famous.   Mr Syme is still well remembered in the town as a fine specimen of the old Scottish gentlemen, clear-headed, warm-hearted, well-cultivated, courteous, full of anecdote and wit ; and, as the fashion then went, devoted to the pleasures of the table, which he never relished so much as when Burns was his cronie.   With them was sometimes associated Dr William Maxwell of Dumfries ;† though, when the trio met, it was generally less as " three merry boys " than as the leading Whigs of the place (for as such they were recognised), to discuss politics over a brimming bowl.   Among Burns's happiest impromptus were those addressed to his friend Mr Syme.   On the poet sending a dozen of porter from the Jerusalem Tavern to Ryedale, he accompanied his present with the lines :—

> " O, had the malt thy strength of mind,
>   Or hops the flavour of thy wit,
>   'Twere drink for first of human kind,
>   A gift that e'en for Syme were fit."

---

* Miss Lewars was afterwards married to Mr James Thomson, writer, Dumfries.   She died in 1855, at the age of seventy-seven, and lies interred in the immediate vicinity of the mausoleum.

† Burns's fervid, emotional nature, strong sense of nationality, and, let us add, *animus* against the Presbyterian clergy, made him at times a Jacobite ; and his abhorrence of arbitrary rule, his sense of justice, and respect for man's natural rights, conspired to make him almost a Jacobin.   His friend, Dr Maxwell, had also sympathies of the same seemingly conflicting nature.   A son of the gallant Kirkconnel Maxwell, who, as noticed in a preceding chapter, went out with Prince Charles in 1745, and became the historian of his expedition, he had a hereditary tendency towards Jacobitism ; but, when studying medicine in France, he caught the revolutionary spirit that was rampant there in 1793, and ever afterwards retained the impression which it produced upon his ardent, youthful mind.   A more congenial companion Burns could not have possessed, and no doubt Maxwell's masculine intellect exercised a large amount of influence over the poet.   In a notice of Dr Maxwell's death, which appeared in the *Dumfries Times* of 22nd Oct, 1834, it is remarked :—" His intimacy with Burns, whose friend as well privately as professionally he was, and of whose last illness he was a faithful and affectionate soother in both capacities, has in some measure rendered the name of Maxwell literary property ; while the liberal principles of the deceased, his visit to Paris during the early days of the first revolution, and the well-known denouncement of him and his presumed designs by Burke, gave him a permanent place in the political history of the country."   It was to this gentleman that Burns, when on his deathbed, presented a pair of pistols as a memorial of their friendship.

On one occasion, when Burns was about to take leave of his host at Ryedale, he was pressed to take another glass ; and he forthwith wrote on the tumbler an answer of consent :—

> " There's death in the cup – sae beware !
> Nay, more—there is danger in touching ;
> But wha can avoid the fell snare ?
> The man and his wine's sae bewitching !"

Towards the close of 1795, the poet, suffering from declining health, wrote in a less mirthful mood, and paid Syme the finest compliment of all, by declining a tempting invitation to dinner at Ryedale, in the following terms :—

> " No more of your guests, be they titled or not,
> And cook'ry the first in the nation ;
> Who is proof to thy personal converse and wit,
> Is proof to all other temptation."

A man of rare worth, Colonel Arentz Schulyer de Peyster, of Mavisgrove, finds merited commemoration in the poet's verse. After honourable service in North America, he retired to Dumfries, the native town of Mrs de Peyster ; and at the stormy period of the French Revolution he turned his military talents to account by embodying and training the 1st Regiment of Dumfries Volunteers, of which Burns was a member. " In his person he was tall, soldier-like, and commanding ; in his manners easy, affable, and open ; in his affections warm, generous, and sincere."[*] He died in 1822, at the advanced age of 96 years or more, regretted by the entire community. The reader will recollect the rhymed epistle which Burns, early in 1796, sent to his commander in answer to some kind inquiries regarding his health. No better thing of the kind has the bard produced than the letter beginning—

> " My honoured Colonel, deep I feel
> Your interest in the poet's weal ;
> Ah ! how sma' heart have I to speel
> The steep Parnassus,
> Surrounded thus by bolus pill,
> And potion glasses." (a)

* Dumfries " Courier."

(a) Mr James D. Law, the Scoto-American author, visited Dumfries in 1902, one of his objects being to make inquiry for Major-General de Peyster of Tivoli, New York, into that gentleman's family associations with this locality and with the poet. He was privileged to examine the library at Magisgrove, and he there obtained several unpublished manuscripts written by Burns. These he published two years later in a large volume entitled "Here and There in Two Hemispheres." The best of the pieces is, he says, "too profane for general circulation." But he had given a copy to Mr W. Stewart Ross ("Saladin"), and that daring "brither Scot" inserted it without abatement in his "Agnostic Journal." The other pieces are "Robert Aitken," two songs—"O Elibanks and Elibraes" is the first line of one, "Ever to be near ye !" the first line of the other ; and verses "To Mr Gow, visiting Dumfries. Air—Tullochgorum." The Robert Aitken ballad consists of six stanzas, four of which are as follow :—

When John Maxwell of Munches,* the greatest agricultural improver of his time near Dumfries, attained to his seventy-first birthday, Burns closed a complimentary address to him with six lines, which have as much of the bard's peculiar manner as any other product of his pen within so small a compass :—

> " Farewell, auld birkie—Lord be near ye !
> And then the De'il he daurna steer ye ;
> Your friends aye lo'e, your foes aye fear ye :
> For me, shame fa' me,
> If neist my heart I dinna wear thee,
> While Burns they ca' me."

In Burns's time the principal brewer at Dumfries was Mr

> When he and she, baith young and auld,
> Were bent on my undoin'
> And tried by lees and scandal bauld
> To drive me clean to ruin,
> Wha never aince withdrew his smile,
> Or listened to the claiken ?—
> Ah, he's a frien' that's worth the while,
> A man like Robert Aitken !
>
> When I tried my rustic pen
> In little bits o' rhymin',
> Wha introduced me but and ben
> And helped me in my climbin' ?
> Wha advertised abroad my name,
> " A minstrel in the makin',"
> Wha fairly read me into fame,
> But lawyer Robert Aitken !
>
> And when wi' muckle qualms I socht
> To get my poems printed,
> While mony " frien's " nae copies bocht
> And some their orders stinted,
> Wha by the dizzen and the score
> The names to me was rakin' ?
> The king o' a' the buying corps
> Was surely Robert Aitken !
>
> The time will come when I'll be deemed
> A poet, grander, greater,
> Than ever prophesied or dreamed,
> The loodest, proodest prater.
> Then let this fact be published too
> That at the bard's awakin',
> The truest, kindest friend he knew
> Was honest Robert Aitken !

We give the complimentary address to the famous fiddler in full :

> Thrice welcome, king o' rant and reel !
> Whaur is the bard to Scotia leal
> Wha wadna sing o' sic a chiel
> And sic a glorious fiddle !
> It's but a weary warl' at best,
> Wauf an' weary—aften dreary—
> It's but a weary warl' at best,
> A wauf and weary widdle !
> It's but a weary warl' at best
> Gang north, or sooth, or east, or west,
> But we will never mak' protest
> When near you and your fiddle.

Gabriel Richardson (provost of the town in 1802 and 1803).
Between the poet's family and that of Mr Richardson there was

> Let prosy parsons pray and preach,
> And wise professors try to teach
> The secrets far beyond their reach
>   As Stradivari's fiddle !
>
> We'll leave them to themsel's to read
> Things sae vexin'—and perplexin'—
> We'll leave them to themsel's to read
>   Life's cabalistic riddle !—
>
> We'll leave them to themsel's to read
> To spin their scheme and mak' their creed ;
> Come, screw your pins and gie's a screed
>   Frae your unrivall'd fiddle !
>
> Nae fabled wizard's wand, I trow,
> Had e'er the magic airt o' Gow,
> When wi' a wave he draws his bow
>   Across his wondrous fiddle !
>
> Sic fays and fairies come and dance—
> Lightly tripping—hopping, skipping—
> Sic fays and fairies come and dance,
>   Their maister in the middle !
>
> Sic fays and fairies come and dance,
> So gently glide and spryly prance,
> And noo retreat and noo advance
>   When he strikes up his fiddle !
>
> In brisk strathspey or plaintive air
> What rival can wi' you compare ?
> O' wha could think a hank o' hair
>   Could thus transform a fiddle ?
>
> What are the notes o' lyre or lute—
> Wizzent, wheezy—slim and sleezy—
> What are the notes o' lyre or lute ?—
>   Inconsequential diddle !
>
> What are the notes o' lyre or lute ?—
> O' pipes, piano, fife, or flute,
> Wi a' that ye can execute,
>   On your enchanting fiddle !
>
> Wha doesna joy to hear the ring
> O' ilka bonny lilt and spring
> That ye frae recollection bring
>   And wheedle through your fiddle !
>
> The sumph that wadna praises gie
> A soulless clod maun surely be ;
> A chiel should never hae to dee
>   That half like you can fiddle !

* "Mr Maxwell," says Robert Chambers, "was grandson's grandson to the Herrieses of Queen Mary's day. One cannot learn without a pleasing kind of surprise that a relation in the fifth degree of one who was Warden of the West Marches in 1544, should have lived to the close of the French Revolutionary War, which was the case of Mr Maxwell, for he died in June, 1814."—Life and Works of Burns, vol. iii., p. 205.

a good deal of intimacy, and the eldest sons of both were sent on the same day to Mr Gray's grammar school together. The provost's son grew up and became a great traveller and naturalist ;* but, as we have heard him humorously state, the first notable expeditions he ever made were on the back of the quadruped that drove a small cotton mill then in full activity at Dumfries, and which Burns notices as follows in a letter to the lady of Woodley Park :— " There is a species of the human genus that I call *the gin-horse class :* what enviable dogs they are ! Round, and round, and round they go. Mundell's† ox that drives his cotton mill is their exact prototype : without an idea or a wish beyond their circle— fat, sleek, stupid, patient, contented ; while here I sit altogether Novemberish, a *melange* of fretfulness and melancholy—not enough of the one to rouse me to passion, nor of the other to repose me in torpor." Burns long predeceased Mr Gabriel Richardson ; but he kept the memory of a worthy man green by writing his epitaph beforehand :—

> " Here brewer Gabriel's fire's extinct,
> And empty all his barrels ;
> He's blest, if as he brew'd he drink,
> In upright, honest morals. "

The poet's daily life in Dumfries is very graphically and fairly described by Robert Chambers in the following passage :— " So existence flows on with Burns in this pleasant southern town. He has daily duties in stamping leather, gauging malt-vats, noting the manufacture of candles, and granting licenses for the transfer of spirits. These duties he performs with fidelity to the King, and not too much rigour to the subject. As he goes about them in the forenoon, in his respectable suit of dark clothes, and with his little boy Robert perhaps holding by his hand and conversing with him on his school exercises, he is beheld by the general public with respect, as a person in some authority, the head of a family, and also as a man of literary note ; and people are heard addressing him as Mr Burns— a form of his name which is still prevalent in Dumfries. At a leisure hour before dinner he will call at some house where there is a piano—such as Mr Newall, the writer's—and there have some young Miss to touch over for him one or two of his favourite Scotch airs, such as the 'Souter's Daughter,' in order that he may accommodate it to some stanzas that have been humming through his brain for the last two or

---

* Sir John Richardson, born at Nith Place, Dumfries, in 1787.

† This was Dr Mundell, who, on retiring from professional service in the Royal Navy, started, in company with some other gentleman, a cotton factory, which flourished for a number of years, till it was injured by the war with America. He was uncle to Mr Mundell of Bogrie. (a)

(a) Tobacconist, and sometime Bailie in Dumfries.

three days. For another half-hour he will be seen standing at the head of some cross street, with two or three young fellows—bankers' clerks or ' writer chiels ' commencing business—whom he is regaling with sallies of his bright but not always innocent wit ; indulging there, indeed, in a strain of conversation so different from what had passed in the respectable elderly writer's mansion that though he were not the same man it could not have been more different. Later in the day he takes a solitary walk along the Dock Green by the river side, or to Lincluden, and composes the most part of a new song : or he spends a couple of hours at his folding-down desk, between the fire and window in his parlour, transcribing in his bold round hand the remarks which occur to him on Mr Thomson's last letter, together with some of his own recently composed songs. As a possible variation upon this routine, he has been seen passing along the old bridge of Devorgilla Baliol, about three o'clock, with his sword-cane in his hand, and his black beard unusually well shaven, being on his way to dine with John Syme of Ryedale, where young Mr Oswald of Auchencruive is to be of the party—or may be in the opposite direction, to partake of the luxuries of John Bushby at Tinwald-Downs. But we presume a day when no such attraction invades. The evening is passing quietly at home, and pleasant-natured Jean has made herself neat, and come in at six o'clock to give him tea—a meal he always takes. The post arrives in Dumfries at eight o'clock at night. There is always a group of gentlemen on the street eager to hear the news. Burns saunters out to the High Street, and waits among the rest. The intelligence of the evening is very interesting. The Convention has decreed the annexation of the Netherlands, or the new treason bill has passed the House of Lords, with only the feeble protest of Bedford, Derby, and Lauderdale. These things merit some discussion. The trades lads go off to strong ale in the closses ; the gentlemen slide in little groups into the King's Arms Hotel or the George.

" As for Burns, he will just have a single glass, and a half-hour's chat beside John Hyslop's fire [at the Globe Tavern], and then go quietly home. So he is quickly absorbed in the little narrow close where that vintner maintains his state. There, however, one or two friends have already established themselves, all with precisely the same virtuous intent. They heartily greet the bard. Meg or John bustle about to give him his accustomed place, which no one ever disputes. And somehow the debate on the news of the evening leads on to other chat of an interesting kind. Then Burns becomes brilliant, and his friends give him the applause of their laughter. One jug succeeds another—mirth abounds—and it is not till Mrs Hyslop has declared that they are going beyond all bounds, and she positively will not give them another drop of hot water, that our bard at length bethinks him of returning home, where Bonnie Jean had been lost in peaceful slumber for three hours, after vainly wondering ' what can be keeping Robert out so late the nicht.' Burns gets to bed a little excited and worn out, but not in a state to provoke much remark from his amiable partner, in whom nothing can abate the veneration with which she has all along regarded him. And though he beds at a latish hour, most likely he is up next morning between seven and eight,* to hear little Robert his day's lessons on Cæsar ; or, if the season invites, to take a half-hour's stroll before breakfast along the favourite Dock Green."†

Early in January, 1796, the poet's stay at the Globe was protracted far into the morning. There was a fell frost in the air, and a deep snow on the ground, as he passed up the close on his homeward way. Hours elapsed, however, before he reached home. Affected by the liquor he had taken, and the freezing cold of the atmosphere, a drowsiness—dread prelude of the sleep of death—overpowered him, and he lay long insensible at the head of the close, where it joins with Shakespeare Street. He had been suffering previously from what Dr Currie calls " an accidental complaint," which, with the strong medicine given to counteract it, disarmed his constitution, so that the merciless air of the month which, thirty-seven years before, " blew handsel in on Robin," pierced through his frame with unresisted and fatal influence. But for this casual incident, the thread of his existence might possibly have been much prolonged ; and better fortune was in store for him had he lived to enjoy it. The political ferment from which he suffered had subsided ; he was acquiring a higher social position—was no longer a suspected person—was in the fair way of obtaining professional advancement—and was being consoled, in some degree, for present poverty by rich foretastes of future fame, which must have been most welcome balm to his proud and wounded spirit. Burns was never fairly himself after that dreadful morning, though, swan-like, he kept singing under the shadow of death.

In a letter addressed some time afterwards to his kind friend and patroness, Mrs Dunlop, he says :—" I have lately drank deep of the cup of affliction. The autumn robbed me of my only daughter and darling child. I had scarcely begun to recover from that shock, when I became myself the victim of a most severe rheumatic fever, and long the die spun doubtful ; until, after many weeks of a sick bed, it seemed to have turned up life, and I am beginning to crawl across my room, and once indeed

* The time should have been a little later. Burns had full sympathy with the sentiment of the old song—

" Up in the morning's no for me,
Up in the morning early."

† Life and Works of Burns, vol. iv., pp. 130-32.

have been before my door in the street." What an object of interest to his sympathising neighbours—the invalided poet, leaning painfully on his staff, yet glad to get a glimpse of the blue heavens once more, and to feel the radiance of the sun, however faint.

Some time in the following month of March, Miss Grace Aiken, daughter of Burns's early patron, Mr Robert Aiken, of Ayr, when proceeding along the streets of Dumfries to visit her friend Mrs Coupland, passed by a tall, gaunt, rather slovenly-looking person of sickly aspect, who uttered an exclamation which made her pause. The voice was the voice of Burns, but the figure seemed to her that of quite another man : so altered was he since, ten years before, she had seen him at her father's house. On being urgently solicited to accompany her to the residence of Mrs Coupland, Burns consented, and there conversed with Miss Aitken and their hostess of other and happier days spent on the banks of Ayr and Doon. Spring came and went without bringing any relief to the doomed bard ; and summer found him lying almost hopelessly prostrate in a humble cottage at Brow, ten miles from Dumfries, on the shores of the Solway, whither he had gone in search of health.*

Before proceeding thither he told Mrs Burns that he thought he was dying, adding the remarkable words—" Don't be afraid ; I'll be more respected a hundred years after I am dead than I am at the present day." On Monday, the 4th of July, he wrote as follows to the Editor of the " Scots Musical Museum :"—" Many a merry meeting this publication has given us, and possibly it may give us more, though, alas ! I fear it. This protracting, slow-consuming illness, which hangs over me, will, I doubt much, my ever-dear friend, arrest my sun before he has reached his middle career. However, hope is the cordial of the human heart, and I endeavour to cherish it as well as I can." This was the last letter save one that the poet dated from Dumfries. After writing it he proceeded

---

* He had some intervals of better health, during one of which, in the middle of April, he was present at a meeting of the St. Andrew's Mason Lodge, to which he belonged. The record of the Lodge contains the following among its entries : 25th Dec., 1791—Burns present. 6th Feb., 1792— Burns present. Philip Ditcher, Esq., of 3rd Regiment of Dragoons, now quartered at Dumfries, admitted apprentice 14th March, 1792—Burns present —Chas. Pye, Captains Walker, Watson, and Pearslow, of 3rd Regiment of Dragoons, all admitted as apprentices. 31st May, 1792—Burns present. 5th June, 1792—Burns present. Ed. Andrews, of the Dragoons, and John Syme, Esq. of Barncailzie, admitted brethren without fees. 22nd Nov., 1792 — Burns present. 30th Nov., 1792—Burns present, and elected Senior Warden. 30th Nov., 1793—Burns present as Senior Warden, Sam Clarke, jun., admitted a member. His name does not appear again till 29th Nov., 1794, and only twice long afterwards, as follows : 28th Jan., 1796—on which night Mr James Georgeson, merchant in Liverpool, appeared, and who, being recom-mended by Brother Burns, was admitted apprentice ; 14th April, 1796, the last minute in which the poet's name occurs.

to Brow, then a hamlet numbering about a dozen houses, the chief
of which was an inn, kept by a Mr Davidson, who willingly
allotted the " chaumer en' " of his little hostelry to Burns as a
lodger.* There was a chalybeate well about a hundred yards from
the poet's residence, that then, as now, drew invalids to the place;
but Brow being then a station on the route between Dumfries
and Carlisle, it was less sequestered than it is to-day. Often
great herds of cattle going south rested for a night in the neighbouring merse, while their drovers proved the best customers that
the clachan inn possessed. Fresh air, sea-bathing, and a powerful
medicinal spring were now placed within the reach of the sorely-
stricken bard ; and they appeared for a day or two to exercise a
beneficial influence upon him. Would that the effect were lasting
and decided! Winds of the South, play with reviving power upon
his haggard cheek ; tide of the Solway, whose praise he sweetly
sang, give vigour to his wasted frame ; waters of the Well, distil
your strongest anodyne to save from an early death the illustrious
sufferer, and become ever after famous in his song ! But a power
stronger than theirs is at work, with which their healing virtues
cannot cope. Mrs Burns states in her memoranda that her husband used to read the Bible to their boys, and that after his death
William was in the habit of remarking, " Mother, I cannot see
those sublime things in the Bible that my father used to see."
During the last sickness of the bard he often pored over the pages
of the sacred volume, and said once to his wife, "If the rest of
them "—meaning Syme and Maxwell—" knew that I was so
religious, they would laugh at me."† One of the few things he
took with him to Brow was an old pocket Bible ; and who shall
rashly venture to say that when studying it, as he did, he found
"no balm in Gilead" when all medicinal influences proved in vain?

Some time after the poet's illness his friendly intercourse with
Mrs Walter Riddel was interrupted ; but it was renewed on Solway
side under circumstances which she has herself narrated. The
lady of Woodley Park was at this time residing in the vicinity of
Brow for the benefit of her health ; and on the second day of the
poet's sojourn there she sent her carriage, with a request that he
would favour her with a visit—all her coldness towards him having
vanished when she heard of his dangerous condition. When he
came, she says, "the stamp of death was imprinted on his features;
and his first salutation was, ' Well, madam, have you any commands for the other world !' " to which she replied, that it seemed
a doubtful case which of them should be there soonest, though she
hoped he would get time to write her epitaph. He showed great
concern about his literary fame, lamenting that he had not put

* The little cabin was remorselessly removed in 1863, as if it had never
been associated with the great poet, and was of no more account than so much
vulgar stone and clay.

† Memoranda, p. xxiv.

his unpublished papers in a state of arrangement, a task which he could not now undertake. Mrs Riddell "had seldom seen his mind greater or more collected" than on this occasion. Her account of the interview closes with the sorrowful intimation— "The next day I saw him again, and we parted to meet no more." Mr James Gracie, banker, Dumfries, having inquired after the poet's health, and offered to send a carriage to bring him home, received an answer which breathed a scintillation of hope. "It would be doing injustice to this place," says the invalid, "not to acknowledge that my rheumatisms have derived great benefits from it already; but, alas, my loss of appetite still continues." He added that he would not require to take advantage of Mr Gracie's kind offer till the beginning of the following week. Next day he wrote a letter to his wife—the last of countless communications in prose and verse sent by him to the faithful sharer of his fortunes. Beautiful in sentiment and diction, it is addressed to "My Dearest Love," tells her that he has reaped benefit from his stay at Brow, expresses happiness on learning from Miss Jessie Lewars that the family are all well, and closes with saying that he would see her on Tuesday next; altogether a beautiful, though unconscious, winding-up of the poet's written intercourse with his Bonnie Jean.

Burns being off duty, his salary was slightly reduced, and, like the "puir tenant bodies" spoken of in "The Twa Dogs," he was sometimes rather "scant o' cash" at Brow. The "halesome parritch, chief o' Scotia's food," was the only dish he could take; and port wine was prescribed for the purpose of recruiting his strength. His landlord, Mr Davidson, did not deal in wines, and on one occasion, it is said, when the bard's stock of money as well as of port was exhausted, he, though ill-fitted to the journey, travelled the distance of a mile to Clarencefield, in order to see if Mr John Burney, who kept an inn there, and who was married to a daughter of Mr Davidson's, would help him in his time of need. Placing an empty bottle on the counter, he asked for a bottle of port wine; and when that was handed to him he whispered to Mr Burney that "the muckle deil had got into his pouch,* and was its only occupant;" but, taking his watch seal in his hand (the veritable seal on which his armorial bearing was engraved†), he

---

* The same idea is expressed in the poem addressed to Collector Mitchell :—

> "Alake, alake ! the meikle Deil,
>   Wi' a' his witches,
> Are at it, skelpin' jig and reel
>   In my puir pouches."

† When Burns, in March, 1793, commissioned Mr Cunningham to get a Highland pebble converted into a watch seal, his directions about the engraving of it were as follows :—"On a field azure, a holly-bush, seeded, proper, in base ; a shepherd's pipe and crook, saltier-wise, also, proper in chief, on a wreath of the colours, a woodlark perching on a sprig of bay-tree, proper, for crest. Two mottoes ; round the top of the crest, ' Wood Notes Wild ;' at the bottom of the shield, in the usual place, ' Better a wee bush

tendered it to the landlord as a security. The landlady, who was standing by, observing that Burns was about to unfasten the seal, stamped indignantly with her foot by way of protest, while her husband, in the same generous mind as herself, pushed the poet gently to the door, making him welcome to the wine without money and without pledge.

Assuming that this anecdote is true, as it has been furnished on good authority, it would be wrong to infer from it that Burns could not have readily obtained as much wine as he required in a different way. A word from him to Mrs Riddell, or to any one of a dozen friends in Dumfries, would have been promptly responded to with a plentiful supply of port, or any other cordial of which he stood in need. It is right for us further to state that when Mr Graham of Fintry heard of the poet's illness, though unacquainted with its dangerous nature, he offered his assistance towards procuring him the means of preserving his health, but the letter, dated on the 15th July, reached its destination when too late to be of service. And it is also worth mentioning, on the authority of Mr Findlater, that Commissioner Graham, regretting his inability to continue the poet's full salary, sent him a private donation of £5, which nearly or totally made up the deficit.

Many kindly attentions were paid to the poet by the people of the neighbourhood. He was invited one evening to tea by Mrs Craig, the wife of the Rev. John Craig, minister of the parish ; and he made an effort to appear at the manse, and to converse in his usual animated manner. Mr Craig being laid aside at the time by ill health, the honours of the house, afterwards so renowned for its hospitality, were done by Mrs Craig and her daughter, Miss Agnes Craig, who subsequently became the wife of the Rev. Henry Duncan, her father's successor.* Miss Craig, who had a fine literary taste, was a warm admirer of the poetry of Burns, and had manifested the deepest interest in the poet since he came to reside in the parish. She was much struck with the debilitated frame and melancholy air of the great man, who was too visibly hastening to the grave : and she remembered ever afterwards the look and tone with which he described himself to her mother as "a poor plucked pigeon." In the desperate game of life, which he had played often wildly and not well, he had been a loser ; and he felt himself utterly bankrupt. Such at

than nae bield.' " We are indebted for the above anecdote to Mr Scott, the intelligent schoolmaster of Clarencefield, to whom it was related by Mrs Burney, some years before her death, which happened about twenty-six years ago. She also gave to Mr Scott the copy of the Bible used by Burns when lodging at Brow, saying that " it was much used by him when there." Mr Burney is still remembered at Clarencefield as a worthy, benevolent gentleman. His house is the fifth in the village ; and besides occupying it as a respectable hotel, he was tenant of a large farm in the parish.

* Afterwards Dr Henry Duncan.

least was the mournful feeling of the hour. In the course of the evening the declining summer sun happened to shine in strongly through the window, and Miss Craig, to save him from supposed annoyance, hastily rose to pull down the blind ; but the dying poet prevented her, saying, " Let the sun shine in upon us, my dear young lady ; he has not now long to shine for me."

Had the poet's mind been kept at ease as regards worldly matters his case might possibly have been redeemed from utter desperation : but during the critical second week of his residence at Brow he received a letter from a Dumfries solicitor, Mr Matthew Penn, requiring payment of a bill, amounting to £7 4s, due to Mr Williamson, draper, for his volunteer uniform. It had been simply placed, with other overdue accounts, in the hands of the legal gentleman, as that seemed the best mode for getting them discharged. It contained no threat ; but Burns's mind was so unhinged by disease that the missive appeared to him the very language of menace. Had he been in health, his knowledge of business would have enabled him to see the real meaning of Mr Penn's letter : as matters stood, it told upon him with over-whelming force. " A rascal of a haberdasher "—thus he wrote to his cousin, Mr James Burnes, at Montrose—" to whom I owe a considerable bill, taking it into his head that I am dying, has commenced a process against me, and will infallibly put my emaciated body into jail. Will you be so good as to accommodate me, and that by return of post, with ten pounds ?" On the same day (12th July) he used similar language in a letter to M⁰ George Thomson :—" After all my boasted independence, curst necessity compels me to implore you for five pounds. A cruel scoundrel of a haberdasher, to whom I owe an account, taking it into his head that I am dying, has commenced a process, and will infallibly put me into jail. Do, for God's sake, send me that sum, and that by return of post." Both of the gentlemen promptly responded to the poet's heart-rending appeal. Burns's health, as we have seen, had slightly improved, and he had penned at Brow the charming lyric—alas, that it was to be his last !—" Fairest maid on Devon's banks," when the receipt of this lawyer's letter provoked a dangerous relapse. " Home, home, home--if only to die !" Such was now the language of his heart.

Allan Cunningham, who was then residing at or near Dumfries,* says :—" The poet returned on the 18th, in a small spring-cart. The ascent to his house was steep, and the cart stopped at the foot of the Mill-hole Brae : when he alighted he shook much, and stood with difficulty ; he seemed unable to stand upright.

* Cunningham was just about twelve years of age at this time, and had come to Dumfries to learn the trade of a mason. When in his apprentice-ship, the future poet and novelist helped to build the Burgh Academy and the Episcopal Chapel in Buccleuch Street, now occupied by the Wesleyans.

He stooped as if in pain, and walked tottering towards his own door : his looks were hollow and ghastly, and those who saw him then expected never to see him in life again."* The same author has given an affecting picture of the state of public feeling in the town during the brief interval between Burns's return and the "last scene of all." Dumfries, he says, "was like a besieged place. It was known he was dying, and the anxiety, not of the rich and the learned only, but of the mechanics and peasants, exceeded all belief. Wherever two or three people stood together, their talk was of Burns, and of him alone. They spoke of his history, of his person, of his works, of his family, of his fame, and of his untimely and approaching fate, with a warmth and an enthusiasm which will ever endear Dumfries to my remembrance. All that he said or was saying—the opinions of the physicians (and Maxwell was a kind and skilful one) were eagerly caught up and reported from street to street. . . . As his life drew near to a close the eager yet decorous solicitude of his fellow-townsmen increased. It is the practice of the young men of Dumfries to meet in the street during the hours of remission from labour, and by these means I had an opportunity of witnessing the general solicitude of all ranks and of all ages. His differences with them on some important points were forgotten and forgiven : they thought only of his genius ; of the delight his compositions had diffused ; and they talked of him with the same awe as of some departing spirit whose voice was to gladden them no more."†

The dying bard was laid in the room to the south on the second floor. Upon the scenes which have, so to speak, localised this little dormitory in the hearts of all the poet's loving votaries, tearful memory often " broods :" his return to it from Brow, so terribly shattered that Mrs Burns was struck nearly dumb with grief : the letter written by him to his father-in-law on the same day—the last words he ever penned—praying for Mrs Armour's presence, as Mrs Burns was daily expecting to be confined, and he felt that his own end was drawing nigh ; the fitful flashes of kindly humour which escaped from him, as when he prayed a brother volunteer not to let the awkward squad fire over him ; the hopeless symptoms that set in on the 19th—a tremor that shook his bodily system, a fever that fired his blood and touched his brain ; the dawn of the 20th, bringing no relief, so that Maxwell begins to despair—Jessie Lewars, however, bearing up heroically while ministering to the dying patient, and Bonnie Jean stealing in every now and then from her own bedroom opposite, to see how he fares ; while Syme, Findlater, and others pass upstairs to take a farewell look of their illustrious friend ; the ensuing night, forerunner of the long starless night of the

* Lockhart's Life of Burns, p. 279.   † Ibid, p. 279.

grave ; the morning of the 21st, when his life came to be measured by moments, for long before meridian the spirit of Burns, recalled from earth, had passed for ever away—his last words, according to the testimony of his eldest son, having been a muttered exe-cration on the legal agent by whom his closing days had been unintentionally embittered and curtailed.*

The local newspaper, published a few days afterwards, con-tained the following intimation of the mournful event :—" Died here, on the morning of the 21st instant, and in the thirty-eighth year of his age, ROBERT BURNS, the Scottish bard. His manly form and penetrating eye strikingly indicated extraordinary mental vigour. For originality of wit, rapidity of conception, and fluency of nervous phraseology, he was unrivalled. Animated by the fire of nature, he uttered sentiments which by their pathos melted the heart to tenderness, or expanded the mind by their sublimity. As a luminary emerging from behind a cloud, he arose at once into notice ; and his works and his name can never die while living divine Poesy shall agitate the chords of the human heart."

These words but inadequately express the loss which Scotland and the world sustained by the premature demise of this gifted, and, with all his defects, still glorious son of song. A sympathy for the varied sufferings he had undergone, a regret for the neglect he had experienced, now mingled with and intensified the

---

* The house in which Burns breathed his last adjoins the premises of the Ragged School, in a niche of which may be seen a memorial bust of the bard, placed there by a most worthy gentleman, the late Mr William Ewart, M.P. for the Dumfries Burghs, with the words, " In the adjoining house to the north lived and died the Poet of his Country and of Mankind, Robert Burns." There are in the lower storey a " but " and a " ben "—in other words, a kitchen and parlour, both used as such when inhabited by Burns, and the latter a fine commodious room, the best in the house : above are two rooms of an unequal size ; the smaller of them an oblong low-ceilinged apart-ment, measuring fifteen feet by nine and a-half, being the one in which he expired. Two attic apartments, used as bedrooms for the children, and a closet nine feet square between the rooms on the second floor, complete the accommodation of the poet's house. (a)

(a) By the will of Colonel William Nicol Burns (executed 18th June, 1858, and witnessed by his brother, Colonel James Glencairn Burns) the house in which the poet died is conveyed to the Dumfries and Maxwelltown Educa-tion Society, which is now represented by the Dumfries and Maxwelltown Industrial School. There is an obligation under the legacy to pay to Mrs Hutchison, the poet's granddaughter, an annuity of £20, and at her decease to continue it to her son during his life ; and there is a further obligation that the house and mausoleum shall be maintained to the satisfaction of a person or persons to be appointed by the Dumfries Burns Club. On the initiative of the Club the Town Council have leased the house, for an annual rent of £20 ; and they have placed it in the care of Mr and Mrs Brown, who reside there with their daughter, Miss Jean Armour Burns Brown. Mrs Brown's father was the poet's eldest son ; and she and her daughter bear a remarkable likeness to the poet. Quite a collection of interesting Burns relics, etcetera, is being accumulated at the house.

homage given to his genius, and caused his faults of life to be overlooked, if not forgotten. Intense was the feeling of sorrow that prevailed in Dumfries and neighbourhood when it was known that the mighty heart of the man who had long given life and lustre to the locality was throbless. He had been, generally speaking, honoured and appreciated by the people of the place ; but when he lay hushed in the sleep of death, he became to them doubly dear. All deplored the loss of such a distinguished citizen, and shared in the general lamentation that so little had been done by the dignitaries and rulers of the nation to keep him in worldly comfort and economise his precious life. And yet, whilst we share this painful feeling, we are inclined to think that Burns's fame has benefited by the pity which his fate awakens. If he had received a greater share of " good things " in this life, been feted, caressed, and pensioned, the world might have not the less admired his productions, but he would have awakened far less of personal interest. We might in that case have liked Burns's poems equally well (though even this is doubtful), but we would not have loved or heeded so much Burns himself. Thus, if this theory be true, his earthly crosses and poverty enriched the heritage of his endless fame, and dowered it as well "by the tears" as by " the praises of all time."

The remains of the bard were removed to the Trades' Hall, in High Street, on the evening of Sabbath, the 24th of July, preparatory to the funeral, which, at the request of his brother volunteers, it was resolved should be conducted with military honours. A regiment of the Cinque Ports Cavalry, and the Fencible Infantry of Angusshire, then quartered in Dumfries, offered their assistance on the solemn occasion ; and the principal inhabitants of the town and neighbourhood signified a wish to take part in the procession. On Monday the 25th, in presence of an immense crowd of tearful sympathisers, the funeral train moved slowly down to St. Michael's cemetery. A party of the volunteers appointed to perform the requisite military service at the interment were stationed in front, with their arms reversed ; the other members of the company supported or surrounded the coffin, on which were placed the hat and sword of their illustrious fellow-soldier ; the civilians were ranged in the rear. In this order the procession moved onward ; whilst the streets through which it passed were lined by the horse and foot soldiers, and the accompanying band played the Dead March in "Saul." Arrived at the place of sepulture, the body was committed to the tomb; three volleys of musketry fired over the grave completing the affecting ceremony. "The spectacle," says Dr. Currie, "was in a high degree grand and solemn, and accorded with the general sentiments of sympathy and sorrow which the occasion had called forth." On the forenoon of this sad day the newly-made widow was seized with the pains of labour, and, just as the grave closed over her husband's dust, gave birth to a son, who died in infancy.

Robert, the eldest son, went to London in 1804, where he held a clerkship in the Stamp Office till 1833, at which date he retired to Dumfries. He possessed a considerable amount of poetical genius, was a good musician, an excellent mathematician and linguist ; and whilst he mentally resembled his father more than either of his brothers, he was the only one of the family in whom the features of the bard were distinctly traceable. Robert's conversational powers were also of a high order, and his company, as may be well supposed, was much sought after and relished by such strangers as his father's fame attracted to Dumfries. William Nichol and James Glencairn, the only other children of the poet who grew up to manhood, obtained commissions in the East India Company's army, each after a highly honourable career attaining the rank of lieutenant-colonel. They resided for many years at Cheltenham, honoured and beloved for their benevolence and amiability. Robert died in 1857 ; James in 1865 ; William in 1871 ; and all three were laid beside their father's dust under the mausoleum.

Mrs Burns continued to reside till her death in the house which has been hallowed by her husband's presence, an object of universal respect on account of her many virtues, and the interest which attached to her as the " Bonnie Jean " of his verse—the uncomplaining, fond, and faithful companion of his wedded life. By the proceeds of a fund raised for the widow, she was enabled to bring up her sons in a creditable way. In 1817, Mr Fox Maule (afterwards Lord Dalhousie) settled a pension on Mrs Burns of £50 a year, after a vain attempt to obtain for her a Government annuity ; this she enjoyed about eighteen months, when her son James, having been promoted to a situation in the Indian Commissariat, made such arrangements for her comfortable maintenance as allowed her to resign the pension, which, if so disposed, she might have retained for life.*

For many years a simple slab of freestone, placed over the poet's grave by his widow, was his only material monument. Eventually, however, a general movement was made for the erection of a mausoleum in some degree worthy of his genius ; and as money flowed in liberally for the scheme, from almost every quarter, and from lowly peasants and mechanics up to Majesty itself, the work

* The poet by his wife, Jean Armour, had nine children –five sons and four daughters ; two of the former, and the whole of the latter, died in childhood. Robert, the eldest son, left a daughter, Eliza, who married Dr Everitt a surgeon in the East India Company's service. She has been long a widow, and now resides, with her only daughter, Miss Everitt, in Belfast. Colonel James G. Burns left a daughter by his first marriage, who married Dr Berkeley Hutchinson. They had a son and three daughters, who, with their mother, still survive. By a second marriage he had one child, Miss Burns, who also

was proceeded with and completed in 1815. (*b*) The mausoleum, in form like a Grecian temple, was designed by Mr. T. F. Hunt of London ; and a mural sculpture for the interior was supplied by an Italian artist named Turnerelli, intended to embody one of the poet's own conceptions--the genius of Coila, finding her favourite son at the plough, and throwing her inspiring mantle over him. The figures were critically inspected by a committee of gentlemen, including the poet's brother, Gilbert, who signified his high satis- faction with the graceful appearance of Coila, and the ethereal lightness of her mantle ; and under the guidance of Gilbert's correct eye and tenacious memory, the sculptor was enabled to render more faithful the likeness of the principal figure. As a whole, however, the statuary is not of the highest class, though it has been sometimes greatly underrated. This much may be said in its favour, that its meaning is intelligible ; and that, if it does not satisfy fastidious art-critics, it appeals successfully to the popular eye and heart.

There being no room at the north corner of the churchyard where Burns was at first buried for the erection of a bulky structure, the mausoleum was built on a site in the south-east, so that the body had to be transported thither—a delicate duty, which was performed with as much privacy as possible. On the 19th of September, Mr William Grierson of Boatford, the zealous secretary to the committee, Mr James Thomson, superintendent of the monument, Mr Milligan, builder, and Mr James Bogie, gardener, Terraughty, " proceeded to the spot before the sun had risen, and made so good use of their time that the imposing ceremony was well-nigh completed before the public had time to assemble, or in fact were aware of the important duty in which the others had been engaged." * Two sons of the poet had been laid beside him—Maxwell Burns, the posthumous child, who died in 1799, and Francis Wallace Burns, who died in 1803, aged fourteen. On opening the grave the coffins of the boys were found in a toler- ably entire state, placed in shells, and conveyed to the vault with the greatest care. As a report had been spread that the principal coffin was made of oak, a hope was entertained that it would be possible to transport it from the north to the east corner of St.

---

survives. Such are the existing descendants of the national bard in 1872. (*a*)

(*a*) Besides his daughter Eliza, there were by another mother born to Robert, the poet's eldest son, a son and daughter. They were brought up in family with him. The daughter is Mrs Brown, who, as already stated, now occupies the Burns House. The son, also named Robert, was married to Mary Campbell, daughter of a schoolmaster in Dumfries, and he and his wife kept a school in Loreburn Street. They had a son, Robert, who became a moulder to trade, and died in early manhood.

(*b*) The foundation stone was laid on 6th June, 1815 ; but the mausoleum was not completed until 1819.

* Picture of Dumfries, p. 85.

Michael's without opening it, or disturbing the sacred deposit it contained. But this hope proved fallacious. On testing the coffin, it was found to be composed of the ordinary materials, and ready to yield to the slightest pressure; and the lid removed, a spectacle was unfolded which, considering the fame of the mighty dead, has rarely been witnessed by a single human being. There were the remains of the great poet, to all appearance nearly entire, and retaining various traces of vitality, or rather exhibiting the features of one who had newly sunk into the sleep of death : the lordly forehead, arched and high, the scalp still covered with hair, and the teeth perfectly firm and white. The scene was so impos- ing that most of the workmen stood bare and uncovered—as the late Dr Gregory did at the exhumation of the remains of the illustrious hero of Bannockburn—and at the same time felt their frames thrilling with some undefinable emotion, as they gazed on the ashes of him whose fame is as wide as the world itself. But the effect was momentary ; for when they proceeded to insert a shell or case below the coffin, the head separated from the trunk, and the whole body, with the exception of the bones, crumbled into dust."* When the remains had been religiously gathered up, they were placed in a new coffin, and interred beside the dust of the two boys. The vault was then closed ; and the party, solemn- ized by their close communion with "the buried majesty" of this Coila-crowned king of song, left the place.

Nineteen years passed by, and the vault of the mausoleum was opened to receive a new inmate—the poet's widow, who died after surviving him the long period of thirty-eight years. How, on the night preceding the interment (30th March, 1834), a number of gentlemen, after receiving due authority, descended into the vault, and obtained a cast of the poet's skull for a phrenological purpose, is well known.† Dr Blacklock of Dumfries, one of the party, drew up a report as to the condition of the cranium, shew-

---

* Picture of Dumfries, p. 86.

† It was Mr James Fraser (afterwards Bailie Fraser) who made the matrix. A cast of the skull, taken from it, having been transmitted to the Phreno- logical Society of Edinburgh, Mr George Combe drew up from it an elaborate paper on the cerebral development of the poet. He laid great stress upon its size, 22½ inches in circumference, and upon the extreme activity of the brain, indicated by other data. Commenting upon the whole, Mr Combe said : " No phrenologist can look upon this head,, and consider the circumstances in which Burns was placed, without vivid feelings of regret. Burns must have walked the earth with a consciousness of great superiority over his associates, in the station in which he was placed—of powers calculated for a far higher sphere than that which he was able to reach—and of passions which he could with difficulty restrain, and which it was fatal to indulge. If he had been placed from infancy in the higher ranks of life, liberally educated, and em- ployed in pursuits corresponding to his powers, the inferior portion of his nature would have lost its energy, while his better qualities would have assumed a decided and permanent superiority."

ing that it was in a high state of preservation. The bones of the
face and palate," he says, " were also sound ; and some small portions of black hair, with a very few gray hairs intermixed, were
observed while detaching some extraneous matter from the
occiput." When the vault was once more opened, for the interment of Burns's eldest son, in May, 1857, the skull of the bard was
found to have altered very little since the cast had been taken
from it. To secure its better preservation, the vacant space of
the enclosing casket was filled with pitch, after which the precious
" dome of thought " was restored to its position, to be no more
disturbed, we trust, till the day of doom.*

---

* The two foregoing chapters, with a preliminary one relating to the
poet's sojourn at Ellisland, have been published by Adam and Charles Black,
Edinburgh, under the title of " Burns in Dumfriesshire : a Sketch of the Last
Eight Years of the Poet's Life."   A second stereotype edition bears date
September, 1870.

CHAPTER LIII.

THE poet's sojourn at Dumfries constitutes a marked era in its history ; and to speak of an event occurring in or about "Burns's time" is still customary in the burgh. Adopting that familiar phraseology, let us briefly notice how educational matters stood with the Dumfriesians in Burns's time. Of established schools for teaching English there were three, the masters of which had amongst them a salary of £20 per annum, and 2s 6d per quarter from each pupil. There was one established grammar school (Latin), the teacher of which had a salary of £20, he receiving no wages from the children of burgesses, but 5s per quarter from others, and Candlemas offerings from all—the scholars numbering about a hundred. Other two schools were endowed by the town : namely, one for arithmetic, book-keeping, and mathematics ; salary, £28 ; wages, 5s per annum from children of burgesses ; 7s 6d from other children, with no offering at Candlemas ; number of pupils about 60 : and one for writing ; salary, £22 ; wages the same as the preceding ; scholars, 70. The grammar school teacher, in addition to his higher salary, had a dwelling-house assigned to him ; an advantage possessed by none of the other masters. By this time the Town Council had cancelled their illiberal edict against adventure schools : so that several of these existed in the burgh, at some of which French, drawing, and dancing were taught ; and there were, besides, two or three boarding schools for girls.

For a long period the endowed schools had no local connec-tion. In order that they might be embraced under one roof a new academy—to be erected by subscription—was projected, and on the 27th of April, 1802, the foundation-stone of the structure was laid near Townhead, by Provost Staig, in presence of a large assembly.* The Academy is a massive and stately building, and extensive additions made to it in 1871 rendered its appearance still more imposing. At first the Academy was managed by a committee of the subscribers ; but in 1814 it was handed over to the paymasters of the teachers, the Town Council, who continued to officiate as its directors till, in accordance with the Education Act of 1872, it was placed under the management of the School Board. The education taught in the Academy at present consists of four departments. One of these, including Latin, Greek, French, and German, is presided over by Mr James Cranstoun,

---

* At the close a numerous company dined in the George Hotel, when Mr (afterwards Dr) Wightman repeated the following verses he had that day written respecting the ceremony :—

" Kind heaven now marks this moment for its own,
    While on the chosen spot that stone is placed,
And dates a course of ages yet unknown,
    In which its memory shall not be effaced.

No ! 'tis a moment this to thousands dear,
    And thousands yet unborn its bliss shall know,
For here fair Science means a fane to rear
    Which ruthless Time will blush to overthrow.

Yes, when Oblivion's mantle shall be thrown
    On all the smiling throng now gathered round,
To learned strangers shall its courts be shown,
    Which while they tread they'll say ' 'Tis classic ground.'

And when this fluttering heart shall beat no more,
    Nor yet this tongue such feeble lines rehearse,
The Muses here some favourite's breast shall store
    With all the treasures of immortal verse.

Through Time's dread vista Fancy darts her view,
    And marks, well pleased, a long and studious train,
Fresh as the morn, and countless as the dew,
    The palm of knowledge eager to obtain.

A line of sages, too, of sire-like mein,
    Glad she can trace, distinguished from the rest,
By Heaven designed in these retreats to reign,
    And stamp instruction ' on the glowing breast.'

Her looks, full-shaded with the olive's wreath,
    On this fair scene Britannia seems to bend,
And, soft as o'er Nith's flowerets zephyrs breathe,
    To say, ' My sons. now to my words attend !

Love well your country, and its laws obey,
    Religion's sacred voice with reverence hear,
And Learning's ample page intent survey—
    Fear God, my sons, and have no other fear.' "

—"Life and Times of the Rev. John Wightman, D.D., late Minister of Kirkmahoe, by his successor, the Rev. David Hogg." A highly interesting work, published by Hodder & Houghton, Paternoster Row, London ; and by J. Anderson & Sons, Dumfries.

B.A., who has acquired distinction by his admirable translations of Catullus and Tibullus : he has the title of rector ; though, strictly speaking, there are few, if any, rectorial duties attached to his office. The salary is £37 11s 10d ; interest of mortified money, £26 8s 2d ; in all, £64. Another, the English department, with numerous collateral branches, is under the able management of Mr Duncan Forbes : salary, £20 8s ; interest, £9 12s ; in all, £30. A third department, mathematics and arithmetic, is well conducted by Mr John Neilson. The salary is £16 6s 6d ; interest, £8 3s 6d : in all, £25. Lastly, penmanship and drawing are efficiently taught by Mr David Dunbar, whose salary is the same as that of the mathematical master. Mr Dunbar is the author of a meritorious volume of poems, published in 1859, and of numerous other poetical pieces with which he has favoured the local newspapers. The salaries of the masters are supplemented by fees and by the interest of £3000, bequeathed for this purpose by Mr Crichton of Friars' Carse, and which became payable on the death of Mrs Crichton, in 1863. At present the interest amounts to £120, of which the English, writing, and mathematical teachers receive £15 each, the remainder going to the rector ; but on condition that he shall keep a well-qualified assistant, and educate ten poor boys gratuitously. The pupils at the Academy have, during the last thirty-four years, been all on the same footing as respects fees ; the exemption in favour of burgess's children having been withdrawn soon after the adoption of the Burgh Reform Act ; and Candlemas offerings having long since gone out of use.

A number of valuable bursaries are attached to the Academy, for which it is indebted to one of its teachers—Mr William Armstrong, of the mathematical department, who died in 1859. By a trust deed, dated 1852, Mr Armstrong conveyed his whole estate to five private friends, as trustees, for payment of his debts, and for behoof of two relatives who were to receive the interest of the same, but who predeceased the testator ; and lastly, were to convey the remainder of his estate " to the provost, bailies, and town clerk of the Burgh of Dumfries, and the rector of the grammar school, and the masters of the mathematical, English, and writing departments of the Academy, and their successors in office, as trustees for the following purposes : namely, to invest the remainder, and apply the annual rent of the whole, in order to establish bursaries in connection with the said Academy, to be called the ' Armstrong Bursaries :' one of the value of £18, another £15, and others £12 each ; and to be awarded to such scholars competing for them as shall, in the opinion of the trustees, rank first, second, third, and so on, in point of regular attendance, general scholarship, and good conduct," at the annual examination of the Academy by its patrons, and who shall have attended its classical and mathematical departments for two years previous to such examinations. Also, that the successful competitors shall not be entitled to receive the bursaries unless they *bona fide* intend to prosecute their studies in the universities of Edinburgh or Glasgow, and attend the mathematical or any other class, during the session immediately subsequent to the award of the said bursaries ; that the bursaries shall be enjoyed for one year only, unsuccessful competitors being permitted to join in any after competitions, if not more than eighteen years of age. The benevolent testator's free estate is worth upwards of £2000 ; so that, besides the fixed bursaries of £18 and £15, enough of interest is left for four or five others of £12 each.

Several men of note, in addition to those named in a previous chapter, have been connected as teachers with the burgh schools, both before and since they were joined into one academy ; these including Dr Dinwoodie, who acted as astronomer to Lord Macartney's Chinese expedition ; Mr James Wait ; the Rev. James Gray (Burns's intimate friend) ; Dr Aglionby Ross Carson, afterwards rector of the High School of Edinburgh, and author of " Exercises on Attic Greek ;" and the Rev. Dr John Wightman of Kirkmahoe, who when a young man acted for three years as usher in the grammar school to Mr Wait. The Academy has long enjoyed the reputation of being a first-class educational establishment. (a)

Our latest direct reference to the Trades bore the date of 1673. How have they fared during the interval between that year and the period we have now reached ? Each of the corporations has increased numerically ; but as respects their internal economy, scarcely any change is noticeable. A minute of 1st September, 1720, reveals the fact that some ordinary shoemakers had dared to "usurp the science of bootmaking," without having first been duly initiated into its mysteries ; and of course these aspiring cordwainers were heavily fined by the rulers of the craft. "Weave truth with trust " was the favourite motto of the websters ; but in March, 1764, some of them proved so far false to their vows of freemanship as to lend " sundry utensils " to unfree weavers, thereby causing " great loss and damage to the incorporation :" fined 3s 4d sterling each. But what was their offence compared with that of John Taylor, who, " though no ways connected with the trade " of habit-making, was actually detected "turning an old coat" for William Crow, silversmith, Dumfries, in that artisan's

(a) The present Academy was erected by the Dumfries School Board on plans prepared by Mr Frank J. C. Carruthers, after competition, and it was opened by Sir R. T. Reid, M.P., in September, 1897. The cost was some £16,000. Under the Board the teaching staff of the Academy has been greatly increased, the salaries advanced, the sources of revenue enlarged – including Government grant for higher education—and the curriculum much extended ; the number of pupils being also increased by means of bursaries obtained in elementary schools in the town and district.

own house ? The box-master and officers of the tailors caught him
" red-handed " in the act, and seizing the ancient garment, they
brought it before a meeting of the body, in proof of his audacity
and their courage. An action of "spulzie and damages" was
raised against the trade by Taylor ; but as the case is not further
noticed in the minute-book, we may assume that it was dismissed
Stay-making in these days was a branch of tailoring, and guarded
with as much jealousy as any other part of it ; yet Elizabeth
Knox, residenter, who was "noways free with the trade, or had
no title to exercise that kind of business," was detected in the
very act of patching up an old pair of stays, and fined 6s 8d
sterling for " the transgression "—the stays being detained till the
money was forthcoming.

On the 17th of December, 1792, the master tailors met, and
" having taken into consideration that the prices charged by them
for work done to their customers has been nearly the same for a
hundred years past, although all other mechanics have increased
their wages," they resolved to form their "log" according to the
following rate of charges, English money :—Making a gentleman's
suit of clothes, 10s ; making a gentleman's greatcoat, 5s 6d ;
mechanics' and livery servants' clothes, 8s ; boy's first suit, 3s ;
mending clothes, per hour, 2d ; ladies' habits, 10s 6d ; ladies'
greatcoats, 5s : any one charging a lower figure, to be fined 10s 6d
for each offence. The first workman's "strike," perhaps, that ever
took place in the burgh is traceable in a minute of the same trade,
dated the 4th of January, 1796. We thus learn that all the
journeymen tailors, stimulated by the example of their masters,
declined to work further, unless their wages were raised from six
pence per day with victuals to ten pence ; and that the employers
offered eight pence a day with victuals—a compromise which was
accepted by the men after they had stood out for a week or more.

Our information respecting the craftsmen has hitherto been
chiefly drawn from the records belonging to each ; but the Seven
Trades had books in which their transactions as a united incorporation were minuted ; and to these, so far as they exist, let us turn
for a little. The oldest ones are a book of accounts beginning in
1714, and a minute-book dating from 1767.* The accounts relate
chiefly to rents drawn from the letting of their hall and lodgings
connected with it, amounting to some £40 sterling at the first of
these periods ; to sales of meal and barley, which the deacons laid
in in large quantities, and sold out to the brotherhood with a
profit ; to charges for repairs on the property, and the expenses
incurred when Riding the Marches, shooting for the Silver Gun, or
at convivial meetings. A few specimens will suffice.

Under date 9th November, 1722, it is stated that the deacons

---

* In the possession of [the late] Mr James Dinwiddie, Irish Street.

and others discussed six bottles of wine "that day we rod the marches," the price being 9s sterling. The Marquis of Annandale having received a ticket of freemanship of the 29th of July, 1723, four bottles of claret were drunk by the fathers of the freemen on the head of it—the rate of charge the same, 1s 6d per bottle. A goodly donation of fifty pounds from the Duke of Queensberry having replenished the box-master's exchequer in November, 1722, his Grace's almoner, "Waterside," was treated to "thrie bottels of whit win" in a change-house—charge, 4s. On the 7th of May, 1727, the following entry occurs:—"Spent at a meeting of the Deacons in the hall anent the Silver Gune shoting, for 5 pynts and half mutchkin brandie, 19s." The chief carousal of the year was on Michaelmas night, when sometimes the Trades spent a ninth part of their entire rental in toasting the health of the newly-elected magistrates : the bill in 1760 running thus :—" 4 pints of spirits [whisky at this date having become a common drink], 16s ; 2 lib. sugar, 1s 8d ; 6 lemons [to flavour the inevitable punch], 9s ; 8 bottles of wine, 16s ; 12 lib. cheese, 3s ; 7 doz. baikes, and 3 six-penny loaves." The Trades were not selfish in their sociality ; money votes to the poor of the town being sometimes given at these festivities, and frequent entries occurring in their books of small sums paid away to poor strangers at the instance of the Convener. The magnitude of their transactions in "victual" may be inferred from the payments made in 1775—£540 10s for oat-meal ; £97 3s for barley ; and £107 2s 8d for herrings. Most of the minutes are too dry or detailed for quotation. They record in brief terms the annual elections ; notice still more briefly the Silver Gun competitions ; and become more communicative after the tide of the Trades has begun to ebb, and their history has lost its early charm.

In 1785 it was resolved that the Silver Gun should be shot for only once in five years ; and ultimately the contest came to be only once in seven. The following are the dates of this great carnival of the Trades, so far as they can be ascertained :—28th March, 1742, Thomas Dickson, glover, convener ; 4th June, 1746, James Aitken, glover, convener ; 4th June, 1762, Thomas Gibson, flesher, convener ; 4th June, 1766, William Crosbie, tailor, convener ; 5th June, 1777, John Paterson, hammerman, convener ; 4th June, 1779, William M'Ghie, squareman, convener ; 4th June, 1781, John Blackstock, shoemaker, convener ; 5th June, 1783, Robert Maxwell, hammerman, convener ; 4th June, 1785, John Ogilvie, shoemaker, convener ; 4th June, 1791, Robert Thomson, hammerman, convener ; 4th June, 1796, William Hayland, hammerman, convener ; 4th June, 1802, Kinloch Winlaw, squareman, convener ; 4th June, 1808, John Fergusson, squareman, convener ; 4th June, 1813, John M'Craken, squareman, convener ; 5th June, 1817, Alexander Lookup, skinner, convener ; 23rd April, 1824, Robert

M'Kinnell, hammerman, convener ; 24th April, 1828, Alexander Howat, flesher, convener ; 8th September, 1831, James Thomson, squareman, convener. *(a)*

During "Burns's time" the Trades were a very powerful body. Taking in master freemen, journeymen, and apprentices, they formed an operative force fully 700 strong, or about a ninth part of the whole population. Those who love precise details will not be displeased with the subjoined statistics, applicable to the year 1790 : Hammermen—40 freemen, 16 journeymen, 14 apprentices ; total, 70. Squaremen (masons, joiners, cabinetmakers, painters, and glaziers)—86 freemen, 84 journeymen, 50 apprentices ; total, 220. Tailors—46 freemen, 20 journeyman, 20 apprentices ; total, 85. Weavers—42 freemen, 15 journeymen, 2 apprentices ; total, 59. Shoemakers—110 freemen, 84 journeymen, 42 apprentices ; total, 236. Skinners and glovers—14 freemen, 5 journeymen, 4 apprentices ; total, 23. Fleshers, 23—all the journeymen free, and, like Harry of the Wynd, killing for their own hand ; apprentices, 10 ; total, 33.

Some time in 1703, the Trades, wishing to get rid of the inconveniences arising from their open-air gatherings, acquired the hall to which reference has been already made. It was a large room above the Meal Market, for which they paid 900 merks. Thirty years afterwards, we find them located in a second hall, near the New Church ; and, before the expiry of another thirty years, their Blue Blanket is seen displayed from another building opposite the Mid-Steeple ; which in its turn was superseded by a new hall erected on the same site in 1804. This, the fourth and last building possessed by the craftsmen of the burgh, cost for mason work £368 5s 6d, less £58, the value of the old materials ; for joiner, plaster, slater, glazier, and plumber work, £838 17s 5d ; a few other items increasing the aggregate to £1167 2s 11d sterling.

On the 4th of June, 1806 (the anniversary of George the Third's birth-day), the new Hall was publicly taken possession of by its owners. At twelve o'clock the colours of the Trades were displayed from the windows ; and in the evening the Blue Blanket, or grand banner of the united Incorporations, was hung from the high front of the building ; while the interior was crowded with a festive company, including the deacons, the magistrates, the officers of the Royal Artillery Company, and of the Dumfriesshire and Troqueer Volunteers, the whole presided over by Convener Samuel Primrose. This was the first of many jovial meetings held in the same hall. At the time of its erection the Trades were in full force. Those who took part in the "house-heating" ceremony that signalled its opening never fancied that theirs was the last

(a) In 1901 the trophy was again shot for. See page 333 (note).

generation in which the freeman's monopoly would be maintained, or that the day was at hand when their convivial gatherings, shooting competitions, and grand Rood Fair processions would cease ; that their property would for the most part be disposed of, and all their goodly paraphernalia, including the Convener's gold chain, the gigantic punch-bowl, and the far-famed Silver Gun, would pass into other hands.

The bacchanalian vessel here referred to was a present from Convener Grainger, and is really a magnificent product of the potter's art. As the meeting at which the bowl was presented was a characteristic one, illustrative in some degree of the Trades and the town when in holiday attire, we copy the account given of it by the local journalist:—"On Tuesday evening last [Hogmanay, 1806], the Convener and Deacons of the Incorporations of this town gave an elegant entertainment in their new Hall to upwards of a hundred gentlemen of the town and county. Convener Fergusson, in name of the Incorporations, presented the freedom of the Trades to John Murray, Esq. of Murraythwaite, vice-lieutenant of the county ; to John Forrest, Esq., Provost of Annan ; and to Colonel John Murray, nephew of the vice-lieutenant, with appropriate addresses to each, to which they made suitable replies. Mr. Robert Grainger, merchant, in a very handsome manner, presented to the Incorporations a most elegant china punch-bowl and silver spoon. The bowl, we understand, will contain ten gallons. On the upper ring in the inside are the words, 'Success to the Wooden Walls of Great Britain !' on the second ring, 'Success to the Incorporations of Dumfries !' on the outside the lion rampant, with the words, 'God keep the King and the Craft !' being the arms and motto of the Incorporations ; and many other emblematical devices. After the bowl was filled by the Convener ['with good rum punch,' says the minute-book], a great number of constitutional and patriotic toasts were given.*

---

* Mr David Dunbar, Dumfries, in whose possession the punch-bowl now is, has published a lengthened poem descriptive of what the Seven Trades' Punch Bowl heard and saw, in which the vessel thus describes its own *debut* at the festive board :—

> " Weel, when I made my first appearance,
> The audience gave their throats a clearance,
> And jumpit bravely to their feet,
> To gi'e me, sir, a welcome meet ;
> Sweet were the sounds that filled each ear
> As cheer stentorian followed cheer ;
> And when the first browst o' my bowl
> Had warmed each heart and fired each soul,
> I think auld Bacchus never smiled
> On sic a scene o' mirth sae wild !
> Toast followed toast, sang followed sang,
> Wild laughter through the hale nicht rang ;
> Time after time my bowl was filled,

The evening was spent with the greatest conviviality and harmony; and, indeed, the manner in which the whole was conducted reflected the highest honour upon the Incorporations of the town." In the same year, the trades were presented with a gilt silver chain and medal, by Deacon Fergusson, "to be worn by the Convener, only on particular occasions;" and by Mr Thomas Boyd, the architect of the new hall, with an elegant chair for the Convener, which piece of furniture was decorated with the arms of the Incorporation, at the expense of another burgess, Mr William Grierson, junior, merchant. The "plenishing" of the hall was further enriched by a beautifully-executed model of a frigate in full sail, placed above the entrance—the gift of Captain Affleck, Aberdeen; and by a capacious snuff-mull, ingeniously constructed out of a ram's head, a present from Captain M'Dowall.

In 1825, when the system, though still seemingly vigorous, was nodding to its fall, the public of Dumfries showed their appreciation of it by subscribing for a magnificent badge of office, to be worn by its chief. On the evening of the 9th of September, that year, the subscribers met with the Trades' officials in the Coffee House, High Street, for the purpose of presenting their gift, which consisted of a massive chain and medal. Provost Thomson officiated as speaker on this occasion. He pointed out the way in which James VI. had recognised the importance of the Dumfries craftsmen, and then said : "The representative of the Trades is justly entitled to such a badge of office as has now been presented to him, not less as a mark of honour and respect than from a consideration that it is proper that one holding so important a situation should be publicly distinguished. Should days of difficulty and confusion at any time arise, no man is able to lend so material aid to the civil authorities as the Convener of the Incorporations ; and round him, with their well-known feelings of loyalty, they will not, in such an event, fail to range themselves, to support the peace of the town, and the laws and religion of the country." After a personal compliment to the recipient of the chain, Convener Allan Anderson, and his immediate predecessor, Mr M'Kinnell, the Provost closed by investing the former with the badge, and begging him to accept it for the Trades, as a token of the esteem in which they were held by their fellow-citizens.* The worthy Convener returned thanks in suitable terms. The chain, a double one, is made up of four hundred and nineteen links ; the

Deep, deep they drank, and muckle spilled ;
The mair they drank, they'd drink the mair,
O' ten fu' bowls they had their share !
Round went the jugs wi' richt gude will,
And nane forgot his glass to fill —
When toast or sentiment was named,
That loyal cheers and bumpers claimed !"
* Seven Trades' Minutes.

medal attached to it is surrounded with beautiful embossed work, and has this inscription engraved on the centre :--" Presented to the Seven Incorporated Trades, by a few of the inhabitants of Dumfries, 9th September, 1825." (a)

On the 5th September, 1812, an institution was founded which was well fitted to exercise a refining influence on the community— we mean the Dumfriesshire and Galloway Horticultural Society. The meeting called for that purpose consisted chiefly of gardeners, and was presided over by Mr William Hood ; Mr William Grierson of Boatford and Mr John Learmont of Dumfries taking a leading part in the proceedings. The society grew at a rapid rate ; and so strong had it become in 1823 that a grand anniversary meeting was held that year, followed by a dinner, at which Colonel Dirom of Mount Annan (distinguished in his day as a great agricultural improver) took the chair, and at which the members presented Mr Grierson with a handsome silver cup, by way of recognising the interest he had taken in the success of the society, and their appreciation of his services in " bringing it to that perfect state at which it had now arrived."

The old jail, which stood on the east side of High Street, was never at its best a very strong building. When, in 1682, two brothers, George and Richard Storie, were consigned to it, charged with murdering Francis Armstrong at Alisonbank, on the Border, the former speedily effected his escape ; and the magistrates, fearing that the latter would do the same, were fain to send him under the sheriff's authority to the " Heart of Mid-Lothian."* In the following year a complaint was made to the Privy Council by Sir Patrick Maxwell of Springkell, that Ludovick Irving, a notorious highwayman, whom he had caused to be followed to Ireland, captured there, and lodged in Dumfries prison, at an expense of £200 sterling, had been allowed to break ward and disappear. The criminal was first put into a " sure vault "—a place that belied its name ; and then consigned " to ane outer room which had no sure posts or doors "—a circumstance which the prisoner soon took advantage of. Sir Patrick claimed his expenses, and demanded the punishment of the magistrates for allowing Irving to get his liberty ; with what success does not appear.† On the 20th of April, 1684, the Privy Council resolved that as " by the throng of prisoners in the Tolbooth of Dumfries, the same has been already broken and is yet in the same hazard," the strong vaults below the Castle should be prepared for the

---

(a) The chain passed into private ownership after the dissolution of the Incorporation. In 1854 it was sold with other properties by public auction. Mr S. Milligan became the purchaser at £35. Two or three years ago the Town Council acquired it by purchase, the price being £34, and it is now a badge of office for the Dean of Guild.

* Privy Council Records.   † Ibid.

reception of prisoners ; and the likelihood is that the vaults would be used for that purpose till the jail was made a little less vulnerable.

"At a much more recent period," says M'Diarmid, "the sister of the celebrated Jeanie Deans, *alias* Helen Walker, was confined in one of the cells of the Dumfries jail, while awaiting her trial for child-murder ; and a female still alive [in 1832], who knew both sisters intimately, stated lately in the presence of her master, Mr Scott, optician, that the individual who wronged "Effie," and afterwards became her husband, frequently visited Dumfries in the evenings, and conversed and condoled with her through the grating.*

In the autumn of 1742, a vagrant woman from the North, named M'Donald, was sent to prison for pilfering a pair of stockings. As she was being consigned to a dark cell, she prayed the jailor to allow her a small bit of candle with which to light up its gloom. The wish was complied with ; and an hour afterwards, just as the ten o'clock bell had ceased to ring, the whole upper part of the prison was in a blaze. With some difficulty the flames were subdued, but not till after the third storey of the building had been consumed, and what was infinitely more pitiful, till the poor miserable prisoner from the Highlands, whose candle had caused the conflagration, had been burned to death. A large portion of the jail had in consequence to be rebuilt, according to the plan of a committee, who recommended that a part of the arch above "the thief's hole," the whole of the upper storey, and the south gable, should be reconstructed, with an addition to the latter of an outer staircase.† So increasingly insecure had the prison become with the lapse of years, and so defective was it in other respects, that the county and burgh authorities resolved in 1801 to erect a new one. It was commenced in the following year, and completed in 1807. The site selected was objectionable on account of its being low and damp, and in a genteel part of the town—Buccleuch Street—to which the prison was no ornament. It contained eight cells for criminals, four small rooms for debtors, and several apartments fronting the street, in what was called the Bridewell division of the building.

The case of Maitland Smith, the first convict who suffered death in front of the new prison, is sufficiently remarkable to deserve a brief notice. Born in the parish of Penpont, working as a cotton spinner in Paisley, enlisting as a soldier to elude a charge of distilling whisky without leave, he, after a long absence, returned to his native district as one of a recruiting party, married, and with his wife's money purchased his discharge, and commenced business as a spirit-dealer in Dumfries. Prosperous,

* Picture of Dumfries, p. 72.   † Town Council Minutes.

acquiring a competency—then suddenly brought to beggary by the bankruptcy of persons deeply indebted to him, "hungry ruin had him in the wind." Under such circumstances poor Smith became wearied of life, and made various attempts at self-slaughter. To meet the urgent demand of some relentless creditors, he abstracted £25 from the cash-box of a mutual relief society, of which he was treasurer; and this, his first serious crime, led to the commission of his last and worst. He only, however, meant to borrow the money: with sundry bills due to him he went out on the 16th of April, 1807, for the purpose of getting them paid, and returning the perilous loan to the box; failing which he meant, by means of pistols which he took with him, to settle all matters under the sun, affecting himself, in another way. Instead of following out his first intention of going to Terregles, where one of his creditors resided, he resolved on visiting his nephew, who lived at Cargen Bridge. The sight of a mounted traveller, who drew up at the neighbouring toll-bar, gave a new colour to his thoughts. Could he only get hold of the stranger's saddle-bags, seemingly lined with gold, he might get rid of all his embarrassments. So whispered the Evil One, and so—giving way to the tempter—responded the man's own heart. At a later stage of the journey, the unsuspecting traveller, who proved to be Alexander Williamson, just returned from England, where he had been on cattle-dealing business for his employer, Mr Corson of Dalwhat, turned into a field at Drumjohn in Kirkgunzeon, to examine some cattle, upon which Maitland Smith, who had joined him previously, fired, and Williamson fell, wounded through the back—dead. No sooner was the murder committed than the miserable wretch would have given worlds to have had it undone. A prey to agonising remorse, he yet plundered the body of his bleeding victim—missing, however, the bags by which his covetousness had been at first inflamed. Apprehension, trial, conviction, followed rapidly, a violent death upon the scaffold finishing the dreadful tale of Maitland Smith, which, when read, may well excite a feeling of pity for his fate, as well as of horror for his crime.*

* There were five other executions at the same place, and two others at the existing prison, built in 1851, the convicts being as follows : – (1) Edward M'Grory, for (in company with another man who escaped) violently attacking and robbing Hugh Gallochar, packman at Corse of Slaiks : date of execution, 8th October, 1820. (2) James Gordon, for beating to death with one of his clogs in Eskdalemuir, and then robbing a half-witted pedlar boy named John Elliot, a native of Hexham : hanged 6th June, 1821. (3) John M'Kenna and (4) Joseph Richardson, for uttering a number of forged guinea notes : executed 16th May, 1823. Hannah Black, wife of M'Kenna, and William Richardson, brother of Joseph, were arraigned on the same charge ; but the former was dismissed *simpliciter* from the bar, and the latter, after being convicted and adjudged to death, had his sentence commuted to transportation for life. (5) James M'Manus, for (in company with James Flinn and Robert Platt)

With this prison is associated the blackest incident in the life of David Haggart, notorious as the smartest thief and most daring burglar and jail-breaker of his day. When, in 1820, occupying the "stone jug" of Dumfries (to borrow a term from his own jargon), he was but a slim youth of twenty-two, yet no fewer than fifteen charges of house-breaking and theft hung over his head. He had escaped from far stronger bastiles than that of Dumfries, and reckoned with confidence on getting outside of it also, by means of false keys which he had managed to fabricate. A fellow-captive named Laurie induced him to throw aside this plan, and adopt the bolder one of knocking down Hunter, the head jailor, with a stone in a "wipe" (piece of cloth), and getting hold of his keys with which to set themselves free. Two other prisoners, Dunbar and M'Grory—the latter lying, heavily ironed, under sentence of death for a murderous assault committed near Gatehouse, were made confederates in the plot ; and the four felons only waited for a favourable opportunity to put it into execution. Dunbar, when in the cage (an erection in the court where prisoners got the benefit of fresh air), had a stone handed up to him by a sympathiser from below ; several iron-cutting implements were conveyed by Haggart to M'Grory ; and when the scheme of the conspirators was quite ripe, they heard with exultation one morning that Mr Hunter had gone to attend the annual races then taking place at Tinwald Downs. The jail-governor absent, they had none left to cope with but Morine the turnkey. A little sharp work with the "chive ;" a well-delivered blow to stun the key-keeper—merely to stupify, not by any means to kill him ; and the jail-birds, so they fancied, would bid farewell to their "cage"—with what peculiar joy in the case of the death-doomed convict, who would flee not for liberty merely, but for life !

In the literal cage three of them were placed on that eventful day ; the fourth, M'Grory, being confined in a separate cell. Haggart, it would seem, could pass out of the cage as easily as if he had had a magic word to open it, like that used by the thieves

knocking down and robbing Andrew Smail, farmer, Becton, while he was returning from Lockerbie Lamb Fair. A verdict of not proven was returned against Flinn and Platt. M'Manus was convicted, and hanged on the 18th of October, 1826. For nearly thirty-six years afterwards Dumfries enjoyed an immunity from the revolting spectacle of a public execution. (6) The next that occurred was at the new jail in Buccleuch Street—that of Mary Timney, a poor ignorant feeble-minded young Irishwoman of excitable temperament, who, in a fit of jealousy, killed Ann Hannah at Carsphad, parish of Kells, with, it is supposed, a wooden mallet or beetle. Great but unavailing efforts were made to obtain a commutation of her death sentence. She was executed on the 29th of April, 1862. The last execution in Dumfries up till this date, and which closed the list of public executions in Scotland, was that of (7) Robert Smith, a young labourer belonging to Eaglesfield, who was hanged on the 12th of May, 1868, for the atrocious crimes of ravaging, murdering, and afterwards robbing a girl named Thomasina Scott, only eleven years old, in a wood between the village of Cummertrees and the town of Annan.

in the Oriental tale ; and when twelve o'clock struck, he was
lying crouching in a closet at the top of a stair that led to the
condemned cell—derned there with deadly weapon—the stone
tied in part of a blanket—and ready to assail the turnkey when
he passed that way.   Morine required to do so : two clergymen
were on a visit to the convict ; Laurie, according to the cue given
him, called on Morine to come up and let out the ministers ; and
whilst the poor man was obeying the treacherous summons, a
murderous blow from Haggart made him stagger and fall.   In a
trice afterwards Haggart was outside the prison ; and heedless of
all his confederates, off he set along Irish Street, round by Shakespeare Street into the King's Arms yard, across High Street, down
the Vennel to the Nith, and then away by the left bank of the
river to Comlongan wood.   The bloodstained fugitive, though
pressed hard by Mr John Richardson, an active criminal officer,
reached Carlisle in safety ; hearing, by the way, to his horror, the
true tidings that Morine had died that night at ten o'clock.
Several months afterwards, however, Haggart was apprehended
in the north of Ireland by Mr Richardson : and, ere many more
weeks elapsed, he was executed in Edinburgh for the murder of
the unfortunate Dumfries turnkey.   The jail which was the
scene of this memorable tragedy was superseded, in 1851, by a
huge, ungainly structure ; possessing, however, excellent interior
arrangements, with accommodation for sixty inmates.

   At a meeting of the Council in 1804, the magistrates were authorised " to lay out the tonnage money now on hand in building the
new quay at Kingholm ; and, if necessary, to borrow money for that
object."   The revenue from tonnage was at this time about £165 a
year, which left but a small surplus ; and, as usual, the bank had to
be drawn upon for the completion of the works ; which was effected
in 1806, the first foreign vessel arriving at Kingholm Quay being
the Clementina, with sugar, on the 16th of September of that year.*
We have already seen how, by the liberality of Mr Maxwell of
Nithsdale, the town became possessed of the ground on which
Glencaple village was built ; and we must now notice how it
acquired the lordship of another hamlet erected nearer home.

   At a meeting of Council held on the 23rd of March, 1812, the
important subject of the moss lands belonging to the burgh was
introduced by Provost Staig.   He stated that a few days ago he
and the other magistrates had visited certain of these mosses situated within the royalty, over which sundry individuals had enjoyed
the liberty of casting turf ; and that as their servitudes had expired, or would soon cease, the property might now be feued or
otherwise disposed of as might seem best.   They had also, he said,
gone to Whinnyhill, where a considerable number of feus had been

taken and several houses built, by which the locality had been greatly improved, and the revenue of the town increased. As Mr Joseph Gass had originated the village, and done much to foster its growth he proposed that it should be called Gasstown, in compliment to its founder. Provost Staig's propositions were cordially approved of. On the 5th of the following September, charters were granted to various persons for twenty-three allotments at a ground rent of from 10s to £1 13s 4d yearly each ; the entire feus amounting £26 12s per annum. In this manner the infant village of Gastown acquired a goodly addition to its size. On the same day fifteen additional feus at Glencaple were let at an aggregate of £13 10s. Thus from these two sources a sum of fully £40 a year was at once added to the revenue of the burgh ; and that in course of time came to be further benefited by the condition imposed on the feuars of " doubling the duty the first year of the entry of every heir or singular successor." *

On the 16th of January, 1810, the Council received from the County Commissioners copies of a bill prepared by them and the Commissioners of the Stewartry, for improving the navigation of the river, and the police regulations of the burgh. Hitherto the Council had been the Neptunes of the Nith ; and now these other bodies desired, by virtue of a new legislative trident, to acquire dominion over its waters, and also sought to intermeddle with the internal affairs of the town. The Provost, Mr Robert Jackson, was not of a temper to tolerate such assumptions ; and in resisting them he was backed by nearly all the Councillors. A conference was brought about between a committee of the latter and the chief promoters of the measure, with the view of coming to a common understanding respecting it ; but as the county authorities stood out for "the bill and the whole bill," those of the town declared war against them, and prepared a bill of their own, based on their existing Tonnage, Ale-duty, and Police Act, passed in 1787, and which had almost run its course.

Both parties made preparations for a Parliamentary campaign, but no real battle ensued. A technical flaw in the burghal measure having endangered its success, its promoters were induced to withdraw it, on condition of receiving payment of their expenses from the other side, amounting to £926 5s 4d. When in the following year (1811), the rival bill was introduced, the Council made strenuous exertions to get it modified, in the belief that it was wiser for them to act thus than to bring up their own measure anew. Mr Maitland of Eccles, who was sent to London to look after the town's interests in the matter, met with considerable success. In reporting the results, he stated that a new arrangement for the first year had been made, which assigned to the magistrates their due place

* Town Council Minutes.

in the Commission; that the original clause in the Act which conferred power to deepen the river as far up as the Caul, and which
in its operation would have endangered the mills and injured the
cattle market, had been so altered as to make the foot of Assembly
Street the boundary of the Trust; and that he had obtained the
insertion of a clause to provide for the improvement of the river
before any of the promoters who had subscribed money towards
accomplishing the purposes of the Act should be allowed to finger
a shilling of their shares.*

It was further reported by Mr Maitland, that though he had
not got the police clause cancelled which "proposed to attach £100
sterling annually during the currency of the bill from the common
funds of the burgh," the town would be virtually relieved from it,
"seeing that he had obtained a bond from Mr Maxwell of Terraughty, a leading promoter of the bill, to free and relieve them from
this most oppressive and unjust assessment." Finally, Mr Maxwell had come under an obligation to re-imburse the town for the
expenses—estimated at upwards of £450—incurred in opposing
the Act.† With some reluctance, the Council acquiesced in the
measure as thus modified, and it was brought into operation in
1812. It was provided that the Commissioners till first of November
that year should consist of the Dumfries magistrates, the deacon-
convener, and certain merchants and county gentlemen who had
each subscribed £100 or more to the fund raised for carrying the
Act; that in future the Commissioners of Supply for Dumfriesshire
and the Stewartry should at their annual Michaelmas meetings
nominate ten of their number each; and that the merchants and
shipowners of Dumfries should, three weeks prior to the first of
November every year, nominate six of their number each to
administer the Act.

As important operations were contemplated on the river, the
rates were made much higher than before. A duty of 1s 2d was
imposed on every ton of goods or merchandise imported or exported
except coals and lime, on which sixpence per ton was levied. A
duty of sixpence per ton register was charged on vessels from
foreign ports entering the river, and of twopence on vessels arriving from the coasts of the United Kingdom; and it was provided
that one penny per ton should be paid by all vessels anchoring at
or near Carsethorn, except such as were chartered to the port of
Dumfries; the limits of the port being from the Nith, opposite the
bottom of Assembly Street, to Southerness, and a point opposite to
it on the other side of the Solway.

Though considerable sums of money had been expended in
improving the river whilst it was under the management of the
Town Council, it had altered little since the time when the Scoto-

Irish ploughed its waters in the curraghs. The new Commissioners of the Nith aimed at making it navigable up to Dockfoot by large vessels; and with this laudable end in view, operations were commenced on a great scale, according to plans furnished by a distinguished civil engineer, Mr Hollingsworth. The works were of a varied nature. In the first instance the course of the stream was rendered less circuitous than before, by an extensive cutting on the Dumfries or Kingholm side, and another corresponding incision on the Galloway side at Nethertown ; secondly, an embankment was formed on both sides for the double purpose of fixing the new channel, and of rendering the adjacent lands less liable to be flooded ; thirdly, the river was deepened by excavations, dredgings, and the reduction by blasting of the annoying stratum of rock that lay right across its bed a little below Castledykes. The proprietor of Nethertown, Major M'Murdo, received no less a sum than £1548 15s as the price of the land given up by him for this undertaking ; and about £800 was paid for the ground taken on the Dumfries side—the town receiving as its share of this sum £246 16s 6d. For the cuttings upwards of £1000 was paid ; and the embankments must have cost at least as much. If to all these sums be added the cost of obtaining the Act of Parliament, £974 ; of survey, £51 ; of levelling, £20 ; of buoys fixed farther down the channel, £90; and of other works bearing on the great object they were all intended to subserve ; the improvements begun in 1812 must, when finished, have cost fully £7000.* The operations were superintended by a committee, of which Mr James M'Whir, merchant, was convener ; and such a high sense was entertained by the Commissioners of that gentleman's services in the matter, that, by way of acknowledgment, they voted him a sum of 250 guineas. When the works were nearly completed, in 1823, Mr M'Whir reported upon them to the Commissioners, and proposed a scheme for liquidating the debt that had been incurred. Mr Hollingsworth, he said, had engaged to secure for them seven feet of water at the Dock for two or three days during the time of spring tides ; which promise had been more than realised, as at such seasons the depth of water at Dockhead was now for four or five days eight feet, and at Dockfoot ten feet. He further explained that by the erection of a small stone jetty at Laghall, opposite Kingholm Quay, the channel there, which could formerly be forded ankle deep, was now eight feet deep at low water. The sum originally subscribed for the works was £9800, of which £7225 had been drawn by the treasurer ; and adding interest for eleven years, and the floating liabilities, about £2000, the total debt on the trust would amount to £13,000. The revenue since 1811 had been £11,367 9s 5d, or an average of £950 a year ; and

---

* Minutes of the Nith Navigation Commissioners.

there was every reason to expect that the annual income would soon reach £1000 or guineas. Mr M'Whir proceeded in his report to show that the best mode of repaying the loan was by borrowing £7000 on the credit of the revenue—a proposal which was adopted and acted upon.* He further stated that, " by the kind exertions of the magistrates," the sum of £400 would be placed at their disposal for the purpose of erecting a commodious harbour in the immediate vicinity of the town ; a vote to that amount having been obtained by ex-Provost Kerr from the Convention of Royal Burghs. Remembering the conflict between the promoters of the new Act and the Town Council, Mr M'Whir rather keenly contrasted the " liberal policy of our present local governors " with what he called " the persecutions formerly experienced " by their predecessors in office. In due time the money granted by the Convention was spent in the erection of a massive harbour wall at Dockhead—which, however, has been of little service to the shipping.

At a more recent date, other embankments were erected between Kingholm Quay and Kelton. The latest work of an extensive kind undertaken by the Nith Commissioners was the construction of a huge sea-dyke below Glencaple Quay, which cost no less a sum than £6000, and though it has had the desired effects of deepening and straightening the channel at that place, it is a matter of question whether these advantages have not been secured at too great an expense, considering how much the revenue has been reduced by the railways, and the difficulty which the shipping of the port have in competing with " the steeds of steam," which carry on the traffic of the district with a speed and regularity that cannot otherwise be rivalled. All the money hitherto spent in improving the Nith has failed to make it a good navigable river. Capacious vessels, drawing seven feet of water or so, can easily come up the estuary to within a few miles of Dumfries ; but after that, in spite of what Mr Hollingsworth and other engineers have done, difficulties commence which are only fairly overcome for the time being when the tidal flux is at least sixteen feet high. For these reasons the shipowners and merchants are beginning to think that, instead of trying to subdue the all but impracticable channel between the town and Glencaple Quay, they ought to connect them, or otherwise reach a deep sea harbour by a railway ; and thus (to use a nautical phrase) splice the perfect mode of land transit on the defective river transit, and secure for the Burgh the full benefits of both. Mr M'Whir, in his report (already quoted from), anticipated that the revenue of the Nith, which had yielded an average of £950 annually from 1811 to 1823, would soon increase to £1000 and upwards. In 1831 it amounted

* Town Council Minutes.

to £1072 17s 4d : it has been occasionally a few pounds higher since ; but as soon as the railway system of the district came into full play, the commerce of the river declined, and it is now in a state of great depression.

Long before " Burns's time," Bridgend had become a populous town ; but even after the beginning of the current century, when it numbered nearly two thousand inhabitants, it had little business and no local government, save what was exercised by the County justices and the superior of the soil. On account of the latter circumstance, the town became tenanted by more than its fair share of lawless characters: wandering tinklers, who, wearied with camp life in Galloway or Annandale, found readily within it welcome rest and refuge ; runners of contraband goods from the Isle of Man, who could usually count on safe lodgings in Bridgend ; while of native poachers and other roughs it reckoned not a few. Being located in a different county, the Dumfries magistrates had no jurisdiction over it whatever. Tam o' Shanter eluded the Alloway witches by putting a running stream between him and them, and burgh delinquents in the same way often effected their escape by wading the Nith at its fords, or crossing it by the bridge, well assured that the officers of justice durst not pursue them into Galloway. When criminals were actually followed into Bridgend by those having the requisite authority, they frequently baffled the beagles of the law by diving into a labyrinth of underground buildings which lay near the river's brink, where whisky was distilled in defiance of the gauger, and where a gipsy gang held rule under their chief, Ryes Aitken, who was nearly as great a local celebrity in his day as Jock Johnston, or even Big Will Bailie.   There was much of exaggeration in the statement attributed to a London magistrate—Sir John Fielding—that the metropolitan detectives could trace a thief over the entire kingdom if he did not get to the Gorbals of Glasgow or Bridgend of Dumfries ; for in that case they had to give up the chase. But the latter was unquestionably a somewhat lawless town till, by its erection, in 1810, into a burgh of barony, under the name of Maxwelltown, it acquired a magistracy of its own. The charter was obtained greatly through the exertions of the late Mr Philip Forsyth of Nithside; and in recognition of his services in this and other respects he had the honour of being elected first provost of the burgh.* Maxwelltown has long been as peaceable a place as

---

* The town, which was long without any proper local government, has now police authorities under Rutherford's Act, as well as a baronial magistracy and council.   In a little tract, entitled " Reminiscences of Maxwelltown," the present Mr Forsyth, son of the gentleman named in the text, thus notices the beneficial changes experienced by the burgh :—" A clean, tidy, thriving town it is now, and worthy sister of mim-mou'd Meg o' Nith, who sits so daintily on the other side ; but in the early years of this century, down till 1810, Bridgend was one of the most disorderly clachans in the kingdom. . . . . ,

any in the British dominions ; and, with its extensive iron foundries (a) and woollen manufactures (of which we shall afterwards speak), and its large timber works and saw-mill (the latter the property of Messrs Gillies & Son), it possesses no inconsiderable extent of trade. Its inhabitants have rapidly increased during the present century, and it is now the most populous town of Kirkcudbrightshire : population in 1871, 4109.

By the establishment of magisterial jurisdiction, and the facility of punishing offenders, the burgh has progressed in the right direction, and it is now not surpassed by any town I know of as regards the general moral character of the inhabitants."

(a) The two founderies were Maxwell's, at Stakeford, and Caldow and M'Kinnell's, off King Street. Both establishments came into the exclusive possession of Mr M'Kinnell ; and they were closed when his business was concentrated in extensive new works erected at Pleasance.

CHAPTER LIV.

THE year 1817 was a melancholy one for Dumfries. It was to the burgh what the day after an exhaustive carouse is to a repentant prodigal. For a hundred years or more the town had been living beyond its means ; and latterly it had been incurring heavy liabilities, which became daily more burdensome and pressing. Great improvements had been effected ; important public buildings had been raised for beauty and use : all these undertakings being excellent in their way—only, they were too numerous and costly for the revenue of the town, even had that been rigidly economised. But frequently the feu duties and rents, of which it was in a considerable measure made up, were badly looked after ; expensive law suits were recklessly entered into ; and every year a good round sum was spent by the authorities on what were delicately called " entertainments," which in plain English meant eating and drinking at the expense of the public. Perhaps the facilities given by Mr Staig for obtaining loans from the Bank of Scotland during the long period in which he was at the head of affairs tended to make the Council additional extravagant. The bank was deemed by them an inexhaustible mine, into which they could never dig too deeply, and a long array of bills bearing heavy discounts bore witness to the persistency with which they drew upon its resources. What with lavish outlays for objects proper and improper, money borrowed at excessive rates, expensive litigation, and losses incurred from defaulting feuars, tenants, and collectors, the burgh was brought to the verge of bankruptcy.

An unfortunate circumstance occurred in the summer of 1816 which precipitated the crisis. The chamberlain or treasurer resigned his office ; and when his accounts came to be examined it was found that he was the town's debtor to the extent of at least £1500, a sum he was unable to refund.* His cautioner or surety, Mr John Maitland of Eccles, was called upon to make up the deficit ; but before he did so the creditors of the burgh became alarmed, and some of them pressed their claims unmercifully—in particular the Humane Society, which, with a rigour at variance

* Town Council Minutes.

with its name, demanded instant payment of £1000 it had lent to the town. Whilst this body clamoured and threatened the trustees of the deceased Robert Wilson, tanner, commenced a process against the Council, without previous warning, for the payment of £800, for which bills had been given. The dilemma into which the authorities were thrown is indicated by the minute of a meeting held by them on the 14th of April. Mr Maitland, it appears, had received notice that unless he paid the money for which he had become bound diligence would be used against him ; and at the above meeting it was announced that no communication had been received from him in reply. It is then stated that as an arrestment had been used in Mr Maitland's hands, at the instance of Mr Wilson's trustees, "the Council authorise the magistrates, or any other members of Council, to enact themselves as cautioners in the Sheriff-Court books to make the arrested funds forthcoming, and thereby obtain letters of loosing the arrestment used in his hands, and in the hands of the town's debtors, tenants, &c. ; and such of the members of Council as grant such bonds of caution, the Council declare the obligation to be for behoof of the town, and the Council become bound to relieve them of their cautionary engagements ; and until this is accomplished the meeting delay giving any directions with regard to the diligence against Mr Maitland."

At another meeting held soon afterwards it was intimated that at least temporary relief had been obtained by Messrs Shortt and Locke, the town clerks, having subscribed a bond of caution for loosing the arrestments ; and that Mr Maitland was about to sell part of an estate belonging to him, so as to be able to satisfy the town. During this breathing time a committee appointed to consider the revenue, for the purpose of introducing more economy into its management, laid before the Council an elaborate and interesting report on the subject. It showed that the total annual revenue of the burgh was £2306 7s 11d, made up as follows :— Permanent feu duties payable by the town's vassals, £124 4s ; rents of lands, houses, cellars, and timber yards, £484 11s 9d ; rents of mills and granaries, £546 15s 3d ; teinds payable out of the lands of Drum and others, including small teinds from town's vassals, £68 11s 2d ; customs payable at the bridge, trone, three ports, &c., the average of which for the last seven years was £656 ; impost on ale, which had yielded on the same average £100 ; fees for admission of burgesses, also on an average of seven years, £50 ; church seats, the rent from which had latterly been £176 5s 9d, but to which the committee proposed an increase of £100. Deducting £13 1s 1d as stipend payable to the minister of St. Michael's Church, the net revenue from all these sources amounted to £2,293 6s 10d.*

The expenditure, as already stated, had been gradually, year after year, getting more out of keeping with the income ; and how to proportion them, so as to let the difference be on the safe side, was the most difficult part of the task assigned to the committee. With the view of securing this desirable result they proposed means for augmenting the revenue as well as reducing the expenditure. The committee stated that the interest on the debts first required to be dealt with : these consisting of sums permanently placed in the town's hands for charitable and useful purposes, and for the greater part of which heritable security was granted betwixt the years 1730 and 1740, over the mills, Milldamhead, Dock, four inclosures of Barkerland, customs at the bridge, and other duties. Of these there were mortified to the Hospital and poor, £2201 6s 6d ; to the schools, £1119 4s 1d ; to two poor individuals under Paterson's deed, £20 : in all, £3340 10s 7d. Then, secondly, there were temporary loans amounting to £18,898 9s ; current bills, £1399 5s 8d ; accounts due to tradesmen, agents, &c., £1422 19s 8d ; interest of these debts up till Whitsunday, 1817, £945 3s 1d ; deducting rents and feu duties in arrear and falling due, £1454 6s 9d ; and computed sum to be owing by the late chamberlain, £1300 ; the debts of the town were £23,252 1s 2d —the interest on which was £1162 12s. The committee's reductions under this head were very trifling, but they suggested various changes in regard to the clerks' fees, salaries of subordinate officials, and outlay for repairs, by which a saving of several hundred pounds a year might be effected. In regard to the municipal feasts, they proposed that " all entertainments be laid aside, excepting the annual dinner at the election of magistrates, and that even considerably restricted in the amount usually contracted."* It was admitted that about £80 a year had been of late spent in this way ; and the committee, after suggesting that the allowance should be restricted to fifteen guineas for the Michaelmas dinner, relented so far as to add five guineas for other festive incidents " of an unavoidable nature."

A mode of letting the small feus so as to be more productive, and several other proposals for increasing the revenue, were embodied in the report ; the annual expenditure as modified being set down as follows :—Interest, £1162 12s ; repairs, £100 ; management, £144 19s 10d ; salaries to ministers, schoolmasters, chamberlain, fiscal, billet-master, jailor, officers, precentor, and bellman, £512 5s 10d : total expenditure, £1919 17s 8d ; which deducted from the revenue, £2293 6s 10d, leaves a surplus of £373 9s 2d ; which balance, however, must be reduced to £250 in order to allow a small contingency fund of £123 9s 2d a year. " This sum of £250," says the committee, " will certainly not speedily

* Town Council Minutes.

produce any important reduction of the debt of the town, but if its operation as a sinking fund be allowed to accumulate annually, it will, with the operation of compound interest, in the course of thirty-three years, fully discharge the whole debts, except what is called the mortified money, amounting to £3340 ; or in twenty-two years and a half one-half of these debts will be discharged." The committee noticed to deplore the embarrassments occasioned by the various law-suits in which the town was unfortunately concerned, and very wisely recommended that in future, whenever practicable, all disputes with other parties should be settled by amicable arrangement or arbitration.

Finally, the committee proposed that the revenues of the burgh should be handed over to trustees for behoof of the creditors ; and that an effort should be made to negotiate a loan on heritable security, with which to pay off such debts as were most pressing. The report, after being slightly altered, was adopted by the Council ; and a committee of the creditors having approved of the proposal for the appointment of trustees, Bailie Barker, his son Mr John Barker, and Mr John Fergusson, ex-convener of the Trades, were named as such, with Messrs Thomson, Johnston, and Miller as a committee of advice from the Council ; and Mr William Gordon, senior agent for the treasurer of the Kirk-Session, the preses of the Humane Society, and any other claimants to the extent of £500 who chose to attend, as a committee of the creditors.* On the death of Mr Fergusson, in 1820, Mr Adam Rankine and Mr James Locke were appointed trustees in his stead. For nearly seven years the public purse was out of the Council's hands ; but at the close of 1824 they recovered hold of it, in virtue of an arrangement with Mr Robert Taylor of Broomlands, whereby he gave them a loan of £20,000 at 3½ per cent., with which they liquidated nearly all the debt, and relieved the trustees of their

---

* By way of security, the trustees obtained sazine of certain properties on the 23d of July, 1817, which are entered as follows in the "Abridgement of Register of Sazines," published under the authority of the 31 and 32 Vic., cap. 34 :—The lands of Kingholm and Powsands (under exception) ; the lands and farm of Milldamhead ; the lands of Upper and Lower Dock, and garden there, and teinds ; the customs and revenues arising from the bridges over the Nith ; the trone and three ports, meal market, flesh market, and weighing machine, with the tolls and customs due to and demandable by the town ; the lands called Greensand-beds, with the banks of the river at the head thereof, and the other bank at or near Pudding Flat, and teinds ; the superiority of the forty shilling land of Over and Nether Netherwood and Langholm, with the mill and salmon fishing of the same, and four acres of land on the north side of the Dovecote of Castledykes ; part of the lands of Whinnyhill (Gastown), with the feu duties thereof ; the old Court-house and Guard-house ; the shop under the old Court-house stair ; a house and timber yard adjoining thereto ; the remaining undivided and unappropriated ground in Locharmoss ; the granary above the meal market, and cellar under the same ; the Back Millhole, and shop and room.

onerous duties.* As we shall soon see, the relief experienced was only of temporary duration : the incubus that had been rolled away soon returning, like the stone of Sisyphus, with redoubled violence, to make wasting havoc of the town's inheritance. As security for the large sum thus advanced, Mr Taylor received a bond over the property and income of the burgh ; it being part of the bargain with him that unless the principal were paid up in five years he would become entitled to the rate of interest then current. In the deeds was embodied a very comprehensive and detailed statement of the town's income and expenditure, which enables us to understand precisely its financial position at the time. We subjoin the substance of the document :—

PROPERTY AND INCOME.

Branch I.—Lands.

1. The farm of Kingholm, about a mile below the burgh, extending to sixty or sixty-one Scots acres ; rent, £150 a year. The property, from its situation on the Nith, and "the intrinsic goodness of the soil," cannot be worth less than £5500.

2. The lands of Milldamhead, lying on both sides of the great turnpike road from Dumfries to Carlisle, twenty acres in extent : rent, £55 ; valued at £1700.

3. The grazing called Dock and Dock Park, containing six acres : let at £55. This property lies on the Nith, immediately below the town, and is "the richest grazing ground in the south of Scotland ; but its value must depend not on that, but on its local situation for warehouses or trade, as it forms the harbour of the town during spring tides. The beauty of the scenery also renders the property valuable for villas, on a part of it at least. Though the burgh would not incline to dispose of it unless under particular circumstances, for the improvement of the place, yet, in the view of the estimate proposed," if offered for sale it would not be worth less than £2000.

4. Garden and houses at Dock Park : rent, £6 10s ; value, £400.

5. Millgreen, on the opposite side of the river : rent, £22 ; value, £650.

6. Garden at the mills : rent, £2 2s ; value, £100.

Branch II.—Feu Duties or Ground Rents.

These are secured on the properties, and amount annually to £119, with teind duties to the extent of £4 7s 4d. In general the owners of the houses built on these feus would be glad to relieve their property from the burden, and to them they are worth at least twenty times the yearly rental ; but they may be entered as valued at £1800.

* Town Council Minutes.

Branch III.—Rents of Buildings.

1. Cellar and granary at Meal Market : rent, £12 ; value, £200.

2. The warehouse and shops in the Mid-Steeple buildings ; rent, £47 5s ; value, £1400.

3. Stable-yard at Sands : rent, £2 ; as for the benefit of the public street the yard ought to be removed, no value is put upon it.

4. Shop and school-room in Bank Street, formerly occupied as a salt-market : rent, £20 ; value, £350.

5. Timber yards on the river : rent, £16 15s. These ought to be removed to afford more accommodation for the cattle market, and therefore they are left unvalued.

Branch IV.—Corn Mills.

1. Flour mill : rent, £220.

2. Barley mill : rent, £60.

3. Oat mill : rent, £171.

4. Waulk and frieze mill : rent, £31 10s ; value of the whole, £7215.

5. Granaries attached to the mills, with ground behind : rent, £57 5s 3d ; value, £855.

Branch V.—Customs and Market Dues.

1. Pontage or bridge dues : rent, £434.

2. Fees levied on goods brought into the markets : let at £47 10s.

3. Fees levied on grain brought into the markets : let at £47 10s.

4. Fees at Flesh Market : let at £21.

5. Fees at weighing-machine : let at £40 10s.

With regard to the first article, it is explained that the right of the burgh to uplift fees from all black cattle going southwards from Galloway, the lower parts of Ayrshire, and the north of Ireland, extends for twenty miles along the river, and therefore commands the whole of such cattle. It is added that the right applies to all horses, sheep, mercandise, &c., and produces a steady rent which must improve with any improvement of the country at large. The value, therefore, cannot be estimated at less than twenty times such rent, namely, £11,800.

Branch VI.—Impost on Ale.

Average annual amount, £104. Deducting ten per cent. for expense of collection, £94 is left ; and the value of the tax, at fifteen times the sum, is £1400.

Branch VII.—Fees Payable on the Admission of Persons to the Freedom of the Burgh or Corporation.

Annual average, £89. " This is a permanent fee, and, according to increased population, must necessarily increase." At fifteen times the present average, the value is £1335.

Branch VIII.—*The Rents of Seats*

In two Established Churches, £300 ; which, fifteen times multiplied, amounts to £4500.

Branch IX.—*Miscellaneous.*

1. The building occupied as the Council Chamber and town clerk's offices, which is proposed to be sold whenever the lease of the old Court-house expires ; value, £500.

2. Green-sands, and other vacant grounds, worth at least £525.

Total amount of the town's annual rent in 1824, £2142 4s 7d. Total value of the town's property and income, £42,230.

Charges, or Outlay.

Branch I.—*Public and Parochial Burdens.*

I. Communion elements, £30 ; stipend to minister of St. Michael's Church, £11 14s 7d ; ditto to minister of Troqueer, £1 19s 6d ; fees to Convention of Burghs and Exchequer, £13.

Branch II.—*Salaries and Miscellaneous Allowances,*

Stated or occasional, amounting in all to £528 16s, including £53 6s 8d to magistrates and conveners for burgess tickets ; £4 18s, " trades' dollars and wines, according to custom of the burgh ;" and £15 15s for annual entertainment at election of magistrates.

Total annual expenditure, £579 10s 1d.

From the foregoing statement very cheering but somewhat fallacious deductions were drawn by the authorities. As the debt, which was upwards of £23,000 in 1817, had now diminished to £20,000, they fancied that they would be able to go on reducing it at even a greater rate. There was an annual revenue of £2142 4s 7d ; the difference between that sum and the annual expenditure as given above was no less a sum than £1542 14s 6d. Deducting from that the interest of Mr Taylor's loan (£20,000) at 3½ per cent., left £862 14s 6d ; and diminishing that still further by allowing £362 14s 6d for new works and repairs, there would still be available £500 a year of surplus, which scrupulously reserved as a sinking fund would be sufficient in forty years or so to sweep away the entire debt, if such should be deemed expedient ; and at all events the Council would be thereby enabled to pay off all pressing creditors without having to part with a single rood of land.*

* Town Council Minutes.

That the retrenchment resolved upon was scrupulously carried out may be inferred from the following Council minute, dated 3rd July, 1827 :—"The said day Mr Barker reported that yesterday he had paid to Mr Taylor £1000 in part of his debt, being two years' saving fund from the revenues of the town." But it unfortunately so happened that the gentleman who had opportunely come to the relief of the town in 1824 now intimated that he wished to have the loan repaid in 1830, as he needed the money.* This demand seems to have thoroughly perplexed and disheartened the Council. Possessed of the loan, they had difficulties enough with which to contend ; deprived of it, they would be overwhelmed with embarrassments, unless they escaped from them by repeating the humiliating expedient—adopted too often by their predecessors—of selling another portion of the burgh's landed property, which it had possessed for ages. They saw no possibility of obtaining a second loan at a moderate rate of interest, to enable them to pay off the existing one ; retrenchment had been carried to the furthest limit ; they could not hope for any such increase of revenue as would afford any sensible relief. "We must therefore," said the Council, "submit to dire necessity, and dispose of the patrimonial acres, as the only means within our reach for removing our difficulties and maintaining the public credit."

Accordingly the sale of certain subjects was resolved upon ; and Mr Brand of Mountainhall and Mr Pagan of Curriestanes, on being appointed to value them, reported to the following effect :— The lands of Kingholm, £7160, if divided into six lots as they suggested ; or if offered whole, the upset might be £6300. Dock Park or Kennedy's Garden, if sold for building lots, £1120 ; gardener's house and offices, £380 ; but if the whole were put up at one lot, the upset might be £1200. The lands of Milldamhead, worth £100 an acre—in all, £1925 ; but as they were burdened with a high stipend of £5 12s, it was suggested that £600 should be the upset price of the portion north of the English road, and £1120 of the part lying on the other side. The two-storey house in Bank Street, built for a salt store, was valued at £200.† On the 19th of July, 1827, the two estates were sold by public auction : Kingholm being bought by Mr John Hannah of Hannah-field, for £6300 ;‡ the north half of Milldamhead, by Mr James Black, for £800 ; and the south half by Mr John Richardson, for

---

* Town Council Minutes. † Ibid.

‡ As showing the value of the same property in 1712, we quote the following Town Council minute, dated on the 26th of September that year :— "The land enclosed in the Kingholm, consisting of forty-two acres of plowable ground or thereby, lately enclosed, together with the houses thereon, was by public roup let to John M'Nish, deacon of the weavers, for three years after Martinmas for twenty-two pounds sterling yearly."

£1120. For the other lots there were no offers ; and fortunately, on this account, the Dock Park remains to this day the property of the town. Some years later the house in Bank Street was sold for £300.* About the same period the six acres of land, with the feus, on which the village of Glencaple is built, passed into private hands, all except a small strip which was sold about nine years ago to ex-Provost Gordon for £50.

It is a matter of lasting regret that the sacrifice of Kingholm and Milldamhead was rendered unavoidable by sheer thriftlessness. Since the date of the sale their market value has been more than doubled ; and were the rents yielded by them poured into the public treasury, the Council would be able to embark in many useful schemes, which, under existing circumstances, they dare not think of. But this lament is vain ; and some consolation arises from the fact that the lavish outlay long indulged in secured not a few lasting improvements, which a timorous financial policy would have left undone. By means of £8220 obtained in the above way, the payment in whole or in part of the sum owing by the ex-chamberlain, and other sums borrowed on the remaining property and on the revenue, the Council paid their principal creditor, and got the town out of the troubled waters in which it was nearly wrecked.

Notwithstanding all the sacrifices of this nature that have been made since the reign of James V., when they are supposed to have commenced, till the present day, Dumfries still possesses no inconsiderable amount of landed property. Most of it is disponed in feu, or is held by parties who have acquired possession on titles originally bad, but which are legalized through prescription, although it is believed there are some who hold burgh land without any title whatever, and whose claims therefore are susceptible of being challenged. A piece of moss at Stoop, about twelve acres in extent, was sold on the 7th of February, 1863, for £52, to the holder of a right of pasturage over it, he being desirous of rendering it by culture more productive. Altogether about 985 acres are held from the town by charter, including not only what was feued as moss, but what was known as the common lands of the burgh. Most of this land is under cultivation of some kind, not more than 101 acres of it being left in its primitive mossy or boggy condition. Besides the chartered and moss lands, there are—(1) The Greensands (formerly called the Upper Sandbeds), including Puddingflat, near Albany Place ; (2) the Academy grounds ; (3) the Dock and Dock-yard ; (4) a portion of the Dock Park, south of Hamilton's feu ; (5) lands at Mills and Mill-green ; and (6) land at the gunpowder magazine below Kingholm quay. The revenue yielded by these subjects varies. For the year ended 15th September,

---

* Town Council Minutes.

1866, it amounted to £65 15s ; from the chartered lands the same year, the sum of £247 19s 11¾d was exigible ; in all £313 14s 11¾d. The revenue under the second head included £7 10s 5d for properties in the town, but exclusive of the feus that lie southward of the Infirmary (these being included in the landward part), and exclusive of what is known as small feus ; and one feu of 2s in the burgh roods, not entered in the chamberlain's books.*

Frequent mention has been made of the money bequeathed to the burgh for educational and charitable purposes. It is usually spoken of as a debt, which it undoubtedly is—only, like the National Debt, the money cannot be called up, but remains in perpetual trust. As a sequel in some degree to the monetary operations just described, the whole of this mortified money, amounting to £4205 14s 1d, was in 1832 formally made over by the magistrates and Council in a bond and disposition to themselves. From this deed† we take the following statement of the bequests :—

1. Robert Johnston, of the parish of St. Ann, Blackfriars', London, by his will dated 30th of September, 1639, left £600 "to be employed in stock or wadsett of lands, for the perpetual yearly maintenance of the aged, blind, lame, and impotent people" of Dumfries.

2. John Raining, of the city of Norwich, bequeathed, on the 28th of March, 1722, £500 to be let out at interest or laid out in the purchase of lands, for the maintenance of six poor widows of the town, sixty years of age or upwards, at the rate of 12s to each, quarterly ; and the surplus to be applied in paying a good capable schoolmaster to teach poor fatherless boys English, Latin, and arithmetic.

3. Mrs Marion Archibald, relict of Dr George Archibald, physician in Dumfries, left, on 20th September, 1733, £60, to be laid out on good security, for the better maintenance of two poor

---

* It is supposed by many that the ancient ceremony of Riding the Marches was designed to show that all the land within the boundary thus described belonged absolutely to the burgh ; but this extreme view admits of question. We think it probable that when the town was royally chartered all the lands within the royalty not in the lawful possession of any one would be granted by the Crown to the burgh ; but the Crown would scarcely prejudice the rights of other superiors, and consequently private parties might have held lands within the marches perambulated ; just as, on the other hand, the burgh held land outside these marches—in Troqueer for instance, where at present some parties hold their lands and possessions as vassals of Dumfries. The Riding of the Marches was, we are inclined to think, originated and continued for the purpose of keeping in remembrance the extent and situation of the territory over which the magistrates had jurisdiction, civil and criminal ; and it may have taken the place of an older practice mentioned by Lord Stair—that of whipping boys at march stones, in order to make them remember the boundary line for life.—*Institutes of the Law of Scotland*, third edition, 1759, pp. 716-17.

† Embodied in the Minutes of Council, 1832.

widows, not under sixty years of age, and relicts of burgesses and inhabitants of the burgh.

4. James and William Moorhead left for the erection of an hospital as already fully set forth in this work.

5. Charles, Duke of Queensberry, gave, on the 11th of October, 1742, £300 for behoof of the said hospital.

6. Mrs Ann Dalzell or Hopkins, relict of Robert Hopkins, left, on the 30th of December, 1768, £100 for the same purpose.

7. James Brand of Drumclyre left, on the 29th of December, 1790, £100 for the same purpose.

8. Miss Lilias Simpson, on the 29th of December, 1790, bequeathed £10 for a like purpose.

9. William Johnston, of Madeira, left £100 for relief of the poor in the parish, as recorded in a Council minute of 30th March, 1801.

10. Mrs Janet Hay or Gillespie left £10 for behoof of the hospital (date not recorded).

11. Samuel Donaldson, of London, left £200, minus legacy duty ; one half for the poor, and the other half for the benefit of a schoolmaster, as recorded in a Council minute of 13th October, 1813.

12. Provost George Bell of Conheath left £100; the interest to be paid to the schoolmaster authorised by the magistrates and Council to teach English, by way of addition to his salary.

All these sums, amounting to £2382 2s, are solely vested in the magistrates and Council ; and those subjoined are intrusted to them in conjunction with other bodies.

13. John Paterson left, on the 22nd of February, 1717, 400 merks Scots, or £22 4s 5⅓d sterling, the ordinary interest of 8000 merks, for maintaining a well-qualified schoolmaster within the burgh "to the end of the world," to teach children in a free school, without receiving from them any fee or reward, in the Latin rudiments, grammar, rhetoric, classic authors, and Greek New Testament. Then, by another later deed, Mr Paterson left 200 merks, or £11 2s 2⅔d sterling, the interest of 4000 merks, for maintaining a well-qualified schoolmaster to teach within the burgh, "to the end of the world," the children of burgesses, indwellers, and burden-bearers, and eight children of the poorest sort of merchant burgesses and burden-bearers of the burgh, in writing, arithmetic, book-keeping, and navigation. An additional sum of 3000 merks was bequeathed by Mr Paterson to enable the magistrates and Council of Dumfries, and ministers of the parish, in whom the principal sums were vested, to uplift the same, as secured by bonds on certain lands, and invest them in some other way if deemed advisable.

14. The before-named George Bell bequeathed £50 to the magistrates, Council, and Kirk-Session for behoof of the hospital.

15. Various legacies, accumulated to £906 10s, were vested in the magistrates, Council, parish ministers, and Kirk-Session, for behoof of the poor in the burgh and parish.

16. By a resolution of the directors of the Hospital, dated 7th March, 1831, £35 17s 3d was set apart from the ordinary funds of that charity.

So much for the mortified money which figures so prominently in the ledger of the burgh, and gives life to some of its chief educational and charitable institutions.

CHAPTER LV.

THOUGH for many years after 1817 the rulers of the town were
much engrossed by matters of finance, they did not neglect other
public questions; and the enterprise of private parties united with
theirs in promoting several beneficial measures. A new approach
was made to the burgh from the north; the site of the cattle
market on the Whitesands was enlarged and paved; a free school
was built on the Greensands in 1821; and the Mid-Steeple and St.
Michael's steeple were each supplied with a new clock, the cost of
both, defrayed by subscription, being about £190. Just when the
monetary shoe might have been supposed to pinch most severely,
the lieges clubbed their shillings and guineas on an expensive
article of luxury with which to decorate their chief, though the
town could barely pay its debts. This was a magnificent double
chain of gold, which cost within a trifle of £150. It was publicly
presented to the Provost, Mr John Kerr, on the 3rd of August,
1822; the Rev. Dr Scott, minister of St. Michael's, making an
eloquent presentation speech in name of the subscribers, and the
Provost responding in appropriate terms. At the next meeting of
Council a minute was adopted recommending his honour to wear
the smaller part of the chain constantly, but to reserve the longer
and heavier part, with a medallion that is attached to it, for
extraordinary occasions." This advice is still acted upon; and on
great days the Provost also wears a rich ermined robe purchased
by the Council in 1862.

The modern part of the town—commenced in the north, after
the building of the new bridge—received an important addition
when the New Assembly Rooms were erected, in 1825; and the
following year was signalised by a great event—the lighting of
the burgh with gas, provided by a company having a capital of
£8000. Almost contemporaneously with this increase of material
illumination, there came into existence a society which has been
the means of diffusing much intellectual light—we refer to the

Dumfries and Maxwelltown Mechanics' Institute. It was started on the 15th of March, 1825, at a meeting held for the purpose in the Trades' Hall, presided over by Provost Thomson ; and in the course of the following year it was in full working order. The members of the original committee are entered in the minute-book as follows:—Provost Thomson, Mr John Gregan, Mr William M'Gowan, Mr Connechie, Dr T. T. Duncan, Mr Grierson, Mr J. Charteris, Convener Anderson, Mr John Gibson, Mr Thomas Roberts, Dr H. Duncan, Mr Barker, Mr Walter Newall, Mr Thomas Watson, and Mr James Wilson. At first the annual subscription was 8s per annum ; for children of members, and apprentices, 4s. When the Institute was ten years old it numbered 150 members· Its fortunes have been very varied : more than once it almost ceased to exist, and was only kept alive by the zealous efforts of Mr William Mundell, grocer ; Mr Thomas Roberts, carver and gilder ; Mr John Bell, ironmonger ; Mr James Charteris, turner ; Mr Alexander Crombie, architect ; Mr William C. Aitken, brass-founder ; Dr W. A. F. Browne, long the able president of the Institute, and others of its early promoters. Fully twenty years ago, when the Institute was in a somewhat sickly condition, Mr Christopher Harkness, afterwards provost of the burgh, became its secretary ; and from that date it has grown in size and im-proved in health. It is now, and has been for a lengthened period, one of the most prosperous societies of the kind in the United Kingdom. There are connected with it an excellent reading-room, a well-selected library of nearly 8000 volumes, a course of lectures during the winter, and classes for young lads whose early education has been neglected. The terms are only 4s a year for adult males, 3s for females, and 2s for apprentices. Usually the membership numbers between 600 and 700. A very elegant and commodious hall, built for the Institute from a design by Mr Alexander Fraser, architect, was opened about the close of 1861. It has sitting accommodation for 1200 persons, and cost about £1500. (a)

(a) Besides the library and reading-room, the Institute supplied the community during the winter months with an attractive lecture or other entertainment every Monday evening ; and the public were also indebted to the committee for two industrial exhibitions. The opening of the Ewart Public Library in 1903 rendered it unnecessary for the Institute to retain its reading-room or continue to lend out books. It was therefore resolved to transfer the whole of these to the Ewart Public Library ; and for the present to restrict the efforts of the committee to the winter course of lectures and entertainments. At the annual meeting in 1905 it was stated that the membership had largely diminished in consequence of the changed conditions, and that the lectures might have to be abandoned—which would certainly be a serious public loss—if they were not better supported. The volumes trans-ferred to the Ewart Public Library consisted of three collections—1, the Mechanics' Institute Library ; 2, the Dumfries Public Library, in the forma-tion of which Burns had taken a part, and which the Institute had acquired ; 3, the collection bequeathed to the Institute by the Rev. W. Dodds—6995

One of the local journalists, writing on the 5th September, 1826, thus notices the improvements to which the introduction of gas formed a sort of climax.   "For a long period," says the writer, " Dumfries was so stationary that it might have been included in the list of what an Irishman calls *finished towns.* But a new spirit has gone abroad.   If we consider the number of streets in Dumfries and Maxwelltown that have been finished, planned, and partly executed within the last few years, the tenements rebuilt, the houses gutted to make shops of, or in other respects remodelled and repaired—the marvels, in a word, worked by Messrs Sinclair and Howat, Newall and Inman, Brown, Hair, and many others, we are quite sure that the original 'shooters of the Siller Gun,' were they to rise from their graves at this moment, would scarcely be able to recognise the ancient burgh they lived, died, and earned their bread in.   The widening of English Street, and the approach by the Townhead, are both very great improvements ; and strangers visiting us from the South and North must now receive favourable impressions of the cleanliness and neatness that characterise Dumfries from the moment they approach the shores of the Nith."

One of the changes involved the removal of a large old pile called the Turnpike, the town house of the Lag family, and in which the noted persecutor Sir Robert Grierson spent the latest years of his life, and died in 1736.   It is pretty generally known that Sir Walter Scott depicted Sir Robert under the title of Redgauntlet, in the romance of the same name ; but the facts are known to few, that the monkey companion of the aged knight, Major Weir, had a veritable existence, and that the " cat's cradle,"

volumes in all, but the majority of them so dilapidated that they had to be discarded.

It was in 1898 that Mr Andrew Carnegie, the munificent millionaire, who had been asked by Provost Glover and others to embrace Dumfries in his scheme for Free Libraries, proffered a sum of £10,000 to the burgh of Dumfries and Maxwelltown, provided they adopted the Free Libraries Act and furnished a site.   The site was immediately forthcoming as a gift from Mr Thomas M'Kie and Miss M'Kie.   The burghs adopted the Act ; and a bill, brought into Parliament by Sir R. T. Reid, was carried to enable burghs and parishes adjoining each other to combine for the purposes of the Act.   Plans, prepared by Mr Alan B. Crombie (son of the Mr Crombie mentioned in the text) were approved of ; and the foundation-stone was laid on the 13th Oct., 1899, by Miss M'Kie.   Mr and Mrs Carnegie, Sir Robert and Lady Reid, were present at the ceremony ; and the day's proceedings, which included the presentation of the freedom of the burgh to Mr Carnegie, were closed with a banquet in the evening, at which the Provost presided.   On the suggestion of Mr Carnegie the building was named after the late Mr W. Ewart, long member for the burghs, and author of the first Free Libraries Act.   At the opening, in 1904—a ceremony which Miss M'Kie gracefully performed—-Mr Ewart's two daughters were present.   The Library is in the management of a committee, appointed by the Town Councils, partly from themselves and partly from the community ; and its admirable catalogue, compiled by the librarian, Mr G. W. Shirley, contains a short history of the foundation.

where the curious creature slept, was a remote turret of the Turnpike that had been built for a place of observation in ancient times.*

The inquiry into the town's pecuniary matters made the circumstances painfully prominent that some of the legal deeds by which its property and privileges were held had been lost or destroyed. Lest injurious results should follow, the burgh's legal agent in Edinburgh was instructed to take steps for obtaining a confirmation of its chartered rights. On the 8th of May, 1827, the Provost (Mr William Thomson) intimated to the Council that the agent had succeeded in procuring, at an expense of £144 15s, "a renewed charter of confirmation by his present Majesty of the former charter granted to this burgh by the sovereigns of this part of the United Kingdom, in which all the privileges, immunities, jurisdiction, and customs pertaining to the burgh were particularly and specially enumerated and confirmed." It was further reported by the Provost that on the 23rd of the preceding month public infeftment had been taken on the new charter at the market cross, a record of which would be duly entered in the registers of sasines for the burgh and county. By the same royal grant the burgh acquired a right of guildry, which it did not previously possess.† The dean, annually elected by the Council, had no extensive jurisdiction; but the charter of 1827, when given effect to, converted him into a dean of guild, increased his powers considerably, and gave him a court and officers of his own. Mr John Barker held the office in its simple form when the new law came into force; and he having resigned it, was thereupon

---

* The Laird of Lag and his favourites are so racily described by Wandering Willie, in Scott's romance of "Redgauntlet," that we must here introduce a portion of the sketch. "There sat the Laird his leesome lane, excepting that he had beside him a great, ill-favoured jackanape, that was a special pet of his, a cankered beast it was, and mony an ill-natured trick it played—ill to please it was, and easily angered—ran about the haill castle, chattering and yowling, and pinching and biting folk, especially before ill-weather or disturbances in the State. Sir Robert ca'd it Major Weir, after the warlock that was burnt; and few folk liked either the name or the conditions of the creature—they thought there was something in it by ordinar'. . . . Sir Robert sat, or I should say lay, in a great armed chair, wi' his grand velvet gown and his feet on a cradle—for he had baith gout and gravel—and his face looked as gash and ghastly as Satan's. Major Weir sat opposite to him in a red laced coat, and the Laird's wig on his head; and aye as Sir Robert girned wi' pain, the jackanape girned too—like a sheep's-head between a pair of tangs : an ill-faured, fearsome couple they were. The Laird's buff coat was hanging on a pin behind him, and his broadsword and his pistols within reach ; for he keepit up the auld fashion of having the weapons ready, and a horse saddled day and night, just as he used to do when he was able to loup on horseback and away after ony o' the hill-folk he could get speerings o'." The Major was literally pistolled by Sir Gilbert, the next laird of Lag, though not (need we add ?) under such circumstances of *diablerie* as are so graphically narrated in the romance.

† Town Council Minutes.

elected as the first dean of guild in Dumfries, at a meeting of Council held on the 31st of July, 1827 ; and at the same time five gentlemen were appointed to co-operate with him, and a clerk and procurator-fiscal were attached to his court, all in terms of the charter. (a)

The crops of 1826 suffered from a protracted drought, which has made the year a memorable one. As a consequence, grain advanced considerably in value : oatmeal, which had formerly been selling in the Queensberry Square market at a moderate figure, rose to fully three shillings per stone—an advance that occasioned much discontent in the town and district, and ultimately led to a serious riot. On Wednesday the 12th of July there was a very welcome fall of rain--the first that had occurred for several weeks—accompanied by a brief but exceedingly violent thunderstorm. Just before the elemental strife commenced, a storm of popular indignation burst forth, provoked by a mealmonger from Maxwelltown, who, seeing that his stock was in great demand, advanced its price to three shillings per stone. When challenged for doing so, he defended his conduct ; and, in exchanging verbal compliments with the dames of the market, he ventured to assail one of them with an epithet which no woman cares about submitting to. Blows followed words, and a dangerous scuffle would have ensued had not the hot-headed man of the meal been apprehended, examined before a magistrate, and committed to prison.

He was unfortunately liberated on bail, and with consummate foolhardiness he resumed his position beside his meal-bags, and vain-gloriously announced to an assembled crowd that "Three-Shilling Rab" was among them once more, and that he must have an additional twopence per stone on account of the trouble he had been put to. " Meal at three and twopence ! Sorrow on ye for a rascally auld skin-flint ! Take that, and that, for yer shamefu' greed !" And with these significant words came a shower of corresponding missiles, directed against " Rab," who, hurriedly retreating from the furious tempest he had reawakened,

(a) By the Burgh Police (Scotland) Act, 1892, Town Councils received the powers of the former Commissioners of Police, and Dean of Guild Courts in those burghs that possessed them were reconstituted. In Dumfries the Dean's Court acquired under this Act considerable additional powers. In Maxwelltown the Town Council and the Police Commission were not only distinct bodies but were elected on distinct franchises ; and the office of Provost, which pertained to the Council, and the office of Chief Magistrate, which pertained to the Police Commission, were not always held by the same person. By the Act of 1892 the Town Council came to be elected on the broader franchise, and acquired the powers of the Police Commission, the title of Chief Magistrate disappearing and that of Provost remaining. There is no Dean of Guild Court in Maxwelltown ; the powers that the court possesses in Dumfries being exercised in Maxwelltown, as in some other burghs, by the Council.

found temporary shelter in the house of Mr Bairden, on the opposite side of the square. From the mouths of the disappointed mob rose sounds which rivalled the bellowing of the thunder that afterwards rolled above the burgh. So violent was the rabble outcry, that in answer to it the trembling refugee had to be turned out ; and when that was done, off he darted down the Long Close into Irish Street, in as great trepidation as Tam o' Shanter with the witches on his track. Less fortunate than that famous wight, he was caught at the foot of the close by a party of the rioters who had taken a ready cut for that purpose ; after they had given him a sound beating, he managed to escape from their hands ; and, all bloody and bruised, he reached with difficulty the Maxwelltown side of the river, where he remained safely hidden for the night. The poor man's house was then visited by the populace, who broke its window panes ; and next, in the madness of their rage, hurried to the houses of other meal-dealers, which they treated in a worse way, though their owners had not sinned after the similitude of "Three-Shilling Rab."

"The scene that now ensued," says the local journalist, "baffles description. Stones and other missiles were flying in all directions ; windows were smashed, doors forced, furniture broken, and even stolen ; and some houses in which not an obnoxious individual resided, soon exhibited an appearance resembling the effects of a bombardment. The damage thus done to many individuals was great ; and one in particular rates his loss at upwards of £20. On the Dumfries side the police and special constables prevented, in a great measure, the fatal results which might have been anticipated ; but in Maxwelltown there was no regular police or public body of sufficient power to suppress such general risings, and hence the fury of the mob raged there almost without control, until it might be said to have exhausted itself merely by its own violence."

A meal-dealer in Church Street had a narrow escape. He was closely besieged in his own premises ; and when doors and windows had been beaten in, he retreated by a back door, and hurrying out for bare life, broke through a thick thorn hedge, and near " the noon of night " presented himself, pale and trembling, at the house of a neighbour, by whom his escape was facilitated. We well recollect seeing, next day, the " cairn " of huge stones, some of them ten pounds in weight, which, piled up in the floor of his shop, seemed in our childish eyes a terrific memorial—and it was really such—of the fury of the rioters. The cause of all the commotion was punished with a fine of two guineas. When returning from the police court he received some verbal abuse, but no actual violence ; and in the afternoon he propitiated the populace, and saved himself from further annoyance, by offering his meal at the reduced rate of two shillings and ninepence per stone.

By far the greatest riot that ever occurred in Dumfries of modern date took place on the 6th of February, 1829. For months before, the deeds of the notorious Burke, who strangled a number of persons and sold their bodies to doctors for dissection, excited the horror of the whole country. He suffered death for his crimes, but his accomplice, William Hare, escaped by turning "king's evidence;" and the authorities in Edinburgh having arranged to send him to his native country, Ireland, he arrived at Dumfries by coach on his way to Portpatrick. The news spread rapidly; and under its excitement a vast crowd, estimated at eight thousand people, collected on the streets—the greatest concourse being in the vicinity of the King's Arms Hotel, where Hare was located, waiting the departure of the Galloway mail. At first, several gentlemen were freely admitted to see him. When, however, the crowd outside increased, and began to use threats of violence, he was removed for greater security to a closet adjoining the tap-room. There he was traced; and a fierce band of intruders, with cries of "Burke him! Burke him!" burst in, who would undoubtedly have made their words good had not several policemen arrived and cleared the room. The time for the Portpatrick mail to start (eleven o'clock a.m.) having come, the inn yard was cleared with difficulty, the horses were yoked, and the coach was drawn out. Hare did not make his appearance. If he had ventured forth, no trembling quadruped with the name he bore ever experienced a worse fate than that which awaited him. The wrath of the "Monument rangers," of the "Kirkgate blades," and all the nameless rabble of the town, from the Moat-brae to the Cat's Strand, was fairly up: they would have torn him to pieces without mercy; and it is scarcely exaggeration to say, in the words of Shakspeare:—

> "Had all his hairs been lives,
> Their great revenge had stomach for them all."

Two passengers were sent forward a few miles in a gig, and the coach started perfectly empty, excepting the guard, driver, and Mr Alexander Fraser, one of the sons of the proprietor. The vehicle literally toiled through the multitudinous living mass that surged and heaved in High Street, and barely opened to let it pass. When at the head of Buccleuch Street the coach was stopped and scrutinised. No one was found inside; and lest Hare, who was a small man, should be secreted in the boot, it too was searched; and the mob being satisfied that the object of their hatred must still be at the King's Arms, permitted the mail to pass on its journey without further harm. According to a statement current at the time, the rioters had arranged to stop the coach a second time at the bridge, and throw Hare over the parapet into the river; and failing that, to "Burke" him at the Cassalands toll-bar, the gates of which had been barricaded by them beforehand

Not having found him in the coach, they returned bent on finding him in the hotel, and making him there feel their vengeance.

Strange to say, many persons were allowed to visit Hare in the afternoon at his quarters in the tap-room, whilst a *posse* of policemen stood at the wide entry to the inn, keeping the angry crowd at bay. " By these successive visitors he was forced to sit or stand in all positions ; and cool, and insensate, and apathetic as he seemed, he was occasionally almost frightened out of his wits. Abuse of every kind was plentifully heaped upon him, as the only fitting incense that could meet his ear ; one woman, it is said, seized him by the collar and nearly strangled him ; while a sturdy ostler who happened to be present, though perhaps not at the same moment, addressed him in these emphatic words :— ' Whaur are ge gaun, or whaur can ye gang to ? Hell's owre guid for the like o' you—the very deevils, for fear o' mischief, wadna daur to let ye in ; and as for heaven, that's entirely out o' the question ! ' "*

How to get rid of the unhappy man became every hour a more pressing question for the magistrates. They saw that on no account must he be kept in the King's Arms till after sunset ; as the mob, favoured by darkness, might resort to desperate measures in order to reach its prey. It was thought if he could by any means be consigned to the prison in Buccleuch Street, its walls would defy any siege to which it might in consequence be subjected ; and, with this end in view, an ingenious device was resorted to. A little before three o'clock a chaise and pair were brought to the door of the inn, to which a trunk was attached and about which a great fuss was made. " Now we'll catch the gallows loon, and gie him't hot and heavy !" roared the exulting rabble. Not so, good Master Mob, bent on a red-handed ministry of retribution ; the chaise you see is but a delusive decoy-duck, and the wretched man you seek for has, under guidance due, leaped from the window of his apartment, crawled like a viper, as he is, along a lengthened line of wall lest his upright form should attract observation, and hurrying into another chaise that stood ready for him at the bottom of the yard, has set off in it at a lightning-like pace.

The postilion, Murdoch by name, plied his whip and managed his team in gallant style. Had he been driving a worthy man instead of a vile miscreant away from a host of foes, he could not have performed his task more heroically. Before reaching his destination he had to make the circuit of half the burgh—down Shakespeare Street ; round Nith Place, the corner of which was turned so sharply that the conveyance ran for a moment on two wheels, and was nearly upset ; up the White Sands. Lashed right and left, how the half-maddened horses did run ! Even if

* Picture of Dumfries, p. 100.

they had flown like the fiery Pegasus, they could not have altogether eluded the vigilance of the Argus-eyed multitude ; and
just as the clattering equipage dashed by the foot of Bank Street,
it was encountered by such a rush of rioters from that thoroughfare and other quarters, that to make way against the cataract
seemed for a while impossible. Many a one in the condition of the
King's Arms Jehu would have compounded for his own safety by
complying with the fierce demand, "Stop and let the murderer
oot !" that greeted him on all sides ; Murdoch, however, neither
stopped nor parleyed, but drove right on, though before he reached
the head of the Sands the crowd, swelled by contributions from
Friars' Vennel and Maxwelltown, had become so dense that he only
made way through it with the utmost difficulty. Several times
the chaise, caught by a score of hands, was brought to a dead
stand ; and had not the mettled steeds plunged forward again the
next minute, Hare would have had no chance. Keeping up the
panel as best he could, cowering in a corner to escape the stones
directed against him, his condition during that terrible ride was
truly pitiable ; though perhaps scant pity was due to the monster
who had without compunction assisted in putting many of his
innocent fellow-creatures to death.

Up Bridge Street ! The mass becomes closer as the passage
grows narrower, and the panting horses make scarcely any progress up the incline. The mob becomes denser and more desperate ;
and the vehicle, wedged in all round, rocks with the heaving multitude as if it would capsize. At this moment, when all hope must
have left both driver and passenger, the crowd suddenly opens up ;
a portion of it withdrawing to the end of the new bridge, to hold
it, in the belief that the route of the chaise lies that way. It
luckily lies in quite an opposite direction. Now, then, postilion,
there is yet a chance left of life and safety ! Handle your ribbons
and lay on whip as you never did before ! And he does by a
marvellous feat in jockeyism clear the corner into Buccleuch Street
almost at a bound ; and then, having a wide thoroughfare before
him, he rapidly leaves the baffled rabble behind, reaches the prison
—the next instant its huge doors opens, and then closes between
the fugitive and those who seek his blood.

His escape raised their fury to a higher pitch than ever. They
forthwith laid regular siege to the jail ; and for hours afterwards
the whole neighbourhood rang with a Babel of noise—the sound of
blows struck against the prison gate, of breaking gas lamps and
window panes, of howls, threats, and curses, by which the "night
was made hideous." For four hours the north-west part of the
town was in full possession of the rioters ; and it was only because
the jail was strong compared with their "munitions of war," that
their pertinacious endeavours to storm it proved unavailing. They
wrenched the ponderous knocker from the massive door, kept up

an incessant battery of large stones against the door itself, while lighter missiles of the same metal—a truly petrifying shower—were poured down into the prison yard, doing much mischief to the buildings. Whether the leaders of the assailing mob had ever heard of the means by which Bruce in 1306 won the Castle of Dumfries, we know not; but when their other appliances failed, they thought like him on that occasion, of resorting to fire. "Tar-barrels and peats!" "Peats and tar-barrels!" they muttered to each other "Ay, ay; let us burn down the door, and roast the wild beast in his den!" responded in louder terms the rank and file; and in all likelihood the incendiary proposal would have been acted upon and much valuable property been laid in ashes, had not a hundred special constables reinforced the police and militia staff at this critical period, and joined them in a bold attempt to clear the ground.

Repeated charges were made by the men of peace for this purpose, and eventually with more success than could have been looked for, seeing that the "insurgents" were so numerous and menacing. Once that the rabble tide began to turn, its waters receded rapidly, and in one short hour afterwards it became manifest that the fearful crisis was over; though a diminished crowd occupied most of the street, and seemed still bent on mischief. When the ten o'clock bell rang, the rioters, congregated outside the ring made by dint of staff and baton, numbered several thousands; but a while before midnight they melted away till only a few hundreds were left; and when the morning of the 7th of February came, cold and bleak, it found not a solitary son of violence astir. Wearied with the work of the wild day and wilder night, the mob dissolved into quiet fragmentary units, was taking its needed rest; and none but the friends of order kept the streets Before day-dawn, Hare was roused from a troubled slumber, and told to prepare for his instant exit: he was rightly looked upon as an Achan in the camp, who for the sake of the town's peace, not less than his own safety, must be thrust out, now that an opportunity for doing so presented itself, before that the populace rose again in wrath, "like a giant refreshed with wine;" and so he was conveyed to the English road by a sheriff's officer and two militiamen, and the tempestuous episode of Hare in Dumfries was brought to a peaceful issue.*

* Hare had, it appears, been smuggled out of Edinburgh jail, muffled in a cloak, and been taken up by the mail coach at Newington. " In his progress to the South his life was repeatedly placed in the greatest jeopardy. Like Cain, a mark was set on his head; yet he finally escaped, and, when the storm blew over, found his way in a coasting vessel to the shores of Ireland. Half a year afterwards, his sister, while returning from the harvest, called for his bundle at the King's Arms Inn, announcing herself in a whisper; and readily obtained an article that was found lying in a corner of the tap-room, like a polluted thing that nobody would appropriate, or even encountered the defilement of throwing away."—*Picture of Dumfries*, p. 102.

CHAPTER LVI.

BEFORE the generation that was contemporary with Burns had
passed away, the very liberality in politics for which he was
tabooed began to prevail, till the once Tory town again became
Whiggish, if not something more. Throughout the country at
large a feeling had risen up against everything that savoured of
monopoly and exclusive privilege. So early as 1818, we find some
faint traces of it in Dumfries, as manifested by the refusal of persons, when made burgesses, to pay the customary fees, and by non-
freemen beginning business within the burgh in defiance of the
deacons and the dean of guild.* No doubt the financial mis-
management from which the town suffered so much tended to
make the inhabitants increasingly dissatisfied with the existing
order of things, and prepared them to join heartily in the national
cry that was soon afterwards raised for Parliamentary and burgh
Reform. Mr David Staig, influenced by failing health, and the
embarrassments of 1817, finally withdrew from public life that
year—the last of the old provosts whose word was law ; and with
him the inveterate Conservatism of which he was at once the
guardian and representative disappeared from the Council.

During his magisterial era the Dumfriesians were accustomed
to look upon the British constitution as perfect, or nearly so, and
the close burgh system as a worthy pendicle to it, which none save
rash fools would interfere with ; but in 1830 such a change had
come over both the people and their rulers, that they with an
almost unanimous voice repudiated the Duke of Wellington's
memorable declaration to his fellow-peers on the 26th of October,
when he said—" I am thoroughly convinced that Britain possesses

* Town Council Minutes.

at this moment a legislature which answers all the good purposes of a legislature in a higher degree than any scheme of government whatever has been found to do in any country in the world ; that it possesses the confidence of the country ; that it deservedly possesses that confidence ; and that its decisions have justly the greatest weight and influence with the people." This anti-Reform manifesto of the Conservative Premier gave a mighty impulse to the popular counter-movement. Enthusiastic meetings to protest against it, and pronounce in favour of the Reform Bill brought into the House of Commons by Lord John Russell, were held all over the country. Annan took the lead in Dumfriesshire ; the county town followed soon after ; and before 1831 was many weeks old all the royal burghs, and numerous other places in the south of Scotland, had given in a hearty adhesion to the Reform cause.

The Dumfries meeting, held in the Court-house on the 2nd of December, 1830, was the greatest political gathering that had ever, up till that date, taken place in the town, at least in modern times. It was densely crowded, comprised most of the principal burgesses, and, to give it increased influence and *éclat*, the Provost, Mr John Fraser, though a Conservative, presided--seemingly not unwilling to be carried with the current of the prevailing tide. The resolutions, eight in number, declared the dissatisfaction of the inhabitants with the existing mode of election, as not affording "a full, free, and equal representation of the people" in the Commons House of Parliament ; and they especially pointed out the defective nature of the Scottish representative system, inasmuch as "the whole number of voters for all the burghs in Scotland was conform to a Parliamentary report of 1825," according to which "the right of voting is exercised by delegates from the several burghs, who are chosen by the Town Council themselves, being self-elected bodies, and uncontrolled by their nominal constituents, the great body of the inhabitants." Among those who took a prominent part in the business were the following gentlemen :—Mr Robert Murray, writer, afterwards provost ; Mr Thomas Harkness, writer ; Mr David Hannay, banker ; Mr William M'Gowan, writer, afterwards provost ; Mr John M'Diarmid, editor of the *Dumfries Courier ;* Mr Benjamin Oney, clothier ; Mr Miles Leighton, merchant, afterwards provost ; Mr William M'Gowan, builder ; Mr Robert Wallace, writer ; Mr James M'Whir, merchant ; Mr Robert M'Harg, merchant ; Mr Archibald Hamilton, writer ; Dr M'Cracken ; and Captain M'Dowall ; making up in themselves—not to name others of the same standing present—no inadequate representation of the worth, intelligence, and material interests of the town. All the resolutions, with a petition to the House of Commons based upon them, were unanimously adopted. Mr Adam Rankine, a gentleman noted for his fervid temperament and public spirit, was so pleased with the meeting that he forwarded an account of it by express to Lord Advocate Jeffrey, the substance of which was communicated by Mr Gibson Craig to a great Edinburgh Reform meeting, and elicited from it a round of cheers in honour of " the judicious resolutions and patriotic example of the citizens of Dumfries."

Patriotic and unselfish the movement certainly was, so far as men of the councillor stamp were concerned. They had long enjoyed a monopoly which gave them exclusive political and municipal power, and trading privileges ; and now they united with their less-favoured fellow-countrymen in demanding its abolition. The Incorporated Trades of Dumfries manifested the same self-denying spirit. The pending Reform Bill was rife with a more sweeping revolution for them than even for the merchants of the guild ; and it would not have been wonderful if they had obstinately opposed the measure, or given to it a sullen, passive resistance. Were the bill to pass, farewell then to their time-hallowed heritage of seven seats at the Council board, with all the political influence, social status, and (more precious than anything else to some) all the pleasant hob-nobbing with nobility which these involved ; whilst, following fast in the wake of the bill, were coming kindred measures by which their ancient incorporation was to be broken up as if it had never been. Rising above such selfish considerations, the Seven Trades met in their own hall on the 4th of March, 1831, under the chairmanship of their chief, Mr James Thomson, convener, and voted a unanimous address to his Majesty, William the Fourth, expressing their sincere approval of, and gratitude for, " the liberal, safe, equitable, and comprehensive Bill of Reform which has been lately introduced into the House of Commons."*

On the 15th of the same month a general meeting of the inhabitants was held, presided over by Provost Fraser, at which the Reform Bill was approved of with the same cordiality and unanimity that characterised the first Dumfries meeting. Mr Robert Murray, after explaining its chief provisions, was warmly cheered when he exhorted those present to be up and doing in support of the Throne and Cabinet at the present crisis ; and he took occasion to pay a high compliment to the Trades, whose address to the King, he said, had been read by him with the liveliest pleasure ; and proud he felt in being the townsman of persons who, unlike the great borough-mongers, were willing to waive their exclusive privileges, and sacrifice their private interests for the good of the public.†

Even the county of Dumfries could not help having its Reform meeting. It took place on the 18th of March—Vice-

---

* Seven Trades' Minutes.   † *Dumfries Courier.*

Admiral Sir Robert Laurie in the chair. A series of resolutions was proposed by Sir William Jardine of Applegarth, and seconded by Mr Leny of Dalswinton, approving of the bill so far as it affected the Scottish burghs, but disapproving of it on the ground that it fixed the franchise for counties too low, and dealt too sweepingly with the English pocket boroughs. Major-General Matthew Sharpe of Hoddom,* "the coming man" for the Dumfries District of Burghs, then stepped forward on behalf of the whole bill, thereby fluttering the timid Volscians of the shire. His amendment to that effect was seconded by Mr Menteath of Close-burn, and lost by the narrow majority of one vote ; eighteen gentlemen having supported the resolutions, and seventeen the amendment.

Three days afterwards the second reading of the bill was carried in the House of Commons by the same small majority of one ; the minority including the member for the Dumfries Burghs, Mr Keith Douglas.† In the following month an amendment was adopted in committee which was deemed fatal to the integrity of the measure. That ministers might appeal to the country on its behalf, Parliament was forthwith dissolved ; and a large majority of members pledged to support the bill were returned. Dumfries was bent on giving a practical rebuke to its peccant representative ; so was Annan. No doubt was entertained as to what these two burghs could and would do in the matter ; but there was no such certainty as regarded the other three "carlines," they being

* General Sharpe was of the old Kirkpatrick line, whose ancestor Ivon held lands in Annandale in the middle of the twelfth century. The Kirkpatricks, as we have seen, possessed the estate of Closeburn for centuries ; but in 1780 it was sold to Mr Menteath by Sir James Kirkpatrick, whose son, Sir Thomas Kirkpatrick, sheriff-depute of Dumfriesshire, married Jane, daughter of Charles Sharpe of Hoddam, descended from John Sharpe, who purchased that estate from the Earl of Southesk in 1690. William Kirkpatrick of Ellisland, grandson of Sir Thomas, married a daughter of Lord Justice-Clerk Erskine ; and their son Charles succeeding to the estate of Hoddam, assumed the name of Sharpe. Burns, in 1791, addressed to Mr Sharpe a humorous epistle under a fictitious signature, enclosing three stanzas written by him to what he calls a charming Scots air of Mr Sharpe's composition, and complimenting him on his being an exquisite violinist (as he was). Mr Sharpe married a daughter of Renton of Lamberton, a lady whose beauty is celebrated in " Humphrey Clinker." Their eldest son was General Sharpe ; their second Charles Kirkpatrick Sharpe, the celebrated wit, artist, and antiquary. Another son, William Sharpe, is the present proprietor of Hoddam. (a)

(a) After the death of Mr W. Sharpe, Hoddam was acquired by Mr Edward Brook, a Yorkshire gentleman, who subsequently purchased the Kinmount estate of the Marquis of Queensberry. Mr Brook, who proved himself to be a singularly generous landlord, greatly improved Hoddam Castle. At his decease Hoddam passed to his elder son Edward, and Kinmount to his son Charles.

† Mr William Robert Keith Douglas was the fifth son of Sir William Douglas of Kelhead, M.P. for the Dumfries burghs, by Grace Johnstone of Lockerbie. He represented the Burghs from 1812 to 1832.

still largely pervaded by the old exclusive leaven. On the 20th of May the Dumfries Council met in their chamber for the purpose of choosing a delegate to vote for them at the ensuing election. As the public were admitted the place was packed to suffocation, and the proceedings were gone through under circumstances of great excitement. General Sharpe was present with the view of promoting the candidature on which he had fairly entered. Mr Keith Douglas was also there to defend his obnoxious vote, and endeavour to placate the fierce opposition which it had aroused. His explanations were received with impatience ; and when he went on to say that he could not engage to support the Reform Bill when next brought forward, the audience greeted the intimation with hisses and groans— sweet music to the honourable gentleman s rival, who on rising afterwards, and giving an unhesitating approval of the bill, received in return a boisterous ovation from the crowd. Bailie Thomson moved that Provost Fraser be appointed delegate, seeing that he had always acted consistently, and would vote for the Liberal candidate, General Sharpe. The motion was seconded by Bailie Corson, and carried unanimously ; not a vote being proffered or voice raised in favour of the Tory candidate, though he had represented the burghs for eighteen years. Bailie Thomson, with the view of preventing any mistake as to the delegate's intentions, begged to ask if he accepted the office on the condition proposed. " Undoubtedly," was Provost Fraser's reply, " I shall be happy to give effect to the intentions of the Council ;"* and with this satisfactory assurance the meeting quietly dispersed.

Annan, with the same unanimity, elected a commissioner pledged to vote for the Reform candidate ; Lochmaben was divided on the subject, but eventually chose a pro-Douglas delegate by a majority of seven votes to six ; and delegates of the same stamp were elected unanimously by Sanquhar and Kirkcudbright : so that, however much the populace might rage and storm, the old member was sure of being once more returned. The parliamentary election took place on Monday, the 23rd of May, at Dumfries, and was preceded by a demonstration which, for numbers, scenic effect, and enthusiasm, was quite unprecedented in the burgh.

At an early hour the Trades and many of the other inhabitants mustered in great force, and with flags, emblematic devices, and music, marched out to Gastown with the view of giving an imposing welcome to General Sharpe, and Mr Scott, banker, the Annan delegate. On the hero of the day being descried advancing in an open carriage, accompanied by several of his friends, a shout was raised which made the welkin ring. Mr Scott, who

* *Dumfries Courier.*

followed with Provost Irving of Annan in another vehicle, was also warmly greeted. As if by magic, the horses were loosed from the carriages, and the latter drawn townwards by a stud of stout lads and men, only too glad to honour in this questionable way the gallant champion of Reform. The procession, with this curious cavalcade in the van, occupied more than a mile of the road, each marcher having a knot of ribbons at his breast of the true-blue colour, whilst no fewer than forty-three banners fluttered overhead. It passed up a portion of English Street, then by Loreburn Street and Townhead into the main thoroughfare. As the magnificent procession defiled down High Street, the voice of the Mid-Steeple bells ringing welcome could scarcely be heard for the deafening cheers with which its leading figure was saluted. After a brief breathing time in the King's Arms Hotel, the General, with a large retinue of supporters, walked to the scene of contest, receiving flattering salutes by the way ; whilst there was none so poor or polite as to do any reverence to the rival candidate as he also passed up to the place of meeting— the Court-house—already filled to overflowing with an impassioned multitude.

The preliminaries are conducted in a pantomimic style ; for no sooner does Mr Keith Douglas take his seat, than a tumultuous uproar begins. Shouts of "Bribery !" "Perjury !" mingle with the inarticulate din ; and as thunder-clouds answer each other, hoarse voices from Buccleuch Street swell responsive to the Babel sounds within. During a slight lull in the tempest, Mr Murray, writer, protests, on technical grounds, against the delegates from Sanquhar and Lochmaben being permitted to vote ; and Mr Patrick Robertson, advocate, who is present with Mr Douglas, contends that their commissions are quite valid, and must be received, which opinion is supported by the Sheriff, who presides. The votes are taken. Provost Fraser of Dumfries and Mr Scott of Annan give their suffrages for General Sharpe, and are loudly cheered. Major Crichton of Sanquhar votes for Mr Keith Douglas ; so do Provost Shand of Kirkcudbright and Mr John J. Henderson of Lochmaben, amid a chorus of hisses and yells. The returning officer thereupon announces, or is understood to announce, that William Robert Keith Douglas, Esquire, has been duly elected as representative of the Dumfries District of Burghs in the Commons House of Parliament. The honourable gentleman must, of course, rise to return thanks. He need not. He may feel grateful to the small majority of the Lochmaben councillors, who sent a commissioner to turn the scale in his favour ; but he owes nothing to the audience he now endeavours to address. They reject him—will have none of his thanks—his eloquence is reduced to dumb, fantastic show ; the noise that greeted him being, says an ear-witness, so terrific that it "would have utterly

overwhelmed the voice of the most stentorian-lunged orator that
ever fretted his hour on the hustings."* On the contrary, the
defeated candidate, though but a poor speaker, is listened to, not
with patience merely, but delight. Though beaten to-day, he sees
with prophetic eye that victory will be his within the next six
months ; and there is tremendous cheering when he makes an
oracular declaration to that effect.

The meeting has put down Douglas, but is not yet done with
him ; for the indomitable Annan delegate rises, intent on giving
him a " heckling." "Will Mr Douglas support those parts of the
ministerial measure, Schedules A and B, which disfranchise the
rotten boroughs ? Let him say yes or no to this plain question.'
The honourable gentleman does not wish to be made further
sport of by the Philistines of Reform. He keeps his seat, and
makes no sign, intending to reserve his answer till a more convenient season, and for the safer latitude of Westminster ; and
the inquisitorial Annanite, on tendering the same question to the
worthy hero of Hoddam, receives a reply that will fall like a
bomb-shell on the camp of the borough-mongers. He means to
give these pestilent gentry no quarter, and goes for the whole
alphabet of Reform, from A and B down to Z ; and thus elicits a
fresh acclamation from the audience. The newly-elected member
now moves as if he wished to speak—under what impulse, none
can tell ; but there is as little disposition as ever to hear him.
He gives up the vain attempt ; and as the Sheriff declares the
business finished, the populace slowly retire, with loud cries of
" Let him no gang back to Parliament and say he is oor member !"
" Bribery and corruption !" " Let us have a look at the Lochmaben delegate !" Mr Douglas, with the commissioners who
voted for him, retired by a back door leading to a street in
the rear of the Court-house, and entering the carriage of Mr
Peter Johnston of Carnsalloch, which was waiting for him, drove
off to that gentleman's residence with the utmost speed. This
arrangement was fortunately kept secret, otherwise the exciting
scenes of the Hare hunt of 1829 might possibly have been repeated
with higher game in view. General Sharpe's procession back to
his hotel was like that of a triumphant conqueror. It was even
more brilliant and imposing than his entry into the burgh on that
eventful day.

Dumfries showed conclusively that it had become Whiggish
once more, as in the period before and long subsequent to the
Revolution. Forty years ago poor Burns was forced to tremble at
his own audacity in hinting that a better "creed of British
liberty " would by-and-bye be obtained than the British Constitution as expounded by De Lolme ; now the member for the

* *Dumfries Courier.*

burghs is ostracised for adhering too closely to De Lolme, and there is an earnest, importunate, all but universal cry raised in Dumfries for an extensive reform of the constitution. In the national agitation for this purpose the burgh, according to its size, took a full share. Every critical stage of Lord John Russell's bill was watched with feverish anxiety : bonfires blazed at the Monument or the Cross when it made any decided advance ; indignant meetings were convened in the Town Hall or the Court-house when its progress was arrested by opposing factions. More especially was the burgh stirred to its utmost depths when, on the 10th of October, 1831, the astounding intelligence arrived that the bill, which had been read a third time in the House of Commons on the 21st of September by a majority of 109, had been rejected in the Upper House by a majority of 41. "Yesterday," says the *Courier* of the 11th, "was a doleful day in Dumfries—by far the most doleful we ever remember. . . . At the post-office and other parts of the town, particularly High Street, the greatest anxiety prevailed to obtain a peep of the newspapers or hear the news. Before eleven o'clock A.M. a number of our townsmen— some of them men of extensive property—had assembled together, each enquiring of his neighbour what was to be done. Despond-ency was altogether out of the question; and in all our experience we never saw men more confident of the high vantage-ground on which they stand. A public meeting was of course determined on, which, having been called by the Provost on a requisition addressed to him, passed a series of strong resolutions regretting the fate of the bill, expressing a hope that his Majesty would still retain the Reform Ministry in office, and that he would take such constitutional steps as they might advise for ultimately securing the success of the measure."

The bill, in a somewhat altered form, was re-introduced next session ; its second reading was carried in the Lower House by 324 to 162, a majority of two to one ; and on the 19th of December it passed its final stage in the Commons by the reduced majority of 116. When, in the following April, the bill was allowed to be read a second time in the Upper House without opposition, the country was agreeably surprised ; but that feeling gave way to indignation when the tactics of the Tory peers came to be under-stood. The Opposition, led by Lord Lyndhurst, opened an ambuscade upon the measure when in committee : they insisted upon deferring the disfranchising clauses till after the enfranchis-ing clauses had been considered—a device which was supported by 151 votes to 116 ; and the result was looked upon as indicative of such inveterate hostility that Earl Grey and his colleagues at once resigned office. Never in modern times has the country been nearer the verge of revolution than during the few days which intervened between the noble lord's surrender of the seals and his re-acceptance after the Duke of Wellington failed in his endeavours to form a Ministry.

In full sympathy with the feeling of the times a Political Union was established in Dumfries " to preserve the peace," " to guard the people from being betrayed into acts of disorder," and to use every effort for the purpose of obtaining " a full and efficient representation of the people " in Parliament ; whilst the Council and the general public voted addresses to the King, urging him to recall Earl Grey, and signed petitions to the Commons, adjuring them to " withhold all supplies " until the Reform Bill should be clothed with the authority of law. Hitherto the political meetings in the burgh had been always closed with a round of cheers in honour of Royalty ; but there was no such sequel to the demonstration in the Court-house on this occasion. The vocation of the gallant officer, Captain M'Dowall, who invariably acted as fugleman, was for once in abeyance. " In anticipation of a different state of things," says the *Courier* of May 15th, " a great dinner was projected for the King's birthday, but the order has been countermanded, and bids fair to be postponed *sine die*. The addresses [adopted at the meeting] were extended as speedily as possible, and in the course of ten hours were signed by 2002 persons ; being 800 more names than were attached to any previous petition, even where they remained for signatures at least an equal number of days."

Dumfries thus manifested its steadfast adhesion to the principles of Reform ; and it is to be regretted that the mob of the town insisted on supplementing the constitutional movement by a manifesto of its own. On the evening of the 14th of May a pot-orator held forth in the market-place ; the burden of his harangue being the iniquity of the borough-mongers, and the threatened ruin of the kingdom by the stubbornness of the anti-Reform King and the Tory peers. So much was the speaker's eloquence relished by the listening crowd, composed mostly of boys, that they paraded him shoulder high through the principal streets ; and then, after dropping him on *terra firma*, they, seized by a destructive impulse, broke the windows of a house in George Street, and of another elsewhere, whose inmates were believed to belong to the unpopular party which the speaker had denounced. This affair, trifling in itself, would have received no notice here, had it not been the prelude of a more serious disturbance. The tribune of the streets having resumed his dangerous vocation next day at dusk, he was, in virtue of a magisterial sentence, committed to "durance vile." On Thursday the good news arrived that the reins of power had been once more put into the hands of Earl Grey ; and whilst the populace were busy burning tar-barrels in honour of this event, the thought of the imprisoned orator—a martyr in the cause of Reform—darted across their minds, and turned their joy into rage. As if with one consent they, to the number of fifteen hundred or more, hurried to Buc-cleuch Street, assailed the prison door with stones, tried to destroy it by fire when the missiles proved ineffectual ; and a fearful night, like that in which Hare was besieged, seemed about to set in, when a powerful body of constables charged the rioters, and off they set, reluctantly leaving the captive demagogue to his fate.

In the course of a few weeks afterwards the burgh presented quite a different aspect with reference to the battle for Reform. The Opposition, overawed by the Prime Minister's resolution to recruit his ranks by an extensive creation of new peers, at length gave way, and allowed the bill to be read a third time, by a majority of 106 to 84, and the royal assent was given to it on the 7th of June. As a necessary pendant to it, the measure for Scot-land was passed by the Lords, and became law in the following month. It increased the number of the Scotch members from forty-five to fifty-three ; but its value consisted chiefly in the change it made in the class of electors, which, as Sir Archibald Alison remarks, " was so great as to amount to a total revolution. The old town councils, in great part self-elected, were succeeded by a host of ten-pound shopkeepers and householders, actuated by different interests, and swayed by different influences ; while the old parchment freeholders, who followed their directing magnate to the poll, were superseded by a multitude of independent feuars in villages, and of tenants in rural districts." As respects the Five Burghs, the bill enlarged the constituency from 93 town councillors to 967 ten-pound householders, the number registered in 1832 ; of which Dumfries furnished 610, Annan 170, Sanquhar 45, Lochmaben 31, and Kirkcudbright 111. The county voters numbered only 72 in 1812 ; in 1830 they had increased to 82 ; and the bill of 1832 advanced the number to 1125, of which 78 were freeholders and 1047 new voters. Having now reached the close of the old representative system and the beginning of the new, we may give here fittingly a list of the members for the Dumfries Burghs from the date of the Union till that of the Reform Act, 1832 :—William Johnstone, 1708 ; (a) John Hutton, M.D., 1710; Sir William Johnstone of Westerhall, 1713 ; Alexander Fergusson of Craigdarroch, 1715 ; William Douglas, yr. of Cavers, 1722 ; Archi-bald Douglas, sen. of Cavers, 1727 ; the Hon. Charles Erskine, 1734, subsequently Lord Advocate, who, being also elected for

(a) This indenture, &c., also returned William Paterson, Esq. ; but by Order of the House, dated 30th November, 1708, all that part of it which related to him was erased.—Note to Return made to an Order of the House of Lords, dated 13th July, 1877, of members of the Parliaments of Great Britain. William Paterson, here referred to, was the founder of the Bank of England.

the county of Dumfries, chose to sit for that constituency, and was succeeded by William Kirkpatrick in 1735 ; the latter was made a clerk of Session in 1738, upon which Sir Robert Laurie was chosen in his room that year; Lord John Johnstone, 1741 ; Sir James Johnstone of Westerhall, 1743—re-elected 1747 ; Colonel Archibald Douglas, 1754 ; the Right Hon. Thomas Miller, Lord Advocate, 1761 ; on being made Lord Justice Clerk in 1766 he was succeeded by the Right Hon. James Montgomery, Lord Advocate ; William Douglas, yr. of Kelhead, 1768—re-elected 1774 ; Sir Robert Herries, 1780 ; Sir James Johnstone of Westerhall, 1784 ; Captain Patrick Miller, yr. of Dalswinton, 1790 ; the Hon. Alex. Hope, Lieut.-Col. of the 14th Regiment, 1796 ; resigned in 1800, when William Hope, Captain, R.N., was returned ; re-elected in 1801 ; the Right Hon. Charles Hope, Lord Advocate, 1802 ; resigned 1803, when Lord Viscount Stopford succeeded him ; the Right Hon. Henry Erskine, Lord Advocate, in 1806, the greatest ornament of the Scottish bar, and by far the most distinguished man that ever represented the Dumfries Burghs ; Sir John Heron Maxwell of Heron and Springkell, 1807 ; William Robert Keith Douglas, son of Sir William Douglas of Kelhead, 1812 ; Mr Douglas was re-elected 1818, 1820, 1822, on being made a Lord Commissioner of the Admiralty, and in 1826, 1830, and 1831.[*]

[*] List of Members for Dumfriesshire during the same period :—Lord James Johnstone, 1708 ; being incapacitated from sitting in the House of Commons, as the eldest son of a peer of Scotland, he was succeeded by William Grierson in 1709 ; Hon. James Murray, 1710 ; (a) Sir William Johnstone of Westerhall, 1713, re-elected 1715 ; Hon. Charles Erskine, 1722, re-elected 1725, 1727, 1734 ; Sir John Douglas of Kelhead, 1741 ; Hon. Lord Charles Douglas, 1747 ; re-elected 1754 ; James Veitch of Eliock, advocate, 1755 ; Lieutenant-General Archibald Douglas of Kirkton, 1761, re-elected 1768 ; Major Robert Laurie, younger of Maxwelton, 1774, re-elected 1780, 1784, 1785 (on appointment as Knight-Marshal of Scotland), 1790, 1796, 1801, 1802 ; Captain William Johnstone Hope, R.N., 1804, re-elected 1806, 1807 (on being made a Lord of Admiralty), 1812, 1818, 1820, 1826, and 1828 (on being appointed Treasurer of Greenwich Hospital) ; John James Hope-Johnstone of Annandale, 1830, re-elected 1831, 1832. (b)

(a) Return amended by Order of the House, dated 22nd February, 1710-11, by erasing the name of William Grierson, Esq. of Lag, and substituting that of Hon. James Murray, Esq.

(b) The following is a list of Members of Parliament for Dumfriesshire from 1831 :—John James Hope Johnstone, 1831 ; re-elected 1832, 1834, 1837, 1841. Viscount Drumlanrig, 1847 ; re-elected 1852. John James Hope Johnstone, 1857 ; re-elected 1859. Sir George G. Walker, 1865. Sir Sydney H. Waterlow, 1868 (declared to be disqualified, as a member of a firm holding a Government stationery contract). Sir George G. Walker, 1869. John James Hope Johnstone (grandson of the former member of the same name), 1874. Sir Robert Jardine, 1880 ; re-elected 1885, 1886. W. J. Maxwell, 1892. Robinson Souttar, 1895. W. J. Maxwell, 1900.

The list for the Dumfries Burghs for the same period is as follows :—W. R. K. Douglas, 1831. General Matthew Sharpe, 1832 ; re-elected 1834, 1837. William Ewart, 1841 ; re-elected 1847, 1852, 1857, 1859, 1865. Sir Robert Jardine, 1868. Ernest Noel, 1874 ; re-elected 1880, 1885. Sir Robert

In order to celebrate the great Reform triumph, a jubilee was resolved upon by the Dumfriesians; and rejoicings worthy of that imposing title were held on the 11th of August. The old town itself was daintily bedizened for the gala-day. Flags floating from windows and pinnacles—garlands crossing from street to street— triumphal arches rising in all the principal thoroughfares, made the place look quite grand and gay. "In walking along the streets it was difficult to get quit of the impression that Birnam or some other woods had mistaken Dumfries for Dunsinane. We have witnessed many anniversaries of Waterloo, but never within our recollection were the gardens and groves laid under contribution to anything like the same extent."* And then there was such a procession! For centuries the Seven Trades had been famed for this sort of pageant; and now, when inaugurating a new political era, fraught with ruin to all their peculiar privileges, they seemed bent on making their last public march under the old close system the most imposing one that had been seen in modern times. The incorporated craftsmen were well supported by other operatives; and the great civic regiment formed by these bodies was wound up by a juvenile company just as eager as their elders to take part in the parade and in the triumph. But this processing through the crowded town, occupying as it did from one o'clock till three, made the marchers hungry and thirsty— ravenous, in fact, for the goodly supplies of meat and drink provided for them at their own firesides, in taverns or public halls; and before gloamin' vanished in the mirk, and for hours afterwards, Convener Grainger's huge punch-bowl was in extraordinary request, and all and sundry were busy refreshing their wearied frames and toasting the good cause in brimming cups, illustrating that connection which, according to the national poet, exists between freedom and whisky.

Besides many private parties, there were at least eight public dinners on the evening of this joyous day. The people were exhilarated to an unexampled pitch by the success that had been achieved, and their faith in a practical Utopia that was to follow in its wake, though it had never yet arrived. In such a rosy and inspiring atmosphere, liberally—we do not say intemperately— moistened with mountain dew, it was natural that they should be hearty in their revels, and also exuberant in their eloquence. We are told by the local chronicler of the jubilee that "never before did Dumfries hear so many speeches spoken—see so many merry hearts met together." The elevated nature of the oratory, which elicited deafening after-dinner plaudits from sympathising

Threshie Reid, 1886; re-elected 1892, 1894 (on being appointed Solicitor-General for England, followed by appointment as Attorney-General), 1895, 1900.

* *Dumfries Courier.*

listeners, may be gathered from the following extract of a speech given by Mr M'Whir, when presiding at the merchants' meeting in the old Assembly Rooms, crowded by the presence of more than a hundred and fifty gentlemen. After shewing that the British people had encountered the conqueror of Napoleon and the hero of a hundred fights, the chairman said : "Such, my countrymen, such was the high and gallant bearing of the men of Britain ; and what is their reward? They have gained a victory and a triumph unparalleled in the history of the world ; and they have gained them in peace. The victory and the triumph they would at all events have gained—no power under heaven could prevent it ; but it might have been a victory won at the cannon's mouth—a triumph cradled on the bloody battle-field. And what are the consequences? Listen, my countrymen—listen to the words of Henry Brougham, thirty months ago, when on his canvass in Yorkshire. 'Take,' says he, 'all broad Scotland—from east to west, from north to south, in her cities and in her provinces—she is one vast rotten burgh !' And what is broad Scotland now? Why, the beams, the radiant beams of the glorious sun of liberty are now shining, and showering, and streaming over every hill and every vale, every mountain, every strath, and every glen in our beloved native land ; and you have the pleasure, the indescribable delight of knowing that, in common with your countrymen, you have secured to yourselves, to your children, to your children's children, those rights and privileges to which as free-born Britons you are justly entitled. And to whom, to whom are you indebted for this mighty boon? You know it well : it is to the high-minded, the united, the brave British people. Pledge me, then, in a flowing, in a brimless bumper, and drain it off to the very lees— to the people, to the brave British people !"*

Pretty good, that ; though it may on cool reflection seem rather too highly poised. But it suited the taste and temperature of the meeting, and the sentiment was rapturously responded to with that highest of festive numbers, "three times three." In a district where such sentiments prevailed, Mr William Robert Keith Douglas, M.P., could expect no more favours. Feeling himself to be foredoomed, he quietly withdrew into private life.

Though this was the case, General Sharpe did not get leave to walk the course. A new rival of liberal politics, Mr David Hannay of Carlinwark House, agent for the National Bank in Dumfries, entered the field and received a considerable amount of support The first election for the Five Burghs under the new Act took place on the 18th of December, 1832. It was a scene of intense excitement. Once more General Sharpe, who continued to be the popular candidate, was met by a grand procession in the English

* *Dumfries Courier.*

road, and escorted to the hustings, which were erected in Queensberry Square. Mr Hannay having also reached the arena, accompanied by a goodly retinue of gentlemen, the business was proceeded with. Provost Corson, seconded by Mr M'Diarmid, proposed General Sharpe ; and the other candidate was nominated
by Mr Sinclair, bookseller, and seconded by the provost of Maxwelltown, Mr John Hairstens. Both candidates addressed the
immense crowd assembled in the Square : but it was long before
Hannay, who was a capital speaker, could command a hearing.
On a show of hands being called for, the presiding officer, Sheriff
Kirkpatrick, said : " It seems almost impossible for me to decide
which party has the majority ; but my impression is that General
Sharpe's is the most numerous." Provost Corson, on being consulted on the point, cried, " Two to one, and far more, in favour of
General Sharpe !"* " Then," said Mr Hannay, " I demand a poll ;"
and accordingly the battle was fought out in the polling booths on
the following Thursday and Friday. From the first it was looked
upon as a matter of certainty by all save a few sanguine Hannay-
ites that Sharpe would be returned ; yet, as the voting went on,
the parties seemed to be well-balanced in the chief burgh ; and
Kirkcudbright, with a clannish feeling for the Galloway candidate,
supported him so well, that had it not been for the powerful
muster made by his Annanite opponents he would have borne
away the prize. But, as on a previous memorable contest,

> " Up sprang Bess o' Annandale,
> And a deadly aith she's taen,
> That she wad vote the Border knight,
> Though she should vote her lane."

So fully and faithfully did the Annan electors carry out this resolution, that they soon and finally decided the wavering balance in
favour of General Sharpe.

At half-past twelve o'clock on Friday, a return was issued as
follows :—For Sharpe, 239 ; for Hannay, 225. This was but a
small majority for the former gentleman ; shortly afterwards,
however, a messenger from the General's citadel burgh, " fiery red
with haste," he having ridden sixteen miles in seventy minutes,
brought a dispatch couched in these terms :—" Annan, half-past
twelve o'clock, Friday.—For General Sharpe, 143; for Mr Hannay,
16 ; majority, 127 ; nine only to poll." This news was not simply
discouraging to Mr Hannay's committee—it was overwhelmingly
crushing. Fight as you may, stout burghers of Kirkcudbright,
you cannot, unless doubled in number, change the fortunes of the
day. Seventy-nine of them supported the squire of Carlingwark ;
twice seventy-nine, with Annan so dead against him, could not
have secured his success. It was known late on Friday night in
Dumfries that not only had Sharpe been returned but that his

* *Dumfries Courier.*

majority was most decided ; and the public sentiment found vent, as usual, in bell-ringing and barrel-burning outside—in convivial gatherings within. Next morning printed returns, which proved to be nearly correct, were issued as follows :—" Close of the poll. For General Sharpe : Dumfries, 275 ; Annan, 144 ; Kirkcudbright, 28 ; Sanquhar, 22 ; Lochmaben, 19. For Mr Hannay : Dumfries, 265 ; Annan, 17 ; Kirkcudbright, 79 ; Sanquhar, 18 ; Lochmaben, 10."* At twelve o'clock, the Sheriff, in the audience of a rejoicing multitude, declared the state of the poll : that in all the burghs General Sharpe had received 487 votes, and Mr Hannay 375 ; and that General Sharpe had been duly elected by a majority of 112.

Thus the honest, unvarnished chief of Hoddom rose to the summit of his earthly ambition. He was worthy of the honour awarded to him, and was proud and grateful for having received it. In tendering his thanks he warmly repudiated the charge brought against him by his opponents, of a want of interest in the county town ; and closed by saying : " Some of my ancestors repose in St. Michael's churchyard ; and as further proof of my alleged want of sympathy, it is my wish that my ashes shall rest in the same spot. Provided I do my duty to the satisfaction of the constituency, I hope some surviving friend, after my course is run, will inscribe on my tombstone—for I can desire no prouder epitaph— ' Here rest the remains of the first representative of the Independent Constituency of the Dumfries District of Burghs.' "†

* The precise figures were – Sharpe : Dumfries, 275 ; Annan, 144 ; Sanquhar, 22 ; Lochmaben, 19 ; Kirkcudbright, 27. Hannay : Dumfries, 255 ; Annan, 17 ; Sanquhar, 18 ; Lochmaben, 10 ; Kirkcudbright, 75.

† The old monument of the Sharpe family, erected at the south-western corner of the cemetery, is enriched with fine carved work, and two mourning cherubs, beautifully executed. General Sharpe died in 1841, and was buried in the churchyard of Hoddam.

CHAPTER LVII.

BEFORE the close of the protracted agitation to which the reader's
attention has just been turned, the fearful malady, cholera
morbus, began to excite alarm throughout the country. It had
long scourged India. In 1831 it appeared in the north-west of
Europe, and after committing sad ravages there, crossed over in
some Hamburgh vessels to Sunderland, first startling that town
with its presence on the 26th of the following October. Next
spring many places far separate from each other were visited by
the fell disease, and the towns that had hitherto escaped awaited
their turn in gloom and terror. Dumfries for the two preceding
years had been more than usually healthy ; but as soon as the
warning note was sounded from Sunderland steps were taken to
improve its sanitary condition, which was admittedly defective.
A vigorous Board of Health was constituted on the 15th of March,
1832,* and under its directing agency, supplemented by private
effort, the houses of the humbler classes were cleansed with hot
lime ; and, what was of more moment, perhaps, supplies of
nourishing soup and other food were served out to many of
their inmates during the winter season. After much had been
done to put the old tenements of the closes, in which hundreds of
families dwelt, in better order, and effect other improvements, the
town was still in a very unsatisfactory state. The scavenging
was deficient ; the drainage merely nominal ; and, worst of all,
the water supply was limited and impure.

With the exception of what was furnished by a few wells and
private pumps, all the water used for domestic purposes was
carried by hand or carted in barrels from the Nith by four old
men, who doled it out in tin pitchers or cans, from door to door,

---

* The Board (constituted by a Privy Council order) consisted of the
following gentlemen :—Provost Corson ; Bailie Robert Armstrong ; Bailie
James Swan ; Mr George Montgomery, dean of guild ; Mr James Thomson,
deacon-convener ; the Rev. Robert Wallace ; Dr William Maxwell ; Mr Archibald Blacklock, surgeon ; Mr James M'Lauchlan, surgeon ; ex-Provost M'Kie ;
ex-Provost Fraser ; Mr John Commelin, agent for the British Linen Company ; Mr John M'Diarmid ; Mr Robert Threshie of Barnbarroch ; and Mr
James Broom, town clerk.

at the rate of five canfuls a penny. The river, when swelled by heavy rains, which was often the case, became thick with mud ; and it was constantly exposed to a more noxious pollution, caused by the refuse poured into it from the town. The quality of the water did not improve by being borne about in barrels of suspicious aspect ; and often, indeed, the liquid drawn from them during summer acquired a taste-me-not repulsiveness by the presence of innumerable little objects, pleasant to no one save an enthusiast in entomology. Besides, the water, whether bad or indifferent, was often not to be had for love or money by the families who depended on the barrels. Sometimes these intermitting fountains stopped running altogether. At such periods portions of the town experienced a water-dearth, thus obtaining a faint inkling, at least, of one leading phase in Oriental life. When the burgh was originally built the houses were massed in closses together, that they might be more easily defended against a foreign enemy ; and when cholera came, as come it did, these places of defence were its chief objects of attack. The town, in fact, as a whole, when looked upon from a sanitary point of view, lay open and exposed to the visitation. A neighbouring city, Carlisle, had a passing call from the disease in July. Coming nearer and nearer, it entered the little village of Tongland Bridge, where it left two victims ; then, after lingering some weeks about the district, doing little harm, but gathering increased power and venom, the fell destroyer burst upon Dumfries.

The first sufferer was a respectable elderly widow, named Paterson, residing in English Street, who was seized on the 15th of September, and died on the following day.* A man in good circumstances, also advanced in life, who resided in an opposite house, hearing of what had occurred, became much alarmed, took ill, and was a corpse before twenty hours elapsed. These were the first prey of the pestilence. For about a week afterwards it seemed to be but dallying with its work, at the rate of only one death per day : a heavy mortality in a population of ten thousand, yet not very alarming, everything considered. "Can this really be cholera ?" many asked ; and some concluded that it was a mere British imitation of the Asiatic disease ; others, that it was the

---

* The second case occurred on the 16th, and the third on the 17th September, in a house of three stories directly opposite to Mary Paterson's house. The names of the sufferers were William Bell and John Paton ; who, being advanced in years, both rapidly sank and died. There were some miserable lodging-houses, for the reception of vagrants from all parts of the kingdom, adjoining Mary Paterson's house ; and such was the anxiety of her neighbours to witness and relieve her sufferings, that two gentlemen, and a town's officer, had to stand at her door till within an hour of her death, to prevent them harassing both her and her medical attendants ; one of whom, Mr M'Cracken, shortly afterwards fell a victim to the disease.—*Note by Dr Blacklock.*

real disorder, but of a mild type, and that the town was going to
get off with a very slight attack. From the 15th of September
till the 24th, inclusive, there were seventeen cases, nine of which
were fatal ; but when, on the 25th, fourteen new cases and
nine deaths were announced, all the people felt that the veritable plague was in their midst, and were filled with fear and
trembling.

This was in Rood-fair week, when the great annual horse
market is held, and the Trades' processions and rejoicings used to
take place. No pageantry in this the closing week of September,
1832, save dismal processions, coming so thick that they jostle
each other as they hurry onward to the tomb : no revelry, but
numerous incidents that might well have figured in Holbein's
fantastic picture, " The Dance of Death." September 26th, nine
new cases, and five deaths ; 27th, thirty-seven new cases, and five
deaths ; 28th, sixty-eight new cases, and nineteen deaths ! The
plague is now holding high carnival ! May God, in His great
mercy, take pity on the poor town, and stay the ravages of the
destroyer ! But it has, as it were, little more than begun its fatal
mission, and speeds on through all parts of Dumfries and the
neighbouring burgh of Maxwelltown, sparing no age, smiting rich
and poor alike, and prostrating the strong nearly as much as
the feeble. At first the humbler classes suffered most severely :
eventually it mattered little whether people sojourned in narrow,
noisome courts, or in spacious squares—in the vilest rookeries of
the Vennel, or in the stately mansions of Buccleuch Street : all
places were freely visited, and no respect of persons was paid.

What rendered the cholera more appalling was the circumstance that every one believed it to be both infectious and
contagious. It was supposed that an affected individual distilled
a poisonous influence all around him ; that there was death in his
touch ; and that the virus of the malady lurked in every article
of his dress. He was counted like a leper of the old Levitical
dispensation, and alas ! too often treated as such ; and when the
cases began to multiply, the town was looked upon as a magazine
of disease—a place devoted to the plague, which no man dared to
enter, and from which many hastened in panic-fear, only, however, in some instances, to fall cholera-stricken in their flight.
Moreover, the disease was very little, if at all, amenable to medical
treatment. It was a mysterious epidemic, which " walked in
darkness," defying all the science and devotedness of the faculty.

> The salutary art
> Was mute ; and, startled at the new disease,
> In fearful whispers hopeless omens gave.
> To heaven, with suppliant rites, they sent their prayers :
> Heaven heard them not. Of every hope deprived,
> Fatigued with vain resources, and subdued
> With woes resistless, and enfeebling fear,
> Passive they sank beneath the weighty blow.

Nothing but lamentable sounds was heard,
Nor aught was seen save ghastly views of death.
Infectious horror ran from face to face,
And pale despair. 'Twas all the business then
To tend the sick, and in their turns to die.
In heaps they fell : and oft one bed, they say,
The sickening, dying, and the dead contained."*

In addition to the resident medical gentlemen, five practitioners were brought from Edinburgh, and two from Castle-Douglas, by the Board of Health. The whole of them, we believe, performed their duty faithfully ; and, sad to tell, two of the native surgeons, Mr William M'Cracken and Mr John M'Ghie, martyrs to their professional zeal, caught the malady and died. No cases were admitted into the Infirmary—a most unwise resolution to that effect having been adopted by a majority of its governors ; and the poorer class of patients, instead of being laid in the well-furnished, well-ventilated, spacious wards of that institution, were crowded into a hospital made out of an old granary, at the foot of English Street. Here they had little chance of recovering ; and their close contact with each other tended to intensify the disease—though the truth is, that there was nearly as great a proportion of deaths among rich persons attacked, and treated in their own houses, as among the poor, one case in every two of both classes having usually a fatal result. The civil authorities of the town, the clergymen, and the influential inhabitants generally, soon rose above the terror which at first seized upon men of all ranks, and co-operated zealously and courageously with the medical practitioners in their efforts to stay the course of the disease.

Direct resistance to it was found to be of little service ; but a plan for withdrawing out of the way those who were peculiarly exposed to an attack was adopted with success. When the head of a poor family was laid low, and the arrows of the pestilence were flying right and left in his homestead, its remaining members were conveyed to rooms in the Academy prepared for their reception, and there comfortably boarded and otherwise cared for. The doors of the High School were closed when the disease became epidemic ; and they were re-opened early in October for heart work rather than head work, that an asylum might be afforded to widows and orphans hurrying away from their ravaged homes and the presence of the destroying pest. By the middle of the month this house of refuge numbered a hundred and twenty inmates, chiefly fatherless children, whose varied wants of mind and body were supplied by a band of " ministering angels ;" and it is gratifying to record that the well-aired lodgings, nourishing food, and warm clothing given to the poor refugees kept them in

* Armstrong's Art of Preserving Health, book iii.

health and strength when the localities they had fled from were still haunted by the destroyer. Good food and comfortable clothing were rightly considered as a species of defensive armour, which sometimes turned away the poisoned shaft when medicine would have been of no avail. A soup kitchen was opened on a liberal scale ; and that in itself, there is every reason to suppose, foreclosed many an attack. Great quantities of tar and pitch were burned in the lanes and streets, making the prevailing gloom more lurid. This was for the purpose of disinfecting the atmosphere ; but the dusky vapour thus sent into it was of no service as compared with the savoury smoke from the generous broth doled out liberally to every applicant. To meet the great expense incurred, a rate was imposed by the Board of Health ; a large fund was raised by voluntary subscription ; and many towns, both in England and Scotland, shewed their sympathy for Dumfries—cholera-stricken more than any town in proportion to its size— by handsome pecuniary contributions for its relief.

Having said this much regarding the means taken to cope with the disease, we must now trace its further progress. Any and every effort to stay its course or propitiate its fury seem, for a while at least, utterly fruitless. September 29th.—The awful visitor is still making fearful havoc : new cases, fifty-two; deaths, thirteen. September 30th.—Worse and worse : no fewer than seventy-three new names are registered, and fourteen deaths occur. October 1st. — Fifty-six new cases, and twenty-three deaths. October 2nd.—Deadliest day of all—" Be thou for ever blotted from the calendar !" The new cases are fifty-five ; the deaths, fourty-four. We dare not pause to reflect upon the scenes of horror which these figures suggest—scenes such as the burgh never witnessed before, though often desolated by the fiend of war ; unless when, in 1623, it was scourged by both plague and famine, which, during the spring and summer of that year, destroyed at least five hundred of the inhabitants. " The bare recollection of them," says the *Courier*, at the time of the crisis, " is enough to quail the stoutest heart : what, then, must have been the dreadful reality ? Hearses plying in every street ; patients seized, and in imminent danger, faster than the bearers were able to remove them, or mourners accompany them to their long home ; the gravedigger's spade in constant requisition ; the strong man stricken down in his pride ; the feeble snatched in a few hours from a sick-bed to the tomb ; the hospital emptied, and as quickly filled again ; for several days scarcely a single recovery ; the faculty fatigued beyond endurance, compelled to ride the shortest distances, and yet unable to answer the incessant calls of suffering humanity ; at other times seriously affected themselves, until relieved by the promptitude and skill of their brethren ; shops for general business shut at noonday ; publicans

warned to close their stores at dusk, that the vicious might be
hampered in their evil propensities ; every vehicle employed in
removing family after family to the country ; the public schools
dismissed ; St. Michael's vacated from the dread of cholera graves,
and divine service performed in the Court-house ; trade suspended, workshops depopulated, and industrious traders gathered
into knots, discussing the fearful extent of the pestilence ; many
requiring medical aid, and paralysed from the force of terror
alone ; every countenance shaded with grief, and a whole community the picture of despair."

October 3rd, when the disease reached its culminating stage,
was market-day ; but when death was mercilessly tithing the
town, no business toll was levied at the bridge. Out of nearly
sixty carriers only one made his appearance. No butter, eggs, or
poultry were offered for sale. Not a solitary bullock was seen on
the Sands, though two thousand cattle at least would have been
there under ordinary circumstances. Next day (October 4th)
brought little abatement of the epidemic ; for though the deaths
fell to twenty-seven, sixty-two new cases were announced. The
report on October 5th was thirty-two new cases, and only eleven
deaths ; and people began to breathe with some degree of freedom. The weather, too, underwent an auspicious change. During
the first ten days of the visitation the sky wore a peculiar aspect ;
and when the suffering town was viewed from the surrounding
heights, a dense mass of cloud appeared hovering over it, which
spectators, with no great stretch of fancy, compared to a vast
funeral pall. " Both burghs" (Dumfries and Maxwelltown), says
Mr Forsyth, " looked as if doomed to destruction : a dense black
canopy enveloped the whole skiey amphitheatre as far as the eye
could reach, fringed by a narrow ray of pinky light along the
horizon, and the sun rarely shedding a ray upon the towns in
which death was so busy."* The pressure of the atmosphere was

---

* Reminiscences of Maxwelltown.

Mr Archibald Forbes, the distinguished correspondent of the *Daily News*
during the Franco-German war, writing to that paper under date "Le Vert
Gallant, 17th January, 1871," respecting the bombardment of Paris, says :
"To-day, atmospherically, has been a day by itself—one of those dull, surly,
yet semi-clear days, that are commoner in summer when thunder is in the air
than in mid-winter. Under such circumstances the aspect which Paris presented was weirdly unique. There is a town in the south of Scotland around
which lingers to this day a ghastly memory, of which the elders shudder when
they speak, and of which the young ones are thankful that they had no personal experience. Dumfries stands in the bottom of a cup, the edges of which
are framed by hills. In 1832 the cholera raged in Britain, and it fastened its
fell fangs on Dumfries. For days, for weeks, for months, it claimed its
victims, till the ill report of the pestilential place was so strong that never a
vender dared enter it with his wares. And all these days—days when the
pest stalked abroad relentless—there hung over the cup, in the bottom of
which stands the town, a dull, heavy film—not dense, indeed, but mystically
altering the sun-rays from bright gold to a lurid orange, and mantling the

felt to be unusually heavy, though that was partly attributable, no doubt, to the circumstance that the nervous system of those who breathed it had lost its wonted tone through the operation of grief and terror. On the 30th of September, after heavy rain on the preceding day, the sky became comparatively bright. The dull, close season returned, however, and continued till the 4th of October, when, about midnight, a tremendous thunder-storm unexpectedly burst over the town ; but though the inhabitants were startled by the peals—sounding "like voice of judgment from the sky"—they operated favourably by dispersing the "cholera cloud," and bringing down copious showers, which helped in their turn to clear the atmosphere. Though this improvement in the weather was short-lived, it exercised a cheering influence : the buoyant air combined with the lightening calendar brought gleams of hope to many a despairing heart—ay, and health to the pulse of many a wasted frame. Then the more sanguine portion of the inhabitants flattered themselves with the idea that the epidemic would decline as rapidly as it had been developed : but, on the 6th, thirty-six new cases and seventeen deaths were reported, as if it had obtained a new lease of power ; and before the cycle of the disease was finished, October had run its course.

As showing the march of the disease for the following fortnight, we quote from a diary published in one of the local newspapers. October 7th (Sabbath).—"To-day the weather was wet and stormy ; the thermometer still lower, and the rain occasionally mixed with hail." New cases, thirty-one ; deaths, four. 8th.— "Another showery and stormy day." New cases, thirty-five ; deaths, twenty-one. 9th.—"The town still unprecedentedly dull and deserted ; many shops remaining closed at noon-day." New cases, fourteen ; deaths, fourteen. 10th.—"Although this is market-day, the town is nearly as dull as it was last week. Only two or three carriers have arrived, and these from a considerable

whole place with its evil shadow, as if some foul and persistent ogre of death were spreading his pinions over the place. As men walked the streets they fell to smell the cholera-breath, so stagnant and rotten was the air, and they went home and wanted graves ere morning. Let any man who would realise how a death-pall like this can hang over a city, read M'Dowall's "History of Dumfries," in the chapter where the author describes the ghastly features of this visitation. As I looked down on Paris to-day there came vividly before me the description I had read of Dumfries in '32. All round it, save on the north side, surged up the foam of the white smoke of the bombardment. Over it hung the dull brown pall of the smoke thrown up by the exploding shells, and the casual conflagrations not large, but frequent, which they occasioned. Underneath—below this brooding demon of brown smoke—the city showed out wondrous clear and plain. At times the sun's rays struggled through the black clouds that underlay the heavens ; fell on the brown pall ; battled through the crannies in it ; and kissed lovingly some white house or metal roof in the beautiful city. Never can I forget the strangely beautiful and yet almost ghastly and utterly abnormal effect."

distance, such as Newcastle, Edinburgh, and Glasgow. Some of the hucksters have procured a small supply of butter, but the price is advanced twenty-five per cent. The Sands is minus a single bullock, and some of the jobbers are anxious that the magistrates should transfer the market to the nine-mile toll-bar. To this advice the authorities demur, and have intimated a hope that in the course of a week or two the panic will die away, and matters proceed in their ordinary course." New cases, sixteen ; deaths, fourteen. 11th.—"The weather dreadful, and contributing, among many other causes, to depress the animal spirits." New cases, fifteen ; deaths, eight. 12th.—"To-day the weather is better ; comparatively few hearses have been seen ; in certain wards scarcely a new case has occurred ; and the whole faculty have evidently profited by one or more nights of sound repose." New cases, thirteen ; deaths, eleven. 13th.—"The weather to-day was delightful ; the medical report, the most cheering that has yet been issued. Nine new cases ; six deaths." 14th.—"There has been one case of cholera in the Infirmary and eight in the Poorhouse. The under jailor and his wife died of cholera some time ago. The head jailor was next attacked, and had hardly recovered when his sister-in-law fell a victim. Some of the prisoners have also been seized." New cases, twenty ; deaths, five. 15th.—"The weather is still close, gloomy, and moist. New cases, twenty ; deaths, eleven." 16th.—"The weather was rather un-promising in the morning, and 'heavily in clouds brought on the day ;' but it improved in the course of the forenoon, and enabled many to brace their nerves, and breathe a purer atmosphere, by strolling a few miles into the country. The medical report was exceedingly cheering, and had an excellent effect on the spirits of the people." New cases, four ; deaths, eight. 17th.—"Another cheering report ; one or two lots of cattle on the Sands ; goodly lots in motion for the markets of the South ; a considerable number of maidens in the egg and butter market ; friends long amissing showing face at last, and the town altogether ten per cent. better than it has been for the last three weeks. The weather good ; the air bracing, and free from moisture ; and everything tending to restore us to, not frighten us from, our propriety." New cases, three ; deaths, three. 18th.—"The medical report still excellent, and several of the stranger practitioners about to leave us. To-day the soup-kitchen was opened under excellent management." New cases, four ; deaths, four. 19th.— "Report to-day not quite so favourable : eight new cases, three deaths, and twenty-eight recoveries. The recoveries, however, are a cheering circumstance ; and we begin to indulge the hope that we will ere long be enabled to announce a clean bill of health. The weather continues delightful, is verging to what it should be during winter, and the remark has become nearly as current as a pass-word, that Dumfries will soon be itself again."

And so, happily, it was, before many more weeks elapsed. For some time one or two fatal cases per day were reported ; and on the 30th of October it was announced, for the first time during the visitation, that not a single death had occurred. The fell destroyer still tarried in the town and suburbs, as if loath to leave a locality where he had acquired such a hecatomb of victims ; but about the middle of November, after a two months' reign of terror, the fiat of an interposing Providence stayed his terrible hand, and, like the overmastered fiend in Bunyan's dream, he "spread forth his dragon's wings, and sped him away." "Few can figure to themselves the pleasure we at length feel," says the *Courier* of the 13th of November, "in announcing that the doors of the cholera hospital have been closed, and that its only occasional inmate is a supernumerary nurse, whose instructions are to keep the pest-house ventilated and free from damp—a precaution which has been adopted in other quarters. During the past week —that is, from Monday the 5th till Monday the 12th current—the new cases were reduced to five, and the deaths to two ; the recoveries within the same period were seven ; and yesterday the patients under treatment were so low as five—most, if not all, of whom are expected to recover."

The entire number of persons attacked by cholera in Dumfries, as officially reported, was 837 ; of whom 380 were males and 457 were females. The deaths reported were 421 : 187 males and 234 females. It was ascertained, however, from the number of coffins made, and the sexton's accounts, that the real deaths exceeded the reputed ones ;* and the probability is, we think, that the mortality was not less than 550. Of the fatal cases 68 occurred in the cholera hospital. Maxwelltown, population considered, suffered about as severely as the sister burgh ; the cases there having been 237, and the deaths 127 ; the first case occurring on the 21st of September, and the last on the 31st of December. A large proportion of those who died in Dumfries were buried in a plot of St. Michael's churchyard set apart for the purpose. Here gangs of gravediggers were busy for weeks together piling the coffined dead tier above tier, and before the pit was finally covered over it had received at least 350 bodies within its dark embrace. The Cholera Mound, as this vast charnel-house is popularly called, lies along the west side of the burial-ground ; and a neat cenotaph tells the fate of those who sleep below, and of their fellow-sufferers, in the following words :—

---

* Pamphlet on Cholera Morbus.   D. Halliday, Dumfries.

IN THIS CEMETERY,
AND CHIEFLY WITHIN THIS ENCLOSURE,
LIE THE MORTAL REMAINS
OF MORE THAN 420 INHABITANTS OF DUMFRIES,
WHO WERE SUDDENLY SWEPT AWAY
BY THE MEMORABLE INVASION OF
ASIATIC CHOLERA,
A. D. MDCCCXXXII.
THAT TERRIFIC PESTILENCE
ENTERED THE TOWN ON 15TH SEPTEMBER,
AND REMAINED TILL 27TH NOVEMBER ;
DURING WHICH PERIOD IT SEIZED
AT LEAST 900 INDIVIDUALS,
OF WHOM 44 DIED IN ONE DAY,
AND NO MORE THAN 415 WERE REPORTED
AS RECOVERED.
THAT THE BENEFIT OF THIS
SOLEMN WARNING
MIGHT NOT BE LOST TO POSTERITY,
THIS MONUMENT
WAS ERECTED, FROM COLLECTIONS MADE IN
SEVERAL CHURCHES IN THIS TOWN.

Ps. xc.—Thou turnest man to destruction ; and sayest, Return, ye children of men. Thou carriest them away as with a flood.

Mat. xxv. 13.—Watch therefore ; for ye know neither the day nor the hour.

CHAPTER LVIII.

As may easily be supposed, the trade of the town was injured for
years by this visitation. The Highland occupation occasioned
directly and indirectly a loss of at least £5000 ; but probably four
times that amount would not cover the expenditure and loss arising from the cholera. Yet, appalling and exhaustive though the
epidemic was, it did good in one respect, by originating a great
sanitary movement, having for its main objects street sewerage
and improved water supply : the former was partially obtained ;
for the latter the town had unfortunately to wait nearly twenty
years. It was very near securing the boon. One of the town
clerks, Mr James Broom, a gentleman of great talent, energy, and
public spirit, whose memory is held dear in Dumfries, was one of
its principal advocates. Provost Corson, Mr James Swan, and
other members of the Town Council, were anxious for it, but somehow or other the efforts put forth by them failed ; and a scheme
prepared by Mr Jardine, civil engineer, in 1833,* for introducing
the water of Nunland springs, from the neighbouring Galloway
hills, figured on paper, but went no farther. It may be a mere
fancy on our part, that the desire for municipal freedom was also
stimulated by the disease ; but we incline to the opinion that the
inhabitants became more anxious to acquire the right of self-
government, from a belief that they would thereby be able so to
improve the town as to render it less likely to be ravaged by
epidemics in future.

Certain it is that they exhibited much zeal in the matter ; and
that their rulers, self-elected though they were, manifested a
praiseworthy desire to get rid of the old close system. On the 5th
of April, 1833, the Council discussed the Burgh Reform Bill, that
had been brought into Parliament by the Lord Advocate. It was
generally approved of ; and the Provost was commissioned to
attend a special meeting of the Convention of Royal Burghs, for
the purpose of expressing the Council's views on the subject.

* Town Council Minutes.

These were extremely Liberal—Radical almost, as shown by the instructions given to Mr Carson. On the motion of Mr Allan Anderson, seconded by Mr David M'Gill, the commissioner was enjoined to move, "That in regard to the qualification clause for voting for Council and magistrates, the whole shall be vested in the resident householders of a certain rent; and the right proposed to be conferred on freemen, and guilders or burgesses, merely as such, shall not form a part of the bill."* This blow at monopoly was followed by another heavier one at class-privilege—Mr William Nicholson (afterwards provost) moving that the commissioner be also instructed to propose, "That in regard to this burgh, and burghs of a similar right and population, the rent qualifying a voter be five pounds"—a motion which, like the first one, was unanimously agreed to.

Whilst the Council called on the legislative Hercules to help the municipal waggon out of the mire, they set their own shoulders manfully to the wheel. Without waiting for Parliamentary action, they, on the 12th of the same month, at the instance of the Provost, resolved with one accord to lay open the privileges of the town to all and sundry.† Since the days of Robert Bruce, if not before, no one could begin business as a merchant or as a trades-man in the town without first being made a burgess or freeman, at considerable expense. If the applicant was the son or son-in-law of a burgess or freeman, he was required to pay a smaller "composition" sum ; but in other cases the "fine," as it was called, was often a serious affair, amounting latterly to £13 6s 8d —a heavy tax on young shopkeepers and craftsmen, and hinder-ing many altogether from commencing business in the burgh. A few days afterwards, at a crowded meeting of the inhabitants, a vote of thanks to the Council was passed, and petitions to Parlia-ment were adopted, praying for the abolition of burgh incorpora-tions in Scotland ; the petitioners setting forth that these had outlived their time ; "that the prosperity of towns where no such incorporations exist, and the decay of towns where they do exist, sufficiently prove that they are equally unprofitable to their mem-bers as to the public ; and that from its local circumstances this truth has been specially exemplified in the case of the town of Dumfries." The chief speech on the occasion was made by the deacon of the shoemakers, "Orator Wilson," a fluent tribune of the people, who did good service in the agitation for Reform. He proclaimed himself to be a Radical politician, eager to lay the symbolic axe at the root of all abuses. He held up to ridicule the idea of people, before they could open shop in the burgh, having to pay down £13 6s 8d for a paltry piece of "sheepskin ;" and he asked how they could petition Parliament to give up the East

* Town Council Minutes.   † Ibid.

India monopoly if the Seven Trades' monopoly was maintained
unbroken ? But the Trades themselves would be as honest as they
were brave, and co-operate with the Council in breaking down
the exclusive system. As for the magistrates and Council of Dumfries, "they will live in the hearts of their townsmen for the noble
concession they have made, and fame will carry their names and
actions to distant posterity. Their fame," continued the speaker,
rising with his subject—"their fame, I say, will be as lasting as
the pyramids of Egypt. Time will never shake it, and imperishable laurels will deck their brow."* Some little laughter mingled
with the applause which greeted this peroration ; but the soaring
eloquence of the worthy deacon did not go a bit too high for the
majority of his hearers. It was a time of vast expectations, as
well as of much excitement ; and big words—what the Americans
term " bunkum," or " tall talk "—were much in vogue.

The Scotch Burgh Reform Bill received the royal assent in
September, 1833, and took effect on the first Tuesday of the
following November. Greatly to the disappointment of the Dumfries Town Council and community, the qualification for voters
was fixed at double the figure they had proposed. Instead of a
five pound rent one of ten pounds was adopted. The new mode
of election was, however, such a vast improvement on the delegate
system that it was warmly welcomed in the burgh ; and the proceedings on the 6th of November, when it was put in force, excited
great interest. Numerous candidates were started, in all the four
wards into which the town had been divided by a royal commission. We append the names of the gentlemen who received the
honour of being the first councillors of the burgh chosen by
popular suffrage. First Ward : Robert Murray, writer, 72 votes ;
Thomas Hairstens, tanner, 57 ; Captain M'Dowall, 47 ; Thomas
Milligan, plumber, deacon of the smiths, 45 ; George Dunbar
cabinetmaker, deacon of the squaremen, 45 ; Samuel Blaind, jun.,
draper, 38. Second ward : William Gordon, writer, 72 ; John
Barker, banker, 71 ; Robert Thomson, merchant, 71 ; James
Walker, wine merchant, 53 ; James Dinwiddie, painter, 50 ; John
Anderson, bookseller, 49 ; Thomas Lonsdale, ironmonger, 32. Third
ward : Robert M'Harg, merchant, 68 ; Robert Scott, hosier, 57 ;
William Nicholson, chair-maker, 46 ; Joseph Beck, coachbuilder,
42 ; Christopher Smyth, writer, 40 ; George Kerr, cabinetmaker,
35. Fourth ward : Robert Kemp, writer, 56 ; Thomas Harkness,
writer, 47 ; Thomas Kennedy, seedsman, 46 ; Alexander Lookup,
skinner, 45 ; Benjamin Oney, clothier, 41 ; Robert Kerr, tanner,
40. As the burgess fine, though condemned, was still exacted,
Captain M'Dowall declined on principle to qualify for his seat by
paying it. A new election for the vacancy was therefore ordered,

* *Dumfries Courier.*

which resulted in the return of Mr George Montgomery, draper. The Council being now quite made up, elected Mr Murray, writer, a gentleman of great ability and moral worth, as the first Reform Provost of Dumfries ; Messrs Kemp, M'Harg, and Harkness were elected bailies ; Mr Walker was appointed dean of guild ; and Mr Barker treasurer and chamberlain. A banquet in the Commercial Hotel appropriately crowned the inauguration of the new municipal system in the burgh.*

By an Act of Parliament passed in 1846, the chief of the exclusive privileges possessed by the Dumfries Trades, and all similar incorporations, were abolished ; and long before that year the Seven Trades had become virtually defunct—a fragment of the body remaining, but all its original spirit gone. The few remaining members continued to hold the property of the Trades, till, in March, 1852, they adopted a unanimous resolution to sell the movable portion of it, except the Silver Gun, which was handed over to the Town Council for preservation. Against this resolution, so far as the convener's gold chain was affected, Mr Adam Rankine, as a subscriber for the badge, applied for an interdict. The case thus raised excited much interest. The sheriff-substitute, Mr Trotter, decided it in favour of the pursuer: Sheriff Napier, on appeal, reversed the decision ; and his interlocutor, on being advocated, was sustained by the Lord Ordinary Rutherford. Accordingly, the chain and the other articles were disposed of by public auction, in the Trades' Hall, on the 8th of April, 1854. Altogether, a melancholy sight it must have been—one that is rather depressing to reflect upon, though it was but the natural sequence of the wise reform that had been effected. Think of these historical relics being knocked down like vulgar chattels ! Even the venerable quarto Bible which the syndic of the craftsmen used at church passed into other hands, and that for the paltry sum of seventeen shillings. The little silver seal with which the documents of the brotherhood had been stamped for nearly two centuries was, for a sorry equivalent of ten shillings, deprived of its official *caste*, so to speak, in spite of its lion, fierce, crowned, and rampant, and its motto, "God save the King and the Craft !" A sword once owned, according to tradition, by the Red Comyn, and seemingly old enough to have been worn by him on the day of his fatal rencontre with Bruce, brought £3 3s. The great Grainger punch-bowl, first brimmed with rum toddy in 1806, under the merry conditions we have previously related, and which so often afterwards replenished glasses that were drained in drinking the toast it bears, "Success to the Incorporations !" lapsed into the moderate seclusion of private life for £2 ; the accompanying silver divider being separated from it, and sold for fifteen shillings. The

* Town Council Minutes, and local newspapers.

wonderful snuff-mull presented by Captain M'Dowall, brought to an unexpected pinch, drew £3 3s. For the ebony staff of office, now that the convener's occupation was gone, £2 18s was realised; and the gold chain of that once powerful, but now impotent, chief of the Trades, became metaphorically dim on this mournful day, though it fell into the hands of a worthy townsman, Mr Samuel Milligan, merchant, for the sum of £35.

The proceeds of the entire sale amounted only to £54 2s 6d ; and it is certainly to be regretted that the principal effects disposed of were not purchased for preservation, instead of being scattered to the four winds. In course of time the Trades' Hall, and the pews in St. Michael's belonging to the Incorporations, were also disposed of ;* Mr Francis Nicholson, merchant, becoming the purchaser of the Hall, in 1847, for £650, but £630 had previously been borrowed on the building.

One of the first fruits of the Reformed Parliament was a General Police Act for such burghs as chose to avail themselves of it. The chief provisions of the measure were adopted at a public meeting held in Dumfries on the 17th of January, 1834 ; and in accordance with it, a rate of one shilling in the pound was imposed, divided as follows :—Paving, independent of road money, 1d per pound, £75 ; watching, 3d per pound, £225 ; lighting, 3½d per pound, £262 10s ; cleansing, 1d per pound, £75; miscellaneous, ½d per pound, £37 10s ; interest and sinking fund, 3d per pound, £225 : total, £900. In allocating these sums it was assumed that the rental assessable would be £18,000.

The mode of supporting the poor of the burgh and parish by church-door collections, and the alms-giving of the benevolent, had long been looked upon as unsatisfactory ; and so greatly had they been increased in number by the cholera visitation, that the adoption of some new plan was felt to be imperative. An endeavour to raise funds by a voluntary assessment having been tried without success, a resolution was adopted by the Town Council and Police Commissioners, in May, to impose a legal rate for the relief of the poor. From the statistics on which they proceeded we learn that the valued rent of the burgh was set down at £18,772 8s ; of the burgh roods, £4450 13s ; and of the landward part of the parish, £7441 15s : in all, £30,664 16s. So fearfully, however, had the epidemic scourge of 1832 depopulated the town, and injured its trade, that a deduction of £670 10s had to be made from the valuation for shops and houses that were standing unlet. The rate was fixed at a maximum of one shilling in the pound, leviable half-yearly : the computation being that, with the rural part of the parish concurring, the first assessment

---

* " It was a curious circumstance," says Mr John Anderson in his manuscript account of Dumfries, " that Selkirk was the name of the deacon of the trade who led the van in the sale of the Kirk seats."

of sixpence would yield £767 ; which, if carefully husbanded, would, it was believed, suffice for more than six months, and reduce the second instalment to fourpence or less.

During this summer (1834) a movement was commenced for obtaining improved market accommodation. From a distant, if not immemorial period, the country damsels belonging to the neighbouring district exposed their butter, eggs, and poultry for sale on a part of High Street adjoining the Mid-Steeple. There they stood every Wednesday, alike in winter as in summer, exposed to the elements, with no shelter or adequate accommodation for their wares, and—however ungallant the phrase may seem—forming a serious obstruction to the traffic of the principal thoroughfare. For their convenience, as well as that of their burghal customers, a proposal was mooted for flitting the fair rural merchants to the building in the east of the town that had been assigned to the corporation of fleshers, in 1760, for the sale of meat, and which had latterly been almost deserted by them for shops in the Vennel and in Maxwelltown, where no dues were exacted. Whilst this scheme was warmly advocated by some members of the Council, others opposed it, chiefly on the plea that the site was far from being a central one. The inhabitants were also greatly divided in opinion on the subject—the *pros* and *cons* were keenly debated ; and it was only when the objectors were unable to point out a better place obtainable at a moderate expense that their opposition was withdrawn and the scheme finally adopted. Its chief promoters were: the Provost, Mr Kemp, elected on the death of Provost Murray, after only six months of service ; Bailies Harkness, M'Harg, and Dinwiddie ; and Councillors Smyth, Beck, and Oney. The building, which belonged to the town, was adapted to its new destination at an expense of less than £500—the builder's contract being £406 10s. It was duly opened for the sale of rural produce in 1835 ; and though rather remote from the centre of the burgh, the New Markets are a decided acquisition. One of the local newspapers, the *Times*, fairly traced their establishment to the operation of municipal reform, and proposed that a name should be given to them commemorative of the fact—a suggestion, however, which was not acted upon. In further accordance with the reforming spirit of the day, the ale-duty, worth £60 to £70 annually, was allowed to lapse ; and the Council, on the motion of Mr William Gordon, writer, long one of the leading Liberals of the burgh, seconded by Bailie Harkness, resolved, by a majority of twelve to six, to abolish a lot of vexatious little dues called the Trone and Three-Port Customs, levied at the entrances of the town, on butter, eggs, cheese, and such like articles, and on grain transmitted through the burgh, and which averaged £45 a year.*

* Town Council Minutes.

At the date of 1780 we gave such a review of past events as might have been taken by an aged Dumfriesian. Now that nearly two other generations have come and gone, a similar retrospect may be given ; and who so fit to furnish it as the senior town-clerk, Mr Francis Shortt of Courance—" a venerable gentleman," says M'Diarmid, writing in 1832, "who retains all his faculties, and a vast fund of local information, at the advanced age of seventy-eight." We cannot now obtain his reminiscences in a literal sense, but we can fancy some of the many changes which he saw during his protracted pilgrimage of more than eighty years. We can suppose this intelligent octogenarian entertaining his more youthful contemporaries with his recollections of how the factious Pyets and Crows ruffled each other's plumage in the famous magisterial contest of 1759 ; of what mutinous mobs he had witnessed—such as the meal riots in 1796, and, a generation afterwards, the popular hydra-headed Nemesis that dogged the heels of the murderer Hare, and the popular tempests which pre-ceded the birth and cradled the infancy of Reform ; of the high Conservatism cherished when Robert Burns, poet and Radical, burst like a meteor on the town, and the ultra Liberalism that came afterwards, and would have made him a demi-god had he not long before prematurely passed away ; of how the bard looked when he was gauging barrels, or handling his arms as a loyal volunteer, or electrifying a social party with his conversational eloquence, or "crooning" some newly-born lyric that was to live for ever—or how, sadly changed, his haggard visage and wasted frame told full surely, in the spring of 1796, that Dumfries was about to lose its most illustrious son—the world, "the greatest poet that ever sprang from the bosom of the people." The aged town-clerk would be able to tell, too, of the building of the New Bridge, the Theatre, the County prison, the Court-house, the Academy, the Assembly Rooms, the New Markets, of the entire new town lying north-west of Friars' Vennel, and of such altera-tions in the shop-architecture of the old town as amounted to a revolution. Of days of darkness and adversity he would also be competent to speak : how a valuable part of the landed inherit-ance of the town had to be sacrificed to keep its head above the waters of bankruptcy ; and how, when the haven of prosperity was reached, a horrible tempest, in the shape of pestilence, over-took and devastated and well-nigh wrecked the devoted burgh. Great as were the historical incidents and material mutations he had seen in his boyhood and prime, the moral revolution effected during his later years was greater and more important. The Dumfries of his childhood had changed before his eyes externally, socially, and politically : it still retained many of its ancient characteristics—the old Old Bridge, the venerable Mid-Steeple, Friars' Vennel (little altered since Burns used to pass down it on his way to Ryedale or Lincluden College), the closes (more's the pity !) of the same pattern as at the date of King James's visit ; and the town still watered by the classic Nith, still overlooked by the "bonnie hills of Galloway," but nevertheless much expanded and modernised. The relics of the Greyfriars' Monastery, of the Castle, and of the New Wark—all of which the old man had gazed upon—had disappeared, with numerous other memorials of mediæval times, and so also had the manners, customs, ideas, and modes of government with which he was long familiar. In the days of his early manhood the close, irresponsible system seemed to be also still in its prime ; and to talk of Parliamentary or municipal reform savoured of treason : now, in his old age, Reform is popular, fashionable, and has already shown its power by sending to the right-about all self-elected or clique-appointed burgh rulers or senatorial representatives.

Of such important incidents and striking changes, occurring within the limits of a life-time, such a faithful witness and "honest chronicler" as we have named could have given, and, we have been assured, often did give, a graphic narrative to his friends. Would that some Boswell had committed the spoken record to paper, or that the local journalists had by other ways and means made their annals more comprehensive and minute. Had this latter course been generally pursued our labour throughout a portion of this work would have been greatly lessened, and the results been rendered more satisfactory. It is but right, however, to add, that, thanks to the newspapers of the town, minute details of the great Reform agitation, and of the dread visit of the epidemic, have been preserved ; and by drawing largely on their columns, we have been enabled to give a copious, and, we trust, an acceptable history of both.

We now, at the close of the old municipal system, stop the general narrative for a little, in order to complete what we have to say respecting the religious denominations, trade, literature, and distinguished men of the burgh.

CHAPTER LIX.

BEFORE the close of the sixteenth century Dumfries was thoroughly Protestant, the Reformation having been radical and
complete. This result was effected chiefly by the great body of
the inhabitants renouncing Roman Catholicism, and in some
degree by the rigorous proscription to which all who adhered to
that faith were liable. It is reported that old St. Michael's Parish
Church was the last place throughout Scotland in which mass
was celebrated before the Presbyterian Establishment was set
up ; and before it was "said or sung" again in the burgh many
generations passed away. During that long interval such few
Romanists as resided in the parish could only take part in public
worship by attending, with some risk to themselves, at the
chapels of Terregles and Kirkconnell : and on more than one
occasion the priests who officiated at the latter place were seized
and sent off to be examined by the Privy Council, on charges of
acting illegally by prosecuting their calling and endeavouring to
proselytize. Two hundred and fifty years after the Reformation
there were only thirty-eight Roman Catholics in the entire parish
of Dumfries.* These were ministered to by Mr John Pepper :
but the body remained without a place of worship till 1811, when
a commodious chapel, dedicated to St. Andrew, was built by
subscription, to which the Terregles and Kirkconnell families
liberally contributed, as also the first clergyman of the congregation, Mr William Reid. It cost, site included, about £2600 ; and
since its erection immense sums have been expended on additions,
internal furnishings, and ornamentation. During a brief interval,
when Mr Reid was stationed in the North, Mr James Carruthers,
author of a "History of Scotland," officiated in his stead ; and on
the removal of Mr Carruthers to Dalbeattie,(a) Mr Reid returned
to his original charge. When he died, in 1845, at the advanced age

---

* Dr Burnside's MS. History.   (a) Newabbey ?

of seventy-eight, he was succeeded by Mr Henry Small, who had previously acted as his assistant for several years. On the death of Mr Small, in 1857, Mr John Strain of Dalbeattie became his successor. In 1858 Mr Strain was appointed President of Blair's College, near Aberdeen ; and in 1864 he was elected Bishop of Abila and Vicar-Apostolic of the Eastern District. Mr Patrick Macmanus, who had formerly officiated as curate to Mr Small, was transferred, in 1858, from Murthly Castle to Dumfries, and after labouring there for about eleven years he received an appointment at Dundee, and was succeeded by Mr Archibald Macdonald, the present priest of St. Andrew's congregation.* A schoolroom with a fine ornamental tower—the latter designed by the Honourable Marmaduke C. Maxwell of Terregles—was built contiguous to the chapel in 1843. Fifteen years afterwards the chapel acquired a still more imposing accompaniment, in the shape of a tall, handsome spire. The lower part is Norman or Romanesque, tinged with Byzantine, and from a design by Mr John H. Bell, architect ; while the upper portion, or spire, which is Early English, and is remarkable for its airy lightness as well as elegance, was designed by Mr Alexander Fraser, architect. Extensive additions were made to the chapel in 1872, according to a design by Mr George Goldie of London ; and it is now, so far as internal appearance goes, one of the most sumptuous places of worship belonging to the Roman Catholic body in Scotland. The additions include a spacious chancel and noble apse, which increase the length of the interior by about fifty feet; and transepts which have a width of seventy-two feet, and are so placed as to give a cruciform aspect to the edifice. All these extensions, with corresponding furnishings and decorations, are due to the munificence of the Hon. M. C. Maxwell. A large family vault was also, at his instance, constructed immediately under the altar. Scarcely was it finished when Mr Maxwell died, after a brief illness at Calais : he did not live to see the completion of the works at the chapel, and he was the first to occupy its chamber of mortality—his remains having been buried there on the 22nd of July, 1872.† The chapel was re-opened for worship on the

* In the chapel of Holy Cross Cemetery, which lies east of St. Michael's Churchyard, there is placed a memorial placard, having upon it the names of the deceased "missionary priests of Dumfries and Terregles," with the dates of their death as follows :—Father John Pepper, 24th March, 1810 ; Rev. James Carruthers, 14th February, 1832 ; Rev. William Reid, 18th March, 1845 ; Rev. W. Grant, 6th February, 1849 ; Rev. John Malcolm, 2nd April, 1852 ; Rev. John Monaghan, 28th June, 1852 ; Rev. James Brown, 10th April, 1856 ; Rev. Henry Small, 16th July, 1857 ; Rev. Alex. Bennet, 25th March, 1865.

† The Hon. M. C. Maxwell was the second son of Marmaduke William Constable Maxwell of Everingham Park, Yorkshire, by Theresa Appolonia, daughter of Edmund Wakeham, Esq., of Beckford. He was born on New-Year's Day, 1806 ; in 1836 he married Mary, only daughter of the Rev.

following 24th of October, by Bishop Strain, assisted by more
than a score of ecclesiastics, among whom was the celebrated
Monsignor Capel, who preached on the solemn occasion. The
number of Roman Catholics in Dumfries, Maxwelltown, and surrounding district, which has been greatly swelled by immigrants
from the sister island, is estimated at 2800. (*a*)

Anthony Marsden of Hornby Castle, Lancashire. Leaving no issue, the
entailed portion of the estates devolved upon a nephew, Frederic, eldest son
of Mr Peter C. Maxwell. The Constables, of Yorkshire, are an old family of
good position. Some of them figured in Border warfare, fighting against the
chiefs of the ancient Scottish house with whom their descendant, William
Haggerstone Constable of Everingham, entered into alliance by marrying
Lady Winifred Maxwell, granddaughter of the Earl of Nithsdale. The Nithsdale and Everingham families having in this way been united, the latter
added the name of Maxwell to their own. In noticing the death of Mr
Maxwell the *Dumfries Standard* says : " Naturally rather retiring, and caring
little about mere parade, he yet kept up something like baronial style at
Terregles, residing in that fine mansion for the greater part of every year, and
with the lady of the manor as fitting helpmate, dispensing hospitality and
charity with no stinted hand. To all his dependants the deceased gentleman
was uniformly considerate and kind ; while his character as a landlord was
excelled by none in the whole country side."

(*a*) On the death of the Rev. Mr M'Donald he was succeeded on the 26th
January, 1877, by the Rev. William Turner, D.D., afterwards Vicar-General
of the diocese of Galloway and Dean of the deanery of St. Ninian, one of its
divisions. On his subsequent appointment as Bishop of Galloway, in 1893,
Dr Turner was succeeded at Dumfries by the Rev. Daniel O'Brien, who had
been for some years curate, and still continues in charge of the mission.

It was in 1878 that the restoration of the Catholic hierarchy of Scotland
took place, and Dumfries became the seat of the bishops of Galloway. This
see, originally that of Whithorn (Candida Casa), was founded by St. Ninian in
397, but was vacant for 320 years—from 1588—and in 1878 it was filled by
the appointment of the Right Rev. John M'Lachlan, D.D., as its first bishop.
He died 16th January, 1893, and was succeeded by the Right Rev. W. Turner,
D.D., who was consecrated 25th July of the same year, the preacher being the
Rev. Sir David Hunter Blair of Dunskey, otherwise known as Fr. Oswald, of
the Benedictine Order at Fort Augustus.

The educational work in connection with the Catholic community in
Dumfries has undergone great change and expansion. In consequence of the
Act of 1872 the original school buildings in Shakespeare Street were found to
be quite inadequate ; and during the incumbency of the Rev. Mr M'Donald
a new school was erected for boys to be placed under the charge of the
teaching Order of the Marist Brothers, and also a community house in which
the teachers might reside. The entire cost of the new premises was borne by
Lord Herries.

After the erection of this school, in Brooke Street—the building being also
intended as a hall for lectures and entertainments—the Marist Brothers
acquired, November, 1873, the Old Infirmary, which the burgh School Board
at one time had been asked to purchase ; and it was converted into a novitiate
for students and a boarding school—St. Joseph's College—for boys. The
Order subsequently acquired the property of Laurel Mount (re-named St.
Michael's Mount), and erected a large building upon it. This, and the mansion, became the novitiate, and St. Joseph's College was exclusively occupied
as a boarding school. The college, under the able direction of the Rev.
Brother James, its principal, has attracted pupils from all parts of the world,
and achieved a remarkable success.

The growing educational wants of Catholics in Dumfries and Maxwell-

Episcopalianism was not quite rooted out of the burgh by the Revolution settlement : though the Presbyterian clergy there, as elsewhere, strove hard to get it extirpated from the country. On the 27th of April, 1703, the Presbytery of Dumfries instructed Mr Veitch "to oppose and protest against" any proposal that might be made in the Commission of Assembly for granting a single grain of toleration to "Black Prelacy," from which they had suffered so much.* About ten years afterwards, however, an Act of Parliament was passed permitting all Episcopal clergymen who should take the oath abjuring the cause of the exiled Stuarts to use the Church of England service in Scotland. In virtue of this just enactment, the Episcopalians of the burgh began soon to exercise their own mode of worship openly; though it was not till 1756 that they were in circumstances to build a chapel. A scheme for erecting a suitable fabric was laid before a meeting of "the Episcopal Society in Dumfries," held on the 22nd of March, 1754, the preamble stating that the society had "long laboured under the very disagreeable necessity of having religious worship in a place very unfit and uncommodious." The proposal in effect was that a chapel should be built at a cost (including site) of £250 to accommodate from 150 to 200 persons— £100 of the sum to be raised by subscription, the rest to be borrowed ; that the minister's stipend should be restricted to £50, "paid out of the profits

town led, in 1896, to the erection of an entirely new school for girls and the junior classes of boys. This—which is also in Brooke Street—was placed under the charge of Sisters of Charity of St. Vincent de Paul, a small community of which Order was established in Dumfries in July, 1892, through the zeal and energy of the present Lady Herries. The sisters were accommodated in the old Presbytery (or priests' house), which had been vacated by the clergy for the community house of the Marist Brothers off Brooke Street, when it was no longer required by them. The new school has room for about 500 children, which is now the average attendance at the Catholic schools in Dumfries. The cost of the edifice was between £5000 and £6000.

The old Catholic Cemetery of Holy Cross having become quite insufficient, ground for a new burial place was acquired in 1903. It occupies a beautiful site on the property of Calside, to the south of Dumfries, and extends to about eleven acres.

Corbelly Hill had often been spoken of as an ideal spot for a park, for the splendid panorama of picturesque country that it commands ; and it is quite possible that Lord Herries, the proprietor, would have parted with it for such a purpose. But he was not approached on the subject, and in 1881 was commenced on the summit the building of a convent of the Benedictine Order of Nuns of the Perpetual Adoration, with a church. This was undertaken through the zeal and energy and mainly at the cost of the late Dowager Lady Herries, her son, Lord Herries, generously gifting the site. Her ladyship unfortunately did not survive to witness the opening in 1884 under a community of nuns from the mother house of the Order in Arras. The original designs of the convent and church were by Mr Peter Paul Pugin ; and successive additions have made the establishment one of the most conspicuous and extensive buildings in the south of Scotland. The nuns also conduct a flourishing boarding school for young ladies.

* Presbytery Records.

of the chappell ;" that the interest of the borrowed money should
be discharged yearly ; that £10 should be taken from the remaining surplus every year, with which to form a sinking fund to
liquidate the debt ; and lastly, that after these deductions, the
sum of £8 6s 8d a year should be allotted for a clerk. This
scheme, on being read over to the meeting, was signed by all
present, numbering twenty-seven, in token of approval ; and a
Committee—consisting of Mr Richard Jameson, minister ; Mr
Charles Stewart of Shambelly, the head of an ancient family long
settled in Kirkcudbrightshire ; Mr William Carruthers, merchant
in Dumfries ; and Mr John Story, writer there—was named to
carry it into effect. In due time the chapel was built on a site*
in Lochmaben-gate ; but though Sir William Grierson of Rockhall
furnished building materials without charge, in the shape of
10,000 bricks, and Sir John Douglas of Kelhead supplied twenty
cart-loads of lime on the same free terms, and though others of
the neighbouring gentry gave liberal subscriptions, the Committee
found that the expenditure exceeded the fund at their disposal
by more than £200.† From the wealthy lord of Staffold Hall
money had to be borrowed, the interest of which was not paid ;
and Mr Lowthian having assigned the bond to his nephew, Mr
Ross, merchant in Dumfries, that gentleman would have raised
diligence upon it had not Mr John Bushby (with whose name all
readers of Burns are familiar) come to the rescue by lifting the
bond—which, however, Mr Stewart had ultimately to discharge.
By pecuniary difficulties such as these the infant congregation
was nearly extinguished : but it struggled through, and survived
them all ; and now, when matured, it is one of the wealthiest in
the burgh. The papers relating to its early history show that the
revival and reorganisation of Episcopalianism in Dumfries were
mainly due to the exertions of Mr Charles Stewart of Shambelly.‡
The chapel in Lochmaben-gate was a plain building, octagonal in
form, with a pavilion roof. A much larger and handsomer place
of worship in Buccleuch Street was occupied by the congregation

---

* At present occupied as a garden by Mr John A. Smyth, solicitor.

† Among the accounts given in to the Committee was one of £3 5s 1½d
from " Painter M'Ghie," as he was familiarly called—the Jacobite whose false
alarm in 1745 sent Prince Charlie in hot haste out of the burgh.

‡ The Shambelly branch of the Stewarts has been settled in that estate
for many hundred years. Captain William Stewart of Shambelly, a gallant
officer who served under Sir Robert Rich in Flanders, died in July, 1745, of
wounds received in action ; and at his death the property devolved upon his
brother-german, Charles Stewart, whose services to the Episcopalian body are
recorded in the text. Charles Stewart was a devoted Jacobite. He occupied
as his town residence the large house in Nith Place which forms part of the
premises that belong to the Mechanics' Institute, and was among the first of
the Dumfriesians to welcome his royal namesake when he entered the burgh
in 1745. The grandson of Charles, Mr William Stewart, succeeded to the
estate in 1844, and is the present head of the family.

from about 1820 till a recent period. The congregation, increasing in size and resources, resolved to erect a more ambitious structure, and accordingly the foundation-stone of a magnificent church, dedicated to St. John the Evangelist, was laid on the 1st of August, 1867, by Mr Gilchrist Clark of Speddoch (acting for Colonel M'Murdo, lay representative of the congregation), in presence of Dr Wilson, Bishop of the Diocese, the clergyman of the congregation, and many of its members. The site, in Lovers' Walk, nearly opposite Dunbar Terrace, is well fitted to set off the massive form and bold details of the fabric—built after a Gothic design supplied by Mr W. Slater and Mr R. H. Carpenter, Regent Street, London, and having a tower, with spire, 120 feet high, the whole being almost Norman in severe simplicity of style. Well-proportioned, chaste, and graceful, the interior is imposing. It is lighted by storied windows, "richly dight" with scriptural subjects ; and the elegant furnishings received valuable additions at Christmas, 1872, in the form chiefly of handsome gas standards, and a grand organ by Hill & Son, of London. The church was consecrated by Bishop Wilson on the 3rd of December, 1868. Sittings have been provided (a hundred of them free) for 450 worshippers. Dr Babington, his son Mr Charles Babington, Mr Farquhar, and Mr Short, have been successively ministers of this congregation ; and the present clergyman is Mr Archibald M'Ewen, M.A., who succeeded Mr Short in 1846. From 600 to 700 souls are connected with the congregation, the communicants numbering 160. During the incumbency of Mr Babington the congregation, originally connected with the Anglican Establishment, was received into full communion with the Scottish Episcopal Church. (*a*)

(*a*) Mr M'Ewen retired in 1883, after having faithfully ministered to the congregation for thirty-seven years. He was succeeded by the Rev. J. R. Denham, who removed to an English charge in 1897, in which year the present rector, the Rev. F. C. Moir, was appointed.

In 1898 the well-built house in Lovers' Walk formerly known as Meadow Bank was bought by the congregation for a rectory. There was a sum of £600 in hand from the sale of the old parsonage in Castle Street, and a further sum of £900 was raised by subscription to cover the cost of the house, which is now called S. John's Rectory. It is close to the church.

S. Ninian's Mission Church in Howgate, Maxwelltown, was erected during the incumbency of Mr Denham, and largely owing to his munificence. It is beautifully furnished, and has accommodation for 120 worshippers. Evening service is held there every Sunday, and other services according to notice.

Rev. A. M'Ewen established a school in connection with the Episcopal Church in a two-roomed dwelling-house in St. David Street in the year 1860. This accommodated only about 100 children, and proved too small. Rev. J. R. Denham, when appointed to the incumbency, made it his first duty to set about building a new school. A site was secured in Rae Street, plans and specifications were approved by the Vestry, and in 1885 the premises were occupied. In 1889 the school was enlarged by the addition of an infant department at a cost of £500. There are 320 children on the roll.

Betwixt 1780 and 1790, Dumfries was repeatedly visited by the apostle of Methodism, John Wesley. He originated a "society" or congregation in the burgh, which seems at first to have been superintended by a Mr Dall. There are several entries in Wesley's journal by which the footprints of the great divine may be traced in the town, and his impressions of it can be obtained. Proceeding from Carlisle on the 13th of October, 1788, he says :—"To-day we went on through lovely roads to Dumfries. Indeed, all the roads are wonderfully mended since I last travelled this way. Dumfries is beautifully situated, both as to wood and water, and gently rising hills, &c. ; and is, I think, the neatest, as well as the most civilised, town that I have seen in the kingdom. Robert Dall soon found me out. He had behaved exceedingly well, and done much good here ; but he is a bold man. He has begun building a preaching-house larger than any in Scotland, except those in Glasgow and Edinburgh ! In the evening I preached abroad in a convenient street on one side of the town. Rich and poor attended from every quarter, of whatever denomination ; and every one seemed to hear for life. Surely, the Scots are the best hearers in Europe !"* Next day Mr Wesley preached in the unfinished meeting-house situated in Queen Street ; and again in the evening, when, he says, the congregation was nearly double, and, if possible, more attentive. "One or two gentlemen, so called," he says, "laughed at first ; but they quickly disappeared, and all were still while I explained the worship of God in spirit and in truth. Two of the clergymen [probably Dr Burnside and Dr Mutter] followed me to my lodging, and gave me a pressing invitation to their houses. Several others, it seems, intended to do the same ; but having a long journey before me, I left Dumfries earlier in the morning than they expected."† Subjoined are other entries, one of them, like our first quotation, being highly complimentary to the Dumfriesians. " May 30th, 1790.—We set out at two [from Glasgow], and came to Moffat soon after three in the afternoon. Taking fresh horses, we reached Dumfries between six and seven, and found the congregation waiting : so, after a few minutes, I preached on Mark iii. 35. Tuesday, June 1st.—Mr Mather had a good congregation at five. In the day I conversed with many of the people : a candid, humane, well behaved people ; unlike most that I have found in Scotland. In the evening the house was filled ; and truly God preached to their hearts. Surely God will have a considerable people here."‡ Methodism did thrive in Dumfries for a considerable period after being initiated there by its founder. It was in its most flourishing condition, perhaps,

---

* Journal of the Rev. John Wesley, A.M., vol. iv., p. 400.

† Ibid, p. 401.

‡ Journal, vol. iv., p. 466.

from 1800 to 1825, including a period (1821-3) when the Rev. Hodgson Casson, an eccentric humourist and good preacher, had charge of the society. Since the latter year, owing greatly to the removal by death of some of the leading Wesleyan families—the Bailiefs, Hinchsliffes, and others—its membership had been much reduced. As one sign of progress, however, it may be mentioned that the chapel in Buccleuch Street, which the Episcopalians vacated when their new chapel was erected, was purchased for, and has since been occupied by, the Wesleyans.

There was no organised body of Dissenters from the Established Church in Dumfries till towards the middle of the eighteenth century. Their first congregation in the town was formed chiefly by numerous parishioners of Troqueer who had deserted their own place of worship under the following circumstances :—The parish having fallen vacant by the death of Mr John Bowie, on the 9th of March, 1732, a royal presentation was issued in favour of Mr James Purcell. When the call came to be moderated in, it was found that most of the people, with the entire Kirk-Session, were opposed to the settlement, their choice having been fixed upon the late minister's assistant, Mr James Ritchie. Seeing this to be the case, the committee of Presbytery who had charge of the case allowed both the presentee of the Crown and the nominee of the majority to be called—all "in terms of the Acts of Assembly anent planting of vacant charges, anno 1732 ;"* and they then remitted the whole matter to the Presbytery. That court declining to meddle with it, sent it to the Synod, by whom it was passed on to the General Assembly ; and the Commission of the latter body, after hearing parties, unanimously sustained the call to Mr Purcell, and enjoined the Dumfries Presbytery to proceed at once with his settlement. The Presbytery, however, declined : with a juster appreciation of popular rights than the supreme court they stood boldly forth as their advocate ; and it was not till an extraordinary amount of pressure was employed against the Presbytery that their "contumacy," as it was called, was overcome. As they refused to proceed with the ordination of the presentee, the Commission of Assembly appointed several ministers and elders "a Committee of Correspondents" to confer with a picked number of the Dumfries ministers ; which mixed body having met in St. Michael's Church, on the 26th of March, adopted a resolution to ordain Mr Purcell with all convenient speed. The Committee, consisting of twelve clergymen and three elders, met

* Troqueer Kirk-Session Records. Those still extant go no further back than 1715. One of the books for 1736-7 is entitled, "Register of the acts and proceedings of the Committee appointed by the Presbytrie of Drumfreis, with sessional power, for managing the affairs of the parish of Troqueir, from June 29th, 1736." From this book of ninety small quarto pages we have taken the account of the Purcell case, by the kind permission of the session-clerk, Mr Joseph Welsh.

accordingly in Troqueer Church on the 29th of April, 1734, to carry out their own decision. "The ordination," we are told, "was gone about peaceably, and with all due solemnity, in the presence of a great multitude of people—so many that the kirk could not contain them."* But the case did not end here. The opposers of the settlement were rendered increasingly indignant by the high-handed manner in which it had been effected ; and the Presbytery, though out-generalled by the Commission, still sympathising with the protesters, declined to hold fellowship with the new minister of Troqueer, or give him a seat in their midst. Again and again the Purcell case came up under one form or another before the General Assembly, till that venerable body, sick of a subject which, if properly dealt with at first, need have given little annoyance, issued a final deliverance, ordering the Presbytery, and also the Synod, to add the name of Mr Purcell to their respective rolls, to support him in his ministry, "to endeavour to make the people of Troqueer submit to it," and to treat them at the same time with all due "tenderness."† The Presbytery, also wearied with the case, which had been pending for four years, submitted to this ultimatum ; and on the 15th of June, 1736, we

---

* Kirk Session Records.

† An illustration of the troubles to which the minister was exposed is supplied by a minute of the sessional committee, dated the 15th of December, 1736. They met in the house of Margaret Fisher, Bridgend : Present—James Purcell (moderator), Robert Wight, and John Scott, ministers, with George Duncan and Thomas Hamilton, elders, to inquire about "a scandal" which the Moderator brought under their notice. It appeared from his statement that on the 26th of the preceding month he went to baptize a child of John Shankland at his house in the village ; that whilst so employed, Ann Wilson, spouse of John Hutton, weaver, "conveened a great number of children, her own among the rest, and set them on to make a tumultuous noise, by laughing, shouting, singing, and mocking all the time ;" that after his departure, "Joseph Hutton and his wife, the said Ann, went into John Shankland's house, quarrelling the said John for allowing Mr Purcell to baptize his child, and saying Mr Purcell was a scandalous person, and that they, viz., Joseph and his wife, would not suffer their house (which John Shankland possessed) to be made a kirk," the said Joseph in particular calling the minister "an unlawful man unlawfully ordained, a scandalous man, and an unclean person ;" that in the evening Hutton had uttered "horrid curses and imprecations" on Mr Purcell and his hearers ; and furthermore, that he had gone to the house of one of them, John Coultart, bent on violence, but the door was bolted in his face by Coultart's valorous spouse, Agnes Yeoman ; upon which the implacable Joseph beat up a window of the house, "and was half way in till he was pulled back by some that were with him," while calling out menacingly for some of Mr Purcell's hearers, especially his precentor, to show face if they dared.

Several sittings were held by the committee on this case, at which witnesses, including Hutton and his better half, were examined—the former denying some of the charges, and pleading the influence of drink in extenuation of the rest. Unable to decide on evidence that was in some degree conflicting, the committee referred the case to the Presbytery, who, we infer, dealt leniently with the offenders, though we are unable to state precisely the conclusion which they arrived at.

find a Committee of their number, invested with "sessional powers," meeting for the first time to co-operate with Mr Purcell in exercising discipline over offenders, and otherwise managing the long-neglected affairs of his parish.* They could not, however, wile back for him those doughty protesters who, shaking the dust from their feet as a testimony against his intrusion, had gone to worship elsewhere. Many of them joined other parochial communions ; while not a few flocked to hear the Seceding preachers, who, under the leadership of Ebenezer Erskine, had separated from the Scottish Church in 1733, and who had opportunely come to visit the district—their Troqueer hearers travelling sometimes as far as Lockerbie for ordinances, turning their backs on both Mr Purcell and the Establishment, and eventually becoming the nucleus of the first Dissenting congregation ever formed in Dumfries. On being thoroughly organised by the Associate Synod of Sanquhar in 1759, they obtained a minister of their own, Mr Thomas Herbertson, who was ordained over them in September, 1761. The congregation enjoyed his services for only eleven months. In 1764 they addressed a call to Mr William Inglis, a native of Leslie, in Fifeshire, who, having accepted it, was ordained early in the following year. While Robert Burns resided in the burgh, he was a seat-holder in Mr Inglis's church, and often sat under his ministry ; and when the poet was asked, in a taunting tone, why he did so, his reply was characteristic, and highly complimentary to the preacher. " I go," said Burns, " to hear Mr Inglis because he preaches what he believes, and practices what he preaches."† On the 22nd of June, 1810, Mr James Clyde, probationer, Perth, was ordained colleague and successor to Mr Inglis. The latter dying in 1826, the entire pastoral duties devolved on Mr Clyde till 1838, when he received Mr David L. Scott of Dalravel, Perthshire, as his assistant and successor. Mr Clyde died on the 7th of March, 1851, in the seventy-fifth year of his age and the forty-first of his ministry ; and Mr Scott continues to be pastor of the congregation, with Mr George Rae, M.A., who was appointed as his colleague and successor, in 1872. Their first place of worship was built about 1760, in Loreburn Street : their present one, a handsome Gothic church, was erected on the same site in 1829. Number of communicants on the roll, 270. (a)

* Kirk Session Records.

† Statement made by the Rev. D. L. Scott, at a soiree held on the evening of the 23rd of December, 1861, to commemorate the centenary of the congregation.

(a) Largely through Mr Rae's efforts the church building was greatly improved, the interior being completely transformed. In 1880 he was translated to Gourock United Presbyterian Church (now Ashton United Free) in succession to the Rev. David MacRae. In March of the next year the Rev. George W. Ure was ordained and inducted colleague to Mr Scott, on

Another body of Seceders from the Established Church, the Relief, took root in the burgh in 1788, planted there by the Relief Presbytery of Glasgow. Mr John Lawson was the first pastor of the congregation, he having been ordained about a year after its formation. On resigning his charge, in 1807, he was succeeded in the following year by Mr Andrew Fyfe, who, with a large number of the congregation, as is elsewhere stated, joined the Established Church in 1835. The next minister was Mr William Adam, ordained in 1837. He remained only a short period in the charge, Mr William Blackwood succeeding him in the spring of 1840, and continuing his oversight of the congregation till 1845. Mr John Hogg, ordained in the following January, demitted in 1850 ; and soon afterwards a call was given to the present minister, Mr John Torrance, whose ordination took place on the 20th of November, 1851. The church built in 1788 bore the following inscription :—" Christo et Ecclesiæ Liberatæ Dicata." It was reconstructed internally in the autumn of 1858, at a cost of about £250. In 1867 the building was purchased for a wool store by Messrs T. & R. Carlyle, Waterbeck ; and two years afterwards a handsome church, in the Pointed Gothic style, from a design by Mr Barbour, was erected for the congregation near the corner where Townhead Street joins with the Lovers' Walk. The design includes a tall spire not yet reared, which is needed to give an aspect of unity to the building. It is seated for 460 persons. Number of communicants, about 230. (a)

About fifty years after the Secession Church had obtained a solid footing in Dumfries, a second congregation was originated there in a singular way. Mr John Lawson of the Relief, having received the present of a gown or cassock, and intimated his intention of wearing it when preaching, not a few of his hearers were dissatisfied. They looked upon the gown as worse than uncalled for ; they considered it an unseemly innovation on the old simple clerical attire, and as savouring in some degree of

whose death, April, 1883, he became sole minister. During this pastorate an organ was introduced, and a spacious hall to the rear of the church was erected. In the summer of 1904 Mr Ure demitted his charge, and on 16th Feb., 1905, the Rev. David R. W. Scott, for eleven years minister of Darvel United Presbyterian Church (now Irvine Bank United Free), was inducted to the charge of Loreburn Street (now United Free) Church. In 1881 the membership was 285 ; at present the membership is 300. An interesting fact in the history of this congregation is that for 140 years, from the induction of Mr Inglis in 1765 till the resignation of Mr Ure, it never had a vacancy in the ordinary sense ; for each new minister was settled as colleague to his predecessor.

(a) Mr Torrance resigned 1879 ; died Oct., 1881. In November, 1880, the Rev. John Cooper was inducted ; died April, 1884. In August of the latter year the Rev. Alex. Smith became minister ; resigned 1893. In July of the same year the Rev. David Mackay was inducted ; resigned October, 1900. In April of 1901 Rev. Peter Wilson was inducted ; resigned February, 1903. The present minister, Rev. Herbert A. Whitelaw, was inducted April, 1904,

that prelatical system which they had learned from their fathers, and with such good reason, to detest. They remonstrated with their minister against his wearing the obnoxious garment without success; and rather than seem to sanction its use, they, in number about a hundred, left his church, and formed themselves into a separate body, assembling in a meeting-house erected on the "Burgher's Brae," Buccleuch Street. The new congregation succeeded in obtaining an able pastor, Mr Walter Dunlop, a native of Haddingtonshire, whom they called in February, 1809, when he was officiating in Liddesdale. He was soon after inducted into his Dumfries charge, and continued to occupy it with success for the remainder of his life. Mr Dunlop was in many respects a remarkable man. He was a good preacher, and eventually became as noted in the neighbourhood for his conversational humour as for his pulpit oratory. The latter, though what would now be deemed old-fashioned and rustic, was highly effective. The manner of it was warm, earnest, and impressive; the matter rich, "sappy," and soundly evangelical. So active and irrepressible was his perception of the ridiculous, and so fond was he of repartee, or of putting down any assumption, or of "shooting folly as it flies," that he was sometimes blamed for indulging in sallies that were out of keeping with his sacred calling. But if in this respect he was not beyond criticism, it is due to his memory to say that he was devotedly attentive at the couch of suffering and the bed of death. His natural temperament might lead him to the house of mirth, but it never caused him to neglect his visits to the house of mourning. Mr Dunlop, when at his best, had a portly, "sonsie" presence, which accorded well with his reputation as a humourist. In 1845, when failing with increased years, the congregation elected as his colleague and successor the Rev. Marshall N. Goold. Mr Dunlop, however, died on the 4th of November, 1846, in the seventy-second year of his age and the forty-second of his ministry, a few months before the ordination of Mr Goold, who has since then continued to be the sole minister of the congregation. An imposing and tasteful new church, according to a Gothic design furnished by Mr Alexander Crombie, architect, Dumfries, was erected by the congregation on the site of their original place of worship in Buccleuch Street. It was opened on the 17th of May, 1863; and is highly ornamental to that fashionable part of the town. Its entire cost was about £2000. There are nearly 400 names on the communion roll. (a).

(a) In 1884 the Rev. John Cairns, M.A., received a call as colleague and successor to Mr Goold, was ordained, and inducted. Eleven years later, on the eve of his jubilee, Mr Goold died, and Mr Cairns became sole minister. In 1885 the new church was internally changed so as to lighten it and render it more comfortable, the cost being £550; in 1887 a harmonium was introduced, and in 1902 this was replaced by an organ at a cost of close upon £500. The trust formed under the will of the late Mr David Johnstone, merchant,

The district which gave Renwick to the Cameronians has always abounded with them since the date of their origin. Richard Cameron himself visited it, accompanied by Cargill, preaching down the Indulgence, which they compared to "a weel-buskit jade," and warning the people against its bewitching snares.* Sometime in 1684 Cameron preached within the barony of Duncow, Kirkmahoe, and soon the village of Quarrelwood, in that parish, became one of the main centres of the body, and for a long period afterwards it was its chief seat in Dumfriesshire. In 1743 the Quarrelwood pastor, Mr John Curtis, took part with three other ministers in constituting the Reformed Presbyterian Church, as the denomination came to be called. The region assigned to the little ecclesiastical capital, Quarrelwood, was a very extensive one, bounded by the Esk on the east, the Urr on the west, by a line from New Galloway to Moffat on the north, and by the Solway on the south. It stretched over between thirty and forty parishes, so that the officiating pastor must have undergone immense toil in ministering to the far-scattered families of his flock, at a time when there were few roads and scarcely a wheeled carriage in the county. Mr James Thomson, ordained in 1796, was the second minister ; and in his day a new church and manse were erected at Quarrelwood, and the congregation multi-plied extensively. In the course of time it became the nursing-mother of new settlements, there being now seven Reformed Presbyterian congregations in the district, all tracing their origin to the little sanctuary at Quarrelwood. It was not till 1826 that a few members of the body began to hold meetings in Dumfries. Increasing in number, they took the George Inn ball-room, and next the Old Assembly Rooms, as temporary places of worship ; and having obtained the services of a regular pastor— Mr James Brown, ordained in November, 1831—they erected their present commodious church in Irving Street, which was opened in May of the following year. On Mr John Jeffray, the minister of the Quarrelwood congregation, proceeding to America, its members, with one accord, connected themselves with the Dumfries congre-gation. Mr Brown's ministry lasted little more than two years. During the cholera epidemic of 1832 he overtasked his strength in visiting the sick, and died young, of consumption, in May, 1834. He was succeeded by Mr John M'Dermid, ordained in October,

had erected frontal premises in Queensberry Street, and an inner court of attractive cottages, the latter for letting to deserving people at less than an economic rent. In 1885 they also erected a Mission Hall at the top of this court, to be worked in connection with the congregation ; the trust providing an annual payment of £50 towards salary of missionary, and the congregation contributing a sum in addition. The congregation, included in the Union of 1900, is now known as Buccleuch Street United Free. Its membership numbers 321.

* Memoirs of Blackadder, p. 264.

1835, who, after ministering acceptably to the congregation for nearly twenty years, accepted a call to the third Glasgow congregation. Mr Alexander Macleod Symington, B.A., son of the distinguished Professor William Symington, was ordained as Mr M'Dermid's successor on the 12th of June, 1856 ; and he continued to officiate as pastor of the congregation till 1867, when he accepted a call from the congregation of St. Andrew's Presbyterian Church, Birkenhead. Mr Robert MacKenna, M.A., is the present minister. The Dumfries congregation possess several interesting relics connecting it with Quarrelwood and the fathers of the Church. These are a set of communion utensils, consisting of two large oval plates, four flagons, four cups, all of pewter, with the words engraved on each, "Belonging to the Old Covenanted Presbyterian Dissenters in Scotland, 1745 ;" also numerous tokens of sheet lead, square shape, initialed "G. M. [General Meeting], 1745," on one side, and "L. S." (Lord's Supper) on the other.* In 1866 the interior of the church was reconstructed, and a spacious hall was added, which is used as a schoolroom and for congregational meetings. The number of communicants is 190.(a)

To the labours and liberality of the Brothers Haldane is traceable the first formation in the burgh of an Independent or Congregational church. The elder of the two, James A. Haldane, carried out a series of preaching tours through Scotland, commencing in 1797 ; and afterwards the younger, Robert, joined in the work. They repeatedly visited Dumfries, where, as was their wont, they held numerous field-meetings, which were addressed by James Haldane, who was a Boanerges in preaching power. Sometimes Mr Charles Simeon, of King's College, Cambridge, and Mr Rowland Hill were associated with the Haldanes in their itinerating home mission. The General Assembly—at that time pervaded by a chilling "moderatism"—sought to check the evangelising enterprise by issuing a "pastoral admonition," in which they warned the people to beware of strange preachers, and debarred Episcopalians or other strangers from occupying the pulpits of the Established Church. This edict caused the Messrs Haldane to secede from the Establishment, and to adopt the Congregational form of ecclesiastical government. Mr Robert

---

* Some of these particulars are taken from a statement made by Mr James Halliday at an annual meeting of the congregation on the 23rd of February, 1865.

(a) Mr MacKenna, formerly of Port-Glasgow, was inducted on 5th Dec., 1867. In 1895 the church was repaired and re-seated at a cost of £400. The late Mr George Henderson of Nunholm left the half of his estate, subject to the payment of a bursary of £10 annually to a Free Church student connected with the district, to found a mission in connection with the congregation. After the union of the R. P. Church with the Free Church in 1876, this congregation assumed the name of Free Martyrs Church. It has adhered to the old forms of worship.

Haldane, at an expense of £30,000, erected or purchased places of worship in Edinburgh, Glasgow, Dundee, Perth, Dumfries, and other towns, in which they might have unrestricted liberty to preach. The chapel thus originated in Dumfries was lost to the Independent body by the brothers who had built it becoming Baptists. In 1814 it was purchased by the County for a Court-house ; and after being re-fronted, was opened as such by the Lords of Justiciary in the spring of 1816. In 1866 it was bought by the Burgh for a Town Hall, at a cost of £1120. About 1810 the Dumfries Independents, then worshipping in a small chapel in Irish Street, gave a call to Mr John Dunn of Berwick-on-Tweed, under whose ministry they increased greatly in number. He was a man of almost apostolic fervour ; and his name, for a series of years, was associated with many philanthropic move-ments in the town and district. Soon after the death of Mr Dunn, in 1820, Mr Thomas Young became pastor of the church ; and on his removal to Garliestown, in 1833, he was succeeded by Mr Robert Machray, M.A. A new Independent chapel, erected in Irving Street, after a neat Italian design, was opened on the 6th of September, 1835 ; and it was enlarged so as to furnish 650 sittings in 1862. In 1842 Mr Machray resigned his charge, that he might proceed to London ; and in 1854 he returned, on invita-tion, to his former pastorate—the duties of which, in the interval, were successively discharged by Mr James Cameron, now of Col-chester ; Mr James Mann, now of Birkenhead ; and Mr Thomas Pullar, who went to Hamilton, and eventually to Canada. Mr Machray, after a lengthened and acceptable ministry, withdrew into private life in 1869, and since the following year Mr John Park has occupied the charge. Number of church members, 120. (a)

(a) The Rev. James Strachan succeeded Mr Machray in 1869, and in the following year he was succeeded by the Rev. John Park, now of London. In 1873 the Rev. Hugh Campbell, M.A., LL.D., succeeded Mr Park ; and since Mr Campbell the succession of ministers has been as follows :—Rev. Frederick Binns, afterwards of Australia, 1877 ; Rev. W. Hanson Pulsford, M.A., after-wards of Chicago, 1883 ; Rev. Robert Mackintosh, B.D., D.D., afterwards professor in the Independent College, Manchester, 1890 ; Rev. Wallace A. M'Cubbin, afterwards of Lewisham, London, 1895 ; Rev. John Murphy, B.D., 1901. During the pastorate of Mr M'Cubbin the congregation purchased a property adjoining the church (formerly the residence of Sir Wm. Broune, writer), and converted it into a suite of halls. During the ministry of Mr Murphy the church has been partly rebuilt, and a debt on the halls paid off.
The Rev. James Strachan continued in Dumfries when he ceased to be pastor of the Irving Street congregation ; and forming another congregation, which met for some years in the Mechanics' Hall, he also engaged very actively in temperance and other work. A site having been acquired for a church in Waterloo Place, the foundation-stone of the new structure was laid in Oct., 1876, by Mr Ernest Noel, M.P. The building, which cost about £1100, was vested in trustees. In 1899 the church and minister were unanimously received into the Congregational Union.

A small body of Baptists existed for a long while in the burgh, without any stated pastor. The members met in the chapel, Irish Street (formerly occupied by the Independents), for worship and mutual exhortation. Last year they differed on the question of strict or free communion, and those who adopted the latter view have since tenanted a smaller house in the same street, where service is conducted by Mr George Anderson. (a)

How much, in matters municipal and social, the burgh has been influenced by the Irvings, we have frequently shown ; and we have now to point out, in a line or two, how one of the greatest of the name, if not " the noblest Roman of them all," set his mark upon its ecclesiastical polity. After Edward Irving—born at Annan, the capital of the district in which his race was cradled—was cast out from the Scottish Church, in 1833, he visited Dumfries, and originated a congregation, holding his peculiar views regarding apostolic gifts, the personal reign of Christ, and the manifestations of the Holy Spirit. After the lapse of several years its members were scattered ; but about sixteen years ago the congregation was reconstructed, and, as far as circumstances would then permit, the ritual of the Catholic Apostolic Church was introduced, that being the name taken by the denomination which Mr Irving originated. The Irish Street chapel was for a while occupied by the body ; but they now possess a small building specially designed for their peculiar service, which was erected at a cost of about £1000, in Queen Street, and opened on the 12th of March, 1865. The style is Norman Gothic, its chief feature a front elevation with tower and pinnacle fifty-eight feet high. The office-bearers of the congregation are of various grades.

Early in January, 1862, a branch of the Evangelical Union Church was formed in Dumfries, chiefly by members of other denominations who had been led to adopt Arminian views of the Atonement. They meet in the Assembly Rooms, expecting, however, soon to occupy a house of their own, which is to be built for them on a good site at the foot of English Street. Mr John Dunlop, ordained 3rd November, 1863, was the first pastor of the congregation : having demitted his charge, he has had as successor Mr James Maconachie and Mr Ninian Galloway, and since the resignation of the latter in 1872, no other minister has yet been

(a) The Baptist congregation now worshipping in the Tabernacle in Newall Terrace was formed in 1872, when they met in a small hall in Loreburn Street. The Rev. Lachlan M'Pherson was their first minister. He was settled in 1876. In 1880 the Rev. T. W. Tooley became pastor. In his ministry the Tabernacle was built. It is an effective piece of architecture, designed by Mr Francis Armstrong, is seated for 450, and cost £2000, including site. After Mr Tooley died, the Rev. W. Muir ministered 1883-4. He was followed in 1885 by Rev. Mr M'Kelwee, M.A., B.Sc. ; in 1889 the Rev. Alex. Bremner was appointed ; and in 1898 the present pastor, the Rev. John Brown Frame.

appointed. The church is Congregational in its form of government : membership fully 100, with a considerable body of adherents. (a)

A movement for a third place of worship in connection with the Established Church was commenced in 1835, under the following circumstances. Mr Andrew Fyfe, minister of the Relief Church, and a large majority of his congregation, presented a petition in that year to the ecclesiastical courts, praying to be admitted within the pale of the Establishment. This prayer was acceded to ; but when the petitioners sought to carry away with them the church and manse from the Relief body, the minority who remained in it successfully resisted the attempt by the aid of the civil courts, and Mr Fyfe and his adherents were left without a place to worship in. That they might not remain long in such a predicament, a subscription was entered into, and so zealously promoted by Major Adair, Captain M'Dowall, Mr John Anderson, bookseller, and other gentlemen, that in the course of a few months a fund of £2520 was obtained, and a fine commanding site for the new ecclesiastical edifice was secured—none other than the celebrated eminence on which Bruce's brother-in-law, Sir Christopher Seton, was executed by command of Edward I., and on which the patriot's widow afterwards erected a chapel dedicated to his memory. On this hallowed mound, granted by the Crown for the purpose, the foundation stone of the building was laid, with Masonic honours, on the 24th of May, 1837 ; and, under the name of St. Mary's Church, it was first opened for public worship on Sabbath, the 17th of November, 1839. Being Gothic in its architecture, it is in keeping with the historical associations of the place, and is altogether a very elegant church. The architect of the building was Mr John Henderson of Edinburgh ; its cost, £2400. Additions by purchase were made to the ground for the formation of a cemetery, which is already mournfully studded with the memorials of a populous race that lie slumbering beneath its turf ; one of its earliest tenants having been the first pastor of St. Mary's, Mr Peter Thomson of Kincardine, Perthshire, who, after a brief but bright ministerial career of nine months, died of fever caught in the course of one of his pastoral visits. Mr Fyfe and some of his friends were rather dissatisfied with the arrangement which, instead of making him the minister of St. Mary's, appointed him as Mr Thomson's colleague, with an annual stipend of only £30, and the privilege of preaching in the evenings, and

(a) The majority of the Evangelical Union joined the Congregational Union in 1896. About a dozen congregations declined to go with the majority, and still continue as the Evangelical Union. Before 1896 the body had become extinct in Dumfries, though it continued for some time after Mr Galloway's ministry under a succession of pastors. The church that was to have been built at the foot of English Street never materialised,

getting the collections then taken by way of supplement. Mr John R. Mackenzie of Inverness was ordained as successor to Mr Thomson, in the summer of 1841 ; and under his ministry the congregation, already large, increased considerably. For the year ending Martinmas, 1841, the rent for sittings, every one of which was taken, amounted to £200 17s ; the collections to £93 ; the minister's stipend being fixed at £180. When the Disruption occurred, in May, 1843, Mr Mackenzie, with the great majority of his people, joined the Free Church. For upwards of two years afterwards no new minister was settled in St. Mary's, its pulpit being supplied fortnightly by the Presbytery. As might have been supposed, the attendance was miserably thin, and the revenue much reduced. For the half-year ending November, 1844, the seat rents and collections amounted to less than £39 ; eventually the sittings were not let at all, and for the next six months, ending in May, 1845, the proceeds of the ladle and the plate were but £9 2s 1d. The congregation reached a zero-point when, one forenoon whilst the air was appropriately cold, they adjourned for service to the vestry, in which there was room enough and to spare after they had all assembled.

The fortunes of the congregation revived soon after Dr Freeland, formerly of Airdrie, became their minister, in July, 1845 ; as a proof of which the seat rents rose to £146 11s for the year ending November, 1846, and the collections to £96. Dr Freeland having been translated to the church and parish of Balmaghie early in 1847, he was succeeded by Mr David Brown, now of St. Enoch's Church, Glasgow. The next minister of St. Mary's was Mr James Stewart ; and he having become settled at Wilton, Mr John Mein Austin, formerly of Johnstone, succeeded him, in May, 1852. Mr Austin's pastorate was signalized by the endowment of St. Mary's, and its erection into a regular parish church. This was effected in 1853, at an expense of £3590, about £1200 of which was obtained by subscription, £800 from the General Assembly's Endowment Committee, whilst the rest was borrowed on the personal security of the trustees of the church ; the principal expenditure having been on the purchase of feu duties, which yield £137 12s 9d a year. Mr Austin became parish minister of St. Mungo in the beginning of 1861 ; and during his last year in St. Mary's the seat rents yielded £121 ; the collections, £78 7s. His successor, Mr William B. Turnbull, formerly of Edinburgh, was ordained in May, 1862. Mr Turnbull, finding that the debt, which amounted to £1500, was a disheartening incubus on both minister and people, resolved, if possible, to get rid of it. By a sale of grave plots, and from other sources, it was reduced to £1200 : by means of a subscription it was further diminished to a little more than £400 ; and by a crowning device, that of a bazaar, held towards the close of 1863, the entire remaining liabilities were swept away, and a small balance was left in the hands of the treasurer. For the year ending November, 1864, the seat rents yielded £148 ; the collections £100 2s ; and the whole revenue of the church amounted to £383 8s. The stipend has ranged from £180—the sum paid to Mr Mackenzie—to £200 and to £320 5s ; the latter amount having been received by Mr Turnbull during the second year of his incumbency. Mr Turnbull accepted the presentation to Townhead Church, Glasgow, in 1866 ; and was succeeded by the present minister, Mr James Mackie, formerly of Partick, Glasgow. The names on the communion roll at the date just given numbered about 480 ; but since then, owing to differences between the minister and his session, the congregation has been much reduced.* (a)

Dumfries took a fair share in the great "ten years' conflict" which ended in the disruption of the National Church on the 18th of May, 1843. A few weeks before that date, the local Presbytery was rent by the withdrawal from it of many members, because the majority, acting according to the prescribed policy of the Moderates, persisting in excluding the names of *quoad sacra* ministers from its roll. Those who retired formed themselves into

* Many of these details are taken from a statement drawn up for the congregation by one of its members, Mr William Milligan, solicitor.

(a) Mr Mackie's ministry, though giving promise at first of great success, soon merged in difficulties with the trustees, Kirk Session, and others, from which till his resignation no effective solution could be found. The first point at issue was one between him and the trustees as to his claim for a free manse, a claim which led to litigation, and his having to quit the manse. Other questions also were brought before the Church courts, and were so long in being settled, and led to so great acrimony, that in 1877 the church was all but empty, had no Kirk Session, no Sunday schools, no organisations of any kind, and the collections and seat rents had fallen to only a few pounds per annum. Only 150 members took part in the election of 1877, some of whom had returned to the church when the vacancy occurred. The present minister, the Rev. A. Chapman, M.A., was ordained and inducted to the charge on the 30th August, 1877, and during his incumbency many changes for the better have taken place. A large scheme of restoration has been carried into effect. A chancel and two vestries have been built, an organ has been introduced, and two costly stained-glass windows have been erected, one in the chancel in memory of Sir James Anderson by his son, the other in the south end in memory of Mr Christopher Harkness by his daughter. The whole work carried out has involved an expenditure of £5000. Fifty years to a day after the first stone of the church was laid, the foundation stone of a church hall was laid with much ceremony on the 24th May, 1887, by Mr Samuel Boyd of Marchmount. Built on a feu granted by Sir James Anderson, it cost about £2400, and was opened free of debt in 1888. Two bequests, one of £300, by Miss Anderson, Park House, the other of £2000 by Mr Matthew W. Boyd, London, have been recently left to secure a manse for the parish. These sums and the small residue of £150 from the former manse fund are as yet made available only for increasing the minister's stipend. The stipend is now very much higher than at any former time, the membership of the church numbers 1143, the number of pupils attending Sunday schools and Bible classes is larger than in any parish in the south of Scotland, and every branch of church work is kept up to a high pitch of efficiency.

a Constitutional or Protesting Presbytery ; and when the Free Church of Scotland was formed, congregations actuated by the same principles as the Presbytery were organised in nearly every parish in the district. The members and adherents of St. Mary's congregation who joined Mr Mackenzie in quitting the Establishment, together with not a few from St. Michael's and the New Church, worshipped as a Free Church congregation for nearly a year in the Old Assembly Rooms, varied by occasional open-air diets in the summer months. Their first communion was dispensed in the Castle Gardens, George Street, on the 27th of August, 1843, in presence of about 3000 persons, and under circumstances which resembled in some respects the great hill-side sacramental assemblages of the olden time. The services throughout were highly impressive, acquiring a tone of subdued enthusiasm, as well as of solemnity, from the character of the conditions with which they were associated. On the preceding day, the foundation stone of a church for the congregation was laid in George Street by the Rev. Dr Candlish ; on the 14th of April, 1844, it was opened for divine service ; and the sacrament of the Supper was dispensed in it on the following Sabbath, to upwards of 600 communicants. The building is plain, but neat, externally ; internally, it is elegant and commodious, affording sitting room for 1000 persons. The cost, including site, was about £1400. A manse adjoining the church was built in 1846. In March, 1847, Mr (now Dr) Mackenzie accepted a call from the Broad Street congregation, Birmingham, in connection with the English Presbyterian Church, and was succeeded by Mr James Julius Wood, M.A., formerly of New Greyfriars', Edinburgh, who was inducted on the 8th of June, 1848. In 1856 he received the degree of D.D. from the University of Glasgow ; and in 1857 Dr Wood had the honour of being elected moderator of the General Assembly of the Free Church of Scotland. This congregation, over which he still ministers, has all along been one of the largest and most flourishing in the town. Number of communicants, fully 600. (a)

(a) Rev. J. Freer, M.A., formerly of St. George's, Glasgow, became colleague and successor to Dr Wood in 1875, and after Dr Wood's death he was sole minister till 1881, when he resigned through failing health. Rev. Charles M'Neil, M.A., succeeded Mr Freer in 1882. He came from the charge in Juniper Green, and still continues.

In 1889 the congregation bought the site of the old Prison in Buccleuch Street. There was some thought of erecting a church at the corner of St. David Street ; but this idea was departed from. A portion of the ground was sold for the new Post Office, and another portion for the new Clydesdale Bank ; and between those two sites a set of handsome halls and offices for congregational and missionary purposes, with two shops to the front, were erected at a cost of £3709.

In 1892 the church was extensively remodelled in the Lombardo-Grecian style of architecture on plans prepared by the late Mr Halliday, and at an outlay of £3450. In 1898 a large organ was presented by the late Miss Brown of Westbourn House. The church, as thus reconstructed and equipped, is

On the opposite bank of the Nith, the results of the Disruption were not less decisive. During the church-extension movement begun by Dr Chalmers, a chapel of ease was erected in Maxwelltown, of which Mr James Begg, now Dr Begg of Edinburgh, was the first minister. Built in 1829, at an expense of £2494, it was destroyed by fire on the evening of Rood-Fair Wednesday, 1842. Next year a new chapel, costing between £1400 and £1500, was erected in its stead ; the congregation—a large one from the first—continuing to prosper for awhile under the ministry of Mr Ranken, till so many of its members and adherents withdrew to constitute a Free Church congregation, that the chapel was nearly emptied, even though its minister thought fit to continue in the Established Church. At first they met for worship in the stackyard at Nithside, the proprietor of which estate, Mr Philip Forsyth, was a staunch member of the Free Church, and did much to promote its principles, as well as to secure the success of the Maxwelltown congregation. On the 28th of August, 1843, the foundation stone of a church for the congregation was laid by him at Laurieknowe ; and so active were the contractors that it was opened for worship on the 19th of November following. On the 2nd of October the congregation gave a unanimous call to Mr William Brown Clark, minister at Half-Morton, who eventually accepted the same, and was inducted on the 5th of April, 1844. In February, 1853, Mr Clark resigned his charge, in order to accept the pastorate of a Presbyterian congregation in Quebec. His successor, Mr David Purves, formerly of Aberdour, Fifeshire, the present minister, to whom a unanimous call was given, was inducted on the 6th of October, 1853. The church being a plain, unpretentious building, the congregation resolved, in 1865, to erect a very handsome new place of worship, with a spire, from a Gothic design by Mr Barbour. It was founded on the 6th of July, that year, Mr Murray Dunlop of Corsock, M.P., performing the ceremony ; and it was occupied for the first time on the 15th of November, 1866, Dr Begg conducting the opening services. The church cost, with site, about £2200 ; of which sum Mr William Milligan of Westpark contributed £300. By repeated efforts on the part of the congregation, the debt—a heavy one—with which they were burdened has been entirely paid off. Present number of communicants, about 500. (*a*)

internally one of the finest, and probably the most spacious, in this district. The congregation have also erected—in 1883 - a Mission Hall at Greenbrae, at a cost of £350, the site being a gift to them.

(*a*) Mr Purves died in 1883, and was succeeded by the Rev. Frank Rae, during whose incumbency the Mission Hall in Old Bridge Street was gifted to the congregation by Lady Ann Ewart, Lincluden. On the removal of Mr Rae to Uddingston, after six years, the Rev. Charles Todd, Ratho, accepted a call to Maxwelltown, where he remained for four years, when he was trans-lated to Aberdeen. The Rev. R. G. Macintyre Birkenhead, succeeded Mr

The Maxwelltown congregation in connection with the Established Church is under the ministry of Mr William Graham, ordained in 1863. Chiefly through his efforts the sum of £1000 was raised in 1865, for the purpose of erecting the charge into a *quoad sacra* parish, which object was realised on the congregation receiving aid from the central fund of the Church to the extent of £1350. Number of communicants, 242.

In 1864 there rose up at the foot of High Street, Dumfries, a beautiful Territorial Church, which is at once the product and memento of an extraordinary religious awakening that took place in the town during the spring of 1861. Some of those who experienced the influence of that revival resolved to put forth a special effort, in order to give permanence to its results, and extend a similar influence to such as were still living in the habitual neglect of religious ordinances. The scheme met with a large measure of success. A congregation was formed under the care of Mr Robert Milligan, now of Dundee ; and Mr Gilbert Laurie, M.A., after ministering to them for two years, was ordained as their pastor in September, 1866—the Free Church Assembly having previously sanctioned the charge. The Territorial Church, built for the congregation through the liberality of Mr Milligan of Westpark, Mr George Henderson of Nunholm, and other friends, was opened for service on the 1st of January, 1865. It cost, with site, fully £2000 : it originally supplied accommodation for 500 sitters ; and about a year ago a gallery was erected, at a considerable expense, capable of holding 250 more. The average attendance is upwards of 400 ; the number of communicants, which was 200 in 1867, has risen to 324. Connected with the Church there is a spacious hall, in which a flourishing school is held, attended by fully 250 children, chiefly of the poorer classes. For the purpose of defraying the debt that had been incurred, a bazaar was held in 1872, which all classes and denominations patronised so liberally that the sum of £500 was realised, with which the congregation cleared off all their pecuniary liabilities, and were enabled to prosecute their evangelising mission with increasing vigour. (*a*)

Todd, and continued for eight years, when he accepted a call to Sydney. The Rev. W. J. Street, the present minister, came from Portsoy, in succession to Mr Macintyre.

(*a*) Mr Laurie accepted a call to Fairbairn Free Church, Glasgow, in 1875. In the same year the Rev. J. D. M'Kinnon, called from Liverpool, was inducted to the vacancy. Two years later, at a meeting of Session, it was resolved that the congregation should take the name of South Free Church. On the death of Mr M'Kinnon the Rev. James Law, Glasgow, received a call, and was inducted in June, 1904. During the ministry of Mr M'Kinnon, who actively engaged in temperance work, more particularly in connection with the order of Good Templars, of which he was repeatedly Grand Chief—Mrs M'Kinnon, who was no less zealous in the cause, being vice chief—considerable improvements were effected in the church. When

As showing, in a single sentence, the progress of Dumfries ecclesiastically considered, it may be mentioned that a hundred and forty-five years ago there was only one congregation in the burgh ; and that at present there are no fewer than sixteen congregations, only two of which are State-endowed, the rest maintaining ordinances and defraying all their other expenses on the voluntary principle. (a)

the Education Act of 1872 came into operation the Territorial Church school was discontinued, and its teacher, Mr Hendrie, entering the service of the Board, became headmaster in St. Michael's School.

(a) It will be gathered from the notes already given to this chapter that some very considerable changes have occurred in the ecclesiastical situation since the text was written.   Others can most conveniently be included in the record at this point.   The half-yearly fast-days have disappeared, and in all the Presbyterian congregations, with one exception, instrumental music has been introduced in the regular service.   The Reformed Presbyterian congregation became a congregation of the Free Church by the Union of 1876 ; and the larger Union of 1900 embraced all the Free and United Presbyterian Churches in the South of Scotland.   This necessitated a re-arrangement of Presbyteries and Synods ; the Presbyteries of Dumfries and Penpont were brought together, and the Synods of Dumfries, Galloway, and Ayr were formed into one great provincial court.

Neither in Dumfries nor in the neighbourhood was there any active opposition to the Union of 1900 ; and the outrageous decision of the House of Lords, in August, 1904, declaring the Free Church remnant who had refused to enter the Union to be the Free Church, entitled to all the property of that Church as before the Union, led to the secession of only a few individuals in this district.   In Dumfries about a score of persons met for worship by themselves as adherents of the Free Church, but they advanced no claim for any of the Church property.   In Galloway the congregations at Cree Bridge and Port-William were ousted by minorities.

As mentioned in note on page 575, the Rev. Dr Paton became minister of St. Michael's Church in 1874.   During his ministry the interior of the church was greatly improved, and in 1890 an organ was placed on one of the lofts.   In 1872 a mission hall was built by the congregation on a site near to the church, with entrances from St. Michael Street and Broom's Road.   The erection of a new manse by the real-rent heritors on a site provided by the congregation on Bankend Road has already been referred to.   It is curious to note, says Dr Paton in his " Book of St. Michael's," the changes of popular opinion in Scotland " even in regard to church furniture and decoration. . . So late as 1875 the Kirk-Session of St. Michael's unanimously resolved, on application being made for leave to erect a marble monument within the church, that no such monuments should be erected, and the monument was erected in the vestibule.   Since then we have seen great changes in such matters.   Eleven stained-glass memorial windows now solemnise and adorn the church, and two marble monuments, three mosaic monuments, and two brasses have been erected "—one to Robert Burns, the other to Thomas Aird. Dr Paton died suddenly when attending the Assembly of 1905, and thus was closed a very active life.

Greyfriars' congregation was one of the first to equip itself with halls for congregational purposes.   These were erected in Irish Street.   In 1873 an organ was presented to the church by Mr Robert Gordon, then of New York, now of London ; and Mrs Davies gifted a house in Castle Street for a manse. The Rev. W. Edie, King Edward's parish, Banffshire, was inducted to Greyfriars in the spring of 1905, in succession to Rev. Mr Weir (see page 569).

On the other side of the river the old parish church of Troqueer has undergone transformation internally and externally. It is no longer the barn-like building that it originally was, but a picturesque object in the landscape. In February of 1876 a vacancy occurred by the death of the Rev. Dr Macfarlane, and in September of the same year the Rev. James A. Campbell was inducted. In 1876 a congregational hall was erected in Church Street at a cost of £2000. In 1887 the church was remodelled on plans prepared by Mr Barbour ; an organ was introduced ; and in a quaint belfry on the eastern gable a bell, the gift of the late Mr J. B. Dinwiddie, solicitor, was placed. To the churchyard a burial ground has been added by the Parish Council, and it is fenced on the river-side by a strong wall with corner towers.

The Salvation Army established itself in Dumfries soon after the movement had extended to Scotland. At first its Sunday processions with instrumental music were regarded with disfavour by the church-going community, and provoked attack by others. This led to interference by the police and an attempt to prohibit the army from parading the town and holding meetings in the streets. The Salvationists were not, however, to be thus deprived of their liberties. Here as elsewhere they maintained their ground ; and now the army is among the religious organisations of the town that are cherished for their work's sake. In the early years of the movement General Booth visited Dumfries ; and it is included in his itinerary for the autumn of this year (1905).

CHAPTER LX.

COMMERCE OF THE PORT—CUSTOM-HOUSE RETURNS—THE CATTLE, SHEEP, AND PIG TRADES OF THE BURGH—HOSIERY—TANNING AND CURRYING —BASKET-MAKING—HORTICULTURE AND THE NURSERY TRADE—RISE AND PROGRESS OF THE TWEED MANUFACTURE—CLOTH FINISHING—THE MAXWELLTOWN IRONWORKS—BUSINESS OPERATIONS IN DUMFRIES.

TWELVE or thirteen vessels were all that the port of Dumfries could boast of in 1790. Three of these traded in foreign wines, or in timber and hides from the Baltic ; the others being employed as coasters, exporting grain and potatoes, and bringing back lime, coal, and merchant goods. Forty years before that time, Dr Burnside tells us, " there was a considerable tobacco trade carried on from Dumfries. At an average of four years, 1250 hogsheads were annually imported. It is alleged, however, that the exportation was considerably greater ; and that, in consequence of some unhappy mistakes of this kind, the trade was discouraged. It has since entirely failed."

The first link in the railway chain by which Dumfries is now united to the great centres of business throughout the country was formed by the opening of the Glasgow and South-Western Company's line from the burgh to Gretna, on the 22nd of August, 1848 : others were supplied when the whole of that railway was completed to Glasgow, in September, 1850, when the Castle-Douglas and Dumfries railway was opened, in November, 1859, and when the burgh was brought within the range of the Caledonian line by the opening of a branch to Lockerbie in September, 1863. These various railways have done much to develop the trade of the burgh and the district ; but, as already noticed, they have seriously reduced the traffic of the port. (a)

(a) A branch line under the Light Railways Act was opened to Leadhills from Elvanfoot on the Caledonian main on 1st October, 1901, and shortly afterwards extended to Wanlockhead ; and in 1905 the Glencairn Railway, leaving the G. & S.-W. main at Holywood, was opened. At Dumfries there have been repeated extensions of the passenger and goods stations, engine-sheds, &c. ; and a well-appointed hotel erected by the Railway Company has been conducted with conspicuous success. When the stage-coach was super-seded by the railway system the King's highways were deemed to have served their time and become for practical purposes parish roads. But there is more of "going to and fro" upon them than ever there was, now that the bicycle has come into universal use, and the motor car arrived with its new terrors for travellers. To a Dumfriesshire mechanic, the late Kirkpatrick M'Millan, Closeburn, we owe the invention which others have developed into the modern bicycle.

In 1831 the Commissioners of Tonnage had an income of nearly £1100 : in 1844, just before the rival mode of transit began to take effect, the revenue had risen to £1212 ; but even then the trust was heavily indebted to the Bank of Scotland—the expenditure including payments for debt and interest to the extent of £1356, and there being a deficit on the year of £144.

In the same year (1844) the tonnage dues inwards were as follows :—1233 tons register, foreign vessels, at 6d, £30 16s 6d ; 27,473 tons, coasting vessels, at 2d, £228 18s 10d ; 6413½ tons of goods, at 1s 2d, £374 2s ; 13,928¾ tons of coals, at 6d, £348 4s 4d ; 212 tons of lime, at 6d, £5 6s. Outwards : 540 tons coasting vessels, at 2d, £4 10s ; 3776½ tons of goods, at 1s 2d, £220 5s 11d ; total revenue, £1212 3s 7d. Forty years afterwards the revenue had fallen to less than one-half of that sum, its whole amount being £554 14s 3d.

In the year last ended (10th June, 1872) the income of the Commissioners was set down as follows :—Inwards : 4334 tons register, coasting vessels, at 2d, £36 2s 4d ; 6636$\frac{4}{10}$ tons of goods, at 10d, £276 10s 4d ; 1747 tons of coals, at 2d, £14 11s 2d ; 339 tons of lime, at 2d, £2 16s 6d. Outwards : 184 tons register, coasting vessels, at 2d, £1 10s 8d ; 3037$\frac{9}{10}$ tons of goods, coasting at 10d, £126 11s 4d. Fines imposed upon merchants for evasion of tonnage duties during year, £131 3s 4d ; total revenues, £589 5s 8d. Expenditure : Harbour-master's expenses (walls, &c., harbours, and quays), £177 6s 5d ; buoys, £58 12s 8d ; management, £44 9s 3d ; embankments, plant, &c., £157 12s 2d ; total, £438 0s 6d, or nearly £623 less than in 1844, before the railways came into operation.

The expenditure in 1871-2 was £438 0s 6d, but this is exclusive of the heavy interest on the sum borrowed for the construction of the sea-dyke between Glencaple Quay and Aird's Point, which, on account of the reduced condition of the trust, has not been paid for several years. (a)

(a) The interest accumulated largely during the course of many ensuing years. Owing to the growing inability of the Commission to provide for its burdens the light at Southerness was extinguished on 1st July, 1867, and in 1875 a further misfortune befell the Trust through an accident in the river to the steam-tug "Arabian," which being made the subject of successful litigation in the Court of Session by the owners of the vessel, practically reduced the Commission to a state of insolvency. The adverse decision was not confined to the question of damages against the Trust, but also involved the Commissioners in personal liability for the expenses of process ; and though this part of the decision was afterwards recalled, the effect upon the Commissioners of Supply of Dumfries and the Stewartry was to render the individual members of these bodies extremely unwilling to accept office when appointed by their respective constituents ; indeed it became their usual course to resign immediately on their appointment. From 1875 onward till 1886 the Commission remained so irregularly constituted as to be almost in a state of abeyance, and the amount of dues collected fell to a very low point. In the year last mentioned, however, the Commission was again regularised,

From the Custom-house point of view the port of Dumfries stretches far beyond the jurisdiction of the Nith Commissioners, extending as it does from the river Sark, the boundary between Scotland and England, to the rivulet or offing of Kirk Andrews Bay, in the Stewartry of Kirkcudbright, and including, as creeks, Annan, sixteen miles, Barlochan, seventeen miles, and Kirkcudbright, twenty-eight miles distant from Dumfries.

In 1790 the vessels entered to the port inwards in this sense numbered 253, with a tonnage of 8982 and 357 men ; while 135 vessels, of 5264 tonnage, with 357 men, entered outwards. Before twenty years had elapsed the trade of the port had doubled in amount, as the following figures for 1809 will show :—Vessels entered inwards, 493 ; tonnage, 18,985 ; men, 1389. Outwards : 287 vessels, 12,090 tonnage, 802 men. As further illustrative of the progress of the port, it may be mentioned that the annual average of five years, ending 1794, shows only 459 vessels, 15,718 tonnage, and 1310 men ; while the average of the quinquennial period ending 1809 exhibits 743 vessels, 29,427 tonnage, and 2069 men. The returns issued for the year ending the 31st of March, 1864, are as follows :—Number of vessels, 117 ; tonnage, 13,139 ; vessels entered inwards, of which 19 were foreign, tonnage, 795 ; outwards, of which 4 were foreign, tonnage, 314. The total duties amounted to £5970, made up thus :—On imports not warehoused, £296 ; on warehoused goods brought from other ports, £5664 : miscellaneous, £20.

Since 1864 a considerable amount of traffic has been withdrawn from the port by the recently-formed wet dock at Silloth, on the Cumberland side of the Solway, where the freights are lower than at Dumfries, and vessels are discharged afloat. Timber can be landed at Silloth, and floated in rafts up the Nith, at much less expense to the importers than if brought direct into the river ; and sometimes, to escape the heavy dues, they get their cargoes landed at Granton, and brought down to Dumfries overland by the Caledonian railway. The Dumfries Custom-house returns for the year ended the 31st of March, 1871, give 1156 coasting vessels, with a tonnage of 14,961 ; 5 vessels (1 British and 4 foreign) entered inwards, with a tonnage of about 960 ; and 2 entered outwards (both British), tonnage, 615 ; duties, £8074.

and Mr James Carmont was appointed clerk and treasurer. In 1894, through the exertions of Mrs Blackett of Arbigland and other public-spirited persons, the light at Southerness was restored. That a period of greater activity has since been entered upon is evidenced by the numerous improvements which have been effected in the port and by a considerable increase in dues collected, which for the year 1904-5 have been upwards of £500, while the liabilities of the Trust have also been largely reduced. The Commissioners from Dumfriesshire and the Stewartry are now appointed by the County Councils ; the other Commissioners are representative as originally of the Town Council, merchants, and shipowners.

The revenue would probably have exhibited a serious decrease, owing chiefly to the late reduction of the tea-duty, had not the Government, since December, 1865, allowed British spirits to be warehoused alongst with foreign spirits, and thereby made the duties more productive. In round numbers, the revenue of the Dumfries Custom-house may be set down at £8000, and its annual expenditure at £640. (a)

Long before the Union a considerable weekly cattle market was held on the Lower Sandbeds, now the White Sands. It took place every Monday till 1659, when, to prevent the desecration caused by the droving of cattle on the preceding Sabbath day, the market was changed, by Act of Parliament, to Wednesday. Taylor, the water-poet, who made a pedestrian journey through Scotland, in 1618, noticed numerous herds of cattle browsing in the south-west of Dumfriesshire as he passed through it ; in Annandale alone he counted " eleven hundred neat, at as good

(a) The rafting of logs of wood to Dumfries, which used to be a picturesque industry on the Solway, has practically ceased. There is perhaps a larger trade in timber than formerly, but it is brought in by rail. The firm of Garland & Roger of Leith have an extensive woodyard here, close to the goods station of the G. & S.-W. ; the Granton Timber Company and Messrs T. & G. Armstrong have woodyards at the Caledonian Railway ; and Messrs Gavin Callander & Son have sawmills at Palmerston.

When the timber duty was removed there remained hardly any dutiable goods to be dealt with on the Nith ; for spirits, wines, teas, and other foreign products operated upon for revenue purposes had already been diverted to the more important ports, and were received in Dumfries by rail, this leading to the construction of extensive warehouses by the railway companies. The re-imposition of a small duty on grain, to be abandoned after a brief experience, produced £70 in 1902 at the port of Dumfries ; the whole being levied on a single cargo.

In 1894 the coasting vessels entered at the port were as follow :—Inwards, 455, having 25,928 of tonnage ; outwards, 457, having 27,936 of tonnage. The foreign trade was represented by 19 vessels of 2289 tons inwards, and 5 vessels of 607 tons outwards.

The Revenue Collection whose central offices are in Dumfries—the old Clydesdale Bank in Irish Street – embraces a very wide circuit. It is divided into four districts—(1) Dumfriesshire and Kirkcudbright ; (2) Kelso, embracing the counties of Berwick, Peebles, Selkirk, and Roxburgh, with part of Edinburghshire ; (3) Langholm, embracing that side of Dumfriesshire and the neighbouring side of Roxburghshire ; (4) Wigtownshire, including part of Ayrshire and part of Kirkcudbrightshire. The Excise returns of the Collection for the year 1904-5 amounted to £67,903, of which the Dumfries and Kirkcudbright district yielded £26,179, the Kelso district £16,529, the Langholm district £10,127, and the Wigtown district £15,068. In the same period house duty for the Collection amounted to £5000 ; land tax to only £4950 ; income tax to £103,022 ; stamps and estate duty to £26,019 ; and Customs to £826.

The smallness of the Customs is explained by the growing practice with local tradesmen of having their dutiable goods sent in by wholesale merchants from bonds in the great commercial centres, such as Glasgow. Messrs David Lennox & Sons have exclusive occupation of the old bonded warehouse on the Whitesands at Dumfries ; and the railway warehouses serve the rest of the merchants who bond on the spot.

grass as ever man did mow ;" but, as in 1655 the custom levied on
live stock and merchandise amounted to only £573 6s 8d Scots,*
it is clear that at that early date the cattle sent to the market
from its chief source of supply, Galloway, must have been few in
number—small as compared with the 30,000 beeves exposed
annually for sale on the Sands in our own day. The two yearly
fairs for horses, one at Candlemas and the other in September,
known as the Rood Fair, are of remote origin, having been confirmed by the charter granted by James VI. in 1621.

The growing importance of the cattle-rearing trade of Galloway was in 1697 marked by a demand for a road whereby the
stock might be driven to the English markets. In June of that
year the matter came before the Privy Council. "It was represented that while there was a customary way between the burgh
of New Galloway and Dumfries, there was no defined or made
road. It was the line of passage taken by immense herds of
cattle which were continually passing from the green pastures of
the Galloway hills into England—a branch of economy held to be
the main support of the inhabitants of the district, and the grand
source of its rents. Droves of cattle are, however, apt to be
troublesome to the owners and tenants of the grounds through or
near which they pass ; and such was the case here."† "Several
debates," the Council record says, " have happened of late in the
passage of droves from New Galloway to Dumfries, the country
people endeavouring by violence to stop the droves, and impose
illegal exactions of money upon the cattle, to the great damage
of the trade ; whereby also riots and bloodsheds have been occasioned, which had gone greater length if those who were employed
to carry up the cattle had not managed with great moderation
and prudence." On a petition from the great landlords of the
district—James, Earl of Galloway ; Lord Basil Hamilton ; Alexander, Viscount of Kenmure ; John, Viscount of Stair ; Sir Andrew
Agnew of Lochnaw, and others—a commission was appointed by
the Privy Council, "to make and mark a highway for droves frae
New Galloway to Dumfries, holding the high and accustomed
travelling way betwixt the said two burghs."

When the Border wars ceased, and cattle were no longer
obtained by "lifting," a great impetus was given to the legitimate
traffic, which was further stimulated by the Union with England.
Soon after that event, the droving trade to the South rapidly progressed, till it became the spring of much wealth to the entire
district. It was speedily felt that the demand was unfailing. The
breeders of Galloway stock in their native district could not send
too many of them to the Sands. A few scores per week were
readily absorbed—the Southern appetite, whetted by the sweetness of the prime Scots beef, still cried for more ; and before the

* Chambers's Domestic Annals.   † Town Council Minutes.

current century was far advanced, some 15,000 head of heavy cattle were annually exported from Dumfriesshire and Galloway for the English market, most of which changed ownership on the Dumfries Sands.* Thirty-five years ago the number had risen to 20,000 ; their value, on an average of years, being not less than £200,000.

The true Galloway is a hardy, well-shaped, profitable beast : the body long, deep, and round ; the back straight and broad ; the leg short and thick ; the foot large ; its coat of hair shaggy and black ; while the circumstance of its being hornless renders it increasingly valuable. Its native fields are in many instances so sheltered as to favour the health of the animal, and the fine meat it yields—doubtless owing in some degree to the quality of the herbage it browses upon, which is rich and sweet, even when scanty. The cattle of this breed driven to the Sands are chiefly two or three years old. On being bought for the London and other English markets, they lay on additional layers of fat in the nourishing pastures of Norfolk before being sent to the shambles. Though for ages the dusky Galloways composed the bulk of the cattle at the Dumfries market, they now occupy the second place in point of numbers ; the picturesque West Highlanders, which Landseer and Rosa Bonheur like so well to paint, and large herds of which were wintered in Galloway, are also diminishing. Ayrshire dairy stock, and crosses, with the shorthorn, have increased ; but the principal change experienced on the Dumfries Sands has been produced by the great immigration of Irish cattle. In 1872 the number of these was 6044, being upwards of 2500 more than in 1870, and surpassing the numbers of both Galloway and Highlanders united. Irish cattle have greatly improved, and they are now nearly all shorthorns of fair quality.

When railways were introduced into the district the beasts, no longer tediously driven along dusty roads, were sent southward by truck —a change which operated beneficially on the Dumfries market ; till, by the opening of the Castle-Douglas railway, in 1859, facilities were afforded for despatching Galloways direct without first sending them to the old central emporium, the White sands. The business of the market was also much changed when, at a mart in the immediate vicinity, Mr Andrew Stewart originated, in 1858, a weekly sale of live stock by auction—an example which has been extensively followed in many other towns. The palmy period of the Dumfries cattle trade was in the earlier half of the present century, it having declined since about 1848 by the operation of various influences ; the chief being the extension of

---

* Pennant, who visited Dumfries in 1772, says :—" The great weekly markets for black cattle are of much advantage to the place ; and vast droves from Galloway and the shire of Air pass through on the way to the fairs of Norfolk and Suffolk."—*Tour*, vol. ii., p. 101.

the railway sytem into Galloway, the establishment of competing markets in the district, and the substitution of sheep for cattle on many farms.

It is still, however, of vast extent—second to none, indeed, on the north side of the Border, as the following statistics for the ten years immediately preceding a severe attack of rinderpest will tend to show :—The number of cattle exposed for sale on the Sands in 1854 was 28,184 ; in 1855, 31,552 ; in 1856, 28,876 ; in 1857, 24,625 ; in 1858, 22,605 ; in 1859, 22,129 ; in 1860, 20,405 ; in 1861, 22,186 ; in 1862, 23,564 ; in 1863, 20,264 ; and in 1864 the number was but 17,974, exhibiting a decline of 2290 head as compared with the preceding year. The cattle plague alluded to did not appear in the district till about the end of autumn, in 1865, but it seriously reduced the supply of stock for the whole year. The disease, during its course of about five months, appeared on forty farms in Dumfriesshire, fifteen of which were in the parish of Dumfries. About 710 cattle died of the disease, and more than 130 were killed in order to assist in checking its ravages : the aggregate value of the animals must have been at least £6000. In consequence of the outbreak, the market was closed on the 8th of November, 1865, and was not re-opened till the 15th of August in the following year. The cattle shown in 1865 numbered only 9605 ; and during the four and a half months of 1866, only 5907. After the cessation of the disease, the numbers of cattle were—15,723 in 1867, 13,256 in 1868, 12,120 in 1869, 12,932 in 1870, 13,340 in 1871, and 15,200 in 1872. The Galloways sold during the summer and autumn of 1872 brought from £7 to £12 ; two-year-olds, £12 to £18 ; three-year-olds, £14 10s to £24. Highlanders : One-year-olds, £6 to £10 10s ; two-year-olds, £11 to £16 10s ; three and four-year-olds, £15 to £24. Ayrshire cows, £12 to £22. Irish cattle, £6 to £16. In 1859 the number of cattle sent from Dumfries by railway was 13,975 : since the opening of the Portpatrick railway, in 1861, a gradual decline has been experienced, only 5362 having been trucked in 1864, 4751 in 1865, and 3470 in 1866 ; the two last years having also been affected by cattle plague. In 1867 there was an increase, 8805 cattle having been sent by railway, and 7456 in the following year.

We can find no traces of a sheep market in Dumfries at an early period. People still living can recollect when the appear ance of so many as a score or two of "bleaters" on the Sands was a rare occurrence; but the rapid increase of turnip husbandry and pastoral farming throughout the county eventually told upon the sheep trade of the town ; and it now surpasses in importance the traffic in cattle. As many as 37,000 sheep, old and young, have been annually offered for sale, taking the average of the five years previous to 1872, their value each year being not less, perhaps, than £70,000 ; the Cheviots, and a breed formed between these hardy mountaineers and the more delicate and heavier fleeced Leicesters, and another formed between the latter and black-faced ewes, constituting the greater portion of the stock.

Every year immense flocks that are never shown on the Sands are sent from the Dumfries railway station, chiefly to Liverpool, Carlisle, Penrith, Appleby, Preston, and Newcastle. The number thus exported was 43,932 in 1859, 39,460 in 1860, 46,007 in 1861, 40,691 in 1862, 37,937 in 1863, 39,811 in 1864, 47,105 in 1865, 35,076 in 1866, 69,620 in 1867, and 65,239 in 1868. As already hinted, much business not included in any of the above figures is done by the hammer of the auctioneer.

Mr Stewart sold, at his mart adjoining the Sands, 1783 cattle, 21,606 sheep and lambs, 143 calves, and 313 pigs in 1870; and 1480 cattle, 24,516 sheep, 150 calves, and 364 pigs in 1871. A second auction mart was opened in Mr Michael Teenan's extensive horse bazaar in 1860, conducted by Mr David Creighton, now of the Royal Bazaar. The sales in 1870 were : 2569 cattle, 17,820 sheep, 277 calves, and 856 pigs ; in 1871, 1424 cattle, 16,987 sheep, 187 calves, and 346 pigs. A third auction mart, called the Royal Bazaar, was opened in 1868, and in 1870 and 1871, when conducted by Mr James Allison, the numbers were—in the former year, 1953 cattle, 22,849 sheep, 489 calves, and 2100 pigs ; and in 1871, 1298 cattle, 15,170 sheep, 431 calves, and 2385 pigs. Since April, 1872, this auction mart has been conducted by Mr D. Creighton.

The entire stock sold at Dumfries, on the Sands and in the marts, numbered 19,237 cattle and 101,125 sheep in 1870 ; and 17,542 cattle and 87,755 sheep in 1871. The rapidity with which the sales by auction are effected contrasts favourably with the old tardy mode of bargain-making, and it is highly probable that the "hammer-in-hand" system of selling stock will come to prevail over every other in all our leading market towns. (a)

For about ninety years pig-feeding has formed one of the industrial features of Dumfriesshire. In 1794, the value of the pork cured in Annandale alone was estimated at £12,000 ; for the whole county, in 1811, the returns were little short of £50,000,* the chief sales taking place on the Dumfries Sands. For many years previous to 1832, upwards of 700 carcasses were sold weekly on the Sands ; the average of which was at least 8000 stones. During the *heat* of the season the amount was often a great deal

---

(a) The revolution which Mr M'Dowall foresaw as the result of the extension of railways and the development of the auction mart system has since taken full effect. The open market on the Sands for sheep and cattle is a thing of the past. The whole trade is conducted in two auction marts, belonging respectively to Messrs Thomson & Laurie and Messrs R. Harrison & Son. The total head of live stock sold in these marts during 1904 (exclusive of some small sales of store stock) was : Cattle, 10,675 ; calves, 2312 ; sheep, 45,779 ; total, 58,766.

* Dr Singer's Survey of Dumfriesshire,

more ; and instances have occurred in which from four thousand
to five thousand pounds' worth of pork have been disposed of in a
single day.   At one period of the war with France, prices rose to
an exorbitant pitch ; and even long after they had settled down,
the sales in Dumfries averaged £50,000 annually.* Formerly,
many hundreds of pigs were fed every year in the burgh ; but as
this was deemed objectionable in a sanitary point of view, it was
finally put a stop to in 1858.   The supply at the market was more
seriously diminished by the same influence that reduced the show
of cattle on the Sands—the extension of railway intercourse to
Castle-Douglas, since which period the falling off has been considerable.   Within these few years an extensive traffic has taken
place in live pigs or porkers—there being now weekly sales of pigs
on Tuesday at the auction marts, the Wednesday sales being confined to cattle and sheep.   These sales of pigs are largely attended
both by local and English buyers. (a)

For these reasons it is not much to be wondered at that the
carcasses of pork sold in Dumfries, which amounted to 13,550 in
1858-9, had dwindled down to 5040 in 1869-70, 7012 in 1870-71, and
7600 in 1871-72, and that there is no chance of the trade ever
reaching its former annual average. Thirty-five years ago, 5s 6d
per stone of 16 lbs. was about the usual price.   More recently a
higher figure has been obtained, rising from 6s to 8s 6d per stone
of 14 lbs., according to quality, and also to size ; carcasses of
twelve or thirteen stones being preferred by curers.   In 1866 as
much as 8s 6d per stone was obtained for best pork ; while in
March, 1869, the very high figure of 8s 10d was obtained ; these
sums being more readily given because of the supply not keeping
pace with the demand.†   The season lasts for nearly five months,

---

* Picture of Dumfries, p. 27.

(a) The open market for pork is also a thing of the past. Carcases are
now delivered to merchants at all times of the year and largely sold as fresh
pork ; and the winter trade for curing is done privately at the business
premises of the purchasers.

† The varying courses of the pork market are shown in the statistics of
the extensive trade carried on by the largest bacon-curer in Dumfries, Mr
William Bell, Provost of the burgh in 1864.   In 1835, Mr Bell bought pork at
3s 2d per stone of 16 lbs. ; and next year, when the imperial stone of 14 lbs.
was introduced, he paid to the same dealer 5s 10d, equal to 6s 8d the heavy
stone.   His transactions on the Sands during the last sixteen years were as
follows :—Season 1856-57 : 15,974 stones ; average price, 7s 2d per stone of
14 lbs.   Season 1857-58 : 11,294 stones ; average, 5s 8d.   Season 1858-59 :
14,478 stones, 13 lbs. ; average, 5s 10½d.   Season 1859-60 : 13,144 stones, 9
lbs ; average, 6s 4½d.   Season 1860-61 : 8455 stones ; average, 7s 0½d.   Season
1861-62 : 12,709 stones, 7 lbs. ; average, 6s 6d.   Season 1862-63 : 14,552
stones, 6 lbs. ; average, 5s 5d.   Season 1863-64 : 12,481 stones, 11 lbs. ;
average, 6s 8¼d.   Season 1864-65 : 14,532 stones, 1 lb. ; average, 6s 9d.   In
season 1865-66, the average rose to the high figure of 7s 3½d ; Mr Bell's
purchases of 13,924 stones 9 lbs. that season costing nearer £6000 than £5000.
Next season (1866-67) pork experienced a sudden downfall, he paying an

beginning in the middle of November, and terminating at the end of March or early in April. When the trade was at its best, fifteen or sixteen years ago, its annual value was at least £65,000; now it is not worth more than £50,000.

A great stimulus has been given to the agriculture of the district by the exhibitions of the Highland and Agricultural Society, held periodically in the burgh or neighbourhood. The first of these took place in 1830, when the cattle shown numbered 180 ; horses, 60 ; sheep, 247 ; swine, 19 ; implements, 18 : total, 524. The second took place in 1837, with the following entries :— Cattle, 181 ; horses, 77 ; sheep, 512 ; articles of dairy produce, 31 ; implements, 36 : total, 841. A third show was held in 1845, when the entries were :—Cattle, 297 ; horses, 75 ; sheep, 537 ; swine, 62 ; poultry, 101 ; dairy produce, 88 ; implements, 143 : total, 1302. A fourth show took place in 1860—the cattle numbered 298 ; horses, 166 ; sheep, 558 ; swine, 54 ; poultry, 216 ; dairy produce, 195 ; and 911 implements : total, 2398. There was a fifth show in 1870, when the entries were :—Cattle, 374 ; horses, 171 ; sheep, 730; swine, 76; poultry, 402; dairy produce, 130; implements, 1874 : total, 3757. (a) Good results have also arisen from the competitions entered into by local farming clubs, and which, joined into a Union Agricultural Society at the suggestion of the Duke of Buccleuch, hold quinquennial exhibitions in Dumfries, which are beginning almost to rival those that take place under the auspices of the parent society. The first Union show was held in 1852 ; at the third, in 1862, the entries included 247 cattle, 112 horses, 177 sheep, 26 swine, and 365 implements ; at the fourth, held on the 1st of October, 1867, there were 232 cattle, 126 horses, 171 sheep, 14 swine, and 138 implements ; and at the fifth, held on the 2nd of

average of 6s 1¼d on 12,912 stones 2 lbs. Season 1867-68 : 12,915 stones 5 lbs. ; average, 6s 6½d. In season 1868-69 pork was scarce, and Mr Bell paid the unprecedented sum of 8s 3d, an average on 6184 stones. In season 1869-70 the price was still high : 9900 stones ; average, 8s 1d. Season 1870-71 : 11,183 stones ; average, 7s 3d. In season 1871-72, the price fell still further, the average on 12,388 stones 8 lbs. being 6s 3d. Most of the Dumfries hams are sent to London for exportation to India, where they are in high repute.

(a) The Highland Society's show was again held in Dumfries in 1878, when the entries were : Cattle, 357 ; horses, 328 ; sheep, 621 ; swine, 39 ; poultry, 303 ; dairy produce, 235 ; implements, 2578. The sum offered in premiums was £2763 ; and the money drawn at the show amounted to £3308. The following are the statistics of the three subsequent shows of the national society held in Dumfries :—Show of 1886—Entries of cattle, 287 ; horses, 312 ; sheep, 505 ; swine, 32 ; poultry, 144 ; dairy produce, 146 ; implements, 1639 ; amount of premiums offered, £2583 ; money drawn, £2314. Show of 1895—Entries of cattle, 269 ; horses, 333 ; sheep, 416 ; swine, 26 ; poultry, 245 ; dairy produce, 114 ; implements, 2265 ; amount offered in premiums, £2456 ; money drawn, £2600. Show of 1903—Entries of cattle, 279 ; horses, 282 ; sheep, 243 ; swine, 42 ; poultry, 419 ; dairy produce, 128 ; wool, 33 ; implements, 1834 ; amount offered in premiums, £3073 ; sum drawn at show, £2917.

October, 1872, there were 257 cattle, 190 Horses, 154 sheep, 10 swine, and 130 implements. (a)

From returns obtained by Government, we learn that in 1866 the whole cattle in Dumfriesshire numbered 45,053 ; the sheep, 371,486 ; the pigs, 18,619 ; and that in 1871 the numbers were :— Cattle, 52,436 ; sheep, 512,670 ; horses, 6840 ; pigs, 19,734. (b)

A considerable hosiery trade existed in Dumfries during " Burns's time," carried on chiefly by Messrs Haining, Hogg, and Dickson, the founders of that branch of business in the town. Among others engaged in it at an early date were Mr James Paterson, Mr John Pagan, Messrs Scott and Dinwiddie, Mr William Milligan (now of Westpark), and Mr William Carson.* At the beginning of the current century, about thirty frames were at work. Then, and for many years afterwards, the narrow frame of a rude construction was alone used, and no such articles as drawers and shirts, which now form the best part of the business, were wrought upon it. Mr M'Diarmid, writing in 1832, says : " Dumfries, in the proper sense of the word, can hardly be called a manufacturing town. In former years, striped or checked cottons were made, but the trade has diminished, and of the cotton weavers found in town and country—amounting to about three hundred in all—by far the largest portions are employed through the medium of agents by the manufacturing houses in Glasgow and Carlisle. Hosiery, on the other hand, has become a staple article of trade, and gives employment to upwards of three hundred hands located in Dumfries and the surrounding villages. Of stockings, socks, drawers, and flannel shirts, from three hundred and fifty to four hundred dozen are fabricated weekly, the value of which may be averaged at the same number of pounds ; and it would thus appear that the capital turned over in this branch of traffic falls little short of £20,000 yearly."†

Of cotton weaving there is now scarcely any ; but the manufacture of hosiery, with its underclothing accompaniments, is still extensively carried on. Much more money than the above sum is

(a) Following upon the last quinquennial show of the Union Agricultural Society, held in 1898, the Dumfries Agricultural Society was formed for the purpose of promoting an annual open show. The first of these was held in 1899, and attended with great success. The purpose of the Union Society being thus superseded, it was shortly thereafter dissolved. The Dumfries Agricultural Society has a membership numbering close upon six hundred. At the show held under its auspices in 1904 the entries numbered 136 cattle, 272 horses, 150 sheep, 74 of dairy produce : total, 632.

(b) The corresponding returns for 1904 were : Horses, 7944 ; cattle, 63,931 ; sheep, 545,156 ; pigs, 9879.

* Mr Carson, who died in 1872, was the oldest operative stocking-maker in Dumfries. He commenced business in 1803, and at that time purchased from Mr James Paterson the first frames (it is believed) that were ever used in the burgh. They were five in number, and cost £80.

† Picture of Dumfries, pp. 9, 10.

now " turned over " in it annually, though it gives employment to fewer weavers than it did forty years ago ; the reason being that many of the frames now in use are so improved that the weaver or knitter can on an average do fully twice as much work with them as with the old narrow machines. The business commenced by Mr William Milligan, in 1805, is still carried on by members of his family, the title of the firm being Milligan & Co. A hosiery business was begun in 1810 by the late Mr Robert Scott, senior (founder of another and much greater trade in the burgh), which is still continued by his son, Mr James Scott, and his son-in-law, Mr Murray, under the designation of Robert Scott & Son ; they and Messrs Milligan & Co. carrying on the largest concerns of this kind that exist in Dumfries. The establishment next in importance is that of Mr William Dinwiddie, at Greenbrae. The hosiery trade gives work to about a hundred and thirty hands in the burgh, and to fully a hundred others who ply the shuttle at their own houses in Gastown, Collin, Lochmaben, Lockerbie, and many other parts of the district ; besides numerous seamers, washers, clerks, and warehousemen (a).

(a) Mr W. A. Dinwiddie and his brother Mr Lauderdale Dinwiddie succeeded to their father's business, as it had been developed by their elder brother Robert in partnership with Mr Halliday. They acquired the works of Messrs Milligan & Co. on the Greensands, and enlarged the factory in King Street, Maxwelltown. It is fitted up with the most modern power frames ; and a very extensive manufacture is carried on of underclothing in the finer qualities of wool and in silk.

Mr Robert M'George, Rosebank, Irongray, employed a few stocking-makers in the first half of the last century, and supplied the trade in Dumfries with frame needles until steel was substituted for iron wire. His son Robert, who had succeeded him at Rosebank, opened a shop in Glasgow Street, Maxwelltown, in 1854, and some years later, in 1863, he went into partnership with Messrs Jamieson & Primrose in hosiery manufacture. They erected a factory in Maxwell Street ; but owing to a deep commercial depression in the country the concern did not prosper. After two or three years the firm was dissolved. Mr M'George retained some of the frames, which he removed to a workshop in Broatch's Close, and he also continued a retail shop which the firm had opened in Dumfries. In 1881 his son, Mr James M'George, purchased the hosiery business of R. Scott & Sons (Messrs Scott & Murray). To make headway in a keen competition it was necessary to obtain the most improved machinery, and this Mr M'George discovered during a special visit of inquiry to Ghent. The Lamb-knitter enabled him to utilise on a larger scale than previously female labour. About 1885 he turned his attention to glove-making ; and by a simple adaptation of the knitter 'a difficulty about working the fingers upon it was overcome. This secret he had to himself for a considerable period, and made good use of the advantage. A knitter was afterwards introduced by the maker to produce a seamless glove, and Mr M'George at once placed an order for a hundred of this machine. It has not been improved upon, and he has need for a much greater number to-day. In 1888 he took into partnership his brother David ; when Messrs Walter Scott & Sons retired from their large mill in St. Michael Street Messrs M'George transferred their industry to the weaving-sheds there ; and in 1902 the senior partner's two sons (Messrs J. and A. M'George) and Mr George Harding joined the firm. They employ from 700 to 800 hands, mostly young women ; and in woollen gloves, knicker-stockings, and ties of silk and

"Some stockings and hats, a small quantity of linens and coarse woollens, and leather on a large scale, are our principal manufactures," said Dr Burnside, writing in 1790.* Fifty years afterwards some two hundred hatters were employed in Dumfries ; but the "heads of the people" give no employment now to local hands in this line, all the hats sold in the burgh being imported. The leather manufacture has been retained and greatly extended. Its annual value was £30,000 in 1832 ; now it cannot be less than £80,000. The "lion's share" of the tanning and currying done in the burgh falls to the lot of Mrs T. D. Currie of Clerkhill ; a large business in the same trades is also transacted by Messrs A. & C. Wallace and by Mr H Murphy ; and a smaller one by Messrs Fallas & Co. (in addition to their saddlery business) : the whole giving labour to nearly 100 hands. About 30,000 hides are transformed into leather yearly by these firms ; the beeves of the district supplying but a small proportion of the raw material, that being chiefly obtained at Liverpool, Birmingham, Newcastle, and Leith. For the finished fabric the principal markets are London and Liverpool (a).

About 1816 basket-making was started in the burgh by an enterprising Yorkshireman, Mr (afterwards Bailie) Hammond. In a short period this seemingly insignificant branch of business grew to such an extent that it became second to none of the same kind in Scotland. Under his successor, Mr James Kennedy, the Dumfries wicker-ware manufacture retains its old repute. Mr Kennedy, like Mr Hammond, grows all his own material, to the

cotton they do a very large trade with home, colonial, and foreign houses. The firm have also a factory at Sanquhar, set up in the old Crichton School-house, and some sixty hands are employed there.

The factory in Maxwell Street was carried on for some time by the late Mr W. Halliday. In 1874 Messrs J. L. Gibson & Co., a firm from Penicuik, acquired the premises for general hosiery work. Since 1878 their business has been chiefly the manufacture of woollen gloves, half hose, and knicker hose, at which they employ some eighty hands. Since the death of Mr J. L. Gibson, his son, Mr W. Gibson, has been sole partner of the firm. Hosiery manufacture is also conducted by Mr James A. Robertson at Saughtrees, and by Mr Robert Hamilton in King Street, Maxwelltown.

* MS. History of Dumfries.

(a) Mr Murphy, who had acquired Watt's tannery in the Mill Hole, subsequently came into possession of Mrs Currie's as well as that of Messrs Wallace. The Dumfries Tanneries Company, formed in 1895, took over those works, and also Mr Fallas's yard. In the hands of the company the entire tanning industry of the town is now concentrated. The premises have been greatly extended, fitted with the latest machinery, and electric lighted. The former firms employed only some score of men, and the company has at present a staff of eighty. Its business is almost exclusively tanning ; the currying branch of the leather trade being so far reduced in Dumfries that it engages only two men. Mr W. A. Dinwiddie is chairman of the company, and Mr Horace Norman has been manager from the first. In a portion of the old tweed mills at Kingholm (acquired by Mr John Charlton) Mr Downes has set up a new industry there—the separation of wool from sheepskins.

culture of which fifteen acres of land are devoted, and the reaping of which gives employment to about a hundred and fifty persons during "the willow harvest." (*a*)

In seeds, flowers, and plants of all kinds, Dumfries has a large and valuable trade. About a hundred acres are laid out as nursery grounds in connection with it, which help to beautify as well as to enrich the burgh. In these about two hundred hands find employment during the busy season, which lasts about six months each year. The most extensive nursery establishment in the town is that of Messrs Thomas Kennedy and Company, established in 1787, and which first acquired a high position through the industry and energy of its head, the late Provost Kennedy. The sole partners at present are Mr Alexander T. Newbigging and Mr Robert Cowan, who have about seventy acres of ground under culture for their products; and give employment in their establishment during the spring months to about a hundred and twenty hands on an average. Their home trade embraces the three kingdoms; and they have business connections with Australia, New Zealand, France, Germany, and Holland. Extensive nursery grounds are also cultivated by two brothers, the Messrs Learmont, whose late father, Mr William Learmont, was, at the time of his death, the oldest market gardener in the burgh.* (*b*)

Twenty-five years ago Dumfries was no more a manufacturing town than it was in 1832; but the nucleus of a great business that was to make it one was formed in 1846, when Messrs Robert Scott and Sons, hosiers, purchased premises that had been occupied as a sawmill at Kingholm village, in order that they might spin yarns for their hosiery business. The largest oak springing from the smallest imaginable acorn would but faintly symbolize the growth of the manufacture that had such a small and simple origin. After the new mill had been in operation for some months

(*a*) Mr Kennedy was succeeded by his nephew, Mr J. Paterson, who continues the business.

* There are large nurseries in several other parts of Dumfriesshire; those of Messrs John Palmer and Son, Annan, which extend to a hundred acres, being the chief.

(*b*) Mr T. K. Newbigging and his brother, John, succeeded their father and Mr Cowan in 1885. In the spring of this year Mr John Newbigging died in the Canaries, where he had gone in the hope of recovering health; and his body was brought for interment at Dumfries. Mr T. K. Newbigging, grandson of the founder of the firm—his mother being a daughter of Provost Kennedy—is thus the sole partner at present. The Learmont family also continue their connection with the nursery trade. Mr John Learmont is sole partner of the firm of W. Learmont & Son, with an extensive nursery at Larchfield; and among the other firms are those of J. Learmont & Co., Welldale Nursery, Maxwelltown; W. Learmont, Glencaple Road; James Service & Sons, Corbelly Hill (the sole partner being Mr Robert Service); John Bogie & Son, Bankend Road; and W. Middleton & Son, Elmgrove Nursery.

its proprietors secured the services of Mr John M'Keachie, (a
a weaver of damask table-covers in Maxwelltown ; and under his
direction an experiment was tried in the construction of tweeds
which proved to be encouragingly successful. The Messrs Scott,
with characteristic shrewdness and sagacity, saw at once that the
germ of the new business thus inadvertently hit upon was worthy
of being fully developed ; and with that enterprise for which
they were also remarkable they invested a very large amount of
capital in the trade. For a year or two it was only of small
extent ; but it rapidly increased afterwards, till it became a
prosperous concern, profitable to its proprietors, and a great
benefit to the burgh and neighbourhood.

Mr Scott, senior, retired from business in 1851, leaving his sons
to prosecute the tweed trade, which they did with unremitting
vigour. Mr John Scott having become proprietor of the Kingholm
establishment in 1857, his brother Mr Robert Scott of Castledykes
joined with another brother, Mr Walter Scott, then of Manchester,
in setting up a second tweed factory. The building, erected in an
orchard between the foot of St. Michael Street and the Dock
meadow, is truly a noble structure : huge, massive, and turreted,
with its chimney stalk rising a hundred and seventy-four feet from
the ground, it is almost palatial in its aspect. In the course of a few
years afterwards, another vast industrial hive, similar in appearance and devoted to the same purpose, rose up almost directly
opposite on the Galloway bank of the river, built for Mr Walter
Scott, he having dissolved partnership with his brother in 1866.
Too often elsewhere town factories are dull, dingy, repulsive-look-
ing erections ; but in pleasing contrast to all this, the Nithsdale
Mills are a decided ornament to the burgh, while the Troqueer
establishment is in every way a great acquisition to the suburbs of
Maxwelltown. For a while Mr Robert Scott wrought the Nithsdale Mills on his own account, after which he leased them to his
nephew, Mr Robert Scott, junior, and Mr. Nixon—an arrangement, however, which was of short duration. Mr. Robert Scott
dying in 1871, the factory was purchased by Mr Walter Scott, who
had in the preceding year become proprietor also of the Kingholm
Mills, where the tweed trade of Dumfries was cradled. The latter
factory has experienced a variety of fortunes. It was disposed of
by Mr John Scott in 1866 to a limited liability company, having a
capital of £80,000, but it did not flourish under this shareholding
management, and after being closed for about a year, it was
re-opened by Mr Walter Scott in 1870. All the three mills are
now carried on by him and his two sons. Twenty-six years ago
the tweed operatives of the burgh numbered only 60, and the
spindels used 1000. By the summer of 1871 the trade had grown

(a) Mr M'Keachie died in November, 1904, at Kirkinner, at a very advanced
age.

to such an extent that the hands at the Kingholm numbered fully 200, spindles 7212; at Nithsdale, 352 hands and 15,864 spindles; and at Troqueer, 532 hands and 10,780 spindles. Continuing still to progress, the figures at the close of 1872 were 1400 workers, with 35,000 spindles and 400 looms—the produce being at the rate of fully 2000 pieces (of 50 yards each) per month. From these statistics some idea may be obtained of the vast extent of the trade carried on by Messrs Walter Scott & Sons. They are the largest manufacturers of tweeds in Scotland, and the character of the firm stands correspondingly high. "The wool used is principally the finer qualities of colonial, a very large portion being Port Philip and New Zealand—sufficient guarantee for the excellence and quality of the goods."* Scotch woollen fabrics have long been the favourite wear of men of all ranks; and Dumfries tweeds have acquired a very high repute in the wholesale trade.† They are sent chiefly to London, Manchester, and Glasgow, from which they find their way to continental Europe, to America, India, and Australia; and large quantities of goods are also sent direct from the mills to many foreign parts, including France, Germany, Russia, and the United States. To estimate the beneficial results that flow to the town from the tweed trade would be no easy task. But for these, and the stimulus given to other occupations by the railways, Dumfries, instead of advancing steadily and rapidly, as it has done during the last twenty-five years, would undoubtedly have retrograded, both as regards population and wealth.(a) A smaller tweed factory was erected by Mr John M. Henderson about five years ago, in which nearly fifty operatives are employed. It is called St. Michael's Mills, from the position which it occupies near the head of that street. (b) In 1862, Mr Thomas Shortridge, who

---

*From a well-written paper on the Scotch woollen trade, communicated to the *Dumfries Standard* by the late Mr David Bell.

† "An old name is still a great power; but, in this age of constant competition, constant progress, and continuous change, the *prestige* of the oldest houses will quickly disappear unless their members are men fully up with the times—marching not only *with* them, but ahead of them. It is because Robert Scott, the father of Dumfries manufacturers, was such a man, and because his sons have been animated by the same spirit, that Dumfries has such a reputation throughout the world for the excellence of her tweeds."— *Paper by Mr D. Bell.*

(a) In 1885 Mr Walter Scott (who died in March, 1892) disposed of the mills to his sons, Charles and Walter Henry, whose partnership lasted for only a few years. About thirteen years ago the parent mill at Kingholm was discontinued and dismantled, and passed into the hands of Mr John Charlton, grain dealer. In 1902 the Nithsdale Mills were sold, a portion being purchased by Mr Charlton, and the portion occupied on lease by Messrs M'George being acquired by them. The firm of Walter Scott & Sons—the partners of which are Mr Walter Henry Scott, Mr Herbert Douglas Scott, Mr Arthur Leonard Scott (his sons), and Mr George Graham—have now the whole of their works concentrated in Troqueer Mills.

(b) In 1880 Mr Samuel Charteries and Mr Robert Spence, the former trained in the commercial department of the tweed trade, the latter in the

has very extensive dye-works stretching from his warehouse at the foot of High Street across to Irish Street, added a branch of cloth-finishing to his other business ; and more recently he begun the manufacture of tweeds. In dyeing, spinning, weaving, and finishing, the firm of Messrs. Shortridge & Son give employment to about fifty hands (a).

Strictly speaking, the burgh has no iron-works, but it is only separated by the Nith from a large foundry which was established about sixty-five years since, called Stakeford, on account of its proximity to the ford of stakes which crossed the river in ancient times ; while a little further inland there is a second foundry, still larger, that of Palmerston, set up in 1818. The proprietor of the latter works, Mr James B. A. M'Kinnel, yr., of M'Murdostown, recently acquired possession of the former also, and he is now making arrangements for locating his business, or the chief part of it, near Milldamhead, on the Dumfries side. (b) With their bands of busy Vulcans, these establishments make the north end of Maxwelltown ring with the clang of trade : the hands employed numbering in all about a hundred and thirty ; and metal to the extent of a thousand tons or more being melted annually by them to take solid shape as rural implements, builders' and joiners' castings, cranes, jennies, railway water tanks, signals and girders, water wheels, gas-works, boilers and steam-engines. For variety and excellence of work the establishments are equally remarkable ; " and," says the " Visitor's Guide," " we believe that, price considered, nowhere in the kingdom can implements for rural

designing room, entered into partnership and took over St. Michael's Mill. The energy and enterprise displayed by this firm have compelled a phenomenal degree of prosperity. In 1885 they purchased the property of Rosefield, contiguous to Troqueer Mills, and proceeded to build the Rosefield Mill. These were designed by the late Mr Alan Crombie, erected at different periods, as an expanding business required, and now present a compact, harmonious whole, with stately elevations to Troqueer Road and to the river, on a frontage of 130 yards. They are electric-lighted, furnished with 180 power-looms, besides dyeing, carding, and spinning machinery, and provide for every operation in the manufacture of cloth from the raw wool to the finished piece. In 1902 the firm (Charteries, Spence & Co.) also leased for the purpose of carding and spinning the front block of Nithsdale Mills. They employ from 600 to 700 hands, and have in addition to their domestic trade an extensive foreign connection. St. Michael's Mills have been turned into dwelling-houses.

(a) The business of Messrs T. Shortridge & Son was transferred to Stakeford, when the foundry there was given up. The senior partner retired a number of years ago, and the concern is wholly in the hands of Mr T. Shortridge, junior, who is efficiently assisted by his sons. On the weaving side of it, as on the dyeing and cleaning, there has been a large extension ; and about a hundred workers are employed. Chemical cleaning was first practised by Mr Shortridge, senior, over sixty years ago ; and it has always been a feature of the firm's work.

(b) The ironworks changed hands at Mr M'Kinnell's death, and after further vicissitude they became the property of Messrs Drummond & Co., by whom they have been carried on for a number of years.

labour be so well obtained—a matter of the first importance to the district around, when we consider that so many of its inhabitants are devoted to the pursuits of agriculture."*

Dumfries does not depend for its prosperity on the surrounding district so much as it did in the ante-railway period, and when there was no tweed manufacture within its bounds ; but it is still, fortunately, the capital of an extensive agricultural province drawing from it a princely revenue, which, distributed amongst its drapers, grocers, ironmongers, jewellers, bakers, confectioners, booksellers, apothecaries, and other shopkeepers or handicrafts-men, assists them to maintain their respective establishments, and both directly and indirectly confers great benefits on the burgh.

To some of them, Wednesday, when the country folks come to market, is as good as any three ordinary days ; to others it is worth the whole secular week ; and this, too, though in some of the towns round about from which customers come, there are now shops which, for appearance and resources, all but rival those of the county town. When, therefore, the farming interest is de-pressed, Dumfries suffers ; and when it is buoyant because "horn, corn, wool, and yarn" are bringing good prices, the burgh sympa-thizingly rejoices with its agricultural neighbours and patrons. Not content, however, with the customers that voluntarily come from country to town, many Dumfries merchants make business raids into the rural districts, from whence they take back more money yearly than even their extensive town trade is worth. All the largest clothiers of the burgh adopt the same plan (begun by the late Mr Kerr in 1813), of travelling for orders to keep their needlemen in better work ; and some of them, stretching their measuring tape far beyond the locality, send back vast quantities of English broadcloth in the form of manufactured garments to the other side of the Western Border (a).

Since the Seven Trades ceased to exist as a united incorpora-tion, in 1834, most of the members then living have been "wede away ;" so that were a Siller Gun wappenschaw to be summoned in this present year of grace, forty men entitled to shoot for the trophy would scarcely be forthcoming. But for all that there is no dearth of craftsmen in the ancient burgh and its sister town, as the following figures, which refer to those working as journey men belonging to the Trades that used to be incorporated, will help to show :—Hammermen, including the smiths and moulders

---

* Visitor's Guide, second edition, p. 63.

(a) This practice of travelling with the tape in the tailoring trade is no longer in vogue in Dumfries. In the grocery business, however, travelling vans carry provisions into all the rural neighbourhood ; and the prevalence of the weekly half-holiday has led to a considerable inflow of country people to the town on Saturday afternoons.

that are employed at the foundries, 226 ; squaremen, 220 ; tailors, 110 ; shoemakers, 100, besides 20 cloggers, or makers of strong shoes with wooden soles ; skinners and tanners, 96 ; fleshers, 24 ; and numerous weavers of hosiery and woollen cloth, as already specified in this chapter, though there is scarcely a vestige left of cotton weaving, which at the beginning of the present century gave employment to about three hundred hands in Dumfries and its immediate neighbourhood.

CHAPTER LXI.

EARLY in the eighteenth century, if not before, there was a printing office in Dumfries. A small quarto of nearly four hundred
pages, entitled "The History of the late Rebellion," written by the
Rev. Peter Rae, issued from the press of his brother Robert Rae
in 1718, and is perhaps the earliest work of an original character
that was printed and published in the burgh. It is a very creditable specimen of typography, being both neat and correct. About
fifty-eight years after that date the town could boast of a weekly
serial in octavo, called the *Dumfries Magazine*, which was also
well got up externally ; but the literary contents were inferior,
and signally lacking in topics of local interest. In 1777, the
printer of the magazine, Provost Jackson, dropped it, and started
a newspaper, under the title of the *Dumfries Weekly Journal*, the
first political broad-sheet published in the town. A glance at
some of the earlier volumes of the *Journal* has left upon us a
favourable impression : the original writing, though very limited,
as was the case in all provincial journals at that time, being
generally vigorous and tasteful. The local news is extremely
scant ; and matters which would in the modern penny-a-lining
style be expanded into columns are disposed of in meagre paragraphs ; while of reporting, strictly speaking, there is none.
Latterly the *Journal* passed into the hands of Mr Carson, writer ;
then it was purchased by the Rev. George Heron ; and when in a
declining state it became the property of Dr Henry Duncan of
Ruthwell, who allowed it to drop in 1833. In April, 1835, its place
as a Conservative organ was occupied by the *Dumfriesshire and
Galloway Herald*.

To Dr Duncan, the *Dumfries and Galloway Courier*—a Liberal
paper that soon acquired more than a district reputation—owes
its origin. It was commenced in 1809—got a good start under his
able editorship ; and when, in 1817, Mr John M'Diarmid became
its conductor it acquired fresh life, and eventually became one of
the most renowned and successful of provincial journals. In the
getting up of his broad-sheet Mr M'Diarmid exhibited commend

able pains and industry. Devoting it more particularly to local
matters, he rendered it a copious weekly record of events occurring
in, or connected with, the three southern counties. It was not the
bare news itself, abundant as that was, which made the *Courier* so
popular ; but it was the style of the composition—so easy, quaint,
and mellifluous--that helped to make it a general favourite. Mr
M'Diarmid was a thorough master of the literary amenities. His
style was usually quiet, playful, and florid ; and it was so
frequently the fitting vehicle of droll stories regarding prodigies
in the earth, air, and waters, or in the fertile fancy of the editor,
that the paper became famous for its wonderful paragraphs, and
was eagerly read by all lovers of the marvellous. The rural
articles penned by him proved also a valuable and attractive
feature, as they not only conveyed information respecting agricultural operations and prices, but embodied illustrative anecdotes
and pleasing scenic sketches, such as Bewick might have engraved
from. Though Mr M'Diarmid was much occupied with his
editorial duties, and in rendering good service as a citizen, he
found leisure to write the "Life of Cowper," "Sketches from
Nature," the "Picture of Dumfries," and to edit the "Scrap Book."
He died, much regretted by the general community of the district,
in 1852 ; since then, the *Courier*, down till a recent date, was well
conducted by his eldest son, Mr William R. M'Diarmid, with Mr
Donald Mitchell as sub-editor, and latterly, the paper has been
carried on under the competent management of Mr Mitchell. (*a*)

The *Dumfriesshire and Galloway Herald* had, as its editor for
a long period, a poet of high rank, Mr Thomas Aird. His
"leaders," especially when of a controversial character, were
exceedingly pointed and pithy—sometimes charged with as much
electric force in a few lines as would serve to invigorate an ordinary editorial column. It is now under the efficient editorship of
Mr William Wallace. The *Herald* was a weekly paper down till
1869, since which it has been issued twice a week. (*a*)

A new Liberal journal, under the title of the *Dumfries Times*,
made its first appearance in 1833. It was for nearly three years
conducted by Mr Robert K. Douglas, a well-trained and accomplished political writer. He was also an eloquent public speaker ;
and in both respects left an impress on the town whilst engaged
upon the *Times*. In 1835 he accepted an engagement as editor of
the *Birmingham Journal*. When in that capacity he penned the
celebrated National Petition, which embodied five of the six
points of Chartism, and is a fine specimen of his style—terse, energetic, and graceful. On Mr Douglas leaving Dumfries the *Times*
became the property of Mr James Broom, town clerk, and Mr
Thomas Harkness ; the latter of whom edited it for a few years, and
then, in 1842, proceeded with the staff and plant of the establish-

ment to Stranraer, and dropping the *Times*, brought out the *Wigtownshire Free Press* in its stead. The present editor of that journal is Mr William M'Ilwraith, under whom it retains its hold of public favour. (*a*)

Early in 1843, the year of the Disruption of the Church of Scotland, a number of the leading Non-intrusionists of the town and district, including Dr Henry Duncan, projected a new weekly journal, which, whilst advocating their views in ecclesiastical matters, should be Liberal in its secular politics. Accordingly, on the 22nd of March, about two months before the Disruption, the first number of the *Dumfries and Galloway Standard* was issued. Dr Duncan took an active part in the management of the paper for some time. Eventually, Mr William Johnstone, a gentleman of decided ability, became its responsible conductor ; and on his removal, in 1846, to Dunfermline, where he presided for many years over a large educational institution, he was succeeded by the present editor of the *Standard*, the author of this History. The paper has been published twice a week since 1855.* (*a*)

(*a*) The *Courier* has since been purchased by the proprietors of the *Herald*, and its publication as a separate newspaper ceased in 1884, its title being transferred to the Conservative bi-weekly, which is now called the *Courier and Herald*. Mr Wallace is assistant editor of the *Glasgow Herald*, and in recognition of his literary labours—which include an elaborate and exhaustive Life of Burns on the scheme adopted by Chambers—he has received the honorary degree of LL.D. from Glasgow University. The last editor of the *Courier*, before it was merged in its Conservative rival, was Mr William M'Ilwraith, transferred from the Stranraer *Free Press*, and now engaged in journalism in Rockhampton, Queensland. The editorial chair of the *Standard* has since the death of Mr M'Dowall, in 1888, been filled by Mr T. Watson ; and the manager in succession to the late Mr George Henderson is Mr Thomas Hunter. A bust of Thomas Aird, subscribed for on occasion of his birth centenary, has been placed in the Public Library. A marble tablet to the memory of Willliam M'Dowall is affixed to the wall in the vestibule of the Town Hall, and a fund was subscribed for an Academy bursary to bear his name.

* Before the "taxes on knowledge" were repealed, there were no local newspapers in the County, except the three published in Dumfries. There are now four others, the *Eskdale and Liddesdale Advertiser*, commenced in May, 1848, published fortnightly (editor and proprietor, Mr Robert M. Rome, Langholm) ; the *Annan Observer*, commenced as a monthly publication, in January, 1857, but published weekly since July, 1861 (editors and proprietors, Mr William Cuthbertson and Son, Annan) ; the *Moffat Times* (present series), commenced in May, 1861, issued weekly (editor, Mr John Brown, author of many vigorous poems in the Scottish dialect ; proprietor, Mr William Muir, Moffat) ; the *Annandale Herald*, originated in August, 1862, issued weekly (editor and proprietor, Mr James Halliday, Lockerbie). The *Kirkcudbright-shire Advertiser*, published weekly at Castle-Douglas, circulates in Nithsdale and Galloway. It was started in July, 1858, by Mr John Stodart, who, in 1860, assumed as his partner Mr John Hunter Maxwell. Mr Stodart died in March, 1867 ; and the *Advertiser* is now edited and published by Mr Maxwell, for himself and the heirs of the late Mr Stodart. (*b*)

(*b*) The *Eskdale and Liddesdale Advertiser* has for some years been published weekly, the present proprietor being Mr Walter Wilson. The

About forty-five years elapsed between the time when the *Dumfries Weekly Magazine* was metamorphosed into the *Dumfries Journal*, and the publication of the next literary serial in the Burgh. The new periodical was a monthly of forty-eight duodecimo pages, printed by Mr J. Swan : the first number of which appeared in July, 1821, under the title of the *Dumfriesshire and Galloway Monthly Magazine.* Its pages were enriched by contributions from Allan Cunningham, John Mayne, Robert Carruthers, and Robert Anderson, the Cumberland poet. The contents were original essays, tales, anecdotes, sketches in prose and poetry, lyrical pieces, and local births, marriages, and deaths; all combining to make up a most useful and interesting miscellany, highly creditable to the literary character of the town. Among the best things in the first and only volume of the work is a series of versified " Dumfries Portraits," ten in number, by Mr (now Dr) Robert Carruthers. Could we have introduced the whole of them, they would have been quite at home in our pages, illustrating as they do some peculiar phases, as well as describing several eccentric characters, of Dumfries life fifty years ago or more. But we can only find space for one of the sketches, which is given on the opposite page.*

Moffat Times was discontinued soon after the death of Mr Brown. Since the death of the founder of the *Annandale Observer*, it has been successfully conducted first by his son, the late Mr W. J. Cuthbertson, and afterwards by his grandsons. Mr J. H. Maxwell, who died in 1889, has been succeeded in the direction of the *Advertiser* by his son and namesake. Another paper, named the *Stewartry Observer*, has been established in Dalbeattie by Mr I. A. Callan.

* The portrait we quote is that of Thomas Wilson, who rang the town bells for sixty-three years, and literally dropped dead at his post just as he had given the first pull to the ten o'clock bell on the night of April 16th, 1825. Having lost his sight when a child, he was familiarly known as "Blin' Tam." Notwithstanding this deprivation, he was famous for his manual dexterity, as well as for his general intelligence.

> " For long and many a year has Tam pursued
> His trade of ringing bells and shaping wood.
> But more than this—a public man is he ;
> Noise in the world he makes, and loyal glee.
> Each king's birth-day the steeple's highest height
> He mounts, and stands triumphant in the light :
> Fires his old gun (which more than thirty years
> He thus has shot, exempt from age's fears),
> And waves his hat – a spectacle might draw
> The admiration of each passing *craw !*
> When Britain's triumphs warmed each generous heart,
> Tam, in his glory, bore a public part ;
> When with each morning news of victory came,
> And British valour fanned the patriot flame,
> Our festive parties Tam essayed to cheer,
> The flag was hoisted and the bells rung clear,
> And fast and merrily he climbed the stair
> To strike the peal and toast the warriors there."

Blin' Tam, in fact, was to the Mid-Steeple what Quasimodo the hunchback was to the belfry of Notre-Dame.

Mr M'Diarmid and a few other gentlemen of a literary turn commenced an important enterprise in the summer of 1825. This was a shilling periodical, octavo size, entitled the *Dumfries Monthly Magazine*. In all, eighteen numbers, forming three thick volumes, were published. Mr William Bennet, who spent his closing years in Burntisland, had the principal charge of the new serial. He was ably supported by Mr M'Diarmid; by Dr John Erskine Gibson, a gifted son of genius, who died in 1833, at the early age of thirty-one; by Dr Robert Carruthers; by Mr Joseph Train, the distinguished antiquary; by Mr Robert Malcolmson of Kirkcudbright; and by Dr Browne, long editor of the *Caledonian Mercury*. Among the casual contributors were Mr William Nicholson, author of the famous "Brownie of Blednoch;" Mr William Burnie, who wrote for it a graphic poem on Dumfries; and Miss Isabella Trotter. So indispensable were the services of Mr Bennet deemed by the proprietors, that on his proceeding to Glasgow, in 1827, to conduct a twice-a-week newspaper there, they dropped the magazine. Six chapters of a History of Dumfries, showing a large amount of research, were contributed by the intelligent editor to its pages; and it is a matter for regret that the narrative was only brought down to the battle of Sark, in 1549. During the infancy of cheap periodical literature, about forty years ago, it was fairly represented in the burgh by *The Southern Mirror*, issued from the press of Mr Robert Palmer, who also, about the same period, published "The Literary Gleaner," a book of choice extracts, which was the best specimen of typography that had up till that date been produced in the district.

Sixty years since the poetical muse was wooed with considerable success on the banks of Nith, if we may judge from a duodecimo volume of original poetry that appeared in 1815, called "The Nithsdale Minstrel," printed at Dumfries "by C. Munro & Co., for Preacher and Dunbar." It comprehends a hundred and twenty pieces, chiefly written by Nithsdale men, and includes several by Burns, Hogg, and Mayne, not previously published. The Rev. Dr Wightman of Kirkmahoe is a contributor to a large extent; the Rev. Dr Duncan of Ruthwell furnishes one poem—a clever parody on "Lochiel's Warning;" Mr Thomas Cunningham, brother of Allan, supplies a charming song—"The hills o' Gallowa';" and no fewer than thirty pieces, some of them exceedingly good, are from the pen of Mr W. Joseph Walter, who was tutor at Terregles during the three years ending in 1815. Walter, in fact, was the Magnus Apollo of the volume: all his productions evince great warmth of fancy, regulated by good taste, and venting itself in verse that flows freely and musically. He is best known by his "Verses on an Evening View of the Ruins of Lincluden Abbey," which, long after the issue of the "Nithsdale Minstrel," went the round of several newspapers as

"an unpublished composition of the poet Burns." Walter's
" Stanzas to Miss —— of —— " are replete with ardent emotion,
expressed in lines which Moore need not have been ashamed of.
The " Minstrel " was edited by the late Rev. William Dunbar of
Applegarth, then a student, and brother of one of the publishers.*
Some even of the nameless bards associated with Walter and the
others we have mentioned in the production of the " Minstrel,"
contribute pieces that are quite worthy of appearing in the same
collection with theirs ; and the book is altogether a credit to the
poetical feeling and literary taste of the locality at the time of
its appearance.

As may have been inferred from the specimens of oratory
already incidentally given, Dumfries, during the early part of the
present century, had a goodly share of speechmakers ; and one of
them, whose name has not yet been mentioned, Mr Henry
Macminn of Lochfield, had a prolific fund of eloquence that
enabled him to dilate easily and effectively on all manner of
subjects. A duodecimo volume of "Speeches on various Public
Occasions during the last Thirty Years " was published by him in
1831 —including, doubtless, his best effusions. Some of them
were delivered on themes and in circumstances that render them
almost historical ; and the book claims a brief notice as being in
other respects illustrative of both the oratory and the literature
of the burgh. Never was the local Demosthenes more fervid and
exalted than when toasting the memory of Burns. At a festive
meeting held in 1822, on the anniversary of the poet's natal day,
Mr Macminn declared that no sooner had the bard reached the
summit of Mount Parnassus "than he was surrounded by the
gods, who with one voice pronounced that Burns should take the
right hand of Jove himself, in the first chariot of fame, as a poet
of the age." Proud ought they to be to have had such a man as
their fellow-citizen ; "and I must confess, gentlemen," said the
speaker in continuation, "that upon this and all occasions you
have proved yourselves to be the friends of genius, the admirers
of literature, and an honour to this quarter of the globe. You
have raised a mausoleum over his ashes : it is magnificent ! you
have done it gloriously ! You have also provided a punch-bowl
to drink to his memory : it is unequalled in any country !—it
would do honour to the table of the greatest potentate on earth !
—the whole navy of Lilliput might fight a pitched battle in it !"
The oration, a lengthened as well as glowing one, closed with a
climax :—" Long was I acquainted with Burns. The more I knew
him the more I admired him : he was friendly, honourable, and
good-hearted. To the mild, the modest, and the good, he was a
shelter from every blast ; but to the forward, the wicked, and the

---

* Also a brother of Mr David Dunbar, sculptor, and of Mr George Dunbar.

impudent coxcomb, his resentment was as a blast from hell !"
Often did the Trades Hall echo with the eloquence of Mr
Macminn. We have heard that on one occasion he eclipsed all
his former eulogiums on the Incorporated Seven by affirming
that their fame extended over the whole earth, savage as well as
civilised ; and that, transcending the bounds of this mundane
sphere, it had pierced the confines of the Dog-star itself. In 1824
he was made a freeman by the grateful Trades ; and in acknowledging the honour done to him, he, among other handsome
things, said that their patriotism and gentlemanly conduct could
not fail to make them "the envy and wonder of a surrounding
world." When Mr Macminn, who was a burgh magistrate for
several years, retired from the bench, at Michaelmas, 1825, his
health was toasted at a convivial meeting of the councillors. In
the course of a characteristic reply, he said : " I retire with
reluctance, because I shall not have the opportunity of associating
so often with such good company as sit round the table—I mean
the Magistrates, Town Council, and Seven Incorporated Trades of
this burgh, who stand so high at present in the scale of being.
Yet, at the same time, I must confess I retire with pleasure,
because I see the present bench is made up of gentlemen of great
respectability and firmness of mind : unshaken in their principles,
uncontaminated by corruption, they are the vice-gerents of
Almighty God on earth, to execute his will." This volume of
speeches is altogether a remarkable one : exaggerations and
bombast it has in abundance ; but with all such drawbacks, it
shows a fertile imagination and a fluency of language, and also at
times a flash, though faint, of genuine poetry, that render it very
readable, and that helped to make the author in his day an
acceptable exponent of public sentiment, on great occasions, in
the little world of Dumfries.

Dumfriesshire has produced many men of note ;* but it is
beyond the province of this work to speak of any except those
who were born in or closely associated with the county town ;
and our notice even of these must be brief. Of Paterson, the
great political economist and projector ; of Miller, the distinguished agriculturist and ingenious inventor ; and of John
Mayne, who wrote charming lyrics in the Scottish dialect before
Burns rose into fame, we have already spoken. Mayne, born in
1757, grew up among the Seven Trades, over whom his genius has
thrown an imperishable lustre. Beginning active life as a printer
in the *Journal* office, Dumfries, he closed it as editor and owner
of the *Star* newspaper of London, after reaching the advanced
age of seventy-eight. The poem of the "Siller Gun," on which his

* For an excellent account of these worthies the reader is referred to a
published lecture on " The Eminent Men of Dumfriesshire," by the Rev.
James Dodds, Dunbar.

literary reputation chiefly rests, was at first a very tiny affair, consisting of twelve stanzas, printed on a single page. In a second edition, which was soon called for, it was expanded considerably, and growing bulkier by degrees, it settled down at length as a five-canto volume. Another member of the " bardic race," still more renowned—Allan Cunningham—was born on the estate of Blackwood, about six miles distant from Dumfries ; and whilst learning to build material structures in the workshop of Mr M'Kaig, mason, he was busy in the " chamber of imagery," composing some of those exquisite ballads which have won for him a niche in the temple of fame. When entertained, in the zenith of his popularity, at a public dinner by the Dumfriesians on the 22nd of July, 1831, "honest Allan " gratefully recognised the ties of love which bound him to the burgh. " I am proud," he said, "that my father* and grandfather were freemen of the town. I am proud that all my earliest and most lasting feelings and associations are connected with a place such as this. I am proud that any little knowledge I possess was gathered amongst you ; and I can never forget the reception I have met with since my arrival in Dumfries." Thirty years ago the poems of Mrs G. G. Richardson, a Dumfries lady, were in much repute, and they are so fine that they ought not to be forgotten : some of them, in fervour of feeling and polish, almost emulating the effusions of Mrs Hemans. The celebrated poet, Mr Thomas Aird, born at Bowden, Roxburghshire, was for nearly thirty years connected with the newspaper press of the town, and is spending in it the autumn of an honoured life. A volume entitled " Flowers from Fatherland, transplanted into English Soil," was published in 1870, which originated with Mr J. P. Trotter, long sheriff-substitute of Dumfriesshire. It consists of songs by Burgher, Schiller, Korner, Uhland, and other German poets, some of them translated by Mr Trotter, the others by Dr A. Mercer Adam, formerly of Dumfries, and Mr George Coltman, B.A., Brazenose College, Oxon., all the pieces being very happily treated. Under the title of " The Bivouac, or Martial Lyrist," Major R. Compton Noake, Dumfries—formerly Adjutant of the First or Royal Dragoons, and subsequently an officer in the Scottish Borderers Militia—

---

* The poet's father, John Cunningham, who was land steward to the ingenious proprietor of Dalswinton, had two other gifted sons ; one of them, Thomas Mouncey Cunningham, author of many fine lyrics akin to those of Allan ; the other, Peter Cunningham, who acquired high reputation and rank as a naval surgeon, while his well-known works, "Two Years in New South Wales," and " Essays on Electricity and Magnetism," bear witness to his remarkable powers of observation, philosophical acuteness, and literary taste. A sister's son of the Cunninghams, Mr William Pagan of Clayton, rendered good service by his writings to the cause of road reform, and gained additional distinction by his book on the genealogy and birth of the projector Paterson. The late Mr James Pagan, a successful journalist, best known as editor of the *Glasgow Herald*, was closely related to the same family.

issued a collection of spirited war songs in 1871, which has already reached a second edition. Mr John M'Diarmid's contributions to general and political literature have been already mentioned ; also those of Dr Robert Carruthers, born at Dumfries in 1799. The *Inverness Courier*, under the management of Dr Carruthers, has acquired merited reputation as one of our ablest provincial journals. He is the author of "The Encyclopedia of English Literature," a "Life of Pope," "The Highland Note-Book," and of a series of lectures on remote periods of Scottish history, which display great research. Another accomplished *litterateur* and journalist, Mr James Hannay, was born within the hearing of the Mid-Steeple bells. Trained as a naval cadet, he, in 1845, settled down on *terra firma*, beginning his literary career as a reporter on the staff of the *Morning Chronicle*, and soon after turning his nautical experiences to a good account in "Biscuits and Grog," "Singleton Fontenoy," and other literary "yarns." When, in 1854, he published a course of lectures on English Humourists, delivered by him in London, and soon after another work of fiction, "Eustace Conyers," he established his claim to be looked upon as one of the cleverest authors of the day. For four years ending in 1864, Mr Hannay was editor of the *Edinburgh Courant*. Returning to London, he produced "A Course of English Literature," a family history called "Three Hundred Years of a Norman House," and contributed numerous articles to the *Pall Mall Gazette*. In 1866 he went abroad to act as British consul, first at Dunkirk, and then at Barcelona, never coming home again, as he died very suddenly at the latter place in January, 1873, aged only forty-six years. Every summer almost, the Titan of the literary world, Mr Thomas Carlyle, a native of Annandale, comes down to Dumfries on a visit to his sister, Mrs Aitken of The Hill, where he frequently meets with his brother, Dr John A. Carlyle, an eminent German and Italian scholar, and best known for his translation of Dante. The great philosopher and historian leads quite a retired life when in the burgh, being anxious to enjoy needed repose during his periodical visits to his native district. (*a*)

(*a*) Thomas Carlyle died at Chelsea, 5th February, 1881. Offer was made by Dean Stanley of burial at Westminster Abbey ; but, in accordance with his express desire, he was buried in the same grave at Ecclefechan with his beloved parents. "He was taken down in the night by the railway," says James Anthony Froude, M.A., in his Life of Carlyle. "I, Lecky, and Tyndall, alone of his London friends were able to follow." Froude's graceless egotism is unconsciously enshrined in the premier position he assumes for himself in that short sentence. But he was guilty of worse faults. He hurried the two volumes of Carlyle's "Reminiscences" into print with indecent catchpenny keenness, and in the most slovenly manner, after Carlyle's death, though his express injunction was that there should be no publication, if any at all, without most careful editing and the lapse of years, so that possible offence to persons still living referred to in the manuscript might be averted.

For nearly half a century preceding 1852, Miss Jean Goldie of Summerhill, a member of the old Craigmuie family, was well known in Dumfries society on account of her active benevolence and literary accomplishments. She had great force of character, and was no less amiable than intelligent. To theological, social, and even political questions, she devoted much attention, expounding her views regarding them in three small volumes, " Faith and Opinion," published in 1840 ; " Family Recollections and National Progress," published in 1841 ; and " Freedom not Lawlessness," which appeared in 1844. Quite in accordance with her philanthropic character, Miss Goldie bequeathed £300 to purchase a public park for the people of Maxwelltown ; but though twenty years have since elapsed, the legacy, now swelled to fully £400 by bank interest, has not yet been given effect to. (a)

Among the minor authors connected with Dumfries who remain to be named are Mr William M'Vittie, who wrote an entertaining work (published in 1825) under the title of " Winter Evening Tales for the Ingle Cheek," and the popular ballad of " Dryfe-Sands ;" Mr Patrick Miller M'Latchie, a young writer's clerk, whose romance of " Douglas, or the Field of Otterburn," has, since its first appearance, nearly sixty years ago, been a great favourite in Dumfries ; and Mr William Miller, who displayed no inconsiderable amount of fancy and taste in his poem of the " Fairy Minstrel," published in 1822.

Dumfries, though rich in architectural products, can boast of only one statue*—a figure of Dr Henry Duncan ; and well does

The ill-feeling that arose over this action of Froude's was resented by him ; and in subsequent executory undertakings—in the four volumes of the Life of Carlyle, and in the three volumes of Memorials and Letters of Jane Welsh Carlyle—by suppression and suggestion, he sought to make or succeeded in making an utterly false impression that Carlyle was inconsiderate, neglectful, and cruel towards his wife, though his tender and chivalrous conjugal devotion is unsurpassed in the history of literary men. Froude's treachery in this matter has been thoroughly exposed in " 'New Letters and Memorials of Jane Welsh Carlyle," edited by Alexander Carlyle, with introduction by Sir James Crichton-Browne, and also in a separate volume, " The Nemesis of Froude," which Sir James produced later in reply to aspersions by partisans of Froude, and which is a singularly brilliant piece of criticism. Sir James Crichton-Browne has distinguished himself in many fields of intellectual effort, but he would still rank with the eminent men of Dumfriesshire if this literary *tour de force* were his only title to do so.

(a) The fund, which had then accumulated to the extent of £828, was invested in 1904 in the purchase of about six acres of land on Nithside estate and laying it out as " The Goldie Park."

* The mausoleum of Burns in St. Michael's burial-ground contains an alto-relievo figure of the poet at the plough ; but Dumfries ought to " decree" him a statue for the ornamentation of Church Crescent, an admirable site which will some day, we doubt not, be able to boast of a fitting memorial of the national bard. (b)

(b) The author's anticipation was fulfilled in 1882, when (on 6th April) the Earl of Rosebery unveiled a marble statue of the poet designed by Mrs D.

he merit that honour from the burgh, as for the greater part of his eminently useful life he did much to promote its moral, social, and economical progress. He was the third son of the minister of Lochrutton (with whose journal relating to the Jacobite occupation of Dumfries the reader is familiar), and was born in the manse of that parish in 1774. He was presented to the parish of Ruthwell in 1799, and there, while faithfully discharging his ministerial duties, he originated various philanthropic schemes, crowning them all by founding a Savings Bank—the invention at once of his marvellously projective mind and benevolent heart, and which proved the prolific parent of similar institutions, countless in number, that are scattered over all parts of the world. About the same time (1810) an Auxiliary Bible Society and a Missionary Society were formed in Dumfries, chiefly owing to the efforts of Dr Duncan.; and, as we have already seen, it was he who started the *Dumfries Courier* in the preceding year, and who originated the *Dumfries Standard* in 1843. His intellect was many-sided : a poet and a political economist, a novelist and a naturalist, an antiquarian and a philosopher ; yet making all his diversified pursuits subordinate or tributary to his mission as a minister of the gospel. Dr Duncan died in 1846.*

From 1775 till the close of that century there was no surgeon in Scotland of higher repute than Dr Benjamin Bell. His grandfather was proprietor of Blackett House, which estate had belonged to the family for many generations ; and his father was a merchant in Dumfries. Benjamin was born there in 1749, educated by Dr George Chapman, rector of the Academy, and apprenticed to Mr Hill, at that time the principal surgeon and apothecary of the burgh. After completing his studies in Edinburgh, he commenced practising in that city, and rapidly rose to the top of his profession. As a skilful operator, a consultiug surgeon, as well as a writer on surgery and cognate subjects, he was equally distinguished. He died in 1806. Another celebrated

O. Hill, Edinburgh, and erected in Church Crescent. The funds, amounting to about £1200, were collected by a committee of Dumfries gentlemen, of which Mr R. Hamilton was chairman ; Mr M'Dowall, secretary ; and Mr H. M'Gregor, treasurer.

* Dr Duncan was twice married. By his first wife, Agnes Craig, daughter of his predecessor in Ruthwell, he had two sons and a daughter. The elder son, the late Rev. George John C. Duncan, D.D., clerk to the English Presbyterian Church, married Miss Belle Clark, a native of Dumfries, authoress of a most ingenious volume entitled " Pre-Adamite Man ;" the younger son, the Rev. William Wallace Duncan, of the Free Church, Peebles, who died in 1864, was married to Mary Lundie, daughter of the Rev. Robert Lundie of Kelso, a deeply interesting and highly popular life of whom, by her mother, the second wife of Dr Duncan, was published soon after her death, in 1840. Barbara Anne, the only daughter of Dr Duncan, is married to the Rev. James Dodds, of the Free Church, Dunbar, a gentleman of great literary acquirements, author of " A Centenary of Church History," " The Eminent Men of Dumfriesshire," " A Memoir of the Rev. Thomas Rosie," and other works.

medical gentleman, Sir Andrew Halliday, spent his closing years
in Dumfries. Born at Copewood, parish of Dryfesdale, in 1782, of
poor parentage, though tracing his descent from "Tom Halliday,
Wallace's sister's son so dear," he earned his first penny fee by
herding cattle ; and before he had seen forty summers he had
acquired wealth, fame, and knightly honours. He was emphatically the friend of the insane ; and to him we are in a great
degree indebted for the ameliorative treatment of these unfortunates that is now in vogue. Sir Andrew Halliday's most useful
life was brought to a close at Huntingdon Lodge, Dumfries, in
1840.

Among the band of heroic explorers that Great Britain has
produced, Sir John Richardson, born at Nith Place, Dumfries, in
1787, holds a conspicuous position. His father was Provost
Gabriel Richardson, whose integrity is commemorated in Burns's
well-known epigram.* As surgeon and naturalist of Sir John
Franklin's overland Polar expedition, the young adventurer
entered first upon his "field of fame." This enterprise was
followed by one of greater range, and still more rife with danger
— the survey of a mysterious line of coast that lay between the
Coppermine and Mackenzie rivers. His triumphant success was
rewarded with a shower of golden honours ; but though past the
meridian of life, he could not settle down to enjoy them when he
learned that Franklin, his fellow voyager, had been lost sight of
in the far north-western regions, prisoned in the pitiless ice—it
might be dead. Under Government auspices, Sir John proceeded
on his chivalrous mission, with the view of saving his friend, or
clearing up the mystery in which his fate was shrouded. Unnumbered risks were gallantly encountered ; but the search,
though protracted over nearly eighteen months, proved of no
avail. Sir John retired in 1855 from active service, to devote the
leisure he had honourably won to the pursuits of science and the
amenities of social life. From his rural retreat at Lancrigg, the
veteran explorer found his familiar way occasionally to Dumfries,
to see his sister, Mrs Wallace, Castledykes, and other relatives.
He died on the 5th of June, 1865. Of Sir James Anderson, another

---

* As already stated on p. 662, Robert Burns was very intimate with the
Richardsons. From 1790 till 1796 the poet was in the habit of spending a
few hours each Sunday evening in Nith Place, and among his admirers there
was none more ardent from youth to old age than he [the future traveller]
who, as a little boy, attracted his attention. Before this period, the metrical
Scripture Paraphrases used along with the Psalms in public worship in Scotland had been revised, and on one occasion Burns pointed out some of those
which he most admired for John to commit to memory. In after life he could
only remember with certainty as among the number the one beginning "How
bright these glorious spirits shine." Richardson was about six years old when
this pleasant Sunday task was assigned to him.—*Life of Sir John Richardson
by the Rev. John M'Ilwraith*, p. 3.

distinguished voyager belonging to Dumfries, also knighted for
his services, we shall speak in a subsequent chapter. (*a*)

Though, as has been shown in the course of this work, the
Dumfriesians were a bold, soldierly race when war was indigenous to
the soil, the town has sent forth few great military captains in these
"piping times of peace;" the only modern native who has acquired
high renown in the tented field being Colonel William Montague
M'Murdo, born in 1819, the favourite officer of his father-in-law,
Sir Charles Napier, the hero of Scinde. He entered the army as
Ensign of the 78th Highlanders in 1837, and proceeding to India
was employed on the staff. From the commencement of the
brilliant operations in Scinde, conducted by Sir Charles Napier,
the great zeal and personal intrepidity manifested by Lieutenant
M'Murdo attracted the notice of his commander, who appointed
him Quarter-Master General, and afterwards gave him his
daughter in marriage. He became Lieutenant-Colonel in 1853,
and Colonel in 1854. During the Crimean War he commanded the
Land Transport Corps ; and subsequently to 1859 he acted as
Inspector-General of the Volunteer forces for a period of five
years. (*b*)

No small amount of lustre from a legal source has been cast
upon the burgh by the present Lord-Advocate, the Right Hon.
George Young. Born at Dumfries, in 1819, he was educated at
the Academy, received his bent as a lawyer from his father, a
shrewd, sagacious gentleman, who officiated many years as procurator-fiscal for the county, passed through the usual college curriculum in Edinburgh, and was called to the bar in 1840. Mr
Young soon attained an extensive practice, and much distinction
as an advocate. He was elected for the Wigtown Burghs in 1865,
the seat for which he still retains. From 1862 till July, 1866, he
officiated as Solicitor-General. In December, 1868, he was again
made Solicitor-General, and he rose to be Lord-Advocate in
October of the following year. He is noted for keen insight,
ready mother wit, lucidity of expression, a rare capacity for dealing with facts, for cool, steady, intellectual force, rather than
ardour or brilliancy, for a·copious vocabulary which never fails
him, and for an industry which never seems to tire. Some
successful lawyers have been poor lawmakers, but Mr Young has
not only risen to the pinnacle of professional greatness, but has

---

(*a*) A distinguished place in the roll of African explorers has been taken
by Mr Joseph Thomson, a native of Thornhill district, who, although cut off
(in 1895) in his thirty-seventh year, achieved much important work, a record
of which is contained in his books, "Through Masai Land" and "Travels in
the Atlas and Southern Morocco."

(*b*) The distinguished officer attained the rank of General, and received
the honour of knighthood in 1881 and the Grand Cross of the Bath in 1893.
He died in 1894, and is commemorated by an altar and retable in St. John's
Church, Dumfries, the gift of members of his family.

had a distinguished Parliamentary career, during which he has
shewn a remarkable genius for legislation and statesmanship.
The comprehensive Scotch Education Act owes its existence to the
Lord Advocate ; and but for his strenuous personal exertions it
would have been stifled at its birth, or strangled at a maturer
stage, so much enmity did it encounter both in and out of Parliament. All the clauses drawn by himself, and written with his
own hand, came before the House in a form so thoroughly matured
that the measure was little altered by the hostile criticism which
it had to endure ; and safe from all danger, it received the royal
assent on the 6th of August, 1872. (a)

Dumfries can boast of some names that are well known in the
world of art ; Mr Robert Thorburn, the great miniature painter,
born in 1818, and Mr William D. Kennedy, who excelled both in
figures and in landscape, being the chief. Thorburn's precocious
talent for drawing was noticed and fostered by Mr John Craik,
writing master in the Academy ; at whose instance he went to
London, where he achieved his present high position. In 1845 he
executed by commission a portrait of the late Prince Consort ; in
1846 one of the Duchess of Mecklenburg-Strelitz ; in 1847 portraits
of the Princess Charlotte of Belgium, and the Duke of Brabant ;
and in the following year a group of the Queen, with the Princess
Helena and Prince Alfred. " He has (says *Men of the Time*) continued to advance in reputation, and his groups of the Hon. Mrs
Norton's family, of the Marchioness of Waterford, and Viscountess
Canning, and of the Duchess of Buccleuch, Ladies Scott and
Balfour, excited special admiration." Mr Kennedy was the son of
a worthy man, Mr Craik's predecessor. After industriously prosecuting his profession as a painter in the British metropolis, he
travelled as a student of the Royal Academy in Italy, and there
acquired a relish for classical landscape, and deepened his love of
brilliant colouring, for which he had always been distinguished.
He died in 1866, at the early age of fifty-two. Mr David Dunbar,
who belonged to a respectable Dumfries family, achieved considerable distinction as a sculptor, his chief works being "The Sleeping
Child " (for which charming production he was made a member of
the Royal Academy of Carrara) ; several busts from the life, and
studies from the antique ; and a statue of Sir Pulteney Malcolm,
erected in the town of Langholm. By instituting a series of fine
art exhibitions, two of which were held in his native town, Mr

(a) Relinquishing his parliamentary career for judicial office, Mr Young
was appointed a judge of the Court of Session in 1874, under the title of Lord
Young ; and the duties of the high position he continued to discharge with
conspicuous ability until 1905, when the burden of his eighty-six years caused
him to resign. He has received numerous academic honours, and been presented with the honorary freedom of Inverness, Dumfries, and Edinburgh—
Dumfries in 1903 ; Edinburgh in 1905.

Dunbar did much to foster the æsthetic faculty amongst his countrymen. He died at Dumfries in 1866. In a walk of his own, illustrative of Scottish rural life, Mr John Currie, sculptor, has displayed no small amount of genius. Born in the neighbouring parish of Lochrutton, he came to Dumfries at a youthful age, and while employed as a journeyman mason he, during leisure hours, indulged his bent for figure-making, which, as manifested in his group of "Dominie Sampson and Meg Merrilees," gained for him great local reputation. He has since produced "Old Mortality and his Pony" (generally deemed Mr Currie's masterpiece), "The Covenanter," "The Cameronian"—all of the same rustic school, the material used being the red sandstone of the district ; also a figure of Dr Henry Duncan, which ornaments the *façade* of the Dumfries Savings Bank ; a marble group representing "Burns Crowned by the Muse ;" besides numerous busts and objects of monumental statuary.

CHAPTER LXII.

WE now proceed, in the briefest possible terms, to notice the
leading events in the history of the burgh, from the date of the
Reform Act till our own day. It was thought at one time that
Toryism would be extinguished by the operation of that measure ;
but this was far from being the case. The Town Council elected
by the ten-pounders contained a fair proportion of Conservatives,
who, under the leadership of Mr John Fraser, grew in strength
till they were able for a while to "turn the tables" upon the
Liberal party. The last save one of the Dumfries provosts under
the old system, he was a member of the first Council under the
new ; and in 1840 he was once more chosen to fill the civic chair.*
Several Conservative provosts have since held rule in the burgh ;
but the Liberals more generally possess a majority in the Council
than their political opponents.

The able and influential agent of Mr William Ewart, elected as
member for the Burghs in 1841, Mr William M'Gowan, writer, was
long recognised as the leader of the Liberals. He was elevated to
the provostship in 1855, and died in office on the 17th of November,
1856. He was preceded and also succeeded by Mr Miles Leighton
(now at the age of eighty-eight years, the oldest merchant in Dumfries), who was a Reformer when to be so was the reverse of
popular. He has been three times chosen as the chief magistrate of
the burgh—a triple distinction conferred on no other burgess since

---

* " Mr Fraser," says the *Dumfries Standard*, in noticing his death, which
took place in 1856, "must have possessed no common ability, when, from
being a perfect stranger, he could in ten years raise himself to the position of
principal magistrate in Dumfries."

the abolition of the old close system. The Conservatives of the Council were strong enough in 1860 to carry the election of one of their number, Mr James Gordon, writer, as provost, who proved so acceptable that he was re-elected in 1863 ; and, as we shall see afterwards, they achieved a similar triumph in 1872.*

After the passing of the Reform Bill, the most exciting occurrence in the town was a contest for the representation of the Five Burghs, at the general election in February, 1835. The same gentlemen who had encountered each other two years before again entered the arena. General Sharpe was proposed by Mr Philip Forsyth of Nithside, and seconded by Mr John M'Diarmid ; and Mr Hannay was nominated by Mr Robert Scott, manufacturer, and seconded by Mr Miles Leighton, merchant. The gallant Laird of Hoddam was re-elected ; but his majority, which was 112 on the first occasion, was reduced to 52.†

An important case, springing from a difference of opinion regarding the extent of the Nith, was brought before Lord Moncrieff and a jury, at Dumfries, on the 30th of April, 1836. Mr R. A. Oswald, and other owners of shore-lands far down the estuary, erected stake-nets upon them ; which Mr James M'Whir, owner of the Nith fishings, held to be within the boundary of the river, and therefore illegal. Mr Maitland, for the defenders, maintained that the nets were in the Solway, and therefore could not be in the Nith ; but Dean of Faculty Hope convinced the jury that the charter of 1395, and sundry statistics which he quoted, gave a range to the river beyond the sandbanks where the nets were planted. A verdict was therefore returned in favour of Mr M'Whir, and the engines were removed forthwith. The salmon fishings of the Nith, once very productive, are now of comparatively little value, yielding not more, perhaps, than £400 a year.‡

A familiar landmark, that long like a gigantic bird flapped its wings on Corbelly Hill, seemed in 1834 about to drop away, fatally disabled by the archer Time, when several gentlemen who took a friendly interest in its fortunes resolved to rescue it by turning it to a new account. The idea was acted upon, and the crazy, weather-beaten windmill was transformed into an Observatory, which, with its accompanying museum, is now one of the great ' lions " of the locality.

On the 10th of January, 1837, some half-a-dozen gentlemen met at the house of Mr David Beveridge, and originated the Dumfries and Maxwelltown Total Abstinence Society. Mr James

* Appendix N.

† The following was the state of the poll :—Sharpe : Dumfries, 220 ; Annan, 135 ; Kirkcudbright, 19 ; Sanquhar, 26 ; Lochmaben, 22 ; total, 422. Hannay : Dumfries, 270 ; Annan, 9 ; Kirkcudbright, 72 ; Sanquhar, 8 ; Lochmaben, 11 ; total, 370.

‡ Lecture on Pisciculture, delivered in Dumfries by Dr Copland,

Broom, its first president,* Mr Beveridge, Mr John M'Intosh, Mr David Halliday, Mr William Gregan, and Mr William F. Johnstone, were among its earliest and most active members. There were no fewer than 1500 names on its roll in January, 1838 ;† and at one time the number reached to at least 2000. (a) The Dumfriesshire and Kirkcudbrightshire Abstainers' Union, formed on the 16th of October, 1867, has superseded the original society. Its first president was Provost Cavan of Kirkcudbright. Dr M'Culloch, Dr James Gilchrist [(of the Crichton Institution), Mr William Gregan, and Mr John Johnstone (merchant), have since officiated in that capacity, the present president being Mr James Rodger. On the roll of the Union there are about 3000 names ; annual income, £300. For promoting the temperance movement the burgh has also three Templars Lodges, and several Bands of Hope. (b)

* Mr Broom died in the meridian of life, on the 18th of January, 1842. From a lengthened tribute paid to his worth in the *Dumfries Times*, we quote the following passage :—" His politics were such as spring from a sensitive mind, which taught him to condemn the encroachments of class privilege on the rights of labour ; and he did not scruple to proclaim, in season and out of season, the title of all to participate in the privileges of freemen. By a bold stand which he made against the drinking usages of the country, he effected an amount of good which few individuals are privileged to perform ; and he was ready to back out the principles which he advocated by the contents of his purse, on all occasions. Whilst assiduous, both by precept and example, to rescue the victims of intemperance, not a few are indebted to him, not only for being drawn from the ensnaring vice, but for assistance and encouragement in beginning life anew. His intellectual powers were of the most versatile description. His reading and literary research took within its range the circle of the belles-lettres, and treatises in all the departments of practical science : the fruits of which, garnered up in his own mind, were given out to others with facile profusion. As a man of business, his shrewdness of penetration and promptitude of decision were unequalled ; and as a speaker, his humour, his earnestness and artlessness, won him golden opinions, and aided in swelling the tide of his popularity."

† *Dumfries Courier.*

(a) The above Society was designed for adults only. In the same year that it was founded—1837—Mr Samuel Welsh set on foot the Dumfries and Maxwelltown Juvenile Teetotal Society. Bands of Hope were introduced at a later period. Mr Welsh, a young pressman in those days, was awarded a silver medal by the Society as the " best speaker and most efficient member." At Walsall, first as a journalist and afterwards as secretary to the Hospital there, the most of his life has been spent in useful work ; and there he continues (1905) to discharge his secretarial duties, enjoying in a ripe old age the confidence and respect of the community.

(b) The Abstainers' Union was dissolved some years ago, and active temperance work in the district is carried on chiefly by the Good Templars, Rechabites, and Bands of Hope. During its existence the operations of the Union were conducted on an extensive scale with great vigour. At one time it had in addition to its honorary office-bearers a salaried secretary, a platform agent, and a periodical, the " Abstainers' Journal," a monthly publication, which also became the recognised organ of the order of Free Templars, and was widely circulated both in England and Scotland. The Free Templar order was a secession from the Good Templar.

Dumfries thirty-five years ago seemed almost on the eve of becoming the seat of a university, by the application towards that object of about £100,000, left to be spent for beneficent purposes by Dr James Crichton of Friars' Carse,* "in any way that his dear wife thought proper," with the approval of other trustees named in his settlement. Mrs Crichton and the trustees would fain have founded such a place of learning, but their attempts to obtain a charter were encountered by so many difficulties that they had to give up the idea; and then, at the instance, it is believed, of Sir Andrew Halliday, the money was applied in establishing and partly endowing a model house for the treatment of the insane. About forty acres of ground, forming part of the estate of Mountainhall, were purchased; and there, in the midst of most beautiful upland scenery, was reared a magnificent edifice, in the Italian style, for the reception of a hundred and twenty patients, which bears the name of the Crichton Royal Institution. Mr Burn of Edinburgh, now of London, was the architect of the building. A large portion of it, costing fully £50,000, was ready for use by 1839, the foundation-stone having been laid in June, 1835. The plan resembles a Greek cross—a low octagonal tower shooting up from the centre, where the nave joins the transepts, being the most noticeable feature, and introduced to give unity and superadded grace to the building. This design was only half carried out in the first instance; and it was departed from to some extent by Mr Moffat, architect, of Edinburgh, who was employed lately to complete the building at an expense which brings the entire outlay up to about £90,000. In 1848 a supplementary structure, termed the Southern Counties Asylum, was erected by the trustees of the Institution for the reception of pauper patients, since which period it has been considerably enlarged, to meet demands for additional accommodation, owing to its having been recognised, by a recent Act of Parliament, as an asylum for the insane poor. At the close of 1871 the number of patients in both establishments was 465, the admissions that year having amounted to 145. When the census was last taken, the entire population, including officers and servants, was found to be 550. The Crichton Institution was fortunate in having for its first medical superintendent Dr W. A. F. Browne, who had devoted much time to the study of mental disease, and was familiar with all the best modes of treating it; and the arrangements which he inaugurated have been continued and developed

---

* Dr Crichton was long in the service of the East India Company. He returned to Scotland in 1808, and next year acquired, by purchase, the classical estate of Friars' Carse, on which he resided until his death, fourteen years afterwards.

with gratifying success by the present resident physician, Dr James Gilchrist. (a)

(a) Since 1883 the institution has been under the direction of Dr James Rutherford, and during that period it has undergone a remarkable process of development. Various purchases of landed property have been made, until the Crichton possesses a compact estate of 750 acres and several detached residences lying immediately round the central institution, and it has also acquired by purchase the country seat of Friars' Carse, where a colony of the better class patients reside. The Second House has been practically re-built ; extensive alterations have been carried out on the First House ; and numerous new buildings have been erected, including model farm steading, laundry and residential blocks, and a sanatorium for consumptive patients. An artesian well was sunk in the lower part of the farm of Rosehall for supply of water to the institution. It yields a continuous supply at the rate of 90 gallons per minute, rising six feet above the surface of the ground. The water is received in a spacious reservoir capable of containing 90,000 gallons, and pumped to a high level reservoir at Maidenbower, with a capacity of 127,000 gallons, from which it is distributed by gravitation. An electric light installation was carried out in 1896. On occasion of the jubilee of the institution in 1889, the directors resolved to provide a place of worship for the large resident population, which should also be a worthy memorial of the gracious foundress. The result was the Crichton Memorial Church, a magnificent building in the Gothic style, erected from the plans of Messrs Sydney Mitchell & Wilson, of Edinburgh, at a cost of approximately £30,000. The original capital fund of the institution, derived from the estate of Dr Crichton, amounted to £94,479. The fixed capital at 11th November, 1904, as appearing in the last published annual report, was £356,417, made up as follows : Land, £75,284 ; premises, £251,177 ; machinery and plant, £14,579 ; furniture, £15,376. The average daily number of patients resident during the preceding year was 775, and of the number under treatment at its close 486 were private or paying patients and 315 were pauper patients, supported by the contributions of Parish Councils. The expenditure chargeable to the floating capital and revenue accounts amounted to £39,662. In this were included grants from the Crichton charitable fund, to the amount of £1711, for reduction of the board of patients whose relatives were in straitened circumstances. The purchases of landed property made on behalf of the institution have been as follows :—In 1884, fields at Mountainhall, £3575, and farm of North Rosehall, £8200 ; in 1889, farm of Midpark, £8000 ; in 1890, farms of Acrehead and South Rosehall, £17,000 ; in 1893, farm of Lochbank, £3800 ; in 1894, farm of Maidenbower, £2000 ; in 1896, estate of Friars' Carse, £22,050. The Crichton Institution was first incorporated by an Act of Parliament passed in 1840, which constituted a board of direction consisting of Mrs Crichton, her two co-trustees (her brother, Colonel Grierson of Barndennoch, and Admiral Johnston of Cowhill), who had power to nominate their successors ; seven noblemen and gentlemen holding official positions, and five co-opted directors. Following upon an agitation initiated in Dumfries County Council and Parish Councils, the directors promoted a bill in the parliamentary session of 1897, which passed unopposed, placing the management on a more representative basis. It constituted a permanent board of fifteen members, viz. :—The Lord Lieutenant of the County of Dumfries ; the Sheriff of Dumfries and Galloway ; the Conveners of the Counties of Dumfries, Kirkcudbright, and Wigtown, and one other representative of each of these counties, appointed by the County Councils ; the Provost of Dumfries ; the Chairman of Dumfries District Lunacy Board ; and five additional members elected by the board of directors, each to serve for a period of three years. Certain members of the old board were also continued as temporary members of the new, viz. :—The Duke of Buccleuch, the Earl of Galloway, the Duke of Hamilton, Mr Dudgeon of Cargen, Mr Johnston of Cowhill Tower, and Mr

How best to minister to minds diseased is the great problem which occupies the attention of Dr Gilchrist and his colleagues ; and it is solved at least as satisfactorily in the Crichton as in any other asylum in Europe. Perhaps the proportion of absolute cures is not greater there than in other well-conducted institutions ; but we know of none in which more is done to soothe and otherwise alleviate the sufferings of the insane. These results are secured by a multiplicity of means involving great care, ingenuity, and thoughtfulness on the part of the officers. Drives into the country to enjoy interesting sights and scenes ; picnic parties ; seaside retreats ; visits to places of public entertainment during the winter evenings : such are some of the outside modes adopted to interest the patients, and make them forego for a while the heavy burden of their cares. The situation of the place, as already hinted, is in the highest degree suitable for such a house : the ground elevated and undulating, charmingly laid out, and commanding a prospect that has some elements in it of the sublime, and many of the beautiful ; whilst the pure atmosphere in which it is swathed, permeated at times by refreshing breezes from the sea, must of itself exercise a beneficial influence on the inmates. Light labour in the gardens, for those able and willing to work ; recreation at cricket and other games, for all who wish to take part in them ; promenades ; festive entertainments on the green grass, when all around is glorious in its summer garniture : these form part of the medicating influences which the establishment itself supplies. Then, when in winter the out-of-door resources are abridged, those inside are multiplied to make up the loss ; and lectures, concerts, balls, and theatricals do much to make the long nights less dreary, and but for which many of the unfortunate patients would feel with Mariana of the Moated Grange, " I am aweary, aweary—I wish that I were dead !" (a)

Graham Hutchison of Balmaghie (the last three being nominated successors of the original trustees), for life ; the Rev. John Paton while he was minister of St. Michael's Parish Church ; and Mr Robinson Souttar, M.P. for Dumfriesshire, during the continuance of the then existing Parliament. An excellent history of the institution has been written by Mr James Carmont, the secretary and treasurer.

(a) The following dedicatory statement and prayer were written by Mrs Crichton on occasion of the laying of the foundation stone of the institution :

JAMES CRICHTON.
ELIZABETH CRICHTON.   A.D.   1835.

It is my earnest wish and desire that this building should be founded on the faith of God. It is built from the funds of my husband, which were acquired solely by the great blessing of God upon his honest industry. From a poor youth he became a rich man, but he ever acknowledged with the deepest feelings of gratitude that to Him who had been his God and his Guide the praise was due.

Deeply impressed by those feelings, it is the sole and most earnest wish of my heart to present this Building and Institution as a humble offering of

General Sharpe having, on account of declining health, retired
from public life in the summer of 1841, Mr William Ewart,* who
had sat for Bletchingly, Liverpool, and Wigan, agreed, at the
request of an influential section of the constituency, to become a
candidate for the representation of the Five Burghs. Another
candidate appeared in the person of Sir Alexander Johnston of
Carnsalloch. Both gentlemen professed to be Liberals ; but most
of the Dumfries Conservatives supported Sir Alexander, in the
belief that he was not so far advanced on the road to Radicalism
as his honourable opponent. There was a large body of Chartists
in the chief burgh, who favoured neither of them, and resolved to
start a candidate of their own—Mr Andrew Wardrop, a clever,
well-informed operative, who could discourse fluently on any
political topic, and had plenty of pluck for the occasion. When
the nomination day arrived (June 20th, 1841), each candidate
appeared with his friends on the hustings in Queensberry Square,
which was occupied by an immense crowd. The knight of Carnsalloch was proposed by Mr Thomas Harkness, and seconded by
Mr Robert M'Harg ; Mr Ewart's nomination was respectively
moved and seconded by Provost Little of Annan and Mr William
Dinwiddie ; while a similar duty was performed for Mr Wardrop
by two working men. Sir Alexander Johnston made a good
speech, that was but indifferently listened to. He was followed

---

gratitude to God, and humbly, and upon my knees, in the presence of Him
who seeth the hearts of all His creatures, I dedicate it to Our Father in
Heaven, humbly and earnestly beseeching Him to turn His eyes from the
sins of her who offers it, and for Christ's sake to hear her prayer : —
     " O Lord God Almighty, I draw near, and with humility and trust I
commit this Asylum to Thy care. I am alone, weak, feeble, and friendless.
But Thou art Almighty. Take it therefore into Thy keeping. Oh bless it
with Thy best blessings. Keep it from corruption, and from sin. Take it
entirely into Thy care ; let not the Devil or Man prevail against it ; and in
everything relating to it, from the greatest to the least, oh ! be Thou its
Director and its keeper, its Guide and its God. Never leave it, never forsake
it. Keep it as the apple of Thine eye. Bless it, O my God, and it shall be
blessed."
     Friars' Carse, 20th June, 1835.

     * Mr Ewart was descended from an old Galloway family, the Ewarts of
Mullock, an estate which John Ewart, merchant, and bailie of Kirkcudbright,
acquired by purchase in 1611. The Rev. John Ewart, a descendant of the
latter, was minister of Troqueer, and father of William Ewart, a successful
Liverpool merchant, who, by his wife, Margaret Jacques, had issue seven
children, one of them being the member for the Burghs. From "Dod's
Parliamentary Companion" we quote the following notice of Mr Ewart,
M.P. : —" Born at Liverpool, 1798. Married, in 1820, his cousin, Mary Ann,
daughter of G. A. Lee, Esq., of Manchester. Educated at Eton, and at
Christchurch, Oxford, where he graduated B.A., 1821 ; gained the university
prize for English verse in 1819. Called to the bar at the Middle Temple,
January, 1827. Sat for Bletchingly from 1828 till 1830, for Liverpool from
1830 till 1832, for Wigan from 1839 till 1841, when he was returned for
Dumfries district."

by Mr Ewart, who, in the course of a telling address, hit his
opponent hard by comparing his progress through the burghs,
gathering support from different sections, to that of a political
Tam o' Shanter :—

> " Now holding fast his auld Whig bonnet,
> Now crooning owre some Liberal sonnet,
> Now glowering round with prudent cares
> Lest Tories catch him unawares."

In the general laughter which followed this sally, the worthy
knight joined heartily. The Chartist candidate had the show of
hands, but did not go to the poll ; though long after he used to
boast good-humouredly that for three days he was M.P. for the
Five Burghs. After a keen, exciting struggle, Mr Ewart was
returned by a majority of 60 votes ;* Annan being mainly instrumental in producing this result—just as General Sharpe twice
owed his election chiefly to that burgh.

In the course of this history we have had to put several food-
riots on record ; and one more—the last—remains to be noticed—a
tremendous meal mob, which broke out on the evening of July 2nd,
1842. Five shops in Dumfries and one in Maxwelltown, belonging
to persons accused of making their bread-stuffs artificially dear,
were damagingly assailed by an indignant rabble, both towns being
thereby thrown into a state of tumult for hours. Twelve of the
ringleaders were captured ; seven of whom on being tried at the
assizes were convicted, and sentenced to three months' imprisonment each.

Towards the close of 1847, a benevolent scheme was mooted,
which had for its object the partial maintenance and the culture of
such poor children in the burgh and district as were growing up in
heathenism and graduating in crime. Thanks chiefly to a devoted
philanthropist, the late Mr David W. Stewart,† the project was
realised ; and the Dumfries Ragged School is the result. Associated
with it there are an Infant School (originated in 1834) and a Common
School, where children of a somewhat higher grade than those cared
for at the Ragged School received education for nothing, or a
merely nominal fee. These three affiliated establishments are maintained and regulated by the Dumfries and Maxwelltown Education
Society, presided over, till his lamented death in June, 1867, by
Mr John Pitcairn Trotter, sheriff-substitute of the county. Its

---

* The poll stood thus :—Ewart : Dumfries, 213 ; Annan, 126 ; Kirkcudbright, 22 ; Sanquhar, 26 ; Lochmaben, 15 ; total, 402. Johnston : Dumfries,
239 ; Annan, 19 : Kirkcudbright, 55 ; Sanquhar, 14 ; Lochmaben, 15 ; total,
342.

† Mr Stewart, who was a younger brother of Mr Charles Stewart of Hill-
side, died on the 21st of May, 1852. In noticing his death, the *Dumfries
Standard* said :—" He was in many respects the Howard of the district ; devoting time, energies, and wealth to the relief of the destitute, and the
reclamation of the depraved."

present chairman is his successor in the sheriffdom, Mr David Boyle Hope. The children at the Ragged School are of two classes : boys who are simply destitute, and against whom no police charge has been brought ; and those who have been sent to the school as a Reformatory, certified under the Act 17 and 18, cap. 74, for begging in the streets, or for petty offences. The smaller proportion of them belong to the former class : they are fed and educated ; while those of the latter class are also lodged and clothed, the Government allowing in their case a small capitation grant for each. One year (1868) there were as many of both classes on the roll as 114 ; but the number has of late been considerably less. In 1871 there were 74, none of whom, when admitted, could either read or write, except six. At the Common School, in the same year, the pupils numbered 119 ; and those at the Infant School 91. The operations of the Education Society are carried on at an expense of about £1,000 annually ; but in 1871 it had advanced to £1,039 12s 7d, owing greatly to a general increase on the price of provisions. For its revenue the Society is mainly dependent on public subscriptions. (a)

Cholera once more ! The dreadful epidemic which decimated the burgh in 1832 visited it again in 1848, attacking about 600 of the inhabitants, of whom 317 died. The first case occurred on the 16th of November : the last during the first week of January, 1849. This visitation did not create so much alarm, nor tell so adversely on the trade of the town, as that of 1832, nor were its ravages so deadly. In Maxwelltown there were 214 cholera cases and 114 deaths : considerably fewer than in 1832, when there were 237 cases, of which 127 proved fatal.

"Waater ! waater !" the ancient "burndrawers" still continued to bawl in 1850, as they perambulated the town, dispensing from their carted barrels a doubtful commodity, which was too often water and something more, and' worse. But the summer of that year saw a legislative measure which silenced the lugubrious cry, and sent the barbarous water-barrel system "to the tomb of all the Capulets." The preamble of a bill to authorise the introduction of water by pipes into Dumfries and Maxwelltown, from Lochrutton Loch, was found proven by a Parliamentary committee on the 10th of May ; and when the news of its success arrived, the bells were rung and bonfires were kindled in the burgh, to manifest the

(a) Legislation which made education first universal and compulsory, then free, has led to a change in the character and work of the Education Society. Its operations are now restricted to the support and management of the Dumfries and Maxwelltown Industrial School, to which truant or neglected children are committed by magisterial warrant. The number of inmates at the close of 1904 was 101. The great value of the school as an agency in social rescue work has been attested by Government inspectors and by returns obtained regarding the after-career of boys who have passed through it. The present chairman of directors is Mr John Primrose, solicitor.

general joy of the inhabitants. Much opposition was given to the measure by interested parties, at every stage of its progress; but zealously promoted by the Town Councils of both burghs (presided over respectively by Provost Nicholson and Provost Maxwell), and by the indefatigable local secretary, Mr Thomson Harkness, it was triumphant in the end; and when carried into effect, proved to be the most valuable material boon acquired by Dumfries in modern times. The first pipe of the water-works was laid on the 16th of January, 1851, by Provost Nicholson, a devoted advocate of the scheme; and on the 21st of October that year, the first instalment of the pure Lochrutton fluid emerged sparkling from the pipes, in presence of a delighted throng. For preliminary work, an expense of £986 7s 4d was incurred; the Act itself cost £1,634 8s 10d; an amendment Act, that was felt to be requisite, cost £267 6s 7d; and for constructing the works there was an outlay of £10,020 15s 9½d : the whole amounting to £12,908 18s 6½d. Towards liquidating this sum, the Act authorised the borrowing of £10,000 on the rates; and £1,500 additional was borrowed on bonds for which the Town Council became collateral security. Originally the pipe for the first mile from the Loch was nine inches in diameter, and for the rest of the distance (nearly four miles) was eight inches; but owing to the growth of the town, a larger main was laid alongside the existing one in 1861. A body of Commissioners, partly chosen by the Councils of the two towns and partly by the ratepayers, manage the scheme. Though the ordinary working expenses are small, a large outlay was incurred by the construction of new filters, as well as pipes, so that the debt is still heavy—nearly £14,000. The revenue is drawn from a public water-rate of sixpence per pound on property, and a similar rate on consumption. It is steadily increasing : for the first year it was £696; five years afterwards it was more than double that amount; and for the year ending the 16th of September, 1872, it was £2,056, nearly threefold—the rate on property for that year yielding £1,140, and for the water consumed, £916. (a)

(a) The public water rate has been reduced to one penny per pound and the domestic consumpt rate to fourpence per pound. The revenue in 1904-5 amounted to £2753. The mortgage debt then stood at £8000, additional capital outlay having prevented a greater reduction.

In the early eighties the condition of the water from the loch became offensive for lack of proper filtration. For seventeen years there had been no increase of filtering area, though the quantity of water passed through had doubled. Various steps were taken to effect a remedy, including the erection of an embankment to cut off the peaty top end of the loch; and finally there was a proposal to go to Parliament for powers to bring in a fresh supply from the Old Water and the Glen Burn. In 1887, at a public meeting, at which the new scheme was explained and criticised, and it was maintained that what the loch required to put it right was better filtration and more of it, on the motion of Mr T. Watson, *Standard*, it was resolved to request the Commission to take a plebiscite. In consequence of the method of voting which the Com-

The good sanitary results of the scheme are incalculable : its
effect in reducing the ravages of fever are especially worthy of
remark.   For many years prior to 1851, the population of the town
and district suffered fearfully from the varied forms of that disease.
From 1823 till 1858, no fewer than 2,481 fever cases were treated
in the Infirmary, and 613 other cases were attended by its officers
according to the home-patient system, abolished in 1833.   During
the fifteen years immediately preceding 1851, this fell enemy of
human life appears to have been particularly virulent : the fever
cases, 1,779 in number, formed one fourth of the entire admissions

missioners instructed, there was another public meeting, at which, again on the
motion of Mr Watson, the ratepayers were advised not to vote at all.
Subsequently, at the last minute, a change in the method by which the
plebiscite was to be taken was made ; but out of a constituency of 2719 only
569 recorded their votes.   Of these 386 were against the scheme, and only 183
for it.   At their next monthly meeting in October, 1887, when the result of
the plebiscite was reported, Mr Joseph Ewing, convener of works, attributed
the chief opposition to the scheme to Mr Watson, whose whole plea, he said,
was merely an alternative project for more filtration.   This, he maintained,
would not meet the case ; and after others had spoken, the majority, including
Provost Lennox, resigned.   Their places were supplied to some extent by their
critics ; a deputation was appointed to visit various towns in England ; and on
their report plans were prepared by Mr Alan Crombie, architect, who was one
of the deputation, for new filter-beds and a thorough aeration of the water.
The result was entirely successful, and at the present time the works, greatly
extended, are among the best in the country.   In 1897 an amending act was
obtained, changing the voting for Commissioners and enabling them to extend
their water service beyond the burghs.   In October, 1901, the jubilee of the
introduction of Lochrutton was celebrated, and, in spite of much chaffing
and caustic criticism, a monumental stone was erected with the names of the
then Commissioners upon it.   But the men who had saved the loch and
removed the cause of complaint were omitted from the jubilation and commemoration.   These proceedings, which included an interesting historical
narrative by the Clerk, Mr J. H. M'Gowan, are reported in the *Standard* of
October 30, 1901, and commented upon.   The omission of the jubilee record
can now in some degree be repaired.   Outside the Commission, as stated by
Mr Ewing, Mr Watson had led the agitation for the retention and purification
of Lochrutton ; while inside the Commission its chief defenders latterly
were Mr James Glover and Mr John Charlton.   The Commissioners who
resigned because of the plebiscite were : Messrs David Lennox (Provost of
Dumfries), Joseph Ewing, John M'Quhae, James Hiddleston, Richard Kirk,
William Lawson, James Maxwell, Wm. Maxwell, J. A. Smith, James Halliday,
James Rennie, A. J. M'Intosh ; there remaining only Messrs J. Glover,
Bell, and Cowan (then Chief Magistrate of Maxwelltown).   The new Com-
missioners were : From ratepayers, Messrs James Scott, shoemaker, and John
Charlton ; and from Town Council of Dumfries, Messrs Wilson (Dean) and
Crombie.   Mr John Luke Scott had just been elected Provost of Dumfries,
and as such he became *ex officio* chairman of the Commission.   On his motion,
when the new Commission met, the following were appointed *ad interim* in
room of certain members resigned : From the Town Council of Dumfries,
Messrs T. Watson, James Currie, Joseph Johnstone Glover (now Provost) ;
from ratepayers, Messrs C. W. Thomson, T. Roddan, John Dickson, and W.
Gordon ; and from Town Council of Maxwelltown, Bailie Herries (now
Provost).   These formed the reconstructed body that retained Lochrutton,
removed all cause of offence from the water supply, and saved the community
from a very costly misadventure.

into the house ; and of these 162 died—a percentage of 31 on the total mortality of the period. In five of the years referred to, ending 1851, there were 861 fever cases, 76 of which proved fatal—an annual average of 172 cases and 15 deaths. Never did the talisman of an Oriental tale exercise a more wonderful influence than the flow of wholesome water into the burgh from its source in Lochrutton : fever, as if awed by an overmastering spell, lost hold of the town when the pure health-giving element became a common beverage in its poorest domiciles. In the very year when the water-works were being constructed, the fever cases in the Infirmary numbered 125 ; next year, when the spell began to take effect, they were reduced to 65 ; in succeeding years, till 1856, the average of attacks annually was only 36, and the deaths 4 ; in two of these years, 1853 and 1855, no fever-stricken patient died in the Infirmary ; in 1858 there were but two fever cases treated in it, and since that period the house and the town have been correspondingly exempt from its deadly ravages. (a)

At least eight centuries have rolled away since the oldest dust that lies within St. Michael's cemetery was organised and alive. We have already related how, about 1160, the churchyard was the scene of a quarrel between two burgesses, that had a fatal issue ; and it may be safely assumed that it existed as a burial-place long before that period. This ancient region of the dead, about two acres in extent, had become so overpeopled by giving sleeping-room to thirty generations of Dumfriesians, that another acre of adjoining ground was added to it in 1850. No provincial town in the United Kingdom possesses a place of sepulture so rich in monumental erections ;* and Burns's mausoleum, its chief attraction, reigns over all, even as he was himself a prince among men, and is of lyrical poets the undying leader and king.

With the view of providing a comfortable retreat for the necessitous poor, and at the same time a check for undeserving applicants, a Workhouse was commenced in the summer of 1853, and completed before the close of the following year, at a cost of fully £5,500. In both of these respects it has operated successfully. The house occupies an airy, healthy site southward of the burgh ; and while

---

(a) There have, of course, been occasional epidemics, as in 1895 and 1904, but these have been of limited range. In the latter year 27 scarlet fever patients, drawn from the town and surrounding district, were under treatment in the Infirmary.

* By the kind assistance of Mr Thomas Watson, monumental mason, we (partly by actual calculation, and to some extent by estimate) have made an enumeration of the stones erected in the old and new grounds of St. Michael's as follows :—First-class monuments, 350 ; table tombstones, 950 ; headstones and erect slabs, 500 ; and other structures, more or less dilapidated, which make up the aggregate number in the cemetery to about 3,000. The oldest stone having any engraving upon it that we have seen, is in the ground belonging to the Couplands of Colliston ; it bears date 1620.

its management appears to strike the golden mean between narrowness and prodigality, the rates since its opening have been considerably reduced. Before that time they were sometimes as high as 2s 6d in the pound ; of late years they have never been more than 1s 6d ; and now that a heavy debt incurred for the erection of the Workhouse has been cleared away, the rates are down to the low amount of 1s 2d—one half payable by proprietors, the other by tenants. The inmates of the Workhouse vary in number from forty to sixty, and the annual outlay for it is about £700. For the year ended 14th of May, 1872, 470 registered poor, with 304 dependants, were relieved ; and 206 casual poor, with 230 dependants. Altogether, for that year the expenditure of the Parochial Board amounted to £4,385 13s 11½d. (*a*)

The spring of 1857 was signalised by another contest for the membership of the burghs. Uninvited by, yet by no means unacceptable to, the Tories of the constituency, Mr James Hannay, son of General Sharpe's opponent, appeared in his native town as a rival candidate to the sitting member, on moderately Conservative principles. So adventurous did Mr Hannay's candidature seem even to his friends, that not one of them had the courage to preside at his first meeting, held in the Theatre ; but he made such a clever taking speech as secured for him many avowed supporters. At the hustings, on the 28th of March, his nomination was moved by Mr Peter Mundell of Bogrie, and seconded by Mr John Stott of Netherwood ; while the re-election of Mr Ewart was proposed by Provost Palmer of Annan, and seconded by Mr Samuel Cavan, afterwards provost of Kirkcudbright. Though Mr Hannay had the show of hands, he was poorly supported at the poll, Mr Ewart having been returned by the overwhelming majority of 321.* In this somewhat romantic episode of his life, Mr Hannay elicited no small praise from his political opponents, on account of his marvellous off-hand eloquence, and opulent intellectual resources of every kind ; and though thoroughly beaten in the contest, he bore the brunt of it creditably, and retired from the field without dishonour.†

(*a*) The accounts of the Parish Council (which has superseded the Parochial Board) for the year ended 15th May, 1905, shew an expenditure of £6465 on the poor law account, the assessment being 1s 1d per pound. The number of poor in receipt of out-door relief at the close of that financial year was 184, and of dependants 192 ; in poorhouse, 64 and 3 dependants ; lunatic poor, 51. For the same period the poor law expenditure of the Parish Council of Troqueer amounted to £2408, the assessment being 1s 2½d per pound, and the numbers of persons chargeable at 15th May, 1905, were : Out-door poor, 100 and 62 dependants ; in poorhouse, 7 ; lunatic poor, 18.

* The numbers were :—Ewart : Dumfries, 279 ; Annan, 103 ; Kirkcudbright, 69 ; Sanquhar, 33 ; Lochmaben, 22 : total, 506. Hannay : Dumfries, 136 ; Annan, 23 ; Kirkcudbright, 18 ; Sanquhar, 0 ; Lochmaben, 8 : total, 185.

† Mr Mark Napier, as Sheriff of Dumfriesshire, was the returning officer

Merry banqueters in the ruined courts of old Carlaverock ! There seems a discrepancy between their dining and cheering, and the desolation to which the castle of the Maxwells is a prey. Yet, when the circumstances of the case are taken into account, there will appear great propriety in the feuars of Carlaverock estate and the tenants of Terregles holding joyous revel in the ancient fortress, and making its walls ring as they drink to the health of the Nithsdale chief, whom the House of Lords had recently recognised as Lord Herries. That was the great object of this festive gathering, which took place on the 6th of July, 1858, and was fittingly presided over by the late Mr Francis Maxwell of Breoch. The title, which its wearer forfeited in the '45, was given to his descendant, William Constable Maxwell of Nithsdale and Everingham, who now takes rank as the tenth Lord Herries.*

A few more months roll round, bringing in the 25th of January, 1859, with a series of *fêtes* and banquets such as was never seen before in the burgh or the Border-land—or, rather we should say, in North Britain—and wherever the sons of Scotia congregate, throughout the world. That day was the centenary

The learned sheriff, high Tory though he is, seems never more in his element than when presiding over a popular assemblage—a duty that he invariably performs with good humour and grace. On the above occasion, Sheriff Napier first made his memorable and often-quoted statement descriptive of a Dumfries outdoor meeting, which, he said, he could not call a mob, as his experience taught him to believe that a Dumfries crowd was the best behaved of any in Scotland.

* On the 26th of July, 1859, Lord Herries manifested his appreciation of the honour conferred upon him by treating his tenants to a grand ball in the Castle (ornamented for the occasion in a highly imposing style), which passed off with entire success. His lordship married Marcia, daughter of the Hon. Sir Edward M. Vavasour, Bart., of Hazlewood, Yorkshire ; and has issue, the Hon. Marmaduke, Master of Herries, six other sons, and eight daughters. (a)

(a) The attainder, in so far as it referred to the title Baron Herries, was as above stated reversed, by Act of Parliament, in 1848, the Earldom of Nithsdale (which was limited to heirs male) not being dealt with in the statute ; and in 1858 William Constable Maxwell was found by the House of Lords to have established his claim to the revived Scotch peerage. Subsequently (in 1884) his son, Marmaduke, eleventh Lord Herries, was advanced to the dignity of a baron of the United Kingdom under the same title. His lordship married Angela-Mary-Charlotte, daughter of the first Lord Howard of Glossop. The two daughters, who were the issue of the marriage, were both married in 1904—the Hon. Gwendoline Constable Maxwell, heiress to the peerage, to the Duke of Norfolk, K.G. ; the Hon. Angela Mary Constable Maxwell to the Hon. James Eric Drummond, brother of the Earl of Perth. In honour of the auspicious double event Lord and Lady Herries entertained their tenantry and a company of distinguished friends to a banquet in Caerlaverock Castle on 8th September of that year. The leading orator of the occasion was another distinguished member of the Maxwell family, the Right Hon. Sir Herbert Eustace Maxwell, Bart. of Monreith, Lord Lieutenant of Wigtownshire, member of Parliament for that county, and a gentleman distinguished as a naturalist and man of letters.

of Burns's birth. Little did those Dumfries gentry who deliberately gave Burns the cold shoulder, on a memorable autumnal evening in 1794, suppose that, sixty-five years afterwards, or at any time, the streets down which they proudly passed would be trophied with garlands, and eloquent with sweet sounds, in honour of the man whom they affected to despise. The old burgh florid with decorations natural and artistic ; a great out-door demonstration, addressed by Mr Washington Wilks : a magnificent procession ; two dinners—one in the Assembly Rooms, presided over by Dr W. A. F. Browne, the other in the Nithsdale Mills, where about a thousand persons assembled—Mr Mundell of Bogrie in the chair—Mr John Hamilton,* of the *Morning Star*, giving in eloquent terms the "immortal memory :" these were the chief, but not by any means the sole features of the centenary celebration in Dumfries. It was in every respect worthy of the town where Burns lived and breathed his last, and where his ashes lie.

Men of all ranks and parties in the burgh cordially wrought together on Burns's day : but the spring of the same year found them broken up into two hostile political camps, over one of which was displayed the unmistakable Reform flag ; from the other flaunted a pennon of doubtful hue, with a somewhat mysterious motto, regarding the meaning of which many of the electors differed—Captain (now Major) Walker of Crawfordton, its owner, affirming that it expressed "strictly independent principles," while his opponents held that if it meant anything at all, it was, "Up with Earl Derby, and down with Lord Palmerston and the Reformers !" Captain Walker proved to be a very formidable antagonist to the Liberal sitting member, Mr Ewart. The fight that ensued was consequently much keener and closer than the contest in 1857. The nomination occurred on the 2nd of May, 1859 ; Mr Ewart being proposed by Provost Leighton, and seconded in an exceedingly trenchant and humorous speech by Dr M'Culloch, while Mr W. R. M'Diarmid, editor of the *Courier*, proposed, and Mr James Saunders of Solway Place, Annan, seconded, Captain Walker. Mr Ewart had the show of hands ; and a poll was demanded on behalf of his opponent. It took place on the 4th of May, and resulted in the re-election of Mr Ewart by the narrow majority of 29.†

Incidental notice has already been taken of the religious

* Mr Hamilton, from being an apprentice in the *Herald* office, Dumfries, fought his way up to a metropolitan editorship. He was cut off before his prime, in 1860 ; and in St. Michael's Churchyard a granite obelisk was erected to his memory by friends and admirers.

† The returns were as follow ·—Ewart : Dumfries, 237 ; Annan, 85 ; Kirkcudbright, 60 ; Sanquhar, 29 ; Lochmaben, 21 : total, 432. Walker : Dumfries, 287 ; Annan, 63 ; Kirkcudbright, 32 ; Sanquhar, 11 ; Lochmaben, 10 : total, 403.

revival experienced in many parts of Dumfriesshire and Galloway in 1861. It was chiefly brought about by the instrumentality of Mr (now Rev.) Edward Payson Hammond, graduate of Williams College, Massachusetts, America. After holding a series of remarkable meetings at Annan, he visited Dumfries ; and there, day and night, laboured as an evangelist from the 27th of January till the 15th of the following month, drawing such continuous crowds to hear him, and making such an impression upon them, as were truly marvellous. Though much of the effect produced seems to have been transient as "the morning cloud and the early dew," the religious public of the burgh and vicinity cherish a grateful recollection of Mr Hammond's devoted services, and there is reason to believe that they have been of lasting benefit to many. (a)

Never before or since, we believe, have the lovely grounds of the Crichton Institution been so crowded with ladies and gentlemen as they were on the 5th of September, 1862. That was the day on which the Dumfries and Galloway Horticultural Society reached the fiftieth year of its existence, and the anniversary was celebrated with a floral jubilee, in the shape of a superb exhibition within the walls of the institution ; a grand procession in which the gardeners, Freemasons, and Oddfellows took a leading part ; a dinner in the Mechanics' Hall, gracefully presided over by Mr Maxwell of Munches ; a fashionable ball in the Assembly Rooms ; and sundry other festive meetings or displays, including the decoration of the chief streets in the burgh with Nature's own drapery—evergreens and flowers. The show was in itself an excellent one ; but the local journals say it paled in brilliancy before the galaxy of lady visitors, "whose bright eyes rained influence" over the scene, and rendered it trebly attractive. For this unique entertainment and its manifold accompaniments the people of the burgh and district were mainly indebted to Mr Miles Leighton, junior. In acknowledgment of his services he was a short time afterwards entertained at supper in the White Hart Hotel (Mr Kirk's)—Bailie Carruthers in the chair—and presented with a handsome silver *epergne* suitably inscribed.*

On the 16th of February, 1862, Major Walker took formal leave of his supporters in Dumfries. Mr Ewart was not on that account left without a rival suitor for the favour of the Five

(a) The South United Free Church (long popularly known as the Territorial Free Church) was an abiding result of the " Revival," as it was called.

* In connection with the floral jubilee there were literary competitions, prizes having been offered for essays on horticulture and poems on flowers. Mr Paterson, gardener, Chester (formerly residing near Dumfries), and another competitor who gave only his initials, were first and second in the prose competitions ; while the prizes for the poetry were awarded to Mr Scott, Minnigaff, teacher, and to Mrs Cuthbertson, Annan.

Burghs. He had been leal and true to them since he first became
the object of their choice, in 1841 ; but another "soldier lad" fell
desperately in love with the Five Carlines when the worthy Laird
of Crawfordton declined to woo them any longer, since their
affections he could not win. Colonel Clark Kennedy of Knockgray, a native of the burgh, and of a good old family, was the new
candidate. In an address to the constituency he expressed his
belief that his political views were more in accordance with the
majority of them than were those of their present representative :
he desired to see an extension of the franchise ; was "decidedly
opposed to the ballot and other extreme measures," was ready "to
give a hearty general support to Lord Palmerston [at that time
Premier], but still as an independent member, following no man
blindly." It was not till more than three years afterwards that
the gallant officer had a complete opportunity of learning to what
extent the Burghs reciprocated his affection ; and meanwhile the
Liberals of Dumfries, by way of encouraging their faithful representative, entertained him at a great banquet in the Assembly
Rooms, which, under the congenial presidency of Bailie William
Bell [afterwards Provost], came off with immense *éclat* on the 30th
of March, 1862. A few weeks before the general election, in 1865,
a keen canvass was commenced by both candidates ; and up till
the nomination day (July 13th), and even afterwards, the friends
of Colonel Kennedy professed to be confident of victory. Mr
Ewart was proposed by Provost Turner of Dumfries, and seconded
by Provost Cavan of Kirkcudbright ; and Mr James Gordon,
ex-Provost of Dumfries, seconded by Provost Graham of Lochmaben, nominated Colonel Kennedy. The show of hands was in
favour of Mr Ewart ; and his early success at the poll, which took
place on the 15th, was so decided that, long ere mid-day, the
Kennedy men learned with consternation that their cause was
hopeless. Mr Ewart was returned by the large majority of 156
votes, made up of a majority in all the burghs.* Far more votes
were recorded than on any former similar occasion, the number
having been 924 ; the next highest was 858, in 1832 ; and the
next, 835, in 1859. Colonel Kennedy conducted his candidature
with courage, ability, and good temper: when acknowledging his
decided defeat, he avowed his resolution to resume his courtship
of the Burghs as soon as a favourable opportunity should arise ;
but the discharge of sterner duties, involving mortal sickness,
interfered. Whilst the gallant officer was in Egypt, on his way
to join the Abyssinian expedition, he was cut off by fever, on the
18th December, 1867, in the very prime of life.

* The poll stood as follows :—Ewart : Dumfries, 328 ; Annan, 101 ;
Kirkcudbright, 54 ; Sanquhar, 32 ; Lochmaben, 25 : total, 540. Kennedy :
Dumfries, 260 ; Annan, 47 ; Kirkcudbright, 42 ; Sanquhar, 17 ; Lochmaben,
18 : total, 384.

In few places is the connection between good sanitary arrangements and a high state of health better understood than in Dumfries. The water scheme was carried by the irresistible force of public opinion ; and the same influence facilitated the adoption of the General Police Act (25 and 26 Victoria, chapter 101). Stoutly opposed for a time, a sweeping majority of seventeen votes to five rendered it triumphant in the Council, when its adoption was moved by Mr James Clarke, and seconded by Mr Richard B. Carruthers, on the 6th of May, 1864. Under its comprehensive provisions, the main drainage has been completed ; the closes have been thoroughly sewered ; and by these and other means the burgh has been made as clean and salubrious as any town of its size in the United Kingdom.

A successful exhibition was held in the Old Assembly Rooms under the auspices of the Dumfries and Maxwelltown Mechanics' Institute, in 1841 ;* and for the purpose of reducing a heavy load of debt, contracted by the erection of the Hall, the committee of the Institute projected a second exhibition, which was opened in that commodious building on the 26th of June, 1865. A number of other gentlemen co-operated with the committee, under the chairmanship of ex-Provost James Gordon, then one of the vice-presidents of the Institute, now its president, and to whom the credit is due of having originated the exhibition. It proved abundantly successful in every sense ; to secure which result, no one laboured more devotedly than Mr William G. Gibson, who, in conjunction with Mr Harkness, acted as secretary to the committee of management. Rich paintings and rare antiquities, ingenious mechanical inventions and curious natural productions, articles of *vertu*, holographs of great men, and relics of Burns about a hundred in number, made up a splendid collection, which afforded crowds of visitors instruction and delight, and (we hope this is no anti-climax) yielded a net profit of nearly £300. (*a*)

On the evening of the 2nd of October, 1866, the same hall was occupied by nearly two hundred ladies and gentlemen, the *élite* of the burgh, met to partake of cake, fruits, and wine, and to witness a unique presentation to Provost Turner. He had, a few months before, acquired an addition to his family ; and, following a precedent set by other towns, the burgesses resolved to provide a silver cradle for the little stranger ; and thereby, says the *Standard*, to manifest "the high esteem in which both Provost and

---

* The joint-secretaries for the exhibition in 1841 were Mr William C. Aitken, now of Birmingham, and Mr William Smith, who has for many years been the editor of a newspaper of high repute, the *Whitehaven Herald*.

(*a*) A successful exhibition on similar lines, and under the same auspices, was held in 1873. A fine art exhibition was held in the new Academy buildings in 1899 ; and on occasion of the opening of it Lord Balfour of Burleigh, Secretary of State for Scotland, was presented with the freedom of the burgh, and entertained at a banquet.

Mrs Turner are held" by the inhabitants. Bailie Newbigging, who liberally provided the entertainment, presided—Mr Martin, the town clerk, officiating as croupier. The chairman, in an able presentation speech, pointed out that the event they had met to commemorate was not only interesting in itself, but unparalleled in the annals of the town. "Let them," he said, "turn over the leaves of the history of Dumfries backwards to the time when a M'Brair wielded power from the civic chair, in 1550, downwards to the comparatively modern time when the word of a Staig was law, and so on till our own day, and they would find no such incident as this recorded in the chronicles of the Burgh." Provost Turner acknowledged the gift in suitable terms.(*a*)

Before the same year (1866) had terminated, the people of Dumfries gave fitting welcome to a distinguished townsman— Captain Anderson of the "Great Eastern," knighted for the share taken by him in laying the electric cable that unites the Old World with the New. Sir James Anderson is the fifth son of a much respected burgess, the late Mr John Anderson, bookseller, and is a fine specimen of the British seaman, well worthy of the honours showered upon him—all which he carries with becoming modesty and grace. He was born in 1824, entered the merchant service in 1840, became connected with the Cunard line of steamers as a commander in 1851, and since his settlement on shore he has taken a very active part in establishing submarine telegraphic lines to India and Australia, and is at present managing director of all the submarine lines that connect Great Britain with India. The reception given to him by the Dumfriesians was of a three-fold kind. On the evening on the 13th of December, he met with the members of the Nithsdale Regatta Club, in order to receive from them an address. The meeting—a most agreeable one—took place in "Prince Charlie's Room," Commercial Hotel, and was presided over by Mr Miles Leighton, junior, commodore of the club, who presented the address, which was enclosed in a silver case—the first piece of plate, Sir James said, he had ever received.* Next day he was made a freeman and burgess, in

---

(*a*) A daughter was born to Provost Glover during his first triennial period of office, and on 5th May, 1898, Mrs Glover and he were the guests of the citizens at a dinner held in the Assembly Rooms, and received a handsome gift of plate, one of the pieces being in the form of the conventional silver cradle. Mrs Glover was also presented with an elegant bracelet and the Provost with a gold medallion as a memento of the diamond jubilee of Queen Victoria, an occasion on which he had the honour to be invited to Buckingham Palace, and in recognition of public services rendered to the burgh.

* Sir James Anderson, in acknowledging the gift, indulged in some pertinent reminiscences of his early life, in connection with a previous regatta club that flourished about thirty years ago in Dumfries. By dint of working overtime when he was serving his apprenticeship as a printer, he was enabled with others to purchase the first boat of the future Regatta Club. It was of iron, and one pound was paid for the boat—all in coppers ! (Laughter.) He

presence of a brilliant company assembled in the Town Hall.
From 1644 till 1795, inclusive, the same privilege was conferred on
2945 individuals, and on how many before and since we cannot
tell ; but we may venture to say that not one of the long list was
more worthy of receiving it than the captain of the "Great
Eastern." Provost Turner, in presenting the burgess ticket
(enclosed in a massive silver box) to Sir James, delivered an effective address, full of historical reminiscences, as became the occasion ; and the young burgess acknowledged the honour conferred
upon him in a few tasteful and feeling remarks. The proceedings
were crowned with a great banquet in the evening—the Provost
in the chair, and Mr W. R. M'Diarmid croupier. It was held in
the large hall of the Assembly Rooms, and attended by about two
hundred gentlemen from the burgh and neighbourhood.

Though a hall was provided for the Town Council in the Mid-
Steeple buildings, they did not occupy it till 1830, it being let by
them for other purposes. During the next thirty-six years it was
used as the Council Chamber ; and since the 9th of November
1866, the burghal authorities have met in what was once the
Court-house, but which they purchased for a Town Hall—a fine,
commodious building, situated in Buccleuch Street—with offices
for the town clerk, the registrar, and the police establishment of
the burgh.

During the three years ending with 1869, the burgh acquired
its three best public buildings, and another one was commenced,
the most imposing of them all : these being the County Court-
house, opened at the spring assizes on the 17th of April, 1866 ; St.
John's Episcopal Church, already described : Greyfriars' Church,
the first stone of which was laid in grand masonic style on the
11th of the following month : and the new Infirmary, which is to
be opened for patients in the spring of the present year. The
Court-house is one of the noblest architectural achievements of
the town ; but its effect would have been much enhanced if,
instead of occupying a low site in Buccleuch Street, it had stood
on a piece of rising ground. Constructed in the Scottish baronial
style, from a design by Mr David Rhind of Edinburgh, its tall
peaked towers and open Italianised parapets gave it at once the
bold characteristics of a castle, and the softer lineaments of a
palace. Wherever these turrets of the edifice are seen mingling

called it after Midshipman Easy's boat, the "Harpy ;" but his friends
christened it "Anderson's Canister." (Great laughter.) With that boat he
succeeded in winning an important race : seeing that he was in the fair way
of losing it, he turned the boat right about, and ran in stern foremost, carrying off the trophy. He could assure the company that ·he went down High
Street with the sovereign he had won, and with the honours he had earned in
that contest, prouder and happier than he could now feel ; because he had
then less care, less responsibility upon his shoulders. (Great cheering.)—
Report in the Dumfries Standard.

in the sky outline of the burgh, they look exceedingly striking
and picturesque ; and the entire building has a superb appearance, whether viewed from the street or surveyed from a distant
height. The new United Presbyterian Church (erected in 1863)
has combined with the Court-House to improve the aspect of
Buccleuch Street ; and the great line of thoroughfare, which
begins at the head of that street, crosses along the New Bridge to
Maxwelltown, and thence along the Galloway road, past the new
Free Church and numerous villas on the same side, is one of the
finest that is to be seen in the town or its environs. (*a*)

Greyfriars', which superseded the New Church, has supplied
the head of High Street with a very imposing edifice. The church
was built by Mr James Halliday, mason, according to a beautiful
Gothic plan prepared by Mr John Starforth of Edinburgh. It
cost £7150, of which sum the Town Council gave £4450, the rest
having been made up by subscriptions. The body of the building,
when viewed .from the front, is rather dwarfed by its colossal
accompaniments of tower and spire ; but seen in perspective, it
looks graceful and imposing. The steeple is unquestionably the
great leading feature of the design : symmetrical in form, and
replete with rich carvings, it rises to the extent of a hundred and
sixty-four feet, challenging notice by its size, and commanding
admiration by its fine proportions. The church is certainly a
great architectural acquisition to the Crescent from which it
springs, and to the main thoroughfare down which it looks.

We have seen how, nearly three centuries since, the Lauries of
Maxwelton sprang from a Dumfries merchant, the progenitor of
Bonnie Annie Laurie ; and their connection with the burgh was, a
few years ago, renewed in a most graceful way when the excellent
lady of the manor, acting under the advice of Major Walker, M.P.,
resolved to devote £5000 towards the erection of a new Infirmary,
on condition that a portion of it should be called "The Laurie
Ward," in memory of her late husband. The old fabric is still in
good repair, but its interior arrangements and means of ventilation do not satisfy the requirements of modern science, so at least
say the medical officers connected with it ; and the governors of
the Infirmary, entering fully into their views, gratefully accepted
Mrs Laurie's princely gift, and took steps for raising by subscription a similar amount—the cost of the new building which they
proposed to erect being, with site and "extras," fully £12,000. Mr
John Starforth, who had already left the impress of his genius on
the buildings of the burgh, supplied the design. That the founda-

(*a*) The architectural character of the street has been still more strikingly
improved by the erection of the Clydesdale Bank, United Free St. George's
buildings, the Post Office, the splendid premises of Messrs Barbour & Sons.
drapers, and, by the bounty of Miss M'Kie of The Moat the broadening and
beautifying of the New Bridge.

tion stone might be laid with due pomp and ceremony, "the sons of light" mustered in great force on the 16th of September, 1869, and, with other corporate bodies, made a grand processional march from the Academy grounds to the site, which is nearly opposite the old house, but is higher and still more salubrious. There the first stone of the New Infirmary was laid with mystic rites by the Provincial Grand Master, Mr Lauderdale Maitland of Eccles. The building, just completed, is in the Northern Italian style of architecture. As seen from St. Michael's Street, where the side elevation and part of the westward front can be taken in at a glance, the effect is very imposing. A central block, three stories high, with wings of two stories, forms the front elevation. The main central doorway is flanked by pilasters, carrying on the second floor two gigantic emblematic figures—the protecting divinities of the house—from the chisel of Mr John Currie. All the windows in the centre and wings are fully architraved, while the large one in the main block is covered by a pointed gable, crock-etted, and capped by a *fleur-de-lis*. With a pierced stone parapet, having terminal ornaments, this principal part of the elevation is completed : a mansard roof rising within, having iron cresting at the summit, and flanked by tall ornamental chimney stalks on each side. Elegant doorways right and left of the main entrance open on verandahs, which conduct respectively to the accident ward and the dispensary. A dormer, opening on the mansard roofing of the wings, enhances their appearance by supplying them with the semblance of an attic storey. The body of the building behind is erected according to the isolated block system, so as to secure thorough ventilation. All the internal arrangements are in fine keeping with the external aspect of the structure ; and the ground connected with it, fully five acres, is to be beautified with shrubs and flowers, which will form a pleasant look-out for the patients, and render the Infirmary increasingly picturesque. The first public building in Dumfries that fell under our notice was a warlike one, meet product of a rude, wild age—the Castle ; the last acquired by the burgh is the fruit of modern civilisation—a house of peace and mercy, a home for the sick and wounded, a tribute of the charitable rich to the afflicted poor, dictated by the humane feeling which "brother to brother binds," and makes "the whole world kin." (*a*)

(*a*) There have since been erected detached blocks for the treatment of infectious disease, for accommodation of the nurses, and a building temporarily utilised (since July, 1900) as a sanatorium for consumptives. Towards the cost of these a sum of £3000 was raised by public subscription on occasion of the diamond jubilee of Queen Victoria in 1897. The Infirmary received a very handsome endowment under the will of Mr Duncan James Kay of Drumpark, who, dying on 7th April, 1903, bequeathed to it the residue of his estate. The total sum ultimately accruing to the institution from this source will be about £34,600, but only about half of it is immediately available, as certain

While this building for the treatment of disease was slowly
acquiring shape an extensive scheme for conserving the public
health, by draining the outlying parts of the burgh, was launched
at the Police Board, and gave rise to much discussion. Before its
appearance all the older streets, with their intersecting closes, had
been sewered ; and the promoters of the scheme wished to extend
the same advantage to the rows or tenements adjoining Queen
Street, in or near to Lovers' Walk, Pleasance, Greystone Flat,
Ramsay Place, Saughtree, Rosevale Cottages, Mein Bank, and the
Parish Workhouse. Some opposed the project because they
thought it was too sweeping, others because the expense, about
£2500, would saddle a heavy tax on proprietors, many of whom
had voluntarily contributed to the expense of previous drainage
schemes. Fortunately, the objections brought against this important piece of sanitary reform were ineffectual : and it was carried
fully out according to the plans (as partially modified) of the
burgh surveyor, Mr Barbour, the works extending over two years,
having been completed in 1871. What Dumfries now needs in the
same direction is a plan to utilise its sewage water for agricultural
purposes, instead of letting it flow into the Nith, where it is worse
than wasted. (a)

annuities have to be provided for. As a memorial of the splendid bequest,
ward No. 10 has been named the Kay Ward, and a pictorial window has been
placed in it. At the time of writing a movement, inaugurated by Mr A. H.
Johnstone-Douglas, Convener of the County of Dumfries, for erection of a
county sanatorium for treatment of phthisis is on the eve of a successful issue.
The purpose of the promoters was to raise £9000 to build and equip the
sanatorium, and to secure annual subscriptions towards its maintenance to
the amount of £2400. The capital sum has already been provided, and a
substantial portion of the requisite annual revenue promised. A corresponding
effort in the county of Kirkcudbright, promoted by Mr W. J. H. Maxwell of
Munches, M.P., Convener of the County, has taken the form of a fund to bear
the cost of sending patients to existing sanatoria and of treating them in their
homes ; and the first annual collection realised the satisfactory sum of £1425.
The Local Government Board having issued what is practically a prohibition
of the treatment of infectious diseases in buildings connected with a general
hospital, arrangements are in progress for the erection of hospitals for such
cases apart from the Infirmary—one for the burgh at Castledykes, one for
Dumfries and Lockerbie districts of the county near Lochmaben.

(a) The sewage of both Dumfries and Maxwelltown has now been intercepted before entering the Nith, not to be utilised as a fertiliser, but to be
subjected to a system of purification by the bacteriological method. The two
Town Councils were constrained to undertake this enterprise through the
action of the Secretary of State for Scotland and the Local Government Board,
who, acting on representations from the County Council of Dumfries and
private individuals, appointed Colonel Gore Booth to conduct an inquiry with
reference to the pollution of the river by the town sewage, and Sir John
Cheyne, K.C., to inquire specially with regard to the want of proper drainage
in the Ryedale district of Maxwelltown. The two Commissioners held a joint
inquiry in April, 1900, when many scientists and engineers were adduced as
witnesses. In fulfilment of an obligation into which they entered during the
sitting of the Commission, the Town Councils constructed extensive purifica-

The year 1867 was opened in Dumfries with a political demonstration by the working classes on a great scale, consisting of a grand procession, in which 1,200 persons took part ; a day meeting on the Dock ; and an evening meeting in Mr Teenan's bazaar : all taking place under the auspices of the local branch of the Scottish Reform League, which numbered about a hundred and twenty members. So successful were the whole proceedings, that one of the speakers from London, after complimenting the Dumfriesians on being the first community to take the field that year in favour of Reform, drew an augury of coming triumph from the manner in which the campaign had been initiated. (*a*)   His anticipations proved to be correct : a persistent agitation for Parliamentary Reform having been rewarded by the enfranchisement of all rate-paying householders before the year had run its course.   In virtue of this concession, the Parliamentary constituency of Dumfries was enlarged from 698 to 1,440, and that of the whole Five Burghs from 956 to 2,378.

In an address to the electors of the burghs dated the 23rd of June, 1868, their veteran representative bade them farewell, after, as he said, "twenty-eight years of willing service on my part, and of generous confidence on yours." For some time previously, Mr Ewart's health had been infirm, and he died on the 29th of January, 1869. Beginning his Parliamentary life as a pupil of Mr Huskisson, he continued throughout a zealous advocate of commercial freedom ; he acquired still more distinction by his success ful endeavours to ameliorate the rigours of our criminal legisla-

tion works, which were brought into operation early in 1905. Those of Dumfries are situated at Castledykes, where a deep excavation had to be made in the rock to secure the necessary low level for the filter beds. Including the price of the land (£5000) and of an intercepting sewer carried along the side of the Nith from the northern boundary of the burgh at Crindau, the cost of the works was a little over £41,000. The site of the Maxwelltown works is on the lands of Troqueer Holm. In addition to the intercepting sewer, starting from the head of College Street, it was necessary to construct a new drain from the Castle-Douglas Road, across the lands of Cassalands, Rotchell, and Ryedale, to serve the south-western portion of the burgh, and this entailed expensive tunnelling. The outlay for the Maxwelltown works reached a total sum of about £28,000. Mr W. Carter, C.E., Edinburgh, was the engineer employed in both cases. The sewage is subjected to the action of microbes in septic tanks and filter beds, and the purified effluent is then discharged into the river.

(*a*) Mr Joseph Tait, baker, now of Toronto, was chairman of the League branch ; the secretary was the late Mr George Barrie Stewart, then a compositor ; and the treasurer, the late Mr T. D. Weir.   On Mr Stewart's removal to England shortly afterwards he was succeeded by Mr T. Watson.   The branch ceased after the election on the new franchise in 1868.   Mr Samuel Cairns, painter (afterwards Bailie Cairns, Maxwelltown), presided at the meeting on the Dock, at which Mr Mantle, the London Radical who was said to "shake the base of the London Monument" with his oratory, was the principal speaker.   At the meeting in the Mart, also presided over by a working-man, Mr Shanks, blacksmith, the chief speakers were Mr George Odger, a London leader of the democracy, and Mr (now Sir) Wilfrid Lawson.

tion, and to promote the cause of popular instruction by means of public libraries and otherwise. Among the statutes which are a transcript of his political creed, and bear lasting testimony to his legislative skill, are the following :—Act abolishing capital punishment for horse stealing, cattle stealing, and stealing in a dwelling-house (1832) ; act abolishing capital punishment for letter stealing, sacrilege, and returning from transportation (1834) ; act providing counsel for defence of indigent prisoners (1835) ; act for establishing free libraries and museums (1850) ; act for facilitating the building of labourers' cottages in Scotland (1860) ; and act for legalising the use of the metric system as a step towards a general international plan of weights and measures (1864).* Mr Ewart's attention to national matters did not render him neglectful of his local duties : these he faithfully discharged, and even such of his constituents as differed from him politically could not but admit that he was an industrious, obliging, and conscientious member. The seat was not actually vacated till the dissolution of Parliament in the following November.

In anticipation of the vacancy, some of Mr Ewart's friends had fixed upon Mr Robert Jardine of Castlemilk, who represented Ashburton from 1865 till its disfranchisement in 1868, as his successor. Prematurely pushing his claims to represent the Dumfries Burghs, they, by so doing, irritated many members of the constituency, especially those working-class voters who had been newly put upon the roll in virtue of the Household Suffrage Act that had just begun to take effect. The result was a mutiny in the Liberal camp, the more advanced section going off to form a new organisation, and taking measures for bringing a candidate of their own stamp into the field. Their views were made known

* We subjoin a brief enumeration of some of the other services rendered by Mr Ewart as a senator. Mr Ewart entered the House of Commons in 1828. He spoke and voted for Catholic emancipation on the 27th of March, 1829. On the 1st of August, 1833, he moved the equalisation of duties on East and West India sugar ; in other words, to establish free trade in that article. 1835-6, moved for, carried, and drew the report of a committee " On the Connection between Arts and Manufactures ;" the result being the establishment of schools of design. 1840, March 5th, moved for the entire abolition of the punishment of death, which motion he repeated in several subsequent years. 1841, April 20th, proposed (and repeated on several other occasions) a motion for appointing a minister of the Crown who should make an annual statement on national education (afterwards adopted and carried into effect by the Government). 1841, April 20th, moved for and carried the opening to the public of Regent's Park, and also an important part of Hampton Court Palace. 1843, June 22nd, moved for the admission of foreign sugar on equal rates of duty with colonial sugar (opposed, but afterwards adopted, by the Government). 1852, May 28th, moved for the examination of candidates for the diplomatic service. 1853, April 8th, repeated the motion (since adopted). 1858, May 7th, moved for, carried, and drew report of select committee on European colonisation in India. Mr Ewart was also a steady and strenuous supporter of the repeal of the taxes on knowledge.

at a crowded meeting held in the Mechanics' Hall, on the evening
of the 10th of July, and responding to them down came Mr Ernest
Noel, from London, whose offer of service was cordially accepted
at another great meeting held in the same place about a week
afterwards. Reference has already been made to the adventurous
candidature of Mr James Hannay. That of Mr Noel was in some
respects still more so, as he was a total stranger, not known even
by name to any of the electors. His attention had been called to
certain resolutions published in the newspapers, which made
known that an advanced Liberal was wanted for the Dumfries
Burghs ; and without any credentials, save what Nature had given
him, he applied personally for the situation at once. He had this
advantage over Mr Hannay, however that he was a free-lance on
the popular side. Of gentle blood, his father being the late Hon.
and Rev. Baptist W. Noel, brother of the Earl of Gainsborough, he
had also a fine address, and proved himself to. be a ready and
eloquent speaker. By the middle of August the split among the
Liberals was complete—the more Radical portion of them in all
the burghs rallying round Mr Noel ; the Whigs, as they were
sometimes called by way of distinction, supporting Mr Jardine,
and being strengthened by many of the Conservatives, who
fancied that the latter was the safer candidate of the two. Mr
Jardine was proposed on the hustings by Provost Cavan of Kirkcudbright, and seconded by Bailie Kerr of Annan. Dr M'Culloch
proposed, and Bailie Fraser seconded, the nomination of Mr Noel.
Each party went to the poll on the 17th of November confident of
success, the Jardinites in general reckoning upon a very decided
majority. They came off victorious, though they did not succeed
in inflicting such a decided blow upon their opponents as they
had expected. For Mr Jardine there voted 1125, for Mr Noel
1083 ; majority for the former, 42.* The defeated candidate,

* The numbers were :—Jardine : Dumfries, 737 ; Annan, 158 ; Kirkcudbright, 79 ; Lochmaben, 118 ; Sanquhar, 34 : total, 1125. Noel : Dumfries, 609 ; Annan, 196 ; Kirkcudbright, 130 ; Lochmaben, 88 ; Sanquhar,
111 : total, 1083. Number of electors on the roll in Dumfries, 1440, of whom
94 did not vote ; in Annan, 384, did not vote, 39 ; in Kirkcudbright, 241,
did not vote, 32 ; in Lochmaben, 159, did not vote, 3 ; in Sanquhar, 155, did
not vote, 11 (a).
    (a) Provost Harkness was agent for Mr Ewart, and made the mistake of
not consulting the Liberal party before inducing Mr Jardine to allow himself
to be brought forward. The opposition originated with the local branch of the
Reform League. It convened a meeting of Trade delegates and others, and
it was resolved to requisition the Provost to call a public meeting to consider
the question of the Parliamentary representation. The resolutions for this
meeting, which was held in the Mechanics' Hall, were previously submitted by
Mr Watson to a small gathering representative of the old voters and the new.
On the suggestion of Dr M'Culloch one of the resolutions, which provided for
a committee of all who wished to be of it, was so altered as to restrict the
number to seventeen. At the public meeting it was attempted to make it
appear that the seventeen would practically exercise the political patronage of

before leaving Dumfries, publicly announced that, if his friends
desired it, he would again visit them in the same capacity whenever a vacancy occurred in the representation of the Burghs
Mr Jardine proved to be a much more consistent and decided
Liberal than many both of his opponents and friends predicted.
He was born in 1826, his father being the late Mr David Jardine
of Muirhousehead, Lockerbie. Though much engaged in managing
an extensive mercantile business, the member for the Burghs
attends industriously and faithfully to his Parliamentary duties.(a)

An election contest for the County ! Such a phenomenon
had not occurred since 1806, though during the last forty years
there have been no fewer than six fights for the representation of
the Burghs. Dumfriesshire, long the Sleepy Hollow of politics,
was thoroughly aroused in the autumn of 1868, the party warfare
that then took place being waged still more fiercely than the
struggle that was going on at the same time for the seat vacated
by Mr Ewart. The Liberal voters of the County had been largely
increased by the Reform Act passed in the preceding year ; and a
pretty general feeling prevailed among their leading men that
they should make a bold, even though ineffectual, dash at the
seat held by Major Walker. It was believed by them that Mr
Gladstone's scheme for the overthrow of the Irish State Church
would form a capital gathering cry, and that by raising it, and
keeping prominently in view also their general principles as a
party, they might muster such a force as would make a creditable
fight ; and that defeat under the circumstances would be less
humiliating than continued inactivity. No one took action in
the matter, however, till some sixty circulars were issued, calling
a private meeting to be held in the *Dumfries Standard* office, for
the purpose of considering what course ought to be pursued, if
any, with the view of initiating a Liberal movement in the
County. About forty electors responded to the invitation, who,
as presided over by Mr Alexander Reid of Newton-Reid, resolved
unanimously that a public meeting on the subject should be
called forthwith. To show what immediately followed, we copy

the burghs. This criticism was, of course, effectively repelled. But there can
be no doubt that had the committee been allowed to be an open one the election
would have been carried by Mr Noel. Not a few who had been with the
opposition in the first instance were estranged when there was no room left for
them on the committee. It was the stir of this contest that stimulated a
Liberal revolt in the County, and led to the amazing success of Sir Sydney
Waterlow there. It also brought into the field a gentleman who was to
achieve unique distinction as a political agent, Mr James H. M'Gowan, who
was one of the committee of seventeen, and subsequently acted professionally
for Mr Noel. The several political associations in this district as we now have
them originated in the contests of 1868.

(a) Sir Robert Jardine—he received the honour of a baronetcy in 1885—
subsequently represented the county of Dumfries from 1880 to 1892. He died
in February, 1905.

a paragraph from a chronological account of the extraordinary contest that set in, and by which the County was convulsed for the next six months :—"September 30 (Rood Fair Wednesday)— Public meeting of electors in Market Hall—nearly six hundred present. Mr Reid, as at the previous meeting, was called to the chair. Resolutions proposed and seconded by Mr Kerr, Brockle- hirst, Mr Reid, Langholm, Mr Douglas of Burnfoot, and Mr Bryden, Lockerbie, declaring that no supporter of the Tory Government could enjoy the confidence of the great body of the constituency, and that an effort should be made to return a repre- sentative of Liberal principles. Resolutions passed unanimously, and with enthusiasm ; and on the motion of Mr Smith, Parkend, seconded by Mr Bell of Carruthers, a committee was named to look out for a suitable candidate." "The hour had come," but where was "the man ?" Not one of the kind wanted turned up in the County. Several local gentlemen were applied to by the committee without success. For about a week County Liberalism lay half despairing, like Rebecca, before the Knight of Ivanhoe came for her deliverance ; till at length, on the 10th of October, a message received by Mr James M'Kie, banker, Dumfries, held out the hope that a veritable London knight, with true blue colours on his lance, would yet enter the lists to do valiant battle on behalf of the forlorn damsel held in captive thrall, as it was said, by the Laird of Crawfordton. Heralded by an ingenious squire, Mr Mays, the expected champion, Sir Sydney Hedley Waterlow, appeared upon the scene ; and, after receiving cordial approval from a crowded meeting held on the 21st of October, over which Colonel Graham of Mossknow presided, Sir Sydney galloped into the arena, throwing down his cartel of defiance, or, in plainer terms, issuing his address as a candidate before another week had expired.* Round the stern reality of his enterprise there gathered a halo of romance : the courage which inspired it was in itself attractive and infectious. He took possession of Prince Charlie's Room and adjoining apartments—not by force, as was done in the '45, but paying mine host of the Commercial a goodly tribute of

* The London correspondent of a local newspaper, writing about Sir Sydney Hedley Waterlow, when he first appeared as a candidate, says :— "While yet a young man, he became a partner in his father's house, the well- known stationery firm of Waterlow & Son, and it is mainly to the adminis- trative ability of himself and brothers that it rapidly became what it is—by far the largest and most perfect establishment of the kind in the United Kingdom. Some fourteen years ago he was elected to the Common Council of the City of London, and very soon rose to the dignities of Alderman and Sheriff. Towards the close of his year of office as Sheriff, Earl Derby advised her Majesty to confer on him the honour of knighthood ; and soon after com- plimented him on his services to the City of London, and especially to the poor of that city, in a manner at once appreciative and emphatic." The candidate for Dumfriesshire, and for a brief period its member, is now Lord Mayor of London.

rent for the same—there, in these classical lodgings, his committee
sat methodising their campaign arrangements, and carrying them
on with extraordinary vigour ; and while hard prosaic work was
being done, the Muse of Song was invoked to glorify the mission
of Sir Sydney by, among others, a clever London Scotsman, Mr
Forbes Robertson, who came as poet laureate in the train of the
" belted knight," and made spirit-stirring speeches as well as
glowing lyrics on his behalf.

These proceedings were at first treated with contempt by the
opposite party. They had so long held unchallenged possession
of the County that they ridiculed the very idea of its being
wrested from them by a Liberal, and a stranger. As the new
movement rolled along, gathering strength from every quarter,
their feelings of scorn gave way to those of anxiety and alarm.
Not till too late did they realise the unpleasant facts that they
had been caught napping, that the enemy whom they had made
light of was thundering at their gates, within reach of the citadel-
seat which they had supposed was impregnable. If, however, the
Conservatives were slow to perceive their imminent peril, they,
when once thoroughly aroused, put forth great and gallant efforts
to confront it, and (if we may change the figure) "out of the
nettle danger to pluck the flower safety." Major Walker rose
with the unexpected crisis, acquitting himself with characteristic
ability and courage ; but the battle was obviously going dead
against him, till on the 3rd of November a damaging blow was
inflicted upon his opponent by a letter which appeared in the
Courier of that date, signed "James Geddes," alleging that Sir
Sydney Waterlow was "a leading Unitarian." On the 7th the
Liberal candidate published a summary of his religious creed in
the *Standard*—"an acceptance of the supreme divinity of our
Saviour Jesus Christ, as the source of all divine truth," which
declaration, however, did less to heal the wound he had received
than the discovery of a plot to make it deeper through the instrumentality of a London spy, who was commissioned from Dumfries
to watch the worshipping whereabouts of Sir Sydney, with the
view of demonstrating that he was thoroughly heterodox. This
" detection of the detective " created a powerful reaction in favour
of the Liberal leader, and before the day of nomination came
round his position was redeemed. That ceremony took place on
the 19th of November, Major Walker being proposed by Mr
Carruthers of Dormont, seconded by Mr Kennedy of Sundaywell ;
while Colonel Graham and Mr M'Call of Caitloch performed a
similar service for Sir Sydney—the latter getting the show of
hands by a majority of five to one.* Wonderful to say, the
promise at the hustings was realised in the polling booths—the

---

* Newspaper Chronology of the Contest.

Liberal leading on the election day, the 21st of November, obtaining a majority of 44 votes, the numbers being 1100 to 1056.*

Sir Sydney Waterlow's triumph was short-lived, though its effects upon the County have not been transient. Sometimes the smallest chink in a warrior's panoply has allowed access to a deadly shaft; and a technical flaw, arising out of the business connections of the Liberal leader, rendered him vulnerable to the enemy whom he had fought and conquered. According to the Act 22, George III., cap. 45, any one engaged as a Government contractor is disqualified from sitting and voting in the House of Commons; and Major Walker, alleging that his opponent still belonged to the stationery firm of Waterlow & Sons, and that they were doing Government work at the date of his election, petitioned against his return, and claimed the seat for himself. "'Twere long to tell, 'twere sad to trace" the various incidents that ensued: enough to say that the petition was eventually withdrawn; that the whole case, as affecting Sir Sydney, was handed over to a Committee of the House of Commons, who, on the 15th of March, found that he was disqualified according to the Act; that he thereupon gave up the seat; and that the conflict was renewed, ending this time in the return of Major Walker. The nomination of candidates took place on the 29th of March, and it is rendered especially memorable from the circumstance that it was the closing ceremony of the kind in Dumfries—the hustings, together with open voting, having since been abolished. Major Walker was proposed by Mr Malcolm of Burnfoot, and seconded by Mr Smith, Dalfibble; Sir S. H. Waterlow was proposed by Colonel Graham, and seconded by Mr Willison, Dalpeddar—there being "a perfect forest of hands held up in favour of the Liberal candidate, and only a few persons forming the right fringe of the multitude pronouncing for his opponent."† At the polling, on the 30th, the Conservatives took the lead, and kept it, carrying their candidate by 1115 votes to 1081—a majority of 34.‡ As has already been stated, the public proceedings in this unparalleled double contest began on a Rood-Fair Wednesday, and they closed precisely six months afterwards, in the midst of another great rural gathering, the March Fair, held on the 31st of that month, when the declaration of the poll was made.

---

* The numbers in the different districts were :—Waterlow : Dumfries, 231 ; Moffat, 135 ; Lockerbie, 190 ; Langholm, 132 ; Thornhill, 147 ; Annan, 265 : total, 1100. Walker : Dumfries, 246 ; Moffat, 81 ; Lockerbie, 160 ; Langholm, 152 ; Thornhill, 197 ; Annan, 220 : total, 1056.

† Newspaper Chronology of the Contest.

‡ The returns from the various districts are subjoined :—Walker : Dumfries, 241 ; Annan, 235 ; Lockerbie, 176 ; Moffat, 85 ; Thornhill, 217 ; Langholm, 161 : total, 1115. Waterlow : Dumfries, 238 ; Annan, 264 : Lockerbie, 179 ; Moffat, 131 ; Thornhill, 144 ; Langholm, 125 : total, 1081.

It only remains for us to add, regarding the political history of the County and Burghs, that Major Walker, who is a gentleman of undoubted ability, announced in March, 1872, that he means to retire at the close of the current Parliament ; that Captain William Hope Johnstone (grandson of Mr Hope Johnstone, long honourably associated with Dumfriesshire as its representative and otherwise) is Conservative candidate for the seat ; that Mr Robert Jardine, resigning the Burgh membership, is his Liberal opponent ; and that Mr Ernest Noel, on again entering the field for the Five Burghs, has been confronted by Sir James Anderson, who is also a Liberal. (a)

(a) The Parliament of 1868 was dissolved in February, 1874, and the composition of its successor gave evidence of a strong Conservative reaction. In the election for the County of Dumfries Mr J. J. Hope-Johnstone of Annandale polled 1453 votes, and Mr Robert Jardine of Castlemilk, 1315; Conservative majority, 138. Sir James Anderson did not proceed with his candidature for the Burghs, and the Conservatives found a champion in Mr M. Carthew Yorstoun of East Tinwald, subsequently Convener of the County. The result of the poll was : Mr E. Noel, 1420 ; Mr Carthew Yorstoun, 1122 ; Liberal majority, 298. At the general election of 1880, when the foreign policy of Lord Beaconsfield was vigorously assailed by Mr Gladstone, Colonel Walker was once more brought forward as Conservative candidate for the county, and Mr Jardine again championed the Liberal cause. The issue of the contest was : Mr Jardine, 1577 ; Colonel Walker, 1505 ; Liberal majority, 72. In the Burghs there was a three-cornered fight. Mr E. Gordon, a London solicitor, was the official Conservative candidate, and Mr T. E. Byrne of Elshieshields also entered the field as an independent Conservative. Mr Noel, the sitting member, polled 1700 votes ; Mr Gordon, 872 ; Mr Byrne, 54; Liberal majority on the gross poll, 774. Colonel Walker received the honour of knighthood in 1892, the rank being that of K.C.B., and was the first Convener of the County under the system of local representative government. He died in 1897.

Before the next general election, which occurred in 1885, the county constituencies had been greatly enlarged by Mr Gladstone's Reform Bill of that year, which created a household franchise. Sir Robert Jardine on that occasion polled 4857 votes, as against 3566 given for the Earl of Dalkeith, eldest son of the Duke of Buccleuch ; Liberal majority, 1291. The young nobleman met a tragic death three months afterwards by the accidental discharge of his gun while he was deer-stalking in the Highlands. In the election of 1885 Mr Noel again held the seat for the Burghs, polling 1546 votes, as against 1363 given for Mr M. Mattinson, barrister ; Liberal majority, 183.

The Parliament elected in November and December, 1885, was dissolved on 26th June of the following year, consequent upon the rejection by the House of Commons of the Irish Home Rule Bill introduced by Mr Gladstone and the cleavage in the Liberal party which that measure occasioned. In the election of 1886 Sir Robert Jardine, again standing for the County, declined to commit himself definitely to Home Rule ; but the Liberal Whip (now Lord Tweedmouth) advised that the Association should adhere to him. Sir Robert knew they had already declared for Home Rule ; and in that knowledge having consented to be their candidate he would probably come all right. This, however, did not satisfy the more advanced and numerous wing of the party, and Mr Thomas M'Kie of Moat House, advocate, was brought forward in the Home-Rule interest. A very peculiar situation was thus created ; for Sir Robert Jardine was the official candidate of the Association, which had pronounced for Home Rule, the Association's machinery was worked for him, the Liberal agent acted for him ; whereas Mr M'Kie, one of the vice-presidents of the

From Dumfriesshire and Galloway Sir Walter Scott borrowed much rare raw material, which his genius transmuted into some of the richest characters and scenes of which his works can boast. If set in processional array, what a marvellous spectacle the latter

Association, and a strong Home-ruler, had to face not only the official organisation, and Sir Robert's Liberal adherents, but also the entire force, official and other, of the Conservative party, who went for Sir Robert. Notwithstanding the great disadvantage that all this implied, Mr M'Kie polled 3252 votes against 4106 for Sir Robert Jardine, whose majority was thus 854. Whether Sir Robert would have been won over to Home Rule had he been returned unopposed we can only conjecture. But the opposition estranged him from Liberalism, and he continued to act with the Conservative party, as a Liberal Unionist.

In the Burghs also Mr Gladstone's Irish policy had a disrupting effect. Dr M'Culloch, the president of the Liberal Association, resigned, and went into opposition. Mr Noel, who had previously advocated the restoration of an Irish Parliament, was now against it. But his attitude being disapproved of by a great meeting in Dumfries, after a speech of his, he did not again seek the suffrages of the Burghs ; and the Liberal candidate was Mr R. T. Reid, Q.C., second son of the late Sir James J. Reid of Mouswald Place, and formerly M.P. for Hereford. Mr Reid received 1547 votes ; Mr M. Mattinson, who was again the Conservative candidate, 1217 ; Liberal majority, 330.

The next general election occurred in 1892. The result of the poll in the County was : Mr W. J. Maxwell, yr. of Munches, Unionist, 4123 ; Mr Thomas M'Kie, Liberal, 3849 ; Unionist majority, 274, this being as much due to an agitation against Disestablishment as to actual antagonism to Home Rule. In the Burghs—Mr Reid obtained 1696 votes ; Sir Andrew Noel Agnew of Lochnaw, 1166 ; Liberal majority, 532. In 1894, on his appointment as Solicitor-General for England, followed shortly afterwards by that of Attorney-General, Sir Robert Reid, as he then became, was returned unopposed, and was also presented with the honorary freedom of Dumfries. Another general election occurred in 1895. The seat for the County was contested by the retiring member and Mr Robinson Souttar, from Oxford. The latter won the day, the figures being : Mr Souttar, 3965 ; Mr Maxwell, 3952 ; Liberal majority, 13. In the Burghs the poll was : Sir Robert Reid, 1785 ; Mr W. Murray of Marraythwaite, 1185 ; Liberal majority, 600.

During the progress of the war with the Boers in South Africa the Prime Minister (the Marquis of Salisbury) advised a dissolution of Parliament, and a general election took place in September and October, 1900. Mr Maxwell recovered the County seat for the Conservatives, receiving 4124 votes, as against 3675 recorded for Mr Souttar, who had offered an uncompromising opposition to the South African policy of the Government; majority, 449. In the Burghs Sir Robert Reid, though he had also condemned, in the House and in the country, Imperial aggressiveness in Africa, and was called in the fashion of the time by the self-styled patriotic party "Little Englander," "Pro-Boer," and other contemptuous names, received 1847 votes ; Mr W. Murray, 1300; Liberal majority, 547.

The general election of 1900 was fought on the footing that the war was practically over, and that it was only right that the Government which had carried it through should fix the terms of peace and arrange for the future settlement of the country. Liberals who had favoured the war were assured that in the new Parliament their principles would not be engaged by any legislation on domestic questions of a controversial character. But, as the event shewed, the war was only half over ; and Liberals who had been induced to remain neutral or to vote for the Government were repaid by a shameful breach of faith ; for the licenses of

could make! Guy Mannering itself might, for such a fancy
pageant, furnish a rich contribution.　Views of Ellangowan Castle
(Carlaverock), of Kippletringan (Annan), of Balcarry Bay, where
Yawkins, the prototype of Dirk Hatteraick, used to land his

English publicans were converted from annual permits into a species of
permanent freehold, from which there could be no ejection without compensation ; the School Board system of England and Wales was destroyed, and
Church and Catholic schools were placed upon the rates without the ratepayers
receiving adequate control of them.　Those measures greatly incensed the
Nonconformists and temperance reformers, and helped to bring about a
reaction of feeling against the Government.

Other influential factors making for their downfall were the financial
situation which their extravagance had created and the audacious attempt to
obtain relief by a return to Protection.　The general election had occurred
when the Marquis of Salisbury was still Prime Minister; and Mr Chamberlain
having gone to South Africa, partly for his health, partly to have a look round
on the havoc produced by his war, Lord Salisbury resigned, and Mr Balfour
became Prime Minister.　Mr Chamberlain professed to be satisfied with this
bit of nepotism successfully performed behind his back, but he never really
settled down on his return to his work of Colonial Secretary under Mr
Balfour.　Without consulting Mr Balfour, he delivered a speech to his own
people of Birmingham in which he declared for a return to Protection.
Then he resigned his position in the Government to conduct an agitation
against Free Trade.　He had first, however, arranged to have his son promoted
to the office of Chancellor of the Exchequer, and there was an interchange of
epistolary compliments, in which Mr Chamberlain thanked Mr Balfour for the
favour extended to his son, and Mr Balfour wished god-speed to Mr
Chamberlain's missionary enterprise.

During ten years of Conservative Government two and a half millions
had been added to the National Debt, and taxes been increased by about
£1 5s per annum per head of the population, man, woman, and child.　This
diminished the spending power of the people to that extent, and produced a
marked depression in the home trade.　The oversea trade, on the other hand,
kept good and continued to grow, and our export trade of manufactures is
now by far the largest on record.

Mr Chamberlain, ignoring the statistics of the Board of Trade, declared
that our export business was being ruined and that in our own domestic
markets the foreigner was reducing prices.　He boldly went in for protective
duties on manufactures and food, with a preference in favour of the colonies,
and the Conservative associations were captured for his propaganda.　Mr
Balfour, observing that the working class wholly and the middle-class mostly
were determined to adhere to Free Trade, that only the great landlords and
certain manufacturing and other interests hoping to profit from the imposition
of taxes on commodities were behind Mr Chamberlain, would give no clear
counsel to his party.　But he allowed all the Free Traders who were of his
Government to leave it rather than break with Mr Chamberlain ; and Mr
Chamberlain appeared to have him in the hollow of his hand.　The position
becoming intolerable, he resigned in the end of December, 1905 and Sir
Henry Campbell-Bannerman was invited to form a Government.　Sir Robert
Threshie Reid was offered and accepted the position of Lord High Chancellor,
and assumed the title of Baron Loreburn of Dumfries, in compliment to the
chief town of the District he had so long and faithfully represented.　Sir
Henry having resolved upon an appeal to the country, there was no bye-
election consequent on acceptance of office.　The general election took place
in January, and resulted in a quite unprecedented Conservative rout.　The
new Parliament contained 385 Liberals and 157 Conservatives, the others
consisting of Nationalists and Labour men.　For the first time a really

contraband wares, and of the Cave at Torrs, near the estuary of
"dark-rolling Dee," which bears the bold smuggler's name ; with
such figures added as Meg Merrilies (Jean Gordon), who, according

effective Labour party, with Mr Hardie for leader, was formed in Parliament.
But on most questions they and the Nationalists could be relied upon by the
Liberal Government, and on the question of Free Trade the Conservative
minority was divided. Mr Balfour lost his seat in Manchester, but a distant
relation made way for him in the City of London.

In the South of Scotland, Dumfriesshire and Kirkcudbrightshire were
won back to Liberalism, and the Dumfries Burghs were, of course, retained.
Provost Glover's descent upon the Burghs as a candidate in opposition to Sir
Robert Reid was a surprise and a sensation. In November of 1903 the
Scottish Liberal Association met in Dumfries, and Mr Morley addressed a
great gathering in the evening. At a luncheon in the afternoon Provost
Glover appeared as a guest ; but no one could then have gathered from what
he said that he had any thought of entering upon a political career. But the
unexpected happens sometimes; and to the astonishment of everybody the
versatile Provost, at a meeting of the Conservative Association in the middle
of the next month, was accepted as prospective candidate. He justified his
candidature by the Chamberlain legend that Free Trade was bringing the
country to ruin, and that it could only be saved by taxing ourselves upon the
importation of those manufactures from abroad which our people were
wanting. On the question of taxation of food, he trimmed in the manner of
Mr Balfour ; as did also Sir Mark M'Taggart Stewart in Kirkcudbrightshire,
where Major M'Micking was to stand for Liberalism. But in Dumfriesshire
Mr J. H. Balfour Browne of Goldilea, who was adopted prospective Conservative candidate in July, 1903—Mr Maxwell of Munches having announced his
intention not to seek re-election—declared himself to be a tariff "whole
hogger" of the school of Mr Chamberlain. In September of the same year
Mr Percy A. Molteno, whose father was the first Prime Minister of Cape
Colony, and who is a partner of the great shipping firm of Donald Currie &
Co., was selected by the Liberal Association.

Sir Robert Reid's accession to the woolsack rendered it necessary for the
Liberals to find a new candidate, and in the month of December they adopted
Mr John W. Gulland, Edinburgh, a gentleman who had helped to found the
Young Scots Society, and had taken an active part in the municipal and
philanthropic life of Edinburgh, as a Town Councillor, a member of School
Board, and in other capacities. The result of the poll, declared 18th
January, 1906, was as follows : Gulland (L), 2035 ; Glover (C), 1402—Liberal
majority, 633. The Kirkcudbrightshire result was declared on the 19th as
follows : M'Micking (L), 2715 ; Stewart (C), 2418—Liberal majority, 297.
The result in Dumfriesshire, declared on the 20th, was as follows : Molteno
(L), 4814 ; Browne (C), 3431—Liberal majority, 1383. On the 24th the
result in Wigtownshire was declared as follows : Viscount Dalrymple (C),
2866 ; Captain Waring (L), 2127—Conservative majority, 739.

The Liberal majority in the Burghs would have been larger than it was
had Sir Robert Reid been the candidate. His past service, his eminence in
Parliament, and his personal relations with the constituency were certain to
make for a record majority in a period of Liberal revival. Much public
sympathy had been elicited by the protracted illness and death of his
wife, a lady who had greatly endeared herself in the wide circle of his friends,
and it was more than regretted that during this trying time the worry of a
prospective contest should have been so early thrust upon him.

Sir Henry Campbell-Bannerman's Ministry was composed mostly of
Scotsmen or gentlemen sitting for Scotch constituencies ; and never until
now had there been at one and the same time Scotsmen as Lord Chancellor,
Prime Minister, leader of the Opposition, Archbishop of Canterbury, and
Archbishop of York.

to the Kippletringan precentor, "was the maist notorious witch
in a' Galloway and Dumfriesshire baith ;" stalwart Dandie Dinmont from Liddesdale, with his four-footed followers ; wily Gilbert
Glossin, the Galwegian John o' the Scales ; and Mr Peter Pleydell,
the clever, rollicking, warm-hearted son of a Dumfries Provost
who might be accompanied by a view of his father's house, the
Woodley Park of Burns's verse, and the Holm of an older day
From Sir Walter's other works might be taken representations of
Old Mortality, with Currie's group of figures, and the tombstone
recently placed over the veteran's remains in Carlaverock Churchyard ;* of sterling Jeanie Deans (Helen Walker), with the
monument raised above her in Irongray Churchyard by Scott
himself ; of Edie Ochiltree, the prince of gaberlunzies, who, as
Andrew Gemmill, was a well-known wanderer in Galloway : of
the famous dominie, Jedediah Cleishbotham, with a picture of
Gandercleuch (the clachan of Penninghame or Newton-Stewart),
in a hostelry of which the said Jedediah drank "mountain dew"
with the exciseman and the landlord ; of witless Madge Wildfire,
the Feckless Fanny of Wigtownshire tradition ; of Wandering
Willie, who, as Willie the Welshman, was long fiddler-in-chief at
all the "merry splores" between Gretna Green and the Braes of
Glenapp ; of the doure Red Gauntlet (Grierson of Lag), with a
picture of his Dumfries town-house, or his ruined tower in the
parish of Dunscore ; of the young Lochinvar, with his runaway

* Mr Joseph Train, the celebrated antiquary, who was several years a
supervisor of Excise in Dumfries, furnished not a few of the Waverley proto-
types.   One of these was Robert Paterson, the "Old Mortality," whom Scott
has made immortal.   Mr Train was never able to ascertain where Paterson
was buried ; and Sir Walter, writing to his correspondent in April, 1829,
expressed regret that the burial-place could not be discovered, as he wished
to erect a monument to the memory of the veteran at his own expense.   A
few years back it was ascertained beyond doubt that Paterson died in the
village of Bankend on the 14th of February, 1801, and was interred in the
neighbouring churchyard of Carlaverock.   While on his way to that burial-
ground, in pursuit of his avocation, he was discovered by Mr Stewart, lessee
of the quarries at the village, in the agonies of dissolution, and immediately
afterwards he expired.   Mr Stewart allowed the remains of Old Mortality to
be laid in a grave-plot of his own ; and the memorial stone which the author
of Waverley desired to set up was erected over the dust of the old worthy in
1870, by Scott's publishers, Messrs Adam and Charles Black.   Mrs Wilson,
wife of Mr Joseph Wilson, schoolmaster, Gasstown, and granddaughter of Mr
Stewart, has often heard her mother—who died in 1858, at the age of seventy-
four—tell the story of Paterson's latter end, and last resting-place, as above
narrated.   The monument is a neat upright slab of a Grecian form, having
carved upon it a mallet and chisel, to indicate his epitaph-restoring pursuits.
It is thus inscribed :—Erected to the memory of Robert Paterson, the Old
Mortality of Sir Walter Scott, who was buried here February, 1801.

          "Why seeks he, with unwearied toil,
              Through Death's dim walls to urge his way—
          Reclaim his long arrested spoil,
              And lead oblivion into day ?"

bride, as chased over Canobie Lea ; of poor Lucy Ashton, the luckless Bride of Lammermoor, whose sad tale was suggested by that of Janet Dalrymple of Stair, wedded against her will to David Dunbar of Baldoon ; and last of all, by glorious Bruce of Annandale, the hero-king of real life, and the hero of Scott's splendid poem, " The Lord of the Isles." Standing in such a close relationship to Scotland's greatest literary son, the district took a commendable part in the national celebration of his centenary. Its chief festive gathering was held in the county town on the evening of the 9th of August, 1871—Mr Thomas Aird presiding, and the croupiers being Dr W. A. F. Browne, Mr Mark J. Stewart of Southwick, Mr J. Gilchrist Clark of Speddoch, and Mr W. R. M'Diarmid. The large hall of the Assembly Rooms was filled on the occasion by nearly a hundred and forty gentlemen, and never has its roof reverberated to a higher strain of eloquence than when " The Immortal Memory of Sir Walter Scott " was proposed by the distinguished chairman.

At the last municipal elections which we have to notice, the ballot was introduced for the first time. The secret mode of voting was proceeded with in a way that seemed tame as com-pared with the keen open contests which had occurred during the preceding forty years. Much interest was felt in the result, however, as the office long so worthily held by Provost Harkness had been rendered vacant by his death on the 10th of October, 1872, and required to be filled up. There were two candidates for the provostship, Mr Thomas Fergusson Smith, and Mr Joseph Ewing, the former a Conservative, the latter a Liberal. When the votes were counted, it was found that all the candidates who sup-ported Mr Smith save one had been elected, and that only one of those who favoured Mr Ewing had escaped defeat : this singular result springing chiefly from the circumstance that the latter had, in 1868, opposed the advanced Liberal candidate for the Burghs, and thereby brought down upon himself the opposition of the more Radical portion of the constituency. As the elections were so decisive, Mr Smith, who is also Chief Magistrate of Maxwelltown, was placed in the civic chair of Dumfries without further opposi-tion. (a) The Council, as now made up, consists of nineteen Liberals and eleven Conservatives. Among other special subjects that have been before the Council for some time are a scheme for

(a) Provost Smith continued to occupy the civic chair until 1878, when he was succeeded by Mr Thomas Shortridge, dyer and manufacturer. Mr David Lennox, merchant, served a double triennial term, from 1881 to 1887. In the latter year the late Mr John Luke Scott, draper, was called to the position, which he resigned on 23rd January, 1896, on account of ill-health, when on the eve of completing his third term of office. Mr Joseph Johnstone Glover, elected interim Provost on 10th February, 1896, had the appointment confirmed by unanimous vote of the Council in November of the same year ; and he had the same happy experience in 1899, 1902, and 1905.

erecting a passenger suspension bridge over the Nith at Dock-head, which is in a forward state ; (a) a movement, originated by Provost Smith, for getting back Kingholm Merse to the burgh, which property, in the absence of an heir to the last owner, has been acquired by the Crown ; (b) and the purchase of the Gas-works in Shakespeare Street, as proposed by Bailie Wood, with the view of supplying cheaper gas to the community. (c)

The sources from which the burgh derives its revenue* are pointed out in chapter fifty-fourth. For the year ending Sep-

(a) An elegant Suspension Bridge was opened on the last day of 1875.

(b) In 1875 the estate of Hannafield, in which Kingholm Merse is included, was conveyed by deed of gift from the Crown as *ultima hæres* to the War Department, with power to use it as a place of encampment and a parade ground for the local militia on occasion of the annual training, and for such other military purposes as they might desire ; subject to which uses the public were to enjoy the right of resorting to the Merse as a place of common recreation. It was also stipulated in the deed of gift that the free revenue of the estate was to be applied in promoting education in Dumfriesshire and Galloway. The Hannahfield Trustees, who administer this fund, are able from its resources to provide continuously three university bursaries of £35 each per annum, one of which falls vacant annually ; and fifteen high school bursaries of £10 each per annum (five falling vacant each year). The lands of Kingholm, as previously mentioned, had been sold by the town in 1827 to Mr John Hannah of Hannahfield, a gentleman who made his fortune in the West Indies. He was succeeded in the property by a nephew, Mr John Wood. Mrs Wood survived her husband, and it was on her death in December, 1869, intestate and without heirs, that the estate lapsed to the Crown. It was understood to have been her intention to bequeath it to the town of Dumfries, and on that ground the Town Council petitioned the Treasury for a gift of it. As already stated, the conveyance to the Magistrates and Council would have been completed but for a negotiation to change the terms of it. Meanwhile the Conservatives came into office, and a representation from the Militia resulted in the gift being made to the War Department.

(c) The Gasworks were purchased by the corporation in 1878 for the sum of £21,000, and since that time they have been entirely reconstructed and greatly extended, the total capital expenditure up to 15th May, 1905 (including the purchase money), having amounted to £59,246. The outstanding loan debt on the works at that date was £32,803. The price of gas has been reduced from 5s 10d per thousand cubic feet, which was charged in the last year of the company's management, to 2s 10d. The Town Council in 1899 obtained a provisional order authorising them to undertake the supply of electricity for light and power within the burgh. This was ultimately transferred to the India Rubber, Gutta Percha, and Telegraph Works Company, Limited, London, under an agreement which secured to the Council the right to purchase the works ; and the company proceeded with the erection of works in Leafield Road, on land leased from the Council, in the spring of 1906.

* A considerable proportion of the revenue is drawn from feu duties, and from dues, customs, and rents, let for the most part annually by public auction. The accounts for last year include the following items :—Feu duties and ground rents, £160 12s 2d ; teinds, £4 0s 2d ; bridge dues, £550 ; market dues, £173 5s ; dean's fees, £26 0s 3d ; rent for property at mills, £384 17s 6d ; for Dock Park, £38 : for shops and houses, £178 10s ; for markets, &c., £64 5s ; for sundries, £6 15s.

tember, 1872, the ordinary income was £1925 13s 6d ; the ordinary expenditure, £1425 6s 5d ; leaving a balance of £500 7s 1d, which, however, was entirely absorbed by the following items of extraordinary expenditure, viz. :—Improvements on slaughter-house, £383 16s 2d ; repairs on manse, &c., £184 18s 6d ; re-seating St. Michael's Church, £49 7s 7d—while there was no extraordinary revenue to counterbalance the deficit. There is a heavy debt owing of £15,219 4s 9d, which, warned by the example of 1817, the Council ought to reduce with all convenient speed. As Police Commissioners, their expenditure (exclusive of the special drainage account) has averaged considerably more than £3000 annually for the last five years, in assisting to meet which bank overdrafts have had to be made, the latter at the close of 1872 amounting to £1700. Roughly speaking, the Council revenue during the last few years has been about £2000 ; that of the Commission, which is from £3000 to £4000 yearly, has a tendency to increase with the size of the town, though, of course, it is affected by the amount of the assessment, which is now 1s per pound, including 2d for road money. The total value of the properties and revenues belonging to the burgh is estimated at about £40,000, In 1746, when Dumfries was appraised for the purpose of raising an assessment connected with the Jacobite tribute money, the value of the houses and public buildings was found to be £34,843 4s ; and if we make adequate allowance for the land that was not valued, we shall arrive at a sum that will fall considerably below the rental of the burgh at the present day. In other words, the valuation of Dumfries for 1871-2 is £40,574,[*] a sum that a hundred and twenty-six years ago would have purchased right out the whole town with the ground it occupied. The annual valuation has risen fully £10,000 within the last ten years. (a)

* This sum is exclusive of railways, and shows an increase of £1607 on the preceding year. The railways within the boundary are rated on an annual valuation of £2580,—*Report of Mr James B. Gemmill, Assessor for the Burgh.* Those in the Parish were valued at £4971 in 1872.

(a) The total revenue of the Town Council for the year ended 15th May, 1905 (the distinction between Town Council and Police Commission having been abolished), was £28,163. In this sum was included £15,865 derived from sale of gas and its bye-products. The various assessments levied by the Council amounted in the aggregate to 2s 6½d per pound of rental, and yielded £8535. The indebtedness of the burgh at the same date amounted to £111,398, and its assets were valued at £174,975, shewing a surplus of £63,577. In addition to its mortgage debts, the Town Council is liable under the Education Act of 1872 for an annual payment of £140 to the School Board towards the maintenance of the Academy ; and in terms of an agreement entered into in 1727 with the Presbytery of Dumfries and the minister of St. Michael's Church, it is under obligation to pay £100 annually to the minister of Greyfriars, as a set-off against which there was assigned to it the right to certain rents from the lands of Drum in Newabbey and excrescent Bishop's tiends, which together yield £66 13s 4d per annum. The Council has also

Considered as a central place in the Post Office system, the town has long stood high, and every year of late its importance from this point of view shews a steady increase. The number of letters, cards, books, pamphlets, and newspapers delivered during four weeks in 1870 was 151,293 ; in the corresponding four weeks of 1871 and 1872, the number respectively was 159,715 and 177,370. The weekly number of such articles passing through Dumfries and Galloway Sorting Tender for head Post Offices has risen from 19,239 in 1870 to 23,549 in 1872. Of telegrams forwarded, received, and transmitted, in 1870 there were 25,987 ; in 1871, 36,342 ; and in 1872, 47,356. The money order transactions show a similar advance, these having numbered 20,536 in 1870, 22,996 in 1871, and no fewer than 26,249 in 1872.*

since 1817 made a further annual payment of £40 " as a free gift " towards the augmentation of the Greyfriars' stipend ; and by resolution adopted in July, 1905, it undertook to continue this contribution during the incumbency of the Rev. William Edie. The annual valuation of the burgh within the original boundaries (including railways) had risen in 1905 to £77,951, being an average increase of over £1000 per annum since Mr M'Dowall wrote ; and in that year the municipal boundary was extended to comprehend the suburbs of Milldamhead, Noblehill, Gasstown, Greenbrae, and Nunfield. This added about two thousand to the burghal population and £6153 to the annual valuation, which thus reached a total of £84,104. The district so annexed continued for parliamentary election purposes to be a part of the county. The valuation of the burgh of Maxwelltown in the same year had increased to £24,757.

     * These statistics were obligingly supplied by the local postmaster, Mr Loudoun. (a)

     (a) Since 1872 there has been a remarkable development of the postal service, in respect both of the extent and variety of its work. Figures for 1904, obligingly supplied by Mr C. S. Chapman, postmaster of Dumfries, shew that in an average week the number of letters and letter packets posted in the town and district is 66,110, giving an annual total of 3,437,720, without taking into account the large amount of extra correspondence dealt with at the Christmas season ; and the weekly delivery reaches a total of 69,573, or an annual total of 3,617,796. Forwarded letters (i.e., passing between other head offices and re-sorted at Dumfries) number 52,609 weekly ; yearly total, 2,735,668. In the Galloway and Irish sorting carriages, which are under the control of the Dumfries postmaster and worked by the Dumfries staff, 85,860 letters are dealt with weekly ; yearly average, 4,464,720. This return brings out a grand total of 14,255,904 per annum. For the parcels department the return is : Posted, 2209 weekly, 114,868 per annum ; delivered, 2071 weekly, 107,692 per annum ; forwarded, 5772 weekly, 300,144 per annum ; in Galloway sorting carriages, 5946 weekly, 309,192 per annum ; grand total, 831,896. About 420 letter mail bags and 240 parcel receptacles are dealt with daily at Dumfries and in the sorting carriages. Of registered letters there were 12,706 delivered during the year, and there were 652 express letter services. Of telegrams there were 47,346 handed in at Dumfries (exclusive of those received at the railway station), 58,593 delivered, 82,732 transmitted (these being messages received from offices not having direct communication with other towns and forwarded from Dumfries to their destination). Telephone calls numbered 11,024. The return of the financial business transacted at the head office shews 101,516 money and postal orders issued and paid, and 3928 savings bank transactions. The head office staff of all grades numbers

As in "Burns's time," Dumfries has a goodly number of volunteers to bid the Gauls and other foreign "loons beware" of venturing to set hostile foot on the Nithsdale portion of "our inviolate island of the brave and free;" and Maxwelltown has also a band of riflemen ready, if need be, to render similar service —" For defence, not defiance."(*a*) The burgh has two verdant arenas, Milldamhead and St. Mary's, on which many a peaceful bowling contest is waged. On the Dock and Greensands the classical *discus*, or quoit, has in season due its modicum of disciples. (*b*) When the Nith is frozen over its surface becomes the scene of many a curling spiel keener than the material on which

89. In addition there are two telegraph engineers and four linesmen located in the premises. The Dumfries district comprises 29 sub-offices, with about sixty postmen or postwomen employed in rural letter and parcel delivery.

(*a*) On occasion of the Boer war, which began in October, 1899, and ended in June, 1902, resulting in the conquest of the Transvaal and Orange Free State, the Dumfriesshire and Galloway battalions of Rifle Volunteers both sent contingents for active service in South Africa. The district militia, now known as the 3rd Battalion King's Own Scottish Borderers, and which had celebrated its centenary in October, 1898, was called up for garrison duty three months after the outbreak of hostilities. The battalion unanimously volunteered for service in the field, and proceeding to South Africa in April, 1900, they formed an integral part of the British field force for two years and five months. The regiment was feted on its return in June, 1902. In October following the freedom of the burgh was conferred on its commander, Colonel James Maxwell Witham, C.M.G., of Kirkconnel; Major Laurie, D.S.O., yr. of Maxwelton (who shortly afterwards succeeded to the command); Major M'Kie, D.S.O., of Bargaly, and the other officers; and they were presented with a silver casket and centre-piece for the regimental mess. Similar honours were conferred on the Volunteers on their departure for the seat of war, and demonstrations of welcome were organised on their return. Large funds were also raised in the district to assist in their better equipment for the campaign and for the relief of their families and of widows and orphans. Officers and men of the Militia who died in South Africa are commemorated by a brass placed in Greyfriars' Church by the officers. A native of Dumfries, Mr William Robertson, while serving with the Gordon Highlanders as Sergeant-Major, was gazetted Lieutenant and received the Victoria Cross for conspicuous bravery in rallying the regiment at Elandslaagte. He subsequently endured the hardships of the prolonged siege of Ladysmith ; and on his return to this country he was, on 24th December, 1900, presented with the freedom of the burgh. A great bazaar in aid of a fund for the better equipment of the Volunteer battalion was held at Dumfries in July, 1898. Viscount Wolseley, then Commander-in-Chief of the Army, visited the town on the occasion and received the freedom of the burgh.

(*b*) There has of recent years been a great development of facilities for open-air sport. The bowling greens mentioned in the text have been superseded by others in Newall Terrace, Dumfries, and Albert Road, Maxwelltown. At Nunholm there are a cricket ground, courts for tennis and hockey, and also a recreation field for the Academy pupils. The royal and ancient game of golf has many votaries. The Dumfries and Galloway Club has a fine course on Summerhill, and a shorter one for ladies adjoins it. Football as a winter sport excites an extraordinary degree of popular enthusiasm. Quoits are no longer played in the public parks, but several clubs foster the pastime.

the competing stones career ; and when summer days are prime, and the icy winter is still far off, the open river is ploughed and splashed by a great array of boaters on recreation bent, or in excited earnestness pulling away bravely at the regatta of the Nithsdale Club.

For indoor recreations there is plentiful provision. The Theatre, built in 1790, and on whose boards strutted Edmund Kean and Macready when starting on the race for fame, still furnishes an occasional season for the lovers of the drama ; the Mechanics' Institute supplies cheap lectures every winter ; and Dumfries, owing to its Border position, is more frequently visited by professional lecturers, musicians, and other "artistes," than many towns in the kingdom twice its size.

Every year the local Burns's Club has a festive celebration of the bard's anniversary ; annual concerts on a great scale are given by the Choral Society, with its vocalists and instrumentalists ; and the published Transactions of the Natural History and Antiquarian Society show that its members know well how to make their learned pursuits useful, attractive, and entertaining.

Of institutions to facilitate the operations of trade and encourage thrift, Dumfries has a creditable proportion. At the date of the Reform Act it had only three or four banking offices ; now it has eight—those of the Bank of Scotland, the Commercial, the British Linen Company, the National, the Clydesdale, the Union, the Royal, and the City of Glasgow ; besides a Savings Bank, with deposits to the amount of £90,000 ; a Benefit and Building Society, commenced in 1857—number of members, 1280 ; a Co-operative Society, dating from 1847—shareholders, 350, subscribed capital, £445 5s, average weekly drawings, £242 ; a branch of Oddfellows, Robert Burns's Lodge—members, 330 ; funds, over £1500 ; and two Foresters' Courts, the Robbie Burns numbering 75, and the Nithside 170. (a)

(a) The City of Glasgow branch was closed in 1878, consequent on the failure of the bank ; but the North of Scotland Bank opened a branch in Dumfries in 1905 ; and the Clydesdale had some time before established a second agency in Maxwelltown. The deposits with the Savings Bank had increased, at the date of the annual balance in the spring of 1905, to the large sum of £301,983, and the bank had also an auxiliary fund of £14,900. The Dumfries and Galloway Benefit and Building Society received during the year 1904-5, in members' subscriptions and payments towards liquidation of loans, £10,648, and paid out to members as withdrawals £5567. Three other building societies, belonging to the federation known as the "Economic," have also been established. The membership of the Co-operative Society has increased to 1415, and it has an annual business turnover of £36,000. The last annual return of the friendly societies shews the Manchester Unity of Oddfellows to have a membership in Dumfries of 445, and the two Courts of Foresters, 579. There have also been formed branches of the Rechabites (a total abstinence and friendly society), Free Gardeners, and Ancient Order of Shepherds.

Some of the burgh's associations for charitable, intellectual, moral, and religious purposes have already been noticed. Several additions to these have been made during the last twenty years, most of which will be found in the following list (those that are exclusively congregational not being included) :—A branch of the National Bible Society—annual revenue, about £70 ; a Home Mission for Dumfries and Maxwelltown, with Ladies' Auxiliary and Agency for Bible Distribution—annual income for them all, about £110 ; a Dorcas Society, which provides ready-made clothing at a cheap rate for the deserving poor of both burghs— revenue, fully £72 ; a Sabbath School Teachers' Union, numbering 291 members ; a Boys' Home (instituted and presided over by Mr William Gregan in 1859), with the adjuncts of a dormitory for orphan apprentice lads, a reading-room with library, a penny savings' bank, a band of hope, and an anti-tobacco society— income for 1872, £171 4s 1d ; and a Medical Mission, begun in 1873, having regard to the spiritual improvement, not less than the bodily health, of the working-classes. To these remains still to be added the "Alms-houses" charity, a cluster of handsome cottages, built at the expense of Mrs Carruthers of Warmanbie, for the reception of "ten or fewer" lame or blind women, natives of Dumfries ; and failing a sufficient number of such, any other needful females whom the trustees may appoint. These institutions, great and small, combined with the Benevolent Society's cheap schools, instituted in 1812, with the Hospital, the Infirmary, and the Education Society, whose enlightened operations have been previously spoken of, show that the burgh recognises in no stinted way the claims of the poor and the destitute, the ignorant and the depraved. (*a*)

(*a*) On the extinction, in 1885, of a life-rent on the estate of the late Mr David Johnstone, writer, Dumfries, it was applied by trustees in terms of his will to the maintenance of "widows, daughters, and sisters of professional men, merchants, and upper class of householders belonging to the burgh of Dumfries or to the village of Lockerbie, who are in reduced and had been formerly in more fortunate circumstances." Eleven villa residences were erected on the Bankend Road, on a property to which the name of Johnstone Park was given. The beneficiaries enjoy the free occupation of these houses and receive annuities of varying amount, the total sum distributed in one year being £277. Under bequests of the late Mr John Martin, printer, and of Mrs Hutton, Langlands, and her sister, Miss Kemp, funds have recently been established for the benefit of the poor of the town. A branch of the Queen Victoria Jubilee Institute for Nurses was formed in Dumfries in 1891, and it maintains two district nurses, whose services are given gratuitously to families in which there is sickness. The Society for Prevention of Cruelty to Children is among the other forms of active benevolence recently developed, and it maintains an inspector for Dumfries and Galloway, who is resident at Dumfries. The Boys' Home associated with the name of Mr Gregan was discontinued after the death of the founder ; and the charity schools have been superseded by the statutory provision now made for education. An important gift of a philanthropic nature was made to the town in 1898, when Miss M'Kie of Moat House erected at her own cost public baths and wash-

It is now, as we saw when commencing our task, a large as well as beautiful town, growing rapidly in size, population, and wealth. How, from a rude, insignificant, timber-built village, it has gradually, during the passage of nine centuries, reached its existing state; and how its civilisation and material improvement have advanced hand-in-hand, we have endeavoured to show. Its earlier streets retain the hoar of antiquity, intermingled with many fresh modern features which wear the dew of youth ; and round about the original burgh there have risen up house-rows and villas sufficient in themselves to constitute no inconsiderable town. In the aspect of Dumfries, as we now find it, there is much to gratify the eye of the antiquarian, and much also to satisfy the advocate of progress. With the old architectural features the new gracefully interblend, just as the charming natural scenery in which they are set contrasts with both, yet makes up with them a harmonious and attractive whole. But the modern portion of Dumfries is increasing at a rapid pace ; and should it go on in the same proportion for the next fifteen years, it will occupy more ground than was embraced by the entire site of the burgh at the date of the Union. The abolition of the close burgh system, the repeal of the corn laws, the con-struction of railways, and the establishment of the tweed trade, have each given a stimulus to the growth of Dumfries. Few provincial towns in Scotland have gone forward during the last thirty-five years with such a gigantic stride ; and its steps in advance have been especially remarkable in the latter half of that period. At the date of the Reform Bill, Albany Place, a row of seven two-storey houses, was the only genteel suburb of which the town could boast ; now it has several which are much more patrician in size and aspect. At the same period the separate country mansions within the royalty numbered about half a dozen ; at present—enriching the view in all directions, on the Moffat Road, by Lovers' Walk, on the Lochmaben Road, on Sir Christopher's Park (opposite St. Mary's Church), at Noblehill, on the Craigs Road, and on the Upper Dock nursery—they number nearly five score, ranging in value from £500 to £2000 each. Many

house on the Greensands for the use of the inhabitants of Dumfries and Maxwelltown. The institution was placed under the management of the Dumfries Town Council. This lady's thoughtful munificence (of which an outstanding example is the widening of the New Bridge) led the Town Council to confer upon her the honorary freedom of the burgh, and in pub-licly receiving this compliment, in September, 1897, she was associated with the Prime Minister of the day, Mr Arthur J. Balfour. Mr Thomas M'Kie, who has been associated with his sister in her philanthropic works, received from the community the gift of two silver loving cups on occasion of his marriage to Miss M. Gordon. Under the will of Mr Matthew W. Boyd, who died in 1902, a sum of £5000 accrues to Dumfries Academy for university bursaries.

of these villas have sprung up within the last ten years ; not a few additional ones are being built, or have been projected. Whether we look to the old parts of the town, or to the new, we see proofs of progress. Buccleuch Street, as already noticed, has undergone a wonderful mutation of late. High Street is still, as in days of yore, the main artery of the burgh : its outward fringe on both sides, however, has been all but completely renewed, every shop in it, save two at most, having been re-built, re-fronted, or extensively remodelled within the last forty years ; yet, in spite of these changes, it is still quaintly picturesque, differing little in general outline from the day when "Bonnie Prince Charlie" rode through it at the head of his kilted Highlanders. Since that period the Mid-Steeple, which juts into the street, has altered for the worse. Sadly weather-worn, it remains neglected by its custodiers ; and though still a fine object, its decayed condition contrasts badly with the tokens of prosperity which surround it on every side—especially since the stylish rival steeple further north has risen up, to look down upon it in a double sense.

One antique tenement, with crow-stepped gable turned to the front, alone remains in Friars' Vennel as representative of its primitive architecture ; the old tavern which includes the kitchen of Devorgilla's Monastery is about to be taken down ; and were any of the Minorite brethren permitted to "re-visit the glimpses of the moon" near their old mundane retreat, they would be strangers in the street that bears their name. Gradually the small one-storey houses, which were long common there and in the other secondary thoroughfares, are disappearing ; the "age of homespun," as typified by a roof of thatch, is nearly at an end. Only a few years back numerous straw-covered cabins were visible in the Vennel, English Street, and the Kirkgate, but the hand of improvement has reduced them to some half-dozen, and planted down stately structures in their stead.* This change for the better is very noticeable in St. Michael Street, which, from being rather a mean-looking outlet southward, has now acquired a respectable aspect, so that the grandeur given to the lower part of it by the Nithsdale Mills, and reflected from the New Infirmary further down, is not out of place.

In a northern direction, Dunbar Terrace and Langlands, both

---

* Thatched buildings on the 1st of February, 1873, as reported to the Police Commission by Mr Barbour, at the instance of Bailie Rennie :—No. 90 Loreburn Street ; 13 and 15 St. Andrew Street ; 19 North Queensberry Street ; 5 King Street ; 11 Burns's Street ; and one, unnumbered, in Robison's Close— seven in all, On receipt of the report, the Commission ordered several of the thatched tenements mentioned therein to be re-built, and the others to have their straw covering replaced by slate. The likelihood, therefore, is that before the current year has run its course, there will not be a single straw-roofed house left in the burgh.

of which are due to the enterprise of Mr George Dunbar, and in another (the south-east), York Place, Victoria Terrace, and many individual mansions, rise up among rural scenes, where recently no houses were visible, or only those of a humbler grade ; and the magnificent station, erected in 1859, supplied a crowning ornament to the south-eastern suburb of the town. The station is exceedingly handsome in itself, and is so set off by a foreground of rare shrubs and flowers as to draw forth the admiration of all visitors, many of whom we have heard declaring that no such beautiful station is to be seen in the United Kingdom. Several ranges of neat two-storey houses, about sixty in number, have been lately formed in the nursery ground, south of Queen Street, supplying accommodation to middle-class families ; but we search in vain for extensive cottage-rows suited for the operative classes, not a few of whom, in the absence of such, are forced to reside in mere hovels, of which there are still too many throughout the burgh. Nowhere within it, perhaps, has the work of reform effected such changes as in the lower part, near the river. How very rustic the Dock Meadow looked about a hundred years ago has already been pointed out. It was little altered when it formed one of Burns's promenades, as " Adown winding Nith " he "did wander, of Phyllis to muse and to sing," and for long afterwards ; but since 1857, the banks and braes of the Nith have acquired new accompaniments ; and the Dock, without losing its natural loveliness, has got, so to speak, fragments of a masonic frame-work which would seem singularly new and strange to all natives of the town returning to it after an absence of fifteen years or more. The acquisition, though artificial, so far from impairing, enhances the attractions of this favourite resort. Indeed, if we desired to give a stranger a good first impression of the burgh, we would conduct him from the vicinity of Castledykes, northward along the river's brim, to catch the varying panorama thus made visible—the stately villas rising in what used to be the Dock nursery on the right, their bright hue (red sandstone) contrasting beautifully with the green garniture by which they are environed ; further on, the magnificent Nithsdale Mills, opposite the sister yet rival structure of Troqueer (*a*)—their tall chimney stalks looking like parts of a huge pillared gateway at the southern entrance of the town ; old St. Michael's familiar steeple ; and the bulk of the town itself, looming finely above and beyond the glorious Dock limes; with the changeless river flowing past, giving freshness and superadded sweetness to the scene. (*b*)

(*a*) Beside which has since been erected the very handsome Rosefield Mills.

(*b*) Since these pages were written the residential quarters around Dumfries and in Maxwelltown have been greatly extended. The tract of land

The fine view from the Observatory, or Corbelly Hill, is described in chapter first. Let us just, when closing, cross over to an opposite point on the railway bridge, at the head of the English road, and take a farewell glimpse of the burgh from that "coign of vantage." Near by, on the right side, rise handsome residences and stately temples; straight over in the valley, which is bounded westward by Criffel and some lesser heights, lies much that is characteristic of Dumfries, old and new, and an element of grandeur is contributed to the scene by its lofty background. Maidenbower Craigs attract attention on the left; following the line from that bold eminence we see modern manufacturing enterprise represented by the Nithsdale Mills; neighbouring the busy haunt lies a quiet necropolis, among whose mortuary tenements we see

> "The last, the hallowed home of one
> Who lives upon all memories,
> Though with the buried gone;"

St. Michael's venerable fane catches the eye at the same time as the Mausoleum; while half a dozen other ecclesiastical buildings crowd upon the view, comprising the modest structure of Troqueer, enriched with Covenanting memories; the spired chapel that reminds us of the ancient Roman faith; the Territorial Church, testifying of successful missionary work among the masses; St. Mary's, enshrined by old patriotic associations; Greyfriars' protruding its charming pinnacle; and the new Church of St. John's, standing like some stalwart Norman baron, unadorned yet stately. Intermingling with all these religious houses, we can individualise numerous marts of trade; trace the body of the burgh to a large extent; notice the far-off Observatory, courting observation; also many nice "bits" of Nature thrown in, as an artist might say, to beautify the effect—the whole landscape being so suggestive that more than half the history of the town might be discoursed from it by way of text. The burgh is keeping pace with the times in these material matters, nor does it lag behind its compeers intellectually. To its progress morally, its declining calendar of crime, and its increasing list of beneficent institutions, alike bear witness; the

lying between Loreburn Street and Dunbar Terrace has, for example, been entirely built upon; and here are two of the most important new buildings of a public nature—the Drill Hall and headquarters of the Dumfriesshire Volunteers, erected in 1890, which is the scene of the larger public gatherings held in the town; and the Ewart Public Library, opened in 1904. The dwelling-house accommodation in the more densely populated part of the town has also been greatly improved. Increase of traffic has necessitated a transformation of the railway station by the erection of a platform and offices on the east side of the main line and contiguous buildings for various railway purposes; but it has still a pretty fringe of shrubbery. A handsome Station Hotel stands in an open space west of the railway.

knowledge of which circumstance makes us pray all the more heartily, with John Home—

> "Flourish, Dumfries ! may Heaven increase thy store,
> Till Criffel sink, and Nith shall glide no more :"

a prayer which will be echoed by all our indulgent readers, "hereabouts or far away ;" and with this benison on the good old burgh, we close our labour of love and bid them respectfully farewell !

APPENDIX.

A, p. 45.—Devorgilla's Bridge.

There is a prevalent belief that this bridge consisted at one time of thirteen arches; and guide books and gazetteers combine in saying that such was the case. The only authority that we have seen in support of this idea is a statement quoted in the "Picture of Dumfries" from Pemberton's "Journey through Scotland," published in 1723, in which the author says: "I passed the river Nith from Galloway to Dumfries over a fair stone bridge of thirteen large arches, the finest I saw in Britain, next to London and Rochester." Nothing can be more explicit than this declaration; but we know from documents that are undoubtedly genuine, that the bridge in 1681 (that is, forty-two years or thereby before Pemberton saw it) had only nine arches; and that in 1747, twenty-four years after 1723, it had still only nine—a picture and description of the bridge given by Grose leaving this point beyond the reach of cavil. The author of "A Tour thro' the whole Island of Great Britain," the sixth edition of which was published in 1761— the tour to which it relates having been made several years sooner—says (vol. iv., p. 115):—"Dumfries was always a good town, with large streets. . . . Over the river Nith is a very fine stone bridge at this place, with nine arches, and so broad that two coaches may go abreast on it." If these varying statements be all correct, then we must come to the strange conclusion that, some time after 1681, four new arches were added to the bridge in order to answer Mr Pemberton's description; and that some time after 1723, and prior to 1747, these four arches were removed, and the bridge reduced till it had only nine arches, as in 1681. The supposition is so incredible that it need not be argued against; and the only right solution of the difficulty that we can see is, to look upon Pemberton's statement about the thirteen arches as one of those mistakes which some travellers— trusting, it may be, to treacherous memories, instead of written notes—are liable. With the view of setting the matter at rest, the street, at the gable of Mr John M'Noe's wine and spirit establishment, was opened at our instance in April, 1866, where the pier of the tenth arch must have been put down, if any tenth arch had ever been in existence. The operation was carefully performed under the direction of an experienced local surveyor, Mr Barbour, who, taking Grose's dimensions of the nine-arch bridge—four hundred feet—added the length of an additional arch, and caused the spot and all around it for a long way to be excavated six feet deep, and probed to a further depth, without finding a trace of any thing resembling the heavy masonic pile of which the other piers consist. The conclusion come to was, that there never had been a tenth pier; and the inference seems to follow, that the bridge never numbered more than nine arches. This experiment, coupled with the other testimony already adduced, has convinced us that the foundation of the other four arches has been laid in the realms of fancy, and not in the solid earth, or shifting sands of the Vennel.

B, p. 45.—Statutes of Devorgilla relating to the Endowment of Balliol College, Oxford.

"Devorgulla de Galweda domina de Balliolo, dilectis in Christo, fratri Hugoni de Hertilpoll et Magistro Wilhelmo de Menyl, salutem in Domino sempiternam. Utilitati filiorum et scholarium nostrorum Oxoniæ commorantium, affectu materno providere cupientes, omnia inferius annotata volumus, mandamus et præcipimus, ab eis inviolabiliter observari; ad honorem scilicet Domini nostri Jesu Christi et Gloriosæ matris suæ Mariæ, necnon et sanctorum omnium. Imprimis, volumus et ordinamus quod scholares nostri omnes et singuli teneantur diebus Dominicis et festis principalioribus, divino interesse officio necnon sermonibus seu prædictationibus in eisdem fastis et diebus; nisi contigerit aliquem ex iis impediri propter urgentem necessitatem vel evidentem utilitatem; cæteris vero diebus diligenter scholas exerceant et studio intendant, secundum statuta Universitatis Oxoniæ, et secundum formam inferius annotatam. Ordinamus etiam quod Scholares nostri teneantur nostris Procuratoribus obedire in omnibus quae ex nostra ordinatione, concessione, commissione ad eorum Regimen et Utilitatem pertinere noscuntur. Item, volumus quod scholares nostri ex semetipsis eligant unum Principalem, cui cæteri omnes humiliter obediant in his quæ officium Principalis contingunt, secundum statuta et consuetudines inter ipsos usitata et approbata; Praedictus autem Principalis, postquam legitime fuerit electus, nostris Procuratoribus præsentetur nec aliquid de suo officio exerceat, antequam ab eis auctoritate nostra in præfato officio fuerit institutus. Cæterum statuimus quod scholares nostri procurent tres missas celebrari singulis annis solenniter pro anima dilecti mariti nostri domini Johannis de Balliol et pro animabus prædecessorum nostrorum omniumque fidelium defunctorum, necnon et pro nostra salute et incolumitate; ita quod prima missa celebratur in prima hebdomada Adventus Domini, et secunda in Hebdomada Septuagesimæ, et tertia in prima hebdomada post octavas Paschæ: et fiant prædictæ missæ de Sancto Spiritu, vel de Beata Virgine, vel pro defunctis, secundum dispositionem Procuratorum. Singulis etiam diebus, tam in prandio quam in cœna dicant benedictionem antequam comedant et post refectionem gratias agant; et orent specialiter pro anima dilecti mariti nostri superius nominati, et pro animabus omnium prædecessorum nostrorum necnon et liberorum defunctorum, pro incolumitate etiam nostra et liberorum, cæterorumque amicorum nostrorum vivorum; item et pro nostris Procuratoribus secundam formam antiquitus usitatam. Et ut melius provideatur sustentationi pauperum, ad quorum utilitatem intendimus laborare, volumus quod ditiores in societate scholarium nostrorum ita temperate studeant vivere, ut pauperes nullo modo graventur propter expensas onerosas; et si contigerit totam communitatem scholarium nostrorum in expensis communibus aliqua septimana excedere portionem a nobis eis impensam, volumus et præcipimus districte quod, ad solutionem illarum expensarum excedentium, nihil omnino recipiatur ultra unum denarium in una septimana ab eis qui, secundum discretionem et arbitrium Procuratorum nostrorum, judicantur, impotentes et insufficienties ad totalem illarum expensarum solutionem faciendam. Si æqualis portio deberet ab omnibus sociis exhiberi, prædicta tamen nolumus extendi ad magnam vacationem quæ durat a Translatione Beati Thomæ Martyris, usque ad festum Beati Lucæ, nec etiam ad septimanas in quibus occurrunt festi Nativitatis Dominicæ, Circumcisionis, Epiphaniæ, Paschæ, et Pentecostes nec in aliis casibus in quibus Procuratores nostri judicaverint illud omittendum: Volumus etiam Procuratores nostros diligentem habere examinationem super præfata Scholarium nostrorum impotentia, et quod scholares ipsi ad Procuratores accedant cum omni confidentia, pro eorum necessitate intimanda. Et si contigerit aliquem vel aliquos de Scholaribus nostris contra ordinationem illam murmurare, aut occasione, istius ordinationis pauperiores verbo vel signo aliquo provocare, volumus quod scholares nostri teneantur sub juramento nobis præstito nomina taliter murmurantium aut provocantium nostris Procuratoribus revelare: qui quidem Procuratores, habita super hoc sufficienti probatione, auctoritate præsentium, sine spe redeundi, ipsum vel ipsos ejiciant indilate. Statuimus etiam quod Scholares nostri communiter loquantur Latinum, et qui passim contra fecerit, a Principali corripiatur; et si, bis aut ter correptus, se non emendaverit, a communione mensæ separetur, per se comedens, et ultimus ominium serviatur: et, si incorrigibilis manserit per hebomadam, a Procuratoribus nostris ejiciatur. Volumus etiam quod qualibet altera hebdoma inter Scholares nostros in eorum domo disputetur unum sophisma et determinetur; et hoc fiat circulariter, ita ut sophistæ opponant et respondeant, et qui in Scholis determinaverint determinent. Si vero aliquis sophista ita provectus fuerit quod merito possit in brevi in Scholis determinare, tunc ei dictatur a Principali quod prius determinet domi inter socios suos. In fine autem cujuslibet disputationis præfigat Principalis diem disputationis sequentis, et disputationem regat et garrulos cohibeat, et assignet sophisma proxime disputandum, opponentem, respondentem et determinatorem, ut sic melius veleant providere. Consimili modo fiat qualibet altera hebdomada de quæstione. Præcipimus etiam Scholaribus nostris firmiter injungentes, ut portatorium, quod eis pro anima dilecti mariti nostri concessimus, diligenter custodiant, nec aliquo modo permittant illud impignorari, vel quocunque titulo alienari. Habeant etiam Scholares nostri unum pauperum Scholarem per Procuratores nostros assignatum, cui singulis diebus reliquias mensæ suæ teneantur erogare, nisi Procuratores nostri illud decreverint omittendum. Ut autem omnia et singula prædicta a nostris Scholaribus in tempore Procuratorum quorumcumque inviolabiliter observentur, præsens scriptum sigilli nostri munimine roboravimus. Datum apud Botel, in Octavis Assumptionis gloriosæ Virginis Mariæ, anno Gratiæ MCC. octogesimo secundo.''

We are indebted for the following translation of the statutes to a young Oxonian, Mr Robert James Muir, Dumfries, recently appointed one of her Majesty's Inspectors of Schools for Scotland:—

"Devorgulla of Galloway, Lady of Balliol, to our brother Hugh of Hertilpool, and Master Wilhelm of Menyl, beloved in Christ, eternal salvation in the Lord. Desiring with maternal affection to provide for the advantage of our sons and scholars resident at Oxford, we will, command, and enjoin all things to be mentioned hereafter, to be by them inviolably observed, to the honour, to wit, of Our Lord Jesus Christ, and His glorious Mother Mary, and eke of all Saints.

"Firstly, we will and ordain that our scholars, all and singly, be bound on Lord's days and on the greater Feasts to be present at the Divine Office, as well as the sermons or preachings on the same feasts and days, unless any of them shall happen to be let by urgent necessity or evident utility; but on other days they shall diligently perform their tasks, and apply themselves to study, according to the Statutes of the University of Oxford, and according to the scheme hereafter mentioned. We also ordain that our scholars be bound to obey our procurators in all things which, according to our ordinances, grant, and commission, are known to belong to their rule and advantage. We also will that our scholars from among themselves elect a principal, whom all the rest shall humbly obey in those matters which belong to the office of principal, according to the ordinary and approved statutes and customs observed among them. But let the aforesaid principal, after he has been lawfully elected, be presented to our procurators, nor exercise aught of his office before he has been by them instituted, by our authority, in the office aforesaid. Furthermore, we decree that our scholars cause three Masses to be duly celebrated every year for the soul of our beloved husband, John, Lord of Balliol, and for the souls of our predecessors, and all the faithful departed, as also for our own weal and salvation, so that the first Mass be celebrated in the first week of the Advent of our Lord, the second in the week of Septuagesima, and the third in the first week after the octave of Easter; and let these aforesaid be Masses of the Holy Ghost, Masses of the Blessed Virgin, or Masses for the departed, according to the arrangement of our procurators. Also, on every day, both at dinner and supper, let them say a blessing before eating, and after meat let them return thanks, and pray specially for the soul of our beloved husband above mentioned, and for the souls of all our predecessors, as also for those of our departed children, for our own salvation and that of our children, and for that of our other living friends, also for our procurators, according to the form of ancient use. And the better to provide for the maintenance of the poor scholars, whose advantage we intend to study, it is our will, that the richer ones in the society of our scholars study to live in such moderation that the poorer ones be not burdened in any way by heavy expenses; and if it shall happen that the common expenses of the whole community, in any one week, exceed the portion by us allowed to them, we will and strictly ordain that for the settling of those extra expenses nothing be received beyond the sum of one penny per week from those who, according to the discretionary choice of our procurators, are deemed straitened and unable to bear total payment of those expenses. If an equal portion should be furnished by all the fellows, nevertheless we are unwilling that the above be extended to the long vacation, lasting from the Translation of Saint Thomas the Martyr to the Feast of Saint Luke, nor again to the weeks in which occur the Feasts of the Nativity of our Lord, Circumcision, Epiphany, Easter, and Pentecost, nor other cases where our procurators think it should be omitted. We will also that our procurators carefully enquire into the above mentioned poverty of our scholars, and that the scholars themselves come to our procurators in all confidence to intimate their necessities. And if it shall happen that any one or more of our scholars murmur against the above ordinance, or on account of that ordinance mock the poor scholars by word or sign of any kind, we will that our scholars be held bound under oath fixed by us to reveal the names of those so murmuring and mocking to our procurators; and the latter shall, on sufficient proof of this being given, without delay expel him or them without hope of return, and this by authority of these presents.

" We also ordain that our scholars generally talk Latin, and let him who once and again does otherwise be corrected by the principal; if, after being twice or thrice corrected, he does not amend, let him be separated from the common table, to eat by himself and be served last of all, and if he remain incorrigible for a week, let him be expelled by our procurators. We will also that on every alternate week one sophism be disputed and determined by our scholars in their own hall; and let this be done in course, so that the disputants may alternately oppose and reply; and let those who shall determine in the Schools determine the argument. But if any disputant be so advanced in merit that he will shortly be able to determine in the Schools, then let the principal make him first determine in the hall among his fellows. At the end of each debate let the principal fix the day for the next debate, let him regulate the debate and restrain the talkative, and let him appoint the question to be next disputed, the proposer, the answerer, and the judge, so that they may the better be able to provide for it. In such manner let the dispute every alternate week be managed. We also command our scholars, with firm injunctions, diligently to preserve the Portatory which we have granted them for the soul of our beloved husband, and neither to suffer it to be impledged nor alienated in any manner. Let our scholars also have one poor scholar appointed by our procurators, for whom on every day they shall be bound to set aside the remains of their table, unless our procurators judge that this may be omitted. And that all and every thing aforesaid may be by our scholars inviolably observed in the time of all procurators whatsoever, these presents we have confirmed by the sanction of our seal.

" Given at Botel, in the Octave of the Assumption of the glorious Virgin Mary, in the year of grace 1282."

C, p. 46.—ESTATE OF DEVORGILLA AT HER DEATH.

DEBTS.—" Laurence of Preston, and John of Milton, of the County of North-ampton; Thomas of Molton, of the County of Cumberland; Master Thomas de Hunsingtone, and Master William de Pothon, of the County of York; William de Fauderleye, and Hugo de Hertwaytone, of the County of Northumberland, have undertaken to make for the King, in regard to the debts of Devorgulla of Balliol, a valuation of the goods and chattels that are now in the King's hand, for the aforesaid debts at Fotheringhay and Hiche. And it was granted that the executors of the said Devorgulla should have full management of the aforesaid goods and chattels, of the lands and tenements similarly held in the King's hand, on the aforesaid occasion. "Of her lands and tenements held in the King's hand."— "Whereas Devorgulla of Balliol owed several sums to the King on the day of her death, payment of which had not yet been made to the King, the Viscount of Essex was instructed to take for the King all the lands and tenements, and also the goods and chattels that belonged to Devorgulla, and to guard them safely, until he should receive other orders from the King. And that he should give notice, on the morrow after Holy Trinity, what lands and tenements, and also what goods and chattels, he took for the King on the aforesaid occasion, and how much they are worth."— Inquisito post mortem—18 Edward I., in Historical Documents, vol. i., pp. 124-5.

D, p. 58.—PRIVILEGES GIVEN TO KIRKCUDBRIGHT BY EDWARD I.

It is appointed by the King and his Council that no passage of wools or of hides, of messengers or of merchants, take place anywhere within the realm of Scotland, excepting in places where are the cocket-seals, and at Kirkcudbright; but before they are exported from Kirkcudbright let the cocket-seal be sent there by the Earl of Warren and by the Council which the King has in Scotland. And that in each place two of the most honest and loyal men of the same place, associated with the keepers of the customs of our lord the King, be appointed and sworn to keep the port so closely by day and night, that no messenger carrying letters or message from abroad pass in any manner without especial warrant from the King, nor any other person carrying closed letters or other suspicious thing, but let such a person be taken and kept in prison until the King shall have ordered his pleasure therein.   And all the mariners who shall pass, every time that they set out, shall swear and be examined, and the merchants shall be free by their oath that they will carry no letters nor message whence mischief might arise to the King or the realm, and that they will bring nothing from abroad by deed or by word, by art or by fraud, which may be hurtful to the King or the realm. And the King wishes that the messengers be closely searched and examined, so that nothing may pass whereby harm or damage may come to the King or the realm.   And if any messenger or other person with a letter or other thing dangerous to the King or the kingdom be found, let him be taken and sent to the King, or let him be kept in prison with his letters until the King shall have told his pleasure.   And let each of the wardens take especial care that no merchant of Lombardy (to whom the passage has already been forbidden, and is so still) pass in anywise.   And should any such come to pass, let him be forthwith taken and safely kept until the King shall have sent his pleasure.—Historical Documents, vol. ii., pp. 131-2.

E, p. 95.—THE SLAUGHTER OF COMYN.

In memory of this deed, the Kirkpatricks of Closeburn assumed as their crest a hand holding a dagger, with the memorable words for motto, "I mak siccar." Lord Hailes, in his "Annals" (vol. ii., p. 242), attempted to show that Sir Roger who slew Comyn was not the representative of the family of Kirkpatrick in Nithsdale; but universal tradition combines with other historians in attributing the ex-Regent's death-blow to the chief of the Closeburn Kirkpatricks, as narrated in the text.   The Rev. Mr Black, of Closeburn, gives the following account of the incident: "In that part of Closburn towards the water of Ayr, by which it is incompassed, is a forty-pound land pertaining to Thomas Kirkpatrick, of Closburn, an ancient family, and chief of that name, having a charter from Alexander K. of Scots, granted to Ivon Kirkpatrick, of the lands and barony of Closburn, before witnesses: Bondington, Cancellario, Rogero de Quency, Waltero filio Alani Senescallo Justiciario Scotiæ, Joanne de Maccuswell Camerario, Rogero Avonell, David Marescallo, Thoma filio Hamil, David de Lindsay, Rogero filio Glay, Roberto de Menyers, dated at Edinburgh, the 15th day of August, and of the said King's reign the eighteenth year. Moreover, the said Laird for his arms and ensign-armorial bears argent a St Andrew's cross azure, on a sheaf of the second three cushions or; above the shield, an helmet befitting his degree, mantled gules, doubled argent. Next is placed on a torse for his crest, a hand holding a dagger distilling drops of blood proper; the motto in an escrole, 'I am sure:' which cast and motto was given by Robert the Bruce, K. of Scots, to Roger Kirkpatrick, upon his killing of the Cumin at the Chappel of Dumfreis."—Sibbald MSS., in Advocates' Library.   In the same manuscript it is stated as a tradition that Bruce, immediately after the slaughter of Comyn, was conducted by Kirkpatrick to a place of refuge among the thick woods of Tynron, where he remained for some time safely hidden; but this vague report is at variance with the statement of Hemingford and other trustworthy historians, that Bruce and his followers gained for themselves an asylum in the Castle of Dumfries.   If there be any truth in the tradition that the bowers of Tynron afforded shelter to the patriot hero, it must have been at a later period, when he was a hunted wanderer in the wilds of Carrick, Galloway, and Dumfriesshire.

F, p. 99.—Dr Arthur Johnstone's Ode.

" Pastor ab Amphryso Drumfrisi pascua cernens
Eminus, Admeti prætulit illa jugis.
Florida tot pingues hic tondent prata juvenci,
Gramina quot verno tempore fundit humus.
Illius externas saturant pecuaria gentes,
Et mensas onerant Anglia sœpe tuas.
Ditior armento seges est, et velifer amnis:
Et mare, quod Zephyri temperat aura levis.
Surgit in hac ædes, cui cedunt templa Dianæ,
Vel venerabilius Græcia si quid habet.
Proditor hic patriæ Brusci virtute Cuminus
Concidit, et sacram sanguine tinxit humum.
Scotia, Drumfrisi reliquis altaria præfer;
Hic tibi libertas aurea parta fuit."

G, p. 103.—Charter of Sir Christopher's Chapel.

Charta Capellani celebrantis pro anima Christopheris de Seton.   Robertus, Die
gratia Rex Scotorum, etc., Christopherus de Seton, miles dilectus noster mortuus
est in servitio nostro, ac Christiana de Brois, sponsa sua sororque nostra dilecta
in loco quo mortem subiit prope Drumfreis, in honorem crucis Dominicæ quandam
Capellam fundavit et extruxit: sciat; propter benevolentiam et affectionem quam
non immerito erga dictum quendam Christophorum habuimus Donavisse Dedisse et
Confirmasse uni Capellano in eadem Capella pro anima dicti Christophorus anïmabus
omnium Fidelium Divina in perpetua celebrare; ac pro nobis et heredibus nostris
Regibus Scotiæ presentando centum solidus Strivilingorum annui reditus per manus
Vicecomitis nostri de Drumfreis, et Balivorum suorum qui pro tempore fuerint de
anno reditu nobis de dicta Baronia de Carlaverock ad criminos Pentecostes et Sancti
Martin, proportionaliter, singulis annis in libereri punam et perpetuam, eleemosynam
recipiendos.   Quare Vicecomiti nostro de Drumfreis et Balivis suis qui pro tempore
fuerint precipimus et mandamus quaternos dictos centum solidos annui reditus
dicto Capellano, ad criminos preditos plenarie persolvant in perpetuum. Quos
quidam centum solidos predicto Vicecomiti et Balivis suis qui pro tempore fuerint
in computis sui annuis volumus pro nobis et heredibus nostris plenius collocares.
In cujus rei fidem, etc., apud Berwica supra Tuedam ultimo die Novembris anni
regni nostri nonoduomo, Robertus Brussius, Scon coronatus erat 1306, mense
Aprilis.—General Hutton's MSS., in Advocates' Library.

H, p. 197.--Robert, Lord Maxwell's Bill for Translating the Scriptures into the Vulgar Tongue.

"The new doctrines concerning religion," says Keith (pp. 36, 37), " had so far
prevailed in Scotland, notwithstanding the severities used against the professors
thereof, in the late King's reign, by the influence of the settled clergy, that, in the
very first Parliament holden after his death, there was a proposal offered by the
Lord Maxwell, on the 15th of March, 1542-3, for a liberty of reading the Bible in
the vulgar tongue: which proposal was received and approved by the Governor
[Arran], and the Lords of the Articles.   And because this was the first public step
towards a Reformation of Religion, perhaps the reader will not be displeased to see
the Act inserted in this history, which is as followeth:—
    "' Anent the Writting gevin in be Robert, Lord Maxwell, in presens of my Lord
Governour and Lordis of Articklis, to be avisit by theim, gif the samin be reasonable or not, of the quhilk the tenor followis:—It is statute and ordaint, that it sal
be leful to all our Soverane Ladyis Leiges to haif the Holy Writ, to wit the New
Testament and Auld, in the vulgar tongue, in Inglis or Scottis, of ane gude and
true Translatioun; and that thai sal incur na Crimes for the hefing and reading of
the samin, provyding alwayis that nae Man dispute or hold oppinyeonis, under the
paines contenit in the Acts of Parliament.   The Lordis of Artícklis beand avisit
with the said Writting, finds the samin reasonable; and therefore thinkis that the
samin may be usit amongis all the Lieges of this Realm, in our vulgar toung, of ane
gude, true, and just Translatioun, because there was na Law shewin nor producit
in the contrair; and that nane of our Soverane Ladyis Leges incur any Crimes for
haifing or reding of the samin in Form as said is, nor sall be accusit therefore in
time coming; and that na Personis dispute, argou, or hold oppunionis of the samin,
under the saidis Painis contenit in the foresaides Act of Parliament.'
    "This draft of the Act having been read, ' ane Maist Reverend Fader in God,
Gawine, Archbishop of Glasgow, Chancelor, for himself, and in name and behalfe
of all the Prelatis of this Realm beand present in Parliament, schew, that ther was
ane Act instantly red in face of Parliament, that the Holy Writ may be usit in our
Vulgar Toung, and that na Crime suld follow thereupon throu the using therof;
and alegit in the said Act that the three Estates concludit the samen: Whilk he,
for himselfe and the Remanent of the Prelates being present, as ane of the three

Estates of the said Parliament, dissassentit thereto simpliciter; but appoint thaime thereto unto the Tyme, that ane provincial Counsel might be had of all the clergy of this Realm, to avis and conclud therupon, gif the samen be necessar to be had in vulgar toung, to be usit amang the Quein's Lieges or not; and therafter to shaw the utter [final] Determination that sal be done in that Behalfe: and therupon askit Instrumentis.'

"But," continues Keith, "notwithstanding this Protestation, the Lord Maxwell's Bill was certainly enacted; seeing that within two days after the Parliament had risen, the Governor, who found himself supported by the adversaries of the established religion, thought fit to cause issue out a Proclamation for notification to all the Lieges of the Act concerning Holy Scriptures. Here follows the orders for the proclamation.

"'GUBERNATORY, Clerk of Register, it is our Will, and we charge you, that ye goe proclaim this Day at the Marcat Crois of Edinburgh the actis made in oure Soverane Ladyis Parliament, that suld be proclaimit and gevin furth to her Lieges; and in speciale the Act made for having the New Testament in Vulgar Toung, with certain additionis; and therefter gif furth the copyis therof aitentick as efferis, to all them that will desyre the samyn; and insert this our Command and charge in the Buiks of Parliament, for youre Warrant. Subscrivit with our Hand, at Edinburgh, the xix. day of Marche, the year of God Jajve, and xlii. yeris.' "

I, p. 223.—THE PROPERTY OF THE M'BRAIRS.

While the M'Brairs were accumulating landed property in all directions, as specified in the text, they were at the same time obtaining by purchase, inheritance, or otherwise, a great many tenements in the Burgh. It has been stated (apparently with exaggerations) that Provost John Corsane, who flourished during the first half of the seventeenth century, owned about one-third of the town over which he ruled; and, judging from a contemporary document which we have had an opportunity of examining, Robert M'Brair, who flourished about fifty years afterwards, appears to have been the next largest proprietor of houses in the Burgh. Of this once opulent local family but faint traces are to be found in the present day: no descendants bearing their name own any property in the town. or live in it as residents, so far as we are aware.

J, p. 243.—CHARTER OF THE COUNTESS OF DOUGLAS.

Two old charters are extant, granting the Bridge Dues to the Greyfriars Monastery—one by Margaret, wife of Archibald, Earl of Douglas, dated 16th January, 1425, the other by her brother-in-law, James, Earl of Douglas, dated 4th January, 1452. They are both nearly in the same terms, and we shall therefore only quote the older of the two:—

"Omnibus hanc cartam visuris vel auditurus Margareta Ducissa Turonie Comitissa de Douglas Domina Galwidie et Vallis Annandie Salutem in Domino sempiternam Noveritis nos in pura et simplici viduitate nostra Dedisse concessisse et hac præsenti carta nostra confirmasse pro salute animæ quondam metuemdissimi Domini et Sponsi nostri Archibaldi Ducis Turonie Comitis de Douglas Domini Galwidie et Vallis Annandie animæ nostræ et animæ quondam carissimi filii nostri Domini Jacobi de Douglas et pro salute animarum progenitorum et antecessorum nostrorum filiorum nostrorum et filiarum nostrarum et pro salute animarum omnium fidelium defunctorum Deo Omnipotenti Beatæ Mariæ Virgini Sancto Francisco ac Gardiano et fratribus minoribus de Drumfres in perpetuum Deo ibidem servituris Totam et integram illan tollam sive custumam quæ per antecessores nostros et nos recipi solebat ad finem pontis De Nith de Drumfres Tenend et habend dictam tollam sive custumam cum pertinentiis dictes Gardiano et fratribus adeo libere quiete integre honorifice bene et in pace in omnibus et per omnia sine aliqua contradictione vel retenemento sicut per antecessores nostros aut nos plenius quietius aut honorificentius tenebatur recipiebatur aut quomolibet possidebatur Reddendo inde annuatim dicti Gardianus et fratres orationum suffragia sanctarum pro omni alio Servitio exactione seculari et demanda quæ de dicta tolla et custuma aliqualiter exigi poterint et requiri Et nos vero Margareta Ducissa supradicta sæpefatam custumam seu tollam dictis Gardiano et fratribus ut predictum est warrantizabimus acquietabimus et in perpetuum defendemus In cujus rei testimonium huic præsenti cartæ Nostræ Sigillum Nostrum apponi præcipimus Testibus Discretis viris magistro Johanne M'Ilhauch rectore de Kirkandre Secretario nostro Domino Willielmo Johnson Capellano nostro Georgio Mur et patricio de Spens cum multis aliis Apud le Treif Decimo sexto die mensis Januarii Anno Domini Millesimo quadringentesimo vicesimo quinto."

K, p. 417.—BRIDGE DUES.

At the Reformation, the superiority and feu duty, with the whole other possessions of the Minorite Friars, Dumfries, fell to the Crown, as being subjects that had no owner, the purpose for which they had been originally given to the

Friars having been declared to be illegal. By a charter dated 23rd April, 1569, King James VI. gave all these possessions to the Burgh of Dumfries, in order that the Burgh might support a hospital and maintain the bridge. This charter narrates that his Majesty considered it his duty to provide that a hospital should be kept up within the Burgh for poor people who were maimed or sick, and for orphans; and also to provide for the safety of his subjects whose business, it bears, made it necessary for them to cross the river, and whose lives would be endangered if the bridge were not kept in repair. It accordingly conveys to the Provost, Bailies, Council, and community of the Burgh, and their successors for ever, all the property and rights whatever which had belonged to the Grey Friars; but, in order that the Friars and other religious persons who were supported therefrom before the Reformation might not be impoverished, the charter reserves to them during their lives the full enjoyment of their income from the subjects conveyed. It erects and incorporates these subjects into one fund or estate, which was to be called "The Royal Foundation of the Hospital of Dumfries," and provides that, so far as the revenues therefrom went, the Burgh should be bound to keep up the bridge and to support the orphans and poor people in the hospital. Owing to some cause or other, however, no charitable institution under this charter has been founded in the Burgh.

Amongst the rights conveyed by that charter, there is specially mentioned the half of the bridge customs falling to the Friars. This would seem to have been merely the 11s 4⅚d of feu duty which had remained with the Friars after they had feued out the customs to John Johnston. The right of superiority itself, to which the feu duty was annexed, appears to have remained with or to have been resumed by the Crown; and in 1591 King James renewed the rights to the bridge dues in favour of John Johnston—a descendant, probably, of the original feuar.

Though the right of the Burgh to levy the bridge dues is recognised in several of its charters, and by the Act of 1681, the amount of the dues is not fixed by any of these deeds, and is regulated only by usage. The Burgh has also a right to certain customs on all goods brought within its liberties for sale, consumption, or otherwise, which customs, in so far as goods and bestial coming across the Nith are concerned, were levied along with the dues, till, in course of time, the two kinds of imposts became intermixed. Tables of both were prepared at various periods—the earliest on record being of date 23d October, 1732. On the 5th of November, 1772, the Town Council passed an Act designed to regulate the bridge and market dues, and directing that some of the latter that used to be uplifted in the market should be uplifted at the ports or entrances of the town instead. A table of bridge dues, based upon this Act, and professing to be framed according to the use and practice then existing, was at the same time published and exhibited at the Old Bridge as the rule of payment; and when the dues were levied at the New Bridge on its erection, the table of 1772 continued to be the guide to the tacksman or lessee in making his charges. The table included also such market dues as were leviable at the bridge. Both kinds of dues were expressed in Scots money, freemen in many cases paying a smaller amount than others. We subjoin a summary of the charges:—

Each horse, cow, or other cattle passing the bridge or the river within the town's privileges, though not presented to market, 2s; when so presented, 8d. Each of these animals brought to market by any of the other ports, 8d; and if not sold, the cattle to have the benefit of other two market days free of duty. Each animal as aforesaid sold in market, 2s, to be paid by the exporter in addition to the 8d levied on the importer. Each animal presented to market, but driven away unsold to England or elsewhere, 2s. Each sheep passing the bridge or river, 4d; each lamb, 2d. Each sheep, hogg, or lamb brought to market by any of the other ports, 4d on entering the market. Each sheep, young or old, sold in market, 4d, paid by the exporter. Each horse, cow, or other cattle passing from the Dumfriesshire to the Galloway side, or for Ireland, or other parts to graze, or cattle flitting from a pasture on the Dumfriesshire to the Galloway side, 1s 4d; each hogg, sheep, or lamb so passing, 2d.

It is then explained that all persons, freemen or unfreemen, who do not reside in the Burgh, but who pay watching, warding, and other portable charges therein, shall pay the same dues as unfreemen; and that all inhabitants, though burgesses, who traffic in cattle, shall pay the same dues as unfreemen, except for single beasts for their own use, which are to pass free.

All corded packs of merchandise that pass or repass, also all packs of wool, skins, lint, oil, wine, tar, and other merchandise, 2s 8d; freemen residenters, 1s 4d. If less than a load, these goods to pay proportionally, except for sheep skins, thirty of which to be charged 8d; freemen, 4d. Each load of meal, bere, barley, wheat, rye, peas, beans, potatoes, and other grain, roots, or fruits, 12d; freemen residenters, 6d. Note.—A load of seed or horse corn, or oats, is ten pecks; a load of bere, barley, meal, peas, beans, wheat, and rye, is eight pecks; and a load of potatoes, roots, and fruits, is four pecks. Each load of butter and cheese, 2s; freemen, 1s; halves or quarters in proportion, except for pieces of butter under four lbs., and single cheeses under half a stone. But no bridge custom is due by freemen residenters for grain, roots, fruit, butter, or cheese, from their own farms, for the use of their families, they paying only custom for what they sell; nor is custom to be levied on grain ground at the town mills, nor on merchant goods bought from freemen in the Burgh, belonging to and exported by the same person, in one day, under four stones weight at a time; such exemptions only to continue, however, during the Council's pleasure.

Each load of fish passing the bridge or river, 1s; each pock or creel of fish, 2d. Each load or creel of clogs or shoes imported, 4d. Each load of coverings, or waulked cloth, 1s; halves and quarters in proportion. Each load of bark above ten pecks, imported, 8d; freemen, 4d. Each corded pack brought in by any of the ports on the town side, if it has not paid duty here, and has not been opened in town, shall, in passing the bridge or river, pay 1s 4d; freemen, 8d; but if opened in town, it shall, on being exported, pay of bridge dues, 2s 8d; freemen, 1s 4d. The tables specifies that no custom is payable by the Nithsdale family, and closes with this "nota bene":—" The double of all the said customs is payable at the public fairs of this Burgh, conform to use and wont.

Such, in brief, is the bridge dues system, as it continued up till a very recent period. Its operation was often complained of by the people of the Stewartry; and more especially when carts or waggons superseded pack-horses, and the charges had to be converted from Scots into sterling money, did it become a source of wrangling and dispute between the tacksman and importers. With the view of facilitating the collection of the dues, the Town Council, on the 16th of October, 1854, issued for the guidance of their tacksman a table defining and explaining the table of 1772; the latter still remaining the authoritative rule of payment for the public. The charges were expressed in sterling money; and, among other changes, the indefinite or uncertain quantities of the old table were transformed into specific measures. Thus, "merchandise," wool, and lint, instead of being charged by the pack, were charged 4d on every 10 cwt.; tar, instead of paying so much per pack, was made liable to 1d per barrel; herrings, though not previously included in merchandise, were subjected to 1d per barrel—quantities of half a cwt. and under to pass free. This comprehensive explanatory sentence was also introduced: " Merchandise includes every thing that is the subject of commerce or mercantile dealing." A peck was represented to contain 7 imperial gallons, weighing 70 lbs. of water; a peck of seed or horse corn, 35 lbs.; a peck of bere, barley, meal, peas, etc., 46 lbs.; and a peck of potatoes, roots, or fruits, 84 lbs.—the charges in each case being adjusted to these measures instead of loads. A load of fish was defined to weigh 2½ cwt.; a load of coverings or waulked cloth was reckoned of the same weight. All the money conversions seem to have been fairly made on the principle that 12d Scots is represented by 1d English; and the Council, in specifying quantities, were, we believe, guided by the best authorities, oral and written, they could obtain. Lime was exempted from bridge dues by the old table; and by that of 1654, coals, and dung purchased by the farmer who was to use it from the person in whose premises it was produced, were also permitted to go free.

Before this new table was drawn up, however, the indiscretion or cupidity of the tacksman in 1854 rendered the impost increasingly obnoxious to the gentlemen of the Stewartry, till, as a result, a number of them united in raising an action for the purpose of having the articles charged upon defined, and the scale of dues determined, or, if possible, getting the dues abolished altogether. It is not necessary that we should give a detailed account of the proximate causes of the litigation, and trace its varied and protracted course through the Court of Session. A brief statement must suffice. On the 5th of February, 1862, an action was brought before the Lord Ordinary (Kinloch) at the instance of Wellwood H. Maxwell of Munches, Mark Sprot Stewart of Southwick, Robert Maxwell Witham of Kirkconnell, Robert Kirkpatrick Howat of Mabie, Wellwood Maxwell of the Grove, Francis Maxwell of Breoch, William Stewart of Shambelly, Patrick Dudgeon of Cargen, Walter M'Culloch of Ardwall, James Biggar of Maryholm, and Alexander Oswald of Auchencruive, against the Provost, Magistrates, and Town Council of Dumfries, in which the pursuers claimed decree of reduction of the tables of 1772 and 1854, and relative Acts of Council, and declarator of the bridge dues, and to have a table of dues prepared; their pleas of law being in effect as follows:—1. The dues enumerated in the tables of 1772 and 1854, and the Acts of the Dumfries Town Council relating to them, not being authorised by statute, charter, or usage, and being altogether without lawful authority, ought to be reduced and set aside. 2. The tables being inconsistent with one another, and unsupported by immemorial usage, ought to be reduced and set aside. 3. The table of 1772 being expressed in Scots money, and in obsolete weights and measures, and having, moreover, fallen into desuetude, and been superseded by usage inconsistent therewith: and the table of 1854 having been merely an unauthorised attempt to revive and explain and extend the application of that obsolete table, no effect can now be given to either of them. 4. In no respect are the defenders entitled to levy higher dues, or from or in respect of persons, bestial, and articles, other than according to the usage which shall be proved to have been immemorial. 5. The defenders are not entitled, under the head merchandise, to levy duty upon articles which have not been subject to it by immemorial usage.

The defenders, under eight different clauses, pleaded their right to levy the duties in question in virtue of their charters, the Act of 1681, immemorial usage, and a prescription extending over more than forty years. They held that the table of 1772, as explained by that of 1854, had been immemorially sanctioned; that there were no sufficient grounds on which the conclusions of reduction could be supported; that the whole material statements of the pursuers, being incorrect in point of fact, the action was unfounded; and that the defenders were therefore entitled to absolvitor, with expenses. Lord Kinloch allowed parties a proof of their respective averments, and to each a conjoint probation; and the same was taken by William Ellis Gloag, Esq., advocate, in the King's Arms Hotel, Dumfries, on the 5th, 6th, 7th, and 8th of April, 1864; and also by adjournment in Edinburgh in the following summer and autumn. With the evidence thus obtained before him, his Lordship pronounced an interlocutor, dated the 30th of June, 1865, to this effect:—He held that the term merchandise, as employed in the table of dues, comprehends all articles which are the subjects of mercantile dealing, and which were in use to be loaded either on a horse or cart; but that it does not comprehend live animals or dead carcases. Also that the said term does not comprehend lime, coal, manure, either natural or artificial, trees or wood, drain-tiles, stones, slates, hay, straw, agricultural implements, furniture, or machinery. He found also that foals, calves, and lambs following their mothers are not chargeable, nor swine, dead or alive; that no charge could be exacted from carriers other than on such articles as the table specifies; that herrings are chargeable as fish, and clogs as shoes; that horses are not chargeable when saddled or in harness; and that the defenders are not entitled to levy double dues at any period. His Lordship further appointed the cause to be enrolled, in order that steps might be taken for having a table of bridge dues framed according to the foregoing finding. In pronouncing the interlocutor, he professed to proceed upon the principle that no dues ought to be levied by the defenders except such as have been sanctioned by immemorial usage.

This decision seriously reduced the revenue of the bridge by its restricted reading of the term "merchandise," and by cutting off several articles which the defenders thought were legally chargeable. The defenders therefore reclaimed, and the case came, by appeal, before the First Division of the Court of Session, on the 1st of June, 1866. All the judges present, the Lord President, the Lords Curriehill, Deas, and Ardmillan, agreed with the Lord Ordinary, whose interlocutor they accordingly adhered to unanimously, with expenses. A new table has since been adjusted, in terms of the judgment of the Court.

Sundry dues, trifling in amount, were also levied at the trone or weigh-house, at the three ports, at the meal market, at the salt market, and at the mills; but all that remained of these were abolished shortly after the adoption of the Burgh Reform Act, 1833.

K,* p. 391.—SUFFERINGS AND LOSSES, 1650-51.

" Ane compt of pairt of the sufferings and losses sustained be the towne of Drumfreis since Septer. 1650.

" Imprimis, Upon the 10th of Decemr., 1650, four trowps of horse under the comand of Major Bethel, surpryzed Drumfries, whair they remained four days upon frie quarters, doing great abuses, the town being no way provyded for them, which losse they estimat to the soume of two hundred pound sterling (£200).

" It., Upon the 17th of Decr., 1650, thair came to Drumfries Leivetenant Collonell Ditton, with a regiment of foot from Cairliell with seven or aught trowps under the comand of Captain Dawson, Major Bethell, Captain Craikenthrop, Captain French, etc., whair the foot remayned for the space of twenty days or thairby upon frie quarters, and the most pairt of the horses; which losse they estimat to the soume of fyve hundred pounds sterling and, above (£500).

" It., Shortly thairafter, about February, 1651, Collownell Harker came to Drumfries with his regiment, whare he with some of his trowps remained upon frie quarters for the most part of the time, till May, which loss, etc., two hundred (£200).

" It., That same yeir, in March and Apryll, came Collounell Allane, whair he remained upon frie quarters till May, at which tyme Collounell Harker and Collounell Allane marched with thair regments towards the army, and ordered the town of Drumfries to buy for thair use a considerable quantity of oats which were come be water fra Ingland, for provisioun for thair horses on thair travill, which losse, etc., ane hundred (£100).

" It., Thairafter, in May, 1651, Collonell Allane returned to Drumfries with his regment, and abode in the cuntrie a short space, at which tyme he caused his trowpes drive away all the beists within and about Drumfries, till the toune sent to him to Hawick ane hundred and fifty punds sterling to releive thair beists (£150).

" It., In July, 1651, Generall Major Harrison come throw Drumfries with about thrie thousand horse and foot, to whom the towne gave in provisions, and they suffered in their corns and other extraordinary losses fourscore punds st. (£80).

" It., In September, 1657, Major Thomas Scot came from Leith with thrie or four trowpes of horses, who constrayned the towne to pay in money ane hundred and fiftie pounds sterling, besyd frie quarters, and greit abundance of corns, which they destroyed for provision for thair horses, which loss and money they estimat at thrie hundred pounds (£300).

" It., Losses sustained by Captain Grimsditch, quarterings by fyve gairds abune his locality, which charges and losses they estimat at one hundred and fifty punds (£150).

" It., The losses they have sustained in August and September, 1656, by the souldiers, who payd almost nothing for thair quarters, and committit many abuses and wrongs, etc., ane hundred punds (£100).

" It., Thair was spent in quarterings since Dec. 1650 till Dec. 1656, Drumfries lying in the roadway betwixt Glasgow, Ayr, Irvine, Galloway, and Ingland, so that all the forces which either went to England, or came from England, to any of these pairts, came throw Drumfries and quartered thair, which loss and damage they estimat five hundred punds (£500).

" Summa of all is £2280 sterling."

L, p. 487.—THE WHITE STEEDS OF THE SOLWAY.

Thousands who never saw the Solway have heard of its rapid northward flight, when swelled by " a flowing sea, and a wind that follows fast," rendered familiar by the line,

" Love swells like the Solway, but ebbs like its tide."

Many fatal accidents have occurred to travellers overtaken by the Solway tides, while endeavouring to cross its sands; and when a " spate " in the Nith conjoins with an unusual flux from the sea, serious inundations ensue, destructive of property, and sometimes also of human life. The oldest recorded flood of this kind took place towards the close of 1627, and is thus described:—" At Blackshaw and portions of the parish of Ruthwell, a deluge was experienced such as ' none then living had seen the like.' It went at least half a mile beyond the ordinary course, and threw down a number of houses and bulwarks in its way, and many cattle and other bestial were swept away with its rapidity; and what was still more melancholy, of the poor people who lived by making salt on Ruthwell sands seventeen perished; thirteen of them were found next day, and were all buried together in the Churchyard of Ruthwell, which, no doubt, was an affecting sight to the relations, widows, and children, etc., and even to all that beheld it. One circumstance more ought not to be omitted. The house of old Cockpool being environed on all hands, the people fled to the top of it for safety; and so sudden was the inundation upon them, that in their confusion, they left a young child in a cradle exposed to the flood, which very speedily carried away the cradle, nor could the tender-hearted beholders save the child's life without the manifest danger of their own. But, by the good providence of God, as the cradle, now afloat, was going forth of the outer door, a corner of it struck against the door-post, by which the other end was turned about, and, going across the door, it stuck there till the waters were assuaged. Upon the whole, that inundation made a most surprising devastation in those parts; and the ruin occasioned by it had an agreeable influence on the surviving inhabitants, convincing them more than ever of what they owed to Divine Providence; and, for ten years thereafter, they had the holy communion about that time, and thereby called to mind even that bodily deliverance."[*] The following is an extract from Mr M'Lellan's manuscript account of Annan:—" The dealers, in former times, passing into England with their horse and cattle for Broughhill and other Cumberland fairs, crossed the Solway Firth from Annan shores, at Booness-Wath ford, during the recess of the tide, with which ford old Joe Brough and other guides were familiar. At this passage many lives have been lost, and dangers incurred, from the rapid ' three-feet-abreast' tidal influx and ebb; and some yet living will remember the unhorsing and drowning of Mr Graham, Cross Keys Inn, Dumfries, about 1818, and how the horse, turning its head to the English side, swam back with the drowned man's son William, who hung on by the hair of its mane."

M, p. 591.—PRINCE CHARLIE'S TRIBUTE MONEY.

We give verbatim the names of the persons who contributed, with the amount of their contributions, as they are entered in the Town Council Minutes.

" From Archd. Maxwell, mert. in Dumfries, thirteen pounds sterline; from Doctor James Hay, physician there, five pounds sterling; and from Joseph Corrie, town-clerk of the sd. Burgh, two hundred and eighteen pounds sterling, for which Wm. Carruthers, Baily, had accepted bills to them; from Winifred Maxwell, relict of Adam Craik, of Duchrae, thirty pounds sterling, for wh. the sd. Wm. Carruthers, and John Dalzell of Fairgirth, had accepted bill to her; from Mr James Hoggan in Comlongon, one hundred pounds twelve shillings sterline; from Wm. Gordon of Campbelltoun, two hundred and fifty-six pounds seven shills. and nihepence ster.; and from Wm. Craik of Arbigland twenty pounds ster.; from the sd. William Gordon of Campbellton, one hundred pounds sterld.; from Wm. M'William, in Greenhead of Caerlaverock, eightie pounds sted.; from John Milligen, mercht. in Kirkcudbright, eightie pounds sterld.; from Sir Robert Laurie of Maxwellton, fourty pounds sted.; from Bryce Blair, late Provost of Annan, one hundred pounds sterline; and from John Goldie of Craigmuie, Commissaire of Drumfries, thirty-two pounds sterld.; and for which sums borrowed from the

[*] Quoted from a contemporary record by Stevenson, in his History of the Church of Scotland.

sd. Mr James Hoggan, the first sum borrowed from Campbellton, and the sum borrowed from Arbigland, the Provost and John Graham, baily, had accepted bills to them—for the sum borrowed from Wm. McWilliam, the Provost, John Ewart, late provost, and Wm. Carruthers, bailey, had accepted bill to him—for the one hundred pounds borrowed from Campbellton, the Provost, Bailys Thos. Gilchrist, Graham, and Carruthers, had accepted bill to him—for the sums borrowed from the sd. Thos. Kirkpatrick, John Milligan, and Sir Robert Laurie, the Provost, Baily Graham, and James Ewart, of Mullock, had accepted bills to them—for the sum borrowed from Mr Blair, the Provost, Baily Graham, and Thomas Kirkpatrick, mert. in this burgh, had accepted bill to him—and for the sum borrowed from the sd. John Goldie, the Provost, and Bailys Graham and Carruthers, had accepted bill to him; and from John Johnston, present provost of Annan, one hundred pounds stg., for wh. the Provost, Baily Graham, and the sd. Thomas Kirkpatrick, mercht. in this Burgh, had accepted bill to him.

As also, that they had borrowed the rest of the sd. two thousand pounds from the persons afternamed, and for which there is yet no security given—viz.: From Wm. Burnet, mercht. sixty-three pounds nine shills.; from James Bell, late baily, five pounds five shills.; from John Graham, present bailie, ninety-four pounds thirteen shills. and threepence; from John Ewart, late provost, eight pounds two shills.; from David Edgar, mertt., ten shills. and sixpence; from Adam Marchbank, deacon of the weavers, one pound; from James Turnbull, schoolmaster, one pound; from Alexr. Wylie, watchmaker, five shillings; from James McNish, taylor, one shillings; from Margaret McNish, five shillings; from James McNish, taylor, one pound one shill.; from Wm. Kellock, inndweller, eighteen shillings; from Robert Baily, officer of Excise, one pound fyve shills.; from James Aiken, convener of the trades, two pounds two shills.; from Mrs Jannet Murray, sister to Dougall Maxwell (alias Murray), of Cowhill, one pound one shill.; from Wm. Reid, deacon of the smiths, ten shills. and sixpence; from Agnes Lewars, weadow. five shillings; from James Neilson, mdssr., ten shills. and sixpence; from Wm. Weish, mert., five shills.; from Mary Reid, widow, five shills.; from John Johnston, mert., two shills.; from James Kennedie, two pounds two shills.; from Wm. Fergusson, mert., one pound; from Wm. Hawthorn, weaver, one pound; from Margaret Corrie, relict of Robert Gordon, seven shills.; from Francis Mitchell, shoemaker, one pound four shills. and sixpence; from Elizabeth Cunningham, widow of Edward Welsh, mertt., two pounds two shills.; from David Kelly, inndweller, five shills.; from Charles Kirkpatrick, mercht.. & Sons, seventeen pounds ten shills.; from Wm. Howell, baxter, seventeen shills.; from Wm. Laurie, mert., one pound ten shills.; from Wm. Johnston, mertt., three pounds seventeen shills.; from Charles Mercer, mathematician, one pound; from Robert Cutlar, late bailie, eighteen pounds five shills.; from Robert Smith, mertt., two pounds two shills.; from Mr George Clerk, of Drumcrief, three pounds; from Ann Johnston, widow of Joseph Johnston, surgeon, two pounds two shills.; from James Kirkpatrick, workman, ten shills. and sixpence; from Jannet Reid, widow of Thomas Edgar, late provost, two pounds two shills.; from James Morison, mertt., sixteen shills.; from David Bean, mercht., six pounds six shills.; from Baily Thos. Gilchrist, one pound one shill.; from Marion Gillison, widow of James Dalgleish, mert., three pounds three shills.; from John Bryon, taylor, five shills.; from John Irving, late provost, two pounds two shills.; from Thos. Wilkie, couper, four shills.; from Wm. Gunzon, mert., five pounds five shills.; from Wm. Hodgeson, tanner, ten shills.; from James Copland, writer, one pound; from Thos, Adamson, weaver, ten shills.; from George Gordon, mert., fourteen pounds; from James Brand, mert., fifty-two pounds ten shills.; from James Clerk, mert., ten pounds; from Robert Edgar, writer, five pounds five shills.; from Elizabeth Dalrymple, Ladie Moriwhat, five pounds; from Thomas Carlyle, writer, four pounds; from Margaret Edgar, widow of John Dobie, ten shills.; from Wm. Clark, writer, eight pounds; from Miss Peggie Maxwell, sister of James Maxwell of Carnsallock, two pounds two shills.; from Thomas Morison, surgeon, five pounds fourteen shills.; from John Beck, innkeeper, ten shills.; from James Douglas, copper-smith, three pounds three shills.; from Matthew Palmer, brewer, one pound one shill.; from Wm. Stothart, mert., six pounds; from James Harley, deacon of the wrights, ten pounds; from James Reid, land-waiter, twenty-five pounds; from Daniel Mason, mert., ten pounds; from Archibald Malcolm, writer, three pounds; from James Corrie, mert., one pound; from John Dalzell of Fairgirth, thirty-two pounds; from Gilbert Paterson, mert., five pounds; from Hugh Lawson, mert., eight pounds; from Alex. Spalding, mert., one pound eleven shills. and sixpence; from Andrew Caird, mert., two pounds; from John Clark, writer, one pound one shill.; from John Riddick, taylor, five shills.; from Samuel Cummine, taylor, one pound one shill.; from Wm. Jardine, vintner, three pounds three shills.; from Alexr. M'Gowan, late Baily, one pound; from Barbara Fingas, widow of Mr Robert Patoun, minister, one pound eleven shillings and sixpence; from Wm. Kerr, shoemaker, one pound one shill.; from Robert Joat, shoemaker, ten shills. and sixpence; from James Cuthbert, stabler, three pounds; from James Swan, innkeeper, four pounds fifteen shills.; from Thos. Davidson, innkeeper, one pound; from Wm. Dod, mert., three pounds: from Elizabeth Maxwell, relict of John Neilson of Chappell, two pounds; from Herbert Kennedy, mert., two pounds two shills.; from Andrew Robison, barber, eight shills.; from George Bell, provost, twenty-five pounds; from James Smith, writer, one pound one shill.; from Jean Braithwait, relict of Wm. Scot, vintner, eleven pounds; from Wm. Carruthers, baily, nine pounds; from Thos. Hidleston, cook, one pound; from James Fairies, mercht., one pound five shills.; from James Maxwell, yr. of Barncleugh, twenty-three pounds; from Robert Grierson, mert.. one pound one shill.; from James Dickson, writer, two pounds two shills.; from John Maxwell, wright, one pound; from Richard Dickson, baxter, ten shills.; from Janet Wilson, widow of John Edgar, baxter, three pounds three shills.; from John Grierson, bookseller, ten shills.; from Mr Richard Louthian of Staffold, thirty pounds; from John Wallace, mert., four pounds; from Thos. Kirkpatrick, mertt., forty-six pounds; from Dr Ebenezer Gilchrist, ten pounds ten shills.; from John Maxwell, mertt., twenty-one pounds four shills. and sixpence; from John McKie, late convener of the trades, two pounds; from Andrew Crosbie, late provost, seven pounds; from John Ewart, vintner, five pounds; from the before-named John Goldy of Craigmuie, one pound; from John Grierson, dyer, one pound one shill.; from Wm. Gardner, gardiner, five pounds; from Charles Edgar, late deacon of the weavers, ten shill. and six-pence; from Wm. Weems, wright, ten shills.; from James Newall, weaver, fyve shills.; and from John Hynd, commissarie clerk, fyve pounds—all the aforesaid sums being sterline money."

N, p. 811.—PROVOSTS OF DUMFRIES.

A complete list of the Provosts, from 1651 till our own day, is furnished by the Books of Council: and from other sources, such as the minutes of the Convention of Royal Burghs, the Acts of the Scottish Parliaments, and unassorted papers in the Record-room, Dumfries, we have been able to carry the list much further back, though in a very incomplete form, and in a few instances names have been intro-duced with some hesitation, as the proof on which we relied was inferential rather than direct. These doubtful cases are indicated by an asterisk. The magisterial elections occurred at Michaelmas (29th September) each year, till the date of the Burgh Reform Bill, in 1833, when they were fixed to take place on the first Friday of November—the provost being chosen for three years, instead of, as before, for one year.

Robert Makbrar or M'Brair	1469	David Bishop	1678-9
*Thomas Welsh	1471	William Craik	1679-80
Robert Makbrar	1472	John Coupland	1680-1
Robert M'Brair	1476	James Kennan	1681-2
Robert M'Brair	1481	John Coupland	1682-3
Robert M'Brair	1518-9	Lord Drumlanrig	1683-4-5-6
Robert M'Brair	1519	John Maxwell of Barncleugh	1687-8
John M'Brair	1552	William Craik	1688-9-90
Rodger M'Brair	1558	Thomas Rome	1691
Archibald M'Brair	1570	Robert Johnstone	1692-3-4
*Herbert Rayning	1572	John Irving	1694-5-6
Robert Rayning	1578	Robert Johnstone	1696
Robert M'Brair	1579	John Irving	1697
Archibald M'Brair	1581	Robert Johnstone	1698
Matthew Dickson	1582	John Irving of Logan	1698-9-1700
John Mareshal	1583	Robert Johnstone	1700-1-2
Simon Johnstoun	1584	Wm. Coupland of Colliston	1702-3-4
John Maxwell of Newlaw	1585	Thomas Rome of Cloudan	1704-5-6
Herbert Rayning	1586	William Coupland	1706-7-8
John Bryce	1587	John Crosbie of Holm	1708-9-10
Roger Gordon	1588-9	Robert Corbet	1710-1-2
Herbert Rayning	1591-2	John Crosbie	1712-3-4
Homer Maxwell of Speddo	1593-4	Robert Corbet	1714-5-6
William Lytle	1595	John Crosbie	1716-7-8
*Herbert Cunninghame	1612	James Corrie	1718-9-20
Herbert Cunninghame	1616	William Craik	1720-1-2
John Corsane	1618	James Corrie	1722-3-4
*Francis Irving	1621	Thomas Edgar	1724-5-6
John Corsane	1622	John Irving	1726-7-8
Roger Kirkpatrick	1623	James Corrie	1728-9-30
*Francis Irving	1626	Thomas Edgar of Reidbank	1730-1-2
*Francis Irving	1629	Andrew Crosbie of Holm	1732-3-4
John Corsane	1639	James Corrie	1734-5-6
John Corsane	1642	John Ewart	1736-7-8
John Corsane	1643	Andrew Crosbie	1738-9-40
John Corsane	1644	George Bell of Conheath	1740-1-2
John Maxwell	1645	John Ewart	1742-3-4
Thomas M'Burnie	1649	George Bell	1744-5-6
Thomas M'Burnie	1651-2-3-4	John Ewart	1746-7-8
Robert Graham	1655-6-7-8-9-60	George Bell	1748-9-50
John Irving	1660-1-2-3-4-5	John Graham	1750-1-2
Thomas Irving	1665-6-7 8	Robert Ferguson	1752-3-4
John Irving	1668-9-70-1-2.3-4	George Bell	1754-5-6
Wm. Craik of Duchrae	1674-5-6-7-8	Robert Maxwell of Cargen	1756-7-8

James Corbet	.. ..	1758–9–60
Robert Maxwell	.. ..	1760–1–2
Ebenezer Hepburn	..	1762–3–4
John Dickson of Conheath		1764–5–6
Robert Maxwell	.. ..	1766–7–8
Ebenezer Hepburn	..	1768–9–70
John Dickson	..	1770–1–2
Robert Maxwell	.. ..	1772–3–4
Edward Maxwell		.. 1774–5
Robert Maxwell	.. ..	1775–6–7
John Clark..	.. ..	1777–8–9
Robert Maxwell	.. ..	1779–80–1
Wellwood Maxwell of Barncleuch		1781–2
David Blair	.. ..	1782–3–4
David Staig	.. ..	1784–5–6
William Clark	.. ..	1786–7–8
David Staig	.. ..	1788–9–90
David Blair	.. ..	1790–1–2
David Staig	.. ..	1792–3–4
John M'Murdo	.. ..	.. 1794–5
David Staig	.. ..	1795–6–7
Robert Jackson	.. ..	1797–8–9
David Staig	.. ..	1789–1800
Robert Jackson	.. ..	1800–1–2
Gabriel Richardson	..	1802–3–4
David Staig	.. ..	1804–5–6
Robert Jackson	.. ..	1806–7–8
David Staig	.. ..	.. 1808–9
Robert Jackson	.. ..	1809–10–1
David Staig	.. ..	1811–2–3
Joseph Gass	.. ..	1813–4–5
David Staig	.. ..	1815–6–7
John Barker	.. ..	1817–8–9
William Thomson	..	1819–20–1
John Kerr ..	.. ..	1821–2–3
William Thomson	..	1823–4–5
John Kerr (died in office)		.. 1825–6
William Thomson..	..	.. 1826–7
William M'Kie	.. ..	1827–8–9
John Fraser	.. ..	1829–30–1
James Corson	.. ..	1831–2–3
Robert Murray (died in office)		.. 1833–4
Robert Kemp	.. ..	1834–5–6–7
David Armstrong	..	1837–8–9–40
John Fraser	.. ..	1840–1–2–3
Thomas Crichton	..	1843–4–5–6
Thomas Kennedy	..	1846–7–8–9

William Nicholson	..	1849–50–1–2
Miles Leighton	.. ..	1852–3–4–5
Wm. M'Gowan (died in office)		1855–6
Miles Leighton	.. ..	1856–7
(Re-elected, 1857–8–9–60.)		
James Gordon	.. ..	1860–1–2–3
(Re-elected 1863; resigned 16th		
January, 1864.)		
William Bell, February 18		1864
William Turner	.. ..	1864–5–6–7
Christopher Harkness	..	1867–8–9
(Re-elected 1869–70–1–2, and died		
in office.)		
Thomas Fergusson Smith		1872–3–4–5
(Re-elected 1875–6–7–8.)		
Thomas Shortridge		1878–9–80–81
David Lennox	.. ..	1881–2–3–4
(Re-elected 1884–5–6–7.)		
John Luke Scott ..	..	1887–8–9–90
(Re-elected 1890–1–2–3; also 1893–4–		
5–6; resigned June, 1896.)		
Joseph Johnstone Glover		1896–7–8–9
(Re-elected 1899–1900–1–2; also		
1902–3–4–5; and in 1905.)		
James Lennox	.. ..	1909–11
James Thomson	..	1911–14
Thomas S. Macaulay	..	1914–23
James Clarke M'George	..	1923–26
David O'Brien	.. ..	1926–29
David Brodie	.. ..	1929–32
David O'Brien	.. ..	1932–35
William James Kelly	..	1935–38
John Lockerbie	.. ..	1938–41
Kirkpatrick Dobie	..	1941–44
Ernest Fyfe	.. ..	1944–47
Thomas Bell	.. ..	1947–53
George Harold Mogerly		1953–56
William Wallace ..	..	1956
George J. MacDowall	..	1956–60
Edward Watt	.. ..	1960–65
E. Robertson	.. ..	1965–
E. Robertson, OBE, JP		1965–75
CHAIRMAN OF NITHSDALE DISTRICT		
COUNCIL:		
Frank H. Young, JP,	..	1974–77
W. Brown Simpson, MBE, JP,		1977–84
K. Cameron, JP,	..	1984–

HISTORY OF DUMFRIES
INDEX

N.B. Page references preceded by the letters 'DUM' relate to the new prefaratory chapter by A.E. Truckell.